The GALE
ENCYCLOPEDIA *of*
CHILDHOOD &
ADOLESCENCE

The GALE
ENCYCLOPEDIA *of*
CHILDHOOD &
ADOLESCENCE

JEROME KAGAN, HARVARD UNIVERSITY, EXECUTIVE EDITOR

Susan B. Gall, Managing Editor

GALE

DETROIT   NEW YORK   TORONTO   LONDON

The Gale Encyclopedia of Childhood and Adolescence

Jerome Kagan, *Executive Editor*
Susan Gall, *Managing Editor*

Gale Research Staff

Kyung Lim Kalasky, *Coordinating Editor*
Mary Beth Trimper, *Production Director*
Evi Seoud, *Production Manager*
Shanna Heilveil, *Production Assistant*
Cynthia Baldwin, *Production Design Manager*

ISBN 0-8103-9884-2
Printed in the United States of America
10 9 8 7 6 5 4 3 2

Library of Congress Cataloging-in-Publication Data
The Gale encyclopedia of childhood and adolescence / Jerome Kagan, executive editor ;
   Susan Gall, managing editor.
       p.   cm.
   Includes bibliographical references and index.
     ISBN 0-8103-9884-2 (alk. paper)
     1. Child development–Encyclopedias.   2. Child psychology–Encyclopedias.   3. Adolescence–
Encyclopedias.   4. Adolescent psychology–Encyclopedias.   I. Kagan, Jerome.
II. Gall,   Susan B.
HQ772.G27   1997
305.231' 03–dc21   97-29270
                                                                                   CIP

Executive Editor
Jerome Kagan

Managing Editor
Susan B. Gall

Editorial Advisors and Reviewers
Nancy Eisenberg, Arizona State University
Robert McCall, University of Pittsburgh
James Perrin, M.D., Massachusetts General Hospital
David Shaffer, M.D., New York State Psychiatric Institute

Contributors

Doreen Arcus
David Axelson, M.D.
Karen Bauman
Karen L. Bierman
Boris Birmaher, M.D.
Hallie Bourne
Cherie Boyer
David A. Brent
Dianne Daeg de Mott
Jill DeVilliers
Janet Fenn
Susan B. Gall
Stanley M. Garn
Jan E. Hasbrouck
Jim Henry
Timothy B. Jay
Jerome Kagan
Mary Anne Klasen
Patricia K. Kuhl

Peter LaFreniere
Michael Lewis
Mary McNulty
Zoran Minderovic
Nancy Moore
Elizabeth Park
Richard H. Passman
Lizette Peterson
Karen L. Rice
Gail B. Slap, M.D.
Laurence Steinberg
Fernando Vidal
Marta Vielhaber, M.D.
Janet A. Welsh
Rosalie Wieder
Michael Windle
Angela Woodward
Janice Zeman

ABOUT THE EDITOR

A prominent researcher in child development, Jerome Kagan is currently Daniel and Amy Starch Professor of Psychology at Harvard University. Professor Kagan received his undergraduate training at Rutgers University, and his Ph.D. in psychology from Yale University.

Kagan's early research, a collaboration with Howard Moss at the Fels Research Institute at Yellow Springs, Ohio, was an evaluation of adults who had been members of a longitudinal study of children from infancy to early adulthood. The question of interest was what factors, if any, predicted later behavior. Their findings, published in 1962 in the book, *Birth to Maturity,* argued persuasively that, although infant characteristics were poor predictors of later outcomes, the child's sex and social class were powerful predictors of adult personality. Kagan applied this observation in later years to point out that social class, not race, was the critical factor in predicting IQ.

Birth to Maturity brought Kagan prominence. The book won the Hofheimer Prize from the American Psychiatric Association in 1963, and Kagan joined the faculty at Harvard University in 1964. He has won numerous honors and awards in the intervening years. He has been an active advocate for children and science through many organizations, including the Social Science Research Council, the National Institute of Child Health and Development, the President's Science Advisory Committee, the National Institute of Education, the National Academy of Sciences, and the Foundation to Improve Television.

A prolific contributor to the field of child development, Kagan has published numerous influential papers on a wide range of topics, including the psychology and physiology of child temperament, determinants of infant attention, the emergence of self, children as witnesses, the measure of personality characteristics, and the contributions of social class to measures of intelligence. He has edited several textbooks in psychology and social science. His published works include *Change and Continuity in Infancy* (1971); *The Growth of the Child* (1978); *Infancy: Its Place in Human Development* (with R. Kearsley and P. Zelazo, 1978); *The Second Year: The Emergence of Self Awareness* (1984); *Unstable Ideas* (1989); and *Galen's Prophecy: Temperament in Human Nature* (1994).

ORGANIZATION OF THE ENCYCLOPEDIA

The *Gale Encyclopedia of Childhood and Adolescence* is a comprehensive reference work addressed to those interested in human development from birth through adolescence, including students of child development, teachers, health care providers, child psychologists, family counselors, education professionals, academics, and parents. Entries were designed to be both accessible to readers with limited knowledge of the subject and authoritative.

Respected child psychologist Jerome Kagan, Daniel and Amy Starch Professor of Psychology, Harvard University, served as executive editor of the encyclopedia. He was assisted in the design of the encyclopedia by a panel of editorial advisors from the fields of education, health care, family counseling, and child psychology, reflecting the diverse fields and disciplines encompassed by the encyclopedia.

Signed entries were prepared by some of the leading experts in child development. Entries range from short to lengthy (over 5,000 words), providing the student or professional in child development with a concise understanding of the subject while still being accessible to the interested general public.

The majority of the entries offer suggestions for further study, including books, periodicals, audiovisual materials, organizations, and in some cases, websites. Entries are illustrated with photos, graphs, charts, or tables where appropriate.

Survey articles cover the primary stages, key theories, and issues in child development. Name entries profile prominent scholars/theorists in child development, with emphasis on their contributions to the field. Other entries define terms and concepts from health care, education, and developmental psychology of interest to people who work with or care for children. Also included are entries on consumer products and mass electronic media aimed at children.

Entries are cross-referenced and thoroughly indexed. A bibliography provides a comprehensive listing of sources for further study on a wide range of topics for further study.

- Entries are alphabetically arranged in a single sequence.
- Length of entries ranges from brief explanations of a concept in one or two paragraphs to longer, more detailed entries on more complex theories and concepts.
- A brief definition of the entry term appears in italics and precedes the body of the entry.
- Illustrations and sidebars accompany many of the entries to enhance the reader's understanding of the subject covered.
- Further study sections are included to point readers to other helpful sources.
- *See also* references are provided at the end of some entries to point readers to related entries.
- Cross-references placed throughout the encyclopedia direct readers to entries that include subjects without their own entries.
- A comprehensive general index completes the work, and guides readers to the people and concepts covered in the book.

CONTENTS

Editors and Contributors. v

About the Editor vii

Organization of the Encyclopedia ix

Illustration Credits xii

Preface xiii

Entries 1

Bibliography. 677

Subject Index 707

ILLUSTRATION CREDITS

American Academy of Orthodontics: Orthodontia; American Academy of Pedicatrics: **Down Syndrome, Hospitalization, Hypertension, Jaundice, Pediatrician, Premature Birth, Safety;** AP/Wide World: **Maria Montessori;** Archives of the History of American Psychology, University of Akron: **Alfred Binet, James McKeen Cattell, Erik Erikson, Anna Freud, Arnold Gesell, Jean Piaget, Philippe Pinel, B. F. Skinner;** Corel Corporation: **Father-child relationships, Gross Motor Skills;** EPD Photos: **Autism, Drawings, Grandparents;** Courtesy of Gallaudet University Press: **American Sign Language;** Courtesy of the Robert Glick family: **Bar/Bat Mitzvah;** Photo by Hornick/Rivlin, Courtesy of Addison-Wesley: **T. Berry Brazelton;** Photo by Peter LaFreniere, courtesy of photographer and Janice Zeman: **Affect, Swimming.**

PREFACE

The development of *Gale Encyclopedia of Childhood and Adolescence (GEOCA)* was directed by one of the most well-respected teachers and researchers in the field of child development, Jerome Kagan of Harvard University (see **About the Editor**, page vii). From a master list of over 1,500 terms prepared under Professor Kagan's direction, the editorial advisors reviewed and selected over 800 terms for inclusion in *GEOCA*. In carrying out this daunting task, the advisors, representing the wide range of disciplines encompassing child development, focused their work on the needs of the target audience for *GEOCA*—parents, librarians, teachers, undergraduate students, health care providers, and social service professionals.

Terms reflect the range of subfields encompassed by the field of child development—from profiles of notable individuals and organizations to essays on childhood illnesses and diseases, to key concepts and theories. The comprehensive bibliography complements the suggestions for further reading that accompany nearly all essays. A comprehensive subject index directs users to topics of interest.

The contributors acknowledge the support and assistance of their own colleagues and staff members who provided guidance and review during preparation of essays for this work. Boris Birmaher, M.D., and David Ax-

elson, M.D., wish to thank Therese Deiseroth for her assistance in the preparation of the entry on depression. Cherie B. Boyer, Ph.D., University of California, San Francisco, wishes to acknowledge the National Institutes of Health, National Institute of Allergy and Infectious Diseases, Sexually Transmitted Disease Branch for their financial support of her work on sexually transmitted diseases. Dr. Boyer would also like to thank Dulce Mohler and Ming Lau for their assistance in preparing the manuscript on the subject for this encyclopedia.

The editors acknowledge with gratitude the support and guidance provided by staff editors at Gale Research: Thom Votteler, who saw the project through its planning stages; Kyung Lim Kalasky, who edited the entries and kept the project moving forward with skill, patience, and intelligence; Christine Jeryan, who supervised the development process; Shanna Heilveil and Evi Seoud, who took the finished product and turned it into a bound volume.

Special appreciation is due to the contributors and advisors, guided by executive editor Jerome Kagan, for their warmth, intelligence, and diligent support through the years of development of *GEOCA*. I hope they will join me in beaming with pride at this bound product of their outstanding efforts.

Susan Gall
Managing Editor
Summer 1997

Abandonment

Legal term describing the failure of a non-custodial parent to provide support to his or her children according to the terms approved by a court of law.

An enduring issue that has received increasing attention since the 1970s, abandonment refers to non-custodial parents who do not fulfill court-ordered financial responsibilities to their children, regardless of their involvement in their children's lives in other ways. Lack of such support is blamed for substantial poverty among single-parent families.

In 1993 it was estimated that up to 27% of children in the United States, representing 11.5 million families, lived in single-parent households headed by women. Fewer than half received any financial support from the non-custodial parent. The income of more than a third of these households fell below the poverty level. The term "deadbeat dads" is often used in discussions about abandonment because most of the parents involved are fathers.

An increasing **divorce** rate and a rise in the number of infants born to unmarried mothers were in large part responsible for forcing the abandonment issue into public consciousness in the 1970s. Traditionally, at least during the 20th century, mothers involved in divorce or unwed births were routinely given physical custody of children, while fathers were granted visitation rights and ordered to pay a certain amount of money to help care for the children's needs. Many men ignored this financial responsibility, forcing some women to get jobs or to seek government support.

States have always taken on the main responsibility for ensuring the welfare of abandoned children. Federal involvement came as early as 1935, when the Social Security Act established the Aid to Dependent Children program, primarily to assist widows. Over subsequent years, federal provisions strengthened the states' mandate. During the early 1970s, when the government's financial burden grew as more and more women turned to welfare, the U.S. Congress began to call for even stronger child-support enforcement provisions.

Enforcement laws vary from state to state. Garnishing wages, attacking bank accounts, and foreclosing on real estate are all used to force payment to affected children. As of 1995, all state enforcement systems were required to be automated, allowing more efficient monitoring of payment and better tracking of violating parents. Some states have begun to deny drivers' and professional licenses to known delinquent parents. "Wanted" posters and other forms of advertising are more unconventional methods used occasionally to locate such parents.

Most states give priority to finding parents whose children, lacking parental support, are receiving government assistance. Some families with independent incomes turn to lawyers or private collection agencies to find offenders and bring them to court for nonpayment. In recent years, hundreds of agencies specializing in child support collection, some of them unscrupulous, have been formed to meet the demand forced by overburdened state agencies. They sometimes charge exhorbitant retainer or contingency fees, substantially reducing the size of the payment recovered by the family.

In the 1990s, the federal government adopted measures to further assist states in the support-collection effort. Military personnel files have become more available, and a program to confiscate federal tax refunds has contributed to keeping the issue in the spotlight. The 1992 Child Support Recovery Act allows courts to impose criminal penalties on parents who cross state lines to avoid child support payments. In 1993, the Department of Health and Human Services gave $1.5 billion to local agencies trying to locate offenders.

Some support exists for consolidating child-support enforcement through the Internal Revenue Service (IRS) rather than the states. Proponents argue that only the IRS can efficiently confiscate deadbeat parents' income and return it to children. Opponents contend that the involvement of the federal bureaucracy would more likely add inefficiency to the enforcement process and only aggravate an already growing problem.

Tardy or absent child support is often coupled with contentious custody battles. A number of family support groups have been formed in recent years to help parents understand their legal rights and alternatives, as well as to lend emotional support. One group—Advocates for Better Child Support (ABC'S), started in 1989 in Massachusetts—has advised up to 10,000 families. It educates custodial parents about their rights, lobbies for legislative reform, works with local enforcement agencies, and offers emotional support to parents. Other groups around the country offer similar services.

The magnitude of the child-support problem will likely continue in the next century. One proposal sure to receive scrutiny calls for "support assurance." Parents obligated to pay child support would make their payments to a federal agency that would funnel the money to recipients and be responsible for collecting delinquent payments. Like other federal entitlement programs, the government would make appropriate payments to children even if their parents do not.

For Further Study

Books

Leonard, Robin, and Stephen Elias. *Family Law,* 3rd ed. Berkeley: Nolo Press, 1994.

Lyster, Mimi E. *Child Custody: Building Agreements That Work.* Berkeley: Nolo Press, 1995.

Warshak, Richard A. *The Custody Revolution: The Father Factor and the Motherhood Mystique.* New York: Poseidon Press, 1992.

Periodicals

Kellman, Susan. "Child Custody and Support: Does the System Serve Children's Best Interest?" *CQ Researcher* 5, January 13, 1995, p. 27.

Van Biema, David. "Dunning Deadbeats." *Time* 145, April 3, 1995, p. 49.

Organizations

ABA Center on Children and the Law
Address: 1800 S Street NW, Suite 200 South
Washington, DC 20036
Telephone: (202) 331-2250

Children's Rights Council (CRC)
Address: 220 Eye St. NE, Suite 200
Washington, DC 20002
Telephone: (202) 547-6227

Joint Custody Association
Address: 10606 Wilkins Ave.
Los Angeles, CA 90024

Parents Sharing Custody (PSC)
Address: 420 S. Beverly Dr., Suite 100
Beverly Hills, CA 90212-4410
Telephone: (310) 286-9171

Ability Grouping

Ability grouping, or tracking, is the practice of separating students into achievement groups and tailoring their curriculum accordingly.

Ability grouping became widely used in American schools of the 1920s as an influx of immigrants entered the school system. IQ tests were administered to determine the ability levels of students, who were then placed in programs that matched their scores. Low-scoring students were given instruction that would prepare them for vocational or unskilled labor, and the high scorers were given college-preparatory work.

Tracking is still the standard practice in most schools in the United States, although current tracking tends to place more emphasis on separating the slower learners from faster learners. Students who need more attention—either because they have trouble keeping up with their schoolwork or because they are ahead of the class and need extra stimulus—are separated and given a curriculum more suited to them. Schools can begin to group students by their abilities at any stage in the educational process. Some schools use psychological and educational testing to group students by their respective abilities before they start kindergarten. Many elementary schools have a loosely organized tracking system of different level reading or math groups that operate within the same classroom. Ability grouping is used most in high schools, where some students follow a college-preparatory track while others take basic skills courses.

Proponents of ability grouping argue that a single, generalized curriculum short-changes both high-achieving and low-achieving students. They point to the advantages it offers to gifted students, who may not thrive unless they are challenged, as well as to slower learners, who may tire of trying and failing to keep up with their peers. But critics of ability grouping cite evidence that students placed on a lower track may be discouraged from achievement. Low-track students are often wrongly placed—a disproportionate number of African American and Latino students end up on a low track. Low-track students can be closed out of educational opportunity because they are not signed up for college-preparatory classes, and they do not realize that they cannot enter college without certain math and languages courses. It can also be very difficult for a student to get out of a low ability grouping once he or she is placed in one. The reasons children are placed in a particular grouping may on occasion be arbitrary, yet the decision has enormous repercussions for individual students. Low expectations for the students placed in a lower track seem to affect these students' confidence, and they are at highest risk for dropping out of school.

Many schools or school systems are trying to eliminate ability grouping. These schools help both the low- and high-track students adjust to one curriculum. For example, high-achieving students can tutor slower students, thus reinforcing their knowledge of a subject. Untracked schools may use more hands-on activities and interdisciplinary projects that students of differing abilities can respond to in different ways.

Untracked schools encourage students to have high expectations for themselves, and let students see how their own educational choices lead to different career paths. Guidance counseling has been shown to be extremely important in untracked high schools. Counselors encourage students to choose courses that will help them meet a specific job-related goal. These schools teach all students what going to college requires in terms of preparatory course work, study skills, and financial planning. Some of these schools have had exceptional results. One program in San Diego decreased its high school drop-out rate by almost 40%, and nearly 100% of the graduates of the program went on to college.

If parents are concerned about ability grouping in their child's school, they may want to meet with school officials and discuss their child's placement. If a school is untracked, parents may need to make sure their child is getting appropriate individualized instruction. Most children will probably benefit from an egalitarian system. But very gifted students may still be unchallenged, and students with learning difficulties may still need extra instruction. Magnet schools or specialized programs may provide more suitable instruction for children with particular educational needs.

For Further Study

Books

Oakes, Jeannie. *Keeping Track: How Schools Structure Inequality,* New Haven, CT: Yale University Press, 1985.

Wheelock, Ann. *Crossing the Tracks: How "Untracking" Can Save America's Schools.* New York, NY: New Press, 1992.

Periodicals

Barko, Naomi."Tracking: Does It Hurt or Help Kids?" *Parents Magazine* 71, January 1996, pp. 125+.

Daniels, Lee A. "Derailing a System." *Emerge* 7, September 1996, pp. 64+.

de Vinck, Christopher. "'I Am Not a Turtle' and Other Tragedies of Tracking." *Education Digest* 59, February 1994, pp. 40+.

Holmes. C. Thomas, and Thomas J. Ahr. "Effects of Ability Grouping on Academic Achievement and Self-Concept of African-American and White Students." *The Clearing House* 67, May–June 1994, pp. 294+.

Audiovisual Recordings

Brandt, Ron, et al. *Tracking: Road to Success or Dead End?* Alexandria, VA: Association for Supervision Curriculum Development, 1992.
(Two 90-minute sound cassettes.)

—A. Woodward

Abortion

Invasive procedure resulting in pregnancy termination and death of the fetus.

Abortion is the final consequence of a woman's decision to terminate her pregnancy. In the U.S., more than 50% of the pregnancies are unintended, and 50% of these end in abortion. More than half (53%) of the unplanned pregnancies happen among the 10% of women who practice no contraception. Most women getting abortions are young: 55% are under 25, including 21% teenagers.

While abortion is practiced throughout society, in all socioeconomic strata, poor women are three times more likely to have an abortion than her well-off counterpart.

White women have 63% of all abortions, but the non-white abortion rate is more than twice the white rate—54 per 1,000 versus 20 per 1,000. About 93% of all abortions are performed for social, not medical, reasons; in other words, most abortions are, from the medical point of view, unnecessary: the mother's health and life and not in jeopardy, and there are no abnormalities which would justify the termination of the fetus's life. Social reasons include fear of motherhood, fear of losing a partner who doesn't want children, fear of parental and social disapproval, financial difficulties, lack of support, and psychological problems, among others.

Abortion is a complex issue which raises a plethora of medical, ethical, political, legal, and psychological questions, and is viewed by proponents and opponents as one of society's fundamental problems. "Abortion," Paul D. Simmons has written (Butler and Walbert, 1992), "is related to life and death, sexuality and procreation—all of which are integrally related in the human psyche." While the "pro-choice" camp defends a woman's right to terminate her pregnancy, "pro-life" forces define abortion as murder. As commentators have noted, dialogue between the two camps has been difficult, seemingly impossible, because opinions are often based on feelings and beliefs. An additional obstacle to dialogue is the fact that the two opposing sides use fundamentally different discourses. Pro-life discourse often draws its strength from the Christian axiom about the sanctity of life, while pro-choice thinking proceeds from the belief that an individual has the freedom to act in her best interest.

While vulnerable to moral condemnation, and even harassment, adult women have the protection of liberal legislation in seeking an abortion (in *Roe v. Wade,* 1973, the U.S. Supreme Court ruled that abortion is a constitutional right). Teenagers, however, are subject to state laws; in 25 states, a minor cannot seek an abortion without parental consent. Traditionally, any medical treatment of a minor requires parental consent, and as the Planned Parenthood Fact Sheet "Teenagers, Abortion, and Government Intrusion Laws" points out, a physician treating a minor without parental consent is committing the common law tort of battery. However, except "in the area of abortion, there have never been criminal penalties for treating a minor on her own consent."

Despite more restrictive legislation, teenage abortions have declined since 1980, according to the 1994 report *Sex and America's Teenagers,* as "fewer teens are becoming pregnant, and in recent years, fewer pregnant teens have chosen to have an abortion." In 1992 in the U.S., there were about 308,000 teen abortions, which amounts to nearly 40% of pregnancies (excluding miscarriages) among teenagers. In general, 61% of teenage abortions are performed with the knowledge of at least one parent, and the informed parents mostly support their daughter's decision to have an abortion.

While the decreased incidence in teenage pregnancy in the U.S. during the last several years, along with the somewhat reduced number of abortions, may seem like an encouraging trend, it is important to point out that teen pregnancy rates are still much higher in the U.S. than in other prosperous countries: twice the rate of Canada, and nine times the rates of the Netherlands and Japan.

For Further Study

Books

Butler, J. Douglas, and David F. Walbert, eds. *Abortion, Medicine, and the Law.* 4th rev. ed. New York: Facts On File, 1992.

Donovan, Patricia. *Our Daughters' Decisions: The Conflict in State Law on Abortion and Other Issues.* New York: Alan Guttmacher Institute, 1992.

Hern, Warren M. *Abortion Practice.* Philadelphia: J. B. Lippincott, 1984.

Sex and America's Teenagers. New York: Alan Guttmacher Institute, 1994.

Periodicals

Darroch Forrest, Jacqueline, and Jennifer J. Frost. "The Family Planning Attitudes and Experiences of Low-Income Women." *Family Planning Perspectives* 28, no. 6, November–December, 1996, pp. 246–55.

"Health Care: Teens Can Go It Alone." *Science* 253, 1991, p. 29.

"Mandatory Parental Consent to Abortion." (Report of the American Medical Association's Council on Ethical and Judicial Affairs.) *Journal of the American Medical Association* 269, no. 1, January 6, 1993, pp. 82–86.

Matthews, Stephen, David Ribar, and Mark Wilhelm. "The Effects of Economic Conditions and Access to Reproductive Health Services on State Abortion Rates and Birthrates." *Family Planning Perspectives* 29, no. 2, March–April 1997, pp. 52-60.

Rogers, James L., et al. "Impact of the Minnesota Parental Notification Law on Abortion and Birth." *American Journal of Public Health* 81, 1991, pp. 294–98.

"Teenagers, Abortion, and Government Intrusion Laws." (Planned Parenthood Fact Sheet). New York: Planned Parenthood Federation of America, October 1992.

Torres, Aida, and Jacqueline Darroch Forrest. "Why Do Women Have Abortions?" *Family Planning Perspectives* 20, no. 4, July–August 1988.

Wattleton, Faye. "Teenage Pregnancies and the Recriminalization of Abortions." *American Journal of Public Health* 80, 1990, pp. 269–70.

—Zoran Minderovic

Abuse *see* **Child Abuse, Physical** and **Child Abuse, Sexual and Emotional**

Academic Curriculum *see* **Curriculum**

Accidents *see* **Childproofing** and **Safety**

Acculturation

The process of adapting to or adopting the practices of a culture different from one's own.

Acculturation is the process of learning about and adapting to a new culture. A new culture may require adjustments in all or some of the aspects of daily living, including language, work, shopping, housing, children's schooling, health care, recreation, and social life. Relocation to a society that is similar to one's own requires less acculturation than moving to a society where cultural norms are unfamiliar. For example, moving to a society where women's roles are different from those of one's home culture can cause feelings of isolation and confusion for the adult women of the family.

Children's well-being and successful adjustment to a new culture is a concern for parents. By about age 11, many children begin to experience feelings of loss when leaving a familiar culture, friends, and comfortable surroundings. Young children adjusting to a new cultural environment take their cues from their parents and teachers. Members of the family who have regular opportunities to interact with their new community—working outside the home or going to school—begin the process of acculturation earlier than those who remain at home.

Acculturation is different in subtle ways from assimilation: assimilation involves being absorbed into the new culture. A popular metaphor for this process was introduced in 1908 by the playwright Israel Zangwill with his work, *The Melting Pot.* Acculturation, on the other hand, is the process of learning the practices and customs of a new culture. People can assimilate without being acculturated. The distinctively dressed Hasidim of Brooklyn or the Mormons of Utah are not completely acculturated to contemporary American society, but they are assimilated. Understanding the distinction between acculturation and assimilation is important for public policy and for society's ability to grow and function smoothly.

A homogeneous consumer culture worldwide has changed the nature of acculturation. People all over the globe watch the same news reports on CNN, rent the same movies, watch the same television programs, eat the same pizzas and burgers from fast food franchises, and many of the world's families have made at least one visit to a Disney theme park. Immigrants to a new country may already be very familiar with the customs and lifestyle of their new home.

Cultural pluralism and multiculturalism

American sociologist Horace Kallen argues that it is unrealistic and counterproductive to force new immigrants to abandon their familiar, lifelong cultural attributes when they arrive in the United States. Instead of the concept of the "melting pot," Kallen prescribed what he called "cultural pluralism." Cultural pluralism interprets U.S. society as a federation rather than a union. Sometimes referred to as multiculturalism, this approach suggests that each group of ethnic Americans has rights, such as representation in government according to their percentage of the total population, and the right to speak and work in their native language, even if it is not the language of their birth. However, English-language culture and social influences continue to dominate, but African American, Hispanic, Jewish, Italian, Asian, and other ethnic influences are certainly apparent.

For Further Study

Books

Apfel, Roberta J. and Simon, Bennett, eds. *Minefields in Their Hearts: The Mental Health of Children in War and Communal Violence.* New Haven: Yale University Press, 1996.

Gordon, Milton Myron. *Assimilation in American Life: The Role of Race, Religion, and National Origins.* New York: Oxford University Press, 1964.

Salins, Peter D. *Assimilation, American Style.* New York: Basic Books, 1997.

Periodicals

Jacobson, Adam R. "Changing With the Times." *Hispanic* 7, March 1994, pp. 20+.

Portes, Alejandro, and Min Zhou. "Should Immigrants Assimilate?" *The Public Interest,* Summer 1994, pp. 18+.

Richey, Marilyn. "Global Families: Surviving an Overseas Move." *Management Review* 85, June 1996, pp. 57+.

Acetaminophen

One of several medications used to reduce fever and other general symptoms of illness, such as body aches and headache.

Acetaminophen, sold without a prescription from a physician, is one of several medications used to treat fever and to relieve pain and general illness symptoms. (Other medications of this type, known as antipyretic, or fever-reducing, agents are **aspirin** and ibuprofen. Aspirin may cause stomach upset, and is associated with Reye syndrome, and is therefore not recommended for children in most situations.) Acetaminophen may be purchased in generic form, and under several trade names, such as Panadol®, Tempra®, and Tylenol®. Dosage of all medications—including acetaminophen—should be determined by a child's weight, not his or her age. However, unless a child is exceptionally under- or overweight for his or her age, it is generally safe to follow the age/weight/dosage charts provided on the acetaminophen product label. In general, babies under the age of three months should not be given acetaminophen—or any other medication—without consulting a physician first. For children, acetaminophen comes in liquid form, in elixir (syrup) form for the toddler, in chewable tablets for the preschool child, and in tablets or capsules to be swallowed for older children and adults.

In the accompanying table, dosages are given in milliliters (ml); 5 ml equals 1 teaspoon (tsp.). Dosage may be repeated every four hours, but should not be given more than five times per 24-hour period.

Acne

A chronic inflammation of the sebaceous glands embedded in the skin.

Acne is the chronic inflammation of the sebaceous glands, normally acquired in **adolescence** between the ages of 14 and 18, that usually resolves itself by the time the individual is 20–30 years old.

RECOMMENDED DOSAGE: ACETAMINOPHEN

Age of child	Weight	Liquid dose	Elixir	Chewable tablets
		80 milligrams of medication in 0.8 ml	160 milligrams of medication in 5 ml	80 milligrams of medication per tablet
0–3 months	6–11 lbs. (2.7–5 kg)	0.4 ml		
4–11 months	12–17 lbs. (5.5–7.7 kg)	0.8 ml	¾ tsp.	1 tablet
12–23 months	18–23 lbs. (8.2–10.5 kg)	1.2 ml	¾ tsp.	1½ tablets
2–3 years	24–35 lbs. (10.9–15.9 kg)	1.6 ml	1 tsp.	2 tablets
4–5 years	36–47 lbs. (16.3–21.4 kg)	2.4 ml	1¾ tsp.	3 tablets
6–8 years	48–59 lbs. (21.8–26.8 kg)	2 tsp.	2 tsp.	4 tablets
9–10 years	60–71 lbs. (27.3–32.3 kg)	2½ tsp.	2½ tsp.	5 tablets
11–12 years	72–95 lbs. (32.7–43.2 kg)	3 tsp.	3 tsp.	6 tablets

Contrary to popular myth, acne is not caused or aggravated by eating greasy foods or chocolate. Acne is associated with heavy sebum secretion caused by **hormones.** Androgens (male hormones) stimulate sebum secretion and estrogen (a female hormone) reduces sebum production.

While the tendency to develop acne is passed from parent to child through genetics, certain practices can aggravate acne outbreak. Acne can be caused by mechanical itrritation, including pulling or stretching the skin, as often happens in athletic activities. Taking steroids can also aggravate acne because steroid drugs contain androgens. Adolescent women who use oil-based cosmetics and moisturizers can also have an aggravated case of acne.

The inflammation that defines acne results from the plugging of the sebaceous ducts, which lead from the sebaceous gland to the surface of the skin. Once plugged, the duct becomes inflamed and pustular. In some individuals the acne pustules are few, infrequent, and isolated. In others the condition is pronounced, with widespread pustule development.

Acne is not a debilitating medical condition, but people find it unsightly and may be unduly embarrassed and worried about their appearance. Since the pustules principally appear on the face, they are quite noticeable. Teenagers tend to be more self-conscious than older people, and so even mild acne can be quite distressing.

Manipulating or squeezing acne pustules can cause deep and permanent scarring. Washing the affected area with a germicidal soap and an abrasive sponge will help dislodge the material plugging the duct. Because estrogen inhibits the development of acne, taking birth control pills may alleviate acne in young women. A topical antibiotic may also prove helpful. For deeper acne, injected antibiotics may be necessary.

For Further Study

Books

Fulton, James E. Jr., and Elizabeth Black. *Dr. Fulton's Step-by-Step Program for Clearing Acne.* New York: Harper and Row, 1983.

Marks, Ronald. *Acne: Advice on Clearing Your Skin.* New York: Arco Publishing, 1984.

Roberts, Jean. *Skin Conditions of Youths 12–17 Years, United States: Prevalence of Facial Acne and Other Skin Condi-*

tions of Youths in the United States by Age, Sex, Race, Geographic Region, and Socioeconomic Background. Rockville, MD: U.S. Dept. of Health, Education, and Welfare, Public Health Service, Health Resources Administration, National Center for Health Statistics, 1989.

Willis, Judith Levine. *Acne Agony.* Rockville, MD: Food and Drug Administration, 1992.

Acting Out

A defense mechanism whereby an individual expresses feelings through behavior rather than word.

The term "acting out" was first coined to describe the behavior exhibited by a patient in expressing inner feelings about his or her psychoanalyst in a psychotherapy session. By the mid-1990s, the expression had acquired a broader definition, and was used to describe any situation where an individual's behavior seemed to reflect the expression of unconscious feelings or conflicts in actions rather than words. Acting out behavior may range from mildly disruptive in a preschool or home setting to dangerous, such as self-harm or suicidal gestures. In children, acting out may result in social isolation and limit his or her ability to engage in and learn from new experiences.

Children may act out as a way to express powerful, painful, and/or confusing feelings that they are unable to verbalize. Parents and teachers dealing with acting out behavior often select a two-pronged approach, depending upon the severity of the situation. The first strategy is aimed at managing the behavior itself: the adult helps the child to learn to substitute an acceptable behavior as an expression of his or her feelings. Secondly, the adult may want to support the child in investigating and dealing with the feelings he or she is expressing in acting out behavior. This investigation often requires the guidance of a trained child psychologist or psychotherapist.

For Further Study

Books

Firestone, Robert W., and Joyce Catlett. *Psychological Defenses in Everyday Life.* New York: Human Sciences Press, 1989.

Kernberg, Paulina F., and Saralea E. Chazan. *Children with Conduct Disorders: A Psychotherapy Manual.* New York: Basic Books, 1991.

Toth, Michele. *Understanding and Treating Conduct Disorders.* Austin, TX: Pro-Ed, 1990.

Periodicals

Yorke, Clifford. "Childhood and the Unconscious." *American Imago* 53, Fall 1996, pp. 227+.

Action for Children's Television

The best-known public interest group aimed at improving the quality of children's television programming in the United States.

The organization Action for Children's Television (ACT) was founded in 1968 in a suburb of Boston by Peggy Charren, a mother concerned about the content of the television programs she saw her children watching at home. Its initial efforts were aimed at advertisers. In 1970 the group filed a petition with the FCC to ban commercials from children's programs altogether, petitioning in subsequent years for more limited concessions, such as a prohibition on advertising specific products, including toys, food, and vitamins. In 1973, largely in response to the actions of ACT, the National Association of Broadcasters adopted revised codes prohibiting the hosts of children's television programs from appearing in commercials aimed at children and limiting the amount of commercial time in children's programming to 12 minutes per hour (a limit that was further reduced two years later to 10 minutes and nine-and-a-half on weekends).

Advocates of better children's television enjoyed further successes in the 1970s, as the networks introduced a substantial amount of educational programming, including Afterschool Specials on ABC and, on CBS, a special newsmagazine program for children modeled on the popular adult program *60 Minutes.* By 1980 the FCC was giving serious consideration to a measure requiring television stations to broadcast a minimum amount of educational programming every day, but it was scuttled when the agency changed hands after Ronald Reagan was elected to the presidency. During the following decade, ACT's major targets included television programs that featured popular **toys**, such as G. I. Joe, and were often referred to as half-hour commercials. It also opposed the proposed introduction of a channel featuring advertiser-based news programming into the schools.

At one point, ACT, with its four-member staff (including Charren), had as many as 20,000 volunteers nationwide working in support of its lobbying, research, and educational efforts. Its annual budget, derived from both public and private sources, was said to be as high as $400,000 or $500,000, which covered the costs of salaries, consulting and legal fees, office rent, publications, transportation, and other expenses. In 1989 the National Academy of Television Arts and Sciences awarded Peggy Charren its prestigious Trustees' Award in recognition of her contribution to the industry, and a counterpart to ACT was launched in Britain. The following year Action for Children's Television saw many of its efforts come to fruition with Congress's passage of the 1990

Children's Television Act, which incorporates two of ACT's long-sought reforms: the legal establishment of advertising limits in children's programming and minimum standards governing the amount of educational programming that must be aired in order for television stations to retain their licenses.

Having accomplished two of its major goals, Action for Children's Television disbanded in 1992, contributing $125,000 of its remaining funds for a lecture series on children and the media at the Harvard University Graduate School of Education, and another $5,000 for graduate school research fellowships. The 63-year-old Charren voiced the hope that people concerned about the future of children's television programming would support organizations such as the Center for Media Education, a public interest group charged with monitoring television stations' compliance with the Children's Television Act.

For Further Study

Books

Alperowicz, Cynthia. *Fighting TV Stereotypes: An ACT Handbook.* Newtonville, MA: Action for Children's Television, 1983.

Fischer, Stuart. *Kids' TV: The First 25 Years.* New York: Facts on File Publications, 1983.

Sarson, Evelyn. *National Symposium on the Effect on Children of Television Programming and Advertising.* Action for Children's Television. New York: Discus Books, 1971.

Schneider, Cy. *Children's Television: The Art, the Business, and How It Works.* Chicago: National Textbook Company, 1987.

Van Evra, Judith Page. *Television and Child Development.* Hillsdale, NJ: L. Erlbaum, 1990.

Winn, Marie. *The Plug-in Drug.* New York: Viking, 1985.

Adaptation

Behavior that enables an organism to function effectively in its environment.

Adaptation describes the process whereby an organism adapts to, or learns to survive in, its environment. The process is crucial to natural selection, enabling those organisms or species best suited to a particular environment to survive. Ethologists, scientists who study the behavior of animals in their natural habitats from an evolutionary perspective, document adaptive behavior.

Adaptation occurs in individual organisms as well as in species. Sensory adaptation consists of physical changes in sense organs in response to the presence or cessation of stimuli. Examples include the adjustment by pupils of the eyes when moving from bright light into a darkened room, or the way in which the sense of touch

becomes accustomed to the sensation of cold after an initial plunge into water. Once a steady level of stimulation (such as light, sound, or odor) is established, the organism's sensors adjust, and no longer respond actively to it. However, any abrupt changes in stimulus require further adaptation.

The adrenalin-produced reactions to environmental dangers, including rapid breathing, increased heart rate, and sweating, are collectively referred to as the "fight or flight" response. These reactions are considered a form of adaptation. The ability to learn new responses, as in **classical** and **operant conditioning,** is another form of adaptation.

The process of adaptation begins in infancy. Infants become more efficient as they nurse and with each year acquire behavior that will enable them to succeed. In the preschool years, the child learns to function or adapt to his environment by emulating and imitating the behavior of others. These adaptive behavior skills are vital to a child's successful development.

For Further Study

Books

Haggerty, Robert J., et al. *Stress, Risk, and Resilience in Children and Adolescents: Processes, Mechanisms, and Interventions.* New York: Cambridge University, 1994.

Harrison, G. A. *Human Adaptation.* New York: Oxford University Press, 1993.

Lorenz, Konrad. *The Foundations of Ethology.* New York: Springer-Verlag, 1981.

Nesse, Randolph M., and George C. Williams. *Why We Get Sick: The New Science of Darwinian Medicine.* 1st ed. New York: Times Books, 1994.

Adaptive Behavior Scale for Infants and Early Childhood (ABSI)

Assesses general maturation, learning, and social adjustment in young children.

The Adaptive Behavior Scale for Infants and Early Childhood (ABSI) is a test of general maturation, learning, and social adjustment for children from birth to six years. It is used as an aid in preschool placement and program planning, and may be used with children who are mentally retarded, developmentally disabled, or physically handicapped. The examiner interviews a parent, teacher, or other adult close to the child to obtain information about the following areas: independent functioning (includes self-help skills such as dressing, eating, and bathing); physical development (locomotion and control of the body); **communication skills**; conceptual skills (such as knowledge of time, shapes, and quantity); play skills; self-direction (including initiative and **attention** span); personal responsibility; and socialization. The ABSI can be used to determine delays in cognitive or communication development, **brain** damage and other sensorimotor problems, and major psychological problems.

For Further Study

Books

Culbertson, Jan L., and Diane J. Willis, eds. *Testing Young Children: A Reference Guide for Developmental, Psychoeducational, and Psychosocial Assessments.* Austin, TX: PRO-ED, Inc., 1993.

McCullough, Virginia. *Testing and Your Child: What You Should Know About 150 of the Most Common Medical, Educational, and Psychological Tests.* New York: Plume, 1992.

Adjustment Disorders

Category of mental disorder featuring significant emotional or behavioral symptoms in response to an identifiable event that precipitated significant psychological or social stress.

Adjustment disorders are maladpative responses to stressful or psychologically distressing life events, such as being placed in **day care** for the first time, being injured in an accident, or experiencing a natural disaster. The diagnosis of an adjustment disorder requires that the inappropriate emotional or behavioral symptoms develop within three months of the stressful event or occurrence.

The **American Psychological Association** (APA) has identified and catagorized several varieties of adjustment disorders, depending on accompanying symptoms and their duration. These subtypes and their related symptoms are as follows:

1.) adjustment disorder with depressed mood, marked by tearfulness and feelings of intense discouragement;

2.) adjustment disorder with **anxiety,** where the individual appears extremely nervous or jittery, or the child displays an unusual or intense fear of being separated from parents, **caregiver**s, or other significant adults;

3.) adjustment disorder with disturbance of conduct, where the major symptom is the breaking of societal norms or rules through vandalism, **truancy**, physical aggression, or other inappropriate behavior.

Two other subtypes, *with mixed anxiety and depressed mood* and *with mixed disturbance of emotions and conduct,* allow for the diagnosis of an individual displaying more than one category of symptoms.

In addition, adjustment disorders can be classified as acute (lasting less than six months) or chronic (lasting more than six months). Adjustment disorders are fairly common; in the mid-1990s, it was estimated that 5–20% of persons seeking outpatient psychological treatment suffered from an adjustment disorder. However, adjustment disorders can occur at any age, and appear to affect males and females equally.

Symptoms of these various adjustment disorders include a decrease in performance at school and withdrawal from social relationships. Adjustment disorders can lead to suicidal thinking or complicate the course of other diseases when, for instance, a sufferer loses interest in taking medication as prescribed or adhering to difficult diets or exercise regimens.

Adjustment disorders can occur at any stage of life. In early **adolescence**, individuals with adjustment disorders tend to be angry, aggressive, and defiant. Temper **tantrums** are common and are usually well out of balance with the event that caused them. Alternatively, adolescents with adjustment disorders may become passive and withdrawn. Older teenagers often experience intense anxiety and **depression**, or what psychologists call "depersonalization," a state in which a person feels he can observe his body interacting with others, but feels nothing.

Many psychological theorists and researchers consider adjustment disorders in adolescents as a stage in establishing an identity. Adolescents may develop adjustment disorders as part of a **defense mechanism** meant to break their feelings of dependence on their parents. This psychological maneuver may precipitate problems in families as adolescents begin seeking individuals outside the family as replacements for their parents. This can be particularly destructive when these feelings of dependence are transferred to involvement with **gangs** or **cults**.

For Further Study

Books

Doft, Norma. *When Your Child Needs Help.* 1st ed. New York: Harmony Books, 1992.

Varma, Ved P. *The Management of Children With Emotional and Behavioural Difficulties.* New York: Routledge, 1990.

Periodicals

Shanok, Rebecca. "Coping with Crisis." *Parents Magazine,* October 1991, p. 169.

Organizations

American Academy of Child and Adolescent Psychiatry
    Address: 3615 Wisconsin Avenue, NW
    Washington, DC 20016-3007
    Telephone: (202) 966-7300

website: http://www.aacap.org
(Profesional organization that provides education about psychiatric disorders affecting children and adolescents.)

The Federation of Families for Children's Mental Health
Address: 1021 Prince Street
Alexandria, VA 22314-2971
Telephone: (703)684-7710
(A national parent-run organization focused on the needs of children and youth with emotional, behavioral, or mental disorders and their families.)

Adler, Alfred (1870–1937)

Psychiatrist known for his theory of individual psychology and for his pioneering work with children and families.

Alfred Adler was born in a middle-class suburb of Vienna, Austria, in 1870 and decided on medicine as his calling at an early age. After graduating from the University of Vienna medical school in 1895, he at first practiced ophthalmology but later switched to psychiatry. In 1902 Adler became part of Sigmund Freud's circle, joining the discussion group that later became the Vienna Psychoanalytic Society and rising in its ranks to eventually become its president and editor of its journal. However, after 1907 Adler's growing disagreement with Freud's theories, especially with their heavy emphasis on the role of sexuality in personality formation, alienated him from the ranks of Freudians.

In 1926 Adler began dividing his time between Vienna and the United States, where he was appointed visiting lecturer at Columbia in 1927. In 1932 he became a lecturer at the Long Island College of Medicine and emigrated to the United States with his wife. Adler died suddenly in 1937 in Aberdeen, Scotland, while on a lecture tour. Today there are more than 100 professional Adlerian organizations and 34 training institutes in the United States, Canada, and Europe.

In 1911, Adler and his followers left the Psychoanalytic Society to form their own group and develop the system of individual psychology, a holistic, humanistic therapeutic approach that views the individual as primarily a social rather than a sexual being and places more emphasis on choices and values than Freudian psychology. At the center of Adlerian psychology is the individual striving toward perfection and overcoming feelings of inferiority (a concept later popularized—somewhat mistakenly—as the "inferiority complex"). During World War I, Adler served in military hospitals for three years. After the war, he became interested in child psychology and established a network of public child guidance clinics in the Vienna school system, offering what was probably the very first family counseling. A therapist would interview family members before a selected audience of parents

and teachers and provide feedback about their situation. There were 28 of these facilities in operation until the Nazis ordered them closed in 1934. Adlerian parent study groups still meet throughout the United States and Canada.

For Further Study

Books

Christensen, Oscar C., ed. *Adlerian Family Counseling: A Manual for Counselor, Educator, and Psychotherapist.* Minneapolis: Educational Media Corp., 1993.

Hoffman, Edward. *The Drive for Self: Alfred Adler and the Founding of Individual Psychology.* Reading, MA: Addison-Wesley Publishing Co., 1994.

Manaster, Guy J., ed. *Alfred Adler, As We Remember Him.* Chicago: North American Society of Adlerian Psychology, 1977.

Rattner, Josef. *Alfred Adler.* New York: F. Ungar, 1983.

Stepansky, Paul E. *In Freud's Shadow: Adler in Context.* Hillside, NJ: Analytic Press, 1983.

—Rosalie Wieder

Adolescence

Sometimes referred to as teenage years, youth, or puberty, adolescence covers the period from roughly age 10 to 20 in a child's development.

> Adolescence is a border between adulthood and childhood, and as such it has a richness and diversity unmatched by any other life stage. ...Adolescents are travelers, far from home with no native land, neither children nor adults. They are jet-setters who fly from one country to another with amazing speed. Sometimes they are four years old, an hour later they are twenty-five. They don't really fit anywhere. There's a yearning for place, a search for solid ground.
>
> —A description of adolescents by Mary Pipher in her 1994 book, *Reviving Ophelia.*

In the study of child development, adolescence refers to the second decade of the life span, roughly from ages 10 to 20. The word adolescence is Latin in origin, derived from the verb *adolescere,* which means "to grow into adulthood." In all societies, adolescence is a time of growing up, of moving from the immaturity of childhood into the maturity of adulthood. Population projections indicate that the percent of the U.S. population between the ages of 14 and 17 will peak around the year 2005.

POPULATION PROJECTIONS		
Year	Population, ages 14–17 (1,000)	Percent of population ages 14–17
2000	15,752	5.7%
2005	16,986	5.9%
2010	16,894	5.7%
2025	17,872	5.3%
2050	21,206	5.4%

Source: U.S. Bureau of Census, Current Population Reports, P25-1130.

There is no single event or boundary line that denotes the end of childhood or the beginning of adolescence. Rather, experts think of the passage from childhood into and through adolescence as composed of a *set* of transitions that unfold gradually and that touch upon many aspects of the individual's behavior, development, and relationships. These transitions are biological, cognitive, social, and emotional.

Puberty

The *biological transition* of adolescence, or **puberty**, is perhaps the most salient sign that adolescence has begun. Technically, puberty refers to the period during which an individual becomes capable of sexual reproduction. More broadly speaking, however, puberty is used as a collective term to refer to all the physical changes that occur in the growing girl or boy as the individual passes from childhood into adulthood.

The timing of physical maturation varies widely. In the United States today, **menarche,** the first menstrual period, typically occurs around age 12, although some youngsters start puberty when they are only eight or nine, others when they are well into their teens. The duration of puberty also varies greatly: eighteen months to six years in girls and two to five years in boys.

The physical changes of puberty are triggered by **hormones**, chemical substances in the body that act on specific organs and tissues. In boys a major change is the increased production of **testosterone,** a male sex hormone, while girls experience increased production of the female hormone **estrogen.** In both sexes, a rise in growth hormone produces the adolescent growth spurt, the pronounced increase in height and weight that marks the first half of puberty.

Perhaps the most dramatic changes of puberty involve sexuality. Internally, through the development of primary sexual characteristics, adolescents become capable of sexual reproduction. Externally, as secondary sexual characteristics appear, girls and boys begin to look like mature women and men. In boys primary and secondary sexual characteristics usually emerge in a predictable order, with rapid growth of the testes and scrotum, accompanied by the appearance of pubic hair. About a year later, when the growth spurt begins, the penis also grows larger, and pubic hair becomes coarser, thicker, and darker. Later still comes the growth of facial and body hair, and a gradual lowering of the voice. Around mid-adolescence internal changes begin making a boy capable of producing and ejaculating sperm.

In girls, sexual characteristics develop in a less regular sequence. Usually, the first sign of puberty is a slight elevation of the breasts, but sometimes this is preceded by the appearance of pubic hair. Pubic hair changes from sparse and downy to denser and coarser. Concurrent with these changes is further breast development. In teenage girls, internal sexual changes include maturation of the uterus, vagina, and other parts of the reproductive system. Menarche, the first menstrual period, happens relatively late, not at the start of puberty as many people believe. Regular ovulation and the ability to carry a baby to full term usually follow menarche by several years.

For many years, psychologists believed that puberty was stressful for young people. We now know that any difficulties associated with adjusting to puberty are minimized if adolescents know what changes to expect and have positive attitudes toward them. Although the immediate impact of puberty on the adolescent's self-image and mood may be very modest, the *timing* of physical maturation does affect the teen's social and emotional development in important ways. Early-maturing boys tend to be more popular, to have more positive self-conceptions, and to be more self-assured than their later-maturing peers, whereas early-maturing girls may feel awkward and self-conscious.

Cognitive transition

A second element of the passage through adolescence is a *cognitive transition.* Compared to children, adolescents think in ways that are more advanced, more efficient, and generally more complex. This can be seen in five ways.

First, during adolescence individuals become better able than children to think about what is possible, instead of limiting their thought to what is real. Whereas children's thinking is oriented to the here and now—that is, to things and events that they can observe directly, adolescents are able to consider what they observe against a backdrop of what is possible—they can think hypothetically.

Second, during the passage into adolescence, individuals become better able to think about abstract ideas.

For example, adolescents find it easier than children to comprehend the sorts of higher-order, abstract logic inherent in puns, proverbs, metaphors, and analogies. The adolescent's greater facility with abstract thinking also permits the application of advanced reasoning and logical processes to social and ideological matters. This is clearly seen in the adolescent's increased facility and interest in thinking about interpersonal relationships, politics, philosophy, religion, and morality—topics that involve such abstract concepts as friendship, faith, democracy, fairness, and honesty.

Third, during adolescence individuals begin thinking more often about the process of thinking itself, or metacognition. As a result, adolescents may display increased introspection and self-consciousness. Although improvements in metacognitive abilities provide important intellectual advantages, one potentially negative by-product of these advances is the tendency for adolescents to develop a sort of egocentrism, or intense preoccupation with the self. Acute adolescent egocentrism sometimes leads teenagers to believe that others are constantly watching and evaluating them, much as an audience glues its attention to an actor on a stage. Psychologists refer to this as the *imaginary audience.*

A fourth change in cognition is that thinking tends to become multidimensional, rather than limited to a single issue. Whereas children tend to think about things one aspect at a time, adolescents can see things through more complicated lenses. Adolescents describe themselves and others in more differentiated and complicated terms and find it easier to look at problems from multiple perspectives. Being able to understand that people's personalities are not one-sided, or that social situations can have different interpretations, depending on one's point of view, permits the adolescent to have far more sophisticated—and complicated—relationships with other people.

Finally, adolescents are more likely than children to see things as relative, rather than absolute. Children tend to see things in absolute terms—in black and white. Adolescents, in contrast, tend to see things as relative. They are more likely to question others' assertions and less likely to accept "facts" as absolute truths. This increase in relativism can be particularly exasperating to parents, who may feel that their adolescent children question everything just for the sake of argument. Difficulties often arise, for example, when adolescents begin seeing their parents' values as excessively relative.

Emotional transition

In addition to being a time of biological and cognitive change, adolescence is also a period of *emotional transition* and, in particular, changes in the way individuals view themselves and in their capacity to function independently.

During adolescence, important shifts occur in the way individuals think about and characterize themselves—that is, in their self-conceptions. As individuals mature intellectually and undergo the sorts of cognitive changes described earlier, they come to perceive themselves in more sophisticated and differentiated ways. Compared with children, who tend to describe themselves in relatively simple, concrete terms, adolescents are more likely to employ complex, abstract, and psychological self-characterizations. As individuals' self-conceptions become more abstract and as they become more able to see themselves in psychological terms, they become more interested in understanding their own personalities and why they behave the way they do.

Conventional wisdom holds that adolescents have low **self-esteem**—that they are more insecure and self-critical than children or adults—but most research indicates otherwise. Although teenagers' feelings about themselves may fluctuate, especially during early adolescence, their self-esteem remains fairly stable from about age 13 on. If anything, self-esteem increases over the course of middle and late adolescence. Most researchers today believe that self-esteem is multidimensional, and that young people evaluate themselves along several different dimensions. As a consequence, it is possible for an adolescent to have high self-esteem when it comes to his academic abilities, low self-esteem when it comes to athletics, and moderate self-esteem when it comes to his physical appearance.

One theorist whose work has been very influential on our understanding of adolescents' self-conceptions is Erik Erikson, who theorized that the establishment of a coherent sense of identity is the chief psychosocial task of adolescence. Erikson believed that the complications inherent in identity development in modern society have created the need for a psychosocial moratorium—a time-out during adolescence from the sorts of excessive responsibilities and obligations that might restrict the young person's pursuit of self-discovery. During the psychosocial moratorium, the adolescent can experiment with different roles and identities, in a context that permits and encourages this sort of exploration. The experimentation involves trying on different personalities and ways of behaving. Sometimes, parents describe their teenage children as going through "phases." Much of this behavior is actually experimentation with roles and personalities.

For most adolescents, establishing a sense of autonomy, or independence, is as important a part of the emotional transition out of childhood as is establishing a sense of identity. During adolescence, there is a movement away from the dependency typical of childhood toward the autonomy typical of adulthood. One can see this in several ways.

First, older adolescents do not generally rush to their parents whenever they are upset, worried, or in need of assistance. Second, they do not see their parents as all-knowing or all-powerful. Third, adolescents often have a great deal of emotional energy wrapped up in relationships outside the family; in fact, they may feel more attached to a boyfriend or a girlfriend than to their parents. And finally, older adolescents are able to see and interact with their parents as people—not just as their parents. Many parents find, for example, that they can confide in their adolescent children, something that was not possible when their children were younger, or that their adolescent children can easily sympathize with them when they have had a hard day at work.

Some theorists have suggested that the development of independence be looked at in terms of the adolescent's developing sense of individuation. The process of individuation, which begins during infancy and continues well into late adolescence, involves a gradual, progressive sharpening of one's sense of self as autonomous, as competent, and as separate from one's parents. Individuation, therefore, has a great deal to do with the development of a sense of identity, in that it involves changes in how we come to see and feel about ourselves.

The process of individuation does not necessarily involve stress and internal turmoil. Rather, individuation entails relinquishing childish dependencies on parents in favor of more mature, more responsible, and less dependent relationships. Adolescents who have been successful in establishing a sense of individuation can accept responsibility for their choices and actions instead of looking to their parents to do it for them.

Being independent means more than merely *feeling* independent, of course. It also means being able to make your own decisions and to select a sensible course of action by yourself. This is an especially important capability in contemporary society, where many adolescents are forced to become independent decision makers at an early age. In general, researchers find that decision-making abilities improve over the course of the adolescent years, with gains continuing well into the later years of high school.

Many parents wonder about the susceptibility of adolescents to **peer pressure**. In general, studies that contrast parent and peer influences indicate that in some situations, peers' opinions are more influential, while in others, parents' are more influential. Specifically, adolescents are more likely to conform to their peers' opinions when it comes to short-term, day-to-day, and social matters—styles of dress, tastes in music, and choices among leisure activities. This is particularly true during junior high school and the early years of high school. When it comes to long-term questions concerning educational or occupational plans, however, or values, religious beliefs, and ethical issues, teenagers are influenced in a major way by their parents.

Susceptibility to the influence of parents and peers changes with development. In general, during childhood, boys and girls are highly oriented toward their parents and less so toward their peers; peer pressure during the early elementary school years is not especially strong. As they approach adolescence, however, children become somewhat less oriented toward their parents and more oriented toward their peers, and peer pressure begins to escalate. During early adolescence, conformity to parents continues to decline and conformity to peers and peer pressure continues to rise. It is not until middle adolescence, then, that genuine behavioral independence emerges, when conformity to parents as well as peers declines.

Social transition

Accompanying the biological, cognitive, and emotional transitions of adolescence are important changes in the adolescent's social relationships, or the *social transition of adolescence*. Developmentalists have spent considerable time charting the changes that take place with friends and with family members as the individual moves through the adolescent years.

One of the most noteworthy aspects of the social transition into adolescence is the increase in the amount of time individuals spend with their peers. Although relations with agemates exist well before adolescence, during the teenage years they change in significance and structure. Four specific developments stand out.

First, there is a sharp increase during adolescence in the sheer amount of time individuals spend with their peers and in the relative time they spend in the company of peers versus adults. In the United States, well over half of the typical adolescent's waking hours are spent with peers, as opposed to only 15% with adults—including parents. Second, during adolescence, peer groups function much more often without adult supervision than they do during childhood. Third, during adolescence increasingly more contact with peers is with opposite-sex friends.

Finally, whereas children's peer relationships are limited mainly to pairs of friends and relatively small groups—three or four children at a time, for example—adolescence marks the emergence of larger groups of peers, or crowds. Crowds are large collectives of similarly stereotyped individuals who may or may not spend much time together. In contemporary American high schools, typical crowds are "jocks," "brains," "nerds," "populars," "druggies," and so on. In contrast to **cliques,** crowds are not settings for adolescents' intimate interactions or friendships, but, instead, serve to locate the adolescent (to himself and to others) within the social structure of the school. As well, the crowds themselves tend to form a sort of social hierarchy or map of the school, and different crowds are seen as having different degrees of status or importance.

The importance of peers during early adolescence coincides with changes in individuals' needs for intimacy. As children begin to share secrets with their friends, a new sense of loyalty and commitment grows, a belief that friends can trust each other. During adolescence, the search for intimacy intensifies, and self-disclosure between best friends becomes an important pastime. Teenagers, especially girls, spend hours discussing their innermost thoughts and feelings, trying to understand one another. The discovery that they tend to think and feel the same as someone else becomes another important basis of friendship.

One of the most important social transitions that takes place in adolescence concerns the emergence of sexual and romantic relationships. In contemporary society, most young people begin dating sometime during early adolescence.

Dating during adolescence can mean a variety of different things, from group activities that bring males and females together (without much actual contact between the sexes); to group dates, in which a group of boys and girls go out jointly (and spend part of the time as couples and part of the time in large groups); to casual dating as couples; and to serious involvement with a steady boyfriend or girlfriend. More adolescents have experience in mixed-sex group activities like parties or dances than dating, and more have experience in dating than in having a serious boyfriend or girlfriend.

Most adolescents' first experience with sex falls into the category of "autoerotic behavior"—sexual behavior that is experienced alone. The most common autoerotic activities reported by adolescents are erotic **fantasies** and **masturbation**. By the time most adolescents have reached high school, they have had some experience with sex in the context of a relationship. About half of all American teenagers have had sexual intercourse by the time of high school graduation.

Estimates of the prevalence of sexual intercourse among American adolescents vary considerably from study to study, depending on the nature of the sample surveyed and the year and region in which the study was undertaken. Although regional and ethnic variations make it difficult to generalize about the "average" age at which American adolescents initiate sexual intercourse, national surveys of young people indicate that more adolescents are sexually active at an earlier age today than in the recent past.

For many years, researchers studied the psychological and social characteristics of adolescents who engaged in premarital sex, assuming that sexually active teenagers were more troubled than their peers. This view has been replaced as sexual activity has become more prevalent. Indeed, several recent studies show that sexual activity during adolescence is decidedly not associated with psychological disturbance.

Although it is incorrect to characterize adolescence as a time when the family ceases to be important, or as a time of inherent and inevitable family conflict, early adolescence is a period of significant change and reorganization in family relationships. In most families, there is a movement during adolescence from patterns of influence and interaction that are asymmetrical and unequal to ones in which parents and their adolescent children are on a more equal footing. Family relationships change most around the time of puberty, with increasing conflict between adolescents and their parents—especially between adolescents and their mothers—and closeness between adolescents and their parents diminishing somewhat. Changes in the ways adolescents view family rules and regulations, especially, may contribute to increased disagreement between them and their parents.

Although puberty seems to distance adolescents from their parents, it is not associated with familial "storm and stress," however. Family conflict during this stage is more likely to take the form of bickering over day-to-day issues than outright fighting. Similarly, the diminished closeness is more likely to be manifested in increased privacy on the part of the adolescent and diminished physical affection between teenagers and parents, rather than any serious loss of love or respect between parents and children. Research suggests that this distancing is temporary, though, and that family relationships may become less conflicted and more intimate during late adolescence.

Generally speaking, most young people are able to negotiate the biological, cognitive, emotional, and social transitions of adolescence successfully. Although the mass media bombard us with images of troubled youth, systematic research indicates that the vast majority of individuals move from childhood into and through adolescence without serious difficulty.

For Further Study

Books

Feldman, S., and G. Elliott, eds. *At the Threshold: The Developing Adolescent*. Cambridge: Harvard University Press, 1990.

Pipher, Mary. *Reviving Ophelia*. New York: Ballantine Books, 1994.

Steinberg, L. *Adolescence*. 4th ed. New York: McGraw-Hill, 1996.

Steinberg, L., and A. Levine. *You and Your Adolescent: A Parent's Guide for Ages 10 to 20.* New York: HarperPerennial, 1991.

—Laurence Steinberg, Ph.D.
Temple University

Adoption

A practice in which an adult assumes the role of parent for a child who is not his or her biological offspring.

An adult assumes the role of parent for a child other than his or her own biological offspring in the process of adoption. Informal adoptions occur when a relative or stepparent assumes permanent parental responsibilities without court involvement. However, legally recognized adoptions require a court or other government agency to award permanent custody of a child (or, occasionally, an older individual) to adoptive parents. Specific requirements for adoption vary among states and countries. Adoptions can be privately arranged through individuals or agencies, or arranged through a public agency such as a state's child protective services. Adoptees may be infants or older children; they may be adopted singly or as sibling groups; and they may come from the local area or from other countries. Adoptive parents may be traditional married couples, but they may also be single men or women or non-traditional couples. Parents may be childless or have other children.

Adoption is a practice that dates to ancient times, although there have been fundamental changes in the process. Ancient Romans, for example, saw adoption as a way of ensuring male heirs to childless couples so that family lines and religious traditions could be maintained. In contrast, modern American adoption laws are written in support of the best interests of the child, not of the adopter.

Modern American adoption laws evolved during the latter half of the 19th century, prompted by changes due to the industrial revolution, large numbers of immigrant children who were often in need of care, and a growing concern for child welfare. Because of the poor health conditions in the tenements of large cities, many children were left on their own at early ages. These dependent children were sometimes placed in almshouses with the mentally ill, and sometimes in foundling homes plagued by high mortality rates. In the 1850s the Children's Aid Society of New York City began to move dependent children out of city institutions. Between 1854 and 1904 orphan trains carried an estimated 100,000 children to the farms of the Midwest where they were placed with families and generally expected to help with farm work in exchange for care.

Massachusetts became the first state to pass legislation mandating judicial supervision of adoptions in 1851, and by 1929 all states had passed some type of adoption legislation. During the early part of the 20th century it was standard practice to conduct adoptions in secret and with records sealed, in part to protect the parties involved from the social stigma of illegitimate birth. After WWI two factors combined to increase interest in the adoption of infants. The development of formula feeding allowed for the raising of infants without a ready supply of breast milk, and psychological theory and research about the relative importance of training and conditioning in child rearing eased the concerns of childless couples about potential "bad seeds." Because of the burgeoning interest in infant adoptions, many states legislated investigations of prospective adoptive parents and court approval prior to finalization of the adoption.

Until about mid-century the balance of infant supply and parent demand was roughly equal. However during the 1950s the demand for healthy white infants began to outweigh the supply. Agencies began to establish matching criteria in an attempt to provide the best fit between characteristics of the child or birth parents and the adoptive parents, matching on items such as appearance, ethnicity, education, and religious affiliation. By the 1970s it was not uncommon for parents to wait 3–5 years after their initial application to a private adoption agency before they had a healthy infant placed with them. These trends resulted from a decrease in the numbers of infants surrendered for adoption following the increased availability of birth control, the legalization of abortion, and the increasingly common decision of unmarried mothers to keep their infants.

In response to this dearth of healthy, same-race infants, prospective adoptive parents turned increasingly to international and transracial adoptions. Children from Japan and Europe began to be placed with American families by agencies after WWII, and since the 1950s Korea has been the major source of international adoptions (except in 1991 with the influx of Romanian children). The one child policy of the Chinese government has provided a new source of infants to American families, and recently many adoptees have come from Peru, Colombia, El Salvador, Mexico, the Philippines, and India.

The civil rights movement of the 1960s was accompanied by an increase in the number of transracial adoptions involving black children and white parents. These adoptions peaked in 1971, and one year later the National Association of Black Social Workers issued a statement opposing transracial adoption. They argued that white families were unable to foster the growth of psychological and cultural identity in black children. Transracial adoptions now account for a small percentage of all adoptions, and these most frequently involve Korean-born children and white American families.

While healthy infants have been much in demand for adoption during the last 50 years, the number of other children waiting for adoptive homes has grown. In response, the US Congress passed the federal Adoption Assistance Child Welfare Act (Public Law 96-272) in 1980, giving subsidies to families adopting children with special needs that typically make a child hard to place. Although individual states may define the specific parameters, these characteristics include older age, medical disabilities, minority group status, and certain physical, mental, or emotional needs.

Types of adoption

Adoption arrangements are typically thought of as either closed or open. Actually, they may involve many varying degrees of openness about identity and contact between the adoptive family and the birth family. At one extreme is the closed adoption in which an intermediary third party is the only one who knows the identity of both the birth and adoptive parents. The child may be told he or she is adopted, but will have no information about his or her biological heritage. When the stigma attached to births out of wedlock was greater, most adoptions were closed and records permanently sealed; however, a move to open records has been promoted by groups of both adoptees and by some birth mothers. Currently about half of the states allow access to sealed records with the mutual consent of adoptee and birth parent, and others have search processes through intermediary parties available. Why search? Some research and clinical observation suggests that, especially during adolescence, healthy identity formation depends on full awareness of one's origins (Where do I get my freckles? Why do I have this musical ability? Why did they give me up?). Other important medical history may be critical to the adoptee's health care planning. For birth mothers, sometimes they simply want to know that their child turned out okay.

The move to open records lead to an increase in open adoptions in which information is shared from the beginning. Open adoptions may be completely open, as is the case when the birth parents (usually the mother) and adoptive parents meet beforehand and agree to maintain contact while the child is growing up. The child then has full knowledge of both sets of parents.

Other open adoptions may include less contact, or periodic letters sent to an intermediary agency, or continued contact with some family members but not others. It can be a complex issue. In the case of an older child who is removed from the family by protective services because of abuse or neglect, the child clearly knows his

birth parents as well as any other siblings. If these siblings are also removed and placed in different adoptive homes, it may be decided that periodic visits between the the children—once every few months, perhaps—should be maintained, but that contact with the abusive parents should be terminated until the child reaches adulthood and may choose to search. Siblings may know each other's placements, but the birth parents may have no knowledge of the children's whereabouts. However, if a child is ultimately adopted by the foster family with whom he or she was initially placed prior to the termination of parental rights or visitation, then the birth parents might have knowledge of the child's placement and whereabouts even though continued contact may not be deemed in the best interests of the child.

Children removed from families for protective issues are sometimes reunited with their parents after a stay in temporary foster homes and after the parents have had the chance to rehabilitate and are able to care adequately for their children. On the other hand, it may be decided that reunification is not a feasible objective for a particular family and a permanent home is then sought. The foster family then plays a major role in the child's transition to his or her "forever family." The desire to provide children with permanent homes and the resulting sense of security and attachment as soon as possible gives rise to another type of adoption, the legal risk adoption.

Legal risk adoptions involve placement in the prospective adoptive home prior to the legal termination of parental rights and subsequent freeing of the child for adoption. In these cases, child protective services are generally involved and relatively certain that the courts will ultimately decide in favor of the adoptive placement. The legal process can be drawn out if birth parents contest the agency's petition for termination. Although there is the risk that the adoption may not be finalized and that the child will be returned to his or her birth parents, social service agencies generally do not recommend such placements unless, in their best judgments, the potential benefits to child and family far outweigh the legal risk.

Whether the child is free for adoption or a legal risk placement, there is generally a waiting period before the adoption is finalized or recognized by the courts. Although estimates vary, about 10% of adoptions disrupt, that is, the child is removed from the family before finalization. This figure has risen with the increase in older and special needs children being placed for adoption. The risk of disruption increases with the age of the child at placement, a history of multiple placements prior to the adoptive home, and **acting out** behavior problems. Interestingly, many children who have experienced disruption go on to be successfully adopted, suggesting that disruption is often a bad fit between parental expectations, skills, or resources and the child's needs. Many agencies conduct parent support groups for adoptive families, and some states have instituted training programs to alert prospective adoptive parents to the challenges—as well as the rewards—of adopting special needs children, thereby attempting to minimize the risk of disruption.

Who gets adopted?

Estimating the total number of children adopted in the United States is difficult because private and independent adoptions are reported only voluntarily to census centers. According to the National Committee for Adoption, there were just over 100,000 domestic adoptions in the US in 1986, roughly an even split between related and unrelated adoptions. Of unrelated domestic adoptees, about 40% were placed by public agencies, 30% by private agencies, and 30% by private individuals. Almost half of these adoptees were under the age of two, and about one-quarter had special needs. There were also just over 10,000 international adoptions, the majority of these children under the age of two and placed by private agencies.

The American Public Welfare Association has collected data through the Voluntary Cooperative Information System on children in welfare systems across the US who are somewhere in the process of being adopted. Of children in the public welfare systems, about one-third had their adoptions finalized in 1988, one-third were living in their adoptive home waiting for finalization, and one-third were awaiting adoptive placements. Key statistics on these adoptions appear in the accompanying table.

Adoptions may be arranged privately through individuals, or a public or private agency may be involved. Although adopting parents may have certain expenses if the adoption is privately arranged, adoptions are assumed to be a gratuitous exchange by law. No parties may profit improperly from adoption arrangements and children are not to be brokered. The objectives of public and private agencies can differ somewhat. Private agencies generally have prospective adoptive parents as their clients and the agency works to find a child for them. Public agencies, on the other hand, have children as their clients and the procurement of parents as their primary mission.

Outcomes of adoption

There is general agreement that children who are adopted and raised in families do better than children raised in institutions or raised with birth parents who are neglectful or abusive. Compared to the general population, however, the conclusions are less robust and the interpretation of the statistics is not clear. Adopted adolescents, for example, receive mental health services more often than their non-adopted peers, but this may be because adoptive families are more likely to seek helping services or because once referring physicians or counselors know that a child is adopted they assume there are likely to be problems warranting professional attention.

STATISTICS ON ADOPTIONS	
Characteristic	**Percent of total adoptees**
White	60%
Black	23%
Hispanic	9%
Adopted by foster family	40%
Adopted by unrelated families	37%
Adoptees with special needs	60%
Adoptees median age	4.8 years

When adjustment problems are manifested by adoptees, they tend to occur around school age or during adolescence. D. M. Brodzinsky and his colleagues have conducted a series of studies from which they conclude that adopted infants and toddlers generally do not differ from non-adopted youngsters, but greater risks for problems such as aggression or **depression** emerge as the 5–7-year-old child begins to understand the salience and implications of being adopted. Still, it should be noted that *the absolute incidence of adjustment problems in adoptees is low even though it may be statistically higher than the corresponding figures for non-adoptees.*

In the course of normal development, adolescence is seen as a time of identity formation and emerging independence. Adopted adolescents are faced with the challenge of integrating disparate sources of identity—their biological origins and their family of rearing—as they establish themselves as individuals. For some this is a difficult task and may result in rebellious or depressive behavior, risks for all adolescents. Many adoption experts feel that families who do not acknowledge the child's birth heritage from the beginning may increase the likelihood that their child will experience an especially difficult adolescence.

Problems associated with adoption may not always be the result of psychological adjustment to adoption status or a reflection of less than optimal family dynamics. **Attention Deficit/Hyperactivity Disorder (ADHD)** was found to be more prevalent in adoptees than non-adoptees, both among children adopted as infants and children removed from the home at older ages. C. K. Deutsch suggests that ADHD in children adopted as infants may be genetically inherited from the birth parents and perhaps reflected in the impulsive behavior that resulted in the child's birth in the first place. In the case of children who have been removed from the home because of the trauma of abuse, the hypervigilance used to cope with a threatening environment may compromise the child's ability to achieve normal attention regulation

Many of the studies addressing the outcomes of adoption fail to consider important factors such as the pre-placement history of the child, the structure and dynamic of the adopting family, or the courses of individual children's development. Many studies are cross-sectional rather than longitudinal by design, meaning that different groups of children at different ages are studied rather than the same children being followed over a period of time. It is also difficult to establish what control or comparison groups should be used. Should adopted children be compared to other children in the types of families into which they have been adopted or should they be compared to children in the types of families from which they have been surrendered? These are complex issues because adoptees are a heterogeneous group, and it is as important to understand their individual differences as it is their commonalities.

For Further Study

Books

Brodzinsky, D. M., and M. D. Schechter, eds. *The Psychology of Adoption.* New York: Oxford University Press, 1990.

Caplan. L. *An Open Adoption.* Boston: Houghton-Mifflin, 1990.

Lancaster, K. *Keys to Adopting a Child.* Hauppauge, NY: Barron's Educational Series, 1994.

Melina, L. R. *Making Sense of Adoption.* New York: Harper & Row, 1989.

National Committee for Adoption (NCFA). *1989 Adoption Factbook.* Washington, DC: National Committee for Adoption, 1989.

Tatara, T. *Characteristics of Children in Substitute and Adoptive Care: A Statistical Summary of the VCIS National Child Welfare Base.* Washington, DC: American Public Welfare Association, 1992.

Periodicals

Brodzinsky, D. M. "Long-Term Outcomes in Adoption." *The Future of Children* 3, 1993, pp. 153–66.

Deutsch, D. K., J. M. Swanson, and J. H. Bruell. "Overrepresentation of Adoptees in Children with Attention Deficit Disorder." *Behavior Genetics* 12, 1982, pp. 231–37.

Stolley, K. S. "Statistics on Adoption in the United States." *The Future of Children* 3, pp. 26–42.

Organizations

AASK (Adopt A Special Kid)
Address: 2201 Broadway, Suite 702
Oakland, CA 94612
Telephone: (510) 451-1748

Adopted Child
Address: P.O. Box 9362
Moscow, ID 83842
Telephone: (208) 882-1794
FAX: (208) 883-8035

Adoptive Families of America
Address: 3333 North Highway 100
Minneapolis, MN 55422
Telephone: toll-free (800) 372-3300; (612) 372-4829
FAX: (612) 535-7808
(Publishes *OURS: The Magazine of Adoptive Families,* a bimonthly magazine.)

American Adoption Congress
Address: 1000 Connecticut Ave., N.W., Suite 9
Washington, DC 20036
Telephone: (202) 483-3399
(Public information center.)

Child Welfare League of America
Address: P.O. Box 7816
300 Raritan Center Pkwy, Edison, NJ 08818-7816
Telephone: toll-free (800) 407-6273; (908) 225-1900
FAX: (908) 417-0482

National Adoption Center
Address: 1500 Walnut Street
Philadelphia, PA, 19102
(Provides information especially with regard to special needs adoption.)

National Adoption Information Clearinghouse
Address: 11426 Rockville Pike
Rockville, MD 20852
Telephone: (202) 842-1919
(Resource for information and referral. Maintains copies of all state and federal adoption laws, including Public Law 96-272, *The Adoption Assistance and Child Welfare Act of 1980.*)

National Council for Single Adoptive Parents
Address: P.O. Box 15084
Chevy Chase, MD 20825
Telephone: (202) 966-6367

—Doreen Arcus, Ph.D.
University of Massachusetts Lowell

Affect

Psychological term often used for observable expression of feelings, but occasionally used for privately experienced emotions.

The expressions of emotion or feelings to others include facial expressions, gestures, tone of voice, and other signs of emotion such as laughter or tears. As a child grows and develops, environmental factors, such as **peer pressure**, and internal factors, such as self-consciousness, help to shape the affect.

What is considered a normal range of affect—display of emotion—varies from **family** to family, from situation

Facial expressions are a key demonstration of a person's affect.

to situation, and from culture to culture. Even within a culture, a wide variation in affective display can be considered normal. Certain individuals may gesture prolifically while talking, and display dramatic facial expressions in reaction to social situations or other stimuli. Others may show little outward response to social environments, expressing only a narrow range of affect to the outside world.

When psychologists describe abnormalities in a child's affect, they use specific terminology. The normal affect—which is different for each child and changes with each stage of childhood—is termed broad affect, to describe the range of expression of emotion that is considered typical. Persons with psychological disorders may display variations in their affect. A constricted affect refers to a mild restriction in the range or intensity of display of feelings; as the display of emotion becomes more severely limited, the term blunted affect may be applied. The absence of any exhibition of emotions is described as flat affect; in this case, the voice is monotone, the face is expressionless, and the body is immobile. Extreme variations in expressions of feelings is termed labile affect. When the outward display of emotion is inappropriate for the situation, such as laughter while describing pain or sadness, the affect is described as inappropriate. Labile affect, also called lability, is used to describe emotional instability or dramatic mood swings.

For Further Study

Books

Ablon, Steven. *Human Feelings: Explorations in Affect Development and Meaning.* Hillsdale, NJ: Analytic Press, 1993.

Bull, Ray. *The Social Psychology of Facial Appearance.* New York: Springer-Verlag, 1988.

Emotions. Alexandria, VA: Time-Life Books, 1994.

Moore, Bert S., and Alice M. Isen, eds. *Affect and Social Behavior.* New York: Cambridge University, 1990.

Tangney, June Price, and Kurt W. Fischer, eds. *Self-Conscious Emotions: The Psychology of Shame, Guilt, Embarassment, and Pride.* New York: Guilford Press, 1995.

Thayer, Robert E. *The Origin of Everyday Moods: Managing Energy, Tension and Stress.* New York: Oxford University Press, 1996.

Demos, E. Virginia, ed. *Exploring Affect: The Selected Writings of Silvan S. Tomkins.* New York: Cambridge University Press, 1995.

Ainsworth, Mary (1913–)

American psychologist specializing in the study of infant attachment.

Mary D. Satler Ainsworth graduated from the University of Toronto in 1935 and earned her Ph.D. in psychology from that same institution in 1939. She is best known for her landmark work in assessing the security of infant **attachment** and linking attachment security to aspects of maternal caregiving.

Ainsworth began her career teaching at the University of Toronto before joining the Canadian Women's Army Corp in 1942 during World War II. After a brief period of post-war government service as the superintendent of Women's Rehabilitation in the Canadian Department of Veteran's Affairs, Ainsworth returned to Toronto to teach personality psychology and conduct research in the assessment of security. She married Leonard Ainsworth in 1950. Since he was a graduate student in the same department in which she held a faculty appointment, the couple decided to move to London where he could finish his degree at University College.

In England Mary Ainsworth began work at the Tavistock Clinic on a research project investigating the effects of early maternal separation on children's personality development. The project director, **John Bowlby,** had studied children's reactions to separations during the war years in England, and brought an evolutionary and ethological perspective to understanding the problems of attachment, separation, and loss. Her work with Bowlby brought Ainsworth's earlier interest in security into the developmental realm, and she planned to conduct a longitudinal study of mother-infant interaction in a natural setting at her earliest opportunity.

That opportunity came when Ainsworth's husband accepted a position in the East African Institute of Social Research in Kampala, Uganda. It was in Uganda that Mary Ainsworth studied mothers and infants in their natural environment, observing and recording as much as possible, and analyzing and publishing the data years later after joining the faculty at Johns Hopkins University in Baltimore.

Based on her original observations in Uganda and subsequent studies in Baltimore, Ainsworth concluded that there are qualitatively distinct patterns of attachment that evolve between infants and their mothers over the opening years of life. Although a majority of these patterns are marked by comfort and security, some are tense or conflicted, and Ainsworth found evidence suggesting that these relationships were related to the level of responsiveness that mothers showed toward their infants from the earliest months. In one study she found mothers who responded more quickly to their infants' cries at three months were more likely to have developed secure attachments with their babies by one year.

How could the security of a relationship be measured? Ainsworth and her colleagues devised a system for assessing individual differences in infants' reactions to a series of separations and reunions with their mothers. This method, the "**Strange Situation**," has become one of the most widely used procedures in child development research.

In this scenario, an observer takes a mother and child of about one year to an unfamiliar room containing toys. There are a series of separations and reunions. For example, mother and child are alone in the room for several minutes, the observer re-enters, remains, and after a few minutes, the mother leaves and returns after a few more minutes. Both observer and mother may comfort the distressed child.

Ainsworth found that key individual differences among children are revealed by the child's reaction to the mother's return. She categorized these responses into three major types: (A) Anxious/avoidant—the child may not be distressed at the mother's departure and may avoid or turn away from her on return; (B) Securely attached—the child is distressed by mother's departure and easily soothed by her on her return; (C) Anxious/resistant—the child may stay extremely close to the mother during the first few minutes and become highly distressed at her departure, only to seek simultaneously comfort and distance from the mother on her return by such behaviors as crying and reaching to be held and then attempting to leave once picked up.

The development of this procedure has spawned an enormous body of literature examining the development of mother-child attachment, the role of attachments to other caregivers, and the correlates and consequences of secure and insecure attachments. Ainsworth's work has not been without controversy. Attempts to replicate her link between response to early crying and later attach-

ment have met with mixed success, and there is much debate about the origins of children's reactions in the Strange Situation. Still, Mary Ainsworth has made a lasting contribution to the study of children's affective growth and the role of supportive relationships in many aspects of development.

See also **John Bowlby.**

For Further Study

Books

Ainsworth, M. *Infancy in Uganda: Infant Care and the Growth of Love.* Baltimore: Johns Hopkins University Press, 1967.

Ainsworth, M., M. C. Blehar, E. Waters, and S. Wall. *Patterns of Attachment: A Psychological Study of the Strange Situation.* Hillsdale, NJ: Erlbaum, 1978.

Periodicals

Karen, Robert. "Becoming Attached: What Experiences in Infancy Will Allow Children to Thrive Emotionally and to Come to Feel That the World of People Is a Positive Place." *Atlantic* 265, February 1990, pp. 35+

—Doreen Arcus, Ph.D.
University of Massachusetts Lowell

Alcoholism

Term encompassing alcohol use, alcohol consumption, alcohol problems, problem drinking, and alcohol dependence.

The concept of alcoholism, in its most general sense, refers to a disease, or disorder, typically characterized by: (a) a prolonged period of frequent, heavy alcohol use; (b) a variety of social and/or legal problems associated with alcohol use (e.g., driving while intoxicated, impaired school/work performance); and (c) the expression of dependency symptoms (e.g., unpleasant withdrawal effects when unable to consume alcohol). Although some adolescents do indeed experience difficulties associated with their use of alcohol at levels of severity so as to be aptly characterized as alcoholic, this subgroup is small relative to the number of children and adolescents who use alcohol at significant, but less severe, levels. Furthermore, there are major differences in the rates of alcohol use across the wide age range constituting childhood and adolescence. Hence, a comprehensive consideration of the role of alcohol in childhood and adolescence necessitates distinctions of what specific features of alcohol-related behaviors are being referred to. Several different features of alcohol-related behaviors (e.g., alcohol use, alcohol problems, beliefs about alcohol) of relevance to children and adolescents are presented here.

Infancy

There is considerable evidence that maternal alcohol consumption during pregnancy may contribute adversely to a baby's development. Abnormalities in offspring associated with maternal alcohol consumption may include prenatal and postnatal growth retardation, neurological deficits (e.g., impaired attentional control), intellectual deficiencies, behavioral problems (e.g., impulsivity), skull or brain malformations, and facial aberrations (e.g., a thin upperlip and elongated flattened midface). These abnormalities, influenced by maternal alcohol consumption during pregnancy, are referred to as fetal alcohol effects (FAEs), or **fetal alcohol syndrome** (FAS) if a sufficient number of effects are manifested by the offspring. Rates of FAS are substantially higher among African Americans relative to Caucasians, and some Native American populations have high rates of FAS. Research studies that have followed infants with FAS and FAEs across time have indicated that many of these children continue to have cognitive difficulties (e.g., lower IQ scores, more learning problems, poorer short-term memory functioning) and behavioral problems (e.g., high impulsivity, high activity level) into childhood and adolescence.

Preschool

While scientifically a relatively new area of study, evidence is accumulating that indicates that most preschool children (ages 3–5 years) can identify alcoholic beverages and have already developed certain cognitive concepts and schemas (i.e., integrated beliefs) about drinking behaviors. In an olfactory (smell) identification task, preschool children were requested to identify substances (e.g., apple juice, coffee, perfume, beer) subsequent to closing their eyes and inhaling odors from jars that contained the various substances. Prior to closing their eyes, the children did not know which substance was going to be presented in the jar. Seventy-nine percent of the preschool children successfully identified at least one alcoholic beverage. In addition, there was a higher rate of alcohol beverage identification among preschool children who had parents who were heavier drinkers. Other findings with preschool children who were and were not children of alcoholics (COAs) indicated significant group differences in beliefs about alcohol consumption. The COA preschoolers, relative to the non-COA preschoolers, were more likely to identify at least one alcohol beverage, to correctly identify a larger number of alcohol beverages (e.g., beer, wine), and to attribute heavier alcohol use to adult men, rather than women. Hence, it appears that the early formation of knowledge structures about and concepts of alcohol use are emerging during the preschool years and, furthermore, that parental drinking practices are associated with these early formative beliefs.

School-age

The acquisition and elaboration of knowledge structures about alcohol use by children continues through the elementary school years. For example, a study indicated that third graders did not know where people typically drink (e.g., at a bar, in their home), but that sixth- and eighth-graders did possess this knowledge. However, a recognition that different concentrations of alcohol were contained in different alcoholic beverages (i.e., beer, wine, and hard liquor) was known by eighth graders, but not by third- or sixth-graders. These knowledge structures by children about alcohol use manifested a cumulative pattern that was also indicated with regard to children's intentions to drink alcohol—a higher percentage of the older children indicated that they intended to use alcohol in the future. Children's intention to drink was also significantly related to parental drinking practices (i.e., the more the parents drank, the more likely that children expressed an intention to drink).

Age differences in the development of alcohol expectancies have also been indicated among children. *Alcohol expectancies* refer to beliefs about anticipated positive and negative consequences associated with drinking alcohol (e.g., "alcohol use increases my social skills and friendliness in group situations"). Alcohol expectancies have been related to higher levels of alcohol consumption and treatment outcome variables (e.g., length of hospital stay, relapse probability) among adolescents and adults, and thus their early origins and development in children are of importance. Findings for alcohol expectancies among school-age children indicated increasingly positive alcohol expectancies across grade levels, with a major increase between the third- and fourth grade. That is, by the fourth grade, children tended to believe that the use of alcohol results in positive outcomes such as higher levels of acceptance and liking by peers and being in a good mood with positive feelings about oneself. These positive alcohol expectancies among fourth graders correspond with findings that at least 25% of fourth graders reported feeling at least some **peer pressure** to consume alcoholic beverages; some level of peer pressure to consume alcoholic beverages increased to approximately 60% among seventh graders.

It is evident that a range of social events (e.g., perceived peer pressure) and developmental processes (e.g., cognitive labeling and knowledge structure elaboration and differentation) about alcohol use are ongoing during the preschool and elementary school years prior to the actual consumption of alcohol. Actual use of alcohol is also initiated by some children during the elementary school years. It has been estimated that 20 to 25% of fourth

WHAT TEENAGERS SAY ABOUT ALCOHOL USE	
Percent of high school seniors who say they've used alcohol	87%
Percent of all wine coolers sold that are consumed by junior and senior high students	35%
Cans of beer consumed by junior and senior high students	1.1 billion
Percent of teens who drink who say they can buy their own alcoholic beverages	66%
Teens under 18 in state-operated juvenile institutions who were under the influence of alcohol when arrested	31.9%
Number of people admitted to state-funded alcohol treatment progerams who were under the age of 21	126,000

graders report having consumed an alcoholic beverage in their lifetime, and this rate increases to slightly more than 50% by eighth grade. Thus, while drinking behavior increases substantially in the next portion of the lifespan to be discussed—adolescence—some of the cognitive foundations (e.g., beliefs and attitudes) for alcohol use and abuse such as intentions to drink, alcohol expectancies, and even initiation have been cultivated or expressed during the preschool and elementary school years.

Adolescence

A number of different indicators have been used to index alcohol-related behaviors during adolescence. One important indicator has been to know approximately how many adolescents have consumed alcoholic beverages in their lifetime, regardless of the quantity consumed or any problems directly associated with alcohol use. The National Institute of Drug Abuse, a federal government agency under the National Institutes of Health, has conducted annual national surveys of teenage substance use for about 20 years. These annual surveillance surveys of substance use among seniors (12th graders) have been completed at the University of Michigan and are collectively referred to as the Monitoring the Future Studies. These studies have been used to monitor historical trends in substance use among adolescents (e.g., increases or decreases in the use of alcohol, cigarettes, and illicit drugs) and to identify new drugs (e.g., "designer" drugs) or new patterns of co-occurring (i.e., combined) sub-

stance use that may be relevant for prevention research efforts and for social policy decision-making.

In addition, the National Council on Alcoholism and Drug Dependence has reported similar findings about the scope of alcohol use by adolescents.

The findings for "ever used alcohol in your lifetime" question among seniors has remained relatively stable from 1993 to 1995, hovering around 80%; the prevalence was somewhat higher in 1991 and 1992, with approximately 88% of high school seniors having used alcohol in their lifetime. However, the percentage of seniors who reported having been drunk in their lifetime has remained largely unchanged from 1991 to 1995, ranging from 62.5 to 65.4%. Furthermore, the number of seniors engaging in "binge drinking," that is consuming five or more drinks in a single setting in the two-week period preceding the survey assessment, has remained unchanged from 1991 to 1995, with a rate of 28–29%. These alcohol use statistics indicate that by their senior year of high school, most adolescents will have used alcohol, over 60% will have been drunk, and over one-quarter will have engaged in binge drinking.

In addition to these alcohol use findings for seniors, there are also some findings for younger age groups. For 8th and 10th graders, "ever used alcohol in your lifetime" was reported by approximately 55% and 71% of children, respectively, across the years 1993 to 1995. Similar to the seniors, the rates of "ever been drunk" were stable across the 1991 to 1995 time period, with a rate of approximately 26% for 8th graders and 47% for 10th graders. Thus, it is significant to note that the majority of children have used alcohol by the time they are in 8th grade, and that one-fourth of them have consumed enough alcohol on a single occasion to characterize themselves as being drunk.

The previous information pertains to indicators of alcohol use across the total sample of adolescents; however, there are some interesting differences for subgroups (e.g., boys and girls) of adolescents. Girls typically begin consuming alcohol at a somewhat later age than boys, but by their senior year, nearly as many girls as boys have used alcohol at some point in their lifetime. Sometimes this has been interpreted to reflect a convergence in drinking practices across the sex groups. Nevertheless, on measures of high-volume (heavy) drinking and alcohol-related problems (e.g., DUI infractions), boys still evidence more alcohol-related difficulties than girls.

Subgroup differences for alcohol use have also been indicated for various racial/ethnic groups. The highest percentage of users of alcohol among teenagers are Caucasians and Native Americans, followed closely by Hispanics. The lowest percentage of users of alcohol among teenagers are reported by African American and Asian

American teenagers. These findings have been replicated in national and state surveys and across different historical time periods. Hence, not all adolescents are equally likely to consume alcohol during the teenage years, as subcultural practices (e.g., beliefs about the negative impact of alcohol use, religious training, dedication to school/career aspirations) among some subgroups may influence the likelihood of consuming alcohol during this period of development. There is some evidence that the parents of African American children more frequently speak to their children about alcohol and substance use than Caucasian parents, and establish clear rules for drug use, including contingent consequences for breaking the rules.

Open parent-child communication about alcohol and drug use and clear guidelines for use (or non-use) appear to be some deterrents of alcohol use among adolescents.

Alcohol-related problems

In addition to knowledge about the number of adolescents who consume alcoholic beverages, a second area of importance pertains to *alcohol-related problems*, that is, major social and personal difficulties that may be associated with the use of alcohol. Three major problem areas have been consistently identified among adolescents who drink alcohol. The first area refers to *adverse social consequences* associated with consuming alcohol and identifies problems in the home, at school, with peers, or with legal authorities. Problems in the home include events such as fighting with parents about drinking or breaking curfew because of drinking. Problems at school include drinking before or during school, or missing school because of drinking. Problems with peers include events such as having a fight with girlfriend or boyfriend about one's drinking. And problems with legal authorities include events such as getting into trouble with the police for fighting or for driving while drinking. Not surprisingly, higher levels of alcohol consumption are associated with higher levels of alcohol problems.

The second alcohol-related problem area refers to *dependency symptoms*. These symptoms refer to behaviors that we often identify with the progressive disease process of alcoholism: doing things while one is drinking and regretting it the next day, thinking about cutting down on drinking, passing out from drinking, getting drunk several days in a row, drinking alcohol to get rid of a hangover, and drinking to forget one's troubles. These behaviors reflect more serious involvement with alcohol to the point that it may severely impact other aspects of daily functioning, including school performance and social interaction. The persistent manifestation of these behaviors suggests that professional assistance is advisable.

The third alcohol-related problem area refers to *escapist drinking coping motives*. That is, when some ado-

lescents feel distressed, due, for example, to conflict with parents or peers, or to an upcoming school exam, they may elect to drink alcohol to relieve (i.e., to escape from) stress associated with these events. This is often referred to as "self-medicating" depressed feelings and often creates problems for two reasons. First, the drinking behavior, in and of itself, does not facilitate problem-solving or other positive coping strategies to ameliorate or eliminate the perceived stressor. Second, if the alcohol consumption is at high levels, it may actually undermine the successful resolution of the conflict by increasing negative mood states and undermining constructive and thoughtful alternatives.

Pharmacologically, alcohol is a central nervous system depressant that is experienced psychologically as a biphasic effect. The initial consumption of alcohol contributes to the suppression, or disinhibition, of some behaviors, and this disinhibition is often experienced positively with regard to mood, that is, it is experienced as the "freeing up" of felt tensions. However, after a period of time (when the alcohol is diluted via metabolic processes), the second phase emerges which consists of a downward spiraling associated with more negative mood states.

Hence, alcohol use may provide temporary relief from the stresses of adolescence, but it does little to resolve stressors and may, in fact, contribute to dysfunctional (avoidance) coping processes. To the extent that this method of (mal)adaption to stress becomes persistent across situations and time, adolescents are at risk for a range of problematic behaviors, including serious alcohol problems or "full-blown" alcoholism.

The three alcohol-related problem areas of adverse social consequences, dependency symptoms, and escapist drinking coping motives are of importance in signifying current major problems, as well as posing potential serious risk for alcoholism and other problem behaviors among children and adolescents as they develop toward young adulthood. Children and adolescents with persistent and pervasive difficulties in these domains are in need of professional assistance, as these are behaviors that portend more dire consequences.

Higher levels of alcohol use and alcohol-related problems among children and adolescents are also associated with a range of other deleterious behaviors that are hazardous to the health and well-being of youngsters. The three major causes of adolescent mortality—accidents (e.g., automobile, boating), homicide, and **suicide**—are highly associated with the use of alcohol among adolescents. Almost 9 out of 10 teenage automobile accidents involve the use of alcohol. Higher levels of alcohol and other substance use have been associated with higher levels of adolescent suicidal ideation (i.e., thinking about committing suicide) and suicide attempts, and alcohol has been found in high concentrations among adolescents who have completed suicide. Higher levels of adolescent alcohol use have also been associated with a number of other adverse health-related outcomes, including sexual precocity, teenage **pregnancy, sexually transmitted diseases**, human immunodeficiency virus (HIV) infection, poor school performance, and school dropout. Alcohol use has often been referred to as the "gateway" substance, preceding the use of marijuana and then other illegal substances (e.g., cocaine, heroin). Thus, heavier alcohol use during adolescence may be symptomatic, or even prognostic, of a range of current and potential future hazardous behaviors among adolescents.

The previous information in this essay has focused on several indicators of alcohol behaviors (e.g., alcohol use, alcohol problems, alcohol expectancies) to address broader societal concerns with child and adolescent alcohol use in the general population. It is important to also recognize that there is a small, but significant, number of adolescents who have quite severe problems with alcohol use and meet clinical criteria for an alcohol disorder. The children and adolescents who meet the clinical criteria for an alcohol disorder typically manifest persistent, high-volume drinking and pervasive adverse social consequences and dependency symptoms. Further, these children typically have a history of childhood behavior problems (e.g., conduct disordered difficulties, attentional deficits), long-term troubled family relations, and a pattern of coexisting substance abuse (e.g., marijuana or cocaine abuse). Prevalence estimates of the number of children and adolescents meeting clinical criteria for an alcohol disorder are not known, though some have speculated that the number may exceed two million.

Risk factors (predictors) of alcohol use and abuse

As the preceding sections have demonstrated, alcohol-related behaviors among children and adolescents occur at a relatively high frequency and can contribute to a host of quite serious health-related outcomes. Given this descriptive information on patterns of alcohol use and the number alcohol-related problems, much attention has been directed toward an understanding of what factors predict alcohol use among children and adolescents. Factors that increase the expectation (or probability) that children or adolescents will use or abuse alcohol are referred to as *risk factors*. Risk factors have been categorized into several useful groups and examples from each of these groups is presented subsequently.

Some *societal-community factors* have been identified as increasing risk for adolescent alcohol use and abuse. For instance, youthful drinking behavior may be fostered via media sources (e.g., television and magazine commercials, movies) and adolescent societal heroes (e.g., athletes, rock stars) that explicitly or implicitly convey the message that alcohol consumption is associated with positively valued characteristics (e.g., popularity with friends). Such societal media images are further fostered by the absence of serious enforcement of established legal standards for underage drinking. Stiff legal penalties for adolescents are often associated with the use, and especially the selling, of substances identified as illegal for adult use (e.g., marijuana, cocaine). Nonetheless, alcohol (which is a legal substance for adults but illegal for adolescents) use by teenagers is not likely to meet with legal enforcement unless there are extenuating circumstances such as a DWI or automobile crash. The absence of legal enforcement of underage drinking may contribute to an atmosphere of implicit tolerance of alcohol use by adolescents. An additional community level factor associated with risk for adolescent drinking is the relative ease of availability of alcoholic beverages. Easy access may occur within the home (e.g., a fully stocked liquor cabinet, refrigerator, or basement supply), or via liquor outlets where minors may either be directly served, or easily request others (e.g., siblings) to purchase alcoholic beverages.

Several aspects of *school functioning* have also been associated with increased risk for adolescent drinking. Early onset, persistent behavior problems including attentional problems, high activity levels, and aggression within the school context have been consistent predictors of high levels of teenage alcohol use. Similar findings have been reported for a low commitment to school achievement and career expectations by adolescents; children and adolescents who do not believe that their educational and career futures are bright tend to associate more with deviant peers and to consume more alcohol. Finally, academic failure (e.g., poor attendance, poor grades, underachievement) is associated with increased risk for heavier alcohol use.

Family factors associated with increased risk for adolescent alcohol use include the drinking practices of other family members (e.g., parents, or sibs' drinking practices), marital conflict, poor family management practices (e.g., failure to monitor children as to where they are, who they are with, etc.), harsh (physically abusive) discipline, physical or sexual abuse, and the lack of a warm, open, nurturing relationship with parents. In brief, highly troubled family relations serve as a springboard for children and adolescents to engage in higher levels of alcohol use and other problem behaviors (e.g., delinquency). Without the emotional warmth and guidance provided by parents and other family members, adolescents from highly troubled families often seek some level of comfort and support with other, often deviant prone, adolescents who are also from troubled family backgrounds. This process of selective association among teenagers from troubled families often results in a progression toward higher levels of alcohol use and other deviant behaviors by these adolescents.

Peer factors are perhaps the single most highly associated risk factor for adolescent alcohol use. Peer selection processes are not random, but rather reflect a tendency for adolescents to select friends and peers according to similarities regarding attitudes, values, and behaviors. Peer groups are frequently identifiable contingent on the shared orientation of constituent members. Thus, peer groups of athletes are often referred to as "jocks" and those peer groups engaged in alcohol and drug use as "heads." The friend and peer context is especially important during adolescence to foster a personal identity or sense of self, and to learn behaviors (e.g., prosocial skills) that are important in young adulthood. The engagement by some adolescents in deviant peer networks may undermine important prosocial skill training and contribute to an alienated sense of self, as well as foster more serious involvement in alcohol use and other deviant behaviors.

Several *individual factors* have also been identified as increasing risk for adolescent drinking behavior. Research on children of alcoholics (COAs) has consistently supported a genetic susceptibility to alcohol among the offspring of alcoholics. COA boys are at four times the risk of an alcohol disorder in adulthood than boys of non-COAs. COAs are also more likely to experience a disrupted family environment and to have more internalizing problems (e.g., depression, anxiety) and externalizing problems (e.g., aggression, **truancy**), and to perform more poorly in school. The personality factors of **alienation** and rebelliousness have also been associated with higher levels of alcohol use. These personality factors are reflected in adolescents being psychologically removed from the normative attitudes and values of society, and not embracing societal values such as educational achievement or law abidance. Poor problem-solving coping skills have also been associated with increases in adolescent alcohol use. Skill deficits in the coping domain may contribute to the adoption of escapist drinking coping motives, or to strategies (e.g., interpersonal aggression) that may foster negative outcomes.

The National Institute on Alcohol Abuse and Alcoholism estimates that 6.6 million children under age 18 live in households with at least one alcoholic parent.

These risk factors for adolescent drinking behavior do not occur in a vacuum, but are often highly interrelated. That is, often adolescents may be at risk not simply because of one factor, but due to the co-occurrence of several of these factors. The engagement by adolescents in consuming alcohol may also maintain or increase the

CHILDREN OF ALCOHOLICS

A number of researchers have studied children of alcoholics (COAs) and their counterparts, children of non-alcoholic parents (non-COAs). These points summarize their findings:

COAs and non-COAs are most likely to differ in cognitive performance: scores on tests of abstract and conceptual reasoning and verbal skills were lower among children of alcoholic fathers than among children of non-alcoholic fathers in one study (Ervin, Little, Streissguth, and Beck).

A research team (Johnson and Rolf) found that both COAs and mothers of COAs were found to underestimate the child's abilities.

School records indicate that COAs are more likely to repeat grades, fail to graduate from high school, and require referral to the school psychologist than their non-COA classmates. (Miller and Jang; Knop and Teasdale)

Researchers (West and Prinz) found that COAs exhibit behavior problems such as lying, stealing, fighting, truancy, and are often diagnosed as having conduct disorders.

level of risk associated with these factors (e.g., increase academic failure) and contribute to a negative spiraling process toward more serious alcohol problems and alcoholism.

Why do children drink?

Various theories have been promulgated as to why children and adolescents initiate alcohol use prior to legal standards established by society. Some suggest that such early onset alcohol use and other problem behaviors (e.g., sexual precocity) represent attempts by adolescents to "try out" or adopt adult social roles. That is, adolescence is sometimes viewed as a time period in the lifespan in which adolescents no longer perceive themselves as children, but rather as "in transition" to adulthood. As a consequence of this perception, adolescents presumably mimic behaviors that adults engage in (e.g., alcohol use, sexual activity) and seek to establish competencies in those domains (e.g., physical attractiveness, romantic involvement) deemed essential to "successful" adult functioning. Engaging in these behaviors thus serves as a training ground for adult behaviors, while simultaneously distancing one's self from the more dependent, parent-offspring relations of childhood. As such, the engagement in alcohol use and other deviant activities during adolescence is viewed as a reflection of adolescents in preparation for adult social roles.

Others have viewed such early onset alcohol use as a symptom of a broader range of problem behaviors reflective of aberrant, or deviance prone, adolescents. These adolescents are proposed to have difficulties not only with early onset alcohol use, but also with poorer school performance, higher use of other illicit substances, higher delinquent activity, more deviant peers, and more troubled family relations. Furthermore, the parents of such adolescents use alcohol and other substances more frequently and are not as disapproving of alcohol and substance use by their offspring as are the parents of adolescents who abstain from or only experiment with alcohol use.

Still others have proposed that alcohol initiation during adolescence is a statistically normative activity (i.e., most teens will try alcohol) characteristic of experimentation in a number of domains during adolescence. According to this perspective, adolescents are responding to a variety of biological (e.g., onset of **puberty** onset) and psychosocial (e.g., transitions to high school contexts) changes in which experimentation is a developmentally common phenomena. In the United States, mixed messages are also conveyed to children and adolescents about alcohol use via various media sources. For example, drinking alcohol is often glamorized by rock stars and is associated with major sporting events (e.g., the Super Bowl).

Many television advertisements convey the message that drinking alcohol is a component of being popular among friends and is central to attracting that "special someone" in your life. It has been estimated that children in the United States will see alcohol consumed an average of 75,000 times (via television, movies, personal observation) prior to reaching the legal drinking age. In addition, many parents allow their underage children to drink alcoholic beverages. Therefore, even though alcohol use among children and adolescents is illegal by societal standards, in practice such messages are poorly conveyed and enforced, and experimentation with alcohol use among adolescents is not surprising.

Warning signs of children's drinking

A frequently posed question by parents and legal guardians of children pertains to "How can I tell if my child is using alcohol or other drugs?" That is, are there any early *warning signs* of child and adolescent substance use and abuse that should serve as red flags of possible problems? The short answer to this query is "Yes." However, prior to reading these warning signs, it is important that caution be exercised before jumping to conclusions about child/adolescent alcohol use because

many of the warning signs may be associated with conditions other than alcohol use.

Many of the warning signs of alcohol use may be symptomatic of other behaviors or problems. For example, disturbed sleeping and eating patterns may be influenced by disruptive family functioning (e.g., marital conflict), the cessation of a romantic involvement, or anxiety about an upcoming examination or poor performance on a recent examination. Likewise, specific physical signs, such as frequent and long-lasting fatigue may reflect a medical disease or psychiatric disorder (e.g., depressive disorder) that is unrelated to alcohol use.

WARNING SIGNS OF ALCOHOL USE

(1) Physical signs could include frequent and long-lasting fatigue, increased health complaints, disturbed sleeping and eating patterns, or confusion in thought processes or ideas.

(2) Psychological and emotional signs could include heightened levels of irritability and mood fluctuations, increases in irresponsible behaviors (e.g., coming home late, forgetting family occasions such as birthdays), increases in seemingly unprovoked hostility and uncooperativeness, a general unwillingness to communicate with parents and other adults (e.g., teachers, school counselors), and increases in depression and withdrawing from interpersonal contact with others (especially adults and other family members).

(3) Social and interpersonal signs could include changes in friends or peer group toward a more deviant social group, the adoption of styles of dress and musical interests that tend toward the deviant subculture, and encounters with legal authorities (e.g., passenger in a car with peers who were stopped for DWI).

(4) School warning signs could include a drop in grades, increases in the number of unaccounted absences and times tardy, and increases in disciplinary problems.

It is important to consider the convergence, or consistency, of several warning signs and to rule out alternative explanations when possible. In addition, it is important to try to distinguish between warning signs indicative of alcohol use or abuse from normative behaviors expressed by most adolescents. For instance, affiliating more with peers and sharing interests in musical tastes and dress is common among adolescents; however, the *choice* of friends, musical interests, and dress, in combination with some of the other warning signs enumerated above (e.g., increased hostility, drop in grades, disciplinary problems), may provide guidelines as to the likelihood that the child/adolescent is engaging in alcohol and substance use.

What to do if you believe your child is drinking

A logical question that follows from the preceding discussion regarding warning signs is "What do I do if I believe that my child is using or abusing alcohol or other substances?" It is important initially to attempt to acquire information and express concerns directly to your child. It is important to remember that this is likely to be a highly sensitive area for your child and that certain tactics are likely to be counterproductive. For example, aggressive verbal attacks or threats are not likely to facilitate open communication with your child, nor is lecturing likely to provide the desired result.

While often difficult because of the sensitivity and importance of this issue for both parents and adolescents, an open discussion, unfettered by parental threats, is likely to yield the most accurate information for subsequent decision making. In addition, if appropriate, it may be useful to provide children with accurate facts about the potential serious problems associated with alcohol use. Such information should be accurate; exaggerated accounts may illicit unwanted fear or parental distrust among children. As noted in previous sections of this essay, even children as young as preschoolers already have some knowledge about alcoholic beverages and drinking practices. However, this knowledge may not be accurate or comprehensive, and may reflect distorted information and myths about alcohol use.

The potential dangers and health risks associated with alcohol use are not likely to be associated with the folklore surrounding youth drinking. This sharing of accurate information about alcohol use may not "solve" the problem associated with adolescent use, but it may facilitate parent-child communication on this topic and may mitigate the probability of escalation of alcohol use by the adolescent.

If more serious alcohol-related problems are indicated, it may be necessary to make decisions about more intensive treatment. There are a wide range of treatment options for adolescent substance abusers, including treatment in a psychiatric hospital, specialized inpatient and outpatient substance abuse treatment programs, educational programs, school-related programs, and mutual help programs such as Alcoholics Anonymous.

The decision to seek more serious treatment for adolescent alcohol and substance abuse is a difficult undertaking. Consultation with your family doctor or pediatrician is advisable, as he/she may be able to provide useful information or refer you to a specialist of adolescent substance abuse problems.

TREATMENT OPTIONS FOR ALCOHOL OR SUBSTANCE ABUSE

The following key issues should be considered in determining which option is the most appropriate for given circumstances:

(1) How severe is the substance abuse problem and is there any evidence (e.g., suicide attempts) to suggest that there may be other problems (e.g., depression)?

(2) What are the credentials of the staff who attend to my child and what form(s) of therapy (e.g., family, group, medications) are to be used?

(3) How will the family be involved in the treatment and how long will it be from treatment entry to discharge? Is there a follow-up phase of treatment?

(4) How will the adolescent continue his/her education during the treatment?

(5) How much of the treatment will our insurance cover and how much will we need to pay "out of pocket?"

For Further Study

Books

Boyd, G. M., J. Howard, and R. A. Zucker, eds. *Alcohol Problems among Adolescents: Current Directions in Prevention Research.* Hillsdale, NJ: Erlbaum, 1995.

Children at the Front: A Different View of the War on Alcohol and Drugs. Washington, DC: Child Welfare League of America, 1992.

Collins, R. Lorraine, Kenneth E. Leonard, John S. Searles, (eds.) *Alcohol and the Family: Research and Clinical Perspectives.* New York: Guilford Press, 1990.

Grosshandler, Janet. *Coping with Alcohol Abuse.* New York: Rosen Pub. Group, 1990.

Schuckit, Marc Alan. *Educating Yourself About Alcohol and Drugs: A People's Primer.* New York: Plenum Press, 1995.

Periodicals

Arenofsky, Janice. "Teens Who Turned Bad Habits into Good Health." *Current Health* 23, May 1997, pp. 6+.

Ervin, C. S., R. E. Little, et al. "Alcoholic Fathering and Its Relation to Child's Intellectual Development." *Alcoholism: Clinical and Experimental Research* 8, no. 4, 1984, pp. 362–65.

Johnson, J. L. and J. E. Rolf. "Cognitive Functioning in Children from Alcoholic and Non-Alcoholic Families." *British Journal of Addiction* 83, 1988, pp. 849–57.

Miller, D., and M. Jang. "Children of Alcoholics: A 20-Year Longitudinal Study." *Social Work Research and Abstracts* 13, 1977, pp. 23–29.

Knop, J., T. W. Teasdale, et al. "A Prospective Study of Young Men at High Risk for Alcoholism: School Behavior and Achievement." *Journal of Studies on Alcohol* 46, 1985, pp. 273–78.

West, M. O. and R. J. Prinz. "Parental Alcoholism and Childhood Psychopathology." *Psychological Bulletin* 102, 1987, pp. 204–218.

Audiovisual Recordings

Alcohol and Alcoholism. Bala Cynwyd, PA: Schlessinger Video Productions, 1991.
(One 37-minute videocassette.)

Alcohol and Drugs. Verona, WI: Attainment Company, Inc., 1994.
(One 30-minute videocassette.)

Teenage Drinking and Drug Use and Back from Drugs. Alexandria, VA: Distributed by PBS Video, 1988.
(One 60-minute videocassette.)

Organizations

Alcoholics Anonymous
See white pages of local telephone book for area groups
website: www.alcoholics-anonymous.org

National Council on Alcohol and Drug Dependence, Inc.
Address: 12 West 21st St.
New York, NY 10010
Telephone: toll-free referrals (800) NCA-CALL [622-2255]; (212) 206-1690

National Institute on Alcohol Abuse and Alcoholism (NIAAA)
Address: National Institutes of Health
Willco Building, 6000 Executive Blvd.
Bethesda, MD 20892-7003
website: www.niaaa.nih.gov

—Michael Windle, Ph.D.
N.Y. State Research Institute on Addictions

Alexia

Inability to read.

Despite acceptable vision and intelligence, children with this condition are unable to read. Sometimes referred to as "word blindness," alexia is a form of **dyslexia.**

See also **Dyslexia**

Alienation

Withdrawal or isolation from other people, rejection of the values of one's family or society, or estrangement from one's own feelings.

Adolescents are the most frequent victims of feelings of alienation. The alienated adolescent has been a familiar cultural figure since James Dean's movies in the 1950s. The alienation often associated with the adolescent quest for identity commonly involves a distrust of adults, a rejection of their values, and a pessimistic world view. Alienated adolescents feel their lives are meaningless and that they have little control over the events that shape their lives. They often feel isolated from adults, their peer group, or even themselves. Teens may feel alienated as a result of **anxiet**y over inadequate social skills or physical attractiveness. Some experts consider alienation as a normal accompaniment to the dramatic physical and intellectual changes and the emotional volatility of the teen years. They view it as a deliberate identity choice, as a teen chooses to withdraw from groups that he or she formerly identified with and reject that group's values. This is especially true in late **adolescence** and early adulthood.

Teenage alienation is viewed as pathological if it accompanies serious psychological disorders, such as **phobias** and obsessions. **Schizophrenia** often involves alienation from both oneself and others, while social alienation characterizes those with antisocial (or psychopathic) personality disorder. Often, persons with **antisocial personality disorder** did not experience normal **attachment** to a parent or caregiver in early childhood, and the normal ability to relate to and identify with others was never developed. Pathological alienation is most often seen in late adolescence.

For Further Study

Books

Adams, Gerald, T. R. Gullotta, and Raymond Montemayor, eds. *Adolescent Identity Formation.* Newbury Park, CA: Sage Publications, 1992.

LeCompte, Margaret Diane. *Giving Up on School: Student Dropouts and Teacher Burnouts.* Newbury Park, CA: Corwin Press, 1991.

Allele

One of a pair of genes.

Genes are arranged in pairs, and each pair influences a specific trait. Alleles are the pairs of genes that control or determine specific traits, such as hair color.

See also **Genetics**

Allergies

A hypersensitive response by the immune system to a foreign substance that is ordinarily harmless.

Allergies account for more office visits to **pediatricians** than any other ailment, besides the common cold, and are responsible for more missed school days than any other medical problem. It is thought that at least one out of every five children has an allergy of some kind. Allergies are often inherited—a child with one allergic parent has a 25–35% chance of developing allergies, and the likelihood rises to between 50 and 65% if both parents have allergies. The substances that cause allergies—such as dust or pollen—are known as allergens (or antigens). In persons with special sensitivities, they produce elevated levels of immunoglobulin E (IgE) antibodies, which in turn unleash chemicals called histamines that produce allergic reactions. Common allergens include pollen, animal dander, house dust, chemicals, feathers, and a number of different foods.

Allergy symptoms affect a number of different body organs. Skin reactions take a variety of forms—including hives, eczema, and other rashes—but whatever their appearance they are almost always accompanied by acute itching. Respiratory symptoms include a runny, congested, or itchy nose and post-nasal drip, as well as the coughing, wheezing, and shortness of breath that characterize **asthma.** Eyes may itch, redden, swell, and water. Other allergic symptoms include itching on the roof of the mouth, clogged ears and gastrointestinal problems (nausea, vomiting, diarrhea). Allergies are usually diagnosed either through observation of symptoms, skin tests, or **elimination diets,** in which different foods are eliminated from the diet in order to discover which ones are causing the problem.

Allergy treatment can be grouped into three broad categories. The simplest is to avoid contact with known allergens. Depending on the type of allergy, this may involve eliminating certain foods from the diet, keeping dust under control by cleaning or by using an air cleaner, making adjustments in pet ownership, or removing trouble-causing items such as feather pillows. The second type of treatment consists of medications, such as antihistamines, that alleviate the symptoms of allergic reactions. A final method is **desensitization,** more familiarly known as allergy shots, a treatment that exposes an allergic person to gradually increasing amounts of certain allergens over an extended time period in hopes of eliminating or reducing sensitivity to them.

Dealing with allergies at different developmental stages

Childhood allergies pose different challenges to parents depending on the age of the child.

Infancy. Some physicians believe babies are especially vulnerable to allergies because their still-developing digestive systems allow excessive amounts of antibody-producing material into the bloodstream. The first five to six months is the period when an infant is most sensitive to allergens. Nursing is often recommended as a way to reduce the likelihood of allergic reactions, since no infant has ever been found to be allergic to her mother's milk. However, traces of whatever the mother eats are passed on to a baby through nursing, so mothers should be alert to possible connections between allergic symptoms in their babies and foods, medication, or even vitamins they have ingested recently. If a mother becomes convinced that her infant is reacting to a particular substance, she should consider eliminating it from her diet while she is nursing.

When an infant under one year of age develops a rash, the most likely cause is the introduction of an unfamiliar food. Physicians often recommend that solid food be introduced gradually to babies who have a family history of allergies. It is recommended that new foods be introduced one at a time, allowing a 7–10 days after each new food before introducing the next. The later a food item is introduced into the diet, the less likely it is to cause an allergic reaction. In addition, allergic reactions tend to be cumulative: the combination of two or more substances may cause an allergic reaction.

Aside from food, dust, harsh soaps or detergents, ingredients in lotions, and other skin preparations also cause allergic reactions. Parents need to make sure that the items they buy for infant care, such as diapers, lotions, shampoos, and detergent, are free of potential allergens. Many dye- and fragrance-free products are currently available on the market.

Toddlerhood. Toddlers are old enough to become anxious about allergic symptoms, a situation that can trigger further allergic attacks, creating a frustrating cycle. It is important for parents to avoid conveying their own anxiety about allergy symptoms to the child. Toddlers are able to take some responsibility for avoiding foods they are sensitive to, particularly if they can recall being sick after eating certain foods. Parental supervision of toddlers is so extensive that it is relatively easy to control the child's food intake during this stage.

Preschool. At the preschool stage, controlling a child's diet becomes more difficult. By this point, he or she may feel stigmatized or left out when made to eat special foods instead of what all the other children are having. In addition to food, parents should also be mindful of other possible allergens that their child may encounter in preschool, such as playdough or papier-mache made from flour or water, which can pose problems for children allergic to wheat.

School age. Parents of school-age children with allergies should make sure their child's teacher is informed of any important restrictions and emergency procedures. If the child needs to take medication and there is no school nurse, another adult should be designated to administer it.

In the following section, the major types of allergies and allergy symptoms are described.

Rhinitis

Many children suffer from the runny nose, sneezing, and watery eyes of allergic rhinitis, which may be either chronic or seasonal. Either kind can be caused by pollen, although the chronic variety is usually caused by dust, food, or other allergens. Seasonal rhinitis, including hay fever, occurs at the same time every year and is caused by the pollen of certain plants, including trees and grass in springtime and ragweed in the late summer and fall. Pollen allergies generally develop between the ages of 6 and 13. Respiratory allergies from dust, animal dander, and molds may occur as early as two or three years of age.

A variety of methods are used to diagnose upper respiratory allergies. One is simple observation: much can be learned by noting, for example, whether allergic attacks occur at a certain time of year or when a child is exposed to a particular environment. Skin testing is often used, although it can produce false positives and, occasionally, allergic reactions. A newer method is the radio-allergosorbent (RAST) blood test, which determines blood levels of the IgE antibodies that trigger allergic reactions.

Antihistamines are the most common treatment for rhinitis. They block the action of histamines, chemicals the body releases in response to allergens. These histamines cause the nasal passage to swell, congestion, and increased mucus production. Antihistamines are usually effective in reducing these symptoms but can cause drowsiness, dizziness, and other side effects. Decongestants offer another method of reducing nasal congestion and swelling, but if decongestant sprays are used for more than three or four consecutive days they can create a dependency on the spray. Cortisone sprays and cromolyn sodium, a spray that prevents symptoms by coating the nasal membranes, have also proven effective in the treatment of rhinitis. While many rhinitis sufferers have been helped by allergy shots, they are costly and time-consuming and do not work for everyone.

Asthma

Asthma is a chronic, reversible respiratory disorder caused by obstruction and swelling of the airways to the lungs. An asthma attack begins when the muscles surrounding the bronchial tubes go into spasm and the tubes become narrow. This stimulates increased mucus production, further blocking the airway, and, finally, inflammation and swelling, which cause even more congestion and discomfort. Symptoms include coughing, wheezing, shortness of breath, fatigue, anxiety, and tightness in the chest. Of the 9–10 million Americans affected by asthma, about half are children under the age of 16. Although asthma is considered an allergy, it is triggered by a variety of both allergic and non-allergic reactions. Some activities that contribute to non-allergic reactions include laughing, crying, and exercises that produce rapid breathing. Other non-allergenic irritants are tobacco smoke, air pollutants, paint, insecticides, and other chemical substances. Allergens that trigger asthma include pollen, animal dander, dust, and foods.

Like other allergies, asthma can be controlled by a combination of avoiding reaction-producing substances, using medications that can prevent attacks or lessen their severity, and administering allergy shots that can, over time, strengthen the body's tolerance to allergens. More than half of all asthmatic children outgrow the condition completely, while another 10% improve to the point where they have only occasional asthma attacks as adults.

Skin allergies

There are three main types of skin allergies: eczema (atopic dermatitis), contact dermatitis, and hives (urticaria). Eczema, which is mainly a condition of infancy and childhood, generally occurs in a cycle that begins with dry, itchy skin, followed by inflammation, "weeping," and crusting, all produced by scratching. At the chronic stage, the affected skin area becomes thickened, leathery, and scaly. Eczema appears most often on the cheeks, ears, and neck, and the inner folds of elbows and knees, but it may affect other parts of the body as well. It is commonly found in allergy-prone families and usually outgrown by the age of six. Aside from avoiding allergens, the most important treatment is to keep the skin lubricated by using hypoallergenic lotions and gentle soaps. (For extremely dry, sensitive skin, Cetaphil lotion may be used as a cleanser instead of soap.) Eczema tends to be aggravated by sweating, food allergies, infections, and emotional stress.

Contact dermatitis—as its name suggests—is caused by topical contact with an irritant, which can be a plant (such as poison ivy), chemical, metal, cosmetic preparation, or other substance. Diaper rash is the most common form of contact dermatitis in infants. The most effective treatment is to avoid contact with known irritants. Calamine lotion, hydrocortisone ointments and creams, and other preparations can help alleviate itching once symptoms occur.

Hives (urticaria) are red, itchy blotches of varying size that can occur anywhere on the body but are especially common on the stomach, chest, arms, hands, and face. A related condition is angioedema, a swelling that may affect the eyelids, lips, mucous membranes, genitals, and other areas. Both of these conditions are treatable with antihistamines, epinephrine, and cromolyn. They are usually acute rather than chronic, although they can sometimes persist for weeks. Intractable cases may be treated with oral cortisone, which should be used sparingly and only as a last recourse because of its side effects.

Food allergies

True food allergies are often confused with intolerance to certain foods. Whereas food allergies, like other types of allergies, are caused by an antibody response, intolerance is produced by a lack of enzymes needed to digest a certain food. For example, people born without the enzyme lactase cannot digest one of the sugars in milk and suffer from gastrointestinal problems when they consume milk and certain milk products. By contrast, an allergy to milk is caused by sensitivity to an allergen (often the protein lactalbumin) in the milk itself. Besides cow's milk, other foods that commonly cause allergic reactions include eggs, grains (often wheat and corn), nuts, fruits (often seeded fruits, especially when served raw), vegetables (especially tomatoes and legumes such as peas, beans, and peanuts), fish and seafood, chocolate, and certain spices and food additives.

Reactions caused by food allergies include hives, swelling of the eyes, lips, and mouth, rashes, abdominal pain and diarrhea, and respiratory symptoms. Reactions to nuts and peanuts (which are actually legumes) can be so severe—even life-threatening—that physicians recommend caution in giving these foods to infants and children in families with a history of allergy. Some school systems are restricting the use of peanuts and peanut butter in lunchrooms or banning them altogether because even touching or smelling these foods can set off a reaction in children with an allergic sensitivity. The best course of action in treating food allergies is to determine which foods a child is allergic to—either by observation, an elimination diet, or skin tests—and then avoiding these foods. If the source of a food allergy cannot be determined, the allergic symptoms may be alleviated with antihistamines. Many food allergies are outgrown as children get older.

Other allergic reactions

About one-fifth of all children are allergic to some type of medication, often penicillin, sulfa drugs, or aspirin. In some cases, tolerance to a drug can be built up through desensitization. Insect venom from bites and stings is another potential cause of allergic reactions. Fortunately, children rarely experience the severe reactions sometimes seen in adults. Offending insects include honeybees, yellow jackets, wasps, hornets, and fire ants (which are found only in the South). Symptoms include hives, itchy eyes, a dry cough, constriction of the throat and chest, nausea, dizziness, and abdominal pain. A severe reaction requires emergency hospital treatment. With honeybee stings, the amount of venom entering the bloodstream can be reduced by removing the stinger (by scraping it off rather than plucking).

It is possible, although rare, for children to experience **anaphylaxis** or anaphylactic shock, the severe—and potentially fatal—allergic reaction (usually to drugs, insect stings, or food) that causes the airways and blood vessels to constrict. An effective emergency measure is an injection of epinephrine, which can control the symptoms until medical care is available.

For Further Study

Books

Feldman, B. Robert. *The Complete Book of Children's Allergies: A Guide for Parents.* New York: Times Books, 1986.

Gershwin, M. Eric, and Edwin L. Klingelhofer. *Conquering Your Child's Allergies.* Reading, MA: Addison-Wesley, 1989.

Postley, John E., and Janet Barton. *The Allergy Discovery Diet: A Rotation Diet for Discovering Your Allergies to Food.* New York: Doubleday, 1990.

Walsh, William. *The Food Allergy Book.* St. Paul, MN: ACA Publications, 1995.

Organizations

American Association of Certified Allergists
Address: 401 East Prospect Avenue, Suite 210
Mount Prospect, IL 60056
Telephone: (312) 255-1024
American Allergy Association
Address: P.O. Box 7273
Menlo Park, CA 94025

Allowance and Money Management

Money given to a child at some regular intervals, to use as the child chooses.

Parents differ in their opinions about giving allowances to their children. Some parents believe that they should provide for the material needs of their children. They think there is no reason a child should have to manage money until they are old enough to understand the working world and mature enough to make responsible purchases. Other parents feel that giving their children allowances is a good way to teach them about money and financial responsibility. If parents decide to give their children allowances, there are several methods of handling the issue. How much they receive, how often they receive it, what they may spend it on, and whether the children must "earn" their allowance by completing **chores** at home are all things for parents to consider.

Children younger than five are generally not mature enough to understand money management. A young child this age usually resists saving money, and will probably want to spend it right way. Older children, on the other hand, can take more responsibility for their money. As they learn math skills at school, they are more able to calculate expenses; they can begin to figure how much they need to save for a desired item, or how much they will have left over after making a purchase. The actual amount of allowance will vary widely from family to family, but one recent survey gives some national averages: six- to eight-year-olds receive on average $2.00 a week; 9- to 11-year-olds just over $4.00; 12- to 13-year-olds $5.82; 14- to 15-year-olds $9.68; and 16- to 17-year-olds $10.80. Some families will give close-in-age siblings the same amount of allowance, but general practice seems to be to give older children more money than younger children.

Saving money is a difficult concept for most children because it is difficult for them to be patient and imagine future wants. If a child wants to buy an item that costs more than his or her allowance, parents can be flexible in their options. They can allot the child some extra-allowance expenditures or help the child figure out how long it would take to save his or her allowance. Parents may offer to provide matching funds—contributing a dollar for every dollar the child saves.

Some parents devise a category system to help their children manage their allowances. The first category is short-term expenses—money the child may spend right away on whatever he or she wants. The second category is saving. Savings may be placed in a special jar, where its slow accumulation is visible. This money is used for items the child wants that cost more than the amount of the weekly allowance. The third category is charity—the church alms plate, or a local cause, for example—or gifts for family members. The parents may determine how a younger child's allowance should be divided among the three categories, or the budgeting may be left up to an older child.

Allowances for teenagers may be a sore topic for many parents. Some parents stop giving allowances to their teenagers at a certain age and encourage them to get a part-time job. Some families put teenagers in charge of all their own expenses, so that they learn to budget. Money can become a difficult issue between parents and children of any age, and learning to be flexible can help each member of the family become more financially responsible.

For Further Study

Books

Drew, Bonnie. *MoneySkills: 101 Activities to Teach Your Child About Money.* Hawthorne, NJ: Career Press, 1992.

Estess, Patricia Schiff, and Irving Barocas. *Kids, Money and Values.* Cincinnati, OH: Betterway Books, 1994.

Godfrey, Neale, with Tad Richards. *A Penny Saved: Using Money to Teach Your Child the Way the World Works.* New York: Simon & Schuster, 1995.

Weinstein, Grace W. *Children and Money: A Parents' Guide.* Rev. ed. New York: New American Library, 1985.

Periodicals

Marcus, Mary Brophy. "Start 'em Young: Kids and Money." *U.S. News & World Report,* March 24, 1997, vol. 122, no. 11, p. 66.

Kramer, Pamela S. "Children and Cash." *Woman's Day,* February 1, 1997, vol. 60, no. 5, pp. 46+.

Bodnar, Janet. "'Dr. T' Tackles Some Toughies: Got Questions About Kids and Money? Dr. Tightwad Has the Answers." *Kiplinger's Personal Finance Magazine,* June 1996, vol. 50, no. 6, pp. 85+.

Cazzin, Julie. "Kids, Cash and Capitalism." *Maclean's,* May 6, 1996, vol. 109, no. 19, p. 40.

—A. Woodward

Alopecia

Hair loss.

Alopecia is partial or total loss of hair as a result of any number of causes, including the normal aging process. In children, alopecia may be a reaction to a drug or therapy (such as chemotherapy or radiation therapy), or may result from a skin disorder or **hormone** imbalance. When hair is lost in patches for unknown causes, the condition is termed *alopecia areata.* When bald spots are the result of compulsive hair-pulling, the condition is termed **trichotillomania.**

Alpha Fetoprotein (AFP) Test

Prenatal test that tests for birth defects.

The Alpha Fetoprotein (AFP) Test is a commonly used prenatal test to monitor the level of AFP—a possible indicator of developmental abnormalities—in the liver of a **fetus** during high-risk pregnancies. The protein is obtained either through amniotic fluid extracted during an **amniocentesis** or from a sample of the mother's blood, usually collected at about the sixteenth week of pregnancy. High AFP levels may indicate abnormal development of the **brain** or spinal cord or problems with the abdominal wall. Elevated levels of AFP are also an indicator of premature delivery and low birth weight. Low levels of AFP can point to chromosomal disorders, including **Down syndrome.** AFP screening is problematical because of the high rate of false positives (over 90% of abnormal readings), creating unnecessary anxiety and necessitating further tests. It is generally recommended that women have two AFP screenings and an ultrasound to arrive at a definitive result. The test is usually indicated only for women with a family history of neural tube defects such as **spina bifida** or other problems.

For Further Study

Books

Blatt, Robin J. R. *Prenatal Tests: What They Are, Their Benefits and Risks.* New York: Vintage Books, 1988.

Charlish, Anne, and Linda Hughey Holt. *Birth-Tech: Tests and Technology in Pregnancy and Birth.* New York: Facts on File, 1991.

Morrison, George S. *The World of Child Development: Conception to Adolescence.* Albany, NY: Delmar Publishers, 1990.

Alternative School

Public or private school that employs a non-traditional structure or curriculum.

An alternative school is one that offers an approach to education that varies from the traditional structure of a group of students in a self-contained classroom learning from a predetermined course of study. Examples of alternative approaches include **nongraded schools,** where students are grouped for reasons other than chronological age or year in school; **curriculum**-based independent study, where each student pursues a unique course of study; and programs designed to manage behavior or other learning difficulties. The majority of alternative schools, according to the National Coalition of Alternative Community Schools (NCACS), are private.

Some public school districts are establishing alternative schools to educate **at-risk** students. For example, in 1982, one public school district outside Baltimore, Maryland, established an alternative public school to educate troubled teenagers. Special programs included a "positive **discipline**" program that awarded students points every period during the school day for behavior, attitude, and academic performance. Points could be redeemed for privileges. The school reportedly has been successful in establishing a disciplined learning environment for students who were likely to drop out or fail to complete high school.

The U.S. Department of Education encourage parents to consider the credentials of teaching faculty and a school's accreditation when selecting a school for their children.

For Further Study

Books

Koetzsch, Ronald E. *The Parents' Guide to Alternatives in Education.* Boston: Shambhala, 1997.

Periodicals

Hiraoka, Leona. "Face It: Alternative Schools for Troubled Youth." *NEA Today* 14, April 1996, pp. 4+.

Organizations

National Coalition of Alternative Community Schools (NCACS)
Address: P.O. Bos 15036
Santa Fe, NM 87506
Telephone: (505) 474-4312

National Association for Legal Support of Alternative Schools (NALSAS)
Address: P. O. Box 2823
Santa Fe, NM 87501
Telephone: (505) 471-6928

National Education Association
Address: 1201 Sixteenth St. N.W.
Washington, DC 20036
Telephone: (202) 833-4000
website: http://www.nea.org

Amblyopia

A common eye problem in which one eye does not develop normal vision.

Amblyopia is also known as lazy **eye.** It occurs when one eye sees better than the other because of injury or because of an underlying eye problem. The child learns to depend on the "good" eye, and sight in the weaker eye atrophies. Amblyopia is children is most commonly a side-effect of **strabismus**—crossed or misaligned eyes. **Cataracts** and astigmatism can also lead to amblyopia. In amblyopia there is nothing organically wrong with the weaker eye. But the **brain** learns to suppress vision in the weaker eye, and if this continues, the eye may lose sight altogether. If amblyopia is diagnosed and treated by the age of three, it is generally quite curable. Treatment usually consists of patching the stronger eye, forcing the child to use the less developed eye so the weaker eye can "catch up." Treatment may last anywhere from weeks to years.

For Further Study

Books

Collins, James F. *Your Eyes: An Owner's Guide.* Englewood Cliffs, NJ: Prentice-Hall, 1995.

Savage, Stephen. *Eyes.* New York: Thomson Learning, 1995.

Showers, Paul. *Look at Your Eyes.* New York: HarperCollins Publishers, 1992.

Zinn, Walter J., and Herbert Solomon. *Complete Guide to Eyecare, Eyeglasses and Contact Lenses.* Hollywood, FL: Lifetime Books, 1995.

Organizations
National Eye Institute
    Address: Building 31, Room 6A32
    Bethesda, MD 20892
    Telephone: (301) 496-5248

—A. Woodward

Amenorrhea

Amenorrhea is the absence of menstruation.

There are two types of amenorrhea, primary and secondary. Primary amenorrhea is delayed **menarche** (the first menstrual period) and is defined as any one of three conditions:

1.) absence of menarche by age 16 with otherwise normal pubertal development (development of breasts and/or pubic hair)

2.) absence of menarche by age 14 with delayed pubertal development

3.) absence of menarche two years after puberty is otherwise completed

Family history should be taken into consideration in any adolescent with primary amenorrhea. Mothers who started to menstruate late will often have daughters who also menstruate late.

Secondary amenorrhea is the absence of menstruation after menarche has taken place. Although it is not uncommon for menstrual periods to be irregular during early **adolescence**, periods usually become regular within 18 months after the first one. After that time, it is considered abnormal for an adolescent to miss three consecutive periods.

Pregnancy

An adolescent with amenorrhea most likely does not have a serious underlying medical problem. Even so, all teenagers with amenorrhea should seek medical care, and an adolescent who has had sexual intercourse even once and then missed a period should assume she is pregnant until a reliable pregnancy test proves otherwise. It should be noted that spotting, or even bleeding, is not unusual during early pregnancy. In addition, it is possible for a girl to conceive before she has had even one period.

Other causes of amenorrhea

If pregnancy is ruled out as the cause of an adolescent's amenorrhea, a doctor will consider several other causes. After pregnancy, the most common reason for amenorrhea (both primary and secondary) is that the ovaries are not receiving appropriate messages from the hypothalamus and the pituitary gland. When this happens, the ovaries do not produce adequate amounts of hormones to trigger **menstruation**.

Less common causes of amenorrhea include pituitary tumor or a problem with the ovaries or uterus. In most cases, however, amenorrhea does not indicate a serious medical problem, and regular periods will resume without any treatment.

Stress

Emotional stress will sometimes prevent the brain from signaling the ovaries properly. It is not uncommon for a woman's period to be delayed when she is having problems with school, work, or relationships. A change in environment (the start of college, for example) can also cause a period to be late.

Physical stress is a common cause of amenorrhea. A girl who is too thin or has too little body fat may not begin to menstruate at the expected age. In girls who have started menstruating, insufficient body fat may cause the periods to stop. Athletes and other women who **exercise** strenuously sometimes experience amenorrhea even when their body weight and body fat levels are within normal ranges.

Diagnosis

One way to determine whether a teenager's ovaries and uterus are functioning is a "progesterone challenge test." In this test, an amenorrheic teenager is given a dose of progesterone, either orally or as an injection. If her ovaries are making estrogen and her uterus is responding normally, she should start a menstrual period within a few days of the progesterone dose. This indicates that the ovaries and uterus are functioning normally, and the cause of the amenorrhea is probably in the brain.

Risks and treatment

The most serious risk associated with amenorrhea is osteoporosis (thinning of the bone) caused by low estrogen levels. Because osteoporosis can begin as early as adolescence, hormone replacement therapy is sometimes recommended for teenagers with chronic amenorrhea.

See also **Menarche, Menstruation**

For Further Study

Books
Bell, Ruth, et al. *Changing Bodies, Changing Lives.* New York: Vintage, 1988.

Organizations

American College of Obstetricians and Gynecologists
Address: 409 12th Street
Washington, DC 20024
(Brochures on menstruation and other topics)

—Gail B. Slap, M.D.
University of Pennsylvania School of Medicine

American Academy of Child & Adolescent Psychiatry

The American Academy of Child and Adolescent Psychiatry (AACAP) represents over 5,000 child and adolescent psychiatrists, all of whom have at least five years of additional training beyond medical school in the fields of general and child and adolescent psychiatry. The members of the Academy actively research, diagnose, and treat psychiatric disorders affecting children and adolescents and their families and support their activities through a variety of programs such as governmental liaison, national public information, and continuing medical education.

The Academy was established in 1953 as the American Academy of Child Psychiatry with fewer than 100 members. Today the AACAP is a dynamic, growing organization whose mission is to direct and respond quickly to new developments in the health care environment, particularly as they affect the needs of children, adolescents, and their families.

The Academy sponsors over 45 committees which work to increase the areas of knowledge for Academy members and the public, and to disseminate information including position statements on various issues such as adolescent psychiatric hospitalization, **pregnancy** prevention, and substance abuse.

The Academy's strong commitment to furthering the understanding and treatment of children and adolescents is also reflected in the wide range of their activities, which include publishing the bi-monthly *Journal* of the American Academy of Child and Adolescent Psychiatry and a quarterly *Newsletter;* promoting support for research careers; providing a national continuing medical education program and participating in the American Medical Association regarding innovations in treatment; and providing public information in the form of published *Facts for Families,* a collection of informational sheets providing the most up-to-date material discussing current psychiatric issues concerning children, adolescents, and their families.

For Further Study

Organizations

American Academy of Child and Adolescent Psychiatry
Address: 3615 Wisconsin Ave., N.W.
Washington, DC 20016
Telephone: (202) 966-7300

American Academy of Pediatrics

Professional association of pediatricians.

The American Academy of Pediatrics (AAP) is a professional association that represents and serves approximately 48,000 **pediatricians** in the United States, Canada, and Latin America, over 34,000 of whom are also board-certified Fellows of The American Academy of Pediatrics (FAAP). Its mission is to promote the attainment of optimal physical, mental, and social health for all infants, children, adolescents, and young adults through advocacy, access to health care, research, service, and public and professional education.

The AAP was founded in June 1930 by a small group of pediatricians who met in Detroit in an attempt to establish an independent pediatric forum to address the special developmental and health needs of children. Its first members wanted to revolutionize children's health care by developing preventive health practices such as **immunizations** and regular health exams. Today these have become standard pediatric health care practices.

Currently the AAP includes 30 committees with such diverse interests as injury and poison prevention, disabled children, sports medicine, nutrition, and child health financing. The Academy also comprises 41 sections consisting of more than 19,000 members who represent the whole spectrum of pediatric specialties as well as 7,000 pediatric residents.

Among the AAP's professional education activities are postgraduate education courses, biannual scientific meetings, seminars, and statements from its committees and sections. In addition, it publishes *Pediatrics,* a monthly professional journal, *Pediatrics in Review,* a continuing education journal, and the *AAP News,* the monthly membership newsletter. Among its public education efforts are manuals on different topics, patient education brochures, *Healthy Kids Magazine,* a series of child care books written by AAP members, and the *Healthy Kids* cable TV show. The Academy also executes original research, promotes its funding, and pursues federal and state legislative advocacy on behalf of children's health needs.

See also **Pediatrician.**

For Further Study

Organizations

American Academy of Pediatrics
    Address: 141 Northwest Point Blvd.
    P.O. Box 927
    Elk Grove Village, Illinois 60009-0927
    Telephone: (708) 228-5005

American Psychiatric Association

Profesional association of psychiatrists.

The American Psychiatric Association is a national medical society whose approximately 38,000 physician and medical student members specialize in the diagnosis and treatment of mental and emotional disorders. The oldest medical specialty society in the United States, the APA was begun in October 1844, when 13 physicians who specialized in the treatment of mental and emotional disorders met in Philadelphia and founded the Association of Medical Superintendents of American Institutions for the Insane. Their goals were to communicate professionally, cooperate in the collection of data, and improve the treatment of the mentally ill.

One hundred fifty years later, the APA's objectives are still designed to advance care for people with mental illnesses: to improve treatment, rehabilitation, and care of the mentally ill and emotionally disturbed; to promote research, professional education in psychiatry and allied fields, and the prevention of psychiatric disabilities; to advance the standards of psychiatric services and facilities; to foster cooperation among those concerned with the medical, psychological, social, and legal aspects of mental health; to share psychiatric knowledge with other practitioners of medicine, scientists, and the public; and to promote the best interests of patients and others actually or potentially using mental health services.

The APA supports psychiatrists and their service to patients through publications such as the *American Journal of Psychiatry,* the oldest specialty journal in the United States, and the *Psychiatric News,* the Association's official newsletter, as well as numerous books, journals, and reports. The APA's annual meeting attracts more than 15,000 attendees and features hundreds of sessions and presenters. Additionally the Association schedules more than 200 meetings each year among its councils, committees, and task forces to further advance the cause

of mental health. The APA also offers a comprehensive continuing medical education program to its members.

For Further Study

Organizations

American Psychiatric Association
    Address: 1400 K Street, NW
    Washington, D.C. 20005
    Telephone: (202) 682-6000

American Psychological Association

Professional association whose members are psychologists worldwide.

The American Psychological Association (APA) was founded in July 1892 by three dozen members. By the 1990s, it was both the world's largest association of psychologists and the major organization representing psychology in the Unites States, including 77,000 members nationally and around the world, 47,000 students, foreign, and high school teacher affiliates, and 48 specialty divisions.

The program of the APA is organized in four domains, each of which contributes to the central goal of seeking ways to increase human wellness through an understanding of behavior. The Science Directorate promotes the exchange of ideas and research findings through conventions, conferences, publications, and traveling museum exhibits. It also helps psychologists locate and obtain research funding. Its science advocacy program works for the enhancement of federal support for psychology, research, and teaching. The Practice Directorate promotes the practice of psychology and the availability of psychological care through legislative advocacy on such issues as health care reform, regulatory activities such as state licensure, and public service such as the pro bono services provided through the Disaster Response Network. The Public Interest Directorate supports the application of psychology to the advancement of human welfare through program and policy development, conference planning, and support of research, training, and advocacy in areas such as minority affairs, women's issues, and lesbian and gay concerns. The Education Directorate serves to advance psychology in its work with educational institutions, professional agencies, and programs and initiatives in education.

The APA's information dissemination efforts include the publication of books as well as more than 24 scientific and professional journals and newsletters such as *APA Monitor* and *American Psychologist.* Since 1970,

PsychINFO, a worldwide computer database, has provided references in psychology and related behavioral and social sciences. The week-long APA annual convention is the world's largest meeting of psychologists, featuring more than 3,000 papers, lectures, and symposia and is attended by more than 15,000 psychologists.

See also **Child Psychologist.**

For Further Study

Organizations

American Psychological Association
  Address: 750 First Street, NE
  Washington, DC 20002-4242
  Telephone: (202) 336-5500

American Sign Language (ASL)

Language of hand gestures and symbols, most of which express an idea or concept rather than a word, used for communication with deaf and hearing-impaired people.

American Sign Language (ASL or Ameslan) is a language of hand gestures and symbols widely used by deaf and hearing-impaired people for communication. ASL has its own grammar rules, and puts words in different order than English. Linguists have studied ASL since the 1960s, and designate ASL as meeting all the requirements of a language—it has grammar rules and uses symbols to express ideas and concepts. ASL uses a single gesture to express many ideas and concepts—it does not require the communicator to reproduce every word in a spoken English-language sentence in gestures. Beginning signers often use ASL signs in the same order as they would words in an English sentence—this is known as "pidgin signing." Most deaf people can understand ASL signed this way. As signers become more fluent in ASL, the appropriate grammar rules and word order become easier to sign. Sign language gestures may be formed with either the left or right hand. When deaf people communicate with each other, they often use ASL; when a deaf person communicates with a hearing person, ASL may be modified to more closely parallel English-language sentence structure.

For Further Study

Books

Cokely, Dennis, and Charlotte Baker-Shenk. *American Sign Language: A Teacher's Resource Text on Curriculum, Methods, and Evaluation.* Washington, DC: Gallaudet University Press, 1990.

A conversation in sign language.

Gallaudet University Press. Wide range of publications for adults and children, including sign language dictionaries. Call (202) 651-5488.

Humphries, Tom, and Carol Padden. *Learning American Sign Language.* Englewood Cliffs, NJ: Prentice Hall, 1992.

Moore, Matthew S., and Linda Levitan. *For Hearing People Only: Answers to Some of the Most Commonly Asked Questions about the Deaf Community, Its Culture, and the "Deaf Reality."* Rochester, NY: Deaf Life Press, 1992.

Audiovisual Recordings

Beginning American Sign Language Videocourse. Salem, OR: Sign Enhancers, 1992.

Practice Sentences: Interpretation, English to ASL. Salem, OR: Sign Enhancers, 1994.
  (videorecording)

Organizations

Publications and visual aids on sign language available from Sign Media, Inc.
  Address: 4020 Blackburn Lane
  Burtonsville, MD 20866-1167
  Telephone: toll-free (800) 475-4756 (voice or TTY)

Amniocentesis

A medical test that involves withdrawing a sample of fluid from the amniotic sac surrounding the fetus in the abdomen of the pregnant woman.

Amniocentesis is a procedure used to detect the presence of genetic disorders such as **Down syndrome** and **spina bifida** in a **fetus**. The primary tool for prenatal diagnosis, it is also used to determine the maturity level of a potentially premature baby. Amniocentesis is normally performed in the 14th–16th weeks of pregnancy in women considered to be at risk of Down syndrome or other problems.

Prior to the development of amniocentesis in the 1950s, there was no way to detect whether a baby might be born with serious health problems. Amniocentesis has changed the nature of pregnancy by offering greater information about the fetus and creating more decisions for the parents. If problems exist with the fetus, the pregnant woman must decide if she will continue the **pregnancy**.

Amniocentesis takes advantage of a wealth of 20th-century technological and medical advances in **genetics,** fetal development, and diagnostic testing knowledge. The procedure is performed by inserting a hollow needle through the abdominal and uterine walls into the amniotic sac. The fluid in the amniotic sac is rich with cells from the fetus, and approximately half an ounce of amniotic fluid is removed.

The fluid is placed in a centrifuge that divides the cells from the liquid. The amniotic liquid and the cells are then analyzed. The amniotic fluid is examined to determine the level of **alpha fetoprotein**, a chemical normally present in the **blood**. High levels of alpha fetoprotein suggest a possible spinal-cord defect such as spina bifida, while low levels of the chemical suggest the possibility of Down syndrome.

The cells, called amniocytes, may also be examined for genetic abnormalities or inborn metabolic errors. Some problems can only be detected after the cells are cultured (the process of growing cells in a laboratory in special material that encourages cell growth).

Amniocentesis is not without some risk to the fetus. About 0.5% of all amniocentesis procedures cause spontaneous **abortion**s. Other possible complications include injury to the fetus and infection of the fetus or the mother. Another disadvantage of the procedure is that it cannot be performed until the 14th week of pregnancy, when the symptom is already well established. Test results cannot be reported for two weeks.

The most common genetic abnormality detected with amniocentesis is Down syndrome. Down syndrome occurs when children are born with 47 chromosomes in each cell instead of the normal 46. Children with this syndrome are mentally retarded and are more likely to have congenital heart disorders and other health problems. Women are at greater risk of giving birth to a Down syndrome child as they grow older. Women 35 and over are generally advised to have an amniocentesis when they are pregnant because the risk of having a Down syndrome child is higher than the risk of losing a baby due to amniocentesis at this stage.

Spina bifida, a serious disorder in which the spine develops abnormally, is another health problem that can be detected by amniocentesis. Spina bifida usually causes some paralysis and may cause other physical disabilities. Inborn metabolic disorders detected by amniocentesis include **Tay-Sachs disease**, a genetic disorder that causes blindness and paralysis. It is fatal in infancy.

Couples at risk for other health problems are also advised to have an amniocentesis. This includes men or women who already have a child with a chromosome abnormality, neural tube defect, or metabolic disorder. A family history of certain genetic problems may also prompt some pregnant women to have an amniocentesis.

The long-term outlook for children born following amniocentesis is positive. A Canadian study compared the health of 1,298 children who had experienced amniocentesis before birth with 3,738 children who had not experienced the procedure. The study, which examined children ages 7–18, found no higher incidence of any health problems in the children who had undergone an amniocentesis.

Experts disagree about whether pregnant women younger than 35 should have amniocentesis. Only 25% of the women who give birth to Down syndrome babies are 35 or older, which means most Down syndrome infants are born to women younger than 35. Some experts have suggested that women 30 and over should have amniocentesis.

Another dispute concerns whether amniocentesis should be used as a tool to select the sex of a fetus. Opinion on the issue has changed among genetics counselors who advise potential parents about genetic testing. In 1975 only 1% of a physicians and technologists polled reported that they would perform amniocentesis for the purpose of sex selection. By 1988 a total of 62% said they would perform the procedure for this purpose.

As knowledge of genetics increases, the scope of information provided through amniocentesis should also increase, creating more choices for pregnant women and their families. Critics say amniocentesis and other prenatal tests have changed pregnancy from a seamless nine months of preparation to a time of uncertainty and important decision-making. While this may be true, amniocentesis has also provided tools for the healthy birth of many infants, including many born to parents whose genetic heritage would have made the birth of healthy offspring unlikely.

For Further Study

Books

Rothman, Barbara Katz. *The Tentative Pregnancy.* New York: Viking Press, 1986.

Merkatz, Irwin R., and Joyce E. Thompson. "Prenatal Diagnosis" in *New Perspectives on Prenatal Care.* New York: Elsevier, 1990.

Wilson, J. Robert, and Elsie Reid Carrington. "Amniocentesis" in *Obstetrics and Gynecology.* St. Louis: Mosby Year Book. 1991.

Periodicals

Baird, P.S., I.M.L. Yee, and A.D. Sadovnick. "Population-Based Study of Long-Term Outcomes after Amniocentesis." *The Lancet* 344, October 22, 1994, pp. 1134–36.

Boss, Judith A. "First Trimester Prenatal Diagnosis: Earlier Is Not Necessarily Better." *Journal of Medical Ethics* 20, 1994, pp. 146–51.

Nicolaides, Kypros, Maria de Lourdes Brizot, Fatima Patel, and Rosalinde Snijders. "Comparison of Chorionic Villus Sampling and Amniocentesis for Fetal Karyotyping at 10-13 Weeks' Gestation." *The Lancet* 344, August 13, 1994, pp. 435–39.

Organizations

American College of Obstetricians and Gynecologists
Address: 409 12th Street
Washington, DC 20024

Anabolic Steroids

Types of drugs that increase strength and muscle growth when ingested by humans.

Anabolic steroids are drugs containing **hormones,** or hormone-like substances, that are used to increase strength and promote muscle growth. They were first developed in the 1930s in Europe to treat undernourished patients and to promote healing after surgery. Competitive weightlifters began using steroids in the 1950s as a way to increase their athletic performance. Use gradually spread throughout the world among athletes in other **sports.**

It has been estimated that at least one in 15 male high school seniors in the United States—more than a half-million boys—has used steroids. Some are athletes attempting to increase their strength and size; others are simply youths attempting to speed up their growth to keep pace with their peers. In some countries, anabolic steroids are available over the counter. In the United States, a doctor's prescription is necessary.

While the effects of steroids can seem desirable at first, there are serious side effects. Excessive use can cause a harmful imbalance in the body's normal hormonal balance and body chemistry. Heart attacks, water retention leading to high blood pressure and stroke, and liver and kidney tumors all are possible. Young people may develop **acne** and a halting of bone growth. Males may experience shrinking testicles, falling sperm counts, and enlarged prostates. Women frequently show signs of masculinity and may be at higher risk for certain types of **cancer** and the possibility of **birth defects** in their children.

The psychological effects of steroid use are also alarming: drastic mood swings, inability to sleep, and feelings of hostility. Steroids may also be psychologically addictive. Once started, users—particularly athletes—enjoy the physical "benefits" of increased size, strength, and endurance so much that they are reluctant to stop even when told about the risks. Major athletic competitions, including the Olympic Games, routinely screen athletes to prevent illegal steroid use.

For Further Study

Books

Dolan, Edward F. *Drugs in Sports.* New York: Franklin Watts, 1986.

Talmadge, Katherine S. *Focus on Steroids.* Frederick, Md.: Twenty-First Century Books, 1991.

Anaclitic Depression

A form of depression in young children that is caused by maternal deprivation.

The concept of anaclitic depression was introduced in 1946 by psychiatrist René Spitz to refer to children who became depressed after being separated from their mothers for a period of three months or longer during the second six months of life. Since these children had no one to "lean on" for the nurturance they required, Spitz coined the term anaclitic (leaning upon) depression to identify their condition. Without an adquate mother substitute, the children exhibited a number of physical and psychological symptoms. They were socially withdrawn and suffered from weight loss, sleeplessness, retarded psychomotor development, and a greater-than-average incidence of physical illness. After three months, some developed physical rigidity.

In those children who were reunited with their mothers within six months, the condition was completely reversed, and they were restored to normal emotional health. However, children who continued without adequate mothering did not improve, eventually exhibiting further signs of deterioration, including agitation, **mental** retardation, or lethargy. In the most extreme cases, their depressed state led to death from marasmus, a condition in which a child wastes away from starvation. The clinical recognition of anaclitic depression as a reaction to maternal separation helped stimulate interest in mothering as an important behavioral and developmental factor in infants.

See also **Attachment; Depression.**

For Further Study

Books

Cytryn, Leon, and Donald H. McKnew. *Growing Up Sad: Childhood Depression and Its Treatment.* New York: Norton, 1996.

Anaphylaxis

Anaphylaxis is a severe, sudden, often fatal bodily reaction to a foreign substance or antigen.

In humans, anaphylaxis is a rare event usually triggered by an antiserum (to treat snake or insect bites), **antibiotics** (especially immunoglobulin), or wasp or bee stings. Certain foods can also trigger these severe reactions, including seafood (particularly shellfish), rice, potatoes, peanuts, egg whites, raw milk, and pinto beans.

In systemic or system-wide cases, symptoms occur just minutes (or in rare cases weeks) after introduction of the foreign substance and include flushed skin, itching of the scalp and tongue, breathing difficulties caused by bronchial spasms or swollen tissues, vomiting, diarrhea, a sudden drop in blood pressure, shock, and loss of consciousness. Less severe cases, usually caused by nonimmunologic mechanisms, may produce widespread hives or severe headache. These less severe cases are called anaphylactoid reactions. Any anaphylactic reaction must be considered a medical emergency and requires immediate professional intervention.

Charles-Robert Richet (1850–1935), a French physiologist, first coined the term to define the puzzling reactions that occurred in dogs following injection of an eel toxin. Instead of acquiring immunity from the toxin as expected, the dogs experienced acute reactions, including often fatal respiratory difficulties, shock, and internal hemorrhaging. While the exact biological process is poorly understood, anaphylaxis is thought to result from antigen-antibody interactions on the surface of mast cells, a connective tissue cell that is believed to contain a number of regulatory chemicals. This interaction damages cell membranes, causing a sudden release of chemicals, including histamine, heparin, serotonin, bradykinin, and other pharmacologic mediators. Once released, these mediators produce the frightening bodily reactions that characterize anaphylaxis.

Because of the severity of these reactions, treatment must begin as soon as possible. The most common emergency treatment involves injection of epinephrine (adrenaline), followed by administration of cortisone, antihistamines, and other drugs that can reduce the effects of the unleashed chemical mediators.

Anaphylactic reactions to food are rare in children, but those who experience them must be taught never to eat that food again. Reading food labels in grocery stores and restaurants and alerting school kitchen personnel are other precautions that help prevent emergencies. In addition, parents need to be aware that vaccines or antibiotics commonly administered to children can in some cases trigger anaphylactic symptoms. It is usually recommended that children remain in the doctor's office near medical care for a period of time after receiving such injections as a precaution.

For people with known reactions to antibiotics, foods, insect and snake bites, or other factors, avoidance of the symptom-inducing agent is the best form of prevention. Anyone, child or adult, who has experienced an anaphylactic episode is advised to wear a Medic Alert bracelet or carry a medical emergency card with them at all times in case of emergency.

For Further Study

Books

How to Take Your Medicine: Nonsteroidal Anti-inflammatory Drugs. Rockville, MD: Department of Health and Human Services, Public Health Service, Food and Drug Administration, Office of Public Affairs, 1990.

It's Spring Again and Allergies Are in Bloom: Anaphylaxis, An Allergic Reaction That Can Kill. Rockville, MD: Department of Health and Human Services, Public Health Service, Food and Drug Administration, Office of Public Affairs, 1990.

Young, Stuart H., et al. *Allergies.* Yonkers, NY: Consumer Reports Books, 1991.

Audiovisual Recordings

It Only Takes One Bite. Virginia: Time Frame Productions, 1993.
(One 18-minute videocassette.)

Anatomical Age

Numerical assessment of a child's physical growth in relation to statistical average.

Using statistical data, the **American Academy of Pediatrics** and the National Institutes of Health in the United States have developed tables to illustrate the growth patterns of children. These tables describe the population of all children of a certain age, with ranges for weight, height, and other physical characteristics. For most children, anatomical age—based on weight and height measurements—is the same as chronological age—based on the number of months or years since birth. However, when a child's physical growth falls outside the range of his chronological age, the child's age will be determined by his growth. For example, if a six-year-old's height and weight falls within the range for five-year-olds, his anatomical age will be given as five.

Androgen Hormones *see* **Hormones**

Androgyny

Having the characteristics of both a man and a woman; not clearly identified as male or female.

Since roughly the 1960s, there have been areas of modern culture where the roles and characteristics of men and women have begun to merge. Supported by legislation that prohibits discrimination because of gender, women assume roles and participate in activities that were formerly reserved—by tradition or law—for men only. Arguments against traditional gender roles are debated in Congress, in the military, and even in the home. A variety of products, such as clothing, bath products, and perfumes, are being marketed to be used by members of both sexes. Androgynynous behavior—dressing in clothing or wearing a hairstyle that is neither masculine nor feminine—is most common in **adolescence** and young adulthood, when the person is establishing his or her identity.

Androgyny in parenting

Androgynous parenting refers to the situation in which a child's mother and father share equally and relatively interchangeably in parenting responsibilities. Some researchers feel that breaking down traditional gender roles in parenting can provide the child with a richer relationship with both parents, a broader role for both mother and father to model, and a more rewarding experience for both parents. Others feel that a strong case should be made against the trend toward androgynous parenting and for the preservation of gender roles in parenting. Among them is researcher David Popenoe, who has analyzed evidence derived from social and biological research. He supports the notion that, for optimal child development, preservation of some aspects of gender roles in parenting results in positive outcomes. Popenoe cites the work of child development expert Urie Bronfenbrenner, who has written extensively on the early stages of human development. Bronfenbrenner and many

others feel that a child must develop a strong **attachment** with one or more persons in order to develop intellectually, emotionally, socially, and morally. In addition, he believes the pattern of interaction and emotional attachment between caregiver and child depends on the involvement of someone else. This third party assists in and encourages the person caring for the child. University of Wisconsin psychologist Willard W. Hartup has also argued that the significance and success of the father's role may be in how his relationship with his children complements the relationship they have with their mother.

For Further Study

Books
Cook, Ellen Piel. *Psychological Androgyny.* New York: Pergamon Press, 1985.

Kovach, Barbara E. *Sex Roles and Personal Awareness.* Lanham, MD: University Press of America, 1990.

Moir, Anne and David Jessel. *Brain Sex: The Real Difference Between Men and Women.* New York: Lyle Stuart, 1991.

Periodicals
Popenoe, David. "Parental Androgyny." *Society* 30, September-October 1993, p. 5+.

Rubinstein, Carin. "Reining in Androgyny." *Psychology Today* 13, March 1980, p. 27+.

Anemia

Deficiency of red cells, or hemoglobin, in the blood.

Anemia is a medical condition in which the quantity of red **blood** cells falls below an acceptable level. Red blood cells, produced in the bone marrow, contain hemoglobin, the component of blood that carries oxygen from the lungs to the body's tissues. Red blood cells circulate in the blood for about 120 days and are then filtered out by the lymphatic system and destroyed, usually in the spleen. When more cells are destroyed than are produced, anemia can result.

Anemia can range from mild to life-threatening in severity, and has a number of causes. The disease can be caused by a single significant blood loss or from a long-term chronic illness. Fetal anemia can develop when the mother's and **fetus**'s blood have **Rh factor** incompatibility. During prenatal tests and newborn examinations, the mother and infant are routinely tested for anemia.

Iron-deficiency anemia

The most common form of anemia results from a deficiency of iron, a key component for the production of hemoglobin. In infancy, iron-deficiency anemia is a problem for infants who are not breastfed, or who are born in developing countries where adequate nutrition or medical attention may not be available. Researchers have discovered that one technique to prevent iron-deficiency anemia among newborns is to wait for about one minute after birth before clamping the umbilical cord. This enables more blood to flow from mother to infant.

Toddlers and young children may develop anemia when they are introduced to solid foods and the variety of their diet becomes important. According to Ibrahim Parvanta, a nutritionist with the Centers for Disease Control and Prevention in Atlanta, Georgia, children ages 6–24 months may have insufficient iron stored in their systems to meet their bodies' needs during this phase of rapid physical growth. He estimates that approximately 9% of children in this age group have at least mild iron deficiency. Symptoms of iron-deficiency anemia are fatigue, paleness, headaches, dizziness, and lowered immunity. In infants and children, iron-deficiency anemia can be a serious condition, resulting in impaired physical and mental development.

Iron requirements increase during periods of rapid growth and at the onset of **menstruation** in girls. Anemia in adolescence is most commonly iron-deficiency anemia. Teenage girls, concerned about their weight, often have diets that are inadequate in iron; an estimated one in four adolescent girls has iron deficiency.

Treatment of iron deficiency usually begins with a doctor's recommendation to increase iron in the diet, or perhaps with a prescription for iron supplements. Iron-rich foods are of two types. The first type of food contains heme iron, which is easier for the body to absorb. These include liver, red meat, poultry, and fish. The second type contains nonheme iron, less easily absorbed by the body, and includes dried apricots, prunes, dates, raisins, beans, tofu, nuts, and leafy green vegetables, such as spinach. Absorption of iron by the body is aided by vitamin C, so adding citrus fruits to an iron-rich meal improves the body's ability to make use of the iron. Using iron cookware to prepare foods also increases the iron content of foods. In general, it is preferable to treat anemia by adding iron-rich foods to the diet, since some people experience nausea when taking iron supplements.

Iron in large quantities is also toxic. The National Capital Poison Control Center at Georgetown University in Washington, DC, reports that from 1988–1992, accidental poisoning from overdose of iron supplements accounted for about 17% of all children's deaths reported to poison control centers. Iron supplements should be considered poisonous, and kept out of the reach of children.

Thalassemia

Thalassemia is a genetic disorder of the blood in which the red blood cells are small and fragile. Thalassemia is found among people of Mediterranean, Middle Eastern, or Southeast Asian descent, and is sometimes re-

RECOMMENDED DIETARY ALLOWANCES (RDAS) FOR IRON

Note: Because iron is stored in the body, the RDAs represent the recommended average intake, not the recommended amount of iron to be consumed daily.

Infants up to 6 months:	6 mg
Children 6 months to 10 years:	10 mg
Females ages 11 to 50:	15 mg
Pregnant women:	30 mg
Women 60 and over:	10 mg
Males ages 10 to 18:	12 mg
Men 18 and over:	10 mg

ferred to as "Mediterranean anemia." The most severe form, known as beta-thalassemia, thalassemia major, or Cooley's anemia, develops during infancy with slow physical growth and **jaundice.** The spleen and bone marrow may become enlarged, causing abnormal skeletal development. If untreated, thalassemia leads to death in later childhood or adolescence. Treatment includes blood transfusions or bone marrow transplants. However, a dangerous side effect of transfusions is build-up of excess iron in the system.

Sickle-cell anemia

Sickle-cell anemia is a genetic disorder that most commonly affects African Americans, but is also found among those of Mediterranean descent. Victims of the disorder have crescent-shaped red blood cells. The unusual shape prevents the cells from carrying oxygen efficiently and causes the cells to become lodged in the capillaries, causing a person intense pain.

Aplastic anemia

Aplastic anemia is characterized by an insufficient supply of all blood cell types, including an abnormal or insufficient production of red cells in the bone marrow. Aplastic anemia, diagnosed in 5,000–6,000 Americans a year, can result from severe viral infections, diseases of the immune system, and hepatitis. It is also associated with **cancer** therapies such as chemotherapy or radiation therapy, both of which adversely affect the bone marrow's ability to produce red blood cells. If not successfully treated, aplastic anemia results in death for about 85% of those afflicted by the condition.

Aplastic anemia is considered a medical emergency, and a bone marrow transplant is performed as quickly as possible after diagnosis. Bone marrow transplantation from a family member is most successful and is recommended for younger patients. Transplantation from unrelated donors has only been achieved in very small children.

Megaloblastic anemia

Megaloblastic anemia is due to a deficiency of certain vitamins, notably vitamin B_{12} and folic acid, which causes the marrow to produce red cells that are larger than normal and have reduced oxygen-carrying ability. These abnormal red blood cells are called macrocytes. Sometimes the deficiency occurs when the person's diet is deficient. Vitamin B_{12} is found in foods of animal origin, such as meat, fish, and dairy products; folic acid is found in green vegetables and liver. In other cases, the deficiency occurs because the person's body is unable to absorb the B_{12}, a condition known as pernicious anemia.

For Further Study

Books

Larkin, Marilynn. *What You Can Do About Anemia.* New York: Dell, 1993.

Periodicals

Krucoff, Carol. "Exercise and Iron." *Saturday Evening Post,* September-October 1996, vol. 268, no. 5, p. 21+.

Purdy, Candy. "Anemia: More Than 'Tired Blood.'" *Current Health* 2, Sept 1994, vol. 21, no. 1 p. 28+.

Raloff, Janet. "Umbilical Clamping Affects Anemia Risk." *Science News,* April 27, 1996, vol. 149, no. 17, p. 263.

Young, Neal S. "Aplastic Anaemia." *The Lancet,* July 22, 1995, vol. 346, no. 8969, pp. 228–32.

Audiovisual Recordings

Rosner, Fred. *The Doctor Talks to You About Anemias.* Bayside, NY: Soundwords, Inc., 1982.

Anesthesia

The loss of feeling or sensation. It may be accomplished without the loss of consciousness, or with partial or total loss of consciousness.

Anesthesiology is a branch of medical science that relates to anesthesia and anesthetics. The anesthetist is a specialized physician in charge of supervising and administering anesthesia in the course of a surgical operation. Depending on the type of operation and procedures used, there are two types of anesthesia: general anesthesia, which causes a loss of consciousness, and local anesthesia, where the anesthetic "freezes" the nerves in the area covered by the operation. In local anesthesia, the patient may be conscious during the course of the operation or given a sedative, a drug that induces sleep.

While the search for pain control during surgery dates back to the ancient world, it was not until 1846 that it went on record that a patient was successfully rendered unconscious during a surgical procedure. Performed in a Boston hospital, the operation used a gas called ether to anesthetize the patient while a neck tumor was removed. In Western medicine, the development of anesthesia has made possible complex operations like open heart surgery and organ transplants. Medical tests that would otherwise be impossible to perform are routinely carried out with the use of anesthesia.

Before the landmark discovery of ether as an anesthetic, patients who needed surgery for either illness or injury had to face the surgeon's knife with only the help of alcohol, opium, or other narcotic. Often a group of men held the patient down during the operation in case the narcotic or alcohol wore off before it was over. Under these conditions many patients died just from the pain of the operation.

Nitrous oxide, another gas still commonly used in dentistry, minor surgery, and some major surgery, was discovered in 1776 by British chemist Joseph Priestly. Another early anesthetic, chloroform, was discovered in 1847 by James Young Simpson. The Scottish gynecologist and obstetrician was searching for an anesthetic that would make bearing children less painful for women. Chloroform use, though, had higher risks than those associated with ether, and it called for greater skill from the physician. Neither ether nor chloroform are used in surgery today.

Anesthesiology as a medical specialty was slow to develop. By the end of the 19th century, ether was administered by "etherizers" who had little medical experience, including students, new physicians, non-medical specialists, nurses, and caretakers. Eventually, nurses began to be used for this job, becoming the first anesthetists by the end of the 19th century.

While the practice of surgery began to make considerable progress by the turn of the century, anesthesiology lagged behind. In the 20th century, though, the need for specialists in anesthesia was sparked by two world wars and advanced surgical techniques. To meet these demands, the American Society of Anesthetists was formed in 1931 and specialists were then certified by the American Board of Anesthesiology in 1937. By 1986, the Board certified 13,145 specialists—physicians and nurses, called nurse anesthetists—in the field of anesthesiology.

Modern anesthesiology can be divided into two types, pharmacological and non-pharmacological. Pharmacological anesthesia uses a wide variety of anesthetic agents to obtain varying degrees of sedation and pain control. The anesthesia is administered orally, by injection, or with a gas mask for inhalation. Examples of non-pharmacological anesthesia are the use of breathing techniques during conscious childbirth delivery (Lamaze method of natural childbirth) and the ancient art of Chinese acupuncture. Non-pharmacological anesthesia requires special skills on the part of its practitioners, and its effects are not as reliable as pharmacological techniques.

Pharmacological anesthesia is described as either general or local. There are three phases to general anesthesia. The anesthetist must first induce the state of unconsciousness (induction), keep the patient unconscious while the procedure is performed (maintenance), then allow the patient to emerge back into consciousness (emergence).

Administration of the anesthetic is usually accomplished by the insertion of a cannula (small tube) into a vein. Sometimes a gas anesthetic may be introduced through a mask. If a muscle relaxant is used, the patient may not be able to breathe on his own, and a breathing tube is passed into the windpipe (trachea). The tube then serves either to deliver the anesthetic gases or to ventilate (oxygenate) the lungs.

During the course of the surgery, the anesthesiologist maintains the level of anesthetic needed to keep up the patient's level of anesthesia to the necessary state of unawareness while monitoring vital functions, such as heart beat, breathing, and blood/gas exchange.

There are a number of possible complications that can occur under general anesthesia. They include loss of blood pressure, irregular heart beat, heart attack, vomiting and then inhaling the vomit into the lungs, coma, and death. Although mishaps do occur, the chance of a serious complication is extremely low. Avoidance of complications depends on a recognition of the condition of the patient before the operation, the choice of the appropriate anesthetic procedure, and the nature of the surgery itself.

Local anesthetics block pain in regions of the body without affecting other functions of the body or overall consciousness. They are used for medical examinations, diagnoses, minor surgical and dental procedures, and for relieving symptoms of minor distress, such as itching, toothaches, and hemorrhoids. They can be taken as creams, ointments, sprays, gels, or liquid; or they can be given by injection and in eye drops.

Some local anesthetics are benzocaine, bupivacaine, cocaine, lidocaine, procaine, and tetracaine. Some act rapidly and have a short duration of effect, while others may have a slow action and a short duration. They act by blocking nerve impulses from the immediate area to the higher pain centers. Regional anesthetics allow for pain control along a wider area of the body by blocking the action of a large nerve (nerve block). Sprays can be used on the throat and related areas for a bronchoscopy, and gels can be used for the urethra to numb the area for a catherization or cystoscopy.

Spinal anesthesia is used for surgery of the abdomen, lower back, and legs. Spinal or "epidural" anesthesia is also used for surgery on the prostate gland and hip. A fine needle is inserted between two vertebrae in the lumbar (lower part) of the spine, and the anesthetic flows into the fluid which surrounds the spinal cord. The nerves absorb the anesthetic as they emerge from the spinal fluid. The anesthetized area is controlled by the location of the injection and the amount of absorption by the spinal fluid.

It is possible to have adverse reactions to local anesthetics, such as dizziness, hypotension (low blood pressure), convulsions, and even death. These effects are rare but can occur if the dose is too high or if the drug has been absorbed too rapidly. A small percentage of patients (1–5%) may develop headaches with spinal anesthesia.

Babies born to mothers who have been administered anethetics during labor and delivery often show anesthetic effects for a period of time after birth. Medication given to women immediately before delivery passes through the placenta to the baby. While the effects of the anesthetic wear off relatively quickly for the mother, it takes the baby's immature system longer to process it out of the body. Affected babies frequently appear lethargic and unresponsive for longer periods of time after birth than babies delivered without maternal medication. While use of anesthetics by the mother is not believed to have any permanent impact on the baby, many pediatricians contend difficulties in breastfeeding and maternal bonding can result from babies' unresponsive behavior in the early days of life.

Special care also must be taken when administering anesthetics to children. Allergic or anaphylactic reactions to a particular medication are difficult to predict, particularly in younger patients who have experienced fewer medical procedures.

Since World War II, many changes have taken place in anesthesiology. Important discoveries have been made with such volatile liquids as halothane and synthetic opiates. The technology of delivery systems has been greatly improved. But with all these changes, the basic goal of anesthesia has been the same—the control of a motionless surgical field in the patient. In the next fifty years it is possible that the goals of anesthesia will be widened. The role of anesthesia will broaden as newer surgical techniques develop in the area of organ transplants. Anesthesia may also be used in the future to treat acute infectious illness, mental disorders, and different types of heart conditions. There may be a wide range of new therapeutic applications for anesthesia.

For Further Study

Books

Barash, Paul G., Bruce F. Cullen and Robert K. Stoelting. *Clinical Anesthesia.* Philadelphia: Lippincott, 1992.

Brazelton, T. Berry. *Doctor and Child.* New York: Delacorte Press/Seymour Lawrence, 1976.

Mckenry, Leda M., and Evelyn Salerno. *Mosby's Pharmacology in Nursing.* Philadelphia: Mosby, 1989.

Anomia

A neurological condition that impairs one's ability to name persons and objects.

Anomia is a type of **aphasia**, a category of disorders caused by damage to the parts of the **brain** that control language and communications. Parts of the brain that may be involved in anomia and other types of aphasia include the auditory cortex, which enables people to make sense of what they hear; Wernicke's area, where words are stored; and Broca's area, which enables the organs of speech to receive the signals sent by Wernicke's area. Aphasia is usually caused by head injuries, tumors, strokes, or infections that affect the brain, particularly the left side of the brain, which controls communication in most people (the concentration of language function in the left brain is less strong for people who are left-handed or have a family history of left-**handedness**).

Anomia is part of the broader category of non-fluent aphasias, in which the person speaks hesitantly because of difficulty naming words and/or producing correct syntax. The non-fluent aphasic may know that he has not found the right word to express what he wants to say or may be unaware that what he is saying is wrong. By comparison, the fluent aphasic produces words readily and abundantly, but they don't make any sense. Non-fluent aphasias generally involve damage to the anterior (front) portions of the brain, while fluent aphasias are associated with the posterior (rear) areas. Aphasias are not necessarily accompanied by any loss of intelligence or **memory** (other than the memory for words). Anomia varies from one person to another. Some have more trouble with "content" words, while others have difficulty with smaller words like "in" and "the." Some have more trouble with proper nouns than common nouns, while others forget them equally.

A person with anomia may be able to drive, work, and perform other activities requiring normal (or even above normal) intelligence as long as they do not require extensive and accurate verbal communication. Many persons (especially young persons) recover from anomia and other aphasias, as long as the condition is not due to a degenerative illness that continues to get worse. Speech therapy may be necessary, as words often cannot be re-learned by the simple repetition through which they were acquired originally. Words can often be more readily recalled if used in common contexts. Another helpful technique for restoring the vocabulary of persons with anomia is to present words in a narrow semantic context, asking them to complete sentences from which only one word is missing.

Researchers have found that persons with normal brains may have problems similar to those of persons suffering from anomia if they are hampered by external forces such as distractions or intoxication.

For Further Study

Books

Teaching Aphasic Children: The Instructional Methods of Barry and McGinnis. Austin, TX: Pro-Ed, 1988.

Sagan, Carl. *Broca's Brain.* New York: Random House, 1979.

Anorexia Nervosa

A psychiatric disorder characterized by a distorted body image leading the person to believe that she is overweight even when she is dangerously underweight.

Anorexia nervosa is a psychiatric disorder in which a person's (usually a girl's) distorted body image leads her to believe that she is overweight even when she is dangerously underweight. Anorectics employ a number of weight-loss strategies, including fasting, dieting, exercise, induced vomiting, and laxative abuse. A girl is considered anorexic when her weight drops below 85% of what is expected for her height and age. Anorexia typically affects adolescent girls; the average age of onset is 13.7 years. Girls with anorexia tend to be perfectionists with a deep-seated need to feel in control. Environmental factors may play a role in the development of anorexia. Although not all anorectics' family situations will fit these generalizations, parents of anorectics tend to be rigid and overprotective, and they often avoid open discussion of problems and tensions.

Physical effects

Anorexia, which is technically starvation, has serious physical effects on a growing adolescent's body. These effects include:

Growth problems. In a young girl who has not finished growing, anorexia can increase the risk of bone deformities or limit eventual adult height.

Delay of sexual maturation. When the percentage of a girl's body fat drops below a certain critical level, a girl will not ovulate or menstruate, and **puberty** will not progress normally.

Gastrointestinal problems. Diarrhea brought about by laxative use can cause dehydration and electrolyte imbalance. Vomiting can cause pancreatic, esophageal, glandular, and dental problems.

Endocrine and metabolic problems. Hypoglycemia (low blood sugar) can cause dizziness and confusion. Malnutrition may result in weakness, fatigue, or muscle cramps. Dehydration is possible.

Skin and hair abnormalities. Anorectics' skin is typically dry and mottled. A fine hair called lanugo grows on the shoulders, back, arms, and face, and pubic and underarm hair becomes thin.

Cardiovascular problems. Anorexia affects heart rate, blood pressure, body temperature, blood volume, and heart size.

Psychological effects

The biological effects of anorexia can compound existing psychological problems as well as contribute to new ones. **Depression**, for example, is a common effect of starvation. As malnutrition depletes a girl's energy stores, her anxiety level may increase because the lethargy she's experiencing makes her feel a loss of control over her body. The anorectic responds to this anxiety by imposing even more stringent restrictions on her diet, which leads to further malnutrition.

Treatment and prognosis

Anorexia nervosa is a life-threatening disease and should be taken seriously. If an adolescent girl exhibits any signs of anorexia, a doctor should be alerted without delay. Effective treatment for anorexia incorporates **psychotherapy**, medical monitoring, and nutrition education. In extreme cases, hospitalization may be necessary.

In many people, abnormal behaviors associated with anorexia (induced vomiting and laxative abuse, for example) will continue in adulthood. More than one quarter of adolescent anorectics will continue to experience **anxiety** or depression as adults, and one in five will continue to be underweight. Anorexia nervosa has one of the highest **suicide** rates of any psychiatric disorder.

See also **Bulimia, Eating Disorders**

For Further Study

Books

Jablow, Martha M. *A Parent's Guide to Eating Disorders and Obesity.* New York: Delta Publishing, 1992.

Maloney, Michael, and Rachel Kranz. *Straight Talk About Eating Disorders.* New York: Facts on File, 1991.

Organizations

National Eating Disorders Organization
   Address: 6655 Yale Avenue
   Tulsa, OK 74136
   Telephone: (918) 481-4044

National Association of Anorexia Nervosa and Associated Disorders (ANAD)
   Address: P.O. Box 7
   Highland Park, IL 60035
   Telephone: (847) 831-3438

Anoxia

Lack of oxygen in the blood supply, also called oxygen starvation.

This term is used to describe a deficiency in, or blockage of, the supply of oxygen in the body. Although not common, anoxia may occur during any stage of fetal development, infancy, or throughout life. *In utero,* the **fetus** may experience anoxia due to a variety of problems related to the mother's **pregnancy.** During prolonged labor and difficult **birth,** neonates (newborn infants) may experience a brief (or sometimes prolonged) cut-off of the supply of oxygen due to such developments as premature separation of the placenta during birth. The growing infant and child are at risk of anoxia mostly in accident-type situations such as **choking**, near-drowning, and near-suffocation. High **fever** may also result in anoxia, although this is rare. In extreme cases, **anemia** may cause the **blood** to be ineffective at carrying adequate oxygen to the body's tissues and organs.

The **brain** is among the organs most susceptible to oxygen starvation. When the brain is affected by anoxia, the special term **hypoxia** is applied. If the brain receives too little oxygen, **developmental disorders** and related **learning disabilities** may result.

Antibiotics

Drugs used to combat bacteria that cause infection.

Antibiotics are substances that combat bacteria, and, as a result, relieve the symptoms of infections caused by bacteria. They have only been available since the end of World War II (1945). There are millions of kinds of bacteria, and the bacteria that harm humans are called "pathogenic bacteria" or pathogens. Some pathogenic bacteria, such as tetanus, cause the human body to produce toxins or poisons as a by-product. These toxins circulate through the body, causing serious illness, or even death. The majority of infections by pathogenic bacteria do not produce these toxins, however. Rather, they cause localized infections, such as an **ear** infection. In babies and young children, antibiotics are used to treat **strep throat**; ear, sinus, and urinary tract infections; **conjunc-**

tivitis; pulmonary infections, such as **bronchitis** and pneumonia; and skin infections, such as impetigo, caused by staph (staphylococcus) bacteria.

Antibiotics work by interfering with the life cycle of bacteria. Some types of antibiotics work by preventing the pathogenic bacteria from multiplying; others work by actually killing the pathogenic bacteria. Antibiotics themselves are produced by certain bacteria and fungi to combat other bacteria and fungi. Scientists have built upon the strengths of naturally occurring antibiotics to develop synthetic versions to target specific strains of bacteria. Different antibiotics are absorbed by the body in different ways. The earliest available antibiotic, a strain of penicillin, is only absorbed by the body through injection.

Physicians prescribe antibiotics according to their diagnosis of the pathogenic bacteria causing the infection. In some cases, a specimen from the infected area (throat swab or urine sample, for example) will be cultured to determine the optimum antibiotic for treating the infection. Antibiotics are powerful, and should be administered with care. It is important to follow the dosage instructions carefully and to take the full course of medication. Discontinuing the antibiotic once the child's condition improves could result in the bacteria flaring up again, having not been fully eradicated. Allergic reactions to antibiotics are not uncommon. Reactions vary from individual to individual, and also depend upon the antibiotic being administered. Reactions range from a mild skin rash to the most severe allergic reactions, including anaphylactic shock, a life-threatening drop in blood pressure that requires immediate attention. Once it has been determined that a child has allergic reactions to antibiotics, it is vital to teach him or her never to take that antibiotic again.

For Further Study

Books

Encyclopedia of Antibiotics. New York: Wiley, 1992.
Handbook of Antibiotics. New York: Little, Brown, 1988.
Lappi, Marc. *When Antibiotics Fail: Restoring the Ecology of the Body.* Berkely, CA: North Atlantic Books, 1995.

Antidepressants

Medications used to treat depression.

Depression in children and adults is similar to the clinical course in adults. It can be reliably diagnosed by a trained mental health professional through clinical interviews with the child or adolescent and outside observers (parents, teachers). Depression causes significant impairment in school, in the family, and in peer relationships. It is associated with other psychiatric disorders, suicidal thoughts, and **suicide** attempts. Both psychotherapy and medication can be effective treatments for depression, either alone or in combination.

The two most common types of antidepressants are tricyclic antidepressants (TCAs) and selective serotonin re-uptake inhibitors (SSRIs). Examples of TCAs include nortriptyline (also known by the brand name Pamelor), imipramine (Tofranil), and desipramine (Norpramin). Examples of SSRIs include fluoxetine (Prozac), sertraline (Zoloft), and paroxetine (Paxil). Clinical studies have shown that some children and adolescents benefit from these medications.

Tricyclic antidepressants (TCAs)

Before using TCAs, it is necessary to have a medical history and examination of the child, including an electrocardiogram (EKG). Not everyone develops side effects when taking TCAs, but the most common side effects include: dry mouth, impaired ability to focus vision at close range, constipation, urinary hesitation, dizziness, weight gain, and sedation. TCAs may produce minor cardiovascular changes such as orthostatic hypotension (low blood pressure when the person stands up, often causing light-headedness), **hypertension**, rapid heart beat, and minor changes in the electrical activity of the heart, which may show in the electrocardiogram (EKG). Most of these side effects can be minimized by slowly increasing or reducing TCA dosage.

During the treatment with TCAs, patients should be monitored by a physician trained in the management of these medications. It is recommended that he or she perform regular blood pressure, heart rate, and EKG monitoring. TCAs may interact with other medications; therefore, parents should inform their children's physicians that the child is taking a TCA. Finally, the TCAs should not be stopped abruptly because doing so may induce mild withdrawal side effects (malaise, chills, stomachache, flu-like symptoms). Though they are safe if carefully monitored and taken as prescribed, TCAs can be lethal if taken in overdose. Therefore parents must be responsible for storing and administering the medication in order to avoid accidental or intentional overdose.

It is important to report that four to five cases of sudden death have been reported in children taking the TCA medication desipramine. (Biederman et al., 1995). However, it is not clear whether the death of these children was due to the medication or other causes.

Selective serotonin re-uptake inhibitors (SSRIs)

The reports that SSRIs are effective in treating adults with major depressive disorder (MDD), together with the findings that SSRIs have a relatively benign side effect profile, low lethality after an overdose, and once-a-day administration, have encouraged the use of SSRIs in children and adolescents.

Several studies have reported 70–90% response rate to fluoxetine or sertraline for the treatment of adolescents with major depressive disorder (MDD), (Birmaher et al., 1996b), but the results of these studies are not conclusive because they have methodological limitations. A recent, large, well-performed investigation showed that fluoxetine was more effective for the treatment of depressed children and adolescents than placebo. Despite the significant response to fluoxetine, many patients had only partial improvement.

Overall, the SSRIs have similar effectiveness and side effects as TCAs. The most common side effects include nausea, stomachache, diarrhea, headaches, mild tremors, sweating, sleep disturbance, sedation, restlessness, lack of appetite, decreased weight, vivid dreams, and sexual dysfunction (inability to have an orgasm or delayed ejaculation). Most of these side effects are temporary and may be diminished by reducing the dose or discontinuing the medication. There are no specific laboratory tests required before administering SSRIs. SSRIs do have potentially harmful interactions with several commonly prescribed drugs; therefore, all physicians should be informed if someone is taking an SSRI.

Children and adolescents who do not respond to treatment

The most common reasons for failure of treatment are inadequate medication dosage or length of medication trial, lack of compliance with treatment, exposure to chronic or severe life events that require different modalities of therapy, existence of other psychiatric disorders (e.g., substance abuse, **anxiety** disorder), and misdiagnosis. There are very few studies of children and adolescents with depressions that are deemed "treatment resistant." In adults with resistant depression, several types of combinations of medications and ECT (electroconvulsive therapy) have been found to be useful.

For Further Study

Periodicals

Biederman, J., S. Farone, E. Mick, and E. Lelon. "Psychiatric Comorbidity Among Referred Juveniles with Major Depression: Fact or Artifact?" *Journal of the American Academy of Child and Adolescent Psychiatry* 34, 1995, pp. 579–90.

Birmaher, B., et al. "Child and Adolescent Depression I: A Review of the Past Ten Years." *Journal of the American Academy of Child and Adolescent Psychiatry* 35, no. 11, 1996a, pp. 1427–39.

Birmaher, B., N. D. Ryan, D. Williamson, D. A. Brent, J. Kaufman (1996b). "Childhood and Adolescent Depression: A Review of the Past Ten Years–Part II." *Journal of the American Academy of Child and Adolescent Psychiatry* 35, no. 12, 1996b, pp. 1575–83.

Kye, C., and N. D. Ryan. "Pharmacologic Treatment of Child and Adolescent Depression." *Child and Adolescent Psychiatric Clinics of North America* 4, no. 2, 1985, pp. 261–81.

Wilens, T., J. Biederman, J. Baldessarini, B. Geller, D. Schleifer, B. Birmaher, and T. Spencer. "The Cardiovascular Effects of Tricyclic Antidepressants in Children and Adolescents." *Journal of the American Academy of Child and Adolescent Psychiatry* 35, no. 11, pp. 1491–1501.

Antisocial Behavior

A pattern of behavior that is verbally or physically harmful to other people, animals, or property, including behavior that severely violates social expectations for a particular environment.

Antisocial behavior can be broken down into two components: the presence of antisocial (i.e., angry, aggressive, or disobedient) behavior and the absence of prosocial (i.e., communicative, affirming, or cooperative) behavior. Most children exhibit some antisocial behavior during their development, and different children demonstrate varying levels of prosocial and antisocial behavior. Some children may exhibit high levels of both antisocial and prosocial behaviors; for example, the popular but rebellious child. Some, however, may exhibit low levels of both types of behaviors; for example, the withdrawn, thoughtful child. High levels of antisocial behavior are considered a clinical disorder. Young children may exhibit hostility towards authority, and be diagnosed with **oppositional-defiant disorder.** Older children may lie, steal, or engage in violent behaviors, and be diagnosed with **conduct disorder.** Mental health professionals agree, and rising rates of serious school disciplinary problems, delinquency, and violent crime indicate, that antisocial behavior in general is increasing. Thirty to 70% of childhood psychiatric admissons are for disruptive behavior disorders, and diagnoses of behavior disorders are increasing overall. A small percentage of antisocial children grow up to become adults with **antisocial personality disorder,** and a greater proportion suffer from the social, academic, and occupational failures resulting from their antisocial behavior.

Causes and characteristics

Factors that contribute to a particular child's antisocial behavior vary, but usually they include some form of family problems (e.g., marital discord, harsh or inconsistent disciplinary practices or actual **child abuse,** frequent changes in primary **caregiver** or in housing, learning or cognitive disabilities, or health problems). **Attention deficit/hyperactivity disorder** is highly correlated with

SCHOOL SOCIAL BEHAVIOR SCALES (SSBS)

The School Social Behavior Scales is one rating scale designed for teachers to assess social competence and antisocial behavior in a K–12 educational setting. Following is a selected list of some of the behaviors it measures:

From SSBS Scale A, Social Competence. These describe prosocial behaviors.

Interpersonal Skills:

Offers help to other students when needed

Effectively participates in group discussions and activities

Understands other students' problems and needs

Invites other students to participate in activities

Exhibits skills or abilities that are admired by peers

Interacts with a wide variety of peers

Is skillful at initiating or joining conversations with peers

Self-Management Skills:

Cooperates with other students in a variety of situations

Remains calm when problems arise

Is accepting of other students

Compromises with peers when appropriate

Follows classroom rules

Academic Skills:

Appropriately transitions between different classroom activities

Completes individual seatwork without being prompted

Listens to and carries out directions from teacher

Asks for clarification of instructions in an appropriate manner

From SSBS Scale B, Antisocial Behavior. These describe antisocial behaviors.

Hostile-Irritable Behaviors:

Blames other students for problems

Teases and makes fun of other students

Is disrespectful or "sassy"

Is easily provoked; has a "short fuse"

Acts "better" than others

Will not share with other students

Has temper outbursts or tantrums

Antisocial-Aggressive:

Takes others' things

Defies teacher or other school personnel

Cheats on schoolwork or in games

Gets into fights

Lies to teacher or other school personnel

Disruptive-Demanding:

Ignores teacher or other school personnel

Is overly demanding of teacher's attention

Is difficult to control

Bothers and annoys other students

---

antisocial behavior. A child may exhibit antisocial behavior in response to a specific stressor (such as the death of a parent or a **divorce**) for a limited period of time, but this is not considered a psychiatric condition. Children and adolescents with antisocial behavior disorders have an increased risk of accidents, school failure, early alcohol and substance use, **suicide,** and criminal behavior. The elements of a moderate to severely antisocial personality are established as early as kindergarten. Antisocial children score high on traits of impulsiveness, but low on **anxiety** and reward-dependence—that is, the degree to which they value, and are motivated by, approval from others. Yet underneath their tough exterior antisocial children have low **self-esteem.**

A salient characteristic of antisocial children and adolescents is that they appear to have no feelings. Besides showing no care for others' feelings or remorse for hurting others, they tend to demonstrate none of their own feelings except anger and hostility, and even these are communicated by their aggressive acts and not necessarily expressed through affect. One analysis of antisocial behavior is that it is a **defense mechanism** that helps the child to avoid painful feelings, or else to avoid the anxiety caused by lack of control over the environment.

Antisocial behavior may also be a direct attempt to alter the environment. **Social learning theory** suggests that negative behaviors are reinforced during childhood by parents, caregivers, or peers. In one formulation, a child's negative behavior (e.g., whining, hitting) initially serves to stop the parent from behaving in ways that are aversive to the child (the parent may be fighting with a partner, yelling at a sibling, or even crying). The child will apply the learned behavior at school, and a vicious cycle sets in: he or she is rejected, becomes angry and attempts to force his will or assert his pride, and is then further rejected by the very peers from whom he might learn more positive behaviors. As the child matures, "mutual avoidance" sets in with the parent(s), as each party avoids the negative behaviors of the other. Consequently, the child receives little care or supervision and, especially during adolescence, is free to join peers who have similarly learned antisocial means of expression.

Different forms of antisocial behavior will appear in different settings. Antisocial children tend to minimize the frequency of their negative behaviors, and any reliable assessment must involve observation by mental health professionals, parents, teachers, or peers.

Treatment

The most important goals of treating antisocial behavior are to measure and describe the individual child's or adolescent's actual problem behaviors and to effectively teach him or her the positive behaviors that should be adopted instead. In severe cases, medication will be administered to control behavior, but it should not be used as substitute for therapy. Children who experience explosive rage respond well to medication. Ideally, an interdisciplinary team of teachers, social workers, and guidance counselors will work with parents or caregivers to provide universal or "wrap-around" services to help the child in all aspects of his or her life: home, school, work, and social contexts. In many cases, parents themselves need intensive training on modeling and reinforcing appropriate behaviors in their child, as well as in providing appropriate **discipline** to prevent inappropriate behavior.

A variety of methods may be employed to deliver social skills training, but especially with diagnosed antisocial disorders, the most effective methods are systemic therapies which address communication skills among the whole family or within a peer group of other antisocial children or adolescents. These probably work best because they entail actually developing (or redeveloping) positive relationships between the child or adolescent and other people. Methods used in social skills training include modeling, role playing, corrective feedback, and token reinforcement systems. Regardless of the method used, the child's level of cognitive and emotional development often determines the success of treatment. Adolescents capable of learning communication and problem-solving skills are more likely to improve their relations with others.

Unfortunately, conduct disorders, which are the primary form of diagnosed antisocial behavior, are highly resistant to treatment. Few institutions can afford the comprehensiveness and intensity of services required to

support and change a child's whole system of behavior; in most cases, for various reasons, treatment is terminated (usually by the client) long before it is completed. Often, the child may be fortunate to be diagnosed at all. Schools are frequently the first to address behavior problems, and regular classroom teachers only spend a limited amount of time with individual students. **Special education** teachers and counselors have a better chance at instituting long-term treatment programs—that is, if the student stays in the same school for a period of years. One study showed teenage boys with conduct disorder had had an average of nine years of treatment by 15 different institutions. Treatments averaged seven months each.

DEALING WITH ANTISOCIAL BEHAVIOR

Listed below are some essential guidelines for dealing with a child who displays antisocial behavior:

- Positively reinforce desired behaviors

- Ignore, or at least not reinforce, undesired behaviors —when possible ignore the behavior, but not the child

- Set firm limits and consequences for violations of limits, but do not ridicule or express hostility in punishing the child

- Provide access to physical outlets, such as dance or sports

- Use touch or physical closeness when appropriate to communicate care, especially to the young child who may have been neglected

- Show affection for the child—do not withhold affection in order to punish

- Accept angry feelings and offer alternatives to aggression as a means of expressing them, such as verbal expression

- Maintain positive expectations for the child's behavior rather than expecting failure—be surprised at failure

- Use physical restraint when necessary to prevent the child or adolescent from hurting someone else. Restraint may also help prevent him or her from having to "save face" by committing further antisocial acts

---

Studies show that children who are given social skills instruction decrease their antisocial behavior, especially when the instruction is combined with some form of supportive peer group or **family therapy.** But the long-term effectiveness of any form of therapy for antisocial behavior has not been demonstrated. The fact that peer groups have such a strong influence on behavior suggests that schools that employ collaborative learning and the mainstreaming of antisocial students with regular students may prove most beneficial to the antisocial child. Because the classroom is a natural environment, learned skills do not need to be transferred. By judiciously dividing the classroom into groups and explicitly stating procedures for group interactions, teachers can create opportunities for positive interaction between antisocial and other students.

See also **Antisocial Personality Disorder, Conduct Disorder, Oppositional-Defiant Disorder, Peer Acceptance.**

For Further Study

Books

Evans, W. H., et al. *Behavior and Instructional Management: An Ecological Approach.* Boston: Allyn and Bacon, 1989.

Landau, Elaine. *Teenage Violence.* Englewood Cliffs, NJ: Julian Messner, 1990.

McIntyre, T. *The Behavior Management Handbook: Setting Up Effective Behavior Management Systems.* Boston: Allyn and Bacon, 1989.

Merrell, K. W. *School Social Behavior Scales.* Bradon, VT: Clinical Psychology Pub. Co., 1993.

Redl, Fritz. *Children Who Hate*: The Disorganization and Breakdown of Behavior Controls. New York: Free Press, 1965.

Shoemaker, Donald J. *Theories of Delinquency: An Examination of Explanations of Delinquent Behavior,* 2nd ed. New York: Oxford UP, 1990.

Whitehead, John T. and Steven P. Lab. *Juvenile Justice: An Introduction.* Cincinnati, OH: Anderson Pub. Co., 1990.

Wilson, Amos N. *Understanding Black Adolescent Male Violence: Its Prevention and Remediation.* Afrikan World Infosystems, 1992.

Antisocial Personality Disorder

A behavior disorder developed by a small percentage of children with conduct disorder whose behavior does not improve as they mature. Also known as sociopathy or psychopathy.

About 3% of males and 1% of females develop antisocial personality disorder, which is essentially the adult version of childhood **conduct disorder.** Antisocial personality disorder is only diagnosed in people over age 18, the symptoms are similar to those of conduct disorder, and the criteria for diagnosis include the onset of conduct disorder before the age of 15. According to the *Diagnostic and Statistical Manual of Mental Disorders (DSM-IV),* people with antisocial personality disorder demonstrate a pattern of antisocial behavior since age 15.

The adult with antisocial personality disorder displays at least three of the following behaviors:

Fails to conform to social norms, as indicated by frequently performing illegal acts, and pursuing illegal occupations.

Is deceitful and manipulative of others, often in order to obtain money, sex, or drugs.

Is impulsive, holding a succession of jobs or residences.

Is irritable or aggressive, engaging in physical fights.

Exhibits reckless disregard for safety of self or others, misusing motor vehicles or playing with fire.

Is consistently irresponsible, failing to find or sustain work or to pay bills and debts.

Demonstrates lack of remorse for the harm his or her behavior causes others.

An individual diagnosed with antisocial personality disorder will demonstrate few of his or her own feelings beyond contempt for others. This lack of affect is strangely combined with an inflated sense of self-worth and often a superficial charm, which tends to mask their inner apathy. Authorities have linked antisocial personality disorder with abuse, either physical or sexual, during childhood, neurological disorders (which are often undiagnosed), and low IQ. Those with a parent with an antisocial personality disorder or substance abuse problem are more likely to develop the disorder. The antisocially disordered person may be poverty-stricken, homeless, a substance abuser, or have an extensive criminal record. Antisocial personality disorder is associated with low **socioeconomic status** and urban settings.

Treatment

Antisocial personality disorder is highly unresponsive to any form of treatment. Although there are medications available that could quell some of the symptoms of the disorder, noncompliance or abuse of the drugs prevents their widespread use. The most successful treatment programs are long-term, structured residential settings in which the patient systematically earns privileges as he or she modifies behavior. Some form of dynamic psychotherapy is usually given along with the behavior modification. The therapist's primary task is to establish a relationship with the patient, who has usually had very few relationships in his or her life and is unable to trust, fantasize, feel, or learn. The patient should be given the opportunity to establish positive relationships with as many people as possible and be encouraged to join self-help groups or prosocial reform organizations.

ANXIETY

See also **Antisocial Behavior, Conduct Disorder, Oppositional-Defiant Disorder, Peer Acceptance.**

For Further Study

Books

Cleckley, Hervey M. *The Mask of Sanity*. Rev. ed. New York: New American Library; St. Louis: Mosby, 1982.

Magid, Ken, and Carole A. McKelvey. *High Risk*. New York: Bantam Books, 1988.

Winnicott, D. W. *Deprivation and Delinquency*. New York: Tavistock Publications, 1984.

Organizations

Antisocial and Violent Behavior Branch
    Division of Biometry and Applied Sciences
    National Institute of Mental Health
    Address: 18-105 Parklawn Bldg.
    5600 Fishers Lane
    Rockville, MD 20857
    Telephone: (301) 443-3728

Anxiety

A condition of persistent nervousness, stress, and worry that is triggered by anticipation of future events, memories of past events, or ruminations about the self.

Stimulated by real or imagined dangers, anxiety affects people of all ages and social backgrounds. When it occurs in unrealistic situations or with unusual intensity, it can disrupt everyday life. Some researchers believe anxiety is synonymous with **fear,** occurring in varying degrees and in situations in which people feel threatened by some danger. Others describe anxiety as an unpleasant emotion caused by unidentifiable dangers or dangers that, in reality, pose no threat. Unlike fear, which is caused by realistic, known dangers, anxiety can be more difficult to identify and alleviate.

A small amount of anxiety is normal in the developing child, especially in adolescents and teens. Anxiety is often a realistic response to new roles and responsibilities, as well as to sexual and identity development. When symptoms become extreme, disabling, and/or when a child or adolescent experiences several symptoms over a period of a month or more, they may be a sign of an anxiety disorder and professional intervention may be necessary. The two forms of childhood anxiety are overanxious disorder and **separation anxiety,** although many physicians and psychologists also include panic disorder and **obsessive-compulsive disorder,** which tend to occur more frequently in adults. Anxiety that is the result of experiencing a violent event, disaster, or physical abuse is identified as post-traumatic stress disorder (PTSD). Most adult anxiety disorders begin in adolescence or young adulthood, and are more common among women than men.

Symptoms

Psychological symptoms of anxiety include tension; self-consciousness; fearfulness; self-doubt; worry; constant need for reassurance; distractibility; feeling as if one is about to have a heart attack, die, or go insane; irritability; and insomnia. Physical symptoms include rapid heartbeat, sweating, trembling, muscle aches (from tension), dry mouth, headache, stomach distress, diarrhea, constipation, frequent urination, hot flashes or chills, throat constriction (lump in the throat), and fatigue. Anxiety symptoms are very similar to those of **depression,** and as many as 50% of children with anxiety will also suffer from depression. Generally, physiological hyperarousal—excitedness, shortness of breath, the "fight or flight" response—characterizes anxiety disorders; whereas underarousal—lack of pleasure and feelings of guilt—characterizes depression. Other signs of anxiety problems are poor school performance, loss of interest in previously enjoyed activities, obsession about appearance or weight, social phobias (e.g., fear of walking into a room full of people), and the persistence of imaginary fears after ages six to eight. Shyness does not necessarily indicate a disorder, unless it interferes with normal activities and occurs with other symptoms. A small proportion of children do experience avoidant disorder, incapacitating shyness that persists for months or more, which should be treated. Similarly, performance anxiety experienced before athletic, academic, or theatrical events does not indicate a disorder, unless it significantly interferes with the activity.

Treatment

Depending on the severity of the problem, treatments for anxiety include school counseling, **family therapy,** and cognitive-behavioral or dynamic psychotherapy, sometimes combined with antianxiety drugs. Therapies generally aim for support—providing a positive, entirely accepting, pressure-free environment in which to explore problems; insight—discovering and working with the child or adolescent's underlying thoughts and beliefs; and exposure—gradually reintroducing the anxiety-producing thoughts, people, situations, or events in a manner so as to confront them calmly. Relaxation techniques, including meditation, may be employed in order to control the symptoms of physiological arousal and provide a tool the child can use to control his or her response.

Parents may also be trained to address their own symptoms, as well as their child's symptoms, if the parents also suffer from anxiety. Creative visualization, sometimes called rehearsal imagery by actors and athletes, may also be used. In this technique, the child writes down (or draws pictures of) each detail of the anxiety-producing event or situation and imagines his or her movements in performing the activity. The child also learns to perform these techniques in new, unanticipated situations.

In severe cases of diagnosed anxiety disorders, anti-anxiety and/or **antidepressant** drugs may be prescribed in order to enable therapy and normal daily activities to continue. Previously, **narcotics** and other sedatives, drugs that are highly addictive and interfere with cognitive capacity, were prescribed. With pharmacological advances and the development of synthetic drugs, which act in fairly specific ways on brain chemicals, a more refined set of antianxiety drugs is now available. Studies have found that generalized anxiety responds well to these drugs (benxodiazepines are the most common), which serve to quell the physiological symptoms of anxiety. Other forms of anxiety such as panic attacks, where the symptoms occur in isolated episodes and are predominantly physical (and the object of fear is vague, fantastic, or unknown), respond best to the antidepressant drugs. Childhood separation anxiety is thought to be included in this category. Psychoactive drugs should only be considered as a last treatment alternative, and extra caution should be used when they are prescribed for children.

For Further Study

Books

Carter, Frank, and Peter Cheesman. *Anxiety in Childhood and Adolescence: Encouraging Self-Help through Relaxation Training.* New York: Croom Helm, 1988.

Kendall, Philip C., et al. *Anxiety Disorders in Youth: Cognitive-Behavioral Interventions.* New York: Pergamon Press, 1991.

Newman, Susan. *Don't be S.A.D.: A Teenage Guide to Handling Stress, Anxiety and Depression.* Englewood Cliffs, NJ: J. Messner, 1991.

Organizations

Anxiety Disorders Association of America
  Address: 6000 Executive Boulevard, Dept. A
  Rockville, MD 20852
  Telephone: (301) 231-9350

National Institute of Mental Health (NIMH)
  Telephone: toll-free information services for panic and other anxiety disorders: (800) 647-2642

NIMH Public Inquiries
  Address: 5600 Fishers Lane, Rm. 7C-02
  Rockville, MD 20857

Apgar Score

An indication of a newborn infant's overall medical condition.

The Apgar score is based on a series of assessments devised by pediatrician **Virginia Apgar** (1909–1974) in 1953, and is standard procedure in many delivery rooms. The primary purpose of the Apgar test is to determine as soon after birth as possible whether an infant requires medical intervention and possibly transfer to a neonatal intensive care unit. The test, which is administered one minute after birth and again four minutes later, evaluates the newborn's heart rate, breathing, muscle tone, color, and reflexes. Each category is given a score between 0 and 2, with the highest possible test score totaling 10. The infant's heart rate is assessed as either under or over 100 beats per minute. Respiration is evaluated according to regularity and strength of the newborn's cry. Muscle tone categories range from limp to active movement. Color—an indicator of blood supply—is determined by how pink the infant is (completely blue or pale; pink body with blue extremities; or completely pink). Reflexes are measured by the baby's response to being poked and range from no response to vigorous cry, cough, or sneeze. An infant with an Apgar score of 8 to 10 is con-

APGAR SCORING SYSTEM			
Rating factor	**Zero**	**1 point**	**2 points**
Color	Blue or pale	Trunk pink, extremities blue	All pink
Heart rate	none	Under 100 beats per minute	Over 100 beats per minute
Muscle tone	Limp	Some movement of limbs	Active movement of limbs
Reflex irritability	No response	Grimace when "poked" in the nose	Cry, cough, or sneeze when "poked" in the nose
Respiratory effort	None	Irregular, with weak cry	Regular, with strong cry

sidered to be in excellent health. A score of 5 to 7 shows mild problems, while a total below 5 indicates that medical intervention is needed immediately.

For Further Study

Books

Apgar, V., and J. Beck. *Is My Baby Alright?* New York: Trident Press, 1972.

McCullough, Virginia. *Testing and Your Child: What You Should Know About 150 of the Most Common Medical, Educational, and Psychological Tests.* New York: Plume, 1992.

Uzgiris, Ina C., and J. McVicker Hunt. eds., *Infant Performance and Experience: New Findings with the Ordinal Scales.* Urbana, IL: University of Illinois Press, 1987.

Apgar, Virginia (1909–1974)

American pediatrician who created a scale for assessing newborn infant health.

Virginia Apgar graduated from Mount Holyoke College in 1929 and earned her M.D. degree from the College of Physicians and Surgeons at Columbia University in 1933. Although she spent her first two years in a surgical internship, Dr. Apgar elected to enter the growing field of anesthesiology. In 1949 she was appointed the first full professor of anesthesiology at Columbia. That same year, after building the department and training program, Dr. Apgar gave up her administrative duties as head of the anesthesiology department and turned to the study of anesthesia and its role in childbirth, assisting in the births of more than 17,000 infants during her career at Columbia.

Apgar published a system for the assessment of newborn health status in 1953. The scoring system that bears her name employs a ten point score based on two points each for healthy heart rate, respiration, muscle tone, reflexes, and color. Typically assessed at one and five minutes after birth, a low Apgar score serves as a quantified signal for further attention or evaluation. For over 40 years the Apgar score has remained the standard method of newborn assessment, prompting one physician to remark, "Every baby born in a modern hospital anywhere in the world is looked at first through the eyes of Virginia Apgar."

During a sabbatical year in 1959, Apgar received a master's degree in public health from Johns Hopkins University. Rather than returning to academic medicine, however, she began working with the National Foundation—March of Dimes and devoted the remainder of her life to the prevention of birth defects through public education and fund raising for research. She continued to lecture in the area of birth defects at Cornell University Medical College and Johns Hopkins School of Public Health. She received many honors and awards for her work, including the Gold Medal for Distinguished Achievement in Medicine from the Columbia College of Physicians and Surgeons' Alumni Association, the first woman to be so honored. She published a popular book for parents with Joan Beck in 1972 entitled *Is My Baby Alright?*

For Further Study

Books

Apgar, V. "Proposal for a New Method of Evaluation of the Newborn Infant." In *Anesthesia and Analgesia* 260, no. 67, 1953, n. p.

Apgar, V., and J. Beck. *Is My Baby Alright?* New York: Trident Press, 1972.

Sicherman, B., and C. H. Green, eds. *Notable American Women: The Modern Period.* Cambridge, MA: Belknap-Harvard, 1980.

—Doreen Arcus, Ph.D.
University of Massachusetts Lowell

Aphasia

A condition, caused by neurological damage or disease, in which a person's previous capacity to understand or express language is impaired.

In aphasia, the ability to understand language and to translate thoughts into words has been impaired by injury to the **brain.** Speaking, listening, reading, or writing capabilities may be affected depending on the type of aphasia involved. In children, head injuries, cerebral tumors, brain infection, or other neurological diseases are the most common causes. (Aphasia is also common among older adults, caused primarily by stroke, brain tumor, or degenerative neurological diseases such as Alzheimer's disease.) Aphasia does not include those neurological problems that affect the physical ability to speak or perform the linguistic functions of reading and writing. Aphasia affects one's capacity to manipulate speech sounds, vocabulary, grammar, and meaning. The understanding of aphasia has been enhanced by the development of diagnostic techniques such as magnetic resonance imaging (MRI).

Most cases of aphasia are caused by damage to the left hemisphere of the brain, which is the dominant language hemisphere for approximately 95% of right-handed people and 60–70% of left-handed people.

CLASSIFICATIONS OF APHASIA

Broca's aphasia. This aphasia is characterized by slow, labored, "telegraphic" speech with prepositions and articles missing ("I went store."), but with little or no effect on comprehension of written and spoken language. It affects the frontal lobe of the left hemisphere of the brain. Known as Broca's area, this part of the brain is named for Paul Broca (1824–1880), a 19th-century French physician who studied the specialized functioning of the left and right sides of the brain.

Wernicke's aphasia. In Wernicke's aphasia, the person's speech is overflowing with words (*logorrhea*) that do not convey the speaker's meaning. The pitch and rhythm of the spoken words sound normal, but the words may either be used incorrectly or are made-up words with no meaning (*aphasic jargon*). Besides their speech difficulties, persons with Wernicke's aphasia also have trouble comprehending language, repeating speech, naming objects, reading, and writing. Wernicke's aphasia results from damage to the upper rear part of the left temporal lobe of the brain, an area that was first described in 1874 by German neurologist Carl Wernicke (1848–1905).

Anomia, or *anomic aphasia.* This form of aphasia results in a failure to remember the names of people, objects, or places, but with comprehension of written and spoken language unaffected.

Global aphasia. This is caused by widespread damage to the dominant cerebral hemisphere, either left or right, and is characterized by an almost total loss of all types of verbal ability—speech, comprehension, reading, and writing.

Dysphasia. This term describes a general loss of language use.

Dysgraphia. Describes a form of aphasia characterized by problems in performing hand writing; *agraphia* describes the complete inability to perform hand writing.

Disconnection aphasias. These are a classification of aphasia caused by damage to the connections of Broca's or Wernicke's areas to each other or to other parts of the brain. *Conduction aphasia* results from damage to the fiber bundles connecting the two language areas and is characterized by fluent but somewhat meaningless speech and an inability to repeat phrases correctly. In *transcortical sensory aphasia,* the connections between Wernicke's area and the rest of the brain are severed, but the area itself is left intact. Persons with this condition have trouble understanding language and expressing their thoughts but can repeat speech without any trouble.

Word deafness. This condition occurs when auditory information is prevented from reaching Wernicke's area of the brain. Persons affected by word deafness can hear sounds of all kinds and understand written language, but spoken language is incomprehensible to them, since the auditory signals cannot reach the part of the brain that decodes them.

There are several different types of aphasia, each with different symptoms and each caused by damage to a different part of the brain.

It is possible for children with moderate aphasia following a head injury or other neurological event to recover some of their language abilities with the aid of a speech pathologist. However, if the damage is severe, there is less chance that language abilities will be recovered.

For Further Study

Books

Eisenson, Jon. *Aphasia and Related Disorders in Children.* 2nd ed. New York: Harper & Row, 1984.

Howard, David. *Aphasia Therapy: Historical and Contemporary Issues.* Hillsdale, NJ: Erlbaum, 1987.

Teaching Aphasic Children: The Instructional Methods of Barry and McGinnis. Austin, TX: Pro-Ed, 1988.

Periodicals

Damasio, Antonio R. "Aphasia." *The New England Journal of Medicine,* February 20, 1992, vol. 326, no. 8, pp. 531+.

Pekkanen, John. "The Boy Who Couldn't Talk." *Reader's Digest,* January 1988, vol. 132, no. 789, pp. 84.

Apnea of Infancy

Cessation of an infant's normal breathing.

Apnea includes a temporary cessation of breathing, where breathing stops and begins again automatically after a few seconds, as well as a prolonged pause, where the baby must be resuscitated.

Apnea usually occurs during sleep and is primarily a disorder of premature infants. Babies born before 34 weeks of gestation do not have a fully developed central nervous system, and they often do not have adequate control of the breathing reflex. The more premature a baby is, the greater the likelihood of apnea. Episodes of apnea are also more problematic for smaller than for larger babies. A small baby stores a smaller amount of oxygen, so the effects of oxygen deprivation are more severe. Apnea usually appears within the first several days after the baby is born. Premature babies are usually kept in an incubator, where their breathing and heart rate are monitored. A drop in the baby's heart rate will sound an alarm, and a nurse can stimulate the baby to resume breathing, if necessary. If apnea is diagnosed, it will probably recur, but most premature babies outgrow the condition by the time they reach their normal due date.

Mild apnea causes no ill effects. The breathing pause is short (10–15 seconds), and the baby starts breathing again on his or her own. In a severe episode, though, breathing may cease for 20 seconds or longer. The infant begins to turn blue because of the lack of oxygen in the blood. The baby retains carbon dioxide and may lapse into unconsciousness unless stimulated to breathe. Rubbing the infant with a finger or striking the soles of the feet may be all that is needed to end a short episode of apnea. If the baby has become unconscious, however, he or she may need to be revived with an oxygen mask. If apnea is frequent or severe, the baby's doctor may decide to treat it by altering conditions in the incubator, such as lowering the temperature, increasing oxygen, or placing the infant in a rocking incubator. Blood transfusions and medication may also be necessary.

Premature babies are also at higher risk for "late apnea," which occurs when the infant is older than six weeks. Late apnea can also affect full-term babies and may be a sign of an underlying problem such as congenital heart disease, infection, **anemia, meningitis,** or seizures. The baby usually recovers from apnea as the underlying disease is treated. Even if no underlying cause is found, late apnea is usually outgrown by the time the baby turns one year old.

There are no specific measures to prevent apnea. It seems to be a sign of developmental immaturity, and it subsides as the baby grows older. Usually a premature baby in an incubator is continually monitored, and hospital staff can easily detect apnea. With late apnea, parents may not notice that the child has stopped breathing in his sleep. If apnea is suspected or diagnosed, parents may install a home monitor until the condition is outgrown. Undiagnosed late apnea can be fatal, and is associated with **sudden infant death syndrome (SIDS).** Parents of premature babies need to be apprised of the possibility of apnea, and should be instructed on how to resuscitate their infant if it occurs. Those particularly worried about late apnea may also wish to be trained in infant first aid. Since apnea usually occurs during sleep, parents may decide to sleep near the baby.

For Further Study

Books

Ince, Susan. *Sleep Disturbance.* Boston: Harvard Medical School, Health Publications Group, 1995.

Johnson, Thomas Scott. *Phantom of the Night: Overcome Sleep Apnea Syndrome and Snoring—Win Your Hidden Struggle to Breathe, Sleep, and Live.* New Technology Publishing, 1995.

Pascualy, Ralph A., and Sally Warren Soest. *Snoring and Sleep Apnea: Personal and Family Guide to Diagnosis and Treatment.* 2nd ed. New York: Demos Vermande, 1996.

Stradling, John R. *Handbook of Sleep-related Breathing.* New York: Oxford University Press, 1993.

Audiovisual Recordings

Getting a Good Night's Sleep. Cleveland, OH: Cleveland Clinic Foundation, 1994.
(One two-hour videocassette. One of a series of seminars called "Health Talks at the Cleveland Clinic" developed by the Department of Patient Education, featuring Wallace Mendelson, M.D., Prakash Kotagal, M.D., Joseph Golish, M.D., Benjamin Wood, M.D.)

Sleep Disorders. Princeton, NJ: Films for the Humanities and Sciences, Inc., 1987.
(One 28-minute videocassette. Discusses sleep disorders and reviews cases of patients suffering from a variety of these disorders.)

—A. Woodward

Appendicitis

Inflammation of the appendix.

Appendicitis occurs when the appendix, a 3–4 in (8–10 cm) worm-like projection of the large intestine, becomes inflamed. The inflammation is caused by hardened feces blocking the appendix channel. Inflammation and infection happen within a matter of hours. If the inflamed appendix bursts, the infection could spread to the abdominal cavity, causing peritonitis or a perforation of the intestine. If a young girl suffers an intestinal perforation, she could develop a severe pelvic infection resulting in sterility.

Appendicitis usually attacks young people between the ages of two and thirty, with teenagers the most likely candidates. One hundred and twenty out of every 100,000 children in the United States undergo appendectomies every year. Some medical professionals believe that many of these surgeries are unnecessary and are making efforts to clarify the diagnostic procedure.

Children of all ages frequently experience stomachaches, and it is often difficult to know when the pain is serious. Appendicitis is characterized by a generalized abdominal pain that gradually increases until the pain is localized in the lower right side of the abdomen. The intensity of the pain may prevent the child from moving, standing, or straightening his or her legs. Fever, nausea, **vomiting,** and/or **constipation** may also be present.

Infants and toddlers rarely suffer from appendicitis. On those rare occasions, diagnosis is exacerbated by the child's inability to verbalize what he or she is feeling. A lack of appetite, immobility, irritability, moaning, keeping the legs flexed, fever, and vomiting could signal appendicitis.

Regardless of its origin, a severe abdominal pain should never be ignored or dismissed. The child should be seen by a physician immediately, regardless of the time of day. The doctor will gently press for tenseness in the abdominal muscles and tenderness on the lower right side. He or she will probably order a blood test to check for high white blood cell count, a signal that there is an infection in the body. Because acute abdominal pain can be caused by other factors, many physicians will order a laparoscopy or ultrasound to confirm whether the appendix is inflamed.

When a child with acute abdominal pain is admitted to the hospital, the medical staff may decide to keep the child under observation for several hours to confirm whether the child is suffering from appendicitis. While this may be upsetting to parents, especially when they are aware of the dangers of perforations, a recent study found that keeping patients under close observation for several hours was not harmful and was effective in reducing unnecessary surgeries.

In virtually all cases, appendicitis is treated by the immediate surgical removal of the appendix in a procedure called appendectomy. Many physicians are using laparoscopic surgery for this purpose. The recovery period is brief, normally three to five days. The physician will likely prescribe antibiotics to prevent infection. If the intestine has been perforated, antibiotic treatment is essential.

For Further Study

Books

Slap, Gail B., and Martha M. Jablow. *Teenage Health Care.* New York: Pocket Books, 1994.

Periodicals

Davenport, Mark. "Acute Abdominal Pain in Children." *British Medical Journal* 312, February 24, 1996, p. 494.

"Observations of Children with Suspected Appendicitis," *American Family Physician* 47, May 1, 1993, p. 1494.

Policoff, Steven Phillip. "Tummy Aches," *Parents Magazine* 68, July 1993, p. 101.

—Mary McNulty

. . . .

Apraxia

Underdevelopment of fine motor skills.

Apraxia is defined by a child's inability to copy shapes, letters, or symbols because he or she cannot control hand movements to produce the proper and necessary sequential movements.

See also **Fine Motor Skills**

. . . .

Arthritis

A term referring to a variety of conditions characterized by inflammation of one or more joints.

Arthritis is commonly regarded as a disease of the elderly, but there are several varieties that primarily affect children, including juvenile rheumatoid arthritis, infectious arthritis, and juvenile ankylosing spondylitis.

Juvenile rheumatoid arthritis (JRA)

The most common form of arthritis in children is juvenile rheumatoid arthritis, also known as JRA or Still's disease. Affecting over 65,000 young people in the United States—roughly 1 in 1,000—it can affect children as young as two years old. The condition occurs in "flare-ups" that can last from a few weeks to several years, alternating with periods of remission. JRA, like other types of arthritis, is thought to be an autoimmune disease, in which antibodies that are supposed to protect the body from foreign invaders turn against its own tissues, primarily the joints. The synovium, a thin membrane surrounding the joints, becomes inflamed, swelling and producing too much fluid. The results are pain, swelling, and stiffness, as well as warmth and redness of the skin. Genetic factors can also play a role in the disease. Its onset—or succeeding flare-ups—can be triggered by infection, injury, or emotional stress. **Birth defects** and diet are not thought to be connected with the disease. There are three types of JRA: pauciarticular onset JRA, polyarticular onset JRA, and systemic onset JRA.

Pauciarticular onset JRA, the least serious type, affects 45% of children who have JRA. Four or fewer joints are involved, and each joint is affected on only one side of the body (i.e., one knee instead of both). Often the affected joints are large ones, such as a knee, hip, or ankle. A small percentage of children with this condition develop an eye inflammation (iritis). Other symptoms include gradual weight gain and fatigue. Pauciarticular onset JRA is usually found in girls under the age of 10 years.

Polyarticular onset JRA affects five or more joints, either large or small, on both sides of the body. About 25% of children with JRA have this more serious form of the disease. It often affects the joints of the hands and fingers. Like pauciarticular onset JRA, it is accompanied by an intermittent low-grade fever, which is generally worse in the evening. Children with this type of arthritis are usually older than those with the pauciarticular onset variety. Other symptoms include a rash, enlarged lymph nodes, and subcutaneous nodules (painless movable lumps under the skin that last up to a few months and then disappear). In addition, children with polyarticular onset JRA—like adults with rheumatoid arthritis—often have an **RH factor** (rheumatoid fator) in their blood. The disease is generally more severe in people with this "RH positive" factor: the symptoms are worse and the joint damage more severe and long-lasting.

Systemic onset JRA is the most serious form of juvenile rheumatoid arthritis. It affects numerous joints as well as other organs, possibly including the liver, spleen, kidneys, lungs, and lymph nodes. It is also accompanied by serious **anemia** and a high ("spiking") **fever** that rises to between 103–105°F (39–41°C) for several hours once or twice a day. Another characteristic symptom is a distinctive salmon-colored rash with irregular borders that can move from one part of the body to another within minutes. This form of JRA can also affect the pericardium (the sac around the heart), causing inflammation and a buildup of fluid.

Treatment

Treatment of juvenile rheumatoid arthritis consists of a combination of medication and physical therapy, which can help control the symptoms and prevent further damage but cannot actually cure the disease itself. In many cases, the preferred medication is **aspirin** in large doses, which decreases the extent of the inflammation. However, side effects rule out this course of treatment for one out of every six children with JRA. Fortunately, a number of other medications belonging to the same general type as aspirin (nonsteroidal anti-inflammatory drugs—NSAIDS) are available to combat the effects of JRA. These include ibuprofen (Advil, Motrin, etc.), Tolectin, Naprosyn, Feldene, Nalfon, and others.

For serious flare-ups that do not respond sufficiently to NSAIDS, various other medications may be used. Cortisone, given orally or as an injection at the site of inflammation, achieves the most dramatic improvement but is used with caution and generally only as a last resort due to potentially serious side effects and the fact that increasingly larger doses are needed in order for the drug to retain its effectiveness. Several slower-acting antirheumatic drugs, including gold salts, d-penicillamine, and hydroxychloroquine, work over a period of months to stop the breakdown of joint tissue. Methotrexate, a commonly prescribed cancer medication, has been effectively used as a fast-acting drug for severe cases of JRA.

Physical therapy is an important part of the treatment for JRA. In the past, children with JRA were kept in bed, sometimes in full body casts, leading to muscle and joint atrophy, as well as other problems—both physical and emotional—caused by immobility and isolation. Even if the arthritis itself was outgrown in adulthood (as it often is) the person was left with lifelong deformities that could only be treated by joint replacement. Today physicians and therapists regard this type of long-term damage as largely preventable through **exercise**—which strengthens and stretches the muscles surrounding the affected joints to prevent them from becoming weak, tight, or shorter from lack of use, and can also prevent a potential bone deformity called contracture. Although exercising can be painful and difficult for a child with stiff and swollen joints, it is extremely important to maintain a regular exercise schedule, either at a physical therapy facility or at home (or a combination of both). Several different types of exercise are helpful. Active exercise, consisting of activities such as knee bends, sit-ups, and toe-touching, strengthens the muscles. Passive exercise, in which another person moves the child's muscle groups through a range of motions, such as flexing and extension, helps maintain flexibility and prevents shortening of the muscles. Strength can also be attained through active resistive exercise in which the child moves a part of the body against resistance from another person. Aerobic exercises such as bicycling, **swimming**, and using rowing machines help maintain endurance. Swimming, as well as other forms of underwater exercise, are especially recommended because they relieve the joints of weight-bearing pressure.

Although exercise is an indispensable part of the treatment for juvenile arthritis, daily periods of rest are also required. As a further treatment measure, heat is applied to relax muscles and help loosen stiff joints. Heat can help children with JRA through the period of morning stiffness they usually experience, and it can reduce pain and spasms from exercise. Moist heat may take the form of a warm bath, whirlpool, hot tub, hot pack, or heated paraffin bath. Saunas, ultrasound, sleeping bags, and diathermy (electrically produced deep heat) are effective sources of dry heat. Heated water beds can also provide comfort for a child with JRA. Some physicians have JRA patients wear a splint or brace to prevent deformity. Often, the brace is worn only at night to decrease interference with daily activities.

School-age children with JRA

Most children with JRA continue to attend school, although some amount of flexibility is necessary on the part of the school and the teacher. Many children with JRA have a hard time moving about early in the day due to morning stiffness and may also need special permission to walk around the classroom for short periods from time to time to avoid further stiffness from inactivity during the day. In other cases, they may need to be excused from certain activities, especially **sports** involving those joints affected by the illness, and may also need to be excused for periods of rest during the school day. Children and adolescents with JRA want and need to participate as much as possible in ordinary activities both in and out of school. In many cases they don't want to tell others about their illness for fear of seeming different from their peers. Counseling can help children with JRA, as well their families, cope with the emotional strain caused by the condition. Many adolescents have been helped by participation in support groups run by local chapters of the Arthritis Foundation.

In approximately 75% of JRA patients, the disease goes into permanent remission by late adolescence or early adulthood. With systemic onset JRA, affected organs such as the liver or spleen do not suffer permanent damage from the condition, and the rash and spiking fever are gone within five years or less. Once the systemic symptoms are over, this type of JRA generally turns into one of the other two types. Children with polyarticular onset JRA are more prone to permanent damage and loss of function than those with the pauciarticular form. It is especially important for these children to follow a regular exercise program to minimize any long-term effects of the disease.

Infectious arthritis

Arthritis in children can be caused by viruses, fungi, or bacteria (usually staphylococci or streptococci) that lodge in a joint. Lyme disease, which is carried by an infected tick, is a form of infectious arthritis. Both infants and older children can contract infectious arthritis. Common symptoms, like those of juvenile rheumatoid arthritis, are pain, swelling, and inflammation of the joints. When the hip joint is involved, as is frequently the case, extensive damage can result, so prompt diagnosis and treatment are essential. The condition is treated with antibiotics and drainage of the affected joints. Arthritis that results from viruses such as influenza, **mumps,** or hepatitis, usually clears up spontaneously when the infection is over. Symptoms may be treated with aspirin and other anti-inflammatory medications.

Juvenile ankylosing spondylitis

Juvenile ankylosing spondylitis primarily affects the spine, although it may first attack the joints and be mistaken for JRA. It is more common in boys than girls and tends to be inherited. Like JRA, treatment can only ease the inflammation and prevent eventual deformity rather than cure the disease itself.

For Further Study

Books

Arthritis Foundation. *Understanding Juvenile Rheumatoid Arthritis.* Atlanta: Arthritis Foundation, 1988.

Brewer, Earl J., and Kathy Cochran Angel. *Parenting a Child with Arthritis.* Los Angeles: Lowell House, 1992.

Thiele, Colin. *Jodie's Journey.* Scranton, PA: HarperCollins, 1988.

Organizations

American Juvenile Arthritis Foundation
Address: 1314 Spring Street, N.W.
Atlanta, GA 30309
Telephone: (404) 872-7100
(Publishes *AJAO Newsletter* quarterly.)

The Arthritis Foundation
Address: 1314 Spring Street, N.W.
Atlanta, GA 30309
Telephone: toll-free (800) 283-7800.

Artificial Respiration

Attempting to restart breathing for someone whose breathing has stopped.

When someone has stopped breathing, medical personnel or trained laypersons may attempt to restart breathing or maintain weak breathing by using artificial respiration. When the procedure is done by mouth-to-mouth resuscitation, it is often referred to as *rescue breathing;* when accomplished by a mechanical device or machine, it is often referred to as *ventilation.* The U.S. Public Health Service recommends that parents receive training in artificial respiration and **cardiopulmonary resuscitation** (CPR) through an agency such as the American Red Cross, YMCA, or other community agency.

For Further Study

Books

American National Red Cross. *Respiratory and Circulatory Emergencies.* Washington, DC: American National Red Cross, 1978.

Audiovisual Recordings

How to Save Your Child or Baby: When Every Second Counts.
Los Angeles, CA: Video Prescriptions, 1987.
(One 40-minute videocassette.)
Seconds Count. Manhattan Beach, CA: Mann Design, 1991.
(One 18-minute videocassette.)

Asbestos

Asbestos is the general name for a wide variety of silicate minerals, mostly silicates of calcium, magnesium, and iron.

The common characteristics of the silicate minerals collectively known as asbestos are a fibrous structure and resistance to fire. Fabricated into corrugated or flat sheets, asbestos has been used as building material in a wide variety of structures, including many schools built before 1970. Formed into cylinders, it has been used for ducts and pipes. Certain types of asbestos with long fibers have been used as components in protective clothing for firefighters, brake and clutch linings for vehicles, electrical insulation, moldings for automobile components, and linings for chemical containers.

Most products manufactured today do not contain asbestos because of the deleterious health effects that have become apparent since the end of World War II. Today scientists know that asbestos can cause a range of respiratory diseases, especially asbestosis (scarring of the lung tissue), lung **cancer**, and mesothelioma (cancer of the chest and abdomen). These problems begin when asbestos fibers enter the respiratory system and become lodged in the interstitial areas—the areas between the alveoli in the lungs. As the fibers continue to accumulate in the lungs, they scar tissue which reduces the flow of air through the respiratory system.

Symptoms develop gradually and include coughing and shortness of breath, weight loss, and **anorexia**. Other respiratory conditions, such as pneumonia and bronchitis, become more common and more difficult to cure. Eventually the fibers may initiate other anatomical and physiological changes, such as the development of tumors and carcinomas.

Individuals most at risk for asbestos-related problems are those continually exposed to the mineral fibers, such as those who work in asbestos mining and processing as well as those who use the product in some other manufacturing line, such as in the production of brake linings. People who smoke cigarettes are particularly susceptible to risk. Some experts believe smokers exposed to asbestos are 90 times more likely to develop cancer than unexposed nonsmokers.

The Environmental Protection Agency (EPA) began to regulate the use of asbestos in the early 1970s when it was declared an air pollutant by the 1970 Clean Air Act. Over the past two decades, mammoth efforts have been made to remove asbestos-based materials from buildings where they are especially likely to pose health risks, such as in school buildings and public auditoriums. Children are especially susceptible to airborne pollutants and, because of their age, carry a greater potential to develop related diseases if exposed. The EPA issued special asbestos-related regulations in 1983 that required school districts to inspect their buildings and monitor air quality. Most school buildings constructed prior to the 1970s contain asbestos.

The removal of asbestos has been the subject of considerable controversy. Critics of removal maintain that, if not done properly, asbestos removal spreads more asbestos fibers into the air than it actually removes. Also, a satisfactory substitute for asbestos has not yet been found. In many cases, encapsulating the asbestos-containing material—with a thick coat of paint, for example—has been deemed a more acceptable preventive measure.

For Further Study

Books

Brodeur, Paul. *Outrageous Misconduct: The Asbestos Industry on Trial.* New York: Pantheon Books, 1985.
Marchok, Janice. *Oh No! Not My Electric Blanket, Too?* Latrobe, PA: The Jetmarc Group, 1991.
Ray, Dixy Lee. *Trashing the Planet.* New York: HarperPerennial, 1990.
Tate, Nicholas. *The Sick Building Syndrome.* Fair Hills, NJ: New Horizon Press, 1994.

Asphyxia Neonatorum

The failure of an infant to breathe at birth.

Babies who are born asphyxiated do not breathe or cry when they are delivered. In mild cases of asphyxia the infant's color is bluish and the limbs may feel stiff. In more severe cases, the skin is gray, and the baby is limp and immobile. Asphyxia neonatorum has been linked to low birth weight, late deliveries, and flattening or twisting of the umbilical cord during labor. Smoking during pregnancy is also considered a risk factor for asphyxia because it tends to produce low birth-weight babies.

Asphyxia requires emergency treatment, preferably in a hospital. **Brain** damage can result if the infant doesn't start breathing within about five minutes. Death can result if the asphyxiation lasts over 10 minutes. Asphyxia can also lead to **seizures,** especially if the baby requires intubation and has a low **Apgar score** five minutes after birth, and if the **blood** from the cutting of the umbilical cord has a high acid content. In older preterm infants (32–36 weeks), asphyxia has been linked to lung and kidney damage as well as brain damage. The first step in treating asphyxia is to remove any liquids blocking the baby's airway. In the hospital, this is done with a special tube, after which the infant is supplied with oxygen. In mild cases of asphyxia, the initial gasp of oxygen is enough to initiate breathing. In severe cases, **artificial respiration** must be performed. If there is brain damage or if the brain is not yet fully developed, the baby may be put on a ventilator for periods of up to several weeks. If asphyxia occurs outside the hospital, a finger should be used to clear any mucus from the baby's throat and gentle mouth-to-mouth resuscitation should be performed.

Identifying infants at risk for asphyxia either before or during labor can prevent the problem or lessen its severity. Obstetricians can identify babies at risk for asphyxia late in pregnancy and advise their patients to deliver in hospitals that have neonatal intensive care units. If an inadequate supply of oxygen from the placenta is detected during labor, the infant is at risk for asphyxia, and an emergency delivery may be attempted either using forceps or by caesarian section.

Today an infant's risk of asphyxia is lower than in the past due to improved prenatal care and awareness of the harmful effects of smoking during pregnancy. However if asphyxia does occur, prompt treatment can assure that the condition will cause no lasting damage.

Aspirin

Common name for acetylsalicylic acid, a common nonprescription drug used to relieve pain and reduce inflammation.

Acetylsalicylic acid, commonly known as aspirin or ASA, is a white, odorless medication available without a doctor's prescription, generally in tablet form. It is a relatively safe drug for adults, but is not recommended for children in most situations. Aspirin has been associated with increased likelihood of developing Reye's syndrome when given to children with viral illness. Although Reye's syndrome is a rare disease affecting the liver and central nervous system, alternate pain relievers are recommended for children with fever or other symptoms treatable with a general pain reliever. Aspirin is used to relieve headache and other general pain, to alleviate the pain of **arthritis,** to reduce fever, and to reduce inflammation and swelling due to injuries. *Side effects:* Aspirin may irritate the lining of the stomach and can cause stomach bleeding.

See also **Acetaminophen.**

Assessment

The evaluation of personality variables, achievement, skill, or ability.

Assessment is used to accomplish different objectives: to learn more about the individual being tested; to rank individuals; for student placement; to identify specific problems and needs; and to improve learning or instruction. Tests of different types are administered and used by teachers, psychologists, and counselors to help students understand themselves and measure their performance against that of their peers. Assessments may be used to evaluate a child's ability or skill at a given point in time; alternatively, they may be used to predict a child's aptitudes or future capabilities.

Traditional standardized tests rely on specific, structured procedures and instructions given to all test-takers by the test administrator (or to be read by the test-takers themselves). With young children, this presents a problem. Young children (preschool and early elementary years) do not have past experience and familiarity with tests and have limited understanding of the expectations of testing procedures. With young test-takers, the test administrator represents a significant factor that influences success. The child must feel comfortable with the test administrator and feel motivated to complete the test exercise. The administrator helps support the test-taker's attention to the test requirements. The testing environment affects all test-takers, but may represent a more significant variable for the youngest test-takers.

Assessment of children is also challenging given the rapid changes in growth experienced during childhood. In childhood, it is difficult to ensure that the test-taker's responses will be stable for even a short period of time. Thus, psychologists, educators, and other test administrators are careful to take the stage of childhood into account when interpreting a child's test scores.

Norm-referenced versus criterion-referenced assessments

In norm-referenced assessments, one person's performance is interpreted in relation to the performance of others. A norm-referenced test is designed to discriminated between individuals in the area being measured. A criterion-referenced assessment allows interpretation of a test-taker's score in relation to a specific standard, or criterion; this type of test is designed to help evaluate whether a person has met a specific level of performance. A timed test of arithmetic facts with a specific performance goal, such as 100 problems answered in 60 seconds with no more than one error, is an example of a criterion-referenced test.

Testing trends

In the 1990s, there has been a trend toward increased use of standardized tests to evaluate performance in U. S. schools. Faced with declining test scores by U.S. students when compared to others around the world, concerned parents and communities have sought ways to measure the performance of schools. Thus, local school districts and some states imposed standardized tests to evaluate knowledge and skills, on the assumption that testing is an effective way to measure outcomes of education. In fact, in the late 1990s the 32-member National Council on Education Standards and Testing appointed by Congress recommended that national achievement standards be created. The council also suggested that a nationwide assessment effort be implemented to measure students' progress.

A shortcoming of standardized testing is that it assumes all students can be evaluated by the same instrument. Because most standardized tests are norm-referenced—the test measures a student's test performance against the performance of other test-takers—students and educators focus their efforts on the test scores, and schools develop curriculum to prepare students to take the test.

Many educators feel that standardized testing does little to improve learning, and they acknowledge that there are no perfect assessment tools that work will for evaluating all students. Researchers have designed and tested alternative assessments, including performance, authentic, and portfolio assessments; journals; interviews; and attitude inventories. All have been criticized for requiring too much time to administer and having imprecise criteria. For schools, the biggest challenge in applying alternative assessments relates to grading, since the alternative assessments are not structured to result in a ranking or traditional grade.

Objectives of assessment

When considering what assessments to use, educators begin by defining the purpose or goal for each test. Examples of a purpose for testing might be to establish rankings for students to comply with mandates for records. Assessment is one way to meet that goal. In addition, psychologists have found that some forms of assessment motivate students because they allow recognition and reward of good performance. Another reason to administer standardized tests is to evaluate students for class placement or **ability grouping.** Improvement of learning and/or instruction may also be a goal of assessment. Students' learning behaviors can be improved if helpful feedback is provided relating to the outcome of the assessment.

Using traditional standardized test results along with results of alternative assessments can provide a comprehensive evaluation of the student. By using more than one source of data, the teacher or psychologist will obtain an objective picture of the student's development.

Alternative methods of assessment

Assessment techniques other than standardized tests are available to the teacher or counselor. These assessment techniques offer students the opportunity to be more closely involved with the recognition of their progress and to discover what steps they can take to improve.

Performance assessment

Performance assessment can be used to evaluate any learning that is skill-based or behavioral. Most often seen in curriculum areas like the arts and athletics, performance assessment requires the test-taker to do something.

Authentic assessment

Authentic assessment was discussed in the mid-1990s and derives its name from the idea that it tests students in skills and knowledge needed to succeed in the real world. Authentic assessment focuses on student task performance and is often used to improve learning in practical areas. An advantage of authentic assessment is that students may be able to see how they would perform in a practical setting, and thus may be motivated to work to improve.

Portfolios

Portfolio assessment was introduced in the 1990s. The portfolio is a collection of examples of the student's work. It is designed to advance through each grade of school with the student, providing a way for teachers and others to evaluate progress. One of the hallmarks of portfolio assessment is that the student is responsible for selecting examples of his or her own work to be placed in the portfolio. The portfolio may be used by an individual classroom teacher as a repository for work in progress or for accomplishments. Portfolios address one of the key concerns raised by critics of standardized tests: portfolios allow the teacher to evaluate each student in relation to his or her own abilities and learning style. The assessment process is controlled by the student, helping to reinforce the idea that he or she is responsible for learning. Portfolios are often shared by the student and teacher with parents during the **parent-teacher conference.**

Interviews

The assessment interview involves a one-on-one or small group discussion between the teacher and student, who may be joined by parents or other teachers. Standardized tests reveal little about the test-taker's thought process during testing. Alternatively, an interview allows the teacher or other administrator to gain an understanding of how the test-taker reached his or her answer. Individual interviews require a much greater time commitment on the part of the teacher than the administration of a standardized test to the entire class at one time. Thus, interviews are most effective when used to evaluate the achievements and needs of specific students. To be successful, interviews require both the teacher and the student to be motivated, open to discussion, and focused on the purpose of the assessment.

Journals

Beginning in elementary school, teachers have used journals as part of the English curriculum since at least the 1980s. In assessment, the journal allows the student to share his or her thoughts on the learning progress. A journal may substitute for or supplement a portfolio in providing a student-directed assessment of achievement and goals.

Attitude inventory

Attitude is one ingredient in the recipe for academic success that is rarely measured objectively. An attitude inventory is designed to reveal both positive and negative (or productive and unproductive) aspects of a student's attitude about school and learning. However, a factor that limits the potential success of such inventories may be the very negative attitude being assessed—the student's negative attitude makes him or her unlikely to participate in any assessment. By demonstrating a sincere interest in addressing student concerns that affect attitude, a school can improve the effectiveness of attitude inventory assessments.

Computer-aided assessment

Computer-aided assessment is being increasingly employed in the 1990s. A key advantage of the use of computers is the capability of an interactive assessment to provide immediate feedback on responses.

Psychological assessment

Psychological assessment of children is used for a variety of purposes. The child's pediatrician, parents, or teacher may ask for psychological assessment to gain a greater understanding of the child's development. Most assessment methods fall into one of three categories: observational methods, personality inventories, or projective techniques.

Types of assessment

There are three basic ways that psychologists can obtain information about a child for assessment purposes: observation; verbal questioning or questionnaire; or assignment of tasks. Psychologists refer to these as the "media of assessment."

Observations are made by a trained professional either in a familiar setting (such as a classroom or playroom), an experimental setting, or during an interview.

Toys, dolls, or other items are often included in the setting to provide stimulus. The child may be influenced by the presence of an observer. However, researchers have reported that younger children often become engrossed in their activities, and thus are relatively unaffected by the presence of an observer. The expectations of the observer, conveyed directly or through body language and other subtle cues, may influence how the child performs and how the observer records and interprets his or her observations. This "observer bias" can influence the outcome of an assessment. For example, the observer may downplay or eliminate specific details of his observation. Alternatively, the observer may interpret his observations in terms of preexisting stereotypes.

Other specific types of observer biases have been identified through study of the assessment procedures. In the "halo effect," the observer evaluates the subject's behavior to confirm his general impression of the subject. For example, the observer believes a particular child is happy and loving. When the observer assesses that child, the child lays a doll face down on the table, an action the observer interprets as parenting. Alternatively, the observer believes another child is angry and hostile. When this child is observed laying the doll face down on the table, the observer interprets the action as aggressive.

Interviews or questionnaires for assessment may be structured with a specific series of questions, or unstructured, allowing the subject to direct the discussion. Interviewers often use rating scales to record information during interviews. A personality inventory is a type of questionnaire used with older children and adults. The personality inventory has questions related to the subject's feelings or reactions to certain scenarios. One of the best known personality inventories for people over age 16 is the **Minnesota Multiphasic Personality Inventory (MMPI),** a series of over 500 questions used to assess a number of personality traits and psychological disturbances.

A projective test is another type of questionnaire requiring a skilled, trained examiner. It presents the test-taker with ambiguous situations to interpret. The reliability of these tests with children is difficult to establish due to their subjective nature, with results varying widely among different examiners. A well-known projective test is the **Rorschach Psychodiagnostic Test,** or inkblot test, first devised by the Swiss psychologist Hermann Rorschach in the 1920s. Another widely used projective test for people ages 14–40 is the **Thematic Apperception Test (TAT),** developed at Harvard University in the 1930s. In this test, the subject is shown a series of pictures, each of which can be interpreted in a variety of ways, and asked to construct a story based on each one. An adaptation administered to children ages 3–10 is the **Children's Apperception Test (CAT).** It is administered to children individually by a trained psychologist to assess personality, maturity, and psychological health.

Assignment of tasks is an assessment method involving the performance of a specific assignment, designed to inform the test administrator about attributes such as the test-taker's abilities, perceptions, and motor coordination.

For Further Study

Books

Handbook of Psychological Assessment. New York: Wiley, 1990.

Meisels, Samuel J. *Developmental Screening in Early Childhood: A Guide.* 3rd ed. Washington, DC: National Association for the Education of Young Children, 1989.

Mitchell, R. *Testing for Learning: How New Approaches to Evaluation Can Improve American Schools.* New York: Free Press, 1992.

Personality and Ability: The Personality Assessment System. Lanham, MD: University Press of America, 1994.

Popham, W. J. *Classroom Assessment: What Teachers Need to Know.* Boston: Allyn & Bacon, 1995.

Stiggins, R. J. *Student-Centered Classroom Assessment.* New York: Merrill, 1994.

Zessoules, R., and H. Gardner. "Authentic Assessment: Beyond the Buzzword and into the Classroom." In *Expanding Student Assessment,* V. Perone, ed. Alexandria, VA: Association for Supervision and Curriculum Development. 1991, pp. 47–71.

Periodicals

Merina, Anita. "Agent of Accountability." *NEA Today* 10, March 1992, p. 9.

Sugarman, Jay, James Allen, and Meg Keller-Cogan. "How to Make Authentic Assessment Work for You." *Instructor* 103, July-August 1993, pp. 66+.

Travis, Jon E. "Meaningful Assessment." *The Clearing House* 69: May-June 1996, pp. 308.

Asthma

A lung disease characterized by spasms and inflammation of the airways, causing wheezing, coughing, and shortness of breath.

Asthma is a lung disease characterized by recurring and sometimes persistent spasms and inflammation of the airways, causing episodic symptoms of wheezing, coughing, and shortness of breath.

Prevalence

A significant medical problem in children of all ages, asthma is the leading cause of school absenteeism and the most common reason for hospitalization of children. In 1993, asthma accounted for an estimated 198,000 hospitalization and 342 deaths among persons under age 25. Approximately 2–10% of children in the United States suffer from asthma; the most recent estimate is 4.3%. Childhood asthma is more common among boys, African Americans, residents of inner cities, and children from low-income families.

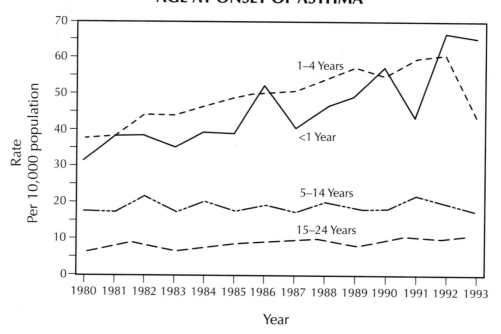

AGE AT ONSET OF ASTHMA

Asthma can arise at any age. Approximately 20% of cases begin in the first year of life. Wheezing due to viral or other infections in the early preschool age group is very common, however, and not all children who wheeze with infection will turn out to have asthma. Less than half of children who have a wheezing episode before age three will be asthmatic at age six. Among children aged 5–14 years of age, the asthma death rate doubled from 1980–93.

The risk factors for asthma are both genetic and environmental. Most children who develop asthma have a family history of **allergies**. Early damage to the lungs caused by **cystic fibrosis**, **premature birth**, artificial ventilation in an intensive care unit, and certain viral illnesses (especially respiratory syncytial virus [RSV]) can also cause a predisposition to asthma.

COMMON TRIGGERS FOR ASTHMA

There are numerous triggers for asthma attacks. The most common ones are as follows:

- animal dander (the shed skin flakes from furry animals)
- aerosol sprays or chemical fumes
- cigarette smoke
- cold, dry air
- exercise
- fireplace smoke
- high pollen counts (trees, grasses, certain weeds)
- household dust (which includes a microscopic insect known as a dust mite)
- molds
- strong perfumes
- viral respiratory infections (common cold, influenza, RSV)

Severity and causes

The severity of asthma varies greatly from child to child. Mild cases may involve only a cough associated with exercise or at night. The milder forms of the disease are the most common, but asthma in its most severe form can result in a catastrophic shortness of breath that leads to death. The severity of asthma can also vary from day to day for the same person. For example, a child with asthma might be entirely well one day and then have a flare-up (attack) several days later.

In addition, asthma has marked diurnal variation in severity, which means that an asthmatic child who is symptom-free in the daytime may experience significant coughing or wheezing at night.

Preventive measures

Many simple steps can be taken to reduce asthma triggers in a child's home. Because children spend many hours asleep in their bedrooms, a number of control measures can be directed toward that room. Mattress and box springs, blankets, books, stuffed toys, clothing, carpeting, and other items in a child's room can gather dust mites. Enclosing mattresses, box springs, and pillows in plastic covers is often helpful, as is washing all bedding (and curtains) in hot water once a week. Eliminating or reducing the number of stuffed toys in a child's room (or at the very least washing them weekly) is a good idea. Removing carpeting from a child's room is very often helpful, because hard floors will gather far less dust than carpets. Vaporizers and humidifiers foster the growth of molds and dust mites and should be used sparingly in an asthmatic child's bedroom.

Other ways of controlling asthma triggers include prohibiting **smoking** anywhere in the house, avoiding smoke-filled areas, and avoiding the use of fireplaces or wood-burning stoves. Heating and air conditioning filters should be changed regularly. High-efficiency particulate air (HEPA) filters are available, which are very effective for removing allergens from household air.

Although there is no way to completely prevent the common cold, children with moderate or severe asthma should receive an annual influenza vaccination. Research is currently underway for an **immunization** to prevent RSV disease.

Treatment

The two main types of asthma medications are *anti-inflammatory medications* and *bronchodilators*. Anti-inflammatory medications decrease the inflammation and swelling of a child's airways, help decrease mucus production, and make the airways less sensitive to irritants. These medications can be used to prevent asthma flare-ups in the long run, as well as to break the cycle of inflammation that prolongs a flare-up.

Anti-inflammatory medications can be divided into two types: *steroids* and *mast-cell stabilizers*. Steroids can be inhaled, swallowed, or injected. *Inhaled steroids* (beclomethasone, triamcinolone, flunisolide), used regularly, can prevent attacks and maintain good lung function in many children with moderate to severe asthma. Used in this way, they may decrease the need for oral or injectable steroids, which have a higher risk of major side effects. *Oral steroids* (prednisone, prednisolone, and methylprednisolone) can be given either in short bursts for several days to hasten the end of a flare-up or, in children with severe, chronic asthma, on a daily or every other day basis in order to prevent flare-ups. *Injected steroids* are commonly used during severe asthma attacks that require hospitalization.

The inhaled *mast-cell stabilizers* (cromolyn, nedocromil) can be used several times a day to prevent attacks.

Bronchodilators relax the airways and increase their diameter, allowing for freer passage of air. The two types of bronchodilators are the *theophyllines* (theophylline and aminophylline, which is metabolized by the body as theophylline) and *beta-adrenergic agents*. Although side effects are fairly common with the theophyllines, in certain patients they can be very useful. The theophyllines are chemically related to caffeine, and the most common side effects are restlessness and insomnia. At higher levels, theophyllines can lead to nausea, **vomiting**, **seizures**, or cardiac arrhythmias. In addition, the theophyllines interact with a number of common medications, so a patient taking theophylline should check with a pharmacist or doctor before taking other medications.

Beta-adrenergic bronchodilators (albuterol, metaproteronol, terbutaline) relax the muscles that surround the airways and provide quick relief of symptoms; however, they have little or no effect on the inflammatory process that sustains an asthma attack, so repeated doses are necessary. In patients with moderate to severe asthma, this cycle can lead to dependency. Bronchodilators can be given orally, by injection, by metered-dose inhaler (puffer), or by nebulizer (aerosol machine).

Many asthma experts recommend a device called a "spacer" to be used along with metered-dose inhalers. The spacer is a tube or bellows-like device held in or around the mouth into which the metered-dose inhaler is puffed. This device enables more medication from a metered-dose inhaler to actually reach the lungs (as opposed to being swallowed).

School-age and older children may also be prescribed *peak flow meters,* simple devices which measure how easy or difficult it is for a child to exhale. With home peak-flow monitoring, it is possible for many children with asthma to discern at an early stage that a flare-up is just beginning and adjust their medications appropriately.

Prognosis

More than half of all asthma cases resolve by young adulthood, but chronic infection, pollution, cigarette smoke, and chronic allergen exposure are factors which make resolution less likely. Small infants and toddlers who have persistent wheezing even without viral infections and those who have a family history of allergies are most likely to have asthma into the school-age years.

For Further Study

Books

Plaut, Thomas, M.D. *Children with Asthma: A Manual for Parents.* 2nd ed. Amherst, MA: Pedipress, 1988.

Audiovisual Recordings

Managing Childhood Asthma: A Parent's Guide. Garden Grove, CA: Medcom. Available from Medcom Inc., P.O. Box 3225, Garden Grove, CA 92642, (800) 877-1443.

Organizations

Asthma and Allergy Foundation of America
Address: 1717 Massachusetts Avenue, NW
Suite 305
Washington, D.C. 20036
Telephone: (202) 727-8462
Mothers of Asthmatics, Inc.
Address: 10875 Main Street, Suite 210
Fairfax, VA 22030

—Marta M. Vielhaber, M.D.

At Risk

Children whose family environment, socioeconomic status, and/ or behavioral history place them at a high probability of failing or dropping out of school.

The term "at risk" is used by educators, social service personnel, and others when referring to children who have a high probability of experiencing failure in school. The child may be at risk for any one or a combination of factors that include family environment, **socioeconomic status,** health, and behavior or emotional problems. Also designated as "at risk" are adolescents who, due to a combination of socioeconomic status, physical and/or mental illness, have a high probability of becoming involved in activities that endanger their psychological health. These activities can include being the perpetrator or victim of violence, engaging in early and unprotected sex, using alcohol and drugs, and becoming truant or delinquent. The set of situations and behaviors associated with failure in school and with later failure to achieve and maintain a productive life are designated "at risk" or "high risk" factors. Evaluative tests for identifying potential dropouts include the Elementary School Pupil Adjustment Scale (ESPAS) for grades K–3, the Dropout Alert Scale (DAS) for grades 4–12, and the Student Sensitivity Index for grades 7–12.

The term "at risk" was popularized with the 1984 publication of the U.S. Department of Education report, *A Nation at Risk: The Imperative for Educational Reform,* which outlined the decline of American students' achievements in science and math as compared to previous generations and as compared to other countries such

RISK FACTORS

The risk factors associated with doing poorly in school are:

- having parents who have not completed high school
- living in a household with annual income below $15,000
- having a brother or sister who is failing in school.

as Japan and Germany. The concept of being at risk was subsequently extended to include students who perform poorly in all school subjects. The relationships between different demographic and social variables associated with failing in school were widely researched. In general usage, the term at risk designates a child or adolescent who is at risk of failing and eventually dropping out of school, but it is used to designate a set of variables in family environment and in the individual's attitudes and activities that are associated with school failure.

Delinquency, drug use, sexual activity, gang activity, and violent and/or criminal behavior are considered at risk or high risk conditions in the sense that they are statistically correlated with failing classes and dropping out of school. The correlates of these situations and behaviors are also isolated and studied—for example, a family's poverty or an adolescent's **depression** places him or her at higher risk for drug use. Drug use places the adolescent at higher risk for dropout. If this does happen, he or she will then be considered at even higher risk for drug use, since teens who are not in school are more likely to use drugs. Thus, children and adolescents can be considered at risk for many problems that interact with the core problem of school failure and dropout.

A 1992 Carnegie Council study found that one-quarter of the 28 million students in middle or junior high schools were considered statistically at risk of failing in school, abusing alcohol and drugs, or engaging in premature and unprotected sexual activity. The report also found a high rate of risk for middle school adolescents being either the perpetrator or the victim of a violent act. Additionally, another quarter (7 million) of the remaining 21 million students were considered at moderate risk due to serious academic, social, or personal problems. A later study by the National Research Council emphasized the importance of home environment in creating risk factors, finding that many home environments failed to provide alternatives to high risk behaviors encountered in the larger community.

A child who has all four risk factors will be four times as likely to fail in school as a child who has only one of them. Thus, even though, according to the National Council on Education Statistics (NCES), the overall dropout rates declined from 15% in 1972 to 11% in 1992 and 1993, the dropout rates for certain groups remained high. In 1993 the dropout rate was 8% for white students, 14% for black students, and 28% for Hispanic students. The dropout rate for students with a high family income level was 3%, whereas the dropout rate for students with a low family income level was 24%.

The concept of "at risk" is a useful tool for identifying individual students with the potential for failure in school, so as to target them for preventive services. Yet critics charge that the term can be used to "label" certain groups, in particular urban minority groups. Such labeling may increase the already at-risk student's problems by creating lowered expectations in the minds of teachers and service providers. Further, the concept does not allow for differences among cultural groups that may account for deviant behaviors in so-called at-risk children.

All students are at risk at some time in their lives. A Phi Delta Kappa study found five situations that lead to students' at-risk behavior: personal pain; academic failure; family socioeconomic factors; family instability, such as fighting, separation, or **divorce;** and family tragedy, such as illness or death. The normal process of development itself imposes high-risk conditions. **Social competence**—making friends and developing social skills—and maturing sexuality places the adolescent in vulnerable positions that can lead to drug use, fighting, early and unprotected sexual activity, and delinquency. **Peer pressure** poses risk factors, though participation in **extracurricular activities** lessens the chance of doing poorly in school or participating in other risky behaviors. Also, urban minorities are not the only high risk socioeconomic groups—rural students are also considered an at-risk group.

Students who are at risk of school failure tend to perceive their teachers as having low interest in them as people. Though critics of the at-risk label cite isolation as a problem, the most successful programs are those that separate at-risk students from the rest of the student body and have low student-teacher ratios. Programs focus on basic academic and survival skills, such as attending to tasks, following directions, raising one's hand to speak, and writing legibly. Successful programs also relate work to education and provide counseling and support services. **Vocational education** programs offer many characteristics of effective at-risk programs, including a hands-on performance orientation, low student-teacher ratios, and a high level of support services.

ADDRESSING THE RISKS

In addition to counseling and career planning, successful at-risk programs address basic psychosocial issues such as self-esteem, **communication skills**, coping skills, and control issues.

Self-concept and self-esteem. Low achievement in school leads to low self-esteem, and the high-risk adolescent turns to other sources to develop a positive self-concept. Contrary to popular conception, at-risk students often have high self esteem based on their participation in deviant or delinquent social groups. Programs such as **peer mediation** promote development of high self-esteem based on prosocial rather than antisocial behavior.

Communication skills. At-risk students learn core social skills necessary to develop relationships with peers and with adults. Working on both speaking and listening skills helps students to communicate effectively.

Coping skills. Coping skills include the use of humor and shift in focus. At-risk students learn such techniques to address disappointment, rejection, fear, anger, and loneliness effectively without using drugs, sex, or violence.

Locus of control. Low-risk students have an internal *locus of control.* They perceive their lives as having an orderliness dependent on their own positive or negative behavior; they believe they have control over their lives. Conversely, at-risk students have an external locus of control, perceiving their lives as under someone else's control. Along with shifting their locus of control, at-risk students must develop the low-risk habits of considering the consequences of their behavior more fully, learning how to delay gratification, and persisting in goal-directed behavior.

For Further Study

Books

Dryfoos, Joy G. *Adolescents At-Risk: Prevalence and Prevention.* New York: Oxford University Press, 1990.

Hamby, J. V. *Vocational Education for the 21st Century.* Clemson, SC: National Dropout Prevention Center, 1992.

Helge, Doris. *Rural, Exceptional, At Risk.* Reston, VA: ERIC Clearinghouse on Handicapped and Gifted Children, 1991.

Kaywell, Joan F. *Adolescents At Risk: A Guide to Fiction and Nonfiction for Young Adults, Parents, and Professionals.* Westport, CT: Greenwood Press, 1993.

Manning, M. L., and L. G. Baruth. *Students At Risk.* Boston: Allyn and Bacon, 1995.

McWhirter, J. J., et al. *At-Risk Youth: A Comprehensive Response.* Pacific Grove, CA: Brooks/Cole, 1993.

National Research Council. *Losing Generations: Adolescents in High-Risk Settings.* Panel on High Risk Youth, Commission on Behavioral and Social Sciences and Education, National Research Council. Washington, DC: National Academy Press, 1993.

Nicolau, Siobhan, and Carmen Lydia Ramos. *Together is Better: Building Strong Partnerships Between Schools and Hispanic Parents.* Washington, DC: Hispanic Policy Development Project, Inc., 1990.

Shirley, L. J., and S. G. Pritz. *The Lifelong Options Program: A Handbook for Implementing and Managing a Vocational Education Program for Youth At Risk.* Clemson, SC: National Dropout Prevention Center, 1992.

Organizations

National Institute on the Education of At-Risk Students
U.S. Department of Education
Address: OERI/At-Risk Room 610
555 New Jersey Avenue, NW
Washington, DC 20208-5521
Telephone: (202) 219-2239

Ataxia

Lack of coordination in the muscles.

Ataxia, an extreme lack of coordination of the muscles, is a symptom of damage to the central nervous system. People with ataxia typically stand with feet planted far apart, and sway while standing, struggling to maintain balance. Jerky eye and head movements are also commonly observed with ataxia. Ataxia may result from a number of causes, including damage to or diseases of the spinal cord or the cerebellum, a part of the brain; tumor on the spinal cord or in the cerebellum; infection affecting the central nervous system; response to **poison** or other environmental factor that causes the central nervous system to stop functioning normally or to degenerate; disease that causes degeneration of the central nervous system, such as multiple sclerosis; or hereditary factors. Hereditary ataxia conditions are rare, and include Friedreich's ataxia, which usually appears between the ages of five and twenty. Friedreich's ataxia is a disabling condition that often causes premature death.

For Further Study

Organizations

Friedreich's Ataxia Group in America (FAGA)
Address: P.O. Box 11116
Oakland, CA 94611
(Organization concerned with Friedreich's ataxia, an ex-

tremely rare inherited form of ataxia involving loss of muscle control, usually of the legs.)

National Ataxia Foundation (NAF)
  Address: 600 Twelve Oaks Center
  15500 Wayzata Boulevard
  Wayzata, MN 55391
  (Publishes *Hereditary Ataxia: The Facts;* a newsletter, *Generations;* and *Hereditary Ataxia: A Guidebook for Managing Speech and Swallowing Problems.*)

National Institute of Neurological Disorders and Stroke (NINDS)
  Address: 9000 Rockville Pike
  Building 31, Room 8A06
  Bethesda, MD 20892

Athletics *see* **Sports**

Attachment Between Infant and Caregiver

An enduring emotional bond that leads the infant to experience pleasure, joy, safety, and comfort in the caregiver's company, and distress when temporarily separated.

Many developmental psychologists view attachment, the special relationship between infant and caregiver, as an important building block for later relationships and adult personality. Because of its central importance to theories of social and emotional development, the scientific study of attachment has remained in the forefront of developmental psychology for the past several decades, beginning with the pioneering work of **John Bowlby** and **Mary Ainsworth.**

The contribution of John Bowlby

Modern attachment theory was developed by John Bowlby as a variant of object-relations theory, itself a variant of Freud's theory that the infant's tie to the mother is the cornerstone of adult personality. While it is true that Bowlby's theory is sometimes referred to as an ethological theory of attachment, Bowlby was not an ethologist, but rather a psychoanalytically trained clinician who integrated a number of approaches, including systems theory and evolutionary theory in formulating modern attachment theory.

Prior to the general acceptance of Bowlby's attachment theory, psychologists viewed attachment as a secondary drive, derived from primary drives like hunger. It was thought that the infant became attached to the mother because she supplied food, and thus became the object of the infant's attachment through association with feeding and the reduction of other primary needs. Assessment of the infant's attachment was based on certain behaviors. A

child was thought to be overly attached if crying and clingy behavior were high in frequency.

In contrast, Bowlby considered the attachment process to be an innate system that evolved in primates through natural selection. Abundant evidence supports this view, including a classic series of studies by Harry Harlow and colleagues during the 1950s and 60s. Using a method involving surrogate "mothers," Harlow was the first to empirically test the notion that attachment to the mother forms as a result of feeding. In one study, Harlow separated infant monkeys from their mothers at birth, then reared them with two surrogate mothers, one made of stiff wire equipped with a bottle for feeding, the other covered with soft terry cloth, but without the bottle. If an infant monkey became attached by associating the mother with food, we would expect to see attachment behaviors exhibited toward the wire surrogate with the bottle. Instead the infant monkeys all showed a clear preference for the soft, cuddly surrogate without the bottle, spending most of their time (when not feeding) clinging to it and leaping into its "lap" when frightened or distressed. While feeding may be an important context for the development of the mother-child bond in natural circumstances, contact comfort was shown to be more central than feeding per se.

Drawing upon classic ethology, Bowlby reformulated the concept of attachment as a dyadic, behavioral system that would be activated automatically when the infant perceived threat in the environment, and remained active until proximity with the caregiver was reestablished. The infant's repertoire of attachment behaviors gradually unfolded in the context of interaction with the caregiver according to a relatively fixed timetable. Initially, the infant is preadapted to engage the caregiver with innate behaviors, such as looking, smiling, crying, and clinging. In time, other behaviors, such as following and complex signaling, emerge with the same goal of remaining in contact with the caregiver. It is not necessary for the adult to specifically teach such behaviors. Rather, the interaction of the caregiver provides a sufficient context for the attachment behaviors of the infant to be expressed. Learning also provides an essential context for shaping the specific qualities of the infant's attachment to a particular caregiver.

The development of the attachment relationship must be distinguished from the appearance of attachment behaviors. Various behaviors can serve the function of attachment, but no particular behavior has primacy. Smiling, crying, or proximity-seeking are common behaviors employed in a variety of contexts to serve a variety of functions. They may be expressed in relation to strangers or even objects. This is one reason why counting the number of behaviors cannot measure an attachment. Attachment refers to how those behaviors are organized with respect to the specific caregiver and the context. The history of the infant's relationship with the caregiver, as well as the emerging cognitive and emotional capacities of the infant, provide the context for the development of this bond. Bowlby characterizes this development in four stages:

Preattachment: birth to six weeks

The preattachment phase, roughly the first six weeks following birth, is characterized by indiscriminate sociability. The key observation in this phase is the lack of differential responsiveness to the primary caregiver. The infant responds positively to a variety of cues regardless of the person providing them. Although there is some evidence that infants may recognize their mother's smell and voice, they do not yet demonstrate a consistent preference for her over others.

Attachment-in-the-making: two to seven months

The next phase of discriminating sociability occurs when the infant is between two and seven months old. In this phase infants can readily distinguish the caretaker from other adults and typically respond to her differently than a stranger. They may smile and vocalize more readily in her presence and quickly settle in her arms when distressed. During this phase the infant begins to learn the natural contingencies of this special relationship and to develop expectations about how the caregiver will respond to various signals. Without any notion of object permanence, the infant does not protest separation during this phase.

Clear-cut attachment: seven to twenty-four months

With the onset of **stranger anxiety** at around seven months of age, the infant has entered the most significant phase of attachment. The hallmark of this phase, which lasts until about age two, is the infant's general tendency to explore from the secure base provided by the mother, or primary caregiver, and to return to her for contact and comfort if threatened or distressed. Separation is actively protested if the infant is on unfamiliar ground.

Goal-corrected partnership: after two years

As the infant moves into toddlerhood around 18 months, the separation protests and proximity-seeking that once characterized the infant's behavior in relation to the attachment figure are on the wane. Toddlers enter a new phase of reciprocal relationship or partnership with the caregiver characterized by negotiation, give-and-take, and the emergence of a new kind of reciprocity. The wise parent recognizes that the hard-fought and new-found autonomy of the two-year-old is but the flip slide of their continued dependence on them for many years to come.

As with most stage theories of development, infants are thought to proceed through the different stages in the same sequence, though the timing may be slightly different among infants. While Bowlby viewed proximity to the caregiver as the goal of the attachment system, later theorists have argued that "felt security" is a more appropriate goal of the system because it prescribes a central role for the emotional qualities of this intimate relationship. By explicitly incorporating an emotional-motivational component into the attachment system, it becomes a more viable model for describing the dynamic stability of this important relationship beyond the period of infancy. The older infants can use many strategies to maintain a sense of security and will require less proximity, even as the attachment relationship to the caregiver deepens.

The contribution of Mary Ainsworth

The first and most important test for Bowlby's theory of attachment was conducted by Mary Ainsworth in a series of naturalistic and laboratory studies. Her first independent research opportunity arose while living in Uganda. She intended to study **weaning** practices in Ganda mothers because they weaned their children by sending them off to stay with their **grandparents**. When she found out that such separations were no longer practiced, she turned her attention to the attachment behaviors described by Bowlby. She observed that the typical Ganda infant formed a specific attachment to the mother, used her to explore the surrounding environment, and protested separation by crying or attempting to follow her. The different stages of their attachment appeared to unfold in a fairly predictable sequence. Her attention to individual differences in the attachment relations she observed in Uganda formed the basis of her contribution to attachment research.

Her first scheme for classifying attachment patterns is presented in *Infancy in Uganda* (1967) and describes a three-fold taxonomy including secure, insecure, and unattached types based on the apparent strength and security of the attachment relation. Later Ainsworth became convinced that all infants became attached but that some showed little felt-security and others attempted to conceal their need for their mothers.

In 1962, Ainsworth conducted her classic Baltimore longitudinal study of mother-infant attachment. She relied upon extensive naturalistic observation of relatively few subjects. Regular four-hour home visits were made to observe 26 families beginning a few weeks after delivery, and continued at three-week intervals until about 54 weeks. Following an ethological model, Ainsworth believed that only extensive naturalistic observation could provide a broad enough, and fine enough, net to capture the details of the attachment process as it was played out in each unique setting. From this inductive approach, involving about 72 hours of observation in each home, together with the cross-cultural observations in Uganda,

AINSWORTH'S 1967 LIST OF ATTACHMENT BEHAVIORS	
1	Differential crying (i.e., with mother compared to others)
2	Differential smiling
3	Differential vocalization
4	Crying when the mother leaves
5	Following the mother
6	Visual motor orientation towards the mother
7	Greeting through smiling, crowing, and general excitement
8	Lifting arms in greeting the mother
9	Clapping hands in greeting the mother
10	Scrambling over the mother
11	Burying the face in the mother's lap
12	Approach to the mother through locomotion
13	Embracing, hugging, kissing the mother (not seen in Ugandan infants but observed frequently by infants in Western societies.)
14	Exploration away from the mother as a secure base
15	Flight to the mother as a haven of safety
16	Clinging to the mother

Ainsworth was able to document an ethogram, or listing, of the typical attachment behaviors shown by the Ganda and American infants, as shown in the accompanying table.

With this descriptive base, Ainsworth was now in a position to develop a laboratory procedure to assess attachment patterns. The impetus for developing such a procedure was provided in part by her failure to observe the secure base phenomenon in the American babies that she saw in the Gandan babies. Ainsworth reasoned that the American infants were comfortable with the familiar routines of the mother coming and going around the house and that she would have to place the infant and mother in a less familiar environment in order to elicit the secure base behavior observed in Africa.

The goal of the procedure was to provide a novel environment that would arouse the infant's motivation to explore while at the same time arouse a certain degree of security seeking. Separation in such an unfamiliar setting would also be likely to activate the attachment system and allow for a direct test of its functioning. The validation of the procedure and its scoring method was grounded in the naturalistic observation of exploration, crying, and proximity seeking in the home.

The strange-situation paradigm, or method, consists of eight episodes which can be construed as involving mild, but cumulative, stress for the one-year-old. The accompanying table presents the eight episodes and the attachment behaviors that can typically be observed.

No single behavior can be used to assess the quality of the infant's attachment to the caregiver. For example, crying in response to separation merely shows that attachment system has been activated, as would the other behaviors listed in the first table accompanying this essay. Infants could differ in the amount and intensity of crying as a function of many factors including age, temperament, or transitory contextual factors like illness. The key to assessing the quality of attachment lies in detecting the organization or pattern of the infant's responses to the changing context, particularly the response to the caregiver.

What are the basic types of infant-caregiver attachment?

Three basic patterns of attachment were described by Ainsworth, and a fourth type has recently been added. Using Ainsworth's original taxonomy, researchers in the United States and Europe have observed a securely attached pattern in approximately 65% of all infants. Two distinct types of less secure anxious patterns were originally described by Ainsworth—resistant attachment (about 10%) and avoidant attachment (about 20%). These percentages vary in different cultures. Finally, a fourth type, disorganized attachment, has been observed by some investigators, though it is observed in less than 10% of all infants.

Secure attachment

These infants show an optimal balance between exploration and play, and the desire to remain near their caregiver in the unfamiliar laboratory context. They typically separate readily from the caregiver, but remain friendly towards her and to the stranger as well. They may, however, be upset during the separation episodes, but their contact with the caregiver upon reunion provides effective relief from this distress. Upon settling, they once again become engaged in play. Infants who show little distress during separation show that they are pleased by greeting their mothers upon their return and

EPISODES IN THE STRANGE SITUATION

Episode number/duration	Event	Attachment behavior observed
1—About 30 seconds	Experimenter introduces parent and baby to playroom and then leaves.	
2—3 minutes	Parent is seated while baby plays with toys.	Parent as secure base
3—3 minutes	Stranger enters, is seated, and talks to parent.	Reaction to unfamiliar adult
4—3 minutes or shorter if baby becomes very upset	Parent leaves room. Stranger responds to baby and offers comfort if upset.	Separation anxiety
5—3 minutes or longer if baby needs more time to calm down and return to play	Parent returns, greets baby, and, if necessary, offers comfort. Stranger leaves room.	Reaction to reunion
6—3 minutes or shorter if baby becomes very upset	Parent leaves room.	Separation anxiety
7—3 minutes	Stranger enters room and offers comfort.	Ability to be soothed by stranger
8—3 minutes or longer if baby needs more time to calm down and return to play	Parent returns, greets baby, if necessary offers comfort, and tries to reinterest baby in toys.	Reaction to reunion

engaging them in social interaction by smiling and sharing discoveries.

Resistant attachment

This pattern is characterized by emotional ambivalence and physical resistance to the mother. The infant is typically reluctant to separate from the mother and quick to show anxiety and distress in the unfamiliar setting. Their general wary attitude extends to the stranger and they become highly distressed by the separation. The key behavioral criterion is the difficulty these infants have settling in the reunion episodes with the mother. The classification is also referred to as anxious-ambivalent because of the anger expressed by these infants towards their mother at the same moment that they are expressing their need for contact and comforting. They often mix contact-seeking with active resistance, squirming, fussing, and even striking out at their mothers when they are upset.

Avoidant attachment

As its label suggests, the key behavioral criterion in this pattern is the active avoidance of the mother when the infant is upset. These infants readily separate from their mothers to explore and may be more friendly towards the stranger than their own mother. Unlike securely attached infants they show little preference for the caregiver and little affective sharing when playing. Their emotional distance from the caregiver becomes more evident following separation. Some infants may begin to seek proximity upon reunion, then suddenly break off the intended movement and turn away. The avoidance of the mother is typically more pronounced following the second separation. These approach-avoidance conflicts sometimes result in displaced behaviors—behaviors which appear out of sequence and have no apparent function. Ethologists interpret such behavior as resulting from the activation of two conflicting motivational systems.

Disorganized attachment

The fourth category reflects a variety of confused and contradictory behaviors on the part of the infant. For example, during reunion with the parent, the infant might look away while being held by the mother or approach her with a blank or even depressed look. Many of these babies convey a dazed or disoriented facial expression. Others may exhibit confusing patterns such as crying unexpectedly after having settled, or displaying odd, frozen postures.

What factors lead to different patterns of attachment?

Bowlby theorized that the interactive history between the infant and the caregiver is the major determinant of the quality of attachment observed at one year. In his view, the infant will come to form an expectation concerning the availability and responsiveness of the caregiver based on the repeated cycles of distress signals and responses throughout the first year of life. These expectations are thought to be revealed in the infant's behavior towards the caregiver in the strange-situation.

Ainsworth's method uses systematic changes of salient aspects of the immediate mother-child context to study interaction patterns in a situation of increasing stress for the infant. From this perspective, active avoidance of the caregiver, or a mixture of approach and resistant behaviors by the infant while under stress, interferes with the contact and comfort typically afforded by attachment figures. Such dysfunctional behaviors are interpreted as a response formulated by the child that reflects a history of emotional unavailability on the part of the caregiver, or inconsistent, chaotic care, respectively. In this sense, the history and quality of the relationship itself may be discerned from a careful analysis of infant behavior in relation to changes in context, particularly the separation and reunion episodes with the caregiver.

Ainsworth rated maternal sensitivity towards the infant at several points over the first year and found that when caregivers had been rated high on sensitivity their attachment relationship with their infants was more likely to be classified as secure. In contrast, caregivers who were rejecting of their infants' desire for contact and comfort were more likely to have anxious attachments with their infants. (Ainsworth, et al., 1978). Ainsworth's basic findings relating quality of care to quality of attachment have been widely replicated. In each study, Ainsworth's sensitivity scale was related to attachment assessments at one year. The link between caregiver rejection and avoidant attachment has also been replicated in several studies.

Various studies have generally shown that emotional availability and other aspects of emotional communication are predictive of security of attachment. For example, infants whose mothers are depressed are often insecurely attached, though not all infants of depressed parents will develop insecure attachments. It is the quality of caregiving, not the depression per se, that is predictive of attachment.

Other factors, such as infant **temperament,** may be indirectly related to attachment, though direct relations are difficult to demonstrate. For example, newborns with neurological problems were not more likely to be classified as insecurely attached, except when this factor was combined with low levels of social and emotional support for caregivers. Similarly, infant proneness to distress was not predictive of anxious attachment, except in combination with high levels of maternal control. Thus, it is reasonable to conclude that infant temperamental characteristics interact with caregiving to increase or decrease the development of an insecure attachment.

Are infants equally attached to fathers and mothers?

Historically, the vast majority of research on parent-infant relationships has involved mothers, so much so that in 1975 Michael Lamb described fathers as "the forgotten contributors to child development." While this situation is gradually changing, it remains true that most research on attachment has focused on the infant's tie to the mother, probably because most fathers spend less time interacting with their babies than mothers do. Nevertheless, the same caregiving qualities that promote secure mother-infant bonds apply equally well to fathers. If the father engages in sensitive caregiving and becomes the object of his baby's affection, he too will begin to serve as a secure base for his infant.

In American families, fathers tend to become increasingly involved with their infants. However, they may not be doing the same things with their infant as mothers do. Typically, mothers devote more time to physical care, holding, soothing, and feeding their baby, whereas fathers are more likely to engage their baby in playful physical stimulation. Considering these different styles, it is not surprising that most infants prefer their mothers when distressed, and look to their fathers for play.

Despite such differences, many infants form the same type of attachment with both their fathers and mothers, though this is not always the case. One study found that about half the infants in the study formed a different pattern of attachment with each parent. In order to determine the father's contribution to the infant's social development, the researchers compared the social responsiveness of infants who were securely attached to one parent only, with infants who were securely attached to both or insecurely attached to both. Not surprisingly, infants who were securely attached to both parents were the most socially responsive.

Do early patterns of attachment influence later relationships?

Attachment theorists have speculated that patterns of co-regulation established within early social relationships provide a working model for later social relations. Some developmentalists believe that the infant's relationship with the primary caregiver(s) lays a foundation for subsequent relationships. Competence in one developmental period can promote adaptation within that period, and prepare the way for the formation of competence in the next.

For Further Study

Ainsworth, M., M. Blehar, E. Waters, and S. Wall. *Patterns of Attachment.* Hillsdale, NJ: Erlbaum, 1978.

Bowlby, J. *A Secure Base: Parent-Child Attachment and Healthy Human Development.* New York: Basic Books, 1988.

Sroufe, L. A. *Emotional Development: The Organization of Emotional Life in the Early Years.* New York: Cambridge University Press, 1996. .

—Peter LaFreniere, Ph.D.
University of Maine

Attention

Concentration on a task.

Attention is concentration, or perceptive awareness, focused on a stimulus, such as a book or worksheet. During such periods of attention, the individual focuses on the stimuli of the task and ignores other environmental stimuli. There are distinct and measurable neurological and physiological aspects of attention, and the ability to achieve a state of attention may be limited by mental or physical dysfunctions. In fact, even short-term illnesses such as the flu can adversely affect the individual's ability to concentrate.

Psychologists use the term "attention span" to refer to the number of separate stimulus elements, or the amount of stimulus, that can be perceived and remembered after a brief presentation. Popularly, "attention span" is used to mean the amount of time that can be continuously spent in a state of attention.

Attention is directed toward a stimulus for any one of a number of reasons: as a conscious decision ("I'm going to practice the piano"); as part of social interaction (engaging in conversation with another person); as a reaction to a direction ("Please read page 35"); or as a reaction to an unexpected event (reaction to a loud noise). During the stages of development, a child's attention

span increases. Researchers believe that even the youngest infants have the ability to focus attention for brief periods in response to visual and auditory stimuli. In fact, the development of attention is nurtured when caregivers provide infants with regular opportunities to focus on auditory and visual stimuli.

A fairly common cognitive disability is the inability to sustain attention or to shift it from one task to another. In children, **attention deficit/hyperactivity disorder** is a frequently diagnosed problem that affects school performance and learning. In some instances, attention deficits indicate a dysfunction in the **brain**'s frontal lobe related to severe head injury or chronic illness. **Memory** and visual perception are likely also to be impaired in a student with an attention deficit.

For Further Study

Books

Barkley, R.A. *Attention Deficit Hyperactivity Disorder; A Handbook for Diagnosis and Treatment.* New York: Guilford Press, 1990.

Hallowell, E.M. and J.J. Ratey. *Driven to Distraction: Recognizing and Coping with Attention Deficit Disorder from Childhood through Adulthood.* New York: Simon and Schuster, 1994.

Hans, James. *The Mysteries of Attention.* Albany, NY: SUNY Press, 1993.

Weiss, G. *Attention Deficit Hyperactivity Disorder.* Philadelphia: W.B. Saunders, 1992.

Periodicals

Auerbach, Sanford H., Keith D. Cicerone, Harvey S. Levin and Daniel Tranel. "What You Can Learn from Neuropsychologic Testing." *Patient Care* 28, July 15, 1994, pp. 97+.

Attention Deficit/ Hyperactivity Disorder

Disorder characterized by attentional deficit and/or hyperactivity—impulsivity more severe than expected for a developmental age.

Attention Deficit/Hyperactivity Disorder (ADHD), which affects 3–5% of school-age children in the United States, refers to a combination of excessive motor restlessness, difficulty in controlling or maintaining attention to relevant events, and impulsive responding that is not adaptive.

For some children hyperactivity is the primary feature of their ADHD diagnosis. These children may be unable to sit quietly in class. They may fidget in their chairs, sharpen their pencils multiple times, flip the corners of the pages back and forth, or talk to a neighbor. On the way up to the teacher's desk they may take several detours.

Most children with ADHD have both attentional and hyperactivity-impulsivity components, and so they may experience difficulties regulating both attention and activity. Although many children who do not have ADHD seem periodically inattentive or highly active, children with ADHD experience these difficulties more severely than others at their same developmental level. Moreover, these difficulties interfere with age-appropriate behavioral expectations across settings such as home, playground, and school.

Psychologists have not always used the label ADHD to describe this constellation of behaviors. In the 1950s and 60s, children exhibiting these symptoms were either diagnosed as minimally brain damaged or labelled as behavior problems. The fourth edition of the ***Diagnostic and Statistical Manual (DSM-IV),*** which is used to classify psychiatric disorders, describes ADHD as a pattern of inattention and/or impulsivity-hyperactivity more severe than expected for the child's developmental level. The symptoms must be present before age seven, although diagnosis is frequently made only following interference with school activities. Symptoms must be present in at least two settings, and there must be clear evidence of interference with academic, social, or occupational functioning. Finally, the symptoms must not be due to other neuropsychiatric disorders such as **pervasive developmental disorder, schizophrenia** or other psychoses, or **anxiety** disorder or other neuroses.

Inattention may be evident in (a) failing to attend closely to tasks or making careless errors, (b) having difficulty in persisting with tasks until they are completed, (c) appearing not to be listening, (d) frequently shifting tasks or activities, (e) appearing disorganized, (f) avoiding activities that require close or sustained attention, (g) losing or damaging items by not handling them with sufficient care, (h) being distracted by background noises or events, or (i) being forgetful in daily activities. According to the *DSM-IV,* six or more of these symptoms must persist for six months or more for a diagnosis of ADHD with inattention as a major component.

Hyperactivity may be seen as (a) fidgety behavior or difficulty sitting still, (b) excessive running or climbing when not appropriate, (c) not remaining seated when asked to, (d) having difficulty enjoying quiet activities, (e) appearing to be "constantly on the go," or (f) excessive talking. Impulsivity may be related to hyperactive behavior and may be manifest as (a) impatience or blurting out answers before the question has been finished, (b) difficulty in waiting for one's turn, and (c) frequent interruptions or intrusions. Impulsive children frequently talk

out of turn or ask questions seemingly "out of the blue." Their impulsivity may also lead to accidents or engaging in high risk behavior without consideration of the consequences. According to the *DSM-IV,* six or more of these symptoms must persist for six months or more for a diagnosis of ADHD with hyperactivity-impulsivity as a major component.

The *DSM-IV* recognizes subtypes of ADHD. The most prevalent type is the Combined Type in which individuals show at least six of the symptoms of inattention as well as of hyperactivity or impulsivity. The Predominantly Inattentive Type and the Predominantly Hyperactive-Impulsive type are distinguished by which of the major pattern of symptoms predominate.

It is important that a careful diagnosis be made before proceeding with treatment, especially with medication. Often symptoms of inattention or hyperactivity may cause parents to seek professional help, but these symptoms may not necessarily indicate the presence of ADHD. Paul Dworkin, a physician with special interests in school failure, reports that out of 245 children referred for evaluation due to parental or school concerns about inattention, impulsivity, or overactivity, only 38% received a diagnosis of ADHD, although almost all (91%) were diagnosed with some kind of academic problem.

Who gets ADHD? Boys outnumber girls by at least a factor of four; studies have found prevalence ranging from four to nine times as many boys with ADHD compared to girls. The family members (first degree relatives) of children with ADHD are more likely to have the disorder, as well as a higher prevalence of mood and anxiety disorders, learning disabilities, and substance abuse problems. Children who have a history of abuse or neglect, multiple foster placements, infections, prenatal drug exposure, or low birth weight are also more likely to have ADHD. Although there is no definitive laboratory test for ADHD nor a distinctive biological marker, children with ADHD do have a higher rate of minor physical anomalies than the general population.

Children may develop problems because of the consequences of ADHD. If the causes of a child's disruptive or inattentive behavior are not understood, the child may be punished, ridiculed, or rejected, leading to potential reactions in the areas of **self-esteem,** conduct, academic performance, and family and social relations. A child who feels that he or she is unable to perform to expectations no matter what type of effort is put forth may begin to feel helpless or depressed. Often, the reaction can exacerbate the inattention or hyperactivity or diminish the child's capacity to compensate, and a vicious cycle can develop.

The course of the disorder may vary. For many ADHD children, symptoms remain relatively stable into the early teen years and abate during later **adolescence** and adulthood. About 30-40% of cases persist into the late teens. Some individuals continue to experience all of their symptoms into adulthood and others retain only some.

What causes ADHD? The exact cause of ADHD is not known. The increased incidence of the disorder in families suggests a genetic component in some cases. Brain chemistry is implicated by the actions of the medications that reduce ADHD symptoms, suggesting that there may be a dysfunction of the norepinephrine and dopamine systems. Brain imagining techniques have been used with mixed success. Positron emission tomography (PET) scans show some reduced metabolism in certain areas (prefrontal and premotor cortex) in ADHD adults, but findings on younger patients are less clear. One complication in conducting these imagining studies is the necessity for patients to remain still for a period of time, something that is, of course, difficult for ADHD children to do.

What can be done? Treatment for ADHD takes two major forms: treating the child and treating the environment. Pharmacological treatment can be effective in many cases. Stimulant medications (Ritalin/**methylphenidate,** Dexedrine/dextroamphetimine, and Cylert/magnesium pemoline) have positive effect in 60–80% of cases and are the most common type of drugs used for ADHD. The benefits include enhancement of attention span, decrease in impulsivity and irrelevant behavior, and decreased activity. Vigilance and discrimination increase and handwriting and math skills frequently improve. These gains are most striking when pharmacological treatment is combined with educational and behavioral interventions.

Stimulant medications, however, may have side effects in some children that may make them inappropriate choices. These side effects include loss of appetite, insomnia, mood disturbance, headache, and gastro-intestinal distress. Tics may also appear and should be monitored carefully. Psychotic reactions are among the more severe side effects. There is some evidence that long-term use of stimulant medication may interfere with physical growth and weight gain. These effects are thought to be ameliorated by "medication breaks" over school vacations and weekends, and the like.

When stimulant medications are not an appropriate choice, non-stimulants or tricyclic **antidepressants** may be prescribed. The use of tricyclic antidepressants, especially, has to be monitored carefully due to possible cardiac side effects. Combined pharmacologic treatment is used for patients who have ADHD in addition to another psychiatric disorder.

It is important that drug treatment not be used exclusively in the management of ADHD. Each child should have an individual educational plan that outlines modifications to the regular mode of instruction that will facilitate the child's academic performance. Teachers need to consider the needs of the ADHD child when giving instructions, making sure that they are well paced with cues to remind the child of each one. They must also understand the origins of impulsive behavior—that the child is not deliberately trying to ruin a lesson or activity by acting unruly. Teachers should be structured, comfortable with the remedial services the child may need, and able to maintain good lines of communication with the parent.

Specialists should devise a series of compensatory strategies that will enable the child to cope with his or her attentional or activity challenges. These strategies might include simple things like checklists of things to do before handing in assignments (name on top, check spelling, etc.), putting a clock on the child's desk to help structure time for activities, or covering the pictures on a page until the child has read the words so that he is not distracted.

Special assistance may not be limited to educational settings. Families frequently need help in coping with the demands and challenges of the ADHD child. Inattention, shifting activites every five minutes, difficulty completing homework and household tasks, losing things, interrupting, not listening, breaking rules, constant talking, boredom, and irritability can take a toll on any family.

Parents may not understand how attention regulation or impulsivity affect daily functioning, and they might not be trained in the kind of techniques that help ADHD children manage their behavior. Siblings may be resentful of what the ADHD child seems to "get away with" or the inordinate amount of attention he or she receives. The ADHD child may be resentful of the younger sibling who is more accomplished at school or never seems to get in any trouble. Family interaction patterns may set up vicious cycles that become destructive and difficult to break.

Support groups for families with any ADHD member are increasingly available through school districts and health care providers. Community colleges frequently offer courses in discipline and behavior management. Counselling services are available to complement any type of pharmacological treatment that the family obtains for its member. There are also a number of popular books that are informative and helpful. Some of these are listed below.

For Further Study

Books

Barkley, R.A. *Attention Deficit Hyperactivity Disorder; A Handbook for Diagnosis and Treatment.* New York: Guildord Press, 1990.

Dworkin, P.H. *Learning and Behavior Problems of School Children.* Philadelphia: W.B. Saunders, 1985.

Hallowell, E.M. and J.J. Ratey. *Driven to Distraction: Recognizing and Coping with Attention Deficit Disorder from Childhood through Adulthood.* New York: Simon and Schuster, 1994.

Weiss, G. *Attention Deficit Hyperactivity Disorder.* Philadelphia: W.B. Saunders, 1992.

Wender, P. *The Hyperactive Child, Adolescent, and Adult: Attention Deficit Disorder through the Lifespan.* New York: Oxford University Press, 1987.

Periodicals

Manuzza, S., R. G. Klein, A. Bessler, P. Malloy, and M. LaPadula. "Adult Outcome of Hyperactive Boys: Educational Achievement, Occupational Rank, and Psychiatric Status." *Archives of General Psychiatry 50*, 1993, pp. 565–576.

Wilens, T. E. and J. Biederman. "The Stimulants." *Psychiatric Clinics of North America.* D. Shafer, ed. Philadelphia: W. B. Saunders, 1992.

Zametkin, A. J. and J. L. Rappaport. "Neurobiology of Attention Deficit Disorder with Hyperactivity: Where Have We Come in 50 Years?" *Journal of the American Academy of Child and Adolescent Psychiatry* 26, 1987, pp. 676–686.

Organizations

Attention Deficit Disorder Association
 Address: P.O. Box 972
 Mentor, OH 44061
 Telephone: toll-free (800) 487-2282
 (Provides educational resources on ADHD)

CHADD
 (Children and Adults with Attention Deficit Disorder)
 Address: 499 NW 70th Ave., Suite 308
 Plantation, FL 33317
 Telephone: (305) 587-3700
 (A national and international non-profit organization for children and adults with ADHD)

—Doreen Arcus, Ph.D.
Univeristy of Massachusetts Lowell

Attribution Theory

An area of cognitive therapy that is concerned with how people explain the causes of behavior, both their own and those of others.

A major concept in the study of attribution theory is **locus of control:** whether one interprets events as being caused by one's own behavior or by outside circumstances. A child with an internal locus of control (also called "an internal") will believe that her performance on a test is governed by her ability or by how hard she studied, whereas an "external" will attribute success or failure by concluding that the test was easy or hard, the teacher graded fairly or unfairly, the room in which the test was administered was too quiet or noisy, or some other rationale. In general, an internal locus of control is associated with optimism and physical health. Children with an internal locus of control also tend to be more successful at delaying gratification in middle childhood than children with an external locus of control, who are less likely to believe that their demonstration of self-control in the present has the ability to influence events in the future. (*See* **Delay of Gratification**)

Internal or external attribution is also made with respect to other people (i.e., is another person personally responsible for a certain event, or is it caused by something beyond his or her control?). We make this sort of attribution when we decide whether to blame a friend for failing to pay back a loan. If we blame it on her personal qualities, the attribution is internal. If we blame it on a problem she is having, then the attribution is external. Three factors influence whether the behavior of others is attributed to internal or external causes: consensus, consistency, and distinctiveness. Consensus refers to whether other people exhibit similar behavior; consistency refers to whether the behavior occurs repeatedly; and distinctiveness is concerned with whether the behavior occurs in other, similar, situations. For example, if a friend consistently fails to repay a loan, an internal attribution may be ascribed.

For Further Study

Books

Douglas, Tom. *Scapegoats: Transferring Blame.* New York: Routledge, 1995.

Hewstone, Miles, ed. *Attribution Theory: Social and Functional Extensions.* Oxford, England: B. Blackwell, 1983.

Lamb, Sharon. *The Trouble with Blame: Victims, Perpetrators, and Responsibility.* Cambridge: Harvard University Press, 1996.

McLaughlin, Mary L., Michael J. Cody, and Stephen Reed, eds. *Explaining Oneself to Others: Reason-Giving in a Social Context.* Hillsdale, NJ: Lawrence Erlbaum Assoc., 1992.

Yussen, Steven R., ed. *The Growth of Reflection in Children.* Oxford, England: Academic Press, 1985.

Auditory Discrimination Test

A diagnostic assessment test for children ages 4–8.

The Auditory Discrimination Test, also called ADT or Wepman's Auditory Discrimination Test, is used to evaluate communication skills and highlight possible reading problems as well as predict certain speech defects. A tester reads 40 pairs of words out loud, one pair at a time, and the child is asked whether each pair is identical or not. The tester covers his or her mouth so that the child cannot distinguish the words visually. The test is often given by a special education teacher or speech language pathologist. Performance is measured on a rating scale with results ranging from "very good development" for the child's age to "below adequate." Different versions of the test are sometimes administered on a follow-up basis to evaluate the effectiveness of remedial instruction.

Authoritarian Parent *see* **Parent-Child Relationships**

Autism

A mental disorder that is characterized by repetitive behavior and a seriously impaired ability to communicate and interact with others.

Childhood autism (sometimes called pervasive developmental disorder) is characterized by a profound difficulty in social relationships. A disorder that appears in early childhood—generally by age three—autism is not completely understood by researchers but is likely to be due to abnormal **brain** development. The disorder differs from child to child, but autism may be first suspected when an infant or toddler fails to develop normal social interactions, such as eye contact with parents. When in the company of others, autistic children may display repetitive movements such as rocking, head banging, or hand twisting. These children also exhibit markedly delayed language or unusual language use, avoidance of eye contact, an obsessional concern for order and sameness, and an aversion to or lack of interest in other persons.

Autism is a rare disorder, occurring in perhaps one in 10,000 births. It can be confused with a form of **mental retardation** caused by a genetic disorder, **fragile X syndrome,** because many symptoms overlap. Research has attempted to characterize the central disorder of autism: is it a cognitive, social, or linguistic deficit? Compounding the picture is the fact that many autistic children are also retarded, though some show normal intelligence on non-verbal tests.

Autism and language development

Approximately 50% of autistic children never learn to talk, or they talk in only the most rudimentary way. Six is the crucial age in this regard, after which the prognosis for dramatic language progress looks bleak. Rigorous behavioral intervention at an early age can often provide such children with a form of communication. Educational programs are willing to try any medium that the child can succeed with: speech, gesture, "**communication board**s" on which the child may point to pictures or sym-

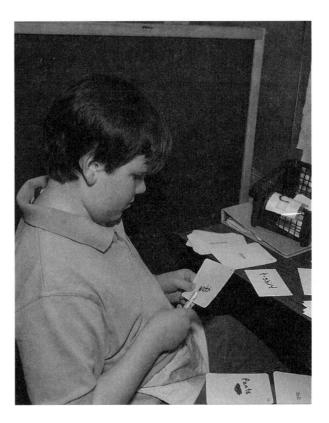

This young man with autism work on a matching game. His desk faces the wall and has partitions on two sides to minimize distractions.

bols, signed languages, and so forth. In the 1990s, there was interest in reaching autistic children via "facilitated communication" in which the child is "helped" by a facilitator's touch to type on a keyboard. This method raised the hopes of many parents and teachers who work with autistic children. However, careful evaluation of the outcomes suggests that the dramatic successes are mostly illusory, and that the child's elaborate, seemingly spontaneous productions were in fact guided unknowingly by the facilitator.

"High-functioning" autistic children can learn to talk, but several features of their language have been highlighted as aberrant. A marked feature of autistic speech is **echolalia,** which is an immediate or delayed repetition of the content and form of another person's speech. The function of echolalia has recently been re-evaluated, with new evidence suggesting that it may be a way for the child to enter or maintain a conversation, in the face of poor spontaneous language skills. The autistic child is also prone to make pronoun substitutions, such as *you* for *I*. The autistic child will say such things as:

Pick you up.

or: You want a hot dog?
when he is clearly making a personal request.

Normal two-year-old children speak this way as well, but only fleetingly. In terms of lexical (vocabulary) development, substantial differences do not seem apparent in the type or variety of vocabulary in normal IQ autistic children. An exception is the autistic child's vocabulary referring to emotions or mental states, such as *think, believe, know,* which is generally impoverished or underdeveloped. Grammar and morphology (inflection and word formation) seem to be developed in an essentially normal way. However, in the area of conversational development, the peculiarities of autism are revealed.

AUTISTICS IN CYBERSPACE

In the late 1990s, a number of sites on the worldwide web offered autistics the opportunity to communicate with each other. One participant offered this explanation of why e-mail communication and online forums work where face-to-face conversation is impossible: "Imagine you are surrounded by ten people rapidly talking to you at the same time, and this goes on for several hours. I'm sure you would want to run into a small room and lock the door....Well, this is how I feel when I'm talking to two people (or one person, sometimes)."

People with autism cannot interpret facial expressions, body gestures, or voice inflection. These intuitive aspects of conversation represent powerful distractions to conversation—which explains the success of electronic communication, where distractions can be minimized or controlled.

Autistic children seem to have a poor grasp of the social functions of language: knowing what is an appropriate topic, or when they should respond. They might initiate inappropriate topics, saying, for example, "I had a shower this morning," as a conversational opener to a visitor to the school.

The child who is autistic may fail to keep up her end of the conversation, or give inappropriate replies to questions. In some cases, it is as if the child does not comprehend the purpose of language as a social skill. In fact, several studies conducted in the 1990s point to the possibility that the autistic child does not develop, or is seriously delayed in developing, an adequate "theory of mind" about other persons. Over the first few years of life—usually by about age four—the normally developing child forms a set of beliefs that help him to understand others around him. He comes to understand that people have ideas and beliefs, desires and fears that may

differ from his own, and that allow him to predict what they will do. Autistic children lack these skills to a degree far beyond what their other mental impairments would suggest. This may be a central deficit of autism, and it may then explain the odd features of autistic language: the failure to understand social interaction, the inattention to language, and the marked lack of reference to emotional or mental states in conversation.

—Jill De Villiers, Ph.D.
Smith College

For Further Research

Books

Bettelheim, Bruno. *The Empty Fortress: Infantile Autism and the Birth of the Self.* New York: Free Press, 1972.

Frith, Uta. *Autism: Explaining the Enigma.* Cambridge, Mass.: Basil Blackwell, 1989 (1990 printing).

Gerdtz, John, and Joel Bregman. *Autism: A Practical Guide for Those Who Help Others.* New York: Continuum, 1990.

Grandin, Temple, and Margaret M. Scariano. *Emergence: Labeled Autistic.* New York: Warner Books, 1996.

———. *Thinking in Pictures and Other Reports from My Life with Autism.* New York: Doubleday, 1995.

Hobson, R. Peter. *Autism and the Development of Mind.* Hillsdale, NJ: L. Erlbaum Associates, 1993.

National Institutes of Health, Public Health Service. *Fact Sheet: Autism.* Washington, D.C.: U.S. Dept. of Health, Education, and Welfare, 1989.

Sacks, Oliver W. *An Anthropologist on Mars: Seven Paradoxical Tales.* New York: Knopf, 1995.

Wing, Lorna. *Autistic Children: A Guide for Parents and Professionals.* New York: Brunner/Mazel Inc., 1985.

Periodicals

Blume, Harvey. "Technology: Autistics, Freed from Face-to-Face Encounters, Are Communicating in Cyberspace." *New York Times* 147, June 30, 1997, p. C6.

Audiovisual Recordings

Prisoners of Silence. PBS Video, 1993.

Autism, Reaching the Child Within. Produced by WHA-TV, Distributed by PBS Video, 1988.

Autoimmune Disorders

Diseases in which the immune system attacks the body's own healthy tissues, forming antibodies in an assault on mistakenly identified "foreign invaders."

Autoimmune disorders occur when the body's immune system loses its ability to recognize the differences between self and nonself tissues. The body then builds antibodies to attack its own tissues and organs, which culminates in a number of different disorders. Some of these become chronic illnesses and may lead to death.

Two of the earliest illnesses identified as autoimmune disorders were systematic lupus erythematosus (SLE) and rheumatoid **arthritis.** Today more than 40 conditions are classified as known or probable autoimmune disorders. It is estimated that autoimmune diseases affect between 5–7% of the population. Most begin during or soon after **puberty**, or when a person reaches his or her forties and fifties. They occur twice as frequently in women as in men.

Rheumatoid arthritis occurs in both children and adults, and is the most common autoimmune disorder. Juvenile rheumatoid arthritis (JRA) affects over 65,000 children and adolescents in the United States, or about 1 in 1,000. In this disorder, the immune system attacks the synovium, a membrane surrounding the joints, resulting in pain, swelling, and stiffness. Like other autoimmune disorders, rheumatoid arthritis is usually episodic, flaring up periodically, subsiding, and then recurring.

There are three distinct types of JRA, differentiated by their severity and by how much of the body is affected. Pauciarticular onset JRA involves fewer than five joints; polyarticular onset JRA affects five or more joints on both sides of the body; and systemic onset JRA affects a large number of joints and other organs as well, such as the lungs, kidneys, liver, spleen, and lymph nodes. Juvenile rheumatoid arthritis is treated with a combination of drugs and physical therapy. The medications of choice are NSAIDS (nonsteroidal anti-inflammatory drugs), especially aspirin in large doses. Physical therapy includes a variety of exercises designed to keep the muscles near the affected joints strong and flexible, prevent them from getting shorter, and prevent bone deformity. JRA goes into permanent remission by late adolescence or early adulthood in approximately 75% of children affected by the disease.

Another serious autoimmune disorder that affects children is Type 1 **diabetes mellitus,** also known as juvenile onset diabetes because symptoms generally appear in early adolescence. Type 2 diabetes mellitus, the most prevalent form of the disease, usually begins in middle age. Diabetes occurs when the pancreas does not produce enough of the hormone insulin, which the body requires to metabolize the blood sugar glucose, a crucial energy source. The condition was first identified as an autoimmune disorder in 1988, when researchers discovered that it is caused by antibodies that attack the insulin-producing cells in the pancreas. Its onset is now thought to be linked to a genetic predisposition combined with a virus or another stressor. In Type 1 diabetes mellitus, the depletion of insulin is so severe that injections of the hormone are necessary. Symptoms of juvenile onset diabetes include extreme thirst, frequent urination, increased appetite together with sudden weight loss, irritability, fatigue, and nausea. In addition to daily insulin injections (which must be continued for life), treatment of diabetes mellitus requires monitoring of the level of glucose in the **blood**, which must also be regulated by adequate exercise and certain dietary measures. Too much glucose can damage the eyes, kidneys, and other organs, and it also presents the risk of a diabetic coma. Too little can produce insulin shock.

Rheumatic fever, which primarily affects children between the ages of four and 18, is an autoimmune disorder that occurs following a strep infection, such as **strep throat** or **scarlet fever.** The antibodies produced to fight the infection attack healthy tissues in the heart, joints, skin, and nervous system. Due to the widespread use of **antibiotics** to combat strep infections, rheumatic fever is rare in developed countries. Symptoms include fever, joint pain and swelling, muscle aches, a rash (possibly intermittent) on the trunk and extremities, nodules in the joints, scalp, or spine, and twitching arms or legs. If the central nervous system is affected, there can also be emotional volatility, muscle weakness, and coordination problems; however, these symptoms are short-lived and temporary, and do not cause lasting damage. Rheumatic fever generally takes between one and four weeks to develop following a strep infection and lasts from two weeks to three months. If the tissues of the heart are inflamed, a condition known as carditis, this can cause permanent damage to the heart valves. Once rheumatic fever is diagnosed, antibiotics are administered if there is still an active strep infection. In addition to anti-inflammatory medications such as **aspirin**, a child whose heart is affected by the disease may be given steroids to reduce inflammation and prevent permanent heart damage.

An autoimmune disorder that primarily affects adults but is also found in children is systematic lupus erythematosus, also known as SLE or lupus. A victim of lupus develops antibodies that attack connective tissues throughout the body. The heart, lungs, and kidneys can be affected, as well as the blood, joints, and central nervous system. Of the estimated 500,000 Americans affected by this disease, some 15% are children, whose symptoms are generally more severe than those of adults. The incidence of lupus in females is nine times that in males.

The most distinctive sign of lupus is a butterfly-shaped rash across the cheeks and the bridge of the nose. However, this only occurs in about a third of those affected by the disease, which can produce a wide variety of symptoms shared by other conditions. This makes diagnosis so difficult that many affected persons suffer from lupus for three to 10 years before being diagnosed. Other symptoms include fever, fatigue, weight loss, **anemia,** swelling and pain in the joints, and sensitivity to cold and light. Once it appears, lupus is never wholly cured; it may go into remission for extended periods of time and then flare up again suddenly. Lupus has traditionally been treated with anti-inflammatory medications, including aspirin and corticosteroids. Currently, most physicians control the disease with small doses of steroids to prevent side effects and use aspirin and other NSAIDS (non-steroidal anti-inflammatory drugs) to relieve pain. In very acute attacks, drugs such as cyclophosphamide that temporarily suppress the immune system may be used.

Another autoimmune disorder that can affect children is psoriasis, often appearing in adolescence or young adulthood, although about 10% of cases occur in children under the age of 10, and it can even appear in infancy. Psoriasis is caused by the excessive growth of certain skin cells called keratinocytes. Its primary symptom is the appearance of red, raised patches of skin called plaques, usually found on the scalp, elbows, knees, arms, legs, back, and genitalia, but can occur anywhere, and may cover up to 80% of the body. When psoriasis begins in infancy, it most frequently appears in the diaper area. In many cases the plaques cause severe itching and soreness, but they may also be painless. The fingernails of up to one half of children with psoriasis are also affected, becoming pitted or showing other changes. In addition to physical discomfort, psoriasis can cause great emotional distress due to its effect on the patient's appearance.

Psoriasis is chronic and incurable. Its symptoms may be alleviated by creams or lotions that help moisturize the skin or that contain cortisone to reduce inflammation. Tar-based creams are also used in some cases. Exposure to ultraviolet light, including sunlight, can also alleviate the symptoms of psoriasis. Immuno-suppressant medications, such as cyclosporine and methotrexate, may be used for very serious flare-ups, but their use is discouraged because of potential side effects.

Of the various types of anemia that can affect children, at least one is an autoimmune disorder. In rare autoimmune hemolytic anemia, red blood cells are attacked by the immune system, which kills the old cells faster than the body can manufacture new ones. Classic symptoms of anemia, including pallor, fatigue, and weakness, appear. Secretion of the destroyed red blood cells can turn the urine red. The condition may appear slowly over a period of days, or the onset may be rapid and life-threatening, with sudden extreme fatigue and **jaundice.** A blood transfusion, the normal emergency treatment for a low blood count, may be impossible for a person with autoimmune hemolytic anemia because the immune system may also attack the red cells of the transfused blood. In most cases, the blood count returns to normal within a relatively short period of time. However, in persons whose blood count drops precipitously and whose bodies reject transfusions, this form of anemia may cause shock, heart failure, and death.

Researchers are not certain what triggers autoimmune disorders. It is thought that certain viruses and bacteria may have evolved to resemble the body's own tissues in an attempt to evade detection by the immune system. When these viruses or bacteria are present, the body's immune system may become confused and attack both the foreign substances and its own tissues. (This would explain why rheumatic fever appears in conjunction with strep infections.) Genetic susceptibility is known to play a role in certain autoimmune disorders, as does **stress**. Stress, though, is thought to bring on relapses of a disease, rather than cause its onset.

As more and more autoimmune disorders are identified, interest has grown in finding ways to prevent or cure them. Increasing attention has been focused on finding ways to isolate and stop harmful antibody activity without suppressing the entire immune system, which makes the body vulnerable to infections and causes dangerous side effects. Cyclosporine, which became available in 1984 and targets only specialized immune cells, called T-cells, increases production of a specific antibody. Cyclosporine has been successfully used to treat a variety of autoimmune disorders, especially psoriasis. It is thought that this type of selective targeting may eventually provide the basis for vaccines that can protect the body by preventing T-cells from manufacturing harmful antibodies.

Another promising research area is a type of treatment known as oral tolerization, based on research showing that tolerance to a particular substance can be increased by administering it orally, and the increased tolerance can prevent or halt an autoimmune reaction. Conditions with known antigens (materials that provoke an autoimmune reaction, such as insulin in diabetics or myelin in persons with multiple **sclerosis**) have responded well to treatments that include oral ingestion of the very substances that are under attack by their own bodies.

Known autoimmune disorders, other than those affecting children, include multiple sclerosis, Graves' disease (a thyroid condition), and Addison's disease (a disorder of the adrenal gland). Disorders in which autoimmune response is suspected include Alzheimer's disease, atherosclerosis, irritable bowel syndrome, and uveitis (an eye inflammation).

See also **Arthritis; Diabetes Mellitus**

For Further Study

Books

Aasend, Nathan. *Autoimmune Diseases.* New York: Venture Books, 1995.

Dwyer, John M. *The Body at War.* Sydney, Australia: Allen & Unwin, 1988.

Nilsson, Lennart. *The Body Victorious.* New York: Delacorte, 1987.

Average

One measure of central tendency in statistics.

The term average is popularly used to refer to a value that is typical of a group. For example, a person may be described as being of average height or average intelligence. Educators and school administrators may describe the average for the population of students in their school. Average always describes a relative value; for example, the average score on a standardized test for students in a particular class may or may not equal the average score for all students in the school. Yet another value will be the average for all test-takers nationwide. Thus, the average is often used as a way to compare attributes of two different groups.

Average is one of the measures of central tendency used in statistics. There are three precise measures of central tendency calculated by statisticians when studying sets of data. The *mean* is calculated by adding together all the numbers in the set being studied, and dividing the total by the number of data points. For example, if the statistician is calculating the mean test score for a group of 27 test-takers, he would add together the scores of all 27 people, and divide the total by 27. Grade-point average, calculated by adding all the numerical values for a student's grades together and dividing by the number of grades received, is an example of a mean. The *median,* or midpoint, for the set of test scores would be the score precisely at the midpoint when the scores are ranked in numerical order. The *mode* is the score that was achieved most often.

Aversive Conditioning

Also referred to as aversion therapy, a technique used in behavior therapy to reduce the appeal of behaviors one wants to eliminate by associating them with physical or psychological discomfort.

In aversive conditioning, the client is exposed to an unpleasant stimulus while engaging in the targeted behavior, the goal being to create an aversion to it. In adults, aversive conditioning is often used to combat addictions such as **smoking** or **alcoholism**. One common method is the administration of a nausea-producing drug while the client is smoking or drinking so that unpleasant associations are paired with the addictive behavior. In addition to smoking and alcoholism, aversive therapy has also been used to treat **nail biting**, sex addiction, and other strong habits or addictions. In the past, electroconvulsive therapy was sometimes administered as a form of aversion therapy for certain disorders, but this practice has been discontinued.

In children aversive conditioning plays a role in one of the most effective treatments for **enuresis** (bedwetting): the bell and pad method. A pad with a wetness sensor is placed in the child's bed, connected to a bell that sounds at the first sign of wetness. When the bell rings, the child must then get out of bed and go to the bathroom instead of continuing to wet the bed. This method is successful in part because it associates bedwetting with the unpleasantness of being awakened and inconvenienced in the middle of the night. A related technique that further reinforces the inconvenience of bedwetting is having the child change his own sheets and pajamas when he wakes up wet at night.

In a variation of aversive conditioning called covert sensitization, the client imagines the undesirable behavior instead of actually engaging in it, and then either imagines or is exposed to an unpleasant stimulus.

See also **Behavior Therapy.**

For Further Study

Books

Doft, Norma. *When Your Child Needs Help: A Parent's Guide to Therapy for Children.* New York: Crown Paperbacks, 1992.

Feindler, Eva L., and Grace R. Kalfus, eds. *Adolescent Behavior Therapy Handbook.* New York: Springer, 1990.

Organizations

American Academy of Child and Adolescent Psychiatry
 Address: 3615 Wisconsin Avenue NW.
 Washington, DC 20016-3007
 Telephone: toll-free (800) 333-7636 or (202) 966-7300

Federation of Families for Children's Mental Health
 Address: 1021 Prince St.
 Alexandria, VA 22314-2971
 Telephone: (703) 684-7710

Association for the Advancement of Behavior Therapy
 Address: 15 W. 36th St.
 New York, NY 10018
 Telephone: (212) 647-1890

B

Babysitter

A person, often a teenager, who provides temporary, occasional child care services.

The term babysitter is usually used to describe someone who provides occasional child care for a few hours at a time. Most families provide the babysitter with general guidelines about bedtime, acceptable activities during the parents' absence, and instructions on who to contact in the event of an emergency. Young people who are interested in providing babysitting services often take advantage of resources available through the public library, community service department, school, or the American Red Cross to learn the basics of babysitting. Books and videotapes are also available, and outline techniques and strategies for safe and successful babysitting.

The American Red Cross provides a certification course for babysitters. Young people over age 11 are eligible to enroll in the eight-hour training course, offered at a variety of community organizations and schools. Some organizations underwrite the cost of the course and offer it free to participants; others charge a fee. The course provides instruction in supervision of children, activity planning for children of all ages, accident prevention, emergency response techniques (including what to do in a **choking** emergency), and job hunting strategies. All participants learn about the role and responsibilities of babysitters, and receive a workbook.

Parents should consider instructing babysitters in the following procedures:

- Ask the babysitter to arrive early, especially for the first assignment, to get acquainted with the child or children

- Review important phone numbers with the babysitter

- Describe the child's routine, including bedtime, approved snacks, toileting habits, comfort objects needed for bedtime

- Set guidelines for the babysitter's personal behavior, such as personal telephone calls or friends visiting

- Describe safety and security procedures, such as what to say when answering the telephone, and how to secure all door locks

- Discuss any situations or behaviors that are likely to cause problems, such as temper **tantrums**, bed/nap time, feeding, etc.

For Further Study

Books

Elliott, Ruth S. *Minding the Kids: A Practical Guide to Employing Nannies, Care Givers, Babysitters, and Au Pairs.* 1st ed. New York: Prentice Hall Press, 1990.

Fogerty, Mary Jayne. *Babysitter's Companion: A Fill-in-the-blank Book for All Names, Numbers, Times, and Places You Want the Babysitter, Mother's Helper, or Anyone Who Takes Care of Your Kids to Know.* Berkeley, CA: Tricycle Press, 1994.

Greene, Caroline. *The Babysitter's Handbook.* New York: Dorling Kindersley, 1995.

The Super Sitter. Washington, DC: U.S. Consumer Product Safety Commission, 1994.

Tauscher, Ellen O. *The Childcare Sourcebook: The Complete Guide to Finding and Managing Nannies, Au Pairs, Babysitters, Day Care, and After-School Programs.* New York: Macmillan, 1996.

Audiovisual Recordings

Baby-sitting the Responsible Way. Charleston, WV: Cambridge Research Group, 1988.
(One 30-minute videocassette and one manual.)

Super Sitters: A Training Course. Niles, IL: United Learning, 1989.
(One 25-minute videocassette, one leader's guide, and one set of duplicating masters.)

Taking Care, the Complete Baby-sitter. Eugene, OR: New Dimension Media, 1988.
(One 23-minute videocassette.)

The Video Guide to Safe Babysitting. St. Louis, MO: Laclede Communication Services, 1988.
(One 34-minute videocassette.)

The bar mitzvah celebrant

Reform Jews revived the traditional bat mitzvah ceremony for girls in the 1940s.

Super Sitters Basics. Milwaukee: Super Sitters, Inc., 1988.
(One 30-minute videocasssette, one 30-page parents' resource guide, one 61-page sitter's guide, and one 63-page emergency care and first aid manual.)

Computer Media

Spengler, George L., et al. *Babysitting Basics.* Kalamazoo, MI: Microcomputer Educational Programs, 1986.
(Two 5-1/4 inch computer disks [for Apple II, II+, IIe, or IIc] and one manual.)

Bar and Bat Mitzvah

Jewish religious ceremony and celebration marking the formal entry into adulthood of boys at age 13 (bar mitzvah) and girls at age 12 (bat mitzvah).

In Hebrew, "bar/bat mitzvah" means "son/daughter of the commandment" or "servant of the commandment." American usage of "bar mitzvah," generally means the occasion itself, and undergoing the bar mitzvah ceremo-

ny is often referred to as "being bar mitzvahed." Technically, though, bar/bat mitzvah is a term referring to the altered status that the young person automatically attains at the age of 12 or 13, with or without a ceremony. Thus, in the true sense of the word, one *becomes* a bar/bat mitzvah. At the age of 13, a boy is traditionally deemed qualified to be counted a part of a *minyan* (the quorum of 10 men needed for public prayer) and can begin wearing *tefillin* (phylacteries), small square leather boxes containing slips inscribed with scriptural passages and worn on the forehead and left arm by Orthodox men during weekday-morning prayers. In addition, the person is considered ready to participate fully in the ritual fast days of the Jewish calendar.

There is evidence that the ages of 12 and 13 attained their current significance as early as the first century A.D., and the Talmud (the authoritative book of commentary on Jewish law) mentions 13 as the age when one becomes fully responsible for obeying the Ten Commandments. The bar mitzvah ceremony itself is thought to have come into existence in Poland and Germany between the 14th and 16th centuries. During a regular Saturday religious service, the boy was summoned to read from the Torah to honor his new status as a full-fledged member of the religious community. Eventually, the event came to be followed by a festive meal.

Throughout most of Jewish history, there was no ceremony for girls that paralleled the bar mitzvah since Jewish women were not called to the Torah until the advent of Reform Judaism in the 19th century. The bat mitzvah was initiated early in the 20th century by Rabbi Mordecai Kaplan, founder of the Reconstructionist Movement. Rabbi Kaplan celebrated the first bat mitzvah—for his daughter, Judith—in 1922. At the time, Reform Judaism had abandoned the bar mitzvah ceremony in favor of a confirmation based on that of the Lutherans, on the grounds that 13-year-olds were too young to be considered adults. When Reform Jews revived the traditional bar mitzvah ceremony in the 1940s, they also adopted the Reconstructionist bat mitzvah, which became widespread by the 1950s. However, Orthodox Jews still do not hold bat mitzvah ceremonies.

Parents usually begin preparing for a bar/bat mitzvah a year or more in advance. A synagogue must be chosen for the ceremony, if the family does not already belong to a congregation. A date must be picked—traditionally the Saturday closest to the bar/bat mitzvah's 12th or 13th birthday, but in practice usually within a month or two of the date, depending on the ability of the synagogue to accommodate the family's request. A space must also be reserved for the party following the ceremony and a guest list drawn up. The date of the ceremony will determine which weekly Torah portion the bar/bat mitzvah will read. Most synagogues offer classes through their religious schools that prepare students for the bar/bat mitzvah ceremony. In addition, many parents hire a private tutor to work with the child on the particular reading he or she will recite. Classes usually begin a year in advance, and tutoring may start anywhere from six to twelve months ahead of the bar/bat mitzvah date.

The bar/bat mitzvah ceremony varies from one synagogue to another. In all cases, the child is called to the pulpit for an *aliyah* (the recitation of blessings for the Torah reading, and the reading itself). Many times, the bar/bat mitzvah reads only a part of the Torah portion; sometimes the entire portion—which may consist of over 100 verses—is read. Often, the child also reads from the corresponding weekly portion of the *haftarah* (readings from the prophets, one corresponding to each weekly Torah portion). Sometimes the role of the bar/bat mitzvah is expanded beyond the Torah (and/or *haftarah*) reading to actually leading the congregation in part of the service itself, speaking in Hebrew, English, or both languages. Relatives of the bar/bat mitzvah are also honored by being called to the Torah to recite blessings and perform other special duties.

Another common part of the ceremony is the *d'rash*, a speech delivered by the bar/bat mitzvah. It may contain an interpretation of the Torah portion, a personal statement of religious belief and dedication, or other sentiments appropriate to the occasion. Traditionally, the father of the bar/bat mitzvah recites the following prayer: *Barukh shepatrani me-onsho shel zeh* (blessed be He Who has relieved me from responsibility for this child). Today, liberal congregations leave out this part of the ceremony. After the bar/bat mitzvah's speech, the rabbi makes a speech (called "the charge") addressed to the young person.

The bar/bat mitzvah ceremony is traditionally followed by a *Kiddush* (blessing recited over a cup of wine) and *seudat mitzvah* (a festive dinner or banquet). In past decades, bar mitzvah parties in the United States attained a reputation for lavishness and ostentation, with families using them partly as an occasion to repay business obligations. Today some families have moved away from the materialism of these extravagant affairs, choosing instead to have a smaller, more personal celebration. Increasingly, the central Jewish tradition of *tzedakah* (charity) has become part of the occasion. Synagogues sometimes have their bar/bat mitzvah classes perform volunteer work in the community as part of their preparation for the occasion, and families may donate a percentage of the money spent on the party dinner to a Jewish charity. In the 1980s a number of American bar/bat mitzvah ceremonies symbolically included a Soviet Jewish "twin" unable to have his or her own ceremony. The Soviet child's name was often printed in the bar/bat mitzvah invitation, and a special certificate was issued in his or her name.

While the great majority of bar/bat mitzvahs are held in synagogues, the ceremony may also take place at home, and the presence of a rabbi is not strictly necessary, as Jewish religious services can be held without one. Some families elect to have the bar/bat mitzvah celebration in Israel, where the ceremony can be held at a site of religious and historical significance. Popular sites include the Western Wall of the Temple in Jerusalem's Old City (the Wailing Wall—for boys only) or the fortification ruins at Masada on the shore of the Dead Sea (for either boys or girls). An innovative modern practice is the celebration of bar/bat mitzvahs by grown men and women who missed having the ceremony at the age of 13— either because they came from non-observant families or they converted to Judaism as adults.

Hasidic Jews (and other traditional-Orthodox sects) have retained the European practice of sending sons who have reached bar mitzvah age to study at yeshivas (religious schools) away from home. They remain at the yeshivas throughout adolescence, boarding at dormitories or with local families.

For Further Study

Books

Diamond, Barbara. *Bat Mitzvah: A Jewish Girl's Coming of Age.* New York: Viking, 1995.

Efron, Benjamin, and Alvan D. Rubin. *Coming of Age: Your Bar/Bat Mitzvah.* New York: Union of American Hebrew Congregations, 1977.

Lanckton, Alice Keidan. *The Bar Mitzvah Mother's Manual.* New York: Hippocrene Books, 1986.

Leneman, Helen. *Bar/Bat Mitzvah Basics.* Woodstock, Vt.: Jewish Lights Publishing, 1996.

Salkin, Jeffrey K. *Putting God on the Guest List: How to Reclaim the Spiritual Meaning of Your Child's Bar or Bat Mizvah.* Woodstock, VT: Jewish Lights Publishing, 1992.

Basal Age

Term used in assessment.

Basal age is the age at which a child can answer all the questions on a specific standardized test correctly and consistently. Sometimes referred to in discussions as simply the "basal," this term is used by psychologists to establish the appropriate testing level for a child. Until the psychologist establishes a child's basal age, it is difficult to begin meaningful testing, especially for children whose performance deviates significantly from the average. The opposite of basal age is ceiling age, the age at which a child fails to answer any item on a standardized test correctly.

Battered Child Syndrome

A group of physical and mental symptoms arising from long-term physical violence against a child.

Battered child syndrome occurs as the result of long-term physical violence against a child or adolescent. An estimated 2,000 children die each year in the United States from confirmed cases of physical abuse and 14,000 more are seriously injured. The battering takes many forms, including lacerations, bruises, burns, and internal injuries. In addition to the physical harm inflicted, battered children are at risk for an array of behavioral problems, including school difficulties, drug abuse, sexual **acting out,** running away, **suicide,** and becoming abusive themselves. **Dissociative identity disorder,** popularly known as multiple personality, is also common among abused children.

Detecting and preventing battered child syndrome is difficult because society and the courts have traditionally left the **family** alone. Out of fear and guilt, victims rarely report abuse. Nearly one-half of child abuse victims are under the age of one and therefore unable to report what is happening to them. The parents or **guardian**s who bring a battered child to a hospital emergency room rarely admit that abuse has occurred. Instead, they offer complicated, often obscure, explanations of how the child hurt himself. However, a growing body of scientific literature on pediatric injuries is simplifying the process of differentiating between intentional and accidental injuries. For instance, a 1991 study found that a child needs to fall from a height of 10 ft (3m) or more to sustain the life-threatening injuries that accompany physical abuse. Medical professionals have also learned to recognize a spiral pattern on x rays of broken bones, indicating that the injury was the result of twisting a child's limb.

Once diagnosed, the treatment for battered children is based on their age and the potential for the parents or guardians to benefit from therapy. The more amenable the parents are to entering therapy themselves, the more likely the child is to remain in the home. For infants, the treatment ranges from direct intervention and hospital care to **foster care** to home monitoring by a social service worker or visiting nurse. Ongoing medical assessment is recommended in all types of treatment. For the preschool child, treatment usually takes place outside the home, whether in a **day care** situation, a therapeutic preschool, or through individual therapy. The treatment includes speech and language therapy, physical therapy, play therapy, **behavior modification**, and specialized medical care.

By the time the child enters school, the physical signs of abuse are less visible. Because these children may not yet realize that their lives are different from those of other children, very few will report that their mothers or fathers are subjecting them to gross physical injury. It is at this stage that psychiatric and behavioral disorders begin to surface. In most cases the children are removed from the home, at least initially. The treatment, administered through either group or individual therapy, focuses on establishing trust, restoring **self-esteem**, expressing emotions, and improving cognitive and problem-solving skills.

Recognizing and treating physical abuse in the adolescent is by far the most difficult. By now the teen is an expert at hiding bruises. Instead, teachers and health care professionals should be wary of exaggerated responses to being touched, provocative actions, extreme aggressiveness or withdrawal, assaulting behavior, fear of adults, self-destruction, inability to form good peer relationships, alertness to danger, and/or frequent mood swings.

HOTLINES

The following organizations operate hotlines or provide advice for family members where there are problems related to physical or other abuse.

- Childhelp National Abuse Hotline
  Telephone: toll-free (800) 422-4453

- National Coalition Against Domestic Violence
  Telephone: (303) 839-1852

- National Council on Child Abuse and Family Violence
  Telephone: toll-free (800) 222-2000

- National Victim Center
  Telephone: toll-free (800) FYI-CALL [394-2255]

- National Runaway Switchboard
  Telephone: toll-free (800) 621-4000

Detection is exacerbated by the fact that all teenagers exhibit some of these signs at one time or another.

Abused teens do not evoke as much sympathy as younger victims, for society assumes that they are old enough to protect themselves or seek help on their own. In truth, all teenagers need adult guidance. The behavior that the abused adolescent often engages in—delinquency, **running away**, and failure in school—usually evokes anger in adults but should be recognized as symptoms of underlying problems. The abused teen is often resistant to therapy, which may take the form of individual **psychotherapy**, group therapy, or residential treatment.

While reporting child abuse is essential, false accusations can also cause great harm. It is a good idea for anyone who suspects that a child is being physically abused to seek confirmation from another adult, preferably a non-relative but one who is familiar with the family. If the second observer concurs, the local child protective services agency should be contacted. The agency has the authority to verify reports of child abuse and make decisions about protection and intervention.

Unlike many other medical conditions, child abuse is preventable. Family support programs can provide parenting information and training, develop family skills, offer social support, and provide psychotherapeutic assistance before abuse occurs.

For Further Study

Books

Ackerman, Robert J., and Dee Graham. *Too Old to Cry: Abused Teens in Today's America.* Blue Ridge Summit, PA: TAB Books, 1990.

Helfer, Ray E. M.D., and Ruth S. Kempe, MD., eds. *The Battered Child.* Chicago: The University of Chicago Press, 1987.

Periodicals

Arbetter, Sandra. "Family Violence: When We Hurt the Ones We Love," *Current Health* 22, November 1995, p. 6.

Organizations

National Committee for Prevention of Child Abuse
Address: 332 S. Michigan Avenue
Chicago, IL 60605
Telephone: (312) 663-3520

—Mary McNulty

Bayley Scales of Infant Development

A comprehensive developmental test for infants and toddlers from 2–30 months of age.

The Bayley Scales of Infant Development measure mental and physical, as well as emotional and social, development. The test, which takes approximately 45 minutes, is administered individually by having the child respond to a series of stimuli. The Mental Scales, which measure intellectual development, assess functions such as **memory,** learning, problem-solving ability, and verbal communication skills. The Motor Scales evaluate the child's ability to sit and stand, perform other activities requiring coordination of the large muscles (**gross motor skills**), and perform more delicate manipulations with fingers and hands (**fine motor skills**). Finally, the Infant Behavior Record (IBR) assesses the child's social and emotional development through a standardized description of his or her behavior during the testing session. Scores are measured against norms for each of the 14 different age groups. Often, the Bayley scales are used to determine whether a child is developing normally and provide for early diagnosis and intervention in cases of developmental delay, where there is significant tardiness in acquiring certain skills or performing key activities. Additionally, they can be used to qualify a child for special services and/or demonstrate the effectiveness of those services. Most recently, the Bayley scales have been used to insure compliance with legislation that requires identification of **at-risk** children and provision of services for them.

For Further Study

Books

Cohen, Libby G., and Loraine J. Spenciner. *Assessment of Young Children.* New York: Longman, 1994.

McCullough, Virginia. *Testing and Your Child: What You Should Know About 150 of the Most Common Medical, Educational, and Psychological Tests.* New York: Plume, 1992.

Walsh, W. Bruce, and Nancy E. Betz. *Tests and Assessment.* 2nd ed. Englewood Cliffs, NJ: Prentice Hall, 1990.

Wortham, Sue Clark. *Tests and Measurement in Early Childhood Education.* Columbus, OH: Merrill Publishing Co., 1990.

Beery-Buktenica Test

Identifies problems with visual perception, fine motor skills (especially hand control), and hand-eye coordination.

The Beery-Buktenica Test, also known as VMI or Developmental Test of Visual-Motor Integration, is a test for ages two through adult that identifies problems with visual perception, **fine motor skills** (especially hand control), and hand-eye coordination. It is usually administered individually but can also be given in groups. The child is given a booklet containing increasingly complex geometric figures and asked to copy them without any erasures and without rotating the booklet in any direction. The test is given in two versions: the Short Test Form containing 15 figures is used for ages 3 through 8; the Long Test Form, with 24 figures, is used for older children, adolescents, and adults with developmental delay. A raw score based on the number of correct copies is converted based on norms for each age group, and results are reported as converted scores and percentiles. The test is untimed but usually takes 10–15 minutes to administer.

For Further Study

Books

Cohen, Libby G., and Loraine J. Spenciner. *Assessment of Young Children.* New York: Longman, 1994.

McCullough, Virginia. *Testing and Your Child: What You Should Know About 150 of the Most Common Medical, Educational, and Psychological Tests.* New York: Plume, 1992.

Walsh, W. Bruce, and Nancy E. Betz. *Tests and Assessment.* 2nd ed. Englewood Cliffs, NJ: Prentice Hall, 1990.

Wortham, Sue Clark. *Tests and Measurement in Early Childhood Education.* Columbus, OH: Merrill Publishing Co., 1990.

Behavior Modification

A treatment approach, based on the principles of operant conditioning, that replaces undesirable behaviors with more desirable ones through positive or negative reinforcement.

Behavior modification is based on the principles of **operant conditioning,** which were developed by Ameri-

can behaviorist B.F. Skinner (1904–1990). In his research, he put a rat in a cage later known as the Skinner Box, in which the rat could receive a food pellet by pressing on a bar. The food reward acted as a reinforcement by strengthening the rat's bar-pressing behavior. Skinner studied how the rat's behavior changed in response to differing patterns of reinforcement. By studying the way the rats "operated on" their environment, Skinner formulated the concept of operant conditioning, through which behavior could be shaped by reinforcement or lack of it. Skinner considered his discovery applicable to a wide range of both human and animal behaviors and introduced operant conditioning to the general public in his 1938 book *The Behavior of Organisms.*

DID SKINNER RAISE HIS OWN CHILD IN A SKINNER BOX?

This famous urban legend was perpetuated by a photo that appeared in *Life* magazine of behavioral psychologist B.F. Skinner's two-year-old daughter standing up in a glass-fronted box. The box was, in fact, a climate-controlled, baby-sized room that Skinner built, called the "aircrib." The aircrib was made of sound-absorbing wood, had a humidifier, an air filter, and was temperature-controlled by a thermostat. Dissatisfied with traditional cribs, Skinner built the box to keep his new daughter warm, safe, and quiet without having to wrap her in clothes and blankets. Skinner was quoted in *New Yorker* magazine as saying his daughter "...spent most of the next two years and several months there, naked and happy." Deborah was so happy in the box, Skinner reported, that she rarely cried or got sick and showed no signs of agoraphobia when removed from the aircrib or claustrophobia when placed inside. The box-like structure and people's misunderstandings about behavioral psychology contributed to the misconception that Skinner was experimenting on his daughter and also probably prevented the crib from becoming a commercial success. People got the impression that Skinner was raising his child in a box similar to the kind he used to study animal behavior—with levers for releasing food.

Today, behavior modification is used to treat a variety of problems in both adults and children. Childhood disorders for which behavior modification has been successfully used include **obsessive-compulsive disorder** (OCD), **attention deficit/hyperactivity disorder**

B. F. Skinner

(ADHD), **phobias**, **enuresis** (bedwetting), and **separation anxiety** disorder (SAD). One behavior modification technique widely used with children is positive reinforcement, which encourages certain behaviors through a system of rewards. Rewards can include items the child wants, such as toys or comic books, or privileges, such as half hours allotted to play video games or watch television. They can be earned in small increments through a system of tokens, such as stickers or stars, that can eventually be exchanged for a specific reward. For example, a child in treatment for social phobia may earn a star for each day he or she greets a certain number of people, or a child with separation anxiety may earn a sticker for not crying when left with a babysitter. In behavior therapy, it is common for the therapist to draw up a contract with the child setting out the terms of the reward system. This positive reinforcement technique has been used to treat a wide variety of disorders in children, ranging from minor adjustment or developmental problems to **autism.**

In addition to rewarding desirable behavior, behavior modification can also discourage unwanted behavior, through either negative reinforcement, or punishment, such as removal of television privileges, or the removal of reinforcement altogether, called extinction. Extinction eliminates the incentive for unwanted behavior by withholding the expected response. A widespread parenting technique based on extinction is the **time-out,** in which a child is separated from the group when he or she misbehaves. This technique removes the expected reward of parental attention.

According to a November/December 1995 *Psychology Today* article, about 300 children were raised in cribs similar to the kind Skinner designed. The writers of the article tracked down about 50 of the people and reported positive results. The parents who used these aircribs liked its safety and convenience, and the children raised in them all exhibited normal health. Skinner's daughter Deborah, far from being mentally unstable (reportedly one of the rumors), married a professor and is a successful artist in England.

See also **Behaviorism.**

For Further Study

Books

Doft, Norma. *When Your Child Needs Help: A Parent's Guide to Therapy for Children.* New York: Crown Paperbacks, 1992.

Koplewicz, Harold S. *It's Nobody's Fault: New Hope and Help for Difficult Children and Their Parents.* New York: Times Books, 1996.

Maag, John W. *Parenting without Punishment: Making Problem Behavior Work for You.* Philadelphia, PA: Charles Press, 1996.

Martin, Garry. *Behavior Modification: What It Is and How to Do It.* Englewood Cliffs, NJ: Prentice-Hall, 1988.

Morris, Richard J. *Behavior Modification with Exceptional Children: Principles and Practices.* Glenview, IL: Scott Foresman, 1985.

Organizations

Association for the Advancement of Behavior Therapy
Address: 15 W. 36th St.
New York, NY 10018
Telephone: (212) 279-7970
American Academy of Child and Adolescent Psychiatry
Address: 3615 Wisconsin Ave. NW
Washington, DC 20016-3007
Telephone: (800) 333-7636 or (202) 966-7300

Behavior Therapy

A goal-oriented, therapeutic approach that treats emotional and behavioral disorders as maladaptive learned responses that can be replaced by healthier ones with appropriate training.

In contrast to the psychoanalytic method of Sigmund Freud (1856–1939), which focuses on unconscious mental processes and their roots in the past, behavior therapy focuses on observable behavior and its modification in the present. Behavior therapy was developed during the 1950s by researchers and therapists critical of the psychodynamic treatment methods that prevailed at the time. It drew on a variety of theoretical work, including the **classical conditioning** principles of the Russian physiologist Ivan Pavlov (1849–1936), who became famous for experiments in which dogs were trained to salivate at the sound of a bell, and the work of American B.F. Skinner (1904–1990), who pioneered the concept of **operant conditioning,** in which behavior is modified by changing the response it elicits. By the 1970s, behavior therapy enjoyed widespread popularity as a treatment approach. Over the past two decades, the attention of behavior therapists has focused increasingly on their clients' cognitive processes, and many therapists have begun to use **cognitive behavior therapy** to change clients' unhealthy behavior by replacing negative or self-defeating thought patterns with more positive ones.

Behavior therapy was used experimentally as early as 1924 to treat **phobias** in a three-year-old. In the 1960s it drew the attention of child psychiatrists and therapists after being used successfully with **institutionalized children** when all other treatment methods had failed. Behavior therapy is especially well suited for use with children whose activities are restricted in ways that make it relatively easy to achieve the environmental control necessary for its success. Also, it is generally completed within a shorter time frame than traditional psychodynamic therapy.

Techniques in behavior therapy

A number of the same techniques that behavior therapists use for adults can also be used successfully with children. The most popular ones fall under the category of **behavior modification,** a term that technically refers only to some of the techniques used by behavior therapists. Based on the operant conditioning principles of B. F. Skinner, behavior modification works by providing clearly specified consequences, either positive or negative, for certain types of actions. Systematic positive reinforcement encourages desirable behavior through a system of rewards, such as a particular toy, or privileges, such as a video rental or an extra half hour of watching television. A system is often established in which tokens, such as stars or stickers, can be accumulated and eventually exchanged for a reward. Often, a contract is drawn up setting forth the terms of the reward system. The opposite of positive reinforcement is either negative reinforcement, such as the withdrawal of a privilege, or simply the removal of the positive reinforcement, a technique known as extinction. An example of extinction is a **time-out** for undesirable behavior, which removes the anticipated reward of attention (even negative attention) from adults and peers, making the behavior in question seem less desirable. Although it is a relatively slow process, extinction is a popular technique for modifying behavior in children.

Other techniques used in behavior therapy include **aversive conditioning,** in which a person is trained to associate an undesirable behavior with an unpleasant effect in order to lessen its appeal; systematic desensitization (exposure therapy), which works by gradually exposing a person to an anxiety-producing object or situation; flooding (implosive therapy), which involves full exposure to an anxiety-producing situation while receiving reassurance from the therapist; and modeling, in which a person watches someone else successfully negotiate an activity or situation that he finds frightening or intimidating (for example, children scheduled for surgery may be shown a video in which a child undergoes and recovers from an operation, in order to help them cope with their fears about the experience). Behavior therapists also use relaxation training consisting of techniques such as deep breathing, progressive muscle relaxation, and guided imagery; hypnosis; biofeedback; social skills training; and paradoxical intention, in which the client is encouraged to actually increase a maladaptive behavior to the point that it becomes unappealing or seems ludicrous. Behavioral approaches such as those mentioned above have been used successfully in family therapy to change long-standing unhealthy patterns of behavior and interaction among family members.

Types of problems treated by behavior therapy

Behavior therapy lends itself favorably to the types of well-defined problems for which children are often treated. A popular treatment for bed-wetting (**enuresis**) that involves aversive conditioning is the bell and pad method. A pad with a sensor that detects wetness is placed in the child's bed or attached to her pajamas. At the first sign of wetness, a bell is activated by the sensor, waking the child. Behavior therapy is also used with children with **separation anxiety** disorder (SAD), a condition in which children four years of age or older experience distress when being separated from their parents or other individuals to whom they are closely attached. In addition to experiencing anxiety and distress at school or in other situations that separate them from their parents, children with this disorder cling to their parents when they are at home, following them around the house, trying to sleep in their bedroom, and resisting being left with babysitters. A behavioral therapist may draw up a contract with a child with SAD, in which the child agrees to very specific goals, such as staying in his own bed at night if the parent promises to read him a story or check on him a specified number of times. The measures specified in the contracts are made very easy at first and then more rigorous as success is achieved. Children with SAD have shown significant improvement after even four weeks of behavior therapy. **Obsessive-compulsive disorder** (OCD) in children also responds well to behavior therapy. Successful techniques include exposure and response prevention, both of which involve preventing the child from engaging in the ritualistic behavior that characterizes this condition, in spite of the anxiety generated. The point is for children to see that nothing bad happens when they don't perform their rituals, and that they can live through the anxiety unharmed.

Behavior therapy is an important part of the treatment for social phobia, the fear of communicating and interacting with other people. It often needs to be combined with medication such as Prozac because children affected by this disorder must have some of their anxiety allayed before they can work with a therapist. In therapy they are taught relaxation techniques, such as guided imagery, in which they imagine themselves succeeding in feared social situations. In addition, they are given a series of small assignments aimed at improving their social skills, such as saying hello to a certain number of people every day, and there is a modest reward for completing each assignment. The therapist and/or the parents also need to coach children with social phobia on how to behave in social situations, even rehearsing what they will say in some cases. Another disorder for which behavior therapy works well is generalized anxiety disorder (GAD), which is characterized by unreasonable and excessive anxiety over a broad range of events or activities. Therapy for this condition generally consists of relaxation training and of finding ways to replace the child's fearful reaction with a normal reaction.

Another childhood disorder that is often treated by behavior therapy is **attention deficit/hyperactivity disorder** (ADHD), the most common childhood psychological disorder, estimated to affect anywhere from 3–9% of all children, the majority of them boys. Although medication with Ritalin or another stimulant is the most effective treatment method, therapy can reinforce the improvements in control and organization. A therapist can also coach the parents of children with ADHD in behavior therapy techniques so that they can exercise control over their children at home in a firm, consistent, and controlled manner.

For Further Study

Books

Doft, Norma. *When Your Child Needs Help: A Parent's Guide to Therapy for Children.* New York: Crown Paperbacks, 1992.

Feindler, Eva L., and Grace R. Kalfus, eds. *Adolescent Behavior Therapy Handbook.* New York: Springer, 1990.

Fishman, Katharine D. *Behind the One-Way Mirror: Psychotherapy and Children.* New York: Bantam Books, 1995.

Kazdin, Alan. E. *Child Psychotherapy: Developing and Identifying Effective Treatments.* New York: Pergamon Press, 1988.

Koplewicz, Harold S. *It's Nobody's Fault: New Hope and Help for Difficult Children and Their Parents.* New York: Times Books, 1996.

Organizations

American Academy of Child and Adolescent Psychiatry
  Address: 3615 Wisconsin Avenue NW.
  Washington, DC 20016-3007
  Telephone: toll-free (800) 333-7636 or (202) 966-7300

Federation of Families for Children's Mental Health
  Address: 1021 Prince St.
  Alexandria, VA 22314-2971
  Telephone: (703) 684-7710

Association for the Advancement of Behavior Therapy
  Address: 15 W. 36th St.
  New York, NY 10018
  Telephone: (212) 647-1890

Behaviorism

A theory of human development initiated by American educational psychologist Edward Thorndike, and developed by American psychologists John Watson and B.F. Skinner.

Behaviorism is a psychological theory of human development that posits that humans can be trained, or conditioned, to respond in specific ways to specific stimuli and that given the correct stimuli, personalities and behaviors of individuals, and even entire civilizations, can be codified and controlled.

Edward Thorndike (1874–1949) initially proposed that humans and animals acquire behaviors through the association of stimuli and responses. He advanced two laws of learning to explain why behaviors occur the way they do: The Law of Effect specifies that any time a behavior is followed by a pleasant outcome, that behavior is likely to recur. The Law of Exercise states that the more a stimulus is connected with a response, the stronger the link between the two. Ivan Pavlov's (1849–1936) groundbreaking work on **classical conditioning** also provided an observable way to study behavior. Although most psychologists agree that neither Thorndike nor Pavlov were strict behaviorists, their work paved the way for the emergence of behaviorism.

The birth of modern behaviorism was championed early in the 20th century by a psychologist at Johns Hopkins University named **John Watson**. In his 1924 book *Behaviorism,* Watson made the notorious claim that, given a dozen healthy infants, he could determine the adult personalities of each one, "regardless of his talents, penchants, tendencies, abilities, vocations and the race of his ancestors." While making such a claim seems ridiculous today, at the time Watson was reacting to emerging Freudian psychoanalytical theories of development, which many people found threatening. Watson's scheme rejected all the hidden, unconscious, and suppressed longings that Freudians attributed to behaviors and posited that humans respond to **punishments** and rewards. Behavior that elicits positive responses is reinforced and continued, while behavior that elicits negative responses is eliminated.

Later, the behaviorist approach was taken up by B.F. Skinner (1904–1990) who deduced the evolution of human behavior by observing the behavior of rats in a maze. Skinner even wrote a novel, *Walden Two,* about a Utopian society where human behavior is governed totally by self-interested decisions based on increasing pleasure. The book increased Skinner's renown and led many to believe that behaviorism could indeed produce such a society.

In the 1950s, however, the popularity of behaviorism began to decline. The first sustained attack on its tenets was made by Noam Chomsky (1928–), a renowned linguist, who demonstrated that the behaviorist model simply could not account for the acquisition of language. Other psychologists soon began to question the role of cognition in behavior.

Today, many psychologists debate the extent to which cognitive learning and behavioral learning affect the development of personality.

See also **Behavior Modification; Behavior Therapy.**

For Further Study

Books

Donahoe, John W., and David C. Palmer. *Learning and Complex Behavior.* Boston: Allyn and Bacon, 1994.

Nye, Robert D. *Three Psychologies: Perspectives from Freud, Skinner, and Rogers.* 4th ed. Pacific Grove, CA: Brooks/Cole Pub. Co., 1992.

Rachlin, Howard. *Introduction to Modern Behaviorism.* 3rd ed. New York: Freeman, 1991.

Staddon, John. *Behaviorism: Mind, Mechanism and Society.* London: Duckworth, 1993.

Todd, James T., and Edward K. Morris. *Modern Perspectives on B.F. Skinner and Contemporary Behaviorism.* Westport, CT: Greenwood Press, 1995.

Todd, James T., and Edward K. Morris. *Modern Perspectives on John B. Watson and Classical Behaviorism.* Westport, CT: Greenwood Press, 1994.

Audiovisual Recordings

Sapolsky, Robert M. *Biology and Human Behavior: The Neurological Origins of Individuality.* Springfield, VA: The Teaching Company, 1996.
(Four audio cassettes and one 32-page manual).

Westen, Drew. *Is Anyone Really Normal?: Perspectives on Abnormal Psychology.* Kearneysville, WV: The Teaching

Company, 1991.
(Four audio cassettes and one 13-page booklet).

Bender Visual Motor Gestalt Test (Bender-Gestalt)

Diagnostic assessment test to identify learning disability, neurological disorders, and developmental delay.

The Bender Visual Motor Gestalt Test is a diagnostic assessment test used with all age groups to help identify possible learning disabilities, neurological disorders, **mental retardation**, or developmental delay. Test results also provide information about specific abilities, including motor coordination, **memory**, and organization. The child is given a series of nine designs, each on a separate card, and asked to reproduce them on a blank sheet of paper. There is no time limit. The test is scored by professionals who consider a variety of factors, including form, shape, pattern, and orientation on the page. The Bender-Gestalt test is often given as part of the **System of Multicultural Pluralistic Assessment (SOMPA).**

For Further Study

Books

Cohen, Libby G., and Loraine J. Spenciner. *Assessment of Young Children.* New York: Longman, 1994.

Culbertson, Jan L., and Diane J. Willis, eds. *Testing Young Children: A Reference Guide for Developmental, Psychoeducational, and Psychosocial Assessments.* Austin, TX: PRO-ED, Inc., 1993.

McCullough, Virginia. *Testing and Your Child: What You Should Know About 150 of the Most Common Medical, Educational, and Psychological Tests.* New York: Plume, 1992.

Wortham, Sue Clark. *Tests and Measurement in Early Childhood Education.* Columbus, OH: Merrill Publishing Co., 1990.

Benton Visual Retention Test

Measures visual perception and visual memory.

The Benton Visual Retention Test is an individually administered test for ages 8-adult that measures visual perception and visual **memory**. It can also be used to help identify possible learning disabilities. The child is shown 10 designs, one at a time, and asked to reproduce each one as exactly as possible on plain paper from memory. The test is untimed, and the results are professionally scored by form, shape, pattern, and arrangement on the paper.

For Further Study

Books

McCullough, Virginia. *Testing and Your Child: What You Should Know About 150 of the Most Common Medical, Educational, and Psychological Tests.* New York: Plume, 1992.

Walsh, W. Bruce, and Nancy E. Betz. *Tests and Assessment.* 2nd ed. Englewood Cliffs, NJ: Prentice Hall, 1990.

··

Bettelheim, Bruno (1903–1990)

Psychologist known for his treatment of emotionally disturbed children, particularly autistic children.

Bruno Bettelheim was born in Vienna in 1903. He was trained as a psychoanalyst, receiving his Ph.D. from the University of Vienna in 1938. In the same year, the Nazis took over Austria and Bettelheim was interned in the Dachau and Buchenwald concentration camps. He was released in 1939 and emigrated to the United States, where he first became a research associate of the Progressive Education Association at the University of Chicago and then an associate professor at Rockford College from 1942–44.

In 1943, Bettelheim gained widespread recognition for his article, "Individual and Mass Behavior in Extreme Situations," a study of human adaptibility based on his concentration camp experiences. In 1944, the psychologist was granted a dual appointment by the University of Chicago as assistant professor and head of the Sonia Shankman Orthogenic School, a residential treatment center for 6–14-year-olds with severe emotional problems, which became the focus of Bettelheim's work with autistic children. Here he successfully treated many children unresponsive to previous therapy, using the technique—which has been both lauded and criticized—of unconditionally accepting their behavior. In addition to relieving the suffering of disturbed children and helping them function in society, Bettelheim was also concerned with the emotional lives and upbringing of normal children and with applying psychoanalytic principles to social problems.

In three decades as an author of works for both scholarly and popular audiences, he covered a broad range of topics. *Love is Not Enough* (1950), *Truants from Life* (1954), and *The Empty Fortress* (1967) are based on his work at the Orthogenic School. *The Informed Heart* (1960) deals with Bettelheim's concentration camp experiences. *Children of the Dream* (1969) analyzes communal childrearing methods on an Israeli kibbutz and their implications for American family life. *The Uses of Enchant-*

ment (1976) argues for the importance of fairy tales in a child's development. Later books include *On Learning to Read: The Child's First Fascination with Meaning* (1981), and *Freud and Man's Soul* (1982). A full professor at the University of Chicago from 1952, Bettelheim retired from both teaching and directorship of the Orthogenic School in 1973. Following the death of his wife in 1984 and suffering a stroke in 1987, he committed suicide in 1990.

For Further Study

Books

Pollak, Richard. *The Creation of Dr. B: A Biography of Bruno Bettelheim.* New York: Simon & Schuster, 1997.

Sutton, Nina. *Bettelheim, a Life and a Legacy.* New York: Basic Books, 1996.

—Rosalie Wieder

··

Bilingualism/Bilingual Education

Use of a language other than English in public school classrooms.

The language rights of ethnic minorities in the United States have been a source of public controversy for close to two decades. The 1970s saw record levels of immigration, bringing an estimated 4 million legal and 8 million illegal immigrants into the country. To accommodate this dramatic surge in the nation's population of foreign language speakers, language assistance has been mandated on the federal, state, and local levels in areas ranging from voting and tax collection to education, social services, disaster assistance, and consumer rights. Today Massachusetts offers driver's license tests in 24 languages; residents of California can choose one of six different languages when they vote; street signs in some parts of Miami are printed in both English and Spanish; and classroom instruction is taught in 115 different languages in New York City schools. Altogether, over 300 languages are spoken in the United States. As of 1990, 31.8 million Americans spoke a language other than English at home, and the country's population included 6.7 million non-English speakers. Nationwide, one-third of the children enrolled in urban schools speak a language other than English at home as their first language. Around 2.6 million schoolchildren throughout the country do not speak English at all.

Organized opposition to bilingualism, which collectively became known as the English-Only movement, began in the 1980s. In 1980 voters in Dade County, Florida, designated English as their official language. The following year, U.S. Senator S.I. Hayakawa of California introduced a constitutional amendment to make English the country's official language. Two influential English-Only lobbying groups were formed: U.S. English, in 1983, and English First, in 1986. In 1986, with the passage of Proposition 63, English became the official language of California. By the mid-1990s, 22 states had passed similar measures. In August 1996, the U.S. House of Representatives, by a margin of 259–169, passed a bill to make English the official language of the federal government. (However, President Bill Clinton vowed to veto the bill if it passed the Senate.) Observers attribute the English-Only movement to backlash against immigration and affirmative action, spurred by fear of competition for jobs and resentment of government spending on bilingual programs.

The government program that has drawn the most fire is bilingual education, which costs taxpayers an estimated $200 million a year in federal funds and billions of dollars in state and local expenditures. Bilingual education programs, which allow students to pursue part of their study in their first language and part in English, were first mandated by Congress in 1968. The constitutionality of bilingual education was upheld in a 1974 Supreme Court ruling affirming that the city of San Francisco had discriminated against 18,000 Chinese-American students by failing to make special provisions to help them overcome the linguistic barriers they faced in school. However, the court did not specify what these provisions should be, and educators have evolved several different methods of instruction for students with first languages other than English. With the immersion (or "sink or swim") approach, nearly all instruction is in English, and the students are expected to pick up the language through intensive exposure. If the teacher is bilingual, the students may be allowed to ask questions in their native language, but the teacher is supposed to answer them in English. The English as a Second Language (ESL) approach, often used in a class where students speak more than one foreign language, takes a more gradual approach to mastering English, using it in conjunction with the student's first language. English-only instruction may be offered, but only in some, rather than all, classes.

The remaining methods rely more heavily on the student's first language. Even though, technically, all teaching methods aimed at meeting the needs of foreign language speakers are considered bilingual education, participants in debates about bilingual education often single out the following methods as targets of praise or criticism. In Transitional Bilingual Education (TBE), students study English but are taught all other academic subjects in their native languages until they are considered ready to switch to English. In some cases, bilingual teachers also help the students improve their skills in

their native language. Bilingual/bicultural programs use the students' native languages not only to teach them the standard curriculum but also for special classes about their ethnic heritage and its history and culture. Two-way or dual language programs enroll students from different backgrounds with the goal of having all of them become bilingual, including those who speak only English. For example, Spanish-speaking children may learn English while their English-speaking classmates learn Spanish.

Critics of bilingual education (or of those methods that rely heavily on the students' native languages) claim that it fails to provide children with an adequate knowledge of English, thus disadvantaging them academically, and they cite high dropout rates for Hispanic teenagers, the group most likely to have received instruction in their native language. They accuse school systems of continuing to promote bilingual programs to protect the jobs of bilingual educators and receive federal funding allocated for such programs. As evidence of this charge, they cite barriers placed in the way of parents who try to remove their children from bilingual programs. Hispanic parents in New York City have claimed that their children are being railroaded into bilingual programs by a system that requires all children with Spanish surnames, as well as children of any nationality who have non-English-speaking family members, to take a language proficiency exam. Children scoring in the bottom 40% are then required to enroll in bilingual classes even if English is the primary language spoken at home. Critics of bilingual instruction also cite a 1994 New York City study that reported better results for ESL instruction than for methods that taught children primarily in their native languages.

In spite of the criticism it has aroused, bilingual education is strongly advocated by many educators. Defenders cite a 1991 study endorsed by the National Academy of Sciences stating that children who speak a foreign language learn English more rapidly and make better overall academic progress when they receive several years of instruction in their native language. A later study, conducted at George Mason University, tracked 42,000 children who had received bilingual instruction and reported that the highest scores on standardized tests in the eleventh grade were earned by those students who had had six years of bilingual education. Programs with two-way bilingual education have had particularly impressive results. Oyster Bilingual Elementary School in Washington, DC, (whose student body is 58% Hispanic, 26% white, 12% black, and 4% Asian) is admiringly cited as a model for bilingual education. Its sixth graders read at a ninth-grade level and have tenth-grade-level math skills. Experts on both sides of the controversy agree that for any teaching method to be successful, the teaching must be done by qualified instructors equipped with adequate teaching materials in appropriately assigned classes with a reasonable ratio of students to teachers.

For Further Study

Books

Chavez, Linda. *Out of the Barrio: Toward a New Politics of Hispanic Assimilation.* New York: Basic Books, 1991.

Crawford, James. *Hold Your Tongue: Bilingualism and the Politics of "English-Only."* Reading, MA: Addison-Wesley Publishing Co., 1992.

Harlan, Judith. *Bilingualism in the United States: Conflict and Controversy.* New York: Franklin Watts, 1991.

Lang, Paul. *The English Language Debate: One Nation, One Language!* Springfield, NJ: Enslow Publishers, Inc., 1995.

Porter, Rosalie Pedalino. *Forked Tongue: The Politics of Bilingual Education.* New York: Basic Books, 1990.

Rodriguez, Richard. *Hunger of Memory: The Education of Richard Rodriguez.* New York: Bantam Books, 1983.

Simon, Paul. *The Tongue-Tied American: Confronting the Foreign Language Crisis.* New York: Continuum, 1980.

Organizations

Multicultural Education, Training, and Advocacy, Inc. (META)
Address: 240A Elm Street, Suite 22
Somerville, MA 02144

National Association for Bilingual Education (NABE)
Address: Union Center Plaza
1220 L Street NW, Suite 605
Washington, DC 20005

U.S. English
Address: 818 Connecticut Ave. NW, Suite 200
Washington, DC 20006

Bilirubin Test

Monitors the liver function of newborns.

The bilirubin test is a blood test to monitor the liver function of newborns. The rapid destruction of red **blood** cells after birth produces more bilirubin than the infant's liver can handle, causing some **jaundice** in about 99% of newborns. The bilirubin test, a normal part of a neonatal screen, monitors levels of this substance in the blood of newborns to make sure that normal degrees of jaundice do not become more severe.

For Further Study

Books

McCullough, Virginia. *Testing and Your Child: What You Should Know About 150 of the Most Common Medical, Educational, and Psychological Tests.* New York: Plume, 1992.

Periodicals

Dundon, Catherine. "Newborn Jaundice." *American Baby* 59, March 1997, pp. 8+.

Alfred Binet

Binet, Alfred (1857–1911)

Founder of experimental psychology in France and pioneer in intelligence testing.

Alfred Binet was born in Nice, France, in 1857. After studying both law and medicine in Paris, he earned a doctorate in natural science. His psychological training—mostly at Jean-Martin Charcot's neurological clinic at the Salpetriere Hospital—was in the area of abnormal psychology, particularly hysteria, and he published books on hypnotism (*Le magnetisme animal,* with C.S. Fere in 1886) and suggestibility (*La suggestibilite,* 1900). From 1895 until his death in 1911, Binet served as director of France's first psychological laboratory, at the Sorbonne. Also in 1895, he established the journal *L'Annee psychologique.* Binet had been interested in the psychology of—and individual differences in—**intelligence** since the 1880s and published articles on emotion, memory, attention, and problem solving in the journal he founded. In 1899 he set up a special laboratory where he devised a series of tests which he used to evaluate the intellectual development of his two daughters. His 1903 book, *L'Etude experimentale de l'intelligence,* was based on his studies of them.

In 1905 Binet and Theodore Simon created the first intelligence test for general use to aid the French government in establishing a program to educate mentally retarded children. In 1908 they revised the test, expanding it from a single scale of measurement to a battery of tests for children in different age groups, with the focus now shifted from identifying retardation to the general measurement of intelligence.

A further test revision in 1911 introduced the concept of mental age. In 1916 the American psychologist Lewis Terman (1877–1956) used the 1908 Binet-Simon test as the basis for the **Stanford-Binet** Intelligence Scale, the best-known and most researched intelligence test in the United States. After developing his pioneering test, Binet co-authored *Les Enfants anormaux (Abnormal Children)* (1907) with Simon and published *Les Idees modernes sur les enfants (Modern Ideas on Children)* in 1909. He died in Paris in 1911.

For Further Study

Books

Wolf, Theta Holmes. *Alfred Binet.* Chicago: University of Chicago Press, 1973.

—Rosalie Wieder

Biological Parent

Male or female whose genes provide the genetic makeup of a child.

The definition of the term *biological parent* has become more complex as medical technology has expanded the parameters of the human reproductive process. Conception of a human **fetus** may be accomplished through sexual intercourse between the male and female parents, through artificial insemination, or through **in vitro fertilization.**

The term *biological parent* is typically used only when a child has more than one set of parents, to distinguish between those who have custody of the child—such as adoptive parents, foster parents, or stepparents—and those who contributed the genetic makeup of the child. The term is legally significant under laws enacted in some states to provide definitions and standards for issues of parentage, especially in those cases involving a paternity suit.

Biopsy

A medical procedure used to diagnose a condition.

Most biopsies involve taking a small piece of skin or muscle under a local anesthetic. When the cells to be analyzed are accessible by needle, the biopsy specimen may be removed with a hollow aspiration needle, which is used to suck out the sample of cells. Aspirations are typically performed with local anesthesia; in addition, ultrasound imagery or other scanning devices may aid in locating the cells of interest. In cases where the cells are not accessible by needle, a longer tube called an endoscope may be inserted into the body with forceps attached for acquiring the specimen. Biopsy analysis is used in diagnosing **cancer** and **muscular dystrophy.**

For Further Study

Books

Talking with Your Child about Cancer. Bethesda, MD: National Cancer Institute, 1994.

Young People with Cancer: a Handbook for Parents. Bethesda, MD: National Cancer Institute, 1982.

Bipolar Disorder

A condition (also called manic depression) characterized by extreme mood swings that alternate between depression and mania (a state of exaggerated elation and euphoria).

According to the National Institutes of Mental Health (NIMH), bipolar disorder affects an estimated 2 million Americans (roughly 1% of the population). The disease usually begins in the teens or early 20s and affects males and females equally. Children with **attention deficit/hyperactivity disorder** (ADHD) are at above-average risk for bipolar disorder: about one in four has or will develop it. Within a 10-year period, a person whose bipolar disorder is not treated with medication usually goes through an average of four **depression**/mania episodes. However, the pattern varies widely: mood swings can occur as frequently as four or more times a month, or as seldom as once every five years.

Bipolar disorder is the depressive illness considered most likely to have a biological cause, thought to be an imbalance in the brain's chemistry. The condition has also been associated with the biological clock that synchronizes one's internal body rhythms with external events. Bipolar disorder is often inherited. In one study, 25% of children with one manic-depressive parent inherited the disorder, and 75% of children with two manic-depressive parents became manic-depressive. An episode of psychotic depression in teenagers is twice as likely to be followed by a manic episode within five years if there is a family history of bipolar disorder. Also, bipolar disorder is often shared by identical **twins.**

The depressed cycle of a person with bipolar disorder has the characteristics of major depression. Symptoms include sadness, apathy, and lack of energy. There may also be significant changes in appetite or weight; slowed-down movements; problems with concentration; feelings of worthlessness; guilt feelings; and suicidal impulses. In the manic state, people with bipolar disorder become euphoric: their thoughts race; their speech is rapid and shifts abruptly from one topic to another; they are constantly occupied, attempting to perform many activities at once, and often have trouble sitting still or sleeping; and they also demonstrate an exaggerated sense of self-confidence, manifested by the belief that they can perform extraordinary feats beyond the ability of the average person. Also common are spending sprees, with excessive sums of money spent on frivolous items, and provocative and/or promiscuous sexual behavior. While in a manic phase, persons with bipolar disorder typically resent any criticism of their behavior, and become irritable or angry when others attempt to calm them down, or when they fail to complete all their projects. Hallucinations or delusions may also occur. A symptom of bipolar disorder especially common among teenagers is extreme mood-lability (rapid changes in mood).

Adolescents with bipolar disorder develop normally until the illness first manifests itself. Their lives are then severely disrupted by the illness. In fact, bipolar disorder is especially disruptive to adolescents, more so than to other age groups: major milestones, such as dating, may be delayed for years until the disease is under control. Schoolwork also suffers because cognitive functioning is affected and concentration impaired. Teens with manic depression are likely to abuse drugs or alcohol to alleviate the anxiety caused by the condition—roughly two-thirds of all persons with bipolar disorder have substance abuse or dependency problems. Unless it is treated, the illness gets worse with each episode and harder to control. In addition, 15% of those who fail to receive adequate treatment for bipolar disorder commit **suicide.** Common misdiagnoses of bipolar disorder include **schizophrenia,** drug or alcohol dependence, unipolar disorder, and personality disorders. It is common to suffer from bipolar disorder for as long as seven to 10 years without having the condition diagnosed and treated.

Bipolar disorder is most effectively treated by lithium, which can halt episodes of both mania and depression. This medication, which works by stabilizing the brain chemicals responsible for mood swings, is 70% effective in alleviating symptoms of mania, sometimes working within hours and usually within one to three weeks. Antipsychotic drugs or benzodiazepines (tranquil-izers) may initially be needed as an emergency measure to treat full-blown mania until lithium can take effect. After manic-depressive symptoms subside, lithium should still be taken as a maintenance drug to prevent future manic episodes. To ensure against toxicity, persons taking the medication must have their blood levels, as well as kidney and thyroid functions, tested regularly. Some manic-depressives are reluctant to give up the "highs" of the manic state and resist taking lithium, or refuse to take the medication because they don't want to become dependent on it. However, discontinuing the medication is risky because lithium treatment can lose some of its effectiveness when it is resumed after being stopped.

Many well-known artists and scientists have suffered from bipolar disorder. According to the NIMH, over one-third of all Pulitzer Prize-winning poets have had symptoms of the disease. Other well-known persons affected by manic depression include painter Vincent van Gogh, writers Sylvia Plath and Virginia Woolf, composers Robert Schumann and Gustav Mahler, and Academy Award-winning actress Patty Duke. In her autobiography, *Call Me Anna,* Duke, who suffered from bipolar disease for many years before it was diagnosed or treated, describes her experience with the illness and her eventual triumph over it.

For Further Study

Books

Clark, Charlotte. *Inside Manic-Depression: The True Story of One Victim's Triumph over Despair.* Sunnyside Press, 1993.

Duke, Patty. *Call Me Anna.* New York: Bantam, 1987.

Ekkehard, Othmer. *Life on a Roller Coaster: Coping with the Ups and Downs of Mood Disorders.* Pia Press, 1989.

Jamison, Kay. *Touched by Fire: Manic-Depressive Illness and the Artistic Temperament.* New York: Free Press, 1993.

Birth

Birth is the process by which a fully developed fetus is expelled from the mother's uterus by the force of strong, rhythmic muscle contractions.

Usually lasting about 16 hours—but in some cases ranging from less than one hour to 48 hours—birth is the culmination of a series of complex physical processes. The length of time between fertilization and birth is called the gestation period. In humans, the gestation period is approximately nine months or 38 weeks.

Birth typically begins at the end of the gestation period when the mother's uterus begins to contract rhythmically, a process called labor. The initiation of labor leading up to birth is the result of a number of hormones, notably oxytocin. Oxytocin is a hormone released from the pituitary gland in the brain, which stimulates uterine contractions and also controls the production of milk in the mammary glands of the breast (a process called lactation). Synthetic oxytocin is sometimes given to women to induce labor. The mechanism that prompts the secretion of oxytocin from the pituitary during labor is thought to be initiated by the pressure of the **fetus**'s head against the cervix, the opening of the uterus. As the fetus's head presses against the cervix, the uterus stretches, and relays a message along nerves to the pituitary, which responds by releasing oxytocin. The more the uterus stretches, the more oxytocin is released. Fetal hormones are also thought to play a role in initiating labor. At the end of gestation, the fetal adrenal glands secrete steroid hormones called corticosteroids, which produce the hormone–like substances known as prostaglandins. Prostaglandins contribute to the contraction of the uterus during labor.

Labor culminating in birth in humans begins with rhythmic contractions of the uterus that dilate the cervix. The cervix is normally tightly closed, and is sealed with a plug of mucus during gestation to protect the fetus from invading microorganisms. During the first stages of labor, the contractions of the uterus dilate the cervix, which widens to about 4 in (10 cm) to accommodate the passage of the fetal head.

In the last weeks of pregnancy, before labor begins, the uterus undergoes irregular contractions, which serve to exercise the muscles of the uterus and may even dilate the cervix. It is not unusual for a woman to go into active labor with a cervix that is already one or two centimeters dilated. During the last weeks of pregnancy, the cervix also thins out (or effaces), which makes dilation easier.

In preparation for birth, the fetus moves further down into the mother's pelvis. When labor begins, the fetus is usually positioned with its head engaged with the top of the cervix. This engagement is called "lightening" or "dropping." When labor begins, the contractions loosen the mucus plug in the cervix, which causes small capillaries in the cervix to break, and the mucus and blood are discharged from the vagina. This discharge is sometimes called "bloody show" and signals the onset of labor.

Another sign that may signal the beginning of labor is the rupturing of the amniotic sac. In the uterus the fetus is encased in a membrane (the amniotic sac) and literally floats in amniotic fluid. When uterine contractions begin, this sac ruptures and the amniotic fluid can leak from the uterus. Not all women experience an abrupt rupturing of the amniotic sac; in some the amniotic fluid gradually leaks out as labor progresses. Once the amniotic sac has ruptured, or the amniotic fluid begins to leak, labor usually progresses more rapidly.

During the first stage of labor, the cervix dilates about 0.5–0.6 in (1.2–1.5 cm) an hour. The uterine contractions are about 5–30 minutes apart, and last for 15–40 seconds. The end of the first stage of labor is associated with the strongest uterine contractions. Contractions are two to five minutes apart, and last for 45–60 seconds. The cervix opens rapidly at this point. This period of labor, sometimes called transition, is usually the most difficult for the mother. The contractions are very strong and close together, and nausea and vomiting are common. After the cervix has dilated to its full width of 4 in (10 cm), the contractions slow down somewhat to about three to five minutes apart. The fetus is then ready to be born, and the second stage of labor begins.

During the second stage, lasting about one to two hours, the mother uses her abdominal muscles to push the fetus through and out of the birth canal. The pushing is actually a reflex action, but if a woman can help the reflex by actively using her muscles, birth goes much faster. As the fetus moves down the birth canal to the vaginal opening, the head begins to appear. The appearance of the head at the opening of the vagina is called crowning. After the head is delivered, first one shoulder is delivered, then the other. The rest of the body follows.

After the baby is born, the umbilical cord that connects the fetus to the placenta is clamped. The clamping cuts off the circulation of the cord, which eventually stops pulsing due to the interruption of its blood supply. The baby now must breathe air through its own lungs.

Before delivery, the placenta separates from the wall of the uterus. Because the placenta contains many blood vessels, its separation from the wall of the uterus causes bleeding. This bleeding, if not excessive, is normal. After the placenta separates from the uterine wall, it moves into the birth canal and is expelled from the vagina. The uterus continues to contract even after the placenta is delivered, and it is thought that these contractions serve to control bleeding.

Today, women have many options for labor and birth. Some women deliver in a hospital with doctors and nurses close by to supervise the birth process. Others choose a nurse-midwife, a person who has been trained to deliver babies but who is not a physician. Still others choose home birth, attended either by a doctor or midwife, or sometimes both. Whatever option a woman chooses, it is important to get good medical care throughout the pregnancy. Periodic prenatal checkups are one of the best ways to avoid birth complications.

Many childbirth experts believe that the more knowledgeable a mother is about the birth process, the less fear and apprehension she will feel giving birth. Many childbirth classes prepare both mother and father for the birth experience and teach relaxation and breathing techniques. The Read method—named after its founder, British physician Grantley Dick-Read—is based on the notion that fear leads to pain. The Read method includes childbirth education, exercises to improve muscle tone, and relaxation techniques. The Lamaze method (developed in the 1940s and named for Dr. Ferdinand Lamaze) takes a psychological approach to managing labor. The Lamaze method teaches women to relax and breathe in response to pain. Another method—the Bradley method—also focuses on deep relaxation and slow, deep breathing.

Regional anesthesia is commonly used during labor and birth. In regional **anesthesia**, drugs are injected to deaden sensation around the spinal nerves that carry sensations from the pelvic region. Controversy about whether these drugs affect the fetus is ongoing, although some kinds of regional anesthesia affect the fetus less than others. General anesthesia, in which the mother is given drugs that put her to sleep, is rarely used today.

For Further Study

Books

Bean, Constance A. *Methods of Childbirth*, 2nd ed. Garden City, New York: Doubleday, 1990.

Bradley, Robert A. *Husband–Coached Childbirth*. New York: Harper and Row, 1981.

Dick-Read, Grantley. *Childbirth Without Fear*. New York: Harper and Row, 1984.

Karmel, Marjorie. *Thank You, Dr. Lamaze*. New York: Harper and Row, 1993.

Knobil, Ernst, and Jimmy D. Neill, eds. *The Physiology of Reproduction*, 2nd ed. New York: Raven Press, 1994.

Mitford, Jessica. *The American Way of Birth*. New York: Dutton, 1992.

Periodicals

"Deciding to Be Born." *Discover* 13, 10 May 1992.

Fischman, Joshua. "Putting a New Spin on the Birth of Human Birth." *Science* 264, May 20, 1994, p. 1082.

Birth Defects

Defects present at birth, resulting from hereditary factors, environmental influences, or maternal illness.

Birth or congenital defects are present at birth and result from hereditary factors, environmental influences, or maternal illness. Such defects range from very minor, such as a dark spot or birthmark that may appear anywhere on the infant's body, to more serious conditions that may result in marked disfigurement or limit the lifespan of the child. A number of factors individually or in combination may cause birth defects. Heredity plays a major role in passing birth defects from one generation to the next. Such conditions as **sickle-cell anemia**, color blindness, deafness, and extra digits on the hands or feet are hereditary. The condition may not appear in every generation, but the defective gene is usually passed on.

Low birth weight is the most common birth defect, with one in every 15 babies being born at less than their ideal weight. Weights between 5 lb, 8 oz (2,500 g) and 3 lb, 5 oz (1,500 g) are considered low. Low birth weight may occur if the baby is born prematurely, before the normal gestation period of 38 weeks has elapsed, or after a normal gestation period. **Premature birth**, other than being a birth defect in itself, may also have accompanying effects. A baby born before the 28th week of gestation, for example, may have great difficulty breathing because the lungs have not developed fully.

Prenatal conditions can cause birth defects. For example, the mother's exposure to chemicals such as mercury or to radiation during the first three months of pregnancy may result in an abnormal alteration in the growth or development of the fetus. The mother's diet may also be a factor. A balanced, healthy diet is essential to the proper formation of the fetus because the developing baby receives all of its **nutrition** from the mother.

Prenatal development of the fetus may also be affected by disease that the mother contracts, especially any that occur during the first trimester (three months) of pregnancy. For example, if a pregnant woman contracts German measles, or **rubella,** the virus may cross the placenta and infect the fetus. The rubella virus interferes with the fetus's normal metabolism and cell movement and can cause blindness (from cataracts), deafness, heart malformations, and **mental retardation**. The risk of fetal damage resulting from maternal rubella infection is greatest during the first month of pregnancy (50%) and declines with each succeeding month.

It is especially important that the mother not smoke, consume alcohol, or take drugs while she is pregnant. Drinking alcohol heavily can result in **fetal alcohol syndrome (FAS)**. Newborns with FAS have small eyes and a short, upturned nose that is broad across the bridge, making the eyes appear farther apart than normal. These babies are also underweight at birth and do not catch up as time passes. They often have some degree of mental retardation and may exhibit behavior problems. A mother who continues to use illicit drugs, such as heroin, crack, or cocaine, will have a baby who is addicted to its mother's drug. The addiction may not be fatal, but the newborn will be physically uncomfortable and disagreeable until the addiction is controlled.

Some therapeutic drugs taken by pregnant women have also been shown to produce birth defects. The most notorious example is **thalidomide**, a mild sedative. During the 1950s women in more than 20 countries who had taken this drug gave birth to more than 7,000 severely deformed babies. These children suffered from a condition called phocomelia, which is characterized by extremely short limbs, often with no fingers or toes.

In 1992, the U.S. Public Health Service published the recommendation that all women of childbearing age consume 0.4 milligrams of folic acid daily to decrease the risk of two common and serious birth defects, **spina bifida** and anencephaly. The Centers for Disease Control estimates that 50–70% of these birth defects could be prevented if this recommendation were followed before and during early pregnancy. All women between 15 and 45 years of age should consume 0.4 mg of folic acid per day because half of U.S. pregnancies are unplanned and because these birth defects occur very early in pregnancy (3–4 weeks after conception), before most women know they are pregnant.

Following are some of the most common birth defects, ranging from those that cause anatomic changes to those that may prove lethal to the newborn.

Clubfoot

Approximately one newborn out of every 400 has a form of clubfoot. In its most serious form, known as equinovarus, the foot is twisted inward and downward and the foot itself is cupped or flexed. If both feet are clubbed in this manner the toes point to each other rather than straight ahead. Often the heel cord or Achilles tendon is so taut that the foot cannot be straightened without surgery.

A milder and more common type of clubfoot is called calcaneal valgus, in which the foot is bent upward and outward in the same way that you would flex your foot at the ankle. Still other forms include talipes cavus, in which the instep is abnormally elevated; talipes valgus, in which the heel is turned outward; and talipes varus, in which the heel is turned inward.

The seriously deformed clubfoot requires surgery to realign the bones and ligaments. The milder forms often can be cured by fitting the baby with corrective shoes to gradually move the bones back into alignment.

Cleft lip and cleft palate

Approximately 7,000 newborns (one of every 700 births) are born with cleft lip and/or cleft palate each year in the United States. **Cleft lip and palate** describe a condition in which a split remains in the lip and roof of the mouth. During growth *in utero* (in the womb) the lip or palate, which develop from the edges toward the middle, fail to grow together. The defect occurs most often among Asians and certain Native American groups, less frequently among whites, and least often among African Americans.

Approximately 25% of infants born with cleft palate have inherited the trait from one or both parents. The cause for the other 75% remains unknown, but is probably a combination of heredity, poor nutrition, drug use, or a disease the mother contracted while pregnant. The cleft may involve only the upper lip, may extend into the palate, or may be located on the back of the palate.

Surgery is especially important to correct the defect in the palate. Feeding a baby with cleft palate is difficult because the food can pass through the palate into the nasal cavity and may be inhaled and cause choking. In the newborn, whose bones have not completely hardened, surgery is relatively simple. As the child ages, however, surgical correction is more difficult and the child will require a speech therapist.

Spina bifida

Spina bifida, or open spine, occurs once in every 2,000 births in the United States. It occurs because, as in cleft palate, the edges of the spine growing around the spinal cord do not meet. An open area remains, which in the worst case of this disease, leaves the spinal cord unprotected. The mildest form of spina bifida may be so slight that the defect does not have any effect on the child and goes undetected until an x ray is taken.

Spina bifida may appear as a cyst, ranging in size from a walnut to a grapefruit, in which some parts of the meninges (layers of connective tissue covering the spinal cord), spinal cord, or both are contained. The lump can be removed surgically. In its most serious form, the lump or cyst has little skin or covering so spinal fluid may leak from it. Roots of the spinal nerves are contained within the cyst and the cyst may be covered with sores. Infection is a serious risk until surgery has been performed and the area has healed. Unfortunately, this leaves the child's legs paralyzed and without feeling. Problems may develop later in control of the bowels and bladder.

Newborns with spina bifida often have a condition called **hydrocephalus**, which means, literally, water in the head. In this condition, cerebrospinal fluid collects in and around the brain and will not drain. Mental retardation can result if the fluid is not drained regularly by implanting a special tube (called a shunt) leading from the brain down into a vein in the child's neck or into the child's chest. Hydrocephaly can also occur in infants who do not have spina bifida. The cause of spina bifida is not known, but a woman can take 0.4 milligrams of folic acid daily to decrease the risk that her child will have this serious birth defect. It can be diagnosed before birth by **amniocentesis** or ultrasound testing.

Heart defects

Congenital heart defects occur in one of every 175 births in the United States. The defect may be so mild that it is not detected for some years or it may be fatal. A baby with a heart defect may be born showing a bluish tinge around the lips and on the fingers. This condition, called cyanosis, is a signal that the body is not receiving enough oxygen. The blue color may disappear shortly after birth, indicating that all is normal, or it may persist, indicating that further testing is needed to determine the nature of the heart defect.

A normal heart has four chambers; two upper, called the atria (singular: atrium), and two lower called the ventricles. Veins returning oxygen-poor blood from the body lead into the upper right chamber, and this blood then flows from the lower right chamber to the lungs. From the lungs vessels carrying oxygen-rich blood flow into the left upper chamber, and the main blood vessel of the body, the aorta, leads out of the left lower chamber. In the womb, this cycle changes because the fetus's blood does not need to flow through its lungs. The fetus receives its oxygen from the mother through the placenta via the umbilical cord. A special shunt in place during fetal development closes at birth so that the blood is cycled in the right direction. Failure of this shunt to close allows blood to back up into the lungs with serious consequences. Surgery is required to close the shunt and restore normal circulation. If it is undetected at birth, a heart defect may impair the growth of a child. Without a sufficient blood supply, children may become breathless at small amounts of exertion and may squat frequently because it is easier to breathe in that position.

Some minor defects may disappear over time as the child grows. A small hole in the wall between the left and right sides of the heart, for example, may close naturally. A larger defect will require surgical patching. Some newborns may have only one upper chamber or only a single lower chamber of the heart. The aorta may be pinched and impair the flow of blood from the heart. Some of the heart valves may not function correctly and occasionally the vessels of the heart may be transposed so that the aorta leads from the right side of the heart.

These are only a few of the heart anomalies that can be present in the newborn. The heart is a complicated organ, and its formation can be influenced by hereditary factors as well as by alcohol consumption or smoking. Fortunately, most heart defects correct themselves over time or can be corrected with surgery.

Other physical deformities

Physical defects in newborns are common. They can affect any of the bones or muscles in the body and may or may not be correctable. Among the more common are the presence of extra fingers or toes (polydactyly), which presents no health threat and can be corrected surgically. Similarly, webbed fingers and toes, a genetic disorder

seen in approximately one of every 1,700–2,000 births, can be treated surgically to resemble normal appendages.

A more serious, though relatively rare, condition is called achondroplasia. This term means without cartilage formation and refers to the supposed lack of cartilage growth plates near the ends of a child's bones. In fact, the plates are present, but grow poorly. Achondroplasia is a type of **dwarfism**. This genetic disorder of bone growth is seen in one in 25,000–40,000 births and is one of the oldest known birth defects. Ancient Egyptian art depicts individuals with this condition. The cause of achondroplasia is not known, nor is there a cure. The child who has this condition will be slow at walking and sitting because of short arms and legs, and this may be interpreted as mental retardation. However, these individuals have normal intelligence.

Hereditary diseases and syndromes

In addition to physical deformities, certain diseases and syndromes are also passed to the infant through the parents' genes. Some of these conditions can be controlled or treated, while others are untreatable and fatal.

Sickle-cell anemia

Sickle-cell anemia is an inherited disease of the blood cells that occurs in one of every 400–600 African Americans. An individual can be a carrier of the sickle-cell anemia gene and not show any active signs of the disease. If two carriers become parents, however, some of their children may have sickle-cell anemia.

In individuals with sickle-cell anemia, one form of hemoglobin transforms into a rigid, sickle shape that deforms the red blood cell. When the cell becomes wedged in a small blood vessel it prevents the flow of blood through the vessel and can initiate what is called a sickle-cell crisis. The lack of blood flow to the tissues being blocked causes pain and degeneration of the tissue.

Abnormal red blood cells are removed from the circulatory system by the spleen, but removal of large numbers of such cells can lead to anemia, a lack of an adequate number of red blood cells. Unfortunately, the breakdown of abnormal red blood cells can in itself cause a serious condition in which excess iron, scavenged from the hemoglobin molecule, is deposited in tissues such as the heart and liver. Although replacement of the destroyed red blood cells could be achieved with blood transfusion, the replacement cells will only add to the iron content of blood. There is no cure for sickle-cell anemia, though scientists are learning how to better control it to prevent sickling of the blood cells.

Tay-Sachs disease

Tay-Sachs disease affects Jews of eastern European origin, the Ashkenazi Jews, and is a condition that is fatal at an early age. A carrier of the disease will have a gene for Tay-Sachs disease and another gene that is normal. If two carriers have children, one in four will be normal, two in four can carry the trait and pass it on without showing any effects, and one in four may have the disease.

The newborn Tay-Sachs child lacks a blood enzyme called hexosaminidase A, which breaks down certain fats in the brain and nerve cells. When born, the baby may appear normal, but over a short period of time, as the brain cells become clogged with fatty deposits, the child will no longer smile, crawl or turn over, and will become blind. Usually the child dies by the age of three or four years.

There is no cure for Tay-Sachs disease, but carriers can be detected by a simple blood test that measures the amount of hexosaminidase A. A carrier will have half the normal amount of the enzyme, and the two carriers can be counseled to explain the probability of producing an offspring with Tay-Sachs disease. Researchers are trying to find a way to provide sufficient levels of the missing enzyme in the newborn, or identify a suitable substitute that could be supplied as the child ages, much like insulin is used to treat **diabetes.** A more technologically advanced line of research is examining the possibility of transplanting a normal gene to replace the defective one in carriers.

Down syndrome

One of every 800–1,000 babies is born with Down syndrome. Down syndrome babies may have eyes that slant upward, small ears that may turn over at the top, a small mouth, and a nose that is flattened between the eyes (at the bridge). Mental retardation is present in varying degrees, but most Down syndrome children have only mild to moderate retardation. Generally, these children can walk, talk, dress themselves, and are toilet trained later than children with normal intelligence. Many attend school and hold jobs.

Down syndrome results when either the egg or the sperm that fertilizes it has an extra number 21 chromosome. If either parent has Down syndrome, the probability of passing the condition on to the offspring is increased. Parents who have had one Down syndrome child and mothers older than 35 years of age are also at increased risk of having a Down syndrome baby.

For Further Study

Books

Down's Syndrome. March of Dimes/Birth Defects Foundation, 1993.

Drinking During Pregnancy: Fetal Alcohol Syndrome and Fetal Alcohol Effects. March of Dimes/Birth Defects Foundation, 1991.

Low Birth Weight. March of Dimes/Birth Defects Foundation, 1991.

Periodicals

Gorman, C. "Thalidomide's Return." *Time* 143, June 13, 1994, p. 67.

Purdy, C. "Birth Defects: Life Goes On." *Current Health* 2, October 1993, pp. 12–13.

Birth Order

The chronological order of sibling birth in a family.

Alfred Adler was a pioneer in the study of birth order, suggesting that social relationships, especially among siblings and between children and parents, significantly impacted the growth and personality of children. Today, birth order research focuses on five ordinal birth positions: first-born, second-born, middle, last, and only-children. Anecdotally, much has been made about the effect of birth order on personality and **intelligence,** and scientific studies seem to support some notions about birth order and certain personality traits. For example, studies have consistently linked first-born children with higher academic achievement when compared to later-born children. In general, first-born children have been found to be responsible, assertive, and task-oriented, often rising to leadership positions as adults. Second-borns and middle children report feeling inferior to older children because they do not possess the older child's advanced abilities. Often, they will choose to focus their energies in areas different from those in which their siblings are already established.

Middle children have been found to succeed in team sports, and both they and last-borns have been found to be more socially adjusted if they come from large families. Last-borns are generally considered to be the family baby throughout their lives. Because of nurturing from many older family members, last-borns from large families tend to develop strong social and coping skills. As a group, they have been found to be the most successful socially and to have the highest self-esteem of all the birth positions. Only children share the "baby" label with last-borns, but differ in that they grow up relating to only adults in the family. They are achievement-oriented and most likely to attain academic success and attend college. On the other hand, only children tend to have difficulties with interpersonal relationships and are the most likely to be referred for help with psychiatric disorders.

A controversial 1996 book by Frank J. Sulloway focused on the impact birth order has on later life. In his *Born to Rebel: Birth Order, Family Dynamics, and Creative Lives,* Sulloway stated that children are molded to a far greater degree by their relationships with their siblings than by their relationships with their parents. They spend more time with them, play, fight, and compete for

SIBLING RIVALRY

Sibling rivalry is a normal part of family life. All children become jealous of the love and attention that siblings receive from parents and other adults. When a new baby is brought home, older children feel betrayed by their parents and become angry, directing their anger first toward the parents and later toward the intruder who is usurping their position. Jealousy, resentment, and competition are most intense between siblings spaced less than three years apart. Although a certain amount of sibling rivalry is unavoidable, there are measures that parents can take to reduce its severity and its potential effects on their children.

An older child should be prepared for a new addition to the family by having the situation explained and being told in advance about who will take care of her while her mother is in the hospital having the baby. The child's regular routine should be disturbed as little as possible; it is preferable for the child to stay at home and under the care of the father or another close family member. If there is to be a new babysitter or other caretaker unknown to the child, it is helpful for them to meet at least once in advance. If sibling visits are allowed, the child should be taken to visit the mother and new baby in the hospital.

Once the new baby is home, it is normal for an older child to feel hurt and resentful at seeing the attention lavished on the newcomer by parents, other relatives, and family friends. It is not uncommon for the emotional turmoil of the experience to cause disturbances in eating or sleeping. Some children regress developmentally, temporarily losing such attainments as weaning, bowel and bladder control, or clear speech, in an attempt to regain lost parental attention by becoming babies again themselves.

There are a number of ways to ease the unavoidable jealousy of children whose lives have been disrupted by the arrival of a younger sibling. When friends or relatives visit to see the new baby, parents can make the older child feel better by cuddling him or giving him special attention, including a small present to offset the gifts received by the baby. The older child's self-esteem can be bolstered by involving him in the care of the newborn in modest ways, such as helping out when the baby is being diapered or dressed, or helping push the carriage. The older child should be made to feel proud of the attainments and responsibilities that go along with his more advanced age—things the new baby can't do yet because he is too young. Another way to make older children feel loved and appreciated is to set aside some "quality time" to spend alone with each of them on a regular basis. It is also important for parents to avoid overtly comparing their children to each other, and every effort should be made to avoid favoritism.

In general, the most stressful aspect of sibling rivalry is fighting. (Physical—as opposed to verbal—fights usually peak before the age of five). It is important for parents not to take sides but rather to insist that the children work out disagreements themselves, calling for a temporary "time out" for feelings to cool down, if necessary. Any form of parental involvement in squabbling by siblings can create a triangle that perpetuates hostilities. Over-insistence that siblings share can also be harmful: to retain a sense of individuality, children need some boundaries from their siblings in terms of possessions, territory, and activities. Furthermore, it is especially difficult for very young children to share their possessions.

Parents should take time to praise cooperation and sharing between siblings as a means of positive reinforcement. The fact that siblings quarrel with each other does not necessarily mean that they will be inconsiderate, hostile, or aggressive in their dealings with others outside the family. The security of family often makes children feel free to express feelings and impulses they are unable to in other settings.

parental attention. Sulloway claimed that sibling rivalry causes siblings to pursue lives that can be dramatically different from each other. He also postulated that younger siblings are often revolutionary thinkers, people capable of altering either the political, artistic, cultural, or intellectual environments of their worlds. These theories caused a considerable stir when they were published and were criticized on many fronts, with opponents citing numerous examples of famous, revolutionary thinkers who were first-borns.

For Further Study

Books

Ames, Louise Bates. *He Hit Me First: When Brothers and Sisters Fight.* New York: Warner Books, 1989.

Dunn, Judy. *From One Child to Two.* New York: Fawcett Columbine, 1995.

Fishel, Elizabeth. *Sisters: Shared Histories, Lifelong Ties.* Berkeley, CA: Conari Press, 1994.

Greenberg, Polly. *What Do I Do When My Children Don't Get Along?* New York: Scholastic, 1997.

McDermott, John F. *The Complete Book on Sibling Rivalry.* New York: Putnam, 1987.

Strean, Herbert S., and Lucy Freeman. *Raising Cain: How to Help Your Children Achieve a Happy Sibling Relationship.* New York: Facts on File Publications, 1988.

Periodicals

Boynton, Robert. "Birth of an Idea," *The New Yorker,* vol. 72, no. 30, October 7, 1996, pp. 72–81.

Brazelton, T. Berry. "First Born, Middle Child, Baby: How to Bring Out Your Child's Best," *Family Circle,* vol. 107, no. 8, June 7, 1994, pp. 42–44.

Brubach, Holly. "Born to be Wild," *New York Times Magazine,* December 15, 1996, p. 67.

Wolfe, Alan. "Up From Scientism: What Birth Order And Darwin Can't Explain." *The New Republic,* vol. 215, no. 26, December 23, 1996, p. 29+.

Bisexuality

Sexual orientation defined as sexual involvement with members of both sexes concurrently (within the period of one year) or any sexual attraction to or involvement with members of both sexes at any time in one's life.

There is no single accepted definition of bisexuality. Some define it narrowly as sexual involvement with members of both sexes concurrently (within a twelve-month period or less). Others define bisexuality more broadly as any sexual attraction to or involvement with members of both sexes at any time in one's life. However, few people qualify as bisexual in its narrow definition. A comprehensive study, "Sex in America," conducted in 1992 by the University of Chicago, found that less than 1% of either males (0.7%) or females (0.3%) had engaged in sexual activity with both males and females within the previous year. While no statistics exist on the numbers of Americans who fit the broad definition of bisexuality, estimates range from the millions to tens of millions.

Sigmund Freud believed that bisexuality was a "disposition" common to all humans. He contended that every individual has a masculine and feminine side, and that each side is heterosexually attracted to members of the opposite sex. Most people, however, according to Freud, repress one side, becoming either hetero- or homosexual. Alfred Kinsey posited a scale for human sexuality ranging from zero, representing exclusive heterosexual behavior, to six, representing exclusive homosexual behavior. Between the two poles is a spectrum of bisexual activity.

Dr. Fritz Klein, a noted psychiatrist, has expanded on Kinsey's work, creating the Klein Sexual Orientation Grid, which takes into account seven different variables and the passage of time in defining one's sexual orientation (see accompanying figure). Klein's variables provide a more detailed look at one's sexuality, examining preferences in attraction, behavior, fantasies, emotional involvement, social involvement, lifestyle, and self-identification. Klein also allows for sexual development over time, an important element missing from Kinsey's work.

Martin S. Weinberg, Colin J. Williams, and Douglas W. Pryor, in their book *Dual Attraction: Understanding Bisexuality,* have developed a simplified version of Klein's grid, exploring only three, rather than seven, variables: sexual feelings, sexual activities, and romantic feelings. Sexual feelings include attraction, fantasies, arousal, etc. Sexual activities are actual behaviors such as kissing, fellatio, and intercourse. Romantic feelings are the experience of "falling in love." Self-identified bisexuals can be more or less hetero- or homosexual in each of these categories.

Some studies of fraternal and identical **twins** show that identical twins are more likely to be bisexual than are fraternal twins, suggesting a genetic basis for bisexual predisposition. These studies have yet to be tested adequately to be considered conclusive, however. The fact is that without a single accepted definition of bisexuality, no single conclusion can be reached concerning its origins.

Debate over why people are hetero-, homo-, or bisexual is a fairly recent phenomenon. Identification by sexual preference only began in the 19th century, and

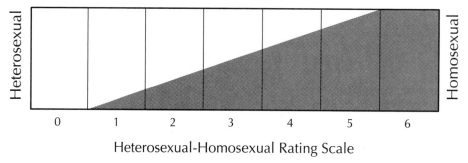

Heterosexual-Homosexual Rating Scale

The above figure shows Albert Kinsey's seven-point rating scale. A "0" rating classifies those who are exclusively heterosexual; a "6" rating classifies those who are exclusively homosexual.

before then, it was rarely discussed. Today, however, there is tremendous pressure for a person to declare a sexual preference. The idea of bisexuality is threatening to some people because sexuality is no longer clearly defined between **homosexuality** and heterosexuality.

Bisexuals are often accused of being "homosexuals in disguise." As a result, they often feel confused about their sexuality. They are considered "too gay" to be straight, and "too straight" to be gay. Few resources exist to help bisexuals understand themselves. Homosexual support groups may reject them if they reveal their heterosexual sides; heterosexuals may reject them if they reveal their homosexual feelings. Many bisexuals remain in the closet, hiding their gender-encompassing feelings from others, and sometimes even from themselves. Others lead dual lives, expressing their homosexual sides with one group of friends, while reserving their heterosexual selves for a totally separate social circle.

Life, and love, can become quite complicated for a bisexual person. The pressures can be tremendous, creating a great deal of stress and pain. A 1989 U.S. Department of Health and Human Services report determined that 30% of teenage **suicide**s occur among gay and lesbian youths, but the number of bisexual victims is unknown. Fortunately, however, a movement has begun in recent years to promote a greater acceptance and understanding of bisexuality. More studies are being done specifically on bisexuality or that include bisexuality as a distinct category.

Unfortunately, concern over the spread of AIDS has caused another backlash against bisexuality, based on the assumption that all bisexuals are promiscuous. Most bisexuals are monogamous for all or part of their lives, and those who engage in promiscuous behavior are not necessarily at greater risk of contracting AIDS. It has been suggested that of women who contract AIDS through sexual intercourse, only 10–20% were infected by bisexual males.

For Further Study

Books

Bass, Ellen, and Kate Kaufman. *Free Your Mind: The Book for Gay, Lesbian, and Bisexual Youth—and Their Allies.* New York: HarperPerennial, 1996.

D'Augelli, Anthony R., and Charlotte J. Patterson. *Lesbian, Gay, and Bisexual Identities Over the Lifespan: Psychological Perspectives.* New York: Oxford University Press, 1995.

Garber, Marjorie. *Vice Versa: Bisexuality and the Eroticism of Everyday Life.* New York: Simon & Schuster, 1995.

Hutchins, Loraine, and Lani Kaahumanu, eds. *Bi Any Other Name: Bisexual People Speak Out.* Boston: Alyson Publications, 1991.

Klein, Fritz, M.D. *The Bisexual Option*, 2nd ed. New York: The Haworth Press, 1993.

Rose, Sharon, et al. *Bisexual Horizons: Politics, Histories, Lives.* London: Lawrence & Wishart, 1996.

Weinberg, Martin S., Colin J. Williams, and Douglas W. Pryor. *Dual Attraction: Understanding Bisexuality.* New York: Oxford University Press, 1994.

Periodicals

Ehrenreich, Barbara. "The Gap Between Gay and Straight." *Time* 141, no. 19, May 10, 1993, p. 76.

Gelman, David. "Tune In, Come Out." *Newsweek* 122, no. 19, November 8, 1993, pp. 70–71.

Leland, John. "Bisexuality." *Newsweek* 126, no. 3, July 17, 1995, pp. 44–50.

—Dianne K. Daeg de Mott

Blood and Blood Disorders

The fluid that carries substances such as hormones, oxygen, and glucose to the tissues of the body and carries carbon dioxide away from the tissues as waste.

Blood is the red-colored fluid that flows through the arteries and veins of the body. Vital to the survival of the body, blood travels through the arteries carrying oxygen from the lungs and glucose from the liver to every cell in the organs and tissues of the body. It returns to the lungs via the network of veins, having exchanged oxygen for carbon dioxide, a waste product. Adults have about six-and-one-half pints (four liters) of blood, which is composed of blood cells (representing slightly less than half of the blood's volume) and plasma.

There are three basic types of blood cells.

- Red blood cells (RBC) contain hemoglobin which carries the oxygen from the lungs. Hemoglobin, made up of protein and iron, is bright red when carrying oxygen. When the oxygen has been delivered to the cells of the body, hemoglobin loses its red pigmentation and takes on a bluish purple color. It then carries the waste product, carbon dioxide, back to the lungs. Red blood cells outnumber white blood cells by around 500:1.

- White blood cells (WBC), also known as leukocytes, are larger but fewer in number than red blood cells. The white blood cells' role is to fight infection or invasion from foreign substances outside the body, such as bacteria or a virus, or a splinter in one's finger.

- Platelets or thrombocytes are cell fragments responsible for the blood's ability to clot. When a body tissue is cut or injured, the platelets begin to join together to form a sticky mass to seal the injured area and stop the flow of blood.

COMPOSITION OF THE FOUR MAIN BLOOD TYPES	
Blood type	**Special protein (antigen) present**
Type A	Type A special protein only
Type B	Type B special protein only
Type AB	Types A and B special proteins both present
Type O	Neither Types A nor B special proteins present

Plasma is about 90% water, with the remaining 10% being composed of dissolved substances, some of which help with the formation of blood clots that seal wounds.

Blood characteristics

Specific proteins, known as antigens, on the surface of the red blood cells and in the plasma differentiate the types of blood. There are two main categories of the special proteins, known as Type A and Type B. Thus, individuals fall into one of four main blood type groups based on combinations of these special proteins. The table illustrates the special protein composition of each blood type. Another feature of blood is the **Rh factor.** The Rh special protein is either present or absent in blood, leading to the labels of Rh positive (protein present) and Rh negative (protein absent). When a pregnant woman and her fetus are of different Rh types, problems in fetal development may occur. The Rh factor is also matched when selecting blood for transfusions.

Blood is collected and stored according to type and Rh factor for use in transfusions. The blood categorized as Type O (neither Type A nor B proteins present) and Rh negative is generally considered to be a universal donor, that is, blood of this type may be accepted by anyone, no matter what their blood type. Because of increased concern over the possibility of contracting a disease through a blood transfusion, individuals may elect to donate their own blood weeks before an elective surgical procedure to ensure compatibility and freedom from new diseases. In many hospital settings, donors may give blood designated for use by a specific patient.

Blood disorders

There are a number of disorders that affect the health and functioning of the blood. Causes of blood disorders range from genetic abnormalities (as in **sickle-cell anemia**) to environmental factors (as in hemorrhage associated with vitamin-C deficiency). Among the most common blood disorders are **anemia,** a condition in which there are too few red blood cells; polycythemia, the counterpart to anemia, where there are too many red blood cells; **leukemia,** a type of cancer in which the blood has too many white blood cells; and thrombosis, a condition where the blood clots too readily. Blood poisoning is a layperson's term for any infection (from mild to life-threatening) affecting the blood or its components. For example, when bacteria invade the blood (often through an injury) and multiply, the condition is known as septicemia. When excessive amounts of toxins are produced, the condition is called toxemia.

For Further Study

Books

Lauer, Ronald M., Richard B. Shekelle, eds. *Childhood Prevention of Atherosclerosis and Hypertension.* New York: Raven Press, 1980.

Audiovisual Recordings

Digestion: Blood and Circulation. Elk Grove, IL: Disney Educational Production, 1995.
    (One 52-minute videotape. Twenty-six minutes are devoted to blood and circulation, with experiments and activities.)
Hemo the Magnificent. Santa Monica, CA: Rhino Home Video, 1991.
    (One 54-minute videotape featuring live and animated characters to tell the story of blood and circulation.)

Organizations

National Heart, Lung, and Blood Institute Information Center
    Address: P.O. Box 30105
    Bethesda, MD 20874-0105
    Telephone: (301) 251-1222
    Website: www.nhlbi.nih.gov/nhlbi/nhlbi.html

Body Image

The perception of one's own body, based chiefly in comparison to socially constructed standards or ideals.

Humans have the unique ability to form abstract conceptions about themselves and to gaze at themselves as both the seer and the object being seen. This can cause conflict when the seer places unrealistic demands on him- or herself, especially on his or her own body. As the advertising and film industries bombard the industrialized world with images of idealized beauty, more and more adolescents are forming negative body images and engaging in self-destructive behaviors to fit an unrealistic ideal.

School-age children

Children begin to recognize themselves in mirrors in meaningful ways at about 18 months and begin perceiving themselves as physical beings in toddlerhood.

School-age children are aware of how their bodies look, though relatively few focus an inappropriate amount of attention on them. Ideally, children learn that their physical appearance is in many ways beyond their control and learn to accept their bodies without judgment. However, children living in the industrialized world are immersed in a culture that creates standards of idealized beauty and then connects those standards to personal worth. Consequently, school-age children can become convinced that they are only worthwhile if they live up to an idealized standard of physical appearance.

Even without the pernicious effects of the media, children face prejudices based on their appearances. Children spend much of their early lives in schools, which are highly social and competitive, with notoriously rigid hierarchies that are often based on physical appearance. Studies have found that teachers are also drawn to the most attractive children, which can further compound a child's poor body image. In a school-age child, a poor body image usually results in social withdrawal and poor **self-esteem.**

Adolescence

As puberty nears, children become increasingly focused on the appearance of their bodies. An adolescent may mature too quickly, too slowly, in a way that is unattractive, or in a way that makes the adolescent stand out in the crowd. Any deviation from the ideal can result in a negative body image, and adolescents may diet or use steroids to counter their own negative self-concept. Distorted body images in adolescence can lead to a number of disorders, such as **anorexia nervosa, bulimia,** or dysmorphic disorder (a severe, clinically recognized illusory body image). These disorders are accompanied by psychological problems, such as **depression** or **anxiety,** as the victim magnifies a slight flaw to such a degree that all other aspects of personality and appearance are ignored. Body-image disorders such as those mentioned have become prevalent in contemporary society, especially among adolescent girls. In 1982 a study concluded that the incidence of anorexia among adolescent girls, for instance, had doubled every 10 years since the 1950s.

For Further Study

Books

Beckelman, Laurie. *Body Blues.* New York : Crestwood House, 1994 [juvenile literature].

Bowen-Woodward, Kathryn. *Coping With a Negative Body-Image.* New York: Rosen Publishing Group, 1989.

Cash, Thomas F. *What Do You See When You Look in the Mirror?: Helping Yourself to a Positive Body Image.* New York: Bantam Books, 1995.

Costin, Carolyn. *Your Dieting Daughter: Is She Dying for Attention?* New York: Brunner/Mazel, 1997.

Ikeda, Joanne P., and Priscilla Naworski. *Am I Fat?: Helping Young Children Accept Differences in Body Size: Suggestions For Teachers, Parents, And Care Providers of Children to Age 10.* Santa Cruz, CA: ETR Associates, 1992.

Periodicals

"Altering Your Body Image: Strategies from the Trenches," *Psychology Today,* January-February, 1997, pp. 30–47.

Audiovisual Recordings

Stewart, Georgiana Liccione. *Developmental Motor Skills for Self Awareness.* Long Beach, NJ: Kimbo Educational, 1973.
(Appropriate for use with the emotionally disturbed, educable mentally handicapped, and multiple-handicapped students.)

Boehm Test of Basic Concepts [Revised (Boehm-R)]

A readiness test for children in grades K-2 that evaluates mastery of basic concepts important for achievement in the early years of school.

The Boehm Test of Basic Concepts can be used as an aid in pinpointing specific areas where a child can benefit from remedial help. The test consists of 50 items and takes 30 minutes to complete. It can be given either individually or in small groups and is hand scored and graded according to a percentile equivalent system. The questions, which mostly involve quantity, space, or time, are administered orally. The child answers them by marking one of several pictures in a multiple-choice picture booklet.

For Further Study

Books

Cohen, Libby G., and Loraine J. Spenciner. *Assessment of Young Children.* New York: Longman, 1994.

Genishi, Celia. ed. *Ways of Assessing Children and Curriculum: Stories of Early Childhood Practice.* New York: Teachers College Press, 1992.

McCullough, Virginia. *Testing and Your Child: What You Should Know About 150 of the Most Common Medical, Educational, and Psychological Tests.* New York: Plume, 1992.

Bonding

The process by which parents form a close personal relationship with their newborn child.

Bonding is the process by which parents form a close personal relationship with their newborn child. The term "bonding" is often used interchangeably with "**attachment**," a related phenomenon. For the purposes of this essay, bonding is confined to the newborn period. Attachment develops over the larger period of infancy and is treated in a separate entry.

The way parents feel about a new child is highly subjective and emotional, and can be very difficult to measure. Some researchers in the United States and elsewhere have attempted to show that there is a "sensitive period" soon after birth, in which the newborn is quietly alert and interested in engaging the mother, and the mother is able to attune to the new child. It is assumed, but not proven, that if mothers are given the opportunity to interact with their infants at this time, they are most likely to become bonded to the child—to begin to respond to him, love him, and take care of him. Fathers who are with their partners at the birth also respond to the infant in characteristic ways immediately after birth.

American pediatricians John Kennell and Marshall Klaus pioneered scientific research on bonding in the 1970s. Working with infants in a neonatal intensive care unit, they often observed that infants were often taken away from their mothers immediately after birth for emergency medical procedures. These babies often remained in the nursery for several weeks before being allowed to go home with their families. Although the babies did well in the hospital, a troubling percentage of them seemed not to prosper at home, and were even victims of battering and abuse. Kennell and Klaus also noted that the mothers of these babies were often uncomfortable with them, and did not seem to believe that their babies had survived birth. Even mothers who had successfully raised previous infants seemed to have special difficulties with their children that had been treated in the intensive care nursery. Kennell and Klaus surmised that the separation immediately after birth interrupted some fundamental process between the mother and the new baby. They experimented with giving mothers of both premature and healthy full-term babies extra contact with their infants immediately after birth and in the few days following birth. Mothers who were allowed more access to their babies in the hospital seemed to develop better rapport with their infants, to hold them more comfortably, smile and talk to them more.

Studies conducted in the 1970s making these claims have come under attack in the 1980s and 1990s. Much of the earlier research has been difficult to duplicate, and many mitigating factors in parent-child relationships make the lasting effects of early bonding experience difficult to pin down with scientific rigor. Nevertheless, bonding research brought about widespread changes in hospital obstetrical practice in the United States. Fathers and family members were allowed to remain with the mother during labor and delivery in many cases. Mothers were allowed to hold their infants immediately after birth, and in many cases babies remained with their mothers throughout their hospital stay. Bonding research has also led to increased awareness of the natural capabilities of the infant at birth, and so has encouraged many others to deliver their babies without anesthesia (which depresses mother and infant responsiveness).

One important factor in the parents' ability to bond with the infant after birth is that the healthy, undrugged newborn is often in what is called a "quiet alert" state for 45 to 60 minutes after birth. Research has demonstrated that immediately after birth the newborn can see and has visual preferences, can hear and will turn his head toward a spoken voice, and will move in rhythm to his mother's voice. Mothers and fathers allowed to interact with their newborns in this time frame often exhibit characteristic behaviors, such as stroking the baby, first with fingertips, then with the palm, looking in the baby's eyes, and speaking to the baby in a high-pitched voice. Researchers have also found physical changes in the mother right after birth, such as hormonal increases triggered by the infant licking or sucking her nipples, and increased blood flow to her breasts when hearing the infant cry. Some scientists speculate that there are instinctual behaviors triggered in the mother in response to the infant immediately after birth that facilitate her bonding with the infant, and thus promote the infant's survival.

Research on the bonding process has been scrutinized. Detractors call attention to the often poor research design of early studies and reject bonding as a scientific fallacy thrust on women to make them feel that they must react to their infants in certain prescribed fashions. Some people have misinterpreted bonding to mean that if the early sensitive period is missed, they cannot become successful parents. Obviously, parents can form close attachments to infants they did not see at birth, either because of medical emergencies or because their children are adopted. Thus, early experience with the newborn is only one factor in the complex relations of parents to children.

Despite some problems with quantifying bonding as a scientific phenomenon, there is a wealth of anecdotal evidence on the positive effects of an after-birth bonding experience. Most hospitals are now much more sensitive to parents' desire to be with their newborn than in the past. Parents-to-be may wish to find out their hospital's policies regarding the period immediately after birth. Questions to ask may include: Will the mother be allowed to hold the baby immediately if there is no problem? If tests are needed, can they be delayed until after the first hour? What family members can be present at the birth? Can family members be present at a cesarean birth? Will the baby stay in the same room with the mother or be sent to a central nursery? Some hospitals reportedly score mothers on how well they seem to bond with their infants, allegedly to flag potential future **child abuse.** This in effect makes early and rapid bonding a test, with failure potentially criminal, and egregiously violates the spirit of the hospital reform that bonding research brought about. If a hospital admits to "testing" for bonding, parents may ask if they may decline the test, or if they can have access to the test results. Ideally, both the birth and the period immediately after should be handled according to the parents' wishes.

For Further Study

Books

Eyer, Diane E. *Mother-Infant Bonding: A Scientific Fiction.* New Haven, CT: Yale University Press, 1992.

Gaskin, Ina May. *Babies, Breastfeeding and Bonding.* South Hadley, MA: Bergin & Garvey, 1987.

Klaus, Marshall H., John H. Kennell, and Phyllis H. Klaus. *Bonding: Building the Foundations of Secure Attachment and Independence.* Reading, MA: Addison-Wesley, 1995.

—A. Woodward

Boredom

A state of weariness with, and disinterest in, life.

Everyone, at one time or another, feels bored. Children, however, may report boredom more frequently because they have not yet learned to alleviate it for themselves. The following essay describes children's sense of boredom at the major developmental stages.

Infants and toddlers

Infants and toddlers rarely experience boredom. Infants spend large blocks of time asleep and much of their waking time feeding. Toddlers have a nearly unlimited curiosity to explore a world that is still new to them. Infants and toddlers, furthermore, have not yet developed the cognitive ability to understand the concept of "having nothing to do."

Preschool and school-aged children

Preschool and school-aged children are fickle in their **attentions**. The child may be engrossed in an activity one minute and, seconds later, lose interest and complain of boredom. This common complaint of preschool and school-aged children can have a variety of meanings, according to psychologists.

Children may complain of boredom when they're anxious because of a change in their environment or schedule. A classic example is the end of the school year. While children have an initial feeling of euphoria at being "set free," many feel apprehensive about having nothing to do all summer. Despite what they say about hating to get up for school every day, children, like most people, crave structure and routine, at least to some extent.

Many psychologists say that it is important to let children try to come up with creative outlets for their anxiety on their own. This helps them realize they can occupy themselves, an ability they may have forgotten after nine months of following a school schedule. Children can also participate in organized group activities, such as a soccer league or bicycling club, which can fill large, empty blocks of time.

Sometimes complaints of boredom mean that the child wants the parent take a more direct interest in his or her life. As Dr. Stephanie Pratola told *Parents* magazine, "When kids feel stressed, they often want your undivided attention. Sit down and have a glass of milk together and let your daughter ramble on or spend a few extra minutes with her before bed." Often, some parental attention will satisfy the child, and she can then occupy herself.

Children may complain of boredom when they are frustrated at being unchallenged by their present activities. Often, children become bored with things that used to challenge them, even before they have achieved what adults might consider mastery. So, a child taking tennis lessons might achieve a level of play that adults may not think is very high, but he or she has lost interest in the game. Many children simply like to try many different things, rather than focusing on mastering a few specific tasks.

In rare instances, children over the age of 10 who repeatedly complain of having nothing to do might be suffering from a clinical condition such as **depression.** In young children, depression is almost always triggered by an emotional upheaval of some sort, such as a family move, death, or **divorce.** Depressed children may withdraw from formerly interesting activities and complain of boredom. The child may need to talk to a psychologist or parent about the factors that are causing the depression.

Adolescents

Boredom is most problematic during adolescence. Adolescents are in the process of defining themselves as being autonomous of their parents and different from the children they were. Activities they enjoyed when they were younger now feel like childish games, but they have not fully developed the interests that will dominate their lives as adults. It is an experimental and stressful time. Adolescents who find themselves unable to navigate the transition from childhood to adulthood sometimes retreat into depression or social pathologies, such as drug use or delinquency.

Boredom in adolescents can also be a sign of a lack of intellectual stimulation in school. More challenging schoolwork can prevent a talented adolescent from becoming bored with school. Boredom can also be effectively alleviated by directing a teen's energy toward creative outlets. Expressing oneself creatively is one of the best methods of coping with boredom and depression because these areas have the potential to seriously engage an adolescent's mind.

For Further Study

Books

Berry, Joy Wilt. *What to Do When Your Mom or Dad Says— "Don't Overdo with Video Games!"* Chicago: Children's Press, 1983 [juvenile literature].

Leckert, Bruce, with L. Weinberger. *Up from Boredom...Down from Fear.* New York: R. Marek, 1980.

Periodicals

Dembling, Sophia. "I'm Bored." *McCall's* 124, July 1997, pp. 103+.

Graham, Janet. "Is Boredom Good for Your Child?" *Working Mother* 18, July 1995, pp. 52+.

Israeloff, Roberta. "There's Nothing To Do," *Parents Magazine* 71, June 1996, pp. 52+.

Wester-Anderson, Joan. "Overcoming Life's Little Doldrums," *Current Health* 19, February 1993, pp. 4+.

 Bowel Disorders

Conditions affecting the small and large intestines.

Children are subject to a wide variety of bowel disorders, including obstructions and infections, as well as malabsorptive, inflammatory, and functional disorders. Causes range from genetic abnormalities to environmental factors such as diet, stress, and exposure to viruses and bacteria. The fully formed gastrointestinal tract is 12–15 ft (4–5 m) long at birth, but all of its components do not function maturely for several months. Intestinal problems resulting from **birth defects** are generally the first to be discovered, often manifesting themselves soon after birth.

Intestinal obstructions are a major type of bowel disorder. If left untreated, they cause malnutrition and other health problems. Some may lead to intestinal ruptures and result in peritonitis, a potentially life-threatening infection of the abdominal cavity. In pyloric stenosis, a common bowel obstruction, the muscle that surrounds the opening between the stomach and the duodenum (part of the small intestine) thickens and becomes stiff, blocking the passage of food to the intestines. The most characteristic symptom is abnormally forceful vomiting (known as projectile vomiting), usually following meals.

The vomiting causes weakness, malnutrition, **constipation,** and dehydration. Treatment consists of surgery to widen the obstructed passageway. Pyloric stenosis is relatively common, occurring in approximately one out of every 250 births and four times more often in boys than girls.

In atresia, another type of bowel obstruction, a portion of either the small or large intestine fails to open properly, impairing normal digestion. This condition is surgically corrected by removing the affected portion of the bowel. Hirschsprung's disease occurs when some of the nerve cells that regulate normal bowel activity are missing, causing a portion of the intestines to contract. This condition is also corrected by surgery. Yet another type of obstruction is intussusception, in which part of the small intestine folds onto itself, in an action that resembles the folding up of a telescope, with one section sliding over another. Intussusception, which occurs most often between the ages of 3–36 months, cuts off circulation in the intestine and can cause an infant to go into shock. It is often associated with an infection, injury, or other problem. It can sometimes be corrected with a special enema, although surgery may be necessary. Intestinal obstruction may also be caused by an inguinal hernia, which occurs when a weakness or opening in the abdominal wall allows part of the intestine to protrude into the groin.

Malabsorptive conditions are disorders in which food cannot pass properly from the small intestine to the rest of the body through the lymphatic or circulatory system. They may be caused by the absence of particular enzymes or by a variety of hereditary or acquired diseases. The most common malabsorptive conditions affecting infants and children in the United States are **cystic fibrosis** and **celiac sprue** disease. Cystic fibrosis, which also causes breathing difficulties and dehydration, hampers normal digestion by preventing the pancreas from functioning normally. Treatment includes replacement of missing pancreatic enzymes with a synthetic substitute and dietary measures to ensure adequate nutrition.

In celiac disease, the small intestine is damaged when the protein gluten (an ingredient of wheat, rye, and other grains) is consumed, preventing proper absorption of essential nutrients. Symptoms of this disorder—which usually appears between the ages of 8–24 months but can begin as late as adolescence—vary but usually include growth retardation, loss of appetite, and irritability. Other possible symptoms include abdominal bloating, **diarrhea,** constipation, vomiting, and excessive bruising. The primary treatment is adherence to a gluten-free diet supplemented, at least initially, by vitamins and minerals to correct the deficiencies caused by the disease. Other causes of malabsorption in children include lactose intolerance, liver disease, disorders of the immune system, milk protein intolerance, and infestations by parasites.

Inflammations of the bowel constitute another category of intestinal disorders. These disorders, collectively known as inflammatory bowel disease (IBD), include ulcerative colitis, Crohn's disease, and bacterial infections. Symptoms include abdominal pain, nausea, and loose stools or diarrhea, which may contain mucus, pus, or blood. As with other conditions that disturb normal intestinal functioning, inflammation of the bowel eventually results in malnutrition and impaired growth and development. In addition, blood loss from the bowel may result in **anemia.** In ulcerative colitis, the mucosal lining of the colon (large intestine) becomes inflamed.

With Crohn's disease, any part of the gastrointestinal tract can be affected, resulting in an inflammation that attacks the intestinal lining and extends deeply into the intestinal wall. The area most commonly affected is the lowest portion of the small intestine (called the terminal ileum), producing chronic abdominal pain. When Crohn's disease affects the colon, it causes diarrhea and severe cramping.

Another cause of intestinal inflammation is the bacterial infection shigellosis, or dysentery, which commonly strikes children between the ages of one and nine. The shigella bacteria are spread by contamination of food, excrement, and hands, and are also carried by flies. As in other forms of inflammatory bowel disease, the lining of the intestine becomes inflamed, causing diarrhea. In serious cases, dehydration may become severe, requiring immediate medical attention. Inflammatory bowel disease caused by infection is treated by administering antibiotics and restoring lost bodily fluids. In ulcerative colitis and Crohn's disease, which have no known treatable cause, anti-inflammatory medications, such as sulfasalazine and corticosteroids, are commonly prescribed. Severe cases may require hospitalization and intravenous feeding.

A bowel disorder experienced by many children is acute viral gastroenteritis, also called stomach or intestinal flu. The disorder is an intestinal infection caused by a virus which penetrates the intestine and damages its lining, interfering with digestion. Unlike bacterial infections, the first symptom of viral infection in the intestine is usually vomiting, which is then followed by diarrhea after one or two days. Other symptoms include appetite loss, abdominal cramps, and, in some cases, fever. Within three to five days, the infection generally runs its course. The primary treatment of gastroenteritis is administration of fluids to prevent dehydration. Breastfed babies with intestinal viruses can continue to nurse; bottle-fed babies should be switched to an oral rehydration product or other clear liquid until they recover. Infants

may temporarily develop lactose intolerance for up to several weeks following an intestinal virus. Viruses are transmitted by food and water, and by direct contact, especially in crowded environments such as schools, daycare centers, and hospitals.

In addition to viral and bacterial infections, bowel disorders also result from infection by parasites or worms. The three most common types are pinworms, roundworms, and hookworms. While people of all ages can be infected by parasites, young children are especially susceptible because of their greater exposure to dirt from playing outdoors, often barefoot, and their tendency to put fingers or other objects in their mouths. After entering the body via the mouth or skin, worms live and/or mature in the intestines and lay their eggs there. Symptoms of parasite infestation can include abdominal pain and distension, nausea, cramps, diarrhea, and loss of appetite. Worms are commonly treated with antihelminthic drugs. For roundworm or hookworm, only the affected person needs treatment; for pinworm, the victim's whole family should be treated.

Irritable bowel syndrome (IBS), a disorder commonly associated with adults, also occurs in children and adolescents. IBS, often called recurrent abdominal pain (RAP), is distinguished from most other bowel problems by the fact that it is caused by an irregularity in digestive functioning, rather than an abnormality in the structure of the bowel itself. Usually in response to stress, the muscles of the colon contract irregularly, interfering with the normal passage of food through the intestine. It may either travel too slowly, causing constipation, or too quickly, causing diarrhea. Persons with IBS often experience both these symptoms regularly, as well as abdominal pain, gas, and bloating.

An estimated 2.5 million children in the United States suffer from irritable bowel syndrome. Symptoms most often begin around the age of 10, although they can start as early as five years of age. The disorder tends to run in families; about 75% of children with IBS have at least one parent or sibling with gastrointestinal problems. Symptoms often disappear in early adolescence and return in the later teen years. Irritable bowel syndrome is a chronic condition that can be managed but not cured. Treatment consists of adding fiber to the diet, both through foods and fiber supplements, and taking measures to reduce and manage stress.

For Further Study

Books

Janowitz, Henry D. *Your Gut Feelings: A Complete Guide to Living Better with Intestinal Problems.* New York: Oxford Univ. Press, 1994.

Scala, James. *Eating Right for a Bad Gut: The Complete Nutritional Guide to Ileitis, Colitis, Crohn's Disease, and Inflammatory Bowel Disease.* New York: Plume, 1992.

Shimberg, Elaine Fantle. *Relief from IBS.* New York: M. Evans, 1988.

Thompson, W. Grant. *The Angry Gut: Coping with Colitis and Crohn's Disease.* New York: Plenum Press, 1993.

Organizations

Crohn's Colitis Foundation of America, Inc.
   Address: 444 Park Avenue South
   New York, NY 10016
   Telephone: (212) 685-3440
Gluten Intolerance Group of North America
   Address: Box 23053
   Seattle, WA 98102-0353
   Telephone: (206) 325-6980
National Digestive Diseases Information Clearinghouse
   Address: Box NDDIC
   9000 Rockville Pike
   Bethesda, MD 20892
   Telephone: (301) 468-6344

Bowlby, John (1907–1990)

English psychiatrist best known for his studies of the effect of maternal deprivation on a child's mental health and emotional development.

The interaction between children and their families is the main focus of British psychiatrist John Bowlby's work. In fact, his study "Maternal Care and Mental Health," published by the World Health Organization (WHO) in 1952, sparked interest and controversy that continues even today. In his research, Bowlby studied children confined to institutions and found them deficient in emotional and personality development. Bowlby's conclusion that maternal deprivation had caused the deficiencies stimulated future studies of infant-mother bonding and the effects of early separation.

John Bowlby was born in 1907, the son of a London surgeon. Following in his father's footsteps, John studied medicine along with psychology at Cambridge and in 1933 completed his medical training in London. He spent five years as an army psychiatrist before beginning an extended tenure at the Tavistock Clinic and the Tavistock Institute of Human Relations in 1946. Serving as a clinician, teacher, and researcher, Bowlby concentrated on child and family psychiatry. His particular fascination with the effects of parents on children stimulated much of his research and led to the renowned WHO report.

It would be difficult to overlook the impact that John Bowlby has had on the field of child development research, especially in the area of **attachment** relations and the social-emotional development of the young child. His 1952 report, for example, led to extensive changes in how children were treated in hospitals and institutions. It is also important to understand how his work departs from traditional psychoanalytic thought and method, although both approaches share an emphasis on early development and the importance of the mother-child relationship.

Bowlby's accounts of the importance of healthy, secure, sustaining attachments in human development are based on observations of children rather than on the retrospective accounts of adult patients. His epic three-volume series, *Attachment, Separation, and Loss,* develops his observations of instinctive attachment behaviors across species, and the role of these behaviors and the mother-offspring relationship in growth and survival, into a theory of attachment and its place in development. According to Bowlby, when attachment behaviors are nurtured by the caregiver, the child develops a sense of security from which exploration of the world and internalization of a positive sense of self can proceed. Rejecting or ambivalent caregivers, on the other hand, provoke insecurity in the child.

How is attachment displayed? Infants demonstrate attachment behaviors, such as seeking and maintaining proximity to the mother, when they are distressed or threatened. Secure attachments are evidenced in the mother's ability to calm her infant and to diminish the threat of external stimuli by her presence. As the child's relationship with his or her mother develops into "a secure base," that child is able to leave the mother and explore the environment, knowing that the mother will be available should that environment become threatening.

Bowlby argues that when the child is separated from the attachment figure, intimate emotional bonds and the associated sense of security are strained and may lead to deviations from normal personality development. The disruption of the attachment system through **death,** and the resulting **depression** and mourning, are even more serious manifestations of the critical role of attachments throughout development.

Many of Bowlby's ideas have spawned lines of research. **Mary Ainsworth** has investigated attachment between mothers and infants cross-culturally; **Robert Hinde** has studied attachments in non-human primates; and Colin Murray Parkes has studied the role of attachments in adult relationships. Numerous other researchers have integrated the concept of attachment into their work, resulting in an enormous, eclectic, and evolving collection of studies and findings.

For Further Study

Books

Bowlby, John. *Attachment and Loss. Vol. 1: Attachment.* New York: Basic Books, 1969.

————. *Attachment and Loss. Vol. 2: Separation: Anxiety and Anger.* New York: Basic Books, 1973.

————. *Attachment and Loss. Vol. 3: Loss: Sadness and Depression.* New York: Basic Books, 1980.

————. *A Secure Base: Parent-Child Attachment and Healthy Human Development.* New York: Basic Books, 1988.

Parkes, C.M., and J. Stevenson-Hinde, eds. *The Place of Attachment in Human Behavior.* New York: Basic Books, 1982.

—Doreen Arcus, Ph.D.
University of Massachusetts Lowell

Brain

Part of the central nervous system located in the skull. Controls mental and physical actions of the organism.

The brain, with the spinal cord and network of nerves, controls information flow throughout the body, voluntary actions, such as walking, reading, and talking, and involuntary reactions, such as breathing and heartbeat. The human brain is a soft, shiny, grayish white, mushroom-shaped structure. Encased within the skull, the brain of an average adult weight about 3 lb (1.4 kg). At birth, the average human infant's brain weighs 13.7 oz (390 g); by age 15, the brain has nearly reached full adult size. The brain is protected by the skull and by a three-layer membrane called the meninges. Many bright red arteries and bluish veins on the surface of the brain penetrate inward. Glucose, oxygen, and certain ions pass easily from the blood into the brain, whereas other substances, such as antibiotics, do not. The four principal sections of the human brain are the brain stem, the diencephalon, the cerebrum, and the cerebellum.

The brain stem

The brain stem connects the brain with the spinal cord. All the messages that are transmitted between the brain and spinal cord pass through the medulla—a part of the brain stem—via fibers. The fibers on the right side of the medulla cross to the left and those on the left cross to the right. As a result, each side of the brain controls the opposite side of the body. The medulla also controls the heartbeat, the rate of breathing, and the diameter of the blood vessels and helps to coordinate swallowing, vomiting, hiccupping, coughing, and sneezing. Another component of the brain stem is the pons (meaning bridge). It conducts messages between the spinal cord and the rest of the brain, and between the different parts of the brain.

Conveying impulses between the cerebral cortex, the pons, and the spinal cord is a section of the brain stem known as the midbrain, which also contains visual and audio reflex centers involving the movement of the eyeballs and head.

Twelve pairs of cranial nerves originate in the underside of the brain, mostly from the brain stem. They leave the skull through openings and extend as peripheral nerves to their destinations. Among these cranial nerves are the olfactory nerves that bring messages about smell and the optic nerves that conduct visual information.

The diencephalon

The diencephalon lies above the brain stem and embodies the thalamus and hypothalamus. The thalamus is an important relay station for sensory information, interpreting sensations of sound, smell, taste, pain, pressure, temperature, and touch; the thalamus also regulates some emotions and memory. The hypothalamus controls a number of body functions, such as heartbeat rate and digestion, and helps regulate the endocrine system and normal body temperature. The hypothalamus interprets hunger and thirst, and it helps regulate sleep, anger and aggression.

The cerebrum

The cerebrum constitutes nearly 90% of the brain's weight. Specific areas of the cerebrum interpret sensory impulses. For example, spoken and written language are transmitted to a part of the cerebrum called Wernicke's area where meaning is extracted. Motor areas of the cerebrum control muscle movements. Broca's area translates thoughts into speech, and coordinates the muscles needed for speaking. Impulses from other motor areas direct hand muscles for writing and eye muscles for physical movement necessary for reading. The cerebrum is divided into two hemispheres—left and right. In general, the left half of the brain controls the right side of the body, and vice versa. For most right-handed people (and many left-handed people as well), the left half of the brain is dominant. By studying patients whose corpus callosum had been destroyed, scientists realized that differences existed between the left and right sides of the cerebral cortex. The left side of the brain functions mainly in speech, logic, writing, and arithmetic. The right side of the brain, on the other hand, is more concerned with imagination, art, symbols, and spatial relations.

The cerebrum's outer layer, the cerebral cortex, is composed of gray matter made up of nerve cell bodies. The cerebral cortex is about 0.08 in (2 mm) thick and its surface area is about 5 sq ft (0.5 sq m)—around half the size of an office desk. White matter, composed of nerve fibers covered with myelin sheaths, lies beneath the gray matter. During embryonic development, the gray matter grows faster than the white matter and folds on itself, giving the brain its characteristic wrinkly appearance. The folds are called convolutions or gyri, and the grooves between them are known as sulci.

A deep fissure separates the cerebrum into a left and right hemisphere, with the corpus callosum, a large bundle of fibers, connecting the two.

The cerebellum

The cerebellum is located below the cerebrum and behind the brain stem. It is butterfly-shaped, with the "wings" known as the cerebellar hemispheres. The cerebellum controls many subconscious activities, such as balance and muscular coordination. Disorders related to damage of the cerebellum are ataxia (problems with coordination), dysarthria (unclear speech resulting from problems controlling the muscles used in speaking), and nystagmus (uncontrollable jerking of the eyeballs). A brain tumor that is relatively common in children known as medullablastoma grows in the cerebellum.

Studying the brain

Researchers have discovered that neurons carry information through the nervous system in the form of brief electrical impulses called action potentials. When an impulse reaches the end of an axon, neurotransmitters are released at junctions called synapses. The neurotransmitters are chemicals that bind to receptors on the receiving neurons, triggering the continuation of the impulse. Fifty different neurotransmitters have been discovered since the first one was identified in 1920. By studying the chemical effects of neurotransmitters in the brain, scientists are developing treatments for mental disorders and are learning more about how drugs affect the brain.

Scientists once believed that brain cells do not regenerate, thereby making brain injuries and brain diseases untreatable. Since the late 1990s, researchers have been testing treatment for such patients with neuron transplants, introducing nerve tissue into the brain. They have also been studying substances, such as nerve growth factor (NGF), that someday could be used to help regrow nerve tissue.

Technology provides useful tools for researching the brain and helping patients with brain disorders. An electroencephalogram (EEG) is a record of brain waves, electrical activity generated in the brain. An EEG is obtained by positioning electrodes on the head and amplifying the waves with an electroencephalograph and is valuable in diagnosing brain diseases such as epilepsy and tumors.

Scientists use three other techniques to study and understand the brain and diagnose disorders:

(1) Magnetic resonance imaging (MRI) uses a magnetic field to display the living brain at various depths as if in slices.

(2) Positron emission tomography (PET) results in color images of the brain displayed on the screen of a monitor. During this test, a technician injects a small amount of a substance, such as glucose, that is marked with a radioactive tag. The marked substance shows where glucose is consumed in the brain. PET is used to study the chemistry and activity of the normal brain and to diagnose abnormalities such as tumors.

(3) Magnetoencephalography (MEG) measures the electromagnetic fields created between neurons as electrochemical information is passed along. When under the machine, if the subject is told, "wiggle your toes," the readout is an instant picture of the brain at work. Concentric colored rings appear on the computer screen that pinpoint the brain signals even before the toes are actually wiggled.

Using an MRI along with MEG, physicians and scientists can look into the brain without using surgery. They foresee that these techniques could help paralysis victims move by supplying information on how to stimulate their muscles or indicating the signals needed to control an artificial limb.

For Further Study

Books

Bear, Mark F., Barry W. Connors, and Michael A. Paradiso. *Neuroscience: Exploring the Brain.* Baltimore: Williams & Wilkins, 1996.

Burstein, John. *The Mind by Slim Goodbody.* Minneapolis, MN: Fairview Press, 1996.

Carey, Joseph, ed. *Brain Facts.* Washington, D.C.: Society for Neuroscience, 1993.

Greenfield, Susan A. ed. *The Human Mind Explained: An Owner's Guide to the Mysteries of the Mind.* New York: Henry Holt, 1996.

Howard, Pierce J. *The Owner's Manual for the Brain: Everyday Applications from Mind-Brain Research.* Austin, TX: Leornian Press, 1994.

Jackson, Carolyn, ed. *How Things Work: The Brain.* Alexandria, VA: Time–Life Books, 1990.

Audiovisual recordings

The Mind. Alexandria, VA: PBS Video, 1988.
(Series of nine 1-hour videocassettes.)

The Nature of the Nerve Impulse. Films for the Humanities and Sciences, 1994–95.
(Videocassette.)

Brazelton Neonatal Test

One of the most extensive techniques available for assessment of newborns.

Developed by psychologist **T. Berry Brazelton** (1918–) in 1979, the Brazelton Neonatal Test is also known as the Neonatal Behavioral Assessment Scale (NBAS), or Brazelton Neonatal Behavioral Assessment Scale (BNBAS). The test is administered when an infant is three days old and again a few days later to check the accuracy of the initial assessment. It is useful not only for assessing an infant's status and detecting any neurological impairment but also as a way for parents to learn more about their newborns and become more effective in aiding their development. Examiners evaluate 20 different reflexes and record the newborn's responses to 26 stimuli and situations including lights, the sound of a rattle, and cuddling. Also assessed are capacities such as attention; orientation to face and voice; ability to be soothed and comforted; smoothness of transitions from one state to another (from crying to alertness, for example); and coordination of motor responses. The NBAS has been used in research to show variance among newborns. In addition, long-term studies that follow one infant from **birth** to preschool age have shown that many traits of the newborn remain stable throughout early childhood. Thus, the Brazelton test has enhanced appreciation by both parents and professionals of each infant as a unique individual. In addition, by watching a skilled tester work with a newborn, parents can learn a great deal about their babies and about how to interact with them.

For Further Study

Books

Brazelton, T. Berry. *Going to the Doctor.* Reading, MA: Addison-Wesley, 1996.

McCullough, Virginia. *Testing and Your Child: What You Should Know About 150 of the Most Common Medical, Educational, and Psychological Tests.* New York: Plume, 1992.

Walsh, W. Bruce, and Nancy E. Betz. *Tests and Assessment.* 2nd ed. Englewood Cliffs, NJ: Prentice Hall, 1990.

Periodicals

Kosova, Weston. "Touchpoints." *Newsweek* 129, Spring-Summer 1997, p. 22.

Brazelton, T. Berry (1918–)

Well-known pediatrician, writer, researcher, and educator.

Like Dr. **Benjamin Spock** (1903–) before him, T. Berry Brazelton has earned a nationwide reputation as a trusted expert on child care, reaching a mass audience through books, personal appearances, newspaper columns, videos, and a cable-TV program. His research on infant behavior and development led him to formulate the Neonatal Behavioral Assessment Scale (NBAS), a series of clinical tests used in hospitals worldwide. Brazelton's efforts on behalf of children have also been extended to

Pediatrician T. Berry Brazelton

the public policy arena through congressional appearances and lobbying efforts.

Thomas Berry Brazelton II was born in Waco, Texas, in 1918. By the sixth grade he had decided on a career in pediatrics. He earned his undergraduate degree from Princeton in 1940 and his M.D. from Columbia in 1943. He remained there another year as an intern and then served for a year in the Naval Reserves. His residency was served at Massachusetts General Hospital in Boston, where he completed an additional residency in child psychiatry at the James Jackson Putnam Children's Center in Roxbury. Brazelton opened his own private practice in Cambridge, Massachusetts, in 1950 and became an instructor at Harvard Medical School the following year. He also began research on newborns, toddlers, and parents with the goal of helping parents better understand and interact with their children. Among other areas, he has focused on individual differences among newborns; parent-infant attachment during the first four months of life; and the effects of early intervention on at-risk infants. Based on his research, Brazelton developed the NBAS, first published in 1973. The test, popularly called "the Brazelton," uses visual, auditory, and tactile stimuli to assess how newborns respond to their environment. It is widely used both clinically and as a research tool.

Brazelton's interest in shifting the focus of pediatric study from disease to infant development led him to found the Child Development Unit at Children's Hospital Medical Center in Boston in 1972, together with Edward Tronick. The unit provides medical students and other professionals the opportunity to research early child development and also prepare for clinical work with parents and children. Brazelton's first book, *Infants and Mothers* (1969), has sold more than a million copies and has been translated into 18 languages. It has been followed by a dozen more, including *Toddlers and Parents* (1974), *On Becoming a Family* (1981), and *Working and Caring* (1984), as well as a series of videotapes on child development. Brazelton also writes a syndicated newspaper advice column and since 1984 has had his own program, *What Every Baby Knows,* on cable television.

—Rosalie Wieder

Breast Development

Breast development is one of the first visible signs of the onset of puberty in girls. It usually begins between the ages of eight and thirteen, shortly before the growth spurt.

Female breast development is measured in stages based on contour (shape), not size. There are five distinct stages of breast development, called Tanner stages: prepubertal—no signs of breast development; early breast budding; elevation of the breast and areola (the pigmented ring surrounding the nipple); projection of the areola and nipple above the breast itself; mature breasts—areola flattened to the level of the breast with only the nipple projecting.

Breast size is not related to sexuality, femininity, or fertility. Nonsurgical means of increasing the size of small breasts (such as creams, pumps, and massage techniques) do not work. Hormonal medications, including oral contraceptives, sometimes cause an increase in breast tissue. **Exercise** can increase the size of chest muscles, but not the breast itself. Although breast size can be increased surgically, serious health problems have been reported in connection with the use of silicone implants.

Abnormally large breasts can result when developing breast tissue is unusually sensitive to estrogen. Very large breasts can lead to a number of problems ranging from neck and shoulder pain to extreme self-consciousness. If such enlargement is physically or psychologically debilitating, a portion of the breast tissue may be surgically removed even before the end of **puberty**.

Asymmetry

In many girls, one breast may develop earlier or faster than the other or one breast may seem firmer or more tender than the other. This asymmetry is most pronounced when the breasts are growing rapidly. In most cases, however, the breasts will resemble each other when they are mature.

Discharge, pain, and masses

The secretion of breast milk is called *galactorrhea*. Milk secretion not related to childbirth or nursing (or occasionally **abortion** or miscarriage) requires medical attention. Galactorrhea accompanied by **amenorrhea** (absence of menstrual periods) could signal the presence of a pituitary tumor.

Breast pain is a normal part of the menstrual cycle and usually subsides as a menstrual period ends. Breast pain or tenderness not associated with menstruation, however, should be reported to a physician. In addition, all adolescent women should learn how to examine their own breasts. Breast examination techniques can be learned from a nurse, a doctor, or even a pamphlet. Although breast cancer is rare in adolescents (less than 1% of lumps discovered in teenagers' breasts are cancerous), any lump that persists for more than a month should be reported to a doctor. One in ten adult women will eventually develop breast cancer, so establishing the habit of monthly self-examination during adolescence may prove lifesaving later on.

For Further Study

Books

Love, Susan M. *Dr. Susan Love's Breast Book*. Reading, MA: Addison-Wesley, 1995.

McCoy, Kathy, and Charles Wibbelsman. *The New Teenage Body Book*. New York: The Body Press (Putnam), 1992.

Organizations

American Cancer Society
Address: 1599 Clifton Road NE
Atlanta, GA 30329
Telephone: 1-800-ACS-2345
(Pamphlets on monthly breast self-examination)

—Gail B. Slap, M.D.
University of Pennsylvania School of Medicine

Breast Enlargement in Adolescent Boys

Male breast enlargement (gynecomastia) is a normal condition that occurs during puberty in more than 60% of boys.

Prevalence

Aproximately 20% of 10½-year-old boys and more than 60% of 14-year-old boys experience gynecomastia (breast enlargement). In addition to swollen breasts, the area around the nipples may feel tender or lumpy. The appearance of gynecomastia can be distressing because it appears at a time when boys are concerned about their sexual identity and development. In 70% of boys, however, it disappears within a year; in less than 8% does it persist for more than two years. Gynecomastia does not indicate disease in most boys, and there is no link between gynecomastia and breast cancer in males.

Cause

It is not clear what causes gynecomastia, but most likely it is related to normal hormonal changes that occur during **puberty**. Levels of both male and female **hormones** increase in boys and girls during puberty. As the levels of these hormones adjust, some female characteristics (such as gynecomastia) may appear in boys, and some male characteristics (such as increased body hair) may appear in girls.

In some cases, gynecomastia is related to medication. If an adolescent boy with gynecomastia is taking medication, or if gynecomastia appears before puberty begins or after it has been completed, a doctor should be consulted.

In some relatively rare instances, gynecomastia may be the result of a chromosomal abnormality, where the male has one or more extra X chromosomes. This condition is known as **Klinefelter's syndrome.**

For Further Study

Books

McCoy, Kathy, and Charles Wibbelsman. *The New Teenage Body Book*. New York: The Body Press (Putnam), 1992.

—Gail B. Slap, M.D.
University of Pennsylvania School of Medicine

Breastfeeding

Also known as nursing, the practice of providing an infant or toddler with nutrition from mother's milk via direct sucking on the breast.

Breastfeeding has nutritional, immunological, and developmental benefits for the child, as well as physiological and emotional benefits for the mother. Breast milk is a unique combination of fats, sugars, minerals, proteins, vitamins, and enzymes that lowers an infant's risk of infections, including diarrheal and urinary tract infections and pneumonia. It has been shown to lower infant susceptibility to atopic diseases, **diabetes,** the **herpes simplex** virus, lymphomas, Crohn's disease, and gastrointestinal problems. Breastfed babies have higher IQs than their bottle-fed counterparts. Women who

BREASTFEEDING PRACTICES WORLDWIDE		
Country	Percent of mothers who	
	start breast-feeding	continue breastfeed-ing for 6 months or longer
Sweden	98	53
Norway	98	50
Poland	93	10
Canada	80	24
Netherlands	68	25
Britain	63	21
United States	57	20

Source: Baby Milk Action, Cambridge, England; Center for Breastfeeding Information, Schaumburg, Illinois, as quoted in *Parenting* (April 1997).

breastfeed recover from childbirth more quickly, return to pre-pregnancy weight sooner, and are better able to space their natural born children due to the suppression of ovulation during lactation. The act of breastfeeding is relaxing for the mother since the hormone prolactin, which is a relaxant, is released when the infant nurses. Women who breastfeed are also less likely to develop pre-menopausal breast **cancer.**

In the United States, very few mothers breastfed their babies from the 1950s to the early 1970s. During the 1970s the natural health movement caused an increase in the number of mothers who breastfed, from 20% in 1970 to 62% in 1982. That figure declined until the early 1990s, when only about half of U.S. mothers breastfed their babies, and only 20% were breastfeeding after six months. Since the late 1980s, both the World Health Organization and UNICEF have been recommending breastfeeding for at least two years. As seen in the accompanying table, this contrasts significantly with practices in European countries.

Currently, all major U.S. organizations promoting children's health agree that breastfeeding provides the best nourishment for the infant. In 1992 the **American Academy of Pediatrics** issued a statement recommending breastfeeding infants through the first year. During the mid-1990s the U.S. Department of Health and Human

Services was working to increase post-partum breastfeeding to 75% and breastfeeding after six months to 50%. To help promote breastfeeding, some states, including California and Florida, have passed laws allowing breastfeeding in public.

The primary deterrents to breastfeeding are infant formula promotion by the media and through hospital samples, and physician, health care provider, and patient misinformation about the benefits of breastfeeding. A national survey found that 25% of physicians did not know the superior nutritive value of breast milk, and 33% were unaware of the immunological benefits of breastfeeding. In individual cases, a new mother's reluctance to breastfeed may derive from the fact that she may not have been taught to breastfeed by her own mother, who had children in an era when breastfeeding was unpopular. While it is a natural practice, breastfeeding is not an instinctive skill, and both mother and infant need to learn how to nurse properly. If breastfeeding is unsuccessful, the baby becomes frustrated and the mother anxious, which worsens the condition. Many mothers give up, thinking they have insufficient milk, a condition that is extremely rare. Most breastfeeding problems involve the frequency and/or efficiency of feedings. A professional lactation consultant can provide advice for mothers who are planning to breastfeed or who are having problems with breastfeeding.

Elements of feeding

Two hormones control breastfeeding: prolactin, which causes the production of milk in the breasts, and oxytocin, which causes the milk ejection or let-down reflex that squirts milk out of the breast. Stimulation of the nipple by the baby's sucking causes the release of both hormones. Breastfeeding should begin as soon as possible after birth, preferably within an hour. For the first three to five days, the breasts will not emit milk but *colostrum*, a thick yellowish fluid high in protein.

Initially, the baby will suck rapidly at the outer end of the nipple. This causes the release of oxytocin and a tingling sensation in the nipple before the milk is ejected. The nipple will elongate and harden, allowing the baby to "latch-on," or pull the rest of the nipple and the entire aureola (the pink or brown area surrounding the nipple) into the mouth against the baby's palate. The baby will then initiate the slower suck-and-swallow rhythm that constitutes nutritive sucking, or milk intake. In addition to the child's active and noisy sucking, signs that the let-down reflex is working are milk dripping from the other breast and uterine contractions.

Feeding sessions should be approximately 20–30 minutes long, with 8 to 10 minutes on the first breast, a change of activity to keep the baby awake, and then 10–15 minutes on the other breast. Feedings should occur about every three hours during the day and every four hours at night during the first six months, equaling 8–12 feedings per 24 hours. The baby should generally be fed on demand, though not more often than every two hours. After a breastfeeding pattern is established, the mother's milk will flow whenever it is about time for a feeding, or when she hears a baby crying.

There are three common breastfeeding positions. Alternating between positions ensures that all milk is drained from the breasts. In the traditional position the mother sits in a comfortable chair with the baby in one arm, the baby's head in the crook of her arm and buttocks in her hand. In the football hold position the mother sits on a sofa or bed with the baby lying next to her, tucked under her arm as in holding a football. In the lying down position mother and baby lie face to face, with one arm under the mother's head and her other arm holding the breast.

Rubber teats or **pacifiers** should not be used within the first few weeks to ensure the baby does not confuse it with the mother's nipple. Initially, babies swallow very little air, and burping is usually not required. (Breastfed babies generally swallow less air than bottle-fed ones.) If burping is necessary, it should be done before switching breasts.

It is normal for a breastfed baby to lose 10% of his birth weight during the first two weeks of life. Thereafter, the baby should gain about an ounce per day, or between one-half and two ounces per day. Signs of adequate nutrition are frequent wet diapers (minimum 6 diapers per day) and loose, yellowish stools. Infrequent urination and dark green stools indicate inadequate intake of milk, and the baby should be taken to the doctor.

If the mother's milk is not expressed, her breasts will become engorged and lactation will stop, even if sucking is still occurring. Milk production can be maintained during breastfeeding problems by artificial expression of the milk using a manual, battery-powered, or electric pump immediately after feedings. The expressed milk will keep the baby healthy and happy while adjustments are being made. Instead of a bottle, a feeding tube or small medicine cup should be used for any supplements so that the baby does not experience problems returning to the breast. (Bottles encourage a passive, not active type of sucking as breastfeeding requires.)

The physician should be contacted whenever the baby is not feeding adequately, sleeps longer than four to five hours per night without feeding during the first two to three weeks, has fewer than six wet diapers per day, has a pale, blue, or yellow complexion, or has a temperature higher than 100.5°F (38°C).

BREASTFEEDING PROBLEMS

The most common problems are caused by poor latching-on, poor milk let-down, and ineffective sucking-and-swallowing.

Latching-On. If the nipple is flat or inverted the baby may not be able to grasp and pull the entire aureola into the mouth. Repositioning is essential until the baby latches on. The football hold is a good position for women with flat nipples. Plastic breast shells can be worn for several hours daily to correct this problem. Nipple shields (Mexican hats) should not be used, as they reduce stimulation to the nipple.

Let-Down. The most common barrier to let-down is the mother's anxiety. Breastfeeding should be done in a relaxing environment. The mother can listen to music and rock, sing to, or stroke the baby. Family support for the practice of breastfeeding and reassurance that the mother and baby will eventually master the process are very important to the success of a new breastfeeder. Sometimes a synthetic form of the hormone oxytocin in the form of a nasal spray will be prescribed by the doctor for temporary failure of let-down.

Ineffective Suck-and-Swallow. If the baby is sucking but not holding the entire aureola inside the mouth and flat against the palate, or is sucking but not swallowing, he or she is not taking in milk. If the baby has not successfully received milk from the breast, he or she may have adjusted to the lack of milk and is only using the breast as a pacifier. It is not recommended to allow a habit of non-nutritive sucking to develop. The baby who sucks while sleeping should be kept awake at the breast by rubbing the head or hands, scratching the soles of the feet, or removing a layer of clothing.

Milk storage

Working mothers with infants under four months should breastfeed as much as possible during off hours, and artificially express milk during the day on a simulated feeding schedule. Studies show these increase production of prolactin, which is necessary for continued milk production. After four months pumping will only need to be done about twice a day. Milk should be pumped and stored under sanitary conditions. Pumping directly into the storage container lessens the chance of contamination. Freshly pumped breast milk will last for several hours at room temperature, and may be kept in a refrigerator for up to 72 hours. Milk may also be stored in a regular freezer for six months or in a deep freezer for 12 months.

Drugs

While every substance the mother ingests will determine the composition of breast milk, many over-the-counter drugs taken in small amounts will not harm the breastfeeding baby. The newer forms of **antidepressants,** such as Prozac and Zoloft, have been found to have no adverse effects over a 12-month period on the breastfeeding baby. Because older types of antidepressants, such as MAO inhibitors, have many side effects on the patient, they may be expected to have adverse effects on a breastfeeding baby. The advantages and disadvantages of taking a particular prescription drug must be weighed against any potential adverse effects on the child. A life-supporting drug may have such a negative effect that breastfeeding is not advised. Ingestion of illegal drugs while breastfeeding endangers the child's health and can lead to the baby's death.

For Further Study

Books

Dana, N., and A. Price. *Successful Breastfeeding: A Practical Guide for Nursing Mothers.* New York: Meadowbrook, 1985.

Division of Maternal and Child Health. *Surgeon General's Workshop on Breastfeeding and Human Lactation.* Washington, DC: Bureau of Health Care Delivery and Assistance, 1991.

Eiger, M. S., and S. W. Olds. *The Complete Book of Breastfeeding,* rev. ed. New York: Bantam, 1985.

Eisenberg, A., et al. *What to Expect the First Year.* New York: Workman Pub., 1989.

Huggins, K. *The Nursing Mother's Companion,* rev. ed. Boston: Harvard Common, 1990.

La Leche League International Staff, eds. *The Womanly Art of Breastfeeding: Thirty-Fifth Anniversary Edition.* New York: NAL-Dutton, 1991.

Organizations

International Childbirth Education Association
Address: Box 20048
Minneapolis, MN 55420
Telephone: (612) 854-8660

International Lactation Consultant Association (ILCA)
Address: 200 N. Michigan Avenue, Suite 300
Chicago, IL 60601
Telephone: (312) 541-1710

La Leche League International
Address: Box 1209, 9616 Minneapolis Avenue
Franklin Park, IL 60131
Telephone: toll-free (800) LA LECHE

Brigance Diagnostic Inventory of Early Development

Evaluates the development of children up to age seven.

The Brigance Diagnostic Inventory of Early Development is an individually administered test that evaluates the development of children up to age seven. It is a popular readiness and screening test and is often used to identify children with developmental delays, aid in designing individualized educational programs for them, and monitor progress over a period of time. Altogether, the 200-item test takes between 30 and 60 minutes to administer, depending on how many of its 11 sections are used with a particular child. Questions are answered by either oral or written response or by pointing to pictures. Two other components of the test are direct observation of the child by the examiner and an interview with the parents to gather additional information about the child's skills. The test evaluates the following skills, in the order in which they are developed: preambulatory, **gross motor, fine motor**, prespeech, speech and language, general knowledge, readiness, basic **reading**, manuscript writing, and basic math skills. Test results are expressed as developmental ages. They can be entered in an individual record book and charted over time as the child's development is monitored.

For Further Study

Books

Cohen, Libby G., and Loraine J. Spenciner. *Assessment of Young Children.* New York: Longman, 1994.

Culbertson, Jan L., and Diane J. Willis, eds. *Testing Young Children: A Reference Guide for Developmental, Psychoeducational, and Psychosocial Assessments.* Austin, TX: PRO-ED, Inc., 1993.

McCullough, Virginia. *Testing and Your Child: What You Should Know About 150 of the Most Common Medical, Educational, and Psychological Tests.* New York: Plume, 1992.

Bronchitis

A lower respiratory inflammation affecting the windpipe (trachea) and bronchial tubes.

Bronchitis can be caused by viruses, bacteria, or **allergies,** and it occurs in both acute and chronic forms, the former usually caused by a virus and the latter by allergies. Acute bronchitis often accompanies upper respiratory tract infections associated with cold viruses that spread to the bronchial tubes, causing inflammation and producing excess secretions. More rarely, bronchitis may be associated with Bordetella pertussis (whooping cough) or mycoplasma (parasitic) infections. In some cases, the larynx, or voice box, is also affected, a condition known as laryngotracheobronchitis.

Acute bronchitis is a common childhood disease, especially before the age of four. It occurs more often in boys than girls and is most prevalent in wintertime. Generally, it is preceded by the upper respiratory symptoms of a cold, including a runny nose, sneezing, congestion, and a low fever. Bronchitis begins with a dry, hacking cough that usually lasts two or three days and then turns into a loose cough that produces thick mucous or sputum. Breathing through the congested airway often produces a wheezing sound and may also cause pain below the sternum, or breastbone. These symptoms may be accompanied by fatigue and appetite loss, but the latter only persist for two or three days, while the respiratory symptoms may last as long as a week or more. The cough usually gets worse at night, interfering with the child's sleep.

Treatment of bronchitis caused by a cold virus consists of controlling the symptoms, since there is no medication that is effective in treating the virus itself. A suppressant such as dextromethorphan may be used for a dry, hacking cough. However, a child with a loose cough needs to be able to expel mucous from clogged airways, and expectorants, such as guaifenesin, aid in this process by thinning the sputum. (However, expectorants are not recommended for children under two years of age.) Cough secretions can also be thinned by drinking plenty of fluids and using a humidifier. Although loose coughs should not be completely suppressed, some amount of cough suppression may be necessary to help a sick child sleep or prevent the excessive throat irritation caused by non-stop coughing. It is important for a child with bronchitis to get adequate rest in order to help the body fight the infection.

A physician should be contacted for any cough that persists longer than four or five days without improvement, or any cough associated with painful breathing. In addition to bronchitis, these may also be symptoms of two other, potentially more serious conditions: pneumonia and bronchiolitis, an inflammation of the bronchioles (small airways from the bronchial tubes to the air sacs of the lungs). If the cause of the bronchial inflammation can be identified as a bacterial infection, **antibiotics** such as erythromycin can be prescribed. Sometimes medicines called bronchodilators are prescribed to open congested airways and stop wheezing, but care should be taken when using them with children because they have a tendency to speed up the heart rate.

In chronic bronchitis, the symptoms of acute bronchitis persist over an extended period of time (more than three or four weeks) or recur frequently. Chronic bronchitis in children is generally caused by allergies (in adults it is often caused by smoking or by repeated attacks of acute bronchitis). Like acute bronchitis, chronic bronchitis is worse in winter, and it may be aggravated by viral and bacterial infections. While the cough can be controlled with suppressants, expectorants, and bronchodilators, the most effective treatment of chronic bronchitis in children is to identify any allergies that may be causing it and treat them by avoiding known allergens (things that trigger an allergic reaction—either foods or substances in the environment). Other treatments include antihistamines to control the body's reaction to allergens and, in the case of certain moderate to severe allergies, a program of **desensitization,** or allergy shots.

For children who are prone to bronchitis, there are measures that can help prevent recurrent attacks. The first is to eliminate smoking from the home. Infants in homes where there are smokers are four times as likely to get bronchitis as infants in non-smoking households. Frequent hand washing can help prevent the spread of germs that may cause acute bronchitis. Avoidance of any substances thought to produce allergic reactions can help prevent chronic allergic bronchitis.

For Further Study

Books

Bellet, Paul S. *The Diagnostic Approach to Common Symptoms and Signs in Infants, Children, and Adolescents.* New York: Lea and Febiger, 1989.

Feldman, B. Robert. *The Complete Book of Children's Allergies: A Guide for Parents.* New York: Times Books, 1986.

Garwood, John, and Amanda Bennett. *Your Child's Symptoms.* New York: Berkeley Books, 1995.

Gershwin, M. Eric, and Edwin L. Klingelhofer. *Conquering Your Child's Allergies.* Reading, MA: Addison-Wesley, 1989.

Brown v. Board of Education

The landmark 1954 Supreme Court decision overruling the constitutionality of the "separate but equal" doctrine that had been the legal basis for racial segregation of the nation's public schools.

Although the **desegregation** of southern schools mandated by the decision was slow in coming, *Brown v. Board of Education* is considered the most significant civil rights court case of the 20th century for the legal precedent it set and for the hope it gave to black people throughout the nation.

Since the turn of the 20th century, the southern states had had a legal justification for requiring black students to attend segregated schools. The Supreme Court's 1896 ruling in *Plessy v. Ferguson* upheld segregated railroad car seating in Louisiana on the grounds that "equal but separate" seating did not violate the black passengers' rights to equal protection under the Fourteenth Amendment to the Constitution. For half a century, this near-unanimous decision (only one justice dissented) served as the legal grounds for racial segregation in virtually all areas of southern life, including education. However, segregated schools in the South, while separate, were definitely not equal, as documented by photographs taken in South Carolina in the 1930s. Whites attended school in brick and stone buildings, while black students were relegated to unheated, overcrowded shacks with crude furniture, inadequate libraries, and underqualified teachers. In 1930 white schools in South Carolina received ten times more money than black schools.

By the 1950s little had changed, and many blacks, believing that the best hope for racial equality lay in education, looked to the NAACP to mount a concerted legal attack on school segregation. A modest beginning had already been made with the organization's victory in a 1938 case in which the Supreme Court ruled that the University of Missouri's grant of an out-of-state scholarship to keep a black student out of its law school denied the student equal protection under the law. After World War II, the NAACP's Legal Defense and Education Fund, under the leadership of future Supreme Court Justice Thurgood Marshall, set its sights on winning a case that would overturn the 1896 *Plessy* ruling. In 1951 the NAACP coordinated the filing of lawsuits challenging segregated schooling in South Carolina, Virginia, Delaware, the District of Columbia, and Kansas.

The Kansas case—under whose name all five were eventually combined and docketed for rehearing by the Supreme Court—was the one that eventually earned a place in the history books. Oliver Brown and the parents of 12 other black children filed a lawsuit against the Topeka Board of Education protesting the city's segregation of black and white students. Brown's eight-year-old daughter Linda was required to take a 21-block bus ride to an all-black school every day when there was a white school within three blocks of the Browns' house. The bus that Linda Brown took arrived at her school before it opened, leaving her waiting outside for half an hour on cold winter mornings. The NAACP argued that segregated schooling had a harmful psychological effect on black children, but the suit was dismissed on the grounds that no law had been broken, as Topeka was legally authorized by the state of Kansas to maintain separate schools for white and black students.

On December 9, 1952, the Supreme Court heard oral arguments on all five of the cases on the Brown docket but postponed its ruling and requested a rehearing, which took place the following year. In the interim, Chief Justice Fred Vinson died and the newly elected President Dwight Eisenhower appointed Earl Warren in his place. Even after a second hearing, the court debated the case for months as Warren negotiated for a unanimous decision which he felt was crucial to ensure southern compliance with what was sure to be an unpopular ruling. Eventually the two dissenting justices were won over but a major compromise was required—agreement that the ruling would be implemented gradually rather than at once, as the NAACP had requested.

The historic ruling was announced on May 17, 1954, by Chief Justice Warren. Stressing the fact that public education was "a right which must be made available to all on equal terms," Warren voiced the court's opinion that separating black children "from others of similar age and qualifications solely because of their race generates a feeling of inferiority as to their status in the community that may affect their hearts and minds in a way unlikely ever to be undone." The crucial reversal of *Plessy* came in the most famous part of the ruling: "We conclude that in the field of public education the doctrine of 'separate but equal' has no place. Separate educational facilities are inherently unequal."

The *Brown v. Board of Education* ruling was jubilantly received by blacks across the nation, and a number of border states, as well as the District of Columbia, took rapid steps to desegregate their school systems. However, the states of the deep South used the gradual implementation decision, announced a year after the initial ruling, as a pretext for years of delay and defiance. The Court had left implementation up to state and local authorities, setting no firm deadlines for compliance and issuing instead the general guideline of a "prompt and reasonable start toward full compliance" and stating that desegregation should occur "with all deliberate speed." The southern states responded with hundreds of laws and resolutions that effectively blocked or limited desegregation. One popular tactic was the pupil-placement law, which gave local school authorities the prerogative of arbitrarily placing students in any school they chose, as long as they maintained that the placement was for psychological, academic, or any other purposes besides race. Other ways of circumventing the desegregation ruling included shutting down schools facing desegregation orders or providing tuition for students who chose to attend segregated private schools.

The southern states remained largely unchecked in their legislative resistance to the Supreme Court ruling in *Brown v. Board of Education,* which received little support from the other branches of the federal government. Southern members of Congress openly incited their states to defy the ruling and even voiced their determination to have the decision reversed. President Eisenhower, a con-servative president courting white southern voters, refused to express support for the *Brown* decision or lobby in any way for its enforcement. Privately, he voiced regret at his appointment of the Supreme Court justice who had been instrumental in obtaining the unanimous ruling.

Legal resistance to *Brown* was accompanied by harassment of black children who did attend newly desegregated schools, to the point that many parents gave up and reenrolled their children in all-black schools. Black children were attacked by shouting, rock-throwing mobs, mistreated by teachers, and tormented by their white classmates. In many communities there was a resurgence of Ku Klux Klan activities and growing membership in the White Citizens' Councils that were a more respectable version of the Klan. Resistance to integration led to a showdown between white extremists and the federal government in 1957 when President Eisenhower was forced to send federal troops to Little Rock, Arkansas, to disperse rioting white crowds preventing nine black students from entering Central High School.

In 1960 only one-sixth of 1% of southern black students attended a desegregated school. By 1964 this figure had risen to 2%, although two years later it remained under 1% for three states in the deep South. Nevertheless, thanks to federal civil rights legislation and tougher federal enforcement of desegregation guidelines, the 1960s eventually saw significant progress in southern desegregation: the number of black students attending desegregated schools rose to 16% in 1967, 20% in 1968, and 58% by 1970. In 1971 the Supreme Court gave district courts the authority to use **busing** for the desegregation of school systems. However, this measure was undermined by decisions later in the decade exempting suburban school districts from participation in efforts to desegregate city schools by busing.

Due to white flight from southern cities to the suburbs and from public to private schools, black enrollment in integrated schools had once again fallen to under 50% by 1980. In 1986 the *Brown v. Board of Education* case was reopened in Topeka on grounds that full integration of the school system had not been achieved. Plaintiffs charged that the school board had provided ways for white parents to avoid sending their children to integrated schools and had drawn boundaries that preserved racially segregated school districts. A federal court eventually ordered the city to produce an integration plan. The urban North had become increasingly segregated as well, with over 60% of black students attending schools that were virtually all-black. By the mid-1990s most black children in the nation still attended schools where less than half the students were white.

The Supreme Court ruling in *Brown v. Board of Education* proved to be only one step in a long and arduous journey toward equality in the nation's schools, but the decision retains an important place in United States history. Legally, it is significant for its reversal of the 50-year-old "separate but equal" doctrine. Symbolically, it supplied hope and inspiration to those involved in the struggle for racial equality in the United States, both during the Civil Rights Movement of the 1950s and '60s and in the years that followed.

For Further Study

Books

Branch, Taylor. *Parting the Waters: America in the King Years, 1954–1963.* New York: Simon & Schuster, 1988.

Greenberg, Jack. *Crusaders in the Courts: How a Dedicated Band of Lawyers Fought for the Civil Rights Revolution.* New York: Basic Books, 1994.

Huckaby, Elizabeth. *Crisis at Central High: Little Rock, 1957–58.* Baton Rouge: Louisiana State Univ. Press, 1980.

Williams, Juan. *Eyes on the Prize: America's Civil Rights Years.* New York: Viking, 1987.

Bulimia Nervosa

An eating disorder marked by episodes of binge eating followed by one or more behaviors to control weight, most commonly self-induced vomiting, laxative abuse, fasting, or excessive exercise.

Bulimia tends to appear in late **adolescence** or early adulthood, and most cases occur among middle- and upper-class females. The binge-purge episodes are almost always kept secret, and they tend to follow a recurrent pattern with at least two episodes per week. Like **anorexia nervosa**, bulimia has its roots in complex social and emotional issues. The family histories of bulimic youth often include emotional chaos, excessive anger, **depression**, substance abuse, and physical or **sexual abuse**.

Physical effects

Although bulimia is not associated with the severe weight loss of anorexia nervosa, it does cause a number of serious health risks, the most significant of which are gastrointestinal. Consequences of frequent **vomiting** include damage to the esophagus, stomach, pancreas, and small intestine. Eventually, a bulimic patient may have trouble keeping down any food for more than a few minutes, and laxative abuse can lead to chronic abdominal pain and **constipation**. Dehydration, kidney stones, **hypoglycemia**, and irregularities in heart rhythm are some of the effects of bulimia. A dentist may notice gum disease, numerous cavities, and damaged tooth enamel caused by the acid content of vomitus.

Psychological effects

Bulimia, like anorexia nervosa, is related to **anxiety** or conflict. However, while the anorectic individual denies she has an eating disorder, the bulimic individual is aware that she has a problem. She feels controlled by food and views her eating habits (and therefore her self) as repulsive to others. She finds comfort in the act of eating, even while dreading the inevitable purge that is to follow.

A bulimic adolescent may experience mood swings, anxiety, or irritability. Normal sleep patterns are often disrupted by amphetamine-induced insomnia, middle-of-the-night eating binges, or bouts of laxative-induced diarrhea. Bulimia is usually marked by secretive behaviors, and bulimic adolescents will often steal food or money to buy food.

Treatment and prognosis

Because a bulimic individual's overall body weight remains normal, it is sometimes years before her family or friends realize that she is struggling with the illness. If an adolescent girl exhibits any signs of an eating disorder, a doctor should be alerted immediately. Effective treatment for bulimia incorporates **psychotherapy**, nutritional counseling, and medical care if physical problems are present. Antidepressant medication is sometimes prescribed to regulate mood, and support groups are often sources of information and encouragement.

Reliable information is not available on the long-term prognosis for adolescents with bulimia. Studies seem to indicate that relapses are fairly common later in life, especially during periods of stress.

***See also* Anorexia Nervosa; Eating Disorders.**

For Further Study

Books

Jablow, Martha M. *A Parent's Guide to Eating Disorders and Obesity.* New York: Delta Publishing, 1992.

Maloney, Michael, and Rachel Kranz. *Straight Talk about Eating Disorders.* New York: Facts on File, 1991.

Organizations

National Eating Disorders Organization
Address: 6655 Yale Avenue
Tulsa, OK 74136
Telephone: (918) 481-4044

National Association of Anorexia Nervosa and Associated Disorders (ANAD)
Address: P.O. Box 7
Highland Park, IL 60035
Telephone: (847) 831-3438

—Gail B. Slap, M.D.
University of Pennsylvania School of Medicine

Bullies

An aggressive child who repeatedly victimizes a less powerful child with physical and/or emotional abuse.

Bullying usually involves an older or larger child (or several children) victimizing a single child who is incapable of defending himself or herself. Although much bullying goes unreported, it is estimated that in the average school an incident of bullying occurs approximately once every seven minutes. Bullying occurs at about the same rate regardless of class size or school size, but, for an unknown reason, rural schools appear to have a higher rate of bullying than urban or suburban schools. Even when bullying is reported, it is not always taken seriously by teachers and parents because many adults believe that children should learn to "stand up for themselves" or "fight back."

Although the stereotypical bully is male, girls engage in bullying behavior almost as often as boys. Their tactics differ, however, in that they are less visible. Boy bullies tend to resort to one-on-one physical aggression, while girls tend to bully as a group through social exclusion and the spreading of rumors. Girls who would never bully individually will often take part in group bullying activities such as "slam books," notebooks that are circulated among the peer group in which comments and criticisms are written about particular individuals.

Bullying begins at a very early age; it is not uncommon to find bullies in preschool classrooms. Up until about age seven, bullies appear to choose their victims at random. After that, they single out specific children to torment on a regular basis. Nearly twice as much bullying goes on in grades two to four as in grades six to eight, and, as bullies grow older, they use less physical abuse and more verbal abuse.

Until about sixth grade, bullies are not necessarily unpopular. They average two or three friends, and other children seem to admire them for their physical toughness. By high school, however, their social acceptance has diminished to the point that their only "friends" are other bullies. Despite their unpopularity, bullies have relatively high **self-esteem.** Perhaps this is because they process social information inaccurately.

For example, bullies attribute hostile intentions to people around them and therefore perceive provocation where it does not exist. "What are you staring at?" is a common opening line of bullies. For the bully, these perceived slights serve as justification for aggressive behavior.

In general, children who become the targets of bullies have a negative view of violence and go out of their way to avoid conflict. They tend to be "loners" who ex-

hibit signs of vulnerability before being singled out by a bully. Being victimized leads these children—who are already lacking in self-esteem—to feel more anxious and thereby increase their vulnerability to further victimization. Being the target of a bully leads to social isolation and rejection by peers, and victims tend to internalize others' negative views, further eroding their self-esteem. Although bullying actually lessens during **adolescence,** that is the period when peer rejection is most painful for victims. In a number of well-publicized cases (in Scandinavia, Japan, and Australia, as well as the United States), adolescents tormented by bullies have been driven to **suicide**.

Evidence indicates that bullying is not a phase a child will outgrow. In a long-term study of more than 500 children, University of Michigan researchers discovered that children who were viewed as the most aggressive by their peers at age eight grew up to commit more (and more serious) crimes as adults. Other studies indicate that, as adults, bullies are far more likely to abuse their spouses and children.

For Further Study

Books

Olweus, Dan. *Bullying at School: What We Know and What We Can Do.* Cambridge, MA: Blackwell, 1993.

Organizations

Bullies and Scapegoats Project

Address: Educators for Social Responsibility
23 Garden Street
Cambridge, MA 02138
Telephone: (617) 492-1764

National School Safety Center
Address: 4165 Thousand Oaks Blvd.
Westlake Village, CA 91362
Telephone: (805) 777-9977

Burns

Contact injuries to the skin and deeper tissues caused by exposure to flames, hot liquids or solids, radiant heat, caustic chemicals, electricity or electromagnetic (nuclear) radiation.

Every year, in the United States, approximately two million people suffer serious burns; of that total, 115,000 are hospitalized and 12,000 die. Children are most commonly burned by scalding liquids in the kitchen or bathroom. Fire is the second most common cause of burns.

Burns are classified as first, second, or third-degree according to their severity.

- First-degree burns damage only the outer layer of skin (epidermis); they cause redness, mild swelling, and stinging pain.

- Second-degree burns affect the second skin layer (dermis); they are more painful and are marked by the appearance of blisters.

- Third-degree burns destroy both the epidermis and dermis and may also damage underlying tissue; the skin appears charred or white and lifeless and may be insensitive to pinprick. Third-degree burns may be less painful than second-degree, due to destruction of nerve endings.

The depth of a burn, its extent (percentage of body surface), and the age of the victim determine its severity. For burns of similar extent and depth, persons under one year and over 40 years of age have a higher mortality rate than those between the ages of two and 39 years. In children, burns affecting 10% of the body require hospitalization.

A reasonably accurate guide to determining the extent of burns is the "Rule of Nine:" head and neck account for 9% of body surface; each arm and hand, 9%; each foot and leg, 18%; anterior and posterior trunk, including buttocks, 18% each; and perineum, 1%.

First aid

First aid for burns requires application of plain cool water as soon as possible after the burn occurs. Soothing ointment may be applied to *minor* burns, but *never* to se-

rious burns. Chemical burns should be washed immediately with copious amounts of cool water, then neutralized with an appropriate chemical agent (e.g., dilute sodium bicarbonate solution for acid burns, vinegar for alkali burns).

Do not apply butter or oil to burns, as they hold in the heat and may damage the skin. Broken blisters can lead to infection, so, if possible, do not break them or allow the child to break them. If the burned area reddens further, oozes, or smells bad, take the child to a doctor immediately.

First and second-degree burns involving less than 10% body surface in children will usually heal well in two weeks. The wounds may be left open to dry or covered with sterile gauze. Burns heal best if the affected part can be immobilized and elevated to decrease the flow of lymph and limit the spread of infection (a major cause of death from burns).

Burns involving 15–25% of the body surface are treated in the hospital, so that intravenous fluids may be administered. These replace lost tissue fluids and provide nutritional support.

Burns of more than 25% of the body surface are generally treated in specialized burn centers, where patients can be kept in sterile wards to avoid complications such as infection, dehydration, pneumonia, and kidney failure. Wounds are covered by skin grafting as soon as possible.

Research is currently underway to grow skin in tissue culture to cover large wounds from small donor sites. Temporary grafts from other humans and pigs can be used. Although they are eventually rejected, these grafts protect the wound until healing occurs. An artificial skin that would serve as a permanent scaffolding for dermal regrowth is being tested.

Deep burns cause extensive scarring that may result in severe disfigurement and limitation of joint motion. Plastic surgery can often reduce the effects of the scars and ameliorate the psychological problems which often occur with serious burn scarring. Children who have suffered disfiguring burns will have difficulty returning to the classroom. Some hospitals have school re-entry programs to prepare the burn survivor's classmates for his or her return. Children need to understand the nature of the child's injuries, any scars or special clothing the child might have, or simply if the burn victim can still play with them. A nurse from the hospital can help children accept the burn survivor by explaining the child's injuries and what the child is going through.

Schools usually have safety programs designed to make children aware of burn and other safety hazards. Parents can reinforce this by warning children about burn dangers such as boiling liquids or chemicals. Small children should never be left alone around potential burn hazards. To prevent scalding in the kitchen, turn pot handles away from the stove's edge. To prevent stove fires, keep all flammable materials (food packages, curtains, towels, potholders, etc.) away from the stove. Check pilot lights on gas stoves to make sure they are working properly. It is also important for a household to have a fire escape plan. Over 50% of burns are considered to be preventable.

For Further Study

Books

American National Red Cross. *First Aid for Burns.* Washington, DC: American National Red Cross, 1977.

Bernstein, Norman R., Alan Jeffry Breslau, and Jean Ann Graham, eds. *Coping Strategies for Burn Survivors and Their Families.* New York: Praeger, 1988.

Munster, Andrew M. and staff of Baltimore Regional Burn Center. *Severe Burns: A Family Guide to Medical and Emotional Recovery.* Baltimore: Johns Hopkins University Press, 1993.

Stouffer, Dennis J. *Journey through Hell: Stories of Burn Survivors' Reconstruction of Self and Identity.* Lanham, MD: Rowman & Littlefield, 1994.

Audiovisual Recordings

Metropolitan Life Insurance Company. *Burns.* Evanston, IL: Journal Films, 1980.
(Videorecording.)

Stein, John M. *The Doctor Talks to You about Burns: A Discussion.* Bayside, NY: Soundwords, 1978.
(One audio cassette. Discusses various kinds of burns,

medical techniques for treating burns, and the development and growth of burn centers. For ages 16 to adult.)

—Karen Bauman

Busing

Transporting students a distance to a school

Since the 1970s, the term busing has come to mean the transporting of students to schools outside their immediate neighborhoods, usually in an attempt to achieve **desegregation.** The federal courts have mandated busing to reflect the goal of racial balance in all schools within a district. Busing is part of a program of involuntary desegregation; voluntary desegregation is characterized by strategies such as magnet schools and district-wide open enrollment, where families are offered incentives of unique curricula or other programs to encourage them to enroll in other-than-neighborhood schools. Supporters of court-ordered or involuntary desegregation have encouraged busing as a key strategy in achieving equal educational opportunity for all students, regardless or racial, ethnic, or religious background. Some critics feel that communities should be allowed to pursue alternative strategies for achieving racial balance before the courts step in with prescriptive orders.

See also **Brown v. Board of Education**

California Achievement Tests (CAT)

Assesses basic academic skills.

The California Achievement Tests (CAT) are among the most widely used tests of basic academic skills. This paper-and-pencil test is available in different forms at 10 overlapping levels covering grades K–12. The CAT is often administered to determine a child's readiness for promotion to a more advanced grade level and may also be used by schools to satisfy state or local testing requirements. Areas covered are reading, spelling, language, reference skills, mathematics, science, social studies, computer literacy, and, on certain tests, study skills. At each level after the kindergarten readiness stage, test results are combined to yield total scores for the first five of these areas (Total Reading, Spelling, Total Language, Reference Skills, and Total Mathematics). The complete battery of California Achievement Tests can take up to 2 hours and 48 minutes depending on the test level. CAT also offers separate tests in specific subjects, such as algebra and chemistry, designed to be given at the end of a course.

For Further Study

Books

McCullough, Virginia. *Testing and Your Child: What You Should Know About 150 of the Most Common Medical, Educational, and Psychological Tests.* New York: Plume, 1992.

Shore, Milton F., Patrick J. Brice, and Barbara G. Love. *When Your Child Needs Testing: What Parents, Teachers, and Other Helpers Need to Know about Psychological Testing.* New York: Crossroad, 1992.

Walsh, W. Bruce, and Nancy E. Betz. *Tests and Assessment.* 2nd ed. Englewood Cliffs, NJ: Prentice Hall, 1990.

Wodrich, David L., and Sally A. Kush. *Children's Psychological Testing: A Guide for Nonpsychologists.* 2nd ed. Baltimore, MD: Brookes Publishing Co., 1990.

Wortham, Sue Clark. *Tests and Measurement in Early Childhood Education.* Columbus: Merrill Publishing Co., 1990.

Cancer

A group of diseases characterized by uncontrollable cell growth.

Cancer is a family of diseases in which cells replicate at an extremely rapid pace. A cancerous, or malignant, tumor begins its growth at a primary site, damaging surrounding tissue and interfering with normal organ function. Eventually, some of the cancerous cells may migrate from the primary tumor to other parts of the body via the bloodstream and form secondary tumors. The specific causes of most forms of cancer are unknown, but researchers have uncovered many probable factors that contribute to the development of the disease, including certain chemicals and forms of radiation, cigarette smoking, diet, and, in some cases, genetic predisposition. Although most cancers occur in adults, cancer is still responsible for more deaths in children than any other disease in the United States, where it is the second leading cause of death—after accidents—in children under the age of 15. Between 7,000 and 8,000 new cases of childhood cancer are diagnosed in the U.S. every year. Like the cancer rate among the adult population, the incidence of cancer in children, especially acute lymphocytic leukemia and brain cancer, is on the rise. However, scientific advances in diagnosis and treatment have dramatically improved short- and long-term survival rates for many childhood cancers.

Pediatric oncologists specialize in the treatment of children with cancer. Childhood cancers are treated with the same three major techniques used for treating cancer in adults: chemotherapy, radiation, and surgery. In chemotherapy, medication is administered orally or intravenously to kill cancer cells, or to stop or retard their growth. Usually a combination of different drugs is used for maximum effectiveness. Chemotherapy agents are powerful drugs that cause unpleasant and sometimes serious side effects, including nausea, hair loss, mouth sores, bleeding, and decreased immune function.

In radiation therapy, high doses of radiation are aimed at the affected area, killing cancer cells. This therapy brings many dangers to the patient. Radiation can kill cells or turn healthy cells into new cancer cells. Whole-body radiation, used to treat cancer that has spread, destroys the body's bone marrow. A matching donor, usually a close relative, must then be found to give marrow for a transplant procedure. Side effects of radiation include fever, irritability, hair loss, headaches, nausea, and appetite loss, in addition to skin irritations at the site where the x rays are aimed. New treatment approaches being developed for children can reduce the side effects of radiation. These include hyperfractionation, which reduces the required dose of radiation, and tailored radiotherapy, which narrows the radiation to only a portion of the affected area. Surgery is the treatment of choice for localized cancers that are detected before they have spread. However, some cancers are more treatable by surgery than others, depending on the accessibility of the tumor. Surgery is often used in conjunction with radiation and/or chemotherapy to prevent a relapse, because if even a single cancer cell is left after the operation, it can lead to renewed abnormal growth and the recurrence of the tumor.

Types of childhood cancers

The most common childhood cancers are **leukemia**, brain cancer, and lymphoma. Leukemia, which accounts for a third of the cancers diagnosed in children every year, affects the tissues that produce blood cells, causing a proliferation of abnormal white cells in the bone marrow. These crowd out the normal cells, interfering with blood clotting, leading to **anemia,** and making the child vulnerable to severe infections. Almost all cases of childhood leukemia, 97%, are acute and progress rapidly. Acute lymphocytic leukemia (ALL) is the most widespread type, accounting for 80–85% of cases in children. Leukemia usually strikes children between the ages of three and five. Symptoms include fatigue, pallor, fever, infections, abnormal bruising, bleeding gums, nosebleeds, and limping. The most effective treatment is chemotherapy to kill the abnormal white blood cells, accompanied initially by blood transfusions and antibiotics. Bone marrow transplants are becoming an increasingly frequent treatment method for this disease. After the diseased marrow is destroyed by radiation or chemotherapy, marrow cells from a compatible donor, usually a sibling, are transplanted into the patient. Treatment advances raised the survival rate for childhood leukemia from 4% in the 1960s to 70% by the 1980s.

Brain tumors are the second most common childhood cancer. Nearly half belong to one particular type,

called an astrocytoma. If the tumor is in an operable location, the prognosis for 10-year survival is 80%. Hodgkin's disease and other cancers of the lymph system, or lymphomas, are also among the most frequent childhood cancers. Symptoms of lymphoma include fever, night sweats, swollen, tender lymph nodes, **jaundice** (yellowish skin and eyes), decreased appetite, and, in the case of Hodgkin's lymphoma, widespread itching. Current survival rates for lymphomas are excellent. With radiation and chemotherapy, the five-year survival rate for Hodgkin's disease is 90%, and the 10-year survival rate is 80%. Non-Hodgkin's lymphoma has a two-year survival rate (with treatment) of 70%, after which relapse is infrequent. With early detection and treatment, the survival rate for non-Hodgkin's lymphoma is as high as 90%.

Children can also develop various types of bone cancer. Two of the most common are osteosarcoma and Ewing's sarcoma. Adolescents, particularly adolescent boys, are especially prone to bone cancer, which tends to develop during growth spurts. The initial symptoms of a bone tumor—pain and swelling—may cause it to be mistaken for a bruise. If the cancer is allowed to progress untreated, it will eventually interfere with use of the affected part of the body—usually an arm or leg—and can make it sensitive to fractures. Although bone cancer is most commonly seen in the limbs, it can also occur in other locations, such as knees, hips, or shoulders. Bone cancer can develop in more than one location simultaneously or can spread from one part of the body to another. Bone tumors are generally diagnosed by a combination of x ray and **biopsy**, in which a small amount of the tumor is removed for laboratory analysis. More sophisticated radiological procedures, such as a bone scan or a CAT scan (computed tomography, or CT), can aid in making a more detailed assessment and deciding on a course of treatment.

Surgery, followed by chemotherapy, is the treatment of choice for osteosarcoma. Usually the affected limb is amputated, although in some cases it is possible to remove only part of the limb, followed by reconstruction through a bone transplant or graft. Ewing's sarcoma is treated with radiation and chemotherapy but not surgery. Due to treatment advances, the prognosis for bone cancer—once considered an almost uniformly fatal illness—has improved dramatically in recent decades. The five-year collective survival rate for bone cancer is now 80%. As many as 50% of Ewing's sarcoma patients are likely to be long-term survivors of the disease. Similarly, the survival rate for osteosarcoma has risen to 50% from only 20% in the 1960s.

Another type of childhood cancer is Wilms' tumor, also known as nephroblastoma. Wilms' tumor is a kidney tumor originating from embryonal kidney cells that is most frequent in children under the age of five. A genetic component has been found in this disease, which is also associated with congenital urinary tract and genital deformities, such as undescended testicles. In most cases, the tumor is first detected as a lump in the abdomen or side. Other symptoms may include swelling, abdominal pain, appetite reduction, weight loss, fever, and urine in the blood. Without the standard treatment of surgery and chemotherapy, the tumor can spread to other organs, including the lungs and liver. Even if the tumor has spread, necessitating the removal of additional tissue besides the affected kidney, recovery from surgery is usually rapid. However, the child's health must be monitored regularly following treatment and recovery, as the tumor may recur, especially in the lungs. Since the 1960s the survival rate for Wilms' tumor has risen from 33% to over 80%.

Emotional and psychological health

In addition to medical treatment, it is important for children with cancer and their families to receive adequate emotional support, which can come from friends, extended family, mental health professionals, support groups, or clergy. In addition to conventional counseling, resources such as play therapy and art therapy can help children cope with emotions such as fear and **depression.** Support groups for children with cancer can also be an important source of reassurance and comfort. In addition, family members of the patient can benefit from individual or group counseling. The serious illness of a child can place a heavy strain on a couple's marriage, and counseling can help parents work through their conflicts and remain healthy emotionally. Childhood cancer is also stressful for siblings, who may feel guilty, depressed, or resentful of the extra parental attention devoted to the brother or sister who is ill. They can also benefit from some form of extra emotional support.

Education is another area of special concern for children with cancer. It is helpful for them to maintain as much of a normal routine as they can, and there are resources available to help them continue their schooling in spite of the interruptions imposed by possibly lengthy hospital stays. Private tutoring is a common option. The Minnesota branch of the American Cancer Society has developed a school reentry program to help make a child's return to school easier following cancer treatment. A pediatric oncology nurse visits the child's school in advance to educate both the school staff and the child's classmates about cancer and its treatment. Special age-appropriate materials, such as coloring books and videos, have been developed for use in the program. These visits can help allay other children's fears about the disease (for example, the idea that it may be contagious) and teachers' anxieties about how to treat a student with cancer.

Although there is still too little certainty about the causes of childhood cancers to make them preventable, there are ways to reduce a child's lifetime chances of developing cancer, based on proven medical findings about factors that contribute to the disease. The most important risk factor is second-hand cigarette smoke. The dangers of passive smoking have been known for years, and there is research establishing a strong link between exposure to smoking during childhood and adolescence and lung cancer in nonsmoking adults. Another area of concern is exposure to toxic substances in and around the home, especially insecticides and weed-killers. Use of household insecticides while a woman is pregnant has been found to nearly quadruple an unborn child's risk of leukemia. Another way to avoid pesticides and herbicides in the home is to eat organically grown fruits and vegetables.

Exposure to radiation in high doses has also been associated with cancer. Radon, a naturally occurring radioactive gas, has been linked to lung cancer by the Environmental Protection Agency (EPA). It is generally recommended that families check the radon levels in their homes against the EPA guidelines for acceptable levels of the gas and take measures to improve sealing and ventilation if the levels are too high.

Another type of radiation that has been linked to cancer is the ultraviolet radiation of the sun, which is the primary cause of skin cancer. Children's skin has less of the pigment melanin than that of adults, making them more sensitive to the sun's rays. A single severe sunburn can increase a child's risk of developing a malignant melanoma later in life, a condition that can be fatal if untreated. In addition, frequent exposure to the sun, even without burning, can increase the chances of developing other types of skin cancer. It is recommended that infants be shaded from strong sunlight by hats, bonnets, stroller covers, and other kinds of protective covering. Active older children can be protected by a sunscreen lotion or cream with a sun protection factor (SPF) of at least 15, applied on all areas exposed to the sun. Direct exposure to the sun can also be limited during the hours between 10 A.M. and 3 P.M. when ultraviolet rays are strongest.

Another risk factor for developing cancer is an unhealthy diet. Certain kinds of cancer are associated with a high level of fat consumption. Fat should only account for 20–25% of the calories consumed daily by those two years of age and older. It is also recommended that both children and adults eat at least five servings of fruits and/or vegetables daily.

For Further Study

Books

Froemer, Margot Joan. *Surviving Childhood Cancer: A Guide for Families.* Washington, DC: American Psychiatric Press, Inc., 1995.

Gaes, Geralyn, Craig Gaes, and Philip Bashe. *You Don't Have to Die: A Family's Guide to Surviving Childhood Cancer.* New York: Villard Books, 1992.

Hyde, Margaret O., and Lawrence E. Hyde. *Cancer in the Young: A Sense of Hope.* Philadelphia: Westminster Press, 1985.

National Cancer Institute. *Tips for Teenagers with Cancer.* Bethesda, MD: U.S. Department of Health and Human Services, 1987.

Trillin, Alice. *Dear Bruno.* New York: The New Press, 1996.

Organizations

American Cancer Society
Address: 777 Third Avenue
New York, NY 10019
Telephone: (212) 371-2900

Cancer Information Service
Address: National Cancer Institute
Building 31, Room 108
Bethesda, MD 20892
Telephone: toll-free (800) 4-CANCER

Children's Hospice International
Address: 1800 Diagonal Rd., Suite 600
Alexandria, VA 22314
Telephone: (703) 684-0330

Ronald McDonald House
Address: Kroc Drive
Oak Brook, IL 60521
Telephone: (708) 575-7418

Carcinogens

Substances capable of causing cancer.

The U.S. Environmental Protection Agency (EPA) classifies many substances on the basis of their potential for causing **cancer.** Classifications are based on results of studies on animals, or with humans. Classification categories refer to epidemiological studies, which are studies to identify the factors controlling the presence or absence of a disease.

Group A or *Human Carcinogens.* There is a relationship between the substance and cancer that has been shown through epidemiological studies on humans.

Group B or *Probable Human Carcinogen.* There are two types of carcinogens in this category. There is sufficient evidence from animal studies and limited epidemiological studies that *B1 carcinogens* cause cancer. *B2 carcinogens* are classified on the basis of sufficient evidence from animal studies only; epidemiological data are inadequate or nonexistent.

Group C or *Possible Human Carcinogens.* Classification in this category is based on limited evidence from animal studies and no epidemiological data.

Group D or *Not Classifiable as to Human Carcinogenicity.* The studies on substances in this category are inadequate or completely lacking, so no assessment of the substance's cancer-causing potential is possible.

Group E or *Evidence of Noncarcinogenicity for Humans.* Substance in this category have tested negative in at least two adequate animal cancer tests in different species and in adequate epidemiological and animal studies.

For Further Study

Books

U.S. Department of Health and Human Services, Public Health Service, *Seventh Annual Report on Carcinogens, Summary 1994.* National Institute of Environmental Health Sciences: Research Triangle Park, North Carolina, 1995. Contact the National Institute of Environmental Health Sciences Publications Office, (919) 541-3419.

Cardiopulmonary Resuscitation (CPR)

Attempting to restart breathing and heartbeat for someone whose breathing and pulse appear to have stopped.

Cardiopulmonary resuscitation (CPR) employs chest compressions in a sequential pattern with **artificial respiration** to restore or maintain weak breathing and heartbeat. Both the U.S. Public Health Service and the **American Academy of Pediatrics** recommend that parents receive training in such first aid techniques from the American Red Cross, YMCA, or other community agency.

For Further Study

Books

American National Red Cross. *Respiratory and Circulatory Emergencies.* Washington, DC: American National Red Cross, 1978.

Audiovisual Recordings

How to Save Your Child or Baby: When Every Second Counts. Los Angeles, CA: Video Prescriptions, 1987. (One 40-minute videocassette.)

Seconds Count. Manhattan Beach, CA: Mann Design, 1991. (One 18-minute videocassette.)

CARCINOGENS

The U.S. Department of Health and Human Services has determined that the following industrial processes, occupational exposures, and chemicals are associated with cancer in humans:

- 4-Aminobiphenyl
- Analgesic mixtures containing phenacetin (used as anti-fever agents)
- Arsenic and arsenic compounds
- Asbestos
- Auramine manufacture
- Benzene (used in nail polish remover, varnishes, airplane dopes, lacquers, and as a solvent)
- Benzidine
- N,N-Bis (2-Chloreothyl)-2-Naphthylamine (Chlomophaozine)
- BIS (chloromethyl) ether and technical grade chloromethyl methyl ether
- Boot and shoe manufacture and repair
- 1, 4-Butanediol dimethanesulphonate (Myleran)
- Certain combined chemotherapy for lymphomas (including MOPP)
- Chlorambucil
- Chromium and certain chromium compounds
- Coal gasification
- Coal tar and coal tar pitch
- Coke production
- Conjugated estrogens
- Cyclophosphamide
- Diethystilbestrol (DES)
- Furniture manufacture
- Isopropyl alcohol manufacture
- Malphalan
- Methoxsalen with ultra-violet A therapy
- Mineral oils
- Mustard gas
- 2-Naphthylamine
- Nickel refining
- Rubber industry (certain occupations)
- Soots, tars, and oils
- Tobacco
- Treosulphan
- Ultraviolet radiation
- Underground hematite mining (with exposure to radon)
- Vinyl chloride

Contact with these substances should be avoided by both children and adults.

Caregiver

Person responsible for meeting the physical and psychological needs of an infant, child, or dependent adult.

A caregiver (alternatively referred to as a caretaker) is the person who has responsibility for meeting the physical and psychological needs of an infant or child. (The term also describes the person responsible for the care of a dependent adult.) The caregiver may be the individual who has legal responsibility for the child—the parent or **guardian**—or may be someone who is hired to assume temporary, short-term, or routine responsibility for the child in the absence of the parent or guardian. A caregiver may also be a member of the household or extended family, such as a **co-parent,** siblings, aunts, uncles, or grandparents. The label caregiver is usually applied to a person taking care of a child or adult at home, although it may be applied to employees in a **day care** setting.

Estimates of the number of people employed as caregivers vary from 14 to 22 million. Only a percentage of these are employed to care for children, but the number is growing. The Children's Defense Fund estimated that in 1990, 6.5 million children under age five whose mothers were employed were cared for by someone other than a parent. For families who wish to hire a caregiver, the process can be emotional and difficult. In 1996, the *Nanny News* reported on hiring practices used to find and employ caregivers for children.

When identifying candidates, interviewing, and hiring, many parents find that the demand for caregivers exceeds the supply. Successful hiring can be accomplished through word-of-mouth, classified ads in the local newspaper, or through placement agencies (fees ranged in 1996 from $1,200 to $3,500 for child caregiver referrals). Before hiring an agency, the parents should investigate its policies and procedures. Parents should ask about how the agency screens references of applicants, and how the agency deals with unsuccessful referrals—does it issue refunds or provide replacements, for example. The International Nanny Association publishes an annual directory of referral services and training programs for nannies.

GLOSSARY OF CAREGIVER TERMS

Au pair: There are two definitions. One describes a foreign person, usually European, who lives with an American family for up to a year to experience American life. Lives as part of the host family and receives a small allowance/salary. Helps with housework and childcare. May or may not have prior childcare experience. Alternatively, an au pair may be a U.S. citizen who lives with a family and provides help with light housework and childcare for 40–60 hours per week. Usually works under the supervision and direction of the parent. May or may not have prior childcare experience.

Babysitter: Provides supervisory custodial care for children on an irregular full- or part-time basis. No special training or background expected.

Governess: A qualified teacher employed by families for full- or part-time at-home education. Work week varies widely. Generally not responsible for physical aspects of childcare.

Mother's (Parent's) Helper: Works for the family to provide full-time childcare and other domestic help for families with one parent at home most of the time. Usually works under the direction and supervision of the at-home parent, but may be left in complete charge for brief periods. No special training is expected.

Nanny: Employed by a family to provide full-time childcare on either a live-in or live-out basis to undertake all tasks related to the care of the children. Duties are generally restricted to childcare and the domestic tasks related to childcare. May or may not have had any formal training, though often has a good deal of actual experience. Nanny's work week ranges from 40–60 hours. Usually works unsupervised.

Nursery Nurse: The title used in the United Kingdom for a person who has received special training and preparation in caring for young children (not limited to in-home care), and has passed the certification examination of the National Nursery Examination Board. May or may not live with the family. Works independently and is responsible for everything related to the care of the children. Duties generally restricted to the childcare and related domestic tasks. Work week ranges from 50–60 hours per week.

Source: Adapted from International Nanny Association's fact sheet, "A Nanny for Your Family...Answers to Questions Parents Often Ask About In-Home Childcare."

Many parents hiring a caregiver on their own for the first time rely on chemistry between the applicant and the family members. Being able to fit in with the family is an important qualification for a caregiver, but experts urge families to do a thorough check of references. Parents should contact the references themselves, and should be wary of false references. For example, prospective employers should never agree to be called by the applicant's references.

Parents can gain access to helpful information about a prospective caregiver's background by hiring an investigation service to do a standard pre-employment screening, which includes checks of criminal records, verification of previous employment, driving records, and a review of workers' compensation claims. In 1996, the cost of such a check was under $100.

Once the hiring decision has been made, parents should remain vigilant about the caregiver's performance. Infants and young children will be unable to communicate problems, but may show signs of anxiety in the caregiver's presence. Parents should be concerned if the child has unexplained injuries or accidents.

Good communication between parents and caregiver ensures that the child's needs in physical and emotional development will be met. Parents should consider creating a structured format—such as a log book or daily conference—that will allow the caregiver to communicate issues, concerns, or accomplishments that come up during the day. In this way, the parents can review what has occurred during the day at a time other than during the hectic rush at the beginning or end of the working day.

For Further Study

Books

Capossela, Cappy, and Sheila Warnock. *Share the Care: How to Organize a Group to Care for Someone Who Is Seriously Ill.* New York: Simon and Schuster, 1995.

Elliott, Ruth and Jim Savage. *The Complete Guide to In-Home Childcare.* New York: Prentice-Hall, 1988.

Kahana, Eva, David E. Biegel, and May Wykle. *Family Caregiving Across the Lifespan.* Thousand Oaks, CA: Sage Publications, 1994.

Lowe, Paula C. *Care Pooling: How to Get the Help You Need to Care for the Ones You Love.* San Francisco: Berrett-Koehler Publishers, 1993.

MacNamara, Roger D. *Creating Abuse-Free Caregiving Environments for Children, the Disabled, and the Elderly: Preparing, Supervising, and Managing Caregivers for the Emotional Impact of Their Responsibilities.* Springfield, IL: C.C. Thomas, 1992.

Neal, Margaret B., et al. *Balancing Work and Caregiving for Children, Adults, and Elders.* Newbury Park, CA: Sage Publications, 1993.

Periodicals

Bell, Alison, and Marian Edelman Borden. "Child-Care Guide." *American Baby* 58, March 1996, pp. 64+.

Field, Anne, and Kate Deely. "A Changing of the Guardian." *Parenting* 9, October 1995, pp. 40+.

Malone, Barbara L. "Finding a Home Caregiver." *Consumers Digest* 36, May–June 1997, p. 86.

Nanny News, six issues per year. For subscription information, call toll-free (800) 634-6266.

Shelton, Sandi Kahn. "Making Child Care Even Better." *Working Mother* 20, January 1997, pp. 32+.

Woodward, Kenneth L., Tom Morganthau, and Sarah Van Boven. "The Great Ages of Discovery." *Newsweek* 129, Spring–Summer 1997, pp. 80+.

Audiovisual Recordings

The Home Care Companion: How to Care for Someone on Bedrest. Healing Arts Communications, 1996. (One 40-minute videorecording.)

Organizations

International Nanny Association
    Address: 900 Haddon Avenue, Suite 438
    Collingswood, NJ 08108
    Telephone: (609) 858-0808
    (Non-profit educational organization for nannies and those who educate, place, employ, and support professional in-home child care providers; publishes a directory of training programs and several fact sheets.)

National Center for the Early Childhood Work Force
    (formerly the Child Care Employee Project)
    Address: 733 15th St., N.W., Suite 1037
    Washington, DC 20005-2112
    [Clearinghouse for information on child care staffing; advocates for better regulation and funding of child care. Also sponsors "Worthy Wage Campaign," a grassroots effort to improve pay for child care workers. Publishes *Mentoring in Early Care and Education: Refining an Emerging Career Path* (59 pp.), and *Breaking the Link: A National Forum on Child Care Compensation* (36 pgs.).]

Cataracts

An opaque formation on the lens at the back of the eye that can block light to the retina and lead to loss of vision.

Cataracts commonly afflict elderly people, but in rare instances an infant may have cataracts in one or both eyes at birth. This condition can result if the mother contracted an infectious disease during pregnancy, and cataracts are sometimes linked with other congenital disorders such as **Down syndrome**. However, there is no known cause for many infant cataracts. The cataract appears as a white spot in the pupil, and the size, shape, and density vary widely. Some can be viewed with a flashlight, others only with special opthalmological instruments when the pupils are dilated. If the cataract is large

or dense enough to obscure vision, the child will need surgery to remove it. If surgery is needed for congenital cataracts, it is usually performed within the first few weeks or months of the child's life. After surgery, the child is fitted with corrective lenses—whether glasses or **contact lenses**. Surgery can be deferred if the cataracts do not seriously interfere with the child's vision.

See also **Eye and Vision Development**

For Further Study

Organizations

American Academy of Ophthalmology
    Address: P.O. Box 7424
    San Francisco, CA 92120-7424

National Eye Institute
    Address: Building 31, Room 6A32
    Bethesda, MD 20892
    Telephone: (301) 496-5248

Catharsis

The release of repressed psychic energy.

The term catharsis originated from the Greek word *katharsis,* meaning to purge, or purgation. In psychology, the term was first employed by Sigmund Freud's colleague Josef Breuer (1842–1925), who developed a "cathartic" treatment for persons suffering from hysterical symptoms through the use of hypnosis. While under hypnosis, Breuer's patients were able to recall traumatic experiences, and through the process of expressing the original emotions that had been repressed and forgotten, they were relieved of their symptoms. Catharsis was also central to Freud's concept of **psychoanalysis,** but he replaced hypnosis with free association.

In other schools of **psychotherapy,** catharsis refers to the therapeutic release of emotions and tensions, although not necessarily unconscious ones such as Freud emphasized. Certain types of therapy in particular, such as psychodrama and primal scream therapy, have stressed the healing potential of cathartic experiences.

For Further Study

Books

Firestone, Robert. *Psychological Defenses in Everyday Life.* New York: Human Sciences Press, 1989.

Hall, Calvin S. *A Primer of Freudian Psychology.* New York: Harper and Row, 1982.

Jenson, Jean C. *Reclaiming Your Life: A Step-by-Step Guide to Using Regression Therapy to Overcome the Effects of Childhood Abuse.* New York: Dutton, 1995.

Psychologist James McKeen Cattell

Cattell Infant Intelligence Scale

Infant intelligence test.

The Cattell Infant Intelligence Scale is one of the oldest infant intelligence tests, originally designed in 1950. The Cattell scale measures mental development from 3–30 months, evaluating motor control and verbalizations. Items at each level cover the preceding period of development. Motor control is assessed by a series of tasks that involve manipulating various objects, such as cubes, pencils, and pegboards. Sample items from the test (with age norms on the Cattell scale) are: lifting a cup (6 months), ringing a bell (9 months), putting a cube in a cup (11 months), and marking with a crayon (12 months). The examiner also takes notes on the infant's attempts to communicate. The test is untimed but usually takes 20-30 minutes. Results are reported in terms of mental age and IQ score. The Cattell scale—which has been modified based on research with the **Gesell**, Minnesota Preschool, and **Merrill-Palmer** scales—is considered an extension of the **Stanford-Binet** intelligence test for younger children. Together, the two tests provide a continuous developmental scale from three months to maturity.

JAMES MCKEEN CATTELL (1860–1944)

After studying with some of the leading European and American research psychologists, James McKeen Cattell focused on what he had learned from Sir Francis Galton in England—that statistics and quantitative methods are powerful research tools. Cattell adopted the practice of testing a large number of research subjects and using statistical analysis to draw conclusions about the resulting data. Cattell is believed to be the first person to use the term "mental test," and he devoted much of his career to the development of an intelligence test. Cattell founded the Psychological Corporation, which did not develop into a successful commercial enterprise until after he left the company.

While Cattell was at Columbia University, more students earned a doctorate in psychology working with him than with any other psychology professor. He cofounded the journal *Psychological Review* with J. Mark Baldwin, and resurrected the journal *Science* after acquiring it from Alexander Graham Bell. Cattell was instrumental in the founding of the American Association for the Advancement of Science.

For Further Study

Books

Cohen, Libby G., and Loraine J. Spenciner. *Assessment of Young Children.* New York: Longman, 1994.

McCullough, Virginia. *Testing and Your Child: What You Should Know About 150 of the Most Common Medical, Educational, and Psychological Tests.* New York: Plume, 1992.

Walsh, W. Bruce, and Nancy E. Betz. *Tests and Assessment.* 2nd ed. Englewood Cliffs, NJ: Prentice Hall, 1990.

Celiac Sprue Disease

A disease characterized by the inability to digest gluten found in many grains. Also called gluten-induced enteropathy or gluten intolerance.

A child suffering from celiac sprue disease is unable to digest gluten, the protein present in wheat, oats, and barley. Gluten intolerance surfaces in one out of every 10,000 Caucasian birth; commonly among people of Irish and Scottish descent. Although the exact pattern is unknown, celiac disease tends to run in families. Parents with the intolerance condition themselves should watch their children closely for symptoms, which generally appear within the first two years of life.

Once the intestines become irritated, the absorption of other nutrients is affected. If unchecked, the child can suffer severe growth impairments. In its advanced state, celiac disease can result in clubbed fingers and delayed tooth developments.

The most telling sign is loose, fatty, foul-smelling bowl movements. In addition, the child may be irritable with little or no appetite. His or her abdomen may be distended. **Vomiting** and dehydration are also common. When the intolerance is present in infants who are eating cereal early, the effects can be life-threatening. These infants need emergency care to replace lost fluids. In most cases, however, by the time celiac disease is diagnosed, the child will have a history of chronic **diarrhea**; his or her height and weight will likely be less than the average. Because frequent diarrhea can also signal intestinal infections or lactose intolerance, the physician may perform a **biopsy** (examination of a small piece of tissue) of the small intestine to determine that celiac disease exists.

Once celiac disease has been diagnosed, all gluten foods should be eliminated from the child's diet. Packaged foods, including baby foods, contain various forms of gluten; any of the following ingredients listed on the package indicate that the food should be avoided: wheat or rye flour, bran, farina, wheat germ, semolina, cereal additives. Based on the results of a 1995 study, some physicians believe that celiac sprue patients can include oat in their diets.

Corn, rice, potato, or soy flour can take the place of the offending grains. A varied diet of unprocessed meats, eggs, milk, cheeses, fish, fruits, and vegetables will provide the child with a nutritionally balanced diet. The child's physician may also recommend that the child take vitamin B and D and iron supplements, and folic acid to aid digestion.

Occasionally a child will develop a temporary sugar intolerance, brought on by the unchecked celiac sprue. In that case, eliminate sugar from the child's diet for four to six weeks until the gluten intolerance is under control. Although the gluten intolerance may subside during **adolescence**, it often reoccurs during adulthood, particularly in the 30s and 40s. Many physicians consider celiac sprue disease as a life-long condition and recommend that the gluten-free diet be followed throughout life.

For Further Study

Books

Braly, James, M.D. and Laura Torbet. *Dr. Braly's Food Allergy and Nutrition Revolution.* New Canaan, CT: Keats Publishing, 1992.

Gluten Intolerance: A Resource Including Recipes. Chicago: American Dietetic Association, 1985.

Wood, Marion N. *Coping with the Gluten-Free Diet.* Springfield, IL: Thomas, 1982.

Organizations

Celiac Disease Foundation
    Address: 13251 Ventura Blvd.
    Studio City, CA 91604-1838
    Telephone: (818) 990-2354
Celiac Sprue Association/USA Inc.
    Address: 120 North 69TH Street
    Omaha, NE 68132-2720
    Telephone: (402) 558-0600
    (Publishes cookbooks and other information.)

—Mary McNulty

Cerebral Palsy

A permanent motor disability caused by brain damage associated with birth.

Cerebral palsy (CP) results from head injury after birth. The primary effects of cerebral palsy range from mild impairment of movement of one part of the body to severe impairment of most **gross** and **fine motor** functions. CP can also cause sight and **hearing** impairments, problems with **depth perception** and balance, **learning disabilities**, and **mental retardation**. Motor problems associated with CP often impair a person's ability to walk, talk, eat, breathe, speak, and control bladder functions, and he or she must receive significant support to perform the daily functions of living.

Cerebral palsy occurs in about 2.5 of every 1,000 live births, so that between 500,00 and 750,000 people in the United States have the disorder. In 30–75% of cases the original cause is unknown. Many birth-related problems associated with CP, such as German measles, RH incompatibility, and asphyxiation during labor, have been nearly eliminated, yet the incidence of CP has not declined accordingly. Some suggest that the relative increase in incidence of CP may be due to increased survival of premature infants. Research has also linked in utero formation of brain cysts with CP.

CP is primarily a problem of planning and controlling movement. Any movement of the human body consists of a delicately timed and coordinated process of muscle contraction (shortening) and expansion (lengthening). For example, to perform the fairly simple act of raising the hand to touch the face, muscles in the front of the arm (biceps) contract and tighten as the muscles in back (triceps) expand and loosen. Lack of coordination of changes in the two muscles results in jerky movement. The act of stopping the movement is as important as initiating and coordinating it. CP is categorized both by the type of muscle affliction and by the location of afflicted muscles.

There are three main types of muscle affliction: *spastic*, *ataxic*, and *athetoid*. In *spastic* CP, the afflicted muscles are extremely tight. People with spastic CP have stiff and jerky movements and difficulty letting go of objects they are gripping. About half of all CP is spastic CP. By contrast, people with the much rarer *ataxic* CP have very loose muscles and experience problems holding onto things. Shakiness and difficulties with depth perception characterize ataxic CP. In *athetoid* CP the afflicted muscles are sometimes too tight and sometimes too loose. Due to random muscle expansions and contractions people with athetoid CP have trouble sitting or standing up and experience involuntary movement of the face, arms, and upper body. About 25% of people with CP have athetoid CP, and another 25% have a combination of forms.

When muscles on all four of the limbs (and usually the trunk and face) are afflicted by cerebral palsy, it is called *quadriplegia*. When only one side of the body is afflicted, it is called *hemiplegia*. When only the legs are afflicted or the leg muscles are more severely impaired than the arms, it is described as *diplegia*. The set of speech problems caused by difficulties moving the jaws, lips, and tongue in persons with quadriplegia is called *dysarthria*.

School-age children with CP

Disabilities associated with cerebral palsy are classified under the Individuals with Disabilities Act, which entitles children ages 3–21 to a "free, appropriate public education" to take place in the "least restrictive environment" (LRE). A team of professionals, including the regular teacher, **special education** teacher, and physical therapists, will perform an initial evaluation of the child's developmental needs and develop an Individualized Educational Plan (IEP) for the child that will be continually updated. Parents usually participate in the planning and evaluation process, and they must approve any changes in the IEP itself. In addition to regular educational goals, objectives for students with CP may include the areas of motor control and perception, augmentative communication, and living and leisure skills.

Increasing adoption of the policy of inclusion—maximum integration of special education students into the regular classroom—requires modification of the environment and the instructional design for students with cerebral palsy. Two of the most important factors in the success of inclusion, also called "mainstreaming," are (1) a high positive attitude on the part of the regular teacher and (2) the presence of an assistant to help the regular teacher modify instructional methods and procedures.

Some important beginning objectives for teachers with students having cerebral palsy are: (1) to modify the classroom environment to accommodate the student's movement, and (2) to become familiar with the student's primary and preferred methods of communication. The quadriplegic student in particular may use a combination of augmentative devices, including a **"communication board"** with symbols, words, and letters on it, a computerized communication device with a keyboard, digital display, and/or voice simulator, and a unicorn stick (strapped to the head) or other pointing device. Communication may be awkward at first, but given a supportive environment the teacher and other students will gradually learn the language of gesture, eye movements, and sound that many students with CP use to communicate.

For Further Study

Books

Aaseng, Nathan. *Cerebral Palsy.* New York: F. Watts, 1991.

Schleichkorn, Jay. *Coping with Cerebral Palsy: Answers to Questions Parents Often Ask.* 2nd ed. Austin, TX: PRO-ED, 1993.

Sanford, Doris. *Yes, I Can!: Challenging Cerebral.* Sisters, OR: Multnomah Press, 1992. [juvenile literature]

Audiovisual Recordings

American Film Institute. *About Annie.* New York: Carousel Film & Video, 1989.
(One 9-minute videorecording about a teenage girl with cerebral palsy.)

Cerebral Palsy: Advances in Treatment and Technology. Cleveland, OH: Cleveland Clinic Foundation, 1992.
(One 2-hour videorecording.)

Organizations

American Coalition of Citizens with Disabilities
   Address: 1346 Connecticut Avenue, NW
   Washington, DC 20036
   Telephone: (202) 785-4265

The Association for the Severely Handicapped
   Address: 7010 Roosevelt Way, NE
   Seattle, WA 98115
   Telephone: (206) 283-5055

United Cerebral Palsy Association
   Address: 7 Penn Plaza, Suite 804
   New York, NY 10001
   Telephone: (800) USA-1UCP
   (A nationwide network of state and local voluntary agencies which provides services and conducts public and professional education programs. Direct services include medical diagnosis, evaluation, and treatment; therapy; assistive technology; information and referral; early intervention; employment; individual and family support; social and recreation programs; community inclusion and independent living; and advocacy and community education.)

Character Education

Education movement to teach morals and values.

Character education, growing in popularity in the 1990s, is the name given to the effort to teach basic values and moral reasoning to primary and secondary school students. Although most character education initiatives in the United States have developed on the local or state level, they reflect a national trend. In 1995, President Bill Clinton and the U.S. Congress declared October 16–22 "National Character Counts Week." Based on the premise that values can be taught, teachers in character education confront students with moral dilemmas and ask them to formulate and defend courses of action. Proponents and supporters include many prominent educators, politicians, and academics.

Parents and educators who are skeptical about the concept of teaching values point out that there is no documented evidence that character education actually improves character. The American Civil Liberties Union bases its opposition to character education on the grounds that it may enable schools to begin teaching religious beliefs. Some religious groups are also hostile to the idea. They feel that public schools, mandated to avoid teaching of religion, will make character a virtue that is anti-religious.

See also **Moral Development** *and* **Values**

For Further Study

Organizations
Center for the 4th and 5th R's (Respect and Responsibility)
   Address: State University of New York—Cortland
   P.O. Box 2000
   Cortland, NY 13045
   Telephone: (607) 753-2011
Character Counts Coalition
   Address: Josephson Institute of Ethics
   4640 Admiralty Way, Suite 1001
   Marina Del Rey, CA 90292
   Telephone: (310) 306-1868
   (Publishes *Ethics in Action* newsletter for members; the stated mission of the Josephson Institute is to improve the ethical quality of society by changing personal and organizational decision-making and behavior.)

Cheating

Intentionally breaking the rules or achieving personal gain through fraud or deceit.

Cheating is defined as the intentional act of breaking the rules, or attempting to achieve personal gain through fraud or deceit. With children, cheating usually refers to academic fraud, such as copying answers from another student while taking an exam, or breaking the rules in a game.

Cheating as a concept is not understood by children until around age seven. Preschoolers often change the rules to a game as they play, innocent of the fact that rules must remain consistent to have any meaning. By seven, however, children have gained an understanding of rules, fairness, and honesty, and cheating then becomes intentional.

Children may cheat for a number of reasons. Some never develop a sense of **guilt,** so they have no internal inhibitors to breaking rules. If they will gain something by breaking a rule, they break it without a qualm. Others experience a thrill in breaking rules, finding it exhilarating to oppose authority. "Getting away with it" gives them a sense of superiority and power over the rule makers and enforcers. Children who lack sufficient challenges in their lives may cheat out of **boredom,** in effect creating a challenge for themselves.

Many children cheat because they feel compelled to measure up to a standard that they do not believe they can reach honestly. Older children and teens are dependent on peer approval and dread exposing themselves as "stupid" or "slow." They will risk the consequences of being caught cheating rather than be humiliated by a poor performance. Parents may put pressure on their children to succeed in school, creating expectations beyond their children's abilities. To avoid disappointing their parents, or to avoid punishment, students will cheat to make good grades. Even those children with a well-developed sense of honesty will sometimes choose to cheat rather than fail.

The tendency to cheat is inversely related to the expectation of success. If a person has experienced repeated successes in a certain area, she will be much less likely to consider cheating in that area than one who has experienced repeated failures. Some early studies of cheating appeared to show that cheating was related to **intelligence,** with "less intelligent" students cheating at a much higher rate than "more intelligent" students. However, the tests used in these early studies were academically oriented, an area in which the better students had experienced repeated success while the poorer students had experienced failures. Therefore, the poorer students were more likely to consider cheating when faced with the academic tests. New studies have been conducted using nonacademic tests with which academically oriented students are unfamiliar. In these studies, "smart" students were at least as likely, if not more likely, to cheat when given the opportunity. In fact, when tests were given that were geared to areas in which poorer academic students had experienced greater success than academically oriented students, the poorer students rarely considered cheating while the academically oriented students cheated.

Studies have also discovered a class (socioeconomic) difference in attitudes toward cheating. Middle- and upper-class children who have been raised with academically oriented values view cheating as a much more serious issue than stealing. The theft of knowledge is considered a greater crime than the theft of money or material goods, for example. In contrast, lower- and working-class children who have grown up in a world that emphasizes material survival, and in which higher education is an unlikely privilege, view stealing as much more heinous than cheating. Therefore, class background must be taken into account when dealing with a child who is cheating.

When a child is caught cheating, adults should not focus primarily on the crime but rather on the cause(s) of it. Sometimes adult expectations are too high for the child's abilities, and the pressure to succeed is too great. If the child is surrounded by peers who are working at a more advanced level than the child can achieve, she may need more attention or a different peer group. Until the underlying causes are determined, no amount of **discipline** will stop the child from cheating.

See also **Moral Development; Self-Conscious Emotions; Values.**

For Further Study

Books

Kurtines, William M., and Jacob L. Gewirtz. *Moral Development: An Introduction.* Boston: Allyn and Bacon, 1995.

Schulman, Michael, and Eva Mekler. *Bringing Up a Moral Child: A New Approach for Teaching Your Child to Be Kind, Just, and Responsible.* New York: Doubleday, 1994.

Sears, William. *The Discipline Book: Everything You Need to Know to Have a Better-Behaved Child—From Birth to Age 10,* 1st ed. Boston: Little, Brown and Co., 1995.

—Dianne K. Daeg de Mott

Chicken Pox

Highly contagious childhood disease caused by the varicella zoster virus, and for which there is a vaccine to provide immunity.

Chicken pox is a highly contagious childhood disease that, until the vaccine became available in the mid-1990s, affected nearly all children under the age of ten years. In the late 1980s, there were a reported 3.9 million cases of chicken pox each year in the United States. The **American Academy of Pediatrics** estimates that more

than 95% of the population contracted chicken pox prior to the availability of the vaccine. Most cases are fairly mild, with the child suffering seven to ten days of discomfort. A small percentage of chicken pox sufferers require hospitalization. Chicken pox is highly contagious. A person with chicken pox is contagious from one to two days before the outbreak of the chicken pox rash, and for six days after the rash erupts. After being exposed, a person will show symptoms of chicken pox within 10–21 days. A person can only get chicken pox once.

Symptoms of the disease include a mild **fever** for one to two days before the appearance of a skin rash (small, watery blisters) that begins on the scalp and body and spreads within three to four days over the entire body. A typical case of chicken pox involves between 250 and 500 blisters over the body. These dry into scabs after three or four days. The blisters are itchy, and children should be discouraged from scratching and their fingernails should be kept very short for the duration of the chicken pox case. There are commercial products available, such as oatmeal baths and calamine lotion, that may help to relieve the itching of chicken pox. Although complications from chicken pox are generally uncommon, the most common one is bacterial infection of the skin, initiated at the site of a chicken pox blister that has broken or was scratched open. Other complications include viral or bacterial pneumonia and **encephalitis** (swelling of the brain). The groups that are at higher risk for developing complications are anyone with a weak **immune system**; children with lung diseases; children with eczema or other skin conditions; infants under one year of age; premature infants whose mothers have not had chicken pox; and newborns whose mothers had chicken pox around the time of delivery. When an adult gets chicken pox, the case is usually more severe and lasts longer. Adults are 10 times more likely than children to require hospitalization from chicken pox. An oral anti-viral drug, acyclovir, may be prescribed for anyone at risk of developing a severe case of chicken pox. Acyclovir is only effective if it is given within 24 hours of the outbreak of the chicken pox blisters. Shingles, known medically as herpes zoster, is a condition of the nerves caused by the chicken pox virus that affects between 10–20% of all people who have ever had chicken pox. Once a person has had chicken pox, the virus remains in his or her nerve roots for the rest of his or her life. The virus most commonly reappears as shingles at age 50 or older, although shingles can occur anytime. Shingles cause numbness, itching, or severe pain in skin areas where the affected nerve root is located, and within about three days, causes clusters of blisters to form along the affected nerve. The blisters last two to three weeks.

For Further Study

Books

Bellet, Paul S. *The Diagnostic Approach to Common Symptoms and Signs in Infants, Children, and Adolescents.* New York: Lea and Febiger, 1989.

Clayman, Charles B., and Jeffrey R. M. Kunz. (eds.) *Children: How to Understand Their Symptoms.* New York: Random House, 1986.

Garwood, John, and Amanda Bennett. *Your Child's Symptoms.* New York: Berkeley Books, 1995.

Organizations

National Institute of Allergy and Infectious Diseases (NIAID)
Address: 9000 Rockville Pike
NIH Building 31, Room 7A50
Bethesda, MD 20892-2520
Telephone: (301) 496-5717
(Arm of the National Institutes of Health that deals with allergies and diseases.)

March of Dimes Birth Defects Foundation
Address: 1275 Mamaroneck Avenue
White Plains, NY 10605
Telephone: (914) 428-7100
(Publishes information sheets on specific birth defects and related topics, including *Chicken Pox During Pregnancy.*)

Child Abuse, Physical

Alternative Terms: Battered Child, Child Maltreatment, Family Violence

Physical child abuse refers to harm to the child inflicted by the **caregiver**. Every year, nearly 1,400 cases of fatal child abuse are reported. Recent information from investigators of child fatality records suggests that the actual number of children killed by their caregivers may be much, much larger. Child Death Review Teams are now being formed in many states to investigate child fatalities that may come from physical abuse. Legal definitions of child abuse vary from state to state, but injuries requiring medical attention are typically regarded as abusive. Nonetheless, the difficulties associated with making these kinds of distinctions are well known, and are often characterized by saying that "one person's 'abuse' is another person's '**discipline**'." Many states explicitly note that spanking "when administered in a reasonable manner" does not constitute abuse. Thus, how severely parents can inflict physical punishment upon their children without it being considered abusive remains subject to interpretation.

Child abuse is costly to society in a number of ways. Medical costs for direct care to children injured by their parents exceed $20 million each year; the bulk of this amount is paid by taxpayers through Medicaid. **Special education** services for abused children cost $7 million per year. The direct costs are small in comparison to the $460 million annual costs of **foster care** for children removed from their home due to parental maltreatment. None of these costs reflect the dysfunction and misery that are seen later in the lives of some abused children.

Physical abuse differs from emotional abuse, in which the child may be ridiculed, blamed or terrorized; sexual abuse, in which the child is subject to sexual behaviors ranging from exposure to intercourse; and child neglect, in which the parents fail to provide the necessities of life or fail to protect the child from harm. However, the factors that place the child at risk for emotional abuse, sexual abuse, and neglect are similar to the factors that lead to physical child abuse. These factors include personality and social class of the parent and the **temperament** of the child. Understanding why these factors increase the risk of child abuse may ultimately help intervention efforts. This entry will consider the impact of physical child abuse across several developmental levels, explore the risk factors for child abuse, and look at methods of treatment and prevention.

The U.S. Department of Health and Human Services collects data on the incidence of child abuse in the United States. The accompanying table on page 140 provides information on the distribution by age.

A Developmental analysis
Infancy

Infants who are premature, mentally retarded, or have physical handicaps are more likely to provoke abuse from their caregiver than are infants without such problems. Similarly, nonhandicapped infants who are nonrhythmic (that is, have uneven sleep and eating patterns) are more likely to be abused. It appears that it is the child's tendency to learn slowly, to be less coordinated, or less affectionate—rather than any physical problem per se—that promotes abuse.

Nonabusive parents are responsive to their infants' emotional cues, and tend to alter their interaction with the infant based on the success of their actions. Abusive parents, in contrast, tend to have rigid patterns of responding, regardless of how their infants react. They become angry when their infant does not respond as they think he or she should. In turn, the infants become wary and fail to become comfortably attached to the mother; when the mother tries to leave them, they either cling to her or display negative affect (e.g., fearful expression, screaming), and when she returns they give conflicted messages, demanding the mother and then pushing her away.

Infants, because of their fragility, are more susceptible to injury from physical discipline than older children. Infants are especially susceptible to head injury from shaking or being thrown. A baby can be fatally injured by being thrown even onto a soft mattress. The ba-

CHILD ABUSE VICTIMS BY AGE, 1994	
Age of child	**Percent of total abuse victims**
Under age 1	7%
1 year	6.2%
2 years	6.6%
3 years	6.8%
4 years	6.7%
5 years	6.5%
6 years	6.3%
7 years	6%
8 years	5.7%
9 years	5.3%
10 years	4.9%
11 years	4.7%
12 years	4.7%
13 years	4.8%
14 years	4.8%
15 years	4.3%
16 years	3.3%
17 years	2.2%
18 years and older	0.8%
Age unknown	2.1%

by's brain hits the back of the skull if thrown with even mild force and intracranial bleeding can result. One expert suggested that the majority of fatal head injuries in infants are inflicted by caregivers.

Toddlerhood

Toddlers are among the most difficult children to control. They make the most demands on parents in terms of efforts to feed them and keep them safe, and are the most attention seeking. All of these attributes contribute to the likelihood of a toddler being abused.

Abusive parents are particularly sensitive to threats to their ability to maintain control over the child. Thus, when their children approach the developmental tasks of the "terrible twos," which involve learning autonomy and beginning control over their environment, their normal behavior is often seen by abusive parents as willfulness

that must be controlled. Because abusive parents often have inaccurate ideas about the capabilities of toddlers, normal soiling of clothes that occur with eating and toileting are seen as deliberate misbehaviors. If the child is punished inconsistently for behaviors that he or she cannot help, the child feels helpless, angry, and confused about how he or she is supposed to respond. With abusive parents as models, the child begins to react aggressively and with a **tantrum** to parental discipline, responses which actually serve to heighten the potential for abuse. It is not surprising that 60% of the major physical injuries inflicted by caregivers occur in children under age 4.

Preschool

Children who have been abused typically show **developmental delays** by the time they are in preschool. It is unclear if these delays occur due to inadequate stimulation and uncertainty in the child about the learning environment, and absence of positive parental interactions that would stimulate language and motor processes, or cumulative neurological damage. These delays, in concert with their parents' higher-than-normal expectations for their children's self-care and self-control abilities, generally provoke additional abuse.

Abused preschoolers respond to peers and other adults with more aggression and anger than do nonabused children. A coercive cycle in which parents and children mutually control one another with threats of negative behavior is evident in many abused preschoolers.

School age

School-age children are expected to function within a variety of social and academic environments. Abused children have more problems within these arenas than do nonabused children. Academic problems are typical, with both poorer grades and poorer performance on standardized achievement tests. Studies that have examined abused children's intellectual performance find lower scores in both verbal and performance (e.g., math, visual-spatial) areas. Abused children also tend to be distractible and overactive, which makes school a very difficult environment.

Peers become increasingly important to school-age children. Abused children are often more aggressive with their peers and are more likely to be socially rejected than other children. They tend to be less mature socially and show difficulty in developing trusting relationships with others.

Abused children are also more disruptive and aggressive within the home, and are frequently viewed by their parents as defiant and noncompliant. Although observational measures confirm their higher levels of disruptiveness, it also appears that the number and intensity of problem behaviors seen by abusive parents in their children may be partially a function of the parents' lower threshold of tolerance for children's noncompliance.

Adolescence

By the time abused children become adolescents, they are more likely to be in contact with the juvenile justice system than children with a comparable family constellation and income level. Many of these children are labeled "ungovernable" for committing such offenses as **running away** and **truancy**, but a higher proportion of abused than nonabused delinquent youth are also involved in crimes of assault.

Follow-up on abused children in later adolescence shows that in addition to having problems with the law, they are more likely to be substance abusers or to have emotional disturbances such as **depression**. Children who are abused are more likely to grow up to be adults who abuse their own children.

Risk factors for physical abuse

Sociocultural factors

Poverty is the sociocultural factor most strongly linked to abuse. Although physical abuse occurs at all income levels, it happens more often in very poor families. It is true that in middle-class families, child injuries are treated by a sympathetic personal physician who may be less likely to diagnose and report abuse-related injuries than the physician in the emergency room who is more likely to treat poor families. Even with such reporting bias, however, poverty seems strongly linked to abuse. It seems that the frustrating effects of poverty on parents are instrumental in creating situations for parents' abuse.

Physical crowding, more likely to occur in poverty, is also associated with abuse. If too many people share a small living space, severe **punishment** of children as a means of maintaining control is more likely.

If a parent lacks social support, abuse is more likely. Having no one to assist with child care and no one to question the use of severe discipline increase the chance that a parent may injure a child.

Caregiver factors

Parents who were themselves abused as children are more likely to abuse their own children. However, not every parent who was abused becomes an abuser; some parents go to great lengths to insure that they never harm their child.

Parents who abuse their children are likely to be younger than the average parent. They are more likely to be single parents. Having emotional problems such as depression or abusing drugs or alcohol also makes a parent more likely to abuse a child.

Child factors

As noted earlier, children from birth to age 4 are the most likely to be injured from abuse. This may be because young children are physically more vulnerable to severe discipline and because children at this age are the most dependent upon the caregiver, the most in need of parental control, and the most provocative (in terms of making messes, saying "no," and other behaviors).

Children who are handicapped and those who are nonrhythmic (that is, with unpredictable eating and sleeping patterns), are more likely to be abused. Similarly, children who are distractible, impulsive, or who have high activity levels are more likely to draw severe physical discipline.

Components to nonabusive parenting skills

Abusive parents socialize differently from nonabusive parents. Nonabusive parents tend to use ignoring or **time-out procedure,** whereas abusive parents tend to shout, threaten, and spank. Some forms of child abuse escalate over time, with the parent spanking harder and more frequently to get the same effect or resorting to abuse to get results. Female caregivers inflict more soft tissue injuries, broken bones, and internal injuries than male caregivers. Severe injuries from a single, explosive incident in which the child is shaken, thrown, or struck are more likely to involve male caregivers.

Awareness of child development

Abusive parents often expect the child to perform behaviors he or she is not yet capable of performing. Parents who abuse their young children expect them to be able to control their impulses, recall and obey complex parental rules, and perform mature chains of behavior such a getting up, washing, and getting dressed by themselves. Nonabusive parents recognize that toddlers and preschool children are incapable of such behaviors. Understanding the limitations of a young child's **memory**, ability to be controlled by words, impulse control, and attention span is essential to developing reasonable expectations for the child. Parents who expect behavior the child cannot deliver are apt to progressively increase their control techniques in order to get the child to comply.

Beliefs and attitudes

Abusive discipline is often the result of the belief that the young child is capable of better behavior and that he or she is deliberately misbehaving to cause the parent difficulty. Such parents often claim that their 18-month-old could stay clean if she wanted to but she dirties her pants just to make more work for the mother. Abusive parents, who believe a child has chosen to misbehave, inflict more punishment on their children than parents who accurately recognize when a child's behavior is not intentional.

Such abusive parents also often believe that effective parenting involves maintaining tight control over the child. A mother who can toilet train her child early and keep the child in line at the grocery store is viewed by abusive parents as a "good" mother. Closely tied to beliefs about the importance of control are aphorisms such as "spare the rod, spoil the child" and "respect comes through fear," which indicate that children learn best through the application of force. Before abusive parents will use skills such as ignoring or time-out, they have to change their beliefs about the importance of control, especially control through physical means.

Another belief abusive parents often hold is that their children should engage in reciprocal parenting. They believe that if they sometimes comfort, wait on, and take care of the child, the child should do the same for them. Such beliefs fit with abusive parents' lack of awareness of children's developmental capabilities and may also stem from the parents' own immaturity and lack of support from other adults. Regardless of the source, when such expectations for children are not met, the parent often responds with anger and hostility.

Emotion

Anger is the most frequent trigger for parental abuse. Abusive parents appear to have a lower threshold for childish behaviors than average parents. Abusive parents are more upset by the same child cues than nonabusive parents. Thus, child behaviors that are merely irritating to average parents are infuriating to abusive parents. Finally, abusive parents may have less control over their anger than nonabusive parents, either because they are unaware of their level of anger, because they are chronically angry, or because they lack anger management skills.

When considering how emotion influences child abuse, it seems important to consider positive emotions as well. Abusive parents experience their children as less rewarding than nonabusive parents. In observation, abusive parents touch their children less, cuddle them less, less frequently call the affectionate names ("honey," "sweetheart"), and smile less at their children. Nonabusive parents respond flexibly to their children, letting the child lead the play interaction. Even in play, abusive parents have expectations that their children seem unable or unwilling to fulfill, making play a disagreeable chore rather than a rewarding endeavor. Abusive parents seem trapped by their own lack of skills, limited developmental understanding, inappropriate expectations, high negative emotion, and low enjoyment of the child.

Altering the parental role

In order to alter abusive parenting, changes need to occur at every level. As abusive parents experience more positive child behaviors, they can respond with praise and rewards to increase the behaviors they like. As positive behaviors increase, negative behaviors decrease. Further, as parents accept the notion that absolute, tight control over the child is not the best goal of parenting, it becomes easier for them to ignore rather than to punish annoying behaviors. If the parent understands that some irritating child behaviors (such as saying "no" or wanting to do it him or herself) are positive and normal developmental behaviors, less anger is directed at the child. Similarly, when the parent's expectations are more in line with what the child can actually do, the parent is not so often annoyed by the child's failure to complete certain tasks, and the parent becomes more competent in requesting appropriate behavior change from the child. When the parent has given up the belief that fear is necessary for children to learn, then the parent is ready to use skills such as ignoring, time-out, and appropriate compliance requests.

Barriers

There are many barriers to change in abusive parental behavior. Most parents' own history suggests that strong physical discipline is the preferred model of parenting. Further, most abusive parents live in families and neighborhoods in which violence is not only condoned but viewed as a necessary vehicle for interpersonal influence. The stresses that are omnipresent in abusive parents' lives assist in maintaining high levels of anger and depression, which block the positive enjoyment of the child. When the parent responds with strong physical discipline, the child's misbehavior typically stops, for that moment at any rate. Thus, the parent is intermittently rewarded for responding abusively. Thus, changing abusive parenting is a challenging task.

It may be preferable to prevent the development of abusive parenting by early interventions to give skills, alter developmental knowledge, change unreasonable parenting expectations, and block the steady build-up of anger and extinguishing of affection for the child. Prevention programs now target teenagers before pregnancy as well as young mothers to try to break the cycle of abuse.

For Further Study

Books

Calam, Rachel, and Cristina Franchi. *Child Abuse and Its Consequences: Observational Approaches.* New York: Cambridge University Press, 1987.

Ludwig, Stephen, and Allan E. Kornberg. *Child Abuse: A Medical Reference.* 2d ed. New York: Churchill Livingstone, 1992.

Owen, Hilary, and Jacki Pritchard. *Good Practice in Child Protection: A Manual for Professionals.* Bristol, PA: Jessica Kingsley Publishers, 1993.

Park, Angela. *Child Abuse.* New York: Gloucester Press, 1988.

Squyres, Suzanne B., Alison Landes, and Jacquelyn Quiram. (eds.) *Child Abuse.* Wylie, TX: Information Plus, 1997.

Tzeng, Oliver C. S., Jay W. Jackson, and Henry H. Karlson. *Theories of Child Abuse and Neglect: Differential Perspectives, Summaries, and Evaluations.* New York: Praeger, 1991.

Walker, C. Eugene, Barbara L. Bonner, and Keith L. Kaufman. *The Physically and Sexually Abused Child: Evaluation and Treatment.* New York: Pergamon Press, 1987.

Audiovisual Recording

Bass, Ellen. *The Courage to Heal.* New York, NY: Caedmon, 1989.
(Two audio cassettes [three hours].)

———. *The Courage to Heal. Part 2, Changing Patterns.* New York: Harper Audio, 1993.
(Two audio cassettes [3 hours].)

Battered Child, Battered Trust. New York: Columbia University Seminars on Media and Society, 1986.
(One 60-minute videocassette.)

Childhood Sexual Abuse. Princeton, NJ: Films for the Humanities and Sciences, 1990.
(One videocassette.)

—Lizette Peterson, Ph.D.
University of Missouri–Columbia

Child Abuse, Sexual and Emotional

Committed acts of sexual or emotional assault or neglect on a child.

See also **Child Abuse, Physical**

Child abuse includes assaults in any of several domains (physical, sexual, or emotional) and may be acts of commission (abuse) or omission (neglect). Congress broadly defines child abuse in Public Law 93-247 as the "physical or mental injury, sexual abuse, negligent treatment, or maltreatment of a child under the age of eighteen by a person who is responsible for the child's welfare under circumstances which indicate that the child's health or welfare is threatened thereby." Many researchers and clinicians view child abuse as a broad collection and range of acts.

Physical abuse

Physical abuse is injury to the child inflicted by a **caregiver**. It is sometimes evidenced by multiple bruises or abrasions, by injuries in soft tissue areas (e.g., upper arm, thigh, buttocks) or by bruises, burns, or other marks in the shape of fingers, hands, or other objects. Unexplained multiple fractures are sometimes detectable on x rays. Trauma to the head or eye is sometimes the result of "the shaken baby syndrome." For more information about this type of abuse, see **Child Abuse, Physical.** The remainder of this essay will discuss sexual and emotional abuse.

Sexual abuse

Children are said to be sexually abused when they experience sexual contact with an adult or older child through coercion or deceptive manipulation at an age and stage of development at which they do not possess sufficient maturity to understand the nature of the acts and therefore to provide informed consent. Often physical force is not necessary since the perpetrator is likely to be someone with whom the child has a trusting relationship and who is in a position of authority over the child.

The type of sexual contact may involve intercourse, touching or fondling the genitals or secondary sex organs with hands, mouth, or objects, or being forced to perform sexual acts with another person. Contact may not involve any actual touching. Children can be coerced into disrobing and exposing themselves, or watching adults disrobe or engage in sexual activity. In some cases, children can be involved in ritualistic sexual abuse as part of **cult** or other belief-driven practice.

Perpetrators go to great lengths to conceal sexual abuse. Children who have been sexually abused may not report the behavior due to threats or to a lack of understanding of what has happened. In addition, they may be confused by the simultaneous physical arousal they may feel and the clearly covert, possibly threatening nature of the event. Evidence of abuse may show in physical symptoms, such as rashes or injuries to the genital area and blood or discharge in bedding or underwear; advanced sexual knowledge for the child's age; provocative or seductive behavior toward others; bedwetting after the child has established the ability to stay dry through the night; declining peer relationships; fear of a person, place, or object associated with the abuse; or changes in school behavior or performance. In addition, older children or adolescents may begin to act out or to withdraw, use drugs or alcohol, or begin to harm themselves or become preoccupied with thoughts of death.

Emotional abuse

Abuse of children is not limited to the physical body. Children who are repeatedly called names, insulted, belittled, intimidated, rejected, criticized, terrorized, or corrupted by those upon whom they are dependent for nurturance have little opportunity to develop any sense of self-worth.

Emotional abuse may also be the result of actions not directed specifically at the child. The prevalence of domestic and community violence exposes children to intimidating and frightening scenes every day. A study at Boston City Hospital found that one in ten children living in an inner city neighborhood had observed a shooting or a knifing by the age of six; half of these incidents occurred in the home and half in the streets. Studies have shown that when children live in homes in which domestic violence is a problem, 75–87% of them witness the violence and 40–60% of them experience abuse themselves, often as a result of being "caught in the middle" of a parental altercation. Children who observe violence react with many of the same psychological symptoms as children who have experienced it directly.

Neglect

Children who are not provided with basic food, shelter, and clothing to the best of their parent's ability are considered neglected. Not surprisingly, neglect is more prevalent in areas of extreme poverty than in other socioeconomic strata. Neglect may be evidenced in undernourishment or **failure to thrive.** Children may not be able to attend or learn in school because of lack of food or sleep. They may develop rashes or infections that go untreated. Failure to send children to school or otherwise provide for their education may also be considered neglect.

What are the outcomes of child abuse?

It is important to remember that there are often multiple factors to consider when discussing the results of child abuse. Abuse seldom occurs in isolation; there may be other problems in the family such as **alcoholism** or the stress of unemployment. Children may also experience multiple forms of abuse. Children may or may not have a supportive relationship with another adult to whom they can turn for support. Children may be abused for an acute period before there is some intervention, or they may experience the trauma chronically and for many years. The child's age and resources, the kind of relationship between the child and the perpetrator, the length and chronicity of the abuse, and the availability of therapy or other intervention services are all factors that contribute to the wide range of long- and short-term outcomes associated with child abuse.

Nonetheless, most children who have been abused experience some symptoms of Post Traumatic Stress Disorder (PTSD). PTSD in children and adolescents may be acute or delayed, that is, the child may experience symptoms immediately or after a period of time has passed, perhaps when the child feels safe. Symptoms may include re-experiencing the abusive episodes at some level, feeling emotionally numb, or becoming physiologically aroused (elevated heart rate, respiration, and so forth). Children may experience disassociation and appear to "space out" when reminded of the abuse or perpetrator. They may have physical symptoms. They may become enraged or feel **guilt** at having provoked the episodes or survived them. They may have invasive

memories, repeated behaviors, or fears related to the abusive situations. They may act out some of their issues in play—punishing the bad guy or victimizing another character while playing with dolls or action figures. In severe cases of chronic trauma, the child may develop serious or prolonged disassociation or **depression.** Severe and chronic abuse has also been implicated in cases of multiple personality disorder.

Once the abuse has stopped, most of these symptoms can be treated with some form of counseling or therapy. Some have argued that full recovery is a lifelong task. Adults who have been abused as children may have to face issues long after the abuse has stopped, when they enter into their own sexual relationships, or when they raise their own children.

Do abused children become abusing adults? The de facto intergenerational transmission of child abuse is not supported by the facts. It appears that the cycle of abuse can be broken, and often is. Social workers David Gil found that only 11% of the abusing parents he studied reported having been abused themselves as children. More importantly, prospective studies of parents who have been abused as children or who were at high risk for abusing their own children found that about 70–80% of parents were able to break the cycle.

Who abuses?

No single causal factor explains who abuses children and who does not. The contributing factors are multifaceted and may be best understood from an ecological point of view, that is, identifying factors that operate in the person, the immediate social environment, and in the culture as a whole. Child abuse is most likely the product of environmental stressors acting upon a person with psychological vulnerabilities in a culture in which violent behavior is an acceptable form of venting the resultant frustrations.

Abusing adults tend to be socially isolated, although it is not clear whether this isolation is due to poor social skills or to circumstance. Some have been abused themselves as children. Abusive incidents are often associated with alcohol consumption and the subsequent blurred judgment and decreased inhibitory control. Parents who abuse their children often overestimate the child's developmental capabilities and interpret behaviors as intentionally directed toward them, even the crying or soiling of young infants.

Although child abuse exists across socioeconomic, racial, and ethnic groups, it is more prevalent in lower-income groups in which the stresses of everyday life are often greater. Job loss and dissatisfaction are often associated with child abuse. Higher rates of abuse exist in military compared to non-military families. It is generally felt that the link between these environmental stressors and abuse is strengthened by the absence of social support networks that might otherwise buffer the family against adversity.

History of social policy

Despite the fact that children have long suffered from intentionally inflicted injuries or death, there have been few organized, comprehensive programs addressing the problem of child abuse. Although certain religions have long prohibited infanticide, and the establishment of asylums and orphanages to rear children whose lives were endangered by family violence or neglect is a practice centuries old, efforts to advocate for the children's basic right to health and safety have been meager and scattered.

Current social policy regarding child abuse in the United States began to take shape with the social work movements in large cities during the latter portion of the nineteenth century. One particular case, that of an 8-year-old girl who was discovered chained, starved, and beaten by her parents in New York City, was brought to the attention of Henry Berg, founder of the Society for the Prevention of Cruelty to Animals. Because no laws existed prohibiting the abuse of children by their parents, the police did not intervene. However, as a result of Berg's efforts, the mother was tried and incarcerated, and the child was removed to an orphanage. The publicity surrounding this case lead to the founding of the Society for the Prevention of Cruelty to Children in 1875.

Until the mid-twentieth century, child abuse was considered a social and legal, but not a medical, issue. Social standards and definitions were used to protect children and intervene as necessary to ensure their welfare. Legal definitions, though often vague, were designed to delineate which perpetrators could be prosecuted and under what conditions children could be made dependents of the state through the removal of parental rights and awarding of custody to the state's child welfare system. Medical definitions were not developed until advances in radiology made the detection of unreported or long-standing injuries possible. When old bone **fractures** became detectable on x ray, physicians began to apply medical diagnoses to cases of child abuse. In 1961, C. Henry Kempe and his colleagues presented a symposium on child abuse to members of the **American Academy of Pediatrics,** and the following year introduced the term "the battered child" in an influential paper.

Current status

The National Center on Child Abuse Prevention Research reported 2.69 million cases of child abuse nationally in 1991. Of these, 25% were physical abuse cases, 15% were sexual abuse, and many involved more than one type of abuse or neglect. In 1992, the number had increased to 2.9 million with 87% of the victims under the age of five years, and 46% under the age of one. Fatalities related to child abuse and neglect were estimated at over 1200 cases, or between three and four children each day.

Is the incidence of child abuse increasing? Since Kempe's influential paper in 1962, the detection and reporting of child abuse has improved. This heightened awareness makes trends difficult to interpret. For example, the U.S. Department of Health and Human Services 1986 national incidence survey found the sexual abuse rate to be 2.8 per 1,000 children, an increase of 300% from 1980, but we cannot be certain whether that increase reflected more abuse, more reporting, or both.

Barriers to dealing with the problem

Why did it take centuries for the medical, social, and legal professions to address this devastating problem? Why is child abuse still prevalent in today's society? There are several possibilities. First, children have long been viewed as the property of their parents. Acceptance of this premise makes it difficult to legislate how one should treat one's own "property" in a culture that values individual rights. Second, certain beliefs about the nature of the child, including many with religious origins, view the child inherently wicked and willful. These views promote the idea that it is for the child's own good that he or she be "disciplined." The related premise, "Spare the rod and spoil the child," equates discipline with physical action and provides justification for some parents to use corporal punishment. David Gil has found that 60% of child abuse is a direct result of corporal punishment. Parents who intend only to spank their child may get carried away with their own anger, may not know their own strength, or may simply hurt their child by accident.

When the line is crossed and punishment turns to what we agree is abuse, our tolerance implodes and our reactions are extremely emotional. Yale University psychologist and child advocate Edward Zigler has suggested three reasons why our general reactions to the subject of child abuse are so emotionally laden. First, our own insecurities are threatened by the notion of a small, helpless child being maltreated by one in whose care he or she is entrusted. Second, the occurrence of abuse stands in direct opposition to the everyday experiences of the majority of parents who are engaged in secure, loving relationships with their children. Finally, the occurrence of abuse threatens the premise of many who hold that a fundamental nurturant, parental instinct exists within the human species. These reasons may also evoke a defensive reaction in people and may contribute to our historical and continued inability to confront the issue.

For Further Study

Books

Garbarino, D., E. Guttman, and J.W. Seeley. *The Psychologically Battered Child: Strategies for Identification, Assessment, and Intervention.* San Francisco: Jossey-Bass, 1988.

Gill, D. *Violence Against Children: Physical Child Abuse in the United States.* Cambridge, MA: Harvard, 1970.

Groves, B.M. "Children Who Witness Violence." In S. Parker & B. Zuckerman (Eds.) *Behavioral and Developmental Pediatrics: A Handbook for Primary Care.* Boston: Little-Brown, 1994.

Periodicals

Hunter, R. S. and N. Kilstrom. "Breaking the Cycle in Abusive Families." *American Journal of Psychiatry* 136, 1979, pp. 1,320-1,322.

Kempe, C., F. Silverman, B. Steele, W. Droegmeuller, and H. Silver. "The Battered Child Syndrome." *Journal of the American Medical Association* 181, 1962, pp. 17-24.

Rodham, H. "Children Under the Law." *Harvard Educational Review* 43, 1973, pp. 487-514.

Zigler, E. "Controlling Child Abuse: Do We Have the Knowledge and/or the Will?" In G. Gerbner, S. L. Kagan, and E. Zigler (Eds.). *Child Abuse: An Agenda for Action.* New York: Oxford, 1980, pp. 3-34.

Zigler, E. and N. W. Hall. "Child Abuse in America." In D. Cicchetti and V. Carlson (Eds.). *Child Maltreatment: Theory and Research on the Causes and Consequences of Child Abuse and Neglect.* New York: Cambridge, 1989, pp. 38-75.

Organizations

The National Adoption Information Clearinghouse
Address: 1400 Eye Street, NW, Suite 600
Washington, D.C. 20005
Telephone: (202) 842-1919
(Maintains resources on adopting children who have been abused.)

The National Clearinghouse on Child Abuse and Neglect
Address: P.O. Box 1182
Washington, D.C. 20013
Telephone: (703) 821-2086
(Collects and disseminates information; provides general publications; and conducts individual research on a particular topic at low cost.)

The National Resource Center on Child Sexual Abuse
Address: 1141 Georgia Avenue
Wheaton, MD 20902
Telephone: (800) 543-7006
(Provides information and resources regarding child sexual abuse; publishes *Round Table Magazine*, and maintains a list of treatment programs in the nation.)

—Doreen Arcus, Ph.D.
University of Massachusetts Lowell

Child Custody Laws

Federal and state laws governing a parent's legal authority to make decisions affecting a child (legal custody) and to maintain physical control over the child (physical custody), as well as the visitation rights of the noncustodial parent.

The responsibilities for care and control of a child are governed in the United States by both federal and state laws. **Custody** may be disputed by both married and unmarried couples with minor children, including married couples who separate but do not divorce. Unmarried parents may claim custody by virtue of their biological rights even if both parents and the child have never lived together as a family. There have also been custody disputes over frozen embryos created before a couple decides to separate.

Temporary custody is often awarded following a preliminary hearing when a couple first separates or files for **divorce.** The custody arrangements are later finalized under a permanent custody or visitation order intended to remain in effect as long as the child is a minor. However, these arrangements may be modified in response to a petition by one parent or an agreement by both parents. Custody decisions in most states favor continued and frequent contact between the child and both parents, and a continued role for both parents in the raising of their children. However, despite any general patterns, custody decisions are strongly influenced by the circumstances of each individual case and their cumulative effect on the welfare of the child.

For custody purposes, parenthood can be legally defined in a number of different ways. A biological, or natural, parent is physically responsible for a child's conception. A stepparent is married to the person who has custody of the child, with whom he has no formal legal relationship. A custodial parent has physical custody of a child; the parent without physical custody is called the noncustodial parent. (Even if parents have joint legal custody, only one usually has physical custody.) Adoptive parents have legally adopted a child, assuming the rights and responsibilities that formerly belonged to the biological parents. An adult who establishes a close emotional bond with a child but is not legally responsible for her care or support is sometimes considered a psychological parent and may, on that basis, be awarded visitation rights in a custody case. Finally, the designation of equitable parent was created to protect fathers who carry out parental duties and form a relationship with a child based on the assumption that they are the child's biological parent but later learn that they are not.

There are several types of custody. Legal custody entails the right to make decisions regarding a child, while physical custody consists of providing a residence for the child and physically taking care of him. In sole custody one parent has both legal and physical custody, while the other has visitation rights. Joint legal custody means that the parents share the responsibility of making decisions about a child; joint physical custody means that they share the responsibility of providing a home for the child. Visitation by a noncustodial parent is generally governed by reasonable visitation orders, which stipulate that the parents work out their own visitation schedule, deciding on reasonable times and places. In some cases, especially where there is significant hostility between the parents, a court may impose a fixed visitation schedule with set times and places for visits by the noncustodial parent. When the court fears that visitation may endanger the child in some way, such as when the parent has a history of violence or abuse, it may order supervised visitation, with an adult other than the custodial parent present throughout each visit (this person may either be someone known to the family or appointed by the court). Grandparents in all states have the right to seek visitation rights with their grandchildren if there is a separation or divorce, or if the family is intact but denies them the right to visit.

The guiding principle in all custody decisions is protecting the best interests of the child. While each custody case has its own combination of circumstances that must be taken into account, certain factors routinely used as criteria are considered so universal that they are often written into state custody laws. In the accompanying table, examples of factors considered in child custody decision are listed with the number of states whose laws include the factor. Of course, any of these factors may (and often do) come into consideration even in those states in which they are not written into the custody laws.

Custody cases can turn ugly when parents begin making accusations of unfitness against each other. Typical accusations against mothers include claims of drug abuse, child abuse or neglect, adultery, open lesbianism, and mental or physical impairment. Some of these accusations are also aimed at fathers, in addition to domestic violence, a history of failure to pay child support, and a significant criminal record. A contesting parent may call witnesses, including relatives, neighbors, babysitters, and teachers, to testify in court, as well as mental health professionals who can provide professional testimony as to the fitness of the parent or the mental and emotional condition of the child. The child may also be asked to testify, although this is usually done in the judge's chambers (*in camera*) so that the child doesn't have to be concerned about alienating either parent, and there is no cross-examination.

It is generally agreed that it is preferable for all concerned if a custody case can be settled out of court. A common means for bringing this about when parents cannot reach an agreement themselves is mediation, a method of solving disputes with the aid of a neutral third party, often a specially trained mediator. Eleven states require mediation in custody or visitation disputes; 19 allow judges to order it at their discretion. Many parents voluntarily seek mediation, a flexible resource that can be used to work out either part or all of a custody agree-

FACTORS CONSIDERED IN CUSTODY DECISION	
Factor	**Number of states that include factor in laws**
Parent's ability to meet the children's needs	28
Parent's ability to insure that children will not be exposed to threats of violence or abuse	37
Quality of the parent-child and other family relationships	28
Preferences of the child (weight given to this factor varies with age of the child)	32
Geographic distance between the parents' homes	13
Stability of the household and the continuity of care	29
Whether the hostility of one parent is undermining the relationship between a child and the other parent or other children in the family	19
Moral fitness and conduct of the parents	12

ment. A skilled mediator can help parents shift their focus from past grievances to the future of the children, clarify vague plans or language, and generate new ideas when an impasse arises. Mediated agreements have to be voluntarily accepted by both sides.

In the 1980s and 1990s, sexual orientation came to play an increasingly significant role in child custody disputes, as gays and lesbians battle for parental rights during a divorce or the termination of a relationship or in response to charges by a third party—usually a grandparent or other relative—challenging their fitness as parents. Custody cases are the most frequent type of litigation involving gays. Court attitudes and actions toward gay parents vary widely. Some judges uniformly act on the principle that living with a homosexual parent is not in the best interests of the child, no matter what the particular situation. Others are more tolerant toward gays who limit their openness about their sexual orientation. A third stance, called the "nexus" approach, considers the possible implications of parental sexual orientation in terms of the child's actual welfare, posing questions about such matters as whether the child will be socially stigmatized because the parent or parents are gay, and whether a child raised by one or two gay parents has an increased likelihood of also becoming gay. Appeals courts in states including New York, Massachusetts, New Jersey, Alaska, and South Carolina have ruled that a parent's homosexuality does not in and of itself constitute a potential cause of harm to a child. However, while the "nexus test" is supposedly the most enlightened approach, it can also be used as a basis for ruling against a gay parent.

Keeping children away from a parent or other guardian who has custody over them constitutes custodial interference. When it occurs with intent to deprive the other parent of custody, it is considered a crime in most states even if the perpetrator also has custody rights. In many states, it is a felony if the child is taken out of state. However, if just cause—such as fear of injury to the child—can be proved, the charges may be dropped or reduced from a felony to a misdemeanor. Efforts by a custodial parent to keep the noncustodial parent from seeing the child on a regular basis constitute visitation interference.

Custody agreements may be modified after the divorce decree with the consent of both parents, with or without court approval. However, the court can't enforce the modifications unless it has approved them. In the absence of an agreed-upon change, one parent can petition the court for a modification. Modifications may be based on factors including changes in either parent's lifestyle, relocation of either parent to another part of the country, or a seriously destabilizing event, such as the arrest or death of either parent or allegations of **child abuse.**

Many of the issues that arise when parents are living in different states or when one has abducted a child to another state are addressed by the Uniform Child Custody Jurisdiction Act, enacted by all states and the District of Columbia, which specifies when a court may award custody and when it must defer to a previous custody decision made in another state. Under this statute, a court may award custody if all of the following conditions can be met: 1) the child has lived in the state for the previous six months or lived there before but was taken to another state by a parent; 2) the child has significant connections with adults in the state—such as grandparents and other relatives, teachers, and doctors—and reliable evidence about the child's care and condition can be provided within the state; 3) the child is in danger of abuse or neglect if he is sent back to the other state; and 4) one of the preceding conditions cannot be met by any other state, or that state has declined to rule on custody of the child.

Custody decisions affect a parent's ability to claim federal income tax deductions and credits. A parent must have physical custody of a child (meaning that the child spends more than 50% of his time with that parent) in order to file as head of household. When parents have joint custody, neither can file as head of household because (at least in theory) the child does not reside with either parent for over 50% of the year. However, if more than one child is involved, each parent can claim 51% for one or more of the children, with the other parent claiming 51% for the other(s). Only custodial parents with income below a certain level are eligible for child care tax credit.

For Further Study

Books

Lamb, Michael E., and Abraham Sagi, eds. *Fatherhood and Family Policy.* Hillsdale, NJ: L. Erlbaum Associates, 1983.

Leonard, Robin, and Stephen Elias. *Family Law,* 3rd ed. Berkeley: Nolo Press, 1994.

Lyster, Mimi E. *Child Custody: Building Agreements That Work.* Berkeley: Nolo Press, 1995.

Musetto, Andrew P. *Dilemmas in Child Custody: Family Conflicts and Their Resolution.* Chicago: Nelson-Hall, 1982.

Pelaka, Beverly. *Don't Settle for Less: A Woman's Guide to Getting a Fair Divorce and Custody Settlement.* New York: Doubleday, 1994.

Shapiro, Robert. *Sharing the Children: How to Resolve Custody Problems and Get On with Your Life.* Bethesda, MD: Adler & Adler, 1988.

Virtue, Doreen. *My Kids Don't Live with Me Anymore: Coping with the Custody Crisis.* Minneapolis: Compcare, 1988.

Warshak, Richard A. *The Custody Revolution: The Father Factor and the Motherhood Mystique.* New York: Poseidon Press, 1992.

Organizations

ABA Center on Children and the Law
Address: 1800 S Street NW, Suite 200 South
Washington, DC 20036
Telephone: (202) 331-2250

Children's Rights Council (CRC)
Address: 220 Eye St. NE, Suite 200
Washington, DC 20002
Telephone: (202) 547-6227

Custody Action for Lesbian Mothers
Address: P.O. Box 281
Narbeth, PA 19072
Telephone: (215) 667-7508

Equality Nationwide for Unwed Fathers
Address: 10606 Wilkins Ave.
Los Angeles, CA 90024
Telephone: (310) 475-5352

Joint Custody Association
Address: 10606 Wilkins Ave.
Los Angeles, CA 90024

Parents Sharing Custody (PSC)
Address: 420 S. Beverly Dr., Suite 100
Beverly Hills, CA 90212-4410
Telephone: (310) 286-9171

Child Prodigy *see* **Genius** *and* **Giftedness**

Child Psychology

Disciplines and theories concerned with the cognitive, psychological, physiological, and social/interpersonal aspects of human development.

Child psychologists study human development from the earliest stages of life through **adolescence** and adulthood. These scientists focus on many areas of growth. In the early years of life they include motor skills, perceptual analysis and inference, language and speech, social behavior, and the emergence of basic emotions of fear, sadness, anxiety, shame, and guilt.

The two important strategies for studying development include the longitudinal study in which a particular group of children is studied over a long period of time, sometimes from infancy through adulthood. The second method, which is more popular because it is less expensive, is called the cross-sectional method. In this strategy a group of children or adolescents at a particular age are studied at that age. In order to compare different ages, different samples would be studied but no group would be studied over time.

The major question that developmental psychologists wish to understand is how the maturational forces that are inevitable interact with experience to produce the behaviors, skills, and motives that we observe. For example, all children will develop an ability to speak and understand language before they are three years of age. However, in some cultural settings, children display this skill soon after the first birthday, while in others it might be delayed until the second or third birthday.

A related problem that puzzles child psychologists has to do with the temperamental factors children inherit that make a contribution to their individual personalities. Here, too, the puzzle is to understand how these inherited temperamental biases and experience in the family and with other children contribute to the traits the child develops.

Prior to Sigmund Freud's writings which became popular after the turn of the century, most Western explanations of the differences among children were attributed to **temperament** or constitution. Freud changed this by arguing that family experience was the more important determinant of differences in children's moods, emotions, and symptoms. Freud believed that those experiences in the family made the child vulnerable to conflicts over hostility and sexuality. The intensity of the conflict and the defenses the child learned to deal with those conflicts were the main determinant of the child's personality. These view were very popular in the United States for the period from 1930 to 1960. However, because of the lack of strong scientific support for these theories, loyalty to these ideas has eroded in a major way.

Erik Erikson substituted for Freud's famous stages on oral, anal, phallic, and genital a more humane set of stages which emphasized the development of **attachment** relations in the first year of life and more generative and creative aspects of human nature, rather than the more narcissistic and destructive.

Jean Piaget's contribution was to motivate child psychologists to pay more attention to the child's intellectual and **cognitive development**.

However, it is fair to say that at the present time there is no overarching theory of child development. Child psychologists are working on a series of problems that cover all of the important areas of growth. It is hoped that as these facts are gathered, brilliant theorists sometime in the future will be able to synthesize this information into a coherent theory that clarifies the child's growth.

—Jerome Kagan
Harvard University

For Further Study

Books

Bee, Helen L. *The Developing Child.* 7th ed. New York: HarperCollins College Publishers, 1995.

Gemelli, Ralph J. *Normal Child and Adolescent Development.* Washington, DC: American Psychiatric Press, 1996.

Kagan, Jerome. *The Nature of the Child.* New York: Basic Books, 1994.

Roberts, Michael C. *Handbook of Pediatric Psychology.* 2nd ed. New York: Guilford Press, 1995.

Sroufe, L. Alan, Robert G. Cooper, and Mary E. Marshall. *Child Development.* New York: Random House, 1987.

Thomas, R. Murray. *Comparing Theories of Child Development.* 3rd ed. Belmont, CA: Wadsworth Publishing Company, 1992.

Vasta, Ross, Marshall M. Haith, and Scott A. Miller. *Child Psychology: the Modern Science.* New York: J. Wiley & Sons, 1992.

Childrearing *see* **Parent-Child Relationships**

Childhood Vaccine Injury Act

U. S. federal law established to provide compensation for injury or death related to a reaction to a vaccine.

In 1986, the U.S. Congress passed the Childhood Vaccine Injury Act to provide compensation to families for injury or death related to complications from an **immunization** while avoiding costly litigation for all parties: the family, the doctor, and the vaccine supplier. The Act was designed, in part, to provide a resolution and compensation in those rare instances where an injury or death occurs in relation to an immunization while not threatening the supply of vaccines. (A manufacturer, faced with lawsuits and costs related to them, could choose to stop manufacturing vaccines; the U.S. government feels the benefits of immunization outweigh the risks, and thus created this program.) The Act covers injury or death related to the DTP vaccine (against **diphtheria,** tetanus**,** and pertussis), the MMR vaccine (against measles**, mumps,** and **rubella**), or polio vaccine. The Act established the National Vaccine Injury Compensation Program (NVICP) to assist with claims following injury or death related to a vaccine. To be eligible for compensation, claims must be submitted to the U.S. Claims Court in Washington, DC, according to guidelines established in the law. A set of guidelines has been established to determine whether the injury or death can be linked to the administration of the vaccine. For example, if the claim is that a child's **seizures** were triggered by administration of a vaccine, the family must demonstrate that the child's first seizure occurred within three days of immunization. Similar guidelines are available for most other injuries believed to be linked to administration of vaccines. If the court rules favorably on the claim, the family is eligible for up to $250,000 (as of 1990), for "present and future pain and suffering, expenses, and projected lost earnings from age 18." The family making the claim can elect to either accept or reject the court's

judgment. By accepting the judgment and compensation, the family gives up the right to take further legal action against the doctor or vaccine manufacturer. If the family rejects the judgment and compensation, they keep the right to pursue other legal action.

See also **Immunization.**

For Further Study

Books

Clayman, Charles B., and Jeffrey R.M. Kunz. eds. *Children: How to Understand Their Symptoms.* New York: Random House, 1986.

Periodicals

"Health Report." *Time* 143, January 3, 1994, p. 28.

Organizations

National Vaccine Information Center
   Address: 128 Branch Road
   Vienna, VA 22180
   (Organization also known as Dissatisfied Parents Together [DPT]. Comprised of parents whose children have had adverse reactions to vaccines, particularly to the DPT vaccine. Publishes *DPT News, Parent Information Packet,* and *The Compensation System and How It Works.*)

National Vaccine Injury Compensation Program (NVICP)
   Address: 6001 Montrose Road, Room 702
   Rockville, MD 20852
   Telephone: (301) 443-6593
   (U.S. government agency that oversees the implementation of the 1986 Childhood Vaccine Injury Act. Provides information packet.)

Childproofing

Refers to the practice of altering an environment in such a way as to maximize the safety of small children.

According to the National Safety Council, 2,100 children, ages four and under, died as the result of home accidents during 1992. Of that total, 400 died by drowning, 100 by poisoning, and 120 in falls. Pediatricians advise parents to start thinking about home safety when their children are around six months old. As soon as the child is even slightly mobile, childproofing the house is a wise practice. Traditionally, this has meant removing breakable objects and storing household chemicals out of reach. In recent years, parents have recognized that **safety** hazards exist in every area of the home. Many parents have installed safety devices throughout the house, including electrical outlet covers, safety gates at tops and bottoms of stairs, and guards over windows. Window protection is vital to avoiding accidental falls. Many types of window guards are available, most of which are permanently affixed to the window sash so that in case of fire, occupants are required to break the glass in order to escape.

The following section describes common precautions that may be taken to avoid accidents in the home:

In the bathroom

- Medicine cabinets should be locked. Razors, scissors, bathroom appliances, and chemicals should be stored in a locked cabinet. (Even iron pills or mouthwash can poison children).

- Medications and cleansers should have child-resistant packaging.

- Toilet locks can be installed to prevent the lid from being lifted by young children. Since children's bodies are top-heavy, they may easily lose their balance, fall over, and drown in as little as one inch of water.

- Faucet protectors prevent bumps and bruises in the tub.

- Water temperature should be lowered to 120°F. Every year, approximately 5,000 children are scalded by tap water, usually in the bathtub.

In the kitchen

- Store household chemicals in locked cabinets.

- Keep appliance cords and tablecloths out of reach. Children who are just learning to walk will reach for anything to help them keep their balance, and may pull appliances down on top of themselves.

- Keep hot foods and beverages, knives, and glassware away from the edges of counters and tables.

- Use only back burners on the stove, if possible, and turn pot handles towards the back of the stove.

In the bedroom

- Make sure baby furniture meets current safety standards. There should be no sharp edges, and slats on cribs and playyards should be no more than 2.5 in (6 cm) apart. If the distance is greater than this, a child may be caught or strangled between the bars.

- The crib mattress should fit snugly into the frame, with no more than two fingers' distance between mattress and crib railing, to avoid strangulation.

- Devices are available to secure dressers and other furniture to walls, as children are often injured by pulling heavy furniture down on top of themselves.

In the pool

- Pools should be fenced, with gates that *lock*. Simple latches are easy for even very young children to open.

- Lock all windows and doors that provide access to the pool area. Alarms may also be installed on these doors, to alert adults if children do slip out.

- Install a phone or keep a waterproof, charged cordless phone near the pool and post emergency numbers on it.

- Prevent unsupervised access to even the smallest plastic wading pool.

While no amount of childproofing can replace vigilant supervision as a means of maintaining child safety, simple and common sense precautions can help prevent many potential accidents.

For Further Study

Books

Dillingham, Maud. *It's 1995. Do You Know How Your Children Are?* Santa Monica, CA: Times Books, 1995.

Periodicals

"Baby-proof Inside and Out." *Prevention* 47, October 1995, pp. 78+.

Children's Apperception Test (CAT)

Assesses personality and maturity level.

An adaptation of the **Thematic Apperception Test** (TAT) for children ages 3–10, the Children's Apperception Test (CAT), individually administered by a trained psychologist, assesses personality and maturity level and is often used for clinical evaluation of psychological health. It is designed to reveal conflicts, emotions, attitudes, stressors, and aggressive tendencies and to assess factors such as control of drives, judgment, and degree of autonomy. The child is shown 10 pictures of animals in various human social contexts and asked to tell a story about each picture and describe how the characters are feeling. There is no numerical score or scale for the test. Results are provided in the form of an examiner's summary of the attitudes, traits, and conflicts illustrated by each of the child's stories.

For Further Study

Books

Knoff, Howard M. *The Assessment of Child and Adolescent Personality.* New York: Guilford Press, 1986.

O'Neill, Audrey Myerson. *Clinical Inference: How to Draw Meaningful Conclusions from Psychological Tests.* Brandon, VT: Clinical Psychology Publishing Co., 1993.

Shore, Milton F., Patrick J. Brice, and Barbara G. Love. *When Your Child Needs Testing: What Parents, Teachers, and Other Helpers Need to Know about Psychological Testing.* New York: Crossroad, 1992.

Wodrich, David L., and Sally A. Kush. *Children's Psychological Testing: A Guide for Nonpsychologists.* 2nd ed. Baltimore, MD: Brookes Publishing Co., 1990.

Chlamydia

Sexually transmitted disease (STD) caused by a bacteria called Chlamydia trachomatis.

Chlamydia, a **sexually transmitted disease**, is more common than **gonorrhea**, affecting 35% and 8% of sexually active adolescents, respectively. Adolescent girls are at especially high risk for infection with chlamydia. Because chlamydia causes no symptoms in half of infected adolescents, it often goes untreated. For this reason, screening for chlamydia should be routine for all sexually active adolescents.

Symptoms

Symptoms of chlamydia may occur in many different parts of the body. In addition to symptoms affecting the genital and anal area, chlamydia is also associated with **conjunctivitis** and **arthritis**. In either sex, chlamydia can cause pain and/or inflammation of the throat, liver, upper abdomen, back, and shoulder. In females, chlamydia can lead to pelvic inflammatory disease (PID), infertility, and ectopic pregnancy. The treatment for chlamydia is prescription of oral **antibiotics** for one to two weeks.

For Further Study

Books
Daugirdas, John T., M.D. *STD, Sexually Transmitted Diseases, Including HIV/AIDS.* Hinsdale, IL: Medtext, 1992.

Organizations
National Sexually Transmitted Disease Hotline
Telephone: (800) 227-8922
(Free information and clinic referrals)

—Gail B. Slap, M.D.
University of Pennsylvania School of Medicine

Choking

Blockage of the throat or windpipe by an object.

Choking is a major cause of death for children under three, and is a hazard for older children as well. Young children explore the world with their mouths, and they will naturally put in their mouths anything that fits. If a small object slips back into the throat and blocks the windpipe, the child may become unable to breathe, and unless the child is helped to eject the object quickly, the child may asphyxiate and die. Food is also a choking hazard, especially for children under three who do not know how to chew food thoroughly. Parents should encourage children to chew, and warn them not to eat while running or playing, or to eat lying down.

Prevention

The common household is full of objects such as coins, tacks, paper clips, buttons, pins, beads, pen caps, bottle tops and nails that pose a choking danger to children. It is of course not possible to rid the house of small items, but parents can take care to keep them out of reach. When **childproofing** the house, parents should view each room from the child's point of view, that is, from down on the floor. By crawling around a rug and looking up at the undersides of furniture, parents can find inconspicuous items that might attract a child's attention but escape the adult's-eye view from above. Crawling babies will go behind and under furniture and worm their way into corners, so even very tight spaces should be checked. Parents should be careful with what they throw in the garbage since toddlers may retrieve small objects that have been thrown away. Egg shells and pull-tabs from beverage cans are both choking hazards commonly found in the garbage.

Toys and parts of toys also pose a danger to young children. Federal law specifies that toys designed for children under three pass a small parts test. Toys or parts for children this age must be able to pass through a tube approximating a child's throat diameter (just over 1 in [3 cm]). However, some children have choked to death on objects that passed the small parts test, and the Consumer Product Safety Commission proposed in 1988 that the test be revised, changing the diameter of the tube to over 1.5 in (4 cm). However, the new diameter has not been adopted and as the test does not apply to toys designed for children over three, parents of several children must be sure that small toys for an older child do not fall into a younger sibling's hands. One solution is to keep toys that are safe for toddlers as well as older children in a general toy box, and keep toys that have small parts in a special area, so that these can be taken down only with adult assistance.

A recent study of the characteristics of objects known to have caused choking deaths in children found that round objects are most dangerous. A small ball or marble can completely seal the windpipe. Round or cylindrical foods are also a particular choking hazard. Round pieces of hot dog, nuts, whole grapes, seeds, and hard candies should not be given to young children, and older children should be watched with care when eating these foods. Another significant choking risk to children of all ages is balloons. Children can inhale a balloon

EMERGENCY PROCEDURE FOR CHOKING

For an infant (child under age one):

- Turn the infant over your forearm, with the head lower than the body.

- Hit the child with the heel of the hand four times between the shoulder blades.

- If the obstruction does not come out, lay the child on his back on the floor. Using two fingers, thrust four times to his chest over the breastbone.

- If the child is still not breathing, open his mouth. If you can see the object, pull it out with a finger. Continue these steps until the child begins breathing or emergency help arrives.

For children older than one year, use the Heimlich maneuver, as follows.

- Standing behind the child, circle your arms around his waist.

- Place one fist against the child's abdomen just under the ribcage. Hold the fist with your other hand and thrust upward until the object pops out.

- If the obstruction does not come out, place the child on his back and deliver abdominal thrusts with the heel of your hand.

- If the object does not come out, open the child's mouth and look for it. If it is visible, pull it out with a finger. Continue these steps until the child begins breathing or emergency help arrives.

while trying to inflate it, or choke on a piece of popped balloon. If children are given balloons, they should be supervised closely.

Treatment

A child who is choking cannot talk or cough. If the airway is completely blocked, the child will turn red, then blue. The parent or caretaker must act immediately to save the child. The accompanying sidebar provides guidelines for what to do in an emergency. All parents and caregivers should become familiar with these procedures, so that they will be ready should an emergency arise. Parents can prepare themselves for choking incidents by taking child safety and first aid classes offered by many community resource centers and health agencies.

For Further Study

Books

American National Red Cross. *Respiratory and Circulatory Emergencies*. Washington, DC: American National Red Cross, 1978.

Oloert, Lois Conrad. *Help! Willie's Choking!: A Young Child's Introduction to the Heimlich Maneuver*. North Aurora, IL: In Quisitor's Publishing Co., 1994.

Periodicals

Rimell, Frank L., et al., "Characteristics of Objects That Cause Choking in Children," *Journal of the American Medical Association*, December 13, 1995, pp. 1763–66.

Audiovisual Recordings

Choking. Evanston, IL: Journal Films, 1980.
    (One 13-minute videocassette.)
How to Save Your Child or Baby: When Every Second Counts. Los Angeles, CA: Video Prescriptions, 1987.
    (One 40-minute videocassette.)
Seconds Count. Manhattan Beach, CA: Mann Design, 1991.
    (One 18-minute videocassette.)

—A. Woodward

Cholesterol

A waxy substance in the chemical family of alcohols synthesized in the liver and used by the body to produce bile, hormones, and nerve tissue

Cholesterol is a critically important compound in the human body. It is synthesized in the liver and used in manufacture of bile, **hormones**, and nerve tissue. High levels of cholesterol have been linked to heart disease.

The liver can manufacture about 600 mg of cholesterol a day, an adequate amount to meet the body's need. But cholesterol is also a part of the human diet, and it is found in many foods. A single egg yolk, for example, contains about 250 mg of cholesterol. Organ meats—like liver and kidneys—are particularly rich in the compound. A 3 oz (85 g) serving of beef liver, for example, contains about 372 mg of cholesterol and a similar-size serving of calves' brain contains about 2,700 mg of cholesterol. Because diets differ from culture to culture, the amount of cholesterol an individual consumes differs widely around the world. The average European diet includes about 500 mg of cholesterol a day, but the average Japanese diet contains only about 130 mg of cholesterol a day. The latter reflects a diet rich in fish rather than meat.

Cholesterol occurs in almost all living organisms with the primary exception of microorganisms. Of the cholesterol found in the human body, about 93% occurs in cells and the remaining 7% in the circulatory system. The brain and spinal cord are particularly rich in the compound. About 10% of the former's dry weight is due to cholesterol. An important commercial source of cholesterol is spinal fluid taken from cattle. Cholesterol is also found in myelin, the material that surrounds nerve strands. Gallstones are nearly pure cholesterol.

How one's body processes cholesterol is affected by both hereditary factors and diet. For most people, when the dietary intake of cholesterol greatly exceeds the body's needs, excess cholesterol will tend to precipitate out of blood and be deposited on arterial linings. The presence of such plaques (clumps) of cholesterol can lead to circulatory disorders such as heart disease. The concentration of cholesterol in human blood also varies rather widely, from a low of less than 200 mg/dL (milligrams per deciliter) to a high of more than 300 mg/dL.

CHILDREN SCREENED WHEN A PARENT HAS HIGH CHOLESTEROL

Parental cholesterol level higher than (mg/dL)	Children screened, %
200 mg/dL	63.5%
220 mg/dL	44.3%
240 mg/dL	25.1%
260 mg/dL	18.1%
280 mg/dL	15.3%
300 mg/dL	13.9%

Source: *Report of the Expert Panel on Blood Cholesterol Levels in Children and Adolescents*, March 1992.

RISK FACTORS FOR HIGH CHOLESTEROL IN CHILDREN

The American Academy of Pediatrics and the National Institutes of Health suggest that children ages 2–19 have their cholesterol checked if they have any one of the following risk factors:

At least one parent who has ever had high blood cholesterol (240 mg/dL or greater).

A parent or grandparent who developed heart disease before age 55.

Parents whose medical history is not known.

Any other risk factors for heart disease, such as cigarette smoking, high blood pressure, obesity, diabetes, or physical inactivity.

Children of any age can be tested to determine the levels of cholesterol in their blood. In fact, many pediatricians believe testing should take place routinely at about ages 2 and 16. Because many children carry the genetic tendency toward high cholesterol levels and heart disease, such screening can pinpoint children early who could benefit from dietary changes. The **American Academy of Pediatrics** has recommended that children older than two follow the same nutritional guidelines as adults, eating no more than 30% of their daily calories from fat and only a small percentage of that from saturated fat. Before the age of two, a higher percentage of calories from fat is required to sustain the rapid growth characteristic of this stage of development

Researchers have attempted to assess which family factors are most likely to predict elevated cholesterol levels in children. Factors that seem likely to predict high cholesterol levels in children are family history of cardiovascular disease and parental cholesterol level. The above table illustrates the percentage of children who would be screened for elevated cholesterol if parental cholesterol level is used as a factor in making the decision when to screen. These percentages represent the results of the Lipid Research Clinics Prevalence Study, reported in March 1992. In general, most pediatricians recommend that all children and adolescents eat a diet low in saturated fatty acid, low in total fat, and low in cholesterol.

For Further Study

Books

Byrne, Kevin P. *Understanding and Managing Cholesterol: A Guide for Wellness Professionals.* Champaign, IL: Human Kinetics Books, 1991.

Eisman, Eugene and Diane Batshaw Eisman. *Your Child and Cholesterol.* Hollywood, FL: Fell, 1990.

Kowalski, Robert E. *Cholesterol & Children.* New York: Harper & Row, 1988.

National Heart, Lung, and Blood Institute. *Cholesterol in Children: Healthy Eating Is a Family Affair.* Bethesda, MD: National Institutes of Health, Publication No. 92-3099, 1992.

Periodicals and Reports

National Cholesterol Education Program. "Report of the Expert Panel on Blood Cholesterol Levels in Children and Adolescents." *Pediatrics* 89, March 1992.

National Institutes of Health. *Update on the Task Force Report (1987) on High Blood Pressure in Children and Adolescents: A Working Group Report from the National High Blood Pressure Education Program.* NIH Publication No. 96-3790, September 1996.

Chores

Household and other tasks of daily living.

Every household has a certain amount of chores that need to get done. Some are more or less daily tasks, like cooking and washing dishes, some are big seasonal jobs, such as shoveling snow or cleaning gutters, others, like dusting or mopping, may only get done depending on how much time you have and how clean you like it. A family may not have an explicit system for assigning chores, but there may be an unspoken agreement or custom. Recent research has shown that women still do the majority of housework in America, even in families where both partners work full time. And resentment over perceived unfairness in the division of housework and child care is a frequent cause of tension in marriages. If children are expected to share in housework, parents may want to come up with a fair and consistent policy of assignment that suits everyone. Not every family will agree that children should share in chores, however. If the children are too young, they may be more hindrance than help. Some parents may feel that schoolwork is the child's job, and housework is for adults. But many families see chores as family work to which each member should contribute. They also believe that assigning chores builds a child's sense of responsibility and teaches a child necessary skills for independent living. How many and what kind of chores a child performs varies with the child's age and ability.

It is important that chores seem to be given out fairly. While young children are often pleased to be given a job, older ones may resent it. One system is to have each family member agree to do certain chores daily, weekly, or at another appropriate interval. Each person's chores are written under his or her name on a chart, and the parent or child can check off the chores as they are completed. The chart makes it clear that every person has work they need to do.

The rotating job wheel is another common approach to assigning chores. In this system, chores are written on the edge of a circle. On an inner circle are the names of family members, divided up like sections of a pie graph. The inner wheel can be turned every week or month, so that every person has a new batch of chores. This is a good way to handle unpopular chores. If chores are few, it may not be necessary to write them down on a chart or rotating wheel. However, it may still be valuable to have a family discussion about chores to help make sure that housework is divided fairly.

Some parents tie their children's **allowance** to completion of chores. The allowance then becomes a paycheck for housework done: if children don't do their chores, they don't get paid. This raises several important issues. If children are not overly motivated by money, they may elect not to do their chores. In such a case, the chore becomes not a family contribution but a monetary transaction. Parents must also determine a fair rate of pay for each chore; harder tasks should pay more than simpler ones. In addition, parents should consider whether they will pay the same rate for a job well done as for one done sloppily or wrong.

Both chores and allowances are frequent areas of tension between parents and children, as children test limits and rebel against parental authority. Some parents use a compromise system of chores and allowance, which gives both parties some flexibility. The parents pay a base allowance that is not tied to completion of chores. On top of this, the child is paid for performing certain extra chores. Even the best thought-out system will have unexpected glitches and complications. Parents should expect to revise the chore list as children mature or as expectations change. Making chore assignments explicit through family discussion can ease tension and resentment.

—A. Woodward

Circumcision

The surgical removal of the foreskin that covers the end, or glans, of the penis.

Until the early 1970s, male infants born in the United States were routinely circumcised. In fact, the National Center for Health Statistics (NCHS) reports that about 90% of boys born in the 1960s and 70s were circumcised. This procedure was done for what were then believed to be hygienic reasons. An estimated 10% of uncircumcised males contract bacterial infections when smegma, a cheese-like secretion of a sebaceous gland, accumulates under the foreskin. Since the mid 1970s, the **American Academy of Pediatrics** (AAP) and the United States Public Health Service have advised that circumcision is not medically necessary. By 1995, the NCHS reported that the rate of circumcision had fallen to about 62%.

Despite the AAP's recommendation that "there are no medical indications for routine circumcision of the newborn," there is no consensus among doctors regarding the procedure. Those physicians who advise parents to circumcise point to research indicating that circumcision reduces the risk of urinary tract infections (UTI), and that uncircumcised men experience higher incidence of penile **cancer,** and have a higher risk of contracting HIV and other **sexually transmitted diseases (STD).** Physicians on the other side of the issue argue that the incidence of UTI, penile cancer, and STDs is too low to justify circumcision.

Most physicians who recommend circumcision suggest that it be done within a week of birth, but at least 12 hours after the birth. The procedure involves removing the foreskin, a flap of skin that covers the glans, or head, of the penis. The baby is swaddled or bound to a board to restrain his arms and legs while the foreskin is cut away.

The pain associated with the procedure is another area of controversy. The pain lasts for about one-half hour after the procedure, but researchers have found a link between the pain of circumcision and the way an infant experiences pain for the next four to five months. Circumcised infants appear to experience more pain during routine **immunizations** than uncircumcised infants.

Some doctors administer a local anesthetic to the base of the penis during circumcision, but this practice carries the risk of possible damage to the nerve endings in the penis. Following circumcision, infants are often given **acetaminophen** to relieve the pain, which continues in lesser intensity for a few days, until the wound around the circumference of the glans is completely healed.

The foreskin will remain firmly attached to the head of the penis of uncircumcised boys until about age three or four; by age five the foreskin is retractable in 90% of uncircumcised males. By that time, parents can begin teaching their son to pull back the foreskin carefully during bathing to clean the glans area.

Phimosis, a rare condition in which the foreskin does not move freely, can cause discomfort during urination and sexual relations. Phimosis can be corrected by circumcision. Another condition, paraphimosis, occurs when the foreskin retracts but does not move back over the glans. The symptomatic pain and swelling can be reduced by applying cold compresses and gentle pressure to move the foreskin back to its normal position. Paraphimosis can also be corrected by circumcision.

Prospective parents should discuss whether to circumcise their child with their doctor before the child is born to evaluate medical opinion and research results. Also influencing the decision are social and religious issues, and the parents' own comfort level with the procedure.

For Further Study

Books

Diamant, Anita. *The New Jewish Baby Book: Names, Ceremonies, Customs.* Woodstock, VT: Jewish Lights, 1993.

Fink, Aaron J. *Circumcision: A Parent's Decision for Life.* Mountain View, CA: Kavanah, 1988.

Romberg, Henry C. *Bris Milah: A Book About the Jewish Ritual of Circumcision.* New York: Feldheim Publishers, 1982.

Romberg, Rosemary. *Circumcision: The Painful Dilemma.* South Hadley, MA: Bergin and Garvey, 1985.

CIRCUMCISION: A TRADITIONAL JEWISH CEREMONY

A *bris milah* is a ceremonial religious circumcision, usually performed at home. According to Jewish tradition, the bris milah, performed on the eighth day after birth, is the beginning of the male infant's Jewish life. The procedure itself is performed by a *mohel*. A mohel is a person who has studied Jewish religious traditions and has been trained in the circumcision procedure. Often, the mohel is a physician. The occasion is one of celebration, with the ritual circumcision carried out with family members and friends in attendance.

Periodicals

Bourland, Julie. "The Circumcision Decision." *Parenting,* February 1997, pp. 103–106.

Audiovisual Materials

Hammond, Tim, producer. *Whose Body, Whose Rights?: Examining the Ethics and the Human Rights Issue of Infant Male Circumcision.* Los Angeles, CA: Dillonwood, 1995. (One 56-minute videocassette. Explores customs, practices, and the human rights issue of infant male circumcision.)

Organizations

National Organization of Circumcision Information Resource Centers (NO-CIR)
  Address: 731 Sir Francis Drake Boulevard
  San Anselmo, CA 94960
  Telephone: (415) 454-5669
National Center for Education in Child and Maternal Health
  Telephone: (202) 625-8400

Claparède, Edouard (1873–1940)

One of the main figures of the child study and progressive education movement in Europe.

Edouard Claparède was one of the leaders in the study and education of children in Europe in the early 1900s. He wrote on numerous subjects, including clinical neurology, perception, animal psychology, hypnosis, hysteria, psychological methodology, the association of ideas, sleep, play, emotions, the empirical control of mediums, the genesis of hypotheses, and the use of film in psychology; he also helped introduce psychoanalysis in the French-speaking world, and pioneered the psychological investigation of judicial testimony.

Claparède's reputation rests on his book *Experimental Pedagogy and Psychology of the Child,* a remarkable synthesis of the history, problems, and methods of the field, and on his creation in 1912 of the Jean-Jacques Rousseau Institute in Geneva, a center for teacher education and developmental research that became a model for similar institutions throughout the world. Claparède's other books in the area dealt with the "school made to measure," aptitude testing, and "functional education;" they were translated into several languages (but not into English). Claparède believed that the school ought to adapt to the child, and that education ought to be based on child psychology. He thus shared, on the whole, the outlook of such American and European psychologists and educators as G. Stanley Hall, **Alfred Binet,** John Dewey, or William Stern.

Claparède was born in 1873 in the French-speaking Swiss city of Geneva, in a distinguished bourgeois Protestant family. In 1901, three years after the end of his medical studies, he created the journal *Archives de psychologie* with his older cousin, the psychologist Theodore Flournoy. In 1908, Claparède succeeded Flournoy as professor of psychology at the University of Geneva, a position he held until his death in 1940.

Claparède's thinking was characterized by a "functional" approach he first elaborated as a critique of associationism. He applied the postulate that behavior has an adaptive function to several psychological problems, including the development of intelligence. An influential notion of his functionalism (it became central in Piagetian psychology) was the "law of the grasp of consciousness." This "law" is based on the idea that the more often a sort of behavior or judgment has been used automatically or by habit, the harder it is to become aware of it. The process of taking cognizance of one's intellectual operations is thus a key in the growth of intelligence.

While trying to synthesize child psychology and education, Claparède enhanced the psychologist's role as expert on mental development, tests, and other aspects of school psychology. Through his publications, his establishment of the Rousseau Institute, and his activities as educational consultant for different countries, he provided a significant impetus to the field of child development in Europe. Jean Piaget, whose career took place for the most part at the Rousseau Institute, was his main intellectual heir.

For Further Study

Books

Claparède, E. "Autobiography." In C. Murchison, ed., *A History of Psychology in Autobiography*, Worcester, MA: Clark University Press, 1930.

Trombetta, C. *Edouard Claparède psicologo,* Rome, Italy: Armando, 1989.

Periodicals

Revue suisse de psychologie 33 (3), special issue, 1974.

—Fernando Vidal
University of Geneva, Switzerland

Class Inclusion *see* **Inclusive Classrooms**

Classical Conditioning

The process of closely associating a neutral stimulus with one that evokes a reflexive response so that eventually the neutral stimulus alone will evoke the same response.

Classical conditioning is an important concept in the school of psychology known as **behaviorism,** and it forms the basis for some of the techniques used in **behavior therapy.**

Classical conditioning was pioneered by the Russian physiologist Ivan Pavlov (1849–1936) in the 1890s in the course of experiments on the digestive systems of dogs (work which won him the Nobel Prize in 1904). Noticing that the dogs salivated at the mere sight of the person who fed them, Pavlov formulated a theory about the relationship between stimuli and responses that he believed could be applied to humans as well as to other animals. He called the dogs' salivation in response to the actual taste and smell of meat an *unconditioned response* because it occurred through a natural reflex without any prior training (the meat itself was referred to as an *unconditioned stimulus*). A normally neutral act, such as the appearance of a lab assistant in a white coat or the ringing of a bell, could become associated with the appearance of food, thus producing salivation as a *conditioned response* (in response to a *conditioned stimulus*). Pavlov believed that the conditioned reflex had a physiological basis in the creation of new pathways in the cortex of the brain by the conditioning process. In further research early in the 20th century, Pavlov found that in order for the conditioned response to be maintained, it had to be paired periodically with the unconditioned stimulus or the learned association would be forgotten (a process known as extinction). However, it could quickly be relearned if necessary.

In humans, classical conditioning can account for such complex phenomena as a person's emotional reaction to a particular song or perfume based on a past experience with which it is associated. Classical (sometimes called Pavlovian) conditioning is also the basis for many different types of fears or **phobias,** which can occur through a process called stimulus generalization (a child who has a bad experience with a particular dog may learn to fear all dogs). In addition to causing fears, however, classical conditioning can also help eliminate them through a variety of therapeutic techniques. One is systematic desensitization, in which an anxiety-producing stimulus is deliberately associated with a positive response, usually relaxation produced through such techniques as deep breathing and progressive muscle relaxation. The opposite result (making a desirable stimulus unpleasant) is obtained through aversion therapy, in which a behavior that a person wants to discontinue—often an addiction, such as **alcoholism**—is paired with an unpleasant stimulus, such as a nausea-producing drug.

For Further Study

Books

Gormezano, Isidore, William F. Prokasy, and Richard F. Thompson. *Classical Conditioning.* 3rd ed. Hillsdale, NJ: L. Erlbaum, 1987.

Lieberman, David A. *Learning: Behavior and Cognition.* Belmont, CA: Wadsworth Publishing Co., 1990.

Mackintosh, N.J. *Conditioning and Associative Learning.* New York: Oxford University, 1983.

Cleft Lip and Palate

Physical defect in the development of the upper part of the mouth, including the lip and palate, or roof of the mouth.

Over 5,000 babies are born each year in the United States with a cleft lip or palate (about 1 in every 700 births). Cleft lip without cleft palate is the third most common congenital malformation among babies born in the United States, and is estimated to occur roughly twice as often in males than in females. Cleft palate without cleft lip is the fifth most common, and it affects roughly twice as many girls as boys. Clefts may be unilateral (affecting the left or right side only) or bilateral (affecting both sides). Left-side clefts represent 70% of all unilateral clefts. Research in the 1980s and 1990s indicated that the incidence of lip and palate clefts was increasing. In the United States, Native Americans have the highest incidence of clefts, at 1 in 278 live births, and African Americans have a lower incidence, at 1 in 3,330 live births. Among whites of European descent, there is a facial cleft rate of approximately 1 in 750 live births.

During the first nine weeks of normal fetal development, the bony and muscular parts of the face, mouth, and throat come together. It is during the fifth through ninth weeks of fetal development that genetic and environmental factors are most likely to affect lip and palate development. Cleft palate occurs when the right and left segments of the palate fail to join properly. Cleft lip oc-

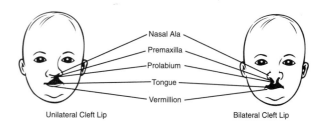

Cleft palate.
Source: Courtesy of the Cleft Palate Foundation.

curs when the lip elements fail to come together. A cleft lip may be complete, extending through the entire length of lip to the floor of the nose. Alternatively, the cleft lip may be incomplete, with some closure in the muscle and lip area between the mouth opening and the nose. The incomplete cleft lip results in less facial distortion because the connected parts of muscle and tissue have a stabilizing effect. In a complete cleft lip, the muscles pull away from the center of the face, resulting in distortion of the nose and mouth.

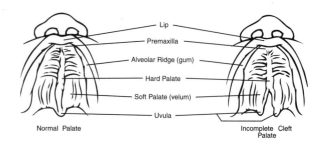

Cleft lip.
Source: Courtesy of the Cleft Palate Foundation.

Causes of clefts are not completely known or understood; in fact, there does not appear to be a single factor that contributes to all clefts. Most scientists believe that clefting is multifactorial, that is, it occurs as a result of a combination of genetic and environmental factors. In the United States and western Europe, researchers report that a family history of facial clefts is present in approximately 40% of all cases. The likelihood of a baby being born with a facial cleft increases if a first degree relative (mother, father, or sibling) has a cleft. Alcohol and drug abuse, lack of vitamins (especially folic acid) during the first weeks of pregnancy, and **diabetes mellitus** in the mother all appear to be related to the occurrence of facial clefts. Researchers from the California Birth Defects Monitoring Program found that women considering pregnancy may be able to reduce the risk of facial clefts (and possibly other birth defects) by taking a multivitamin containing folic acid for one month prior to becoming pregnant and for at least the first two months after conception.

Although some types of clefts can be detected during pregnancy by an ultrasound test, many are not discovered until birth. Generally, within the first few days following birth of an infant with a facial cleft, a team will be assembled to prepare a plan for treatment of the cleft. The interdisciplinary team usually includes representatives from several medical or psychological disciplines, including pediatrics, plastic surgery, otolaryngology, orthodontia, prosthodontics, oral surgery, speech and language pathology, audiology, nursing, and psychology. It is common for one team member, often a nurse with specialized training, to coordinate service and communication between the team members and the family. The cleft defect is corrected by a series of surgeries, the first of which may be performed within the first days after birth. Other aspects of physical and psychological development for a child with a cleft lip or palate are managed by other members of the team.

Children with clefts of the palate are at risk for ear infections, since the palatal muscles may not function efficiently to open the small tubes connecting the throat to the middle ear (eustachian tubes). For this reason, an otolaryngologist (ear, nose, and throat or ENT specialist) is included on the team. An audiologist will also participate in the infant's early care, testing his hearing using special audiometric equipment designed for use with infants and toddlers.

Related to the increased vulnerability of the ears is a greater risk of speech development problems. A speech pathologist with knowledge about cleft lip and palate should evaluate the infant in the first six months of life, and at least once a year after that. Approximately 80% of children with cleft palate develop normal speech after the cleft is closed, although development may be slower than normal. For 20%, additional surgery and speech therapy will be necessary.

Infancy

Infants with cleft lip or cleft soft palate generally have few feeding problems. However, when the cleft involves the hard palate, the infant is usually not able to suck efficiently. For these infants, caregivers must experiment with various feeding techniques, such as specially shaped nipples or alternate feeding positions. The infant with a cleft should be held in nearly a sitting position (at least at a 45-degree angle) during feeding to minimize the chance that the breastmilk or formula will flow back into the nose. In addition, the infant should be burped frequently, approximately every three or four minutes. The sucking reflex is strong in all infants, and should be encouraged in infants with facial clefts even if the sucking is inefficient, since the reflex appears to contribute to later development of speech. It is important to keep the cleft

DEALING WITH CLEFT LIP OR PALATE

Parents of a newborn baby with a cleft lip or palate are often confused and afraid of the impact the defect will have on their child's life. These feelings can be alleviated by learning about the cleft and the processes required to correct it. They also must communicate with family, siblings, and friends about what they are learning about clefts. It is important for people who come into contact with the child to realize that a cleft is not a wound, although it may give the impression that it is tender or sore. Parents can help others to understand that the cleft does not hurt, and that it will be repaired. To ensure normal psychological and speech development, parents should interact with their infant—talking, singing, taking photographs—as they would any newborn in the family, and should encourage others to do the same.

As the child with a cleft grows and develops, he or she will certainly experience many good and bad reactions from adults and children. Other children may tease the child or use the term "harelip." It may be helpful for parents of a child with a facial cleft to meet with his classmates and teachers to explain the history of the term "harelip." Although a facial cleft was once referred to as a "harelip" to reflect its similarity to the mouth of a rabbit, the term is considered rude and insulting today. Educating adults and children about cleft lip and palate is the best way to relieve others' anxiety about the defect and lessen any negative psychological effects that bad reactions might have on the child.

clean, and not to allow formula, mucous, or other matter to collect in the cleft.

Toddlerhood

As the child moves from infancy to toddlerhood, speech and hearing development continue to be monitored. Additional surgeries may be performed to continue to correct and refine the cleft. In addition, a pediatric dentist cares for the newly developing teeth. An appliance to help with speech development, known as an obturator, may also be prepared by a prosthodontic specialist to support the development of normal speech.

If a child is enrolled in a preschool program, teachers and staff should be briefed on the child's situation, the progress that has been made in correcting the cleft, and the special support the child may need as he or she begins the first organized school experience. If the child has difficulty adjusting psychologically to the cleft and to the reactions of others, a psychologist can be consulted to help the child cope with his feelings.

School-age years

Beginning elementary school is an exciting time for all children and their families. In most cases, the surgeries required to close the cleft have been completed by this time. Speech therapy and counseling continue through these years. At around the time the child is ready to enter school, the cleft palate team, in consultation with the family, may consider the need for additional surgery to improve the physical appearance of the cleft. These surgeries usually involve improving the symmetry and appearance of the nose and lips. The child's face will continue to grow and develop—for boys until about 16–18 years of age, for girls until about 14–16. The decision to undergo surgeries for improvement of appearance must take further growth and psychological factors into consideration. Consultation with members of the cleft palate team will help the parents and child decide when to do the final touch-ups.

School-age children may also need reconstructive work to improve the appearance and function of the teeth and gums. When the cleft goes through the upper gum, there may be insufficient bone to support the permanent teeth, and a bone graft may be recommended. A small piece of bone, usually from the child's hip, ribs, or leg, is removed and grafted into the gum area at the front of the mouth near the teeth. Orthodontic treatment is usually necessary either prior to or after the graft.

With advances in surgical techniques and with more complete repair of facial clefts at an early age, it is realistic to expect 80% of children with clefts to have normal speech development by the time they enter school. Continuation of speech therapy will result in continuous improvement for most common speech problems.

Adolescence

Adolescents face universal challenges in forming their own identities. It appears that teenagers with cleft lip or palate are just as likely to be emotionally healthy as their peers. The primary problems related to cleft lip and palate that persist into adolescence affect appearance and speech. During adolescence, facial growth is nearly complete, making it possible to perform any refinements to the nose and mouth areas, if necessary or desirable. Speech problems such as misarticulation (mispronouncing words) and hypernasality (nasal tone of voice) may still appear in adolescence, even though speech therapy may have successfully controlled both. These two problems increase with fatigue, and an adolescent's lifestyle may regress speech improvement. In some cases, the re-

paired palate may not be growing at a sufficient rate to prevent nasality from developing. The cleft palate team can assess the adequacy of the palate for speech functioning and suggest a strategy for treatment. In adolescence, the palate may need some additional minor repair, or the teen may be instructed to use a prosthetic device to improve palate closure until the palate growth is sufficient.

Some adolescents may want to join a support group of people with clefts of the lip or palate. Most of these groups are locally organized by parents of children with cleft lip or palate. The Cleft Palate Foundation is a national association that provides interested adolescents and their families with information about social or educational groups in their area.

For Further Study

Books

Berkowitz, Samuel. *The Cleft Palate Story: A Primer for Parents of Children with Cleft Lip and Palate.* Chicago: Quintessence Books, 1994.

Moller, Karlind T., Clark D. Starr, and Sylvia A. Johnson. *A Parent's Guide to Cleft Lip and Palate.* Minneapolis: University of Minnesota Press, 1990.

Powers, Gene R. *Cleft Palate.* Austin, TX: PRO-ED, 1986.

Starr, Philip. *Cleft Lip and/or Palate: Behavioral Effects from Infancy to Adulthood.* Springfield, IL: Charles C. Thomas, 1983.

Wicka, Donna Konkel. *Advice to Parents of a Cleft Palate Child.* 2d ed. Springfield, IL: Thomas, 1982.

Wynn, Sidney K. and Alfred L. Miller, editors. *A Practical Guide to Cleft Lip and Palate Birth Defects: Helpful, Practical Information and Answers for Parents, Physicians, Nurses, and Other Professionals.* Springfield, IL: Thomas, 1984.

Audiovisual Recordings

Cleft Lip and Palate—Feeding the Newborn.
Available from: Cleft Lip and Palate Program
Address: Hospital for Sick Children
555 University Avenue
Toronto, Ontario, Canada M5G 1X8
Telephone: (416) 813-7490

Organizations

AboutFace
In the United States: 1002 Liberty Lane
Warrington, PA 18976
Telephone: (800) 225-FACE (800-225-3223)
FAX: (215) 491-0603
In Canada: 99 Crown's Lane
Toronto, Ontario, Canada M5R 3PR
Telephone: (416) 944-FACE (416-944-3223)
FAX: (416) 944-2488
(International information and support organization for individuals with facial abnormalities and their families). Publishes pamphlets, booklets, and manuals, including a cleft care kit for parents.

American Cleft Palate Craniofacial Association (ACPCA) and
Cleft Palate Foundation (CPF)
Address: 1218 Grandview Avenue
Pittsburgh, PA 15211
Telephone: "Cleftline" (800) 24-CLEFT; [(800) 242-
5338]
(Operates the "Cleftline," an information line providing
names of cleft palate specialists and support groups).

American Speech-Language-Hearing Association
Address: 10801 Rockville Pike
Rockville, MD 20852
(Publishes a directory of speech pathologists).

Wide Smiles
Address: P.O. Box 5753
Stockton, CA 95285-8153
(Publishes *How Different Is Anthony?*, a read-aloud book
about a boy who was born with a cleft lip and palate. Good
for all ages, especially those aged 4–8).

Cliques

A group of people who identify with each other and interact fre-
quently. An exclusive social group.

The term clique has two levels of significance. In its
neutral usage by social researchers it denotes a group of
people who interact with each other more intensively
than with other peers in the same setting. In its more popular form it has negative connotations, and is used to describe a social group that excludes others on the basis of
superficial differences, exercising greater than average
amount of **peer pressure** upon its members. The numerous terms teenagers use to describe themselves and others—such as jocks, druggies, populars, brains, nerds,
normals, rappers, preps, stoners, rockers, punks (punx),
freaks (phreaks), and skaters—exemplify both levels of
meaning in the word "clique." These terms both accurately refer to the activities or qualities the group members share as well as to the exclusiveness of the groups.

A clique consists of a particular group of people
within a particular location. Cliques are characterized by
a pattern of relationships in which each member is either
directly or indirectly connected with every other member, and in each pair relationship the members exchange
social overtures (phone calls, get-togethers, etc.) on a
fairly equal basis. Joining cliques, having the desire to
join a particular clique, and being excluded from cliques
are considered a normal part of adolescent development.
Joining cliques helps children to develop, identify, and
regulate social interaction. Generally children begin to be
more aware of differences and form cliques in late elementary school, between the ages of 8 and 10 years old.
As they begin to separate emotionally from their parents,
young adolescents' identification with their peers is

greatly exaggerated between ages 10 and 12 years old,
when a child's clique may change on a daily basis.

The issue of belonging is extremely important during middle school and high school, and membership in
cliques can have a strong effect on the adolescent's sense
of self-worth. During high school, cliques become more
consistent, though their composition may change. Research shows that the way an adolescent or teen behaves
is better predicted by the behavior of cliques in which he
is a part than by the behavior of individual friends.

Most cliques are fairly complex and have a mixture
of positive and negative qualities. Cliques may be judged
according to the degree to which they exert positive or
negative peer pressure, accept diversity among members,
and appreciate individuality. Even if a group exerts positive peer pressure—to perform academically or to avoid
drugs, for example—it may also be exerting negative peer
pressure by being exclusive on the basis of race, class, religion, sexual orientation, or ethnicity. Cliques may also
be exclusive on the basis of activities surrounding a particular interest, such as a type of music or sport. Extremely exclusive cliques may be led by authoritarian
adolescents who wield power by alternately praising and
criticizing members, or changing superficial values and
opinions, which effectively keep members wondering
about their status in the clique.

For Further Study

Books

Berenstain, Stan. *The Berenstain Bears and the In-Crowd.* New
York: Random House, 1989. [juvenile]

Elkind, David. *All Grown Up and No Place to Go: Teenagers in
Crisis.* Reading, MA: Addison-Wesley, 1984.

Peck, Lee A. *Coping with Cliques.* New York: Rosen Publishing Group, 1992.

Sciacca, Fran. *Cliques and Clones: Facing Peer Pressure.*
Grand Rapids, MI: Zondervan, 1992.

Shellenberger, Susie. *Lockers, Lunch Lines, Chemistry, and
Cliques.* Minneapolis, MN: Bethany House Publishers,
1995.

Cognitive Behavior Therapy

A therapeutic approach based on the principle that maladaptive
moods and behavior can be changed by replacing distorted or
inappropriate ways of thinking with thought patterns that are
healthier and more realistic.

Cognitive therapy is an approach to **psychotherapy**
that uses thought patterns to change moods and behaviors. Pioneers in the development of cognitive behavior
therapy include Albert Ellis (1929–), who developed rational-emotive therapy (RET) in the 1950s, and Aaron
Beck (1921–), whose cognitive therapy has been widely

used for **depression** and **anxiety.** Cognitive behavior therapy has become increasingly popular since the 1970s. Growing numbers of therapists have come to believe that their patients' cognitive processes play an important role in determining the effectiveness of treatment. Currently, almost 70% of the members of the Association for the Advancement of Behavior Therapy identify themselves as cognitive behaviorists.

Like behavior therapy, cognitive behavior therapy tends to be short-term (often between 10 and 20 sessions), and it focuses on the client's present situation in contrast to the emphasis on past history that is a prominent feature of Freudian **psychoanalysis** and other psychodynamically oriented therapies. The therapeutic process begins with identification of distorted perceptions and thought patterns that are causing or contributing to the client's problems, often through detailed record keeping by the client. Some self-defeating ways of thinking identified by Aaron Beck include all-or-nothing thinking; magnifying or minimizing the importance of an event; overgeneralization (drawing extensive conclusions from a single event); personalization (taking things too personally); selective abstraction (giving disproportionate weight to negative events); arbitrary inference (drawing illogical conclusions from an event); and automatic thoughts (habitual negative, scolding thoughts such as "You can't do anything right").

Once negative ways of thinking have been identified, the therapist helps the client work on replacing them with more adaptive ones. This process involves a repertoire of techniques, including self-evaluation, positive self-talk, control of negative thoughts and feelings, and accurate assessment of both external situations and of the client's own emotional state. Clients practice these techniques alone, with the therapist, and also, wherever possible, in the actual settings in which stressful situations occur (*in vivo*), gradually building up confidence in their ability to cope with difficult situations successfully by breaking out of dysfunctional patterns of response.

Today cognitive behavior therapy is widely used with children and adolescents, especially for disorders involving anxiety, depression, or problems with social skills. Like adult clients, children undergoing cognitive behavior therapy are made aware of distorted perceptions and errors in logic that are responsible for inaccurate or unrealistic views of the world around them. The therapist then works to change erroneous beliefs and perceptions by instruction, modeling, and giving the child a chance to rehearse new attitudes and responses and practice them in real-life situations. Cognitive behavior therapy has been effective in treating a variety of complaints, ranging from minor problems and developmental difficulties to severe disorders that are incurable but can be made somewhat more manageable. It is used either alone or together with other therapies and/or medication as part of an overall treatment plan.

Cognitive behavioral therapy has worked especially well, often in combination with medication, for children and adolescents suffering from depression. It can help free depressed children from the pervasive feelings of helplessness and hopelessness that are supported by self-defeating beliefs. Children in treatment are assigned to monitor their thoughts, and the therapist points out ways that these thoughts (such as "nothing is any fun" or "I never do anything right") misrepresent or distort reality. Other therapeutic techniques may include the completion of graded task assignments, and the deliberate scheduling of pleasurable activities.

Cognitive behavioral therapy is also used for children with **conduct disorder,** which is characterized by aggressive, antisocial actions, including hurting animals and other children, setting fires, **lying,** and theft. Through a cognitive behavioral approach (which generally works better with adolescents than with younger children because of the levels of thinking and control involved), young people with this disorder are taught ways to handle anger and resolve conflicts peacefully. Through instruction, modeling, **role playing,** and other techniques, they learn to react to events in socially appropriate, nonviolent ways. Other childhood conditions for which cognitive behavior therapy has been effective include generalized anxiety disorder and **attention deficit/hyperactivity disorder.** It can help children with ADHD become more controlled and less impulsive; often, they are taught to memorize and internalize the following set of behavior guidelines: "Stop—Listen—Look—Think—Act."

Cognitive behavioral therapy has also been successful in the treatment of adolescents with **eating disorders,** who, unlike those with conduct disorders, hurt themselves rather than hurting (or attempting to hurt) others. The cognitive approach focuses on the distorted perceptions that young women with **anorexia** or **bulimia** have about food, eating, and their own bodies. Often administered in combination with medication, therapy for eating disorders needs to be continued for an extended period of time—a year and a half or longer in the case of anorexia.

Cognitive therapy is generally not used for disorders, such as **schizophrenia** or **autism,** in which thinking or communication are severely disturbed.

For Further Study

Books

Beck, Aaron. *Cognitive Therapy and the Emotional Disorders.* New York: International Universities Press, 1976.

Dryden, Windy, ed. *The Essential Albert Ellis: Seminal Writings on Psychotherapy.* New York: Springer, 1990.

Feindler, Eva L. *Adolescent Anger Control: Cognitive-Behavioral Techniques.* New York: Pergamon Press, 1986.

Fishman, Katharine Davis. *Behind the One-Way Mirror: Psychotherapy and Children.* New York: Bantam Books, 1995.

Mahoney, Michael J., ed. *Cognition and Psychotherapy.* New York: Plenum Press, 1985.

Martorano, Joseph T., and John P. Kildahl. *Beyond Negative Thinking: Breaking the Cycle of Depressing and Anxious Thoughts.* New York: Insight Books, 1989.

Wolpe, Joseph. *Life Without Fear.* Oakland, CA: Harbinger, 1988.

Organizations

American Academy of Child and Adolescent Psychiatry
> **Address:** 3615 Wisconsin Avenue NW
> Washington, DC 20016
> **Telephone:** (202) 966-7300

American Society for Adolescent Psychiatry
> **Address:** 4330 East West Highway, Suite 1117
> Bethesda, MD 20814
> **Telephone:** (301) 718-6502

Association for Advancement of Behavior Therapy
> **Address:** 15 West 36th St.
> New York, NY 10018
> **Telephone:** (212) 279-7970

Albert Ellis Institute (formerly the Institute for Rational-Emotive Behavior Therapy)
> **Address:** 45 East 65th St.
> New York, NY 10021
> **Telephone:** (212) 535-0822
> **Website:** http://www.rebt.org

Cognitive Development

The development of thought processes, including remembering, problem solving, and decision-making, from childhood through adolescence to adulthood.

Historically, the cognitive development of children has been studied in a variety of ways. The oldest is through intelligence tests, such as the widely used **Stanford Binet Intelligence Quotient**, or IQ, test first adopted for use in the United States by psychologist Lewis Terman (1877–1956) in 1916 from a French model pioneered in 1905. IQ scoring is based on the concept of "mental age," according to which the scores of a child of average **intelligence** match his or her age, while a gifted child's performance is comparable to that of an older child, and a slow learner's scores are similar to those of a younger child. IQ tests are widely used in the United States, but they have come under increasing criticism for defining intelligence too narrowly and for being biased with regard to race and gender. In contrast to the emphasis placed on a child's native abilities by intelligence testing, learning theory grew out of work by behaviorist researchers such as **John Watson** and B. F. Skinner

(1904–1990), who argued that children are completely malleable. Learning theory focuses on the role of environmental factors in shaping the intelligence of children, especially on a child's ability to learn by having certain behaviors rewarded and others discouraged.

The most well-known and influential theory of cognitive development is that of French psychologist **Jean Piaget.** Piaget's theory, first published in 1952, grew out of decades of extensive observation of children, including his own, in their natural environments as opposed to the laboratory experiments of the behaviorists. Although Piaget was interested in how children reacted to their environment, he proposed a more active role for them than that suggested by learning theory. He envisioned a child's knowledge as composed of *schemas,* basic units of knowledge used to organized past experiences and serve as a basis for understanding new ones. Schemas are continually being modified by two complementary processes that Piaget termed assimilation and accommodation. Assimilation refers to the process of taking in new information by incorporating it into an existing schema. In other words, we assimilate new experiences by relating them to things we already know. On the other hand, accommodation is what happens when the schema itself changes to accommodate new knowledge. According to Piaget, cognitive development involves an ongoing attempt to achieve a balance between assimilation and accommodation that he termed equilibration.

Piaget's stages of cognitive development

At the center of Piaget's theory is the principle that cognitive development occurs in a series of four distinct, universal stages, each characterized by increasingly sophisticated and abstract levels of thought. These stages always occur in the same order, and each builds on what was learned in the previous stage. During the first, or sensorimotor, stage (birth to 24 months), knowledge is gained primarily through sensory impressions and motor activity. Through these two modes of learning, experienced both separately and in combination, infants gradually learn to control their own bodies and objects in the external world. The ultimate task at this stage is to achieve a sense of object constancy, or permanence—the sense that objects go on existing even when we cannot see them. This developing concept can be seen in the child's keen enjoyment of games in which objects are repeatedly made to disappear and reappear.

The preoperational stage (ages two to six years) involves the manipulation of images and symbols. One object can represent another, as when a broom is turned into a "horsey" that can be ridden around the room, and a child's play expands to include "pretend" games. Language acquisition is yet another way of manipulating symbols. Key concepts involved in the logical organization of thoughts—such as causality, time, and perspective—are still absent, as is an awareness that substances retain the same volume even when shifted into containers of different sizes and shapes. The child's focus remains egocentric throughout both the preoperational and sensorimotor stages.

During the third, or concrete operational, stage (six or seven to 11 years of age), children can perform logical operations, but only in relation to concrete external objects rather than ideas. They can add, subtract, count, and measure, and they learn about the conservation of length, mass, area, weight, time, and volume. At this stage, children can sort items into categories, reverse the direction of their thinking, and think about two concepts, such as length and width, simultaneously. They also begin to lose their egocentric focus, becoming able to understand a situation from the viewpoint of another person.

The fourth, or formal operations, stage begins in early adolescence (age 11 or 12) with the development of the ability to think logically about abstractions, including speculations about what might happen in the future. Adolescents are capable of formulating and testing hypotheses, understanding causality, and dealing with abstract concepts like probability, ratio, proportion, and analogies. They become able to reason scientifically and speculate about philosophical issues. Abstract concepts and moral values become as important as concrete objects.

Modern views

In the decades since Piaget's theory of cognitive development became widely known, other researchers have contested some of its principles, claiming that children's progress through the four stages of development is more uneven and less consistent than Piaget believed. It has been found that children do not always reach the different stages at the age levels he specified, and that their entry into some of the stages is more gradual than was first thought. However, Piaget remains the most influential figure in modern child development research, and many of his ideas are still considered accurate, including the basic notion of qualitative shifts in children's thinking over time, the general trend toward greater logic and less egocentrism as they get older, the concepts of assimilation and accommodation, and the importance of active learning by questioning and exploring.

The most significant alternative to the work of Piaget has been the information- processing approach, which uses the computer as a model to provide new insight into how the human mind receives, stores, retrieves, and uses information. Researchers using **information–processing theory** to study cognitive development in children have focused on areas such as the gradual improvements in children's ability to take in information and focus selectively on certain parts of it and their increasing attention

spans and capacity for **memory** storage. For example, they have found that the superior memory skills of older children are due in part to memorization strategies, such as repeating items in order to memorize them or dividing them into categories.

Today it is widely accepted that a child's intellectual ability is determined by a combination of heredity and environment. Thus, although a child's genetic inheritance is unchangeable, there are definite ways that parents can enhance their children's intellectual development through environmental factors. They can provide stimulating learning materials and experiences from an early age, reading to and talking with their children and helping them explore the world around them. As children mature, parents can both challenge and support the child's talents. Although a supportive environment in early childhood provides a clear advantage for a child, it is possible to make up for early losses in cognitive development if a supportive environment is provided at some later period, in contrast to early disruptions in physical development, which are often irreversible.

For Further Study

Books

Bruner, Jerome S. *Studies in Cognitive Growth: A Collaboration at the Center for Cognitive Studies.* New York: Wiley, 1966.

Ginsburg, Herbert, and Sylvia Opper. *Piaget's Theory of Intellectual Development.* 3rd ed. Englewood Cliffs, NJ: Prentice-Hall, 1988.

Lee, Victor, and Prajna Das Gupta., eds. *Children's Cognitive and Language Development.* Cambridge, MA: Blackwell Publishers, 1995.

McShane, John. *Cognitive Development: An Information Processing Approach.* Oxford, Eng.: B. Blackwell, 1991.

Piaget, Jean, and Barbel Inhelder. *The Growth of Logical Thinking from Childhood to Adolescence.* New York: Basic Books, 1958.

Sameroff, Arnold J., and Marshall M. Haith, eds. *The Five to Seven Year Shift: The Age of Reason and Responsibility.* Chicago: University of Chicago Press, 1991.

Cold Sores

Popular name for mouth sores caused by a type of herpes simplex virus (HSV).

Cold sores, also sometimes referred to as fever blisters or oral herpes, form around the mouth. Caused by a virus known as herpes simplex type 1, cold sores are contagious; direct contact with an infected person may result in contracting the virus.

*See also **Herpes Simplex.***

Coles, Robert Martin (1929–)

American psychiatrist and author.

Psychiatrist and author Robert Coles pioneered the use of oral history as a method of studying children. His five-volume series of books called *Children in Crisis*, published from 1967–1978, won a Pulitzer Prize in recognition of its wide-ranging examination of children throughout the world and how they cope with war, poverty, and other crises. Trained as a pediatrician as well as a psychiatrist, Coles became a professor of psychiatry and medical humanities at Harvard University Medical School in 1978. His lifelong interest in children has generated more than 50 books.

Coles was born in 1929 in Boston to parents who encouraged him to read what he has called "spiritually alert" novelists such as Tolstoy and George Eliot. His mother was a lifelong community worker; his father's values were exemplified in his work from the mid-1960s to the mid-1980s as an advocate for poor, elderly residents of Boston. Coles studied medicine and psychiatry in Boston before serving two years as a U.S. Air Force physician. During advanced training in **psychoanalysis** in New Orleans, Coles reached a turning point. Deeply moved by the sight of a young black girl being heckled by white segregationists, in 1960 Coles began his examination of children and their hopes and fears by studying school desegregation in New Orleans. "History had knocked on the city's door—a city whose people were frightened and divided. Had I not been there, driving by the mobs that heckled six-year-old Ruby Bridges, a black first-grader, as she tried to attend the Frantz School, I might have pursued a different life," Coles writes in the introduction to *The Spiritual Life of Children*. "I had planned until then to enter the profession of psychoanalytic child psychiatry. Instead, I became a 'field worker,' learning to talk with children going through their everyday lives amid substantial social and educational stress."

Traveling from the Deep South to Appalachia, from New Mexico to Alaska, Coles eventually traveled overseas to Europe, Africa, Central and South America, and the Middle East. His wife, Jane, and their three sons began to share in some of the research, as they talked to children of all races and social status about religion, race, poverty, and war. During his career, Coles has written for various medical, psychiatric, and psychoanalytic journals, in addition to seeing patients when possible. He has also volunteered as a tutor in a school for underprivileged children. Besides *Children in Crisis*, Coles's prominent books include *The Moral Life of Children*, *The Political Life of Children*, *The Spiritual Life of Children*, and *Women of Crisis*.

For Further Study

Books

Coles, Robert. *The Mind's Fate: A Psychiatrist Looks at His Profession.* Boston: Little, Brown and Co., 1975.

Periodicals

Gordon, Mary. "What They Think About God." *The New York Times Book Review*, November 25, 1990, p.1+.

Gray, Francine du Plessix. "When We Are Good We Are Very, Very Good." *The New York Times Book Review*, November 21, 1993, p. 9.

Colic

Intense abdominal discomfort typically affecting infants under three months of age and whose cause is unknown.

In the first weeks and months after birth, an estimated 10% of all infants exhibit symptoms of intense abdominal pain, accompanied by the passage of gas. Often signalled by uncontrollable crying, body tension, and drawing up of the legs toward the abdomen, this condition, referred to as colic, typically peaks during the late afternoon and evening hours. The cause of colic is not known. It is slightly more common among first-born children, and more male infants exhibit signs of colic than females.

Some strategies for dealing with colic include wrapping the infant snugly in a light blanket, offering the infant a pacifier, rubbing his back while he lies face down across your lap, or holding the infant over your shoulder and rocking or walking continuously while talking or singing in a soothing voice. If the baby is being fed with formula, switching the formula may help. However, in all likelihood, the colic will continue until the baby's system adjusts and she outgrows it at around three to five months of age. There does not seem to be any connection between colic and any long-range health problems.

For Further Study

Books

Schneider, Phyllis. *Parents Book of Infant Colic.* New York: Ballantine Books, 1990.

Taubman, Bruce. *Curing Infant Colic: The 7-Minute Program for Soothing the Fussy Baby.* New York: Bantam Books, 1990.

Weissbluth, Marc. *Crybabies: Coping with Colic.* New York: Arbor House, 1984.

Young, Carol. *Crying For Help: How to Cure Your Baby of Colic.* New York: Thorsons, 1986.

College Entrance Examinations *see* **SAT**

Comfort Habits *see* **Security Objects; Thumb Sucking**

Communication Board

A device for use in communicating with people who have no or impaired communication skills.

A communication board is a device designed to facilitate communication between two individuals, one or both of whom have verbal communication difficulties. Communication boards and related aids are used by people who have difficulty using speech to communicate, or whose speech cannot be understood by others. Such devices are often successful in helping people with **aphasia, autism, mental retardation** and other brain dysfunctions, voice, hearing, or visual problems, or neurological disorders. The communication board allows an individual to point to the word or pictorial representation of the appropriate concept he or she wants to communicate.

Communication board

A communication board is not a substitute for speech, but provides support for basic communication. Communication boards are often custom-made by the user or his friends, teachers, or family members, sometimes using a purchased kit designed for the purpose. Commercial kits for making communication boards include mat boards with packages of stickers representing familiar words or concepts encountered during the activities of daily life. Stickers may feature either words or simple drawings to represent the concepts to be used in communication. Some communication boards can be written on with a marker; these have an erasable surface, usually white, that is sometimes referred to as "china board."

Variations on the communication board

Some communication boards have advanced programmable features that incorporate spoken language as well as visual depictions of the concepts. For example, using a programmable, purchased device, a parent could develop a custom communication board for the child to use in choosing food at mealtime. The photos could feature selected food items that the child likes. In response to the question "What would you like for lunch?" the child touches a pressure-sensitive picture of pizza, and the pre-programmed voice says "I would like cheese pizza, please." Such devices allow the child to simulate simple spoken communication. Although the devices with voice responses are more costly than the simple printed communication board system, computer technology has made them easier to use and affordable for many schools and families.

Portable communication boards are available in wallet-like cases to help the nonverbal child communicate at school, in restaurants, and elsewhere. The creative use of communication boards and voice-response devices enable the child with limited speech to share his ideas, needs, wants, and feelings with those around her.

For Further Study

Books

Ross, Linda M., ed. *Communication Disorders Sourcebook: Basic Information About Deafness and Hearing Loss, Speech and Language Disorders, Voice Disorders, Balance and Vestibular Disorders, and Disorders of Smell, Taste, and Touch.* Detroit, MI: Omnigraphics, 1995.

Communication Skills and Disorders

The skills needed to use language (spoken, written, signed, or otherwise communicated) to interact with others, and problems related to the development of these skills.

Experts in child development generally agree that all babies develop skills for spoken and written language according to a specific developmental schedule, regardless of the language being learned. Although the milestones follow one another in roughly the same sequence, there is significant variability from child to child as to when the first word is spoken and the first sentence is composed.

The accompanying table illustrates the developmental milestones for communication.

Language employs symbols—words, gestures, or spoken sounds—to represent objects and ideas. Communication of language begins with spoken sounds combined with gestures, relying on two different types of skills. Children first acquire the skills to receive communications, that is, listening to and understanding what they hear (supported by accompanying gestures); next,

COMMUNICATION MILESTONES

Age	Milestone
0–12 months	• Responds to speech by looking at the speaker; responds differently to aspects of speaker's voice (such as friendly or angry, male or female). • Turns head in direction of sound. • Responds with gestures to greetings such as "hi," "bye-bye," and "up" when these words are accompanied by appropriate gesture by speaker. • Stops ongoing activity when told "no" when speaker uses appropriate gesture and tone. • May say two or three words by around 12 months of age, although probably not clearly. • Repeats some vowel and consonant sounds (babbles) when alone or spoken to; attempts to imitate sounds.
12–24 months	• Responds correctly when asked "where?" • Understands prepositions *on, in,* and *under;* and understands simple phrases (such as "Get the ball."). • Says 8–10 words by around age 18 months; by age two, vocabulary will include 20–50 words, mostly describing people, common objects, and events (such as "more" and "all gone"). • Uses single word plus a gesture to ask for objects. • Refers to self by name; uses "my" or "mine."
24–36 months	• Points to pictures of common objects when they are named. • Can identify objects when told their use • Understands questions with "what" and "where" and negatives "no," "not," "can't," and "don't." • Responds to simple directions. • Selects and looks at picture books; enjoys listening to simple stories, and asks for them to be read aloud again. • Joins two vocabulary words together to make a phrase. • Can say first and last name. • Shows frustration at not being understood.
36–48 months	• Begins to understand time concepts, such as "today," "later," "tomorrow," and "yesterday." • Understands comparisons, such as "big" and "bigger." • Forms sentences with three or more words. • Speech is understandable to most strangers, but some sound errors may persists (such as "t" sound for "k" sound).
48–60 months	• By 48 months, has a vocabulary of over 200 words. • Follows two or three unrelated commands in proper order. • Understands sequencing of events ("First we have to go to the grocery store, and then we can go to the playground"). • Asks questions using "when," "how," and "why." Talks about causes for things using "because".

COMMUNICATION MILESTONES	
Age	**Milestone**
60–72 months	• By 60 months, can identify rhyming words. • There are few obvious differences between child's grammar and adult grammar. • Still needs to learn subject-verb agreement, and may not have mastered all irregular verbs. • Can carry on a conversation. • Communicates with family, friends, and strangers, and responds with information appropriately.

Source: U.S. Department of Health and Human Services.

they will begin experimenting with expressing themselves through speaking and gesturing. Speaking will begin as repetitive syllables, followed by words, phrases, and sentences. Later, children will acquire the skills of reading and writing, the written forms of communication. Although milestones are discussed for the development of these skills of communication, many children begin speaking significantly earlier or later than the milestone date. Parents should refrain from attaching too much significance to either deviation from the average. When a child's deviation from the average milestones of development cause the parents concern, a pediatrician or other professional may be contacted for advice.

Spoken language problems are referred to by a number of labels, including language delay, language disability, or a specific type of language disability. In general, experts distinguish between those children who seem to be slow in developing spoken language (**language delay**) and those who seem to have difficulty achieving a milestone of spoken language (**language disorders**). Language disorders include **stuttering**; articulation disorders, such as substituting one sound for another (tandy for candy), omitting a sound (canny for candy), or distorting a sound (shlip for sip); and voice disorders, such as inappropriate pitch, volume, or quality. Causes can be related to hearing, nerve/muscle disorders, head injury, viral diseases, **mental retardation**, drug abuse, **cleft lip** or **palate**.

In the past, most parents, pediatricians, and educators recommended giving the child time to outgrow a difficulty with spoken language. As of the late 1990s, research had shown that early speech and language disorders could lead to later difficulties in learning to read, write, and spell. Thus, many professionals recommended evaluation by a speech-language pathologist for toddlers who demonstrated language delay. However, not all speech-language specialists agree on early evaluation

and therapy. Those who feel early intervention is unnecessary cite the results of research by Rhea Paul at Portland (Oregon) State University. She found that about two-thirds of children who were not talking at age two showed continued delays until age three, and one-half were still behind the typical language development schedule at age four. But by kindergarten, only one-fourth of those children had not caught up with their peers.

Parents and their pediatrician should communicate frequently about a child's spoken **language development**, and should consider all factors related to spoken language delay when considering whether to have a specialist evaluate and treat the delay. Such factors as the possible stigma attached to labeling a child with language difficulties versus whether intervention will prevent social and educational difficulties should be considered in making the decision.

For Further Study

Books

Berko-Gleason, J. *The Development of Language*. New York: Macmillan, 1993.

de Villiers, P., and J. de Villiers. *Early Language*. The Developing Child series. Cambridge, Mass.: Harvard University Press, 1979.

Fletcher, P., and B. MacWhinney. *The Handbook of Child Language*. Cambridge, MA: Blackwell Publishers, 1995.

Goodluck, H. *Language Acquisition: A Linguistic Introduction*. Cambridge, MA: Blackwell Publishers, 1991.

Landau, B., and L. Gleitman. *Language and Experience: Evidence from the Blind Child*. Cambridge, MA: Harvard University Press, 1985.

Pinker, S. *The Language Instinct*. New York: Morrow, 1994.

Periodicals

Bates, Elizabeth, and Jeffrey Elman. "Learning Rediscovered." *Science* 274, December 13, 1996, pp. 1849+.

Cowley, Geoffrey. "The Language Explosion." *Newsweek* 129, Spring-Summer 1997, pp. 16+.

Organizations

American Speech-Language-Hearing Association

Address: 1801 Rockville Pike

Rockville, MD 20852

Telephone: toll free voice or TTY (800) 638-8255; voice or TTY (301) 897-8682

e-mail: ircasha.org

website: www.asha.org

(Publishes brochures, booklets, and fact sheets on speech-language pathology.)

National Institute on Deafness and Other Communication Disorders

Address: National Institutes of Health

Bethesda, MD 20892

e-mail: webmaster@ms.nih.gov

website: www.nih.gov/nidcd/

....

Computers in Education

Electronic devices used to enhance, facilitate, or support learning activities.

Since the 1980s, computers have been widely available in schools, libraries, and a growing percentage of U.S. households. In fact, the percentage of U.S. public schools that had computers grew from 77.7% in the academic year 1984–85 to 97.5% in 1993–94. For the same two academic years, the number of students per computer dropped from almost 63 in 1984–85 to 11 in 1993–94. The National Center for Education Statistics tracks data on computer use by students, both at school and at home.

A summary of their findings for 1984 and 1993 appears in the accompanying table.

Experts in education are actively involved in developing ways for students to use technology to improve education. There is no single application that is universal to all classrooms. In some settings, students use computers for simple word processing—that is, to type reports and other documents and to print out the results. This application allows students to revise and edit easily. Educators have observed that some students are more likely to produce revisions when working on a computer, since a computer makes it much easier to redraft a sentence and produce a new printout when compared with producing a handwritten copy. Some parents and educators express concerns about the impact of computers on handwriting; students who use computers don't get as much practice in the skills required for legible handwriting.

Another classroom application of computers is for information gathering and research. Encyclopedias and other reference works are available on CD-ROMs, which can be searched by the student using the computer in his or her classroom or school library. With increased usage of computers, many students are learning to type at an earlier age. Traditionally, students learned to type in high school or later, but the students of the 1990s begin "keyboarding" as soon as they have access to a computer, often in the preschool years. Formal keyboarding skills are taught in elementary schools, beginning in the second or third grade.

Another application of computers in classrooms is for so-called computer-aided instruction (CAI). Interactive programs provide practice in such basic skills as

PERCENT OF STUDENTS USING COMPUTERS			
	Use computers at school	**Use computers at home**	**Use computers at home for school work**
1984			
—Percent of total, 1984	27.3%	11.5%	4.6%
1993			
—Percent of total	59.0%	27.0%	14.9%
—Percent of pre-K and kindergarten students	26.2%	15.6%	0.6%
—Percent of students in grades 1–8	68.9%	24.7%	10.8%
—Percent of students in grades 9–12	58.2%	28.7%	20.9%

Source: U.S. Center for Education Statistics, *Digest of Education Statistics,* 1994.

spelling, math computation, and word recognition. Other programs capitalize on student's curiosity and motivation to use computers to teach such curriculum subjects as history, archaeology, geology, and cultural history. For example, a program may allow a student to type in a phrase and have it translated to hieroglyphics; another offers an opportunity to explore digitally the studio of French Impressionist painter Claude Monet.

Educators have identified the following advantages for the use of technology in teaching: many students enter school with a strong familiarity with technology; technology allows information to be presented in short segments, using visual and audio stimuli, which addresses the short attention span of young learners; using technology more closely approximates the way humans learn through experiences. Some disadvantages or barriers to the use of CAI in schools are: computer equipment is expensive; the individualized nature of computer use limits small-group or full class instruction possibilities.

For Further Study

Books

Alessi, Stephen M. and Stanley R. Trollip. *Computer-Based Instruction: Methods and Development.* 2nd ed. Englewood Cliffs, NJ: Prentice Hall, 1991.

Bitter, Gary G., Ruth A. Camuse, and Vicki L. Durbin. *Using a Microcomputer in the Classroom.* 3rd ed. Boston: *Allyn and Bacon,* 1993.

Bright, George W. *Microcomputer Applications in the Elementary Classroom: A Guide for Teachers.* Boston: Allyn and Bacon, 1987.

Cannings, Terence R. and LeRoy Finkel. *Technology Age Classroom.* Wilsonville, OR: Franklin, Beedle & Associates, 1992.

Hoot, James L. (ed.) *Computers in Early Childhood Education: Issues and Practices.* Englewood Cliffs, NJ: Prentice-Hall, 1986.

Kepner, Henry S., Jr., (ed.) *Computers in the Classroom.* 2nd ed. Washington, DC: National Education Association, 1986.

Gayeski, Diane M. (ed.) *Multimedia for Learning: Development, Application, Evaluation.* Englewood, NJ: Educational Technology Publications, 1993.

Geisert, Paul and Mynga K. Futrell. *Teachers, Computers, and Curriculum: Microcomputers in the Classroom.* 2nd ed. Boston: Allyn and Bacon, 1995.

Holton, Felicia Antonelli. *Compukids: A Parent's Guide to Computers and Learning.* New York: New American Library, 1985.

Kommers, Piet, A.M. Scott Grabinger, and Joanna C. Dunlap, (eds.) *Hypermedia Learning Environments: Instructional Design and Integration.* Mahwah, NJ: L. Erlbaum Associates, 1996.

Keizer, Gregg. *The Family PC Guide to Homework.* New York: Hyperion & Family PC, 1996.

Lengel, James G. and Diane S. Kendall. *Kids, Computers, and Homework.* New York: Random House, 1995.

Papert, Seymour. *The Children's Machine: Rethinking School in the Age of the Computer.* New York: Basic Books, 1993.

———. *The Connected Family: Bridging the Digital Generation Gap.* Atlanta, GA: Longstreet Press, 1996.

Protheroe, Nancy, Elizabeth Wilson, Lorene Kluge. *The Internet Handbook for School Users.* Arlington, VA: Educational Research Service, 1994.

Ryba, Ken, and Bill Anderson. *Learning with Computers: Effective Teaching Strategies.* Eugene, OR: International Society for Technology in Education, 1990.

Tison, Cindra and Mary Jo Woodside. *The Ultimate Collection of Computer Facts & Fun. A Kid's Guide to Computers.* Carmel, IN: SAMS, 1991.

Audiovisual Recordings

The Imagination Machines. An Explanation of the Role of Computer Technology in Arts Education and the Impact of the Arts on New Electronic Learning Tools. Santa Monica, CA: Getty Center for Education in the Arts, 1991. (One 1-hour videotape.)

Concept Formation

Learning process by which items are categorized and related to each other.

A concept is a generalization that helps to organize information into categories. For example, the concept "square" is used to describe those things that have four equal sides and four right angles. Thus, the concept categorize things whose properties meet the set requirements. The way young children learn concepts has been studied in experimental situations using so-called artificial concepts such as "square". In contrast, real-life, or natural, concepts have characteristic rather than defining features. For example, a robin would be a prototypical or "good" example of the concept "bird." A penguin lacks an important defining feature of this category—flight, and thus is not as strong an example of a "bird." Similarly, for many children the concept "house" represents a squarish structure with walls, windows, and a chimney that provides shelter. In later development, the child's concept of house would be expanded to include nontypical examples, such as "teepee" or "igloo," both of which have some but not all of the prototypical characteristics that the children have learned for this concept.

Natural concepts are often learned through the use of prototypes, highly typical examples of a category—like the robin cited above. The other major method of concept learning is through the trial-and-error method of testing hypotheses. People will guess or assume that a certain item is an instance of a particular concept; they then learn

SELECTED READINGS ABOUT THE INTERNET

The Internet and World Wide Web comprise vast resources of information that students may want to access, using their computer at school or home. Here are some resources for parents and educators interested in learning ways to use these electronic links to enhance education.

How-to References

Bix, Cynthia Overbeck. *Kids Do the Web.* Adobe Books, 1996.

Barron, Ann E., and Karen S. Ivers. *The Internet and Instruction: Activities and Ideas.* Englewood, CO: Libraries Unlimited, 1996.

Cotton, Eileen Giuffri. *The Online Classroom: Teaching with the Internet.* Bloomington, IN: ERIC Clearinghouse on Reading, English, and Communication: Edinfo Press, 1996.

Cummins, Jim and Dennis Sayers. *Brave New Schools: Challenging Cultural Illiteracy Through Global Learning Networks.* New York: St. Martin's Press, 1997.

Lasarenko, Jane. *Wired for Learning.* Indianapolis, IN: Que Corp., 1997.

Valauskas, Edward J., and Monica Ertel. (eds.) *The Internet for Teachers and School Library Media Specialists: Today's Applications, Tomorrow's Projects.* New York: Neal-Schuman Publishers, 1996.

Ryder, Randall J., and Tom Hughes. *Internet for Educators.* Upper Saddle River, NJ: Merrill, 1997.

Williams, Bard. *The Internet for Teachers.* 2nd ed. Foster City, CA: IDG Books, 1996.

Internet/World Wide Web Safety

Carlson, Matt. *Childproof Internet: A Parent's Guide to Safe and Secure Online Access.* New York: MIS Press, 1996.

Distefano, Vince, Gregory Giagnocavo, Dorissa Bolinski, and the staff of Classroom Connect. *Child Safety on the Internet.* Lancaster, PA: Classroom Connect, 1997. (Book and computer disc.)

Audiovisual Recordings

Wiese, Michael, executive producer. *Kids on the Internet.* Studio City, CA: Internet Video Partners, 1996. (One 30-minute videocassette.)

Internet for Educators: A Step-by-Step Guide to Help Educators Understand and Use the Internet. Seattle, WA: White Rain Films, 1996. (One 66-minute videocassette and booklet.)

---

more about the concept when they see whether their hypothesis is correct or not.

People learn simple concepts more readily than complex ones. For example, the easiest concept to learn is one with only a single defining feature. The next easiest is one with multiple features, all of which must be present in every case, known as the conjunctive concept. In conjunctive concepts, *and* links all the required attributes. For example, the concept square is defined by four sides *and* four 90-degree angles. It is more difficult to master a so-called disjunctive concept, when either one feature or another must be present. People also learn concepts more easily when they are given positive rather than negative examples of a concept (e.g., shown what it is rather than what it is not).

For Further Study

Books

Bruner, Jerome S. *Studies in Cognitive Growth: A Collaboration at the Center for Cognitive Studies.* New York: Wiley, 1966.

Ginsburg, Herbert, and Sylvia Opper. *Piaget's Theory of Intellectual Development.* 3rd ed. Englewood Cliffs, NJ: Prentice-Hall, 1988.

Lee, Victor, and Prajna Das Gupta. (eds.) *Children's Cognitive and Language Development.* Cambridge, MA: Blackwell Publishers, 1995.

McShane, John. *Cognitive Development: An Information Processing Approach.* Oxford, Eng.: B. Blackwell, 1991.

Piaget, Jean, and Barbel Inhelder. *The Growth of Logical Thinking from Childhood to Adolescence.* New York: Basic Books, 1958.

Sameroff, Arnold J., and Marshall M. Haith. (eds.) *The Five to Seven Year Shift: The Age of Reason and Responsibility.* Chicago: University of Chicago Press, 1991.

Conditioning *see* **Aversive Conditioning; Classical Conditioning; Operant Conditioning**

Condom

A thin, elastic covering worn on a man's penis during sexual intercourse to catch semen and protect against sexually transmitted diseases (STDs).

When used properly in combination with a vaginal spermicide, a condom is a relatively effective form of **contraception.** In addition, except for abstinence, condoms are the only effective way to decrease the risk of infection with **sexually transmitted diseases** (STDs). Many health officials recommend that sexually active adolescents use a condom every time they have sexual intercourse, even when another method of contraception is used. Condoms made of latex are the most effective against STDs.

The combination of a vaginal spermicide and a condom reduce the risk of pregnancy to less that 10%, but a condom alone should not be considered reliable contraction. A condom should always be checked for holes before use, and never used more than once. Before any genital contact, a condom should be unrolled all the way to the base of the penis, allowing a half inch (about 1.25 cm) of empty space at the tip to catch the semen. To create this empty space, the tip of the condom can be pinched as the condom is rolled on. Pinching the tip also prevents air from entering the condom, which can lead to tearing. After intercourse, a man should hold the rim of the condom while withdrawing his penis to prevent semen from spilling.

The only lubricants that can safely be used with a condom are water-based lubricants such as K–Y jelly or contraceptive gels. Oil-base lubricants such as petroleum jelly or baby oil will diminish a condom's effectiveness. A condom in an unopened package will remain effective for several years if not exposed to heat.

Conduct Disorders

A childhood antisocial behavior disorder characterized by aggressive and destructive actions that harm other human beings, animals, or property, and which violate the socially expected behavior for the child's age.

Along with **anxiety** and **depression,** conduct disorder is one of the most frequently diagnosed childhood psychological disorders. Depending on the population, rates of the disorder range from 6–16% in males and 2–9% in females and are expected to increase as antisocial behavior increases. Symptoms of conduct disorder include aggression**,** destruction of property, deceitfulness or theft, and serious violations of rules. The specific manner in which these activities are carried out may vary with age as cognitive and physical development occur. The child may exhibit opposition to authority (characteristic of **oppositional-defiant disorder**) during early childhood, gradually adopt the more serious behaviors of **lying,** shoplifting, and fighting during school age years, and then develop the most extreme behaviors such as burglary, confrontative theft, and rape during puberty and teenage years. Males tend to demonstrate more confrontative behaviors, such as fighting, theft, vandalism, and discipline problems, than females, who are more likely demonstrate lying, **truancy,** substance abuse, and prostitution.

Depending on the age it first appears, two forms of conduct disorder are identified: childhood-onset type and adolescent-onset type. In childhood-onset conduct disorder, the individual, usually a male, will have exhibited at least one criteria for the disorder before age 10 and will usually have full-blown conduct disorder by puberty.

These children are more likely to develop adult **antisocial personality disorder.** Adolescent-onset conduct disorder tends to be milder, with no exhibiting symptoms before age 10. Adolescents with this type of conduct disorder are only slightly more frequently male than female, have more normal peer relationships, and are less likely to progress to antisocial personality disorder as adults. Their antisocial behaviors may be much more marked when in the presence of others.

Diagnosis

According to the ***Diagnostic and Statistical Manual of Mental Disorders (DSM IV),*** conduct disorder is present when a child or adolescent (1) repetitively violates the rights of others or violates age-appropriate social norms and rules, and (2) this pattern of behavior causes significant impairment in social, academic, or occupational functioning. Three or more of the following criteria must have been present within the past 12 months, with one present within the past six months:

Aggression
The child or adolescent:
- bullies, threatens, or intimidates others;
- initiates physical fights;
- uses a weapon with potential to cause serious harm;
- is physically cruel to people;
- is physically cruel to animals;
- steals while confronting the victim (mugging, extortion, robbery);
- forces another person into sexual activity.

Destruction of Property
The child or adolescent:
- deliberately engages in fire-setting with the intention of doing serious damage;
- deliberately destroys others' property (other than by fire).

Deceitfulness or Theft
The child or adolescent:
- breaks into someone else's house, building, or car;
- lies to obtain goods, favors, or to avoid obligations;
- steals objects of non-trivial value without confronting the victim.

Serious Violations of Rules
The child or adolescent:
- stays out late at night against parental prohibition before age 13;
- runs away once for a lengthy period of time or twice overnight;
- is truant from school before age 13.

Because children and adolescents with conduct disorder often attempt to minimize the seriousness of their behavior, diagnosis is based on observations by parents, teachers, other authorities, peers, and by victims of the child's abuse. Generally, the child will present an exterior of toughness which actually conceals low **self-esteem,** and will demonstrate little empathy for the feelings of others or remorse for his or her actions. The disorder is associated with early sexual activity, substance abuse, reckless acts, and suicidal ideation. Chronic health problems, **attention deficit/hyperactivity disorder,** poverty, family conflict or a family history of alcohol dependence, mood disorders, antisocial disorders, and **schizophrenia** are also linked to the disorder.

There is some concern that the behaviors associated with conduct disorder may potentially be considered "normal" responses in the context of certain highly violent social conditions, for example war-zones (a concern when treating some immigrants) and high-crime urban neighborhoods. In these areas, the routine threats posed to life and property may encourage aggressive and deceptive behaviors as protective responses. Thus, the social and economic context in which the behaviors occurred should be taken into account, and in some cases a model based on trauma may be helpful.

A majority of children with conduct disorder no longer exhibit the extreme behaviors by the time they reach adulthood, but a substantial number do go on to develop antisocial personality disorder. For information about treatment, see entry on antisocial behavior.

See also **Antisocial Behavior, Oppositional-Defiant Disorder**

For Further Study

Books

Kazdin, Alan E. *Conduct Disorders in Childhood and Adolescence.* Newbury Park, CA: Sage Publications, 1995.

Kernberg, Paulina F., et al. *Children with Conduct Disorders: A Psychotherapy Manual.* New York: Basic Books, 1991.

Sholevar, G. Pirooz, ed. *Conduct Disorders in Children and Adolescents.* Washington, DC: American Psychiatric Press, 1995.

Organizations

American Academy of Child and Adolescent Psychiatry
Address: 3615 Wisconsin Avenue, NW
Washington, DC 20016-3007
Telephone: (202) 966-7300
Website: http://www.aacap.org
(A professional association whose mission includes educating parents and families about psychiatric disorders affecting children and adolescents, educating child and adolescent psychiatrists, and developing guidelines for treatment of childhood and adolescent mental health disorders.)

The Federation of Families for Children's Mental Health
Address: 1021 Prince Street
Alexandria, VA 22314-2971
Telephone: (703)684-7710
(A national parent-run organization focused on the needs of children and youth with emotional, behavioral, or mental disorders and their families.)

Conflict Resolution

The process of defusing antagonism and reaching agreement between conflicting parties, especially through some form of negotiation. Also, the study and practice of solving interpersonal and intergroup conflict.

"Conflict" from the Latin root "to strike together" can be defined as any situation where incompatible activities, feelings, or intentions occur together. Conflict may take place within one person, between two or more people who know each other, or between large groups of people who do not know each other. It may involve actual confrontation between persons, or merely symbolic confrontation through words and deeds. The conflict may be expressed through verbal denigration, accusations, threats, or through physical violence to persons or property. Or the conflict may remain unexpressed, as in avoidance and denial.

A given conflict may be defined in terms of the *issues* that caused it, the *strategies* used to address it, or the *outcomes* or consequences that follow from it. Preschool and early elementary school-aged children tend to have conflict over property issues, and they tend to use physical strategies to resolve them, like taking a toy they want from another child. As children grow older the causes of conflict are more frequently about social order, and they are more likely to use verbal strategies as solutions.

Strategies for resolving or preventing the development of conflict can be classified as avoidance, diffusion, or confrontation. Turning on the TV rather than discussing an argument is a form of avoidance. Two teen athletes talking to their peers or counselors after a dispute on the football field is an example of diffusion. Insulting another student's girlfriend or arranging to meet after school to fight are examples of confrontation. Courtroom litigation, like the trial and indictment of a juvenile who has violated the law, also represents a form of confrontation.

The phrase conflict resolution refers specifically to strategies of diffusion developed during the second half of the 20th century as alternatives to traditional litigation models of settling disputes. Based on the idea that it is better to expose and resolve conflict before it damages people's relationships or escalates into violence, methods of conflict resolution were developed in business management and gradually adopted in the fields of international relations, legal settings, and, during the 1980s, educational settings. According to the principles of conflict resolution, the only true solution to a conflict is one that attempts to satisfy the inherent needs of all the parties involved.

Most conflict resolution programs employ some form of negotiation as the primary method of communication between parties. In the negotiation process, parties with opposing interests hold conversations to settle a dispute. Negotiation can be distributive, where each party attempts to win as many concessions to his or her own self-interest as possible (win-lose), or integrative, where parties attempt to discover solutions that embody mutual self-interest (win-win). Research on games theory and the decision-making process suggest that the face-to-face conversation involved in direct negotiation may actually influence people to act in the interest of the group (including the opposing party), or some other interest beyond immediate self-interest. Certainly the simple act of talking with the opposition sends a message that the parties are committed to positive resolution, and face-to-face negotiation inherently tends to be integrative in its consequences.

The success of a given instance of conflict resolution depends on the attitudes and skills of the disputants and of the mediator or arbitrator. The elementary skills that have been identified as promoting conflict resolution overlap to a high degree with those that reflect social competence in children and adolescents. They include:

• Awareness of others

• Awareness of the (not necessarily obvious) distinctions between self and others

• Listening skills

• Awareness of one's own feelings and thoughts, and the ability to express them

• Ability to respond to the feelings and thoughts of others

A child or adolescent will employ the basic skills of conflict resolution to varying degrees in responding to a conflict. Responses can be graded according to the level of cooperativeness they reflect, i.e., the level of integration the child experiences between his own self-interest and the interest of the opposing party. Thus, threatening the other party reflects a slightly more integrated, constructive response to conflict than an immediately aggressive response such as hitting. Examples of progressively more cooperative responses to conflict are: withdrawing from a conflict; demanding or requesting the opposing party to concede; providing reasons the op-

posing party should concede (appealing to norms); proposing alternatives to the opposing party; and proposing "if" statements, suggesting willingness to negotiate. Perspective taking, or articulating and validating the feelings and thoughts of the other party ("I see that you want...."), reflects the higher orders of conflict resolution skills. Integration of interests ("We both want...") reflects the highest level, leading to a consensual settlement of negotiations.

Conflict resolution in education

Conflict resolution in education includes any strategy that promotes handling disputes peacefully and cooperatively outside of, or in addition to, traditional disciplinary procedures. The rise of violence and disciplinary problems, along with an increasing awareness of need for behavioral as well as cognitive instruction, spurred the development of conflict resolution programs in schools during the 1980s. These programs received national attention in 1984 with the formation of the National Association for Mediation in Education (NAME). By the late 1990s most major cities had instituted some form of large-scale conflict resolution program. According to a 1994 National School Boards study, 61% of schools had some form of conflict resolution program.

Conflict resolution programs differ widely in terms of who participates, the quantity of time and energy they require, and levels of funding they receive. Funding is usually provided by an outside source such as the state, a university program, or a local non-profit organization. Programs can be classroom-wide, school-wide, or district-wide, and can include any of the following components:

• Curriculum and classroom instruction

• Training workshops for faculty, staff, students, and/ or parents in conflict management skills, negotiation, and mediation

• Peer education and counseling programs where students either train each other in conflict resolution skills and/or actually carry out dispute resolution

• Mediation programs in which students, staff, or teachers carry out dispute resolution

Some conflict resolution programs provide a venue for actual dispute resolution, while others only provide only training and instruction. For example, after attending an in-service training on conflict resolution a teacher may decide to include the principles as curriculum for the students or to implement a new classroom policy that actually employs the principles of conflict resolution in maintaining discipline. School-wide or district-wide peer counseling and **peer mediation** programs carry out actual dispute resolution on a larger scale. Peer mediation, where students are trained in a step-by-step mediation process in order to provide ongoing mediation service for other students, is the most popular form of conflict resolution program. While these "applied" programs are more expensive than strictly curriculum-based programs, they appear to be significantly more effective. One study demonstrated that curriculum by itself does not change students' behavior in conflict situations, whereas the structured format of peer mediation program did change the way students addressed conflict.

For Further Study

Books

Deutsch, M. *The Resolution of Conflict: Constructive and Destructive Processes.* New Haven, CT: Yale University Press, 1989.

Girard, K., and S. Koch. *Conflict Resolution in the Schools: A Manual for Educators.* San Francisco: Jossey-Bass, Inc., 1996.

Kreidler, W.J. *Creative Conflict Resolution: More Than 200 Activities for Keeping Peace in the Classroom—K–6.* Glenview, IL: Scott, Foresman, 1984.

Lam, J.A. *The Impact of Conflict Resolution Programs on Schools: A Review and Synthesis of the Evidence.* 2nd edition. Amherst, MA: National Association for Mediation in Education, 1989.

Organizations

American Friends Service Committee
Address: 1501 Cherry St.
Philadelphia, PA 19102

Community Relations Service (CRS)
Address: U.S. Department of Justice
5550 Friendship Blvd.
Chevy Chase, MD 20815

Institute for Mediation and Conflict Resolution (IMCR)
Address: Automation House, 4th Floor
49 East 68th St.
New York, NY 10021

National Institute for Dispute Resolution
Address: 1726 M Street, NW, Suite 500
Washington, DC 20036
Telephone: (202) 466-4764

Conformity

Adaptation of one's behavior or beliefs to match those of the other members of a group.

Conformity describes the **adaptation** of behavior that occurs in response to unspoken group pressure. It differs from compliance, which is adaptation of behavior resulting from overt pressure. Individuals conform to or comply with group behavior in an attempt to "fit in" or to follow the norms of the social group. In most cases, conforming to social norms is so natural that people aren't even aware they are doing it unless someone calls it to their attention or violates the norms.

Researchers have studied conformity using controlled experiments. The first classic experiment in conformity was carried out in the 1930s by Muzafer Sherif. It made use of an optical illusion called the autokinetic phenomenon—the fact that a small stationary point of light in a darkened room will appear to move. The autokinetic phenomenon affects individuals differently, i.e., the amount of movement experienced by different people varies. In Sherif's experiment, several subjects were placed together in a room with a stationary light. Each was asked to describe its movement aloud. As the individuals listened to the descriptions of others, their answers became increasingly similar as they unconsciously sought to establish a group norm. The power of social norms was demonstrated even more strikingly when the subjects continued to adhere to the norm later when they were retested individually. Sherif's experiment demonstrates one of the important conditions that produces conformity: ambiguity. There was no clear-cut right answer to the question asked of the subjects, so they were more vulnerable to reliance on a norm.

In the 1950s another researcher, Solomon Asch, devised a conformity experiment that eliminated the ambiguity factor. Subjects were asked to match lines of different lengths on two cards. In this experiment, there was one obvious right answer. However, each subject was tested in a room full of "planted" peers who deliberately gave the wrong answer in some cases. About three-fourths of the subjects tested knowingly gave an incorrect answer at least once in order to conform to the group.

Asch's experiment revealed other factors—notably unanimity and size of the majority—that influence conformity even when ambiguity isn't an issue. Unanimity of opinion is extremely powerful in influencing people to go along with the group. Even one dissenter decreases the incidence of conformity markedly. Individuals are much more likely to diverge from a group when there is at least one other person to share the potential disapproval of the group. People who follow the lead of an initial dissenter may even disagree with that person and be dissenting from the group for a totally different reason. However, knowing there is at least one other dissenting voice makes it easier for them to express their own opinions.

Individual differences also determine the degree to which conformity will occur. Although the ambiguity and unanimity of the situation are powerful contributors to the incidence of conformity, they are not the sole determinants. Personal characteristics and the individual's position within the group play a role as well. Individuals who have a low status within a group or are unfamiliar with a particular situation are the ones most likely to conform. Thus, students who are new to a class, new members of a study or activity group, or new residents to a community are more likely to be affected by the pressure to conform. Personality traits, such as concern with being liked or the desire to be right, also play a role.

Cultural factors are also influential. Certain cultures are more likely than others to value group harmony over individual expression. In fact, school administrators, organization managers, and even parents can establish an atmosphere or "culture" that either fosters conformity or allows for dissension and individuality.

For Further Study

Books

Feller, Robyn M. *Everything You Need to Know About Peer Pressure.* New York: Rosen Publishing Group, 1995.

Friar, Linda and Penelope B. Grenoble. *Teaching Your Child to Handle Peer Pressure.* Chicago: Contemporary Books, 1988.

Goldhammer, John. *Under the Influence: The Destructive Effects of Group Dynamics.* Amherst, NY: Prometheus Books, 1996.

Congenital Defects *see* **Birth Defects**

Conjunctivitis

Conjunctivitis is an infection or inflammation of the conjunctivae, *the thin layer of cells which covers the surface of the sclerae (whites) of the eye and also the inside of the lids.*

Conjunctivitis can be caused by a number of conditions, varying with the age of a child. In the newborn period, several types of conjunctivitis can be acquired through the birth canal, most commonly gonorrheal conjunctivitis and chlamydial conjunctivitis. Gonorrheal conjunctivitis generally produces a profuse, pus-like discharge. Left untreated, it can lead to blindness. Chlamydial conjunctivitis in the newborn period produces symptoms which are much more subtle, namely a mild redness and eye discharge several days or weeks after birth. Chemical (silver nitrate) or antibiotic eye drops are routinely administered in most hospital nurseries to prevent gonorrheal and chlamydial conjunctivitis. The silver nitrate drops used to prevent gonorrheal conjunctivitis often produce a mild chemical conjunctivitis of their own, characterized by redness of the conjunctivae and swelling of the lids. This form of conjunctivitis is harmless and usually clears up on its own.

A common type of conjunctivitis in the later newborn period is associated with lacrimal duct stenosis (blocked tear duct). If the tear duct (which drains tears from the eye into the nose) is congenitally blocked or not formed, the tears will drain poorly, and that eye will be more prone to minor conjunctival infections. Most blocked tear ducts open on their own in the first year of life. If they do not, they can be opened surgically in the second half of the first year. In preschool-age children, bacterial conjunctivitis can sometimes occur with ear infections.

The causes of conjunctivitis in school-age and older children are similar to those in adults, most commonly **allergies** and viruses. Allergic conjunctivitis—whose primary symptoms are itchiness of the eyes, redness of the lids, and a stringy, clear discharge—can be present year-round (perennial allergic conjunctivitis) or only when spring or fall pollens are in the air (seasonal allergic conjunctivitis). Direct infection with viruses, especially a group of viruses called adenoviruses, constitutes the other major cause of conjunctivitis in older children. Sometimes these can become secondarily infected. Styes of the lid can also cause a secondary conjunctival irritation. A less common cause of conjunctivitis is **herpes simplex** virus, which is usually introduced to the eye after touching an active herpes lesion. In addition, severe chemical conjunctivitis can result from alkaline detergents in the eye.

The lay term for conjunctivitis, "pinkeye," is very nonspecific. A number of diseases can cause "pinkeye" that is not technically conjunctivitis. Danger signs requiring prompt medical attention are eye irritation in a contact lens wearer (especially one who wears soft contact lenses), severe swelling of the eye or eyelids, severe pain, photophobia (sensitivity to light), a foreign body sensation in the eye, persistent blurred vision, a bulging eye, a pupil that is unreactive to light, or symptoms that become worse despite several days of treatment.

—Marta M. Vielhaber, M.D.
Kaiser-Permanente, Cleveland

Conscience *see* **Moral Development**

Constipation

Difficulty with producing a bowel movement, or infrequent bowel movements.

Constipation, a condition that can affect the human digestive system at any stage of life, is rarely serious or chronic. Because bowel functions vary from individual to individual, the individual's own normal pattern should be taken into consideration when constipation is suspected. For this reason, it is important for parents and caregivers to be familiar with the bowel patterns of their infants and young children. Although constipation may cause considerable discomfort, a return to normal bowel function is usually accomplished within a day or two.

Constipation is caused when the muscles at the end of the large intestine restrict the fecal material from passing through and out of the body. A tendency toward constipation seems to be hereditary. The longer the fecal material is "stalled" in the large intestine, the drier it becomes, making it more difficult and even painful to pass. For children, the discomfort associated with passing a dry stool may cause them to avoid the process, thereby exacerbating the problem.

Infants

With young infants, constipation is rare, and it is not typically experienced until the infant begins solid foods. In an infant whose diet includes solid foods, constipation may be suspected if at least one bowel movement is not produced each day, or if the stool seems unusually firm or dry. An infant experiencing repeated or chronic bouts of constipation should be seen by a pediatrician, who can assess whether a digestive disorder is the cause. Constipation in breastfed babies is uncommon and almost always related to something other than diet.

One possible cause of constipation in infants under the age of one year is the switch from formula to cow's milk. Cow's milk is more likely than formula to cause constipation, and temporarily switching back to formula may alleviate the constipation. If the infant has started solid foods, an increase in dietary fiber may relieve the infant. High-fiber foods suitable for infants include prunes, apricots, plums, peas, beans, and broccoli. Cutting back on bananas and rice, both of which contribute to constipation, may also help.

Toddlers

When a child begins **toilet training**, it is important to establish regular, healthy bowel habits. Parents and caregivers should monitor the child's bowel function, which should include at least one bowel movement each day. If the child's bowel movements are infrequent, high-fiber foods, such as prunes, apricots, peas, beans, broccoli, and whole-grain breads, should be added to his diet. Increasing fluids, particularly water, may also help.

Retention of stool may become a problem between the ages of two and five. A child may avoid moving his bowels on the toilet during toilet training. By the next day, the retained stool is harder, drier, and therefore painful to pass. This discomfort encourages the child to avoid having bowel movements, and a cycle is established. Laxatives, stool softeners, and enemas should not be administered without consulting a pediatrician.

Treatment for this type of chronic constipation includes a healthy diet high in fiber, with the possible addition of mineral oil until the child's system functions normally and without discomfort. A pediatrician will design a strategy to help cope with the preschool child's constipation.

School-age children

School-age children may experience problems having bowel movements away from home. As with infants and toddlers, school-age children who withhold bowel movements will have harder and drier stool. In some cases, the fecal material accumulates, stretching the rectum and nullifying the normal urge to have a bowel movement. Sometimes watery fecal material leaks out, appearing like diarrhea on the child's underwear. A pediatrician's advice will be required in restoring the lower digestive tract to normal function. Reestablishing a regular bowel routine will be necessary to correct this most severe example of constipation.

See also **Bowel Disorders; Digestive Disorders;** *and* **Encopresis**

For Further Study

Books

Schaefer, Charles E. *Childhood Encopresis and Enuresis: Causes and Therapy.* Northvale, NJ: Jason Aronson, 1993.
Schuster, Marvin. *What Is Constipation?* Washington, DC: National Digestive Diseases Information Clearinghouse, U.S. Dept. of Health and Human Services, Public Health Service, National Institutes of Health, National Institute of Arthritis, Diabetes, & Digestive and Kidney Diseases, 1986.

Contact Lenses

Clear or slightly colored plastic lenses worn directly on the eyeball to correct vision problems, held in place over the cornea by a thin layer of tears.

The concept of corrective lenses that sit directly on the eyeball was developed in the ninth century, but it was not until the late 20th century that manufacturing and grinding techniques for contact lenses were perfected. Originally contact lenses were made of glass, then later of hard plastic, and still later of flexible, highly oxygen-permeable soft plastic. Today, the majority of lenses worn are of two basic types: rigid gas permeable (so-called "hard" lenses) and soft lenses. Hard lenses are smaller and more durable, but require a longer period of adjustment for the wearer. Hard contact lenses can correct some vision problems, like astigmatism, that the soft lenses cannot. The soft lenses are slightly larger than hard lenses. They are more comfortable and less expensive, but can be easily torn. The latest generations of contact lenses are extended wear and disposable soft lenses. Extended wear lenses are intended to be worn for several weeks at a time, while disposable lenses are thrown away every day or every few weeks, or in the newest versions, every day. The Contact Lens Council reports that 26 million Americans wear contact lenses. Among contact lens wearers, approximately 80% wear the soft type and 18% wear rigid gas-permeable lenses. The Council reports that about 11% of contact lens wearers, approximately 2.8 million people, are under 18.

Infants

There are few instances when corrective lenses—eyeglasses or contacts—are prescribed for infants. However, when an infant develops **cataracts**, a condition known as infantile aphakia, contact lenses may be prescribed following surgery. In 1993, the *Journal of the American Medical Association* reported that contact lenses were safe and effective for use with infants following cataract surgery. Routine care of the lenses was easily learned by the baby's parents or caregivers.

Preschool and school-age children

Contact lenses are a significant improvement over eyeglasses for children and adolescents who participate in sports or outdoor activities.

Contact lenses are recommended for most athletes who need corrective eyewear. Often, a single pair of lenses is less expensive than the combined cost of glasses and prescription goggles. Swimmers especially can benefit from being able to see underwater while wearing regular goggles over their contact lenses. Because contact lenses tend to dry the eye, swimmers and all athletes should take care to blink several times before and after an activity session in order to assure natural cleansing. If any pool water enters a swimmer's eyes, the lenses should be thoroughly disinfected as soon as possible to remove pool contaminants. Children who like spending time looking into a telescope, microscope, or binoculars may also prefer contacts over eyeglasses.

The primary drawback to wearing contact lenses, especially for children, is the requirement that they be cleaned and disinfected daily in order to prevent an infection, which could result in permanent damage to the eye. Careful choice of lenses and consistent lens care will minimize the risk of infection. Wearers of hard lenses are the least prone to infection but the lenses are much less comfortable, more expensive, and can pop out of the eye more easily than soft lenses. Daily wear soft lenses put the wearer at a slightly higher risk of infection because they absorb more external liquids and airborne contaminants. Extended wear soft lenses in particular pose a much greater risk than daily wear soft lenses. Though extended-wear lenses are extremely thin and allow some oxygen—necessary for healthy eyes—to reach the cornea, they are worn continuously, including at night while the eyelid is closed. Bacteria can easily grow more easily under these conditions. Twenty-one in 1,000 extended lens wearers develop infections as opposed to 4 in 1,000 daily soft lens wearers. To reduce this risk, eye care professionals now recommend removing extended wear lenses at night. In addition, newer versions of extended wear lenses being developed may offer increased oxygen exchange and pose less risk. Disposable lenses may also help to prevent infection, since the wearer is guaranteed a clean pair of lenses every few weeks or every day.

For Further Study

Organizations
Contact Lens Council
> **Address:** 8201 Corporate Drive, Suite 850
> Landover, MD 20785
> **Telephone:** (800) 884-4252

Contraception

Contraception (birth control) is the prevention of conception (pregnancy).

In the United States, 60% of boys and 50% of girls between the ages of 15 and 19 are sexually active, yet only half of these adolescents use contraception the first time they have intercourse. Approximately one million adolescent girls become pregnant in this country each year, and **sexually transmitted diseases (STDs)** are becoming more prevalent. Because sexual exploration will be a fact of life for many adolescents, knowledgeable adults should be available to discuss contraceptive alternatives with them *before* such exploration begins.

Male condom

Condoms are inexpensive and easy to obtain. Because the condom is the only known way to reduce the spread of STDs (including AIDS), a condom should always be used during sexual intercourse, even when another contraceptive method is used. For contraceptive purposes, a condom alone should never be relied on for protection against **pregnancy**. For adolescents who use condoms alone, the odds of becoming pregnant within a year are one in five.

Female condom

The female condom, a new form of contraception, is less effective than the male condom at preventing pregnancy and STD infection. Like the male condom, the female condom can be easily obtained in pharmacies.

CONTRACEPTIVE RELIABILITY

Contraceptive type	Estimated effectiveness	Risks	STD protection	Convenience	Availability
Male condom	85%	Irritation or allergic reaction (rare)	Latex condoms help protect, especially against herpes and AIDS	Applied immediately before intercourse; used only once and discarded	Nonprescription
Female condom	74–79% ·	Irritation or allergic reaction (rare)	May protect; not as effective as male condom	Applied immediately before intercourse; used only once and discarded	Nonprescription
Spermicide alone	70–80%	Irritation or allergic reaction (rare)	Unknown	Applied no more than one hour prior to intercourse	Nonprescription
Sponge	72–82%	Irritation or allergic reaction (rare); difficulty in removal; toxic shock syndrome (very rare)	None	Can be inserted hours before intercourse and left in place up to 24 hours; used only once and discarded	Nonprescription
Oral contraceptive	97–99%	Blood clots, heart attack and stroke, gallbladder disease, liver tumors, water retention, hypertension, mood changes, dizziness and nausea; not for smokers	None	Must be taken on a daily schedule, regardless of frequency of intercourse	Prescription
Implant	99%	Menstrual cycle irregularity; headaches, nervousness, depression, nausea, dizziness, change of appetite, breast tenderness, weight gain, enlargement of ovaries and/or fallopian tubes, excessive growth of body and facial hair, may subside after first year	None	Effective 24 hours after implantation for approximately 5 years; can be removed by physician at any time	Prescription; minor outpatient surgical procedure
Injection	99%	Amenorrhea, weight gain, and other side effects similar to implant	None	One injection every three months	Prescription

CONTRACEPTIVE RELIABILITY					
Contraceptive type	Estimated effectiveness	Risks	STD protection	Convenience	Availability
Diaphragm with spermicide	82–94%	Irritation and allergic reactions (rare); bladder infection; toxic shock syndrome (very rare)	None	Inserted before intercourse; can be left in place 24 hours, but additional spermicide must be inserted if intercourse is repeated	Prescription
Cervical cap with spermicide	At least 82%	Abnormal Pap test; vaginal or cervical infection; toxic shock syndrome (very rare)	None	Can remain in place for 48 hours, not necessary to reapply spermicide for repeated intercourse; may be difficult to insert	Prescription

Source: *FDA Consumer,* September 1993.
Note: For comparison, 60–85% of sexually active women using no contraception would be expected to become pregnant in a year.

Spermicides

Spermicides are available as foam, jelly, cream, suppositories, or a two-by-two-inch (50-by-50 mm) sheet of film. They are easy to use, widely available, and inexpensive. When used in conjunction with condoms, spermicides are an effective means of preventing pregnancy.

Oral contraceptives

Commonly known as "the pill," oral contraceptives are the most effective method available to adolescents. Taken correctly, the pill provides 99.5% protection against pregnancy. (It provides no protection against STDs, however.) Although the pill has a number of side effects, the most serious risks associated with its use are rare in adolescents. Minor side effects which are usually not serious include vaginal bleeding between periods, nausea, weight gain, breast tenderness, **amenorrhea,** changes in skin or hair, and mood changes. Oral contraceptives are not recommended for women who smoke more than fourteen cigarettes per day.

Hormone implants (Norplant)

These contraceptive devices, which consist of hormone (progestin) capsules inserted under the skin on a woman's upper arm, can prevent pregnancy for several years. Hormone implants are associated with significant side effects and provide no protection against STDs.

Hormone injection (Depo-Provera)

Depo-Provera, injected into the upper arm once every three months, provides 99% protection against pregnancy. It provides no protection against STDs, however, so a condom should still be used every time intercourse occurs.

Sponge

The vaginal sponge, like condoms and vaginal spermicides, can be purchased without a prescription. The sponge is only about 85% effective at preventing pregnancy, however, so it should be used in combination with a condom. Once inserted in the vagina, the sponge remains effective for twenty-four hours, no matter how many times intercourse occurs. Because of an association with toxic shock syndrome (TSS), another method should be used during **menstruation.**

Diaphragm

The diaphragm is used in conjunction with spermicidal cream or jelly and has the potential to be more than 95% effective when used correctly and consistently. The main problem associated with the diaphragm is a high failure rate due to nonuse or improper use. A woman must be fitted for a diaphragm by a health-care professional. Because of an association with toxic shock syndrome (TSS), another method should be used during menstruation.

Cervical cap

The cervical cap is similar to a small diaphragm and is also used with spermicidal cream or jelly. Like the diaphragm, it must be fitted by a health-care professional. Also like the diaphragm, there is some risk of toxic shock syndrome (TSS).

See also **Condom**

For Further Study

Books

Corbett, Margaret-Ann and Jerrilyn H. Meyer. *The Adolescent and Pregnancy.* Boston: Blackwell Scientific Publications, 1987.

Kilby, Donald. *Manual of Safe Sex.* Philadelphia: Decker, 1986.

Shapiro, Howard I. *The New Birth-Control Book: A Complete Guide for Men and Women.* New York: Prentice Hall Press, 1988.

Periodicals

Goldberg, Merle S. "Choosing a Contraceptive." *FDA Consumer* 7, September 1993, pp. 18–25.

Audiovisual Recording

American Medical Communications. *Contraception: Know Your Options.* Newark, NJ: Parade Video, 1993.
(One 39-minute videocassette.)

Armstrong Information Services. *Teenage Birth Control: Why Doesn't It Work?* Pleasantville, NY: Sunburst Communications, 1986.
(One 31-minute videocassette and one teacher's guide.)

Milner-Fenwick, Inc. *Teen Contraception.* Van Nuys, CA: AIMS Media, 1989.
(One 13-minute videocassette.)

—Gail B. Slap, M.D.
University of Pennsylvania School of Medicine

Conventional Stage *see* **Moral Development**

Convergent Thinking

The ability to narrow the number of possible solutions to a problem by applying logic and knowledge.

The term convergent thinking was coined J. P. Guilford, a psychologist well-known for his research on **creativity.** Guilford posited that a prime component of creativity is **divergent thinking,** the capacity to arrive at unique and original solutions and the tendency to consider problems in terms of multiple solutions rather than just one. Convergent thinking, which narrows all options to one solution, corresponds closely to the types of tasks usually called for in school and on standardized multiple-choice tests. In contrast, creativity tests designed to assess divergent thinking often ask how many different answers or solutions a person can think of to a specific question or problem. Some researchers have claimed that creative achievement actually involves both divergent and convergent thinking—divergent thinking to generate new ideas and convergent thinking to "reality test" them in order to determine if they will work.

For Further Study

Books

Amabile, Teresa M. *Growing Up Creative: Nurturing a Lifetime of Creativity.* New York: Crown Publishers, 1989.

Guilford, J. P. *The Nature of Human Intelligence.* New York: McGraw-Hill, 1967.

Conversation Board *see* **Communication Board**

Convulsions *see* **Seizures**

Co-Parent

Term for persons who share in child care activities.

The term co-parent is applied to several different parenting scenarios. A co-parent may be a person who does not have legal **custody** of a child but who shares in the child care with the custodial parent. A person sharing a household with a parent and his or her child is an example of a co-parent. A co-parent may also be a step-parent who has not legally adopted the stepchildren. Homosexual couples use co-parent to describe the partner of the parent who has legal custody of the children (through **adoption** or biological **birth**).

Coparenting is also used to describe the situation where two parents cooperate as closely as possible in sharing all facets of child rearing. In addition to having both joint legal and physical custody, the parents arrange to divide responsibility for the day-to-day tasks involved in child care, such as chauffeuring the children, attending school activities and teacher conferences, purchasing clothing and other necessities, and taking the children to doctor appointments.

For Further Study

Books

Gold, Lois. *Between Love and Hate: A Guide to Civilized Divorce.* New York: Plenum Press, 1992.

Lansky, Vicki. *Vicki Lansky's Divorce Book for Parents: Helping Your Children Cope with Divorce and Its Aftermath.* New York: Penguin Books, 1989.

Shapiro, Robert. *Sharing the Children: How to Resolve Custody Problems and Get On with Your Life.* Bethesda, MD: Adler & Adler, 1988.

Warshak, Richard A. *The Custody Revolution: The Father Factor and the Motherhood Mystique.* New York: Poseidon Press, 1992.

Organizations

Joint Custody Association (JCA)
Address: 10606 Wilkins Ave.
Los Angeles, CA, 90024
Telephone: (310) 475-5352

Parents Sharing Custody (PSC)
Address: 420 S. Beverly Dr. Suite 100
Beverly Hills, CA 90212-4410
Telephone: 310-286-9171

Copralalia *see* **Tourette's Syndrome**

Core Curriculum

The course of study taken by all students in a specific academic group.

This term describes, in a broad example, those courses taken by all students in a particular high school, or, more narrowly, those courses taken by all students pursuing a clerical course of study. Most commonly, the term "core curriculum" is used to describe the courses that form the common denominator for a particular student body.

See also **Curriculum**

Core Knowledge Foundation

Nonprofit organization founded by American educator E. D. Hirsch, Jr. to promote the implementation of a nationwide shared academic curriculum for U.S. students.

Founded by University of Virginia professor E. D. Hirsch, Jr. in 1988, the Core Knowledge Foundation is a nonprofit organization dedicated to the goal of designing a course of study for U.S. schools that will result in a core of shared knowledge by all students. Hirsch, an English professor, was inspired by the positive response to his 1987 best-seller, *Cultural Literacy: What Every American Needs to Know,* and decided to apply his ideas toward the education of U.S. students. In working toward that goal, he founded the Core Knowledge Foundation to offer publications, workshops, and other resources for schools interested in incorporating the basic knowledge that Hirsch and his followers believe are crucial to success in U.S. society. Under Hirsch's direction, the Core Knowledge Foundation developed and published a sample curriculum, known as the *Core Knowledge Sequence,* for students in kindergarten through grade six. The Foundation worked with teachers, curriculum specialists, parents, and subject-matter experts to prepare the *Sequence,* which features specific content guidelines designed to form the basis for about 50% of a school's curriculum.

The *Sequence* offers a planned progression of specific knowledge in six content areas, namely history, geography, mathematics, science, language arts, and fine arts. Where state or school district curricula provide general guidelines concerning skills to be learned at each grade level, the Core Knowledge Sequence recommends specific content. In addition, the *Sequence* is a plan that builds from year to year, which its supporters say helps to prevent repetitions and gaps in instruction.

Critics of the "core knowledge" approach feel that it focuses too strongly on European American history, giving too little attention to other ethnic and cultural influences in American history. Another criticism is that the *Sequence* does not provide for individual differences in learning rates, interests, and abilities.

As of 1997, the *Core Knowledge Sequence* had been implemented or was being phased in for kindergarten through grade six by over 200 schools in 36 states. A draft of a *Core Knowledge Sequence* for grades seven and eight was completed, and in 1997 was being reviewed by teachers, parents, and curriculum specialists. The Core Knowledge Foundation expects the draft to be available in final form in the late 1990s.

Following the successful experiences of educators in Europe in applying curriculum-based instruction in preschool, the Core Knowledge Foundation has initiated development of a preschool sequence as well.

For Further Study

Books

Hirsch, E. D., Jr., Joseph Kett, and James Trefil. *Cultural Literacy: What Every American Needs to Know, What Literate Americans Know.* New York: Vintage Books, 1988.

Hirsch, E. D., Jr., William G. Rowland, Jr., and Michael Stanford, eds. *A First Dictionary of Cultural Literacy: What Our Children Need to Know.* 2nd ed. Boston: Houghton Mifflin, 1996.

Hirsch, E. D., Jr. *The Schools We Need and Why We Don't Have Them. Books to Build On: A Grade-By-Grade Resource Guide For Parents and Teachers.* New York: Delta, 1996.

———— and John Holdren. *What Your Kindergartner Needs to Know: Preparing Your Child for a Lifetime of Learning.* New York: Doubleday, 1996.

————. *What Your First Grader Needs to Know: Fundamentals of a Good First Grade Education.* New York: Doubleday, 1997.

———. *What Your Second Grader Needs to Know: Fundamentals of a Good Second Grade Education.* New York: Dell, 1993.

———. *What Your Third Grader Needs to Know: Fundamentals of a Good Third Grade Education.* New York: Delta, 1992.

———. *What Your Fourth Grader Needs to Know: Fundamentals of a Good Fourth Grade Education.* New York: Doubleday, 1994.

———. *What Your Fifth Grader Needs to Know: Fundamentals of a Good Fifth Grade Education.* New York: Doubleday, 1993.

Organizations

Core Knowledge Foundation
Address: 2012 B Morton Dr.
Charlottesville, VA 22903-6803
Telephone: (804) 977-7550
FAX: (804) 977-0021
website: www.coreknowledge.org

Counterconditioning

An aspect of behavior therapy that involves weakening or eliminating an undesired response by introducing and strengthening a second response that is incompatible with it.

The type of counterconditioning most widely used for therapeutic purposes is systematic desensitization, which is employed to reduce or eliminate fear of a particular object, situation, or activity. An early example of systematic desensitization was an experiment that is also the first recorded use of **behavior therapy** with a child. In a paper published in 1924, Mary Cover Jones, a student of the pioneering American behaviorist **John Watson,** described her treatment of a three-year-old with a fear of rabbits. Jones countered the child's negative response to rabbits with a positive one by exposing him to a caged rabbit while he sat some distance away, eating one of his favorite foods. The boy slowly became more comfortable with the rabbit as the cage was gradually moved closer, until he was finally able to pet it and play with it without experiencing any fear.

In the 1950s South African psychiatrist Joseph Wolpe (1915–) pioneered a prototype for systematic desensitization as it is generally practiced today. Like Cover's experiment, Wolpe's technique involved gradually increasing the intensity of exposure to a feared experience. However, instead of countering the fear with a pleasurable stimulus such as food, Wolpe countered it with deliberately induced feelings of relaxation. He had the client imagine a variety of frightening experiences and then rank them in order of intensity. The client was then trained in deep muscle relaxation and instructed to practice it as he pictured the experiences he had de-

scribed, progressing gradually from the least to the most frightening. Today systemic desensitization of the type pioneered by Wolpe is widely used with both adults and children. In adults its uses range from combating **phobias,** such as a fear of snakes or flying, to increasing tolerance of pain from chronic illnesses or natural childbirth. In children, it is used to overcome a wide variety of fears, such as fear of certain animals or fear of the dark. The relaxation techniques most often used with children are deep breathing exercises and visual imagery (through which a calming effect is obtained by vividly imagining a peaceful or appealing scene). A typical sequence of treatment for a child afraid of dogs would be to pair the relaxation response first with very low-key exposures, such as being shown pictures of dogs, and then progressing to actual exposure to and finally interaction with them.

Another type of counterconditioning is **aversive conditioning,** which makes a particular behavior less appealing by pairing it with an unpleasant stimulus. Aversive conditioning has been used in adults to break addictions to substances such as tobacco and alcohol. Alcoholics are sometimes given an alcoholic drink together with a drug that induces nausea to weaken the positive feelings they associate with drinking. A common use of aversive therapy with children is the bell and pad treatment for **enuresis** (bedwetting), in which a wetness sensor placed in the bed activates a bell at the first sign of bedwetting.

Crawling

A major means of mobility in infancy, consisting of forward motion with weight supported by the infant's hands (or forearms) and knees.

Crawling is the primary form of mobility achieved by infants before they learn to walk. Babies have a primitive crawling reflex at birth, which is instinctively activated when they are placed on their abdomens. Their legs flex, and they move forward, raising their heads to free them for motion. However, this reflex disappears during the early weeks of life, and true crawling is not learned until the second six months, normally around the same time that an infant is able to sit up alone for extended periods of time. The learning process, which occurs gradually, is usually completed by the age of nine to ten months.

Even before they can crawl, infants find other methods of moving about. For most babies, creeping—wriggling or slithering forward on one's stomach—comes before crawling, typically by the age of seven months. Infants also find that they can cover quite a bit of distance simply by rolling from place to place. Especially on smooth floors, it is fairly easy for them to move forward using only their arms or elbows and pulling their legs along, which are held out straight behind them. Infants can also get around while remaining in a seated position and pulling themselves along with one or both arms, a form of mobility sometimes called "hitching" or "bottom shuffling." From the infant's perspective, it actually has several advantages over crawling: it can leave one arm free, it allows better visibility, and the baby is already in a sitting position when she reaches her destination. In many cases, these alternate means of mobility are so convenient that the child never learns to crawl, proceeding directly to pulling herself upright and learning to walk. This is perfectly normal and not a cause for concern. **T. Berry Brazelton** discounts as myth the idea that a failure to crawl is associated with later coordination problems. He stresses the fact that crawling is not one of the necessary developmental milestones.

Learning to crawl involves a gradual trial-and-error learning process. When infants first get up on their hands and knees, they will make modest attempts at movement, rocking or swaying in the direction they want to go. When they try to move, their balance is unstable and they have trouble coordinating their movements, frequently moving an arm or leg and toppling over. One source of difficulty is the fact that, neurologically, control over the arms and shoulders develops faster than control of the legs. This is also the reason that once the infant is finally able to make real progress, it is often in a backwards direction, because she is able to push harder with her hands and arms than with her feet. To her dismay, the newly crawling infant may find that the toy she is going after is actually getting farther and farther away. Although parents can provide temporary assistance by firmly placing their hands against the baby's feet, propelling them into forward motion in spite of themselves, backwards crawling typically persists for several weeks until the infant's coordination is better developed.

Once an infant can crawl, the parent needs to provide a safe, spacious area for her to explore. The baby is at the beginning of one of the most intense periods of educational development of her life and needs to satisfy her natural curiosity and her enormous capacity to learn by exploring. Rather than restrict her to a small area, it is recommended that parents "childproof" the home and keep it that way for the next two to three years. The greatest dangers to an inquisitive infant include uncovered electrical outlets, ungated stairways, and household cleaners, medications, and other potentially toxic substances. Other childproofing precautions include eliminating or securely anchoring light-weight furniture, hiding or securing electrical cords that could be pulled on, keeping valuable items or small objects that could be ingested on high shelves out of the baby's reach, keeping crib bars raised as high as possible, and strapping the infant securely into high chairs and strollers.

Even in a safe environment, expert opinion varies on whether a crawling infant should be left unsupervised at any time.

For Further Study

Books

Eckert, Helen M. *Motor Development.* 3rd ed. Indianapolis, IN: Benchmark Press, 1987.

Thomas, Jerry R., ed. *Motor Development in Childhood and Adolescence.* Minneapolis, MN: Burgess Publishing Co., 1984.

. . . .

Creativity

The ability to create inventions, produce works of art, or solve problems using an original, novel, or unconventional approach.

Although many people equate creativity and **intelligence,** the two terms are not synonymous, and it is not necessary to have a genius-level IQ in order to be creative. While creative people do tend to have average or above-average scores on IQ tests, beyond an IQ of about 120 there is little correlation between intelligence and creativity. Researchers have found environment to be more important than heredity in influencing creativity, and a child's creativity can be either strongly encouraged or discouraged by early experiences at home and in school.

In the 20th century psychologists, educators, and other social scientists have proposed numerous theories of creativity. The psychoanalytic framework of Sigmund Freud emphasized the role of unconscious processes in creativity. Freud introduced the idea that creative achievements in the arts, sciences, and other fields result from a sublimation of libidinal (sexual) impulses. He also drew attention to the relationship between creativity in the adult and play in the child. Subsequently, the behaviorist school of psychology has focused on the relationship between creativity and external positive reinforcement (rewards, praise, honors, etc.), while cognitive theorists have analyzed the mental components of the creative process.

Another approach has been the attempt to understand creativity by studying the lives of famous innovators in a variety of fields, such as Albert Einstein, Charles Darwin, and Pablo Picasso. Howard Gruber, the major proponent of this approach, found certain broad common characteristics among a number of creative individuals: 1) they engaged in a variety of activities within their chosen fields; 2) they had a strong sense of purpose about their work; 3) they had a profound emotional attachment to their work; and 4) they tended to conceptualize problems in terms of all-encompassing images. In a more recent version of this approach, Harvard psychologist Howard Gardner has extended his influential work on multiple intelligences to the field of creativity, analyzing the lives of seven famous creative figures in the arts and sciences who were born in the latter half of the 19th century and helped inaugurate and define the modern era during the first part of the 20th. Focusing in each case on a single significant discovery or breakthrough, Gardner rejects the traditionally monolithic view of creativity in favor of a pluralistic one that encompasses a wide variety of skills and abilities. According to this view, people are creative within a specific domain (or domains) rather than creative "in general." In addition, they show creativity regularly during the course of a lifetime and introduce innovations that are considered unorthodox at first but eventually become widely accepted within their culture.

The theories of J. P. Guilford regarding creativity have strongly influenced the field of education. First becoming popular in the 1950s, his psychometric approach (i.e., one that views creativity as measurable by testing) is based on the concepts of convergent and divergent thinking. **Convergent thinking**—the type usually displayed on traditional intelligence tests—involves narrowing the number of possible solutions to a problem, while **divergent thinking**—the type that Guilford associated with creativity—entails the ability to envision multiple solutions to a problem. As put forward by Guilford, divergent thinking has three major characteristics: fluency, flexibility, and originality. Fluency is the ability to rapidly envision a number of different ways to solve a problem. Flexibility refers to the ability to consider various alternatives at the same time. Originality denotes the degree to which a person's ideas differ from those of most other people.

Since the development of Guilford's psychometric approach to creativity, a variety of tests have been devised to assess creativity. A number of these—geared toward measuring divergent thinking—have been based on how many different solutions an individual can propose to a specific problem and on the extent to which a person's answers differ from those of most other test takers. Typical questions asked on such tests include "Try to imagine the range of consequences that might follow if all national and local laws were suddenly abolished" and "Name as many uses as you can think of for a brick." Creativity tests—like standard intelligence tests—have been found to have a high degree of reliability in that an individual is likely to have similar scores on a variety of these tests. However, questions have arisen over their validity in terms of the usefulness of what they measure. One study found little correlation between the scores of

both elementary and secondary students on divergent thinking tests and their actual achievements in high school in such creative fields as art, drama, and science. Many researchers have concluded that divergent thinking, while important to the creative process, is not the sole element necessary for creative achievement and that creative accomplishment requires both divergent and convergent thinking. Besides being original, the successful solution to a problem must also be appropriate to its purposes, and convergent thinking allows an individual to evaluate his or her ideas and reject them if they do not withstand further scrutiny.

In an attempt to go beyond the psychometric approach to creativity pioneered by Guilford, other researchers have studied the personality traits and motivation of creative people, focusing on their contemporaries rather than on historical figures. Personality traits have been assessed based on how creative individuals describe themselves or on their responses to tests such as the Rorschach, or inkblot, test. A Berkeley-based study found that creativity is often accompanied by personality traits such as independence, self-confidence, unconventionality, easy access to unconscious processes, and dedication to work. In addition, studies of people known for their creative accomplishments show that certain personality traits that may be impossible to measure on a test—such as motivation, initiative, ambition, tolerance for ambiguity, perseverance, and independent judgment—are commonly associated with creativity.

In the 1980s social psychologist Teresa Amabile focused on the importance of intrinsic motivation in creativity, arguing that a prime component in defining creativity is the pursuit of an activity purely for its own sake rather than for external rewards, such as money or recognition. In a variety of studies, items created by people who were told that their work would be judged and possibly rewarded for creativity have been found to be less creative than the results produced by those who were simply asked to work on a project with no prospect of external reward. Amabile has posited a three-part definition of creativity. In addition to intrinsic motivation, the other two essential criteria for creative achievement are expertise in a specific field ("domain skills"), which must be learned, and creative skills, including divergent thinking.

A 1962 study by Graham Wallas produced a widely used four-stage breakdown of the creative process based on data obtained from scientists and other innovators. First is the preparation stage, which consists of articulating the problem, obtaining background information, and considering it carefully in light of one's research. In the incubation stage, subconscious ideas about the problem are allowed to emerge as it enters a dormant period, during which there is no active progress, although one may periodically "mull it over." Next comes the illumination stage, in which an important insight is gained, often suddenly and intuitively. Finally, in the verification stage, the idea is tested and judged.

Environment appears to play a greater role than heredity in the development of creativity: identical twins reared apart show greater differences in creativity than in intellectual ability. Family environments with certain characteristics have been found to be more conducive to creativity than others. One of these characteristics is a relaxed parental attitude rather than one that is overly anxious or authoritarian. On the whole, the families of creative children discipline them without rigid restrictions, teaching them respect for values above rules. Similarly, they emphasize achievement rather than grades. The parents in such homes generally lead active, fulfilling lives themselves and have many interests. Finally, they reinforce creativity in their children by a general attitude of respect and confidence toward them and by actively encouraging creative pursuits and praising the results. It has been found that creativity in both children and adults is affected by positive reinforcement. In one study, four-year-olds produced more original block arrangements when their efforts were praised by adults and reverted to less imaginative patterns when reinforcement was withheld. Positive reinforcement has also been shown to boost fifth graders' scores on creativity tests, help sixth graders write more original stories, and lead college students to produce novel word associations. Studies have also found that positively reinforcing one kind of creative activity encourages original thinking in other areas as well.

Just as certain actions and attitudes on the part of parents can encourage creativity, others have been found to discourage it. Devising restrictive guidelines or instructions for an activity reduces its potential as a creative experience. Unrestricted, imaginative play is central to creativity in children—exposure to new objects and activities stimulates the senses, reinforces exploratory impulses, and results in the openness to new experiences and ideas that fosters creative thinking. In addition, anything that takes the focus away from the creative act itself and toward something external to it can be damaging. For example, knowing that one's efforts are going to be evaluated tends to restrict the creative impulse, as does knowing of the possibility of a prize or other reward. Competition creates yet another type of external focus that can stifle creativity.

Schools as well as families can encourage creativity by offering children activities that give them an active role in their own learning, allow them freedom to explore within a loosely structured framework, and encourage them to participate in creative activities for the sheer enjoyment of it rather than for external rewards.

For Further Study

Books

Amabile, Teresa. *The Social Psychology of Creativity.* New York: Springer-Verlag, 1983.

———. *Growing Up Creative: Nurturing a Lifetime of Creativity.* New York: Crown Publishers, 1989.

Bean, Reynold. *How to Develop Your Children's Creativity.* Los Angeles: Price Stern Sloan, 1992.

Briggs, John. *Fire in the Crucible: The Alchemy of Creative Genius.* New York: St. Martin's Press, 1988.

Gardner, Howard. *Creating Minds.* New York: Basic Books, 1993.

Guilford, J. P. *The Nature of Human Intelligence.* New York: McGraw-Hill, 1967.

Hubbard, Ruth. *A Workshop of the Possible: Nurturing Children's Creative Development.* York, ME: Stenhouse, 1996.

Creativity Tests

Tests designed to measure creativity in children or adults.

Creativity tests, mostly devised during the past 30 years, are aimed at assessing the qualities and abilities that constitute creativity. These tests evaluate mental abilities in ways that are different from—and even diametrically opposed to—conventional intelligence tests. Because the kinds of abilities measured by creativity tests differ from those measured by **intelligence quotient (IQ)** tests, persons with the highest scores on creativity tests do not necessarily have the highest IQs. Creative people tend to have IQs that are at least average if not above average, but beyond a score of 120 there is little correlation between performance on **intelligence** and creativity tests.

Most creativity tests in use today are based at least partially on the theory of creativity evolved by J. P. Guilford in the 1950s. Guilford posited that the ability to envision multiple solutions to a problem lay at the core of creativity. He called this process **divergent thinking** and its opposite—the tendency to narrow all options to a single solution—**convergent thinking.** Guilford identified three components of divergent thinking: fluency (the ability to quickly find multiple solutions to a problem); flexibility (being able to simultaneously consider a variety of alternatives); and originality (referring to ideas that differ from those of other people). Early tests designed to assess an individual's aptitude for divergent thinking included the Torrance (1962) and Meeker (1969) tests.

The most extensive work on divergent thinking was done under Guilford's direction at the University of Southern California by the Aptitudes Research Project (ARP), whose findings between the 1950s and 1970s produced a broad structure-of-intellect (SI) model which encompassed all intellectual functions, including divergent thinking. A number of the ARP divergent thinking tests, which were originally devised as research instruments for the study of creativity, have been adapted by a variety of testing companies for use by educators in placing gifted students and evaluating gifted and talented programs. The ARP tests are divided into verbal and figural categories. Those that measure verbal ability include:

- *Word Fluency*: writing words containing a given letter

- *Ideational Fluency*: naming things that belong to a given class (i.e., fluids that will burn)

- *Associational Fluency*: writing synonyms for a specified word

- *Expressional Fluency*: writing four-word sentences in which each word begins with a specified letter

- *Alternate Uses*: listing as many uses as possible for a given object

- *Plot Titles*: writing titles for short-story plots

- *Consequences*: listing consequences for a hypothetical event ("What if no one needed to sleep?")

- *Possible Jobs*: list all jobs that might be symbolized by a given emblem

The figural ARP tests, which measure spatial aptitude, include the following:

- *Making Objects*: drawing specified objects using only a given set of shapes, such as a circle, square, etc.

- *Sketches*: elaborating on a given figure to produce sketches of recognizable items

- *Match Problems*: removing a specified number of matchsticks from a diagram to produce a specified number of geometric shapes

- *Decorations*: using as many different designs as possible to outline drawings of common objects

Divergent thinking tests are generally evaluated based on the number and variety of answers provided; the originality of the answers; and the amount of detail they contain (a characteristic referred to as elaboration). A number of creativity tests currently in use include sections that measure divergent thinking. The Creativity Assessment Packet (ages 6–18) is composed of Test of Divergent Thinking as well as Divergent Feelings Test that measures traits including imagination, curiosity, risk-taking, and complexity. A Divergent Production subtest is part of the Screening Assessment for Gifted Elementary Students (SAGES) (ages 7-13), together with a Reasoning subtest that emphasizes the identification of relationships and a multiple-choice School Acquired Information subtest. The goals of the Test of Creative Potential (TCP) (ages 2–adult) are described using the language of divergent thinking theory: fluency, flexibility, and elaboration. Like the ARP tests, it has a figural section (Picture Decoration) to measure nonverbal ability, as well as a verbal section and a symbolic section. Among the oldest of the divergent thinking tests are the Torrance Tests of Creative Thinking (TTCT) (ages 5–adult), which also have both verbal and figural sections and measure fluency and other standard categories.

Rather than ways of thinking, some creativity tests evaluate attitudes (based on the child's answers), behavior (based on descriptions by an observer familiar with the child, usually a parent or teacher), creative perception, or creative activity. The Creativity Attitude Survey (CAS) (grades 4–6), composed of 32 statements for which the child indicates agreement or disagreement, assesses confidence in one's own ideas; appreciation of fantasy; theoretical and aesthetic orientation; openness to impulse expression; and desire for novelty. The Preschool and Kindergarten Interest Descriptor (PRIDE) (ages 3–6) is one of the tests completed by an observer rather than by the person being evaluated. It includes 50 items that assess children's behavior in the following areas: Independence-Perseverance, Imagination-Playfulness, Originality, and Many Interests. The Scales for Rating the Behavioral Characteristics of Superior Students (SRBCSS) (child and adolescent) include 95 questions by which teachers evaluate students in such areas as motivation, leadership, art, music, dramatics, and both precise and expressive communication. The Creativity Checklist (CCL) (grades K–graduate school) is also filled out by an observer; it measures resourcefulness, constructional skill, ingenuity or productiveness, independence, and positive self-referencing behavior, as well as the more standard fluency, flexibility, and complexity that are common to divergent thinking tests.

Some creativity tests specifically address the problem of assessing creativity in minority populations, who are at a disadvantage in tests that place a strong emphasis on verbal and semantic ability. The SOI-Learning Abilities Test (ages 2–adult) includes such categories as constancy of objects in space; auditory attention; psychomotor readiness; auditory concentration for sequencing; and symbolic problem-solving. The use of creativity tests such as this can aid in identifying gifted minority students, who, as a group, do not perform as well on standard IQ tests as non-minority students and are thus overlooked in the allocation of resources for talented students. (In one minority-populated school in Florida, only four out of 650 students were labeled as gifted according to aptitude standard tests.) The Eby Gifted Behavior Index (all ages) reflects the growing view of creativity as specific to different domains. It is divided into six talent fields: verbal, social/leadership, visual/spatial, math/science problem-solving, mechanical/

technical, and musical. The Watson-Glaser Critical Thinking Appraisal, for adolescents and adults, is a more analytical assessment of giftedness based on five components of critical thinking: inference, deduction, interpretation, awareness of assumptions, and evaluation of arguments.

Creativity tests have been found reliable in the sense that one person's scores tend to remain similar across a variety of tests. However, their validity has been questioned in terms of their ability to predict the true creative potential of those who take them. In one study, there was little correlation between the scores of both elementary and secondary students on divergent thinking tests and their actual achievements in high school in such creative fields as art, drama, and science. Creativity tests have also been criticized for unclear instructions, lack of suitability for different populations, and excessive narrowness in terms of what they measure. In addition, it may be impossible for any test to measure certain personal traits that are necessary for success in creative endeavors, such as initiative, self-confidence, tolerance of ambiguity, motivation, and perseverance. Tests also tend to create an anxiety-producing situation that may distort the scores of some test takers. Teresa Amabile, a well-known researcher in the field of creativity, has advocated assessing creativity by observing a child's creative activities in a natural setting, such as painting or storytelling.

Critiques of tests that involve divergent thinking have also been based on the conclusion of many researchers that creative accomplishment actually requires both divergent and convergent thinking. Besides being original, the successful solution to a problem must also be appropriate to its purposes, and convergent thinking allows one to evaluate one's ideas and reject them if they cannot withstand further scrutiny.

For Further Study

Books

Amabile, Teresa. *The Social Psychology of Creativity.* New York: Springer-Verlag, 1983.

————. *Growing Up Creative: Nurturing a Lifetime of Creativity.* New York: Crown Publishers, 1989.

Guilford, J. P. *The Nature of Human Intelligence.* New York: McGraw-Hill, 1967.

Sternberg, R. J. *The Nature of Creativity.* New York: Cambridge University Press, 1988.

Torrance, E. P. *Guiding Creative Talent.* Englewood Cliffs, NJ: Prentice-Hall, 1962.

—Rosalie Wieder

Crib Death *see* Sudden Infant Death Syndrome

Critical Period

A time span generally in early development during which an organism is uniquely sensitive to specific stimuli. Also referred to as the optimal or sensitive period.

Although the term "critical period" is used in a variety of contexts, it is most closely associated with ethology, the study of innate and learned behavior in the natural environment. The critical period plays an important role in the concept of imprinting, first described by Konrad Lorenz in connection with the earliest process of social attachment in young animals. Imprinting also applies to any irreversible behavioral response acquired early in life. In the most famous example of imprinting involving goslings, Lorenz demonstrated that exposure to an appropriately maternal object during a critical period would activate the "following" instinct; he successfully had a group of goslings follow him after he "impersonated" their absent mother. This concept was popularized in 1996 in the feature film Fly Away Home.

Other examples of critical periods include the initial four months of life during which puppies must be exposed to humans in order to make good pets and the early months in which birds must be exposed to the characteristic song of their species in order to learn it. The study of critical periods in animal behavioral development eventually led to the search for and analysis of critical periods in human development.

Critical periods in human development

Critical periods, although not as precisely limited in humans as in other species, have been described for behaviors such as smiling, infant-mother **attachment,** and **language development.** Researchers such as **Maria Montessori** described critical, or sensitive, periods for certain aspects of human development. In developing her **Montessori method** of education, Montessori defined distinct but overlapping "sensitive periods" that were conducive to development in specific areas. For example, from ages one to five, development and learning are conducive through sensory stimulation. Thus, it is important during this period of childhood for children to experience sensory input whenever possible. A related sensitive period described by Montessori is that for language development, occurring between the ages of three and about five months. During this stage, children are sensitive to sounds and able to discriminate between them and thus should be given auditory stimulation to foster successful language development.

The concept of the critical period appears to be supported by studies of the so-called "wild" or **feral child**ren who were deprived of human society for an extended period. These children, although relatively few in number, have been shown to be unable to recover their full language development when they missed the necessary sensory and auditory stimulation during the critical period.

For Further Study

Books

Candland, Douglas Keith. *Feral Children and Clever Animals: Reflections on Human Nature.* New York: Oxford University Press, 1993.

Denny, M. Ray. *Comparative Psychology: Research in Animal Behavior.* Homewood, IL: Dorsey Press, 1970.

Lillard, Paula Polk. *Montessori Today: A Comprehensive Approach to Education from Birth to Adulthood.* New York: Schocken Books, 1996.

Lorenz, Konrad. *The Foundation of Ethology.* New York: Springer-Verlag, 1981.

Crying and Fussing in an Infant

Crying in infants is a normal, healthy means of expression and communication. The average six-week-old baby cries for two-and-a-half hours every day. Infants cry because they are hungry, uncomfortable, in pain, overstimulated, tired, or even just bored. A new mother can distinguish her infant's crying from that of other babies within three days, and some fathers can make this distinction as well. Infants have several distinct cries. A hungry cry begins softly and then becomes loud and rhythmic; an angry cry is similar to a hungry cry but louder. A cry of pain has a distinctive pattern, beginning with a single shriek followed by a short silence and then continuous loud wailing. Neglected or abused infants have a high-pitched cry that is difficult for adults to tolerate. This type of cry is characteristic of babies born to crack-addicted mothers and has been linked to abnormalities in the central nervous system. An infant's crying patterns and ability to be comforted are important indicators of **temperament**, both in infancy and even in later years.

The most common way to comfort a crying infant is to hold her close to one's chest. Some infants are soothed by the motion of a cradle, rocking chair, stroller, swing, or automobile. Sucking on a **pacifier** is another universal comforter. Other methods include a warm bath, a massage, music, or some type of background noise, such as the sound of a hair dryer, a washing machine, or fan. There are also special recordings that reproduce sounds similar to those the infant heard while in the mother's womb. Some infants are hypersensitive to stimuli, and their crying will actually get worse if they receive any more than a minimum of comforting, such as parental holding or cuddling. A sign of healthy emotional development is the degree to which an infant learns to comfort herself, either with the aid of an object such as a stuffed toy or blanket, or by certain patterns of behavior.

A common cause of persistent crying in infants is **colic,** a pattern of regular crying spells that usually occur in the late afternoon and evening in infants between the ages of about three weeks and three months. Although its exact cause is not known, it is thought to be related to gastrointestinal distress or, in some cases, hyperactivity. Other causes of excessive crying include hypersensitivity and **depression.** Hypersensitive infants cry in response to new experiences and situations that don't normally upset other babies; ordinary comforting measures, such as holding, rocking, feeding, or swaddling, don't work and may even make the crying worse. Hypersensitivity can be a matter of temperament or it can be influenced by the behavior and attitude of the parents, especially if they have ambivalent feelings toward the infant because of their previous life experiences. An infant or toddler who doesn't respond to being comforted may also be depressed, although this condition is rare at this stage of life. The symptoms of childhood depression resemble those of depression in adults: sadness, fatigue, eating and sleep problems, lack of pleasure in formerly enjoyable activities, and social isolation. Some children who are neither depressed nor hypersensitive get into the habit of excessive crying as a way of demanding parental attention. The parents of such children are generally overprotective, not giving them the chance to develop independence and resourcefulness by solving problems on their own.

Excessive crying may also be the sign of a medical problem (although even loud wailing is not necessarily a sign that an infant is critically ill.) Among the most common physical reasons for crying are earaches, flu, and other causes of low-grade fever. Teething also causes increased crying. Medical attention may be required if an infant is crying more than usual or the cries themselves sound different—if, for example, they are weaker or more high-pitched than usual.

For Further Study

Books

Ayllon, Ted. *Stopping Baby's Colic: The New Program Designed to Relieve Most Infants' Persistent Crying in 3–7 Days.* New York: Perigee Books, 1989.

Barns, Rebecca Beall, ed. *20 Ways to Calm a Crying Baby.* Charlottesville, VA: Thomasson-Grant, 1994.

Jones, Sandy. *Crying Baby, Sleepless Nights.* Harvard, MA: Harvard Common Press, 1992.

Sammons, William A. H. *The Self-Calmed Baby: A Liberating New Approach to Parenting Your Infant.* Boston: Little, Brown, 1989,

Sears, William. *Keys to Calming the Fussy Baby.* New York: Barron's, 1991.

Cults

Groups of people intensely devoted to a person, idea, or movement.

Traditionally, "cult" was a term used for any new religious movement. A number of currently well-established religious groups, including the Methodists, Mormons, Christian Scientists, and Seventh-Day Adventists, were considered cults when they were first formed, and Christianity itself began as a cult that broke away from Judaism. Since the 1960s, the term "cult" has taken on a new significance as groups with a wide variety of belief systems and customs have attracted members (often young people) who abandon mainstream lifestyles to devote themselves to these new cults and their leaders.

Although the philosophies and activities of cults vary, most of them have certain characteristics in common, most notably allegiance to a charismatic leader believed to have transcendent or divine qualities who commands complete devotion and strict obedience from cult members. Other common features include unquestioning belief in a body of teachings propounded by the group's leader and adherence to a set of practices based on these teachings. Cults are also known for the high degree of conformity demanded of their members, whose behavior is closely monitored and publicly censured when it departs from accepted behavioral norms. Cult members are commonly expected to sacrifice for the good of the group, often devoting their time to earning money for its support. One of the main ways that cults retain close control over their members is by alienating them from their families and other contacts in the outside world. In some cases, families have fought back by hiring professional "deprogramming" experts to break the psychological control that cults have gained over their children Some cults also isolate members by moving to a remote location. Cult membership is typically associated with an all-encompassing conversion experience or emotional revelation that makes people experience the world differently and can even change their physical perceptions. Cults tend to attract troubled, alienated individuals drawn by the social acceptance and security they offer.

Several of the most popular and best-known cults that have gained followers in the United States in recent decades originated in Asia or have had leaders born in Asia. The oldest is the Hare Krishna movement (officially, the International Society for Krishna Consciousness), which became popular in the 1960s and 1970s. Its members are highly visible in their long robes, chanting, danc-ing, passing out pamphlets, and collecting money. The men's heads are shaved, with an unshaved strand hanging from the crown. Krishna followers live in strictly run communes, where they spend much of their time meditating. Another Asian-inspired cult popular in the '60s and '70s was the Divine Light Mission imported to the United States from India by the young Guru Maharaj Ji when he was 13 years old. His followers, called "premies," numbered as many as 50,000 in the United States at the height of his popularity. The Unification Church led by the Korean-born Reverend Sun Myung Moon is unusual among Asian-inspired cults in that it is more closely related to Christianity than to Eastern religions. However, its philosophy combines Christianity with Buddhism and Taoism, and its stated goal is control of the world by a single supreme religion. Members are known as "Moonies."

In stark contrast to the asceticism traditionally associated with religious movements and their founders, leaders of modern cults have often amassed great personal wealth. Guru Maharaj Ji was known for his luxurious lifestyle; at the height of his popularity, his organization had an income of about $3 million a year. In the early 1980s the holdings of Reverend Moon's Unification Church were estimated at $100 million and included real estate in New York and California and ownership of two newspapers. Moon himself was living on a sumptuous Hudson River estate valued at $700,000. Federal and local tax authorities contested the Unification Church's claims to tax exemption as a religious organization, and Moon was convicted of tax evasion for failing to report $112,000 in interest on a $1.6 million personal savings account at the Chase Manhattan Bank.

In recent decades, two cults have been associated with major tragedies resulting in multiple deaths. Both were led by mentally unbalanced men in whom grandiosity, paranoia, and an uncanny ability to manipulate an entire community of people proved to be a disastrous combination. In the late 1970s, Jim Jones, a Protestant clergyman, led hundreds of the followers of his People's Temple to a commune in Guyana, a small South American country. After a United States congressman and three journalists investigating the cult were killed, the entire community of over 900 persons committed mass suicide under orders from Jones. In 1993, David Koresh, leader of the Branch Davidian cult, also led his followers to their death after a confrontation with the outside world—in this case, a 51-day standoff between the group and federal forces surrounding the Davidian compound in Waco, Texas. Over 80 cult members, including Koresh, died when the compound burned down, probably in a deliberate mass suicide.

Many children and adolescents have been affected by cults, either because their parents are members or because they themselves join. Young children have been physically, sexually, and psychologically abused in cults. Reports of child abuse were among the factors that convinced the federal government that it would have to storm the Branch Davidian compound in Waco. Children who survived the fire recounted incidents of corporal punishment by a special team of paddle-wielding "mighty men" in a special "whipping room" and told of sexual abuse by cult leader Koresh. By the age of 12, children were separated from their parents and segregated by sex, and Koresh pursued additional psychological strategies to undermine their **attachment** to their parents so that he could strengthen his control over them.

Since the early 1980s, reports by survivors of satanic cults have led to the identification of a pattern of abuse labeled SRA (sadistic ritual abuse). Victims include children, adolescents, and adults. The abuse, which is intended to initiate the victim into satanic beliefs and practices, usually occurs over an extended period of time. It may involve incest, torture, animal mutilation or killing, drug use, death threats, cannibalism, or "marriage" to Satan. Often, survivors (especially those who were under the age of six when the abuse occurred) cannot remember these episodes without the aid of a psychotherapist, either because they were drugged or hypnotized at the time or because of dissociation mechanisms, including multiple personality disorder, that enable them to cope with these traumatic experiences. Once memories of the abuse are brought to the surface, they often result in **depression** and suicidal feelings.

Although people of all ages join cults, the majority are young adults, and many are adolescents. Cults appeal to adolescents' naiveté and idealism and offer them a way to rebel against their parents. They also offer young people structure, security, and peer acceptance at an unsettling time in their lives. Adolescents who are drawn to cults often have a poor self-image, are heavily reliant on peer approval, and are not having their emotional needs adequately met by their families. Signs of cult involvement among teenagers include secretive or defiant behavior, withdrawal from family activities, odd hours, changes in friends, and a chronic shortage of money.

The surrender of autonomy that cult membership demands makes it difficult for members to decide to leave on their own, and many might not leave were it not for outside assistance, usually by their families. Well-known mind-control expert Ted Patrick invented the term "deprogramming" for the process of breaking down an individual's allegiance to a cult. Often the person must be physically removed from the cult against his or her will by either being tricked or kidnapped. Undoing the effects of the mind control imposed on cult members requires several stages. At first, cult members refuse to talk with those trying to help them and concentrate on resisting

them and trying to escape. Eventually, when they become willing to listen and respond to arguments, the deprogrammer begins presenting evidence that discredits the cult and its leader.

Once cult members become convinced that they have been manipulated, deprogrammers focus on restoring their normal thought processes. The full deprogramming process can take weeks. Often cults contact renegade members to try winning them back, and some do return when they find it too hard to readjust to life on the outside. A failed deprogramming attempt makes it even harder for the cult member to leave again. Full readjustment to society by former cult members can take months or even longer, with health, energy levels, decision-making ability, interpersonal relationships, and other facets of life affected.

For Further Study

Books

Deikman, Arthur J. *The Wrong Way Home: Uncovering the Patterns of Cult Behavior in American Society.* Boston: Beacon Press, 1991.

Galanter, Marc. *Cults: Faith, Healing, and Coercion.* New York: Oxford Univ. Press, 1989.

Johnson, Joan J. *The Cult Movement.* New York: Franklin Watts, 1984.

Melton, J. Gordon. *Encyclopedia Handbook of Cults in America.* Garland, 1986.

—Rosalie Wieder

Culture-Fair Test

An intelligence test in which performance is not based on experience with or knowledge of a specific culture.

Culture-fair tests, also called culture-free tests, are designed to assess **intelligence** (or other attributes) without relying on knowledge specific to any individual cultural group. The first culture-fair test, called Army Examination Beta, was developed by the United States military during World War II to screen soldiers of average intelligence who were illiterate or for whom English was a second language. Beginning in the postwar period, culture-fair tests, which rely largely on nonverbal questions, have been used in public schools with Hispanic students and other non-native-English speakers whose lack of familiarity with both English language and American culture have made it impossible to assess their intelligence level using standard IQ tests. Culture-fair tests currently administered include the Learning Potential Assessment Device (DPAD), the Culture-Free Self-Esteem Inventories, and the Cattell Culture Fair Series consisting of scales one to three for ages four and up. The Cattell scales are intended to assess intelligence independent of cultural experience, verbal ability, or educational level. They are used for **special education** placement and college and vocational counseling. The tests consist mostly of paper-and-pencil questions involving the relationships between figures and shapes. Parts of scale one, used with the youngest age group, utilize various objects instead of paper and pencil. Activities in scales two and three, for children age eight and up, include completing series, classifying, and filling in incomplete designs.

Culture-fair testing is a timely issue given current debate over bias in intelligence and educational testing as it affects students who can speak and write English, but who are unfamiliar with white middle-class culture. Bias in intelligence testing has a historical precedent in early tests designed to exclude immigrants from Southern and Eastern Europe from admission to the United States on grounds of mental inferiority. Critics of current tests claim that they discriminate against ethnic minorities in similar ways by calling for various types of knowledge unavailable to those outside the middle-class cultural mainstream. To dramatize the discriminatory nature of most intelligence testing, Professor Robert L. Williams devised the Black Intelligence Test of Cultural Homogeneity that requires a command of vocabulary items widely known among African Americans but not familiar to most whites (such as "do rag" and "four corners") and a knowledge of black history and culture ("Who wrote the Negro National Anthem?"). Williams claimed that the difficulties faced by white persons attempting to take this test are comparable to those that confront many blacks taking standardized IQ tests.

Critics of standardized tests claim that minority test takers are also penalized in ways other their unfamiliarity with specific facts. A pervasive negative attitude toward such tests may give children from minority groups less motivation than whites to perform well on them, further reduced by low levels of trust in and identification with the person administering the test. In addition, students from a minority culture may be more likely to interpret and answer a question in ways that differ from the prescribed answer. (In the field of **educational psychology,** this phenomenon is referred to as **divergent thinking** and also tends to penalize gifted children.) Studies have shown that culture-fair tests do reduce differences in performance between whites and members of minority groups. However, they lag behind the standard tests in predicting success in school, suggesting that in their quest for academic success, members of minority groups must overcome cultural barriers that extend beyond those encountered in IQ tests.

For Further Study

Books

Fraser, Steven. *The Bell Curve Wars: Race, Intelligence, and the Future of America.* New York: Basic Books, 1995.

Herrnstein, Richard J., and Charles Murray. *The Bell Curve: Intelligence and Class Structure in American Life.* New York: Free Press, 1994.

Mensh, Elaine, and Harry Mensh. *The IQ Mythology: Class, Race, Gender, and Inequality.* Carbondale, IL: Southern Illinois University Press, 1991.

Seligman, Daniel. *A Question of Intelligence: The IQ Debate in America.* New York: Birch Lane Press, 1992.

Curriculum

The course of study, developed to be presented in sequence and to meet specific goals, offered by an educational institution for its students.

The curriculum of a school or other educational institution is the structured course of study its students follow. Public, independent, and parochial schools, while differing in their respective approaches to education and classroom format, each establish a formal statement of educational goals or mission and develop a plan to meet those goals. The plan is generally comprised of specific learning objectives achieved through study of subjects such as science, mathematics, literature, and history.

In the United States, there has never been a national curriculum established, although many countries have such a curriculum. Since 1983, when the Department of Education published *A Nation at Risk,* the following basic high school curriculum has been recommended: four years of English; three years of mathematics; three years of science, including physical and biological science; one-half year of computer science; and two years of foreign-language study for students planning to go to college.

School districts may offer more than one type of curriculum depending on the needs, interests, and abilities of the students for whom the curriculum is designed. For example, the student who intends to apply to college will need to follow an academic curriculum; alternatively, the student who plans to enter the workforce after high school may select a vocational curriculum. Other students may choose a general curriculum. Some schools cover the same material, but at different rates, across all curricula. For example, the academic curriculum for students who are college-bound might cover material in two years that students taking the general curriculum will cover in three years. An Individualized Education Plan (IEP) is a curriculum of study developed to meet the special interests of a student with a disability.

JAMES MADISON CURRICULUM FROM U.S. DEPARTMENT OF EDUCATION

Subject	Kindergarten–Grade 3	Grades 4–6	Grades 7 and 8
English	Introduction to reading and writing	Introduction to critical reading	Grade 7: Survey of elementary grammar and composition
			Grade 8: Survey of elementary literary analysis
Social studies	Introduction to history, geography, and civics	Grade 4: U.S. history to the Civil War	
		Grade 5: U.S. history since 1865	
		Grade 6: World history to the Middle Ages	
Mathematics	Introduction to mathematics	Intermediate arithmetic and geometry	Two from among these courses: algebra, pre-algebra, or general math
Science	Introduction to science	Grade 4: Earth science	Grade 7: Biology
		Grade 5: Life science	Grade 8: Chemistry and physics
		Grade 5: Physical science	
Foreign language	Optional	Introduction to foreign language	Formal language study
Fine arts	Music and visual art	Music and visual art	Music appreciation and art appreciation
Physical education/ health	Physical education and health	Physical education and health	Physical education and health

Every state publishes guidelines for its schools districts to follow in designing their curricula. In most cases, citizens of the state may receive a copy of the state guidelines by contacting the office of the education in the state government. In the states that administer proficiency or achievement tests to all students, the tests are generally devised to evaluate each student's ability. A curriculum may then be selected according to those abilities.

An independent (private) or parochial school may offer special courses, such as religious studies, as part of its overall curriculum. According to the National Association of Independent Schools, there are no general guidelines or structured curricula followed by the independent schools in the United States.

For Further Study

Books

Drake, Susan M. *Planning Integrated Curriculum: The Call to Adventure.* Alexandria, VA: Association for Supervision and Curriculum Development, 1993.

English, Fenwick W. *Deciding What To Teach and Test: Developing, Aligning, and Auditing the Curriculum.* Newbury Park, CA: Corwin Press, 1992.

Borman, Kathryn M. and Nancy P. Greenman, eds. *Changing American Education: Recapturing the Past or Inventing the Future?* Albany: State University of New York Press, 1994.

Gunter, Mary Alice, Thomas H. Estes, and Jan Schwab. *Instruction: A Models Approach.* 2nd ed. Boston: Allyn and Bacon, 1995.

McNeil, John D. *Curriculum: A Comprehensive Introduction.* 4th ed. Glenview, IL: Scott, Foresman/Little, Brown Higher Education, 1990.

Posner, George J. and Alan N. Rudnitsky. *Course Design: A Guide to Curriculum Development for Teachers.* 4th ed. New York: Longman, 1994.

Tanner, Laurel N., ed. *Critical Issues in Curriculum.* Chicago: University of Chicago Press, 1988.

Organizations

Association of Supervision and Curriculum Development
Address: 1250 North Pitt Street
Alexandria, VA 22314-1453
Telephone: (800) 933-2723; (703) 549-9110
website: http://www.ascd.org; e-mail: infor@ascd.org
(Organization of 180,000 educators and others dedicated to improving education; publishes the journal *Educational Leadership;* newsletters; and sponsors conferences.)

National Association of Independent Schools (NAIS)
Address: 1620 L Street NW
Washington, DC 20036
Telephone: (202) 973-9700
(Publishes *Principles of Good Practice* for K–12, which includes general guidelines for curriculum development.)

Cursing *see* Undesirable Language

Custody

The legal arrangement for the guardianship of children whose parents divorce or do not marry.

Custody involves the authority to make decisions governing children's welfare, the responsibility of caring for them, and the provision of visitation rights if there is a noncustodial parent.

Types of custody

The parenting arrangements of divorced or unmarried couples usually fall into one of four categories. In *sole custody*, one parent (the custodial parent) is largely responsible for the care of the children. Although decisions about visitation schedules, holidays, and other such matters can be jointly decided by both parents, the custodial parent has ultimate authority to make decisions concerning the child (unless these decisions violate the custody agreement itself). The noncustodial parent has visitation rights. In the past, sole custody arrangements traditionally consisted of having children live with one parent and visit the other on alternate weekends. Today the trend is toward having children spend more time with the noncustodial parent, which relieves some of the burden placed on the custodial parent and allows for a stronger relationship between the children and the noncustodial parent. Since the noncustodial parent has usually been the father, modern practice also acknowl-

edges the fact that many fathers want to play a greater role in their children's lives.

Joint custody involves two different considerations: who has authority to make decisions governing the children, and where the children will live. Joint legal custody means that parents share equally in making decisions affecting their children, but it does not necessarily dictate where the children will live. Within the joint custody agreement, a separate designation of joint *physical* custody stipulates that parents will share the residential responsibility for their children, even if the time spent living in the two residences isn't equally divided between them.

In *split custody* (as its name implies), the children are split up, with each parent taking primary responsibility for one or more of the siblings. Each child has an established visitation schedule with the noncustodial parent. Split custody can actually take place under either of two legal arrangements. Each parent can have sole custody of the children who live with him or her, or both parents may share joint custody of all the children and be appointed only as the primary physical custodian of the children in their care. Split custody is the least common custody arrangement.

Coparenting (not a legal term) describes a situation in which two parents cooperate as closely as possible in sharing all facets of child rearing. In addition to having both joint legal and physical custody, the parents arrange to divide responsibility for the day-to-day tasks involved in child care, such as chauffeuring the children, attending school activities and teacher conferences, purchasing clothing and other necessities, and taking the children to doctor appointments.

Historical background

Legal customs regarding the awarding of custody have changed with diverging social conditions and attitudes. Before the 19th century, custody was considered a simple property arrangement and, since very few women owned property, men received custody of the children when a couple divorced. In the 19th century, as attitudes toward children became more sentimental, the prevailing legal attitude toward custody was revolutionized by the "tender years" doctrine—the idea that young children have special needs that can only be filled by their mothers. This notion was reinforced by the idealization of motherhood that accompanied 19th-century industrialization, with its "separation of the spheres," wherein men were increasingly employed outside the home, while women were expected to confine their aspirations and activities to the domestic sphere.

At first, mothers were awarded custody of children up to the ages of about five or six, after which point the children were returned to their fathers. Eventually, however, the "tender years" were extended upward until, by the early 20th century, mothers were routinely awarded permanent custody of both younger and older children. As the century progressed, the theories of Sigmund Freud and other psychologists gave renewed support to the mother in custody decisions. In the early 1950s, the famous British psychoanalyst **John Bowlby** reinforced this preference through his studies of maternal deprivation in European war orphans. By the 1960s, a father had to prove that his wife was mentally incompetent, abusive, or addicted to drugs or alcohol in order to gain custody of his children.

Two developments in the 1970s set the stage for a shift in the prevailing attitude toward child custody. The women's movement, with its challenge to gender stereotypes both at work and at home, helped instigate a reassessment of the prevailing practice of gender-based custody settlements. At the same time, clinical researchers began paying unprecedented attention to the role of fathers in their children's lives and to their effect on child development.

By the early 1990s, joint custody had become the most common custody arrangement. The number of states with joint custody statutes grew from three in 1980 to 48 in 1992. Today joint custody is the preferred arrangement in 19 states. In 24 states, it can be requested by the parents, and in five states it can be decreed by a judge. Today many couples draw up a parenting plan that includes a legal custody arrangement but goes further to outline how they will cooperate in specific areas of child rearing, including routine care, residence, holidays, and financial support, and how they will resolve impasses when these occur.

Residential arrangements

While it is clear that children benefit from custody arrangements that enable them to maintain close relationships with both parents, there is still controversy about the merits of joint physical custody. There has not been sufficient research to determine the effects of alternating residences compared with having one primary residence. Similarly, there is little conclusive evidence as to whether one type of schedule is preferable to another (i.e., half a week at each parent's house compared with alternating weeks). Experts agree, however, that a true spirit of cooperation between the parents is necessary in order for joint physical custody to work, and that it is not beneficial if there is intense conflict and hostility between the parents.

Children's developmental needs should also be taken into account in deciding on a residential arrangement and schedule.

Infancy and toddlerhood

Very young children need frequent contact with both parents for bonding to occur. On the other hand, frequent overnight visits can threaten the continuity and stability that are also primary needs at this stage. When the infant or toddler does spend time in two different households, it is important to maintain consistency in feeding schedules, nap times, and other aspects of care so that the child will feel that the world is a stable and predictable place. Overnight visits can become more frequent as the child gets older, and the telephone can also be an important source of contact. Weekend visits generally work out well for toddlers.

Preschool

Children of preschool age need to feel that they are important to the parent of the opposite sex while at the same time obtaining reassurance that the same-sex parent hasn't rejected them. **Divorce,** in particular, produces fears of abandonment in children at this age, increasing their natural need for stability and reassurance. Preschoolers are able to manage longer separations from the primary caregiver than infants or toddlers. Joint physical custody is often workable with preschoolers if care has been shared by both parents prior to the divorce. Alternation of residence should be for short blocks of time, generally about half a week. A common schedule is Wednesday-Saturday and Sunday-Tuesday with parents alternating Saturday nights.

School age

At this age, school continuity and access to friends become important considerations for the child. Boys in the primary school grades have a strong need to maintain regular contact with their fathers, even if they no longer live in the same home. School-age children tend to be very concerned and literal-minded about the fairness of custody arrangements. Joint physical custody can be successful if both parents continue to live in the same neighborhood. Although living in two households is difficult for the child, the effort required is balanced by the value of maintaining close contact with both parents.

Adolescence

Teenagers aren't as dependent as younger children on their parents. In adolescence, involvement with peers and social activities becomes a priority, and the young person becomes preoccupied with carving out an independent identity. Many children who have alternated residences while they were in grade school go back to having one primary home base when they enter their teens. It is important to spend time regularly with the nonresidential parent, but the emphasis should be on the quality rather than the quantity of that time. Adolescents need to have a say in planning their residential and visitation arrangements, and parents need to remain flexible in dealing with their teenaged children.

Custody problems

Custody arrangements, which are difficult even when parents cooperate with each other, can lead to serious problems in families where parents are preoccupied with their own feelings of hostility toward each other, especially when access to children becomes a tool for revenge. Custodial parents may deny visitation to their exspouses in order to punish them or because of disagreements over parenting practices. On the other hand, some divorced parents fail to meet even the minimum visitation requirements of the divorce agreement. However, if a parent keeps up child support payments, there are few legal consequences for failure to stick to the visitation schedule.

Allegations of either physical or sexual abuse on the part of a parent can be an effective way to have custody or visitation rights revoked. It is not uncommon for such allegations to be made falsely for revenge motives, and defense against these accusations is difficult. Another extreme expression of parental conflict is the kidnapping of children by noncustodial parents. Most kidnappings involve children between the ages of three and nine and occur shortly before or after a divorce. There is a link between domestic violence and parental kidnapping, and the kidnapping is often preceded by threats. Parental kidnapping is a federal offense, and, in accordance with the Federal Uniform Child Custody Jurisdiction Act, custody and visitation orders issued anywhere in the United States must be honored in all 50 states. However, there are no international agreements that cover parental kidnapping, and parents who take their children out of the country can avoid prosecution.

See also **Child Custody Law**

For Further Study

Books

Galper, Miriam. *Long Distance Parenting: A Guide for Divorced Parents.* New York: Signet, 1989.

Gold, Lois. *Between Love and Hate: A Guide to Civilized Divorce.* New York: Plenum Press, 1992.

Lansky, Vicki. *Vicki Lansky's Divorce Book for Parents: Helping Your Children Cope with Divorce and Its Aftermath.* New York: Penguin Books, 1989.

Shapiro, Robert. *Sharing the Children: How to Resolve Custody Problems and Get On with Your Life.* Bethesda, MD: Adler & Adler, 1988.

Virtue, Doreen. *My Kids Don't Live with Me Anymore: Coping with the Custody Crisis.* Minneapolis: Compcare, 1988.

Warshak, Richard A. *The Custody Revolution: The Father Factor and the Motherhood Mystique.* New York: Poseidon Press, 1992.

Organizations

Children's Rights Council (CRC)
Address: 220 Eye St. NE, Ste. 200
Washington, DC 20002
Telephone: (202) 547-6227

Fathers Rights and Equality Exchange (FREE)
Address: 701 Welch Rd., Suite 323
Palo Alto, CA 94304
Telephone: (415) 853-6877

Joint Custody Association (JCA)
Address: 10606 Wilkins Ave.
Los Angeles, CA, 90024
Telephone: (310) 475-5352

Parents Sharing Custody (PSC)
Address: 420 S. Beverly Dr. Suite 100
Beverly Hills, CA 90212-4410
Telephone: (310) 286-9171

Parents Without Partners
Address: 8807 Colesville Rd.
Silver Spring, MD 20910
Telephone: (301) 588-9354

Cystic Fibrosis

A genetic disorder that causes a thick mucus to build up in the respiratory system and in the pancreas, a digestive organ. People with cystic fibrosis are highly susceptible to respiratory infections and are typically malnourished due to the malfunctioning of the pancreas.

One of every 25 babies born in the United States is affected with cystic fibrosis, the most common fatal genetic disease in the nation. The average life expectancy of people with cystic fibrosis is 29 years. Only 10% of people with the disease survive into their 30s. Ninety-five percent of cystic fibrosis deaths are caused by lung complications; the other 5% are due to liver failure.

Most cases of cystic fibrosis are caused by a defective gene that must be carried by both parents to produce a child with cystic fibrosis. It is estimated that one in every 20 Americans carries the defective gene. When two carriers have a child, there is one in two chance the child will carry the gene but not have cystic fibrosis, one in four chance the child will not even have the gene, and one in four chance the child will have cystic fibrosis. In most cases, cystic fibrosis is diagnosed by the age of three. Repeated colds and respiratory infections, coughing, and abnormally low weight gain may be present from birth. Other problems such as pneumonia or asthma may precede the diagnosis. Some children become very ill and survive for only a few years.

In 1989, a team of researchers located the defective cystic fibrosis gene, which causes production of a defective version of an important protein called the CF transmembrane conductance regulator (CFTCR), which performs a crucial function in airway and pancreas cells. The protein works as a pump within the cell membrane, regulating the movement of sodium and chloride (the components of salt) in and out of cells. In people with cystic fibrosis, however, this pump does not work and water is retained within the cells, depriving the tissues of much-needed moisture. A dry, sticky mucus builds up in the airway and the pancreas, obstructing breathing and interfering with digestive processes. The mucus also clogs sweat glands and salivary glands.

People afflicted with cystic fibrosis have trouble breathing and are highly susceptible to bacterial infections of the lungs. Normally, bacteria are expelled from the lungs by coughing and the movement of thin mucus up the airways to the throat where the bacteria are expelled. But in people with cystic fibrosis the mucus is too thick to be moved and bacteria are able to inhabit the lungs and cause infection. Children with cystic fibrosis often become infected with such bacteria as *Streptococcus pneumoniae*, *Hemophilus pneumoniae*, and *Staphylococcus aeureus*. Adults are most susceptible to *Pseudomonas aeurginosa*. A rare type of bacteria, *Pseudomonas cepacia*, currently infects people with cystic fibrosis at alarming rates. *P. cepacia* causes a severe infection and hastens lung damage, leading to earlier death.

In addition to lung disease, people with cystic fibrosis have digestive disorders due to the thick mucus that clogs the pancreas. The pancreas secretes enzymes during digestion that break down food so that the body can absorb nutrients. But with cystic fibrosis, this function is impaired. People with the disease are typically thin and malnourished due to malabsorption of nutrients. Liver disease and **diabetes** may also occur with cystic fibrosis.

Cystic fibrosis is diagnosed with a "sweat test," a simple procedure that measures the amount of salt in the patient's perspiration. A high level of salt indicates cystic fibrosis. Currently no definitive cure for cystic fibrosis exists. Treatment of the disease focuses on alleviating symptoms caused by the build-up of mucus.

To combat the lung infections that accompany cystic fibrosis, many people with the disease periodically take courses of antibiotics as a preventive measure. Some people undergo a course of antibiotics four times a year. Mucus in the lungs can also be broken down by drugs called mucolytic agents. These agents can be taken as pills but some are manufactured in the form of aerosols and are inhaled.

Clearing the thick mucus from the lungs can also be accomplished by physiotherapy. Physiotherapy includes breathing exercises and percussion, the administration of blows to the back and chest to loosen the mucus. Some people with cystic fibrosis perform percussion on themselves but it is most effective when performed by someone else. In patients who can tolerate it, vigorous exercise has been shown to improve fitness and well-being, as it also loosens the thick secretions.

To control the malabsorption of nutrients, people with cystic fibrosis take pancreatic enzymes in pill form with every meal. A diet high in fat, protein, and carbohydrates is also recommended to boost the nutrients that a cystic fibrosis sufferer receives. Multi-vitamins can also help prevent deficiencies of certain vitamins. When these methods do not result in adequate weight gain, some people supplement their diets with tube feedings in which a nutrient-rich solution is infused through a tube placed in the stomach.

Researchers hope that the discovery of the gene responsible for cystic fibrosis will lead to a genetic approach to curing the disease. In gene therapy, a normal gene is inserted into cells to replace the defective gene. The lung and pancreas cells are most affected by the disorder and must receive the new gene. Once inside, the normal gene encodes for the correct protein. In most gene therapy experiments, cells from an affected organ are removed from the body and infected with a virus that has been induced to carry the normal gene. The newly infected cells are then put back into the body. In treating cystic fibrosis, however, this method has failed, and researchers are currently working on an approach in which the patient inhales the gene-carrying virus directly.

In 1994, researchers successfully transferred a virus containing the normal CFTCR gene into four cystic fibrosis patients. The patients inhaled the virus into the nasal passages and lungs. An adenovirus, the virus used to carry the gene, is considered relatively harmless to human beings. Nevertheless one patient in this experiment developed viral-infection symptoms, including headache, fatigue, and fever. Data is currently being collected on whether the experiment affected the mucus production in the lungs of the subjects.

Before gene therapy for cystic fibrosis is perfected, researchers must overcome several obstacles. The most important obstacle is the use of viruses as carriers for the normal genes. Some scientists contend that using viruses is simply too dangerous, especially for patients who already have a chronic debilitating disease. Furthermore, the genetic material of viruses is small compared to human genetic material and thus can mutate quickly. If a virus undergoes a mutation, a small chance exists that the mutation could result in an extremely dangerous disease, such as **cancer**. In the future, the genes may be transferred within liposomes, spheres consisting of a fatty substance called lipid.

Currently, the test for the cystic fibrosis gene is 85% effective in detecting the gene in a person's blood, cheek scrapings, or saliva. Some researchers believe that this effectiveness rate is still too low and that testing should be performed only on persons who have a familial history of cystic fibrosis. Others argue that because the test is relatively inexpensive, easy to perform, and the effectiveness rate acceptable, the test should be offered to everyone. First-trimester prenatal testing for the disease has been available since 1986. Studies have shown that only a small percentage of parents take advantage of the test, and many parents who have had one child with cystic fibrosis simply have no more children.

For Further Study

Books

Shapiro, Burton L. and Ralph C. Heussner, Jr. *A Parent's Guide to Cystic Fibrosis.* Minneapolis: University of Minnesota Press, 1990.

Periodicals

Brock, David J.H. "Prenatal Screening for Cystic Fibrosis: 5 Years' Experience Reviewed." *The Lancet* 347, January 20, 1996, p. 148.

"Gene Therapy for CF Reaches Human Lungs." *Science News* 146, September 3, 1994, p. 149.

Jedlicka-Kohler, Ilse, Manfred Gotz, and Irmgard Eichler. "Utilization of Prenatal Diagnosis for Cystic Fibrosis over the Past Seven Years." *Pediatrics* 94, July 1994, p. 13.

Johnson, Larry G. "Gene Therapy for Cystic Fibrosis." *Chest* 107, February 1995, pp. 775–815.

Koch, Christian, and Holby Niels. "Pathogenesis of Cystic Fibrosis." *The Lancet* 3341, April 24, 1993, p. 1065.

Norvell, Candyce. "The Facts on Cystic Fibrosis." *Current Health* 21, May 2, 1995, p. 22.

Samuelson, Wayne M. "Cystic Fibrosis: A Newer Outlook." *Medicine* 74, January 1995, pp. 58–63.

Webb, A.K., and T.J. David. "Clinical Management of Children and Adults with Cystic Fibrosis." *British Medical Journal* 308, February 12, 1994, pp. 459–63.

Audiovisual Recordings

Alex: The Life of a Child. Bethesda, MD: Cystic Fibrosis Foundation, 1986 (produced by ABC-TV). (One 95-minute video.)

CF Gene Therapy: A Medical Revolution. Bethesda, MD: Cystic Fibrosis Foundation, 1997. (One sixteen-minute videocassette.)

The Effect of Ibuprofen on CF Lung Disease. Bethesda, MD: Cystic Fibrosis Foundation, 1995. (One 8-minute videocassette.)

From Molecules to Miracles. Bethesda, MD: Cystic Fibrosis Foundation, 1995. (One 56-minute videocassette.)

A Guide for Parents and Children. Bethesda, MD: Cystic Fibrosis Foundation/McNeil Pharmaceutical, 1988. (One 38-minute videocassette.)

Solving the CFTR Protein Puzzle. Bethesda, MD: Cystic Fibrosis Foundation, 1996. (One 14-minute videocassette.)

Organizations

Cystic Fibrosis Foundation
Address: 6931 Arlington Rd.
Bethesda, MD 20814
Telephone: toll-free (800) FIGHT-CF; (301) 951-4422
e-mail: infor@cff.org

Day Care

Care for infants, preschool, and school-aged children in institutional facilities and private (family) homes.

In the mid-1990s, it was estimated that nearly 50% of all American children will spend at least part of their childhood in a single-parent home, due to the rise in out-of-wedlock births and **divorce**. In addition, the number of single-parent families and families where both parents are employed grew dramatically from 1965 to 1995. As a result, finding quality, affordable child care is a process faced by over half of all U.S. families.

Day care and family day care centers

Day care centers have emerged as an important option for care of infants, preschool, and school-age children. Day care facilities are mainly classified into two categories: the day care center, which is located in a public facility and equipped with a staff; and the family day care center, which is run in a home setting by a private caregiver. It is difficult to generalize about day care centers of either type, because structure, focus, and quality of care varies greatly. To help families in selecting day care, most states have regulations for licensing day care centers. A license is not a guarantee of quality care, but it does signify that the day care center meets certain standards of safety, group size, ratio of adults to children, and staff qualifications.

In 1990, the National Child Care Survey found that 49% of U.S. parents interviewed preferred institutional child care in contrast to home-based care (21%) or care by a relative (12%). Child care by relatives has been on a steady decline since 1965.

Effects of day care on child development

Much research has studied the effects of day care on emotional and **cognitive development**. When family factors, parents' personality traits, the child's **temperament**, and the number of different child care arrangements the child has experienced are all taken into account, most researchers conclude that day care has little or no effect on the child's emotional and cognitive development. In other words, it is difficult both to evaluate the effects of day care objectively because of the wide variation in day care experiences; and to separate the effects of day care from the complex interaction of other factors such as the child's temperament and other family factors.

Day care centers

The National Association for the Education of Young Children (NAEYC) is a professional membership organization dedicated to the healthy development of young children. It issues recommendations relating to the structure and organization of day care centers, particularly those that accept infants and toddlers. These recommendations are considered to be the minimum standards a day care center should observe; a lower ratio of children to caregivers is always encouraged.

- A maximum of four infants (birth to 12 months) per caregiver, and a maximum of eight infants and two caregivers per group.

- A maximum of four young toddlers (12–24 months) per caregiver, and a maximum of twelve young toddlers and three caregivers per group.

- A maximum of six older toddlers (24–36 months) per caregiver, and a maximum of twelve older toddlers and two caregivers per group.

Day care centers offer parents reliable, consistent care from early morning to early evening. (Parents employed in weekend or evening shift positions are largely unable to secure institutional day care. Employers, such as hospitals, that rely on around-the-clock employee shifts, are increasingly being pressured to offer child care on their premises for employees.) Day care centers provide young children with experience in social interaction through structured activities. Most day care centers are staffed with full-time and part-time workers, all or some of whom may have received training in child development, first aid, and safety procedures. Many communities require staff training as part of the day care center licensing procedure.

Disadvantages of day care centers may include neglect of the child as an individual due to over-enrollment, and the possibility that the center management will bypass or fail to meet licensing regulations (including safety standards). In addition, while the bulk of day care center staff are hired with some specialized training, some are not. Staffing challenges are amplified by high turnover rates due to generally low wages and poor (or no) employee benefits such as medical insurance, paid vacations, and sick leave.

Family day care

Family day care centers, where children are cared for by a caregiver in her home, are often registered or licensed by their communities. The licensing procedure serves as a referral to prospective clients, because families seeking day care can request a listing of licensed family day care centers in their neighborhood. Advantages of family day care include the home-like setting, offering comfort to both parents and child; potential for greater scheduling flexibility; and lower overall number of children being cared for.

The National Association for Family Day Care (NAFDC), a professional membership organization, offers these minimum standards for family day care settings:

- No more than six children per family day care provider, including the provider's own children.

- No more than two of the children in a family day care group should be under age two.

- The family day care provider should be at least 18 years old.

- The family day care provider should have completed basic training in first aid, safety, and child development.

One of the key differences between day care centers and family day care (or care by an individual) is the consistency and reliability of care. Individual caretakers and relatives are less able to provide for a substitute caretaker in the event of an emergency, sickness, or schedule conflict. On the other hand, an individual caretaker or relative may develop a stronger, more nurturing bond, with the children she (or less often, he) cares for, and may be able to accommodate a family's need for care outside the normal business day.

The decision to use day care—whether in a facility or home setting—is highly individualized. Parents should observe the activities at more than one center before making their day care choice. State and community agencies can provide guidance in identifying nearby centers to consider. Ultimately, the parents must evaluate what factors are important to them, and which staff seems to reflect the parent's own temperament, child-rearing style, and values.

For Further Study

Books

Berezin, Judith. *The Complete Guide to Choosing Child Care.* New York: Random House, 1990.

Schmittroth, Linda. *Statistical Record of Children.* Detroit: Gale Research, 1994.

Zigler, Edward F. and Mary E. Lang. *Child Care Choices: Balancing the Needs of Children, Families, and Society.* New York: The Free Press, 1991.

Periodicals

Broberg, Anders G., Holger Wessels, Michael E. Lamb, and C. Philip Hwang. "Effects of Day Care on the Development of Cognitive Abilities in 8-Year-Olds: A Longitudinal Study." *Developmental Psychology,* January 1997, vol. 33, no. 1, pp. 62–69.

Organizations

National Association for the Education of Young Children (NAEYC)
Address: 1509 Sixteenth Street N.W.
Washington, DC 20036
Telephone: (202) 232-8777

National Association for Family Day Care (NAFDC)
Address: 725 Fifteenth Street, N.W., Suite 505
Washington, DC 20005
Telephone: (202) 347-3356

Daydreaming

Temporary escape from daily reality by forming mental pictures.

In daydreams—exercises of imagination—the person forms a mental image of a past experience or of a situation that he or she has never actually experienced. Some psychologists use the acronym TUIT (Task-Unrelated Images and Thoughts) to describe episodes of daydreaming. A daydream may be triggered by a situation, a **memory**, or a sensory input (sight, taste, smell, sound, touch).

Psychologists estimate that one-third to one-half of a person's thoughts while awake are daydreams, although a single daydream rarely lasts more than a few minutes. Daydreaming is generally not harmful, unless the daydreaming episodes interfere with activities of daily living. When the daydreamer's daily routine is disrupted—a student does not hear the teacher assigning homework; for example, he or she may be using daydreams as a **defense mechanism.** In extreme situations, the daydreamer begins to confuse mental images with reality, and the daydream is referred to as a hallucination.

Daydreaming first occurs for most people during childhood, sometime before age three. Daydreaming patterns established in childhood often carry into adolescence and adulthood. Children who have positive, happy daydreams generally continue these types of mental images into adulthood; these daydreamers are most likely to benefit from the positive aspects of mental imagery. On the other hand, children whose daydreams are negative, scary, or visualize disasters establish a pattern of **anxiety** that will carry over into adulthood as well.

A child may talk or act out the scenario envisioned during his or her daydreams. Many young children include an **imaginary playmate** in the mental images of daydreaming. After around 10, however, the process of internalizing daydreaming begins; these older children and adolescents create private mental images, and are less likely to talk or physically participate in their daydreams. Researchers have examined changes in daydreaming habits over time among intellectually gifted children and adolescents. Findings suggest that content of daydreams may change over time, but frequency of daydreaming was fairly stable, diminishing somewhat during adolescence.

Athletes, musicians, and other performers use a form of daydreaming known as visualization. As the individual prepares for a competition or performance, he or she forms a mental picture of him- or herself executing and completing the task with the desired successful outcome.

For Further Study

Periodicals

Henderson, Bruce B., et al. "Individual Differences in IQ, Daydreaming and Moral Reasoning in Gifted and Average Adolescents," *International Journal of Behavioral Development,* vol. 7, June 1984, pp. 215–30.

Hogan, John, "Daydreaming: Experiments Reveal Links Between Memory and Sleep," *Scientific American,* October 1994, pp. 32+.

Seligson, Susan V., "What Your Daydreams Really Mean," *Redbook,* July 1995, pp. 51.

Gold, Steven R. and Bruce B. Henderson, "Daydreaming and Curiosity: Stability and Change in Gifted Children and Adolescents," *Adolescence,* vol. 25, Fall 1990, pp. 701–08.

Deafness *see* Hearing Development and Impairment

Death and Mourning

Understanding and adjusting to death and loss at various stages of life.

Almost every child or adolescent faces the death of someone close—a relative, friend, or even a pet—at some point in his or her life. In fact, it is estimated that about 5% of children under age 15, or about 1 in 20, will lose one or both parents.

Parents, **caregivers,** and teachers can provide support and minimize fear by answering a child's questions about death honestly. Encouraging communication will help the child through the essential grieving period. At one time, well-meaning adults felt that it was in the child's best interests to avoid discussing death. However, research has shown that children cope more successfully with a loss or death if they feel included in the group that has experienced the loss, and share in grieving and mourning.

When listening to a child's observations about death, adults must keep an open mind. A child may respond to the death of a grandmother, who used to make cupcakes for her, by observing that there will be no more cupcakes for dessert. This response could be interpreted as selfish, but it is in fact an expression of the child's loss in her own, very personal, terms. When a child learns of the accidental death of a playmate, he may ask to go out to play. This too may be an expression of the loss, as the chid might want to remember his friend by engaging in the activity the two of them shared. The child's response to loss can be misunderstood by adults, especially by those who are also grieving. By passing judgment on the child's reactions ("I can't believe you said that! Don't you feel sad that Grandma died?"), adults undermine the child's feelings and make the loss even more difficult for the child to handle.

In the days, weeks, and months that follow a death or loss, adults should refrain from criticizing or reacting negatively to the child's feelings. When the child seems to repeat the same questions over and over, the same answers, as open and honest as possible, must be repeated patiently. Young children may express concern, either directly or through behavior, about being abandoned or neglected, or that they may have in some way caused the death. Changes in appetite, complaints of feeling sick, and changes in activity patterns can be indications that the child is worried or anxious. Adults can help a child deal with these fears by acknowledging them and by reassuring the child that he will still be cared for, and that no one can cause a death by thoughts and feelings.

When the death or loss was unanticipated, as in a case of accident or violence, children may grieve longer and more intensely. Sad feelings may resurface over the years when the child experiences the loss anew, such as on holidays or other occasions. When a parent is deeply affected by the death of a loved person, the child may need the steady support of another adult. Books about illness and death can also be helpful. Adults should review the books in advance or ask a librarian, teacher, or counselor for advice. Issues of concern include age-appropriateness, situation-appropriateness, and religious point of view.

Preschool and school-age years

By the time a child is about two and a half or three, he will be able to acknowledge that a death has occurred, but he will not really understand the reality of death. Research indicates that by ages five to seven, children begin to understand that death is permanent. They also begin to acknowledge the universality of death, that it happens to everyone. Around this age, children are often ready to be part of rituals of death, such as visits with the deceased's family, the wake, funeral, or memorial service. Prior to participating in a visit or funeral, it is helpful to prepare the child for the experience, and to explain the purpose of the visit—to grieve and help the family. If a child expresses reluctance to participate in any aspect of the rituals of death, adults should accept his feelings and not exert pressure.

School-aged children can understand what death means, but they may be so overwhelmed that they act as if nothing has happened. Unexpressed feelings may surface as physical symptoms such as stomachache, headache, and unusual complaint of tiredness. Behavior may also change, demonstrated by reluctance to go to school, daydreaming in class, or a decline in academic performance.

Children will both grieve alone and share their grief with others. Families can take a number of actions to support emotional healing, such as openly acknowledging the death, letting children participate in the rituals, and maintaining familiar routines such as school and bedtime activities. Parents should also let children see them grieve. Rather than avoid any mention of the deceased, it may help to display a photograph in a prominent place as a way of letting family members maintain memories. The visual reminder provides a way to help the child understand that it is okay to talk about the person who died.

Adolescence

Teenagers have an adult understanding of death, but may find it even more difficult than younger children to deal with their sorrow. Behavior problems, dropping out of school, physical complaints such as headache or chest pain, sexual promiscuity, and even **suicide** attempts may result from their feelings of pain and loss. Oftentimes, teenagers are reluctant to talk to adults who may help them through their grief.

The death of a peer—even someone they hardly knew—affects adolescents differently than the death of an older person. They must cope not only with the shock of life's unpredictability, but their own mortality. Families who find that one or more members are having seri-

ous trouble coping with a death after a reasonable period of grieving should seek advice from a family physician, counselor, or religious leader.

For Further Study

Books

Buckingham, R. W. *Care of the Dying Child: A Practical Guide for Those Who Help Others.* New York: Continuum, 1989.

Kubler-Ross, E. *On Children and Death.* New York: Macmillan, 1983.

Smilansky, S. *On Death: Helping Children Understand and Cope.* New York: Peter Lang Publishing, 1987.

Webb, N. B., ed. *Helping Bereaved Children: A Handbook for Practitioners.* New York: Guilford Press, 1993.

Periodicals

Essa, Eva L., Colleen I. Murray, and Joanne Everts. "Death of a Friend." *Childhood Education,* Spring 1995, vol. 71, no. 3, p. 130.

Smith, Karen, and Karen Boardman. "Comforting a Child When Someone Close Dies." *Nursing,* October 1995, vol. 25, no. 10, pp. 58+.

Veciana-Suarez, Ana, and Julie Bourland. "A Death in the Family." *Parenting,* October 1995, vol. 9, no. 8, p. 80(6).

Westmoreland, Paula. "Coping with Death: Helping Students Grieve." *Childhood Education,* Spring 1996, vol. 72, no. 3, p. 157(4).

Witten, Matthew. "Talking About Death." *Parents Magazine,* January 1997, vol. 72, no. 1, p. 75(2).

"What Happens When We Die?" *Woman's Day,* June 27, 1995, vol. 58, no.11, p. 114.

Selected Children's Books About Death

Brown, M. W. *The Dead Bird.* New York: Harper and Row, 1985.

Clifton, L. *Everett Anderson's Goodbye.* New York: Holt, Rinehart & Winston, 1983.

DePaola, Tomie. *Nana Upstairs and Nana Downstairs.* New York: Putnam, 1973.

McGraw, S. *Love You Forever.* Scarborough, Ontario: Firefly Books, 1986.

Tresselt, A. *The Dead Tree.* New York: Parents' Magazine Press, 1972.

Zolotow, Charlotte. *My Grandson Lew.* New York: Harper and Row, 1974.

Deductive Reasoning

Way of thinking that relates ideas to one another in reaching conclusions.

Deductive reasoning is a way of reasoning that relates two or more general concepts or conditions to a specific case. For example, a child learns that birds fly south in October, and that a robin is a bird, he will use deductive reasoning to conclude that a robin will fly south in

October. Deductive reasoning is often confused with **in-ductive reasoning,** which uses a specific observation to reach a general conclusion.

Defense Mechanisms

Unconscious strategies for avoiding or reducing threatening feelings, such as fear and anxiety.

The concept of the defense mechanism originated with Sigmund Freud (1856–1939) and was later elaborated by other psychodynamically oriented theorists, notably his daughter Anna Freud (1895– 1982). Defense mechanisms allow negative feelings to be lessened without an alteration of the situation that is producing them, often by distorting the reality of that situation in some way. While they can help in coping with stress, they pose a danger because the reduction of stress can be so appealing that the defenses are maintained and become habitual. They can also be harmful if they become a person's primary mode of responding to problems. In children, excessive dependence on defense mechanisms may produce social isolation and distortion of reality and hamper the ability to engage in and learn from new experiences.

Defense mechanisms include denial, repression, suppression, projection, displacement, reaction formation, regression, fixation, identification, introjection, rationalization, isolation, sublimation, compensation, and humor. *Denial* and *repression* both distort reality by keeping things hidden from consciousness. In the case of denial, an unpleasant reality is ignored, and a realistic interpretation of potentially threatening events is replaced by a benign but inaccurate one. Either feelings or events (or both) may be denied. In very young children, a degree of denial is normal. One way of coping with the relative powerlessness of childhood is for young children to sometimes act as if they can change reality by refusing to acknowledge it, thereby ascribing magical powers to their thoughts and wishes. For example, a child who is told that her parents are divorcing may deny that it is happening or deny that she is upset about it. Denial has been shown to be effective in reducing the arousal caused by a threatening situation. In life-threatening or other extreme situations, denial can temporarily be useful in helping people cope, but in the long term painful feelings and events must be acknowledged in order to avoid further psychological and emotional problems. Related to denial is avoidance, which involves avoiding situations that are expected to elicit unwanted emotions and impulses.

In repression, painful feelings are conscious initially and then forgotten. However, they are stored in the unconscious, from which, under certain circumstances, they can be retrieved (a phenomenon Freud called "the return of the repressed"). Repression can range from momentary memory lapses to forgetting the details of a catastrophic event, such as a murder or an earthquake. Complete amnesia can even occur in cases where a person has experienced something very painful. The Oedipus complex by which Sigmund Freud explained the acquisition of **gender identity** relies on a child's repression of incestuous desires toward the parent of the opposite sex and feelings of rivalry toward the parent of the same sex. Other situations may also occasion the repression of hostile feelings toward a loved one (especially a parent). Possibly the most extreme is **child abuse,** the memory of which may remain repressed long into adulthood, sometimes being deliberately retrieved in therapy through hypnosis and other techniques.

A third defense mechanism, related to denial and repression, is *suppression,* by which unpleasant feelings are suppressed through a conscious decision not to think about them. Suppression differs from repression and denial in that the undesirable feelings are available but deliberately ignored (unlike repression and denial, where the person is completely unaware of these feelings). Suppression generally works by replacing unpleasant thoughts with others that do not produce stress. This may be done instinctively, or it may be done deliberately in a therapeutic context. **Cognitive behavior therapy** in particular makes use of this technique to help people combat negative thought patterns that produce maladaptive emotions and behavior. For example, a child may be instructed to block feelings of fear by thinking about a pleasant experience, such as a party, an academic achievement, or a victory in a sporting event. Suppression is considered one of the more mature and healthy defense mechanisms.

Projection and *displacement* allow a person to acknowledge anxiety-producing feelings but transfer them to either another source or another object. In projection, the undesirable feelings are attributed to another person or persons. An angry person believes others are angry at her; a person who is critical of others believes they are critical of him. Very young children are especially prone to projection because of their egocentric orientation, which blurs the boundary between themselves and others, making it easier to also blur the distinction between their feelings and those of others.

Displacement is a defense by which an impulse perceived as dangerous is displaced, either through redirection toward a different object or replacement by another impulse. In the first type, known as object displacement, anger or another emotion is initially felt toward a person against whom it is unsafe to express it (in children, for example, toward a parent). Displacement functions as a means by which the impulse can still be expressed—allowing a catharsis of the original emotion—but toward a safer target, such as a sibling, peer, or even a toy. In the second type of displacement, known as drive displacement, the object of the emotion remains the same but the emotion itself is replaced by a less threatening one.

Reaction formation, another defense mechanism, involves behavior that is diametrically opposed to the impulses or feelings that one is repressing. For example, a parent who is repressing feelings of resentment or rejection toward a child may overcompensate by appearing to be lavishly generous and solicitous of the child's welfare. In this type of situation, the child generally senses the true hostility underlying the parent's behavior. A child who is being toilet trained may show an exaggerated sense of fastidiousness to counter conflicts over controlling elimination. The Freudian stage of sexual latency in middle childhood is yet another example of reaction formation: in order to repress their sexual feelings, children at this age evince a strong sense of indifference or even hostility toward the opposite sex. Sometimes a distinction is drawn between feelings that are diametrically opposed to a repressed impulse and the actual behavior that expresses them, with the former called reaction formation and the latter referred to as undoing.

Two defense mechanisms—*regression* and *fixation*—are associated with developmental disturbances in children. In regression, a child, confronted with a situation that produces conflict, anxiety, or frustration, reverts to the behavior of an earlier stage of development, such as **thumb-sucking** or bed-wetting, in an attempt to regain the lost sense of safety that characterized the earlier period. In fixation, the child doesn't lose any previously gained developmental ground but refuses to move ahead because developmental progress has come to be associated with anxiety in some way.

Identification, which is basic to human development and an essential part of the learning process, can also serve as a defense mechanism. Taking on the characteristics of someone else can enable a person to engage in impulses or behavior that she sees as forbidden to her but acceptable for the person with whom she is identifying. Another motive for identification is a fear of losing the person with whom one identifies. One particularly well-known variety of identification is identification with the aggressor, where someone who is victimized in some way takes on the traits of the victimizer to combat feelings of powerlessness. This type of projection occurs when a child who is abused by his parents abuses others in turn. In some cases, however, this type of projection may occur in response to aggression that is imagined rather than real and create a self-perpetuating cycle by actually eliciting in others the aggression that was only imaginary initially. In *introjection,* which is related to

identification, only a particular aspect of someone else's personality is internalized.

Rationalization, another type of defense mechanism, is an attempt to deny one's true motives (to oneself or others) by using a reason (or rationale) that is more logical or socially acceptable than one's own impulses. Typical rationalizations include such statements as "I don't care if I wasn't chosen for the team; I didn't really want to play soccer anyway" and "I couldn't get my homework done because I had too many other things to do." Adolescents, caught between their own unruly impulses and adult expectations that seem unreasonable, are especially prone to rationalizing their behavior. Their advanced cognitive development makes many adolescents adept at this strategy.

Like rationalization, *isolation* is a rather complicated defense. It involves compartmentalizing one's experience so that an event becomes separated from the feelings that accompanied it, allowing it to be consciously available without the threat of painful feelings. Isolation can take on aspects of a *dissociative disorder,* with children separating parts of their lives to the point that they think of themselves as more than one person (for example, a good child and a bad one who only appears under certain circumstances). By compartmentalizing they can be relieved of feeling responsible for the actions of the "bad child."

Sublimation, one of the healthiest defense mechanisms, involves rechanneling the energy connected with an unacceptable impulse into one that is more socially acceptable. In this way, inappropriate sexual or aggressive impulses can be released in sports, creative pursuits, or other activities. Undesired feelings can also be sublimated into altruistic impulses, from which one may derive the vicarious pleasure of helping others. Other defense mechanisms generally viewed in a positive light include *compensation*—devoting unusual efforts to achievement in order to overcome feelings of inferiority—and the use of *humor* as a coping device.

For Further Study

Books

Firestone, Robert W., and Joyce Catlett. *Psychological Defenses in Everyday Life.* New York: Human Sciences Press, 1989.

Freud, Anna. *The Ego and the Mechanisms of Defense.* New York: International Universities Press, 1966.

Freud, Sigmund. *An Outline of Psychoanalysis.* New York: Norton, 1987.

Goleman, Daniel. *Vital Lies, Simple Truths: The Psychology of Self-Deception.* New York: Simon and Schuster, 1985.

Delay of Gratification

The ability to forgo an immediate pleasure or reward in order to gain a more substantial one later.

The acquisition of the ability to delay gratification is part of a child's social and **emotional development**. One of the developmental differences between preschoolers and toddlers is the greater ease with which preschoolers can be persuaded to delay gratification. On the whole, however, they need adult encouragement in order to maintain this behavior. Left to their own devices, few five-year-olds will pass up something attractive even if they know they will be rewarded later on. When children this age are given the choice between a modest treat (such as a small dish of ice cream) and a more substantial one later (an ice cream sundae), few will hold out for the delayed one unless they are pressured or closely monitored by adults.

The ability to delay gratification increases markedly between the ages of 5 and 12. When kindergartners in one study were offered a choice between being given a small candy bar immediately or a larger one later, 72% chose the smaller candy bar. This number decreased to 67% among first and second graders and 49% for third and fourth graders. By the fifth and sixth grades it had fallen to 38%, nearly half the rate for kindergartners. Although all children show an improved ability to delay gratification as they get older, some are more successful at it than others.

Generally, the children who are most successful in delaying gratification in middle childhood are those with an internal **locus of control** (a strong belief that their actions can influence events). By contrast, children with an external locus of control are less likely to believe that it is worth exerting self-control in the present because they doubt their ability to influence events in the future.

Delayed Speech *see* **Language Development**

Delinquency *see* **Truancy**

Democratic Parenting *see* **Parent-Child Relationships**

Dendrite

Nerve cell fibers that receive signals from other cells.

The nerve cell, or neuron, has two types of fibers to send and receive signals. Dendrites are short, threadlike fibers that extend from the cell body of a nerve cell to receive signals. The other fibers, the axons, send or transmit signals to other nerve cells. Dendrites receive electrochemical signals, which are known as postsynaptic potentials, from the axons of other neurons. The information contained in these signals is fired across a synaptic gap a billionth of an inch wide and transmitted toward the cell body, with the signals fading as they approach their destination. A single neuron can have many dendrites, each composed of numerous branches; together, they comprise the greater part of the neuron's receptive surface.

The number of axons and dendrites increases dramatically during infancy and childhood. Scientists believe this increase in nerve growth may occur to facilitate the rapid development experienced during this stage of human growth. Alternatively, the number of axons and dendrites decreases in early **adolescence.** Thus, a child of six has more dendrites than an adult.

For Further Study

Books

Barr, Murray Llewellyn. *The Human Nervous System: An Anatomical Viewpoint.* 6th ed. Philadelphia, PA: Lippincott, 1993.

Resetak, Richard M. *Receptors.* New York: Bantam Books, 1994.

Audiovisual Recordings

Messengers. Princeton, NJ: Films for the Humanities, 1985.

Nerves at Work! Part of *The Living Body* series. Princeton, NJ: Films for the Humanties, 1985.

Denial of Reality *see* **Defense Mechanisms**

Dental Development

Process of development of the permanent teeth.

Dental development begins in the first trimester of prenatal life, when the tips or cusps of the primary or deciduous teeth start to form, and it ends (in most individuals) when the root ends of the third permanent molars fully calcify and finally close. From start to finish, development and exfoliation (shedding) of the 20 deciduous teeth and the development of the 32 permanent teeth occupies a period of more than two decades.

"Teething," the emergence of the deciduous teeth, begins in the middle of the first year of life, and ends in the second year with the emergence of the second deciduous molars (symbolized as "dm2"). Some discomfort is associated with the piercing of the gums, especially so for the large deciduous molars; the permanent teeth may also cause some discomfort in the course of emergence through the gums, especially the permanent molars, which have no predecessors to pave the way.

There are in all 20 deciduous teeth, i.e., 2 incisors, one canine, and two deciduous molars in each of the four jaw quadrants of the jaw. The successional or permanent teeth (typically 32 in number) are also shown relative to the occlusal level (horizontal line) and the midline of the face.

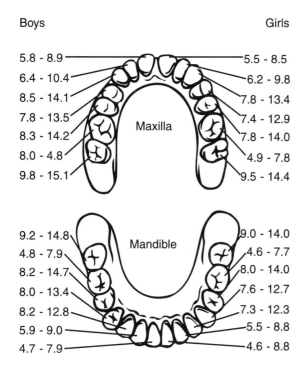

Boys   Girls

Boys		Girls
5.8 - 8.9		5.5 - 8.5
6.4 - 10.4		6.2 - 9.8
8.5 - 14.1		7.8 - 13.4
7.8 - 13.5	Maxilla	7.4 - 12.9
8.3 - 14.2		7.8 - 14.0
8.0 - 4.8		4.9 - 7.8
9.8 - 15.1		9.5 - 14.4

Boys		Girls
9.2 - 14.8		9.0 - 14.0
4.8 - 7.9		4.6 - 7.7
8.2 - 14.7	Mandible	8.0 - 14.0
8.0 - 13.4		7.6 - 12.7
8.2 - 12.8		7.3 - 12.3
5.9 - 9.0		5.5 - 8.8
4.7 - 7.9		4.6 - 8.8

Except for the earliest stages of prenatal dental development and with the possible exception of the third permanent molar (M3), girls are advanced over boys in dental development, by as much as six percent or so. Girls also have slightly smaller tooth crowns and slightly shorter tooth roots, allowing sex identification of cadavers and skeletalized material.

To a larger extent, both dental development and tooth size are under genetic control, as shown in twin and sibling comparisons, and there are population differences both in developmental timing and in crown size and shape. Dental development is also affected by such endocrine disorders as hypopituitarism and hypothyroidism. Dental development is slightly advanced in **obesity** and slightly retarded in chronic malnutrition.

Some teeth may fail to form, a condition known as agenesis, especially so for the third molar (M3) and—sometimes—the lateral (2nd) incisors, i.e., I2. When M3 and especially I2 are missing, the remaining teeth tend to be reduced in size and late developing as well. Supernu-

MOUTH PROTECTORS

The American Dental Association, in cooperation with the Academy of Sports Dentistry, recommends that all participants in contact sports wear protective mouth gear. Since 1962, high school and college-level football players have been required to wear faceguards and mouth protectors during practice sessions and in competition, preventing an estimated 200,000 injuries per year. Many experts go beyond contact sports, to recommend that mouth protectors be worn during any recreational sport where there is danger of mouth injury, including surfing, basketball, skateboarding, gymnastics, racquet sports, and field hockey.

The ADA recommends wearing a mouth protector when participating in these sports:

- Acrobatics, gymnastics, skateboarding, and skydiving
- Basketball and volleyball
- Boxing, martial arts, weightlifing, and wrestling
- Discus throwing and shotputting
- Field hockey, football, rugby, and soccer
- Handball, lacrosse, racquetball, and squash
- Ice hockey and skiing
- Surfing and water polo

There are three types of mouth protectors: the ready-made (one size fits all) mouth protector; the mouth-formed mouth protector; and the custom-made protector. The preferred design covers only the upper teeth. This is more comfortable for the athlete and protects the most often injured. In addition, since the upper teeth overlap the lower teeth for most people, the mouth guard offers some protection for the lower teeth as well.

Young athletes who wear removable orthodontic appliances, such as retainers, should remove them when playing contact sports.

merary (extra) teeth also exist, though rarely, usually as relatively shapeless pegs, but in some cases there may be a complete extra molar (M4) that is fully formed.

Traditionally, the emergence of the first deciduous or baby tooth was taken as an indication to extend the infant's diet beyond breast milk alone. (Nowadays cereals and other foods are introduced much earlier then in the past.) In turn, completion of the deciduous dentition was taken as a readiness for solid foods, now introduced far earlier than the end of the second year of life. Traditionally also, emergence of the second permanent molars was considered evidence of the ability to perform "adult," rigorous labor.

The major disorders of the dentition during childhood are dental caries (cavities), malocclusion (malpositioning of the teeth), and less commonly, accidental injury. The incidence and prevalence of dental caries increased rapidly during the 19th century until the middle of the 20th century, consistent with increased consumption of sucrose. Addition of fluorides to the water supply and the use of topical fluorides reversed the incidence of caries, and many dental schools have been closed as a consequence.

Malocclusions are now ubiquitous, with over 90% of children affected to some degree. Though the actual cause of malocclusion is not known, satisfactory dental alignment can be achieved by orthodontic intervention.

Many accidental injuries occur during participation in contact sports. Most injuries of this type can be prevented by the use of mouthguards and protective headgear.

See also **Fluoridation, Orthodontia.**

For Further Study

Books

Ardley, Bridget. *Skin, Hair, and Teeth.* Englewood Cliffs, NJ: Silver Burdett, 1988.

Gaskin, John. *Teeth.* London; New York, NY: F. Watts, 1984.

Gillis, Jennifer Storey. *Tooth Truth: Fun Facts and Projects.* Pownal, VT: Storey Communications, 1996.

Lauber, Patricia. *What Big Teeth You Have!* New York: T.Y. Crowell, 1986.

Shoesmith, Kathleen A. *Do You Know About—Teeth?* London: Burke Books, 1982.

Periodicals

Garn, S.M., J.M. Nagy, S.T. Sandusky, and F. Trowbridge. "Economic Impact on Tooth Emergence." *American Journal of Physical Anthropology* 32(2), 1973, pp. 233-370.

Garn, S.M. "Genetics of Dental Development." In: *The Biology of Occlusal Development.* Proceedings of a sponsored symposium honoring Professor Robert E. Moyers. J.A. McNamara (eds.). The Center for Human Growth and Development, Ann Arbor, Michigan, 1977.

Garn, S.M., R.H. Osborn, and K.D. McCabe. "The Effect of Prenatal Factors on Crown Dimensions." *American Journal of Physical Anthropology,* vol. 51, pp. 665–77.

Garn, S.M. and B.H. Smith. "Developmental Communalities in Tooth Emergence Timing." *Journal of Dental Research* vol. 59, no. 7, 1980, p. 1,178.

Organizations

American Dental Association
    Bureau of Health Educaiton and Audiovisual Services

Address: 211 East Chicago Avenue
Chicago, IL 60611

—Stanley A. Garn, Ph.D.
University of Michigan

Deoxyribonucleic Acid *see* **DNA**

Dependent Personality Disorder

A lack of self-confidence coupled with excessive dependence on others.

Persons affected by dependent personality disorder have a disproportionately low level of confidence in their own intelligence and abilities and have difficulty making decisions and undertaking projects on their own. Their pervasive reliance on others, even for minor tasks or decisions, makes them exaggeratedly cooperative out of fear of alienating those whose help they need. They are reluctant to express disagreement with others and are often willing to go to abnormal lengths to win the approval of those on whom they rely. Another common feature of the disorder is an exaggerated fear of being left to fend for oneself. Adolescents with dependent personality disorder rely on their parents to make even minor decisions for them, such as what they should wear or how they should spend their free time, as well as major ones, such as what college they should attend.

Dependent personality disorder occurs equally in males and females and begins by early adulthood. It may be linked to either chronic physical illness or **separation anxiety** disorder earlier in life. The primary treatment for dependent personality disorder is **psychotherapy,** with an emphasis on learning to cope with anxiety, developing assertiveness, and improving decision-making skills. Group therapy can also be helpful.

For Further Study

Books

Costa, Paul T., and Thomas A. Widiger, eds. *Personality Disorders and the Five-Factor Model of Personality.* Washington, DC: American Psychological Association, 1994.

Friedland, Bruce. *Personality Disorders.* New York: Chelsea House, 1991.

Depression

An emotional state or mood characterized by one or more of these symptoms: sad mood, low energy, poor concentration, sleep or appetite changes, feelings of worthlessness or hopelessness, and thoughts of suicide.

Until recently, it was thought that children and adolescents could not suffer from clinical depression. It was assumed that children were not physically or psychologically mature enough to develop symptoms of depression and that adolescents with mood difficulties were simply going through "growing pains." However, several investigations have shown that if appropriately evaluated, children and adolescents do suffer from depression. We will refer to clinical depression that presents with severe symptoms as major depressive disorder (MDD) and depression that has moderate, chronic symptoms as dysthymic disorder (see below for specific criteria). Depression is relatively common; the prevalence (number of cases in one year) of MDD and dysthymic disorder combined is approximately 2% for children and 6% for adolescents.

Clinical features

Every child and adolescent can be occasionally and appropriately sad. However depression is more than just having a sad mood for a while. Children and adolescents with depression have a pervasive change in mood as well as a number of other clinical characteristics. There are four types of depression that child psychiatrists diagnose in children and adolescents: major depressive disorder (MDD), dysthymic disorder, adjustment disorder with depressed mood, and bipolar depression. **Bipolar disorder** (previously called manic-depressive illness) is another type of mood disorder consisting of periods of mania and depression. The diagnostic criteria and clinical presentation of the depressed phase of bipolar disorders is similar to that of MDD.

Major depressive disorder (MDD)

MDD is the most severe form of depression and has the most prominent clinical symptoms. Symptoms of MDD include:

1) persistent depressed or irritable mood most of the day (easily annoyed, angry, sad, anxious, hopeless; sometimes described as not having any emotion)

2) markedly diminished interest or pleasure in all or almost all activities (not able to enjoy activities that were previously fun, easily bored, sits around and does not do much)

3) significant weight loss or gain

4) sleep disturbance (trouble falling asleep, staying asleep, waking up too early, or sleeping more than usual)

5) psychomotor retardation (appearing to have slowed-down thinking and movements) or agitation (new onset of restless activity, pacing, unable to stay still)

6) fatigue or loss of energy (frequent complaints of feeling tired or having to push hard to do usual activities)

7) feelings of worthlessness or excessive guilt (very self-critical, blaming self for minor transgressions)

8) difficulty concentrating (distractible, unable to focus on challenging tasks, forgetful, indecisiveness)

9) thoughts of death or **suicide**, or attempting suicide

According to the **American Psychiatric Association**, to be diagnosed with MDD, the child or adolescent must have at least five of the above symptoms nearly every day for at least two weeks, and one of those symptoms must be either: (1) depressed or irritable mood; or (2) loss of interest and pleasure. These symptoms must represent a change from previous functioning and produce impairment in relationships with others or in performance of usual activities. The symptoms and change in mood cannot be attributed to abuse of drugs, use of medications, certain severe psychiatric illnesses, bereavement, or medical illness.

Overall, the clinical picture of childhood MDD parallels the symptoms of adult MDD, with some minor differences. In children, symptoms of anxiety (including **phobias** and trouble separating from caretakers), physical complaints, and behavioral problems seem to occur more frequently. Adolescents tend to have more sleep and appetite disturbances, psychosis (hallucinations or delusions), and impairment of functioning than younger children. In addition, the incidence and severity of suicide attempts increase after puberty.

Dysthymic disorder

Dysthymic disorder consists of a persistent, long-term change in mood which is generally less intense than in MDD. The associated symptoms of dysthymic disorder are not as severe as MDD. To be given a diagnosis of dysthymic disorder, the child or adolescent must have depressed mood or irritability on most days for most of the day over a period of one year, as well as at least two of the following symptoms: (1) change in appetite; (2) sleep disturbance; (3) low self-esteem; (4) poor concentration or difficulty making decisions; (5) decreased energy; or (6) feelings of hopelessness. In addition, they may have other symptoms, such as feelings of being unloved, anger, somatic complaints (such as stomach aches, nausea, or headaches), **anxiety**, and sometimes disobedience.

Adjustment disorder with depressed mood

Sometimes children and adolescents experience an excessive change in mood in response to a very stressful event or a series of stressful events. If they develop a persistently depressed mood (often with tearfulness and hopelessness) and impairment of functioning within three months of the stressor(s), but do not meet criteria for MDD or dysthymic disorder, then they would receive a diagnosis of an adjustment disorder with depressed mood. An adjustment disorder does not have the associated symptoms of MDD or dysthymic disorder. It is important to emphasize that MDD or dysthymic disorder may be precipitated by stressful events, so that if a child or adolescent has the appropriate symptoms, they should receive a diagnosis of MDD or dysthymic disorder. The prevalence, clinical course, and treatment of adjustment disorder with depressed mood have not been well studied in children and adolescents; a few studies indicate that it lasts for approximately six months and usually does not recur.

Presentation to outside observers

The diagnosis of depression can be difficult because the depressed and irritable mood often makes the child and adolescent less able and willing to share how they are feeling. Some of the symptoms of depression are difficult for others to observe because they are related to how the person is feeling inside. Parents and teachers may only notice that the depressed child or adolescent has become withdrawn, whiny, or moody. Little things make them angry or tearful, and they tend to view many situations as negative or overwhelming. They interact less with others and withdraw from favorite activities such as sports, social events, or extracurricular activities. Their school performance often declines, and the child may start to get into trouble at school or skip classes. However when clinically assessed, the depressed child or adolescent will often report sad mood, low energy, poor concentration, sleep or appetite changes, feelings of worthlessness or hopelessness, and thoughts of suicide. This underscores the necessity of gathering information from both outside observers and the child herself when assessing for depression.

Coexisting psychiatric disorders

Forty to 70% of children and adolescents with clinical depression also have other coexisting psychiatric diagnoses, such as disruptive behavior disorders (**conduct disorder**, **oppositional-defiant disorder,** and **attention deficit/hyperactivity disorder**), anxiety disorders, abuse of drugs and/or alcohol, and **eating disorders** (**bulimia** and **anorexia nervosa**). Identification and treatment of the coexisting psychiatric disorders may be important for the overall treatment of the depression.

Clinical course

MDD episodes tend to last approximately 7–9 months, and about 90% of the major depressive episodes end by 1.5–2 years after the onset. Between 6 and 10% of MDD episodes become chronic. Depression is a recurrent disorder; a child or adolescent experiencing a first episode of MDD has a 40% probability of developing another depressive episode within the next two years and 70% chance within the next five years.

Follow-up studies of depressed adolescents have found that 20–40% of adolescents with MDD are at risk to develop bipolar disorder within a five year period after the onset of the depression. Characteristics associated with the conversion from MDD to bipolar disorder include the presence of psychomotor retardation and psychosis during the depression, family history of bipolar disorder or strong family history for mood disorders, and the development of agitation, high energy, or euphoria when taking **antidepressant** medications.

Furthermore, over a period of five years, approximately 70% of the children and adolescents with dysthymic disorders will develop an episode of MDD. Once these children have developed MDD, the course of their mood disorders follows the natural course of MDD. Therefore it may be very important to identify and treat childhood dysthymic disorder early.

The most severe complications of depression are suicidal ideation and suicide attempts. The adolescent suicide rate has quadrupled since 1950 (from 2.5 to 11.2 per 100,000), and currently represents 12% of the total mortality in this age group. Beyond depression, predisposing factors for suicidality include the existence of anxiety, disruptive, bipolar and personality disorders, and substance abuse. In addition, family history of depression or bipolar disorder, family history of suicidal behavior, exposure to family violence, impulsivity, and availability of methods (e.g., firearms at home) have been associated with an increased risk for suicide.

Children and adolescents with clinical depressions are at high risk for suicide, homicide, abuse of alcohol/drugs, physical illnesses, poor academic and psychosocial functioning. Moreover, after remission, previously depressed children may continue to show significant problems. These psychosocial problems tend to improve with time unless the depression develops again. The existence of other psychiatric disorders, family problems, and environmental stresses influences the risk for recurrent depression and suicide attempts.

Causes of clinical depression

Several factors are associated with the onset, duration, and recurrence of early onset MDD. Studies assessing relatives of depressed children and children of depressed parents have concluded that clinical depression runs in families. Investigations of **twins** who have been raised in separate families and other **adoption** studies have provided evidence that genetic factors predispose a person to develop clinical depression. Environmental factors such as exposure to negative events (e.g., deaths, **divorce**, medical illnesses), lack of support, family conflict, and aversive experiences in early childhood (neglect, death, abuse) may also contribute to the development of depression.

Several biological abnormalities, including changes in the secretion of the growth **hormone** and cortisol, have been linked to children and adolescents with depression. However there are no laboratory tests that diagnose MDD or dysthymic disorder. The most useful tools in diagnosing depression are (1) a thorough evaluation of depressive symptoms through interviews and observation of the child, and (2) interviews with parents and other key figures, such as teachers.

Treatment

Several treatment strategies, including different forms of **psychotherapy** and medication, have been developed for the treatment of MDD and dysthymic disorder in adults. Unfortunately, there has been relatively little research conducted with children and adolescents.

Psychotherapy for the acute treatment of MDD

Several types of psychotherapies have been used to treat MDD and dysthymic disorder in children and adolescents, including: psychodynamic psychotherapy, cognitive-behavioral therapy (CBT), **family therapy**, interpersonal therapy (IPT), social skills training, and group therapy. Though the manner of performing the different types of psychotherapy may vary, the overall goal of these therapies is to reduce the symptoms of depression. In addition, they generally try to improve the child's coping skills, problem-solving abilities, academic functioning, parent-child and peer relationships, and, at times, understanding of internal psychological processes. Cognitive-behavior therapy has been the most frequently studied psychotherapy in childhood and adolescent depression; it appears to be effective in the treatment of acute depression, prevention of relapses, and prevention of the onset of new depressions. However, studies of other forms of psychotherapy (IPT, family therapy, social skills training, group therapy) have shown that these forms of therapy are potentially effective as well in treating childhood depression.

It may also be important to include parents in the treatment process because: (1) children are dependent on their parents; (2) depressed youth frequently come from families with high rates of depression or high degree of conflicts; and (3) parent psychopathology and family conflict may predict a poor outcome to treatment and increase risk for depressive recurrences.

Medication interventions for the acute treatment of MDD

Most of the studies published so far have evaluated the effects of the tricyclic antidepressants, such as nortriptyline (brand name Pamelor), imipramine (Tofranil), desipramine (Norpramin), and the selective serotonin reuptake inhibitors (SSRIs), such as fluoxetine (Prozac), sertraline (Zoloft), and paroxetine (Paxil) in treating clinical depression. The studies show that some children and adolescents benefit from these medications.

Medications for treating depression differ in some ways from medications that people take for other medical illnesses. Though some people with depression notice a reduction in symptoms in a few days, most of the time there is a delay of up to 4–6 weeks for the medications to have an effect. The symptoms of depression usually do not improve all at once, but instead show a gradual and, at times, uneven improvement. Once the depression has improved, there is evidence, at least in adults, that people with depression should keep taking medication for a period of time to prevent recurrence. Lastly, all antidepressants carry a small risk of triggering a manic or hypomanic (milder form of mania) episode in vulnerable patients. (For more information on medications, please refer to **Antidepressants**).

Prevention

Relapse and recurrences

Very few investigations of depression have addressed the prevention of relapses (reappearance of depression within two months of symptom resolution) and recurrences (a new episode of depression). After successful treatment with psychotherapy or medication, most patients have a relapse or recurrence. Therefore, to prevent relapses, it is recommended that psychotherapy and/or medication treatments continue. In adults, medication (with same dose that was used to cure the depression) may be continued for at least 16–20 weeks after achieving full remission of depressive symptom. In addition, various forms of psychotherapy can be used during the continuation period to help patients cope with the psychological and social difficulties produced by the depression and to manage the stress and conflicts that may trigger a depressive relapse or diminish medication compliance.

To prevent recurrences, the length of therapy depends on several factors, such as severity of the depression, number of depressive episodes, chronicity, presence of psychotic symptoms, other psychiatric disorders, family psychopathology, and presence of an adequate support system. In adults, three to five years of psychotherapy and/or medication can significantly reduce the occurrence of additional MDD episodes. Community studies of adolescents have shown that group cognitive-behavioral therapy combined with relaxation and group problem-solving therapy may prevent recurrences of depression for up to 9–24 months after treatment.

Education and primary prevention

Prevention of depression for children and adolescents at high risk to develop depression, such as the offspring of depressed parents and children with some depressive symptoms, may be of prime importance. Recent studies of high school adolescents and school children with some symptoms of depression, but not clinical depression, showed that cognitive interventions were effective in reducing depressive symptomatology and lowered the risk for developing depression for up to two years after the intervention. The prevalence and morbidity of depression in children and adolescents underscore the need for improved public awareness about depression, early detection and prompt treatment of depressed youths, and more research on the prevention and treatment of these disorders.

—Boris Birmaher, M.D. and David Axelson, M.D.
Department of Psychiatry
University of Pittsburgh School of Medicine
Western Psychiatric Institute and Clinic

For Further Study

Periodicals

Birmaher, B., N. D. Ryan, D. Williamson, D. Brent, J. Kaufman, R., J., P., and B, Dahl. "Child and Adolescent Depression I: A Review of the Past Ten Years." *Journal of the American Academy of Child and Adolescent Psychiatry* 35, no. 11, 1996a, pp. 1427–39.

Birmaher, B., N. D. Ryan, D. Williamson, D. A. Brent, J. Kaufman(1996b). "Childhood and Adolescent Depression: A Review of the Past 10 Years - Part II." *Journal of the American Academy of Child and Adolescent Psychiatry* 35, no. 12, 1996b, pp. 1575–83.

Jaycox, L. H., K. J. Reivich, J. Gillham, and M. E. P. Seligman. "The Prevention of Depressive Symptoms in School Children." *Behaviour Research and Therapy* 32, no. 8, 1994, pp. 801–16.

Kovacs, M., T. L. Feinberg, M. A. Crouse-Novak, S. L. Paulauskas, and R. Finkelstein. "Depressive Disorders in Childhood. I. A Longitudinal Prospective Study of Characteristics and Recovery." *Archives of General Psychiatry* 41, 1984b, pp. 229–37.

Kovacs, M. "Presentation and Course of Major Depressive Disorder during Childhood and Later Years of the Life Span." *Journal of the American Academy of Child and Adolescent Psychiatry* 35, no. 6, 1996, pp. 705–15.

Lewinsohn, P. M., G. N. Clarke, H. Hops, and J. Andrews. "Cognitive-Behavioral Group Treatment of Depression in Adolescents." *Behavior Therapy* 21, 1990, pp. 385–401.

Rao, U., N. D. Ryan, and B. Birmaher. "Unipolar Depression in Adolescents: Clinical Outcome in Adulthood." *Journal of the American Academy of Child and Adolescent Psychiatry* 34, 1995, pp. 566–78.

Rohde, P., P. M. Lewisohn, and J. R. Seeley. "Are Adolescents Changed by an Episode of Major Depression?" *Journal of the American Academy of Child and Adolescent Psychiatry* 33, 1994, pp. 1289–98.

Depth Perception

Ability to determine visually the distance between objects.

The ability to perceive depth seems to exist early in life. Research with infants has revealed that by two months of age, babies can perceive depth. Prior to that, they may be unable to do so in part because of weak eye muscles that do not let them use binocular depth cues.

Monocular Depth Cues. Psychologists have identified two different kinds of monocular cues. One comes into play when we use the muscles of the eye to change the shape of the eye's lens to focus on an object. We make use of the amount of muscular tension to give feedback about distance.

A second kind of monocular cue relates to external visual stimuli. Artists use these visual cues to make two dimensional paintings appear realistic. These cues may seem obvious to us now, but artistic renderings from earlier than about the sixteenth century often seem distorted because artists had not yet developed all the techniques to capture these visual cues.

Binocular Cues. Binocular cues require that we use both eyes. One cue makes use of the fact that when we look at a nearby object with both eyes, we bring our eyes together; the muscle tension associated with looking at close objects gives us information about their distance. The second binocular cue involves retinal disparity. This means that each eye (or, more specifically, the retina of each eye) has a slightly different perspective. The slight difference in appearance of an object in each eye when we gaze at it gives us further information about depth. Children's Viewmasters produce a three-dimensional image that has depth because of a slightly different picture that is delivered to each eye. In the natural world, because of the relatively small distance from one pupil to another (about 2.5 inches or 6.5 centimeters) binocular cues are effective only for objects that are within about 500 yards (455 m) of the viewer.

Desegregation

A process whereby policies and practices of racial segregation are undone through legislative action, social change, school reorganization, and educational programs.

Desegregation is a difficult concept to define, and social scientists, educators, and activists have struggled to formulate a consistent, unified definition. There seems to be general agreement that the concept "desegregation" denotes the legal and actual abolition of racial segregation, particularly in education. The terms "desegregation" and "integration" are often used interchangeably, but many writers clearly distinguish these two terms, emphasizing that "integration" implies a higher level of social cohesion which desegregation does not necessarily guarantee.

Desegregation is a relatively recent phenomenon. As late as the 1950s, segregation was legal, upheld by a 1896 U.S. Supreme Court ruling in *Plessy* v. *Ferguson*. In what has been defined as a blatant violation of the Fourteenth Amendment, the Supreme Court permitted racial segregation of public—including educational—facilities. Aimed at the African Americans, the largest non-white minority in the country, this legislation provoked many protests, particularly among black educators, who accurately perceived segregated education as a mechanism to maintain inferior academic standards for the black population. In the early 1950s, the NAACP launched a campaign against segregation, attacking its supporting legislation. The legal battle for desegregation scored a great victory in 1954, when the Supreme Court, overturning the 1896 ruling, declared in **Brown v. Board of Education** that racial segregation is unconstitutional.

Unfortunately, as proponents of desegregation soon realized, the court ruling covered just one aspect of this multi-faceted phenomenon. In fact, the legal victory was a necessary, but not sufficient, condition for successful desegregation. Having cleared the legal hurdle, the desegregation process now had to confront a variety of formidable obstacles: court battles, political opposition, prejudices, and racism—unconscious and intended. Even with desegregation officially sanctioned and formally implemented, segregation can be practiced in subtle, almost unnoticeable ways. For example, as Ellis Cose has written, according to a study of New York public schools, minority parents are often not informed about special programs, while the white parents are automatically given that information.

In addition to dealing with efforts to subvert and undermine desegregation, supporters of the process have also had to contend with the learned skepticism of experts who view desegregation as a huge effort yielding dubious results. Melvin Seeman, for example, has observed that because people have great expectations, desegregation is often condemned when its benefits, though evidently tangible, fail to cause a stir. In other words, people tend to reject desegregation because it leads to modest, not spectacular, improvements. In addition, as Seeman explains, critics sometime focus on short-term effects of desegregation, paying little attention to long-term effects. For example, while lowered **self-esteem** among minority students can be a short-term effect of a desegregated classroom, students can eventually regain and develop a greater sense of self-esteem. Finally, academic failure due to extraneous factors is sometime blamed on desegregation. However, as proponents of

desegregation have argued, desegregation needs to be understood in a wider social context: often, when desegregation and integration fail, the failure, far from implying that desegregation is not a viable social process, reflects the objective—economic and political constraints—and subjective—prejudice and racism—forces which strive to preserve racial discrimination.

Often difficult to identify, resistance to desegregation assumes a variety of forms. A combination of skepticism and apathy, while not necessarily indicating racism, may reflect a pessimistic attitude toward the idea of social and psychological change. In some cases, prosperous minority parents who identify with their social class, but not with their race, give little thought to the importance of desegregation, and therefore ignore the whole process. In other cases, parent might accept the idea "but not for my child," the reasoning being that desegregated schools provide inferior education, particularly in Washington, as Jack E. White has observed (White, 1996), where many black teachers and school officials keep their children outside the public school system. White views this attitude as catastrophic, asserting that the black school officials and educators who neglect the schools they run "have betrayed the best of the African-American tradition, which values education above all else, and have given whites who never believed in integration an easy excuse for abandoning it." Sometimes resistance to desegregation stems from racist attitudes which people inherit or form independently. For example, in a study of group attitudes, William T. Smelser and Neil J. Smelser quote research indicating that white children from punitive and authoritarian families are likely to develop negative attitudes toward blacks. Finally, simple ignorance can undermine the desegregation process. For example, a black child may feel totally alienated in an "integrated" school where black culture is completely ignored (Gussin Paley, 1995).

There seems to be general agreement among researchers that the desegregation process has not transformed public education to satisfy the needs—academic, cultural, and psychological—of minority students. On the one hand, desegregation may have fallen short of its promise; on the other, for a significant segment of the population, abandoning desegregation is not a rational option. First of all, as proponents of desegregation have affirmed, even a less-than-stellar track record can hardly be dismissed as a failure. If integrated classrooms are not meeting minority students' needs, as Constance Johnson reports (Johnson, 1994), perhaps this is due to insufficient desegregation, which means that desegregation must be pursued more energetically.

As an ongoing social process, however, desegregation has benefited from the insights of educators and activists who have approached it as an attainable social project. It is important, as White has remarked, to remember "that integration's real purpose was not to produce Norman Rockwellish racial brotherhood." Rather, one goal is for all children to be guaranteed the same educational opportunity, which White defines as "the same quality of instruction, textbooks, and facilities." Cose cites the example of University of Texas professor Philip Uri Treisman, who has successfully encouraged minority students to excel in mathematics. As Cose reports, Treisman's formula for success combines interracial study groups, hard work, and individual attention. In study groups, students can directly experience the fact that everybody, regardless of race, struggles with challenging intellectual problems, exerting his or her intellectual—not racial or cultural—power. If small groups under optimal conditions have no trouble gaining the insight that race is not a factor in intellectual accomplishment, there is no reason, proponents of desegregation contend, this insight cannot be extended to larger groups and to society as a whole.

For Further Study

Books

Ogbu, John. *The Next Generation.* 1974.

————. *Minority Education and Caste: The American System in Cross-Cultural Perspective.* 1978.

Ravitch, Diane. *The Schools We Deserve: Reflections on the Educational Crises of Our Time.* New York: Basic Books, 1985.

St. John N. H. *School Desegregation: Outcomes for Children.* New York: Wiley, 1975.

Periodicals

Cose, Ellis. "The Realities of Black and White: Jim Crow Is Long Dead, But the Promise of Integration Remains Unfulfilled." *Newsweek* 127, no. 18, April 29, 996, p. 36.

Gussin Paley, Vivian. "Their Voices Didn't Come Through." *New York Times Book Review,* February 19, 1995, p. 11.

Johnson, Constance. "The Sad Way Kids Look at Integration." *U.S. News and World Report* 116, no. 20, May 23, 1994, p. 33.

Meier, Kenneth J., Joseph Stewart, Jr., and Robert E. England. *Race, Class, and Education: The Politics of Second-Generation Discrimination.* Madison: University of Wisconsin Press, 1989.

Seeman, Melvin. "Intergroup Relations." In *Social Psychology: Sociological Perspectives,* edited by Morris Rosenberg and Ralph H. Turner, pp. 378–410. New Brunswick, NJ: Transaction Publishers, 1992.

Smelser, William T., and Neil J. Smelser. "Group Movements, Sociocultural Change, and Personality." In *Social Psychology: Sociological Perspectives,* edited by Morris Rosenberg and Ralph H. Turner, pp. 625–52. New Brunswick, NJ: Transaction Publishers, 1992.

White, Jack E. "Why We Need to Raise Hell." *Time* 147, no. 18, April 29, 1996, p. 46.

—Zoran Minderovic

Desensitization

A long-term form of allergy treatment involving gradual exposure to small doses of allergens over a period of several years. Also known as immunotherapy and allergy shots.

Desensitization is a form of **allergy** treatment that involves the periodic injection of small amounts of allergens over a period of several years. Allergens such as dust and pollen cause certain people to produce elevated levels of immunoglobulin E (IgE) antibodies, which in turn unleash chemicals called histamines that produce allergic reactions. By introducing allergens into the body in a highly diluted form, desensitization is designed to increase the immune system's tolerance to these substances so that they no longer cause such allergic reactions as **asthma,** sinus congestion, sneezing, and red, watery eyes. Allergy shots are effective for many of the approximately six million Americans who receive them regularly. However, the desensitization process is long, time-consuming, and expensive and doesn't work for everyone. In addition, it is not recommended for all types of allergies.

Each course of treatment is individually tailored: a person receives injections containing small portions of only those allergens to which he or she has demonstrated sensitivity. The initial doses are extremely low. If tolerated, they are gradually increased until they reach a maintenance level at which they may be continued for years. Children are usually given a shot in the arm once a week and required to remain in the allergist's office for 20–30 minutes afterwards in case of a serious reaction, either local or systemic. Local reactions may be limited to a feeling of warmth at the injection site or they may be more serious, involving pain and swelling. The weekly schedule is typically maintained for a period of four to eight months, after which the shots are given at increasingly longer intervals. The shots are generally continued until allergic symptoms have been absent for about a year and a half. In most cases, it takes three to five years to reach this point.

While desensitization has proven successful in promoting **immunization** against some allergens—notably tree and grass pollens, dust, ragweed, and molds—it is not recommended for use against food allergies. Because of the long-term effort and expense involved, it is considered appropriate only for moderate to severe allergies and it is usually undertaken only if an allergy doesn't respond to medication. The major types of allergies for which desensitization is recommended are rhinitis (both seasonal and chronic) and asthma. Rhinitis is the inflammation of the mucous membranes that causes a runny nose, sneezing, and nasal irritation. The seasonal variety (also called hay fever) occurs at the same time every year and is a reaction to specific plants (trees and grass in springtime, ragweed in late summer and fall). The chronic variety may be caused by plants but also by dust, food, or other allergens. The more limited the range of allergens, the better desensitization will work. Allergy shots have also proven effective in treating asthma, in which swelling and congestion of the bronchial tubes cause coughing, wheezing, and shortness of breath. Desensitization is not recommended for skin allergies, such as hives and eczema.

Allergic reactions to insect stings have been successfully treated by desensitization to the venom of particular insects. Such treatments have been demonstrated to be almost 100% effective for reactions that are systemic (rather than limited to the location of the sting), involve either the respiratory or cardiovascular system, and include either a decline in blood pressure or obstruction of an airway. In addition, best results are obtained when the patient has tested positive for insect venom either by skin testing or the radioallergosorbent (RAST) blood test. In almost all cases, the injection causes either no reaction or a local reaction limited to redness, swelling, or discomfort at the injection site. Severe systemic reactions, including anaphylactic shock, a potentially fatal constriction of airways and blood vessels, are possible, so it is important to follow the general desensitization precautions by remaining at the doctor's office for at least 20 minutes after the shot.

For Further Study

Books

Feldman, B. Robert. *The Complete Book of Children's Allergies: A Guide for Parents.* New York: Times Books, 1986.

Gershwin, M. Eric, and Edwin L. Klingelhofer. *Conquering Your Child's Allergies.* Reading, MA: Addison-Wesley, 1989.

Organizations

American Association of Certified Allergists
    Address: 401 East Prospect Avenue, Suite 210
    Mount Prospect, IL 60056
    Telephone: (312) 255-1024
American Allergy Association
    Address: P.O. Box 7273
    Menlo Park, CA 94025

Developmental Age *see* **Developmental Quotient**

Developmental Delay

Any delay in a child's physical, cognitive, behavioral, emotional, or social development, due to any number of reasons.

Developmental delay refers to any significant retardation in a child's physical, cognitive, behavioral, emo-

tional, or social development. The two most frequent reasons for classing a child as having developmental delay involve those psychological systems for which there are good norms. This is especially true for motor development and language development. Because it is known that all children begin to crawl by eight months of age and walk by the middle of the second year, any child who was more than five or six months delayed in attaining those two milestones would probably be classified as developmentally delayed and the parents should consult the **pediatrician.**

Most children begin to speak their first words before they are eighteen months old and by three years of age the vast majority are speaking short sentences. Therefore, any child who is not speaking words or sentences by the third birthday would be considered developmentally delayed and, as in motor development delay, the parent should consult the pediatrician.

The other developmental problems that children show are more often called disabilities rather than delays. Thus, the small group of children with autism do not show normal social development but these children are usually called disabled or autistic rather than developmentally delayed. Similarly, most children are able to read single words by the second grade of elementary school. Children who cannot do that are normally labeled dyslexic or learning disabled, or in some cases academically delayed, rather than developmentally delayed.

Physical development is assessed by progress in both fine and gross motor skills. Possible problems are indicated by muscles that are either too limp or too tight. Jerky or uncertain movements are another cause for concern, as are abnormalities in reflexes. Delays in motor development may indicate the presence of a neurological condition such as mild **cerebral palsy** or **Tourette's syndrome.** Neurological problems may also be present when a child's head circumference is increasing either too fast or too slowly. Although physical and cognitive delays may occur together, one is not necessarily a sign of the other.

Important cognitive attainments that physicians look for in infants in the first 18 months include object permanence, an awareness of causality, and different reactions to strangers and family members. Cognitive delays can signal a wide variety of problems, including **fetal alcohol syndrome** and brain dysfunction. Developmental milestones achieved and then lost should also be investigated, as the loss of function could be sign of a degenerative neurological condition.

Delays in social and emotional development can be among the most difficult for parents, who feel rejected by a child's failure to respond to them on an emotional level. They expect such responses to social cues as smiling, vocalization, and cuddling, and may feel angry or frustrated when their children do not respond. However, a delay in social responses can be caused by a number of factors, including prenatal stress or deprivation, prematurity, birth difficulties, including oxygen deprivation, or a hypersensitivity of the nervous system (which creates an aversion to stimuli that are normally tolerated or welcomed).

Many physicians routinely include developmental screening in physical examinations. Parents concerned about any aspect of their child's development are generally advised to seek the opinion of a pediatrician or appropriate specialist. Specific assessment instruments such as the **Gesell Development Scales** and the **Bayley Scales of Infant Development** are used to help determine whether an infant is developing at a rate appropriate to the child's age.

For Further Study

Books

Haskell, Simon H. *The Education of Children with Motor and Neurological Disabilities.* New York: Nichols, 1989.

Sugden, David A. *Problems in Movement Skill Development.* Columbia, SC: University of South Carolina Press, 1990.

Developmental Psychology

The field of psychology that studies the ways in which people develop physically, emotionally, intellectually and socially over the course of their lives.

Developmental psychologists are concerned primarily with how the human mind/personality changes over the course of a lifetime, from its conception and intrauterine development through childhood, adolescence, adulthood, and old age. The field envelops nearly all aspects of life and seeks to understand the factors that influence personality, **intelligence,** and behavior. Initially, developmental psychologists focused primarily on childhood development, believing that with adulthood came a kind of personality stasis. One of the first to question this notion was Erik Erikson (1902–1979) in his landmark 1950 book *Eight Ages of Man,* laying out a schema whereby human personality continues to change and evolve throughout the life-cycle. It was chiefly due to Erikson's work that developmental psychology expanded its view, taking on what is referred to within the field as the lifespan approach.

Sigmund Freud (1856–1939), the first theorist to link childhood experience with adult behavior, proposed what is perhaps the most widely known but least understood theory of childhood development. He saw personality development as consisting primarily of a conflict between biology and culture; that is, between the geneti-

cally programmed needs of the infant/child and the ability or willingness of the parents to satisfy those needs. Freud laid out a blueprint of development consisting of four stages: the oral, the anal, the phallic, and latency. At each stage of development, which Freud believed occurred at varying ages, infants and children had different needs, all biologically determined. What Freud saw as significant was the degree to which those needs were either met or frustrated by the parents: extremes at either end, frustration of gratification, resulted in fixation which stunted development.

Freud's ideas were, and continue to be, highly controversial, mainly because he attributed feelings of sexuality to infants, but also because of his focus on male concepts and imagery to explain his theory. Later developmental psychologists would expand on Freud's work, or propose new schemes of development. One such theorist was the Swiss zoologist and psychologist **Jean Piaget,** who revolutionized developmental psychology with his theories of intellectual, or cognitive, development. Piaget's first contribution was to define intelligence as a process of volitional, cognitive endeavor a person undertakes to make sense of the world. He theorized that as a person passes through each of these stages she struggles to internalize or understand the novelties inherent in each stage. This process has three phases: assimilation, accommodation, and equilibrium. The stages consist of the sensorimotor (0-2 years), the pre-operational (2-7 years), the concrete operational (7-11 years), and the formal operational (11-15 years). Each stage requires the mastery of the skills and understanding of the previous stage, and not everyone reaches every stage.

Erik Erikson, as earlier noted, also contributed significantly to the field of developmental psychology. One of Erikson's main tenets was the idea of crisis: a significant moment when a person's existing understanding of himself and his place in the world becomes untenable. The identity crisis, a term Erikson coined, is the most widely known such crisis. **Erikson's theory** of development is also based on his belief that biology, or genetics, requires that humans pass through these stages. Once pushed into them, however, culture takes over and the social/family environment greatly determines the success of the crisis resolution. Erikson's stages are laid out as a series of conflicts, thus underlining his concept of crisis. These stages, which occur at varying ages, are: basic trust versus mistrust; autonomy versus shame and doubt; initiative versus guilt; industry versus inferiority; identity versus role confusion; intimacy versus isolation; generativity versus stagnation; integrity versus despair.

Another area within the field of developmental psychology which has gained interest in recent years is **moral development** as pioneered by Lawrence Kohlberg (1927–1987). In a series of investigations in which children were presented with moral dilemmas, Kohlberg found that moral reasoning develops through three distinct levels occurring between the ages of seven and adolescence. As with all the other theories discussed, the ages at which individuals arrive at the stages vary, and, like Piaget's stages, not everyone arrives at the "highest" stage of moral development. For more information, see **Kohlberg's theory of moral reasoning.**

For Further Study

Books

Anderson, Clifford. *The Stages of Life: A Groundbreaking Discovery: The Steps to Psychological Maturity.* New York: Atlantic Monthly Press, 1995.

Bee, Helen L. *Lifespan Development.* New York: HarperCollins Publishers, 1994.

Burman, Erica. *Deconstructing Developmental Psychology.* New York: Routledge, 1994.

Kail, Robert V., and John C. Cavanaugh. *Human Development.* Pacific Grove, CA: Brooks/Cole, 1996.

Gauvain, Mary, and Michael Cole. *Readings on the Development of Children.* New York: Scientific American Books, 1993.

Zigler, Edward, and Matia Finn-Stevenson. *Children in a Changing World: Development and Social Issues.* 2d ed. Pacific Grove, CA: Brooks/Cole Publishing Company, 1993.

Periodicals

Nash, J. Madeleine. "Fertile Minds," *Time,* February 3, 1997, pp. 49–56.

Developmental Quotient

The developmental norm used to express a child's physical, behavioral, and language development.

The developmental quotient is a norm used to express aspects of a child's development as measured by the **Gesell Development Schedules.** These tests were created by Arnold Gesell (1880–1961), the United States's foremost authority on child rearing in the 1940s and early 1950s. Gesell was among the first to outline standard stages of child development, which he considered to be governed more by biological than environmental factors. He envisioned both mental and physical development in infants, children, and adolescents as comparable, orderly processes, with every child passing through a sequence of predictable stages, although at varying ages.

The Gesell Development Schedules, which are still published as part of the Gesell Preschool Test produced by the Gesell Institute, were originally designed for use with children between four weeks and six years of age. They measure development in a wide range of areas—in-

cluding motor and **language development,** adaptive behavior, and personal-social behavior—both qualitatively and quantitatively. The results of the test are expressed first as developmental age (DA) and then converted into developmental quotient (DQ). A separate developmental quotient may be obtained for each area represented on the scale.

In the 1940s and 1950s, developmental quotients were widely used by educators and mental health professionals to assess children's **intelligence.** Eventually, Gesell's ideas were supplanted by theories that stressed the importance of environmental rather than biological elements in child development, notably those of Jerome Bruner (1915–) and **Jean Piaget.** The developmental quotient is no longer accepted as a valid measure of intellectual ability. However, it is still used to assess the behavioral, emotional, and physical development of children between the ages of 2 1/2 and 6. Included among the abilities assessed by the Gesell Preschool Test are eye-hand coordination, attention span, ability to understand and follow directions, visual perception, short-term memory, recognition of similar shapes, language comprehension, and gross motor skills.

For Further Study

Books

Ames, Louise Bates. *Arnold Gesell: Themes of His Work.* New York: Human Sciences Press, 1989.

Developmental Reading Disorder

A condition in which reading ability is significantly below the norm in relation to chronological age and overall intellectual potential.

Also referred to as reading disability, reading difficulty, and **dyslexia,** developmental reading disorder is the most commonly diagnosed **learning disability** in the United States. Estimates of its prevalence vary widely, ranging from 4% of children (given by the **American Psychiatric Association**'s *Diagnostic and Statistical Manual*) to 20%, the figure given by a 1995 study directed by Sally E. Shaywitz of Yale University. (According to the latter figure, some 10 million children in the United States have some form of reading disability.) Reading disabilities are diagnosed up to five times more frequently in boys than girls, although some sources claim that this figure is misleading because boys are more likely to be screened for learning disabilities due to their higher incidence of disruptive behavior, which draws the attention of educators and other professionals. Most reading disabilities were formerly grouped together under the term dyslexia, which has largely fallen out of favor with educators and psychologists because of confusion over widespread and inconsistent use of the term in both broad and narrower contexts. Developmental reading disorder is distinct from **alexia,** which is the term for reading difficulties caused by brain damage from injury or disease. However, neurological studies of alexia have helped researchers better understand reading disabilities.

Types of and causes of reading disorders

Reading disabilities have been classified as either dyseidetic, dysphonetic, or mixed. Children with the dyseidetic type are able to sound out individual letters phonetically but have trouble identifying patterns of letters when they are grouped together. Their spelling tends to be phonetic even when incorrect ("laf" for "laugh"). By comparison, dysphonic readers have difficulty relating letters to sounds, so their spelling is totally chaotic. They are able to recognize words they have memorized but cannot sound out new ones to figure out what they are. They may be able to read near the appropriate grade level but are poor spellers. Children with mixed reading disabilities have both the dyseidetic and dysphonic types of reading disorder.

Specific problems that can be involved in a reading disability include reversals and other errors involving letter position (the classic symptoms of dyslexia); bizarre spelling; omissions and additions; repetitions; failure to recognize words; hesitant oral reading; difficulty repeating or recalling polysyllabic words or sequences of letters or digits; word-by-word rather than contextual reading; and too much or too little reliance on contextual cues. In addition, children with developmental reading disorder often have a history of late speech development and generally demonstrate slowness in processing information.

A variety of causes have been advanced for developmental reading disorder. Researchers favoring a biological explanation have cited heredity, minimal brain dysfunction, delays in neurological development, and failure of the right and left hemispheres to function properly together.

Developmental reading disorder is often identified in the first grade, when reading instruction begins. Children with reading disabilities lag behind their peers in reading progress and have serious spelling problems. They also tend to have trouble writing (many have poor handwriting), have an unusually small vocabulary, and favor activities that do not require verbal skills. Also, like children with other learning disabilities, those with developmental reading disorder often earn poor grades and dislike school, reading, and homework. Even at the preschool stage, there are certain problems, such as trouble sounding out words and difficulty understanding words or concepts, that may foreshadow a reading disability.

Remedial reading techniques

Reading disabilities are diagnosed on the basis of individualized testing. Schools are required by law to provide specialized instruction for children with learning disabilities, including developmental reading disorder. The child may receive special help from his or her teacher within the regular classroom setting ("corrective reading"). Preferably, however, she will work with a reading specialist ("remedial reading"), either privately or in a small group that meets in a special classroom, generally called a resource room, reading center, or reading lab. (Reading specialists are certified in many states.) A variety of teaching methods are used; in many cases if one approach isn't successful with a particular child, the teacher will try another one. The synthetic **phonics** method, which was once the mainstay of reading instruction nationwide, is often used for remedial reading instruction. Children start by learning basic consonant and vowels sounds, first separately and then in combination (usually starting with consonants and short vowels and progressing from there to three-letter words), and vocabulary words are only introduced when all the letter sounds have already been studied. Students are taught to sound out unfamiliar words one letter or letter-group at a time based on their sounds. With the opposite approach—the whole-word or analytic method—students first acquire a basic vocabulary of words they know by sight and then study the relationships of letters and sounds by analyzing how they operate within these words. Initially a few phonetic units are taught, beginning with consonants and short vowel sounds, and the sounds are combined in a particular sequence, with tracing, writing, and spelling used as supplementary activities.

Another remedial reading technique is the kinesthetic approach (also known as the Orton-Gillingham method), in which new words are taught using a procedure nicknamed VAKT for the four senses that are involved: visual, auditory, kinesthetic, tactual. It is basically a phonetic approach that teaches individual letter sounds, then blends them into words. What is unique is the multisensory component, which involves writing each new letter, sound, or word on an oversize card and having the child trace it with her finger while pronouncing it. This activity is followed by several other steps over a period of weeks, including visualization and memorization. In contrast to the Orton-Gillingham method—which is most helpful for children with a dyseidetic reading disorder, who learn letter sounds more easily than whole words—the Fernald method uses a kinesthetic approach but emphasizes whole words. In addition to tracing, writing, and saying selected words, the child uses them in sentences and stories, keeping a collection of new words in a special file box.

The language experience, or **whole-language approach,** which has aroused controversy since its adoption in the regular reading curriculums of many schools since the 1980s, is also used for remedial reading. A whole-word approach whose main emphasis is on motivation and creativity, it attempts to get the child involved in reading by introducing words through colorful, imaginative stories. Other approaches to remedial reading include the color-coding method (which associates letters with specific colors that are then blended to create sounds) and the neuropsychological approach, which utilizes the findings of advanced brain research to devise activities targeting certain types of neurological functioning.

The outcome of treatment for reading disabilities varies, depending on the quality of the remedial program, the severity of the disorder, and the motivation and intelligence of the child. Given the proper remedial help, some children with reading disabilities have been able to successfully complete high school, college, and even graduate school, while others have been forced to limit their vocational choices to fields that do not demand strong literacy skills. Factors that have been found to contribute to the success of treatment include early intervention (elementary rather than secondary school); an IQ over 90; instruction by qualified reading specialists; and a total of over 50 hours of instruction.

For Further Study

Books

Goldsworthy, Candace L. *Developmental Reading Disorders: A Language-Based Treatment Approach.* San Diego: Singular Publishing Group, 1996.

Lipson, Marjorie Y., and Karen K. Wixson. *Assessment and Instruction of Reading Disability: An Interactive Approach.* New York: HarperCollins, 1991.

Manzo, Ula C. *Literacy Disorders: Holistic Diagnosis and Remediation.* Fort Worth: Harcourt, Brace Jovanovitch, 1993.

Organizations

The Learning Disabilities Association of America
Address: 4156 Library Rd.
Pittsburgh, PA 15234
Telephone: (412) 341-1515

Dyslexia Research Foundation
Address: 600 Northern Boulevard
Great Neck, NY 11021
Telephone: (516) 482-2888

Nation Center for Learning Disabilities, Inc. (NCLD)
Address: 99 Park Ave., 6th Floor
New York, NY 10016
Telephone: (212) 687-7211

Orton Dyslexia Society
Address: 8600 LaSalle Road
Chester Building, Suite 382
Baltimore, MD 21286–2044
Telephone: (410) 296-0232; toll-free information line: (800) ABC–D123

Developmental Test of Visual Perception *see* Frostig Developmental Test

Diabetes Mellitus

A serious disorder caused by an absence of or insufficient amount of insulin in the bloodstream.

Insulin is a hormone produced by the pancreas in varying amounts, depending on the concentration of glucose (sugar). When the pancreas is unable to secrete enough insulin to maintain a normal concentration of glucose in the blood, the blood-glucose concentration becomes elevated. Large amounts of glucose are then excreted in the urine. Insulin allows glucose to be absorbed by the liver and fat cells, where it is stored as glycogen. In times of stress, exercise, or an emergency, the glycogen is reconverted back to glucose. It also sends glucose to the muscle cells where it is then converted to energy.

More than 12 million Americans are affected by diabetes. There is a 5–6% increase in the number of those affected each year by the disease, primarily due to the population's increased rate of longevity. A rising rate of obesity, a prime cause for incidences of diabetes over the age of 40, also contributes to the increasing frequency of diabetes. It is estimated that for each reported new case of diabetes, there is an unreported one because symptoms of the early stages of adult diabetes tend to go unrecognized. Symptoms usually progress from mild to severe as the disease progresses.

Approximately 300,000 deaths each year are attributed to diabetes. Its prevalence increases with age, from about 0.2% in persons under 17 years of age to about 10% in persons aged 65 years and over. Females have a higher rate of incidence for the disease, while higher income groups in the United States show a lesser incidence than lower income groups. The incident rate is markedly different among ethnic groups; it is 20% higher in non-Caucasians than in Caucasians. However, for reasons as yet unknown, the rate of diabetes in ethnic groups such as Native Americans, Latin Americans, and Asian Americans is especially high and continues to rise.

There are two forms of diabetes mellitus. Type I is called insulin-dependent and type II, non-insulin-dependent. (In June 1997, an Expert Committee of the American Diabetes Association recommended changing the categories of diabetes to Type 1 [formerly Type I-insulin-dependent diabetes mellitus] and Type 2 [formerly Type II-non-insulin-dependent diabetes mellitus]. This essay uses the conventional terminology, which was widely used at the time of publication.)

Insulin-dependent diabetes (type I) generally starts in childhood, affects approximately 700,000 Americans, and is characterized by severe insulin deficiency. It is probably due to the destruction of the insulin-secreting cells of the pancreas, which is often caused by an autoimmune disorder. Without insulin, the person develops ketoacidosis, a condition where high levels of ketone bodies are present in the blood. When the body is deprived of glucose, which can occur as a result of insulin deprivation or fasting, the body begins to break down fat for fuel. Ketones are the result of this lipid metabolism. The resulting lowered blood pH value leads to the acidosis.

Ketoacidosis is a serious condition and can lead to confusion, unconsciousness, and death if not treated. It can be diagnosed by urine tests which detect ketones in the urine. Untreated or uncontrolled diabetes will lead to ketosis, but fasting or starvation also produces ketones. Other symptoms of ketoacidosis include vomiting, abdominal pain, loss of appetite, and nausea. A very high blood glucose level in insulin-dependent diabetes can also lead to heart failure and coma.

Genetics plays a major role in Type I diabetes. There is also some evidence that children infected with certain viruses—rubella and coxsackie B in particular—may be susceptible to the disease. Diabetes in newborns can result from low birth weight as well as genetic predisposition. Some infants experience temporary diabetes, which may recur later in life.

Non-insulin-dependent diabetes (type II) usually occurs in people over age 40, and affects approximately 15.3 million Americans. This group comprises about 80% to 85% of the diabetic population. Even though they may have more than normal levels of insulin, they are resistant to its action. Unlike those with type I diabetes, people with type II diabetes rarely have ketoacidosis. Instead, insulin action can be impaired by obesity. Therefore, people who gain too much weight and ethnic groups that have changed to higher carbohydrate diets appear to be particularly prone to type II diabetes.

Pregnancy can also elevate a woman's glucose level. This condition is known as gestational diabetes and complicates approximately four percent of all U.S. pregnancies. Although their glucose levels may return to normal after they give birth, these woman may be at risk of developing type II diabetes in the future.

For those people who are in a high risk group for getting diabetes (those who have had relatives with diabetes, adults over the age of 40 who are overweight, and women who have had babies weighing nine pounds or more at birth), there is a quick and simple screening test that requires a drop of blood from the finger and takes about one to two minutes to complete. The test shows if there is a high or low blood-sugar level in the blood. After the results of the screening test, other tests can be done, if necessary. If the screening test shows blood-sugar levels that are either too high or too low, a fasting plasma glucose test can be given. One or more samples of blood are taken after the individual fasts for 10 to 16 hours. Blood-glucose levels of less than 115 milligrams per decaliter (mg/dl) are normal. Fasting plasma glucose levels of more than 140 mg/dl indicate diabetes. The oral glucose tolerance test also starts with a fast but adds a glucose drink taken after the fasting plasma glucose is tested. It is followed by several other tests to determine blood glucose levels. There are other tests used to monitor the condition, including self-tests. The presence of circulating islet antibodies is a good predictor of insulin-dependent diabetes. Research is being done on genetic tests to predict the risk of developing diabetes.

Deaths from ketoacidosis and diabetic coma have decreased over the years. However, long-term complications from diabetes began to increase as diabetics' life span increased. Some of these complications are kidney failure, heart disease, blindness, and nervous system disorders, all of which are believed to be the results of elevated blood-glucose levels. Today, glucose levels are controlled by injecting a rapidly absorbed insulin just before each meal. Added to this dosage, the slowly absorbed insulin can then be injected or pumped in by a prosthetic implant device between meals to maintain low insulin concentrations. The amounts required are determined by frequent blood-glucose measurements.

For overweight, non-insulin-dependent diabetics, controlling diet, avoiding foods high in sugar and carbohydrates, and encouraging weight loss may be sufficient treatment. A regular program of physical exercise is also recommended as an important part of diabetes treatment. Exercise utilizes surplus blood glucose and helps a person to both lose and maintain weight. In addition, non-insulin-dependent-type oral drugs may stimulate the pancreas to secrete additional insulin. It may be necessary to give injections of insulin.

Diabetes can be particularly difficult to manage during **adolescence,** when elevated levels of certain growth hormones make controlling blood glucose levels difficult. In addition, adolescents sometimes resist the dietary restrictions and close monitoring necessary to maintain good health. The most serious problem diabetic children face is **hypoglycemia,** or low blood glucose. Common symptoms in young children include misbehavior and irritability, although symptoms can vary from episode to episode. Hypoglycemia is easily treated by eating a sweet food. Parents are advised to inform teachers about symptoms and to enlist their help in maintaining the routines necessary to manage diabetes, including frequent testing of blood glucose levels, eating snacks before exercise, careful diet, and close monitoring of insulin dosage.

A relatively new treatment for type II diabetes is the drug Glucophage (generic name: metformin). Glucophage affects how the body handles its own insulin, increasing its effectiveness. With only a few side effects (diarrhea, nausea, bloating) that fade after the body adjusts to the medication, Glucophage offers an alternative to those who don't respond to changes in diet and exercise.

For Further Study

Books

Davidson, Mayer B. *Diabetes Mellitus: Diagnosis and Treatment.* New York: Churchill Livingstone, 1991.

Gordon, Neil F. *Diabetes: Your Exercise Guide.* Dallas: Human Kinetics, 1993.

Periodicals

Anstett, Patricia. "Newly Approved Drug Controls Most Common Type of Diabetes." *Detroit Free Press,* May 5, 1995, pp. 1A-2A.

Clements, G.B. "Coxsackie B Virus Infection and Onset of Childhood Diabetes." *The Lancet* 346, July 22, 1995, p. 221.

"Insulin Resistance in Puberty." *The Lancet* 337, May 25, 1991, p. 1259.

"The Last Word on Childhood Diabetes." *Diabetes Forecast* 49, March 1996, p. 43.

U.S. House of Representatives. "Diabetes Mellitus: An unrelenting Threat to the Health of Minorities." 102nd Congress, April 16, 1992. Report on hearings before the select committee on aging.

Organizations

American Diabetes Association
Address: 1660 Duke Street
Alexandria, VA 22314
website: www.diabetes.org

Diagnostic and Statistical Manual of Mental Disorders (DSM-IV)

A reference work developed by the American Psychiatric Association and designed to provide guidelines for the diagnosis and classification of mental disorders.

The American Psychiatric Association publishes the *Diagnostic and Statistical Manual of Mental Disorders,* widely referred to as *DSM-IV,* a reference work designed to provide guidelines for psychologists and others to use in the diagnosis and classification of mental disorders.

The latest edition, *DSM-IV,* serves as a reference to psychiatrists, other physicians and mental health professionals, psychologists, social workers, and others in clinical, educational, and social service settings.

First published in 1917, each new edition of *Diagnostic and Statistical Manual of Mental Disorders* has added new categories. With the third edition, published in 1980, the *DSM* began recommending assessment of mental disorders according to five axes, or dimensions, that together establish an overall picture of a person's mental, emotional, and physical health, providing as complete a context as possible in which to make a proper diagnosis. The diagnostician evaluates the patient according to criteria for each axis to produce a comprehensive assessment of the patient's condition; the multiaxial system addresses the complex nature of more mental disorders.

Axis I lists 14 major clinical syndromes. These include disorders usually first diagnosed in childhood or **adolescence** (hyperactivity, **mental retardation, autism**); dementia, amnesia, and other cognitive disorders; substance-related disorders; **schizophrenia** and other conditions characterized by abnormalities in thinking, perception, and emotion; and sexual and gender identity disorders. Also listed in Axis I are mood, **anxiety,** somatoform, dissociative, eating, **sleep,** impulse control, and **adjustment disorders**, as well as factitious (false) disorders.

Axis II is for assessment of personality disorders—lifelong, deeply ingrained patterns of behavior that are destructive to those who display them or to others. Some examples are narcissistic, dependent, avoidant, and antisocial personality types. This axis also includes developmental disorders in children.

Axis III considers any organic medical problems that may be present. The fourth axis includes any environmental or psychosocial factors affecting a person's condition (such as the loss of a loved one, sexual abuse, **divorce,** career changes, poverty, or homelessness).

In Axis V, the diagnostician assesses the person's level of functioning within the previous 12 months on a scale of 1 to 100.

One notable feature of *DSM-IV* is that it dispenses with two previously ubiquitous terms in the field of psychology—"neurosis" and "psychosis"—because they are now considered too vague. The term "neurosis" was generally used for a variety of conditions that involved some form of anxiety, whereas "psychosis" referred to conditions in which the patient had lost the ability to function normally in daily life and/or had lost touch with reality. Conditions that would formerly have been described as neurotic are now found in five Axis I classifications: mood disorders, anxiety disorders, somatoform disorders, **dissociative identity disorders,** and sexual disor-

DSM-IV CLASSIFICATION SYSTEM	
Axis	Disorders covered
Axis I	Clinical Disorders: Includes disorders usually diagnosed in childhood
Axis II	Personality Disorders and Mental Retardation
Axis III	General Medical Conditions
Axis IV	Psychosocial and Environmental Problems

ders. Conditions formerly referred to as psychotic are now found in Axis I as well. Besides diagnostic criteria, the *DSM-IV* also provides information about mental and emotional disorders, covering areas such as probable cause, average age at onset, possible complications, amount of impairment, prevalence, gender ratio, predisposing factors, and family patterns.

DSM-IV contains the results of a comprehensive and systematic review of relevant published literature, including earlier editions of *DSM*. In cases where the evidence of a literature review was found to be insufficient to resolve a particular question, data sets were reanalyzed and issue-focused field trials were conducted. These literature reviews, data reanalyses, and field trials that form the basis of *DSM-IV* have been fully documented, condensed, and published separately as a reference record in a five volume set entitled *DSM-IV Sourcebook*. The *DSM-IV Sourcebook* also contains executive summaries of the rationales for the final decisions relative to inclusion in *DSM-IV*.

For Further Study

Books

Diagnostic and Statistical Manual of Mental Disorders, 4th edition. Washington, DC: American Psychiatric Association, 1994.

DSM-IV Sourcebook. Washington, DC: American Psychiatric Association, 1994. In five volumes, contains documentation of all work leading to criteria published in *DSM-IV*, and includes executive summaries of the rationales for final decisions made in compiling the work.

. . . .

▌ Diaper Rash

A non-contagious irritation of an infant's buttocks, upper thighs, and genitals caused by soiled diapers.

Diaper rash is a localized outbreak of rash, redness, and inflammation caused by contact with urine, feces, and bacteria. Diaper rash can be triggered by prolonged exposure of skin to wetness from urine or loose stools, and is most common in the first few weeks following birth. This skin disorder is characterized by an irritation of the skin covered by the diaper, especially the buttocks, upper thighs, and genitals.

The area of skin covered by the diaper remains constantly warm and damp, creating an environment where irritation from urine and feces can lead to inflammation. Leaving the baby's skin exposed to air for an extended period of time during each diaper change will help minimize the risk of skin irritation. There does not seem to be any correlation between the use of either cloth or disposable diapers and the development of diaper rash.

Treatment requires keeping the area dry and exposed to air as much as possible. For at least one hour each day, the infant should be allowed to rest without a diaper. To absorb urine, the infant can be placed on several layers of diaper or toweling. Ointments such as zinc oxide or other diaper rash creams will provide protection from irritation, and should be applied to affected areas at every diaper change. In cases where diaper rash is persistent, the baby's skin may be sensitive to materials in the diaper. Switching from cloth to disposables, or vice versa, may solve the problem.

To prevent diaper rash, the following steps can be taken:

- Change diapers frequently.

- Allow the baby to remain naked, with the diaper area exposed to air, for as long as possible during each diaper change.

- Rinse the skin in the diaper area with clear water at each diaper change.

- Wash hands thoroughly before and after every diaper change to avoid spread of bacteria.

- If using cloth diapers, rinse diaper thoroughly before laundering, and put the diapers through an extra rinse cycle when laundering.

If diaper rash persists with no improvement for more than a week, a pediatrician should be consulted.

For Further Study

Books

Gewirtzman, Garry. *Smooth as a Baby's Bottom: A Dermatologist's Complete Guide to Your Child's Skin.* Hollywood, FL: Frederick Fell, 1988.

Periodicals

Brown, Carol Deasy. "In the Red." *Parenting* 8, March 1994, p. 106.

Eden, Alvin N. "Diaper Rash." *American Baby 57,* August 1995, p. 12+.

Locker, Hilary. "Caring for Your Baby's Skin." *American Baby* 58, June 1996, p. 52+.

Stern, Loraine. "Caring for Children's Skin." *Woman's Day* 57, April 26, 1994, p. 34.

Diarrhea

An increase in the frequency and/or fluidity of bowel movements.

Children in the United States average one or two bouts of diarrhea a year. The primary danger associated with diarrhea is dehydration from the excess fluid lost through bowel movements, especially if the diarrhea is accompanied by fever and /or vomiting. Diarrhea-inducing diseases such as cholera are associated with the deaths of 4 million children in developing countries every year. Although the problem is much less severe in industrialized countries such as the United States, it is estimated that 500 children die annually as a result of diarrhea, mostly in low-income, single-parent, African American families. Diarrhea has a wide variety of causes, including bacterial and parasitic infections, viruses, inflammatory bowel disease, reactions to medications, congenital defects, food poisoning, **allergies,** malabsorptive conditions, and stress. It occurs in both chronic and acute forms and may be accompanied by vomiting, stomachaches, and abdominal cramps. A physician should be contacted if a child shows signs of dehydration, which include dry mucus membranes, decreased urination, dry lips, and a decrease in or absence of tears. Diarrhea is a special concern in very young infants, in whom it can cause both dehydration and acidosis (a drop in the alkaline content of the blood and body tissues) within hours.

Acute diarrhea

The primary cause of acute diarrhea in older infants and children is infectious gastroenteritis or stomach flu, usually caused by a virus. This condition usually lasts only a few days, although a small percentage of children develop lactose intolerance for several weeks. In a small percentage of cases, gastroenteritis is caused by bacterial infections, including shigella, campylobacter, yersinia, and pathogenic *E. coli.* Bacterial gastroenteritis generally produces more severe symptoms than viral infection, including more frequent and bloody stools and severe cramping. Bacterial gastroenteritis also lasts longer. Diarrhea may persist for up to a week, as opposed to two to three days for viral infections. Bacterial gastroenteritis is associated with food poisoning caused by foods contaminated with a bacterium such as staphylococcus aureus. Food poisoning causes intense but short-lived symptoms which usually end within 12–24 hours.

Other causes of acute diarrhea in children include overeating, reactions to antibiotics, laxatives, toxins, carbohydrate intolerance, and inflammatory bowel disease.

The protein in milk can cause an autoimmune reaction, or allergy, in some infants, resulting in acute diarrhea. Other symptoms of this disorder include bloody stool, vomiting, appetite loss, irritability, and excessive crying. Allergies to the proteins contained in cow's milk, goat's milk, or soy milk initially resemble infectious gastroenteritis, for which it is frequently mistaken. Diagnosis is confirmed when symptoms respond to a formula that does not contain the offending protein. Most babies outgrow milk protein allergy by the time they are one year old.

Chronic diarrhea

Diarrhea sometimes persists over an extended period of time, with the child having several loose stools every day. It is not uncommon for infants and children between the ages of six months and three years to have chronic diarrhea for which no apparent medical cause can be found. This condition, which some equate with irritable bowel syndrome in older children and adults, is known as nonspecific diarrhea of infancy and childhood. The gastroinestinal tract of a child suffering from this condition appears to continue functioning normally in spite of the loose stools. As long as medical causes are ruled out by a physician and the child continues to thrive, this type of diarrhea is not considered dangerous to a child's health.

Chronic diarrhea may also be caused by malabsorptive conditions, which interfere with the normal digestive function of the intestines and threaten the child's health, primarily through various manifestations of malnutrition. These conditions include celiac disease, in which the intestinal lining is damaged by foods containing the protein gluten; **cystic fibrosis,** in which the absorption problem is caused by a lack of digestive enzymes normally produced by the pancreas; secondary lactose intolerance; and disaccharidase deficiency, which prevents the digestion of some sugars. Another cause of chronic diarrhea is multiplication of the bacterium *Clostridium difficile* when a child is taking antibiotics. This bacterium, which is usually present in small amounts, can produce a toxin that damages the lining of the colon and causes mild to severe diarrhea. Fortunately, *Clostridium difficile* can itself be eradicated by various antibiotics, including Vancomycin, metronidazole, and bacitracin. Infection by the parasite *Giardia lamblia* is another cause of chronic diarrhea.

Ulcerative colitis and Crohn's disease—together known as inflammatory bowel disease (IBD)—also cause chronic diarrhea. In ulcerative colitis, inflammation of the mucosal lining of the colon prevents proper absorption of water, causing diarrhea, abdominal pain, and often blood in the stool. Other symptoms include loss of appetite and weight loss. Crohn's disease is an inflammatory disorder that can involve any portion of the gastrointestinal tract. When it affects the colon, it produces symptoms similar to those of ulcerative colitis.

Treatment

The most significant modern advance in the treatment of dehydration from diarrhea is oral rehydration therapy (ORT). The therapy is a fluid containing water, carbohydrates, and a combination of mineral salts that restore the body's electrolyte balance, which is necessary for the proper functioning of many organs and becomes disturbed by a loss of fluids. This treatment, first developed in the 1950s to combat the devastating effects of diarrhea in developing nations, is recommended by the **American Academy of Pediatrics** (AAP), to rehydrate children who have significant fluid loss and as a preventative measure when there are no signs of dehydration. Fluids for ORT are available in various brands, such as Pedialyte, Naturalyte, and Rehydralyte, all regulated by the Food and Drug Administration (FDA) as medical foods.

AMERICAN ACADEMY OF PEDIATRICS (AAP) GUIDELINES FOR REHYDRATION TO TREAT DIARRHEA

- Diarrhea with no dehydration: Normal food intake and supplemental rehydration fluids administered at home within four to six hours of each episode of diarrhea. If the problem persists, call a doctor.

- Diarrhea with mild dehydration: See a physician. Administration of oral rehydration fluids at the doctor's office, repeated at home.

- Diarrhea with moderate or severe dehydration: Treatment at a health care facility. Oral rehydration for moderate cases, intravenous fluids for severe cases.

In addition to the use of rehydration fluids, current AAP guidelines for the treatment of diarrhea caused by gastroenteritis, or stomach flu, differ in other ways from the traditional "starve a fever" school of treatment still practiced by many pediatricians. The AAP rejects the time-honored practice of withholding solid food for 24 to 48 hours because it has been found that food can actually reduce diarrhea by helping the intestine absorb water. The current guidelines advocate eating as soon as possible (no later than 6 hours) after each bout of diarrhea. Also recommended is the ingestion of a normal, balanced variety of foods as opposed to the traditional low-fiber

diet once favored for use in treating intestinal problems. (The best-known variant for children was commonly called the BRAT diet—bananas, rice, applesauce, and toast.) Still recommended, however, is avoidance of foods high in sugar or salt, and of milk for the first day or two. Many doctors caution against taking over-the-counter diarrhea medication, which can prolong the illness that is causing the diarrhea by slowing down the purgation process and giving bacteria or viruses more time to grow.

A 1991 study published in the *Journal of the American Medical Association* found that some families do not use oral rehydration fluids because they find the cost prohibitive. Name brands cost as much as $6 per liter. However, it is possible to purchase generic brands for as little as $2 per liter. It is important to remember that ORT does not treat the intestinal disorder itself—it merely prevents the occurrence of dehydration as the illness runs it course. In cases where diarrhea is accompanied by frequent vomiting, the child may be unable to keep enough of the ORT fluid down for it to be effective, and intravenous rehydration may become necessary.

For Further Study

Books

Janowitz, Henry D. *Your Gut Feelings: A Complete Guide to Living Better with Intestinal Problems.* New York: Oxford University Press, 1994.

Patel, Nalin M. *The Doctor's Guide to Your Digestive System.* Champaign, IL: N.M.P. Publishing, 1988.

Phillips, Sidney F. *Diarrhea: Infectious and Other Causes.* Washington, D.C.: National Digestive Diseases Information Clearinghouse, U.S. Dept. of Health and Human Services, 1995.

Scala, James. *Eating Right for a Bad Gut: The Complete Nutritional Guide to Ileitis, Colitis, Crohn's Disease, and Inflammatory Bowel Disease.* New York: Plume, 1992.

Organizations

Crohn's Colitis Foundation of America, Inc.
Address: 444 Park Avenue South
New York, NY 10016
Telephone: (212) 685-3440

National Digestive Diseases Information Clearinghouse
Address: Box NDDIC
9000 Rockville Pike
Bethesda, MD 20892
Telephone: (301) 468-6344

American Academy of Pediatrics
Address: 141 Northwest Point Boulevard
Elk Grove Village, IL 60007
Telephone: toll-free (800) 433-9016; (708) 228-5005

Diet *see* **Nutrition**

Digestive Disorders

Disorders that affect one or more of the organs and glands that make up the digestive system.

The digestive system consists of organs—the mouth, esophagus, stomach, and small and large intestines—and glands—salivary glands, liver, gall bladder, and pancreas. The glands secrete digestive juices containing enzymes that chemically break down food into smaller, more absorbable molecules. In addition to providing the body with the nutrients and energy it needs to function, the digestive system also separates and disposes of waste products ingested with the food.

Digestive disorders in infancy

Congenital defects

Malformation of any one of the digestive organs can disrupt digestive functions. Surgery is required to correct most of these conditions. The intake of food can be disrupted by orofacial clefts, commonly known as **cleft lip** or **palate.** This condition is usually corrected by surgery within the first three months following birth, and may be corrected within the first days after birth. Infants with cleft lip or palate may have difficulty feeding because they are unable to suck efficiently enough to nurse or bottle feed. Special bottles that direct the flow of formula to the back of the mouth are used in these cases.

Another congenital disorder, an abnormal closure in an opening of one of the digestive system organs called atresia, requires surgery as soon as possible after birth to allow normal function of the digestive system. Abnormal closures may also affect the intestines. An imperforate anus is completely closed off, and surgery to create an opening is required immediately after birth.

Abnormal narrowing of a digestive system passageway, stenosis, typically affects the stomach or intestines. In pyloric stenosis, the pyloric sphincter between the stomach and small intestine is too small to allow food to pass through it. A symptom of pyloric stenosis is projectile vomiting following every feeding, usually within 15 to 30 minutes. Most infants with pyloric stenosis begin to exhibit projectile vomiting sometime between two weeks and four months. The **vomiting** may develop gradually while the parents and pediatrician try various strategies for relieving a newborn's "spitting up." Pyloric stenosis may occur as often as one in every 250 births, and is most common in male, white, first-born babies. Like most narrowing or closures of digestive system organs, pyloric stenosis is serious and must be corrected with surgery. Similarly, in anal stenosis, the anus is too small to allow the passage of fecal material.

Infants with chronic vomiting may also have a condition that results when the esophogeal sphincter, the valve between the esophagus and stomach, allows the stomach contents to flow back into the esophagus. This problem, usually outgrown within the first year, can be alleviated by burping the infant frequently and by leaving the infant in an upright or semi-upright position for at least 30 minutes following a feeding. For bottlefed babies, thickening the formula with baby cereal may help.

Digestive disorders in toddler, preschool, and school years

After the first few months of life, the most common causes of digestive disorders are infections caused by a virus or, less commonly, bacteria or parasites. An intestinal infection, referred to as gastroenteritis, is spread by unsanitary water or food supplies. A pediatrician should be consulted when a young child experiencing abdominal pain exhibits any of these warning signs: vomits blood or greenish bile; exhibits strenuous or repeated vomiting, or vomiting that lasts more than 24 hours; complains of harsh abdominal pain or has a swollen abdomen; exhibits symptoms of dehydration, such as decreased or lack of urination; is unable to take fluids; or seizure.

When an infant or young child is vomiting, it is important to keep his head turned to the side or face down over a basin or towel to minimize the possibility that the vomitus (material being vomited) be inhaled into the lungs. A key concern whenever a young child is vomiting and unable to keep anything in her stomach is dehydration. About one to two hours after the last vomiting episode, offer the child a few sips of cool water. Follow this every half hour with a few sips of water or other clear liquid such as sugar water or gelatin water (one-half to one teaspoon of sugar or flavored gelatin in about four ounces of water). There are also commercial electrolyte solutions that your pediatrician may prescribe to counteract the potential for dehydration during a bout with vomiting. Gradually return the child to a normal diet over the next 24 hours, while continuing to encourage his intake of fluids. If your child is unable to keep fluids down, and continues to vomit for more than 24 hours, notify your pediatrician. He may order diagnostic blood, urine, and other tests. In rare instances, a hospital stay may be required.

After age five, emotional upset—either distress or excitement—sometimes triggers abdominal pain and even vomiting. If your child exhibits recurring abdominal pain and vomiting accompanied by change in behavior, emotional triggers for the digestive problems should be considered. Your pediatrician, your child's teacher, or a child psychologist can help diagnose the root of the emotional upset.

Inguinal hernia

Inguinal hernia, present in 5% of all children and more commonly in boys than girls, occurs when an open-

NORMAL FUNCTION OF THE DIGESTIVE SYSTEM

Food is taken into the mouth where the teeth break it down into smaller pieces. The tongue rolls these pieces into balls (boluses). The sensations of sight, taste, and smell cause the salivary glands, located in the mouth, to produce saliva which then pours into the mouth to soften the food. Amylase, a type of enzyme in the saliva, begins the breakdown of carbohydrates (starch) into simple sugars. Ptyalin, one of the main amylase enzymes found in the mouth, is also secreted by the pancreas.

The moistened and partially digested food is maneuvered to the back of the mouth (pharynx) by the tongue, where it is then swallowed. In the throat, rings of muscles force the food into the esophagus, which moves the food from the throat to the upper part of the stomach with wavelike muscular contractions. Known as peristalsis, this muscle action consists of the alternate contraction and relaxation of the smooth muscles of the esophagus. At the junction of the esophagus and stomach, the powerful esophageal sphincter muscle acts as a valve to keep food, stomach acids, and bile from flowing back into the esophagus and mouth.

Digestion in the stomach

Chemical digestion begins in the stomach, where food is broken down by the action of gastric juice containing hydrochloric acid and a protein-digesting enzyme called pepsin. The stomach lining also secretes mucus to protect itself from being irritated by the gastric juices. The gastric juices break the food into smaller molecules, which, in turn, stimulate the stomach lining to release the hormone gastrin into the bloodstream.

Stomach muscles churn the food into a fine semi-liquid paste called chyme. The pyloric sphincter between the stomach and the duodenum (the first section of the small intestine) controls the flow of chyme from the stomach.

The small intestine or small bowel is a long, narrow tube about 20 ft (6 m) long. Coiled and twisted between the stomach and the large intestine, the small intestine's lining, the mucosa, contains millions of glands that aid in the digestive and absorptive processes. Muscle action moves the chyme toward the large intestine through the three sections of the small intestine—the duodenum, the jejunum, and the ileum. Upon entering the duodenum, chyme undergoes further enzymatic digestion and is subjected to pancreatic juice, intestinal juice, and bile. There are three enzymes in pancreatic juice which digest carbohydrates, fats, and proteins. The gall bladder secretes bile containing bile salts and other substances that help to emulsify (dissolve) fats which are otherwise insoluble in water.

Chyme passing from the duodenum next reaches the 3-ft (1-m) jejunum of the small intestine, where the digested breakdown products of carbohydrates, fats, proteins, and most of the vitamins, minerals, and iron are absorbed. The inner lining of the small intestine is composed of up to five million tiny, finger-like projections called villi. The villi increase the rate of absorption of the nutrients into the bloodstream by extending the surface of the small intestine to about five times that of the surface area of the skin. The last section of the small intestine is the ileum.

Absorption and elimination in the large intestine

The large intestine, or colon, is wider and heavier then the small intestine, but much shorter—only about 4 ft (1.2 m) long. It rises up on one side of the body (the ascending colon), crosses over to the other side (the transverse colon), descends (the descending colon), forms an S-shape (the sigmoid colon), reaches the muscular rectum, about 5 in (13 cm) long, where the feces is expelled through the anus, which has a large muscular sphincter that controls the passage of waste matter. Fecal matter contains undigested food, bacteria, and cells from the walls of the digestive tract.

Gallbladder

The gallbladder lies under the liver and is connected by various ducts to the liver and the duodenum. Its main function is to store bile until it is concentrated enough to be used by the small intestine. Bile contains cholesterol dissolved in the bile acids.

Pancreas

The pancreas, in its digestion function, secretes pancreatic juices when food reaches the small intestine. In its endocrine function, a group of cells within the pancreas secrete the hormone insulin. Insulin targets liver and muscle cells, and allows them to take excess sugar from the blood and store it in the form of glycogen.

ing in the lower abdominal wall allows the child's intestine to squeeze through. Most hernias are not painful, and they are discovered when the child, parent, or pediatrician notices a bulge in the groin area. A hernia develops when the large sac that surrounds the abdominal organs, known as the peritoneum, does not close properly prior to birth. Openings in the peritoneum can allow small section of the intestine to push through into the groin (in boys or girls) or the scrotum (in boys).

In a small percentage of hernias, the section of intestine becomes trapped, causing a condition known as incarcerated hernia. When there is tenderness or swelling associated with a hernia, it may be incarcerated. All hernias require medical attention, but the presence of pain or swelling make it urgent that you seek treatment.

Digestive disorders in adolescence

Eating disorders, such as **anorexia nervosa** and **bulimia,** affect mostly young women in adolescence. Not digestive disorders per se, eating disorders can contribute to physical problems centerd in the digestive system.

Stomach ulcers are sores that form in the lining of the stomach. Ulcers are rare in children and uncommon in adolescents. People who are at most risk for ulcers are those who smoke, middle-age and older men, chronic users of alcohol, and those who take anti-inflammatory drugs, such as aspirin and ibuprofen.

For Further Study

Books

Maryon-Davis, Alan and Steven Parker. *Food and Digestion.* New York: F. Watts, 1990.

Peikin, Steven R. *Gastrointestinal Health.* New York: Harper-Collins, 1991.

Thompson, W. Grant. *The Angry Gut: Coping with Colitis and Crohn's Disease.* New York: Plenum Press, 1993.

Audiovisual Recordings

Gut Feelings: Health Talks at the Cleveland Clinic. Cleveland, OH: Cleveland Clinic Foundation, 1996.
(Two-hour video on digestive disorders.)

Organizations

American Digestive Disease Society
Address: 7720 Wisconsin Avenue, NW
Bethesday, MD 20814
Telephone: (301) 223-0179
(Organization for people with digestive diseases. Provides information and referral; offers counseling; publications include *Living Healthy,* a magazine; booklets and books on special diets to manage various digestive disorders.)

See also **Appendicitis; Bowel Disorders; Colic; Constipation; Diarrhea; Eating Disorders; Encopre-** sis; Kidney Function and Urological Disorders; Liver Development and Function

Diphtheria

An acute bacterial infection characterized by the formation of a gray or yellowish-white membrane over the throat and nasal passages.

Diptheria can affect any of the body's mucus membranes, causing swelling of the neck and inflammation of the heart and nervous system, and certain strains can result in widespread organ damage. Diphtheria is also a possible cause of croup, an inflammation of the membranes lining the trachea, larynx, or bronchial tubes. The disease usually strikes children between the ages of one and 10. Symptoms include low-grade fever, headache, sore throat, general malaise, and, in some cases, swollen lymph nodes in the neck. Diphtheria is rare in Western industrialized nations, where most children are vaccinated against it. In the United States, diphtheria **immunization** is part of the DPT vaccine, which also protects against pertussis and tetanus. It is administered to children at the ages of two, four, and six months, again between 15 and 18 months, and one last time at age four to six. Adult booster shots are recommended every 10 years.

While there are few chances for a child to contract diphtheria in the United States, children who travel to other countries with their parents can still be exposed to the disease. It is highly contagious and can be spread by coughing, sneezing, talking, or through the expelled breath of an infected person. The bacteria that cause diphtheria, *Corynebacterium diphtheriae,* incubate for one to six days after exposure, after which symptoms gradually appear. The disease is treated with **antibiotics** and antitoxins. Although the risk of contagion is eliminated almost immediately following the beginning of treatment, full recovery takes longer, requiring bed rest and sometimes hospitalization. Diphtheria can be fatal, so prompt diagnosis and treatment are essential. When antitoxins are administered within three days of the onset of illness, full recovery is probable.

For Further Study

Books

Bennett, Claire L. *Communicable Diseases Handbook.* New York: Wiley, 1982.

Organizations

National Institute of Allergy and Infectious Diseases (NIAID)
Address: 9000 Rockville Pike
NIH Building 31, Room 7A50
Bethesday, MD 20892-2520

Telephone: (301)496-5717
(Arm of the National Institutes of Health that deals with allergies and diseases.)

Discipline

Actions or methods used to achieve controlled behavior.

Discipline used as a noun means orderly, controlled behavior. The verb "to discipline" means different things to different people. Most definitions of "to discipline" fall into two general camps: 1) to control, punish, and correct; or 2) to teach, guide, and influence. The majority of studies today show that the second definition is more effective in producing the desired behavior.

The word discipline is often used as a synonym for **punishment,** but this is incorrect. Discipline is a system of actions or interactions intended to create orderly behavior. There are a variety of disciplinary systems which show varying degrees of success. Some disciplinary systems use punishment as a tool; others shun punishment, believing it is at best ineffective, at worst destructive (or counterproductive).

Punitive systems have been the norm in the West for centuries. Judaeo-Christian religion has traditionally been seen to promote authoritarian parenting: "Spare the rod, spoil the child" is an oft-quoted pseudo-Biblical injunction (the only actual words similar to this in the Bible are "He who spares the rod hates his son, but he who loves him is diligent to discipline him"—Proverbs 13:24, Revised Standard Version). Some conservative Christians and Jews continue to hold to this style of discipline in the belief that punishment is the only way to teach children proper submission and obedience to parents, other adults, and ultimately God.

Other systems of discipline reject harsh, physical violence. Practices of "logical consequences" and "**time-out**" are two well-known examples. Both are behavior modification techniques that are used to train a child to behave in socially, or parentally, acceptable ways. Rewards and punishments are used to control a child's actions. This can be effective in modifying external behaviors, but it does little to change underlying motivations or attitudes. In fact, attempts to control a child actually prevent any lasting influence from occurring. Children instead simply rebel against the imposed limitations, resist authority, and resort to **lying,** evasion, or manipulation to get their needs and desires met.

Harshly punitive measures of discipline have been shown to create anxiety, fear, anger, hatred, apathy, **depression,** obsessiveness, paranoia, sadomasochism, domestic violence, **aggression,** crime, and apocalyptic religious views, none of which promotes stable, orderly,

socially creative behavior. When children are punished harshly, they remember only the pain and humiliation of the punishment, not the reason for the discipline. They lose trust in their parent(s) and become less likely to accept their authority in the future. Physically violent discipline actually promotes further violence by teaching a child that force is a means to gain control, and that violence is acceptable in "loving" relationships. Perhaps the biggest problem with punitive systems of discipline, whether violent or nonviolent, is that eventually the parent runs out of means of control. As the child grows, physical force is less and less effective, and the child continually learns new ways to evade other forms of punishment. At some point, the child becomes immune to discipline.

Despite this reality, however, Western culture remains wedded to punitive discipline in the vast majority. A survey conducted in 1980 by Murray Straus, Richard Gelles, and Suzanne Steinmetz showed that 70% of parents randomly sampled viewed slapping or spanking children as "necessary"; 77% viewed these forms of discipline as "normal"; and 71% viewed them as "good." Nearly three-fourths (73%) of the parents had used some form of physical discipline on their child at some time in that child's life. Those parents who spanked their child did it more than once every other month (7.2 times per year). Of the children in the survey, 86% of three-year-olds, 82% of five-year-olds, 54% of those 10–14 years old, and 33% of those 15–17 years old had experienced physical punishment. Millions of children have been kicked, bitten, or punched by a parent (between one and two million in 1975 alone), some even beaten up. It is clear from these statistics that punitive discipline is common and frequent in Western society today.

In the 1980s and 1990s, however, a shift has begun away from punitive discipline toward a more relational style based on **attachment,** mutual trust and respect, and equality. This has occurred for a number of socio-cultural reasons. First of all, the increasing frequency of self-destructive and socially destructive behaviors on the part of increasingly younger children is clear evidence that common forms of discipline now in use are not working. The rise in crime, drug and alcohol abuse, school dropout rates, and **suicide** show a dangerous lack of discipline among children. Punitive measures, such as the "war on drugs," or "getting tough on crime," have been ineffective, if not counterproductive. In response, therefore, a number of adults have begun to explore alternative systems of discipline that do not rely on control or punishment.

Another factor in the shift away from punitive discipline is the historical movement in favor of greater democracy throughout Western culture that has led different subgroups to seek social equality. Today, chil-

STAGES OF MORAL DEVELOPMENT

Childhood is often divided into 5 approximate stages of moral development:

- Stage 1 = infancy—the child's only sense of right and wrong is what feels good or bad;

- Stage 2 = toddler years—the child learns "right" and "wrong" from what she or he is told by others;

- Stage 3 = preschool years—the child begins to internalize family values as his or her own, and begins to perceive the consequences of his or her behavior;

- Stage 4 = ages 7-10 years—the child begins to question the infallibility of parents, teachers, and other adults, and develops a strong sense of "should" and "should not";

- Stage 5 = preteen and teenage years—peers, rather than adults, become of ultimate importance to the child, who begins to try on different values systems to see which fits best; teens also become more aware of and concerned with the larger society, and begin to reason more abstractly about "right" and "wrong."

dren and youth are striving for equality as well, refusing to be treated as inferior to adults. Many of today's parents grew up in this atmosphere of increased equality for children and now view their own children as equals.

The cultural trend toward isolated nuclear **family** units rather than multigenerational extended families that has been underway since World War II (1939-1945) has also created a significant change in the dynamics of childrearing. Today's children are raised by only one or two parents in relative isolation. Long-standing cultural traditions and behaviors are lost as the cultural community disappears. Demands on parents' time and energy force them to leave their children with other **caregivers** who may not share their cultural background. Children are further exposed to a much wider range of traditions, values, beliefs, and attitudes today through the media as well. All this makes them less inclined to accept, without question, what their parents tell them. Children are coming to question their parents', and others', authority at a younger and younger age. Reduced supervision has also given children more freedoms.

A basic tenet of successful democracy is that with freedom comes responsibility. Equality-based disciplinary systems are not permissive; rather, parents seek to guide children to responsible choices. Parenting is authoritative (authority based on experience and expertise) rather than authoritarian (authority based on force). Children cannot be taught to take responsibility unless responsibility is given to them. Therefore, appropriate amounts of freedom to choose, and to experience the consequences of those choices, are granted to children according to their developmental level.

These stages determine the type of guidance given to a child by the adult caregiver, and the amount of self-determination the child is allowed. Ideally, the parent or other adult caregiver develops an intimate knowledge of the child, a connection based on close awareness and attachment, so that the adult can provide the guidance needed by that particular child.

No two children are exactly alike, so no one method of discipline can be applied to all children with equal success. Neither will the same form of discipline work with the same child in every situation at every age. Good discipline, therefore, is contingent upon the right relationship between adult and child, not the right techniques. It is also imperative that adults be self-disciplined teachers. Children learn from modeling, so parents must model disciplined behavior. Self-discipline involves self-esteem, self-acceptance, and self-respect. A parent's relationship with her or himself, therefore, is as important to good discipline as is the parent's relationship with the child.

Clearly, nonpunitive discipline is a complex endeavor that requires a good deal of maturity and knowledge on the part of the parent. Many books and videos are available to help parents develop the skills necessary to provide their children with effective discipline. *Parents* magazine, a popular and well-respected parenting journal, and the Children's Television Workshop both produced guides to effective equality-based discipline in 1990. Experiential programs such as Parent Effectiveness Training (PET), developed in 1962 by Thomas Gordon (who went on to create Teacher Effectiveness Training, or TET, a few years later), also exist for more direct education. For in-depth research, an abundance of scholarly works present statistical analyses and studies of the effectiveness of a variety of disciplinary systems, most of which show equality-based discipline to produce the best results.

See also **Punishment**

—Dianne K. Daeg de Mott

Displacement *see* **Defense Mechanisms**

FOR FURTHER STUDY

Further reading in different approaches to discipline:

Equality-Based Discipline

Bjorklund, Barbara R., and David F. Bjorklund. *Parents Book of Discipline*. New York: Ballantine Books, 1990.

Gootman, Marilyn E. *The Loving Parents' Guide to Discipline: How to Teach Your Child to Behave—With Kindness, Understanding and Respect*. New York: Berkley Books, 1995.

Gordon, Thomas. *Discipline that Works: Promoting Self-Discipline in Children*. New York: Plume, 1991.

Grisanti, Mary Lee, Dian G. Smith, and Charles Flatter. *Parents' Guide to Understanding Discipline: Infancy Through Preteen*. New York: Prentice Hall, 1990.

Nelsen, Jane. *Positive Discipline*, rev. ed. New York: Ballantine Books, 1996.

Sears, William. *The Discipline Book: Everything You Need to Know to Have a Better-Behaved Child—From Birth to Age 10*, 1st ed. Boston: Little, Brown and Co., 1995.

Wyckoff, Jerry. *How to Discipline Your Six-to-Twelve Year Old: Without Losing Your Mind*, 1st ed. New York: Doubleday, 1991.

Behavior Modification

Clark, Lynn. *The Time-Out Solution: A Parent's Guide for Handling Everyday Behavior Problems*. Chicago: Contemporary Books, 1989.

Dobson, James. *Dare to Discipline*. Wheaton, IL: Tyndale House, 1981. *The New Dare to Discipline*. Wheaton: Tyndale, 1992. (Conservative Christian approach to control-based discipline. Other books by Dobson include *Parenting Isn't for Cowards: Dealing Confidently with the Frustrations of Child-Rearing* [Waco, Texas: Word Books, 1987], *Children at Risk: The Battle for the Hearts and Minds of Our Kids* [Dallas: Word Pub., 1990], and *Life on the Edge* [Dallas: Word Pub., 1995].).

Dreikurs, Rudolf. *Logical Consequences: A New Approach to Discipline*. New York: Dutton, 1990.

Wright, Logan. *Parent Power*. New York: William Morrow, 1980.

Scholarly Analyses

Greven, Philip. *Spare the Child: The Religious Roots of Punishment and the Psychological Impact of Physical Abuse*. New York: Vintage Books, 1990.

McCord, Joan, ed. *Coercion and Punishment in Long-Term Perspectives*. Cambridge/New York: Cambridge University Press, 1995.

Straus, Murray, Richard Gelles, and Suzanne Steinmetz. *Behind Closed Doors: Violence in the American Family*. New York: Anchor Press/Doubleday, 1980.

▌ Dissociative Identity Disorder/Multiple Personality Disorder

A disorder in which a person's identity dissociates, or fragments, creating additional, distinct identities that exist independently of each other within the same person.

Persons with dissociative identity disorder (DID) adopt one or more distinct identities. Each identity or personality is distinct from the other(s) in specific ways. There are cases in which a person will have as many as 100 or more identities, while some people only exhibit the presence of one or two. ("Co-presence" is the term used to describe the situation that exists when two or more personalities are simultaneously present with or without knowledge of each other's existence or current presence.)

Prior to the publication of the *Diagnostic and Statistical Manual of Mental Disorder-IV* (*DSM-IV*), dissociative identity disorder was referred to as multiple personality disorder (MPD); the birth personality was referred to as the original personality, and the condition was referred to as "split personality." With the publication of *DSM-IV*, these terms are now considered imprecise and are no longer used. The *DSM-IV* lists four criteria for diagnosing someone with dissociative identity disorder:

• The presence of two or more distinct "identities or personality states;"

• At least two personalities must take control of the person's identity on a regular basis;

• Exhibits aspects of amnesia, that is, the person forgets routine personal information;

• The condition must not have been caused by "direct physiological effects," such as drug abuse or head trauma.

Persons with DID usually have one personality that controls the body and its behavior. Psychiatrists refer to this personality as the "host." This is generally not the person's original personality or birth personality. The host is often initially unaware of the other identities and typically loses time when they appear. The host is the identity that most often initiates treatment, usually after developing symptoms, such as **depression.** The personality that seeks treatment—whether the host or not—is referred to as the "presenting personality."

The *DSM-IV* uses the term "alter" to describe the distinct identities or personality states that the client or patient with DID experiences. To be classified as a "personality state," the following conditions must be met: a consistent and ongoing set of response patterns to given stimuli; a significant confluent history; a range of emotions available (anger, sadness, joy, and so on); a range of intensity of **affect** for each emotion (for example, anger ranging from neutrality to frustration and irritation to anger and rage).

Psychiatrists refer to the phase of transition between alters as the "switch." The number of alters in any given case can vary widely. Alters are often of different genders, i.e., men can have female alters and women can have male. A 1986 study found that in 37% of patients diagnosed with then-MPD, alters demonstrated different **handedness** from the host. The physical changes that occur in a switch between alters is one of the most difficult aspects of dissociative identity disorder for psychiatrists to understand. People assume whole new physical postures, voices, and vocabularies.

Terminology of dissociation

Dissociative amnesia, referred to as psychogenic amnesia in *DSM-III-R*, is one of the dissociative disorders described in *DSM-IV*. Its diagnostic criteria are:

1) One or more episodes of inability to recall important personal information, usually of a traumatic or stressful nature, that is too extensive to be explained by ordinary forgetfulness;

2) The disturbance does not occur exclusively during the course of another mental disorder, and is not due to the effects of a substance or a neurological and/or other general medical condition.

The symptoms of DID cause clinically significant distress or impairment in functioning. Memory disturbances, collectively known as amnesias, may be localized, selective, generalized, continuous, and/or systematized. For individuals with DID, the existence of amnesia is not necessarily the same in every personality state or personality fragment. For example, when one personality is aware of another but the other has no similar awareness, the condition is described as one-way amnesia. When neither personality is aware of the other, the condition is described as two-way amnesia.

Dissociative fugue (in *DSM-III-R,* psychogenic fugue) is given these diagnostic criteria in *DSM-IV* and is usually triggered by traumatic, stressful, or overwhelming life events:

• Sudden, unexpected travel from home or work, with the inability to recall some or all of one's past;

• Confusion about personal identity or assumption of a new identity;

• The disturbance does not occur exclusively during the course of DID and is not due to the effects of a substance or general medical condition;

• The symptoms cause clinically significant distress or impairment in functioning.

Dissociative disorders in children

There are no reliable figures on the prevalence of this disorder in children, although it has been reported with increased frequency during the 1990s. In diagnosing children, leaders in the field distinguish between children pretending to be other people, or trying out different roles during normal developmental. When behavior in young children becomes intensified, often following a trauma, the result may go beyond the trying out of roles to the creation of alter personality states.

The average age of onset of DID is in early childhood, generally by the age of four. The disorder is far more common among females than males (estimates range as high as 9 to 1). Once established, the disorder will last a lifetime if not treated; even with treatment, the prospects of complete cure are unlikely. According to available statistics, individuals with DID have an average of 15 identities. New identities can accumulate over time as the person faces new types of situations. Switching, the process of changing from one alter to another, may be triggered by outside stimuli such as an event, or by internal stimuli, such as feelings or memories. Switching is usually observable by others, with characteristic changes in posture or facial expression, voice tone or speech patterns, and mood or behavior.

An example of a trigger might be the first experience with sexuality in **adolescence.** An identity may emerge to deal with this new experience. People with DID tend to have other disorders as well, such as depression, substance abuse, borderline personality disorder and **eating disorders.** Many individuals with DID also have post-traumatic stress disorder (PTSD); in fact, researchers sometimes describe DID as complex and/or chronic PTSD. (In PSTD by definition, the individual has experienced a traumatic event that involved actual or threatened death or serious injury, or a threat to the physical integrity of self or others, and the person's response involved intense fear, helplessness, or horror.) In nearly every case of DID, horrific instances of physical or sexual **child abuse** was present. It is believed that young children,

TESTS TO DIAGNOSE DID

Dissociative Experiences Scale (DES)

Developed by Frank W. Putnam and Eve B. Carlson, the Dissociative Experiences Scale (DES) is an assessment instrument that can be completed by a client in about 10 minutes. It asks the respondent to indicate the frequency with which certain dissociative or depersonalization experiences occur.

Dissociative Disorder Interview Schedule (DDIS)

A structured 30–45 minute interview developed to standardize the diagnosis of DID. The DDIS has shown that DID is a valid diagnosis with a consistent set of features. Developed by Ross, Heber, Norton and Anderson, the DDIS has been used in several research studies and has good clinical validity.

Structured Clinical Interview for DSM-IV Dissociative Disorder (SCID-D)

Developed by Marlene Steinberg, this structured interview enables a trained interviewer to assess the nature and severity of dissociative symptoms.

Mapping

Mapping is a technique used to learn about an individual's internal personality system. The client is asked to draw a map or diagram of his or her personality states. As therapy progresses, the client is asked to update the map. Also known as personality mapping or system mapping.

faced with abuse and neglect, create a fantasy world in order to escape.

Treatment of dissociative identity disorder is a long and difficult process, and the successful integration of all identities into one is unlikely. A 1990 study of 20 DID clients revealed that only five were successfully treated. Some therapists use a technique of "talking through" to one or more personality states that are not in control. For example, a therapist may address the client's personality states as if they were a group: "I want everyone inside to listen." Treatment also involves having DID clients recall the memories of their childhood, sometimes under hypnosis. This procedure requires skill and caution, however, since the recovered memories may be so traumatic that they cause further harm. The recovery of suppressed memories, a crucial component in DID, is controversial. Many psychologists and psychiatrists with expertise in memory believe that it is unlikely that memories can be recovered for events that occurred before the age of three.

Another cause for the skepticism is the dramatic increase in reports of the disorder since 1980. Eugene Levitt, a psychologist at the Indiana University School of Medicine, noted in an article published in *Insight on the News* (1993) that "in 1980, the disorder [then known as multiple personality disorder] got its official listing in the *DSM*, and suddenly thousands of cases are springing up everywhere."

Although there is yet no scientific evidence to support their claim, there are some in the field of psychiatry who feel that DID is an iatrogenic illness, i.e., one that is caused by or aggravated by the actions of a psychotherapist. These researchers contend that the client produces DID symptoms to meet the expectations of a therapist.

For Further Study

Books

Steinberg, Marlene. *Handbook for the Assessment of Dissociation: A Clinical Guide.* Washington, DC: American Psychiatric Press, 1995.

Periodicals

Arbetter, Sandra. "Multiple Personality Disorder: Someone Else Lives Inside of Me." *Current Health* November 2, 1992, p. 17.

Mesic, Penelope. "Presence of Minds." *Chicago,* September 1992, p. 100.

Sileo, Chi Chi. "Multiple Personalities: The Experts Are Split." *Insight on the News*, October 25, 1993, p. 18.

"When the Body Remembers." *Psychology Today*, April 1994, p. 9.

Divergent Thinking

The ability to come up with original and unique ideas and to envision multiple solutions to a problem.

The concept of divergent thinking was developed in the 1950s by psychologist J. P. Guilford, who saw it as a major component of **creativity** and associated it with four main characteristics: fluency (the ability to rapidly produce a large number of ideas or solutions to a problem); flexibility (the capacity to consider a variety of approaches to a problem simultaneously); originality (the tendency to produce ideas different from those of most other people); and elaboration (the ability to think through the details of an idea and carry it out). Guilford, whose research was oriented toward testing and measurement (psychometrics), believed that creative thinkers are at a disadvantage when taking standard intelligence tests, which penalize divergent thinking and reward its opposite, **convergent thinking**—the ability to narrow all possible alternatives down to a single solution (the type of thinking required by multiple choice tests).

Over a number of years, the Aptitudes Research Project at the University of Southern California, under Guilford's leadership, devised an extensive sequence of tests to measure intellectual abilities, including creativity. Some of the ARP divergent thinking tests have been widely adapted for use in placing students in gifted programs and evaluating the success of such programs. They include a number of different assessment techniques that measure the key characteristics of fluency, flexibility, and originality. Among the fluency tests are word fluency, which asks test-takers to think of as many words as they can that contain a given letter, and ideational fluency, which involves naming things that belong to a specific category, such as fluids that will burn. Other tests included listing all the possible jobs that might be represented by a specific emblem and writing titles for short stories after having been told their plots. The part of the ARP test sequence that has been the most widely adapted for assessing creativity in children is the alternate uses test, which asks the child to name as many uses as possible for an everyday object, such as a paper clip or a brick. Another popular creativity test derived from the ARP project is the consequences test, in which a person is asked to list the possible consequences of an imaginary event ("What would happen if everyone were immortal?"). In addition to these verbal tests, ARP also devised tests to measure spatial aptitude, which include such tasks as drawing objects using geometrical shapes.

Although creativity is associated with the highest levels of achievement in many fields and presumably valued by society, the educational system often penalizes divergent thinkers. The typical standardized measure of intelligence is the multiple-choice test, which is diametrically opposed to the divergent thinker's problem-solving process. To a creative thinker, it may seem more productive to try finding reasons why *all* the choices on a multiple-choice question could be correct than to select the preferred answer. In addition, most classroom teaching is heavily biased toward the learning style of convergent thinkers, a fact that helps explain the dismal school performance of such legendary geniuses as Albert Einstein and Thomas Alva Edison, who was considered retarded and expelled from school. Creative children easily become bored in situations where uniform responses are expected and the product of intellectual effort is emphasized over the process. Instead of answering questions correctly, divergent thinkers are likely to provide additional answers of their own or even challenge the questions themselves, responses that teachers may consider inconvenient, uncooperative, and a threat to their authority.

For Further Study

Books

Amabile, Teresa M. *Growing Up Creative: Nurturing a Lifetime of Creativity.* New York: Crown Publishers, 1989.

Bean, Reynold. *How to Develop Your Children's Creativity.* Los Angeles: Price Stern Sloan, 1992.

Guilford, J. P. *The Nature of Human Intelligence.* New York: McGraw-Hill, 1967.

Divorce

The legal termination of a marriage.

The unprecedented rise in the U.S. divorce rate over the past 30 years has had significant consequences for the nation's children, over a million of whom are affected by divorce every year. The U.S. Bureau of the Census has predicted that 40% of children growing up in America in the 1990s will experience the breakup of parental marriages.

Common childhood and adolescent reactions to parental divorce include a continuing desire for the parents to reunite; fears of desertion; feelings of guilt over having been responsible for the divorce; developmental regression; sleep disorders; and physical complaints. While researchers have found that some children recover from the trauma of divorce within one to three years, recent long-term studies have documented persistent negative effects that can follow a child into adolescence and beyond, especially with regard to the formation of intimate relationships later in life. The effects of parental divorce have been linked to phenomena as diverse as emotional and behavioral problems, school dropout rates, crime rates, physical and sexual abuse, and physical health and well-being. However, mental health professionals continue to debate whether divorce is more damaging for children than the continuation of a troubled marriage.

Infancy and toddlerhood

During these stages, children's reactions to divorce stem from interference with the satisfaction of their basic needs. The removal of the noncustodial parent or increased work hours for the custodial parent can cause **separation anxiety**, while the parents' emotional distress tends to be transmitted to children at these ages, upsetting their own emotional equilibrium. The inability of infants and toddlers to understand the concept of divorce on an intellectual level makes the changes in their situation seem frighteningly unpredictable and confusing. The child may revert to an earlier development stage in such areas as eating, sleeping, **toilet training**, motor activity, language, and emotional independence. Other signs of distress include anger, fearfulness, and withdrawal.

Preschool

At this stage, the child's continued egocentric focus, coupled with a more advanced level of cognitive development, leads to feelings of guilt as he becomes convinced that he is the reason for his parents' divorce. Children at this age are also prone to powerful fantasies, which—in the case of divorce—can include imagined scenarios involving abandonment or punishment. The disruption that follows divorce, particularly in the relationship with the father, also becomes an important factor for children at this stage of development. Developmental regression may take the form of insisting on sleeping in the same room or bed as the parent; refusing to eat all but a few types of food; stuttering or reverting to baby talk; disruptions in toilet training; and developing an excessive emotional dependence on a parent.

School-age

By the early elementary grades, children are better able to handle separation from the noncustodial parent. Their greater awareness of the divorce situation, however, may lead to elaborate and frightening fantasies of abandonment or of being replaced in the affections of the noncustodial parent. Typical reactions at this stage include sadness, **depression**, anger, and generalized anxiety. Disruption of basic developmental progress in such areas as eating, sleeping, and elimination is possible but less frequent than in younger children. Many children this age suffer a sharp decline in academic performance, which often lasts throughout the entire school year in which the divorce takes place. One effective means of helping early elementary children cope with their feelings is communication by displacement, in which a doll or story character acts out feelings and fantasies the child is reluctant to claim as his or her own.

Children in the upper elementary grades are capable of understanding the divorce process on a relatively sophisticated level. At this stage, the simple fears and fantasies of the younger child are replaced by more complex internal conflicts, such as the struggle to preserve one's allegiance to both parents. Older children become adept at erecting **defense mechanisms** to protect themselves against the pain they feel over a divorce. Such defenses include denial, intellectualization, displacement of feelings, and physical complaints such as fatigue, headaches, and stomachaches. Children in the upper elementary grades are most likely to become intensely angry at their parents for divorcing. Other common emotions at this stage of development include loneliness, grief, anxiety, and a sense of powerlessness.

Adolescence

For teenagers, parental divorce is difficult because it is yet another source of upheaval in their lives. Teenage behavior is affected not only by recent divorces but also by those that occurred when the child was much younger. One especially painful effect of divorce on adolescents is the negative attitude it can produce toward one or both parents, whom they need as role models but are often blamed for disappointing them.

Adolescents are also prone to internal conflicts over their parents' divorce. They are torn between love for and anger toward their parents and between conflicting loyalties to both parents. Positive feelings toward their parents' new partners come into conflict with anxiety over the intimacy of these relationships, and the teenager's close affiliation with the custodial parent clashes with his or her need for increased social and emotional independence. Although children at all ages are distressed by parental divorce, by adolescence it can result in potentially dangerous behavior, including drug and alcohol abuse, precocious and/or promiscuous sexual activity, violence, and delinquency.

Helping children cope with divorce

Psychologist Judith S. Wallerstein, an internationally recognized authority on the effects of divorce on children, has proposed that children whose parents divorce face special psychological tasks in addition to the normal developmental tasks all children must accomplish. She outlines the following sequence of seven steps: 1) attaining a realistic understanding of the divorce; 2) achieving enough distance from the situation to continue with their lives; 3) absorbing the loss of the original family unit and of the noncustodial parent; 4) handling their anger; 5) dealing with guilt feelings; 6) facing the fact that the divorce is permanent; and 7) remaining optimistic about their own chances for healthy relationships in the future.

Experts agree that it is important for parents who are divorcing to avoid involving their children in their disputes or forcing them to choose sides, and are often advised to avoid criticizing their former mates in front of their children. In order for children to heal from the emotional pain of parental divorce, they need an outlet for open expression of their feelings, whether it be a sibling, friend, adult mentor or counselor, or a divorce support group. Extended families can be a significant source of support for children, providing them with stability and with the reassurance that others care about them. Although parental divorce is undeniably difficult for children of all ages, loving, patient, and enlightened parental support can make a crucial difference in helping children cope with the experience both immediately and over the long term.

For Further Study

Books

For adults

Kalter, Neil. *Growing Up with Divorce: Helping Your Child Avoid Immediate and Later Emotional Problems.* New York: Free Press, 1990.

Lansky, Vicki. *Vicki Lansky's Divorce Book for Parents: Helping Your Children Cope with Divorce and Its Aftermath.* New York: Penguin Books, 1989.

Wallerstein, Judith S. *Second Chances: Men, Women, and Children a Decade after Divorce.* New York: Ticknor & Fields, 1989.

Wallerstein, Judith, and Joan Kelly. *Surviving the Break-Up: How Children Cope with Divorce.* New York: Basic Books, 1980.

For children

Blume, Judy. *It's Not the End of the World.* Scarsdale: Bradbury, 1972.

Bolick, Nancy O'Keefe. *How to Survive Your Parents' Divorce.* New York: Franklin Watts, 1994.

Brown, L., and M. Brown. *The Dinosaurs Divorce.* Little, Brown. (For ages 4–8)

Gardner, Richard. *The Boys and Girls Book About Divorce.* Northvale, N.J.: Aronson, 1992.

Hamm, Diane Johnston. *Second Family.* New York: Macmillan, 1992.

Krementz, Jill. *How It Feels When Parents Divorce.* New York: Knopf, 1984. (For ages 8–14)

Organizations

Children's Rights Council (CRC)
> **Address:** 220 Eye St. N.E., Ste. 200
> Washington, DC 20002
> **Telephone:** (202) 547-6227

Joint Custody Association (JCA)
> **Address:** 10606 Wilkins Ave.
> Los Angeles, CA 90024
> **Telephone:** (310) 475-5352

DNA

An organic substance that encodes and carries genetic information and is the fundamental element of heredity.

The thousands of genes that make up each chromosome are composed of deoxyribonucleic acid (DNA), which consists of a five-carbon sugar (deoxyribose), phosphate, and four types of nitrogen-containing molecules (adenine, guanine, cytosine, and thymine). The sugar and phosphate combine to form the outer edges of a double helix, while the nitrogen-containing molecules appear in bonded pairs like rungs of a ladder connecting the outer edges. They are matched in an arrangement that always pairs adenine in one chain with thymine in the other, and guanine in one chain with cytosine in the other. A single DNA molecule may contain several thousand pairs. As the transmitter of inherited characteristics, DNA replicates itself exactly and determines the structure of new organisms, which it does by governing the structure of their proteins.

The specific order and arrangement of these bonded pairs of molecules constitute the genetic code of the organism in which they exist by determining, through the production of ribonucleic acid (RNA), the type of protein produced by each gene, as it is these proteins that govern the structure and activities of all cells in an organism. Thus, DNA acts as coded message, providing a blueprint for the characteristics of all organisms, including human beings. When a cell divides to form new life, its DNA is "copied" by a separation of the two strands of the double helix, after which complementary strands are synthesized around each existing one. The end result is the formation of two new double helices, each identical to the original. All cells of a higher organism contain that organism's entire DNA pattern. However, only a small percentage of all the DNA messages are active in any cell at a given time, enabling different cells to "specialize."

Many viruses are also composed of DNA, which, in some cases, has a single-strand form rather than the two strands forming the edges of a double helix. Each particle of a virus contains only one DNA molecule, ranging in length from 5,000 to over 200,000 subunits. (The total length of DNA in a human cell is estimated at five billion subunits.) Radiation, thermal variations, or the presence of certain chemicals can cause changes, or "mistakes," in an organism's DNA pattern, resulting in a genetic mutation. In the course of evolution, such mutations provided the hereditary blueprints for the emergence of new species.

History

The Swiss researcher Frederick Miescher first discovered DNA in 1869. He extracted a substance (that he called nuclein) containing nitrogen and phosphorus from cell nuclei. The question of whether nucleic acids or proteins, or both, carried the information that make the genes of every organism unique was not answered, however, until the molecular structure of DNA was determined in 1953. This pioneering work was accomplished by an American biochemist, James D. Watson, and three British scientists—Francis Crick, a biochemist, Maurice Wilkins, a biophysicist, and Rosalind Frank, a microchemist.

Since the 1970s, scientists have furthered their understanding of the molecular structure of genes through experiments with recombinant DNA. As its name suggests, this technique combines fragments of DNA from two different species, allowing an experimenter to purify, or clone, a gene from one species by inserting it into the DNA of another, which replicates it together with its

PRACTICAL APPLICATIONS OF DNA RESEARCH

In the late 1990s, news reports focused on applications of DNA research. For example, medical researchers focused on finding ways to use DNA replication to repair damaged tissue, such as spinal cord, heart muscle, and brain, that is unable to repair itself or regenerate after injury. Other researchers sought ways to stop the uncontrolled growth of cancer cells by understanding the DNA replication process.

In 1997, a 7-month-old lamb named Dolly was introduced to the world by researcher Ian Wilmut of the Roslin Institute in Scotland. Dolly's life began as a speck of DNA from another female sheep, of which she is now a perfect genetic copy. This was the first successful cloning of a mammal from an adult of its species. Debate over ethical and moral issues of cloning will continue for years to come.

DNA analysis was also reportedly gaining increased application. Forensic laboratories used by police departments to analyze crime evidence were using complex DNA analysis on blood samples taken from crime scenes. The DNA from the blood evidence was analyzed and compared to blood samples taken from suspects.

In commerce, some manufacturers were considering implanting DNA into clothing products to fight against the production of illegal copies. DNA is used as a unique identification "tag" in fabric. The DNA molecule is attached to an inorganic base, and can be detected using a special handheld scanner. Counterfeiters would find it difficult to detect and copy the DNA marker in a clothing item, such as a pair of jeans.

own genetic material. The term "recombinant DNA" also refers to other laboratory techniques where a specific portion of DNA is artificially rearranged or reproduced. Although controversial, gene cloning is an important scientific accomplishment that has enabled researchers to produce an unlimited number of gene copies gathered from a variety of organisms, including human ones.

For Further Study

Books

Gribbin, John. *In Search of the Double Helix.* New York: McGraw-Hill, 1985.

▌Down Syndrome

Also referred to as Down's syndrome or Down's, a genetic disorder present at birth that is caused by an abnormality in the number of chromosomes.

Down syndrome occurs with equal frequency in people of different nationalities, social backgrounds, and economic classes, averaging 1 in about every 600 births. In the United States, over 400,000 people have the condition. Women over 35 are at greater risk of bearing a child with Down syndrome than younger women. One in 1500 children with Down syndrome is born to a mother under 30; for mothers over 45, this figure rises to one in 65. Altogether, though, 80% of all Down infants are actually born to women under 35. According to recent studies, the age of the father may play a role as well. Prenatal detection of Down syndrome is possible through **amniocentesis** and chorionic villus sampling and is recommended for pregnant women over the age of 35.

John Langdon Haydon Down, a British physician, first described Down syndrome in 1866. In 1959, French pediatrician Jerome Lejeune found that it is caused by a genetic abnormality: an extra chromosome in the 21st pair of chromosomes (**trisomy** 21). People with Down syndrome have a total of 47 chromosomes instead of the normal 46. The main symptom of Down syndrome is mild to severe mental and motor retardation. Motor, speech, and sexual development are delayed, and cognitive development may not peak until the age of 30 or 40. Most people who have the disorder are severely retarded, with an IQ of between 20 and 49, and prone to a number of physical problems, including hearing and heart defects, poor vision, cataracts, and low resistance to respiratory infections. In the past it was common for children with Down syndrome to die of pneumonia before reaching adulthood. They have a greater than average likelihood of developing **leukemia,** and many die of a neurological condition similar to Alzheimer's disease by the age of 35. In spite of the discovery of antibiotics and other medical advances, people with Down syndrome still have an average life expectancy of only 16 years and seldom live past the age of 50.

Individuals with Down syndrome have a short, stocky build, with a short neck and a smaller than average skull, usually flat in back. Their most distinctive facial features are the upward-slanting, almond-shaped eyes on which an early name used for the condition—mongolism—was based. Other facial characteristics include a small nose with a flat bridge; a fold of skin (the epicanthal fold) at the inner corner of the eye; a large, protruding tongue (which makes normal speech difficult); and light spots at the edge of the iris (Brushfield spots). The outer ear and chin are generally small. The

Children with Down syndrome are capable of participating in most aspects of family life.

hands are small, with short fingers, a curved little finger, and a line on the palm called the Simian line. Children and adults with Down syndrome tend to have sweet and docile temperaments; they are generally cheerful, cooperative, affectionate, and relaxed.

Infancy

Wide variations occur in the developmental sequence for children with Down syndrome. On the whole, they go through the same developmental stages as other children but often at a delayed rate. One common characteristic that hampers development in infants with Down syndrome is low muscle tone (hypotonia), characterized by floppy, overly relaxed muscles. Proper muscle tone can be developed eventually with the aid of physical therapy. At the age of one year, most Down infants are able to roll over, sit up by themselves, and support their own weight from a standing position; they can also reach for and pick up objects. Teething may be delayed, and when they do come in, their teeth often appear in an unpredictable order, in contrast to those of most other infants.

Toddlerhood

By the end of their second year, infants with Down syndrome can usually crawl (although many progress straight to walking without crawling at all). Most can stand unassisted and take at least a few steps on their own. They communicate enthusiastically through gestures and simple expressions such as "da-da" and "ma-ma" and imitate the activities of those around them.

Preschool

At three years, most children with Down syndrome can climb stairs with some support, walk backwards, sit in a chair, and throw a ball. Many are toilet trained. They enjoy a variety of games, including make-believe games, although their attention span is shorter than that of other children. While language comprehension is good at this age, verbalization is still quite limited. Most children can recognize pictures in their favorite books. By four years of age, most will be able to feed themselves, however messily, and handle much of their own personal care (hand and face washing, most dressing and undressing, toilet routines). The development of increased independence is accompanied by tantrums when they do not get their way or cannot find someone to play with.

Between the ages of three and five, children with Down syndrome can benefit by attending a nursery school, either in a program for children with special needs or in a mainstream classroom. They can be assisted

DEVELOPMENTAL MILESTONES - AVERAGE AGE (IN MONTHS)		
Milestone	Average age of accomplishment (in months)	
	Children with Down syndrome	"Normal" children
Smiling	2	1
Rolling over	8	5
Sitting alone	10	7
Crawling	12	8
Standing	20	11
Walking	24	13
Talking	16	10

with self-help skills, social skills, and both gross and fine motor coordination. Children with Down syndrome also need assistance with playing, as they have difficulty developing their own games without help from an adult or another child. Around the age of four or five a marked advance in language development occurs, with an increase in vocabulary and in the ability to link words together.

School age

Many children with Down syndrome have little difficulty adjusting to school, especially if they have been enrolled in a preschool and the family environment has not been overprotective. Integration into mainstream schooling may take a variety of forms. With total integration, children with Down syndrome spend the entire school day in regular educational settings but have assistance from personnel trained in aiding special students. In partial integration, students divide their time between a regular educational environment and a special class. At the elementary school level, it is important for educators to provide help with communication and socialization skills, motor skills, and self-help skills as well as academics.

Most children with Down syndrome can master some reading skills. One developmental program that began with children as young as 30 months and stressed positive parent-child communication eventually enabled Down syndrome children to read at a second-grade level.

Instances of affected children reading at close to a fourth-grade level have also been documented. Some children do best in a reading program with an emphasis on specific functional purposes, such as reading menus in restaurants or signs in supermarkets. Other areas of focus in a functional reading program include banking, budgeting, following simple recipes, and using the telephone directory. Children with Down syndrome generally do less well at mathematics than at reading.

Adolescence

In adolescents with Down syndrome, the normal teenage conflicts between the desire for independence and the need for security are magnified. Like other teens, they become concerned with their appearance and with **peer acceptance,** and they need encouragement and support to prevent feelings of inferiority and possible social withdrawal. The growth spurt and sexual maturation experienced by all teens can be especially baffling to these young people, and they need to have these changes described and explained in advance in order to help cope with them. Teenage girls with Down syndrome, who usually begin to menstruate at the same age as their peers, need careful instruction on what to expect and how to take care of themselves. Boys need to understand that **masturbation** is a normal but private activity. Sexual activity and **contraception** need to be discussed with teens of both sexes.

The secondary school experience for teenagers with Down syndrome continues the emphasis of earlier grades on developing socialization and self-help skills. **Role playing** can be an important tool in learning appropriate behavior in a number of different social situations. At this stage, students need preparation to function in the community as independently as possible as adults and need practice and skills in such diverse areas as shopping, meal planning, health and safety, and money management.

A very important educational experience for adolescents with Down syndrome is the opportunity to function in an employment setting for at least a few hours per week. This type of experience encourages maturity and independence and helps young people form concrete ideas about the types of jobs they would like to have in the future. These temporary job placements can also help in the development of social skills and good work habits.

Although until the 1970s most people with Down syndrome were institutionalized, those with only moderate retardation are capable of achieving some degree of self-sufficiency, whether moving to a group home or apartment or remaining in the parental home. Today, with changed social attitudes and expanded educational opportunities, many lead productive, fulfilling lives. "Life Goes On," a dramatic series about a family with a

Down syndrome teenager (played by Chris Burke, an actor who has Down syndrome), premiered on network television in 1989.

For Further Study

Books

Cunningham, Cliff. *Down's Syndrome: An Introduction for Parents.* Cambridge, MA: Brookline Books, 1988.

Pueschel, Siegfried. *Down Syndrome: Toward a Brighter Future.* Baltimore: Paul H. Brookes, 1990.

Stray-Gundersen, ed. *Babies with Down Syndrome: A New Parents Guide.* Woodbine House, 1986.

Organizations

National Down Syndrome Congress
   Address: 1800 Dempster Street
   Chicago, IL 60068
   Telephone: (312) 823-7550; toll-free (800) 232-NDSC

National Down Syndrome Society
   Address: 141 Fifth Avenue, Suite 75
   New York, NY 10010
   Telephone: (212) 460-9330

Draw-A-Person Test

Used to measure nonverbal intelligence or to screen for emotional or behavioral disorders.

Based on children's drawings of human figures, this test can be used with two different scoring systems for different purposes. One measures nonverbal **intelligence** while the other screens for emotional or behavioral disorders. Drawings obtained from a child during a single administration may be used with both systems. During the testing session, which can be completed in 15 minutes, the child is asked to draw three figures—a man, a woman, and him- or herself. Draw a Person:QSS (Quantitative Scoring System) assesses intellectual ability by analyzing 14 different aspects of the drawings, such as specific body parts and clothing, for various criteria, including presence or absence, detail, and proportion. In all, there are 64 scoring items for each drawing. A separate standard score is recorded for each one, and a total score for all three. The use of a nonverbal, nonthreatening task to evaluate intelligence is intended to eliminate possible sources of bias by reducing variables like primary language, verbal skills, communication disabilities, and sensitivity to working under pressure. However, test results can be influenced by previous drawing experience, a factor that may account for the tendency of middle-class children to score higher on this test than lower-class children, who often have fewer opportunities to draw. Draw a Person:SPED (Screening Procedure for Emotional Disturbance) uses the test's figure drawings as a means of identifying emotional problems. The scoring system is composed of two types of criteria. For the first type, eight dimensions of each drawing are evaluated against norms for the child's age group. For the second type, 47 different items are considered for each drawing.

For Further Study

Books

Chandler, Louis A., and Virginia J. Johnson. *Using Projective Techniques with Children: A Guide to Clinical Assessment.* Springfield, IL: C.C. Thomas, 1991.

Mortensen, Karen Vibeke. *Form and Content in Children's Human Figure Drawings: Development, Sex Differences, and Body Experience.* New York: New York University Press, 1991.

Wortham, Sue Clark. *Tests and Measurement in Early Childhood Education.* Columbus: Merrill Publishing Co., 1990.

Drawings

Children use art for both for enjoyment and as a means of expression. The art of children is individualistic and revealing. Instruction in the technique and interpretation of art is a component of the **curriculum** in most schools. In addition, classroom teachers can employ drawing as one component of activities designed to allow students to develop skills of reflection and expression. Narrative drawings—drawings that tell a story—can be incorporated into writing lessons, or used independently to strengthen skills of observation and description. Drawings are also effective tools of communication for students with limited verbal and written communication.

Drawings can help a psychologist determine a child's personality characteristics. A number of tests, such as **Draw-A-Person Test,** and **Goodenough-Harris Drawing Test,** are based on the notion that the ability to accurately draw human figures is one nonverbal measure of intelligence. For individuals with behavior and other personality disorders, art therapy is one of the tools available to explore and treat the symptoms and causes of the disorder. Art therapy is frequently employed in the treatment of **eating disorders,** in coping with chronic illness or long-term hospitalization, and in the education of autistic children.

For Further Study

Books

Dalley, Tessa. *Art as Therapy: An Introduction to the Use of Art as a Therapeutic Technique.* New York: Routledge, 1994.

Krampen, Martin. *Children's Drawings: Iconic Coding of the Environment.* New York: Plenum Press, 1991.

Levens, Mary. *Eating Disorders and Magical Control of the Body: Treatment Through Art Therapy.* New York: Routledge, 1995.

A drawing by an autistic student.

Levich, Myra F. *They Could Not Talk and So They Drew—Children's Styles of Coping and Thinking.* Springfield, IL: C.C. Thomas, 1983.

Linesch, Debra Greenspoon. *Adolescent Art Therapy.* New York: Brunner/Mazel, 1988.

Malchiodi, Cathy A. *Breaking the Silence: Art Therapy with Children from Violent Homes.* New York: Brunner/Mazal, 1990.

Mortensen, Karen. *Form and Content in Children's Human Figue Drawings: Development, Sex Differences, and Body Experience.* New York: New York University Press, 1991.

Santoy, Claude. *Interpreting Your Child's Handwriting and Drawings Toddler to Teens.* New York: Paragon House, 1991.

Thomas, Glyn V. Anghle M.J. *An Introduction to the Psychology of Children's Drawings.* New York: New York University Press, 1990.

Waller, Diane Elizabeth. *Art Therapy: A Handbook.* Milton Keynes, PA: Open University Press, 1992.

Working with Children in Art Therapy. New York: Routledge, 1990.

Periodicals

Evans, Sara, and Patricia McCormick. "Paint Power!" *Parents Magazine* 68, August 1993, pp. 104+.

Trudeau, Garry. "Out of the Crayons of Babes." *The New York Times Magazine,* January 22, 1995, pp. 34+.

Audiovisual Recordings

Squiggles, Dots, and Lines. Newton, MA: Kidvids, 1989. (One 25-minute videocassette, featuring Ed Emberley's simple tools for drawing.)

Dropout *see* **School Phobia and Refusal**

Drug Therapy

Drug therapy encompasses the wide variety of medications administered to combat or regulate diseases and conditions such as **cancer**, *psychiatric illnesses, and seizures.*

Use of drug therapy in treating children is a relatively new field. Many drugs prescribed for similar conditions in adults are not FDA-approved for children, and some are only approved for children over the age of 12. When drug therapy has been prescribed for a child, it is imperative that the parents or caregivers learn about the proper dosages, possible side effects, and harmful interactions with other medications. If the medications are to be administered at home, extra precaution should be taken to keep them in a safe and secure place.

An estimated 12 million children in the United States suffer from some form of psychiatric illness, including **attention deficit/hyperactivity disorder (ADHD)**, major **depression**, **schizophrenia**, **Tourette's syndrome,** anxiety disorders, and **autism**. Because research has shown that many psychiatric illnesses are biological in origin, drug therapy is often the prescribed treatment. However, the medications can evoke side effects such as irritability, agitation, nausea, and headaches. The stimulants used to control ADHD can suppress growth, particularly weight gain. Schizophrenia is treated with antipsychotic agents such as chlorpromazine, thioridazine, haloperidol, and thiothlxene. Long-term use can produce tardive dyskinesia, an involuntary tongue and mouth movement disorder, stiffness, and tremors. Clomipramime, an antidepressant effective in the treatment of **obsessive-compulsive disorder** in adolescents, can produce dry mouth, blurred vision, constipation, rapid heartbeat, and urinary retention. Muscle stiffness often accompanies the drug haloperidol when it is taken for Tourette's syndrome.

Chemotherapy, a short-term program of drug therapy prescribed after cancer surgery to delay or stop the growth of cancerous cells, typically causes serious side effects. This is due to the fact that healthy cells are destroyed as well. The most common side effects are hair loss, nausea, and fatigue. Sometimes side effects disappear over time. In other cases, additional medication is prescribed to minimize side effects of other drugs.

Possible drug interaction is a concern. Recently it was found that the antibiotic oral rifampin prescribed for the prevention of the meningoccal virus in children can interfere with drugs the child may be taking for seizure prevention. Under the Omnibus Reconciliation Act of 1990, pharmacists are strongly encouraged to maintain patient files for effective drug therapy management. Parents should make sure that their local pharmacy has a record of their child's drug history.

Some physicians and pharmacists believe the time of day a drug is taken can determine its effectiveness. Because body temperature, blood pressure, and pulse rate are at their lowest in the pre-dawn hours, asthmatics often suffer attacks in the early hours when lung power is diminished. Therefore, many physicians prescribe a long-acting beta-agonist that can be taken at bedtime and last 12 hours.

Many parents also worry that their children will become addicted to medications. While antidepressants and antipsychotic drugs are not addictive, benzodiazepines and stimulants can be, and they should be monitored carefully.

For Further Study

Periodicals

Cardoni, Alex S. "Drug Therapy of Psychiatric Disorders in Children." *American Druggist* 208, September 1993, no. 4, p. 65.

DSM-IV see **Diagnostic and Statistical Manual of Mental Disorders**

DTP vaccine *see* **Immunization**

Dwarfism

Term applied broadly to a number of conditions resulting in unusually short stature.

While dwarfism is sometimes used to describe achondroplasia, a condition characterized by short stature and disproportionately short arms and legs, it is also used more broadly to refer to a variety of conditions resulting in unusually short stature in both children and adults. In some cases physical development may be disproportionate, as in achondroplasia, but in others the parts of the body develop proportionately. Short stature may be unaccompanied by other symptoms, or it may occur together with other problems, both physical and mental. Adult males under 5 ft (1.5 m) tall and females under 4 ft 8 in (1.4 m) are classified as short-statured. Children are considered unusually short if they fall below the third per-

centile of height for their age group. In 1992 there were about five million people of short stature (for their age) living in the United States, of which 40% were under the age of 21.

Some prenatal factors known to contribute to growth retardation include a variety of maternal health problems, including toxemia, kidney and heart disease, infections such as **rubella,** and maternal malnutrition. Maternal age is also a factor (adolescent mothers are prone to have undersize babies), as is uterine constraint (which occurs when the uterus is too small for the baby). Possible causes that center on the **fetus** rather than the mother include chromosomal abnormalities, genetic and other syndromes that impair skeletal growth, and defects of the placenta or umbilical cord. Environmental factors that influence intrauterine growth include maternal use of drugs (including alcohol and tobacco). Some infants who are small at birth (especially twins) may attain normal stature within the first year of life, while others remain small throughout their lives.

The four most common causes of dwarfism in children are achondroplasia, **Turner syndrome,** inadequate pituitary function, and lack of emotional or physical nurturance. Achondroplasia (short-limbed dwarfism) is a genetic disorder that impairs embryonic development, resulting in abnormalities in bone growth and cartilage development. It is one of a class of illnesses called chondrodystrophies, all of which involve cartilage abnormalities and result in short stature. In achondroplasia, the long bones fail to develop normally, making the arms and legs disproportionately short and stubby (and sometimes curved). Overly long fibulae (one of two bones in the lower leg) cause the bowlegs that are characteristic of the condition. In addition, the head is disproportionately large and the bridge of the nose is depressed. Persons with achondroplasia are between 3–5 ft (91–152 cm) tall and of normal intelligence. Their reproductive development is normal, and they have greater than normal muscular strength. The condition occurs in 1 out of every 10,000 births, and its prevalence increases with the age of the parents, especially the father. Achondroplasia can be detected through prenatal screening. Many infants with the condition are stillborn. Turner syndrome is a chromosomal abnormality occurring only in females in whom one of the X chromosomes is missing or defective. Girls with Turner syndrome are usually between 4.5–5 ft (137–152 cm) high. Their ovaries are undeveloped, and they do not undergo puberty. Besides short stature, other physical characteristics include a stocky build and a webbed neck.

Endocrine and metabolic disorders are another important cause of growth problems. Growth can be impaired by conditions affecting the pituitary, thyroid, parathyroid, and adrenal glands (all part of the endocrine system). Probably the best known of these conditions is growth hormone deficiency, which is associated with the pituitary and hypothalamus glands. If the deficiency begins prenatally, the baby will still be of normal size and weight at birth but will then experience slowed growth. Weight gain still tends to be normal, leading to overweight and a higher than average proportion of body fat. The facial structures of children with this condition are immature, making them look younger than their actual age. Adults in whom growth hormone deficiency has not been treated attain a height of only about 2.5 ft (76 cm). They also have high-pitched voices, high foreheads, and wrinkled skin. Another endocrine disorder that can interfere with growth is hypothyroidism, a condition resulting from insufficient activity of the thyroid gland. Affecting 1 in 4,000 infants born in the United States, it can have a variety of causes, including underdevelopment, absence, or removal of the thyroid gland, lack of an enzyme needed for adequate thyroid function, iodine deficiency, or an underactive pituitary gland. In addition to retarding growth, it can cause **mental retardation** if thyroid hormones are not administered in the first months of an infant's life. If the condition goes untreated, it causes impaired mental development in 50% of affected children by the age of six months.

About 15% of short stature in children is caused by chronic diseases, of which endocrine disorders are only one type. Many of these conditions do not appear until after the fifth year of life. Children with renal disease often experience growth retardation, especially if the condition is congenital. Congenital heart disease can cause slow growth, either directly or through secondary problems. Short stature can also result from a variety of conditions related to inadequate nutrition, including malabsorption syndromes (in which the body is lacking a substance—often an enzyme—necessary for proper absorption of an important nutrient), chronic inflammatory bowel disorders, caloric deficiencies, and zinc deficiency. A form of severe malnutrition called marasmus retards growth in all parts of the body, including the head (causing mental retardation as well). Marasmus can be caused by being weaned very early and not adequately fed afterwards; if the intake of calories and protein is limited severely enough, the body wastes away. Although the mental and emotional effects of the condition can be reversed with changes in environment, the growth retardation it causes is permanent. On occasion, growth retardation may also be caused solely by emotional deprivation.

Since growth problems are so varied, there is a wide variety of treatments for them, including nutritional changes, medications to treat underlying conditions, and, where appropriate, hormone replacement therapy. More than 150,000 children in the United States receive growth hormone therapy to remedy growth retardation caused by endocrine deficiencies. Growth hormone for therapeutic purposes was originally derived from the pituitary glands of deceased persons. However, natural growth hormone, aside from being prohibitively expensive, posed health hazards due to contamination. In the 1980s, men who had received growth hormone therapy in childhood were found to have developed Kreuzfeldt-Jakob disease, a fatal neurological disorder. Since then, natural growth hormone has been replaced by a biosynthetic hormone that received FDA approval in 1985.

For Further Study

Books

Crandall, Richard, and Thomas Crosson, eds. *Dwarfism: The Family and Professional Guide.* Irvine, CA: Short Stature Foundation and Information Center, 1994.

Deluca, Helen R. *Mountains to Climb.* Huron, OH: Cambric Press, 1983. (Biography)

Kuklin, Susan. *Thinking Big: The Story of a Young Dwarf.* New York: Lothrop, Lee & Shepard Books, 1986. (Illustrated book for young people.)

Organizations

Short Stature Foundation and Information Center
    Address: 17200J Jamboree Rd.
    Irvine, CA 92714
    Telephone: (714) 474-4554

Dysfunctional Family

A family whose interrelationships serve to detract from, rather than promote, the emotional and physical health and well-being of its members.

Although this term is used casually in popular culture, health care professionals define dysfunctional family as one where the relationships among family members are not conducive to emotional and physical health. Sexual or physical abuse, alcohol and drug addictions, delinquency and behavior problems, **eating disorders**, and extreme aggression are some conditions commonly associated with dysfunctional family relationships.

The concept of the dysfunctional family is based on a systems approach to mental health diagnosis and treatment, where the individual's symptoms are seen in the context of relationships with other individuals and groups, rather than as problems unique to the client. There is no strict definition of a "dysfunctional family," and especially in popular usage the term tends to be a catchall for many different relational disorders that take place within the family system and its subsystems (parents, children). Mental health care providers and institutions increasingly recognize family and couples therapy as effective methods of treating diverse mental health disorders, especially where children are involved.

Some of the characteristics of dysfunctional family systems are as follows:

- Blaming; failure to take responsibility for personal actions and feelings; and invalidation of other family members' feelings.

- Boundaries between family members that are either too loose or too rigid. For example, the parent may depend excessively on the child for emotional support (loose boundaries) or prevent the child from developing autonomy by making all the decisions for the child (rigid boundaries).

- Boundaries between the family as a whole and the outside world may also be too loose or too rigid.

- A tendency for family members to enact set roles—caregiver, hero, scapegoat, saint, bad girl or boy, little prince or princess—that serve to restrict feelings, experience, and self-expression.

- A tendency to have an "identified patient"—one family member who is recognized as mentally unhealthy, who may or may not be in treatment, but whose symptoms are a sign of the inner family conflict. Often the identified patient's problems function to disguise the larger family issues. For example, a child may be regarded as a bully and a troublemaker in school and labeled a "problem child," when he may in fact be expressing conflicts and problems, such as abuse from home, by acting out and being "bad."

Family therapists, like other therapists, take many different treatment approaches—psychodynamic, behavioral, cognitive, or a combination of these therapies. They may talk to members individually, together, and in subgroups. They may ask family members to reenact situations, or to do "homework" by modifying elements of their behavior and responses. As with individual therapy, one of the goals of family counseling is to reframe problems so that family members can see specific events and behaviors more clearly in a broader systems perspective.

For Further Study

Books

Annunziata, Jane, and Phyllis Jacobson-Kram. *Solving Your Problems Together: Family Therapy for the Whole Family.* Washington, DC: American Psychological Association, 1994.

Kaslow, Florence W., ed. *Handbook of Relational Diagnosis and Dysfunctional Family Patterns.* New York: John Wiley, 1996.

Minuchin, Salvador, and H. Charles Fishman. *Family Therapy Techniques.* Cambridge, MA: Harvard University Press, 1981.

Dyslexia

A reading disability that is not caused by an identifiable physical problem (such as brain damage, visual or auditory problems).

Dyslexia is a specific **learning disability** characterized by a significant disparity between an individual's general **intelligence** and his or her language skills, usually reflected in school performance.

Estimates of people with dyslexia range from 2% to the National Institutes of Health figure of 15% of the U.S. population. It is a complicated disorder with no identifiable cause or cure, yet it is highly responsive to treatment in the form of special instruction. The most obvious symptoms of the dyslexic show up in reading and writing, but listening, speaking, and general organizational skills are also affected. The dyslexic may have trouble transferring information across modalities, for example from verbal to written forms. The dyslexic's characteristic reversal of letters, confusion between similar letters such as "b" and "d," omission of words when reading aloud, trouble sounding out words, and difficulty following written instructions were first thought to be the result of vision and perceptual problems—i.e., a failure of taking in the stimulus. Only a small percentage of dyslexics have vision disorders, however, and it is now generally agreed by physicians, researchers, and educators that dyslexia is primarily a language disorder. Whereas the non-dyslexic intuitively learns phonic (sound) rules while learning to read, the dyslexic needs specific, methodical drill and practice to learn the visual-auditory associations necessary for reading comprehension and written expression.

Originally it was thought that dyslexia affected more boys than girls (in a ratio of 5:1), but later studies found boys to be only slightly more likely than girls to be dyslexic. Figures for diagnosed child dyslexics are skewed because for various reasons boys tend to be referred more frequently for **special education**. Diagnosis is complicated by the fact that anywhere from 20% to 55% of dyslexics also suffer from **attention deficit/hyperactivity disorder (ADD),** a behavioral disorder which can aggravate reading problems. There are many different theories about the causes and classifications of different types of dyslexia, but few hard conclusions. It is definitely familial, and about 40% of boys and 20% of girls with a dyslexic parent show the disorder. Several genetic studies have found gene linkages which demonstrate heterogeneous (multiple methods of) transmission. Dyslexics have average or above average intelligence, and it is speculated that they have heightened visual-spatial and motor awareness. Thomas Edison, Albert Einstein, Woodrow Wilson, General George Patton, and Auguste Rodin are thought to have been dyslexic.

Diagnosis

Children who demonstrate a reading level greater than two SE's below expected level for their age, intelligence, and education are generally diagnosed as dyslexic. Once reading problems are identified, a comprehensive series of tests of neuropsychological function (vision, hearing, and speech), intelligence, and achievement (word and letter recognition) will determine the existence of visual and auditory problems, behavior problems, or sub-normal intelligence, all of which may have symptoms similar to dyslexia.

While teachers and physicians are trained to recognize some language problems, many symptoms of dyslexia will be noticeable to parents. Contrary to popular thought, a child's mirror writing (writing backwards), reversal of letters, and confusion over which hand to use are not necessarily symptomatic and may only indicate lack of development. Indicators of dyslexia include:

- Lack of awareness of sounds
- Delayed speech
- Difficulty understanding spoken words
- Difficulty reading single words
- Extreme difficulty spelling words
- Extreme difficulty with handwriting
- Difficulty with locational and time indicators: up/down, right/left, yesterday/tomorrow
- Lack of enjoyment of reading
- Difficulty transferring information across modalities: writing down thoughts or speech, reading out loud

A child normally develops phonological awareness—the ability to differentiate between speech sounds and recognize their written symbols—while learning to read. The ability to sound out nonsense words (for example, from Lewis Carroll's poem "Twas brillig and the slithy toves/ Did gyre and gimble in the wabe") is a strong indicator of phonological awareness. In cases where the dyslexic has compensated for the disability by paying special attention to context or simply by rote memorization, a nonsense-word test may reveal the reader's underlying phonological disability despite his academic success.

Until they are diagnosed, dyslexics tend either to compensate—doing relatively well in school until they reach a situation where their phonological disabilities cannot be ignored (for example, in high school or college, where the work load is significantly increased)—or they fail to compensate, focusing their attention elsewhere, and are labeled as lazy by teachers and parents. If caught early, especially before the third grade, dyslexia is highly treatable through special education. Dyslexia is categorized as a learning disability under the national **Education for All Handicapped Children Act** passed in 1975. Dyslexic children are entitled to a comprehensive evaluation by a team of educational specialists, to an Individualized Treatment Plan (IEP), and to ongoing evaluation. Parents or caretakers may request the initial evaluation, may participate in all levels of the process, and must give their consent before the treatment plan begins.

Treatment

There are many treatment approaches available to the public, ranging from visual stimulation to diets to enhancement of regular language education. But it is generally agreed that specialized education is the only successful remedy, and the American Academy of Ophthalmology, the **American Academy of Pediatrics,** and the American Association for Pediatric Ophthalmology and Strabismus have issued a policy statement warning against visual treatments and recommending a cross-disciplinary educational approach. In fact the first researcher to identify and study dyslexia, Dr. Samuel Torrey Orton, developed the core principles of such an approach in the 1920s. The work of three of his followers—teachers Bessie Stillman, Anna Gillingham, and Beth Slingerland—underlies many of the programs in wide use today such as project READ, the Wilson Reading System, and programs based on the Herman method. These and other successful programs have three characteristics in common. They are:

(1) Sound/symbol based. They break words down into their smallest visual components: letters and the sounds associated with them.

(2) Multisensory. They attempt to form and strengthen mental associations among visual, auditory, and kinesthetic channels of stimulation. The student simultaneously sees, feels, and says the sound-symbol association; for example, a child may trace the letter or letter combination with his finger while pronouncing a word out loud.

(3) Highly structured. Remediation begins at the level of the single letter-sound, works up to digraphs, then syllables, then into words and sentences in a very systematic fashion. Repetitive drill and practice serve to form necessary sound-symbol associations.

Whatever remediation program is used, the IEP itself should define the student's specific problems and learning objectives, rather than make vague or general recommendations such as "John needs more support in reading comprehension." A good example of a specific learning objective would be "Max will be able to identify the following sound/symbol association in nonsense words: consonants, short and long vowels, and blends." When

ADD is co-diagnosed with dyslexia, special care should be taken to identify specific reading problems, and to define cognitive as well as behavioral learning objectives.

For Further Study

Books

Bowler, Rosemary F., ed. *Annals of Dyslexia.* Baltimore, Md.: The Orton Dyslexia Society, 1983.

Galaburda, A., ed. *Dyslexia and Development: Neurobiological Aspects of Extraordinary Brains.* Cambridge, MA: Harvard UP, 1993.

Miles. T. R. *Dyslexia.* Philadelphia: Open University Press, 1990.

Periodicals

Lytle, Vicky. "Edison, Rockefeller, Rodin, and the Reading Problem: Detecting Dyslexia in Students." *NEA Today* 4, October 1985, pp. 10–11.

Rooney, Karen. "Dyslexia Revisited: History, Educational Philosophy, and Clinical Assessment Applications." *Intervention in School and Clinic* 31, no. 1, 1995, pp. 6–15.

Rumsey, Judith M. "The Biology of Developmental Dyslexia: Grand Rounds at the Clinical Center of the National Institutes of Health." *JAMA* 19, no. 7, 1992, pp. 912–16.

Organizations

Council for Learning Disabilities
Address: P.O. Box 40303
Overland Park, KS 66204

Foundation for Children with Learning Disabilities
Address: 99 Park Avenue
New York, NY 10016

Orton Dyslexia Society
Address: 8600 LaSalle Road
Chester Building, Suite 382
Baltimore, MD 21286–2044
Telephone: (410) 296-0232; toll-free information line: (800) ABC–D123

Ear

The human ear is the anatomical structure responsible for hearing and balance.

The ear consists of three parts: the outer, middle, and inner ears. The outer ear collects sounds from the environment and funnels them through the auditory system. The outer ear is composed of three parts. The pinnas, the two flap-like structures on either side of the head commonly called ears, are skin–covered cartilage, not bone, and are therefore flexible. The second part of the outer ear, the external auditory canal, is a passageway in the temporal lobe of the skull, which leads from the outside of the head and extends inward and slightly upwards. In the adult human, it is lined with skin and hairs and is approximately 1 in (2.5 cm) long.

The third part of the outer ear, the tympanic membrane or eardrum, is a thin, concave membrane stretched across the inner end of the external auditory canal much like the skin covering the top of a drum. The eardrum marks the border between the outer ear and middle ear. The eardrum transmits sound to the middle ear by vibrating in response to sounds traveling down the external auditory canal. The middle point of the tympanic membrane is attached to the stirrup, the first of three bones contained within the middle ear.

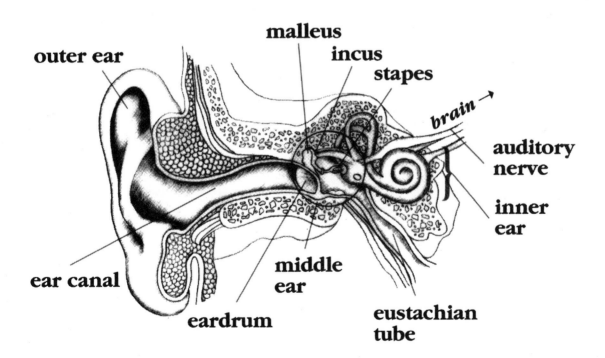

The human ear. Sound is captured by the outer ear and is transmitted to the middle ear by the eardrum.

The middle ear transmits sound from the outer ear to the inner ear and is the site of one of the most common infections in infants and young children, otitis media. The middle ear consists of an oval, air–filled space approximately 2 cubic cm in volume. The tympanic membrane is on one end and the back wall, separating the middle ear from the inner ear, has two windows, the oval window and the round window. The eustachian tube connects on one side, the brain lies above, and the jugular vein lies below. The middle ear is lined entirely with mucous membrane (similar to the nose) and is surrounded by the bones of the skull.

The eustachian tube connects the middle ear to the nasal passage. This tube is normally closed, opening only as a result of muscle movement during yawning, sneezing, or swallowing. The eustachian tube allows for air pressure equalization, permitting the air pressure in the middle ear to match the air pressure in the outer ear. The most noticeable example of eustachian tube function occurs when there is a quick change in altitude, such as when a plane takes off. Prior to takeoff, the pressure in the outer ear is equal to the pressure in the middle ear. When the plane gains altitude, the air pressure in the outer ear decreases, while the pressure in the middle ear remains the same, causing the ear to feel "plugged." In response to this the ear may "pop." The popping sensation is actually the quick opening and closing of the eustachian tube, and the equalization of pressure between the outer and middle ear.

Three tiny bones, the hammer (malleus), the anvil (incus), and the stirrup (stapes), conduct sound waves from the outer ear to the inner ear, which is responsible for interpreting and transmitting sound sensations and balance sensations to the brain. The inner ear is small (about the size of a pea) and complex in shape, and its series of winding interconnected chambers has been compared with (and called) a labyrinth.

Otitis media—the common ear infection—occurs when bacteria or viruses invade the middle ear through the eustachian tube and cause a swollen or inflamed eardrum. It is estimated that at least 60% of infants experience at least one ear infection before their first birthday, and 70% by the age of two. At least half of these children will have three or more. Most children outgrow their susceptibility to ear infections by the age of five as their bodies grow and their immune systems become more able to handle viruses.

Parents suspect ear infection when infants become irritable, possibly run a **fever**, and tug at their ears. Usually very painful, otitis media is responsible for at least 30% of visits to pediatricians each year. Diagnosis is often difficult because of the small size of children's ears. Treatment typically has consisted of antibiotics, although there has been much disagreement in recent years about their effectiveness. Some studies suggest that many cases of otitis media resolve themselves without treatment, particularly those caused by viruses. Many pediatricians contend that overdispensing antibiotics has reduced their effectiveness as bacteria develop resistance to them.

A more serious type of ear infection, otitis media with effusion (OME), occurs when fluid accumulates to block the eardrum. OME often causes no symptoms and, if left untreated for an extended period, can seriously compromise a child's ability to hear. Subsequent learning and **language development** may also be affected. Again, there are varying recommended treatments. Many doctors do not intervene in the early stages of OME, believing most cases resolve themselves within a few months. **Antibiotics** and surgery—to implant tubes that drain the fluid away from the eardrum—are other options. Some physicians theorize that frequent episodes of otitis media cause OME.

Permanent hearing loss is one possible consequence of ear infections in infants and children. While many are believed to originate with colds and upper respiratory infections that are difficult to prevent, there are some suggestions for reducing the incidence. First, some studies have shown that **breastfeeding** during the first 4–6 months of life dramatically reduces the number of ear infections. Breastfed babies often are fed in a more upright position than bottle-fed babies, which may prevent fluid from escaping into the ear and providing a breeding ground for bacteria. It is also believed that mothers transmit certain antibodies that help babies combat infection-causing bacteria. Parents are also advised to reduce infants' exposure to environmental risks, such as second-hand cigarette smoke, which may increase the incidence of ear infections. Frequent close contact with other children, such as in group **day care** situations, may also increase the likelihood of contracting ear infections.

Hearing loss in infants and children can result from other factors as well, particularly noise exposure. Loud music heard through earphones is a particular concern for adolescents. **Toys** such as **video games** and walkie/talkies present risks for children of all ages. It is recommended that infants be tested for hearing impairment before they are discharged from the hospital after birth, and definitely within the first six months of life. Low birth weight, use of a ventilator after birth, and family history of hearing loss are all considered potential risk factors.

For Further Study

Books

Mango, Karin. *Hearing Loss.* New York: Franklin Watts, 1991.

Martin, Frederick. *Introduction to Audiology.* 4th ed. New Jersey: Prentice Hall, 1991.

Periodicals

"Breast-feeding Prevents Ear Infections." *Tufts University Diet & Nutrition Letter* 11, August 1993, p. 8.

Brooks, Adrienne C. "Questioning Children's Ear Infection Treatment*." Consumer's Research Magazine* 78, February 1995, p. 19.

"Hearing Hazards of Toy Cellular Phones and Walkie-Talkies." *Child Health Alert* 13, July-August 1995, p. 3.

Mestel, Rosie. "Pinna to the Fore." *Discover* 14, June 1993, pp. 45–54.

Early Childhood Education

Educational programs for children prior to their entering elementary school.

Any educational program servicing children in the preschool years, employing trained adults, and administering a program designed to enhance later school performance might be considered an example of early childhood education (ECE). However, the original impetus behind what is now a heterogeneous collection of programs was the desire to provide young children living in poverty—and sometimes their families—with assistance to minimize the risks to their later academic growth and development. Probably the most well-known public early childhood program in the United States is the **Head Start** Program. Many others fall under the auspices of Title I of the Elementary and Secondary Education Act.

Title I preschool (i.e., prekindergarten) programs operate under a system of federal, state, and local cooperation. Local educational agencies apply to state agencies for program approval, and programs are funded with federal money. Local programs are monitored by state agencies but have the freedom to choose their own educational approaches. Head Start programs are funded by the federal Department of Health and Human Services, providing grants directly to community organizations. Private centers are tuition-based and may receive assistance from private foundations, or hold contracts to serve a certain number of children through Title I or other need-based programs.

There are several models of service delivery. Some programs are *child centered*, offering educational programs to groups of three- to five-year-olds in schools or other centers. Adjunct social services may also be available. Specialized services (e.g., health, speech-language therapy, occupational therapy) may be administered through the local public school (*see **Education for all Handicapped Children Act***) or through other providers. Head Start programs, for example, are mandated to provide education, health and social services, and parent services.

Another type of program is one that is more *family focused*. Such programs provide family support services often through home visits or parent education centers. Their goal is to educate and nurture parents to provide more appropriate stimulation and care for the child at home.

Still other programs attempt to meet both *child- and family-centered* goals. They may provide center-based care and education for children while parents attend school themselves or obtain job training. A major objective of these programs is to help families move out of poverty, ameliorating some of the risk factors that necessitated early childhood education in the first place .

What evidence is there to suggest that ECE offers children a "head start" in their academic careers? Several model programs around the United States—the Abecedarian Project in North Carolina, Houston Parent Child Center, Milwaukee Project, and Syracuse Family Development Research Program, for example—have provided some answers. Studies indicate improvement in IQ scores and achievement among children who attend model programs compared to their peers who do not. At least in some projects, gains in IQ persist into adolescence when children had been enrolled in programs offering full-day educational child care. The most uniform effects, however, tend to be in areas of school performance.

Graduates of ECE programs are more likely to progress through their subsequent school years without being retained in grade (i.e., repeating), are less likely to be enrolled in **special education** classes, and appear to be more likely to graduate from high school compared to other children from similar backgrounds who did not attend early childhood programs They also are judged by their elementary school teachers to be better adjusted and seem to show more pride in their achievements compared to their unenrolled peers.

Of course, these results are from model programs. Do the benefits extend to programs that are more typical of what is available in most communities? Studies indicate that they do when the community programs meet basic guidelines for quality (e.g., teacher to child ratio, staff training), but the benefits—while still sizable—are somewhat dampened. Ellen Frede has reported that the most effective programs are those that offer small class size, ongoing support to teachers, ongoing communication with parents or guardians, and curriculum content and methods that are not too different from what the child will encounter in their early school years.

Doris Entwisle has pointed out that experience in elementary school contributes substantially to sustaining the benefits of early childhood education. Even a temporary cognitive boost can enable a child to take full advantage of experiences in the primary grades, prevent placement in lower tracks, avoid grade **retention**, improve the expectations of teachers, and generally smooth the transition to the early school years. The effects begin to accumulate and may be enhanced by schools that provide supports such as small class size in the early grades, which has been shown to offer advantages to students that persist even when they move into larger classes in later grades.

Changes in the lives of children and families have contributed to the expansion of ECE efforts in recent years. Increasing numbers of single parent families and families in which both parents are employed have prompted the need for more private programs. In 1990, an estimated 60% of children in wealthy families were enrolled in some type of preschool education.

Children of wealth, however, are not the ones who will benefit most from their ECE experiences. Wealthy families frequently have resources to provide their children with educational advantages right in the home, including stimulating toys, games, books, computer programs, and access to play spaces, as well as basic **safety**, **nutrition**, and health care. Families who are living in poverty, however, often do not have such resources. In fact, these families frequently face multiple risks stemming from their poverty, including neighborhood violence, less than adequate nutrition, and poor health care. Therefore, it is not surprising that early childhood education offers the most to children of poverty, those who otherwise have the least.

While the need for further investment in public programs is becoming increasingly evident due to the continuing increase in the number of children living in poverty, 1993 saw only about 35% of children from poor families enrolled in ECE programs. According to Donald Hernandez, the number of children under the age of five living in poverty remained at about 25% from 1949 through the 1970s. By 1993, however, the number of preschoolers living in poverty had climbed to 33% with another 15% of these children living in near poverty conditions, while the Head Start program was able to serve less than one-third of eligible children.

Although there is resistance to providing full funding for federal early childhood initiatives, W. Steven Barnett points out that the estimated national cost of failing to offer two years of quality ECE is approximately $100,000 for each child born into poverty, or $400 billion for all impoverished children under the age of five. By comparison, Barnett estimates the cost of full ECE funding at $25 or $30 billion per year, a substantial portion of the annual federal budget, but a fraction of the eventual costs of not offering ECE to each poverty-stricken child who may benefit from it. The demographic trends suggest that early childhood education has become—and will continue to be—an important aspect of achieving an educational standard applicable to all youth.

For Further Study

Books

Consortium for Longitudinal Studies. *As the Twig Is Bent: Lasting Effects of Preschool Programs.* Hillsdale, NJ: Earlbaum, 1983.

Hernandez, D. J. *America's Children: Resources from Government, Family, and the Economy.* New York: Russell Sage Foundation, 1993.

Schorr, L. *Within Our Reach: Breaking the Cycle of Disadvantage.* New York: Doubleday, 1988.

Woodill, G. A., Bernhard, J., and Prochner, L., eds. *International Handbook of Early Childhood Education.* New York: Garland, 1992.

Zigler, E., and S. Muenchow. *Head Start: The Inside Story of America's Most Successful Educational Experiment.* New York: Basic, 1992.

Periodicals

Alexander, K. L., and D. Entwisle. *Achievement in the First Two Years of School: Patterns and Processes.* Monographs of the Society for Research in Child Development, Serial No. 218, 53, 2, 1988 .

Barnett, W. S. "Benefit-Cost Analysis of Preschool Education: Findings from a 25-Year Follow-Up." *American Journal of Orthopsychiatry* 63, 1993, pp. 500–508.

Frede, E. C. "The Role of Program Quality in Producing Early Childhood Program Benefits." *The Future of Children* 5, 1995, pp. 115-133.

Early Intervention

Therapeutic services provided from birth to age three.

Early intervention programs provide children from birth to age three with therapeutic services designed to prevent disorders that may stem from genetic conditions or adverse circumstance and to ameliorate **developmental delays** at as early a point as possible. **Down syndrome, cerebral palsy, cleft palate,** and hearing and vision impairments are all conditions identifiable at birth or soon thereafter. Children with any of these conditions—or any combinations of them—are typical of the children referred to early intervention programs. Other children, who may not have such obvious conditions, may be referred because of significant delay in speech, language, motor, or **cognitive development**—often by the pediatrician or a community-based screening program.

Children begin early intervention with an assessment by members of a multidisciplinary team. Composition of the teams may vary, but often include an **early childhood education** specialist, a speech-language pathologist, an occupational therapist, a social worker, and a health care provider.

School districts often administer programs, typically in a multi-district collaborative arrangement. Other programs may be based in hospitals, clinics, or community centers. There are several, often overlapping, models of service delivery.

Center-based programs bring infants and children in for group sessions that often involve teaching stimulation strategies to parents, and promoting interaction among young children. Depending on the needs of the child, a classroom component may be offered. Home visits may supplement the center-based care to allow providers to assess the needs of the child and family in their own environment and to promote transfer of skills from the center to the real world.

Home-based programs offer support and teaching in the infant's home. Teachers, nurses, therapists, social workers, or some team combination of these, make weekly visits to the infant and family to provide suggestions and model behaviors that encourage stimulating and responsive parent-infant interaction.

Some early intervention programs are aimed at reducing social stresses that might lead to negative consequences for the child in families who are **at risk** (e.g., infants born to young adolescent mothers) or who have a history of negative parenting (e.g., abusive parents). Teaching parenting skills, educating parents about child development, and providing a support network for parents who face daily multiple stresses have been shown to be effective in enhancing family functioning and child development.

A central feature of early intervention programs is the involvement of both parents and infants or young children. Children born with seriously handicapping conditions may need remedial and preventive services for their own skill development, but parents also need support and guidance in understanding their child's condition, identifying ways of dealing with consequences of the condition at home, and coping with their own feelings of loss, guilt, or helplessness. Once intervention has been successful with parents, they are better able to nurture their child's optimal development, not just in a weekly visit, but through the everyday experiences of living.

—Doreen Arcus, Ph.D.
University of Massachusetts Lowell

Eating Disorders

Eating disorders are characterized by an obsessive preoccupation with food and/or body weight.

Eating disorders are rooted in complex emotional issues that center on **self-esteem** and pervasive societal messages that equate thinness with happiness. Eating dis-

orders usually surface in **adolescence**, and more than 90% of sufferers are female, although the incidence among males appears to be growing. Because eating disorders are neither purely physical nor purely psychological, effective treatment must include both medical management and **psychotherapy**. The earlier a diagnosis is made and treatment is started, the better the chances of a successful outcome.

See also **Anorexia Nervosa, Bulimia**

For Further Study

Books

Jablow, Martha M. *A Parent's Guide to Eating Disorders and Obesity*. New York: Delta Publishing, 1992.

Maloney, Michael and Rachel Kranz. *Straight Talk About Eating Disorders*. New York: Facts on File, 1991.

Organizations

National Eating Disorders Organization
Address: 6655 Yale Avenue
Tulsa, OK 74136
Telephone: (918) 481-4044

National Association of Anorexia Nervosa and Associated Disorders (ANAD)
Address: P.O. Box 7
Highland Park, IL 60035
Telephone: (847) 831-3438

—Gail B. Slap, M.D.
University of Pennsylvania School of Medicine

Ebonics

Alternate terms: Black English; African American Vernacular English.

The form of English spoken by many black Americans, especially those living in urban, inner-city neighborhoods.

Ebonics (derived from "ebony" and "**phonics**") gained nationwide attention at the end of 1996, when the Oakland, California, school board passed a controversial resolution recognizing it as a separate language distinct from standard English. The school board's action, taken in response to declining academic performance by the district's black students, was aimed at improving the quality of teaching by offering special workshops to ensure that teachers understood Ebonics and respected its African linguistic roots. There was also speculation that by classifying its black students as speakers of a second language, Oakland might qualify to receive Federal funds for bilingual education programs, such as those offered to Hispanic and Asian students. However, the United States Department of Education has continued to maintain that Ebonics is a dialect of English rather than a distinct language.

Linguists have traced the grammar and syntax patterns of black English to West African and Niger-Congo languages. Distinctive elements of black speech include the use of "to be" in place of "is" and "are" ("He be home today.") or its omission altogether ("He not coming."). The "s" is commonly omitted from third-person singular verbs ("He play football every day.") and may be dropped from other words as well ("Sometime he be too busy."). It can also be added to words where it would not appear in standard English ("That candy mines."). A final "th" in a word is often replaced by an "f" sound ("I going wif you."). Other features include the double subject ("My sister she went to the store.") and the pronunciation of "ask" as "ax."

The formal recognition of Ebonics by the Oakland school board ignited a nationwide controversy involving issues of education and race. Some African Americans considered the Oakland measure a gesture of respect toward their cultural and linguistic heritage; others were offended by the perceived implication that blacks were incapable of speaking their native language without special assistance. Still other critics held that the recognition accorded to Ebonics would further disenfranchise blacks by endorsing their linguistic isolation from mainstream white culture.

For Further Study

Books

Baugh, John. *Black Street Speech: Its History, Structure, and Survival.* Austin: University of Texas Press, 1983.

Orr, Eleanor Wilson. *Twice as Less: Black English and the Performance of Black Students in Mathematics and Science.* New York: Norton, 1987.

Smitherman, Geneva. *Talkin and Testifyin: The Language of Black America.* Detroit: Wayne State University Press, 1986.

Taylor, Hanni U. *Standard English, Black English, and Bidialectism: A Controversy.* New York: P. Lang, 1989.

Periodicals

Baron, Dennis. "Ebonics Is Not a Panacea for Students At Risk." *The Chronicle of Higher Education* 43, January 24, 1997, p. B4+.

Gibbs, W. Wayt. "A Matter of Language." *Scientific American* 276, March 1997, pp. 25+.

Title: McMillen, Liz. "Linguists Find the Debate Over 'Ebonics' Uninformed." *The Chronicle of Higher Education* 43, January 17, 1997, pp. A16+.

Echolalia

Repetition of another person's words or phrases.

Using a mechanical, robotlike speech pattern, an individual with certain mental disorders may repeat words or phrases spoken by others. Known as echolalia, this behavior is observed in children with **autism, Tourette's syndrome, schizophrenia,** and certain other brain disorders.

Education for All Handicapped Children Act

Known as Public Law 94-142, a federal law mandating that all handicapped children have available to them free public education suited to their needs.

The Education for All Handicapped Children Act seeks to assure equal opportunity in education for all handicapped children between the ages of five and eighteen, and in most cases for children 3–5 and 18–21 as well. Handicapped children may not be excluded from public school because of their disability and school districts are required to provide special services to meet the needs of handicapped children. The law requires that handicapped children be taught in a setting that resembles as closely as possible the regular school program, while also meeting their special needs. Programs vary according to the individual needs of the special student. Some handicapped children may be placed in a regular classroom, but have special resources available to them; other students may need training at a special school. The law provides for screening so that children with special needs are recognized and treated accordingly. The law also requires that an Individualized Education Program (IEP) be developed for each special needs student, with input from the student and student's parents. Students must have access to specialized materials and equipment if necessary, such as Braille books for blind students. Handicapped students are also entitled to have specially trained teachers to meet their particular needs. The law provides for ongoing monitoring of the handicapped student's program and an appeals process for both the school and the parents of the handicapped child, so that no child is put in or kept out of special education without the consent and agreement of parents and teachers.

The first step in the **special education** process is to identify children with various educational handicaps. States and school districts operate programs to find children with disabilities, and to make their parents aware as soon as possible the resources available to them. Children with a wide range of handicaps are eligible for special education. Blind, deaf, or physically handicapped children are eligible, as are children who may have a mild speech disorder such as a stammer, a learning disability that makes it very difficult for a child to learn to read, or a behavioral or emotional problem that interferes with learning. In some cases, the parents may identify the child as having a problem that needs further evaluation; in others, the teacher may alert the parents.

If parents or school officials note a possible problem in a child, the child is referred for an evaluation. The law requires that parents be notified in writing, in their native language, of the reason for the referral, and be given a description of the evaluation process. The parents' written consent is required before a child can undergo the evaluation. The parents may also request, in writing, that their child be evaluated.

The next step in the process is evaluation. The law specifies that the evaluation be done by a multidisciplinary team, and not by a single person. Different states have different teams, but they usually include a social worker, a psychologist, and the child's classroom teacher. The parents must be a part of the evaluation team by law. The law recognizes that parents know the child best, and their input is essential. The child will usually be given a variety of standardized tests to determine specific aptitudes and weaknesses. The evaluation team may also observe the child in the classroom, review his or her classroom work, and consult with a guidance counselor, tutor, or other school staff who has worked closely with the child.

If the child is found to need **special education,** the parents will be asked to meet with a special team to help draw up an Individualized Education Plan (IEP). This team is separate from the evaluation team, though it may include some of the same school district staff. The child may be transferred to a special school, or allowed to work with a specialist in the school, depending on what the team decides will help the child most. Parents must give their written consent before the IEP is implemented.

The law requires that the IEP be reviewed by the IEP team at least once a year. Also, all students in special education must be reevaluated at least once every three years. If the parents or the school requests it, the reevaluation may be conducted sooner.

For Further Study

Books

Shore, Kenneth. *The Special Education Handbook: A Comprehensive Guide for Parents and Educators.* New York: Teachers College Press, 1986.

Organizations

National Information Center for Children and Youth with Disabilities
Address: P.O. Box 1492
Washington, DC 20013
Telephone: toll-free (800)884-8200; (202) 695-0285

—A. Woodward

Educational Age

A feature of test scoring where a student's test scores are compared to others.

Educational age is one measure of how a student's score on a standardized test compares to others in various chronological age categories. Education age is a type of norm used in achievement tests or other types of tests. For example, a group of six-year-olds may be given a standardized test. Each student will receive an individual score, which can then be compared to a table of scores linked to ages. Some children's scores may correlate with scores of children younger, others with children who are older. Thus, a child may be six years, five months old, and have an educational age (as measured by one test) of six years, zero months. Alternatively, a six-year-old's educational age may be seven years, six months.

Educational Psychology

The study of how people, especially children, learn and which teaching methods and materials are most effective.

Educational psychologists create achievement tests, develop learning aids and curricula, study cognitive development, and investigate psychological issues in the classroom, including adjustment problems and teacher–pupil interaction. Research in educational psychology encompasses such diverse topics as gender differences in mathematical ability; ways to help dyslexics read and learn better; the effects of **anxiety** on education; identifying and working with gifted children; the effects of television on school work; and **creativity** in children of a certain age or grade level.

Since educational psychology began to develop as a distinct field, its practitioners have tended to focus either on school and curriculum reform or measurement and learning theory. Early pioneers of the first approach were William James (1842–1910) and John Dewey (1859–1952) in the 1890s. James, whose functionalist philosophy focused on how consciousness helps human beings adapt to their environment, thought that educational problems should be studied in their natural environment—the classroom—rather than the laboratory. He was one of the first authorities in the field to regard classroom observation as a legitimate source of scientific data. The ideas of John Dewey have had a major influence on education in the United States. An advocate of active learning, Dewey stressed the importance of learning by doing as opposed to the rote memorization and authoritarian teaching methods that had long been the norm in most schools. He experimented with educational curricula and methods and advocated parental participation in the educational process. His first major book on education, *The School and Society* (1899), was based on lectures he had given to parents of pupils enrolled in his experimental school at the University of Chicago, founded to develop new educational methods.

The first important figure of the more theoretical branch of educational psychology was Edward L. Thorndike, often called "the father of educational psychology." Where James and Dewey were concerned with the practical application of psychology in the classroom, Thorndike, who had a background in animal research, did pioneering theoretical work in areas including conditioning and scientific measurement. He applied the principles he had discovered in his research to such topics as **language development,** reading instruction, and mental testing. His accomplishments included a book *(Introduction to the Theory of Mental and Social Measurements)* that provided statistical data about test results. In spite of his theoretical orientation, Thorndike directly influenced the nation's educational policies, notably the abandonment of the traditional classical Latin and Greek high school curriculum, which occurred after Thorndike's research established the fact that the major assumption behind classical education—that progress in one subject automatically leads to progress in others—was false. In addition to Thorndike, important early innovators in the area of measurement and testing include **G. Stanley Hall** and his students Arnold Gesell (1880–1961), whose Developmental Schedules are still used today and who was widely regarded as the nation's foremost authority on child rearing and development in the 1940s and 1950s, and Lewis Terman (1877–1956), who introduced **Alfred Binet**'s intelligence test to the United States in 1916 together with the concept of the **intelligence quotient (IQ).**

In addition to representing two different areas of research, the traditions of Dewey and Thorndike are also related to contrasting teaching paradigms, which have periodically been the focus of clashes within the educational establishment. The first paradigm, sometimes referred to as constructivism, is related to the emphasis that Dewey and other innovators early in the century placed on meaningful learning that relies on active engagement in such tasks as planning, problem-solving, communicating, and creating rather than on rote memorization and repetitive drills. The basic philosophy underlying this view is that knowledge must be presented in a meaningful context in order to be effectively assimilated. The second, contrasting paradigm has been called the transmission model because it emphasizes the act of transmitting information from the teacher to the student, a process in which the student plays an essentially passive role and is the object of stimulus-response strategies, such as being rewarded for correct answers. This model

is based on associationism and **behaviorism**—schools of psychology associated with Thorndike and B. F. Skinner.

Examples of these contrasting approaches are found in current controversies surrounding the teaching of reading. The **whole-language approach** introduced in schools around the country over roughly the past 15 years has come under attack by parents and educators who claim that it doesn't work, and that students need traditional **phonics** instruction to really learn how to read. Whole language is thoroughly constructivist: meaning is emphasized by instruction through stories and poems, and students take an active role in learning by producing their own texts (sometimes even their own spellings). By comparison, phonics corresponds closely to the transmission model: it relies on learning the sounds of letters and letter combinations (which, by themselves, have no meaning) by rote and memorizing them through repeated drills, a process that allows for little creativity. While some participants in the controversy have advocated teaching reading primarily through phonics, others in the field recommend combining the two approaches, a strategy already applied in some form by many teachers.

One researcher whose work has become influential in the classroom in recent years is Harvard psychologist Howard Gardner, whose theory of multiple intelligences (MI) is at the forefront of current research on the nature of intelligence. In his 1983 book *Frames of Mind,* Gardner posited the existence of seven different types of intelligence: 1) linguistic; 2) logical-mathematical; 3) spatial; 4) interpersonal (ability to deal with other people); 5) intrapersonal (insight into oneself); 6) musical; and 7) bodily-kinesthetic (athletic ability). Each type of intelligence includes a separate set of problem-solving skills, and every person has all the types, although some may be developed far more fully than others. Gardner has critiqued traditional education for emphasizing the linguistic and logical-mathematical intelligences almost exclusively, and he believes that IQ tests predict school performance only because they correspond to school curricula in their emphasis on these skills to the exclusion of other aspects of human intelligence. In recent years, a number of schools throughout the country have instituted curricula, teaching methods, and methods of assessment based on Gardner's theory of multiple intelligences. According to the theory, every subject and concept can (and should) be covered in ways that involve all the different types of intelligence, reflecting the fact that children have a variety of different learning styles. MI-based programs are especially effective with diverse student populations and in classrooms that include special-needs students. Another characteristic of these programs is that they are student- rather than teacher-driven in their emphasis on hands-on experience and active inquiry by students.

The education of those with special needs is a growing area of concern for educational psychologists. Current psychological theory and practice favor mainstreaming disabled or emotionally troubled children and teenagers—that is, including them in classrooms with their nondisabled peers—to give them a fuller educational experience and help reduce barriers between the general population and those with special needs. The application of educational psychology to special-needs education encompasses a variety of areas, including guidelines for classifying children and teenagers as retarded or deviant; teaching methods for **special education** instructors; and, where necessary, creation of intervention programs and individualized educational plans.

Division 15 of the **American Psychological Association** is devoted to educational psychology. Most of its members teach at universities, although some work in school settings. Professional journals in the field include *Journal of Educational Psychology, Educational Psychologist, Educational Researcher, Review of Educational Research,* and *American Educational Research Journal.*

For Further Study

Books

Brown, Ann L. *Psychological Theory and the Study of Learning.* Urbana, IL: Bolt Beranek and Newman, 1985.

Bruner, Jerome. *On Knowing: Essays for the Left Hand.* Cambridge, MA: Belknap Press, 1979.

Carter, Maggie. *Training Teachers: A Harvest of Theory and Practice.* Redleaf Press, 1994.

Cattell, Raymond B. *Personality and Learning Theory.* Springer Publishing, 1979.

Gardner, Howard. *The Unschooled Mind: How Children Learn and How Schools Should Teach.* New York: Basic Books, 1991.

———. *Multiple Intelligences: The Theory in Practice.* New York: Basic Books, 1993.

Electric and Magnetic Fields

Referred to as EMF, the fields of energy surrounding electric power wires and other current-carrying devices.

Electric power lines, household wiring, and appliances all carry electric current. Since the late 1970s, concerns have been raised about the link between electric and magnetic fields, the invisible lines of force that surround all electrical devices, and **cancer.** Alternating current (AC), the form of electric power used in the United States, produces fields that induce weak electric currents in objects that conduct electricity, including humans. Direct current, the form of current produced by batteries, is unlikely to induce electric current in humans. The currents induced by AC fields have been the focus of most research on how EMFs may affect human health.

Some studies in **epidemiology** (studies with humans to understand the cause and progression of disease) have suggested a possible link may exist between exposure to power-frequency electric and magnetic fields (EMFs) and certain types of cancer, primarily **leukemia** and brain cancer.

From 1979 to 1993, 14 studies analyzed the possible association between proximity to power lines and types of childhood cancer. Of these, eight have reported correlation between proximity to power lines and some form of cancer. Four of the 14 studies showed a statistically significant association with leukemia.

As of 1995, there is no scientific consensus about EMF and its relation to cancer. However, in 1992, the Energy Policy Act in the United States provided $65 million to fund the five-year program of EMF Research and Public Information Dissemination Program (EMF RAPID). The EMF RAPID program reported its findings to the U.S. Congress in 1997.

For the typical homeowner, identifying and measuring sources of EMF exposure is complex: EMF fields change constantly, depending on the power usage in the person's environment, and his or her proximity to the power source. People living close to large power lines tend to have higher overall exposures to electric fields, since fields close to transmission lines are much stronger that those surrounding household appliances. Magnetic fields, on the other hand, are stronger in close proximity to household appliances than directly beneath power lines. These magnetic fields decrease in strength with distance from the source more quickly than do electric fields.

To find out about EMFs from a particular power line, homeowners may contact the utility that operates the power line. Most utilities will conduct EMF measurements for customers at no charge. Other options are to hire an independent technician (often listed in the yellow pages of the telephone directory under "Engineers, environmental"), or to purchase a gaussmeter for self-monitoring of EMF levels.

Strategies for minimizing exposure to EMF are: increase the distance between yourself and the EMF source (keep appliances and electronics at arm's length); avoid unnecessary proximity to high EMF sources (don't play under power lines or on top of power transformers for underground lines); and reduce the time appliances operate (for example, turn computer monitor off when not in use).

For Further Study

Books

EMF in Your Environment: Magnetic Field Measurements of Everyday Electrical Devices. Washington, DC: U.S. Environmental Protection Agency (EPA), 1992.

National Institute of Environmental Health Sciences and U.S. Department of Energy. *Questions and Answers about EMF: Electric and Magnetic Fields Associated with the Use of Electric Power.* Washington, DC: U.S. Government Printing Office, 1995.

Possible Health Effects of Exposure to Residential Electric and Magnetic Fields. Washington, DC: National Academy Press, 1997.

Periodicals

"Electromagnetic Fields: No Evidence of Threat." *Consumers' Research Magazine* 79, December 1996, pp. 23+.

Schneider, David. "High Tension: Researchers Debate EMF Experiments on Cells." *Scientific American* 273, no. 4, October 1995, p. 26(3).

Wartenberg, Daniel. "EMFs: Cutting Through the Controversy." *Public Health Reports* 111, May–June 1996, pp. 204+.

Organizations

U.S. Department of Energy
Electric and Magnetic Fields (EMF) Research and Public Information Dissemination (RAPID) Program
Telephone: 202/586-5575
(Information on the five-year national research and risk assessment program on EMF.)

U.S. EPA Public Information Center
Address: 401 M St., SW
Washington, DC 20460
Telephone: toll-free EMF Infoline (800) 363-2383

Elimination Diet

A systematic approach for diagnosing food allergies.

An elimination diet is the systematic elimination of different foods and food groups from the diet as a means of diagnosing food **allergies.** While people of all ages can develop an allergic sensitivity to certain foods, such allergies are especially common among children. In the United States, one child in six develops an allergic reaction to certain substances, and foods are among the prime offenders. (Many food allergies are outgrown during adolescence.) Common symptoms of food allergies include hives, angioedema (swelling), respiratory congestion, and gastrointestinal problems. Food allergies are also known to play a secondary role in many chronic conditions, such as **asthma, acne,** ear infections, eczema, headaches, and hay fever. The most effective means of treating food allergies is to avoid the foods that produce allergic reactions.

There are two main ways of diagnosing food allergies by the elimination method. A casual approach involves eliminating, one at a time, foods from the diet suspected of causing allergic reactions, and observing the allergic person to see if there is a reduction in symptoms in the absence of particular foods. The more rigorous method (which is a true elimination diet) reverses this strategy by eliminating many foods at the outset and then adding suspected allergens (allergy-producing substances) one at a time. Elimination diets often include a rotation component, by which even the limited foods allowed at the beginning are allocated in such a way that no single food is eaten more than once within a three-day period. This feature has two purposes. First, it alleviates the monotony of a limited diet. Second, it allows for the possibility that some persons may even be allergic to the relatively safe foods allowed initially. If there is an allergic reaction at this stage, rotating foods makes it possible to identify the cause of the problem.

An elimination diet is divided into two parts: the elimination and reintroduction phases. During the elimination phase, which generally lasts between one and two weeks, as many known allergy-producing foods as possible are eliminated from the diet. Foods commonly known to cause allergies include citrus fruits, corn, chicken, oats, eggs, wheat, soy products, milk, vinegar and other products of fermentation, coffee and tea, cane sugar, chocolate, tomatoes, peanuts and other legumes, and food additives. In one very strict diet, the elimination phase includes only two foods known to be virtually allergy-proof: lamb and rice. Another, more liberal, diet allows a range of 56 different foods (although 12 of the items on the list are spices and a number of the others are relatively uncommon foods such as tapioca, carob, millet, rhubarb, and artichokes).

During the elimination phase of the diet, which clears the body of allergens, ingredient labels for all processed foods should be carefully scrutinized to make sure that none of the proscribed foods make their way into the diet. Persons with chronic food allergies should see their symptoms subside during this phase of the diet unless they happen to be sensitive to any of the normally non-allergenic foods allowed on the list at this point. A child with food allergies may breathe more easily and feel more energetic. Red, itchy eyes may improve, and congestion may clear up. Different diets handle the reintroduction phase differently. In some cases, the "test" foods are introduced at three-day intervals. In one diet, a new food is reintroduced every day for 15 days. Foods should be reintroduced in as pure a form as possible (for example, cream of wheat rather than bread) for maximum certainty that the resulting effects are produced by the substance in question rather than by some other ingredient added during the manufacturing process.

In a less rigorous diagnostic diet, food intake remains normal except that one suspected food or food group at a time is eliminated for a period of one to two weeks and the reaction observed. A strict elimination diet should not be undertaken without the supervision of a physician. The elimination phase of the diet should not last more than two weeks, since this restricted regimen will lack some essential nutrients. Another way to identify food allergies is to keep a food diary, recording everything eaten for a period of three or four weeks and noting any allergic reactions during that period.

For Further Study

Books

Cook, William. *Tracking Down Hidden Food Allergies.* Jackson, TN: Professional Books, 1980.

Feldman, B. Robert. *The Complete Book of Children's Allergies.* New York: Times Books, 1986.

Postley, John E., and Janet Barton. *The Allergy Discovery Diet: A Rotation Diet for Discovering Your Allergies to Food.* New York: Doubleday, 1990.

Walsh, William. *The Food Allergy Book.* St. Paul, MN: ACA Publications, 1995.

Yoder, Eileen Rhude. *Allergy-Free Cooking: How to Survive the Elimination Diet and Eat Happily Ever After.* New York: Addison-Wesley, 1987.

Organizations

American Allergy Association
Address: P.O. Box 7273
Menlo Park, CA 94025
American Dietetic Association
Address: 430 North Michigan Avenue
Chicago, IL 60611

Embryo

The developing human organism from the implantation of the fertilized ovum in the uterus, about two weeks after conception to the eighth week after conception.

The embryonic period of fetal development is one of rapid growth when the major organ systems begin forming and the main external features first appear. It is also a critical time for prenatal health and development—the most sensitive of all the stages of human development. During this period miscarriages or **birth defects** can be caused by a variety of factors, including maternal illness or use of alcohol and other drugs, and exposure to radiation. An enormous amount has been learned about embryos through ultrasonography and the study of miscarried embryos.

At the beginning of the embryonic period, a structure known as the embryonic disc is formed from the inner cells of the fertilized egg. The outer cells, collectively known as the trophoblast, have begun to form the protective substances, including the amniotic fluid, placenta, and umbilical cord, that will surround and nourish the developing organism during the prenatal period. Also formed by the trophoblast is the yolk sac, which produces blood cells for the embryo until it can manufacture its own and then disappears. The embryonic disc, which begins as a flat structure, separates into three distinct layers: the ectoderm, or outer layer, which will turn into the skin and nervous system; the mesoderm, or middle layer, from which the circulatory, excretory, and reproductive systems, as well as the muscles and bone, will be formed; and the endoderm, or inner layer, which will become the lungs and digestive system. The embryo's growth follows two general patterns of development: cephalo-caudal (from the head downward) and proximo-distal (inner to outer). In the third week, the head and blood vessels begin to develop, as does the notochord, a rod-like structure along the back of the embryo that will later become the spine, spinal cord, and brain. During the fourth week, the heart begins beating, and the eyes, ears, nose, and mouth start to form. The first signs of arms and legs appear, as do the tissues from which the lungs, liver, and pancreas will later be formed. By the end of the first month, the embryo is about 5 mm (0.2 in) long and weighs about 0.02 g (0.0007 oz). However, it is already 7,000 times the size of the zygote that was formed immediately upon conception four weeks earlier.

Between the fifth and eighth weeks, the brain begins to regulate the functioning of the internal organs, which continue to develop. The arms and legs begin to extend and take on a definite shape, developing according to the cephalo-caudal and proximo-distal patterns: first the arms, hands, and fingers, followed by the legs, feet, and toes. By the end of the fifth week, the embryo has doubled in size and has grown a tail-like structure that will become the coccyx, or lowermost tip of the backbone. By the seventh week it is about 2 cm (1 in) long and facial features are visible. By the eighth week, the embryo has grown to about 4 cm (1.5 in), weighs about 1 g (0.04 oz), and has begun to take on a recognizably human shape. The facial features are fully formed, the heart has assumed its final shape, and all the other basic organs have begun forming, except for the reproductive organs. The fingers and toes, which had been webbed, are separate, and elbows and knees have formed as well. From the end of the eighth week on, the developing infant is known as a fetus.

Embryology—the study of embryos—has yielded a substantial amount of information about human development, including important discoveries about congenital abnormalities. In recent times, important ethical questions have been raised by the scientific use of human embryos for research and such techniques as *in vitro* fertilization and cryotechnology. Louise Brown, the first "test tube baby," was born in July of 1978 with the help of *in vitro* fertilization, which is performed outside the mother—in a test tube or petri dish—using her eggs and the father's sperm. The fertilized egg, or zygote, after undergoing some initial development, is implanted in the mother's uterus. In the past 10 years, cryotechnology has made it possible to freeze human embryos indefinitely at extremely cold temperatures, a process that individuals may use for a variety of reasons. The disclosure in early 1997 that both an adult sheep and a monkey had been cloned from embryos further complicated the ethical issues surrounding embryology by raising the specter of human cloning. In March 1997 President Clinton issued an order prohibiting the use of federal funds for research on human cloning. This followed previous legislative and executive measures banning federal funding of embryo research, which is seen as controversial because of its possible links to the abortion issue and to the debate over whether the embryo—which contains the entire "genetic program" needed to produce a human being—represents the beginning of human life.

For Further Study

Books

Doran, Kevin. *What Is a Person: The Concept and the Implications for Ethics.* Lewiston, NY: E. Mellen Press, 1989.

Lejeune, Jirtma. *The Concentration Can: When Does Human Life Begin?* San Francisco: Ignatius Press, 1992.

Singer, Peter. *Making Babies: The New Science and Ethics of Conception.* New York: C. Scribner's Sons, 1985.

Vaughan, Christopher. *How Life Begins: The Science of Life in the Womb.* New York: Times Books, 1996.

Wolpert, L. *The Triumph of the Embryo.* Oxford: Oxford University Press, 1991.

EMF *see* **Electric and Magnetic Fields**

··
Emotional Development

The process by which infants and children begin developing the capacity to experience, express, and interpret emotions.

The study of the emotional development of infants and children is relatively new, having been studied empirically only during the past few decades. Researchers have approached this area from a variety of theoretical perspectives, including those of social constructionism, differential emotion theory, and **social learning theory**. Each of these approaches explores the way infants and children develop emotionally, differing mainly on the question of whether emotions are learned or biologically predetermined, as well as debating the way infants and

children manage their emotional experiences and behavior.

Early infancy (birth–six months)
Emotional expressivity

To formulate theories about the development of human emotions, researchers focus on observable display of emotion, such as facial expressions and public behavior. A child's private feelings and experiences cannot be studied by researchers, so interpretation of emotion must be limited to signs that can be observed. Although many descriptions of facial patterns appear intuitively to represent recognizable emotions, psychologists differ on the their views on the range of emotions experienced by infants. It is not clear whether infants actually experience these emotions, or if adults, using adult facial expressions as the standard, simply superimpose their own understanding of the meaning of infant facial expressions.

Between six and ten weeks, a social smile emerges, usually accompanied by other pleasure-indicative actions and sounds, including cooing and mouthing. This social smile occurs in response to adult smiles and interactions. It derives its name from the unique process by which the infant engages a person in a social act, doing so by expressing pleasure (a smile), which consequently elicits a positive response. This cycle brings about a mutually reinforcing pattern in which both the infant and the other person gain pleasure from the social interaction.

As infants become more aware of their environment, smiling occurs in response to a wider variety of contexts. They may smile when they see a toy they have previously enjoyed. They may smile when receiving praise for accomplishing a difficult task. Smiles such as these, like the social smile, are considered to serve a developmental function.

Laughter, which begins at around three or four months, requires a level of cognitive development because it demonstrates that the child can recognize incongruity. That is, laughter is usually elicited by actions that deviate from the norm, such as being kissed on the abdomen or a **caregiver** playing peek-a-boo. Because it fosters reciprocal interactions with others, laughter promotes social development.

Later infancy (7–12 months)
Emotional expressivity

During the last half of the first year, infants begin expressing fear, disgust, and anger because of the maturation of cognitive abilities. Anger, often expressed by crying, is a frequent emotion expressed by infants. As is the case with all emotional expressions, anger serves an adaptive function, signalling to caregivers of the infant's discomfort or displeasure, letting them know that something needs to be changed or altered. Although some infants respond to distressing events with sadness, anger is more common.

Fear also emerges during this stage as children become able to compare an unfamiliar event with what they know. Unfamiliar situations or objects often elicit fear responses in infants. One of the most common is the presence of an adult stranger, a fear that begins to appear at about seven months. The degree to which a child reacts with fear to new situations is dependent on a variety of factors. One of the most significant is the response of its mother or caregiver. Caregivers supply infants with a secure base from which to explore their world, and accordingly an exploring infant will generally not move beyond eyesight of the caregiver. Infants repeatedly check with their caregivers for emotional cues regarding safety and security of their explorations. If, for instance, they wander too close to something their caregiver perceives as dangerous, they will detect the alarm in the caregiver's facial expression, become alarmed themselves, and retreat from the potentially perilous situation. Infants look to caregivers for facial cues for the appropriate reaction to unfamiliar adults. If the stranger is a trusted friend of the caregiver, the infant is more likely to respond favorably, whereas if the stranger is unknown to the caregiver, the infant may respond with anxiety and distress. Another factor is the infant's **temperament.**

A second fear of this stage is called **separation anxiety.** Infants seven to twelve months old may cry in fear if the mother or caregiver leaves them in an unfamiliar place.

Many studies have been conducted to assess the type and quality of emotional communication between caregivers and infants. Parents are one of the primary sources that socialize children to communicate emotional experience in culturally specific ways. That is, through such processes as modeling, direct instruction, and imitation, parents teach their children which emotional expressions are appropriate to express within their specific sub-culture and the broader social context.

Socialization of emotion begins in infancy. Research indicates that when mothers interact with their infants they demonstrate emotional displays in an exaggerated slow motion, and that these types of display are highly interesting to infants. It is thought that this process is significant in the infant's acquisition of cultural and social codes for emotional display, teaching them how to express their emotions, and the degree of acceptability associated with different types of emotional behaviors.

Another process that emerges during this stage is **social referencing.** Infants begin to recognize the emotions of others, and use this information when reacting to novel situations and people. As infants explore their world, they generally rely on the emotional expressions of their mothers or caregivers to determine the safety or appropriateness of a particular endeavor. Although this process has been established by several studies, there is some debate about the intentions of the infant; are infants simply imitating their mother's emotional responses, or do they actually experience a change in mood purely from the expressive visual cues of the mother? What is known, however, is that as infants explore their environment, their immediate emotional responses to what they encounter are based on cues portrayed by their mother or primary caregiver, to whom they repeatedly reference as they explore.

Toddlerhood (1–2 years)
Emotional expressivity

During the second year, infants express emotions of shame or embarrassment and pride. These emotions mature in all children and adults contribute to their development. However, the reason for the shame or pride is learned. Different cultures value different actions. One culture may teach its children to express pride upon winning a competitive event, whereas another may teach children to dampen their cheer, or even to feel shame at another person's loss.

Emotional understanding

During this stage of development, toddlers acquire language and are learning to verbally express their feelings. In 1986, Inge Bretherton and colleagues found that 30% of American 20-month-olds correctly labeled a series of emotional and physiological states, including sleep-fatigue, pain, distress, disgust, and affection. This ability, rudimentary as it is during early toddlerhood, is the first step children in the development of emotional self-regulation skills.

Although there is debate concerning an acceptable definition of emotion regulation, it is generally thought to involve the ability to recognize and label emotions, and to control emotional expression in ways that are consistent with cultural expectations. In infancy, children largely rely on adults to help them regulate their emotional states. If they are uncomfortable they may be able to communicate this state by crying, but have little hope of alleviating the discomfort on their own. In toddlerhood, however, children begin to develop skills to regulate their emotions with the emergence of language providing an important tool to assist in this process. Being able to articulate an emotional state in itself has a regulatory effect in that it enables children to communicates their feelings to a person capable of helping them manage their emotional state. Speech also enables children to self-regulate, using soothing language to talk themselves through difficult situations.

Empathy, a complex emotional response to a situation, also appears in toddlerhood, usually by age two.

The development of empathy requires that children read others' emotional cues, understand that other people are entities distinct from themselves, and take the perspective of another person (put themselves in the position of another). These cognitive advances typically are not evident before the first birthday. The first sign of empathy in children occurs when they try to alleviate the distress of another using methods that they have observed or experienced themselves. Toddlers will use comforting language and initiate physical contact with their mothers if they are distressed, supposedly modeling their own early experiences when feeling upset.

Preschool (3–6 years)

Emotional expressivity

Children's capacity to regulate their emotional behavior continues to advance during this stage of development. Parents help preschoolers acquire skills to cope with negative emotional states by teaching and modeling use of verbal reasoning and explanation. For example, when preparing a child for a potentially emotionally evocative event, such as a trip to the doctor's office or weekend at their grandparents' house, parents will often offer comforting advice, such as "the doctor only wants to help" or "grandma and grandpa have all kinds of fun plans for the weekend." This kind of emotional preparation is crucial for the child if he or she is to develop the skills necessary to regulate their own negative emotional states. Children who have trouble learning and/or enacting these types of coping skills often exhibit **acting out** types of behavior, or, conversely, can become withdrawn when confronted with fear or anxiety-provoking situations.

Beginning at about age four, children acquire the ability to alter their emotional expressions, a skill of high value in cultures that require frequent disingenuous social displays. Psychologists call these skills emotion display rules, culture-specific rules regarding the appropriateness of expressing in certain situations. As such, one's external emotional expression need not match one's internal emotional state. For example, in Western culture, we teach children that they should smile and say thank-you when receiving a gift, even if they really do not like the present. The ability to use display rules is complex. It requires that children understand the need to alter emotional displays, take the perspective of another, know that external states need not match internal states, have the muscular control to produce emotional expressions, be sensitive to social contextual cues that alert them to alter their expressivity, and have the motivation to enact such discrepant displays in a convincing manner.

It is thought that in the preschool years, parents are the primary socializing force, teaching appropriate emo-

tional expression in children. Moreover, children learn at about age three that expressions of anger and aggression are to be controlled in the presence of adults. Around peers, however, children are much less likely to suppress negative emotional behavior. It appears that these differences arise as a result of the different consequences they have received for expressing negative emotions in front of adults as opposed to their peers. Further, this distinction made by children—as a function of social context—demonstrates that preschoolers have begun to internalize society's rules governing the appropriate expression of emotions.

Carolyn Saarni, an innovator in the exploration of emotional development, has identified two types of emotional display rules, prosocial and self-protective. Prosocial display rules involve altering emotional displays in order to protect another's feelings. For example, a child might not like the sweater she received from her aunt, but would appear happy because she did not want to make her aunt feel badly. On the other hand, self-protective display rules involve masking emotion in order to save face or to protect oneself from negative consequences. For instance, a child may feign toughness when he trips in front of his peers and scrapes his knee, in order to avoid teasing and further embarrassment. In 1986 research findings are mixed concerning the order in which prosocial and self-protective display rules are learned. Some studies demonstrate that knowledge of self-protective display rules emerges first, whereas other studies show the opposite effect.

There also has been research done examining how children alter their emotional displays. Researchers Jackie Gnepp and Debra Hess in 1986 found that there is greater pressure on children to modify their verbal rather than facial emotional expressions. It is easier for preschoolers to control their verbal utterances than their facial muscles.

Emotional understanding

Beginning at about age four or five, children develop a more sophisticated understanding of others' emotional states. Although it has been demonstrated that empathy emerges at quite a young age, with rudimentary displays emerging during toddlerhood, increasing cognitive development enables preschoolers to arrive at a more complex understanding of emotions. Through repeated experiences, children begin to develop their own theories of others' emotional states by referring to causes and consequences of emotions, and by observing and being sensitive to behavioral cues that indicate emotional distress. For instance, when asked why a playmate is upset, a child might respond "Because the teacher took his toy" or by reference to some other external cause, usually one that relates to an occurrence familiar to them. Children of this age are also beginning to make predictions about others' experience and expression of emotions, such as predicting that a happy child will be more likely to share his or her toys.

Middle childhood (7–11 years)
Emotional expressivity

Children ages seven to eleven display a wider variety of self-regulation skills. Sophistication in understanding and enacting cultural display rules has increased dramatically by this stage, such that by now children begin to know when to control emotional expressivity as well as have a sufficient repertoire of behavioral regulation skills allowing them to effectively mask emotions in socially appropriate ways. Research has indicated that children at this age have become sensitive to the social contextual cues which serve to guide their decisions to express or control negative emotions. Several factors influence their emotion management decisions, including the type of emotion experienced, the nature of their relationship with the person involved in the emotional exchange, child age, and child gender. Moreover, it appears that children have developed a set of expectations concerning the likely outcome of expressing emotion to others. In general, children report regulating anger and sadness more to friends than mothers and fathers because they expect to receive a negative response—such as teasing or belittling—from friends. With increasing age, however, older children report expressing negative emotions more often to their mothers than their fathers, expecting dads to respond negatively to an emotional display. These emotion regulation skills are considered to be adaptive and deemed essential to establishing, developing, and maintaining social relationships.

Children at this age also demonstrate that they possess rudimentary cognitive and behavioral coping skills that serve to lessen the impact of an emotional event and in so doing, may in fact alter their emotional experience. For example, when experiencing a negative emotional event, children may respond by employing rationalization or minimization cognitive coping strategies, in which they re-interpret or reconstruct the scenario to make it seem less threatening or upsetting. Upon having their bicycle stolen or being deprived of television for a weekend, they might tell themselves, "It's only a bike, at least I didn't get hurt" or "Maybe mom and dad will make up something fun to do instead of watching TV."

Emotional understanding

During middle childhood, children begin to understand that the emotional states of others are not as simple as they imagined in earlier years, and that they are often the result of complex causes, some of which are not externally obvious. They also come to understand that it is possible to experience more than one emotion at a time, although this ability is somewhat restricted and evolves slowly. As Susan Harter and Nancy Whitsell demonstrated, seven-year-old children are able to understand that a person can feel two emotions simultaneously, even if the emotions are positive and negative. Children can feel happy and excited that their parents bought them a bicycle, or angry and sad that a friend had hurt them, but they deny the possibility of experiencing "mixed feelings." It is not until age ten that children are capable of understanding that one can experience two seemingly contradictory emotions, such as feeling happy that they were chosen for a team but also nervous about their responsibility to play well.

Displays of empathy also increase in frequency during this stage. Children from families that regularly discuss the complexity of feelings will develop empathy more readily than those whose families avoid such topics. Furthermore, parents who set consistent behavioral limits and who themselves show high levels of concern for others are more likely to produce empathic children than parents who are punitive or particularly harsh in restricting behavior.

Adolescence (12–18 years)
Emotional expressivity

Adolescents have become sophisticated at regulating their emotions. They have developed a wide vocabulary with which to discuss, and thus influence, emotional states of themselves and others. Adolescents are adept at interpreting social situations as part of the process of managing emotional displays.

It is widely believed that by adolescence children have developed a set of expectations, referred to as scripts, about how various people will react to their emotional displays, and regulate their displays in accordance with these scripts. Research in this area has found that in early adolescence, children begin breaking the emotionally intimate ties with their parents and begin forming them with peers. In one study, for instance, eighth-grade students, particularly boys, reported regulating (hiding) their emotions to (from) their mothers more than did either fifth- or eleventh-grade adolescents. This dip in emotional expressivity towards mothers appeared to be due to the boys' expectations of receiving less emotional support from their mothers. This particular finding demonstrates the validity of the script hypothesis of self-regulations; children's expectations of receiving little emotional support from their mothers, perhaps based on past experience, guide their decisions to regulate emotions more strictly in their mothers' presence.

Another factor that plays a significant role in the ways adolescents regulate emotional displays is their heightened sensitivity to others' evaluations of them, a sensitivity which cans result in acute self-awareness and self-consciousness as they try to blend into the dominant social structure. David Elkind has described adolescents as operating as if they were in front of an imaginary audience in which every action and detail is noted and evaluated by others. As such, adolescents become very aware of the impact of emotional expressivity on their social interactions and fundamentally, on obtaining peer approval. Because guidelines concerning the appropriateness of emotional displays is highly culture-specific, adolescents have the difficult task of learning when and how to express or regulate certain emotions.

As expected, gender plays a significant role in the types of emotions displayed by adolescents. Boys are less likely than girls to disclose their fearful emotions during times of distress. This reluctance was similarly supported by boys' belief that they would receive less understanding and, in fact, probably be belittled, for expressing both aggressive and vulnerable emotions.

For Further Study

Periodicals

Bretherton, Inge and Janet Fritz, et al. "Learning to Talk about Emotions: A Functionalist Perspective," *Child Development* 57, 1986, pp. 529–48.

Gnepp, Jackie, and Debra Hess. "Children's Understanding of Verbal and Facial Display Rules," *Developmental Psychology* 22, no. 1, 1986, pp. 103–08.

Malatesta, Carol Zander, and Jeannette Haviland. "Learning Display Rules: The Socialization of Emotion Expression in Infancy." *Child Development* 53, 1982, pp. 991–1003.

Zahn-Waxler, Carolyn, and Marian Radke-Yarrow, et al. "Development of Concern for Others," *Developmental Psychology* 28, no. 1, 1992, pp. 126–36.

—Janice Zeman
University of Maine

Empiricism

The theory that all knowledge is acquired through experience.

Empiricism is the theory proposed by philosophers and psychologists that all knowledge and behavior are acquired through experience, and are not at all attributable to inborn or innate characteristics or traits. The English philosopher John Locke (1632–1704) developed the early ideas of empiricism, publishing in 1690 his *Essay Concerning Human Understanding*. He believed that infants are born with no innate moral sense, attitudes, or knowledge in any form. Locke envisioned the human mind at birth as a blank slate (*tabula rasa*), on which experience will record knowledge.

The psychologist **John Broadus Watson** expanded on the ideas of Locke when he formed his theory of **behaviorism**. Watson believed that a healthy infant could be taught to do anything. He did not acknowledge the existence of any inborn talents or abilities that would influence such learning.

Since the 1970s, there has been considerable research into the contribution of a child's **temperament** to his or her development, and most modern experts disagree with Locke and Watson. They believe instead that temperament is a source of individual differences in emotions that are innate to the individual. Temperament is a predisposition that allows two individuals to experience the same objective event very differently within the range of normal behavior and development.

Nativism is the theory that expresses the point of view opposite to empiricism.

For Further Study

Books

Buckley, K.W. *Mechanical Man. John Broadus Watson and the Beginnings of Behaviorism.* New York: Guilford Press, 1989.

Carruthers, Peter. *Human Knowledge and Human Nature: A New Introduction to an Ancient Debate.* New York: Oxford University Press, 1992.

Deleuze, Gilles. *Empiricism and Subjectivity: An Essay on Hume's Theory of Human Nature.* New York: Columbia University Press, 1991.

Slater, John G., ed. *Bertrand Russell, 1927–42: A Fresh Look at Empiricism.* New York: Routledge, 1996.

Encephalitis

An inflammatory disease of the brain caused by a virus that either has invaded the brain, or a virus appearing elsewhere in the body that has caused a sensitivity reaction in the brain. Encephalitis infects the brain tissue itself and has serious consequences.

Among the many forms of encephalitis are those that occur seasonally, those that affect animals, and a form that is carried by a mosquito. Viruses that have been directly implicated in causing encephalitis include the arbovirus, echovirus, poliovirus, and the **herpes simplex** virus. Encephalitis occurs as a complication of, for example, **chicken pox**, polio, and vaccinia, which is a cowpox virus used in smallpox vaccinations, as well as the common flu virus. Other implicated causes include the herpes simplex virus, responsible for the common cold sore, eczema, and genital herpes; the measles (**rubeola**) virus; some of the 31 types of echoviruses that also cause a paralytic disease or an infection of the heart muscle; the coxsackie virus responsible for infections of the heart and paralysis; the mumps virus; and the arboviruses that normally infect animals and can be spread by mosquito to humans.

The virus responsible for encephalitis can invade the cranium and infect the brain via the circulatory system. The blood-brain barrier, a system that protects the brain from certain drugs and other toxins, is ineffective against viruses. Once it has gained entrance into the brain the virus infects the brain tissue. The immediate reaction is an inflammation that causes the brain to swell and activates the immune system. The tightly closed vault of the cranium leaves little room for the brain to enlarge, so when it does expand it is squeezed against the bony skull. This can result in loss of neurons, or nerve cells, which can result in permanent post-infection damage, depending upon the location of the damage.

The individual who is developing encephalitis will have a fever, headache, and other symptoms that depend upon the affected area of the brain. He may fade in and out of consciousness and have **seizure**s resembling epileptic seizures. He may also have rigidity in the back of the neck. Nausea, **vomiting,** weakness, and sore throat are common. Certain viruses may cause symptoms outside the nervous system as well. The **mumps** virus will cause inflammation of the parotid gland (parotitis), the spleen, and the pancreas as well as the brain, for example. An infection by the herpes virus can cause hallucinations and bizarre behavior.

Treatment of encephalitis is difficult. It is important that the type of virus causing the infection be identified. Drugs are available to treat a herpes virus infection, but not others. The death rate can be as high as 50% among patients whose encephalitis is caused by the herpes virus. Infection by other viruses, such as the arbovirus, may have a mortality rate as low as 1%. Reduction of fever, as well as treatment for nausea and headache, is needed. Unfortunately, even those who survive viral encephalitis may have remaining neurologic defects and seizures.

Reye's syndrome is a special form of encephalitis coupled with liver dysfunction seen in young children and adolescents. Invariably, children who develop Reye's syndrome have had an earlier viral infection from which they seemingly have recovered. Hours or days later, however, they will begin to develop symptoms such as vomiting, convulsions, delirium, and coma. A virus such as the influenza virus, varicella (measles), and coxsackie virus are responsible. For reasons unknown, giving a child **aspirin** tablets to reduce fever accompanying a cold or flu can trigger Reye's syndrome. At the time the nervous system begins to show signs of infection, the liver is also being affected. Fatty deposits begin to replace functional liver tissue, and similar fatty tissue can be found in the heart muscle and the kidneys. The relation-

ship between the viral effects on the brain and the parallel liver damage is not known.

Treatment is not specific to the virus, but is directed at relieving pressure on the brain and reducing symptoms. The head of the bed can be elevated and the room left very cool. Care is taken to maintain normal levels of blood sugar and other blood factors such as sodium and potassium.

The mortality rate for Reye's syndrome can be as high as 25–50%. Early diagnosis and initiation of treatment play an important part in keeping the mortality low. Other factors, including age and severity of symptoms, affect the outcome. Some children who survive Reye's syndrome will show signs of brain damage such as impaired mental capacity or seizures.

It is important that children who contract one of the common childhood diseases of viral origin, such as mumps, measles, or chicken pox, be watched closely to ensure that they do not develop symptoms of a brain infection from the same virus.

For Further Study

Periodicals

Adams, R.M. "Meningitis and Encephalitis: Diseases that Attack the Brain." *Current Health* 21, October 1994, pp. 27–29.

Encopresis

Repeated involuntary or inappropriate bowel movement in children age four or older.

Encopresis is defined as repeated involuntary defecation somewhere other than a toilet by a child age four or older that continues for at least one month. Soiling, fecal soiling, and fecal incontinence are alternate terms used for this behavior. When there is no physical cause for encopresis, psychiatrists classify problems with urination and defecation as elimination disorders. Because bowel control is usually easier for a child to achieve than bladder control, problems with soiling are less common than those associated with wetting. In addition, encopresis is more likely to be a symptom of emotional problems or dysfunction in the **parent-child relationship**. In such cases, parents are likely to need the advice of a professional to devise a strategy for dealing with encopresis.

For some children, the cause of the inappropriate bowel movement is biological, requiring medical attention. Pediatricians refer to this problem as organic encopresis. Inappropriate defecation may be accompanied by withholding of feces, which can lead to bowel problems.

Bowel habits, although necessary to physical health, are private and rarely discussed openly. As a result, bowel problems such as **constipation** and encopresis are often ignored or left untreated for a long period of time. Parents wait and hope for the child to "grow out of it." When a child is learning appropriate toilet habits during toddlerhood and preschool years, involuntary or inappropriate bowel movements are common, and do not constitute encopresis. When parents treat a bowel problem as a cause for embarrassment or shame, they may unintentionally aggravate or prolong it. It may be reassuring to most parents to realize that encopresis rarely persists beyond late childhood.

When there is no physical cause for the soiling, psychological or emotional factors are often at work. The child may have received inadequate **toilet training,** or she may be using bowel movements as a display of hostility, anger, or frustration. Other emotional problems sometimes exhibited by children with encopresis include short attention span and hyperactivitiy, low tolerance of frustration, and lack of coordination. Encopresis may also be triggered by a change in the child's environment, such as the birth of a sibling, parents' **divorce,** move to a new home, or other serious family problems.

Treatment

Before beginning treatment for encopresis, the pediatrician will first look for any physical cause for the inappropriate bowel movements. If none is found, he or she will then work with a counselor or psychiatrist to analyze the variables that characterize the encopresis. For example, the following questions may be investigated:

Was the child ever consistently toilet trained?

Is the soiling random or does it occur in response to specific environmental or emotional triggers?

Have there been any changes in diet or physical growth and development that correspond to the onset of soiling?

Is soiling part of a pattern of problems reported by a parent?

Psychotherapy may be needed to help the child deal with emotional conflicts, while parents are simultaneously reinforcing appropriate toileting behaviors. Psychoanalysis focuses on the underlying psychological causes of encopresis. Advocates of this approach believe that encopresis is a symptom of an underlying conflict experienced by the child. Psychoanalytic therapy is usually carried out over a prolonged period of time, and it may be carried out simultaneously with **behavior therapy** focusing on the soiling itself. The therapist, the child, and his/her family concentrate on modifying the inappropriate soiling behavior while investigating the emotional conflicts that may trigger it.

See also **Enuresis**

For Further Study

Books

Galvin, Matthew. *Clouds and Clocks: A Story for Children Who Soil.* New York: Magination Press, 1989. [juvenile fiction]

Schaefer, Charles E. *Childhood Encopresis and Enuresis: Causes and Therapy.* Northvale, NJ: Jason Aronson, 1993.

Audiovisual Recordings

Understanding Incontinence. Cleveland, OH: Cleveland Clinic Foundation, 1994.
(Two-hour videotape covering urinary and fecal incontinence.)

English as a Second Language *see* **Bilingualism/Bilingual Education**

Enuresis

Also known as bedwetting, the inability to control urination during periods of sleep.

Sometime around the age of three, children typically begin to exhibit bladder control during the day and make the transition from diapers to toileting. For most children, nighttime bladder control follows. The term enuresis—often thought of as the technical term for bedwetting—refers to the continued involuntary passage of urine after an age at which control is expected.

When daytime wetting persists beyond the age of four, or nighttime wetting persists beyond the age of six, the child is considered to have *primary enuresis.* When the ability to stay dry has developed normally and without intervention but is followed by a period of wetting that lasts for three months or more, the child is considered to have *secondary enuresis.* The distinction between these two types is based on the child's physiological ability to control his or her urinary output. In cases of primary enuresis, this ability is usually compromised. In cases of secondary enuresis, the child often has no physical problems impairing bladder control, but may be reacting to some emotional or psychological issues. Most cases of enuresis—about 90%—are of the primary type.

Enuresis may interfere significantly with social and emotional aspects of normal development. Consider the plight of the 10-year-old who still wets the bed regularly. He or she may avoid activities such as camping out or attending pajama parties because of the potential humiliation of wetting in the presence of friends and acquaintances. Bedwetting may also present a stressor to family functioning with daily loads of sheets, blankets, and pajamas to be washed. Limited laundry facilities or crowded living conditions can make this extra task even more difficult.

Children may also develop a sense of failure and helplessness with regard to the inability to control night-time wetting. In fact, some studies have shown that bed-wetters show lower scores on indices of **self-esteem** and tend to underachieve compared to non-bedwetting peers. More importantly, these same studies showed that successful treatment of enuresis is associated with increased self-confidence and outgoing behavior at school.

Who becomes enuretic? Approximately 10% of six-year-old children wet their beds. By age 10, about 5% of children have primary enuresis, and 2% continue to show the disorder after puberty with cases persisting into adulthood. Genetics probably play a role in who becomes enuretic. Most children with primary enuresis have a relative—either a parent or an aunt or uncle—who wet the bed as a child. Many parents report that their bedwetting child is an extremely sound sleeper compared to their other children, an observation not supported by recent studies that suggest that parents' impressions may be due to the fact that they are not *trying* to wake their other children during the night. In fact, bedwetting may occur in any stage of sleep.

What causes enuresis? On occasion, enuresis turns out to be the result of a serious medical condition that causes increased urinary output, such as **diabetes** or **sickle-cell anemia.** A small number of enuretic children have a history of snoring and may have episodes of sleep **apnea** (interrupted breathing) that contribute to their bedwetting. Most cases of primary enuresis, however, are caused by smaller than normal functional bladder capacity and bladder irritability.

Functional bladder capacity is the number of fluid ounces that can be held in the bladder before one feels an urge to urinate as the result of wavelike contractions of the bladder. These contractions push fluid down past the inner sphincter muscle, a ring-like muscle that keeps the bladder closed when it is tensed. Normally, contractions are triggered when the bladder is full. However, in children with small functional bladder capacity, contractions are triggered by a smaller amount of fluid. Children who also have irritable bladders experience more and stronger contractions than normal at this lower volume. Both bladder contractions and the action of the inner sphincter are involuntary, that is, they are not under conscious control.

Only the action of the outer sphincter muscle is under voluntary control. We normally use this muscle to hold back urination in between the first urge of bladder contractions and the time that we are able to get to a bathroom. In deep sleep states, however, voluntary muscles relax. If a child reaches his or her functional capacity and experiences bladder contractions while the outer sphinc-

ter is relaxed in deep sleep, bedwetting may occur. This is not a problem for a child with normal bladder capacity. However, the enuretic child with a small functional bladder capacity and an irritable bladder is unable to hold the fluid that accumulates during a 10-12 hour nighttime sleep. When this child's functional bladder capacity is reached and many intense contractions push fluid beyond the relaxed outer sphincter, bedwetting occurs.

Although the most common causes of primary bedwetting are physical, psychological factors may also be involved. It can become a complex cycle as the child and family react to the bedwetting in ways that might exacerbate the problem.

The causes of secondary enuresis can be more difficult to pinpoint. It is a common reaction in children who have experienced trauma and may persist even after the incidents of physical, sexual, or emotional abuse have ceased. Even normal developmental changes in the family or the child's situation may result in a period of secondary enuresis, such as the bedwetting associated with the birth of a younger sibling or a child's entry to kindergarten. Bedwetting will resolve in most cases when the underlying emotional issues have been adequately addressed.

Can primary enuresis be treated? Yes. Many myths have surrounded the challenge of treating enuresis, dating from A.D. 77 when Pliny the Elder recommended feeding supplements of boiled mice to enuretic children. Fortunately, modern research has clarified factors that contribute to the causes of enuresis, thereby outlining the components of sound treatment.

Unfortunately, old myths occasionally appear in contemporary professional advice and health plan policy. One such myth is "Enuresis is a self-limiting condition, and treatment is not necessary." While some children do grow out of enuresis, without intervention a substantial number remain enuretic into adolescence and a smaller number into adulthood. "Don't drink anything after dinner." While the enuretic child should not drink a quart of soda before bedtime, excessive curtailing of liquids can be counterproductive by prompting an urge to urinate at even lower volumes of bladder pressure. Another common myth is "He could stay dry if only he tried harder." While *motivation* must be a part of any thorough treatment program, it is difficult for effort alone to accomplish anything when one is fast asleep.

No treatment plan should begin without a thorough evaluation designed to identify factors contributing to the problem. The basic assessment should include a complete physical examination, urinalysis and a urine specific gravity, evaluation of the urinary stream, neurologic examination, the assessment of bladder habits (e.g., the amount and frequency of urine produced each day, whether leakage occurs with laughter or effort) and bedtime habits (e.g., evening consumption of products such as caffeinated colas or chocolate that may act as a diuretic, whether the child is overtired at bedtime), and urodynamic studies as needed.

The treatment program that follows may include the use of wetness alarms to heighten the child's awareness of the signals that his or her bladder is full, exercises to increase sphincter control and bladder capacity, pharmacological interventions for short-term use, and psychological support. The use of wetness alarms combined with exercises to improve sphincter control and increase bladder capacity provides the best long-term treatment results; reported success rates have ranged from 65–85%.

Wetness alarms condition the child to awaken at the sensation of impending urination, especially when they are paired with sphincter control exercises. By awakening the child with a loud noise immediately upon urinating, the child eventually awakens prior to the sound and is able to urinate in the bathroom. The alarm can also be used during daily exercises as a signal to interrupt the stream of urination, helping the child to learn an association between "hearing the buzzer" and "holding it."

Increasing functional bladder capacity by consuming a large amount of fluid and then waiting as long as possible before urinating is another component to being able to sleep through the night and remain dry. How much fluid should a child be able to retain? A child's normal bladder capacity in ounces may be estimated by adding two to the child's age in years. Martin Scharf recommends measuring the child's output during bladder stretching exercises twice weekly to chart improvement in the bladder capacity. Long-term success in treating enuresis is always accompanied by significant increase in bladder capacity that is evidenced in decreased frequency of daytime urination regardless of the type of treatment program used.

Pharmacological agents have been used to treat enuresis, which provide good results in the short-term while the child is taking the medication, but poor effectiveness once the drug is removed. Desmopressin acetate (DDAVP) is an antidiuretic hormone that is administered by nasal spray. One drawback to DDAVP is that it is effective when nasal passages are clear and absorption is maximal, making it useless during cold and flu season. Imipramine (Tofranil) is an **antidepressant** that also has anticholinergic effects, that is, it suppresses the body's response to the neurochemical acetylcholine, thereby reducing bladder irritability. Both DDAVP and Imipramine have spontaneous success rates of about 70–75%, and are often prescribed for children going on camping trips or in need of a short-term treatment. As with any drug, there

SUPPLIERS OF WETNESS ALARMS

Alarms are often available at drug stores, pharmacies, or medical supply stores. There are several different types, and a range of prices. Product descriptions may be obtained from the following companies:

Koregon Enterprises, Inc.
Address: 9535 SW Sunshine Ct., Suite 100
Beaverton, OR 97005
Telephone: (800) 544-5240
(Manufacturers of Nite Train'r)

Nytone Medical Products, Inc.
Address: 2424 S. West
Salt Lake City, UT 84119
Telephone: (801) 973-4090
(Manufacturers of Nytone.)

Palco
Address: 1595 Soquel Dr.
Santa Cruz, CA 95065
Telephone: (408) 476-3151
(Manufacturers of Wet-Stop.)

can be side effects, warranting careful monitoring of dosage and administration.

Finally, treatment programs must attend to the psychological needs of the child and family. Providing information, setting realistic goals, structuring reinforcement, and addressing any of the child's negative feelings engendered by his or her experience with enuresis will enhance the effectiveness of any treatment method. Richard Ferber stresses the need for responsibility training and reinforcement in helping the child take responsibility for staying dry through reinforcement rather than punishment. With reinforcement and support, the child is able to take pride in his or her accomplishments as wetness begins to decrease in amount and frequency.

Successful treatment of enuresis is seldom an overnight event. Progress is often slow and hampered by relapses. Parents who are well informed and able to maintain positive attitudes in support of their child are better able to help the entire family cope with the problem of enuresis.

For Further Study

Books

Azrin, N. H. and V. A. Besalel. *A Parent's Guide to Bedwetting Control.* New York: Pocket Books, 1981.

Ferber, R. *Solve Your Child's Sleep Problems.* New York: Simon & Schuster, 1985.

Schaefer, C. K. *Childhood Encopresis and Enuresis.* New York: Von Nostrand Reinhold, 1979.

Scharf, M. B. *Waking Up Dry.* Cincinnati: Writer's Digest Books, 1986.

Periodicals

Koff, S. A. "Estimating Bladder Capacity in Children." *Urology* 21, 1988, p. 248.

Kolvin, I., R. C. MacKeith, and S. R. Meadow, Eds. *Bladder Control and Enuresis.* London: Heinemann Medical Books, 1973. (Especially the following chapters: "How Children Become Dry"; "Conditioning Treatment of Nocturnal Enuresis: Present Status"; and "Nocturnal Enuresis: The Importance of a Small Bladder Capacity.")

Rushton, G. "Enuresis." *Clinical Pediatric Urology.* P. O. Kelalis, L. R. King, and A. B. Belman. Eds. Philadelphia: W.B. Saunders, 1992.

—Doreen Arcus, Ph.D.
University of Massachusetts Lowell

Epidemiology

The study of patterns and possible causes of diseases in humans.

Epidemiologists study short-term outbreaks of disease, called epidemics, and long-term diseases such as **cancer** and heart disease. The challenge in epidemiology is to determine whether a true relationship exists between the cause being studied and the resultant disease. Epidemiologists must assess possible effects of factors other than those specifically being studied (called "confounders"). Epidemiologists seek "statistically significant" evidence that a relationship exists between the factor being studied and the incidence of disease. To be "statistically significant" the relationship must be due to more than just chance.

Epilepsy

A condition affecting people regardless of age, sex, or race, where a pattern of recurring malfunctioning of the brain is present.

Epilepsy, from the Greek word for **seizure**, is a recurrent demonstration of a brain malfunction. The outward signs of epilepsy may range from only a slight smacking of the lips or staring into space to a generalized convulsion. It is a condition that can affect anyone of any age, sex, or race.

The number of people with epilepsy is not known. Some authorities say that up to 0.5% of the population are epileptic, but others believe this estimate is too low. Many cases of epilepsy, particularly those with very subtle symptoms, are not reported. The most serious form of epilepsy is not considered an inherited condition, though parents with epilepsy are more prone to have children with the disease. On the other hand, an epileptic child may have parents who show no sign of the condition, though they will have some abnormal brain waves.

Though the cause of epilepsy remains unknown, the manner in which the condition is demonstrated indicates the area of the brain that is affected. Jacksonian seizures, for example, which are localized twitching of muscles, originate in the frontal lobe of the brain in the motor cortex. A localized numbness or tingling indicates an origin in the parietal lobe on the side of the brain in the sensory cortex.

The recurrent symptoms, then, are the result of localized, excessive activity of brain cells or neurons. These can be seen on the standard brain test called the electroencephalogram (EEG). For this test electrodes are applied to specific areas of the head to pick up the electrical waves generated by the brain. If the patient experiences an epileptic episode while wired to the EEG, the abnormal brain waves can easily be seen and the determination made as to their origin in the brain. Usually the patient does not experience a seizure and no abnormalities are found.

Grand mal seizures are those that are most characteristic of epilepsy. Immediately prior to the seizure, the patient may have some indication that a seizure is imminent. This feeling is called an aura. Very soon after experiencing the aura the patient will lapse into unconsciousness and experience clonic seizures, which are generalized muscle contractions that may distort the body position. Thrashing movements of the limbs shortly ensue and are caused by opposing sets of muscles alternating in contractions (hence, the other name for grand mal seizures: tonic-clonic seizures). The patient may also lose bladder control. When the seizures cease, usually after three to five minutes, the patient may remain unconscious for up to half an hour. Upon waking, he or she may not remember having had a seizure and may be confused for a time.

In contrast to the drama of the grand mal seizure, the petit mal may seem inconsequential. The patient interrupts whatever he or she is doing and for up to about 30 seconds may show subtle outward signs such as blinking eyes, staring into space, or pausing in conversation. After the seizure previous activities are resumed. Petit mal seizures are associated with heredity, and they never occur in people over the age of 20 years. Oddly, though the seizures may occur several times a day, they do so usually when the patient is quiet and not during periods of activity. After **puberty** these seizures may disappear or they may be replaced by the grand mal type of seizure.

A serious form of seizure, status epilepticus, indicates a state in which grand mal seizures occur in rapid succession with no period of recovery between them. This can be a life-threatening event because the patient has difficulty breathing and may experience a dangerous rise in blood pressure. This form of seizure is very rare, but it can be brought on if someone abruptly stops taking medication prescribed for the epilepsy. It may also occur during alcohol withdrawal.

Most children who experience seizures are not epileptic because the seizures occur only once. Epileptic children frequently suffer more from the misconceptions that accompany the condition than from the seizures themselves. While medication can control most of the symptoms, it cannot educate other children and adults who mistakenly believe epilepsy is a sign of below-average intelligence or even **mental retardation**. Over-protective parents often attempt to hide their child's condition from others or limit their activities unnecessarily.

Some types of epilepsy are characteristic of children. Benign rolandic epilepsy, which involves seizures that commonly occur at night or during sleep, usually starts after three years of age and disappears, with or without treatment, by adolescence. Juvenile myoclonic epilepsy, or epilepsy of Janz, begins in late childhood or adolescence and is characterized by jerking of the arms or legs that occurs while drifting off to sleep or upon awakening. It is easily controlled by medication and is believed to be genetic in origin.

Infantile spasms, sometimes incorrectly diagnosed as **colic**, usually begin between four and eight months of age and disappear by the age of four years. Most children with infantile spasms have impaired mental capabilities and subsequently develop Lennox-Gastaut syndrome, another form of epilepsy that includes falling down and multiple seizures.

A number of drugs are available for the treatment of epilepsy. The oldest is phenobarbital, which has the unfortunate side effect of being addictive. Other commonly used drugs include phenytoin, carbamazepine, and sodium valproate. All have the possibility of causing such undesirable side effects as drowsiness, nausea, or dizziness. Several new drugs are being studied to determine their efficacy and safety.

The epileptic patient needs to be protected from self-injury during an attack. Usually for the patient having a petit mal seizure, little needs to be done. Occasionally these individuals may lose their balance and need to be helped to the ground to avoid hitting their heads, but otherwise need little attention. The individual in a grand mal seizure should not be restrained, but may need some help to avoid striking his limbs or head on the floor or nearby obstruction. If possible, the patient should be rolled onto his side. This will maintain an open airway for breathing by allowing the tongue to fall to one side.

Epilepsy can be a recurrent, lifelong condition. Medication can control seizures in a substantial percentage of patients, perhaps up to 85% of those with grand mal manifestations. Some patients will experience seizures even with maximum dosages of medication, and these individuals need to wear an identification bracelet to let others know of their condition.

For Further Study

Books

Freeman, John M., et al. *Seizures and Epilepsy in Childhood: A Guide for Parents.* Baltimore: The Johns Hopkins University Press, 1990.

Periodicals

Glanz, J. "Do Chaos-Control Techniques Offer Hope for Epilepsy?" *Science* 265, August 26, 1994, p. 1174.

Hahn, Jin S. "New Antiepileptic Drugs for the Treatment of Childhood Epilepsies." *The Western Journal of Medicine* 162, April 1995, p. 353.

Organizations

American Epilepsy Foundation
Address: 638 Prospect Avenue
Hartford, CT 06105-2498
Telephone: (203) 232-4825
Epilepsy Foundation of America
Address: 4351 Garden City Drive
Landover, MD 20785
Telephone: (800) 332-1000

Erikson's Theory

Influential theory of lifelong psychological development by child psychologist Erik Erikson.

The German-born child development expert Erik Erikson (1902–1994), who emigrated to the United States in the 1930s, published his theory of developmental stages in the 1950 volume *Childhood and Society.* Erikson broke with traditional Freudian psychologists in attributing major developmental significance to stages of life beyond early childhood and also in his emphasis on the role of the ego. In addition, Erikson, like other psychodynamic theorists after Freud, did not give sexuality the preeminent place it occupied in the work of his famous predecessor. In contrast to Freud's psychosexual stages, the stages of development outlined by Erikson are called *psychosocial* stages. Erikson is also known for formulating the concept of the adolescent identity crisis.

Erik Erikson

Erikson's developmental framework consists of eight stages that cover the entire life span. At each stage, the individual is faced with a central conflict and the task of overcoming it.

Infancy

Trust vs. mistrust. In infancy, the quality of basic trust—the sense that one's needs will be met, especially by the mother—must be established or the individual will learn to mistrust the world. The sense of trust is rooted in the quality of an infant's care and the relationship with the primary caregivers.

Toddlerhood

Autonomy vs. shame and doubt. The central task of toddlers is the acquisition of autonomy, manifested by making choices and learning self-control. Confidence in being able to do things for oneself must surmount feelings of shame and doubt brought on by the difficulty of adapting to society's rules and restrictions, including requirements for self-control such as toilet training.

Preschoolers

Initiative vs. guilt. Between the third and fifth year, the child actively begins to explore her environment and initiate activities on her own. This is the stage at which a sense of purpose is developed, along with the ability to pursue goals in spite of the guilt that may come with asserting oneself and also despite the knowledge that one may fail.

School age

Industry vs. inferiority. During the school years, the child's ability to master new tasks and skills successfully depends on overcoming feelings of inadequacy. The overall goal at this stage is the development of competence. Progress though the first four stages of Erikson's framework is cumulative. Together, these stages create a foundation for negotiating the following ones. Difficulty with any of the stages will hinder future development.

Adolescence

Identity vs. role confusion. The central task of **adolescence** is carving out a new identity amidst the physical and emotional upheavals of this period. Erikson was the first to use the term "identity crisis" in connection with this stage of life, referring to the confusion and **anxiety** engendered by the need to choose from among a variety of alternatives and to make commitments to a specific set of goals and values. Confronted with physical growth and sexual maturation as well as imminent choices about education and careers, teenagers must meet the challenge of integrating their past experiences and characteristics into a stable sense of self. Some common ways young people deal with the insecurity of adolescence include forming **cliques**, becoming preoccupied with older role models and mentors, and falling in love. Young people who lack the stability or self-awareness to solve their identity conflicts risk identity diffusion, an inability to make defining choices about themselves, which can later block their development as adults.

Adulthood

Early adulthood (intimacy vs. isolation). The central task at this stage is the ability to commit oneself to another person in an intimate relationship. The alternative is a sense of isolation and abandonment.

Middle age (generativity vs. stagnation). In middle age, the ability to devote oneself to the creation of something that will last—either through parenting, work, or other activities—becomes paramount. The alternative is to become self-centered and apathetic.

Maturity (integrity vs. despair). A person who has mastered the psychological tasks and resolved the conflicts of previous stages can approach old age with the strength and wisdom to face physical frailty and approaching death without despair.

Erikson's theory of psychosocial stages has been profoundly influential. In the 1970s, journalist Gail Sheehy popularized and extended Erikson's concept of

ERIKSON'S IDENTITY CRISIS

Erikson's theory about identity crisis and identity confusion is based, in part, on his own life experience. He was born to Danish parents and was told that his parents separated before he was born. When he was three-years-old his mother married his pediatrician, Dr. Theodore Homburger, who adopted him and gave him his name. When he was a teenager his mother confessed that he was, in fact, the child of an extramarital affair. He never knew his birth father or his mother's first husband. This confusion was complicated by the fact that his adoptive father was Jewish and his Danish heritage clearly showed in his features. He was ostracized by his Jewish friends and mistreated by anti-Semitic schoolmates. According to some sources, he became introverted and often withdrew into a fantasy world. After graduating from high school, he decided to travel rather than go to college.

In the late 1920s, Erikson underwent psychoanalysis with Anna Freud, whom he met when he was employed as a tutor to the children of an American woman studying with Sigmund Freud in Vienna. Erikson described the analysis as liberating, although painful at times. Around this time he changed his name to Erik Homburger Erikson, which perhaps reflects his attempt to resolve his childhood identity crisis. In 1933 he completed his own formal training in psychoanalysis and left Vienna with his wife to avoid the Nazis and to make a physical and philosophical break with the Freuds.

Erikson's many accomplishments included an appointment at the Harvard Medical School, a Pulitzer Prize for his book on Gandhi, a professorship at Yale's medical school, and the founding of a center, named after him, at Harvard Medical School's Cambridge Hospital. Erikson's accomplishments give credence to his theory that the ills of childhood can be healed in adulthood-- that an identity crisis is a normal and healthy part of becoming an adult. After a turbulent childhood and adolescence, Erikson went on to become one of the most innovative and creative thinkers of the 20th century.

developmental stages in adulthood in her best-selling *Passages: Predictable Crises of Adult Life.* Erikson, who died in 1979, won both the Pulitzer Prize and the National Book Award for his publications.

For Further Study

Books

Erikson, Erik H. *Childhood and Society.* New York: Norton, 1950.

———. *Identity and the Life Cycle.* New York: International Universities Press, 1959.

Sheehy, Gail. *Passages: Predictable Crises of Adult Life.* New York: E. P. Dutton, 1976.

Stevens, Richard. *Erik Erikson: An Introduction.* New York: St. Martin's, 1983.

. . . .

Ethics

Personal rules for behavior.

Ethics are rules for behavior, based on beliefs about how things should be. Ethical statements involve: 1) assumptions about humans and their capacities; 2) logical rules extending from these assumptions; and 3) notions of what is good and desirable.

Ethical systems (sets of rules for acceptable behavior) concern the "shoulds" and "should nots" of life, the principles and **values** on which human relations are based.

The assessment of whether a behavior is ethical is divided into four categories, or domains: consequences, actions, character, and motive. In the domain of consequences, a behavior is determined to be "right" or "wrong" based on the results of the action, whereas the domain of actions looks only at the act itself. The domain of character looks at whether a person's overall character is ethical; a person who is deemed as "virtuous" has consistently ethical behavior. The motive domain evaluates a person's intentions, regardless of the consequences. It considers whether the person intended to do good, even if the result was bad. A behavior may be deemed "ethical" according to one domain of assessment, but appear "unethical" according to another. For example, a poor person steals a small amount of food to feed her starving child from a wealthy, well-fed person who does not even notice that the food is missing. This act would be considered ethical in the domain of consequences, since the child can be fed, and motive, since the person is caring for her child, but unethical in the domain of actions, because stealing in itself is wrong. The poor person's general behavior would have to be evaluated to determine whether she is ethical in the domain of character.

Ethics can also be divided into two main schools, absolutism and relativism. Absolutists believe that ethical rules are fixed standards (for example, stealing is always wrong, no matter what the circumstances). Relativists, on the other hand, believe that all ethics are subject to context (for example, stealing may be wrong in certain circumstances but not in others). Few people are actually pure absolutists or pure relativists, but rather fall somewhere along the spectrum between the two extremes, tending towards one or the other. Most who tend towards absolutism will allow for special circumstances and bend the rules on occasion, while those who tend towards relativism will admit to some universal standards that form a "bottom line" of behavior.

In order to develop ethical maturity, people must have moral awareness and moral agency (or autonomy). Moral awareness is the ability to recognize the ethical element of a given situation. For some, eating beef is simply an act of appetite and habit, with no thought given to its ethical implications. For others, whether to eat beef is a complicated moral question involving the ethics of land use (grazing cattle vs. growing food crops), conservation (the destruction of rainforests to increase grazing grounds), and the global economy (the transformation of underdeveloped countries into cattle farms for Western industrialized nations). Moral agency or autonomy means the freedom to choose between alternative behaviors. A person cannot develop ethical maturity without being able to choose from alternatives. Without moral awareness and moral agency, ethics become meaningless because behaviors are simply automatic, or forced.

The question of moral agency becomes complicated by the tendency to equate ethical behavior with obedience. Because humans first learn ethics as small children from adult authority figures, our initial understanding of ethics is "obeying." When we do what adults want us to, we are told we are "good." If we disobey, we are "bad." Some people never outgrow this, continuing throughout life to believe that being "good" means obeying external authorities. These people have never developed a sense of moral agency, even though they are capable of making choices. A prime example of this dilemma is the numerous soldiers and citizens who carried out or assisted in the torture and murder of millions of Jews, Russians, gays, and others in the Holocaust of World War II. Do their claims that they were "just following orders" exempt them from ethical responsibility? Likewise, in situations of oppression where people have been traumatized into blind obedience to their oppressors, are the oppressed ethically responsible for their actions, or do they lack moral agency? These are difficult questions with no clear answers, but they do illuminate the essential character of freedom to choose in the development of ethical maturity.

Ethical maturity involves accepting full responsibility for one's ethical choices and their consequences. An ethically mature person obeys her or his own, inner authority (or conscience), rather than an outside authority figure. Moving from the infantile state of externally determined obedience to the mature state of self-determina-

tion is a long and difficult process, however. In her 1994 book, psychologist Elizabeth McGrath presents nine stages of ethical development.

- Stage 1 = The person sees the world in polar terms of we-right-good versus they-wrong-bad. Right answers for everything are known to an authority whose role is to mediate or teach them.

- Stage 2 = The person perceives diversity of opinion and uncertainty and accounts for these as confusion engendered by poorly qualified authorities or as exercises designed to encourage individuals to find their own system.

- Stage 3 = The person accepts diversity and uncertainty as legitimate, but only as temporary conditions in areas for which the authority has not yet found an answer. The perceived uncertainty on the part of the so-called experts makes the person anxious. Therefore, this stage does not last long.

In Stages 1–3, ethical choices are based completely on obedience to external authorities. A person in these stages of ethical development is rigid in their beliefs and defensive when challenged, because there is no internal sense of confidence. The person's ethics are not grounded in any self-determined understanding of right and wrong, but rather in the dictates of outside authorities. When the infallibility of those authorities comes into question, the anxiety produced either pushes the person on to Stage 4, or back to the unquestioning stance of Stage 1. Some people never progress beyond the first three stages of ethical development.

The biggest shift in ethical understanding comes between Stages 3 and 4, if the person chooses to progress rather than regress. At this point, blind obedience to absolute, externally determined codes of behavior is thrown off and replaced with extreme relativism. As the person matures further, this extreme relativism is gradually modified. In McGrath's words:

- Stage 4 = The person perceives that legitimate uncertainty and diversity of opinion are extensive and concludes that all people have a right to their own opinions. The person rejects ethical authorities in favor of a thoroughgoing relativism in which anyone's opinion, including the individual's, is as good, true, or reliable as anyone else's.

- Stage 5 = The person perceives all knowledge and values, including those of formerly recognized ethical authorities, as contextual and relativistic and relegates dualistic right-wrong functions to a subordinate status by placing them in context.

In other words, Stage 4 reasoning makes "right" and "wrong" meaningless with a completely relativistic, anything-goes ethical stance. In Stage 5, however, "right" and "wrong" return, not as absolutes as in the first three stages, but as contextual concepts.

The next steps in ethical maturity involve taking responsibility for one's own ethical choices, leading eventually to a solid, well-reasoned, ethical self-determination.

- Stage 6 = The person recognizes that he or she must orient himself or herself in a relativistic world through a personal commitment, as distinct from unquestioned or unconsidered commitment to simple belief in certainty.

- Stage 7 = The person makes an initial, limited commitment.

- Stage 8 = The person experiences the initial implications of commitment and explores the subjective issues of responsibility.

- Stage 9 = The person assumes responsibility for his or her beliefs and realizes that commitment is an ongoing, unfolding activity.

The ethically mature person understands that ethical maturity is not a final achievement but a lifelong process of growth and development.

Ethics are acquired from the day of our birth until the day of our death. At first, ethics are absorbed through **parent-child relationships** and the imitation of adult behavior. Children should interact with warm, caring, ethically mature adults during their first years of life to promote positive ethical development. Parents and teachers have a strong impact on children through the tenor of their relationships with children and with each other. Adults most often try to promote ethical behavior in children by establishing rules and codes of behavior through rewards and punishments. However, experts have found that this is much less effective than modeling and personal interaction.

Ethics are also acquired through labeling and sexual roles. People most often live up to the labels they are given, especially children. If a child is labeled "delinquent," she or he will incorporate that label and behave accordingly. If, on the other hand, a child is labeled "well-behaved," he or she will fulfill that expectation. Sexual roles also confer labels; "masculine" and "feminine" carry distinct expectations in nearly every culture, which children learn to conform to or rebel against early on. To become ethically mature, a person must struggle past assigned labels and roles to develop a freely chosen sense of identity, from which will grow the ethical code.

Two other important sources of ethical development are the practice of ethical behaviors and social interaction. Adults can help promote positive ethical development in children by creating opportunities for the children to make age-appropriate ethical choices and ex-

perience the consequences of those choices. It is also important to create a safe, supportive social environment so that children can learn to value others and identify with their community. Empathy is an essential element in positive ethical behavior; unless a person identifies with others and values them, she or he will have no qualms about causing others pain or suffering.

Finally, to reach full ethical maturity, a person must create his or her own ethical systems, born out of a sense of connection with all humans and other forms of life. Children must be given the opportunity to ground themselves in a sense of safety and community, out of which they can develop a responsible code of ethics that will carry them creatively through life.

See also **Moral development**

For Further Study

Books

McGrath, Elizabeth Z. *The Art of Ethics: A Psychology of Ethical Beliefs.* Chicago: Loyola University Press, 1994.

Messerly, John G. *An Introduction to Ethical Theories.* Lanham, MD: University Press of America, 1995.

Pojman, Louis P. *Ethics: Discovering Right and Wrong.* Belmont, CA: Wadsworth Publishing, 1990.

Terkel, Susan Neiburg. *Ethics.* New York: Lodestar Books, 1992.

—Dianne K. Daeg de Mott

Ethnic Identity

An individual's feeling of belonging to a particular ethnic group.

The adjective *ethnic* is derived from the Greek noun *ethnos*, which means *race, people, nation,* and *tribe.* Although the modern term has a narrower connotation, denoting primarily *people,* vestiges of the older, more inclusive meaning still remain, particularly in types of discourse where the concepts of race and nationality are used interchangeably. Matters get even more complicated when the concept of *identity* is introduced, because, strictly speaking, a person's identity is a sum of essential attributes, and ethnicity, as researchers have asserted, is not necessarily an essential attribute of personal identity.

Students of children's ethnic identity have to work in the context of the child's developing, evolving self. Because of this fact, insights provided by studies of adult feelings of ethnic identity are not very helpful. As children mature, their perception of ethnicity undergoes profound transformation. This transformation is concomitant with cognitive development. For example, as Frances Aboud and Anna-Beth Doyle explain (Aboud and Doyle,

1983), in the stage of **cognitive development** which Jean Piaget named *pre-operational* (between the ages of 2 and 7), children show a strong tendency to identify with a group perceived as their own, while rejecting those seen as different. With the onset of the operation phase, children, who are now capable of rational thought, generally grow more tolerant toward "others," also showing empathy and understanding toward children who are viewed as different. This finding shows that the development of ethnic consciousness, although related to cognitive development, does not mirror the child's intellectual growth. However, with cognitive maturation, ethnicity, which is initially experienced as an image, or a set of physical attributes, becomes a mental construct which includes language, customs, cultural facts, and general knowledge about one's own ethnic group. Thus, to a four-year-old Mexican American child, ethnic identity is formed on the basis of his or her recognition of certain physical traits (Bernal, Knight, Ocampo, Garza, Cota, 1993). Later, as the child becomes aware of ethnicity as an idea, ethnic identity is experienced as an inner quality, or, as Aboud and Skerry note in a study that compared ethnic self-perception in kindergarten, second grade, and university students (Aboud and Skerry, 1983), internal attributes replace external attributes as the determinants of ethnic identity.

It has been assumed that the family plays a crucial role in the process of ethnic identity formation. Undeniably, family members are a traditional source of historical, cultural, and mythological information about one's own ethnic group, but, as Richard D. Alba (Alba, 1990) explains, the family's effectiveness as an inculcator of ethnic identification is, if not problematic, rather difficult to assess. Contrary to the traditional image of the father as the, so to speak, link between the child and his or her ethnic history, Alba has found that, in many cases, a child's perceived interest in his or her own ethnicity is the result of the family's wishful thinking. Defined from a psychological point of view as a mental construct, ethnic identity seems based on a set of elements which includes historical/cultural knowledge, oral traditions, and mythology. Children (and adults) often have a hard time differentiating between history and mythology. Sadly, in adults, a mythology-based ethnic identity may lead to dangerous, potentially violent, delusions, such as the idea of the "superiority" of a particular race (e.g., the Nazi myth of an "Aryan" race) or an ethnic group justifying genocide. Children's "ethnic fantasies" are more benign. For example, Erik Erikson (Erikson, 1980), in a work originally published in 1959, discusses a case of a high school student's "confabulatory reconstruction" of her origin. Born of American parents and living in Central Europe, the adolescent girl literally created a Scottish childhood, replete with copious, and precise, biographi-

cal data for herself. When confronted by Erikson, who wanted to know the purpose of this ethnic reconstruction, the young girl answered that she needed a past. Indeed, history is the key ingredient of ethnic identity, real or imagined. Significantly, the fact that ethnic identity is past-oriented renders it fragile, as it depends, to a large extent, on information that cannot be easily verified. In his seminal work *Wirtschaft und Gesellschaft*, originally published in 1922 (Weber, 1978), the sociologist Max Weber describes ethnic identity as a subjective belief: "We shall call 'ethnic groups' those human groups that entertain a subjective belief in their common descent because of similarities of physical type or of customs or both, or because of memories of colonization and migration; this belief must be important for the propagation of group formation; conversely, it does not matter whether or not an objective blood relationship exists. Ethnic membership (*Gemeinsamkeit*) differs from the kinship group precisely by being a presumed identity, not a group with concrete social action, like the latter. In our sense ethnic membership does not constitute a group; it only facilitates group formation of any kind, particularly in the political sphere. On the other hand, it is primarily the political community, no matter how artificially organized, that inspires the belief in common ethnicity."

For Further Study

Books

Aboud, Frances E., and Anna-Beth Doyle. "The Early Development of Ethnic Identity and Attitudes." In *Ethnic Identity: Formation and Transmission among Hispanics and Other Minorities*, edited by Martha Bernal and George P. Knight. Albany: State University of New York Press, 1993, pp. 47-59.

Alba, Richard D. *Ethnic Identity: The Transformation of White America*. New Haven: Yale University Press, 1990.

Bernal, Martha E., George P. Knight, Katheryn A. Ocampo, Camille A. Garza, and Marya K. Cota. "Development of Mexican American Identity." In *Ethnic Identity: Formation and Transmission among Hispanics and Other Minorities*, edited by Martha Bernal and George P. Knight. Albany: State University of New York Press, 1993, pp. 31–46.

Erikson, Erik. *Identity, Youth and Crisis*. New York: W. W. Norton, 1968.

———. *Identity and the Life Cycle*. New York: W. W. Norton, 1980.

Phinney, Jean S. "A Three-Stage Model of Ethnic Identity Development in Adolescence." In *Ethnic Identity: Formation and Transmission among Hispanics and Other Minorities*, edited by Martha Bernal and George P. Knight. Albany: State University of New York Press, 1993, pp. 61–79.

Weber, Max. *Economy and Society: An Outline of Interpretive Sociology*. Vol 1. Berkeley: University of California Press, 1978.

Periodicals

Aboud, Frances E., and Shelagh A. Skerry. "Self and Ethnic Concepts in Relation to Ethnic Constancy." *Canadian Journal of Behavioural Science* 15, no. 1, 1983, pp. 14–26.

Hall, Thomas D., Christopher Bartalos, Elizabeth Mannebach, and Thomas Perkowitz. "Varieties of Ethnic Conflict in Global Perspective: A Review Essay." *Social Science Quarterly* 77, no. 2, June 1966, pp. 445–52.

Ocampo, Katheryn A., Martha E. Bernal, and George P. Knight. "Gender, Race , and Ethnicity: The Sequencing of Social Constancies." In *Ethnic Identity: Formation and Transmission among Hispanics and Other Minorities*, edited by Martha Bernal and George P. Knight. Albany: State University of New York Press, 1993, pp. 11–30.

Piaget, J., and A. M. Weil. "The Development in Children of the Idea of the Homeland and of Relations to Other Countries." *International Social Science Journal* 3, 1951, pp. 561–78.

—Zoran Minderovic

Exercise

Methodical and repetitive physical activity benefiting a person's health.

Traditionally, exercise has been a concern of adults, the reasoning being that children are naturally active and do not need any structured program of physical activity. Scientists and physicians now generally agree that regular exercise is beneficial to a child's health. Exercise, **pediatricians** argue, is needed to counteract such alarming trends as childhood obesity, resulting from, among other factors, poor nutritional habits and a sedentary lifestyle. While the **American Academy of Pediatrics** has stated that exercise classes do not benefit children under the age of three, there is general agreement that moderate aerobic exercise (e.g., running, walking, cycling, or swimming), in addition to strengthening the child's cardiovascular system, establishes healthy exercise habits which will positively affect long-range health. However, according to *Fitness for Life*, children may not be getting the right kind of exercise in school, as school programs emphasize competitive sports, such as soccer and football, which develop skills and endurance, without providing the benefits of an aerobic workout.

Experts have noted that younger children need parental supervision while exercising; in fact, parental participation is recommended, as children often need direction for structured activities. Furthermore, children, because of their short attention span, need brief exercise periods. As Bob Glover and Jack Shepherd have observed, children are easily discouraged if adults attempt to impose their own style of exercising. Since children may perceive longer exercise periods as boring, it is important to make simple aerobic exercise fun. This can be done by organizing hikes and games of tag or hide-and-seek; dancing to music is also good aerobic exercise. Experts generally agree that school-age children need about 30 minutes of aerobic exercise three or four times a week. The President's Council on Physical Fitness, however, suggests at least 30 minutes of daily exercise.

In addition to better physical health, researchers have found that exercise can foster a child's intellectual and spiritual development as well. In fact, University of Toronto physiology professor Roy J. Shephard has found that students who spend an extra hour in gym class improve their academic performance. Subsequent research seems to confirm Shephard's original findings (Olsen, 1994).

Exercise also plays an important therapeutic role for children suffering from various physical and mental conditions. Muscular disorders, such as **muscular dystrophy**, neurological disorders, such as **cerebral palsy**, and various physical injuries are not an obstacle to exercise, and many handicapped children successfully participate in races, games, exercise programs, even competitive sports. Notable among the fitness programs for handicapped children is the Achilles Track Club Youth Program in New York City, which offers physical education enabling handicapped youngsters to participate in races. Researchers have found that children with handicaps can actually engage in quite demanding types of physical activity such as judo. Jorge M. Glaser and Joseph Y. Margulies studied a group of seven blind and mentally retarded children with associated psychiatric disorders. Using a modified form of judo, the researchers organized a biweekly training program for these children. When the six-month program was completed, the scientists found improvements in the children's physical fitness, **gross** and **fine motor skills**, and psychological disposition.

Exercise is also an important therapeutic tool in the field of child psychiatry. According to research done at the San Diego Center for Children, which offers treatment to children with serious emotional and behavioral problems, exercise may decrease aggressiveness. A special form of exercise used for children with psychiatric conditions is dance movement therapy (DMT), which the American Dance Therapy Association defines as "the psychotherapeutic use of movement as a process which furthers the physical and psychic integration of an individual." In DMT for children, the therapist uses movement as a symbolic communication system which will enable the child to express his or her emotional difficulties. In contrast to verbal psychotherapy, DMT relies on nonverbal symbols and behavior; often, this is an advantage for traumatized children who are unable to talk about their distress. In addition, DMT, which also uses verbal metaphors when appropriate, works well for children with limited or inhibited verbal skills.

For Further Study

Books

Fitness for Life: Childhood to Maturity. Alexandria, VA: Time-Life Books, 1989.

Glover, Bob, and Jack Shepherd. *The Family Fitness Handbook.* New York: Penguin Books, 1989.

Stanton-Jones, Kristina. *An Introduction to Dance Movement in Therapy in Psychiatry.* London: Routledge, 1992.

Periodicals

Gleser, Jorge M., Joseph Y. Margulies, et al. "Physical and Psychosocial Benefits of Modified Judo Practice for the Blind, Mentally Retarded Children: A Pilot Study." *Perceptual and Motor Skills* 74, June 1992, pp. 915–25.

Olsen, Eric. "Fit Kids, Smart Kids." *Parents* 69, no. 10, October 1994, p. 33.

Welsh, M. Cay, and Elise E. Labbé. "Children and Aerobic Exercise: A Review of Cognitive and Behavioral Effects." *Journal of Experimental Child Psychology* 58, no. 3, December 1994, pp. 405–17.

—Zoran Minderovic

Externalizing Disorders

Behavior problems that affect how a child relates to his or her environment.

In contrast to internalizing disorders—the other broad category of childhood behavior disorders—externalizing disorders are manifested in children's outward behavior rather than (or in addition to) their internal thoughts and feelings. These disorders include problems of control, such as **conduct disorder,** and problems of inattention and impulsivity, such as **attention deficit/hyperactivity disorder** (ADHD). Internalizing disorders include **depression** and various types of **anxiety,** such as **separation anxiety** disorder and generalized anxiety disorder. Some disorders, such as **autism,** are not categorized as either internalizing or externalizing disorders.

Extracurricular Activities

Activities sponsored by and usually held at school, but that are not part of the academic curriculum.

Extracurricular activities, programs offered by a school system that do not form part of the academic curriculum, range from sports to newspaper editing to music and theater. Many, like football and drama, enjoy extreme longevity, serving as a part of their school's pro-

gram over a number of years. Others, like recycling club or writer's workshop, may be offered for a shorter timespan to reflect a community interest or involvement by a particular sponsoring faculty member. For many students, extracurricular activities present an opportunity to practice social skills and to experiment in activities that may represent a career interest.

Extracurricular activities also help to form the student's profile for consideration in college admissions. A student's academic record and scores on standardized tests form the core of his or her college application profile. However, admissions officers consider other factors, such as a demonstrated talent and participation in athletics or the arts, or leadership in school or extracurricular activities.

For Further Study

Books

Miracle, Andres and C. Roger Rees. *Lessons of the Locker Room.* New York: Prometheus Books, 1994.

Periodicals

"Knock for Jocks." *Psychology Today* 27, November–December 1994, pp. 12+.

Townsend-Butterworth, Diana. "It's 3:15—Is Your Child Having Fun Yet?" *Family Circle* 108, September 1, 1995, pp. 60+.

Extroversion

A term used to characterize children and adults who are typically outgoing, friendly, and open toward others.

Extroverts are people who are often leaders, work well in groups, and prefer being with others to being alone. Other personality traits often associated with extroversion include optimism, risk taking, and love of excitement and change. Children who are extroverts prefer having company to playing alone and tend to have many friends.

Extroversion is generally defined in comparison to its opposite, **introversion,** which is used to describe people who are quieter, more reserved and sensitive, and more comfortable in solitary pursuits. The two tendencies can be regarded as opposite ends of a continuum, with most people falling somewhere in between. Nevertheless, many children and adults have traits that clearly place them closer to one end than to the other. Both extroversion and introversion in some people are thought to be the result of inborn tendencies–called **temperament**—that are shaped by environmental factors. The psychologist Hans Eysenck has suggested that the temperamental foundation involves the ease with which the cerebral cortex becomes aroused. Eysenck notes that in introverts some parts of the brain are very sensitive to arousal and are easily overstimulated, causing them to prefer quiet surroundings and calm situations. The extrovert, on the other hand, can tolerate a higher level of cortical arousal and thus seeks out social interaction and exciting situations for stimulation.

Tendencies toward extroversion or introversion often lead children to develop and cultivate contrasting strengths, sometimes referred to in terms of contrasting types of **intelligence.** Extroverts more readily develop *inter*personal intelligence, which has to do with making friends easily, demonstrating **leadership** ability, and working effectively with others in groups. In introverts the more highly developed traits are more likely to be those associated with *intra*personal intelligence, such as the deeper awareness of one's feelings and the ability to enjoy extended periods of solitude. All children have both types of intelligence, but in many children one is stronger than the other, depending on whether the child is an introvert or an extrovert.

For Further Study

Books

Eysenck, Hans J., and Michael Eysenck. *Personality and Individual Differences.* New York: Plenum Press, 1985.

Campbell, Joseph, ed. *The Portable [Carl] Jung.* New York: Viking, 1971.

Eye and Vision Development

The infant eye is only partially developed at birth. Newborns are generally very far-sighted—they can see light and shapes and notice movement, but the eyes focus only 8–15 in (20–38 cm) away. This corresponds to about 20/400 vision. Eye movements are not coordinated in the newborn, and the eyes may not begin to move together until four weeks or after. Binocular vision develops between two and six months of age, and by five months, the infant's vision has generally improved to about 20/100. By the age of two, a normal child's vision is still only about 20/60, and 20/20 vision is not approached until the child is between four and five years old, or later.

The newborn eye appears different from the adult eye. The iris lacks pigment, so many babies are born with grayish blue eyes—the mature eye color does not develop for at least six months. The cornea of the infant eye is also relatively large compared to the adult eye. The sclera (the white outer part of the eye) is thin and undeveloped in the newborn and may appear bluish until the scleral fibers develop and thicken. In rare instances, infant **cataracts** may be present in one or both eyes. The lachrymal glands, which produce tears, generally do not begin to function until the child is about four weeks old, so a newborn may cry without tears. The size and shape of the eyeball changes rapidly during the first years of life, and the optic nerve and the visual parts of the brain are also developing.

Before an infant develops the muscular coordination to move the eyes together, the eyes may move randomly, and the baby may appear intermittently cross-eyed. This is normal for a child under the age of two months. Between two and three months, the infant's eyes begin to move together, and can track a moving object. At around four months, the infant can usually detect and reach for a nearby object. The infant can usually distinguish between objects by six months. Vision improves during the next six months as control of binocular vision develops. In binocular vision, the information transmitted from each eye to the brain along the optic nerve is transformed into a single image. Binocular vision depends on the ability of the eyes to align properly. Precise movement of the eyes is controlled by small muscles around the eye. Common eye problems may result from problems in these muscles (**strabismus, amblyopia**), defects of a part of the eye itself (retinal disorders, corneal disorders), or structural defects of the eye (near-sightedness, far-sightedness, astigmatism).

A pediatrician will normally examine a child's eyes as part of a regular health check-up. A parent should also be alert to signals of possible eye problems, including: crossed eyes, red or swollen eyes or eyelids, drooping eyelids, squinting, shutting or covering one eye, holding the head at an angle, sensitivity to light, holding objects close to the eye, or random or jerky eye movements (in a child older than two months). An older child may complain of inability to see clearly, seeing double, or headaches or nausea after doing close work, and these all may be signs of an eye or vision problem. If a parent or pediatrician suspects any problems with a child's vision or eye health, the child should be examined by an ophthalmologist.

The ophthalmologist examines a child's eyes externally, noting size and position of the eyes, position and condition of the eyelids, and any obvious defects. The eyes may also be examined internally using special magnifying instruments. The child's pupils may be dilated by eyedrops for this part of the exam. An infant's vision can be tested by noting how the child's eyes move to track a moving light or toy. The examiner may cover the child's eyes one at a time. If one eye has better vision than the other, the child will usually resist having the good eye covered. An older child's vision can be tested using Allen cards or E cards. The Allen cards show pictures of familiar objects in graduated sizes. The E cards show the letter E in different orientations and in graduated sizes.

The child is asked to point to the direction the feet of the E are turned: up, down, left or right. If a young child is unable to concentrate on the vision test in the ophthalmologist's office, the parents may be given cards so that they can do a test at home. The ophthalmologist will also perform refraction tests to measure the child's eyes for corrective lenses, if necessary.

For Further Study

Books

Collins, James F. *Your Eyes: An Owner's Guide.* Englewood Cliffs, NJ: Prentice-Hall, 1995.

Savage, Stephen. *Eyes.* New York: Thomson Learning, 1995.

Showers, Paul. *Look at Your Eyes.* New York: HarperCollins Publishers, 1992.

Zinn, Walter J., and Herbert Solomon. *Complete Guide to Eyecare, Eyeglasses and Contact Lenses.* Hollywood, FL: Lifetime Books, 1995.

Organizations

American Academy of Ophthalmology
Address: P.O. Box 7424
San Francisco, CA 92120-7424

National Eye Institute
Address: Building 31, Room 6A32
Bethesda, MD 20892
Telephone: (301) 496-5248

—A. Woodward

Eyelid Problems

Conditions or diseases that affect the eyelid.

There are a few common conditions that can affect a child's eyelids. A stye is a common problem that is easily treated. It appears as a red bump on the edge of the eyelid, and is caused by a bacterial infection in a hair follicle or sweat gland on the lid margin. Warm, moist compresses applied several times a day are a successful treatment. If the stye is stubborn, a **pediatrician** may prescribe an antibiotic ointment.

A chalazion is an inflammation of an oil gland in the underside of the eyelid. It appears as a small bump beneath the eyelid, accompanied by redness and mild discomfort. Like styes, chalazions can be treated with application of warm, moist compresses. Prescription antibiotic ointment or drops may also be necessary. Chalazions often recur, and if they are problematic, a pediatrician may recommend surgery to remove the affected gland.

Ptosis is a condition in which the eyelid or eyelids droop. In some cases it is present from birth, as the result of incomplete development of the muscles which hold up the lid. Rarely, it is the result of trauma to the cranial nerves at birth. Ptosis may also develop after birth because of some trauma to the eyelid, or because of an underlying disease such a myasthenia gravis. Ptosis may appear as a droopy, partially lowered lid, merely as a heavy or enlarged upper lid, or the lid may completely cover the eye. In the rare case of congenital ptosis in which the drooping lid covers the entire eye or pupil, the child may need immediate surgery to correct the condition, or else vision will not develop normally. In a milder case, surgery is also the advised treatment, but it is usually not done until the child is three or four years old.

For Further Study

Books

Collins, James F. *Your Eyes: An Owner's Guide.* Englewood Cliffs, NJ: Prentice-Hall, 1995.

Savage, Stephen. *Eyes.* New York: Thomson Learning, 1995.

Showers, Paul. *Look at Your Eyes.* New York: HarperCollins Publishers, 1992.

Zinn, Walter J., and Herbert Solomon. *Complete Guide to Eyecare, Eyeglasses and Contact Lenses.* Hollywood, FL: Lifetime Books, 1995.

Organizations

American Academy of Ophthalmology
Address: P.O. Box 7424
San Francisco, CA 92120-7424

National Eye Institute
Address: Building 31, Room 6A32
Bethesda, MD 20892
Telephone: (301) 496-5248

—A. Woodward

Failure to Thrive (FTT)

Failure of an infant, toddler, or child to grow at a normal rate. Related terms include malnutrition, growth hormone deficiency, low birth weight, and short stature.

Failure to thrive (FTT) occurs when an infant, toddler, or child fails to grow at a normal rate, either due to organic (genetic) or environmental causes. Growth is measured as a combination of factors, including age, weight, height, and sometimes bone age. The height and weight of a child can vary widely at a particular age and still be considered normal. According to the National Center for Health Statistics standards, FTT is formally diagnosed when the child's weight is below the fifth percentile for his age (i.e., he or she is smaller than 95% of others his age) or when the weight drops more than two percentile groups. Low height alone or slightly low height with proportional weight may only indicate short stature. Whenever a child's weight or height falls below the tenth percentile he or she should be observed for other symptoms.

Many factors can cause a child's failure to thrive and grow normally. Traditionally the syndrome is broken down into the categories of organic failure to thrive (OFT) and inorganic or non-organic failure to thrive (NOFT). Organic FTT is caused by a genetic or biological disorder such as **diabetes** or enlarged adenoids, or most commonly **digestive** (gastrointestinal tract) **disorders**. Non-organic FTT is diagnosed when organic causes have been ruled out and some combination of environmental factors prevents the infant or child from taking in sufficient food or nutrients; for example, when infant formula is prepared incorrectly.

Most cases of FTT can be traced to both biological and environmental factors, and the distinction between organic and non-organic FTT is sometimes seen as useless or even harmful because the designation "non-organic" leads people to blame the parents—who may or may not be contributing to their child's disorder. Rather, the

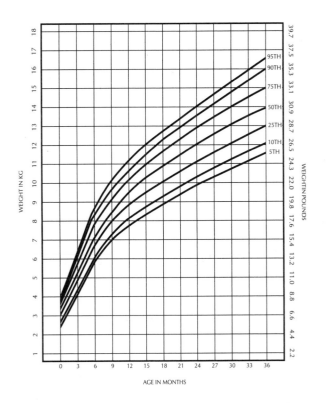

Girls' weight by age percentiles, from ages birth to 36 months.

point is to determine the combination of causes. For example when a child suffers from a biological problem that goes unnoticed, the parent reacts by being more forceful at feeding time, and then, as the child begins to avoid food, a vicious cycle develops that has both biological and environmental causes (and solutions). This is the case with children who suffer from oral hypersensitivity.

Whatever the combination of causes, FTT is a medical condition that is always accompanied by malnourishment. Malnourishment, especially within the first two years of life, causes serious cognitive and behavioral problems in later life, and can lead to **mental retardation**. While the factors in non-organic FTT can be diffi-

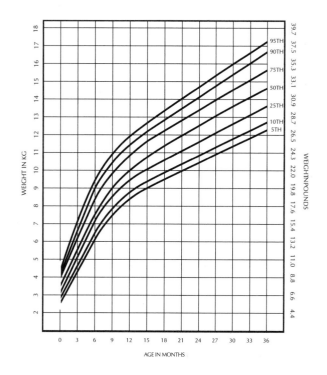

Boys' weight by age percentiles, from ages birth to 36 months.

cult to isolate, it is highly responsive to treatment, frequently solved by a period of close observation and subsequent changes in feeding habits. When organic causes exist, the doctor will treat the underlying problem and perhaps give compensatory **nutrition**.

The first step in treatment is to determine whether a child's weight is in fact below normal. If a child's weight is below 90% of the median weight for age (i.e., the 50th percentile), there is mild FTT. A weight between 75%–60% of the median signifies moderate FTT and below 60% severe FTT. First a child's weight will drop, then his height, so it is essential to know the pattern of weight change over time. The age that FTT first occurs can indicate its causes:

Newborn FTT is frequently organic, often caused by gastrointestinal tract problems such as reflux, parasites, milk intolerance, **diarrhea**, or another metabolic problem such as diabetes. Incorrect or too infrequent breast-feeding or overdilution of formula can also lead to FTT. Sometimes a mother and child do not bond well, due to postpartum **depression** or other causes, which leads to feeding problems.

Onset of FTT at around *4 months old* often indicates underfeeding, caused by inadequate feeding patterns or circumstances (no highchair, lack of resources for food, etc.).

Onset at around *7–9 months* is sometimes a product of struggles over the child's autonomy. Struggles with

the child over feeding might be exaggerated due to the parents' overconcern and **anxiety**. Food intolerance may also occur as solid foods are introduced. Also, the presence of food in the child's bottle can inhibit intake.

Onset in *toddlers* may again be a struggle over autonomy, and/or a result of the child being able to walk and to be more easily distracted from feeding.

At any age food **allergies** may be a problem, though just as often parents contribute to deficiencies by diagnosing food "allergies" and withholding certain nutritious foods. Also, excessive drinking of liquids other than formula or milk can constitute empty calories and cause nausea. Watch for signs of organic problems by looking at the skin, nails, and oral cavities for abnormalities. Besides a weight history, the doctor will require a record of exactly what, when, where, and how the child eats and drinks (the dietary history). In addition to digestive problems, the doctor will also test for infections, kidney problems, **tuberculosis**, and sometimes HIV infection or **cystic fibrosis**. Tests may also be done for toxins such as **lead poisoning**, and deficiencies such as those of iron and zinc. After other factors are ruled out, the level of growth hormone in the body may also be measured.

Treatment

To diagnose FTT and assess its causes in a child are significant steps towards treating the syndrome. The immediate goal of treatment is to encourage or induce *catch-up growth*, defined as a growth rate of 2–3 times the average for the child's age. The feeding and/or eating problems that were identified in diagnosis should be corrected, the child's food should be calorically enriched, and a multivitamin given to make up for deficiencies caused by rapid growth. Infant formula may be concentrated up to no more than 24 calories per ounce (one 13 oz. can plus 8 oz. water). For catch-up growth the child should consume between 120–180 calories per kilogram of weight per day. The desired growth should occur within the first month.

More serious cases of FTT may require immediate hospitalization and artificial feeding/nutrition, followed by the usual testing for organic causes, along with an extensive assessment of the child's total caloric intake and eating or feeding circumstances at home. Medical, nutritional, and social factors should all be observed, preferably in their natural settings, by a "grow" team of a doctor, nurse, social worker, nutritionist, and possibly a psychologist.

For cases of FTT caused by parental neglect, mistreatment, or dysfunctional family dynamics, extensive education and/or therapy is required for the parents. Children who experience catch-up growth while being treated may relapse into malnutrition when they return home or intervention services cease. FTT in these cases is not quickly resolved. Studies have found that, even when corrected for race, gender, and socioeconomic factors, statistical figures indicate that children are at high risk for this type of FTT (non-organic) when they come from families where the parents fight or argue, where there are three or more older siblings, and where very low resources are devoted to care for the child (i.e., compared to the spending habits of other families with the same income). Parents of children who suffer from non-organic FTT due to abuse tend to be more unresponsive, disorganized, harsh, and aggressive with their children than other parents of the same race, gender, and **socioeconomic status**. Whether it is the cause or effect of FTT, infants and children with non-organic FTT caused by abuse tend also to have withdrawn and irritable **temperaments**.

For Further Study

Books

Drotar, Dennis, ed. *New Directions in Failure to Thrive: Implications for Research and Practice.* New York: Plenum Press, 1985. Based on the Proceedings of the National Institute of Mental Health Workshop held October 9–10, 1984.

Periodicals

Frank, Deborah A., Robert Needlmen, and Mary Silva. "What to Do When a Child Won't Grow (Treating Failure to Thrive)." *Patient Care* 28, May 1994, pp. 107–22.

Goldson, E. "Neurological Aspects of Failure to Thrive." *Developmental Medicine and Child Neurology* 31, 1989, pp. 821–26.

Phelps, LeAdelle. "Non-Organic Failure to Thrive: Origin and Psychoeducational Implications." *School Psychology Review,* January 1, 1991, pp. 417–29.

Organizations

The MAGIC Foundation for Children's Growth
   Address: 1327 N. Harlem Avenue
   Oak Park, IL 60302
   Telephone: (708) 383-0808
   (National non-profit organization providing support services for families of children afflicted with chronic and/or critical disorders, syndromes, and diseases that affect a child's growth.)

Fairy Tales

Simple narratives, typically involving supernatural beings or improbable events, settings, or characters, either of folk origin or individually authored in a style reminiscent of the folk tradition.

Fairy tales and folk tales fall into six major categories, such as cumulative tales, based on a repetitive action that builds to a climax (as in "The House That Jack Built") and *pourquoi tales,* which purport to explain the origin of certain customs or traits (for example, "how the leapard got his spots"), as well as those containing supernatural elements, which are usually called fairy tales. One of the standard categories of folktale is the "realistic tale," which implies that all the other types—not just fairy tales—contain some measure of fantasy. For example, one of these categories, the beast tale, by definition includes **fantasy** elements. Even if they are not unique in their inclusion of magical and other wondrous elements, fairy tales are distinguished from most other folktales by their greater length and complexity and by their inclusion of romance and adventure. The designation of "fairy tale" is also applied to the "literary folktales" of such authors as Hans Christian Andersen.

Fairy tales typically have simple, direct plots, even when they involve multiple episodes and themes. They take place in the past ("once upon a time"), and the time, setting, and central conflict are quickly established at the beginning with little time devoted to description. The conflict is usually resolved soon after the climax of the story in a brief and usually happy ending (". . . and they lived happily ever after"). Characterization is two-dimensional, with characters being either completely good or completely evil. Attention is maintained through suspense and repetition, a frequent plot element, often in series of threes (as in the three "huff and puff" sequences enacted by the wolf in "The Three Little Pigs").

Common narrative devices include magical powers, spells that induce extended sleep, magical objects and transformations, wishes, and trickery. A single fairy tale generally exists in multiple variants throughout the world; over 500 have been recorded for the Cinderella story. Scholars have accounted for variants of folktales by theories of both monogenesis (origin in a single culture that was then diffused among different peoples) and polygenesis (simultaneous origin in various cultures reflecting universal beliefs and emotions). The Russian scholar Vladimir Propp reduced the plot elements in all folktales to 31 identifiable actions that recur in different combinations but in predictable sequences, for example, "family member leaves home," "the villain causes harm or injury to a member of the family," "the hero or heroine returns," and "the villain is punished".

The current versions of many well-known fairy tales date back to their preservation in written form by European writers as far back as the 17th century, when the Italian Giambattista Basile included "Snow White," "Sleeping Beauty," and other tales in a collection. The first major compilation of this type was Charles Perrault's 1697 *Contes de ma mère l'oye (Tales of Mother Goose),* which included "Cinderella," "Little Red Riding Hood," and other perennial favorites. The best-known transcription of oral folktales remains the *Kinder- und Hausmärchen* published between 1812 and 1815 by Jacob and Wilhelm Grimm, popularly known as *Grimm's Fairy Tales.* Although their collections are sometimes called "literary fairy tales," both Perrault's tales and those of the Brothers Grimm were intended to remain as faithful as possible to the original oral versions. However, numerous other purveyors of fairy tales, right up through the Disney studios in our own time, have softened the grislier aspects of fairy tales to avoid offending adult audiences or frightening juvenile ones. For example, Engelbert Humperdinck's opera *Hansel and Gretel* is based not on the Grimms' tale but on the bowdlerized version by Ludwig Bechstein that was far more popular in 19th-century Germany. Bechstein changed the wicked stepmother into a biological parent torn by feelings of guilt, turned the terrifying witch into a quasi-comic figure, and made the dark and fearful forest into a scene of contemplation and prayer. Such alterations are opposed by some modern commentators, who argue that instead of making fairy tales more appropriate for children, the changes actually rob them of much of their literary and psychological value.

Most experts reserve the "literary" label for original narratives modeled on the style and formulas of folk tales, such as those by Hans Christian Andersen, the most famous and successful writer in this genre and author of such classics as "The Ugly Duckling," "The Snow Queen," "The Little Mermaid," "Thumbelina," and "The Red Shoes." Although his earliest tales were based on folk sources, his later works are entirely original, and some are even said to contain autobiographical elements. Other 19th-century authors who tried their hand at literary fairy tales include the German Romantic authors Johann Wolfgang von Goethe, E. T. A. Hoffmann, and Clemens Brentano, and George MacDonald, John Ruskin, and Oscar Wilde. Modern writers of original fairy tales include poet Carl Sandburg (*The Rootabaga Stories*), humorist James Thurber (*The Thirteen Clocks* and *Many Moons*), novelist John Gardner (*Dragon, Dragon and Other Tales, Gudgekin the Thistle Girl*), and storyteller Jane Yolen (*The Girl Who Loved the Wind, The Girl Who Cried Flowers and Other Tales*).

Fairy tales as children's literature

Fairy tales are a valuable form of children's literature for several reasons. First of all, their simplicity, drama, and pacing make them attractive to children, fostering a delight in storytelling in particular and literature in general. In addition, their fantasy elements help foster an active imagination. Fairy tales are also an important part of every child's cultural legacy—as stories alluded to in many other contexts and as examples of many basic narrative and symbolic elements that appear in other, more complex literary forms.

In addition to providing an important key to one's own culture, they are also a way of learning about and appreciating the cultures of others. Fairy tales also give children, who are relatively powerless in most areas of their lives, an opportunity to join vicariously in the triumph of the underdog in a world where the smallest animal, the poorest peasant, or the youngest daughter often prevails over those larger, richer, older, and more powerful. The role that fairy tales play in a child's emotional life received its most wide-ranging and famous analysis in Bruno Bettelheim's 1976 study *The Uses of Enchantment,* in which Bettelheim described how fairy tales, through their embodiment of fundamental psychological dramas, can help children confront and resolve conflicts in their own lives.

In another analysis, F. André Favat has claimed that fairy tales appeal to young children because of qualities that can be related to characteristics outlined by psychologist **Jean Piaget.** The preoperational stage of development (ages two to six), which corresponds roughly to the age at which children first come to know and love fairy tales, is, according to Piaget, characterized by "magical thinking," an attribution of unexplained powers to objects and forces in the external world and of consciousness to inanimate objects that resembles the workings of the world in fairy tales. Favat also points out that the centrality of the heroes and heroines to their fairy tale world corresponds to the egocentric focus of the child during the preoperational stage. Finally, Favat points out that fairy tales appeal to the young child's moral sense as described by Piaget in that they generally reward the good and punish the wicked.

A child's interest in fairy tales begins at the pre-reading stage and continues through most of elementary school, peaking between the ages of 8 and 10. The simplest fairy tales, such as *The Three Little Pigs* or *The Red Hen,* can be appreciated by preschoolers, with more complex tales introduced in the primary or intermediate grades. Tales by Hans Christian Andersen, Oscar Wilde, and Eleanor Farjeon are among those recommended for older children. Among their other virtues, fairy tales lend themselves well to an interdisciplinary educational approach. A fairy tale unit in the primary grades can encompass a variety of art projects, such as drawing one's most liked or disliked fairy tale character, producing "before and after" pictures for characters who undergo magical transformations, or mapping the action of a fairy tale. Children can dramatize tales using simple puppets they create themselves. Language skills can be promoted by listing special words and rhymes found in the tales. Children can also create and illustrate their own fairy tales.

For Further Study

Books

Adler, Bill, Jr. *Tell Me a Fairy Tale: A Parent's Guide to Telling Magical and Mythical Stories.* New York: Penguin, 1995.

Andersen, Hans Christian. *Andersen's Fairy Tales.* Translated by L. W. Kingsland. Oxford: Oxford University Press, 1985.

Bauer, Caroline Feller. *New Handbook for Storytellers.* Chicago: American Library Association, 1993.

Bettelheim, Bruno. *The Uses of Enchantment: The Meaning and Importance of Fairy Tales.* New York: Knopf, 1976.

Bottigheimer, Ruth B. *Fairy Tales and Society.* Philadelphia: University of Pennsylvania Press, 1986.

Hamilton, Virginia. *The People Could Fly: American Black Folktales.* New York: Knopf, 1985.

Haviland, Virginia, ed. *The Fairy Tale Treasury.* New York: Dell, 1986. [Preschool-grade 4]

Mallet, Carl-Heinz. *Fairy Tales and Children.* New York: Schocken, 1984.

Phelps, Ethel Johnston. *The Maid of the North: Feminist Folk Tales from Around the World.* New York: Holt, 1981.

Rockwell, Anne. *The Three Bears and 15 Other Stories.* New York: HarperCollins, 1975. [Preschool-grade 1]

Yolen, Jane, ed. *Favorite Folk Tales from Around the World.* New York: Pantheon, 1986. [Grades 6 and up]

Familial Retardation

(Also called sociocultural or cultural-familial retardation)

Mild mental retardation attributed to environmental causes and generally involving some degree of psychosocial disadvantage.

The majority of persons suffering from **mental retardation** fall into the category of familial retardation rather than that of clinical retardation, which usually has neurological or other organic causes. Persons with familial retardation typically have IQs ranging from 55–69 and show no signs of physical disability. Environmental causes thought to contribute to familial retardation include the quality of the mother's prenatal care, maternal and child nutrition, family size, the spacing of births within a family, disease, and health risks from environmental toxins such as lead. The 1994 publication of *The Bell Curve*, an analysis, by Richard J. Herrnstein and Charles Murray, of the relative importance of heredity and environment in determining IQ scores, and the 1995 release of the most in-depth study to date on retardation among school children both renewed public interest in familial retardation and its causes.

Familial retardation is usually not detected until a child enters school and has academic difficulties, at which point the teacher recommends psychological evaluation. Unlike the parents of clinically retarded children, who generally seek out help for their youngsters, the parents of those with familial retardation may take offense when their children are labeled mentally retarded and deny that there is a problem, especially since their children are often able to function competently in their daily lives outside school. Some studies have shown that educators are more likely to classify poor and/or minority children as mentally retarded, while labeling white middle-class children with comparable IQ scores as learning disabled. Other critics have pointed out that familial retardation may be diagnosed in children who are simply unprepared to cope with the demands of school because of cultural and linguistic isolation.

Familial retardation may be reduced by nutritional, health, and educational intervention at an early age. In a study conducted in the 1970s, educators selected mother-child pairs from among a group of women with IQs under 75 living in the poorest section of Milwaukee, Wisconsin, while establishing a control group of mothers in the same neighborhood with IQs over 100. For the first five years of the children's lives, the targeted group of mothers and their children received instruction in problem-solving and language skills, as well as counseling to motivate them to learn and succeed. The mothers and children in the control group received no form of environmental enrichment. At the age of five, the children in the target group had IQ scores averaging 26 points higher than those of the children in the control group. At the age of nine, their average IQ was 106 (slightly above the universal norm of 100), while that of the other children was only 79. (Later results, however, were somewhat disappointing, as the mothers' motivation to continue the program became difficult to maintain over the long term.)

In 1995, an Atlanta study conducted jointly by the Centers for Disease Control and Prevention and Emory University found important new evidence linking mild retardation to social and educational deprivation. It was found that 8.4 out of every 1,000 10-year-olds were mildly retarded (defined as an IQ of 50–70), while 3.6 of every 1,000 suffered severe retardation due to such conditions as **cerebral palsy** or **Down syndrome.** The incidence of mild retardation was 2.6 higher in blacks than whites, although this difference was halved when socioeconomic factors were taken into account. Children of all races were four times as likely to be mildly retarded if their mothers had not finished high school. The incidence of mental retardation was also slightly higher for children of teenage mothers. The Atlanta study also confirmed earlier claims that teachers are more likely to seek IQ testing for minority children from poor families. Based on the findings of this sur-

STATISTICS ON FAMILIES, 1980, 1990, 1995						
Type of household	1980 Number in 1,000	1990 Number in 1,000	1995 Number in 1,000	1980 percent of total	1990, percent of total	1995, percent of total
All families	59,550	66,090	69,305	71%	71%	86%
—with children under 18	31,022	32,289	34,296	35%	35%	52%
Married couple families	49,112	52,317	53,858	56%	54%	67%
—with children under 18	24,961	24,537	25,241	26%	25%	40%
Single father with children under 18	616	1,153	1,440	1%	1%	2%
Single mother with children under 18	5,445	6,599	7,615	7%	8%	10%

Source: U.S. Bureau of Census, *Current Population Reports*, P25-1129.
*Percents calculated from Bureau of Census projections.

vey, the federal government launched a pilot program to improve health and education for disadvantaged mothers and children, with special emphasis on providing a more intellectually stimulating home environment for at-risk youngsters through reading programs and other activities.

As adults, socioculturally retarded individuals live in a variety of settings, including their parental homes, group homes, and their own independent residences. Very few are institutionalized. Most make a satisfactory adjustment to adult life in their communities, although their adjustment in early adulthood is likely to be more difficult than that of the average person. Often they must learn from their own life experiences lessons that others learned (or at least were introduced to) at home. Eventually, however, most become responsible and self-supporting members of their communities with the ability to meet adult responsibilities and commitments.

For Further Study

Books

Fraser, Steven. *The Bell Curve Wars: Race, Intelligence, and the Future of America.* New York: Basic Books, 1995.

Herrnstein, Richard J., and Charles Murray. *The Bell Curve: Intelligence and Class Structure in American Life.* New York: Free Press, 1994.

Family

Two or more people related to each other by genetics, adoption, marriage, or in some interpretations, by mutual agreement.

Family is broadly defined as any two people who are related to each other through a genetic connection, **adoption,** marriage, or by mutual agreement. Family members share emotional and economic bonds. The term *nuclear family* is used to refer to family members who live together and share emotional, economic, and social responsibilities. The nuclear family is often comprised of a married couple who are parents to their biological or adopted children; all members live together in one household. This type of nuclear family is increasingly referred to by social scientists as an *intact family,* signifying that the family had not been through a divorce, separation, or death of a member. The U.S. Bureau of Census statistics on families are presented in the accompanying tables.

In addition to the nuclear family, other complex and diverse combinations of individuals lead to what social scientists call blended or nontraditional families. When a family has experienced divorce or death leaving one parent to be primarily responsible for raising the children, they become a *single-parent family.* (The terms *broken family* and *broken home* are no longer widely used because of their negative connotations.)

STATISTICS ON FAMILIES, PROJECTIONS						
Type of household	2000 Number in 1,000	Percent of total*	2005 Number in 1,000	Percent of total	2010 Number in 1,000	Percent of total
All families	71,669	100%	74,733	100%	77,895	100%
—with children under 18	33,117	46%	32,699	43%	32,203	41%
Married couple families	55,496	77%	57,371	77%	59,308	76%
—with children under 18	24,686	34%	23,958	32%	23,126	29%
Single father with children under 18	1,694	2.4%	1,797	2.4%	1,888	2.4%
Single mother with children under 18	6,737	9.4%	6,944	9.3%	7,189	9.2%

Source: U.S. Bureau of Census, *Current Population Reports*, P25-1129.
*Percents calculated from Bureau of Census projections.

Following the end of one marriage, one or both of the ex-spouses may enter a new marriage. Through this process of remarriage, stepfamilies are formed. The second spouse becomes a stepparent to the children from the first marriage. In the family formed by the second marriage, the children from each spouse's first marriage become step-siblings. Children born or adopted by the couple of the second marriage are half-siblings to the children from the first marriage, since they share one parent in common.

In some cases, a stepparent will legally adopt his or her spouse's children from a previous marriage. The biological father or mother must either be absent with no legal claim to **custody**, or must grant permission for the stepparent to adopt.

In situations where a single parent lives with someone outside of marriage, that person may be referred to as a **co-parent.** Co-parent is also the name given to the partner in a homosexual relationship who shares the household and parenting responsibilities with a child's legal adoptive or biological parent.

The home which was owned by the family prior to a divorce or separation is referred to as the *family home* in many state laws. In court settlements of divorce and child custody issues, the sale of the family home may be prohibited as long as the minor children are still living there with the custodial parent. The sale of the home may be permitted (or required to pay the noncustodial parent his or her share of its value) if the custodial parent moves or remarries, or when the children leave home to establish their own residences.

The term *extended family* traditionally meant the biological relatives of a nuclear family; i.e., the parents, sisters, and brothers of both members of a married couple. It was sometimes used to refer to the people living in the household beyond the parents and children. As family relationships and configurations have become more complex due to **divorce** and remarriage, extended family has come to refer to all the biological, adoptive, step-, and half-relatives.

Government agencies and other statistics-gathering organizations use the term *head of household* to refer to the person who contributes more than half of the necessary support of the family members (other than the spouse); in common usage, the head of household is the person who provides primary financial support for the family.

For Further Study

Books

Bernardes, Jon. *Family Studies: An Introduction.* New York: Routledge, 1997.

Elkind, David. *Ties That Stress: The New Family Imbalance.* Cambridge, MA: Harvard University Press, 1994.

Eshleman, J. Ross. *The Family: An Introduction.* 7th ed. Boston: Allyn and Bacon, 1994.

Kephart, William M. and Davor Jedlicka. *The Family, Society, and the Individual.* 7th ed. New York: HarperCollins, 1991.

Strong, Bryan and Christine DeVault. *The Marriage and Family Experience.* 4th ed. St. Paul: West Publishing Co., 1989.

White, James M. *Dynamics of Family Development: A Theoretical Perspective.* New York: Guilford Press, 1991.

Audiovisual Recordings

Ohio Cooperative Extension Service. *Changing Families, Challenges and Opportunities.* Columbus, OH: Ohio Cooperative Extension Service: The Ohio State University, 1988.
(Four sound cassettes, covering the subjects of latchkey families, single-parent families, strengthening step-families, and two-income families.)

Organizations

Family Service Association of America (FSA), formerly the Family Welfare Association of America)
Address: 11600 West Lake Park Drive
Milwaukee, WI 53244
Telephone: (414) 359-1040; toll-free (800) 221-3726
(Organization providing information services for families related to social functioning and mental health. Publications include *The Family Guide to Child Care: Making the Right Choices.*)

Step Family Foundation (SFF)
Address: 333 West End Avenue
New York NY 10023
Telephone: (212) 877-3244
(Disseminates information on step families, provides counseling and training service, and published informational materials.)

Family Therapy

The joint treatment of two or more members of the same family in order to change unhealthy patterns of communication and interaction.

Family therapy is generally initiated because of psychological or emotional problems experienced by a single family member, often a child or adolescent. These problems are treated as symptomatic of dysfunction within the family system as a whole. The therapist focuses on the interaction between family members, analyzing the role played by each member in maintaining the system. Family therapy can be especially helpful for dealing with problems that develop in response to a particular event or situation, such as **divorce** or remarriage, or the birth of a new sibling. It can also be an effective means to draw individuals who feel threatened by individual therapy into a therapeutic setting.

Family therapy has a variety of origins. It is related to the long-standing emphasis of **psychoanalysis** and other psychodynamic approaches on the central role that early family relationships play in the formation of personality and the manifestation of psychological disorders. Family therapy also grew out of the realization that progress made by patients staying in treatment centers was often reversed when they returned to their families. As a result, a number of therapists became dissatisfied treating clients individually with no opportunity to ac-

tively address the harmful family relationships that were often the source of their clients' problems.

Family therapy, either alone or in conjunction with other types of treatment, has been effective in the treatment of children suffering from a variety of problems, including **anxiety**, **enuresis** (bed-wetting), and **eating disorders**, and also in working with victims of **child abuse**. In addition to alleviating the child's initial complaint and improving communication within the family unit, family therapy can also help reduce stress and conflict by helping families improve their coping skills.

There are a number of approaches to family therapy. Perhaps the best known is structural family therapy, founded by Salvador Minuchin. A short-term method that focuses on the present rather than the past, this school of therapy views a family's behavior patterns and rituals as central to the problems of its individual members. Poor communication skills play a key role in perpetuating destructive interactions within families, such as the formation of alliances among some family members against others. The goals of structural family therapy include strengthening parental leadership, clarifying boundaries, enhancing coping skills, and freeing family members from their entrenched positions within the family structure. Minuchin divided families' styles of interacting into two basic types—enmeshed and disengaged, considering behavior at either extreme as pathological, with most families falling somewhere on a continuum between the two. Minuchin believed that the functioning of family systems prevented individuals from becoming healthier emotionally, because the family system relied on its troubled member to play a particular role in order to function in its accustomed way. This stability is disrupted if an individual changes significantly.

Psychodynamically oriented family therapy emphasizes unconscious processes (such as the projection of unacceptable personality traits onto another family member) and unresolved conflicts in the parents' families of origin. The lasting effects of such traumatic experiences as parental divorce and child abuse are explored. This type of therapy focuses more on family history and less on symptoms, resulting in a lengthier therapeutic process. Therapists who employ an object relations approach emphasize the importance of having the parents in a family work out conflicts with their own parents. Some practitioners include grandparents in their work with families in order to better understand intergenerational dynamics and deeply rooted behavior patterns. Ivan Boszormenyi-Nagy, a well-known proponent of this orientation, would only treat families when members of three generations could participate in therapy sessions.

Behavioral family therapy views interactions within the family as a set of behaviors that are either rewarded or punished. The behavioral therapist educates family members to respond to each others' behavior with positive or negative reinforcement. A child might be discouraged from repeating a negative behavior, for example, by losing some privileges or receiving a "time-out." Positive behavior might be rewarded with the use of an incentive chart on which points or stickers are accrued and eventually exchanged for a reward. Behavioral approaches sometimes involve the drawing up of behavioral "contracts" by family members, as well as the establishment of rules and reinforcement procedures.

Several other family therapy approaches, including that of Virginia Satir, are primarily concerned with communication. Satir's system combines the teaching of family communication skills, the promotion of self-esteem, and the removal of obstacles to the emotional growth so that family members can have full access to their innate resources.

For Further Study

Books

Boyd-Franklin, Nancy. *Black Families in Therapy.* New York: Guilford Press, 1989.

Minuchin, Salvador. *Family Therapy Techniques.* Cambridge: Harvard University Press, 1981.

Nichols, Michael P., and Richard C. Schwartz. *Family Therapy: Concepts and Methods.* Boston: Allyn and Bacon, 1991.

Satir, Virginia. *Conjoint Family Therapy.* Palo Alto, CA: Science and Behavior Books, 1983.

Walters, Marianne, et. al. *The Invisible Web: Gender Patterns in Family Relationships.* New York: Guilford Press, 1988.

Organizations

American Assocation for Marriage and Family Therapy
    Address: 1717 K Street N.W., Suite 407
    Washington, DC 20006
    Telephone: (202) 452-0109
American Family Therapy Association
    Address: 2020 Pennsylvania Avenue, N.W., Suite 273
    Washington, DC 20006
    Telephone: (202) 994-2776

Fantasy

The creation of imaginary persons, objects, or events in response to a psychological need.

Fantasy plays an important role in the lives of children, especially in their play. Because of their egocentric focus, children, unlike healthy adults, can have trouble distinguishing their fantasies from reality. In addition to developing **creativity,** fantasy can serve the important function of helping a child confront her **fear**s and desires in a safe context that she can control.

The most common form of childhood fantasy is the **imaginary playmate** or friend, which often appears in early childhood, most commonly at the age of three or four. Naturally, an imaginary playmate is invisible (as opposed to a toy or another object that the child invests with life). Rather than a sign of disturbance, imaginary friends are generally a sign of mental health. They are one of the most important ways that a child can exercise the imagination, which develops at around the age of three. Imaginary friends serve as an important emotional outlet that children can use to safely act out aggressive, controlling, rebellious, or other potentially threatening impulses. They also serve as a means of exploration, helping a child establish her identity by "trying out" different ways to be, including different genders. Finally, imaginary friends give children a zone of **privacy** at a time when there are few areas of their lives free from intrusion by others. As long as a child maintains a healthy balance between private time with her imaginary friend and social time with peers, an imaginary friend is an asset to mental health and development between the ages of three and six.

While fantasies often serve as a means of wish fulfillment, they can also express fears. Of all fantasies, fantasies about death are most frequent in children, adolescents, and the elderly. Several psychologists have theorized that the frightening fantasies of children express a universal fear that their parents, who are so much larger and more powerful than they, will kill them, or that they will kill their parents.

In addition to the fantasies that they create on their own, fantasy provided through **fairy tales** and other narratives can play an important role in helping children interpret events in their lives and deal with fear, **anxiety,** anger, jealousy, and other frightening emotions.

For Further Study

Books

Bettelheim, Bruno. *The Uses of Enchantment: The Meaning and Importance of Fairy Tales.* New York: Vintage Books, 1977.

Bloch, Dorothy. *So the Witch Won't Eat Me: Fantasy and the Child's Fear of Infanticide.* New York: Grove Press, 1978.

Clark, Cindy Dell. *Flights of Fancy, Leaps of Faith: Children's Myths in Contemporary America.* Chicago: University of Chicago Press, 1995.

Paley, Vivian. *Bad Guys Don't Have Birthdays: Fantasy Play at Four.* Chicago: University of Chicago Press, 1988.

Father–Child Relationships

Interaction between a father and the children he is parenting.

The traditional roles of the father in our society have been that of the bread-winner and the disciplinarian. As more and more mothers work outside the home, the fathers' role in the family is changing. Parents today expect to share more child-rearing responsibilities. The single father and the house-husband are not rare these days, and society seems less ready to stigmatize men who care for their young children. One sign of this attitude change is the fact that fathers are now routinely allowed—even encouraged—to come into labor and delivery rooms to watch the **birth**s of their children, and are allowed to hold their children in their first moments after birth. This is a huge departure from the image of the expectant father nervously pacing the waiting room, then peering at the newborn infant through the nursery window.

Research indicates that fathers play an important role in shaping children's perceptions about their own masculinity or femininity.

FATHER-CHILD HOUSEHOLD

In June 1997, the U.S. Census Bureau reported that the number of single fathers with children under 18 grew from 400,000 in 1970 to 1.7 million in 1995. That same year, government data shows that 2.5 million children lived with just their fathers—48% of whom were divorced, 28% were never married, 18% were married but not living with their wives, and 5% were widowed.

For children living with their father only:

- Median family income was $23,155 (1994)
- Percent that were classified as poor: 26%
- Six out of ten lived with at least one sibling.
- Percent of fathers with high school diplomas: 76%
- Percent of fathers with a bachelor's degree or more: 12%
- Percent with a father who was working: 79%
- Five out of 10 lived in rental housing.

For children living with both parents:

- Median family income was $46,195 (1994)
- Percent that were classified as poor: 11%
- More than eight out of ten lived with at least one sibling.
- Percent with at least one parent with a high school diploma: 86%
- Percent with at least one parent with a bachelor's degree or more: 29%
- Percent with at least one parent working: 85%
- Less than 3 out of 10 lived in rental housing.

Nurturing the infant

A man's relationship with his child begins before birth. **Fetus**es can hear voices from outside the womb by the sixth month of development. A father-to-be may enjoy talking to the unborn child. Newborns seem to recognize their mother's voice immediately after birth, and will respond to their father's as well, if it is already familiar to them.

A father is allowed to witness the birth of this child in most modern American hospitals. More and more, fathers participate in the birth as a breathing coach or moral supporter. Even in the case of a Caesarean birth, the father is often allowed to attend the surgery. Being present at a child's birth allows a father to show his commitment to the child and the child's mother. Fathers seem to feel more comfortable with their babies and take more interest in caring for them if they have participated in the birth and held their babies right away.

If the birth has no complications, the infant is usually quiet and alert right after birth. The newborn can see faces that are 8–12 inches (20–30 cm) away, and will seek out a person's eyes and stare. The newborn can hear well, and will turn her head or eyes toward a familiar sound. These early minutes of the newborn's life are often extremely rewarding for new parents, and many studies indicate that both mothers and fathers feel more secure with their babies and more confident caring for them if they have had time alone with the newborn right after birth (*see* **Bonding**).

Unless the father is the primary **caregiver**, a child under the age of two is likely to be more attached to his or her mother than father. The father may feel rejected or defeated in his attempts to take his share of the child-rearing if the young child is cold to him or pushes him away when upset. A father's bond with a young child can be stronger if there is some special time when he has the child alone. The father may develop special games and songs that only he does with the child. If there is some routine for father-child interaction, such as a nightly bathtime or bedtime ritual, the child is more likely to be comfortable with both parents.

Gender identity

According to research, the father typically plays a larger role than the mother in shaping his children's perceptions about their own masculinity or femininity. The father may consciously or unconsciously reward what he considers gender-appropriate behavior. For example, he may be visibly unsettled by a boy playing with dolls or wearing his sister's dress. A man who wished for a boy may encourage his daughter's tomboy tendencies, or he may expect his son to share his interest in certain masculine activities.

Children also pick up cues to gender roles by observing how their father treats their mother, and vice versa. Some children will respond positively to their father's expectations of their gender-appropriate behavior. But if the father's expectations clash with the child's **temperament** or desires, he may alienate the child. At such times, it may be necessary for the father to reevaluate his expectations and find new ways to interact with his child.

For Further Study

Books

Cath, Stanley H., Alan R. Gurwitt, John Munder Ross, eds. *Father and Child: Developmental and Clinical Perspectives.* Hillsdale, NJ: Analytic Press, 1994.

Geiger, Brenda. *Fathers as Primary Caregivers.* Westport, CT: Greenwood Press, 1996.

Laskin, David. *Parents Book for New Fathers.* New York: Ballantine Books, 1988.

Parke, Ross D. *Fatherhood.* Cambridge, MA: Harvard University Press, 1996.

Sears, William. *Keys to Becoming a Father.* Hauppage, New York: Barron's Educational Series, 1991.

Sulzberger, C. L. *Fathers and Children.* New York: Arbor House, 1987.

Audiovisual Recordings

The Dad Film. Boston, MA: Fanlight Productions, 1989. (One 28-minute videocassette.)

—A. Woodward

Fear

An aversion to a person, place, activity, event, or object that causes emotional distress and often avoidance behavior.

Fear is defined as emotional reaction related to a person, place, activity, event, or object. Symptoms of fear may include stiffening and crying in the newborn; crying and avoidance of the feared person or object in toddlers; bodily symptoms such as a stomachache or headache in children or adolescents (especially regarding school or separation anxieties); anger, avoidance, and denial of the fear in adolescents and teens; and panic reactions—sweating, trembling, fast heartbeat. While normal fears tend to be experienced in phases and tend to be outgrown by adulthood, abnormal fears are those that are persistent and recurrent, or fears that interfere with daily activities for at least a month. Abnormal fears, including extreme **separation anxiety**, **school phobia** (being afraid to go to school), or extreme social fears, may indicate an **anxiety** disorder.

More than 50% of children experience normal phobias (fear of a specific object) or anxieties (more general worries) before they are 18 years old. For adults it may be helpful to distinguish between rational fears, such as fear of snakes or guns, which are survival mechanisms and serve to protect a person from danger, and irrational fears (**phobias**) which cannot be traced to any reasonable cause. Many childhood fears fall somewhere between the rational and irrational, occurring in phases as the child or adolescent is exposed to new experiences and as both cognitive reasoning and the capacity for imagination develop. Whether a child's fear is considered normal generally depends on his or her age, background, and most importantly by how much it interferes with his or her normal daily activities. Fear of water may be considered normal in a child who has never learned how to swim, but it might be considered abnormal in the adolescent son of a coastal fisherman.

There are many avenues that parents, guardians, and teachers can follow in responding to childhood or adolescent fears. The first step is to assess whether the fear is age-normal. Following are some normal fears and their approximate ages of occurrence.

INFANCY, TODDLERHOOD, AND PRESCHOOL YEARS

Infants—Fear of being dropped or of falling; most are also afraid of loud noises.

Toddlerhood/Preschool—Fear of strangers, animals, bugs, storms, darkness, people with masks, monsters, "bad" people; fear of being separated from parents or attachment figures (i.e., age-appropriate separation anxiety); fear of being left alone, especially at night.

School-age years—Separation anxiety; fear of death and violence (war, murder, kidnapping); anxiety about school achievement.

Adolescence—Anxiety about school achievement; fear of social rejection and related worries; sexual anxieties.

Other fears not associated with any specific age are fear of visiting the doctor or dentist; fear of traveling by car, boat, or plane; and fear of going to school, sometimes called school phobia. School phobia often results in a refusal to attend school and is caused either by a deeper separation anxiety or fear of some aspect of the school environment. Many children experience a mild, temporary form of school phobia. If refusal to attend school lasts longer than three days in a row, however, parents might want to seek the help of a school counselor in addressing the underlying problem(s). In earlier grades the many new experiences of school may contribute to the phobia—being with strange authority figures, older children, submitting to a new rule system, publicly performing or speaking. In later grades the social and academic or extracurricular pressures may create additional fears.

The most significant factors in overcoming fear are identifying the fear, developing a sense of control over the feared environment (autonomy), and envisioning alternatives to the feared negative outcomes. Forcing children to perform activities they are afraid to do destroys, rather than builds, autonomy and self-confidence. If a child refuses to do something or explicitly voices fear, it should be taken seriously and explored through questioning and discussion. Ask the child or adolescent what

change can be made to accommodate the fear and make him or her feel more in control.

Some theories hold that reading scary picture books functions as a courage-building tool for children and helps them face their fears in a controlled environment—they are free to turn the page or to remind themselves that the monster is not real. Horror stories or movies may serve the same purpose for teens (though children do not have the same level of choice in leaving the theater and should not be exposed to disturbing movies). Controlled exposure—i.e., gradually introducing the child to the source of fear—often provides the necessary structure for addressing most fears. For instance, treating a child's fear of water might begin by incrementally filling the bathtub higher and working up to wading in a small stream or baby pool. Treating or preventing school phobias may require repeated short visits to the school accompanied by the parent, and brief meetings or gatherings with teachers and/or groups of other children before leaving the child alone.

Before, during, and after exposure to the source of fear, the child can begin to imagine controlling the environment and his own reactions in other ways. Creative visualization can be used, for example, to imagine a switch the child can use to control his fear when visiting the doctor or dentist. A comforting ritual, a familiar object, or thoughts of a beloved person can be used as a good luck charm before embarking on a scary trip or performing a task such as speaking in class or sleeping alone. Relaxation techniques can also be taught.

For Further Study

Books

Brown, Jeffrey. *No More Monsters in the Closet: Teaching Your Child to Overcome Everyday Fears and Phobias.* New York: Crown Paperbacks, 1995.

Joseph, Stephen M. *Mommy! Daddy! I'm Afraid: Help Your Children Overcome Fears That Hold Them Back in School and at Play.* New York: Collier Books, 1979.

Kellerman, Jonathan. *Helping the Fearful Child: A Parent's Guide to Everyday and Problem Anxieties.* New York: Norton, 1981.

Lobby, Ted. *Jessica and the Wolf : A Story for Children Who Have Bad Dreams.* New York: Magination Press, 1990.

Sanders, Pete. *Feeling Safe.* New York: Gloucester Press, 1988.

Warren, Paul, and Frank Minirth. *Things That Go Bump in the Night : How to Help Children Resolve Their Natural Fears.* Nashville, TN: T. Nelson Publishers, 1992. (This book also addresses Christian aspects of fear.)

Note: For titles of children's picture books on specific fears, look under the subject *bibliotherapy* at your local library or bookstore.

Feral Children

Lost or abandoned children raised in extreme social isolation, either surviving in the wild through their own efforts or "adopted" by animals.

The term "feral" means wild or undomesticated. Psychologists have studied feral children—children reared in complete or nearly complete isolation from human contact—to gain insights into aspects of human socialization and development. When feral children enter human society after their developmental years in isolation, they often continue to be seriously retarded. Researchers seek to answer the question of whether the abnormalities existed before their removal from society or developed because of their isolation.

Interest in feral humans began as early as the 1700s and continues to modern times. When Swedish naturalist and physician Carl Linnaeus (1707–1778) developed the system of scientific classification for plants and animals, he included the classification of *loco ferus*—"feral" or "wolf" men, characterized as four-footed, nonspeaking, and hairy. The 1994 film *Nell* was based on the true story of a young woman introduced to society after living for years in near-isolation.

Victor, the "wild boy of Aveyron," is the most famous case of a human being surviving in total isolation for an extended period of time. Discovered in 1799, Victor had been lost or abandoned in childhood, apparently surviving on his own in the wild up to the age of approximately 11. Philippe Pinel (1745–1826), pioneering French psychiatrist and director of the Bicêtre asylum in Paris, declared Victor an incurable idiot. But Jean-Marc-Gaspard Itard (1775–1838), a physician and teacher of the deaf, undertook to educate Victor. Although he remained almost totally unable to speak, Victor showed great improvements in socialization and cognitive ability in the course of several years spent working with Itard. In 1807, Itard published *Rapports sur le sauvage de l'Aveyron (Reports on the Wild Boy of Aveyron)*, a classic work on human educability, detailing his work with Victor between the years 1801–05.

Another well-known historical case involves a young man named Kaspar Hauser who appeared in Nuremberg, Germany, in 1828. He had apparently been locked up in isolation for an extended period, but without being totally deprived of human care. A 17-year-old with the mentality of a child of three, Hauser was reeducated over the next five years. His development had been stunted by extreme social and sensory deprivation, but the process of reeducation enabled Hauser to communicate verbally, although his speech was substandard.

Despite the persistence and popularity of stories about children reared by animals throughout history, well-documented cases of such children are very rare. In most cases the documentation begins with the discovery of the child, so that virtually nothing is known about the time actually spent in the company of animals. The best-known modern case of zoanthropy (humans living among animals) is that of the so-called "wolf children of Midnapore" (India). In 1920, two young girls, Kamala (about age 8) and Amala (about one and a half), were observed living with wolves in India. When they were discovered, their "rescuers" actually removed them from the embrace of a pair of wolf cubs in order to take them back to society. Not only did they exhibit the physical behavior of wolves—running on all fours, eating raw meat, and staying active at night—they displayed physiological adaptations to their feral life, including modifications of the jaw resulting from chewing on bones. The girls were taken to an orphanage where they were cared for and exposed to human society. Amala died within two years, but Kamala lived there for nine years, achieving a moderate degree of socialization.

The study of feral children has focused on some of the central philosophical and scientific controversies about human nature. Researchers have engaged in debates about nature vs. nurture, which human activities require social instruction, whether there is a critical period for language acquisition, and to what extent education can compensate for delayed development and limited **intelligence**. Itard's pioneering work with the "wild boy of Aveyron" has had an impact on both education of the disabled and early childhood education. Educators like **Maria Montessori** have taken the study of feral children seriously. In 1909, Montessori wrote that she felt the work of Itard provided a foundation for her own work with young children.

For Further Study

Books

Candland, Douglas Keith. *Feral Children and Clever Animals: Reflections on Human Nature*. New York: Oxford University Press, 1993.

Audiovisual Recordings

Secret of the Wild Child. Boston, MA: WGBH Educational Foundation, Boston, MA: 1994.

Fetal Alcohol Effect (FAE) and Fetal Alcohol Syndrome (FAS)

The adverse and chronic effects of maternal alcohol abuse during pregnancy on her infant.

The effects of heavy maternal alcohol use during pregnancy were first described as fetal alcohol syndrome

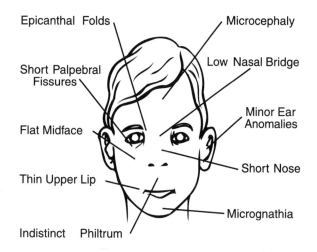

Epicanthal Folds

Short Palpebral Fissures

Flat Midface

Thin Upper Lip

Indistinct Philtrum

Microcephaly

Low Nasal Bridge

Minor Ear Anomalies

Short Nose

Micrognathia

Facial features of fetal alcohol syndrome.

(FAS) in the United States in 1973. An estimated one to three babies of every thousand births in the United States has FAS, making FAS the leading cause of **mental retardation.** It is also one of the few preventable causes of mental retardation and other **birth defects.** The U.S. Public Health Service estimates that between two and five of every thousand babies born in the United States exhibits one or more effects from fetal alcohol exposure. Although the precise amount of alcohol that must be consumed to cause damage is not known, it is believed that both heavy, consistent alcohol consumption and occasional binge drinking can produce FAS. In April 1997, the Centers for Disease Control and Prevention released the results of a study it had conducted in 1995. In a survey of 1,313 pregnant women, 3.5% said they "drank frequently" during pregnancy. (The agency defined "frequently" for the survey as having seven or more drinks per week, or binging on five or more drinks once within the previous month.)

Why some fetuses are affected and others are not is not completely understood. However, researchers believe that a combination of genetic and environmental factors work together to determine whether maternal alcohol consumption will affect the development of the **fetus.** Research has suggested that the genetic makeup of members of some racial and ethnic groups makes them less able to physically break down alcohol in the liver, and as a result, they are more susceptible to alcohol's adverse effects. When alcohol passes from the mother's bloodstream across the placenta to the developing fetus, the developing organs are unable to process it and thus are vulnerable to damage or arrested growth.

Women who drink heavily during **pregnancy** have a significantly higher risk of spontaneous **abortion** (known as miscarriage); their risk of miscarriage or

stillbirth is at least twice that of nondrinkers. For the woman who carries the fetus to term (or near-term), researchers speculate that, in addition to genetic factors, her nutritional status and general health will affect her ability to tolerate alcohol. Due to these and other factors, an estimated 40% of women who drink heavily during pregnancy will give birth to an infant with FAS; all women who drink large amounts of alcohol during pregnancy risk giving birth to an infant with fetal alcohol effects (FAE). FAE describes the condition where the visible physical effects of alcohol are less pronounced than with FAS, but where the learning and psychosocial characteristics are still pronounced. Both FAS and FAE produce lifelong effects that can be managed and treated but not cured.

FAS encompasses a range of physical and mental birth defects:

- prenatal growth retardation (low birth weight, length, and head circumference)

- low Apgar scores at birth

- postnatal growth retardation (failure to gain weight and develop normally)

- intellectual and attention deficiencies

- behavioral problems

- skull or brain malformations

- distinctive facial features (one or more):

  - small head (microcephaly)

  - small eyes with folds in the skin near the nose (epicanthal folds) and short horizontal eye openings (palpebral fissures)

  - underdevelopment of the upper lip with flat philtrum (ridges extending vertically between the upper lip and nose)

  - small jaw (micrognathia)

Infancy

There are two issues when dealing with the effects of maternal alcohol consumption on the newborn infant. First, a woman who drank heavily during pregnancy is likely to continue to drink after the baby is born. Second, the infant, born with low birth weight and length, may continue to display slow growth. **Bonding** with the mother is weaker than normal, and the baby may never establish regular feeding and sleeping patterns. Some FAS/FAE babies also display symptoms of **failure to thrive.** Babies with FAS/FAE may also be subjects of abuse or neglect, with inconsistent home and parenting environments.

When FAS/FAE is diagnosed during infancy, support services for parent and infant can be implemented.

These include treatment for alcohol abuse, stimulation for the infant, and counseling to improve parenting skills.

Toddlerhood

The FAS/FAE toddler may display signs of hyperactivity and distractibility. He or she may also show signs of **developmental delay,** such as delayed walking, poor coordination, delayed **language development,** and problems with **toilet training.** FAE/FAS toddlers may be prone to irritability and temper **tantrums.** Children with FAS/FAE will benefit from enrollment in **Head Start** or other preschool programs for children whose risk of failure in school is increased. FAS/FAE children may require more time to achieve developmental milestones that their normal peers.

School-age children

FAS/FAE children are at risk of experiencing failure early in their school career. Because their developmental problems are often undiagnosed, these students may not be provided with support and **special education** services that are available. By around fourth grade, when most school curriculums require higher cognitive processes, FAS/FAE children may begin refusing to go to school. They may have difficulty making and keeping friends, and may be viewed as intrusive "pests" by their peers. Appropriate social behavior is difficult for the FAS/FAE student to learn, further compounding problems of social isolation.

Early experimentation with drugs and alcohol is not uncommon. Other **antisocial behaviors,** such as arson, shoplifting, **lying,** defiance of authority, and destructiveness may develop in later elementary years and early adolescence.

Counseling and treatment for behavior and learning problems are best sought from professionals with experience in FAS/FAE. A coordinated program of family counseling and support of the child will bring the greatest likelihood of success.

Adolescence

Teachers and parents dealing with an FAS/FAE adolescent must adjust expectations to reflect the teen's actual abilities and maturation level. Researchers have found that FAS/FAE adolescents may not achieve the maturity of a normal 18-year-old until about age 25. Thus, the transition to adulthood will be slower and is best handled within a safe, controlled environment, with supportive adults to provide guidance and set limits.

FAS/FAE adolescents often become involved in inappropriate or unsafe sexual situations, brought about by physical maturity and emotional immaturity. FAS/FAE young adolescents, seeking approval, are easily victimized by sexual abusers; in addition, emotional immaturity may cause the FAS/FAE adolescent to abuse younger children sexually. Like many individuals who experience repeated failures in school, ostracism for behavior problems, and social isolation, sexual activity sometimes assumes a disproportionately significant role in the FAS/FAE adolescent's life.

Adolescents with FAS/FAE may benefit from involvement in vocational education and training programs, structured social situations (like clubs and organized recreational activities), and ongoing counseling about relationships, behavior management, and prevention of substance abuse.

FAS/FAE is a lifelong condition that, depending on its severity, will limit the individual's ability to function productively in the adult world. Early diagnosis and intervention with support and education services are the keys to success in social and vocational settings.

For Further Study

Books

Blume, Sheila B. *What You Can Do to Prevent Fetal Alcohol Syndrome: A Professional's Guide.* Minneapolis: Johnson Institute, 1992.

Davis, Diane. *Reaching Out to Children with FAS/FAE: A Handbook for Teachers, Counselors, and Parents Who Work with Children Affected by Fetal Alcohol Syndrome and Fetal Alcohol Effects.* West Nyack, NY: Prentice Hall, 1994.

Dorris, Michael. *The Broken Cord.* New York: Harper and Row, 1989.

Edelstein, Susan B. *Children with Prenatal Alcohol and/or Other Drug Exposure: Weighing the Risks of Adoption.* Washington, DC: CWLA Press, 1995.

McCuen, Gary E., ed. *Born Hooked: Poisoned in the Womb.* 2nd ed. Hudson, WI: G.E. McCuen Publications, 1994.

Nevitt, Amy. *Fetal Alcohol Syndrome.* New York: Rosen Publishing Group, 1996.

Stratton, Kathleen, Cynthia Howe, and Frederick Battaglia. *Fetal Alcohol Syndrome: Diagnosis, Epidemiology, Prevention, and Treatment.* Washington, DC: National Academy Press, 1997.

Periodicals

"More Women Report Alcohol Use in Pregnancy." *New York Times,* April 25, 1997, p. A13.

Steinmetz, George. "The Preventable Tragedy, Fetal Alcohol Syndrome." *National Geographic Magazine,* vol. 11, no 2, February 1992, pp. 36–39.

Audiovisual Recordings

Fetal Alcohol Syndrome (FAS) and Effects: What's the Difference? Evanston, IL: Altschul Group, 1989. (For information: 1-800-421-2363) (One 24-minute videocassette.)

Fetus

The unborn child from the start of the ninth week after conception to the time of birth.

Prenatal development is defined by two stages. The first stage involves the formation of the **embryo** from the fertilized egg. During this stage, the embryo's cells multiply and differentiate rapidly at an exponential rate. The embryo develops a primitive nervous and circulatory system. In the second stage of prenatal development the child-to-be is referred to as the fetus. Embryologists begin calling the embryo a fetus once the first bone cells appear, which is at about the eighth week after conception. The fetus is unlike the embryo in that it begins to become much more active. In the first trimester the fetus can kick its legs and move its arms. At this stage the heartbeat is strong enough to be detected by ultrasound.

For Further Study

Books

Johnson, Robert., ed. *Mayo Clinic Complete Book of Pregnancy and Baby's First Year.* New York: William Morrow, 1994.

Simkin, P., J. Whalley, and A. Keppler. *Pregnancy, Childbirth, and the Newborn: The Complete Guide.* New York: Meadowbrook Press, 1991.

Fever

An elevated body temperature.

While the standard for normal body temperature is 98.6°F (37°C), normal body temperatures actually fluctuate within a range of one to two degrees, making it impossible to formulate a precise definition of fever based on a specific temperature. Children's temperatures are generally higher than those of adults and fluctuate more widely. They may vary depending on the time of day, the child's emotional state or level of physical activity, the amount of clothing worn, or the surrounding room temperature. In general, temperatures under 100°F (37.7°C) are considered "subfebrile" (i.e., not indicating fever). Rectal temperatures of up to 100.4°F (38°C) may be considered normal.

A part of the **brain** called the hypothalamus acts as the body's thermostat, keeping its temperature at or close to 98.6°F (37°C). When there is an infection (or certain other types of disease), the body's white blood cells produce specific proteins (endogenous pyrogens) that reach the brain through the bloodstream and stimulate the hypothalamus, which signals the body to increase its metabolic rate and consume oxygen faster, resulting in a higher body temperature. Fever is one of the ways the body defends itself against infections. It is commonly caused by viral and bacterial infections, including colds, earaches, and flu. When fever is present, the production of infection-fighting white blood cells is increased, and their effectiveness is enhanced. More serious potential causes of fever include pneumonia, urinary tract infections, **appendicitis,** and **meningitis**. Fever can also be caused by non-infectious conditions that produce inflammation—such as juvenile rheumatoid **arthritis,** Crohn's disease, and lupus—as well as overexertion, dehydration, allergic reactions, insect bites and stings, and toxic reactions.

A child's temperature can be taken in several ways. Rectal temperatures are about half a degree higher than oral ones. A rectal reading is considered more accurate than an oral one, which may be affected by previously eaten hot or cold foods or by a child's breathing. Underarm temperatures are considered reliable for young infants, and new electronic thermometers can measure temperature through the ear. Although fever is generally a cause for concern among parents, high fevers are not necessarily a sign of serious illness. Unlike adult temperatures, the level of a child's temperature does not necessarily indicate the severity of an illness. A mild cold may produce a fever as high as 105°F (40.5°C), while the fever accompanying pneumonia may only be 100°F (37.7°C). The temperatures of newborn infants are particularly unreliable because the baby's temperature control mechanism is not yet adequately developed.

Although fevers are generally not dangerous, they are treated because they cause discomfort and can prevent children from getting the sleep and nourishment they need in order to get well. **Aspirin** was the medication most commonly used to lower fevers until 1980, when researchers found that the use of aspirin to treat children's fevers caused by influenza and **chicken pox** was associated with Reye's syndrome, a dangerous condition that causes liver impairment and brain damage and can result in coma and eventual death. Since then, **acetaminophen**s (sold under such brand names as Tylenol) have become the most widely recommended drugs for treating fever in children. Acetaminophens, which are available in liquid form, tablets and capsules for oral use, and as suppositories, are effective in treating fever but do not share aspirin's inflammation-reducing properties. Ibuprophen (Advil, Nuprin, etc.) is an effective fever reducer that is also an anti-inflammatory. However, it has not been on the market as long as acetaminophens and has been known to produce allergic and gastrointestinal side effects. A fever can also be reduced one or two degrees by sponging a child with room-temperature water (about 70°F [21°C]) while he or she sits in a tub filled with water up to waist level.

One frightening aspect of fever in infants and young children is that it can lead to a type of seizure called a febrile convulsion. These convulsions occur in 3–5% of all children and appear to be linked to an existing predisposition rather than to the severity of the fever or how quickly it has risen. Febrile seizures recur in approximately half the children who have them; about a third experience a second recurrence. Alarming as they are, there is no evidence that febrile convulsions cause any permanent damage or lead to **epilepsy.** They usually last only a few minutes (sometimes only seconds). While the seizure is happening, the child's head should be protected from injury and the airways kept open. Keeping the head turned to the side will prevent choking in case of vomiting. If the seizure lasts more than five minutes, an ambulance should be called. Whether or not emergency treatment is needed, a physician should be notified. It is important to determine that the seizure was due only to fever, rather than meningitis.

Most experts agree that a doctor should be notified immediately when fever appears in an infant under the age of eight weeks. Children at this age are susceptible to serious, even life-threatening, infections that can come on suddenly and need immediate attention. For children up to the age of three years, a doctor should be notified of any fever over 103°F (39.4°C). In older children, a fever of 105°F (40.5°C) or over requires prompt medical attention, as does any fever that lasts longer than four or five days. Medical attention should also be sought for any fever accompanied by unusual irritability or sleepiness, listlessness, pain, a stiff neck, difficulty breathing, reduced urination, or any other symptoms that arouse suspicion.

For Further Study

Books

Berry, James R. *Why You Feel Hot, Why You Feel Cold: Your Body's Temperature.* Boston: Little, Brown, 1973.

Brace, Edward R., and John P. Pacanowski. *Childhood Symptoms: Every Parent's Guide to Illnesses.* New York: HarperPerennial, 1992.

Garwood, John, and Amanda Bennett. *Your Child's Symptoms.* New York: Berkeley Books, 1995.

Kluger, Matthew J. *Fever: Its Biology, Evolution, and Function.* Princeton, NJ: Princeton University Press, 1979.

Periodicals

Chong, C.Y., and D.M. Allen. "Childhood Fever." *Singapore Medical Journal* 37, February 1996, pp. 97–100.

Figure-Ground Perception

The ability to visually differentiate between a sensory stimulation and its background.

A person's ability to separate an object from its surrounding field is referred to as figure-ground perception. Visual figure-ground perception is the ability to distinguish an object from the background field. Auditory figure-ground perception is the ability to hear the voice of one speaker over the background noise (conversations, music, air conditioning) of the environment. The object that a person focuses on is called the figure; everything else is referred to as background, or simply ground.

Children who are easily distracted are often unable to focus on one object while ignoring or blocking out the background. Children with **attention deficit/hyperactivity disorder** or attention span difficulties often benefit from a learning environment that minimizes background distractions. While a classroom with lots of visual and auditory stimulus may be exciting to some students, the easily distracted child finds it overwhelming. He or she is unable to focus on any one aspect of the environment, and spends all his or her time processing the stimuli. This student is unable to distinguish the important stimuli for learning from all other sensory inputs.

To study figure-ground discrimination ability, psychologists have created different kinds of assessment stimuli. Some stimuli involve simple ambiguous figures, like the famous face-vase figure that can be interpreted as two faces looking at one another or as one goblet, depending on what aspect a person focuses on. Complex stimuli, such as the so-called "Magic Eye" pictures that became popular in the 1990s, can also be used to demonstrate figure-ground relationships. These complex pictures require concentration and control to relax the muscles of the eyes to see a three-dimensional figure emerge from the background.

Psychologists have also demonstrated figure-ground principles with auditory stimuli, and have developed exercises for students to improve their ability to hear a speaker above background noise.

For Further Study

Books

Bregman, Albert S. *Auditory Scene Analysis: the Perceptual Organization of Sound.* Cambridge, MA: MIT Press, 1990.

Coren, S., and L.M. Ward. *Sensation and Perception.* 3rd ed. San Diego: Harcourt Brace Jovanovich, 1989.

Dance, Sandy. *Picture Interpretation: A Symbolic Approach.* River Edge, NJ: World Scientific, 1995.

Graham, Norma Van Surdam. *Visual Pattern Analyzers.* New York: Oxford University Press, 1989.

Handel, Stephen. *Listening: An Introduction to the Perception of Auditory Events.* Cambridge, MA: MIT Press, 1989.

Pavel, Monique. *Fundamentals of Pattern Recognition.* 2nd ed. New York: M. Dekker, 1993.

Fine Motor Skills

Skills involving control of the fingers, hands, and arms.

Fine motor skill involves deliberate and controlled movements requiring both muscle development and maturation of the central nervous system. Although newborn infants can move their hands and arms, these motions are reflexes that a baby cannot consciously start or stop. The development of fine motor skills is crucial to an infant's ability to experience and learn about the world and thus plays a central role in the development of intelligence. Like **gross motor skills**, fine motor skills develop in an orderly progression, but at an uneven pace characterized by both rapid spurts and, at times, frustrating but harmless delays. In most cases, difficulty with certain fine motor skills is temporary and does not indicate a serious problem. However, medical help should be sought if a child is significantly behind his peers in multiple aspects of fine motor development or if he regresses, losing previously acquired skills.

Infancy

The hands of a newborn infant are closed most of the time and, like the rest of her body, she has little control over them. If her palm is touched, she will make a very tight fist, but this is an unconscious reflex action called the Darwinian reflex, and it disappears within two to three months. Similarly, the infant will grasp at an object placed in her hand, but without any awareness that she is doing so. At some point her hand muscles will relax, and she will drop the object, equally unaware that she has let it fall. Babies may begin flailing at objects that interest them by two weeks of age but cannot grasp them. By eight weeks, they begin to discover and play with their hands, at first solely by touch, and then, at about three months, by sight as well. At this age, however, the deliberate grasp remains largely undeveloped.

Hand-eye coordination begins to develop between the ages of 2¾ and 4¾ months, inaugurating a period of trial-and-error practice at sighting objects and grabbing at them. At four or five months, most infants can grasp an object that is within reach, looking only at the object and not at their hands. Referred to as "top-level reaching," this achievement is considered an important milestone in fine motor development. At the age of six months, infants can typically hold on to a small block briefly, and many have started banging objects. Although their grasp is still clumsy, they have acquired a fascination with grabbing small objects and trying to put them in their mouths. At first, babies will indiscriminately try to grasp things that cannot be grasped, such as pictures in a book, as well as those that can, such as a rattle or ball. During the latter half of the first year, they begin exploring and testing objects before grabbing them, touching them with an entire hand and, eventually, poking them with an index finger.

One of the most significant fine motor accomplishments is the pincer grip, which typically appears between the ages of 12 and 15 months. Initially, an infant can only hold an object, such as a rattle, in his palm, wrapping his fingers (including the thumb) around it from one side, an awkward position called the palmar grasp, which makes it difficult to hold on to and manipulate the object. By the age of eight to ten months, a finger grasp begins, but objects can only be gripped with all four fingers pushing against the thumb, which still makes it awkward to grab small objects. The development of the pincer grip—the ability to hold objects between the thumb and index finger—gives the infant a more sophisticated ability to grasp and manipulate objects, and also to deliberately drop them. By about the age of one, an infant can drop an object into a receptacle, compare objects held in both hands, stack objects, and nest them within each other.

Toddlerhood

Toddlers develop the ability to manipulate objects with increasing sophistication, including using their fingers to twist dials, pull strings, push levers, turn book pages, and use crayons to produce crude scribbles. Dominance of either the right or left hand usually emerges during this period as well. Toddlers also add a new dimension to touching and manipulating objects by simultaneously being able to name them. Instead of only random scribbles, their drawings include patterns, such as circles. Their play with blocks is more elaborate and purposeful than that of infants, and they can stack as many as six blocks. They are also able to fold a sheet of paper in half (with supervision), string large beads, manipulate snap toys, play with clay, unwrap small objects, and pound pegs.

Preschool

The more delicate tasks facing preschool children, such as handling silverware or tying shoelaces, represent more of a challenge than most of the gross motor activities learned during this period of development. The central nervous system is still in the process of maturing sufficiently for complex messages from the brain to get to the child's fingers. In addition, small muscles tire more easily than large ones, and the short, stubby fingers of preschoolers make delicate or complicated tasks more difficult. Finally, gross motor skills call for energy, which is boundless in preschoolers, while fine motor skills require patience, which is in shorter supply. Thus, there is considerable variation in fine motor development among this age group.

By the age of three, many children have good control of a pencil. Three-year-olds can often draw a circle, although their attempts at drawing people are still very primitive. It is common for four-year-olds to be able to use scissors, copy geometric shapes and letters, button large buttons, and form clay shapes with two or three parts. Some can print their own names in capital letters. A human figure drawn by a four-year-old is typically a head atop two legs with one arm radiating from each leg.

School age

By the age of five, most children have clearly advanced beyond the fine motor skill development of the preschool age. They can draw recognizably human figures with facial features and legs connected to a distinct trunk. Besides drawing, five-year-olds can also cut, paste, and trace shapes. They can fasten visible buttons (as opposed to those at the back of clothing), and many can tie bows, including shoelace bows. Their right- or left-**handedness** is well established, and they use the preferred hand for writing and drawing.

Encouraging fine motor development

Encouraging gross motor skills requires a safe, open play space, peers to interact with, and some adult supervision. Nurturing the development of fine motor skills is considerably more complicated. Helping a child succeed in fine motor tasks requires planning, time, and a variety of play materials. Fine motor development can be encouraged by activities that youngsters enjoy, including crafts, puzzles, and playing with building blocks. Helping parents with everyday domestic activities, such as baking, can be fun for the child in addition to developing fine motor skills. For example, stirring batter provides a good workout for the hand and arm muscles, and cutting and spooning out cookie dough requires hand-eye coordination. Even a computer keyboard and mouse can provide practice in finger, hand, and hand-eye coordination. Because the development of fine motor skills plays a crucial role in school readiness and cognitive development, it is considered an important part of the preschool curriculum. The Montessori schools, in particular, were early leaders in emphasizing the significance of fine motor tasks and the use of learning aids such as pegboards and puzzles in early childhood education. The development of fine motor skills in children of low-income parents, who often lack the time or knowledge required to foster these abilities, is a key ingredient in the success of programs such as **Head Start.**

See also **Gross Motor Skills**

For Further Study

Books

Eckert, Helen M. *Motor Development.* 3rd ed. Indianapolis, IN: Benchmark Press, 1987.

Lerch, Harold A., and Christine B. Stopka. *Developmental Motor Activities for All Children: From Theory to Practice.* Dubuque, IA: Brown and Benchmark, 1992.

Thomas, Jerry R., ed. *Motor Development in Childhood and Adolescence.* Minneapolis: Burgess Publishing Co., 1984.

Fluoridation

The process of adding fluoride to drinking water or another substance in order to reduce the occurrence of tooth decay.

Fluoridation was first introduced into the United States in the 1940s in an attempt to combat the serious problem of tooth decay. Today, more than half of the U.S. population drinks fluoridated water from public water supplies.

Tooth decay occurs when food acids dissolve the protective enamel surrounding each tooth and create a hole, or cavity, in the tooth. These acids are present in food, and can also be formed by acid-producing bacteria that convert sugars into acids. There is overwhelming evidence that fluoride can substantially reduce tooth decay. When ingested into the body, fluoride concentrates in bones and in dental enamel, which makes the tooth enamel more resistant to decay. It is also believed that fluoride may inhibit the bacteria that convert sugars into acidic substances that attack the enamel.

Opponents of fluoridation have not been entirely convinced of its effectiveness, and are concerned by possible side effects. They are also disturbed by the moral issues of personal rights that are raised by the addition of a chemical substance to an entire city's water supply. The decision to fluoridate drinking water has generally rested with local governments and communities and has always been a controversial issue.

Fluoride is present in most water supplies at low levels and nearly all food contains traces of fluoride. Toothpaste and mouthwash also contain added fluoride.

Infants who do not receive adequate amounts of fluoride in the water or formula they drink routinely have been given fluoride supplements beginning at about one month of age. In 1995, the **American Academy of Pediatrics** (AAP) recommended delaying such supplements until six months of age. Along with the American Dental Association, the AAP also revised downward the minimum level of fluoride at which supplementation is necessary. Studies now suggest that too much fluoride has resulted in an increase in the incidence of fluorosis, a discoloration or mottling of the teeth. While fluorosis can be unsightly, there is no evidence it weakens the positive effects of fluoride. Recent research also suggests that direct application of a fluoride gel to teeth with braces can ease bleeding of the gums and plaque buildup.

The issue of fluoridation was particularly controversial in the 1950s and 1960s, when heated debate surrounded the issue across the country. Critics pointed to the known harmful effects of large doses of fluoride that led to bone damage and to the special risks for people with kidney disease or those who were particularly sensitive to toxic substances. Between the 1950s and 1980s, some scientists suggested that fluoride may have a mutagenic effect (that is, it may be capable of causing human **birth defects**). Controversial claims that fluoride can cause **cancer** were also raised. Today, some scientists still argue that fluoridation is not without health risks.

Up until the 1980s the majority of research into the benefits of fluoridation reported substantial reductions (50–60% on average) in the incidence of tooth decay where water supplies had fluoride levels of about one ppm (parts per million). By the end of the decade, however, the extent of this reduction was being viewed more critically. By the 1990s, even some fluoridation proponents suggested that observed tooth decay reduction, directly as a result of water fluoridation, may only have been at levels of around 25%. Other factors, such as education and better dental hygiene, could also be contributing to the overall reduction in tooth decay levels. Fluoride in food, salt, toothpastes, rinses, and tablets has undoubtedly contributed to the drastic declines in tooth decay during the twentieth century. It also remains unclear what, if any, side-effects are of one ppm levels of fluoride in water ingested over many years. Although it has been argued that any risks associated with fluoridation are small, these risks may not necessarily be acceptable to everyone. The fact that only about 50% of U.S. communities have elected to adopt fluoridation is indicative of people's cautious approach to the issue. In 1993, the National Research Council published a report on the health effects of ingested fluoride and attempted to determine if the maximum recommended level of four ppm for fluoride in drinking water should be modified. The report concluded that this level was appropriate but that further research may indicate a need for revision. The report also found inconsistencies in the scientific studies of fluoride toxicity and recommended further research in this area.

For Further Study

Books

Martin, B. *Scientific Knowledge in Controversy: The Social Dynamic of the Fluoridation Debate.* Albany, New York: State University of New York Press, 1991.

National Research Council Committee on Toxicology. *Health Effects of Ingested Fluoride.* Washington, DC: National Academy Press, 1993.

United States Department of Health and Human Services Committee to Coordinate Environmental Health and Related Programs. Ad Hoc Subcommittee on Fluoride. *Review of Fluoride Benefits and Risks: Report of the Ad Hoc Subcommittee on Fluoride.* Washington, DC: Public Health Service, Department of Health and Human Services, 1991.

Whitford, G.M. *The Metabolism and Toxicity of Fluoride.* Basel, New York: Karger, 1989.

Periodicals

"Fluoride Facts and Fallacies." *Medical Update* 18, July 1994, p. 2.

"Fluoride in the Water and Toothpaste?" *Child Health Alert* 12, November 1994, p. 5.

"Fluoride Supplementation for Children: Interim Policy Recommendations." *Pediatrics* 95, May 1995, p. 777.

Hileman, B. "Fluoridation of Water." *Chemistry and Engineering News* 66, August 1, 1988, pp. 26–42.

"The Latest on Fluoride." *Pediatrics for Parents* 16, March 1995, p. 12.

Lee, Yun. "Healthy Braced Teeth: Fluoride Gel Cuts Cavities for Orthodontic Wearers." *Prevention* 47, November 1995, p. 46.

Foster Care

Foster care is full-time substitute care of children outside their own homes by people other than the biological parents.

Children are placed in foster care for a number of reasons. Some are being protected from abuse at home; others have been neglected by their parents, or have parents who are unable to take care of them. A small percentage of children are in foster care because their parents feel unable to control them, and their behavior may have led to delinquency. In all cases, the child's natural parents temporarily give up legal custody of the child. A child may be placed in foster care with the natural parents' consent. In a clear case of abuse or neglect, a court can order a child into foster care without the parents' consent. Foster care does not necessarily mean care by strangers. If a government agency decides a child must be removed from her home, the child may be placed with relatives or with a family friend. Children may also be placed in a group home, where several foster children live together. State social service agencies are usually in control of foster care decisions, though they may also work with private foundations.

Federal money supports most foster care programs, and a federal law governs foster care policy. This law, the Adoption Assistance and Child Welfare Reform Act of 1980, emphasizes two aims of foster care. One is to preserve the child's biological family if at all possible. Children are placed in foster care only after other options have failed, and social service agencies work with the biological family to resolve its problems, so that children can return to their homes. The second aim of the Child

Welfare Reform Act is to support the so-called "permanency planning." This means that if a child must be removed from her home, the social service agency handling the case can decide quickly whether the child will ever be returned. If it seems likely that parents will not be able to care for their children again, their parental rights may be terminated so that the child is free to be adopted. This policy is articulated in this law in order to prevent children from living too long in an unstable situation. Today about half of all children in foster care are returned to their original homes within six months. Nevertheless, another estimated 25% of children in foster care remain in foster care for at least two years.

There are close to 400,000 children in foster care in the United States. About one third of these children are from poor families. Poor children are more likely to be in foster care than middle-class children because their families have fewer resources. Illness or loss of a job may be devastating to a poor family with no savings and no relatives who can afford to assist them. African American children make up about 40% of all children in foster care. They are also more likely to stay in foster care longer, or to have been in foster care since infancy. Also, children of alcoholics or drug addicts are at high risk for neglect or abuse, and so they are often placed in foster care.

In most cases, children who have been placed in foster care have been subjected to some form of abuse or neglect, and being removed from familiar surroundings is, in itself, usually highly traumatic. Children in foster care may have nightmares, problems sleeping or eating, and may be depressed, angry, and confused. Many young children in foster care are unable to understand why they have been taken from their parents. Even if a child is in some sense relieved to be out of a home that was dangerous to her, she may still miss her parents, and imagine that there is something she must do to get back to them. Though there is evidence that children from abusive and neglectful homes start to feel better in foster care, separation is almost always difficult for children.

Foster care can be difficult for foster parents as well. A child who has been neglected or abused suffers psychological damage that may make the child withdrawn, immature, aggressive, or otherwise difficult to reach. Foster placements sometimes fail because the parents simply cannot handle the demands of a troubled foster child. Despite the stress of foster parenting, about 100,000 homes in the U.S. take in foster children. A foster parent may be a single person, and in some areas, single mothers make up a large proportion of foster parents.

Foster parents must be licensed by the agency that handles foster care in their area. The foster parent or parents' home must pass an inspection for health and safety, and in most states, the parents must attend training sessions covering issues of foster care and how to deal with problems. When a child is placed, the foster family has responsibility for feeding and clothing the child, getting the child to school and to appointments, and doing any of the usual things a child's parents might be called to do. The foster parents might also need to meet with the foster child's therapist, and will meet regularly with the child's caseworker as well. The foster parent aims to help the foster child develop normally in a family situation.

Foster parents usually receive money for taking in foster children. With this money they are expected to buy the child's food and clothing, and take care of incidental expenses. Most of the foster parent's responsibilities toward the foster child are clearly defined in a legal contract. Foster parents do not become the guardians of foster children; legal guardianship remains with the state agency. Foster placements may last for a few days or weeks, or even years. If the biological parents give up their rights or their rights to their child are severed, the foster family may wish to adopt the foster child. Foster parenting is meant to be an in-between stage, while a permanent placement for the child is settled. As such, it is stressful and uncertain, but for many families very rewarding.

For Further Study

Books

Davies, Nancy Millichap. *Foster Care.* New York: Franklin Watts, 1994.

—A. Woodward

Fracture

A break in the normal structure of a bone.

Bone fractures most often result from an accidental injury, although they may be caused by repeated stress from such activities as walking, dancing, or marching, or by medical conditions that weaken the bones. They are commonly divided into two major types: closed fractures, in which the ends of the bones remain in place under the skin, and open fractures, in which they protrude through the skin. Children's fractures are often less severe than those of adults and heal more quickly because their bones are softer and more resilient. (It is possible for a child's bone to bend more than 45 degrees without breaking.) Cracks, hairline, and "greenstick" fractures, in which the bone splits on one side, are common. Other types of fractures include the buckle fracture, in which the bone has been compressed and part of it is raised or bulging; the complete fracture, in which the bone is broken into separate pieces; and the dislocation fracture, in which the bone is both broken and dislocated.

About three-fourths of all children's fractures occur in the upper extremities, often as a result of a fall onto an outstretched hand, elbow, or side of the shoulder. This type of fall can also break the clavicle, or collarbone, the bone most often fractured by children. Elbow fractures, which account for about 10% of all children's fractures, must be treated promptly to prevent possible deformity and nerve damage. The femur, or thighbone, is another common site for childhood fractures, often caused by falling from a height or by an automobile accident. Also common are fractures of the bones in the lower leg—the tibia, or shinbone, and the fibula—which can be caused by a seemingly minor impact, such as jumping off a chair. These fractures are usually more serious in older children than in toddlers, damaging nerves and blood vessels.

Like other types of head injuries, skull fractures are not uncommon among children. Because their skulls are still relatively flexible, infants and young children can tolerate brain swelling after a head injury better than older children and adults. However, prompt medical attention is crucial; an untreated head injury can result in **mental retardation** or **seizures.** A trauma that causes excessive force to the neck or back, such as a severe shaking or whiplash, can result in a neck or spinal fracture. These fractures are among the most serious childhood injuries because they can damage the spinal cord, resulting in paralysis.

The primary symptom of a fracture is pain at the site of the injury, usually accompanied by swelling, discoloration, and a limited range of motion and/or inability to bear weight in the affected area. There may be visible deformity of the bone and, in common fractures, bone ends may be visible through the skin. A child with a fracture may experience numbness or tingling in an affected extremity and may become pale. An infant or toddler with a fracture will become fussy and irritable. Signs of a neck or spinal fracture include neck or back pain, numbness or paralysis, and holding the head or neck at an odd angle.

When a fracture is suspected, the child should be taken to a hospital emergency room. The injured area should not be moved and should not bear any weight until the child is examined by a physician. A limb in which a fracture is suspected can be immobilized using a makeshift splint made from a pillow, folded newspaper, or other support. Elevating and applying ice to the injured area can alleviate pain by minimizing swelling. No food should be consumed in case general **anesthesia** is necessary to reset the bone. It is especially important not to move a child with a suspected skull, neck, or spinal fracture. If pain and swelling from an apparent sprain or other musculoskeletal injury fail to lessen within a day or two, the child should be examined for a possible fracture.

A fracture diagnosis is made or confirmed by x-ray examination. Treatment varies depending on the type of fracture, the affected bone, and the age of the child. Realignment of the bone, also called fracture reduction, is often unnecessary in children, and immobilization in a plaster or plastic cast is usually sufficient. A fractured long bone in an arm or leg commonly takes from six to 12 weeks to heal in an adult and less time in a child. Some fractures may require immobilization by traction, pins, wires, screws, or plates. There may be complications if the growth plate at the end of a long bone (in an arm or leg) is injured. Damage to the growth plate can halt normal development, shortening bones and resulting in deformity of bones and joints.

Parents can take steps to reduce the likelihood of childhood fractures by installing safety gates in the home and using car seats for children weighing up to 40 pounds (18 kg). Strollers, carriages, tricycles, and bicycles should be sturdy and well designed, and children should be trained in bicycle safety. Padded surfaces under jungle gyms and other playground structures can reduce the incidence of fractures in children, and protective helmets used for activities such as bicycling and rollerblading can protect against skull fractures.

For Further Study

Books

Clayman, Charles B., ed. *The Human Body: An Illustrated Guide to Its Structure, 1st American ed.* New York: Dorling Kindersley, 1995.

Hall, Katy. *Skeleton! Skeleton!* New York: Platt and Munk, 1991.

Wolff, Angelika. *Mom! I Broke My Arm!* New York: Lion Press, 1969.

Fragile X Syndrome

A genetic disorder that causes mental retardation.

Fragile X syndrome is a genetic disorder that occurs in all ethnic groups, and one out of 700 pregnant women carries the fragile X defect. In 1992, a new test was announced for determining whether a woman carries the fragile X genetic defect. When a woman learns that she carries this defect, she may then elect to undergo **amniocentesis** or chorionic villus tests to determine whether her fetus also carries the fragile X defect. The incidence of fragile X syndrome is estimated to be approximately one in every 2,000 to 3,000 births; the estimates include one per 1,500 males and one per 2,500 females.

Fragile X appears to be caused by an abnormal number of repeats of a genetic sequence on a segment of the X chromosome. (It was initially characterized as the Martin-Bell syndrome.) Because fragile X has been observed in all ethnic groups, it may be considered one of the most frequent single-gene disorders in humans. It is difficult to diagnose in infants, but the features slowly become evident as the child grows.

Developmental delay and **mental retardation** are the most significant features of fragile X syndrome. In fact, fragile X syndrome is a common cause of mental retardation—researchers estimate that 20% of all boys with IQ levels between 30 and 55 (severely to moderately retarded) have fragile X syndrome. Overall, the population with fragile X syndrome ranges in mental retardation from profound (IQ below 25) to borderline, with an average IQ **(intelligence quotient)** in the moderately retarded range (35–55).

Before the onset of puberty, boys with the syndrome have delayed developmental milestones and may display some avoidance behavior similar to **autism.** They may also exhibit hyperactivity and **attention deficit/hyperactivity disorder. Language delay** is frequently observed; absence of speech is rare, but a playful, repetitive speech pattern is common.

An adult male with fragile X syndrome is likely to have the following characteristics: a long, narrow face with head circumference above the 50th percentile; prominent jaw and forehead; large and slightly malformed ears; hyperextending joints; high arched palate, and enlarged testicular volume.

In girls, the symptoms appear to be milder than in boys. The mental retardation is less severe, with most female patients falling in the mild-to-borderline retarded range. Emotional problems are reportedly more common in females with fragile X syndrome. An adult female with fragile X syndrome has facial characteristics similar to an adult male—prominent jaw and forehead and large, protruding ears.

Mental retardation caused by fragile X syndrome (or any other cause) often requires that the individual receive lifetime custodial care.

For Further Study

Organizations

National Fragile X Foundation
    Address: 1441 York St., Suite 303
    Denver, CO 80206
    Telephone: (303) 333-6155; toll-free (800) 688-8765
    (U.S. callers only)
    FAX: (303) 333-4369
    (Seeks to increase awareness of the characteristics and treatment of fragile X syndrome among members and the general public. Operates 74 resource centers, 14 outside the United States, and the Fragile X Project, providing funding for education, genetic screening and counseling, and treatment programs. Publishes *National Fragile X Foundation Newsletter* quarterly.)

Friendship

Companions or peers with whom one has common interests, emotional bonds, and social relationships.

Why have friends? "To have somebody to play with," responds the 9-year-old. "So you won't be alone. To have someone to back you up, to stand by you," answers the 12-year-old. These two replies reflect a developmental perspective on friends and friendships that appears to be characteristic of children in diverse cultures and societies.

Although children have many peers in playgroups, classrooms, and neighborhoods, they have a more select group of friends and an even smaller number of "best" friends. Carollee Howes noted that friendships in preschools emerge out of mutual social attraction and a "climate of agreement," in which children find it easy to be with each other and to engage in the sort of activities they both enjoy. These early friendships provide children with opportunities to cooperate and communicate with others. Consequently, children who have formed stable friendships are more able to complete complex activities with each other than with peers who are not friends. Friendships are often among children of the same sex.

The likelihood that children's close friendships are with members of the same sex rises to near certainty during middle childhood so that by age 12, nearly all American children identify a same sex peer as their "best friend." In addition to activities of mutual interest, friends tend to talk to each other—about themselves, their teachers, their families, and especially peers. In fact, Parker and Gottman (1989) concluded that gossip was a fundamental aspect of friendships in the middle childhood years when children's awareness of hierarchical social standing and popularity highlight their own relative status in comparison to others. Gossip among friends seems to serve the function of exploring those relative relationships and ascertaining one's own status.

Although best friends tend to be of the same sex, boys and girls are certainly not segregated altogether during middle childhood years. Contact in schools and neighborhoods may often be in groups of male friends meeting groups of female friends, sometimes for joint activities and sometimes for teasing or other provocations, often involving "who likes whom."

By **adolescence** the intimate nature of friendship has emerged, especially for girls. Even by age 12, friends are described as someone special, someone who stands by you and "backs you up." Compared to the friendships of middle childhood, based largely on mutual interests and activities, adolescent friendships also reflect each other's attitudes, values, and beliefs. Adolescents report spending more time with friends than with their family and tend to value friends for their understanding and the sense of identity they reflect. Whereas boys tend to spend time with a group of friends, girls tend to spend time with a smaller number of closer friends.

Robert Selman believes that there is a further shift in the concept of friendship from early to later adolescence. The earlier emphasis on developing mutual intimacy and support changes as more mature adolescents develop an appreciation of friends' needs to establish relations with others without interpreting that need as a threat to the original relationship. Selman has also examined the growth of perspective-taking ability, and has found that the sophistication of one's ability to take on the perspective of others is correlated to one's level of friendship development. Further, children with clinical problems often have impaired social relations, poorly developed friendships, and difficulties with perspective taking.

Friendships are special relationships, and needs to be distinguished from general peer relations. Clare Stocker and Judith Dunn, for example, have studied the sibling, peer, and friendship relations of 5- to 10-year-olds. Although they found no patterns linking sibling and peer relationships, they found that children who had the most conflictual relationships with their siblings were described by their mothers as having closer and more positive best friendships compared to children with more positive sibling relationships. Stocker and Dunn suggest that children may compensate for conflictual family relationships by investing in their friendships. On the other hand, hostile, controlling relationships with siblings may provide the child with sufficient experience to be particularly adept at other intimate social relationships. What is clear, however, is that these relations do not hold for same age peers in general, but only for close friends, an indication that, among children's social relations, friendships assume a privileged status.

For Further Study

Books

Parker, J. G., and J. M. Gottman. "Social and Emotional Development in a Relational Context: Friendship Interactions from Early Childhood to Adolescence." In T. J. Berndt, and G. W. Ladd, eds. *Peer Relationships in Child Development.* New York: Wiley, 1989.

Selman, R. "The Child as Friendship Philosopher." In S. R. Asher, and J. M. Gottman, eds. *The Development of Children's Friendships.* Cambridge: Cambridge University Press, 1981 .

Periodicals

Howes, C. "Peer Interaction of Young Children." Monographs of the Society for Research in Child Development, Serial No. 217, 1987, no. 53, p. 1.

Stocker, C., and J. Dunn. "Sibling Relationships in Childhood: Links with Friendships and Peer Relationships." *British Journal of Developmental Psychology* 8, 1990, pp. 227–244.

Frostig Developmental Test of Visual Perception

Assesses visual perception and hand-eye coordination.

The Frostig Developmental Test of Visual Perception is also known as the Marianne Frostig Developmental Test of Visual Perception and the DTVP. It is a test widely administered to children in pre-kindergarten through third grade to diagnose possible **learning disabilities** or neurological disorders by assessing perceptual skills (visual perception and hand-eye coordination). Children are generally referred for the test by **special education** teachers, occupational therapists, or psychologists. The DTVP can be administered individually or in groups. It consists of 41 tasks arranged in order of increasing difficulty on demonstration cards and is designed to evaluate the child's visual skills in the following areas: eye-motor coordination (drawing continuous straight, curved, or angular shapes); **figure-ground perception** (detecting embedded figures); constancy of shape (distinguishing common geometric shapes); position in space (identifying reversed position); and spatial relations (connecting dots to form shapes and patterns). Test results are evaluated in relation to standard first-grade reading skills. Raw scores for each subtest are converted to age scores and scaled scores. The scaled scores for all five subtests are then combined for a total test score, which is divided by the child's age to produce a perceptual quotient. Guidelines are provided for scores considered necessary to first-grade readiness. While the DTVP can be an indicator of learning disabilities, the test by itself is not a definitive indicator of learning disorders, nor do high scores on it rule them out. Young children may need more than one session to complete the test, which has also been adapted for the hearing-impaired and non-English-speaking children.

For Further Study

Books

Cohen, Libby G., and Loraine J. Spenciner. *Assessment of Young Children.* New York: Longman, 1994.

Hart, Diane. *Authentic Assessment: A Handbook for Educators.* Menlo Park, CA: Addison-Wesley, 1994.

McCullough, Virginia. *Testing and Your Child: What You Should Know About 150 of the Most Common Medical, Educational, and Psychological Tests.* New York: Plume, 1992.

Wortham, Sue Clark. *Tests and Measurement in Early Childhood Education.* Columbus: Merrill, 1990.

G

Gambling, Pathological

Uncontrollable impulse to gamble, regardless of the problems caused in daily life.

Pathological gambling, a pattern of repeated gambling and preoccupation with gambling, often begins in **adolescence** in males, and somewhat later in females. Individuals with this disorder often experience a progression in their gambling, becoming increasingly preoccupied with gambling, increasing the amounts wagered, and often continuing to gamble despite attempts to stop or control the behavior.

See also **Impulse Control Disorders.**

Gangs

A group of people recognized as a distinct entity and involved in antisocial, rebellious, or illegal activities.

A youth gang is a group of young people whose members recognize themselves as a distinct entity and are recognized as such by their community. Their involvement in antisocial, rebellious, and illegal activities draws a negative response from the community and from law enforcement officials. Other characteristics of gangs include a recognized leader; formal membership with initiation requirements and rules for its members; its own territory, or turf; standard clothing or tattoos; private slang; and a group name. In a document published by Boys and Girls Clubs of America, the U. S. Department of Justice has divided gangs into several types. Territorial ("turf" or "hood") gangs are concerned with controlling a specific geographical area. Organized, or corporate, gangs are mainly involved in illegal activities such as drug dealing. Scavenger gangs are more loosely organized than the other two types and are identified primarily by common group behavior.

Since the 1980s, teen gang activities have become an increasing cause for concern in many areas of the United States. It is estimated that hundreds of thousands of young people—perhaps upwards of a million—belong to thousands of gangs in major urban centers, suburbs, small cities, and even in rural areas. A study conducted at the University of Southern California found gang activity in 94% of the country's major cities and over 1,000 cities altogether. The number of gang members in Los Angeles County alone was estimated at 130,000 in 1991. In the same year there were an estimated 50 gangs in New York City, 125 in Chicago, and 225 in Dallas. Today's gangs are more involved in serious criminal activities than their predecessors. Gang-related violence has risen sharply, involving ever-younger perpetrators who are increasingly ready to use deadly force to perpetuate rivalries or carry out drug activities. In addition, the scope of gang activities has increased, often involving links to drug suppliers or customers in distant locations.

Youth gangs are found among virtually all ethnic groups. Mexican American gangs, whose members are sometimes referred to as *cholos*, have long been active in the Southwest and are now spreading to other parts of the country. Today these groups include not only the traditional Mexican American membership but also new immigrants from Central American countries such as El Salvador. The most visible Hispanic gangs on the East Coast have traditionally been the Puerto Rican gangs in New York City, originally formed by the children of immigrants who came to this country in the 1940s and 1950s. African American gang affiliations often center around the Crips and Bloods, Los Angeles gangs that are bitter rivals, or the Vice Lords and Folk Nation, which are Chicago gangs. Chinese gangs, which began in New York in the 1960s and 1970s, prey on the Asian community, extorting money in return for protection. With the wave of immigration from Southeast Asia following the Vietnam war, Vietnamese and Cambodian gangs have formed, also terrorizing their own communities.

The most visible white gangs are the skinheads (named for their close-shaven heads), who typically embrace a racist, anti-Semitic, and anti-gay philosophy, often involving neo-Nazi symbolism and beliefs. There are thought to be between 3,000 and 4,000 skinheads in the United States, including such groups as the Aryan Youth Movement, Blitz Krieg, and White Power. Skinhead activities have included painting racial slurs on buildings, damaging synagogues and the homes of Jews and blacks, and sometimes fatal assaults on members of minority groups. The white Spur Posse, a gang of white high school athletes in California, received media attention in the late 1990s for sexually molesting teenage girls.

A variety of factors have been cited as causes for teen involvement in gangs. Social problems associated with gang activity include poverty, racism, and the disintegration of the nuclear family. Some critics claim that gangs are glamorized in the media and by the entertainment industry. On a personal level, adolescents whose families are not meeting their emotional needs turn to gangs as substitute families where they can find acceptance, intimacy, and approval. Gangs can also provide the sense of identity that young people crave as they confront the dislocations of adolescence. Teenagers also join gangs because of social pressure from friends. Others feel physically unsafe in their neighborhoods if they do not join a gang. For some youths, the connection to a gang is through family members who belong—sometimes even several generations of a single family. Yet another incentive for joining is money from the gangs' lucrative drug trade. Drug profits can be so exorbitant as to dwarf the income from any legitimate job: teenagers in one suburban high school in the early 1990s were handling $28,000 a week in drug money, with individual profit averaging $5,000.

The basic unit in gangs, whatever their origin or larger structure, is a **clique** of members who are about the same age (these groups are also called posses or sets). A gang may consist entirely of such a clique, or it may be allied with similar groups as part of a larger gang. The Crips and Bloods consist of many sets, with names such as the Playboy Gangster Crips, the Bounty Hunters, and the Piru Bloods. It is to their clique or set that members feel the greatest loyalty. These neighborhood groups have leaders, who may command as many as 200 followers. In groups affiliated with larger gangs, these local leaders are accountable to chiefs higher up in the gang hierarchy. At the top is the kingpin, generally an adult, who has the ultimate say in how the gang conducts its financial operations and oversees its members.

The lowest level on which a young person may be associated with a gang is as a lookout—the person who watches for the police during drug deals or other criminal activities. Lookouts, who are commonly between seven and twelve years old, can be paid as much as three hundred dollars a week. At the next level are "wannabes," older children or preteens who identify themselves with a gang although they are still too young for membership. They may wear clothing resembling that of the gang they aspire to and try to ingratiate themselves with its members. Sometimes they cause trouble in or out of school as a way of drawing the gang's attention. Once wannabes are being considered for entrance into a gang they undergo some form of initiation. Often it includes the commission of a specified crime as a way of "proving themselves." In addition, gangs generally practice certain initiation rituals, such as "walking the line," in which initiates have to pass between two lines of members who beat them. In other cases, initiation brutalities follow a less orderly course, with a succession of gang members randomly perpetrating surprise beatings that initiates have to withstand without attempting to defend themselves. Other rituals, such as cutting initiates and mixing their blood with that of older members, are also practiced.

Gangs adopt certain dress codes by which members show their unity and make their gang affiliation visible both to members of other gangs and to the community at large. Gang members are usually identifiable by both the style and color of their clothing. Latino gangs traditionally wore khaki pants, white T-shirts, and plain cotton jackets, but today black pants and jackets are favored, often worn with black L.A. Raiders caps. The Crips are strongly associated with the color blue, typically wearing blue jackets, running shoes with blue stripes and laces, and blue bandannas, either tied around their heads or hanging prominently from a back pocket. (The color of the rival Bloods is red.) Two rival African American gangs in Chicago wear hats tilted in different directions to signal their affiliation. With the increased use of deadly force by today's gang members, gang clothing codes can be very dangerous: nonmembers have been killed for accidentally wandering onto gang turf wearing the colors of a rival group. In addition to their clothing, gang members express solidarity by adopting street names and using secret symbols and codes, often in graffiti spraypainted in public places.

Although most gang members are male, young women do join gangs—either mixed-gender or all-female gangs (which are sometimes satellites of male gangs and sometimes independent of them). Traditionally they have played a subservient role in mixed gangs, assisting the males in their activities and forming romantic attachments within the gang, but generally not engaging in criminal activities more serious than shoplifting or fighting girls from other gangs. To be initiated into a mixed-sex gang, female members have often been required to have sex with multiple gang members. Today girl gang members are more apt than in the past to participate in serious violence, such as drive-by shootings, armed robbery, and "wildings," savage group attacks on innocent victims in public places, often involving sexual assault.

Perhaps the most troubling feature of gang activity in the 1980s and 1990s is its increased level of violence, which often victimizes not only gang members themselves but also innocent bystanders who unwittingly find themselves in its path. Thousands of young people with no gang connections have been killed because they were in the wrong place at the wrong time. Most gang-related killings are linked to fights over turf (including drug turf), "respect" (perceived threats to a gang member's status), or revenge. In Los Angeles County, the number of gang-related slayings soared from 212 in 1984 to 803 in 1992. Nationwide, the total number of teenagers murdered every year has risen 55% since 1988, an increase thought to be closely linked to the growth of gang activity. In 1991 over 2,000 people were injured or killed in drive-by shootings, 90% of which are thought to be committed by gang members. A major factor that has raised the level of gang violence is easy access to such weapons as automatic rifles, rapid-fire pistols, and submachine guns.

A common feature of membership in youth gangs is the difficulty encountered by young people who want to quit. They are virtually always punished in some way, ranging from ritualized beatings (mirroring the initiation ceremony) to murder. Sometimes the member's entire family is terrorized. Many young persons—and sometimes even their families—have had to relocate to another city in order to safely end gang affiliations. In some cities, there are organizations (some staffed by ex-gang members) that help young people who want to leave gangs.

Possible signs indicating that a teenager has joined a gang include the following: lower grades and disciplinary problems in school; nervous, hostile, or uncommunicative behavior at home; new friends who are not introduced to the family; reduced amounts of time spent at home; unexplained possession of money; and possession of a weapon.

For Further Study

Books

Greenberg, Keith Elliot. *Out of the Gang.* Minneapolis, MN: Lerner Publications, 1992.

Gardner, Sandra. *Street Gangs in America.* New York: Franklin Watts, 1992.

Knox, Mike. *Gangsta in the House: Understanding Gang Culture.* Troy, MI: Momentum Books, 1995.

Monti, Daniel. *Wannabe: Gangs in Suburbs and Schools.* Cambridge, MA: Blackwell, 1994.

Oliver, Marilyn Tower. *Gangs: Trouble in the Streets.* Springfield, NJ: Enslow Publishers, 1995.

Webb, Margot. *Coping with Street Gangs.* New York: Rosen Publishing Group, 1992.

Organizations

National School Safety Center
Address: 4165 Thousand Oaks Blvd., Suite 290
Westlake, CA 91362
Telephone: (805) 446-4264

National Youth Gang Information Center
Address: 4301 Fairfax Dr., Suite 730
Arlington, VA 22203
Telephone: (800) 446-4264

Gates-MacGinitie Reading Tests (GMRT)

Measures reading achievement.

The Gates-MacGinitie Reading Tests measure reading achievement in grades K–12. The GMRT is a timed multiple-choice test administered in groups. It is used to place students in remedial or accelerated reading programs, evaluate the programs themselves, and aid in advising students and monitoring their progress. There are seven different levels covering grades 1–12 and two additional early levels for kindergarten and first grade. Level PRE (Pre-Reading evaluation) can aid in identifying concepts with which beginning readers may need extra help. It provides scores in five areas including Literacy Concepts, Oral Language Concepts, and Letters and Letter-Sound Correspondences. Level R is designed to assess the reading skills of children who make less than average progress in reading by the end of the first grade. Level R scores include Initial Consonants, Final Consonants, Vowels, and Use of Context. Test results for these early levels can help in making decisions about whether a child will benefit from a modified reading program and also aid in choosing reading materials and instructional methods for an entire reading group. Levels 1 through 10/12 have three scores each: Vocabulary, Comprehension, and a Total Score. These levels can identify which children need special help with comprehension, vocabulary, or other aspects of reading, and/or further evaluation.

For Further Study

Books

Hart, Diane. *Authentic Assessment: A Handbook for Educators.* Menlo Park, CA: Addison-Wesley Pub. Co., 1994.

McCullough, Virginia. *Testing and Your Child: What You Should Know About 150 of the Most Common Medical, Educational, and Psychological Tests.* New York: Plume, 1992.

Gates-McKillop-Horowitz Reading Diagnostic Tests

Assesses oral reading, spelling, and writing abilities.

The Gates-McKillop-Horowitz Reading Diagnostic Tests are individually administered reading skills test that assess the oral reading, spelling, and writing abilities of children in grades one to six. It is generally used for group placement in classes and can also identify reading difficulties in older students. The 11-part test covers the following areas: oral reading; recognition of isolated words; knowledge of word parts; recognizing and blending common word parts; reading words; giving letter sounds; naming letters; identifying vowel sounds; auditory blending and discrimination; and writing (by means of an informal writing sample). Not all parts of the test are used with all students. The test is untimed but usually takes about an hour.

For Further Study

Books

McCullough, Virginia. *Testing and Your Child: What You Should Know About 150 of the Most Common Medical, Educational, and Psychological Tests.* New York: Plume, 1992.

Gay/Gay Community *see* Homosexuality

Gender Bias in Education

Treating boys and girls differently at school.

Gender bias in education means treating boys and girls differently at school. This can include how teachers respond to students, what students are encouraged to study, and how textbooks represent gender roles. Education researchers have studied gender bias in the schools for the past 20 years, but the subject did not receive widespread publicity until the early 1990s, with the publication of several landmark studies. A study commissioned by the American Association of University Women (AAUW) in 1991 entitled "Shortchanging Girls, Shortchanging America," synthesized much earlier research and concluded that the average school is biased against girls in a number of ways. The study claimed that girls do not receive as much attention from teachers as boys, boys are called on to answer more abstract and complex questions than girls, teachers encourage boys to think for themselves more than girls, and many school books continue to present stereotypical images of women or ignore women's achievements. While elementary school girls report high **self-esteem**,

once they reach junior high, many girls think less well of themselves consciously. The findings of the AAUW study were amplified in a further report in 1992, called "How Schools Shortchange Girls," and in a book published in 1994 by two of the major researchers included in the earlier studies—Myra and David Sadker's *Failing at Fairness: How America's Schools Cheat Girls.* The Sadkers' work quantified classroom behavior and found, for example, that on average, boys are 12 times more likely than girls to talk in class and five times more likely to get the teacher's attention. Educational researchers are concerned that such bias against girls contributes to many adolescent girls' self-esteem. Compared to boys, girls think less of their academic skills and shy away particularly from math and science.

In spite of the conclusions of the AAUW studies, other experts point out that girls continue to have considerable success in school. Girls stay in school longer, cut classes less than boys, and on average earn better grades than boys. Though boys, on average, outperform girls on standardized math and science tests, girls score higher than boys on standardized reading and writing tests. Girls, on average, take more academic courses than boys, are more likely than boys to finish high school, and are more likely to go to college. The percentage of female students in medical school continues to rise—to nearly 50%—which seems to contradict the idea that girls are discouraged from pursuing scientific careers.

The importance of conscious reports of self-esteem is another controversial aspect of the gender bias debate. Some writers point out the discrepancy between girls' high grades and reported low self-esteem. Another study suggests that self-esteem is not a good indicator of academic achievement or future success. Students may think well of their abilities and perform poorly, or vice versa. The Educational Testing Service, which administers the **Scholastic Assessment Test (SAT)** and other tests, has found simply that students who spend more time on math homework do better on math tests. It is difficult to quantify the effects of self-esteem in such a direct way.

Bias in standardized tests is another issue that has been scrutinized in the 1990s. Some advocacy groups have claimed that standardized tests are written with biased language, in that they refer to men much more than women. According to other research, girls tend to perform better on essay tests than on multiple choice tests. Another concern is that colleges often base scholarships on test scores. A girl with higher or equal grades but lower test scores than a boy is less likely to receive a college scholarship.

Some school districts have experimented with single-sex classrooms, offering all-girl math, science, and engineering classes. Others have separated all academic classes into boys or girls only. Some research suggests that girls in single-sex schools excel academically and have higher self-confidence; however, single-sex education within a co-ed public school is still experimental, and some have suggested that it may violate Title IX of the federal Education Amendments of 1972, which prohibits discrimination on the basis of sex.

If parents are concerned about gender bias, they should visit their child's school and discuss perceived problems with other parents, teachers, and administrators, and encourage their children to be more sensitive to gender stereotypes.

For Further Study

Books

Sadker, David, and Myra Sadker. *Failing at Fairness: How America's Schools Cheat Girls.* New York: Scribner's, 1994.

—A. Woodward

Gender Constancy

A child's realization that gender is fixed and does not change over time.

The concept of gender constancy, influenced by the **cognitive development** theory of **Jean Piaget,** was introduced by Lawrence Kohlberg (1927–1987). Addressing the formation of gender identity in terms of cognitive development, Kohlberg advanced the idea that the development of sex roles depends in large part on a child's understanding that gender remains constant throughout a person's lifetime. Children realize that they are male or female and are aware of the gender of others by the age of three. However, at these ages they still do not understand that people cannot change genders the way they can change their clothes, names, or behavior. Kohlberg theorized that children do not learn to behave in gender-appropriate ways until they understand that gender is permanent, which occurs at about the age of seven. At this point they start modeling the behavior of members of their own sex. Although it has been supported by some research studies, Kohlberg's theory has also been criticized on the grounds that children do show certain types of gender-associated behavior, such as toy and playmate selection, by the ages of two or three. This points to the fact that there are others factors, such as parental reinforcement, that influence the adoption of sex-typed behavior.

Gender Identity

The sense of identification with either the male or female sex, as manifested in appearance, behavior, and other aspects of a person's life.

Influenced by a combination of biological and sociological factors, gender identity emerges by the age of two or three and is reinforced at **puberty.** Once established, it is generally fixed for life.

Aside from sex differences, other biological contrasts between males and females are already evident in childhood. Girls mature faster than boys, are physically healthier, and are more advanced in developing oral and written linguistic skills. Boys are generally more advanced at envisioning and manipulating objects in space. They are more aggressive and more physically active, preferring noisy, boisterous forms of play that require larger groups and more space than the play of girls the same age. In spite of conscious attempts to reduce sex role stereotyping in recent decades, boys and girls are still treated differently by adults from the time they are born. The way adults play with infants has been found to differ based on gender—girls are treated more gently and approached more verbally than boys. As children grow older, many parents, teachers, and other authority figures still tend to encourage independence, competition, and exploration more in boys and expressivity, nurturance, and obedience in girls.

A major step in the formation of gender identity occurs at about the age of three when children first become aware of anatomical differences between the sexes, usually through observation of siblings or peers. The awareness of physical difference is followed by awareness of the cultural differences between males and females and identification with the parent of the same sex, whose behavior the child begins to imitate. The most famous 20th-century theory about the acquisition of gender identity at this stage of life is the Oedipus complex formulated by Sigmund Freud (1856–1939). Like its female counterpart, which Freud termed the Electra complex, the Oedipus complex revolves around a child's wish to possess the parent of the opposite sex, while simultaneously wishing to eliminate the parent of the same sex, who is perceived as a rival.

In the Oedipus complex, the young boy develops incestuous desires toward his mother, while regarding his father as a rival for her affections. Fearing that the father will cut off his penis in retaliation—a phenomenon Freud called castration anxiety—the boy represses his forbidden desires and finally comes to identify with the father, internalizing his values and characteristics, which form the basis for the child's superego. In the female version of this theory, the young girl's discovery of sexual difference results in penis envy, which parallels castration anxiety in boys. The girl blames her mother for depriving her of a penis, and desires her father because he possesses one. As in the Oedipus complex, the girl eventually represses her incestuous desires and identifies with the same-sex parent (in this case, the mother).

The Oedipus complex has been widely criticized, especially by feminist critics who reject its assumption that "anatomy is destiny." One respected feminist theory is that of Nancy Chodorow, for whom the central factor in gender identity acquisition is the mother's role as primary **caregiver,** which leads to a greater sense of interrelatedness in girls, who identify with the mother and go on to reproduce the same patterns of mothering in their own adult lives, while boys, needing to identify with the parent of the opposite sex, acquire a defining sense of separateness and independence early in life. This "reproduction of mothering," being both biologically and sociologically determined, is at least theoretically open to the possibility of change if patterns of parenting can be altered.

The formation of gender identity has been approached in different terms by Lawrence Kohlberg (1927–1987), who formulated the concept of **gender constancy,** the awareness that gender remains fixed throughout a person's lifetime. Kohlberg noted that while children are aware of their own gender and the gender of others by the age of three, they do not really begin assuming appropriate gender-based behavior until the age of about seven, when they first understand that gender is permanent—that they cannot change gender the way they can change their clothes or their behavior. Kohlberg believed that children do not start systematically imitating the behavior of members of their own sex until that point.

While most children follow a predictable pattern in the acquisition of gender identity, some develop a gender identity inconsistent with their biological sex, a condition variously known as gender confusion, gender identity disorder, or **transsexualism,** which affects about 1 in 20,000 males and 1 in 50,000 females. Researchers have found that both early socialization and hormonal factors may play a role in the development of gender identity disorder. Children with gender identity disorder usually feel from their earliest years that they are trapped in the wrong body and begin to show signs of gender confusion between the ages of two and four. They prefer playmates of the opposite sex at an age when most children prefer to spend time in the company of same-sex peers. They also show a preference for the clothing and typical activities of the opposite sex: transsexual boys like to play house and play with dolls. Girls with gender identity disorder are bored by ordinary female pastimes and prefer the rougher types of play typically associated with boys, such as contact sports.

Both male and female transsexuals believe and repeatedly insist that they actually are, or will grow up to be, members of the opposite sex. Girls cut their hair short, favor boys' clothing, and have negative feelings about maturing physically as they near adolescence. In childhood, girls with gender identity disorder experience less overall social rejection than boys, as it is more socially acceptable for a girl to be a tomboy than for a boy to be perceived as a "sissy." About five times more boys than girls are referred to therapists for this condition. Teenagers with gender identity disorder suffer social isolation and are vulnerable to **depression** and **suicide.** They have difficulty developing peer relationships with members of their own sex as well as romantic relationships with the opposite sex. They may also become alienated from their parents.

Most children eventually outgrow gender identity disorder. About 75% of boys with gender identity disorder develop a homosexual or bisexual orientation by late adolescence or adulthood, but without continued feelings of transsexuality. Most of the remaining 25% become heterosexuals (also without transsexuality). Those individuals in whom gender identity disorder persists into adulthood retain the desire to live as members of the opposite sex, sometimes manifesting this desire by cross-dressing, either privately or in public. In some cases, adult transsexuals (both male and female) have their primary and secondary sexual characteristics altered through a sex change operation, consisting of surgery followed by hormone treatments.

For Further Study

Books

Chodorow, Nancy. *The Reproduction of Mothering: Psychoanalysis and the Sociology of Gender.* Berkeley: University of Berkeley Press, 1978.

Diamant, Louis, and Richard D. McAnulty, eds. *The Psychology of Sexual Orientation, Behavior, and Identity: A Handbook.* Westport, CT: Greenwood Press, 1995.

Golombok, Susan, and Robyn Fivush. *Gender Development.* Cambridge: Cambridge University Press, 1994.

Kohlberg, Lawrence. *Child Psychiatry and Childhood Education: A Cognitive-Developmental View.* New York: Longman, 1987.

Lloyd, Barbara B. *Gender Identities and Education: The Impact of Starting School.* New York: St. Martin's Press, 1992.

General Educational Development *see* **Test of General Educational Development**

Genetic Disorders

Conditions with a link to the individual's genetic make-up.

Genetic disorders are conditions that can be traced to an individual's heredity. Many of these disorders are inherited and are governed by the same genetic rules that determine dimples and red hair. However, some genetic disorders result from a spontaneous mutation during embryonic development. If one parent can transmit the genetic information (in genes) that causes a child's disorder, then the disorder is said to be genetically dominant. However, if both parents lack the disorder and pass the disorder's gene to a child, then the genetic disorder is said to be recessive. But not all genetic diseases are completely determined by genes alone; some are promoted by environmental factors such as diet. Disorders that result from both genes and environment are called multi-factorial genetic diseases. In addition, some genetic disorders occur predominantly in males or females, due to the nature of the sex chromosomes, X and Y. Although many genetic diseases, such as **cystic fibrosis** and **sickle-cell anemia**, do not occur often, some more common genetic diseases include **hypertension, diabetes**, and certain forms of **cancer.**

Genetic inheritance

The principles of genetic inheritance can seem complicated to non-scientists. Basically, genetic information is organized into chromosomes in the cellular nucleus. Human cells have 46 chromosomes each—except for sperm and eggs (reproductive cells), which each have 23 chromosomes. Each person receives 23 chromosomes from their mother's egg and 23 chromosomes from their father's sperm. All but one of the 23 chromosomes are called autosomes, or non-sex chromosomes. These 22 chromosomes do not determine gender. The remaining chromosome is the sex chromosome and is either an X or a Y. Females have two Xs (XX), and males have one of each (XY). Females can only pass an X to their offspring, and males can pass either an X or a Y. Hence, the male sperm is responsible for gender selection. Because of their two X chromosomes, females can carry a disease gene on one X chromosome but not exhibit the disease since they have another X chromosome to compensate. However, males only have one X chromosome and can be affected by the same disease. Such genetic disorders are called X-linked.

The 44 autosomes have parallel coded information on each of the two sets of 22 autosomes, numbered 1 through 22, called homologous pairs. This coding is organized into genes. Individual genes are made of deoxyribonucleic acid (DNA), and code for particular proteins. Proteins play numerous critical structural and functional roles in the body. Each gene has a set locus, or position, on a particular chromosome. The genes with the same locus on corresponding chromosomes are called alleles. So, conventional terminology would describe one person as having two alleles of the same gene. Humans are called diploid organisms, because we have two alleles of each autosomal gene.

Genotype

A shorthand is used to portray alleles that make up a person's genotype for a single locus. Genotypes are usually written as lower or upper case letters of the alphabet (such as AA, aa or Aa), where capital letters define dominant genes and lower case letters define recessive genes. When an allele can be one of many types, several letters can represent the same gene. Genotypes are either homozygous or heterozygous. Having two identical alleles, such as AA or aa, makes a person homozygous for that locus. Having different alleles (for example, Aa) at a locus makes someone heterozygous. The actual trait observed in a person is called the **phenotype**. Examples of phenotypes include dimples, brown eyes, and tongue-curling. Some traits are dictated by a single gene; whereas other are the result of multiple genes (multi-genic). This is true whether the trait is disease-related or not.

Genetic dominance describes the ability of a single allele to control phenotype. However, this concept does not explain all genetic observations. For example, sickle-cell anemia is a genetic recessive disease characterized by abnormal hemoglobin production. However, sickle-cell heterozygous people also produce some abnormal hemoglobin, although they usually do not experience illness, due to their normal hemoglobin. The production of both allelically encoded forms is an example of codominance. Therefore, this phenotype is said to be codominant. Incomplete dominance also occurs. Height is a example of this type of dominance, where the offspring can have a height between the heights of their parents (which is not the same height as either parent). Height, however, is also determined by a number of other factors such as diet (environment) and hormonal regulation (genetic). Thus, it is apparent that several factors can contribute to final phenotype in a number of traits; this is also true for various diseases.

The autosomes can be distinguished from one another in size and staining patterns. Chromosomal analysis can be performed on cell samples from one person. Corresponding chromosomes 1 through 22 and the sex chromosomes can be lined up and visually inspected for abnormalities. Any obvious flaw can indicate or explain a diseased state. Sometimes it is apparent that a part of one chromosome was incorrectly combined with a different chromosome during cellular division. When other than two autosomes 1 through 22 are present, the aberrant result is called aneuploidy. Most aneuploidies are trisomies (three homologous autosomes), or the presence of extra sex chromosomes.

Dominant genetic disorders

If one parent has an autosomal dominant disease, then offspring have a 50% chance of inheriting that disease. There are roughly 2,000 autosomal dominant disorders (ADDs) with effects that range from inconvenience to death. These diseases may manifest early or late in life. ADDs include **Huntington's disease** (HD), polydactyly (extra toes or fingers), Marfan's syndrome (extra long limbs), achondroplasia (a type of **dwarfism**), some forms of glaucoma, most forms of porphyrias, and hypercholesterolemia (high blood cholesterol). In most ADDs, the homozygous genotype elicits a more severe disorder; however, this is not true for Huntington's disease.

HD is one of the most debilitating ADDs. It is characterized by progressive chorea (involuntary, rapid, jerky motions) and mental deterioration. HD usually appears in affected individuals between the ages of 30 and 50, and leads to dementia and eventual death in about 15 years.

Marfan's syndrome, or arachnodactyly, is an ADD characterized by long, thin arms, legs, and fingers. People with Marfan's also tend to be stoop-shouldered and have blue sclera of the eyes. In addition, these individuals have a high incidence of eye and aortic heart problems. Statistics show some correlation between older fathers and offspring with Marfan's. Not all people with Marfan's inherit it from a parent; about 15% of Marfan's cases are caused by a fresh mutation in the same locus. Abraham Lincoln is believed to have been afflicted with Marfan's.

Recessive genetic disorders

Recessive genetic disorders (RGD) result from the acquisition of two recessive alleles of a gene—one from each parent. When both parents carry a harmful, recessive trait, one or both of them may be unaware that they are carriers. Hence, the birth of a child with the recessive disease may be a shock to the healthy parents. The probability of two heterozygous parents having an affected child is 25% each time they conceive. The chance that they will have a heterozygous (carrier) child is 50% for each conception, and the chance of having an unaffected homozygous child is also 25% for each pregnancy. About 1,000 confirmed RGDs exist with the better known diseases, including cystic fibrosis, **phenylketonuria (PKU),** galactosemia, retinoblastoma (Rb), albinism, sickle-cell anemia, thalassemia, **Tay-Sachs disease, autism**, growth hormone deficiency, adenosine deaminase deficiency (ADD), and Werner's syndrome (juvenile muscular dystrophy).

A number of eye disorders are RGDs, and are usually associated with a mutant gene on chromosome 13. The Rb gene was the first human gene to be located and identified as causing retinoblastoma, cancer of the retina. Most retinoblastomas are hereditarily transmitted; however, in some case, a heterozygous person develops a mutation of one gene, which makes them homozygous for the disease. Other recessive eye disorders include myopia (nearsightedness), albino eyes, day blindness, displaced pupils, and dry eyes. Some RGDs affect people of one particular ethnic background more than the rest of the population. Three such RGDs are cystic fibrosis (CF), sickle-cell anemia (SCA), and Tay-Sachs disease (TSD). CF is one of the most common autosomal recessive diseases in caucasian children in the U.S. About 4–5% of caucasians carry this recessive gene on chromosome 7, which causes exocrine mucus-producing glands to secrete an unusually thick mucus that clogs ducts and collects in lungs and other body areas. CF patients usually die before the age of 20, while some individuals live to the age of 30. SCA usually appears in the world's black and Hispanic populations; however, some cases also occur in Italian, Greek, Arabian, Maltese, southern Asian, and Turkish people. About 1 in 12 blacks carry the SCA gene. SCA is caused by mutations in two hemoglobin genes. Hemoglobin carries oxygen in red blood cells to tissues and organs throughout the body. SCA patients have red blood cells that live only a fraction of the normal life span of 120 days. The abnormal blood cells have a sickled appearance, which led to the disease's name. SCA patients also die early, before the age of 30. The TSD gene is carried by 1 in 30 Ashkenazi Jews. Children born with TSD seem normal for the first 5 months, but eventual cerebral degeneration progresses to blindness and death before the age of four.

Galactosemia and phenylketoniuria (PKU) are examples of metabolic RGDs that are caused by a defective gene important in metabolism. People with galactosemia cannot metabolize galactose, the sugar found in milk, and **mental retardation** may result if normal milk is not avoided by people with this rare disease. People with PKU cannot convert phenylalanine to tyrosine. The build-up of phenylalanine leads to severe mental retardation. PKU is carried by 1 in 50 caucasians. It is one of the few severe genetic disorders that can be controlled by diet. A phenylalanine-free diet containing sufficient amino acids is available for people diagnosed with PKU. Since 1961, a test has been available to readily screen newborns for PKU from a blood test, and most states perform this test routinely.

ADD is one of few "curable" genetic diseases. ADD is caused by a single mutation on chromosome 20 in an enzyme important to the immune system. Not only are bone marrow transplants hopeful treatments, but now gene therapy has been successful at replacing these patients' defective gene with a healthy gene which enables their immune system to function effectively.

X-linked genetic disorders

X-linked genetic disorders (XLGDs) can be either dominant or recessive. Dominant XLGDs affect females, are usually lethal, and are severely expressed in those males that survive; a high percentage of male embryos with dominant XLGD will spontaneously abort in a miscarriage. Dominant XLGD's include: Albright's hereditary osteodystrophy (seizures, mental retardation, stunted growth), Goltz's syndrome (mental retardation), cylindromatosis (deafness and upper body tumors), oral-facial-digital syndrome (no teeth, cleft tongue, some mental retardation), and incontinentia pigmenti (abnormal swirled skin pigmentation).

Recessive XLGDs are passed to sons through their mothers, who are known or unknown carriers. Often, a carrier mother will have an affected male relative. Major XLGDs include: severe combined immune deficiency syndrome (SCID), color blindness, hemophilia, Duchenne's muscular dystrophy (DMD), some spinal ataxias, and Lesch-Nyhan syndrome. Roughly one third of these XLGDs result from a spontaneous mutation. Of these disorders, color blindness is the most benign.

Hemophilia is a more serious XLGD caused by failure of one of the clotting proteins that routinely prevent an injured person from bleeding to death. Hemophilia A, the most severe form of this disease, is characterized by extreme bleeding. It primarily affects males, although a few females have had hemophilia A (the offspring of a hemophiliac father and a carrier mother).

Other usually fatal XLGDs affect the immune, muscular, and nervous systems. SCID is an immune system disorder characterized by a very poor ability to combat infection. This illness is very rare, and its only likely cure is a near-match bone marrow transplant. DMD afflicts young boys and is apparent by age three or four; it is characterized by wasting leg and pelvic muscles. DMD victims are usually wheelchair bound by the age of 12, and die before the age of 20, often due to heart problems. Some spinal ataxias are XLGDs marked by degeneration of the brain and spinal chord.

Multifactorial genetic disorders

Statistics and studies of **twins** are often used to determine the genetic basis for multi-factorial genetic disorders (MFGDs). Because environment can play an important role in the development of these diseases, identical and fraternal twins who have been raised in different and identical homes are evaluated for these MFGDs. If fraternal twins have a higher than normal incidence and identical twins show an even higher rate of the disease, then genetic inheritance is believed to contribute to causing the disease. These disorders include some disorders associated with diet and metabolism, such as obesity, diabetes, **alcoholism**, rickets, and high blood pressure. Also included is the tendency to contract certain infections such as measles, scarlet fever, and tuberculosis. In addition, **schizophrenia** and some other psychological illnesses are strong MFGD candidates. Congenital hip, club foot, and cleft lip are also MFGDs. Various cancers are also correlated with genetic vulnerability.

Certain breast, colon, skin, and small-cell lung cancers have a genetic link. Familial breast cancer usually affects younger women, whereas some other types of breast cancer do not appear until later in life. Although familial breast cancer shows a very high degree of genetic dominance, it does not target every female relative and is thought to have another environmental or other unknown factor contribution. Familial colon cancer is attributed to polyposis—colon polyps that become cancerous. Some malignant melanomas of the skin are also highly heritable.

The tendency of some people to be more susceptible to a particular MFGD and not another is characteristic of human genetics. Although all healthy humans have a similar body form with very similar physiological functions, there is a tremendous diversity among humans that results from a diverse gene pool, which explains why certain groups of people with some genotypes in common would be more prone to a particular disease, while others would have resistance to the same disease. This diversity buffers the human race from being annihilated by a single agent.

Other genetic-linked disorders

The two most common aneuploidies, trisomies and extra sex chromosomes, can be due to maternal or paternal factors, including advanced age. A number of aneuploidies can be attributed to dispermy—where two sperm fertilized one egg. The resulting genetic disorders can occur due to a spontaneous mutation, and a familial tendency towards these disorders cannot always be found. Trisomies make up to 52% of chromosomal abnormalities, with trisomies 14, 15, 16, 18, 21, and 22 being the most frequent. Live-born children with autosomal aneuploidies have **trisomy** 13, 18, or 21, and all have some mental retardation. Trisomy 13 (Patau's syndrome) is characterized by retarded growth, **cleft lip,** small head and chin, and often polydactyly. Trisomy 18 (Edward's syndrome) is marked by severe, variable abnormalities of the head, thumbs, ears, mouth, and feet. Trisomy 21 (**Down syndrome**) occurs equally in all ethnic groups, and is closely related to increased maternal age. Children with Down syndrome can have poor muscle tone, a flattened face, extra folds of skin at the eyes, low-set ears, visible (Brushfield) spots on the iris of their eyes, and a single crease along the palm of their hands.

Aneuploidy of the sex chromosomes can cause abnormal genital development, sterility, and other growth problems. The most common such aberration are multiple X syndromes. Triple X females can bear normal children. Males with an XXY aneuploidy are afflicted with **Klinefelter's syndrome**, have small testes and cannot produce sperm. Men with XYY aneuploidy are born more frequently (about 1 in every 200–1,000 males) than most aneuploidies, and controversy exists as to whether these individuals have a higher criminal tendency than the rest of the male population.

Genetic testing and counseling

Tests exist that reveal varying degrees of genetic information. Most of these tests are performed by isolating chromosomes from cellular nuclei, or by measuring a detectable product linked with a known genetic disorder. These tests can be used prior to conception, to determine a couple's risk of having an affected child; during pregnancy, to identify possible genetic disorders; and at birth or later in life, to assess an individual's probability of developing a disorder.

The most successful widespread test for a genetic disorder is newborn testing for PKU, a condition treatable with a special diet. Newborn screening for hypothyroidism and galactosemia is also done in several states. Prenatal tests in embryos and fetuses include chorionic villus sampling (CVS), **amniocentesis**, and ultrasound. CVS can detect Down syndrome, hemophilia, DMD, CF, SCA, and sex chromosomal aberrations. Amniocentesis can detect Tay-Sachs disease, Down syndrome, hemophilia, spina bifida, and other abnormalities. Ultrasound is used to visualize the developing baby; it can detect spina bifida, anencephaly (no brain), and limb deformities.

Genetic counseling and testing can help people find out if they carry the gene for some disorders, or whether they will develop a late-onset genetic disorder themselves. Genetic probes can identify the genes for Huntington's disease, cystic fibrosis, Tay-Sachs, sickle-cell anemia, thalassemia, and abnormalities associated with growth hormones. Genetic testing capabilities increase each year as additional genetic disorder loci are found. Genetic disorders that are determined by multiple loci are more difficult to pin down for testing.

For Further Study

Books

Plomin, R. *Nature and Nurture*. Pacific Grove, CA: Brooks/ Cole Publishing, 1990.

Stine, G., ed. *The New Human Genetics*. Dubuque, IA: Wm. C. Brown, 1989.

Genetics and Genetic Counseling

A branch of science that attempts to understand the fundamental biologic makeup of organisms by examining the genetic blueprints in each cell.

The nucleus of every cell holds the key to nearly every visible and invisible feature of the human body, from the color of hair to the pumping capacity of the heart. In each nucleus of every cell there are 23 pair of chromosomes (46 total). One pair of these chromosomes determines the sex of the child while the other 22 pair determine all the other components of the human body. Chromosomes contain genes which influence the production of proteins and thus influence all aspects of body structure and function. There is a tremendous amount of information encoded in the nearly 100,000 genes in each cell. Geneticists and molecular biologists work to identify the variations that exist between animals or humans by studying the changes that occur during the cell's division. The alterations that take place during the development of any organism may include mutations, insertions, deletions, or translocation during the copying of genetic material from one cell to the other. These changes are the basis for chromosomal abnormalities such as in **Down syndrome** or **trisomy** 18, where there is an extra or missing chromosome material in the embryo, or in single-gene disorders like **sickle-cell anemia** and **cystic fibrosis,** which are caused by a small change on a single gene called a point mutation.

The study of human genetics is less than 100 years old and yet in the last century scientists have identified over 400 genes that cause a variety of diseases from sickle-cell anemia and Down syndrome to high **cholesterol** and **depression**. In addition science has been able to elucidate the inheritance pattern of disease in certain families.

Genetic counseling

A genetic counselor works with a person concerned about the risk of an inherited disease. In 1975, the American Society of Human Genetics clarified the role of genetic counseling. As a communication process, genetic counseling attempts to 1) accurately diagnose a disorder, 2) access risk of recurrence in the concerned family members and their relatives, 3) provide alternatives for decision-making, and 4) provide support groups that will help the family members cope with the recurrence of a disorder.

The role of the genetic counselor is to facilitate the exchange of information regarding a person's genetic legacy. The genetic counselor does not prevent the incidence of a disease in a family but can help family members assess the risk for certain hereditary diseases and offer guidance. At present there are less than 2,000 ac-

GENES AND BEHAVIOR

Is a child's athletic ability inherited, or simply a product of training? If one parent has **schizophrenia**, will his child acquire the disease? The genetic foundations of behavior are studied by behavior genetics, an interdisciplinary science which draws on the resources of several scientific disciplines, including genetics, physiology, and psychology. Because of the nature of heredity, behavior geneticists are unable to assess the role played by genetic factors in an *individual's* behavior: their estimates by definition apply to *groups*. There are 23 pairs of chromosomes in each human cell (a total of 46 chromosomes—each with approximately 20,000 genes). Genes from both members of a pair act in concert to produce a particular trait. What makes heredity complex and extremely difficult to measure is the fact that human sperm and eggs, which are produced by cell division, have 23 unpaired chromosomes. This means that one half of a person's genes comes from the mother, and the other half from the father, and that each individual, with the exception of his or her identical twin, has a unique genetic profile.

Scientists are currently working on the Human Genome Project, which will map the estimated 100,000 genes in the human DNA. So far, they have been able to identify genes responsible for a variety of diseases, including Huntington's disease, Down syndrome, cystic fibrosis, **Tay-Sachs disease,** and a number of **cancer**s. Genetic information about a particular disease constitutes a crucial milestone in the search for a cure. For example, **phenylketonuria (PKU)** is a disease caused by a recessive gene from each parent; PKU's genetic basis is clearly understood. A child with PKU is unable to metabolize phenylalanine, an amino acid found in proteins. The phenylalanine build-up afflicts the central nervous system, causing severe brain damage. Because the genetic processes underlying PKU are known, scientists have been able to develop a screening test, and thus can quickly diagnose the afflicted children shortly after birth. When diagnosed early, PKU can be successfully controlled by diet.

While genetic research can determine the heritability of a some diseases, the genetic foundations of behavior are much more difficult to identify. From a genetic point of view, physical traits, such as the color of a person's hair, have a much higher heritability than behavior. In fact, behavior genetics as-

sumes that the genetic bases of an *individual's* behavior simply cannot be determined. Consequently, researchers have focused their efforts on the behavior of groups, particularly families. However, even controlled studies of families have failed to establish conclusive links between genetics and behavior, or between genetics and particular psychological traits and aptitudes. In theory, these links probably exist; in practice, however, researchers have been unable to isolate traits that are unmodified by environmental factors. For example, musical aptitude seems to recur in certain families. While it is tempting to assume that this aptitude is an inherited genetic trait, it would be a mistake to ignore the environment. What is colloquially known as "talent" is probably a combination of genetic and other, highly variable, factors.

More reliable information about genetics and behavior can be gleaned from twin studies. When compared to fraternal (dizygotic) **twins**, identical (monozygotic) twins display remarkable behavioral similarities. (Unlike fraternal twins, who develop from two separate eggs, identical twins originate from a single divided fertilized egg.) However, even studies of identical twins reared in different families are inconclusive, because, as scientists have discovered, in many cases, the different environments often turn out to be quite comparable, thus invalidating the hypothesis that the twins' behavioral similarities are entirely genetically determined. Conversely, studies of identical twins raised in the same environment have shown that identical twins can develop markedly different personalities. Thus, while certain types of behavior can be traced to certain genetic characteristics, there is no genetic blueprint for an individual's personality.

Twin studies have also attempted to elucidate the genetic basis of **intelligence**, which, according to many psychologists, is not one trait, but a cluster of distinct traits. Generally, these studies indicate that identical twins reared in different families show a high correlation in IQ scores. No one questions the genetic basis of intelligence, but scientists still do not know how intelligence is inherited and what specific aspects of intelligence can be linked to genetic factors.

credited genetic counselors practicing in the United States. This figure is expected to increase in response to the enormous changes taking place both in the scientific community and society. There are limitations to the power of genetic counseling, though, since many of the diseases that have been mapped offer no cure for such disorders as Down syndrome or **Huntington's disease**. Although a genetic counselor cannot predict the future unequivocally, he or she can discuss the occurrence of a disease in terms of probability. A genetic counselor, with the aid of the patient or family, creates a detailed family pedigree that includes the incidence of disease in first-degree (parents and siblings) and second-degree relatives (aunts and uncles). Before or after this pedigree is completed, certain genetic tests are performed using DNA analysis, x ray, ultrasound, urine analysis, skin biopsy, and physical evaluation. For a pregnant woman, prenatal diagnosis can be made through **amniocentesis** (the withdrawal of amniotic fluid during pregnancy) or chorionic villus sampling (the biopsy of chorionic villus tissue).

Concerns about genetics research is an issue that will become increasingly relevant to families trying to embark on uncovering their genetic risks towards common diseases such as breast **cancer,** heart disease, **asthma,** depression, and **diabetes.** Even as each month brings a new gene discovery, barriers still remain between the concerned person and the wealth of information that lies in one's DNA. Access to genetic centers and counseling may be further hampered by insurance companies that do not reimburse patients for testing and counseling.

For Further Study

Books

Jorde, L., J. Carey, and R. White. *Medical Genetics.* St. Louis: Mosby, 1995.

Milunsky, Aubrey. *Choices Not Chances: An Essential Guide to Your Hereditary and Health.* Boston: Little, Brown, 1989.

Plomin, R. *Nature and Nurture.* Pacific Grove, CA: Brooks/Cole Publishing, 1990.

Stine, G., ed. *The New Human Genetics.* Dubuque, IA: Wm. C. Brown, 1989.

—Elizabeth Park

Genital Herpes

Genital herpes is a sexually transmitted disease (STD) usually caused by herpes simplex virus (HSV) type 2.

Herpes is a family of viruses that causes various types of infections, one of which is genital herpes. In the United States, one-half million new cases of genital herp-es are reported every year. Oral herpes, which causes **cold sores** of the mouth or lips, is caused by a different type of herpes virus (HSV type 1) and is not sexually transmitted.

Symptoms

Many people with herpes have no symptoms and do not know they are infected. A genital herpes infection in the active state is characterized by genital lesions (sores or blisters), discharge, pain, and itching; painful urination; swollen glands in the groin; fever; and fatigue. After this symptomatic episode, the virus becomes dormant, sometimes for years, until some type of stress precipitates another attack.

Transmission

Genital herpes can be spread only when it is in the active state. HSV type 2 is usually transmitted through sexual contact, although the virus can live for a time on objects such as towels and toilet seats. Strict personal hygiene during an active episode can prevent spread of the virus. There should be no sexual activity until all sores are completely healed (one to four weeks), and a person infected with genital herpes should always use a condom and spermicides.

Treatment

There is no cure for genital herpes. A medication called acyclovir may be prescribed to accelerate healing during an initial attack. Warm baths, ointments, and pain medication can help alleviate symptoms during an attack, but the virus itself does not disappear when symptoms subside.

See also **Cold Sores; Herpes Simplex**

For Further Study

Books

Daugirdas, John T., M.D. *STD, Sexually Transmitted Diseases, Including HIV/AIDS.* Hinsdale, IL: Medtext, 1992.

Organizations

National Sexually Transmitted Disease Hotline
    Telephone: (800) 227-8922
    (Free information and clinic referrals)

—Gail B. Slap, M.D.
University of Pennsylvania School of Medicine

Genius

A state of intellectual or creative giftedness.

There are differences in intellectual attainment among children. Some children make strides in learning and **creativity** that are well beyond what would normally be expected and are called geniuses or gifted students. Although definitions of genius, or **giftedness,** are inevitably culture-bound and subjective, psychologists are trying to determine what factors might contribute to its emergence in children.

Infancy and preschool

Because it is impossible to tell which infants will become gifted children, it is extremely difficult to study environmental influences on giftedness from infancy. So researchers generally study gifted children only in later years, relying solely on unscientific methods such as self-reports and memories of parents and teachers. While this is not the most reliable method of study, it does offer some insight into the development of geniuses.

Psychologist William Fowler has done extensive research in this area and has found that parental intervention is by far the most important determinant of intellectual giftedness. In a 1981 study, Fowler surveyed decades of scientific inquiry into the making of genius. He found that in one important study, 87% of the gifted children studied had been given substantial, intensive training by their parents at home, focusing on speech, reading, and mathematics—all highly structured avenues. The parents of these gifted children had ambitious and sometimes very specific plans for their children. The parents were nearly all from the professional class, allowing them the time and the money to devote such resources to the intellectual development of their children.

Many psychologists suggest reading to infants and preschoolers can be beneficial in their later acquisition of linguistic competency. Of course, infants have no understanding of the content of what is being read to them, but the rhythmic patterns of formal writing, as opposed to the haphazard, often jumbled, syntax of human speech, is craved by the developing brain, which seeks to order all the sensory information it is receiving. This also helps explain the beneficial effects of classical music, which is also highly ordered and full of patterns, repetition, and variations, just like language. Other findings indicate that gifted children tend to be firstborns or only children, and that they come from cohesive families with a stable socioeconomic status.

One major study tracked a large pool of children, beginning in infancy, with the intention of discovering what factors led to the development of giftedness as shown by high IQ test scores. The Fullerton Longitudinal Study, completed in the early 1990s, was a breakthrough study in this area. Its results supported the findings of other researchers, namely that parental intervention in a child's education was by far the most significant factor in the development of genius. The study also suggested ways to recognize the propensity for genius in early infants, something that psychologists have debated for some time. It

found that infants who became gifted "show[ed] significantly greater goal directedness, object orientation, attention span, cooperativeness, positive emotional tone, and responsivity to test materials." It also found that potentially gifted children may be identified by their ability to pay attention, while maintaining a positive attitude, to the sometimes difficult tests researchers use. So even if an infant or very young child scores well in only one area, the fact that she was able to maintain her attention for the duration of the test may be of more significance in predicting later giftedness than her poorer scores on other tests.

Psychologists have examined various home-tutoring techniques and have found that there appears to be no single kind of stimulation that might turn a normal child into a gifted child. All methods seem to work, provided they center on language or math. It has even been suggested that the method matters little because the child is responding to the quantity of attention rather than to the content of what is being taught.

School-age and adolescence

When a child reaches school age, it becomes possible to measure his or her **intelligence** more reliably. Intelligence tests are the subject of intense debate among psychologists, educators, and the general public. Most standardized tests measure logical-mathematical, linguistic, and spatial intelligence. However, the idea of multiple intelligences was formulated by psychologist Howard Gardner, who defined six components of intelligence: linguistic, logical-mathematical, spatial, musical, bodily-kinesthetic, and personal. Today, many people regard intelligence as comprising different types of skills and talents. Most school systems, however, continue to measure intelligence, and giftedness, according to test results measuring logical-mathematical, linguistic, and spatial intelligence. Gifted children are often identified by their unusually high scores on traditional intelligence tests.

Gifted children usually become bored in the regular classroom. When a gifted child is placed in the highest track and is still bored, educators may promote the child a year or two to challenge her academically. However, most psychologists believe that the social costs of skipping grades probably outweigh the intellectual benefits, especially in young children. Learning social skills is just as much a part of school as academic advancement.

If a gifted child is not promoted or sent to another school, there are various activities that can facilitate the child's intellectual development. Parents and teachers can devise after-school and weekend projects. Many community colleges offer evening and weekend classes that gifted adolescents can attend. Libraries and museums offer lectures and programs by visiting scholars and curators, which gifted children might find highly stimulating. Older teens can work part-time after school at tutoring centers or in college laboratories. During summer breaks, many specialized "camps" offer advanced instruction in a variety of disciplines, from foreign language studies to music to computer programming.

For Further Study

Books

Gottfried, Allen W., et al. *Gifted IQ: Early Developmental Aspects.* New York: Plenum Press, 1994.

Howe, Michael J.A. *The Origins of Exceptional Abilities,* Cambridge, MA: Basil Blackwell, 1990.

Periodicals

Allman, Arthur. "The Anatomy of a Genius." *U.S. News and World Report,* October 25, 1993.

Begley, Sharon. "The Puzzle of Genius." *Newsweek,* June 28, 1993.

Genotype

Describes the underlying genetic makeup of an individual.

Genotype is the complete description of an individual's genetic traits. Its companion—the phenotype—describes the observable traits, or outcome, of the genotype. The genotype includes information about inherited conditions and syndromes that are recessive and may not be apparent in the phenotype. For example, a child may have a recessive gene for blue eyes in his genotype, while having brown eyes in his phenotype. Understanding and analyzing the genotype are important in the diagnosis of genetically transmitted diseases or syndromes caused by recessive genes.

See also **Phenotype**

German Measles *see* **Rubella**

Gesell Development Schedules, Preschool Test, and School Readiness Test

Evaluates the physical, emotional, and behavioral development of infants and young children.

The Development Schedules are a set of four timetables devised by Arnold Gesell (1880–1961) at Yale University to evaluate the physical, emotional, and behavioral development of infants, toddlers, and preschoolers. They describe typical behavior at specified ages in the following areas: ability to adapt; motor functioning; use of language; and social interaction. The Development Schedules are useful to pediatricians, child

Psychologist Arnold Gesell

psychologists, and other professionals who work with children. They also serve as the basis for evaluating a child's performance on the Gesell tests. The Preschool Test, which is administered individually to children between the ages of 2½ and 6, consists of a variety of tasks and activities. Oral sections measure language skills, attention span, and accuracy of personal knowledge. Besides talking about themselves and their families, children are asked to name animals and discuss their favorite activities. A paper-and-pencil section assesses dominance, neuromuscular development, fine motor skills, and task-appropriate behavior. Children are asked to write their names, copy geometric figures, write numbers, and complete a drawing. A building-block section, which involves building increasingly complex structures with a set of cubes, measures fine motor skills, hand-eye coordination, and attention span. Other tasks included in the Preschool Test are repeating numbers, recognizing shapes, and discriminating among prepositions.

The Gesell School Readiness Test, used for screening older children (ages 4½ to 9) for placement in kindergarten through third grade, consists of the Preschool Test plus additional tasks including visual exercises, matching and drawing tests, and a labeling and naming exercise to assess right and left orientation. A child's performance on the Gesell tests is evaluated based on the Development Schedules, and he or she is assigned an overall "development age" (DA). Although the Gesell test and schedules are widely used, critics claim that children with undiagnosed visual or other perceptual problems can be assigned disproportionately low DAs and be penalized in terms of school placement.

For Further Study

Books

Cohen, Libby G., and Loraine J. Spenciner. *Assessment of Young Children.* New York: Longman, 1994.

Hart, Diane. *Authentic Assessment: A Handbook for Educators.* Menlo Park, CA: Addison-Wesley Pub. Co., 1994.

McCullough, Virginia. *Testing and Your Child: What You Should Know About 150 of the Most Common Medical, Educational, and Psychological Tests.* New York: Plume, 1992.

Walsh, W. Bruce, and Nancy E. Betz. *Tests and Assessment.* 2nd ed. Englewood Cliffs, NJ: Prentice Hall, 1990.

Wortham, Sue Clark. *Tests and Measurement in Early Childhood Education.* Columbus: Merrill Publishing Co., 1990.

Gestation Period and Gestational Age

The period that the fetus develops from conception to birth.

The human gestation period—the period of time between conception and labor—is approximately forty weeks (280 days), measured from the first day of the mother's last menstrual period. A gestation period of thirty-eight weeks (266 days) is calculated for women who are pregnant by a procedure such as **in vitro fertilization** or artificial insemination that allows them to know their exact date of conception. The gestational period is divided into three major periods called trimesters. The first trimester last from weeks one through twelve, the second from weeks thirteen through twenty-seven, and the third from weeks twenty-eight to forty. The gestational age of a fetus or newborn infant corresponds to how far along it is in the gestation period, usually measured in weeks and days from the first day of the mother's last menstrual period.

The gestation period may also be calculated by an ultrasound examination, which is most reliable for this purpose between the eighth and eighteenth weeks of pregnancy. This is the method used by most doctors to determine a woman's due date and the gestational age of the fetus. Due dates for women who conceive naturally are only approximations and are precisely accurate for only one pregnancy out of twenty. Even estimations based on an ultrasound examination can be off by ten to fourteen days. Babies delivered anywhere from three weeks early to two weeks late are considered normal full-term babies. Knowledge of the gestational age is important in assessing whether or not a pregnancy is progressing normally and also in evaluating the health status of a newborn. Standard criteria for size, growth, and maturation are available for all infants, whether they are delivered prematurely, at term, or later than term, to determine whether their physical condition is appropriate for their gestational age (AGA). For a full-term infant, the length appropriate for gestational age is forty-eight to fifty-three centimeters and the weight is between 2700 and 4000 grams. Gestational age is also used as a baseline to identify babies who are at risk because of their small size—small for gestational age (SGA) or small for date (SFD). No matter how early or late they are delivered, infants are considered small for their gestational age (SGA) if their size and weight at birth are below the tenth percentile of the appropriate range. Such infants are at increased risk for numerous health problems, including short stature, certain infections, respiratory problems, and **sudden infant death syndrome**.

For Further Study

Books

Cherry, Sheldon. *Understanding Pregnancy and Childbirth,* 3rd ed. New York: Macmillan, 1992.

Grunfeld, Nina. *Pregnancy Week by Week.* New York: Smithmark, 1995.

Giftedness

Above-average intellectual or creative ability or talent in a particular area, such as music, art, or athletics.

Intellectual giftedness is generally indicated by an IQ of at least 125 or 130 (found in about 2% of all children). Children who are extremely creative are also considered gifted, although their giftedness can be hard to identify by academic performance or standardized tests. Giftedness has been defined not only in terms of specific talents and academic abilities, but also by general intellectual characteristics (including curiosity, motivation, ability to see relationships, and long attention span) and personality traits such as leadership ability, independence, and intuitiveness. In general, gifted children are creative, innovative thinkers who are able to envision multiple approaches to a problem and devise innovative and unusual solutions to it.

In the early days of intelligence testing it was widely thought that a person's mental abilities were genetically determined and varied little throughout the life span, but it is now believed that nurture plays a significant role in giftedness. Researchers comparing the behavior of parents of gifted and average children have found significant differences in childrearing practices. The parents of gifted children spend more time reading to them and encouraging creative types of play and are more involved with their schooling. They are also more likely to actively encourage **language development** and expose their children to cultural resources outside the home, including those not restricted specifically to children, such as art and natural history museums. The involvement of fathers in a child's academic progress has been found to have a positive effect on both boys and girls in elementary school in terms of both grades and achievement test scores. Within the family, **grandparents** can also play a positive role as mentors, listeners, and role models. A disproportionately large percentage of high-achieving women have reported that at least one grandparent played a significant role in their lives during childhood. (The anthropologist Margaret Mead named her paternal grandmother as the person with the single greatest influence on her life.) Even within a single family, giftedness can be influenced by such environmental factors as **birth order,** gender, differences in treatment by parents, and other unique aspects of a particular child's experiences.

Parents and teachers can often identify gifted children informally by observing their behavior. However, for formal purposes standardized intelligence tests—most often the **Stanford-Binet** or **Wechsle**r tests—almost always play a role in assessing giftedness, even though such tests have been criticized on a variety of grounds, including an overly narrow definition of intelligence, possible racial and cultural bias, and the risk of unreliability due to variations in testing conditions. Critics have questioned the correlation of IQ scores with achievement later in life, pointing out that standardized tests don't measure many of the personal qualities that contribute to professional success, such as independence, motivation, persistence, and interpersonal skills. In addition, the **creativity** and intuition that are hallmarks of giftedness may actually lower a child's scores on tests that ask for a single solution to a problem rather than rewarding the ability to envision multiple solutions, a trait—called **divergent thinking** by psychologists and educators—that often characterizes giftedness.

Care at home rather than in an institutionalized **day care** setting is generally considered preferable for a child's intellectual development until at least the age of two, especially during the first six months of life. At home the child can receive a level of attention, stimulation, and encouragement that is not possible in an institutionalized day care environment. Eventually, though, the variety of stimulation that preschools provide can be highly beneficial to a child's intellectual development. Experts have criticized the trend toward academic saturation in preschool, nicknamed "hothousing," that has become popular since the 1980s—especially in major cities—with parents seeking a competitive edge to help their youngsters get into top private schools and, eventually, universities. While defenders view this phenomenon as tapping the great learning potential of young children, detractors criticize the surfeit of structured activities that characterizes such programs at the expense of creativity, play, and emphasis on **emotional development.** One variation on the hothousing phenomenon is "double-schooling," a trend that involves enrolling preschool children in two different half-day programs.

Enrollment in special programs

Parents seeking to enroll gifted youngsters in a preschool program need to consider how well it promotes social and emotional as well as intellectual growth, and whether it gives children time for the unstructured activities that "let them be children" and also promote creativity and independence. It is recommended that they take into consideration the institution's physical environment (amount of space, kinds of toys, scheduling); how the children and teachers interact; teaching methods and philosophies; and curriculum content. A common academic route for gifted children is early kindergarten admission. Although state legislatures generally set a minimum age of five for starting kindergarten, at least one-third of the states have provisions allowing local school districts to make exceptions and enroll children who show school readiness early (usually as young as four). Parents who suspect that their child may benefit from early kindergarten admission can have an IQ test privately administered by a trained psychologist to help them and local educators assess whether early admission is indicated. Other signs of readiness for acceleration include early evidence of reading skill, a large vocabulary, and general knowledge levels beyond what is average for the child's age group. In addition to intellectual level, other factors, such as the child's social skills, gross motor development, size, level of emotional maturity, and gender—girls are ready for early admission more often than boys—are important in deciding whether acceleration will be a successful experience. In spite of popular horror stories about school acceleration, gifted children who have a good level of all-around school readiness at an early age generally do well, both academically and socially, when admitted to kindergarten early. In addition, early kindergarten admission avoids the disruption that is caused when acceleration takes the form of skipping grades later on.

Special challenges for gifted children

Gifted children face a variety of different educational settings once they are in school. In some cases, there is no special provision for gifted education, and they participate in regular classes with peers their own age. This option is often unsatisfactory, as gifted children generally cover the course material faster than their classmates, often becoming bored and developing a negative attitude toward school. Once this negative attitude appears, underachievement in school is a common result. In addition, gifted children often feel compelled to hide their talents in order to fit in socially with their peers. An alternative to full-time schooling in the regular classroom is the "pull-out" gifted program, in which gifted students leave the class for several hours a week to join a special group for advanced instruction. While such programs can be an improvement over the instruction offered in the regular classroom, the gifted student who leaves class for several hours each week may feel self-conscious or ostracized (and this routine can make the pupils who don't leave feel bad as well.)

One type of program that is optimal but not often available is a non-structured individualized approach, in which gifted children at different grade levels work independently and in groups, with the teacher gearing each child's assignments to her individual needs. Another successful approach is the placement of gifted children at a particular grade level in a separate, self-contained class, preferably combining whole-class activities with some group or individualized instruction to meet the needs of children who are highly gifted in a particular area, such as math. Yet another alternative in gifted education is acceleration other than early kindergarten admission. This may take a variety of forms, including skipping one or more grades or individualized work in which the student advances at his own pace with the help of a tutor. Entire gifted classes have even been known to collectively skip a grade. At the secondary level, options include simultaneous enrollment in high school and college; early college entrance; and advanced placement (AP) high school classes, which are available in a variety of subjects. Students who take an AP course and subsequently score well on an independently administered standardized test may receive college credit for the course.

Although giftedness has the potential to enrich a child's life in many ways, certain characteristics and personality traits common to gifted children can also create a variety of problems and challenges for youngsters and their parents and teachers. The independent thinking habits associated with giftedness can lead children to question authority in ways that create disciplinary problems and alienate teachers. In gifted boys, in particular, a high degree of natural curiosity and energy often combines with a lag in developmental maturity, resulting in underachievement and causing them to be labeled as difficult by their teachers. Many gifted children prefer working alone to working in groups, and, in some cases, they fail to develop adequate social skills (although the stereotype of the isolated loner—the "egghead" or "nerd"—is an exaggerated one that is not typical of most gifted children,

many of whom are distinguished by their leadership abilities). The long attention span and intense powers of concentration typical of gifted children may make it hard for them to shift from one activity to another, and they may miss instructions and other important information imparted when they are intensely absorbed in a task. Sometimes gifted children develop an unusually wide or narrow range of interests, either of which can pose problems. Another trait common to gifted children is a heightened degree of emotional sensitivity, which may cause unusually strong reactions to events that would be less traumatic for other children. **Perfectionism** is another frequent challenge to the emotional well-being and academic success of gifted children.

Despite increasingly enlightened social and parental attitudes toward gender differences in recent decades, gifted girls still face certain unique obstacles to academic and personal development. From infancy, girls still receive many messages, either subtle or overt, that impart the traditional expectation that women will place personal relationships and nurturance above academic and professional achievement. Boys still spend much more time than girls playing with toys that they can take apart and put back together, enhancing their skills at spatial relations and their feelings of mastery and accomplishment, and it is still easier to find male than female role models to look up to and emulate in many fields. In many classroom situations, boys, with their high activity level, tend to draw more of the teacher's attention than girls (even if it is negative attention). By adolescence, many gifted girls are concerned that if they appear too competitive intellectually, boys will not be attracted to them. This concern is reflected in the fact that teenage girls are more assertive and competitive in single-sex educational environments than they are in mixed-gender groups. Especially in the areas of math and science, girls' interest and self-confidence (as well as their test scores) decline after the age of 11. It has also been found that gifted adolescent girls are especially prone to develop eating disorders, which are typically associated with certain qualities common to gifted children, especially perfectionism and a strong tendency toward self-criticism.

Recommendations for helping gifted girls develop their talents free of the limitations of gender stereotypes include enrolling them in preschools that actively resist sex role stereotyping in their activities and in the attitudes of their staffs (and that have both male and female teachers to counter the idea that only women teach and care for the young); choosing nonsexist toys and encouraging them to engage in types of play that develop visual-spatial problem-solving skills; exposing them to successful professional women, both personally and through books and other media; and encouraging feelings of mastery and self-confidence over perfectionism and fear of failure.

For Further Study

Books

Alvino, James, and the editors of *Gifted Children Monthly*. *Parents' Guide to Raising a Gifted Child: Recognizing and Developing Your Child's Potential*. Boston: Little, Brown, 1985.

———. *Parents' Guide to Raising a Gifted Toddler: Recognizing and Developing the Potential of Your Child from Birth to Five Years*. Boston: Little, Brown, 1989.

Goland, Susan K. *The Joys and Challenges of Raising a Gifted Child*. New York: Prentice Hall Press, 1991.

Clark, Barbara. *Growing Up Gifted*, 3rd ed. Columbus, Oh.: Merrill Publishing Co., 1988.

Elkind, David. *The Hurried Child: Growing Up Too Fast Too Soon*. Reading, MA: Addison-Wesley, 1988.

Perry, Susan. *Playing Smart: A Parent's Guide to Enriching, Offbeat Learning Activities for Ages Four to Fourteen*. Minneapolis, MN: Free Spirit Publishing, 1990.

Rosen, Marcia. *Test Your Baby's I.Q.* Englewood Cliffs, NJ: Prentice-Hall, 1986.

Smutny, Joan F., Kathleen Veenker, and Stephen Veenker. *Your Gifted Child: How to Recognize and Develop the Special Talents in Your Child from Birth to Age Seven*. New York: Facts on File, 1989.

Sternberg, Robert J., and Janet E. Davidson, eds. *Conceptions of Giftedness*. London: Cambridge University Press, 1986.

Glaucoma

An eye disease characterized by build up of fluids within the eye.

Glaucoma is most often a disease of older people, but in rare instances, a child is born with the condition or develops it before the age of two. Because of abnormal development of the drainage mechanisms within the eye, the eye is unable to rid itself of fluids, and the resulting pressure within the eye can cause tissue and nerve damage. Untreated glaucoma can lead to tunnel vision or permanent blindness. An infant with congenital glaucoma may have enlarged, hazy corneas; show signs of being extremely sensitive to light; and have very teary eyes. The eye may also seem enlarged or bulging. Treatment for glaucoma is surgery to provide a route to drain fluid from the eye. Surgery is successful in controlling glaucoma in about 75% of cases.

Goiter

Goiter is a swelling in the neck, caused by a malfunction of the thyroid gland.

The thyroid gland, located in the base of the neck, absorbs iodine from the blood and uses this to produce **hormones** that regulate many body functions, including

EXAMPLES OF IODINE-RICH FOODS		
Food	**Serving size**	**Micrograms of iodine**
Cod or haddock, cooked	3-½ oz (100 g)	175
Chocolate milkshake (fast food)	1 average	158
Homemade meatloaf	3-½ oz (100 g)	123
Lima beans, boiled	½ cup (90 g)	104
Chocolate ice cream	1 cup (133 g)	94
Corn grits, cooked	½ cup (120 g)	86
Chocolate milk, low-fat	1 cup (250 g)	83
Yogurt, low-fat	1 cup (227 g)	73
Milk, low-fat	1 cup (244 g)	66
Milk, skim	1 cup (246 g)	64
Milk, whole	1 cup (244 g)	61

Source: FDA's Total Diet Study (1982–1984).

growth, nerve function, and absorption of vitamins and calcium. If the thyroid gland does not receive enough iodine from the blood, the gland may enlarge, causing a goiter. A goiter can also develop if the thyroid gland does not produce enough thyroid hormones, a condition called hypothyroidism. Goiter is also present in hyperthyroidism, when the gland produces too much thyroid hormone.

A common cause of goiter around the world is lack of iodine in the diet. The thyroid needs iodine to produce thyroid hormones, and if sufficient iodine is not available, the gland enlarges because it is working harder. The main dietary sources of iodine are grains and vegetables grown in iodine-rich soil, and saltwater fish and seafoods. The Recommended Daily Allowance (RDA) for iodine for adolescents and adults is 150 micrograms per day. To combat iodine deficiency in the U.S., iodine has been added to salt since 1924. The body needs only very small amounts of iodine for healthy thyroid function, so iodized salt usually provides an adequate dietary amount.

There are two forms of thyroid disorder, however, that affect children regardless of diet. Congenital hypothyroidism is a disorder in which a child may be born with an underactive thyroid gland. Symptoms appear when the baby is six to twelve weeks old, and include cool, mottled or yellowish skin, coarse hair, and a dull appetite. The baby's neck will look unusually short and fat. The facial features are also affected: the bridge of the nose is underdeveloped, so the nose appears flat and the eyes seem widely spaced, and the tongue is thick and protrudes.

Hypothyroidism slows the baby's growth and development, and the child may have weak muscles and slow reflexes. If untreated, this condition can lead to **mental retardation**. Hypothyroidism can also begin later in life, in a child born with normal thyroid function. It usually begins when a child is between 11 and 14 years old. Onset of this disease is not related to diet, but it may be a side effect of an auto-immune disease that attacks the thyroid. Children with this disease may develop dry, coarse hair and skin, poor circulation, and low blood pressure. Goiter may appear, along with the facial characteristics of the hypothyroid baby. The disease slows the child's growth, and **puberty** is usually delayed. All the symptoms of acquired hypothyroidism can be treated with medical intervention, and the condition does not lead to mental retardation. Diagnosis is made with a simple blood test, and treatment involves replacing the deficient thyroid hormones. The goiter may need to be removed surgically.

Hyperthyroidism, or overproduction of thyroid hormones, usually affects older women, and only rarely affects children. In children with this condition, goiter may develop, and the eyes may bulge out. Just the opposite of hypothyroidism, the hyperthyroid child grows faster than normal and may have flushed, warm skin, and increased heart rate. The child may be restless and irritable, unable to concentrate, and tire easily. All these symptoms can be reversed by medical treatment. Treatment usually involves medication that blocks the excess hormone production. Surgery may be needed to remove the thyroid gland or reduce its size.

The symptoms of thyroid malfunction are usually obvious, and can be confirmed with a blood test. Pediatricians normally keep careful records of a child's growth and weight gain, and can use these to diagnose the slowed or increased growth symptomatic of thyroid disease. Any swelling on a child's neck should be given prompt medical attention. Treatment of thyroid problems, especially if undertaken promptly, are usually successful and without serious side effects.

For Further Study

Books

Bayliss, Richard I. S., and W. M. G. Tunbridge. *Thyroid Disease: The Facts.* New York: Oxford University Press, 1991.

Wood, Lawrence C., David S. Cooper, and E. Chester Ridgway. *Your Thyroid: A Home Reference.* 3rd ed. New York: Ballantine Books, 1995.

Periodicals

Zamula, Evelyn. "Thyroid Disorders Often Unsuspected." *FDA Consumer* 26, December 1992, pp. 34–39.

—A. Woodward

Gonorrhea

Gonorrhea is a sexually transmitted disease (STD) caused by a bacteria called Neisseria gonorrhoeae.

Gonorrhea is most common among females ages 15–19 and males ages 20–24. Although most males experience symptoms, 50% of females have no symptoms. For this reason, gonorrhea in adolescent girls often goes untreated. Therefore, screening cultures for gonorrhea should be routine for all sexually active adolescents.

Symptoms

Most males (95%) with gonorrhea will experience a yellow discharge from the urethra. In females, gonorrhea can affect the cervix, uterus, and fallopian tubes. In addition to symptoms affecting the genital and anal area, gonorrhea can affect the liver, throat, skin, joints, blood, and brain. In addition, gonorrhea can cause a severe form of **conjunctivitis** in infants born to infected mothers. The most common complication of untreated gonorrhea is pelvic inflammatory disease (PID). Less common is a complication called disseminated gonococcal infection (DGI), where the bacteria travels through the blood to distant sites such as skin or joints.

Treatment

Gonorrhea is treated with **antibiotics**, either injected or taken orally. After treatment, repeat cultures should always be performed to be certain the infection has been cured.

For Further Study

Books

Daugirdas, John T., M.D. *STD, Sexually Transmitted Diseases, Including HIV/AIDS.* Hinsdale, IL: Medtext, 1992.

Organizations

National Sexually Transmitted Disease Hotline
Telephone: (800) 227-8922
(Free information and clinic referrals)

—Gail B. Slap, M.D.
University of Pennsylvania School of Medicine

Goodenough-Harris Drawing Test

Assesses intelligence without relying on verbal ability.

The Goodenough-Harris Drawing Test is assumed to assess **intelligence** without relying on verbal ability. It is administered individually or in groups to children aged 3–15 and consists of Draw-a-Man and Draw-a-Woman Tests and an optional Self-Drawing Test. (The **Draw-a-Person Test**, which consists of the same tasks, is a separate test with a different scoring system and is available in two different versions, either as a psychological test for emotional disorders (SPED) or a measure of mental ability (QSS). In contrast, the Goodenough-Harris Drawing Test is used *only* as an intelligence test.) The Goodenough-Harris test is untimed but usually takes about 15 minutes. For all subtests, the child is asked specifically to draw the entire body rather than just the head and shoulders. He or she can erase and start over and, when the test is given individually, talk to the examiner about any of the drawings. The test is evaluated on the basis of 73 scorable criteria, with separate norms for males and females. Raw scores for the Draw-a-Man and Draw-a-Woman tests (but not for the Self-Drawing Test) are converted to standardized scores.

For Further Study

Books

Cohen, Libby G., and Loraine J. Spenciner. *Assessment of Young Children.* New York: Longman, 1994.

McCullough, Virginia. *Testing and Your Child: What You Should Know About 150 of the Most Common Medical, Educational, and Psychological Tests.* New York: Plume, 1992.

Mortensen, Karen Vibeke. *Form and Content in Children's Human Figure Drawings: Development, Sex Differences, and Body Experience.* New York: New York University Press, 1991.

Goodness of Fit

Term used by statisticians to describe a formula for measuring how well a theoretical hypothesis fits a set of observations.

In 1900, Karl Pearson published a paper describing a statistical test—known as chi-square test of goodness of fit—that measures how closely a researcher's hypothesis matches the observations he or she collects during an ex-

periment. The concept behind this test is relatively simple—in rolling dice, one may assume that each die will fall equally often on each of its six faces. By applying the chi-square goodness of fit test, a researcher can then test whether the hypothesis—that the die will fall equally on all sides—fits what was recorded in the experimental data. Pearson's chi-square test is one measure of how well the hypothesis and data match, and is especially useful where the data falls into discrete categories, called "cells" by statisticians.

Child psychiatrists Alexander Thomas and Stella Chess used the test for goodness of fit in their study in the late 1950s that examined inherent individual differences in children, and the ways these differences contributed to developmental difficulties. Thomas and Chess followed over 100 children from infancy through early adulthood. Their data, gathered from interviews, contained details about children's behavior and parents' values and expectations. They focused on nine characteristics of behavior, including activity level, rhythmicity or regularity in biological functions like eating and sleeping, the tendency to approach or withdraw, adaptability, threshold of responsiveness (degree of stimulation required to evoke a response from the child), intensity or energy level of reactions, quality of mood, distractibility and attention span, and persistence. Thomas and Chess emphasized that goodness of fit—the extent to which the child's temperament fit with the values, expectations, and style of the child's family—was an important factor in the child's growth and development.

For Further Study

Books

Dorr-Bremme, Donald W. *Ethnography and Evaluation: The Goodness of Fit.* Los Angeles: Graduate School of Education, UCLA, 1983.

Periodicals

Hacking, Ian. "Trial by Number; Karl Pearson's Chi-Square Test." *Science* 5, November 1984, pp. 69+.

Grade Equivalent *see* **Assessment**

Grand Mal Seizures *see* **Epilepsy** *and* **Seizures**

Grandparents

The parents of one's mother and father.

Grandparents can play an important role in children's lives, providing love and comfort, as well as stability and a sense of **family** identity. There are about 50 million grandparents in the United States today, and they are playing an increasingly important role in American families. Modern medical advances have given grandparents better health and longer life expectancy, allowing them to participate more fully in the lives of their grandchildren, leading to greater closeness and a larger impact on their lives. In the past, many adults didn't live long enough to spend much, if any, time with their grandchildren. Today, for the first time in history, adults in this country usually have the chance to know most of their grandchildren, and children usually know most of their grandparents. In 1900 there was only a 25% chance that all four grandparents of a newborn child would be alive, and the odds decreased to 2% by the child's fifteenth birthday. By comparison, children born in 1976 had a one in six chance of having all four grandparents alive by the time they turned 15 and a 50% chance of having three out of four still living.

Grandparents have a unique role to play in the life of a family. They can provide their grandchildren with comfort and companionship in a relaxed atmosphere removed from most of the disciplinary tensions that are often unavoidable between parents and children. Grandparents can be a source of refuge and strength in times of crisis. They can also help relieve some of the everyday stress faced by working couples by offering babysitting, advice, and other forms of assistance. Their own work commitments keep some grandparents in their forties and fifties as busy as their children. In other cases, though, a grandparent may have precious extra time—often lacking in busy dual-career families—to spend with grandchildren, talking with and reading to them, listening to their thoughts, and perhaps accompanying them on outings, such as a trip to the movies or the zoo. Grandparents can also help diffuse tensions between parents and children. If they are able to avoid taking sides, they can serve as sympathetic and insightful listeners.

In addition to increased longevity, another major factor that has led to an increased role for many grandparents is the rising **divorce** rate. Many older people will see at least one of their grown children divorce. A divorce can bring grandparents closer to both their children and grandchildren. They may be called on for help ranging from moral support, advice, and babysitting, to financial assistance and a place to live. In most cases, maternal grandparents become closer to the children following a divorce, while the children's contact with paternal grandparents often decreases. Sometimes grandparents on the noncustodial side are placed in the uncomfortable position of trying to maintain good relations with the custodial parent—at the risk of alienating their own child—to ensure continuing contact with the grandchildren. In the past, grandparents had few legal rights when it came to their grandchildren and could be denied contact at the

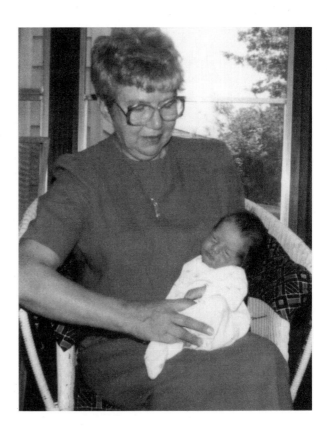

Longer life expectancy allows grandparents to enjoy more years with their grandchildren.

whim of a daughter- or son-in-law who had **custody.** Today grandparents in all 50 states can petition for visitation rights in the event of a divorce. Such rights may be formally included in the final divorce settlement by the parents' lawyers or granted in court by the judge. In some states grandparents also have the right to petition for custody if a court finds both parents unfit to care for a child. However, the granting of such rights is rare and generally limited to extreme cases. Also, like other aspects of custody law, laws pertaining to grandparents vary from one state to another.

In addition to those few who are legally granted custody in divorce cases, an increasing number of grandparents are informally taking over the primary responsibility for raising their grandchildren due to parental neglect, abuse, or abandonment, or following the death of a parent. The number of grandparents assuming full-time responsibility for their grandchildren rose 41% between 1980 and 1994. Today over three million children in the United States live with their grandparents. Suddenly finding themselves with young children at home at a time when they had expected to have leisure in their lives is difficult for both middle-aged and elderly grandparents. Younger grandparents may find themselves "sandwiched" between taking care of their grandchildren and caring for their own aging parents. A network of support groups for grandparents who are their grandchildren's primary caretaker, Grandparents As Parents, was begun in California in the 1980s and has spread throughout the country.

Another current demographic trend that poses a challenge for grandparents is geographic mobility, which makes for many long-distance grandparenting relationships. There are a variety of ways that grandparents who live too far away for regular visits can still remain an active and visible part of their grandchildren's lives. Occasional visits both to and from one's grandchildren are, of course, the best means for establishing and maintaining a close relationship. Whether or not this is possible, there are other ways that contact can be maintained, including letters and audio or videotapes. Imaginative ideas for keeping in touch include joint projects, such as having a grandparent and grandchild plant matching gardens and compare their progress, or take turns composing a joint story and mailing the latest installment back and forth. Parents can mail or fax the children's drawings and keep grandparents up to date on the youngsters' latest interests so they can treat them to appropriate small gifts from time to time.

One of the most important roles a grandparent can fulfill is that of historian, passing on to grandchildren a sense of family history and identity. Even seemingly ordinary details of grandparents' lives, such as descriptions of everyday life when they were young or of famous historical events they remember, can be fascinating to children. Grandparents can also share family stories. Often they remember stories the children's own parents are familiar with but have never thought of telling their children. Grandparents can leave their grandchildren (and future generations) a unique legacy by creating a record of their recollections, either written or on tape. An enhanced sense of history can be imparted by including photographs, old letters, and other souvenirs, and also by recording lullabies or other songs that are part of the family's traditions. Yet another way that a grandparent can help keep the family in touch with its roots is by creating a family tree, complete with pictures, if possible.

For Further Study

Books

Carson, Lillian. *The Essential Grandparent: A Guide for Making a Difference.* Deerfield Beach, FL: Health Communications, 1996.

Dodson, Fitzhugh. *How to Grandparent.* New York: Harper & Row, 1981.

Kornhaber, Arthur. *Grandparent Power! How to Strengthen the Vital Connection Among Grandparents, Parents, and Children.* New York: Crown Publishers, 1994.

Organizations

AARP Grandparent Information Center
    Address: American Association or Retired Persons (AARP) Headquarters
601 E St., NW
Washington, DC 20049
    Telephone: (202) 434-2296

Grandparents As Parents (GAP)
    Address: P.O. Box 964
Lakewood, CA 90714
    Telephone: (310) 924-3996

Grandparents United for Children's Rights
    Address: 137 Larkin St.
Madison, WI 53705
    Telephone: (608) 238-8751

Gray Oral Reading Test (GORT-R)

Diagnoses reading problems and measures progress in oral reading.

The Gray Oral Reading Test (GORT-R) is an individual, timed test that diagnoses reading problems and measures progress in oral reading. The test is used with children and adolescents aged 7–17 and is usually administered by a **special education** teacher or reading specialist. A series of 13 increasingly difficult passages is read aloud, and the examiner records errors and notes the child's reading style. When a certain number of errors is made in two successive passages, the reading portion is ended, and the child is then asked several comprehension questions about each passage. The test takes 15–30 minutes depending on how much of it is completed. A separate score is derived for each passage based on reading rate and errors, and the passage scores are combined to yield a total score and then converted to standard scores and percentiles. GORT-R is useful in diagnosing specific problems such as skipping words, mispronunciation, and adding words. However, since it is a timed test, slower readers are penalized.

Gross Motor Skills

The abilities required in order to control the large muscles of the body for walking, running, sitting, crawling, and other activities.

Motor skills are deliberate and controlled movements requiring both muscle development and maturation of the central nervous system. In addition, the skeletal system must be strong enough to support the movement and weight involved in any new activity.

Once these conditions are met, children learn new physical skills by practicing them until each skill is mastered.

Gross motor skills, like **fine motor skills**—which involve control of the fingers and hands—develop in an orderly sequence. Although norms for **motor development** have been charted in great detail by researchers and clinicians over the past 50 years, its pace varies considerably from one child to the next. The more complex the skills, the greater the possible variation in normal children. The normal age for learning to walk has a range of several months, while the age range for turning one's head, a simpler skill that occurs much earlier, is considerably narrower. In addition to variations among children, an individual child's rate of progress varies as well, often including rapid spurts of development and frustrating periods of delay. Although rapid motor development in early childhood is often a good predictor of coordination and athletic ability later in life, there is no proven correlation between a child's rate of motor development and his intelligence. In most cases, a delay in mastering a specific motor skill is temporary and does not indicate a serious problem. However, medical help should be sought if a child is significantly behind his peers in motor development or if he regresses, losing previously acquired skills.

Infancy and toddlerhood

The sequence of gross motor development is determined by two developmental principles that also govern physical growth. The cephalo-caudal pattern, or head-to-toe development, refers to the way the upper parts of the body, beginning with the head, develop before the lower ones. Thus, infants can lift their heads and shoulders before they can sit up, which, in turn, precedes standing and walking. The other pattern of both development and maturation is proximo-distal, or trunk to extremities. One of the first things an infant achieves is head control. Although they are born with virtually no head or neck control, most infants can lift their heads to a 45-degree angle by the age of four to six weeks, and they can lift both their heads and chests at an average age of eight weeks. Most infants can turn their heads to both sides within 16 to 20 weeks and lift their heads while lying on their backs within 24 to 28 weeks. By about 36 to 42 weeks, or 9 to 10 months, most infants can sit up unassisted for substantial periods of time with both hands free for playing.

One of the major tasks in gross motor development is locomotion, or the ability to move from one place to another. An infant progresses gradually from rolling (8 to 10 weeks) to creeping on her stomach and dragging her legs behind her (6 to 9 months) to actual crawling (7 months to a year). While the infant is learning these temporary means of locomotion, she is gradually becoming able to support increasing amounts of weight while in a standing position. In the second half year of life, babies

During a child's first two years, development of gross motor skills represents significant milestones.

begin pulling themselves up on furniture and other stationary objects. By the ages of 28 to 54 weeks, on average, they begin "cruising," or navigating a room in an upright position by holding on to the furniture to keep their balance. Eventually, they are able to walk while holding on to an adult with both hands, and then with only one. They usually take their first uncertain steps alone between the ages of 36 and 64 weeks and are competent walkers by the ages of 52 to 78 weeks. By the age of two years, children have begun to develop a variety of gross motor skills. They can run fairly well and negotiate stairs holding on to a banister with one hand and putting both feet on each step before going on to the next one. Most infants this age climb (some very actively) and have a rudimentary ability to kick and throw a ball.

Preschool

During a child's first two years, most parents consider gross motor skills a very high priority; a child's first steps are the most universally celebrated developmental milestone. By the time a child is a preschooler, however, many parents shift the majority of their attention to the child's cognitive development in preparation for school. In addition, gross motor activity at these ages requires increasing amounts of space, equipment, and supervision. However, gross motor skills remain very important to a child's development, and maintaining a youngster's instinctive love of physical activity can make an important contribution to future fitness and health.

By the age of three, children walk with good posture and without watching their feet. They can also walk backwards and run with enough control for sudden stops or changes of direction. They can hop, stand on one foot, and negotiate the rungs of a jungle gym. They can walk up stairs alternating feet but usually still walk down putting both feet on each step. Other achievements include riding a tricycle and throwing a ball, although they have trouble catching it because they hold their arms out in front of their bodies no matter what direction the ball comes from. Four-year-olds can typically balance or hop on one foot, jump forward and backward over objects, and climb and descend stairs alternating feet. They can bounce and catch balls and throw accurately. Some four-year-olds can also skip. Children this age have gained an increased degree of self-consciousness about their motor activities that leads to increased feelings of pride and success when they master a new skill. However, it can also create feelings of inadequacy when they think they have failed. This concern with success can also lead them to try daring activities beyond their abilities, so they need to be monitored especially carefully.

School-age

School-age children, who are not going through the rapid, unsettling growth spurts of early childhood or adolescence, are quite skilled at controlling their bodies and are generally good at a wide variety of physical activities, although the ability varies on the level of maturation and the physique of a child. Motor skills are mostly equal in boys and girls at this stage, except that boys have more forearm strength and girls have greater flexibility. Five-year-olds can skip, jump rope, catch a bounced ball, walk on their tiptoes, balance on one foot for over eight seconds, and engage in beginning acrobatics. Many can even ride a small two-wheeler bicycle. Eight- and nine-year-olds typically can ride a bicycle, swim, roller-skate, ice-skate, jump rope, scale fences, use a saw, hammer, and garden tools, and play a variety of sports. However, many of the sports prized by adults, often scaled down for play by children, require higher levels of distance judgment and hand-eye coordination, as well as quicker reaction times, than are reasonable for middle childhood. Games that are well suited to the motor skills of elementary school-age children include kick ball, dodge ball, and team relay races.

In adolescence, children develop increasing coordination and motor ability. They also gain greater physical strength and prolonged endurance. Adolescents are able to develop better distance judgment and hand-eye coordination than their younger counterparts. With practice, they can master the skills necessary for adult sports.

For Further Study

Books

Eckert, Helen M. *Motor Development.* 3rd ed. Indianapolis, IN: Benchmark Press, 1987.

Hoppert, Rita. *Rings, Swings, and Climbing Things.* Chicago: Contemporary Books, 1985.

Lerch, Harold A., and Christine B. Stopka. *Developmental Motor Activities for All Children: From Theory to Practice.* Dubuque, IA: Brown and Benchmark, 1992.

Thomas, Jerry R., ed. *Motor Development in Childhood and Adolescence.* Minneapolis, MN: Burgess Publishing Co., 1984.

Group Norms

The rules by which a group has agreed, implicitly or explicitly, to follow.

Culture is a set of **values,** norms, symbols, language, and way of life shared by a group of people. Culture is passed on from generation to generation. Group norms—the rules of daily living that members of the group adhere to—represent one aspect of culture. Homogeneous cultures, where all the members share language, lifestyle, and racial make-up, have a clear, well-defined set of norms that the group follows. Members of heterogeneous cultures represent a number of subcultures and do not necessarily have one language, lifestyle, and race in common. Thus, such cultures have fewer rules that all members voluntarily live by and tolerate a wider range of lifestyles, languages, and values. This loosening of norms is necessary within the larger culture to avoid conflict between members of the subcultures.

Groups norms are passed down to the next generation beginning in the earliest stages of life. As members of the group interact with a newborn infant, he or she is learning about the group's cultural practices and norms. Cultural institutions, such as schools and religious institutions, continue the transfer of group norms; parochial schools use the curriculum to reinforce religious group norms; public schools reinforce the societal norms or government norms.

Group norms also apply to small groups of people, whenever individuals are affiliated with each other for some common purpose. Examples of groups where norms function to establish standards for behavior are sports teams, a student's peer group, or the group of students in a self-contained classroom. Group norms exert powerful positive or negative forces in motivating students' academic performance and behavior.

Members of a cultural group interact with others from a variety of perspectives. Ethnocentricism describes an attitude of a person who regards his or her own culture as the best. Cultural relativism describes an attitude of a person who is open to understanding other cultures by trying to learn about them. Stereotyping is the making of broad generalizations about individual members of a cultural group, assigning qualities to him or her simply because he or she is a member of the cultural group. An example of a stereotype is "All Germans love beer."

Group norms are a form of **peer pressure,** and educators and parents try to help children embrace groups norms that are positive and promote good health, such as the norm to perform well academically or to develop good health. Equally powerful are group norms that reward disruptive behavior in the classroom or that value risk-taking, such as engaging in petty crime or using drugs or alcohol to achieve status in a group.

For Further Study

Periodicals

Triandis, Harry C. "The Psychological Measurement of Cultural Syndromes." *American Psychologist* 51, April 1996, pp. 407–15.

Research Reports

Ricks, Julie J., and Cassandra L. Collara. *"One of Us Is Not As Powerful As All of Us": Building a Community for Teaching and Learning Mathematics.* East Lansing, MI: Center for the Learning and Teaching of Elementary Subjects, Institute for Research on Teaching. Research Report, 1993.

Guardian

A non-biological parent who assumes legal responsibility for a minor.

An adult who becomes legally responsible for a minor child that is not his or her biological child is called a guardian; the minor is referred to in legal terms as the *ward.* A guardian is the person who assumes legal responsibility for the child's financial support, and for any education, medical treatment, or other activities required by law. The guardian may, but does not necessarily, have **custody** of the child. The guardian may or may not be involved in the child's daily activities and care.

Experts advise parents to name a guardian for their minor children in a legal will. If parents die without having made provisions for the guardianship of their chil-

dren, the court will appoint a guardian. An ideal candidate to serve as guardian should have the following characteristics: close relative or friend of the family; known and respected by both parents and children; willingness to serve as guardian; young enough to carry out the responsibilities of childrearing; lifestyle that is compatible with the needs of children; education and interests similar to those of the family; and living near the family, or willingness to relocate if necessary.

When a guardian has been chosen, and the guardian has agreed to accept the responsibility, family members and others close to the family should be apprised of the relationship. This will avoid any challenges to the guardianship relationship later on.

For Further Study

Books

Goldstein, Joseph, et al. *The Best Interests of the Child: The Least Detrimental Alternative.* New York: Free Press, 1996.

Krause, Harry D. *Child Law: Parent, Chld, and State.* New York: New York Universty Press, 1992.

Guilt

An emotional state produced by thoughts that we have not lived up to our ideal self and could have done otherwise.

Guilt is both a cognitive and an emotional experience that occurs when the child realizes that he or she has violated a moral standard and is responsible for that violation. Typically, among American children, the violations include hurting another person, disobedience, or seizing of someone else's property. A guilty conscience results from thoughts that we have not lived up to our ideal self. Guilt feelings may also inhibit us from falling short of our ideal again in the future. Individual guilt is an inner reflection on personal wrongdoing, while collective guilt is a shared state resulting from group—such as corporate, national, or community—wrongdoing.

Guilt serves as both an indicator and inhibitor of wrongdoing. Healthy guilt is an appropriate response to harming another and is resolved through atonement, such as making amends, apologizing, or accepting punishment. Unhealthy guilt, sometimes called neurotic or debilitating guilt, is a pervasive sense of responsibility for others' pain that is not resolved, despite efforts to atone. Healthy guilt inspires a person to behave in the best interests of him- or herself and others and make amends when any wrong is done. Unhealthy guilt stifles a person's natural expression of self and prohibits intimacy with others.

Unhealthy guilt can be instilled when a child is continually barraged with shaming statements that criticize the child's self, rather than focusing on the specific harmful behavior. A statement such as, "It is wrong to take someone else's things without permission—please return my book," creates an appropriate awareness in the child of healthy guilt for doing wrong. Saying, "Give me my book back! I can't trust you with anything!" shames the child, declaring that he or she is by nature untrustworthy and will never be better than a thief, regardless of future behavior. Consequently, the child sees his or her identity as defective, and may feel powerless to atone for any wrongdoings. This identity can be carried into adulthood, creating a sense of debilitating guilt.

An important difference between shame and guilt is that in the former, the child does not feel he could hae avoided the action; in guilt, he feels responsible. Guilt can be used to manipulate someone into behaving in a certain way. This is known as a "guilt trip." Provoking another's sense of guilt in order to obtain something that he or she might not otherwise have offered is a manipulation of internal motivations. If a teenager asks permission to go out for the evening and the single parent responds, "Go ahead and go to the movie, dear . . . don't worry about me . . . I'll be fine here all by myself in this big old house all evening with nothing to do . . . ," the teenager will be made to feel guilty for the parent's loneliness. If the guilt trip is heavy, the teenager may decide to stay home with the parent, even though he or she really wants to go to the movie. It is appropriate to let people know when they have unnecessarily or intentionally hurt others, or have ignored their responsibilities to others. This will instill fair guilt that will help a person be less hurtful in the future.

Although conclusive studies have yet to be conducted, it is likely that the sense of guilt changes along with a person's cognitive and social development.

These stages have yet to be thoroughly documented and are still open to critique, particularly the early stages. Some people believe that infants and young children feel a great deal of empathy for others and could conceivably experience guilt over causing them harm.

Guilt can be deactivated, the conscience "turned off." Some people never seem to develop a healthy sense of guilt in the first place, through a failure to develop empathy or a lack of appropriate limits, while others choose to turn theirs off. Guilt can be deactivated in two different ways:

1) The person convinces him- or herself that the act was not a violation of what is right.

2) The person reasons that he or she has no control over the events of life and is therefore not responsible for the outcome. With no sense of personal responsibility, there can be no sense of guilt.

When guilt is reduced, internal limits on behavior disappear and people can act without remorse.

STAGES OF GUILT DEVELOPMENT

The researcher M. L. Hoffman has proposed the following stages of guilt development:

Infancy—Because infants have no clear sense of separate identity or the effect of their behavior on others, it would be impossible for them to feel true guilt over hurting another.

Early childhood—Young children understand themselves as physically separate from others, but do not yet have a deep understanding of others' inner states; therefore, they feel guilt over hurting another person physically, but not over doing emotional damage.

Middle childhood—With the increased understanding of others' inner states, children develop a sense of guilt over inflicting emotional pain on others or failing to act on another's behalf.

Adolescence to adulthood—Cognitive development now allows the young adult to perceive abstract, universal concepts of identity and suffering and, therefore, to feel a sense of guilt over more general harm, such as world hunger, poverty, oppression, etc.

See also **Moral Development; Self-Conscious Emotions**

For Further Study

Books

Greenspan, P. S. *Practical Guilt: Moral Dilemmas, Emotions, and Social Norms*. New York/Oxford: Oxford University Press, 1995.

Hoffman, M. L. "Development of Prosocial Motivation: Empathy and Guilt." In *The Development of Prosocial Behavior*, edited by N. Eisenberg, pp. 218–231. New York: Academic Press, 1982.

Kurtines, William M., and Jacob L. Gewirtz, eds. *Moral Development: An Introduction*. Boston: Allyn and Bacon, 1995.

Middleton-Moz, Jane. *Shame and Guilt: Masters of Disguise*. Deerfield Beach, FL: Health Communications, 1990.

Schulman, Michael, and Eva Mekler. *Bringing Up a Moral Child: A New Approach for Teaching Your Child to Be Kind, Just, and Responsible*, rev. ed. New York: Main Street Books/Doubleday, 1994.

Wechsler, Harlan J. *What's So Bad About Guilt? Learning to Live With It Since We Can't Live Without It*. New York: Simon and Schuster, 1990.

—Dianne K. Daeg de Mott

Guthrie Test *see* **Phenylketonuria**

H

Habituation

The reduction in response level that occurs when an infant has become accustomed to a particular stimulus.

Habituation, the reduction in response to a stimulus over time, has been the subject of research on infant perception. Researchers have studied habituation by measuring infant response levels based on fluctuations in heart rate, intensity of sucking on **pacifiers,** and concentration of gaze. When an infant is exposed to a new stimulus, these activities speed up or become intensified. However, when the exposure continues for a certain period of time, responsiveness drops and will only rise again if the stimulus is withdrawn and reintroduced (or a new one is presented). Habituation has been widely used in infant research because it can assess an infant's ability to discriminate between similar stimuli. For example, it can be used to determine if a baby can hear different pitches by exposing her to a single pitch until her level of physiological or behavioral response drops and then seeing if it rises when a new pitch is introduced.

Researchers have also found that some aspects of the interaction between mothers and infants are instinctively based on the habituation process. In order to remain stimulated by the mother's gaze, the infant periodically turns away from it, and the level of stimulation rises again with each new exposure.

Haemophilus Influenzae Type B

Bacteria that can cause several serious illnesses in unvaccinated individuals.

Haemophilus influenzae type B (HiB) is a bacteria that can cause serious infections, including **meningitis** and epiglottitis. Although the word influenzae may imply a relation to influenza, or the "flu," the two diseases are unrelated. Influenza is caused by a virus, not bacteria. Other less common infections caused by *H. influenzae* type B include pneumonia and infections in the blood, bones, joints, skin, and the membrane covering the heart. Before the availability of the *Haemophilus influenzae* type B (HiB) vaccine, thousands of children under the age of five became seriously ill with meningitis and epiglottitis. Meningitis describes any infection of the membranes that cover the spinal cord and brain, whether caused by a virus, or more seriously, by bacteria such as *H. influenzae* type B. Prior to availability of the vaccine, about 12,000 cases of meningitis in children under five occurred in the United States each year; one in 20 of those infected died from the disease, and one in four developed permanent brain damage. Vaccines for this bacteria are available, and new ones were being developed as of the late 1990s. The **American Academy of Pediatrics** issues recommendations and advice on new vaccines as they become available.

For Further Study

National Institute of Allergy and Infectious Diseases (NIAID)
Address: 9000 Rockville Pike
NIH Building 31, Room 7A50
Bethesda, MD 20892-2520
Telephone: (301) 496-5717

Hair-Pulling, Compulsive
see **Trichotillomania**

Hall, Granville Stanley (1844–1924)

American psychologist.

Granville Stanley Hall played a decisive role in the organization of American psychology. He invited Sigmund Freud and Carl Jung to America, thus contributing to the diffusion of **psychoanalysis.** Above all, he gave a crucial impetus to the study of the child and the life cycle (his last psychological book dealt with senescence, the process of becoming old). Hall stressed the social relevance of empirical developmental research, and authored the first major treatise on adolescence. His theories and methods have since been superseded, but the life-span, stage-based perspective typical of this thinking became a central component of modern psychology.

Hall was born in 1844 in rural Massachusetts, the son of educated farmers. He studied at Williams College and at the Union Theological Seminary; in 1878 he received a Ph.D. from Harvard University for a thesis on the role of muscular sensations in space perception. He then studied with Wilhelm Wundt and Hermann Ludwig Ferdinand von Helmholtz in Germany. He joined Johns Hopkins University in 1884, set up one of the first psychology laboratories in the U.S., and established the *American Journal of Psychology* to promote experimental psychology. In 1889, he became the first president of Clark University, which awarded many of the early American doctorates in psychology. He led a popular child-study and educational reform movement, which he supported through his journal *Pedagogical Seminary*. He inspired and was the first president of the American Psychological Association. Hall died in 1924.

Hall studied childhood by means of questionnaires (a method he pioneered) on topics such as children's play, lies, fears, anger, language, and art. He distributed them among teachers, thus amassing huge amounts of data. The backbone of Hall's thinking was the concept of recapitulation, according to which individual development repeats the history of the species. As supposedly apparent in children's games, childhood reflected primitive humanity. The following, "juvenile" stage corresponded to an age when humans were well adjusted to their environment and displayed tribal inclinations; it was therefore suited to the formation of groups adapted to the child's "social instinct." **Adolescence** was a "new birth" that brought forth ancestral passions, an age of "storm and stress" characterized by conflicting moods and dispositions, a capacity for religious conversion, and an unlimited creative potential. Hall claimed that it was essential to channel these energies (especially sexual), and that it was "the apical stage of human development" and the starting point "for the super anthropoid that man is to become." His idealized and lyrical depiction of adolescence synthesized common nineteenth-century ideas about youth into a evolutionary framework and, while conveying nostalgia for a lost closeness to nature, provided an increasingly urban and industrialized society with a confident image of its own future.

For Further Study

Books

Hall, G. S. *Adolescence: Its Psychology and its Relations to Physiology, Anthropology, Sociology, Sex, Crime, Religion and Education.* 2 vols., New York: Appleton, 1908.
———. *Life and Confessions of a Psychologist.* New York: Appleton, 1923.
Ross, D. G. *Stanley Hall: The Psychologist as Prophet.* Chicago: University of Chicago Press, 1972.

Hallucinogens

Substances that cause hallucination—perception of things or feelings that have no foundation in reality—when ingested.

Hallucinogens, or psychedelics, are substances that alter users' thought processes or moods to the extent that they perceive objects or experience sensations that in fact have no basis in reality. Many natural and some synthetic substances have the ability to bring about hallucinations. In fact, because of the ready market for such chemicals, they are manufactured in illegal chemical laboratories for sale as hallucinogens. LSD (lysergic acid diethylamide) and many so-called designer drugs have no useful clinical function.

Hallucinogens have long been a component in the religious rites of various cultures, both in the New and Old Worlds. Among the oldest are substances from mushrooms or cactus that have been in use in Native American rites since before recorded history. Hallucinogenic mushrooms have been used for centuries in rites of medicine men to foresee the future or communicate with the gods. The mushroom is consumed by eating it or by drinking a beverage in which the mushroom has been boiled. The effects are similar to those experienced by an LSD user—enhancement of colors and sounds, introspective interludes, perception of nonexistent or absent objects or persons, and sometimes terrifying, ominous visions.

Another ancient, natural hallucinogenic substance is derived from the Mexican peyote cactus. The flowering head of the cactus contains a potent alkaloid called mescaline. Hallucinogenic substances can be found in a number of other plant species.

In the 1960s, hallucinogens were discovered and embraced by the hippie movement, which incorporated drugs into its culture. In addition, artists, poets, and writers of the time believed that the use of hallucinogens enhanced their creative prowess.

Use of LSD, the most widely known hallucinogen, declined after large numbers of users experienced serious, sometimes fatal, effects during the 1960s. In the United States, LSD was classified as a Schedule I drug according to the Controlled Substance Act of 1970. That designation is reserved for those drugs considered unsafe, medically useless, and with a high potential for abuse.

LSD made a comeback in the 1990s, becoming the most abused drug of people under 20 years of age. Its low cost ($1 to $5 per "hit"), ready availability, and a renewed interest in 1960s culture are blamed for the resurgence. A 1993 survey reported that 13% of 18- to 25-year-olds had used hallucinogens, in most cases LSD, at least once.

Drugs such as LSD are often differentiated from less potent psychedelics, which have the primary effect of inducing euphoria, relaxation, stimulation, relief from pain, or relief from anxiety. This group of drugs is exemplified by marijuana, which is available worldwide and constitutes one of the primary money crops in the United States. Opiates such as heroin or morphine, phencyclidine (PCP), and certain tranquilizers such as diazepam (Valium) also belong to this category.

LSD was first synthesized in 1938 by Dr. Albert Hofmann, a Swiss chemist who was seeking a headache remedy. Years later, he accidentally ingested a small, unknown quantity, and shortly afterward he was forced to stop his work and go home. Hofmann lay in a darkened room and later recorded in his diary that he was in a dazed condition and experienced "an uninterrupted stream of fantastic images of extraordinary plasticity and vividness...accompanied by an intense kaleidoscope-like play of colors."

Three days later, Hofmann purposely took another dose of LSD to verify that his previous experience was the result of taking the drug. He ingested what he thought was a small dose (250 micrograms), but which is actually about five times the amount needed to induce pronounced hallucinations in an adult male. His second hallucinatory experience was even more intense, and his journal describes the symptoms of LSD toxicity: a metallic taste, difficulty in breathing, dry and constricted throat, cramps, paralysis, and visual disturbances.

LSD is one of the most potent hallucinogens known, and no therapeutic benefits have been discovered. The usual dose for an adult is 50–100 micrograms. (A microgram is a millionth of a gram.) Higher doses will produce more intense effects and lower doses will produce milder effects. The so-called "acid trip" can be induced by swallowing the drug, smoking it (usually with marijuana), injecting it, or rubbing it on the skin. Taken by mouth, the drug will take about 30 minutes to have any effect and up to an hour for its full effect to be felt, which will last 2 to 4 hours.

The physiological effects of LSD include blurred vision, dilation of the pupils of the eye, muscle weakness and twitching, and an increase in heart rate, blood pressure, and body temperature. The user may also salivate excessively and shed tears, and the hair on the back of his arms may stand erect. Pregnant women who use LSD or other hallucinogens may have a miscarriage, because these drugs cause the muscles of the uterus to contract. Such a reaction in pregnancy would expel the fetus.

To the observer, the user usually will appear quiet and introspective. Most of the time the user will be unwilling or unable to interact with others, to carry on a conversation, or engage in intimacies. At times even moderate doses of LSD will have profoundly disturbing effects on an individual. Although the physiological effects will seem uniform, the psychological impact of the drug can be terrifying. The distortions in reality, exaggeration of perception and other effects can be horrifying, especially if the user is unaware that he has been given the drug. This constitutes what is called the "bad trip."

Among the psychological effects reported by LSD users is depersonalization, the separation from one's body, yet with the knowledge that the separated mind is observing the passing scene. A confused body image (the user cannot tell where his own body ends and the surroundings begin) also is common. A distorted perception of reality is also common. For example, the user's perception of colors, distance, shapes, and sizes is inconsistent and unreliable. In addition, the user may perceive absent objects and forms without substance. He may also taste colors or smell sounds, a mixing of the senses called synesthesia. Sounds, colors, and taste are all greatly enhanced, though they may constitute an unrealistic and constantly changing tableau.

The user often talks incessantly on a variety of subjects, often uttering meaningless phrases. But he may also become silent and immobile for long periods of time as he listens to music or contemplates a flower or his thumb. Mood swings are frequent, with sudden alternations between total euphoria and complete despair.

Some users will exhibit symptoms of paranoia. They become suspicious of persons around them and tend to withdraw from others. Feelings of anxiety can also surface when the user is removed from a quiet environment and exposed to everyday stimuli. Activities such as standing in line with other people or walking down a city sidewalk may seem impossible to handle. Users have been known to jump off buildings or walk in front of moving trucks.

How LSD and other hallucinogens produce these bizarre effects remains unknown. The drug attaches to certain chemical binding sites widely spread through the brain, but what ensues thereafter has yet to be described. A person who takes LSD steadily with the doses close together can develop a tolerance to the drug. That is, the amount of drug that once produced a pronounced "high" no longer is effective. A larger dose is required to achieve the same effect. However, if the individual keeps increasing his drug intake he will soon pass over the threshold into the area of toxicity.

Discontinuing LSD or the other hallucinogens, especially after having used them for an extended period of time, is not easy. The residual effects of the drugs produce toxic symptoms and "flashbacks," which are similar to an LSD "trip."

Currently, the most common form of LSD administration is by licking the back of a stamp torn from a perforated sheet of homemade stamps. The drug is coated on the back of the sheet of stamps or is deposited as a colored dot on the paper. Removing one stamp, the user places it on his tongue and allows the LSD to dissolve in his saliva. Because a tiny amount can produce strong effects, overdoses are common.

Teens often experiment with LSD or other hallucinogens in reaction to poor family relationships and psychological problems. Others are prompted by curiosity, peer pressure, and the desire to escape from feelings of isolation or despair. Typical physical signs of hallucinogen use include rapid breathing, muscle twitching, chills and shaking, upset stomach, enlarged pupils, confusion, and poor coordination.

For Further Study

Books

Robbins, Paul R. *Hallucinogens*. Springfield, NJ: Enslow, 1996.

Periodicals

Fernandes, B. "The Long, Strange Trip Back." *World Press Review* 40, September 1993, pp. 38–39.

Monroe, Judy. "Designer Drugs: CAT & LSD." *Current Health* 21, September 1994, p. 13.

"The Negative Side of Nostalgia." *Medical Update* 17, July 1993, p. 3.

Porush, D. "Finding God in the Three-Pound Universe: The Neuroscience of Transcendence." *Omni* 16, October 1993, pp. 60–62.

Handedness

A person's preference for one hand when performing manual tasks.

The term handedness describes a characteristic form of specialization whereby a person by preference uses one hand for clearly identified activities, such as writing. For example, a person who uses his or her right hand for activities requiring skill and coordination (e.g., writing, drawing, cutting) is defined as right-handed. Roughly 90% of humans are right-handed. Because left-handed children who are forced to write with their right hand

sometimes develop the ability to write with both hands, the term ambidexterity is often used in everyday parlance to denote balanced handedness.

An often misunderstood phenomenon, handedness is a result of the human brain's unique development. While the human mind is intuitively understood as a single entity, research in brain physiology and anatomy has demonstrated that various areas of the brain control different mental aptitudes, and that the physiological structure of the brain affects our mental functions. The brain's fundamental structure is dual (there are two cerebral hemispheres), and this duality is an essential quality of the human body. Generally speaking, each hemisphere is connected to sensory receptors on the opposite side of the body. In other words, the right hand is controlled by the left hemisphere of the cerebral cortex. When scientists started studying the brain's anatomy, they learned that the two hemispheres are not identical. In fact, the French physician and anthropologist Paul Pierre Broca (1824-1880) and the German neurologist and psychiatrist Carl Wernicke (1848–1905) produced empirical evidence that important language centers were located in the left hemisphere. Since Broca's findings were based on right-handed subjects, and since right-handedness is predominant in humans, psychologists felt prompted to develop the notion of the left hemisphere as the dominant part of the brain. Furthermore, Broca formulated a general rule stating that the language hemisphere is always opposite of a person's preferred side. In other words, the left hemisphere always controls a right-handed person's language abilities. According to Broca rule's, left-handedness would indicate a hemispheric switch. Handedness research, however, uncovered a far more complex situation. While Broca's rule works for right-handers, left-handed people present a rather puzzling picture. Namely, researchers have discovered that only about two out of 10 left-handers follow Broca's rule. In other words, most left-handed people violate Broca's rule by having their language center in the left hemisphere. Furthermore, the idea of clearly defined cerebral dominance seems compromised by the fact that some 70% of left-handed people have bilateral hemispheric control of language.

While hemispheric dominance can be observed in animals, only humans have a clearly defined type of dominance. In other words, while animals may be right or left "pawed," only humans are predominantly right-handed. The American developmental psychologist Arnold Gesell (1880-1961), known for his pioneering work in scientific observation of child behavior, noted that as early as the age of four weeks infants display signs of handedness. At that age, according to Gesell, right-handed children assume a "fencing" position, right arm and hand extended; by the age of one, right-handedness is clearly established, the child using the right hand for a variety of operations, and the left for holding and gripping. Predominant right-handedness in humans has led researchers to define right-handedness as genetically coded. If left-handedness also had a genetic basis, was it possible to establish inheritance patterns? However, empirical studies, even studies of identical twins, have failed to establish left-handedness as a genetic trait. For example, a person with two left-handed parents has only a 35% chance of being left-handed.

In the past, left-handedness was associated with mental deficiency, as well as emotional and behavioral problems, which led to the popular belief, strengthened by folklore, that left-handed people were somehow flawed. In addition, left-handedness has also been associated with immunological problems and a shorter life span. While not devoid of any foundation, these ideas are based on inconclusive, and sometimes even deceptive, evidence. For example, statistics may indicate a shorter life-span for left-handers, but what statistics omit is the fact that higher mortality should probably be attributed to accidents in an often dangerous right-hand world.

An even greater challenge than right-handed scissors and can openers is what psychologist Stanley Coren calls "handism," the belief that right-handedness is "better" than left-handedness. The idea that left-handers need to conform to a dominant standard has traditionally been translated into punitive educational practices whereby left-handed children were physically forced to write with their right hand. While there is a growing awareness among educators and parents that left-handedness should not be suppressed, the left-handed child is still exposed to a variety of pressures, some subtle, some crude, to conform. These pressures are reinforced by a tradition of maligning left-handed people. Major religious traditions, such as Christianity, Buddhism, and Islam, have described left-handedness in negative terms. Current language is also a rich repository of recorded animosity toward left-handers. For example, the word left evolved from the Anglo-Saxon lyft, which means weak. The Latin word sinister, meaning left and unfavorable, is still used to denote something evil, and gauche, the French word for left, generally indicates awkwardness. The numerous expressions which imply that left is the opposite of good include a left-handed compliment.

Being a left-handed child still has many disadvantages, despite the efforts made to accept left-handedness. Even children whose parents and teacher tolerate their left-handedness often suffer in school. For example, a left-handed student's paper may be down-graded for being "sloppy" because of the teacher's unconscious reaction to handwriting that just doesn't seem "right." In addition, art and science projects may receive unfair criticism because the teacher did not realize that the left-handed student was struggling with instruments and

equipment designed for the right-handed majority. In essence, as advocates of left-handers have pointed out, it is not enough just to tolerate left-handedness: the right-handed world should become user-friendly for individuals exhibiting all the varieties of handedness.

For Further Study

Books

Coren, Stanley. *The Left-Hander Syndrome: The Causes and Consequences of Left-Handedness.* New York: Vintage Books, 1993.

Temple, Christine. *The Brain.* London: Penguin Books, 1993.

Periodicals

Tabak, Lawrence. "A Change of Hands." *Parenting* 8, no. 7, June–July 1994, p. 149.

—Zoran Minderovic

Hand-Eye Coordination

The ability to coordinate vision with fine motor skills.

Hand-eye coordination begins developing in infancy. Although it is an instinctive developmental achievement that cannot be taught, parents can hasten its progress by providing their children with stimulating toys and other objects that will encourage them to practice reaching out for things and grasping them.

Until the age of eight weeks, infants are too nearsighted to see objects at distances farther than about eight inches from their faces, and they have not yet discovered their hands, which are kept fisted throughout this period. By the age of two to two-and-a-half months, the eyes focus much better, and babies can follow a moving object with their gaze, even turning their heads to keep sight of it longer. However, when a child this age drops an object, she will try to find it by feeling rather than looking for it, and although she plays with her hands, she does it without looking at them.

By three months, most infants will have made an important hand-eye connection; they can deliberately bring their hands into their field of vision. By now they are watching their hands when they play with them. They also swipe at objects within their view, a repetitive activity that provides practice in estimating distance and controlling the hands. Attempts to grab onto things (which usually fail) consist of a series of tries, with the child looking at the object and then at his hand, moving his hand closer to it, and then re-sighting the object and trying again.

At the age of four or five months, hand-eye coordination is developed sufficiently for an infant to manipulate toys, and she will begin to seek them out. By the age of six months, she can focus on objects at a distance and consistently follow them with her eyes. At this point, the infant can sight an object and reach for it without repeatedly looking at her hand. She senses where her hand is and can lead it straight to the object, keeping her eyes on the object the entire time. By the final months of her first year, an infant can shift her gaze between objects held in both hands and compare them to each other.

Toddlerhood

The toddler stage brings further progress in hand-eye coordination, resulting in the control necessary to manipulate objects with increasing sophistication. The ability to sight and grasp objects accurately improves dramatically with the acquisition of the "pincer grasp." This ability to grasp objects between the thumb and forefinger develops between the ages of 12 and 15 months. Around the same time, children begin stacking objects on top of each other. Most can stack two blocks by the age of 15 months and three by the age of 18 months. At this age they also begin emptying, gathering, and nesting objects, or placing one inside another. Toddlers can also draw horizontal and vertical pencil lines and circular scribbles, twist dials, push levers, pull strings, pound pegs, string large beads, put a key in a lock, and turn book pages. Eventually, they are able to stack as many as six blocks, unwrap small objects, manipulate snap toys, and play with clay. Between the ages of 15 and 23 months there is significant improvement in feeding skills, such as using a spoon and a cup.

Preschool years

During the preschool period, hand-eye coordination progresses to the point of near independence at self-care activities. A four-year-old is learning to handle eating utensils well and button even small buttons. Four-year-olds can also handle a pencil competently, copy geometric shapes and letters, and use scissors. By the age of five, a child's hand-eye coordination appears quite advanced, although it will still continue to be fine-tuned for several more years. He approaches, grasps, and releases objects with precision and accuracy. He may use the same toys as preschoolers, but he manipulates them with greater skill and purpose and can complete a familiar jigsaw puzzles with lightning speed. An important milestone in hand-eye progress at this stage is the child's ability to tie his own shoelaces. At the age of six, a child's visual orientation changes somewhat. Children of this age and older shift their gaze more frequently than younger children. They also have a tendency to follow the progress of an object rather than looking directly at it, a fact that has been linked to the practice of some six-year-olds using their fingers to mark their places when they are reading.

Even when absorbed in tasks, they look away frequently, although their hands remain active.

School-aged children

Hand-eye coordination improves through middle childhood, with advances in speed, timing, and coordination. By the age of nine, the eyes and hands are well differentiated, that is, each can be used independently of the other, and improved finger differentiation is evident as well. Nine-year-olds can use carpentry and garden tools with reasonable skill and complete simple sewing projects.

See also **Fine Motor Skills, Motor Development**

For Further Study

Books

Eckert, Helen M. *Motor Development.* 3rd ed. Indianapolis, IN: Benchmark Press, 1987.

Lerch, Harold A., and Christine B. Stopka. *Developmental Motor Activities for All Children: From Theory to Practice.* Dubuque, IA: Brown and Benchmark, 1992.

Harlow, Harry F. (1905–1981)

American psychologist whose major contributions to psychology arose from his work with rhesus monkeys.

Experimental and comparative psychologist Harry Harlow is best known for his work on the importance of maternal contact in the growth and social development of infants. Working with infant monkeys and surrogate mothers made of terrycloth or wire, Harlow concluded that extended social deprivation in the early years of life can severely disrupt later social and sexual behavior. Harlow also conducted important studies involving the behavior of prisoners of war during the Korean War, as well as work concerning problem-solving and learning among primates.

Harlow was born in 1905 in Fairfield, Iowa. Following his education at Stanford, where he earned his bachelor's degree and a Ph.D. in 1930, he began a long academic career at the University of Wisconsin. His teaching career spanned 44 years, beginning in 1930. He also served as director of the university's Regional Primate Center from 1961–71. In his work with primates, Harlow developed what he called a "uniprocess learning theory," which describes how primates learn through a succession of incorrect responses to stimuli.

When Harry Harlow began his famous studies of attachment behaviors in rhesus monkeys, he was able to pit two competing theories of the development of affiliative behaviors against each other. Drive-reduction approaches were based on the premise that bonds between mothers and children were nurtured by the fact that mothers provided food and warmth to meet the infant's biological needs. Attachment theorists, on the other hand, felt that the provision of security through contact and proximity were the driving factors in the development of **attachment**.

Harlow devised a series of ingenious studies in which infant rhesus monkeys were raised in cages without their natural mothers, but with two surrogate objects instead. One surrogate "mother" was a wire form that the monkey could approach to receive food. Another form offered no food, but was wrapped in terry cloth so the infant could cling to a softer and more cuddly surface. What happened when a large, threatening mechanical spider was introduced into the cage? The infant monkeys ran to the terry cloth surrogates, demonstrating that contact comfort was more important than just meeting basic hunger needs for the establishment of a relationship from which the infant might derive security.

In a series of related experiments, Harlow studied the effects of maternal and contact comfort deprivation across the monkey's lifespan, uncovering unexpectedly harmful effects of such deprivation on the monkeys' own childrearing abilities at maturity. Later, Harlow's student Stephen Suomi and his colleagues demonstrated that these longstanding effects could be improved by introducing a nurturant "foster grandmother."

Harlow's conclusions about maternal bonding and deprivation, based on his work with monkeys and first presented in the early 1960s, later became controversial, but are still considered important developments in the area of **child psychology**.

Harlow served for many years as editor of the *Journal of Comparative and Physiological Psychology*. In 1960, he received the Distinguished Scientific Contributions Award from the **American Psychological Association**, and in 1967, he was awarded the National Medal of Science.

For Further Study

Books

Harlow, Harry. *Learning to Love.* New York: Aronson, 1974.

—Doreen Arcus, Ph.D.
Harvard University

Head Lice

Parasitic insects that live on hair.

Infestation with head lice, also called pediculosis, is a common occurence in schools and day care centers.

Head lice are parasitic insects that live on hair. The adults feed on blood from the scalp, causing intense itching, and lay their eggs (nits) on the hair shaft. Lice do not fly or hop like fleas, but they are quite easily passed from child to child. Playmates can pass them along through close physical contact, sharing hats or hair brushes, or lying on bedding or furniture on which lice-infested hair has fallen. If a few children in a school group have head lice, an epidemic may quickly build. Treatment is not difficult, but it may be drawn out if not all the nits are caught, or if the child is reinfested.

Symptoms of head lice include intense itching of the scalp, but some children may have the lice and not itch. If a child's playmates have head lice, it is best to check the child's hair immediately. The adult lice can be seen crawling through the hair. They may appear clear or whitish, or if engorged with blood, they may be dark brown. The nits look like tiny clear globs, and may be found anywhere along the hair shaft, but are more common on the hair at the top of the head, at the nape of the neck, and above the ears.

To treat a child for head lice, the adult insects must be killed with an insecticide shampoo and the nits removed with a special fine-toothed comb. Insecticide shampoo is available over the counter, or by prescription. The main ingredient in most lice shampoos, gamma benzene hexachloride, is a central nervous system toxin, so the shampoo must be used with care. Consult a doctor before treating a young child for head lice. After shampooing, comb through the child's hair with a fine-toothed comb (usually included with the shampoo package), and inspect the child's hair under a bright light or in strong sunlight to make sure all the nits are combed out. At the same time the child is treated, the child's bedding and clothing should be washed in hot water with regular detergent. Combs and hairbrushes can be treated simply by soaking in very hot water for 10 minutes.

A second shampoo treatment may still be necessary in seven to ten days if any nits survived. The child may also become reinfested from other children. Parents will need to inspect the child's head regularly if head lice are still a problem at the child's school or day care.

For Further Study

Books

Copeland, Lennie. *The Lice-Buster Book: What To Do When Your Child Comes Home With Head Lice!* Mill Valley, CA: Authentic Pictures, 1995.

—A. Woodward

Head Start Programs

A preschool program for three- to five-year-old children from low-income families. Its aim is to prepare children for success in school through an early structured learning program.

Head Start began in 1965 as part of the War on Poverty program launched by the administration of president Lyndon B. Johnson. Nearly half the nation's poor people were children under age 12, and Head Start was developed to respond to the needs of poor children as early as possible. A few privately funded pre-school programs for poor children in inner cities and rural areas had shown marked success in raising children's intellectual skills. Many low-income children also had unrecognized health problems and had not been immunized. Head Start was envisioned as a comprehensive program that would provide health and nutritional services to poor children, while also developing their cognitive skills. The program aimed to involve parents as well. Many parents of children in the program were employed as teacher's aides, so that they would understand what their children were learning, and help carry on that learning at home.

The program was political from its inception. Head Start was launched with much fanfare by Lady Bird Johnson, Lyndon Johnson's wife, and presidents from Lyndon Johnson to Bill Clinton have praised the program and taken credit for its successes. Measuring the program's actual success is not a simple matter, however. Head Start is said to save taxpayers' money, because children who attend Head Start are more likely to graduate high school and get a job than their peers who do not attend Head Start. However, the precise long-term benefits of Head Start are difficult to gauge, and researchers disagree even about the short-term benefits. Nevertheless, one government publication states that, in the long term, $6 are saved for every $1 invested in the Head Start program. Other studies merely suggest that Head Start graduates are more likely than their peers to stay in the proper grade level for their age in elementary school.

Head Start presently serves approximately 700,000 children across the nation. Most programs are half-day, and include lunch. The curriculum is not the same in every program, but in most cases school readiness is stressed. Children may be taught the alphabet and numbers, and to recognize colors and shapes. Health care is an important aspect of the program, and children in Head Start are monitored to keep them up to date on their **immunizations;** testing is also available for hearing and vision. Many programs are integrated to include children with special needs such as a physical or mental handicap. Class size is limited to between 17 and 20 children, with two teachers. Parents are encouraged to volunteer their time in the classroom, or to work as teacher aides. Most

programs are aimed at four-year-olds, who attend Head Start for one year, before starting kindergarten. Some programs are for two years, and others are for infants and toddlers, who participate with their parents. Eligibility in Head Start is limited to families at or below the federal poverty level.

For Further Study

Books

Zigler, Edward, and Susan Muenchow. *Head Start: The Inside Story of America's Most Successful Educational Experiment.* New York: Basic Books, 1992.

Organizations

National Head Start Association
   Address: 201 N. Union Street, Suite 320
   Alexandria, VA 22314
   Telephone: (703) 739-0875

—A. Woodward

Head Turning Reflex *see* **Neonatal Reflexes**

Hearing Development and Impairment

Hearing begins in the womb—pregnant women have reported feeling the fetus move in response to loud noises at 31 weeks (7 weeks before full-term delivery). Newborns are sensitive to the location, frequency, pitch, and volume of sounds. Loud sounds startle them, while rhythmic, repetitive sounds tend to soothe them. During the second month of life, they become sensitive to a wider range of sounds, reacting to a variety of medium-range sounds that can affect them differently depending on their mood. (For example, a child at this age may enjoy the sound of a vacuum cleaner when she is feeling happy and become upset by it when she is in an irritable mood.) It has been found that infants can hear higher frequencies than adults can (a fact that may be related to the adult instinct to produce "baby talk" at higher pitches than those of their normal speaking voices). In addition, babies can detect a broad range of pitches and discriminate among different speech sounds (better, in some cases, than adults). At the age of six months, they can tell the difference between sounds that differ as little as 10 decibels in loudness.

Parents can test the hearing of a young infant at home by clapping or making some other loud noise and seeing if it elicits a startled response. By the age of six months, infants will look around for the source of the noise. Hearing should also be evaluated regularly by a child's pediatrician. Infants and children can have their hearing tested by audiometry, in which frequency perception is assessed by listening to sounds through earphones in a soundproof room; tympanometry, which works by measuring sound waves bouncing off the eardrum with a special probe inserted into the ear; and brainstem auditory-evoked response (BAER), which measures brain waves through a test that is similar to an electroencephalogram (EEG).

Approximately 1% of all children sustain some degree of hearing impairment, with 2 out of 1,000 suffering profound hearing loss. About 65% of these children are born deaf, and an additional 12% become deaf before the age of 3. A hearing loss delays speech and language acquisition, interferes with cognitive development, and disrupts progress in school. Even with the modern technology and level of health care available in the United States, hearing losses in children sometimes go undetected or unconfirmed for months or even years—significant hearing losses have gone undiagnosed in children as old as six. Early detection and intervention are crucial in preventing or minimizing developmental and educational delays.

Hearing loss is most commonly categorized by which parts of the ear are affected. Conductive hearing loss is caused by a problem in the middle or outer ear that interferes with the conduction of sound to the inner ear, while sensorineural hearing loss involves an abnormality of the cochlea or auditory nerve in the inner ear. Mixed hearing loss indicates a combination of both of these types. Hearing impairments are also classified as prelingual (before a child can learn to speak) or postlingual (after language acquisition has occurred), and genetic or nongenetic (based on whether it is inherited). Yet another way hearing loss is classified is by severity. Normal hearing is generally defined as the ability to hear sounds of 15 decibels (dB) or less. A child with a mild hearing loss can only hear sounds that are between 15 and 40 or 45 dB or louder. At this level of hearing loss, speech and conversation are unaffected, but there is some difficulty hearing distant sounds. A moderate hearing loss means that only sounds registering 40 to 60 or 70 dB can be heard. At this level, the ability to hear normal conversation and form sounds is affected. With severe hearing loss, a child can only hear sounds that register 60 to 90 dB and needs a hearing aid to be able to discern more than an occasional word of conversation. A profound hearing loss is defined as the inability to hear sounds that are under 90 dB, meaning that only very loud sounds—louder than those used in conversation—can be heard. A child with profound hearing loss may hear better with a hearing aid but will still generally be unable to articulate words normally.

The most frequent cause of hearing impairment in children is otitis media, or infection of the middle ear, which is very common in children between the ages of 6 months and 2 years (and can occur in older and younger children as well). Ordinarily it causes a mild to moderate, temporary conductive hearing loss that disappears when the condition clears up. However, persistent or recurrent infections may cause an ongoing moderate hearing loss that can interfere with speech and language development. Common treatment methods for this problem include prolonged low doses of antibiotics and an outpatient procedure called a myringotomy, in which a small tube is inserted through the eardrum to drain fluid and equalize the pressure between the middle ear and the ear canal. Certain physical conditions are associated with conductive hearing loss from middle ear infections. These include **cleft palate,** which impairs middle ear drainage through the eustachian tubes, leading to conductive hearing loss in 30% of children with this condition; other head and facial abnormalities, such as Treacher-Collins syndrome; and **Down syndrome,** which is characterized by narrow ear canals that are conducive to middle ear infections. About 80% of children with Down syndrome sustain some degree of hearing loss.

Another cause of conductive hearing loss is excessive build-up of earwax, which can keep sound waves from reaching the eardrum. Earwax, which protects the ear from dust and other foreign matter, is produced by glands in the outer ear canal and normally works its way out of the ear naturally. However, sometimes excessive amounts can build up and harden in the outer ear canal, causing a gradual decrease in hearing and, in some cases, irritating the canal. Earwax can usually be removed at home (with a doctor's instructions) by flushing out the ears with water after using special drops to soften the wax. If necessary, the doctor can remove earwax by suction or with a metal probe.

Sensorineural hearing loss has a variety of causes, including over 70 known genetically inherited conditions, which account for approximately half of all severe sensorineural hearing losses. Problems occurring during birth or shortly afterward (such as asphyxia, where the baby fails to breathe) can cause inner ear or nerve damage. Hearing loss may also result from intrauterine infections during pregnancy, the best-known of which is **rubella** (German measles) contracted during the first trimester of pregnancy. Other viruses known to cause sensorineural hearing loss include toxoplasmosis, herpes, and cytomegalovirus (CMV). Bacterial infections in infancy (such as **meningitis**) are another cause of hearing impairment. It is also thought that the noise from incubators may affect the hearing of premature infants.

A variety of hearing aids are available for children. The postauricular, or behind-the-ear, hearing aid fits behind the ear and is connected to a plastic earmold, which is custom-fitted to each child. (These must be replaced frequently in rapidly growing young children.) An older child with sufficient residual hearing can use the less noticeable in-the-ear or in-the-canal hearing aids, in which the entire apparatus fits inside the ear. In addition to these traditional hearing aids, recent technological advances have made several newer devices available. The transposer changes high-pitched sounds inaudible to many hearing-impaired persons into lower-pitched sounds they can hear. Hearing aids that can be programmed by computer are custom-fitted to an individual's particular type of hearing loss. The new device that has received the greatest degree of attention is the cochlear implant, which, attached directly to the cochlea in a surgical procedure, functionally "replaces" the damaged hair cells of persons with sensorineural hearing loss. The implant itself, consisting of electrodes implanted into the cochlea through a hole drilled in the mastoid bone, works together with two external components: a speech processor, which is commonly worn on the belt or carried in a pocket, and a microphone. Unlike hearing aids, which can only help children who have some residual hearing, cochlear implants can help those whose hearing is completely destroyed. Over 1,000 children worldwide have been fitted with these devices. While cochlear implants do not restore full normal hearing, they offer potentially substantial improvement in speech recognition and production, as well the ability to hear and identify common sounds such as car horns and doorbells.

Today a variety of educational approaches are used with hard of hearing and deaf children. A variety of systems, known as oral approaches, utilize spoken rather than sign language for all communication needs. They may rely on lipreading or on the extension of residual hearing made possible by today's powerful hearing aids and cochlear implants, or on a combination of both methods. One of these, the auditory-verbal approach, relies on enhanced residual hearing, teaching children to speak by having them listen to spoken language. Its ultimate goal is to enable children with hearing loss to attend regular schools and participate fully in the life of the hearing world around them. Another method, Cued Speech, supplements lipreading skills with a set of eight phonetically based handshapes. Each handshape represents several combinations of consonant sounds in order to help children learn how words and letters sound. (Vowel sounds are represented by a series of diagrams showing different placements in and around the mouth.) The phonetic mastery made possible by Cued Speech can enable hearing-impaired children to become familiar with a variety of dialects besides their own and learn spoken foreign languages as well.

In contrast to oral methods, the Bilingual-Bicultural (or Bi-Bi) approach treats the hearing impaired as a separate culture with its own language (American Sign Language, or ASL). With this approach, ASL is taught as the primary language and standard English (written only) as a secondary one. In addition, children learn about the history, contributions, and customs of deaf culture, and their parents are encouraged to learn ASL and become active in the deaf community. A contrasting approach that incorporates signing is called Total Communication, which is based on a philosophy of inclusiveness that embraces all forms of communication that can help a hearing-impaired child communicate and learn, including hearing amplification, signs, gestures, lipreading, and finger-spelling. However, unlike the Bilingual-Bicultural approach, Total Communication uses signing systems based on English (collectively referred to as Manually Coded English or MCE) rather than American Sign Language, which is a separate language system distinct from English. Manually Coded English systems include Signed English, Seeing Essential English and its spin-off, Signing Exact English, and Contact Signing (formerly called Pidgin Sign English).

For Further Study

Books

Jeffrey, Lorraine. *Hearing Loss and Tinnitus.* New York: Sterling Publishing, 1995.

Maxon, Antonia. *The Hearing-Impaired Child: Infancy through High School Years.* Boston: Andover Medical Publishers, 1992.

Roush, Jackson, and Noel D. Matkin, eds. *Infants and Toddlers with Hearing Loss: Family-Centered Assessment and Intervention.* Baltimore: York Press, 1994.

Schwartz, Sue, ed. *Choices in Deafness: A Parents' Guide to Communication Options.* 2nd ed. Bethesda, MD: Woodbine House, 1996.

Organizations

Alexander Graham Bell Association
   Address: 3417 Volta Place, NW
   Washington, DC 20007
   Telephone: (202) 387-5220
Deafness Research Foundation
   Address: 9 E. 38th Street
   New York, NY 10016
   Telephone: (212) 684-6556
Hearing Aid Helpline
   Address: 20361 Middlebelt Rd.
   Livonia, MI 48152
   Telephone: toll-free (800) 521-5247; (313) 478-2610
National Association for Hearing and Speech Action
   Address: 10801 Rockville Pike

Rockville, MD 20852
Telephone: toll-free (800) 638-8255; (301) 897-8682

Heart

The organ that pumps the blood for circulating throughout the human body.

The human heart is a pulsating, four-chambered organ that circulates blood through the body. Though the heart appears to be a simple organ, it requires a complex series of nerve stimulations, valve openings, and muscle contractions to adequately achieve its purpose.

The human heart on the average weighs about 10.5 oz (300 g). Cone-shaped and about the size of a closed fist, it lies in the mid-thorax, under the breastbone (sternum). Nestled between the lungs, the heart is covered by a fibrous sac called the pericardium. This important organ is protected within a bony cage formed by the ribs, sternum, and spine.

In its ceaseless work, the heart contracts some 100,000 times a day to drive blood through about 60,000 miles (96,000 km) of vessels to nourish each of the trillions of cells in the body. Each contraction forces about 2.5 oz (0.075 liter) of blood into the circulation, which adds up to about 10 pints (4.7 liters) of blood every minute. On the average, the heart will pump about 2,500 gallons (9,475 liters) of blood in a day, and that may go up to as much as 5,000 gallons (18,950 liters) with exertion. In a lifetime the heart will pump about 100 million gallons of blood.

Oxygen-depleted blood returns to the right atrium—or holding chamber—of the heart, from which it passes through the tricuspid or right atrioventricular valve into the lower right chamber, the ventricle. The tricuspid valve is so named because it has three cusps, or flaps, that open and close to control the flow of blood. When the right ventricle contracts, blood is forced from the heart into the pulmonary artery through the pulmonary semilunar valve. The thin, fibrous flaps of the semilunar valve have strong fibers attached to them. These fibers are also attached to the wall of the ventricle. These cords prevent the valve from ballooning up into the atrium when the ventricle contracts.

The blood flows through the pulmonary artery, the only artery in the body that carries unoxygenated blood into the lungs, where it loses carbon dioxide and other impurities and picks up oxygen. The freshly oxygenated blood then returns to the left side of the heart through the four pulmonary veins, which empty into the left atrium. The contents of the atrium then pass through the left atrioventricular, or mitral, valve into the left ventricle.

The left ventricle has the hardest task of any chamber in the heart. It must force blood from the heart into the body and head. For that purpose, it has a much thicker wall, approximately three times thicker than the right ventricle wall. When the left ventricle contracts, blood passes through the aortic semilunar valve into the largest artery in the body (the aorta) to be carried and distributed to every area of the body.

The wall that divides the right and left sides of the heart is the septum. Occasionally, the septum is imperfectly formed, and may have an opening in it that allows blood from the right and left sides to mix. If this septal defect is minor, there are usually no serious medical consequences. However, a larger opening that allows too much blood to mix, thus preventing the left ventricle from applying sufficient pressure, will require surgery. A patch can be placed over the opening to seal it and ensure normal function.

The heart muscle is unique in that it is not under voluntary control, and must work incessantly. The heart muscle, or myocardium, requires considerable nourishment, and the arteries that feed the myocardium are the first to branch off from the aorta. These are the coronary arteries that pass down and over the heart to provide a copious and uninterrupted blood supply to it. Any interruption of blood flow through these arteries can trigger a heart attack.

This coordinated pattern of chambers filling and emptying in sequence is controlled by a system of fibers providing the electrical stimulus to trigger contraction of the heart muscle. The initial stimulus is provided by a small node of specialized tissue in the upper area of the right atrium. This is called the sinoatrial node, or SA node. Under the influence of this node, the heart beats at a sinus rhythm, which is normal. The SA node fires an electrical impulse that spreads across the atria, causing them to contract. The signal also reaches another node, the atrioventricular or AV node, lying near the bottom of the right atrium just above the ventricle. This node receives the electrical signal from the SA node, and sends out its own electrical impulse. The AV impulse travels down a specialized train of fibers into the ventricular muscle. This causes the ventricles to contract and expel their contents. Thus, the contraction of the atria is made to occur slightly before the contraction of the ventricles. The heart's electrical activity can be measured by a device called the electrocardiograph (ECG or often abbreviated EKG).

Variations in the electrical system can lead to serious, even dangerous, consequences. When that occurs, an artificial electrical stimulator called a pacemaker must be implanted to take over the regulation of the heartbeat. A small pacemaker can be implanted under the skin near the shoulder, and long wires from it are fed into the heart and implanted in the heart muscle. The pacemaker can be regulated for the number of heartbeats it will stimulate per minute. Newer pacemakers can detect the need for increased heart rate when the individual is under exertion or stress, and will respond.

Heart disease is the leading cause of death among older Americans. Heart attacks—blockage of a coronary artery—and atherosclerosis or "hardening of the arteries"—deposits of fat on coronary artery walls—are two of the most common conditions that lead to impaired health and fatalities. Both are preventable in most cases, particularly by closely monitoring the health of children and adolescents and by teaching young people to care for their health.

Smoking, high blood pressure, obesity, high **cholesterol** levels and diabetes are all risk factors in heart disease. Young people who eliminate bad habits such as smoking, and try to eat nutritious, low-fat diets, and exercise regularly have a greater chance of maintaining healthy hearts throughout their adult years. Many physicians advocate periodic checks of blood cholesterol levels beginning at the age of two, particularly for children with a family history of heart disease. Up to 15% of children in the United States are believed to have high cholesterol levels which, left untreated, can lead to heart disease. All teens are encouraged to have their blood pressure checked periodically, particularly if they are overweight and have a family history of high blood pressure, **diabetes,** or stroke.

"Hypertrophic cardiomyopathy," an extreme thickening of the walls of the heart's chambers, occurs mainly in young athletes. It is a rare condition that garners much publicity. Athletes are usually stricken during intense physical exercise, sometimes during competitions. Fainting and complete heart failure can result. Young athletes are encouraged to get complete physicals that include chest X-rays, which can detect the otherwise silent condition.

Less than one percent of infants are born with congenital heart defects or other heart-related problems. While they are difficult to predict, some risk factors have been identified, including: congenital heart disease in either or both parents, sibling or relative; maternal diabetes; alcohol or drug abuse by the mother during pregnancy; rubella, toxoplasmosis, or HIV infection of the mother; exposure of the mother to certain medications during pregnancy.

Doctors are able to detect many heart problems soon after birth and often before birth. Some can be treated prenatally. Common problems include structural defects that hinder the normal circulatory pattern of the blood, connection problems between the main arteries and veins and the heart itself, malformed or missing heart valves, and other defects that block the blood flow through the vessels.

For Further Study

Books

Davis, G. P., and E. Park, eds. *The Heart: The Living Pump.* Washington, DC: U. S. News Books, 1981.

Katz, A. M. *Physiology of the Heart.* New York: Raven Press, 1992.

Texas Heart Institute. *Heart Owner's Handbook.* New York: John Wiley & Sons, 1996.

Zaret, B., et al, eds. *Yale University School of Medicine Heart Book.* New York: Hearst Books, 1992.

▌ Hepatitis B Virus

Virus, also known as serum hepatitis virus, that may lead to chronic infection of the liver in unvaccinated children.

Hepatitis B virus (HBV) causes serious illnesses, notably chronic infection of the liver or liver **cancer,** especially if the virus is acquired during childhood. The virus is transmitted in several ways, including from mother to infant at birth. During the first five years of life, children are susceptible to the virus, and can contract it from carriers of the virus with whom they come into close contact. The most common ways that HBV virus is spread in adults is through sexual intercourse or through shared intravenous drug needles or ear-piercing equipment.

Not everyone exposed to the virus contracts hepatitis; many people are carriers of the virus without even anoint it. Immunization for infants and young children is important because early infection with HBV greatly increases the likelihood that the virus will cause liver failure in adulthood. All mothers who are at risk of carrying HBV, such as health care workers, are tested for HBV at the time of giving birth. Babies whose mothers test positive for HBV must receive the first dose of vaccine at or immediately after birth. In addition, those babies receive a dose of hepatitis B immune globulin (HBIG), and receive the other two recommended doses of the vaccine on an accelerated schedule. No serious adverse reactions are linked to the hepatitis B vaccine. The mild effects that may occur include fussiness, soreness, swelling, or redness at the site of the injection. These symptoms, when they occur, begin within 24 hours of receiving the vaccine and are gone with 48–72 hours.

For Further Study

National Institute of Allergy and Infectious Diseases (NIAID)
Address: 9000 Rockville Pike

NIH Building 31, Room 7A50
Bethesda, MD 20892-2520
Telephone: (301) 496-5717

Hermaphroditism

An organism with both male and female reproductive organs that produce both male gametes (sperm) and female gametes (ova).

In some animals, the simultaneous hermaphrodites, both male and female organs are functional at the same time. In other animals, the sequential hermaphrodites, one sex develops at one time, which later develops into the other sex. Examples of both strategies are found in nature, especially in the invertebrates, and for many creatures, hermaphroditism is the only method of reproduction.

Many experts believe that true hermaphroditic humans do not exist, but some scientists consider true human hermaphrodites as those who possess one testis and one ovary, even though only one of the two function. Pseudohermaphroditism is a condition in which an individual has both male and female external genital organs, but the gonads are of one sex. Female embryos exposed to high levels of androgens (male hormones) develop female internal reproductive organs but male external genitalia. Alternately, genetic defects cause children to be born with female external genital organs, which change at puberty with the development of a penis and the closure of the false vagina.

Some experts estimate that up to four percent of human births involve some form of variation from what is considered normal male or female morphology. Such infants are usually treated with hormonal medication and surgical intervention as soon as possible to avoid the social and emotional stigma attached to sexual deviation.

For Further Study

Books

Elia, Irene. *The Female Animal.* New York: Henry Holt, 1988.

Periodicals

Berreby, D. "Sex and the Single Hermaphrodite." *Discover* 13, 1992, pp. 88–93.

Fausto-Sterling, Anne. "Focus on Only Two Sexes Is Narrow." *The Brown University Child and Adolescent Behavior Letter* 10, July 1994, p. 1.

Heredity *see* **Genetics and Genetic Counseling**

Herpes Simplex

Virus that causes blister-like open sores, usually on the mouth or genitals of the infected person.

Herpes simplex virus (HSV) exists in two known forms. HSV type 1 causes sores to erupt near the mouth; HSV type two causes sores to erupt on the genitals. HSV type 1 sores are referred to as oral herpes, **cold sores,** or fever blisters. Oral herpes is one of the most common viral diseases of childhood.

Prenatal stage. Prior to birth, fetuses of mothers with genital herpes are at risk for birth defects. An active genital herpes sore at the time of birth can cause extremely serious results, including blindness, birth defects, and even death. Cesarean section is advisable for mothers with active herpes eruptions at the time of delivery.

Newborn infants. Newborn babies have their mother's antibodies providing them immunity against herpes simplex virus until around six months of age.

Infancy, toddlerhood, and school- age children

Children who come into direct contact with a person with HSV may develop symptoms of HSV within two days to two weeks. Direct contact with a person with HSV is the only way the virus is spread. If a child contracts HSV, he or she should be kept away from other children and adults to avoid further spread of the disease. Early symptoms of HSV infection include pain and swelling of the gums, headache, fever, and increased saliva. Within a few days, red bumps may begin to appear in and around the mouth. Over the course of two to three weeks, the sores will develop into blisters or open sores and then crust over and heal. The first eruption of sores from HSV is termed the primary episode. As of the mid-1990s, there was no cure for HSV. The HSV virus remains dormant in the infected person's body forever, and may reactivate periodically. Future episodes are usually milder. Although there is some question about what triggers the virus to activate, stress, fatigue, allergies, some types of injuries, and sunburn seem to contribute.

Adolescence

Adolescents, like younger children, can contract oral herpes, and the course of the infection will be the same as it is in younger children. In adolescence, if the young person becomes sexually active, the risk of contracting any **sexually transmitted disease (STD),** including genital herpes, obviously increases. Both HSV type 1 and HSV type 2 can cause sores to form in the genital area, and in any other part of the body that might come into contact with the mouth or genitals of the infected person. As with oral herpes, genital herpes is spread by contact with an infected person around the time that sores have appeared.

Treatment. Discomfort from symptoms of HSV may be relieved with **acetaminophen**. Patients should avoid acidic beverages if sores are in and around the mouth. Whether on the mouth, genitals, or elsewhere, sores can be treated with acyclovir ointment. Ointments containing steroids, such as cortisone, contribute to the spread of HSV and should not be used.

For Further Study

Organizations

Herpes Resource Center (HRC), an affiliate of American Social Health Association
Address: Box 100
Palo Alto, CA 94302
(Organization of and for people with genital herpes.)
National Institute of Allergy and Infectious Diseases (NIAID)
Address: 9000 Rockville Pike
NIH Building 31, Room 7A50
Bethesda, MD 20892-2520
Telephone: (301) 496-5717

Hinde, Robert A. (1923–)

British biologist.

Robert A. Hinde, trained as a biologist, is best known for his studies of the effects on infants of short-term separation from their mothers. During the late 1950s, Hinde established a colony of rhesus monkeys to serve as his laboratory. There he conducted extensive research that led to new information on human interpersonal relationships. Later he concentrated on children ages three to six and their relationships both with their mothers and their peers.

Hinde earned an undergraduate degree at Cambridge University and a doctorate at Oxford University. In 1950, he became curator of the Ornithological Field Station of the Sub-Department of Animal Behavior. Later he was named Royal Society research professor and honorary director of a medical research council unit. His early work centered on ethology, the study of animal behavior. During the 1960s, his interests expanded to include the relations between ethology and other disciplines, particularly psychology, and the mother-child bond.

Among Robert Hinde's more influential studies were those that showed that an infant's attainment of independence was largely a function of maternal behavior. He observed that rhesus mothers encouraged independence in their infants before the infants themselves appeared to seek it. Hinde also demonstrated that an infant's presence affected the mother's relationship to other adults and argued that an **attachment** relationship more likely reflected the contributions of both the mother and infant, rather than that of the infant alone. The dynamics of relationships, therefore, reflected an ongoing interplay between the traits of the individuals involved and the nature of the relationship.

For Further Study

Books

Hinde, Robert. *Animal Behaviour: A Synthesis of Ethology and Comparative Psychology.* New York: McGraw Hill, 1966.
——. *Biological Bases of Human Social Relationships.* New York: McGraw-Hill, 1974.
——. *Toward Understanding Relationships.* London: Academic Press, 1979.

—Doreen Arcus, Ph.D.
University of Massachusetts Lowell

Hold Back *see* **Retention in School**

Homeless Children

Children and adolescents living without a permanent residence, with or without parent or guardian.

Homeless children face a daunting range of problems. A 1992 U.S. Department of Education report, *Serving Homeless Children,* stated: "...homeless children may have special social and emotional needs resulting from a destabilized, disrupted, or confused family life. These needs may be amplified in situations where homeless children are ridiculed and stigmatized at school."

Researchers have noted a range of problems among the population of homeless children, including:

- physical problems: hunger and poor **nutrition**; lack of or inadequate access to medical and dental care; lack of or inadequate **immunization,** leading to susceptibility to disease; lack of or inadequate hygiene; lack of or inadequate **sleep**; and susceptibility to illness and infection.

- behavior problems: **antisocial behavior,** disruptive behavior, and inadequate social skills such as the inability to share and the tendency to develop inappropriate relationships with adults.

- academic problems: irregular attendance at school; lack of an appropriate study space where homework can be done; lack of access to library resources or reference books at home.

EDUCATING HOMELESS CHILDREN

Prior to 1987, school districts and communities enforced local laws that barred homeless children from enrolling in school—without a permanent residence they were ineligible for enrollment in public schools. In July 1987, the Stewart B. McKinney Homeless Assistance Act was passed by the U.S. Congress, stating that "homelessness alone should not be sufficient reason to separate students from the mainstream school environment." In addition to providing emergency assistance for people without a safe residence, the Act requires states to provide homeless children and adolescents with access to public education. Communities and school systems complete a grant application to receive assistance for their homeless population. Despite the passage of this statute, homeless children still face many challenges in getting an education, such as gaining access to bus transportation and meeting immunization and other requirements for enrollment. To address these issues, in 1990 Congress passed amendments to the Act that required states to actively support the education of homeless children. However, by 1997, experts estimated that only a small percentage of communities that were providing education to homeless children were receiving economic assistance under the provisions of the McKinney Act.

In 1989, U.S. Department of Education estimated that 220,000 school-age children were homeless; in 1990, the National Law Center on Homelessness and Poverty estimated that 450,000 children (of all ages) were homeless; in 1994, the U.S. Department of Education estimated that 317,000 school-age children were homeless; but the Children's Defense Fund estimated the number of school-aged homeless children to be much higher—1.6 million.

Adolescents

Adolescents who are homeless are often runaways or "throwaways" (adolescents who have left home with the encouragement or tacit approval of their parent). They cannot stay in shelters set up for homeless families because they have no parent, and they are not allowed to stay in shelters for adults because of their age. Thus, adolescents are often drawn to settings where they will come into contact with drug and alcohol abusers. Researchers estimate that a quarter of homeless adolescents in large cities engage in prostitution, trading sex for money or drugs.

See also **Running Away**

For Further Study

Books

Anderson, Leslie M., et al. *An Evaluation of State and Local Efforts to Serve the Educational Needs of Homeless Chldren and Youth.* Washington, DC: U.S. Department of Education, 1995.

Mark, Mary Ellen. *A Cry for Help: Stories of Homelessness.* New York: Simon and Schuster, 1996.

Schwartz, Wendy. *A Guide to Promoting Children's Education in Homeless Families.* New York: ERIC Clearinghouse on Urban Education, 1995.

———. *School Programs and Practices for Homeless Students.* New York: ERIC Clearinghouse on Urban Education, 1995.

Stonge, James H. ed. *Educating Homeless Children and Adolescents: Evaluating Policy and Practice.* Newbury Park, CA: Sage, 1992.

Periodicals

Bassuk, E. "Homeless Families." *Scientific American,* December 1991, pp. 66–74.

Eddowes, E. Anne. "School Providing Safer Environments for Homeless Children." *Childhood Education* 70, Annual 1994, pp. 271+.

Reganick, Karol A. "Prognosis for Homeless Children and Adolescents." *Childhood Education* 73, Spring 1997, pp. 133+.

Serving Homeless Children: The Responsibilities of Educators. Washington, DC: U.S. Department of Education, 1992.

Swick, Kevin J. "Teacher Strategies for Supporting Homeless Students and Families." *The Clearing House* 69, May–June 1996, pp. 293+.

Woods, Cyndy Jones, and Darwin Harrison. "A Magnet for Homeless Students: The Thomas J. Pappas Regional Education Center." *The Clearing House* 68, November–December 1994, pp. 123+.

Organizations

National Center for Missing and Exploited Children
Address: 2101 Wilson Blvd., Suite 550
Arlington, VA 22201
Telephone: toll-free (800) THE-LOST [843-5678]; (703) 235-3900

National Clearinghouse on Runaway and Homeless Youth
Address: P.O. Box 13505
Silver Spring, MD 20911-3505
Telephone: (301) 608-8098

National Law Center of Homeless and Poverty
Address: 918 F St., NW, Number 412
Washington, DC 20004
Telephone: (202) 638-2535

National Network of Runaway and Homeless Youth Services
Address: 1319 F St., NW, Suite 201
Washington, DC 20004
Telephone: (202) 783-7949

Home Schooling

Teaching children at home, rather than sending them to a public or private school.

Home schooling is perhaps the fastest growing trend in education in this country. According to the Department of Education, about 500,000 students, or about 1% of the total school age population, were taught at home in 1996. Home schooling organizations put the estimate much higher, at close to 1.2 million. The Department of Education's figures jumped 30% over five years, and some researchers say the number of home-schooled children is growing at about 25% annually. Home schooling is now legal in every state, though requirements vary. Some states require parents who teach their children at home to have teacher's certificates or college degrees; some require extensive monitoring by public school officials. Some states have specific curriculum and testing requirements, while others only ask that parents notify the school district that they plan to teach their children at home.

Before the mid-19th century, home schooling was common. Public schools became widespread in the United States in the 1830s, though many rural families found it inconvenient for their children to travel long distances to school. The first compulsory education law was passed in 1852 and by the turn of the century, children in most communities were required to attend school, usually through eighth grade. Home schooling became, for the most part, obsolete. But dissatisfaction with public education led some parents and educators back to the home school option in the 1970s. The writings of Raymond Moore, a former U.S. Department of Education official, and John Holt, author of several books on education, gave credence and national presence to a growing home school movement. The number of families schooling at home grew tremendously in the 1980s with the majority composed of fundamentalist Christians. The rise in home schooling led to numerous legal confrontations, but through changes in state laws and precedent-setting legal cases, many barriers to home schooling dropped by the early 1990s. Simultaneously, many studies of home-schooled children demonstrated that they scored consistently better or equal to their peers in traditional schools.

Some legal obstacles still remain for parents who home school. For instance, some parents who teach their children at home have sued school districts for denying access to school equipment or extra-curricular activities. While some public and private schools have accommodated home-schooled children with access to science labs and participation in sports teams, others have resisted. Many parents who have opted to home school vilify public schools, while educators often stress that home-schooled children are not fully socialized because they are not exposed to children of different backgrounds and abilities. Though there is a negative stigma attached to children who've been home schooled, a recent University of Michigan study of home-schooled children found them to be well-adjusted socially.

Reasons for schooling children at home differ from family to family. The majority of families choose home schooling for religious reasons. About 80% of families who home school identify themselves as Christian, with many coming from fundamentalist or evangelical sects. Many Christian families prefer to home school because they fear public schools foster a moral environment at odds with their own. Furthermore, they may disagree with the curriculum, or fear the influence of non-Christian students on their children. Interestingly, the growth of home schooling in the 1970s and 1980s coincided with a surge of fundamentalism in the political arena. Yet a growing number of families home school for non-religious reasons. Some parents believe that children should be allowed to learn at their own pace. Raymond Moore claims that children are not ready for formal academic learning until age eight or ten, or even older. Home-schooled children need not follow a regular school curriculum, which teaches reading in first grade, for example, and multiplication in the third grade. The home school parent and child might determine together when the child is ready to read or multiply. Other parents choose to home school because their children are bored in school. Home schooling is most popular in the primary grades, and about one-third of all home-schooled students eventually return to conventional schools, usually for high school.

Home schooling involves a tremendous commitment from the parents. At least one parent must be willing to work closely with the child, plan lessons, keep abreast of requirements, and perhaps negotiate issues with the school district. The most common home school arrangement is for the mother to teach while the father works out of the home. There are a variety of educational materials geared for the home school, published by dozens of suppliers. Some are correspondence courses, which grade students' work, some are full curricula, and some are single topic workbooks or drill materials in areas such as math or phonics. Many of the curriculum providers are indentifiably Christian, including several major home school publishers such as Bob Jones University Press, Alpha Omega Publications, and Home Study International. A major non-religious provider of home school materials is the Calvert School in Baltimore. Figures vary as to how many home schools use published curricula or correspondence courses, but the Department of Education estimates that it is from 25 to 50%; the rest use a curriculum the parents and/or child have devised. Education writer John Holt, a champion of home schooling, suggested that no particular area of study was essential. He advised parents to use real life activities such as work in a family business, writing letters, bookkeeping, observing nature, and talking with old people as meaningful academic lessons. Home schools might fall anywhere on this spectrum, between the tightly planned study of a formal curriculum to Holt's free-form, experiential learning.

Parents interested in teaching their children at home need to find out what laws apply to their state and school district. Many resources are available through the organizations listed below.

For Further Study

Books

Guterson, David. *Family Matters: Why Homeschooling Makes Sense.* New York: Harcourt Brace Jovanovich, 1992.

Moore, Raymond, and Dorothy Moore. *The Successful Homeschool Family Handbook.* Nashville: Thomas Nelson Publishers, 1994.

Pedersen, Anne, and Peggy McNamara, eds. *Schooling at Home: Parents, Kids, and Learning.* Santa Fe: John Muir Publications, 1990.

Organizations

National Homeschool Association
    Address: P.O. Box 157290
    Cincinnati, OH 45215-7290
    Telephone: (513) 772-9580

Home School Legal Defense Association
    Address: P.O. Box 159
    Paeonian Springs, VA 22129
    Telephone: (540) 338-5600

Holt Associates "Growing Without Schooling"
    Address: 2269 Massachusetts Ave.
    Cambridge, MA 01240
    Telephone: (617) 864-3100

Homosexuality

Enduring emotional, romantic, or sexual attraction to individuals of one's own gender.

For most of history, open discussions about homosexuality—sexual attraction to people of one's own gender—have been taboo. Men and women with a homosexual orientation are referred to as gay, while the term lesbian refers to women only. Homosexuality was classified as a mental disorder until 1973, when the **American Psychiatric Association** removed "homosexuality" from the *Diagnostic and Statistical Manual of Mental Disorders.* Two decades later, bias and discrimination against gays and lesbians still exists, but sexual orientation is discussed more openly.

There are no reliable statistics on the number of people who are homosexual. The American researcher Alfred C. Kinsey conducted extensive surveys on sexual behavior in the 1950s, and estimated that about 4% of men and 3% of women were exclusively homosexual; however, his research found that 37% of men and 28% of women had had some sexual experience with a person of their own gender. Most researchers in the 1990s estimate the percentage of the population with homosexual orientation at about 5%, while recognizing that the estimate is based on projections, not hard statistics.

The four components of human sexuality are biological sex, gender identity (the psychological sense of being male or female), sexual orientation, and social sex role (adherence to cultural norms for feminine and masculine behavior). Sexual orientation refers to enduring emotional, romantic, sexual, or affectionate feelings of attraction to individuals of a particular gender. Sexual orientation may or may not be reflected by the individual in his or her behavior, because feelings of attraction may be repressed or ignored for any number of reasons.

Three sexual orientations are commonly recognized: homosexual, attraction to individuals of one's own gender; heterosexual, attraction to individuals of the opposite gender; bisexual, attractions to members of either gender.

Through history, various theories have been proposed regarding the source and development of sexual orientation. Many scientists believe that sexual orientation is shaped for most people at an early age through complex interactions of biological, psychological, and social factors. In most cases, sexual orientation emerges for most people in early adolescence without any prior sexual experience. Many reports have been recorded by people recounting efforts to change their sexual orientation from homosexual to heterosexual with no success. For these reasons, psychologists believe that sexual orientation is not a conscious choice that can be voluntarily changed. In addition, scientific research over 30 years confirms that homosexual orientation is not associated with emotional or social problems. Based on research conducted in the 1960s, psychologists, psychiatrists, and other mental health professionals concluded that homosexuality is not an illness, mental disorder, or emotional problem.

The process of identity development for lesbians and gay men, usually called "coming out," has been found to be strongly related to psychological adjustment. Being able to discuss one's sexual orientation is a sign of positive mental health and strong **self-esteem** for a gay man or lesbian. But even for those gays and lesbians who have adjusted psychologically to their sexual orientation, false stereotypes and prejudice make the process of "coming out" challenging. Lesbian and gay people must risk rejection by family, friends, co-workers, and religious institutions when they share their sexual orientation.

In addition, violence and discrimination are real threats. In a 1989 national survey, almost half of the gay and lesbian people surveyed reported being the target of some form of discrimination or violence during their lifetime. Legal protection from discrimination and violence for gay and lesbian people is important. Some states categorize violence against an individual on the basis of her or his sexual orientation as a "hate crime" with more stringent punishment. Eight U.S. states have laws against discrimination on the basis of sexual orientation.

There is no scientific evidence to support the idea that sexual orientation can be changed through therapy. Some well-meaning parents have sought therapy to help their child change his or her sexual orientation, especially when the admission of homosexuality seems to be causing the child great emotional pain. In fact, there have been reports of cases where such therapy was successful; however, several factors in these reports cause psychologists to question the results. First, none of these cases have been reported on by objective mental health researchers; rather, many of the reports about sexual orientation being changed through therapy have been generated by organizations who are ideologically opposed to homosexual orientation. In addition, the reports have not allowed for a realistic follow-up period. In 1990, the American Psychological Association stated that scientific evidence does not support conversion therapy; in fact, the evidence reveals that it can actually be psychologically damaging to attempt conversion. Sexual orientation is a complex component of one's personality not limited to sexual behavior. Altering sexual orientation is to attempt to alter a key aspect of the individual's identity.

Like people of other sexual orientations, a percentage of gays and lesbians seek counseling. They may see a therapist for any of the reasons many people seek help—coping with grief, anxiety, or other mental health or relationship difficulties. In addition, they may seek psychological help in adjusting to their sexual orientation and in dealing with prejudice, discrimination, and rejection. Families who are adjusting to the news that one of their members is homosexual may also seek counseling to help with the complex feelings and prejudices that such news may elicit.

Since sexual orientation emerges in adolescence—already a stage of challenging emotional, social, and physical development—families of adolescent gays and lesbians should learn as much as they can about sexual orientation. Educational materials and support and discussion groups exist for both adolescents and their family members.

For Further Study

Books

Bass, Ellen, and Kate Kaufman. *Free Your Mind: The Book for Gay, Lesbian, and Bisexual Youth—and Their Allies.* New York: HarperPerennial, 1996.

Dynes, Wayne R., et al. *Encyclopedia of Homosexuality.* New York: Garland, 1990.

Garnets, L. D. and D. C. Kimmel. *Psychological Perspectives on Lesbians and Gay Male Experiences.* New York: Columbia University Press, 1993.

Gonsiorek, J.C., and J.D. Weinrich. *Homosexuality: Research Implications For Public Policy.* New York: Sage Publications, 1991.

Goodchilds, J. D., *Psychological Perspectives on Human Diversity in America.* Washington, DC: American Psychological Association, 1993.

Michale, Robert T., et al. *Sex in America: A Definitive Survey.* Boston: Little, Brown, 1994.

Miller, Deborah A., and Alex Waigandt. *Coping with Your Sexual Orientation.* New York: Rosen, 1990. [For adolescents]

Rafkin, Louise, ed. *Different Daughters: A Book by Mothers of Lesbians.* Garden City, NY: Doubleday, 1989.

Schulenburg, Joy. *The Complete Guide to Gay Parenting.* Garden City, NY: Doubleday, 1985.

Periodicals

Garnets, L. D., et al. "Issues in Psychotherapy with Lesbians and Gay Men." *American Psychologist* 46:9, pp. 964–72.

Organizations

American Psychological Association
    Address: Office of Public Affairs
    750 First St., N.E.
    Washington, DC 20002-4242
    Telephone: (202) 336-5700
    Email: public.affairs@apa.org

Federation of Parents and Friend of Lesbians and Gays
    Address: P.O. Box 27605
    Washington, DC 20038
    Telephone: (202) 638-4200

National Federation of Parents and Friends of Gays
    Address: 8020 Eastern Avenue NW
    Washington, DC 20004
    Telephone: (202) 726-3223

National Gay and Lesbian Task Force
    Address: 1734 14th Street, NW
    Washington, DC 20009
    Telephone: (202) 332-6483

National Institute of Mental Health
    Address: 5600 Fishers Lane, Room 7C02
    Rockville, MD 20857
    Telephone: (301) 443-4513

Parents and Friends of Lesbians and Gays
    Address: 1012 14th Street, NW, Suite 700
    Washington, DC 20005
    Telephone: (202) 638-4200

Sex Information and Education Counsel of the United States
Address: 130 W. 42nd Street, Suite 2500
New York, NY 10036

Hormone Therapy *see* **Anabolic Steroids**

Hormones

Biochemical agents that transmit messages between components of living organisms.

Hormones are biochemical messengers that regulate physiological events in living organisms. More than 100 hormones have been identified in humans. Hormones are secreted by endocrine (ductless) glands such as the hypothalamus, the pituitary gland, the pineal gland, the thyroid, the parathyroid, the thymus, the adrenals, the pancreas, the ovaries, and the testes. Hormones are secreted directly into the blood stream, where they travel to target tissues and modulate digestion, growth, maturation, reproduction, and homeostasis. Hormones do not fall into any one chemical category, but most are either protein molecules or steroid molecules. These biological managers keep the body systems functioning over the long term and help maintain health. The study of hormones is called endocrinology.

Hypothalamus

Most hormones are released into the bloodstream by a single gland. Testosterone is an exception, because it is secreted by both the adrenal glands and by the testes. The major site that keeps track of hormone levels is the hypothalamus. A number of hormones are secreted by the hypothalamus, and they stimulate or inhibit the secretion of hormones at other sites. When the hypothalamus detects high levels of a hormone, it reacts to inhibit further production. When low levels of a hormone are detected, the hypothalamus reacts to stimulate hormone production or secretion. The body handles the hormone estrogen differently. Each month, the Graafian follicle in the ovary releases increasing amounts of estrogen into the bloodstream as the egg develops. When estrogen levels rise to a certain point, the pituitary gland secretes luteinizing hormone (LH) which triggers the egg's release into the oviduct.

The major hormones secreted by the hypothalamus are corticotropin releasing hormone (CRH), thyrotropin releasing hormone (TRH), follicle stimulating hormone releasing hormone (FSHRH), luteinizing hormone releasing hormone (LHRH), and growth hormone releasing hormone (GHRH). CRH targets the adrenal glands. It triggers the adrenals to release adrenocorticotropic hormone (ACTH). ACTH functions to synthesize and release corticosteroids. TRH targets the thyroid where it

functions to synthesize and release the thyroid hormones T3 and T4. FSH targets the ovaries and the testes where it enables the maturation of the ovum and of spermatozoa. LHRH also targets the ovaries and the testes, helping to promote ovulation and increase progesterone synthesis and release. GHRH targets the anterior pituitary to release growth hormone to most body tissues, increase protein synthesis, and increase blood glucose.

The hypothalamus also secretes other important hormones such as prolactin inhibiting hormone (PIH), prolactin releasing hormone (PRH), and melanocyte inhibiting hormone (MIH). PIH targets the anterior pituitary to inhibit milk production at the mammary gland, and PRH has the opposite effect. MIH targets skin pigment cells (melanocytes) to regulate pigmentation.

Pituitary gland

The pituitary has long been called the master gland because of the vast extent of its activity. It lies deep in the brain just behind the nose, and is divided into anterior and posterior regions. Both anti-diuretic hormone (ADH) and oxytocin are synthesized in the hypothalamus before moving to the posterior pituitary prior to secretion. ADH targets the collecting tubules of the kidneys, increasing their permeability to and retention of water. Lack of ADH leads to a condition called diabetes insipidus characterized by excessive urination. Oxytocin targets the uterus and the mammary glands in the breasts. Oxytocin also triggers labor contractions prior to birth and functions in the ejection of milk. The drug pitocin is a synthetic form of oxytocin and is used medically to induce labor.

The anterior pituitary (AP) secretes a number of hormones, including growth hormone (GH), ACTH, TSH, prolactin, LH, and FSH. GH controls cellular growth, protein synthesis, and elevation of blood glucose concentration. ACTH controls secretion of some hormones by the adrenal cortex (mainly cortisol). TSH controls thyroid hormone secretion in the thyroid. In males, prolactin enhances testosterone production; in females, it initiates and maintains LH to promote milk secretion from the mammary glands. In females, FSH initiates ova development and induces ovarian estrogen secretion. In males, FSH stimulates sperm production in the testes. LH stimulates ovulation and formation of the corpus luteum, which produces progesteronein females, whereas LH stimulates interstitial cells in males to produce testosterone.

Thyroid gland

The thyroid lies under the larynx and synthesizes two hormones, thyroxine and tri-iodothyronine. This gland takes up iodine from the blood and has the highest iodine level in the body. The iodine is incorporated into the thyroid hormones. Thyroxine has four iodine atoms and is called T4. Tri-iodothyronine has three iodine atoms and is called T3. Both T3 and T4 function to increase the metabolic rate of several cells and tissues. The brain, testes, lungs, and spleen are not affected by thyroid hormones, however. T3 and T4 indirectly increase blood glucose levels as well as the insulin-promoted uptake of glucose by fat cells. Their release is modulated by TRH-RH from the hypothalamus. When temperature drops, a metabolic increase is triggered by TSH. Chronic stress seems to reduce TSH secretion which, in turn, decreases T3 and T4 output.

Depressed T3 and T4 production is the trademark of hypothyroidism. If it occurs in young children, this decreased activity can cause physical and **mental retardation**. In adults, it creates sluggishness—mentally and physically—and is characterized further by weight gain, poor hair growth, and a swollen neck. Excessive T3 and T4 cause sweating, nervousness, weight loss, and fatigue. The thyroid also secretes calcitonin, which serves to reduce blood calcium levels. Calcitonin's role is particularly significant in children whose bones are still forming.

Parathyroid glands

The parathyroid glands are attached to the bottom of the thyroid gland. They secrete the polypeptide parathyroid hormone (PTH), which plays a crucial role in monitoring blood calcium and phosphate levels. Calcium is a critical element for the human body. Even though the majority of calcium is in bone, it is also used by muscles, including cardiac muscle, for contractions, and by nerves in the release of neurotransmitters. Calcium is a powerful messenger in the immune response of inflammation and blood clotting. Both PTH and calcitonin regulate calcium levels in the kidneys, the gut, bone, and blood.

PTH deficiency can be due to autoimmune diseases or to inherited parathyroid gland problems. Low PTH capabilities cause depressed blood calcium levels and neuromuscular problems. Very low PTH can lead to tetany or muscle spasms. Excess PTH can lead to weakened bones because it causes too much calcium to be drawn from the bones and to be excreted in the urine. Abnormalities of bone mineral deposits can lead to a number of conditions, including osteoporosis and rickets. Osteoporosis can be due to dietary insufficiencies of calcium, phosphate, or vitamin C. The end result is a loss of bone mass. Rickets is usually caused by a vitamin D deficiency and results in lower rates of bone formation in children. These examples show the importance of a balanced, nutritious diet for healthy development.

Adrenal glands

The two adrenal glands sit one on top of each kidney. Both adrenals have two distinct regions. The outer region (the medulla) produces adrenaline and noradrenaline and is under the control of the sympathetic nervous system. The inner region (the cortex) produces a number of steroid hormones. The cortical steroid hormones are derived from cholesterol and include mineralocorticoids (mainly aldosterone), glucocorticoids (mainly cortisol), and gonadocorticoids. Aldosterone and cortisol are the major human steroids in the cortex. However, testosterone and estrogen are secreted by adults (both male and female) at very low levels.

Aldosterone plays an important role in regulating body fluids. It increases blood levels of sodium and water and lowers blood potassium levels. Cortisol secretion is stimulated by physical trauma, exposure to cold temperatures, burns, heavy exercise, and anxiety. Cortisol targets the liver, skeletal muscle, and adipose tissue, and its overall effect is to provide amino acids and glucose to meet synthesis and energy requirements for metabolism and during periods of stress. Because of its anti-inflammatory action, cortisol is used clinically to reduce swelling. Excessive cortisol secretion leads to Cushing's syndrome, which is characterized by weak bones, obesity, and a tendency to bruise. Cortisol deficiency can lead to Addison's disease, which has the symptoms of fatigue, low blood sodium levels, low blood pressure, and excess skin pigmentation.

The adrenal medullary hormones are epinephrine (adrenaline) and nor-epinephrine (nor-adrenaline). Both of these hormones serve to supplement and prolong the "fight or flight" response initiated in the nervous system. This response includes increased heart rate, peripheral blood vessel constriction, sweating, spleen contraction, glycogen conversion to glucose, dilation of bronchial tubes, decreased digestive activity, and low urine output.

Pancreas

The pancreas secretes the hormones insulin, glucagon, and somatostatin, also known as growth hormone inhibiting hormone (GHIH). Insulin and glucagon have reciprocal roles. Insulin promotes the storage of glucose, fatty acids, and amino acids, while glucagon stimulates mobilization of these constituents from storage into the blood. Insulin release is triggered by high blood glucose levels. It lowers blood sugar levels and inhibits the release of glucose by the liver in order to keep blood levels down. Insulin excess can cause **hypoglycemia** leading to convulsions or coma, and insufficient levels of insulin can cause **diabetes mellitus,** which can be fatal if left untreated. Diabetes mellitus is the most common endocrine disorder.

Glucagon secretion is stimulated by decreased blood glucose levels, infection, cortisol, exercise, and large protein meals. Among other activities, it facilitates glucose release into the blood. Excess glucagon can result from tumors of the pancreatic alpha cells, and a mild diabetes seems to result. Some cases of uncontrolled diabetes are also characterized by high glucagon levels, suggesting that low blood insulin levels are not necessarily the only cause in diabetes cases.

Female hormones

The female reproductive hormones arise from the hypothalamus, the anterior pituitary, and the ovaries. Although detectable amounts of the steroid hormone estrogen are present during fetal development, at puberty estrogen levels rise to initiate secondary sexual characteristics. Gonadotropin releasing hormone (GRH) is released by the hypothalamus to stimulate pituitary release of LH and FSH, which propagate egg development in the ovaries. Eggs (ova) exist at various stages of development, with the maturation of one ovum taking about 28 days. The ova are contained within follicles that are support organs for ova maturation. About 450 of a female's 150,000 germ cells mature to leave the ovary. The hormones secreted by the ovary include estrogen, progesterone, and small amounts of testosterone.

As an ovum matures, rising estrogen levels stimulate additional LH and FSH release from the pituitary. Prior to ovulation, estrogen levels drop, and LH and FSH surge to cause the ovum to be released into the fallopian tube. The cells of the burst follicle begin to secrete progesterone and some estrogen. These hormones trigger thickening of the uterine lining, the endometrium, to prepare it for implantation should fertilization occur. The high progesterone and estrogen levels prevent LH and FSH from further secretion—thus hindering another ovum from developing. If fertilization does not occur, eight days after ovulation the endometrium deteriorates, resulting in menstruation. The falling estrogen and progesterone levels that follow trigger LH and FSH, starting the cycle all over again.

In addition to its major roles in the menstrual cycle, estrogen has a protective effect on bone loss, which can lead to osteoporosis.

Hormones related to pregnancy include human chorionic gonadotrophin (HCG), estrogen, human chorionic somatomammotrophin (HCS), and relaxin. HCG is released by the early embryo to signal implantation. Estrogen and HCS are secreted by the placenta. As birth nears, relaxin is secreted by the ovaries to relax the pelvic area in preparation for labor.

Male hormones

Male reproductive hormones come from the hypothalamus, the anterior pituitary, and the testes. As in females, GRH is released from the hypothalamus, which stimulates LH and FSH release from the pituitary. Testosterone levels are quite low until puberty. At puberty, rising levels of testosterone stimulate male reproductive development including secondary characteristics. LH

stimulates testosterone release from the testes. FSH promotes early spermatogenesis. The male also secretes prostaglandins. These substances promote uterine contractions which help propel sperm towards an egg during sexual intercourse. Prostaglandins are produced in the seminal vesicles, and are not classified as hormones by all authorities.

For Further Study

Books

Little, M. *The Endocrine System*. New York: Chelsea House Publishers, 1990.
Parker, M., ed. *Steroid Hormone Action*. New York: IRL Press, 1993.

Hospitalism *see* Anaclitic Depression

· ·

Hospitalization

Admittance to a hospital as a patient.

Whether planned or on an emergency basis, hospitalization causes disruption in the life of any child. However, with the special accommodations that modern hospitals usually make for both children and their parents, a stay in the hospital need not be a traumatic event. If children receive proper support from the hospital and their families, hospitalization can even make them feel good about themselves for having successfully negotiated a challenge to their maturity, self-discipline, and courage. Because no one can predict when a child may face an emergency hospital stay, it is a good idea for all parents to spend some time talking to their children about hospitals.

Children should be carefully prepared for prearranged hospitalizations. Before they can reassure their children, parents need to deal with their own fears about the impending experience, which can be easily communicated to a child. They should describe and explain, as honestly and thoroughly as possible, what will happen to the child while she is in the hospital. A toy doctor kit can help psychologically prepare a child for the experience. There are also a number of books written especially for this purpose that parents can read to children. There are various symbolic steps parents can take to reassure young children, with their limited concept of time, that the hospital stay will be temporary. They can plan a party afterward or read a storybook part way through and mark the place where it will be resumed once the child comes home.

For preschool children, explanations should be simple and concrete. Trying to explain that the child will undergo a series of tests or that he will spend three weeks in the hospital will not ease the child's anxiety. Instead, the

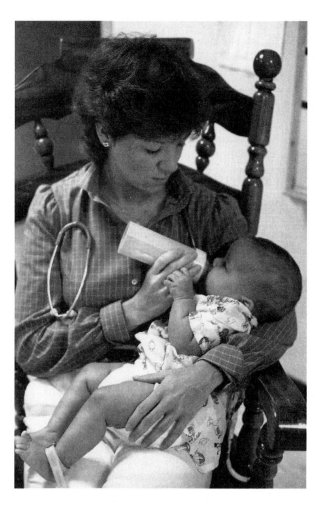

The furnishings and staff of the children's floor in most hospitals are selected to be more home-like than other areas.

BOOKS AND VIDEOS FOR CHILDREN AGES 2 TO 8

Books

DeSantis, Kenny. *A Doctor's Tools*. New York: Dodd, Mead, 1985.

Hautiz, Deborah. *A Visit to the Sesame Street Hospital*. New York: Random House, 1985.

Rey, Margaret, and H.A. Rey. *Curious George Goes to the Hospital*. New York: Scholastic Books Services, 1974.

Videos

The Hospital Adventures of Jimmy, Judy, and AC. (Videorecording). Fairlawn, NJ: Balducci Productions, 1993.

Steedman, Julie. *Emergency Room—An ABC Tour*. (Ages 2 to 10). McLean, VA: Windy Hill Press, 1974.

Stein, Sara Bonnett. *A Hospital Story*. (Ages 3 to 10). New York: Walker and Co., 1974.

parent might indicate the part or parts of the body that are to be "fixed," using a doll or stuffed animal. By the ages of five or six years, children can understand hospitalization on a more sophisticated level. They will be familiar with some medical instruments and concepts and better able to grasp the time frame involved. A special concern with children this age is the possibility that they will feel like they are going to the hospital because they have done something wrong, and parents need to reassure the child that this is not true. Overall, the best reassurance parents can give children of any age is the promise that they will be there to help them through the experience, even if they cannot be physically present during the entire ordeal.

Many hospitals allow parents and children to tour their pediatric facilities, further reassuring the child. Children may be shown rooms similar to those in which they will stay. They may also be shown the unit's playroom, become familiar with some of the hospital equipment they will see frequently during their stay, or meet some of the nursing staff. It is best for parents to be present during these tours, so the child can see that they approve of the facilities and trust the care providers. When it comes time to help the child pack for the hospital, it is helpful to take old, familiar, comforting pajamas, toys, and other belongings.

Children's floors in many hospitals are staffed by at least some nurses who specialize in caring for infants and children and understand their special needs. In addition, it is common for the staff to include a children's activities specialist with a background in child development and therapeutic play. When a child is admitted, a nurse will probably consult with the parents to learn about any dietary restrictions or preferences. As with adult hospitalization, there will usually be daily menu choices available. Once in the hospital, a child usually shares a room with one or more other children, which is usually a positive experience. A typical feature of children's hospitals or children's areas in hospitals is a playroom where children can interact with others who are undergoing similar experiences.

Even with preparation and support, it is normal for children to experience certain fears when they are hospitalized. The most common is **separation anxiety.** The hospital is a frightening place full of unfamiliar sights, sounds, and people, and the child's primary source of security and reassurance is a parent. Many young children have never spent even a single night away from their parents, and if the parents leave for the night, especially at the beginning of a hospital stay, a child can easily fear that they will never return. Even a parent's short absence during the day can prove upsetting to a child. It is becoming increasingly common for parents to stay with a hospitalized child overnight, at least initially, either in a special nearby unit or on a cot or chair in the child's room. Once the child has become familiar with the hospital environment and personnel, the parents can encourage attachments to particular staff members or playmates to prevent the child from feeling abandoned during periods when the parents must be away.

In addition to separation anxiety, it is common for hospitalized children to fear mutilation or even death. Children may or may not verbalize these fears. Besides comforting their children simply by their presence, parents can also help them cope with the sense of helplessness that brings on such fears by trying as much as possible to help them feel they have some control over things. They may be able to decide what they will eat or wear, or what toys they will play with.

Children may cope with the emotional turmoil of hospitalization by social withdrawal, aggression, or an unnatural degree of obedience stemming from the fear that if they are "bad," even worse things will happen to them. All of these are normal and generally transient reactions that do not cause any long-lasting emotional harm. It is also common for children to experience some developmental regression in response to being hospitalized, either during the experience or after they come home. Often, they temporarily lose a recent advance, such as staying dry at night or overcoming certain fears. It can be helpful for children to cope with their feelings about hospitalization once they are home by playing with dolls and other toys. A doctor kit bought to help prepare for the hospitalization is sometimes very helpful in replaying children's reactions once they are home again.

For Further Study

Books

Azarnoff, Pat, ed. *Preparation of Young Healthy Children for Possible Hospitalization: The Issues.* Santa Monica: Pediatric Projects, 1983.

Organizations

Association for the Care of Children's Health
   Address: 7910 Woodmont Ave., Suite 300
   Bethesda, MD 20814
   Telephone: (301) 654-6549

Human Papilloma Virus (HPV)

Genital human papilloma virus (HPV) is a sexually transmitted disease (STD), the most common symptom of which is genital warts.

Of the more than 60 types of human papilloma virus (HPV), 20 are associated with genital infections. Five of these are associated with cervical **cancer**.

In addition to visible growths or warts in the genital area, HPV often causes microscopic lesions on the vagina, cervix, penis, or rectum. Because HPV is often detected by routine Pap smear, sexually active adolescent girls should have annual Pap tests.

Treatment for HPV varies depending on the site of the infection. Genital warts can be treated by topical medications in a doctor's office or clinic. If this treatment is not successful, a wart might be removed by freezing or laser.

For Further Study

Books

Daugirdas, John T., M.D. *STD, Sexually Transmitted Diseases, Including HIV/AIDS.* Hinsdale, IL: Medtext, 1992.

Organizations

National Sexually Transmitted Disease Hotline
   Telephone: toll-free (800) 227-8922
   (Free information and clinic referrals)

—Gail B. Slap, M.D.
University of Pennsylvania School of Medicine

Huntington's Disease

A hereditary disease of the central nervous system.

Huntington's disease, also called Huntington's chorea, causes intellectual impairment, emotional disturbances, and the uncontrollable arm, leg, and body movements that are its most characteristic feature. It is named for George Huntington, an American physician who first wrote about the disease in 1872. As a child, he had heard the condition described by his physician father and seen some patients affected by it. The incidence of Huntington's disease is estimated at between 4 and 10 out of every 100,000 births. About 25,000 Americans have been diagnosed with the disease, and over 100,000 are thought to have a family history that puts them at risk. Onset is usually between the ages of 35 and 45 but can occur in individuals younger than 20 and over 60. In the United States Huntington's disease became familiar to many people when popular folk singer Woody Guthrie became ill with the disease in the 1950s. Guthrie died in 1967 after being hospitalized for nearly 15 years.

Although the disease is known to be genetically transmitted, its exact cause is unknown. Physiologically, it is characterized by the death of **brain** cells (which cannot be replaced) and subsequent deterioration of the brain that follows a consistent pattern. The part of the brain that controls motor activity shrinks severely, the cells that carry nerve impulses to the brain are destroyed, and the balance of certain brain chemicals is disturbed. In autopsies, the brains of Huntington's patients have been found to weigh 150 to 500 grams less than normal brains. Genetically, Huntington's disease is an autosomal dominant disorder that can be passed on through either the mother or father. As a dominant genetic disorder, it cannot be passed on by individuals who don't have it themselves. The gender of the parent with Huntington's tends to affect the age of onset; persons with early onset usually inherit the disease from their fathers, those with later onsets from their mothers. A DNA marker for Huntington's disease was discovered by Dr. James Gusella in 1983, making it possible to test for the disease before the symptoms become apparent, although the tests require blood samples from at least two relatives of the person being tested. Prenatal testing has been available since 1986.

Unless there is a known familial history of the disease, Huntington's disease usually goes undiagnosed for years after its onset, as the lives of its victims and their families gradually deteriorate. The initial symptoms are often vague feelings of nervousness and restlessness. The victim's temperament undergoes a seemingly inexplicable change, as he or she becomes moody and irritable, and has periods of temper and depression that frighten and alienate family members. This behavior, together with the early signs of involuntary movement, is often mistaken for **alcoholism,** with the tragic result that people suffering from the disease are stigmatized by family and community just when they are most in need of help and emotional support. Because of the mental and emotional impairment associated with the disease, Huntington's victims become unable to function effectively at work, eventually losing their jobs or businesses. Many then drift from job to job. Even if alcoholism is not suspected, they may be shunned due to suspicions of insanity.

Between 5 and 10% of persons with Huntington's disease begin showing symptoms of the disease before the age of 20 (usually in adolescence). The symptoms tend to be more severe in children and adolescents than in adults, and the disease progresses more rapidly, often resulting in death within eight years. **Epilepsy** is especially common in young people with Huntington's and contributes to the frequent misdiagnosis of their condition, as does the onset of **mental retardation.** Another distinctive feature of the disease in children and adolescents is that the involuntary physical movements ("chorea") are often replaced by rigidity, either at the onset or later, thus resembling an unusual form the disease sometimes takes in adults, called the Westphal variant.

Although the number of children and adolescents who suffer from Huntington's disease is quite small, it strongly affects the lives of the far greater number of young people whose parents have been stricken with it and who may or may not go on to develop it themselves in later life. In addition to facing the knowledge that they may have Huntington's themselves (only a small percentage of family members take advantage of the available testing), these youths must cope with the disruption that any serious illness creates in a family. They may have the responsibility of caring for the ailing parent or contributing to the family income. Emotionally, they face the stigma associated with a disease that involves both physical handicaps and the appearance of insanity in the affected parent. A special problem associated with Huntington's is the danger that the parent's neurologically based emotional turbulence will lead to physical abuse, which it often does.

While there are no medications that can reverse or arrest the disease itself, **drug therapy** can help reduce the involuntary physical movements. Medication is sometimes prescribed for the mood disorders that accompany Huntington's disease, and counseling can often help relieve the chronic depression that is one of the hallmarks of the disease (it is estimated that as many as 25% of Huntington's patients commit **suicide**). Regular exercise as well as physical, occupational, and recreational therapy can also help combat mental, emotional, and physical deterioration. Because Huntington's disease affects the mind, body, and emotions, a broad spectrum of professional help is needed to manage this illness, and a team approach has been recommended for this purpose. Huntington's patients can benefit not only from the services of physicians and nurses, but also from the work of physical, occupational, music, and speech therapists, as well as a variety of home health care personnel.

For Further Study

Books

Folstein, Susan E. *Huntington's Disease: A Disorder of Families.* Baltimore: Johns Hopkins University Press, 1989.

Phillips, Dennis H. *Living with Huntington's Disease: A Book for Patients and Families.* Madison: University of Wisconsin Press, 1981.

Organizations

The Huntington's Disease Society of America, Inc.
Address: 140 West 22nd St., 6th floor
New York, NY 10011
Telephone: (212) 242-1968

Hereditary Disease Foundation
Address: 606 Wilshire Blvd., Suite 504
Santa Monica, CA 90401
Telephone: (213) 458-4183

Hurler's Syndrome

A severe genetic disorder that causes skeletal deformity and mental retardation.

Hurler's syndrome belongs to the broader category of mucopolysaccharidosis (MPS), a type of disease caused by an excess accumulation of certain substances (mucopolysaccharides) found in connective tissue. There are six major types of mucopolysaccharidosis, all produced by various enzyme deficiencies that cause mucopolysaccharides to be stored in cells. It is possible to screen for these conditions because the stored mucopolysaccharides leak into the urine. MPS occurs in an estimated 1 in 25,000 live births.

Hurler's syndrome, named for Gertrud Hurler (1889–1965), the German pediatrician who first identified the condition in 1919, is one of the more common forms of mucopolysaccharidosis. Like most other types of MPS, it is an autosomal recessive trait. Caused by a deficiency in the enzyme alpha-L-iduronidase, it is characterized by mental and growth retardation, short, broad bones, a humpback, joint stiffness, and limited joint function. Children with Hurler's syndrome have slow growth during the second six months of life and generally stop growing altogether by the age of two. The corneas become clouded, and facial deformities develop, including a prominent forehead, coarse features, thick earlobes, a sunken nasal bridge, excessively full lips, and upturned nostrils. The spine becomes shortened, the liver and spleen enlarged, the chest deformed, and the abdomen protruding. After the age of three, the mouth is usually held open. Children afflicted by Hurler's syndrome usually die by the age of 10 from heart failure or pneumonia. Recently, physicians have had some success in treating the condition with bone marrow transplants. Prenatal screening for Hurler's syndrome may be done through either **amniocentesis** or chorionic villus sampling by testing for levels of the associated enzyme in cultured fetal cells.

Hydrocephalus

Term describing a condition in which fluid collects inside the skull.

Hydrocephalus, which means literally "water on the brain," is a condition in which excessive cerebrospinal fluid (CSF) collects inside the skull. This fluid is normally found in the brain, although excessive amounts of CSF may build pressure to levels that cause brain damage and subsequent disability.

The brain rests within the natural bony vault of the cranium. There it is protected by the skull and by layers of fibrous material that help to stabilize it and to contain the fluid that surrounds it. The brain itself is a very soft, gelatinous material that requires substantial protection. Three layers of connective tissue line the skull and surround the brain. The pia mater (which means literally "tender mother") lies directly on the brain, following its contours and continuing along the spinal cord as it descends through the spine. The second layer is the arachnoid (resembling a spider's web), a very thin, fibrous membrane without blood vessels. It, too, lies close to the brain but does not follow its every contour. The space between the pia mater and the arachnoid, called the subarachnoid space, contains the arteries and veins that circulate blood to the brain and the cerebrospinal fluid that bathes the nervous tissues. The outermost layer, the dura mater ("hard mother"), is a two-layered, leathery, tough membrane that adheres closely to the inside of the skull.

The CSF that bathes the brain and spinal cord is manufactured and secreted in the brain by a structure called the choroid plexus. Cerebrospinal fluid is a colorless, clear fluid that contains oxygen, some proteins, and glucose (a form of sugar). Normally, the fluid will circulate through the cranium and down the spinal column. It will be absorbed by special structures called villi in the arachnoid tissue or it will drain from one of several outlets. Excessive fluid accumulates because the brain is manufacturing too much CSF or the drainage routes are blocked and the fluid cannot drain properly.

The capacity of the ventricles in the brain and the space around the spinal cord is approximately 125 milliliters (0.26 pints). The choroid plexus manufactures from 500 to 750 milliliters (1.1 to 1.6 pints) of fluid each day. The pressure of the CSF within the nervous system, therefore, is related to the rate of manufacture versus the rate of drainage of the fluid. Fluid pressure can be measured by inserting a needle between two of the lumbar vertebrae into the spinal canal. The needle is then connected to a meter that indicates the fluid pressure.

The choroid plexus is composed of specialized cells that line the ventricles of the brain. The ventricles are four small, naturally formed cavities in the brain that act as reservoirs for CSF. Overproduction of fluid or its failure to drain can enlarge the ventricles and press the brain against the bony vault of the skull.

Newborn babies who have hydrocephalus will often develop grossly swollen heads. The bones of the skull have not fused and the pressure of the fluid inside the skull can expand the disconnected bony plates.

The two types of hydrocephalus are called communicating and noncommunicating. Communicating hydrocephalus is caused by overproduction of fluid by the choroid plexus. The fluid, which overwhelms the absorption capacity of the arachnoid, collects inside the ventricles as well as outside the brain. This is the most common form of hydrocephalus occurring in adults and is the result of injury or infection such as **encephalitis**. At the onset of the condition the patient will become clumsy in walking and appear tired. Other signs will develop indicating a brain injury. To diagnose communicating hydrocephalus the physician will review the patient's recent history to determine whether an infection or head injury has occurred. In addition, such diagnostic measures as a magnetic resonance image (MRI) of the skull can reveal the presence of excess fluid. This condition is readily treatable.

Noncommunicating hydrocephalus is the most common form of the condition in childhood. Usually it will be diagnosed immediately after birth, when signs such as a swollen cranium are seen. Here the problem lies in a narrowing of a drainage aqueduct that inhibits passage of the CSF out of the cranium. The ventricles enlarge greatly and the fluid pressure begins to push the brain against the skull. In this case a shunt can be implanted in the skull to drain the fluid into a vein to relieve the pressure.

Unfortunately, shunts are often subject to complications such as blockage, infection, and overdrainage, necessitating multiple surgeries. A new procedure, third ventriculostomy, may offer freedom from shunt dependency. Third ventriculostomy involves a process in which cerebrospinal fluid within the ventricle is diverted elsewhere in an attempt to relieve pressure on the brain without using a shunt. A tiny (one millimeter) perforation is made in the wall of the third ventricle, thus allowing movement of CSF out of the blocked ventricle. This surgery was performed as early as 1922, but it was considered too risky. Now with the use of new technologies, such as MRI and endoscopic guidance, risks have been minimized and ventriculostomy has become more accepted.

Noncommunicating hydrocephalus is associated with a congenital condition called meningomyelocele. A newborn with this condition is born with the spinal cord and its superficial coverings exposed. The spinal canal, the opening through which the spinal cord passes, has not fused, so the cord can protrude through the open side. Almost always, the surgical repair of the meningomyelocele will result in hydrocephalus, which will in turn require surgical correction. Noncommunicating hydrocephalus can also occur in an adult and generally is the result of the formation of a tumor that blocks the drainage area.

All forms of hydrocephalus can be treated surgically, so it is important that diagnosis be made as soon as possible after the condition is detected. With excessive fluid pressure inside the skull, brain damage can occur, leading to various forms of disability that can be avoided if treatment is timely.

Hyperglycemia

A condition caused by abnormally high levels of glucose, or blood sugar, in the blood, usually as the result of diabetes mellitus.

Also known as diabetic ketoacidosis, hyperglycemia develops over a period of a few days as the blood sugar levels of a diabetic child gradually rise. The first signs are frequent urination and increased thirst. The child may then show any of the following symptoms, including flushed face, dry skin, dry mouth, headache, nausea, vomiting and abdominal pain, drowsiness and lethargy, blurry vision, fruity-smelling breath, rapid heartbeat, and deep and labored breathing. Without treatment, the child can lapse into a diabetic coma and die. Treatment for hyperglycemia includes an injection of insulin, usually in combination with administration of intravenous fluids and salts.

Occurrences of hyperglycemia can be prevented by careful monitoring of the blood sugar levels, insulin injections, and a proper diet. Diabetic adolescents are especially susceptible to hyperglycemia, since hormonal levels are in flux and many adolescents exhibit erratic eating and sleeping patterns. Athletic activities can be beneficial since exercise makes use of surplus blood glucose.

For Further Study

Books

Siminerio, Linda M., and Jean Betschart. *Children with Diabetes.* Alexandria, VA: American Diabetes Association, 1986.

Slap, Gail B., and Martha M. Jablow. *Teenage Health Care.* New York: Pocket Books, 1994.

Audiovisual Recordings

Children with Special Health Needs. Cleveland, OH: Cleveland Clinic Foundation, 1993.
(One 2-hour videocassette. This video-taped program covers human growth, asthma, diabetes, teenagers and mental health.).

Managing Diabetes. Cleveland, OH: Cleveland Clinic Foundation, 1993.
(One 2-hour videocassette.)

Organizations

The American Diabetes Association
Address: P. O. Box 25757
1660 Duke Street

Alexandria, VA 22314
Telephone: (800) 232-3472
The Joslin Diabetes Center
Address: One Joslin Place
Boston, MA 02215
Telephone: (617) 732-2400
The Juvenile Diabetes Foundation
Address: 432 Park Avenue South
New York, NY 10016
Telephone: (800) 223-1138

Hypertension

Also known as high blood pressure, a condition in which too much force is exerted by the blood as it travels through the body's arteries.

There are two types of hypertension: primary and secondary. Primary, or essential, hypertension is caused by external factors; secondary hypertension is related to an underlying disorder, such as a congenital heart defect or kidney disease. Factors that increase the risk of high blood pressure include age (the likelihood of hypertension increases with age), race (hypertension is two to three times more common in blacks than in whites), heredity, and being overweight.

About 60 million Americans have high blood pressure. Of this number roughly 2.7 million are children between the ages of six and 17. Secondary hypertension occurs in only about 10% of the diagnoses—in the majority of cases the condition has no known cause. However, serious hypertension in infants and young children is usually of the secondary variety. Secondary hypertension also occurs (although less frequently) in adolescents, in whom it can signal a hormonal imbalance, kidney disorder, or other condition. In contrast, primary hypertension is not unusual among adolescents and is also found, though infrequently, in children. Of the two types, secondary hypertension is easier to detect because the symptoms of the underlying condition alert the child and parents that something is wrong. Primary hypertension usually produces no symptoms, a fact that makes it important for children to have their blood pressure tested regularly starting at the age of three. Children and adolescents with high blood pressure have an increased risk of developing hypertension in adulthood.

Blood pressure in children is measured the same way as in adults—with the familiar inflatable cuff and meter known as a sphygmomanometer (although a special smaller cuff is used for children). Two figures are used to describe blood pressure. The top figure—known as systolic blood pressure—refers to the level of pressure when the heart contracts to circulate the blood. The lower number—called the diastolic pressure—is based on the reading when the heart is resting. The total pressure is the systolic over the diastolic pressure, expressed in millimeters of mercury (a typical blood pressure reading might be 120 over 80). High blood pressure in adults is defined as a reading higher than 140 over 90. The blood pressure of children is lower than of adults and steadily increases as the child grows older. For example, a normal reading for a three-year-old would be 98 over 64. High blood pressure is diagnosed in children if the average of three readings is higher than that for 90% of children in the same age group. Aside from age, size itself is a factor—larger children have higher blood pressure than smaller ones, whatever their age (a fact taken in account when their blood pressure is assessed). Children should not have their blood pressure taken when they are nervous or agitated. Adolescents should be careful not to ingest any stimulants, such as caffeine, nicotine, or alcohol, in the hours preceding a blood pressure reading.

When a child is found to have elevated blood pressure, blood and urine tests and kidney x rays are commonly taken to rule out any underlying disorder. If the diagnosis is primary hypertension, common treatment measures include a program of increased exercise and dietary modifications to cut down on sodium, especially salt, which is abundant in many foods favored by young people, such as french fries, pizza, potato chips, hot dogs, and hamburgers. Some substitution of healthy snacks such as fruit can help reduce the amount of salt in the diet. If the child is overweight, dietary changes may focus on weight loss. Even a modest reduction in weight can help reduce blood pressure. If other measures do not sufficiently alleviate the hypertension, a medication may be prescribed, usually a diuretic which cuts down on water retention by increasing the amount eliminated through urination.

For a child with a family history of heart disease or stroke, careful monitoring of blood pressure and treatment of hypertension can help reduce the risk of these conditions. According to the National High Blood Pressure Education Program, the treatment of hypertension early in life can also reduce the risk of heart and kidney failure and promote longevity. It is recommended that children and adolescents with high blood pressure have their blood pressure checked twice a year.

For Further Study

Books

Caris, Timothy N. *Understanding Hypertension: Causes and Treatments.* New York: Basic Books, 1986.

Rees, Michael K. *The Complete Family Guide to Living with High Blood Pressure.* Englewood Cliffs, NJ: Prentice-Hall, 1980.

Salander, James M. *Hypertension: Reducing Your Risk.* New York: Bantam, 1993.

BLOOD PRESSURE LEVELS FOR THE 90TH AND 95TH PERCENTILES OF BLOOD PRESSURE FOR BOYS AGE 1 TO 17 YEARS BY PERCENTILES OF HEIGHT

Age	Height Percentiles*→ BP† ↓	Systolic BP (mm Hg)							Diastolic BP (mm Hg)						
		5%	10%	25%	50%	75%	90%	95%	5%	10%	25%	50%	75%	90%	95%
1	90th	94	95	97	98	100	102	102	50	51	52	53	54	54	55
	95th	98	99	101	102	104	106	106	55	55	56	57	58	59	59
2	90th	98	99	100	102	104	105	106	55	55	56	57	58	59	59
	95th	101	102	104	106	108	109	110	59	59	60	61	62	63	63
3	90th	100	101	103	105	107	108	109	59	59	60	61	62	63	63
	95th	104	105	107	109	111	112	113	63	63	64	65	66	67	67
4	90th	102	103	105	107	109	110	111	62	62	63	64	65	66	66
	95th	106	107	109	111	113	114	115	66	67	67	68	69	70	71
5	90th	104	105	106	108	110	112	112	65	65	66	67	68	69	69
	95th	108	109	110	112	114	115	116	69	70	70	71	72	73	74
6	90th	105	106	108	110	111	113	114	67	68	69	70	70	71	72
	95th	109	110	112	114	115	117	117	72	72	73	74	75	76	76
7	90th	106	107	109	111	113	114	115	69	70	71	72	72	73	74
	95th	110	111	113	115	116	118	119	74	74	75	76	77	78	78
8	90th	107	108	110	112	114	115	116	71	71	72	73	74	75	75
	95th	111	112	114	116	118	119	120	75	76	76	77	78	79	80
9	90th	109	110	112	113	115	117	117	72	73	73	74	75	76	77
	95th	113	114	116	117	119	121	121	76	77	78	79	80	80	81
10	90th	110	112	113	115	117	118	119	73	74	74	75	76	77	78
	95th	114	115	117	119	121	122	123	77	78	79	80	80	81	82
11	90th	112	113	115	117	119	120	121	74	74	75	76	77	78	78
	95th	116	117	119	121	123	124	125	78	79	79	80	81	82	83
12	90th	115	116	117	119	121	123	123	75	75	76	77	78	78	79
	95th	119	120	121	123	125	126	127	79	79	80	81	82	83	83
13	90th	117	118	120	122	124	125	126	75	76	76	77	78	79	80
	95th	121	122	124	126	128	129	130	79	80	81	82	83	83	84
14	90th	120	121	123	125	126	128	128	76	76	77	78	79	80	80
	95th	124	125	127	128	130	132	132	80	81	81	82	83	84	85
15	90th	123	124	125	127	129	131	131	77	77	78	79	80	81	81
	95th	127	128	129	131	133	134	135	81	82	83	83	84	85	86
16	90th	125	126	128	130	132	133	134	79	79	80	81	82	82	83
	95th	129	130	132	134	136	137	138	83	83	84	85	86	87	87
17	90th	128	129	131	133	134	136	136	81	81	82	83	84	85	85
	95th	132	133	135	136	138	140	140	85	85	86	87	88	89	89

*Height percentile determined by standard growth curves.
†Blood pressure percentile determined by a single measurement.

The blood pressure check is a routine part of most physical examinations. An estimated 2.7 million children between the ages of six and 17 have high blood pressure.

BLOOD PRESSURE LEVELS FOR THE 90TH AND 95TH PERCENTILES OF BLOOD PRESSURE FOR GIRLS AGE 1 TO 17 YEARS BY PERCENTILES OF HEIGHT

Age	Height Percentiles*→ BP†	Systolic BP (mm Hg)							Diastolic BP (mm Hg)						
		5%	10%	25%	50%	75%	90%	95%	5%	10%	25%	50%	75%	90%	95%
1	90th	97	98	99	100	102	103	104	53	53	53	54	55	56	56
	95th	101	102	103	104	105	107	107	57	57	57	58	59	60	60
2	90th	99	99	100	102	103	104	105	57	57	58	58	59	60	61
	95th	102	103	104	105	107	108	109	61	61	62	62	63	64	65
3	90th	100	100	102	103	104	105	106	61	61	61	62	63	63	64
	95th	104	104	105	107	108	109	110	65	65	65	66	67	67	68
4	90th	101	102	103	104	106	107	108	63	63	64	65	65	66	67
	95th	105	106	107	108	109	111	111	67	67	68	69	69	70	71
5	90th	103	103	104	106	107	108	109	65	66	66	67	68	68	69
	95th	107	107	108	110	111	112	113	69	70	70	71	72	72	73
6	90th	104	105	106	107	109	110	111	67	67	68	69	69	70	71
	95th	108	109	110	111	112	114	114	71	71	72	73	73	74	75
7	90th	106	107	108	109	110	112	112	69	69	69	70	71	72	72
	95th	110	110	112	113	114	115	116	73	73	73	74	75	76	76
8	90th	108	109	110	111	112	113	114	70	70	71	71	72	73	74
	95th	112	112	113	115	116	117	118	74	74	75	75	76	77	78
9	90th	110	110	112	113	114	115	116	71	72	72	73	74	74	75
	95th	114	114	115	117	118	119	120	75	76	76	77	78	78	79
10	90th	112	112	114	115	116	117	118	73	73	73	74	75	76	76
	95th	116	116	117	119	120	121	122	77	77	77	78	79	80	80
11	90th	114	114	116	117	118	119	120	74	74	75	75	76	77	77
	95th	118	118	119	121	122	123	124	78	78	79	79	80	81	81
12	90th	116	116	118	119	120	121	122	75	75	76	76	77	78	78
	95th	120	120	121	123	124	125	126	79	79	8C	80	81	82	82
13	90th	118	118	119	121	122	123	124	76	76	77	78	78	79	80
	95th	121	122	123	125	126	127	128	80	80	81	82	82	83	84
14	90th	119	120	121	122	124	125	126	77	77	78	79	79	80	81
	95th	123	124	125	126	128	129	130	81	81	82	83	83	84	85
15	90th	121	121	122	124	125	126	127	78	78	79	79	80	81	82
	95th	124	125	126	128	129	130	131	82	82	83	83	84	85	86
16	90th	122	122	123	125	126	127	128	79	79	79	80	81	82	82
	95th	125	126	127	128	130	131	132	83	83	83	84	85	86	86
17	90th	122	123	124	125	126	128	128	79	79	79	80	81	82	82
	95th	126	126	127	129	130	131	132	83	83	83	84	85	86	86

*Height percentile determined by standard growth curves.
†Blood pressure percentile determined by a single measurement.

Hypoglycemia

Abnormally low levels of glucose in the blood.

Hypoglycemia, or insulin shock, is brought on by abnormally low levels of glucose in the blood. The condition is common among individuals with **diabetes mellitus** who are administering their own insulin injections. An inadequate diet, minor illnesses, or excessive activity without adequate sustenance can contribute to the condition. If unchecked, hypoglycemia can lead to unconsciousness. In very rare cases, the victim may suffer a **seizure.**

A hypoglycemic child will appear irritable, sweaty, shaky, and confused and may complain of being very hungry. In most cases, a snack will remedy the situation quickly. A child who is **vomiting** or unable to retain liquids needs immediate medical attention.

Hypoglycemia can occur repeatedly in diabetic children whose insulin dosage is too high. While rare in non-diabetic children, hypoglycemia occasionally occurs when a child's diet is abnormally high in carbohydrates. Teenagers who follow fad diets or lose weight too quickly can experience episodes of hypoglycemia. Hypoglycemia can often be prevented if children eat five or six high protein meals and snacks a day.

For Further Study

Books

Saunders, Jeraldine, and Harvey M. Ross. *Hypoglycemia: The Disease Your Doctor Won't Treat.* New York: Pinnacle Books, 1980.

Service, F. John, ed. *Hypoglycemic Disorders: Pathogenesis, Diagnosis, and Treatment.* Boston: G.K. Hall, 1983.

Slap, Gail B., and Martha M. Jablow. *Teenage Health Care.* New York: Pocket Books, 1994.

Weller, Charles, and Brian Richard Boylan. *How to Live with Hypoglycemia.* Garden City, NY: Doubleday, 1968.

Hypoxia

Lack of oxygen to the brain.

When the cells of the **brain** receive little or no oxygen, irreversible damage is often the result. Hypoxia is the term applied to oxygen starvation of the brain; when the lack of oxygen is more generalized in the whole body, the term **anoxia** is used. Hypoxia may affect the **fetus** prior to **birth**, or may occur during the birth process itself. Premature separation of the placenta is one of the primary reasons for the oxygen supply to be cut off to a fetus during birth. Hypoxia is believed to be a contributing factor in **cerebral palsy** and other developmental disorders.

Idiot Savant *see* **Savant Syndrome**

Imaginary Playmate

Companion created by imagination or daydreaming.

An imaginary playmate is a friend or companion created by the child in his imagination or daydreams. Imaginary playmates are common during the preschool years: experts estimate that about half of all children create such a playmate. By the early elementary school years at around age six, most imaginary playmates disappear from the child's imagination.

The type of interaction the child engages in with his or her imaginary playmate varies. The playmate generally has a name and a clear identity. Parents and teachers do not need to discourage children from playing with imaginary friends, if they have them. The imaginary playmate relationship nurtures the child's imagination and can provide practice of social skills.

John Caldeira and his colleagues conducted a study to examine the relationships between children's play with imaginary playmates, children's general **creativity** and positive social interaction, and television viewing patterns at home. The activities of 141 three- and four-year-olds were observed and rated eight times over one year by trained observers. According to parents' reports, 55% of the children in the study had imaginary playmates at home. The researchers found that the children with imaginary playmates at home were more likely to engage in imaginative play in school. They were also more likely to demonstrate positive affect, social interaction, cooperativeness, and greater use of verbal skills. Boys who did not have imaginary playmates at home were more likely to demonstrate aggressive behavior. The parents who reported that their children did not have an imaginary playmate also reported that their child watched television more frequently.

For Further Study

Periodicals

Caldeira, John, et al. "Imaginary Playmates: Some Relationships to Pre-Schoolers' Spontaneous Play, Language, and Television-Viewing." ERIC document ED 174303.

Cassidy, Anne. "The Power of Pretend Friends." *Working Mother* 18, October 1995, pp. 92+.

Epstein, Robert. "The Creative Spark." *Working Mother* 17, February 1994, pp. 58+.

Levine, Karen. "Telling Tales: What Your Child's Never-Ending Stories Say About His Inner Life." *Parents Magazine* 71, October 1996, p. 139.

Immune System

The body's defenses against the microorganisms that cause disease.

The immune system provides the human body with protection from the microorganisms that cause disease. Traditionally scientists viewed the immune system as a defensive network that protected the "self" from infectious "non-self" invaders. In the mid-1990s, some immunologists modified this view of the immune system, creating a new model of the body's immune system that is able to discriminate between beneficial "non-self" invaders (food or helpful bacteria) and threatening invaders. One of the leading scientists investigating the functioning of the immune system in the 1990s was Polly Matzinger of the National Institute of Allergy and Infectious Diseases in Bethesda, Maryland. Matzinger proposed a model of the immune system that responds to invaders only when cells of the body are injured or damaged.

No matter what model is used, immunologists generally agree that the immune systems consists of three lines of defense. The first line is made up of the physical barriers—the skin and mucous membranes—that prevent microorganisms from entering the body. The next line of defense, the innate or non-specific immunity, features responses from cells that surround and digest invaders, and from chemicals like histamine and serum proteins that help to destroy bacteria. The final defense is slower acting but more specific to the invader. This specific immunity calls into action the lymphocytes or white blood cells produced by the thymus and bone marrow.

The human body is constantly bombarded with microorganisms, including viruses (such as those that cause colds and influenza), bacteria (such as those that cause pneumonia and food poisoning), parasites, and fungi. The immune system efficiently wages a daily battle to rid the body of harmful organisms. When the immune system is unable to function because of injury or damage, the consequences are severe. For instance, Acquired Immune Deficiency Syndrome (AIDS) is caused by a virus—human immunodeficiency virus (HIV)—that attacks a key immune system cell, the helper T-cell lymphocyte. Without these cells, the immune system cannot fight off the harmful microorganisms. Eventually, the person succumbs to infections that a healthy immune system would effortlessly neutralize.

Organs of the immune system

The organs of the immune system either make the cells that participate in the immune response or act as sites for immune function. These organs include the lymphatic vessels, lymph nodes, tonsils, thymus, Peyer's patches, and spleen. Lymphatic fluid (or lymph) circulates through the lymph nodes via the lymphatic vessels. The lymph nodes are small aggregations of tissues located throughout the lymphatic system. White blood cells (lymphocytes) that function in the immune response are concentrated in the lymph nodes where foreign cells of microorganisms are detected and overpowered.

The tonsils and Peyer's patches contain large numbers of lymphocytes. Located at the back of the throat and under the tongue (tonsils) and in the small intestine and appendix (Peyer's patches), these organs filter out potentially harmful bacteria that may enter the body via the nose, mouth, and digestive system.

The thymus gland, located within the upper chest region, weighs about 15 grams or one-half ounce at birth. It continues to grow until, by the time the child has reached age 12, the thymus has roughly doubled in size. During childhood, the thymus makes large numbers of the lymphocytes known as T-lymphocytes or T-cells. Around puberty, T-cell production is taken over by the lymph nodes and spleen, and the thymus begins to shrink. By adulthood, it is sometimes impossible to detect in x rays. Prior to **puberty**, removal of the thymus due to disease or injury in a child may have a negative effect on both physical growth and the development of immunity to certain organisms.

Bone marrow, found within the interior of bones, also produces lymphocytes that migrate out of the bone marrow to other sites in the body. Because bone marrow is an integral part of the immune system, certain bone **cancer** treatments that require the destruction of bone marrow are extremely risky, because without bone marrow, a person cannot make lymphocytes. People undergoing bone marrow replacement must be kept in strict isolation to prevent exposure to viruses or bacteria.

The spleen destroys worn-out red blood cells and acts as a reservoir for blood. Any rupture to the spleen can cause dangerous internal bleeding, a potentially fatal condition. The spleen also contains lymphatic tissue and produces lymphocytes.

Overview of the immune system

For the immune system to work properly, two things must happen: first, the body must recognize that it is being threatened by foreign microorganisms. Second, the immune response must be quickly activated before many body tissue cells are destroyed by the invaders.

Barriers: skin and mucous membranes

The skin and mucous membranes act as effective barriers against harmful invaders. The surface of the skin is slightly acidic which makes it difficult for many microorganisms to survive. In addition, the enzyme lysozyme, present in sweat, tears, and saliva, kills many bacteria. Mucous membranes line many of the body's entrances, such as those that open into the respiratory, digestive, and uro-genital tract. Bacteria become trapped in the thick mucous layers and are thus prevented from entering the body.

In the upper respiratory tract, the hairs that line the nose also trap bacteria. Any bacteria that are inhaled deeper into the respiratory tract are swept back out again by the cilia—tiny hairs—that line the trachea and bronchii. One reason why smokers are more susceptible to respiratory infections is that hot cigarette smoke disables the cilia, slowing the movement of mucus and bacteria out of the respiratory tract.

Non-specific immune defenses

Non-specific lymphocytes carry out "search and destroy" missions within the body. If these cells encounter a foreign microorganism, they will either engulf the foreign invader or destroy the invader with enzymes. The following are non-specific lymphocytes:

Macrophages are large lymphocytes that engulf foreign cells. Because macrophages ingest other cells, they are also called phagocytes (*phagein*, to eat + *kytos*, cell).

Neutrophils are cells that migrate to areas where bacteria have invaded, such as entrances created by cuts in the skin. Neutrophils digest microorganisms and release microorganism-killing enzymes. Neutrophils die quickly; pus is an accumulation of dead neutrophils.

Natural killer cells kill body cells infected with viruses by punching a hole in the cell membrane, causing the cell to lyse, or break apart.

Fever response is a non-specific response to bacterial or viral invasion. The body responds by increasing its internal temperature, creating conditions that are hostile to the growth of the virus or bacteria.

The inflammatory response is an immune response confined to a small area. When a finger is cut, the area becomes inflamed—red, swollen, and warm. These signs are evidence of the inflammatory response. Injured tissues send out signals to immune system cells, which quickly migrate to the injured area. These immune cells perform different functions: some engulf bacteria, others release bacteria-killing chemicals. Other immune cells release a substance called histamine, which causes blood vessels to become wider (dilate), thus increasing blood flow to the area. All of these activities promote healing in the injured tissue.

When the body's immune system reacts to pollen (a harmless substance) as if it were a bacterium, an immune response is prompted. Histamine is released which dilates blood vessels, causes large amounts of mucus to be produced, and stimulates the release of tears. To combat these reactions, many people take antihistamines, drugs that deactivate histamine.

Specific immune defenses

The specific immune response is activated when microorganisms survive or get past the non-specific defenses. Two types of specific defenses destroy microorganisms in the human body: the cell-mediated response and the antibody response. The cell-mediated response attacks cells which have been infected by viruses. The antibody response attacks both "free" viruses that haven't yet penetrated cells and bacteria. Most bacteria do not infect cells, although some do, such as the *Mycobacteria* that cause **tuberculosis**. The specific immune response depends on the ability of the immune lymphocytes to identify the invader and create immune cells that specifically mark the invader for destruction. Bone marrow produces an amazing array of lymphocytes, each of which is capable of recognizing one specific molecular shape called an antigen.

Two kinds of lymphocytes operate in the specific immune response: T lymphocytes and B lymphocytes, (T lymphocytes are made in the thymus gland, while B lymphocytes are made in bone marrow). B and T lymphocytes are individually configured to attack a specific antigen. For example, the blood and lymph of humans have T-cell lymphocytes that specifically target the chicken pox virus, T-cell lymphocytes that target the

diphtheria virus, and so on. When T-cell lymphocytes specific for the chicken pox virus encounter a body cell infected with this virus, the T-cell multiplies rapidly and destroys the invading virus.

After the invader has been neutralized, some T cells remain behind. These cells, called memory cells, impart immunity to future attacks by the virus. Once a person has had **chicken pox**, memory cells quickly stave off subsequent infections. This secondary immune response, involving memory cells, is much faster than the primary immune response. When a human is immunized against a disease, the vaccination injects whole or parts of killed viruses or bacteria into the bloodstream, prompting memory cells to be made without a person developing the disease.

Helper T cells are a subset of T-cell lymphocytes present in large numbers in the blood and lymphatic system, lymph nodes, and Peyer's patches. When one of the body's macrophage cells ingests a foreign invader, it displays the antigen on its membrane surface. These antigen-displaying-macrophages, or APCs, are the immune system's distress signal. When a helper T cell encounters an APC, it immediately binds to the antigen on the macrophage. This binding unleashes several powerful chemicals called cytokines. Some cytokines stimulate the growth and division of T cells, while others play a role in the fever response. Still another cytokine, called interleukin II, stimulates the division of cytotoxic T cells, key components of the cell-mediated response. The binding also "turns on" the antibody response. Any disease, such as HIV, that destroys helper T cells destroys the immune system.

Antibodies are made when a B cell specific for the invading antigen is stimulated to divide. The dividing B cells, called plasma cells, secrete antibodies composed of a special type of protein called immunoglobin (Ig).

T cells

T-cell lymphocytes are the primary players in the cell-mediated response. When an antigen-specific helper T cell is activated, the cell multiplies. The cells produced from this division are called cytotoxic T cells. Cytotoxic T cells target and kill cells that have been infected with a specific microorganism. After the infection has subsided, a few memory T cells persist, so conferring immunity.

Chemical signals activate the immune response; likewise, chemical signals must turn it off. When all the invading microorganisms have been neutralized, special T cells (called suppressor T cells) release cytokines that deactivate the cytotoxic T cells and the plasma cells, and the cells of the body return to normal functioning.

Immune system disorders

Sudden Infant Death Syndrome

In 1994, researchers reported in the medical journal *The Lancet* that abnormal immune response in the respiratory system may contribute to **sudden infant death syndrome (SIDS)**. Two to three times as many T-lymphocytes were found in lungs of children who died from SIDS that in those who died from other causes. In addition, the number of B-lymphocytes appears to be higher in SIDS infants than in others.

The World Resources Institute in Washington, DC, issued a report in 1996 linking the increased exposure to chemical pesticides in the environment and immune system disorders. Developing nations are at the greatest risk, since they often do not regulate pesticide use. The Institute cited the former Soviet republic of Moldova, where, from 1960 to the late 1980s, pesticides were used in concentrations nearly 20 times the average used elsewhere in the world. Eighty percent of children known to have been exposed to the pesticides appear to have irregularities in their immune systems. Because the interpretation of the study results is difficult, more research is needed.

For Further Study

Books

Almonte, Paul. *The Immune System.* Crestwood House; Maxwell Macmillan Canada; Macmillan International, 1991.

Cook, Allan R. *Immune System Disorders Sourcebook: Basic Information for the Layperson.* Detroit, MI: Omnigraphics, 1996.

Edelson, Edward. *The Immune System.* New York: Chelsea House, 1989.

Schindler, Lydia Woods. *The Immune System: How It Works.* Bethesda, MD: U. S. National Institutes of Health, 1993.

Periodicals

Engelhard, Victor H. "How Cells Process Antigens." *Scientific American* 271, August 1994, p. 54.

Kedzierski, Marie. "Vaccines and Immunisation (sic)." *New Scientist* 133, February 8, 1992, p. S1.

Kisielow, Pavelrod. "Self-Nonself Discrimination by T Cells." *Science* 248, June 15, 1990, p. 1369.

Miller, Jacques. "The Thymus: Maestro of the Immune System." *BioEssays* 16, July 1994, p. 509.

Radesky, Peter. "Of Parasites and Pollens." *Discover* 14, September 1993, p. 54.

"Special Issue: Life, Death, and the Immune System." *Scientific American* 269, September 1993.

Strange, Carolyn. "Rethinking Immunity." *BioScience* 45, November 1995, pp. 663+.

Travis, John. "Tracing the Immune System's Evolutionary History." *Science* 261, July 9, 1993, p. 164.

▮ Immunization

Vaccine administered, usually to a baby or child, to prevent infection with a specific serious illness.

People are given immunizations to protect them from serious illnesses. The vaccines used in immunization are actually weakened doses of the organism that causes the disease. These organisms trigger the person's own **immune system** to produce antibodies against the disease. In this way, if the person ever comes into contact with the disease, his body will be prepared to fight it. Immunization schedules vary widely from country to country. In the Unites States, the **American Academy of Pediatrics (AAP)** issues recommendations for immunization of babies and young children. Eight major childhood diseases are covered by this schedule: polio, measles, **mumps,** German measles **(rubella),** whooping cough (pertussis), **diphtheria,** tetanus (lockjaw), and **meningitis** and other haemophilus infections. Although in most developed countries these diseases are not very common, any one of them could cause disability or death. Immunizations should be taken seriously. Children traveling to other countries should be immunized according to the recommendations of public health officials familiar with the country the child will be visiting. All families should maintain records, signed by a doctor, regarding their schedule of immunizations. The Childhood Vaccine Injury Act was passed in 1986 to provide compensation to families for injury or death related to complications from immunizations.

DTP Vaccine

The DTP vaccine, immunizing against diphtheria (D), tetanus or lockjaw (T), and pertussis or whooping cough (P), is given in five injections, usually in the buttocks, upper thigh, or upper arm. The DTP vaccine is recommended for almost all young children. All 50 U.S. states require that children be immunized against diphtheria before entering school; nearly all require immunization against tetanus, and roughly 35 require immunization against pertussis. The first three doses are given at two, four, and six months of age. The next two are given at around 18 months and between four and six years of age, usually before the child enters school. If a child has ever experienced a **seizure,** the **pediatrician** may administer only the diphtheria and tetanus portions of the vaccine.

Side effects. Some infants experience mild side effects, such as a low-grade fever (less than 102°F or 38.9°C), irritability, listlessness, and redness and sensitivity in the area where the injection was given. These symptoms may be treated with acetaminophen, but should not be treated with aspirin. About one child in every 100–1,000 receiving the DTP vaccine may experience more serious side effects, such as constant crying for more than three hours, high **fever** (105°F or 40.6°C), or high-pitched, scream-like crying. Even more rare (about one for every 1,750 cases) are seizure (jerking, staring episode, usually associated with high fever) or collapse (limp, pale, and unresponsive). A pediatrician should be notified immediately if a baby or child exhibits any symptoms beyond the mild side effects after receiving the DTP vaccine. Although there has been some controversy about the DTP vaccine because of the side effects, the American Academy of Pediatrics strongly recommends this immunization for most children on the grounds that the benefits far outweigh the slight risk.

Related vaccines include DTaP (diphtheria, tetanus acellular, pertussis) vaccine, which is less likely to cause even the mild side effects of DTP and may be used for the 4th or 5th doses of DTP immunization; and DT (diphtheria tetanus) vaccine, which does not provide immunization against pertussis, and is not recommended for most healthy children.

MMR vaccine

The MMR vaccine, immunizing against mumps, measles (rubeola), and German measles (rubella), was licensed by the Food and Drug Administration in the United States in 1971. It is normally administered at about 15 months of age.

Side effects. Most children do not experience side effects from the MMR vaccine. Occasionally, beginning seven to ten days after the immunization, the child may have one or more of these reactions: mild skin rash, slight swelling of the lymph nodes in the neck or groin, low-grade fever (less than 102°F or 38.0°C), sleepiness, or slight pain in the joints. One special note about side effects, however, is that eggs are used in the manufacture of the MMR vaccine, and the pediatrician should be aware of any allergic reaction to eggs the child may have exhibited prior to the administration of the vaccine.

Polio vaccine

Polio (poliomyelitis) is a disease caused by a virus. In mild cases, the person will experience fever, sore throat, nausea, and pain and stiffness in the spine and legs. In more severe cases, known as paralytic polio, the disease can cause paralysis of some muscles of the body and can cause death in its most serious cases. Fortunately, the incidence of polio has become rare since vaccines became widely available in the 1950s. The most common vaccine in use in the late 1990s was developed by Albert Bruce Sabin in the late 1950s. It is the oral, live-virus vaccine, referred to as Oral Polio Vaccine (OPS) or Sabin oral vaccine. OPV is given in four doses, at two and four months of age, between six and eighteen months, and be-

tween four and six years of age. (A fifth dose may be prescribed if the child lives in or is traveling to a country where polio is more prevalent than it is in the United States.) The advantages of OPV are that it provides a strong, permanent immunity to polio, and can be painlessly administered orally.

Side effects. The oral, live-virus vaccine is, as its name implies, a live virus. Therefore, the polio virus will be present in the infant's or child's stools for several days after the vaccine is given. A nonimmunized individual coming into contact with the stool could be infected. If a parent of **caregiver** is not immunized against polio, the pediatrician should be informed before the vaccine is given. Other individuals who could be susceptible to the live virus include anyone with a compromised immune system such as children with **leukemia,** those being treated with long-term steroids, receiving treatment for any kind of **cancer,** or those infected with HIV. In these cases, inactivated polio virus (IPV) is the safe choice for immunization against polio.

The OPV was not the first vaccine to be developed against polio. An alternative, the inactivated polio vaccine or IPV, was developed by Jonas Salk and was first available to the public in 1954. The IPV is given by injection in the leg or arm, rather than administered orally, and provides less vigorous immunity than the OPV.

Side effects: Individuals who are allergic to the drugs neomycin or streptomycin should not receive IPV. Pregnant women can safely receive either OPV or IPV.

Haemophilus influenzae type B conjugate vaccine

The *Haemophilus influenzae* type B (HiB) conjugate vaccine provides immunity to bacterial infections cause by the *Haemophilus influenzae* B bacteria. Examples of these infections are meningitis and epiglottitis.

Hepatitis B virus vaccine

The hepatitis B vaccine provides immunity against the hepatitis B virus (HBV) which can cause serious illness, especially chronic liver disease. Immunization for infants and young children is important because early infection with HBV greatly increases the likelihood that the virus will cause liver failure in adulthood. All mothers are tested for HBV at the time of giving birth. Babies whose mothers test positive for HBV must receive the first dose of vaccine at or immediately after birth. In addition, those babies receive a dose of hepatitis B immune globulin (HBIG), and receive the other two recommended doses of vaccine on an accelerated schedule.

Side effects. No serious adverse reactions are linked to the hepatitis B vaccine. The mild effects that may occur include fussiness, soreness, swelling, or redness at the site of the injection. These symptoms, when they oc-

RECOMMENDED IMMUNIZATION SCHEDULE FOR INFANTS AND CHILDREN

Age	Recommended immunizations
4 months	Diphtheria, tetanus, and pertussis (DTP) Polio (OPV or IPV) Hepatitis B (HBV) *Haemophilus influenzae* type B (HiB) (1)
6 months	Diphtheria, tetanus, and pertussis (DTP) Hepatitis B (HBV) *Haemophilus influenzae* type B (HiB)
12–15 months	*Haemophilus influenzae* type B (HiB) Tuberculosis test (2)
12–18 months	Diphtheria, tetanus, and pertussis (DTP) Polio (OPV or IPV) Varicella zoster (chicken pox) vaccine (VZV)
15 months	Measles, mumps, and rubella (MMR) vaccine Hepatitis B (HBV)
4–6 years	Diphtheria, tetanus, and pertussis (DTP) Polio (OPV or IPV) Measles, mumps, and rubella (MMR) vaccine (3)
12–14 years	Varicella zoster (chicken pox) vaccine (VZV) (4)
14–16 years	Tetanus-diphtheria booster (5)

Notes:

(1) Three HiB (*Haemophilus influenzae* type B) conjugate vaccines have been licensed in the United States for use with infants. There are slight variations in the recommended sequence of immunizations.

(2) In the United States, no routine immunization for tuberculoses is recommended. All children are tested for tuberculoses with a skin-prick test on the forearm, often through the schools. Children with positive skin test results are investigated further to determine whether treatment is required.

(3) The second MMR vaccine is recommended at either 4–6 years or 11–12 years; however, it may be administered anytime, provided one month has elapsed since the administration of the first dose.

(4) Children who have not been vaccinated previously and who lack a reliable history of chicken pox should be vaccinated by age 13. VZV can be administered anytime after 12 months of age; children under 13 years receive a single dose; persons 13 and older should receive two doses administered 4–8 weeks apart.

(5) Lifelong immunization to tetanus and diphtheria requires inoculations—so-called "booster shots"—of vaccine theoretically every 10 years. In practice, only the tetanus booster is routinely given because the risk of contracting tetanus is significant enough to warrant it. Diphtheria has been nearly eradicated in the United States, so boosters are only prescribed in communities where cases of diphtheria have been reported.

Adapted from *Recommended Childhood Immunization Schedule, United States, January–June 1997,* approved by the Advisory Committee on Immunization Practices (ACIPT), American Academy of Pediatrics (AAP), and the American Academy of Family Physicians (AAFP).

cur, begin within 24 hours of receiving the vaccine and are gone with 48–72 hours.

Varicella zoster (chicken pox) vaccine (VZV)

The varicella zoster vaccine to protect children against the common childhood disease known as chicken pox was approved for use in the United States in the early 1990s. It was tested in Japan in the 1970s, and in the United States during the 1980s in over 9,400 healthy children and 1,600 adults. The VZV is 70–90% effective in preventing chicken pox. If a vaccinated child does contract chicken pox, his or her case will be generally mild, with fewer skin lesions (15–30), a lower fever, and quicker recovery. Vaccinated children who get chicken pox are contagious, and can infect others with the disease. As of the mid-1990s, a booster for the VZV is not recommended, but studies were underway to determine how long immunity from the vaccine lasts.

Side effects. Most children experience only mild side effects from this vaccine. These include redness, tenderness, swelling, or a mild rash of several small pimples where the injection was given; tiredness, fussiness, mild fever, and nausea. The rash or pimples may also appear elsewhere on the body, and can occur up to one month after the injection was given. The VZV can be given at the same time as other recommended childhood vaccines, including DTP, polio, hepatitis B, and *Haemophilus influenzae* type B. It can also be given at the same time as the MMR vaccine. If the VZV and MMR are not given together, however, there should be at least a one-month interval between the two vaccines.

Other vaccines may be recommended for specific situations, and the pediatrician's advice should be sought and followed. Travel to tropical countries may require immunization for one or more diseases, such as cholera, typhoid fever, and yellow fever. Side effects from these vaccines are more severe than for the routine immunizations of childhood, and must be weighed against the necessity of the travel. Certain children with special needs may also be given the vaccines against influenza, pneumoccus, and **rabies.**

For Further Study

Books

Bellet, Paul S. *The Diagnostic Approach to Common Symptoms and Signs in Infants, Children, and Adolescents.* New York: Lea and Febiger, 1989.

Garwood, John, and Amanda Bennett. *Your Child's Symptoms.* New York: Berkeley Books, 1995.

Organizations

American Academy of Pediatrics, Division of Publications
  Address: 141 Northwest Point Blvd., P. O. Box 927
  Elk Grove Village, IL 60009-0927
  (Publishes brochures on most immunizations and childhood diseases, and a 24-page booklet for parents that includes forms for tracking immunizations and other health-related information.)

National Institute of Allergy and Infectious Diseases (NIAID)
  Address: 9000 Rockville Pike
  NIH Building 31, Room 7A50
  Bethesda, MD 20892-2520
  (Arm of the National Institutes of Health that deals with allergies and diseases.)

National Vaccine Information Center
  Address: 128 Branch Road
  Vienna, VA 22180
  (Organization also known as Dissatisfied Parents Together [DPT]. Comprised of parents whose children have had adverse reactions to vaccines, particularly to the DTP vac-

cine. Publishes *DPT News, Parent Information Packet,* and *The Compensation System* and *How It Works.*)

Impulse Control Disorders

A psychological disorder characterized by the repeated inability to refrain from performing a particular action that is harmful either to oneself or others.

Impulse control disorders are thought to have both neurological and environmental causes and are known to be exacerbated by stress. Some mental health professionals regard several of these disorders, such as compulsive gambling or shopping, as addictions. In impulse control disorder, the impulse action is typically preceded by feelings of tension and excitement and followed by a sense of relief and gratification, often—but not always—accompanied by **guilt** or remorse. Researchers have discovered a link between the control of impulses and the neurotransmitter serotonin, a chemical agent secreted by nerve cells in the brain. Selective serotonin reuptake inhibitors (SSRIs), medications such as Prozac that are used to treat **depression** and other disorders, have been effective in the treatment of impulse control disorders. The **American Psychiatric Association** describes several impulse control disorders: **pyromania, trichotillomania** (compulsive hair-pulling), intermittent explosive disorder, **kleptomania, pathological gambling,** and other impulse-control disorders not otherwise specified. The first three of these disorders are known to affect children and/or adolescents.

Pyromania involves the repeated setting of fires for no specific reason (such as sabotage or revenge). Rather, the pyromaniac is someone who tends to have a fascination with fire itself, often expressed as an interest in firefighters and their procedures and equipment. It is not uncommon for a pyromaniac to set a fire, report it himself, and then watch as firefighters put it out, even offering to assist them. Pyromania can occur in a child as young as age three, although it is rare at any age and even rarer in childhood. While children and adolescents account for over 40% of those arrested for arson in the United States, only a small percent of fires set by young people indicate the presence of pyromania. Juvenile fire-setting is usually attributed to more generalized conditions characterized by a broad range of impulsive and/or antisocial behavior, such as **conduct** or **adjustment disorders** or **attention deficit/ hyperactivity disorder** (ADHD).

Of those persons diagnosed with pyromania, the vast majority—some 90%—are male. Pyromaniacs have feelings of sadness and loneliness that eventually give way to rage, for which setting fires serves as an outlet. Some researchers have linked pyromania to victims of **child** abuse. Persons affected by this disorder often suffer from other behavioral problems and also tend to have **learning disabilities** and attention disorders. Often, children who set fires also have a history of cruelty to animals. Some common biological characteristics have been discovered in pyromaniacs, including abnormalities in the levels of the neurotransmitters norepinephrine and serotonin, which may be related to problems with impulse control, and low blood sugar levels.

Pyromania has responded to behavioral treatment designed to increase a person's awareness of the emotions that lead up to a fire-setting episode and provide alternate ways of dealing with them. Often this type of therapy is followed by a more psychodynamically oriented approach that deals with the deeper underlying problems that arouse the negative emotions associated with the disorder. **Family therapy** has been particularly successful with children, as have community-based intervention programs, some of which have the youngsters spend some time with firefighters who can serve as positive role models and help build their **self-esteem**. Selective serotonin reuptake inhibitors (SSRIs) are also used to treat pyromania. Childhood pyromania responds well to treatment and is eradicated in about 95% of children who demonstrate signs of the disorder.

Trichotillomania is the name given to compulsive hair-pulling not caused by any other condition, such as **schizophrenia**. In children, it occurs equally among males and females; in adults, it is much more common in females. Statistics on the incidence of trichotillomania are scant, for most people affected by it do not seek professional help. However, a well-documented survey taken on a college campus found between 1–2% of students affected by this disorder, with the incidence in females as high as 3.4%, more than twice that in males. Another study found trichotillomania to be about one-fifth as prevalent as nail-biting, a habit practiced by 20% of Americans, which would place the incidence of trichotillomania at 4% of the population. The primary ages of onset are between 5–8 years of age and 13. Many young children exhibit harmless hair-pulling (often in conjunction with **thumb-sucking**) that stops by the age of six. However, some continue to revert to this habit in times of stress, a tendency that can eventually lead to trichotillomania. In some individuals the condition is episodic, while in others it continues steadily for long periods of time.

In trichotillomania, hair is most often pulled from the scalp, resulting in bald patches, but it can also be pulled from the eyebrows, eyelashes, beard, torso, armpits, or pubic area. The hair may be pulled in short repeated episodes or for hours at a time. Hair-pulling is often accompanied by other actions, including chewing on or swallowing the pulled hair, called tricophagia. Trichotillomania has been associated with **depression**, anxiety, and **obsessive-compulsive disorder** (OCD), but it is still recognized as a disorder distinct from these conditions. It has been linked neurologically to distinctive patterns of glucose metabolization and is thought to have a genetic component. Effective drug treatments include selective SSRIs (particularly Prozac), lithium, and SSRIs in combination with the drug pimozide (Orap), which affect the brain chemical dopamine. **Psychotherapy** has proven more effective in children with the condition than in adolescents or adults. In some cases, hypnosis is used to break the habit and explore any underlying emotional problem that may be at its root.

Intermittent explosive disorder was only recently recognized as an impulse-control disorder. It is characterized by violent and aggressive outbursts of temper that are significantly disproportionate to the events that trigger them. These outbursts often result in property damage and/or personal injury. Occurring mostly in teenagers and young adults, it is four times as common in men as in women and appears to have a genetic component, as evidenced by multigenerational family histories of violence. The outbursts of temper that characterize intermittent explosive disorder, like the symptoms of other impulse control disorders, are often followed by feelings of relief and eventual remorse. Treatment consists of both therapy and medication. Antipsychotic drugs, anticonvulsants, beta-blockers, lithium, and benzodiazepines have all shown to alleviate the symptoms of this disorder.

A condition not listed by the American Psychiatric Association that some experts consider an impulse-control disorder is repetitive self-mutilation, in which people intentionally harm themselves by cutting, burning, or scratching their bodies. Other forms of repetitive self-mutilation include sticking oneself with needles, punching or slapping the face, and swallowing harmful substances. Self-mutilation tends to occur in persons who have suffered traumas early in life, such as sexual abuse or the death of a parent, and often has its onset at times of unusual stress. In many cases, the triggering event is a perceived rejection by a parent or romantic interest. Characteristics commonly seen in persons with this disorder include perfectionism, dissatisfaction with one's physical appearance, and difficulty controlling and expressing emotions. It is often seen in conjunction with schizophrenia, post-traumatic stress syndrome, and various personality disorders. Usual onset is late childhood or early adolescence; it is more frequent in females than in males.

Those who consider self-mutilation an impulse control disorder do so because, like the other conditions that fall into this category, it is a habitual, harmful activity. Victims often claim that it is accompanied by feelings of excitement, and that it reduces or relieves negative feelings such as tension, anger, anxiety, depression, and loneliness. They also describe it as addictive. Self-mutilating behavior may occur in episodes, with periods of remission, or may be continuous over a number of years. Repetitive self-mutilation often worsens over time, resulting in increasingly serious forms of injury that may culminate in suicide. Treatment includes both psychotherapy and medication. The SSRI Clomipramine (Anafranil), often used to treat obsessive-compulsive disorder, has also been found effective in treating repetitive self-mutilation. Behavioral therapy can teach persons with this disorder certain techniques they can use to block the impulse to harm themselves, such as spending more time in public places (because self-mutilating behavior is almost always practiced secretly), using music to alter the mental state that leads to self-mutilation, and wearing protective garments to prevent or lessen injury. In-depth psychodynamic therapy can help persons with the disorder express the feelings that lead them to harm themselves.

For Further Study

Books

Gaynor, Jessica, and Chris Hatcher. *The Psychology of Child Firesetting: Detection and Intervention.* New York: Bruner/Mazel, 1987.

Koziol, Leonard F., Chris E. Stout, and Douglas H. Ruben, eds. *Handbook of Childhood Impulse Disorders and ADHD: Theory and Practice.* Springfield, IL: C.C. Thomas, 1993.

Rider, Anthony Olen. *The Firesetter: A Psychological Profile.* Washington, D.C.: Federal Bureau of Investigation, U.S. Department of Justice, 1984.

Stein, D. J., ed. *Impulsivity and Aggression.* Chichester, NY: Wiley, 1995.

In Loco Parentis

Latin, translated "in place of the parents."

In loco parentis is a term used in situations where another individual or agency is acting in place of a parent on behalf of a minor. The term is used in legal settings to assign the rights, duties, and responsibilities of a parent to another person or agency. Alternatively, the term has been used in less formal references to describe the role played by an educational institution, such as a boarding school, college, or university, in supervising minors and young adults.

In Vitro Fertilization

Laboratory procedure in which an egg is fertilized by sperm in a specimen dish outside the woman's body.

In vitro fertilization (IVF) is a medical procedure that combines a human egg (ovum) and **sperm** in a laboratory dish to increase the possibility of conception. Two days after successful fertilization, the fertilized egg or embryo is placed in the woman's uterus, where it remains for a normal pregnancy and **birth**. Louise Brown became the first "test-tube baby" conceived using this procedure when she was born in England on July 25, 1978. Since then about 100,000 successful births have resulted from in vitro fertilization, but the procedure still has a relatively low success rate. When measured by the number of pregnancies achieved by the number of egg retrieval attempts, the overall IVF success in the United States is about 18%. (In other words, 18 pregnancies can be expected from 100 attempted egg retrievals.)

The procedure

In vitro fertilization consists of four distinct steps. In the first step, the woman receives daily injected doses of **hormones** to stimulate the ovaries to produce multiple eggs. The effect of the hormone doses on maturation of the eggs is monitored closely for about two weeks by the fertility clinic through blood tests and ultrasound tests of the ovaries. If the woman's body has responded by producing several mature eggs, she and her partner prepare for the next step: removal of the eggs from the ovary. (Research has shown that the success rate of in vitro fertilization can be improved by fertilizing three or four eggs. A woman's normal monthly cycle produces just one egg.)

Exactly 36 hours before egg retrieval, the woman receives an injection of the hormone human chorionic gonadotropin (HCG) to prepare her body for pregnancy. Following egg retrieval, she will receive daily injections of progesterone for about two weeks to further prepare her uterus for pregnancy. The egg retrieval takes place in the clinic. Ultrasound is used to guide a thin, hollow needle into the vagina, through the vaginal wall, and into the ovary. The eggs are sucked, one by one, into the needle.

The next step in the IVF process is fertilization of the eggs in the laboratory. A few hours before egg retrieval, the woman's partner provides the lab with a semen sample. The sperm and eggs are placed together in a laboratory dish.

The final step is the transfer of embyos into the woman's uterus. Two days after retrieval, the eggs are checked for evidence of fertilization. Three or four embryos are transferred into the woman's uterus. Although it is unlikely that all the embryos will survive, twins and triplets occur in about one-third of in vitro fertilization pregnancies. If more than that number of eggs have been successfully fertilized, the couple, together with their doctor, must decide whether to freeze the extra embryos, discard them, make them available for research, or donate them to another infertile couple. Most couples elect to freeze their embryos with the intention of using them in future pregnancy attempts.

In two weeks, a pregnancy test will show whether IVF has been successful. If it has, the couple prepares for a pregnancy that is subject to the same risks of miscarriage and **birth defects** as any pregnancy. If IVF has failed, the couple may choose to repeat the procedure. Most clinics discourage repeating IVF more than four times.

Couples electing IVF know that the odds are against them, and that the procedure is costly, both financially and emotionally. In the mid-1990s, the cost of an IVF procedure was estimated to be $7,500 to $10,000. In many cases, health insurance will not cover this procedure. Physically, the woman must be prepared for some discomfort and the possibility of serious side effects from the massive hormone doses. Both the woman and the man can expect to have their ordinary work and home lives disrupted by the IVF regimen. To help couples cope psychologically, many clinics have therapists on staff. Despite these challenges, about 40,000 infertile couples invest millions of dollars in IVF each year.

Ethical issues

Since 1978, IVF has gained acceptance among physicians, the public, and all major religious groups, and is no longer considered an experimental medical procedure. Troubling ethical issues arise, however, when multiple embryos are produced.

Almost all couples elect to freeze extra embryos. As of the mid-1990s, tens of thousands of frozen embryos existed in the United States alone. Ideally, the couple decides in advance what to do with the embryos in the event of death or divorce. In a few well-publicized cases, however, couples have fought for "custody" of the embryos. The existence of frozen embryos is also troubling for those who believe that these tiny beings deserve some consideration as potential humans. Additionally, it is not uncommon for the couple who elected to store the embryos to lose contact with the clinic once they have completed their fertility treatment. In 1991, a law was passed in the United Kingdom placing a five-year time limit on storage of frozen embyos. Under this law, 3,300 fertilized human eggs were disposed of, having reached their time limit in August 1996.

Multiple embryos transferred into a woman's body, if most or all survive, also force a difficult decision. Carrying more than twins greatly increases the odds of a difficult pregnancy and premature birth. To prevent such outcomes, physicians encourage women carrying three or more fetuses to consider fetal reduction, also known as selective termination. In this procedure, excess fetuses are aborted with a chemical injection. Fetal reduction is usually done prior to the third month of pregnancy.

New scientific breakthroughs involving IVF continue to pose ethical questions. It is possible for an egg donated by one woman to be fertilized by an infertile woman's husband's sperm and implanted into the infertile woman. This procedure challenges common notions of motherhood. Is the mother the woman who gave birth or the woman who contributed the egg? Couples and the health care community will continue to struggle to balance the couple's desire for parenthood with the developing technologies, costs, and ethical issues of fertility treatments.

For Further Study

Books

Silber, Sherman J. *How to Get Pregnant with the New Technology.* New York: Warner Books, 1991.

Periodicals

Adler, Jerry. "Clone Hype." *Newsweek,* November 8, 1993, p. 60.

Gibbs, Wayt, and Tim Beardsley. "Fertile Ground: IVF Researchers Pioneer the Bioethical Frontier." *Scientific American,* February 1994, p. 26.

Grady, Denise. "How to Coax New Life." *Time Special Issue: Frontiers of Medicine* 148, no. 14, Fall 1996, p. 36.

Hopkins, Ellen. "Tales From the Baby Factory." *New York Times Magazine,* March 15, 1992, p. 40.

Lemonick, Michael D. "Sorry, Your Time Is Up: A Controversial British Law Targets 3,000 Human Embryos for Disposal." *Time* 148, no. 8, August 12, 1996, p. 41.

Incest *see* **Child Abuse, Sexual and Emotional**

Inclusive Classrooms

Alternative terms: Inclusion, Mainstreaming

General education settings in which students identified as having disabilities (e.g., learning disabilities; mild/moderate/severe mental retardation; serious emotional disturbance; orthopedically, visually, hearing impaired) are placed to receive instruction for all or part of their educational program.

In 1975, the U.S. Congress passed Public Law 94-142, popularly known as the **Education for All Handicapped Children Act,** that required every school district in the country to insure that students with disabilities are educated alongside their non-disabled peers to the maximum extent appropriate. It decreed that "special" classes or schools be used only when **special education** students cannot achieve satisfactorily in general education settings. This law was reenacted as the Individuals with Disabilities Education Act (IDEA) (PL 101-476) in 1990.

The current inclusion movement that has come to be known as the "Regular Education Initiative" (REI) was triggered by Madeline Will's call for general and special educators to assume a "shared responsibility" for educating children with learning problems. REI proposes more integrated general and special educational systems in order to provide effective and appropriate education to the full range of students in the context of general education classrooms. As a result of the inclusive movement, growing numbers of students with disabilities, especially **learning disabilities,** are being placed at least part-time into regular classrooms.

STEPS FOR EFFECTIVE INCLUSION

The National Information Center for Children and Youth for Disabilities (NICHCY) has identified these steps for effective inclusion:

- Include teachers, parents, and building administrators in planning the inclusion process.

- Train teachers in instructional practices for disabled students.

- Use support professionals (special education teachers, physical therapists, school psychologists, etc.) to assist classroom teachers.

- Change the school curriculum as necessary to accommodate the needs of students with physical and cognitive disabilities.

- Evaluate program results in relation to targeted outcomes.

In 1992, *Oberti v. Board of Education of the Borough of Clementon School District* established that placement in inclusion classrooms can offer substantial benefits and must be considered a right of all students, rather than a privilege for selected children. Based on verdicts reached in two separate cases, the decision to remove a special education student from a general education classroom must be based on evidence that the student cannot be effectively educated in that setting. PL 94-142 requires that the educational program of children with disabilities be determined individually for each child and documented in a written plan called the Individualized Education Program (IEP). Factors used to determine whether a student's IEP should be implemented in general or special education classes include the severity of the child's disability, including potentially disruptive behavior, and whether the costs of providing a student's education in a regular classroom significantly affects the resources of the district to educate other students.

Debate on inclusion

The implementation of inclusion has triggered intense debate among both special and general educators, as well as among parent/student advocacy groups representing children with different disabilities. Proponents of inclusion cite several benefits that can be gained by placing special students in general classrooms. They include increased positive social contact with peers, reduced stigma related to special placements, and exposure to the traditional curriculum. The most adamant inclusion supporters call for "full inclusion," full-time placement of all students with disabilities into general education classrooms, regardless of the severity of the disability. The Association for Persons with Severe Handicaps (TASH) and the Association of Retarded Citizens (ARC) are two advocacy groups that have called for implementation of full inclusion practices.

Concerns about inclusion have been raised by supporters of the special education system and professional and disability advocacy organizations, including the Council for Exceptional Children (CEC), the Learning Disabilities Association of America (LDA), and the Council for Children with Behavior Disorders (CCBD). These groups question the ability of the general education system to meet the needs of the wide range of instructional, emotional, and behavioral needs of all students. General classroom teachers are trained to develop and implement instructional programs for children who fall within the "average" range of abilities. Their preparation does not include substantive training in curriculum modification for low-performing and low-skilled students, or in dealing with the behaviors often displayed by children who are severely emotionally disturbed. Others maintain that many special students primarily need to learn functional life-skills or basic academic skills, rather than informational learning, which is the focus of most general education curricula.

Effective inclusion

While the debate on inclusion continues, the practice of placing disabled students into general education programs continues. Various groups are examining the still scant but growing research on inclusion and have developed some guidelines for schools implementing inclusion programs.

For Further Study

Books

Block, Martin E. *A Teacher's Guide to Including Students With Disabilities in Regular Physical Education.* Baltimore: Brookes, 1994.

Clark, Catherine, Alan Dyson, and Alan Millward, eds. *Towards Inclusive Schools?* New York: Teachers College Press, 1995.

Cook, Ruth E., Annette Tessier, and M. Diane Klein. *Adapting Early Childhood Curricula for Children in Inclusive Settings.* 4th ed. Englewood Cliffs, NJ: Merrill, 1996.

Moore, Lorraine. *Inclusion, A Practical Guide for Parents: Tools to Enhance Your Child's Success in Learning.* Minnetonka, MN: Peytral Publications, 1996.

Westwood, Peter S. *Commonsense Methods for Children with Special Needs: Strategies for the Regular Classroom.* 2nd ed. London; New York: Routledge, 1993.

Wood, Judy W. *Adapting Instruction for Mainstreamed and At-Risk Students.* 2nd ed. New York: Maxwell Macmillan, 1992.

Periodicals

Fuchs, D., and L. Fuchs. "Inclusive Schools Movement and the Radicalization of Special Education Reform." *Exceptional Children* 60, 1994, pp. 294–309.

Katsiyannis, A., G. Conderman, and D. J. Franks. "State Practices on Inclusion: A National Review." *Remedial and Special Education* 16, 1995, pp. 279–87.

Kauffman, J. M. "How to Achieve Radical Reform of Special Education." *Exceptional Children* 60, 1993, pp. 6–16.

Schumm, J. S., and S. Vaughn. "Getting Ready for Inclusion: Is the Stage Set?" *Learning Disabilities Research & Practice* 10, 1995, pp. 169–79.

Will, M. C. "Educating Students with Learning Problems: A Shared Responsibility." *Exceptional Children* 52, 1986, pp. 411–15.

Zigmond, N. "An Exploration of the Meaning and Practice of Special Education in the Context of Full Inclusion of Students with Learning Disabilities." *Journal of Special Education* 29, 1995, pp. 109–15.

Audiovisual Recordings

Facing Inclusion Together. Reston, VA: Council for Exceptional Children, 1993.
   (One 50-minute video depicting collaboration between special educators and classroom teachers.)

Regular Lives. Reston, VA: Council for Exceptional Children, 1990.
   (One 30-minute video narrated by actor Martin Sheen showing the inclusion of students with mental and physical disabilities into regular classrooms.)

Two Faces of Inclusion: The Concept and the Practice. Reston, VA: Council for Exceptional Children, 1993.
   (One 50-minute video presents the inclusion debate.)

Organizations

Council for Exceptional Children (CEC)
   Address: 1920 Association Drive
   Reston, VA 22091-1589
   Telephone: (800) 232-7323

National Center on Educational Restructuring and Inclusion (NCERI)
   Address: Room 1530, Graduate Center CUNY
   33 West 42nd St.
   New York, NY 10036
   Telephone: (212) 642-2656.

The National Information Center for Children and Youth for Disabilities (NICHCY)

   Address: P.O. Box 1492
   Washington, DC 20013
   Telephone: (800) 695-0285

Research on inclusion is being conducted by:
Dr. Naomi Zigmond
   Address: University of Pittsburgh, 4K38Q
   Pittsburgh, PA 15260
Dr. Jeanne Shay Schumm and Dr. Sharon Vaughn
   Address: University of Miami
   P.O. Box 248065
   Coral Gables, FL 33124-2040

—Jan E. Hasbrouck, Ph.D.
Texas A&M University

Inductive Reasoning

Way of thinking that uses comparisons to reach conclusions.

When a child uses inductive thinking or reasoning, he or she engages in the evaluation and comparison of facts to reach a conclusion. Inductive reasoning progresses from observations of individual cases to the development of a generality. (Inductive reasoning, or induction, is often confused with **deductive thinking;** in the latter, general principles or conditions are applied to specific instances or situations.) If a child puts his or her hand into a bag of candy and withdraws three pieces, all of which are red, he or she may conclude that all the candy is red. Inductive reasoning, or induction, is the process by which a general conclusion is reached from evaluating specific observations or situations.

Infant Mortality

The statistical rate of infant death up to the age of one year, expressed as the number of such deaths per 1,000 live births for a specific geographical area over a given time period.

Infant mortality is the incidence of death that occurs in the first year after birth, expressed in relation to every 1,000 live births. Infant mortality is commonly divided into two categories: neonatal deaths (occurring during the first 27 days after birth) and postneonatal deaths (occurring from the age of 28 days to one year). Infant mortality is considered an important indicator of the general level of health for a given population.

Toward the end of the 19th century, before the widespread recognition that bacteria was a major cause of illness, rates of infant mortality throughout the world were much higher than they are today. It was common for 20% or more of all infants in many populations to die before they reached their first birthday, and often mortality rates were even higher for children between the ages of one and five. In the last years of the 19th century, large areas of Russia had an infant mortality rate of nearly 28%. In 1901, the infant mortality rate in England, birthplace of the industrial revolution and capital of a global empire, was 16%. By 1930 the number of infant deaths had declined dramatically in many countries as the causes of infection came to be understood. Most progress up to this point was due to precautions such as hand washing and sterilization of milk rather than to actual medical advances, since **antibiotics** and sulfa drugs—the first medications that were really effective in fighting infection—were not developed until the late 1930s and 1940s. Although data on infant mortality in the developing nations is much less complete than the figures for the developed world, it is clear that the world's poorer countries have made dramatic progress in lowering infant mortality in the 20th century, due in large part to public health programs, especially those that have combated malaria through mosquito control. Availability of medication and **immunization** have also played a major role in improving infant health in developing nations.

In 1993 the infant mortality rate worldwide was 69 deaths per 1,000 live births, according to figures released by the United Nations Population Fund (the U.S. Census Bureau figures are slightly lower). The U.N. also reported an average infant mortality rate for the world's industrialized nations of 12 deaths per 1,000 live births. According to the U.S. Census Bureau's *World Population Profile,* the highest ratio of infant deaths (177 per 1,000 live births) was found in the Western Sahara and the lowest (four per 1,000) in Japan. The 1993 infant mortality rate in the United States was 8.4 per 1,000, ranking it twenty-second among the world's developed nations (a rank it maintained over the following two years, according to preliminary data for 1994 and 1995). The relatively high rate of infant deaths in the U.S. compared to Japan and Western Europe is largely accounted for by high infant mortality rates among low-income minority populations. Overall, the rate of infant mortality for blacks is more than twice that for whites (16.5 per 1,000 as opposed to 6.8 in 1993). In addition to the difference in the mortality figures themselves, the figures for blacks have declined at a disproportionately slower rate than those for whites. In 1950 the infant mortality rate for blacks was 1.6 times as high as that for whites; in 1991 it was 2.2 times as high. The 1993 statistics for infant mortality in the U.S. list the following as the 10 leading causes of death: 1) **birth defects;** 2) **sudden infant death syndrome** (SIDS); 3) respiratory distress syndrome; 4) disorders associated with prematurity and low birth

weight; 5) pregnancy complications that affect newborns; 6) oxygen deprivation, either before or during birth (**hypoxia** and **asphyxia neonatorum,** respectively); 7) infections present during the period of birth; 8) accidents; 9) complications during birth; and 10) pneumonia or influenza. The first four causes collectively accounted for 54% of all infant deaths.

A cluster of interrelated environmental factors is associated with infant mortality in the United States. These include poverty, inadequate prenatal care, cutbacks in federal programs, a high rate of teenage pregnancies, and use of drugs, alcohol, and tobacco during pregnancy. The factor most often cited as responsible for the lower rates of infant mortality in other developed nations is the universal availability of free prenatal and maternal health care. According to the U.S. Department of Health and Human Services, in 1990 only 61% of African American women received prenatal care in the first trimester of pregnancy. Even when free care is available, low-income women often face significant barriers in obtaining it. They may be unable to take time off work for the lengthy waits that clinic visits often require.

The principal way environmental factors such as poor prenatal care affect infant health is through birth weight. Low birth weight—defined as weight under 5.5 pounds—is responsible for 75% of neonatal deaths and 60% of postneonatal deaths. (Advanced medical technology makes it possible to save many more low-birth-weight babies than could have been saved in the past.) In addition to being considered a leading cause of infant mortality in its own right, low birth weight is also associated with the top three other causes—congenital anomalies (birth defects), sudden infant death syndrome, and respiratory distress syndrome. Thirty-one other countries have a lower incidence of low-birth-weight deliveries than that of the United States. Known risk factors for low birth weight are smoking, drug and alcohol consumption during pregnancy, and teen pregnancy. (In Japan, which has the world's lowest rate of infant mortality, under 1% of mothers are teenagers, compared with 13% in the United States.) Other factors thought to be associated with the relatively high levels of low birth weight among infants born in the U.S. include lower levels of social support, including marital support.

For Further Study

Books

Boone, Margaret S. *Capital Crime: Black Infant Mortality in America.* Newbury Park: Sage, 1989.

Institute of Medicine. *Preventing Low Birthweight.* Washington, DC: National Academy of Sciences Press, 1985.

Sears, William. *SIDS: A Parent's Guide to Understanding and Preventing Sudden Infant Death Syndrome.* Boston: Little, Brown, 1995.

Tinker, Anne. G., and Marjorie A. Koblinsky. *Making Motherhood Safe.* Washington, DC: World Bank, 1993.

U.S. Congress, House Select Committee on Hunger. *An Examination of Barriers to Pre- and Postnatal Care for High-Risk Women and Infants.* Washington, DC: Government Printing Office, 1992.

Organizations

National Black Womens' Health Project
   Address: 1237 Abernathy SW
   Atlanta, GA 30310
   Telephone: (404) 758-9590

Women's Health Network
   Address: 1325 G Street NW
   Washington, DC 20005
   Telephone: (202) 347-1140

Information Processing Theory

A strategy for the study of cognitive development.

Information processing theory was developed to help **social learning** theorists and others understand how humans learn and solve problems. In information processing theory, the human being is analogous to a computer. In applying information processing theory to child development, researchers examine the maturation of mental processes to explain changes in problem-solving behavior, decision-making, information gathering and storage, and other cognitive processes.

In 1954, D. E. Broadbent formulated the first information processing theory, known as Broadbent's theory of attention. Broadbent based his theory on research that involved a listening task: subjects in Broadbent's study were presented with pairs of digits, one in each ear, and later asked to recall them. Subjects found it easier to repeat the numbers if they could first list all digits presented to one ear, and then list the digits presented to the other ear. The task of integrating the two lists was much more difficult.

In the early 1980s, information processing pioneer Robert Siegler suggested that children's ability to reason improved with age, and that an older child is able to draw upon a greater variety of mental processes than a younger child.

Information processing theorists liken the sensory input to humans to the input functions of a computer. The processes of thinking—perception, problem solving, and **memory**—are similarly compared to the computer's data reading, data processing, and storage capabilities. The

actions taken by humans are likened to a computer output.

While the computer analogy is limited and limiting, information processing theory has provided a structure for the study of cognitive processes in children.

Inhelder, Bärbel (1913–1997)

Swiss psychologist and educator.

Bärbel Inhelder is permanently linked to **Jean Piaget** as a remarkable instance of scientific collaboration. Inhelder started working with Piaget in the early 1930s; by the 1940s, as she recalled, Piaget told her he needed her "to counter his tendency toward becoming a totally abstract thinker." Piaget never lost sight of his epistemological goals, while Inhelder was much more of a psychologist.

Inhelder was born in 1913 in the German-speaking Swiss city of St. Gall, the only child of cultured parents. In 1932, she moved to Geneva to study at Edouard Claparède's Rosseau Institute. At Piaget's suggestion, she examined children's comprehension of conservation of quantities. The book they published together on the subject in 1941 was the first of many other collaborations. In her dissertation, using conservation tests as diagnostic tools, Inhelder confirmed Piaget's claim that the sequence of developmental stages is invariant, and showed how mentally retarded children were fixated at a certain stage. In exemplary Piagetian fashion, she did not focus on test results alone, but on how subjects arrived at their answers; this allowed her to determine their general cognitive skills as well. In 1943, after finishing her dissertation, Inhelder settled in Geneva for good; she became a professor at Geneva University in 1948, and retired in 1983. She died in 1997.

In the 1950s, after investigating children's conceptions of geometry and probability with Piaget, Inhelder devised a series of clever situations to study the development of inductive reasoning. In one of them, subjects were asked to discover the factors (length, thickness, and so forth) that make metal rods more or less flexible. This work led to the definition of the developmental stage of "formal operations," characterized by the capacity for hypothetico-deductive thinking. This study resulted in two influential books, *The Growth of Logical Thinking from Childhood to Adolescence* (1958) and *The Early Growth of Logic in the Child* (1969). In both, Inhelder conducted the psychological research, while Piaget elaborated logical models for describing mental structures. Inhelder's later work with Piaget and others dealt with mental imagery and memory (both shown to depend on the subject's developmental level), the effects of training on cognitive development, and the impact of malnutrition on early intellectual development. Since the 1970s, Inhelder analyzed problem-solving behavior in children and adolescents, with the goal of understanding their strategies and implicit theories.

Inhelder was the first to use Piagetian tests as a diagnostic tool; today, most test batteries include Piagetian items. She also created several of the most widely replicated experiments of developmental research. By the nature of her thinking, which was more focused than Piaget's on the specifically psychological processes of cognitive development, as well as by her close personal contacts with American researches, Inhelder played a crucial role in turning the Piagetian approach into a mainstream paradigm of cognitive **developmental psychology**.

For Further Study

Books

Inhelder, B. "Autobiography," in G. Lindzey, ed. *A History of Psychology in Autobiography*, vol. 8. Stanford: Stanford University Press, 1989.

———. *The Diagnosis of Reasoning in the Mentally Retarded* [1943]. Trans. W. B. Stephens et al. New York: J. Day, 1968.

Institutionalization/ Institutionalized Children

Children who are cared for in a facility outside their family home, also referred to as residential care.

Institutionalization is the placing of emotionally or physically handicapped children in a therapeutic facility outside of the home. In 1990, the American Public Welfare Association estimated that just over 400,000 children were living in residential care in the United States. However, three-quarters of those children are in **foster care.** Only 16%, or 65,000, are in group homes, residential treatment centers, or psychiatric hospitals. Group homes may have as few as four children; residential treatments may have 100 or more young people housed in groups of 8–12 and supervised by house parents or childcare personnel.

Child welfare experts differ widely on the long-term effects of institutionalization. A shortage of research funds means that little solid evidence exists to support one side or the other. While laws exist to provide out-of-home placement, the legal system often discourages it. Although many improvements have been made in the

quality of residential care, some experts believe that incidence of neglect or below-standard care still exist. Of particular concern is the lack of proper staff training. Fortunately, the traditional training school with a custodial shift-work staff is being replaced by smaller group homes with a family-type atmosphere and a highly skilled staff who live with the young residents.

With an emphasis on rules, chores, schedules, neatness, cleanliness, and order, the best institutional care offers emotionally and physically handicapped children a better chance at life. They can learn new skills, improve behavioral and psychological problems, and develop **self-esteem.** In a protected environment abused children can learn to think of adults as kind and dependable.

In choosing the proper residential treatment, parents should look for these criteria: a nurturing live-in adult staff; a family-style arrangement; low youth-to-adult ratios; high rates of positive interactions between youths and adults; psychologically informed treatment planning; ongoing evaluation and formalized after-care plans. Whenever possible, the child should be involved in his or her assessments.

Physically handicapped children and those with mild emotional or behavior problems benefit from a therapy protocol that minimizes the fact of institutionalization. However, severely disturbed children require a highly controlled environment. Safety is of primary importance so that the children are protected from abuse, drugs, and **suicide** attempts. Opportunities for **running away** must be minimized. Bedroom doors should open into the hallway to prevent barricades.

Institutionalization for emotionally disturbed children and adolescents is usually not meant to provide long-term treatment. The average stay ranges from several months to two years. Physically handicapped children generally remain in residential care until they are able to live on their own, or for the rest of their lives, depending on the severity of the handicap. In any case, the institution should stay in close contact with the child's parents and encourage visitation.

When the child is institutionalized to protect him from abusive parents, it is not unusual for him to enter a mourning period. Regardless of what pain the parents have inflicted, the child will often remain staunchly loyal to them. Social workers and group home parents should not challenge this loyalty in any way. Social service workers often feel angry or resentful towards the abusive parents, which further complicates the worker's mandated goals: reunite the family while protecting the child.

Deciding to place a child in a treatment center is fraught with emotion. Parents may face criticism from friends and other family members. It is helpful to know that hospitalization is necessary when the child becomes a threat to himself or to others.

For Further Study

Books

Ainsworth, Frank, and Leon C. Fulcher, eds. *Group Care for Children: Concept and Issues.* New York: Tavistock, 1981.

Blomquist, Geraldine M. *Coping as a Foster Child.* New York: Rosen Publishing, 1992. [For children]

Periodicals

Ayres, Carole Briggs. "Tough Choice." *The Exceptional Parents* 23, no. 4, p. 24, April–May 1993.

Weisman, Mary Lou. "When Parents Are Not in the Best Interests of the Child." *Atlantic Monthly* 274, no. 1, p. 42, July 1994.

Organizations

The Children's Defense Fund
    Address: 25 E Street N.W.
    Washington, DC 20001
    Telephone: (202) 628-8787
Child Welfare League of America
    Address: 440 1st Street N.W., Suite 310
    Washington, DC 20001
    Telephone: (202) 638-2952
    FAX: (202) 638-4004
National Association of Homes and Services for Children
    Address: 1701 K Street N.W., Suite 200
    Washington, DC 20006
    Telephone: (202) 223-3447

Intelligence

A term referring to a variety of mental capabilities, including the ability to reason, plan, solve problems, think abstractly, comprehend complex ideas, learn quickly, and learn from experience.

Throughout the 20th century scientists have debated the nature of intelligence, including its heritability and whether (and to what extent) it exists or is measurable. The 1994 publication of Richard J. Herrnstein and Charles Murray's volume *The Bell Curve* brought these debates to the forefront of public attention by discussing links between social class, race, and IQ scores, despite the fact that many have questioned the validity of IQ tests as a measurement of intelligence or a predictor of achievement and success.

Although the assessment of mental abilities through standardized testing has had many detractors, especially over the past 30 years, the notion that intellect is a measurable entity—also called the psychometric approach—lies at the heart of much modern theorizing about the nature of intelligence. A rudimentary forerunner to 20th-century intelligence testing was developed in the 1860s by Charles Darwin's younger cousin, Sir Francis Galton, who, inspired by *On the Origin of Species,* set out to prove that intelligence was inherited, using quantitative studies of prominent individuals and their families. Galton's work was followed in 1905 by that of French psychologist **Alfred Binet,** who introduced the concept of mental age, which would match chronological age in children of average ability. It would exceed chronological age in bright children and would be below in those of lesser ability. Binet's test was introduced to the United States in a modified form in 1916, and with it the concept of the **intelligence quotient** (mental age divided by chronological age and multiplied by 100).

In the meantime, one of the central concepts of the psychometric approach to intelligence had been introduced in England in 1904 by Charles Spearman, who had noted that people who perform well on one type of intelligence test tend to do well on others also. Spearman gave a name to the general mental ability that carried over from one type of cognitive testing to another—*g* for general intelligence—and ultimately decided that it consisted mainly of the ability to infer relationships based on one's experiences. Although the concept of *g* has the disadvantage of being based solely on a particular statistical analysis rather than direct observation, it has remained an important part of psychometric research.

Psychometrics is still considered by many to be a valid scientific area of inquiry, but it has been challenged by researchers who approach intelligence in different ways. Instead of studying the structure of intelligence (i.e., what it is) some scientists have focused on the processes involved (how it works). A leader in this information-processing approach is Robert Sternberg, whose triarchic theory of intelligence not only addresses internal thought processes but also explores how an individual uses them to solve problems within his or her environment. The first part of Sternberg's theory, like psychometric theories, is concerned with the internal components of intelligence, although its emphasis is on process rather than structure. It analyzes the processes involved in interpreting sensory stimuli, storing and retrieving information in short- and long-term memory, solving problems, and acquiring new skills. The second part of the triarchic theory addresses the interaction between mental processes and experience, centering on the fact that, while a new experience requires complex mental responses, as it becomes increasingly familiar, the required response gradually becomes routine and automatic. In the third part of his theory, Sternberg analyzes the way that people use their intelligence to survive in the "real world" by either adapting to their environments, modifying them, or abandoning them in favor of new ones.

Another approach is Howard Gardner's theory of multiple intelligences, which replaces the general intelligence factor (*g*) with seven different types of intelligence: linguistic; logical-mathematical; spatial; interpersonal (ability to deal with other people); intrapersonal (insight into oneself); musical; and bodily-kinaesthetic (athletic ability). According to Gardner, each of these areas of competence includes a separate set of problem-solving skills that can be mobilized by various symbolic systems. Every person has all the different types of intelligence, although some may be developed far more fully than others. (The most dramatic example of this is found in **savants,** mentally retarded people with exceptional abilities in a few highly specialized areas, usually involving calculations.)

Gardner regards his theory as radical in its rejection of *g* and in its reliance on psychometric premises. He claims that *g* (a purported general intelligence factor enabling people to perform fairly consistently on different types of mental tests) is an artificial construct made possible by the fact that standard IQ tests assess only the first three of the seven types of intelligence, ignoring the others. He also argues that IQ tests can predict school performance only because formal education emphasizes those abilities measured by the tests, rather than truly assessing all aspects of human intelligence. In recent years, Gardner's theory has become popular among educators, and a number of schools have instituted programs based on his ideas.

Another focus for recent studies of intelligence has been the evolutionary development of the **brain.** Scientists with this research orientation are interested in the ways that human mental capacities developed over hundreds of thousands of years or more in response to changing problem-solving challenges in the environment. From this perspective, the *g* factor of the psychometricians could be viewed as a specialized ability that has evolved in response to our expanded exposure to tests of all kinds rather than an innate ability that enables us to deal with them. An evolutionary perspective on the phenomenon of similar performance in a variety of cognitive tests might also take into account the selective pairing of cognitively matched couples that has resulted from the modern freedom to marry for love, producing children whose abilities are more and more likely to be uniformly high or low across a series of different cognitive tasks.

For Further Study

Books

Eysenck, H. J. *The IQ Argument: Race, Intelligence, and Education.* Library Press, 1971.

Fraser, Steven. *The Bell Curve Wars: Race, Intelligence, and the Future of America.* New York: Basic Books, 1995.

Gardner, Howard. *Frames of Mind: The Theory of Multiple Intelligences.* New York: Basic Books, 1983.

Goleman, Daniel. *Emotional Intelligence.* New York: Bantam, 1995.

Herrnstein, Richard J., and Charles Murray. *The Bell Curve: Intelligence and Class Structure in American Life.* New York: Free Press, 1994.

Kline, Paul. *Intelligence: The Psychometric View.* London: Routledge, 1991.

Sternberg, R. J. *Beyond IQ: A Triarchic Theory of Human Intelligence.* Cambridge, Eng.: Cambridge University Press, 1985.

Intelligence Quotient (IQ)

A measurement of intelligence based on standardized test scores.

Although IQ tests are still widely used in the United States, there has been increasing doubt voiced about their ability to measure the mental capacities that determine success in life. IQ testing has also been criticized for being biased with regard to race and gender. In modern times, the first scientist to test mental ability was **Alfred Binet,** a French psychologist who devised an intelligence test for children in 1905, based on the idea that **intelligence** could be expressed in terms of age. Binet created the concept of "mental age," according to which the test performance of a child of average intelligence would match his or her age, while a gifted child's performance would be on par with that of an older child, and a slow learner's abilities would be equal to those of a younger child. Binet's test was introduced to the United States in a modified form in 1916 by Lewis Terman. The scoring system of the new test, devised by German psychologist William Stern, consisted of dividing a child's mental age by his or her chronological age and multiplying the quotient by 100 to arrive at an "intelligence quotient" (which would equal 100 in a person of average ability).

The **Wechsler Intelligence Scales,** developed in 1949 by David Wechsler, addressed an issue that still provokes criticism of IQ tests today: the fact that there are different types of intelligence. The Wechsler scales replaced the single mental-age score with a verbal scale and a performance scale for nonverbal skills to address each test taker's individual combination of strengths and weaknesses. The **Stanford-Binet** and Wechsler tests (in updated versions) remain the most widely administered IQ tests in the United States. Average performance at each age level is still assigned a score of 100, but today's scores are calculated solely by comparison with the performance of others in the same age group rather than test takers of various ages. Among the general population, scores cluster around 100 and gradually decrease in either direction, in a pattern known as the normal distribution (or "bell") curve.

Although IQ scores are good predictors of academic achievement in elementary and secondary school, the correspondence between IQ and academic performance is less consistent at higher levels of education, and many have questioned the ability of IQ tests to predict success later in life. The tests don't measure many of the qualities necessary for achievement in the world of work, such as persistence, self-confidence, motivation, and interpersonal skills, or the ability to set priorities and to allocate one's time and effort efficiently. In addition, the **creativity** and intuition responsible for great achievements in both science and the arts are not reflected by IQ tests. For example, creativity often involves the ability to envision multiple solutions to a problem (a trait educators call **divergent thinking**); in contrast, IQ tests require the choice of a single answer or solution to a problem, a type of task that could penalize highly creative people.

The value of IQ tests has also been called into question by recent theories that define intelligence in ways that transcend the boundaries of tests chiefly designed to measure abstract reasoning and verbal comprehension. For example, Robert Steinberg's triarchical model addresses not only internal thought processes but also how they operate in relation to past experience and to the external environment. Harvard University psychologist Howard Gardner has posited a theory of multiple intelligences that includes seven different types of intelligence: linguistic and logical-mathematical (the types measured by IQ tests); spatial; interpersonal (ability to deal with other people); intrapersonal (insight into oneself); musical; and bodily-kinaesthetic (athletic ability).

Critics have also questioned whether IQ tests are a fair or valid way of assessing intelligence in members of ethnic and cultural minorities. Early in the 20th century, IQ tests were used to screen foreign immigrants to the United States; roughly 80% of Eastern European immigrants tested during the World War I era were declared "feeble-minded," even though the tests discriminated against them in terms of language skills and cultural knowledge of the United States. The relationship between IQ and race became an inflammatory issue with the publication of the article "How Much Can We Boost IQ and Scholastic Achievement?" by educational psychologist Arthur Jensen in *the Harvard Educational Review* in 1969. Flying in the face of prevailing belief in the effects of environmental factors on intelligence, Jensen argued that the effectiveness of the government social programs of the 1960's War on Poverty had been limited because the children they had been intended to help had relatively low IQs, a situation that could not be remedied by government intervention. Jensen was widely censured for his views, and standardized testing un-

derwent a period of criticism within the educational establishment, as the National Education Association called for a moratorium on testing and major school systems attempted to limit or even abandon publicly administered standardized tests. Another milestone in the public controversy over testing was the 1981 publication of Stephen Jay Gould's best-selling *The Mismeasure of Man,* which critiqued IQ tests as well as the entire concept of measurable intelligence.

Many still claim that IQ tests are unfair to members of minority groups because they are based on the vocabulary, customs, and values of the mainstream, or dominant, culture. Some observers have cited cultural bias in testing to explain the fact that, on average, African-Americans and Hispanic-Americans score 12–15 points lower than European-Americans on IQ tests. (Asian-Americans, however, score an average of four to six points higher than European-Americans.) A new round of controversy was ignited with the 1994 publication of *The Bell Curve* by Richard Herrnstein and Charles Murray, who explore the relationship between IQ, race, and pervasive social problems such as unemployment, crime, and illegitimacy. Given the proliferation of recent theories about the nature of intelligence, many psychologists have disagreed with Herrnstein and Murray's central assumptions that intelligence is measurable by IQ tests, that it is genetically based, and that a person's IQ essentially remains unchanged over time. From a sociopolitical viewpoint, the book's critics have taken issue with *The Bell Curve*'s use of arguments about the genetic nature of intelligence to cast doubt on the power of government to remedy many of the nation's most pressing social problems.

Yet another topic for debate has arisen with the discovery that IQ scores in the world's developed countries—especially scores related to mazes and puzzles—have risen dramatically since the introduction of IQ tests early in the century. Scores in the United States have risen an average of 24 points since 1918, scores in Britain have climbed 27 points since 1942, and comparable figures have been reported throughout Western Europe, as well in Canada, Japan, Israel, Australia, and other parts of the developed world. This phenomenon—named the Flynn effect for the New Zealand researcher who first noticed it—raises important questions about intelligence testing. It has implications for the debate over the relative importance of heredity and environment in determining IQ, since experts agree that such a large difference in test scores in so short a time cannot be explained by genetic changes.

A variety of environmental factors have been cited as possible explanations for the Flynn effect, including expanded opportunities for formal education that have given children throughout the world more and earlier exposure to some types of questions they are likely to encounter on an IQ test (although IQ gains in areas such as mathematics and vocabulary, which are most directly linked to formal schooling, have been more modest than those in nonverbal areas). For children in the United States in the 1970s and 1980s, exposure to printed texts and electronic technology—from cereal boxes to video games—has been cited as an explanation for improved familiarity with the types of maze and puzzle questions that have generated the greatest score changes. Improved mastery of spatial relations has also been linked to video games. Other environmental factors mentioned in connection with the Flynn effect include improved nutrition and changes in parenting styles.

For Further Study

Books

Bridge, R. Gary. *The Determinants of Educational Outcomes: The Impact of Families, Peers, Teachers, and Schools.* Cambridge, MA: Ballinger Publishing Co., 1979.

Eysenck, H. J. *The Intelligence Controversy.* New York: Wiley, 1981.

Fraser, Steven. *The Bell Curve Wars: Race, Intelligence, and the Future of America.* New York: Basic Books, 1995.

Herrnstein, Richard J., and Charles Murray. *The Bell Curve: Intelligence and Class Structure in American Life.* New York: Free Press, 1994.

Kline, Paul. *Intelligence: The Psychometric View.* London: Routledge, 1991.

Sternberg, R. J. *Beyond IQ: A Triarchic Theory of Human Intelligence.* Cambridge, Eng.: Cambridge University Press, 1985.

Intermittent Explosive Disorder

Uncontrollable episodes of aggression, where the person loses control and assaults others or destroys property.

Persons with this disorder experience episodes of aggressive or violent behavior that result in assault of a person or animal or the destruction of property. These intense episodes occur spontaneously, not in response to provocation or threat, and individuals often express regret as soon as the episode ends. Usually he or she does not exhibit aggressive tendencies between episodes. This disorder can appear at any age, but is more common in adolescence through the 20s, and is more common in males. This disorder is believed to be rare, and reliable statistics on the frequency of occurrence are not available.

See **Impulse Control Disorders.**

Introversion

A commonly used term for adults or children who are quiet, reserved, thoughtful, and self-reliant and who tend to prefer solitary work and leisure activities.

Individuals who are quiet, reserved, thoughtful, and self-reliant are often referred to as "introverts." They are likely to prefer solitary work and leisure activities. In comparison with extroverts, who draw most of their energy from social interaction and respond to external stimuli immediately and directly, introverts tend to mull things over before formulating a reaction, and their energy is regenerated by time spent alone.

Carl Jung was the first psychologist to use the terms *introversion* and *extroversion*, which literally mean "inward turning" and "outward turning." More recently, researchers in the field of personality, most notably Hans Eysenck, have popularized these terms. Eysenck claims a biological basis for introversion and **extroversion**, rooted in differences in sensitivity to physical and emotional stimulation. Eysenck claims that introverts are more sensitive to cortical arousal and thus more likely to be overwhelmed by external stimuli while extroverts, who are less sensitive to arousal, are more likely to actually seek out additional stimuli. Eysenck also created a system of personality types combining introversion and extroversion with degrees of emotionality and stability to arrive at four types corresponding to the classical four **temperaments** first delineated by Hippocrates. These types (together with Eysenck's formulations) are melancholic (emotional and introverted); phlegmatic (stable and introverted); choleric (emotional and extroverted); and sanguine (stable and extroverted).

Introversion is observable even in early childhood. An introverted child is able to entertain herself alone for extended periods of time, while extroverts need company most of the time. When it comes to socializing, introverts are likely to focus their attention on only one or a few best friends rather than a larger social group. Like introverted adults, children who are introverts like to "look before they leap," observing situations before they are ready to participate, and thinking things over before they speak. They are independent, introspective thinkers, turning inward to formulate their own ideas about things. They are more likely than extroverts to act differently in public than they do at home because they feel less at ease among strangers. They prefer to concentrate on a single activity at a time and dislike interruptions. On an emotional level, they are likely to become absorbed by their own emotions and pay less attention to those of the people around them. They may also be more reluctant than extroverted children to talk about their feelings.

The personality traits that characterize introversion overlap at several points with those often seen in gifted children, such as independence of thought, the ability to spend extended periods of time absorbed in solitary pursuits, and heightened sensitivity to social interactions. The association between introversion and **giftedness** has been reinforced by the findings of Dr. Linda Silverman at Denver University's Gifted Child Development Center, who found that an unusually high percentage of introverted children are gifted.

Although introversion and extroversion are observable, documented personality tendencies, people generally do not conform completely to either description. This fact is reflected, for example, in the Myers-Briggs Type Indicator, which treats introversion and extroversion as two ends of a continuum, with most people falling somewhere in between. Some scores come out very close to either end, while others are virtually at the half-way mark. However, it is possible for Myers-Briggs test results to change over time as people change.

See also **Self-Conscious Emotions; Shyness; Temperament**

For Further Study

Books

Eysenck, Hans J., and Michael Eysenck. *Personality and Individual Differences.* New York: Plenum Press, 1985.

Campbell, Joseph, ed. *The Portable [Carl] Jung.* New York: Viking, 1971.

Kagan, J., and N. Snidman. "Biological Bases of Childhood Shyness." *Science* 240, 1988, pp. 167–171.

Shapiro, Kenneth Joel. *The Experience of Introversion.* Durham, NC: Duke University. Press, 1975.

Invulnerables

Term used to describe children who deal well with adversity.

Invulverables are children who seem to be unaffected by adverse home and socioeconomic environmental conditions in which they live. These children are subjected to family and economic stresses, and yet exhibit remarkable coping skills. Psychologists have frequently targeted this group for study, since the so-called invulnerables provide opportunities to study the psychosocial and parental factors, along with personality characteristics, that enable them to succeed despite adverse home environments. Psychologists have attempted to identify what factors enable these children to succeed despite their seeming lack of support and opportunity. Research-

ers have been more successful in identifying factors that lead to a child's lack of success in school than in identifying those complex personality and environmental factors that contribute to resilience in the face of adversity. Among the factors that appear to contribute to an invulnerable's success is one significant, supportive relationship with an older adolescent or adult.

Iowa Tests of Basic Skills (ITBS)

Measures the development of basic skills needed for academic success.

The Iowa Tests of Basic Skills is one of the most widely administered standardized tests measuring the development of basic skills needed for academic success. It can be used to identify individual strengths and weaknesses, monitor a student's progress from year to year, and aid in evaluating the effectiveness of classroom instruction. ITBS is available in several alternate forms on 10 levels covering grades K–9. It is one of the tests often chosen to fulfill state or locally mandated testing requirements. Areas covered include vocabulary, **reading,** language, spelling, capitalization, punctuation, usage, work and study skills, use of visual and reference materials, mathematical concepts, problem solving, computation, and, in some cases, listening, work analysis, science, and social studies. Test scores are reported in a number of different forms, including grade equivalents, standard scores, local and national norms, and even specially normed scores for Catholic or private schools or certain socioeconomic brackets. Some forms of the ITBS include tests of the ability to read maps and interpret graphs. There is also a version of the Iowa test for students in grades 9–12, the Iowa Tests of Educational Development (ITED). These emphasize more complex material and more advanced skills, including critical analysis, comprehension of scientific material, distinguishing between different literary styles, and using common informational tools.

For Further Study

Books

Hart, Diane. *Authentic Assessment: A Handbook for Educators.* Menlo Park, CA: Addison-Wesley Pub. Co., 1994.

McCullough, Virginia. *Testing and Your Child: What You Should Know About 150 of the Most Common Medical, Educational, and Psychological Tests.* New York: Plume, 1992.

Jaundice

Refers to the yellowing of skin, sclera (white of eyes), mucous membranes, and of body fluids such as urine and blood plasma.

Jaundice is caused by excess bilirubin in the blood stream. The skin, sclera (whites of the eyes), mucous membranes, urine, and blood plasma have a yellowish cast when a person has jaundice. Jaundice is not a disease, but a symptom of an underlying disease or condition.

Most bilirubin, which is a reddish pigment, is a byproduct of red blood cells. When a red blood cell dies after a lifespan of about 120 days, its components are either recycled for other uses or discarded by the body as waste. During this process, the **liver** combines bilirubin with another chemical to make it water soluble and discards it into the bile. The bile is then transported by the intestine out of the body.

There are several ways in which a person can become jaundiced. The most common is obstruction of bile flow through the biliary system. For example, a gallstone, a liver tumor, or a pancreatic tumor can block a biliary duct. Hemolytic jaundice occurs when the liver is overloaded with bilirubin due to **anemia**, incompatible **blood** transfusion, or extreme heat or cold. Liver cells that are damaged by hepatocellular disease (hepatitis, cirrhosis), toxins, tumors, or inflammatory conditions are unable to process bilirubin, thus preventing normal excretion.

Neonatal jaundice, especially in premature infants, is common. In fact, almost all premature infants and two-thirds of full-term babies experience jaundice. Most newborns have a higher concentration of red blood cells than older infants and children. These red blood cells have a shorter lifespan, which leads to a larger amount of bilirubin available to be processed by the liver. The bilirubin accumulates—and the infant's skin yellows—as the immature liver struggles to keep up and develop the capaci-

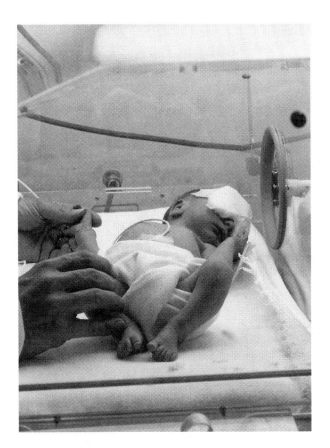

Jaundice in infancy, a common occurrence, is treated with phototherapy, or exposure to light. The infant's eyes are covered during the procedure.

ty to handle it. In addition, some infants develop jaundice because of an incompatibility with the mother's blood.

Jaundice is not considered particularly dangerous for infants. Some physicians advocate no treatment because the liver matures rapidly after birth and the condition usually resolves itself within days. Others believe that, because extremely elevated bilirubin levels can cause kernicterus, an often fatal **brain** disease, treatment is advised. Generally, infants with jaundice are treated with phototherapy, or exposure to light, which causes bilirubin near the skin's surface to decompose and become water soluble without the liver's help. The infant's eyes are covered during the procedure. Extreme cases of neonatal jaundice are treated with exchange transfusion, in which the infant's blood is gradually replaced with unaffected donor blood.

For Further Study

Periodicals

Caglayan, Suat, et al. "Superiority of Oral Agar and Phototherapy Combination in the Treatment of Neonatal Hyperbilirubinemia." *Pediatrics* 92, July 1993, p. 86.

Dennery, Phyllis A., William D. Rhine, and David K. Stevenson. "Neonatal Jaundice–What Now?" *Clinical Pediatrics* 34, February 1995, p. 103.

Dundon, Catherine. "Newborn Jaundice." *American Baby* 57, July 1995, p. 8.

Lazar, Leora, Aviva Litwin, and Paul Merlob. "Phototherapy for Neonatal Nonhemolytic Hyperbilirubinemia...." *Clinical Pediatrics* 32, May 1993, p. 264.

Pellman, Harry. "Newborn Jaundice, or Why It's O.K. to Be Mellow Yellow." *Pediatrics for Parents*, June 1992, p. 4.

Junk Food *see* Nutrition

Juvenile Delinquency *see* Truancy

K

Kaufman Assessment Battery for Children (KABC)

Intelligence and achievement test.

The Kaufman Assessment Battery for Children (KABC) is an **intelligence** and achievement test for children ages 2-1/2 to 12-1/2. It consists of 16 subtests, not all of which are used for every age group. A distinctive feature of the KABC is that it defines intelligence as problem-solving ability rather than knowledge of facts, which it considers achievement. This distinction is evident in the test's division into two parts—intelligence and achievement—which are scored both separately and together. The Mental Processing (or intelligence) portion of the test consists of two series of subtests. Sequential Processing primarily assesses short-term memory and includes number recall, repetition of a sequence ("work order"), and repetition of hand movements. Simultaneous Processing evaluates pattern detection and nonverbal reasoning. Its subtests include completing a drawing ("gestalt closure"); spatial memory (reproducing layout of objects on a grid); placing a series of photos in correct chronological order; and, for younger children, face recognition and "magic window" (identifying a picture through a slit). The KABC Achievement subtests include naming famous people and places from photos; an arithmetic test; riddles; reading letters and single words; acting out a printed command to demonstrate reading comprehension; and (for younger children) naming objects from pictures. Test scores may be converted to competitive rankings (percentiles and age or grade equivalents). The KABC is often used to assess learning disabilities and **mental retardation**, but it can also aid in identifying **giftedness**.

KABC's strong emphasis on **memory** and lesser attention to verbal expression are intended to offset cultural disparities between black and white children. While whites score an average of 15 points higher than blacks on most intelligence tests, the differences on the KABC

for children under 8 amount to less than 2 points on Sequential Processing, 6 on Simultaneous Processing, and 8 on the Achievement section. At later ages, these point differences are 7, 12, and 12 points, respectively. In addition, the test may be given to non-native speakers in their first language and to the hearing impaired using **American Sign Language**.

For Further Study

Books

Gifford, Bernard R., and Mary Catherine O'Connor. (eds.) *Changing Assessments: Alternative Views of Aptitude, Achievement, and Instruction.* Boston: Kluwer Academic Publishers, 1992.

Kingore, Bertie W. *Portfolios: Enriching and Assessing All Students, Identifying the Gifted Grades K-6.* Moines, IA: Leadership Publishers, 1993.

McCullough, Virginia. *Testing and Your Child: What You Should Know About 150 of the Most Common Medical, Educational, and Psychological Tests.* New York: Plume, 1992.

Kibbutz

A type of community in Israel where the residents work cooperatively and share responsibilities, including child-rearing.

A kibbutz is an Israeli rural community in which the residents share equally in the work and profits. Kibbutzim are self-governing under a system of direct participatory democracy. Elected officers are responsible for the day-to-day operations.

When they were first established in the early 1900s, kibbutzim were agricultural collectives. Adults had separate sleeping quarters, but children by and large lived in a communal area and were raised by the group. Now most children live with their parents at least until the age of 13 or 14, when they move into the dormitories.

Today there are more than 200 kibbutzim in Israel, with several hundred members in each. The nature of kibbutzim has changed. Many have privatized their businesses, and hire workers and professionals from the outside. In addition to the traditional farm, many kibbutzim also have factories producing goods from furniture to computer chips to animated films.

Equal education for all is a hallmark of kibbutz life. Although major educational decisions are made by the general assembly, instruction is now conducted by professional teachers, child care workers, and psychologists. Group child care begins early in the kibbutz child's life. The newborn stays with her mother for one to two months and then moves into the babies' house during the day. The mother returns to work on a part-time basis initially so that she can still feed and bathe her infant. However, by the time the child celebrates her first birthday, the mother is working full-time again. Between the ages of three and four, the child enters kindergarten. Many parents visit their young children once or twice during the day.

At the age of six, formal education begins. Although a few kibbutzim still run their own elementary schools, none of them operates an independent high school. In most cases, the children attend a regional consolidated school in which the kibbutz is a partner. The school curriculum is guided by the Israeli Ministry of Education. Kibbutz children spend one day of each school week working on the kibbutz, usually on the children's farm or zoo, occasionally in the kitchen or dining hall. By the time they graduate from high school, each student has achieved proficiency in at least one aspect of kibbutz operations. All Israeli students enter the Army after high school. Men serve for three years; women for two.

When kibbutzim were first established, young adults were expected to return to work the kibbutz after military service. University education was not an option. Over the years, this has changed, primarily due to pressure from the younger generations. Now most kibbutzim provide tuition for a university education after the military requirement has been satisfied. Many kibbutzim also offer adult education opportunities.

Kibbutzim offer short residential programs for under-privileged children and Jewish children living outside Israel. These are usually work-study programs for adolescents that last from two weeks to one year. Participants work on the kibbutz during their stay.

For Further Study

Books

Lavi, Zvi. *Kibbutz Members Study Kibbutz Children*. New York: Greenwood Press, 1990.

Spiro, Melford E. *Children of the Kibbutz*. Cambridge, MA: Harard University Press, 1975.

Organizations

Kibbutz Program Center
Address: 110 East 59th Street, 3rd floor
New York, NY 10022
Telephone: (212) 318-6130
FAX: (212) 832-2597
e-mail: kibbutzdsk@aol.com

The Joint Authority for Jewish Zionist Education
Telephone: 212/339-6081

Young Kibbutz Movement
Address: 27 W. 20th Street
New York, NY 10011
Telephone: (212) 675-1168

Kidney Function and Urological Disorders

Functioning of the body's systems to filter wastes.

The kidneys filter waste materials and excess fluid from the **blood** and also produce hormones that are important for blood formation, blood pressure, and bone formation. Entering the kidneys through the renal artery, blood is processed in tiny tubes called nephrons and returned to circulation through the renal veins. The waste substances that are filtered out are turned into urine, which collects in the central part of the kidney (called the renal pelvis) and passes through the ureters to the bladder. When a half pint or more of urine has collected in the bladder, it is emptied from the body through the urethra.

The kidneys and ureters begin to form when an **embryo** is about four or five weeks old and are complete, in a rudimentary form, by the eighth week. However, they still need to travel to their correct place in the lower back, an activity that occurs throughout the rest of the prenatal period. Urine is produced and excreted before birth, forming part of the amniotic fluid, but it is the mother's placenta that filters out most of the waste products produced by the fetus. Upon birth, the baby's kidneys, which weigh about half an ounce each, have to take over this function on their own.

Most infants urinate for the first time within 24 hours of birth and between 8 and 20 times or more a day after that. Infants' urine generally ranges from clear to pale yellow in color, although foods, vitamins, and even urate (one of the salts contained in the urine) may cause it to change color. The urine of infants under the age of two has practically no odor but then becomes stronger due to higher concentrations of ammonia (especially when it is allowed to collect in a diaper for a while). Children cannot control urination until the sphincter muscles and the nerves at the base of the bladder are sufficiently developed, which does not occur until at least the age of two.

Most children learn to control their bladders during the daytime by the age of three. However, **enuresis** (bedwetting) may occur in a healthy child (especially one who is a sound sleeper) until the age of four or five.

Congenital abnormalities

A number of congenital kidney abnormalities may occur in children, often originating during that part of the prenatal period when the kidneys are moving into their permanent position. Often these defects do not cause symptoms and require no medical attention. Some children are born with only one kidney (renal agenesis), a condition that poses no health threat as long as the remaining kidney stays healthy. An ectopic kidney—one that is in the wrong place—generally functions normally, although it may cause a malformation of the ureter, obstructing the flow of urine. A horseshoe kidney, one of the more common abnormalities, consists of two kidneys that are joined to each other, forming a U-shaped structure that lies lower than the normal position. The joint kidney may or may not act as a single organ. A malrotated kidney is one that faces the wrong direction but still functions properly. Kidneys may also be underdeveloped (hypoplastic) or develop abnormally (dysplastic), conditions that are not necessarily debilitating if they affect only one kidney. With two hypoplastic kidneys, however, renal failure eventually occurs.

Other abnormalities include supernumerary kidneys (two normal kidneys with an extra renal pelvis); multicystic kidney (one kidney filled with cysts, which doesn't function normally and may become cancerous); polycystic kidney (numerous cysts in both kidneys, which become enlarged and fail to function normally); double ureters (two ureters—instead of the normal one—draining one or both kidneys); and ureteropelvic junction obstruction, or UPJ (a narrowing of the place where the renal pelvis and ureter join, blocking the flow of urine to the bladder and usually requiring surgery).

Kidney disorders

Nephrotic syndrome is a disorder that affects the ability of the glomeruli (the kidney's filtering units) to retain protein in the blood. Protein is excreted through the urine, creating a protein deficiency that leads to fluid retention. Symptoms are swelling around the eyes and in the feet and other parts of the body, as well as weight gain from the excess fluid and a dramatic decline in urine output. While this condition often follows an infection or other illness elsewhere in the body, its exact cause is not known. It is treated with steroids, which reduce the amount of protein in the urine (the dosage of these drugs is reduced as soon as possible to avoid potential side effects). Although nephrotic syndrome tends to recur after the initial episode, it disappears by the late teens or before and causes no lasting damage in over three-fourths of the children affected by it.

Nephritis is the general name for inflammation of the kidneys, of which there are several different types. Although they can potentially lead to kidney failure, they are all treatable. Glomerulonephritis, or inflammation of the glomeruli, occurs in both acute and chronic forms. The acute form generally occurs after a bacterial infection, such as streptococcus, when antibodies accumulate in the glomeruli and damage them. Symptoms include blood in the urine, swelling from fluid retention, high blood pressure, headaches, and blurred vision. Although glomerulonephritis usually resolves on its own, it is necessary to monitor the child for high blood pressure, fluid retention, and other potentially dangerous symptoms. Sometimes this monitoring is done in the hospital, where a special high-protein, low-salt diet may also be administered. In addition, kidney failure may occur, requiring temporary dialysis.

In pyelonephritis, unlike glomerulonephritis, the kidneys are directly infected by bacteria that enter from the lower urinary tract. In addition to infections, a variety of disorders can cause nephritis, including lupus and other diseases that weaken the immune system, and reactions to medication. Alport's syndrome, a progressive condition that often leads to kidney failure, is a hereditary disease that results in chronic nephritis due to a genetic defect in the glomeruli. It is often associated with nerve deafness and, in some cases, with eye problems as well.

Other portions of the urinary tract besides the kidneys may become inflamed. Cystitis is a bladder inflammation produced by infection or by other causes, including drugs and radiation. Symptoms include frequent urination, a burning sensation when urinating, and pain in the lower abdomen. When caused by infection, cystitis is treated with **antibiotics**. Urethritis is an inflammation of the urethra, with symptoms similar to those of cystitis.

A kidney tumor known as Wilms' tumor (also called nephroblastoma) is one of the most common forms of childhood **cancer**. It occurs most frequently in children under the age of five (especially under the age of two), but it is also found in adolescents. A hereditary component has been found for this disease, which is also associated with congenital urinary tract and genital deformities, such as undescended testicles. The first sign of the tumor is often a lump in the abdomen or side; symptoms may include blood in the urine, abdominal pain, swelling, loss of appetite, weight loss, and fever. With surgery and chemotherapy, the two-year survival rate for Wilms' tumor is 80% (up dramatically from 33% in the 1960s).

The tumor may spread to other organs, including the lungs and liver, necessitating the removal of additional tissue besides the affected kidney. However, even if the tumor has spread, children usually recover rapidly from surgery for this disease. Since the cancer may recur, children who have had Wilms' tumor need to be monitored carefully following treatment and recovery. Mesoblastic nephroma is another kidney tumor found in children (usually very young infants) and requires removal of the kidney to ensure long-term survival.

Kidney stones, which are most often found in adults, can also occur in children. These usually pebble-sized pieces of crystallized mineral (including phosphates, calcium, urates, or other substances) are often passed out of the body through the urinary tract but sometimes obstruct the flow of urine, damage the kidney, or lodge in the ureters, causing severe pain. They can also trigger infections. Treatment to dissolve the stone depends on its composition, which can be analyzed from a urine sample in which fine grains of the stone are contained. Sometimes surgery is indicated. Another option is removal of the stone with special calipers. Once the nature of the stone is determined, dietary modifications may be recommended to prevent a recurrence.

Kidney failure

Kidney failure—when the kidneys are no longer able to adequately eliminate waste materials from the blood—does not generally happen until the kidneys lose 70% or more of their function, since they normally have considerably more capacity than is needed. In acute kidney (or renal) failure, the kidneys stop functioning suddenly. It usually has a cause other than kidney disease, such as blood loss, dehydration, a drug reaction, or a variety of other serious conditions. Symptoms include decrease in urination, swelling, drowsiness, and irregular heartbeat. Chronic kidney failure, which can be caused by a variety of kidney disorders, occurs gradually. Many types of kidney disease have few symptoms in their early stages, allowing significant deterioration to take place before kidney failure becomes apparent. Often, fatigue is the first symptom of chronic kidney failure, followed by loss of appetite, low urine output, and thirst. Other symptoms include pallor, headaches, nausea, cramps, facial puffiness, and dry or itchy skin. Kidney failure also slows growth and can even stop it altogether. The first measures in treating kidney failure include dietary changes, oral nutritional supplements, and medications that lower the levels of phosphate absorbed into the blood from the intestine. Blood pressure must also be controlled. In most cases, the condition progresses to end-stage renal disease (deterioration to 5–10% of normal capacity), and dialysis or transplantation often becomes necessary.

There are several types of dialysis. Hemodialysis is a means of filtering the blood through a machine—often called an artificial kidney—that performs the functions of a normally working kidney. Blood is pumped from the body into an artificial membrane that performs a filtering operation similar to that of the kidney's own glomeruli while a special dialysis solution, called dialysate, helps regulate the blood's chemical content and remove waste and excess fluids. The patient, who often has a shunt surgically implanted in an arm or leg artery to simplify the connection process, undergoes dialysis sessions two or three times a week in the hospital, at a special dialysis center, or at home with proper medical supervision. Each session lasts about four hours.

Instead of using an external machine, peritoneal dialysis uses the small blood vessels in the membranes of the patient's own peritoneal cavity as a filtering agent for the blood. A catheter is inserted into the abdomen, and a fluid similar to that used for hemolytic dialysis is infused through it, providing the body with needed electrolytes and carrying waste materials with it when it drains. Peritoneal dialysis may be administered several different ways. The intermittent form, which is repeated every hour for 24 to 48 hours, is generally used for acute renal failure that is not expected to require long-term treatment. Continuous ambulatory peritoneal dialysis (CAPD) is performed four or five times a day, and the dialysis fluid is left inside the patient between sessions, for periods of four to six hours. Continuous cycling peritoneal dialysis is performed at night while the child sleeps. During this period, the peritoneal cavity is filled and flushed several times.

A child with end-stage renal failure is also a candidate for a kidney transplant, one of the most successful and frequently performed transplant operations. Although the body has a natural tendency to reject all foreign matter, it is less likely to reject the transplanted kidney if the tissue of the donor closely matches that of the recipient. The most compatible donor organs are those from siblings and parents, in that order. If a kidney from a relative isn't available, transplant centers throughout the country are contacted for a compatible kidney from an accident victim or other recently deceased donor. The operation, which is not a complicated one, takes about four hours, followed by up to six weeks in the hospital. The medication cyclosporine, which suppresses the body's immune system, is commonly taken by transplant recipients, with the dose lowered sharply after the first year following surgery, since an immune system suppressant also impairs the body's ability to fight infections.

The first two years are the most crucial period for acceptance or rejection of the new kidney. A kidney donated by a sibling has a two-year success rate of 90–95%; a kidney transplant from a nonrelative has a success rate between 65 and 80%.

For Further Study

Books

De Wardener, H.E. *The Kidney: An Outline of Normal and Abnormal Function.* New York: Churchill Livingstone, 1985.

National Institutes of Health. *What You Need to Know about Wilms' Tumor.* National Institutes of Health, Public Health Service, U.S. Dept. of Health and Human Services, 1983.

Schrier, Robert W. *Diseases of the Kidney.* 4th ed. Boston: Little, Brown, 1988.

Organizations

American Association of Kidney Patients (AAKP)
Address: 1 Dan's Boulevard, Suite LL1
Tampa, FL 33505
Telephone: (813) 251-0725

American Kidney Fund
Address: 6110 Executive Boulevard, Suite 1010
Rockville, MD 20852
Telephone: toll-free (800) 638-8299

American Urological Association
Address: 1120 North Charles Street
Baltimore, MD 21201
Telephone: (301) 727-1100

National Institute of Diabetes, Digestive, and Kidney Diseases
National Institutes of Health
Address: 9000 Rockville Pike, Building 31, 9A04
Bethesda, MD 20892
Telephone: (301) 496-3583

National Kidney Foundation, Inc.
Address: 30 E. 33rd Street
New York, NY 10016
Telephone: (212) 889-2210

Kleptomania

Overwhelming impulse to steal.

Persons with kleptomania experience a recurring and irresistable urge to steal. They do not steal for the value of the item, for its use, or because they cannot afford the purchase. Stolen items are often thrown or given away, returned, or hidden. Kleptomania can begin at any age, and is reported to be more common among females. Kleptomania is distinguished from deliberate theft or shoplifting, where the individual is motivated by a desire to acquire the item, or to fulfill a dare from peers. Shoplifting is more common than kleptomania; it is estimated that less than 5% of individuals who shoplift exhibit symptoms of kleptomania.

See also **Impulse Control Disorders**

Klinefelter's Syndrome

A condition affecting males that is caused by the presence of extra X chromosomes.

Klinefelter's syndrome, also known as primary micro-orchidism, affects males only. A normal male has one pair of sex chromosomes made up of one X and one Y. In Klinefelter's syndrome, one or more extra X chromosomes are present. (The extra chromosomes identified as Klinefelter's syndrome fall into one of the following categories: 47XXY, 48XXYY, 48XXXY, 49XXXY, or 49 XX/XXY.

Although individuals with Klinefelter's syndrome appear to be more likely to experience learning difficulties, the syndrome often remains undiagnosed. At **puberty**, a boy with more than one extra X chromosome may tend to develop enlarged breasts, a condition that can be treated with medication. In addition, the testes remain very small, and most males with Klinefelter's syndrome produce little or no sperm. In fact, it is during tests for infertility that Klinefelter's is most frequently diagnosed.

For Further Study

Books

Berch, Daniel B., and Bruce G. Bender. *Sex Chromosome Abnormalities and Human Behavior: Psychological Studies.* Boulder: Westview Press, 1990.

Strom, Charles. *Heredity and Ability: How Genetics Affects Your Child and What You Can Do About It.* New York: Plenum Press, 1990.

Therman, Eeva. *Human Chromosomes: Structure, Behavior, and Effects.* New York: Springer-Verlag, 1993.

Knee-Jerk Reflex *see* **Neonatal Reflexes**

Kohlberg's Theory of Moral Reasoning

Theory featuring six stages of moral development advanced by American psychologist Lawrence Kohlberg.

Lawrence Kohlberg (1927–1987), an American psychologist, pioneered the study of **moral development** in the late 1950s. Kohlberg's theory of moral reasoning involved six stages through which each person passes in order, without skipping a stage or reversing their order. His theory states that not all people progress through all six stages.

In the 1950s, science as a whole held to the positivist belief that scientific study should be free of moral values, maintaining instead a purely "objective," value-free stance. Western psychology at that time was dominated by behaviorists who focused on behavior rather than reasoning or will. In 1958, Lawrence Kohlberg published a study that broke with both the positivists and behaviorists by presenting a theory of moral development (bringing together science and moral values) based on cognitive reasoning (rather than behavior). Kohlberg's theory initiated an entirely new field of study in Western science that gained momentum in the 1960s and 1970s and continues to inspire new research today.

Kohlberg's theory of moral development expands upon **Jean Piaget**'s work in the 1930s concerning cognitive reasoning. Piaget proposed three *phases* of **cognitive development** through which people pass in a loose order. In contrast, Kohlberg posited six *stages* (in three levels, with two stages each) of moral development, based on cognitive reasoning, through which each person passes in unvarying and irreversible order. According to Kohlberg, every person begins at Stage 1 moral reasoning and develops progressively to Stage 2, then Stage 3, etc. Not everyone makes it through all six stages; in fact, people who use Stage 5 or 6 moral reasoning are quite rare. Kohlberg claimed that his stages of moral development are universal, applying equally to all human beings across cultural divisions.

In brief, Kohlberg's theory of moral development presents three levels: the preconventional, conventional, and postconventional. Each level contains two stages. Stages 1 and 2 in the preconventional level involve an "egocentric point of view" and a "concrete individualistic perspective" in which the person makes choices based on the fear of **punishment** and the desire for rewards. In Stages 3 and 4 of the conventional level, persons make choices from a "member-of-society" perspective, considering the good of others, the maintenance of positive relations, and the rules of society. Persons in the final stages of the postconventional level, Stages 5 and 6, reason from a "prior-to-society" perspective in which abstract ideals take precedence over particular societal laws.

To measure the level at which persons are operating morally, Kohlberg developed a highly refined interview process in which hypothetical situations are presented that involve a moral dilemma. The person's answers to questions surrounding that dilemma determine the stage at which he or she is reasoning. One of the best-known examples of hypothetical moral dilemmas presented in Kohlberg's interview is that of an impoverished man who needs a certain medicine for his wife who is ill: is the man justified in stealing the medicine from the pharmacy when he does not have enough money to pay for it? Why or why not? The details of the hypothetical situation can then be altered slightly to bring out the nuances of a person's moral reasoning (e.g., does it depend on how ill the wife is, how poor the husband is, whether it is a small,

family-owned corner drugstore or a large, nationwide chain, etc.).

Kohlberg also developed a method of moral education based on an expanded form of the interview process. He believed that participation in moral discussions spurs growth in moral reasoning. The "just community" approach to education that Kohlberg helped create has three basic aims: 1) to encourage moral development through discussions of moral issues; 2) to develop a culture of moral norms through community-building and the democratic establishment of rules; and 3) to create a context where students and teachers can *act* on their moral decisions. Just Community programs were put into effect in a number of public schools, with a fair amount of success (see Power, Higgins, and Kohlberg 1989).

However, there have been many criticisms of Kohlberg's theory of moral development and his methods. Some critics claim that the use of hypothetical situations skews the results because it measures abstract rather than concrete reasoning. When children (and some adults) are presented with situations out of their immediate experience, they turn to rules they have learned from external authorities for answers, rather than to their own internal voice. Therefore, young children base their answers on rules of "right" and "wrong" they have learned from parents and teachers (Stages 1 and 2 according to Kohlberg's theory). If young children are presented with situations familiar to them, on the other hand, they often show care and concern for others, basing their moral choices on the desire to share the good and maintain harmonious relations, placing them in Stage 3 or 4 (which Kohlberg claimed was impossible at their age).

Kohlberg's emphasis on abstract reasoning also creates confusing results in which habitual juvenile delinquents can score at a higher stage of moral development than well-behaved children. Because behaviors are not considered and reasoning is determined through hypothetical situations, children who behave in immoral ways may be able to answer hypothetical moral dilemmas in a more advanced fashion than better-behaved children who think less abstractly. Early criticisms of Kohlberg's lack of attention to behaviors led Kohlberg to add an emphasis on moral action to his Just Community educational program. For those who are looking for concrete help in developing moral values in children, however, Kohlberg's theory is still of little practical use.

Another strong criticism of Kohlberg's theory is that it devalues the morality of care and community. Carol Gilligan was the first to attack this aspect of Kohlberg's theory, relating it to gender differences between men and women (all of Kohlberg's original subjects were male, as was Kohlberg himself). Although Gilligan's critique has weaknesses of its own, her assessment of Kohlberg's theory as incomplete has many supporters, though others relate the absence of communitarian morality to class rather than gender differences.

Kohlberg, as a member of the educated, elite, white, male, Western culture, viewed individual autonomy and justice as the premier moral values. He even went so far as to equate morality with justice (ignoring other moral values such as courage, self-control, empathy, etc.). Members of the working and rural classes, however, tend to have a more communitarian approach to life, viewing the common good as the highest value, promoting care and harmonious relationships over individual justice. (Women, having been relegated to "lower class" status for centuries, may have developed a more communitarian approach to life for that reason, rather than simply because they are female.) Non-Western and tribal societies also frequently see the community as more important than the individual.

According to Kohlberg's upper-class Western view of moral reasoning, communitarian morality is doomed to rest forever at a lower stage of development (Stages 3 and 4). This view disregards the possibility that communitarian morality may be as advanced as individualistic morality, if not more so. It also places Western culture at the top of the scale, with little room for cross-cultural inclusion. Although Kohlberg insisted that his theory was culturally inclusive, he found little empirical evidence to back this up. In all of his interviews, only a few people showed Stage 5 reasoning, and nearly all were well-educated Westerners. Stage 6 reasoning was never substantiated in interviews; Kohlberg created it as an "ideal" and pointed to examples such as Gandhi to support its existence. After a tremendous amount of criticism over the fact that Stage 6 was purely hypothetical, Kohlberg removed it from the empirical stages but retained it as a "theoretical construct in the realm of philosophical speculation." Despite equally heavy criticism, Kohlberg refused to remove Stage 5 from his system.

With all its possible flaws, however, Kohlberg's theory of moral development was the first of its kind and remains the springboard for all subsequent research into moral reasoning. Critiques of Kohlberg's theory have led, and continue to lead, to more expansive and inclusive understandings of the development of moral reasoning. Kohlberg's Just Community program also yielded significant results and led to the ongoing creation of other similar alternative education programs.

For Further Study
Books

Crittenden, Paul. *Learning to Be Moral: Philosophical Thoughts About Moral Development.* New Jersey: Humanities Press International, 1990.

Gilligan, Carol. *In a Different Voice: Psychological Theory and Women's Development.* Cambridge, Massachusetts: Harvard University Press, 1982.

Kohlberg, Lawrence. *Essays on Moral Development, I: The Philosophy of Moral Development: Moral Stages and the Idea of Justice.* San Francisco: Harper & Row, 1981.

———. *Essays on Moral Development, II: The Psychology of Moral Development.* San Francisco: Harper & Row, 1984.

———. *Child Psychology and Childhood Education: A Cognitive-Developmental View.* New York: Longman, 1987.

Kurtines, William M., and Jacob L. Gewirtz, eds. *Moral Development: An Introduction.* Boston: Allyn and Bacon, 1995.

Power, F. C., Ann Higgins, and Lawrence Kohlberg. *Lawrence Kohlberg's Approach to Moral Education: A Study of Three Democratic High Schools.* New York: Columbia University Press, 1989.

Schulman, Michael, and Eva Mekler. *Bringing Up a Moral Child: A New Approach for Teaching Your Child to Be Kind, Just, and Responsible,* rev. ed. New York: Main Street Books/Doubleday, 1994.

—Dianne K. Daeg de Mott

Kohs Block Design Test

Intelligence test.

The Kohs Block Design Test is a cognitive test for children or adults with a mental age between 3 and 19. It is mainly used to test persons with language or hearing handicaps but also given to disadvantaged and non-English-speaking children. The child is shown 17 cards with a variety of colored designs and asked to reproduce them using a set of colored blocks. Performance is based not just on the accuracy of the drawings but also on the examiner's observation of the child's behavior during the test, including such factors as attention level, self-criticism, and adaptive behavior (such as self-help, communication, and social skills). The Kohs Block Design Test is sometimes included in other tests, such as the **Merrill-Palmer** and Arthur Performance scales.

For Further Study

Books

McCullough, Virginia. *Testing and Your Child: What You Should Know About 150 of the Most Common Medical, Educational, and Psychological Tests.* New York: Plume, 1992.

Walsh, W. Bruce, and Nancy E. Betz. *Tests and Assessment.* 2nd ed. Englewood Cliffs, NJ: Prentice Hall, 1990.

L

Lamaze Method *see* **Birth**

Landau's Reflex *see* **Neonatal Reflexes**

Language Acquisition Device (LAD)

Notion that some knowledge about language is built into the brain of the human child.

Learning theorists argue that the environments of young children everywhere are supportive of learning. All young children are surrounded by speech from the beginning: parents and others address remarks to babies, respond to their vocalizations and heap praise on their earliest attempts to say words. People adjust their own speech to accommodate the young child's needs, simplifying their vocabulary, shortening their sentences, and talking about the here-and-now, usually in a special speech "register." This **motherese** or parentese that cues the child that this is talk meant for the child's ears.

There are some theorists who argue that this environmental support gives the child everything necessary to "figure out" the rules of language. In other words, the child is like a miniature linguist, collecting evidence to decide among hypotheses about the grammar. But mathematical linguists have determined that any set of sentences is compatible with an infinite set of possible grammars. In 1968 a startling proof showed that human language is unlearnable in a finite amount of time: there are too many potential rule systems that could have generated the set of sentences a learner has heard at any one time.

One solution is to argue that the child receives accurate corrective feedback about his hypotheses. Under this kind of condition, language would be learnable in a finite time. But evidence for reliable and consistent corrective feedback in the average child's environment is very weak. When it comes to grammar, most parents notice only the superficial mistakes made by their children, and these only when the child is "old enough to know better," e.g., saying *foots* or *comed* when in grade school. Parents do provide some feedback about the clarity or truth of their children's sentences, but studies reveal that adults do not provide reliable feedback on the grammaticality of children's sentences. Explicit correction seems to be too rarely and inconsistently used to "train" the child to speak grammatically.

The alternative solution is to claim that the child has some preconceived ideas, or innate knowledge. Learning language is possible in a finite amount of time if the learner already knows the range of possibilities existing in universal grammar. Linguistic approaches to language acquisition assume that some knowledge about language is built into the human child.

Linguistic theory states that languages are deeply similar in ways that have only just begun to be uncovered. All languages seem to make use of the same small inventory of categories for the construction of sentences: noun phrases, verb phrases, sentences, and the like. In addition, there are principles that seem to be universal and which constrain the forms that sentences can take. Currently many people are persuaded that these facts might be part of the assumptions that the child brings to the language acquisition task. The child may in fact "know" that sentences are built from the abstract categories, and know in advance the principles that dictate that the rules are going to have a limited range of possible forms. These central ideas were introduced by Noam Chomsky in 1965 and have motivated much work on **language development.** Chomsky proposed that children are born with a Language Acquisition Device (LAD) that contains hypotheses that guide their language learning.

To demonstrate the subtlety of the abstract principles on which these arguments depend, consider the following short story:

Once there was a boy who loved climbing trees in the forest. One afternoon he slipped and fell to the ground. He picked himself up and went home. That night when he had a bath, he saw a big bruise on his arm. He said to his dad, "I must have hurt myself when I fell this afternoon."

Now comes the question:

a) *When did the boy say he hurt himself?*

Notice there are two possible answers, either to when he said it, or to when he hurt himself. That is, the "when" question could be connected to the "say" or to "hurt." Research shows that three-year-olds also allow both answers: sometimes giving one, sometimes the other. But now consider the subtle variant:

b) *When did the boy say how he hurt himself?*

Suddenly, the ambiguity is gone, and only one answer seems right: "that night in the bath." Three-year-olds also only give that answer to b). They seem to know already the constraint that question words may not "move" over another question word: a constraint that is embedded in universal grammar.

For a learning theory account to be viable, the two-year-old would have to have the ability to sift through evidence of this subtlety to arrive at the appropriate generalization. The problem that then arises is the rarity of such sentences. In hundreds of hours of recorded conversations between several young children and their **caregivers**, there are typically only a couple of dozen examples, and of course never the close contrasting pairs described above. It does not seem plausible that the child learns the contrasts for himself.

Instead, it is argued, the child is in possession of considerable pre-existing knowledge about the forms that rules can take. There is still considerable scope for learning theories. Even if the starting point is not a "blank slate" but a LAD, the child has to learn the meaning of every word in her language: no one has argued that words are innate! Furthermore, the child has to use the evidence of conversation to make a multitude of choices about the rules of her language (and their irregularities). The doctrine of innate ideas may have a relatively limited role to play except in defining the boundaries within which learning can take place.

For Further Study

Books

Berko-Gleason, J. *The Development of Language.* New York: Macmillan, 1993.

de Villiers, P., and J. de Villiers. *Early Language.* The Developing Child series. Cambridge, Mass.: Harvard University Press, 1979.

Fletcher, P., and B. MacWhinney. *The Handbook of Child Language.* Cambridge, Mass.:Blackwell Publishers, 1995.

Goodluck, H. *Language Acquisition: A Linguistic Introduction.* Cambridge, Mass.: Blackwell Publishers, 1991.

Pinker, S. *The Language Instinct.* New York: Morrow, 1994.

—Jill De Villiers, Ph.D.
Smith College

Language Delay

Term used to describe a problem in acquiring a first language in childhood on a normal schedule.

The milestones of child **language development**—the onset of babbling, first words, first sentences—are quite variable across individuals in a culture, despite the universal similarity in the general ages of their development. In one study of 32 normally developing children at 13 months, the average number of words reported by parents was 12, but the range was 0 to 45. The two-word-sentence stage was reached anywhere from 16 to 28 months in the same sample. In addition, differing styles of language development are now recognized.

Some children fit the classic pattern of first speaking one word "sentences," such as "truck," then joining two words "truck fall," and then three, "my truck fall." But other children speak in long unintelligible babbles that mimic adult speech cadence and rhythm, so the listeners think they are just missing some important pronouncement. The first is called a *referential* style, because it also correlates with attention to names for objects and event descriptions. The second, with less clearly demarked sentence parts, is called *expressive* style. Such a child is quite imitative, has a good rote memory, and often is engaged in language for social purposes—songs, routines, greetings, and so forth. The expressive child seems to be slightly slower at cracking the linguistic code than the referential child, but the long term differences between the two styles seem nonsignificant. Given this range of individual pace and style, how can one tell if a child is really delayed in language development, and what are some of the causes?

Monolingual vs. bilingual

A child growing up with two or more languages is often slower to talk than a monolingual child. This is not surprising given the amount of analysis and code-cracking necessary to organize two systems simultaneously, but the life-long advantage of knowing two native languages is usually considered an appropriate balance to the cost of a potential delay. **Bilingualism** in children and adults is the norm throughout the world: monolinguals are the exception. The learning of each language proceeds in the bilingual child in much the same way as it does in the monolingual child. Some mixing may be observed, in which the child uses words or inflections from the two languages in one utterance. Some report that the bilingual child initially resists learning words for the same thing in the two languages: for instance, a child who learned Spanish and English together learned *leche* but then would not say *milk*, a French/English bilingual used *bird* but refused to use *oiseau*.

Language delay and hearing loss

Children with a hearing loss, either from birth or acquired during the first year or two of life, generally have a serious delay in spoken language development, despite very early diagnosis and fitting with appropriate hearing aids. However, in the unusual case that sign language is the medium of communication in the family rather than speech, such a child shows no delay in learning to use that language. Hearing development is always one of the first things checked if a pediatrician or parent suspects a language delay. The deaf child exposed only to speech will usually begin to babble in "canonical syllables" (ba-ba, gaga) at a slightly later point than the hearing child, and recent work suggests that the babbling is neither as varied nor as sustained as in hearing children. However, there is often a long delay until the first words, sometimes not until age two years or older.

Depending on the severity of the hearing loss, the stages of early language development are also quite delayed. It is not unusual for the profoundly deaf child (greater than 90 decibel loss in both ears) at age four or five years to only have two-word spoken sentences. It is only on entering specialized training programs for oral language development that the profoundly deaf child begins to acquire more spoken language, so that the usual preschool language gains are often made in the grade school years for such children. Many deaf children learning English have pronounced difficulties in articulation and speech quality, especially if they are profoundly deaf, though there is great individual variation. A child who has hearing for the first few years of life has an enormous advantage in speech quality and oral language learning than a child who is deaf from birth or within the first year.

Apart from speech difficulties, deaf children learning English often show considerable difficulty with the inflectional morphology and syntax of the language that marks their writing as well as their speech. The ramifications of this delayed language are significant also for learning to read, and to read proficiently. The average reading age of deaf high school students is often only at the fourth grade level.

For these reasons, many educators of the deaf now urge early compensatory programs in signed languages, because the deaf child shows no handicap in learning a visually based language. Deaf children born to signing parents begin to "babble" in sign at the same point in infancy that hearing infants babble speech, and proceed from there to learn a fully expressive language. However, only 10% of deaf children are born to deaf parents, so hearing parents must show a commitment and willingness to learn sign language, too. Furthermore, command of at least written English is still a necessity for such children to be able to function in the larger community.

Language delay and mental retardation

Mental retardation can also affect the age at which children learn to talk. A mentally retarded child is defined as one who falls in the lower end of the range of intelligence, usually with an IQ (**intelligence quotient**) lower than 80 on some standardized test. There are many causes of mental retardation, including identified genetic syndromes such as **Down syndrome**, **Williams syndrome,** or **fragile X syndrome.** There are also cases of retardation caused by insults to the **fetus** during pregnancy due to alcohol, drug abuse, or toxicity, and disorders of the developing nervous system such as **hydrocephalus.** Finally, there are environmental causes following birth such as **lead poisoning, anoxia,** or **meningitis.** Any of these is likely to slow down the child's rate of development in general, and thus to have effects on language development. However, most children with very low IQs nevertheless develop some language, suggesting it is a relatively "buffered" system that can survive a good deal of insult to the developing brain.

For example, in cases of hydrocephalus it has been noted that children who are otherwise quite impaired intellectually can have impressive conversational language skills. Sometimes called the "chatterbox syndrome," this linguistic sophistication belies their poor ability to deal with the world. In an extreme case, a young man with a tested IQ in the retarded range has an apparent gift for acquiring foreign languages, and can learn a new one with very little exposure. For example, he can do fair translations at a rapid pace from written langages as diverse as Danish, Dutch, Hindi, Polish, French, Spanish, and Greek. He is in fact a **savant** in the area of language, and delights in comparing linguistic systems, though he cannot live independently.

Adults should not consider retarded children to be a uniform class; different patterns can arise with different syndromes. For example in hydrocephalic children and in Williams syndrome, language skills may be preserved to a degree that is discrepant from their general intellectual level. In other groups, including Down syndrome, there may be more delay in language than in other mental abilities.

Most retarded children babble during the first year and develop their first words within a normal time span, but are then slow to develop sentences or a varied vocabulary. Vocabulary size is one of the primary components of standardized tests of verbal intelligence, and it grows slowly in retarded children. Nevertheless, the process of vocabulary development seems quite similar: retarded children also learn words from context and by incidental learning, not just by direct instruction.

Grammatical development, though slow, does not seem particularly deviant, in that the morphology comes in the same way, and in the same order, as it does for normal IQ children. The child's conversation may be marked by more repetition and routines than creative uses, however. By the early teens, the difference in the variety of forms used in a sample of conversation may be more striking in some groups. There may be important differences among types of retarded children in their grammatical proficiency. As of the 1990s, these differences are just beginning to be uncovered. The Down syndrome adolescent with an IQ of around 50 points does not seem to progress beyond the grammatical level of the normally intelligent child at three years, with short sentences that are quite restricted in variety and complexity. Children with Down syndrome are also particularly delayed in speech development. This is due in part to the facial abnormalities that characterize this syndrome, including a relatively large tongue, and also is linked to the higher risk they appear to suffer from ear infections and hearing loss. Speech therapy can be a considerable aid in making such a child's speech more intelligible. Despite the delay, children with Down syndrome are often quite sociable and interested in language for conversation.

Language delay and blindness

Children who are blind from birth sometimes have other neurological problems, which makes it difficult to assess the effect of blindness itself on cognitive and linguistic development. However, in the cases where blindness seems to be the only condition affecting the child, some initial language delays are noted. On average, blind children seem to be delayed about eight months in the onset of words. In general, though, detailed longitudinal studies have revealed that the blind child learns language in much the same way as the sighted child, with perhaps more reliance on routines and formulas in conversation. Linguists are interested in the process by which blind children learn to use words such as see and look given their lack of experience with sight, but these words were found to come in quite normally, with the appropriately changed meaning of "touch" and "explore tactilely."

For Further Study

Books

Landau, B., and L. Gleitman. *Language and Experience: Evidence from the Blind Child.* Cambridge, Mass: Harvard University Press, 1985.

Periodicals

Nelson, K. "Individual Differences in Language Development: Implications for Development and Language." *Developmental Psychology* 17, 1981, pp. 170–87.

—Jill De Villiers, Ph.D.
Smith College

Language Development

The process by which children acquire their first language in early childhood.

Human infants are acutely attuned to the human voice, and prefer it above all other sounds. In fact, they prefer the higher pitch ranges characteristic of female voices. They are also attentive to the human face, particularly the eyes, which they stare at even more if the face is talking. These preferences are present at birth, and some research indicates that babies even listen to their mother's voice during the last few months of pregnancy. Babies who were read to by their mothers while in the womb showed the ability to pick out her voice from among other female voices.

Infancy

Since the early 1970s, it has been known that babies can detect very subtle differences between English *phonemes* (the functional units of speech sound). For example, they can detect the difference between "pa" and "ba," or between "da" and "ga." Of course, they do not attach meaning to the differences for 12 months or more. The original technique of investigating this capacity capitalized on babies' innate ability to suck on a nipple. The nipple is linked to a device that delivers sound contingent on the baby's sucking. Babies introduced to this device suck vigorously to hear the sound, even when it is a repetitive "ba ba ba ba." Because babies also get bored with repetition, they stop sucking hard after a few minutes. At that point the researcher can change the sound in subtle ways, and see if the baby shows renewed interest. For example, it might be a different example of "ba," perhaps one with a bit more breathiness. Or, it could play a sound that would fall into a new phoneme class for adults, like "pa." Babies ignore the first kind of change, just as adults would, but they suck with new vigor for the new phoneme.

Babies have finely tuned perception when it comes to speech sounds, and, more importantly, they seem to classify many sounds the same way adult speakers would, a phenomenon known as *categorical perception*. These sounds that they perceive as indivisible categories are generally those that form the basis for many speech systems in the world's languages, rather than those that are used only rarely, like "th." Infants come into the world already predisposed to make certain distinctions and classifications: apparently they are not driven to make them by language exposure.

Babbling

At the beginning of infancy, vegetative noises and crying predominate. Observers note that by the age of four months, the baby's repertoire has expanded in more interesting ways. By this point babies are smiling at **caregivers** and in doing so they engage in a cooing noise that is irresistible to most parents. When the baby is being fed or changed, she will frequently lock gazes with her caregiver and coo in a pleasant way, often making noises that sound like "hi," and gurgles. It is common for the caregiver to respond by echoing these noises, thereby creating an elaborate interchange that can last many minutes. This may not happen universally, however, as not all cultures take the baby's vocalization so seriously. The nature of the sounds made at this stage is not fully speech-like, though there are open mouth noises like vowels, and an occasional "closure" akin to a consonant, but without the full properties that normally make a syllable out of the two.

At some point between 4 and 10 months, the infant begins producing more speech-like syllables, with a full resonant vowel and an appropriate "closure" of the stream of sound, approaching a true consonant. This stage is called "canonical babbling."

At about six to eight months, the range of vocalizations grows dramatically, and babies can spend hours practicing the sounds they can make with their mouths. Not all of these are human phonemes, and not all of them are found in the language around them. Research has shown that Japanese and American infants sound alike at this stage, and even congenitally deaf infants babble, though less frequently. These facts suggest that the infant is "exercising" her speech organs, but is not being guided very much, if at all, by what she has heard.

By age 10 or 12 months, however, the range of sounds being produced has somewhat narrowed, and now babies' babbling in different cultures begin to take on sound characteristics of the language that surrounds them. The babbling at this stage often consists of reduplicated syllables like "bababa" or "dadada" or "mamama." So it is no accident that most of the world's languages have chosen, as names for parents, some variant of "papa," "mama," "dada," "nana": these coincide with articulations that baby can make most easily at the end of the first year.

Toddlerhood

The first words make their appearance any time between 9 and 15 months or so, depending on the child's precocity and the parent's enthusiasm in noticing. That is, the baby begins making sounds that occur fairly reliably in some situations AND are at least a vague approximation to an adult-sounding word.

What the baby "means" by these sounds is questionable at first. But before long, the baby uses the sounds to draw a caregiver's attention, and persists until she gets it, or uses a sound to demand an object, and persists until it is given to her. At this point the first words are being used communicatively as well. There is a fairly protracted period for most babies in which their first words come and go, as if there is a "word of the week" that replaces those gone before. One of the characteristics about these first words is that they may be situation-specific, such as the case of a child who says "car" only when looking down on the roofs of cars from her balcony. But after several months of slow growth, there is an explosion of new words, often called the "word spurt." This usually coincides with an interest in what things are called, e.g., the child asking some variant of "What's that?" Vocabulary climbs precipitously from then on—an estimated nine new words a day from ages 2 to 18 years. These developments are noted in all the cultures that have been studied to date.

The nature of the child's first 50 words is quite similar across cultures: the child often names foods, pets, animals, family members, toys, vehicles and clothing that the child can manipulate. Most of what is named can either move or be moved by the child: she generally omits words for furniture, geographical features, buildings, weather and so forth. Children vary in that some develop an early vocabulary almost exclusively of "thing" words and actions, whereas others develop a social language: words for social routines, and expressions of love, and greetings. Researchers differ as to whether these are seen as different styles inherent in the child or whether their social environment encourages them in different ways. Researchers agree that the child learns most effectively from social and interactive routines with an accomplished talker (who may be an older child), and not, at least at the start, from passive observations of adults talking, or from radio or TV shows. Experiments and observations show that children pick up words at this stage most rapidly when the caregiver uses them to name or comment on what the child is already focused on.

Word meanings

The meanings of the child's first words are not necessarily the same as those of the adults around her. For instance, children may "overgeneralize" their first words to refer to items beyond their usual scope of application. A child might call all men "Daddy," or all animals "doggie," or all round objects "ball." Others have pointed out that "undergeneralization" also occurs, though it is less likely to be noticed. For instance, a child might call only her own striped ball "ball," and stay silent about all the rest, or refer to the family dog and others of the same type as "doggie" but not name any others. The child may also use a word to refer to a wide variety of objects that hold no single property in common. A child who learned "moon" for the full moon later used it for street lamps, house lights (lights in common), doorknobs and the dial on the dishwasher (shape in common), and toenail clippings on a rug (related shape). Put into a class, these objects share nothing in common except a shifting form of resemblance to the original moon. It has been argued that children's first word meanings have only a family resemblance rather than a common thread. In fact, there are philosophers who argue that such is the nature of many adult words as well.

It has long been recognized that words are inherently ambiguous even when an object is being pointed at: does the word refer to the object, or its color, shape, texture, function, shadow? Recent work on word learning has also drawn attention to the biases the child brings to word learning. One such bias is the *Whole-Object assumption,* that is, children assume a new word refers to the object itself rather than a property. However, a competing constraint is *mutual exclusivity*: if a child already knows a word for an object, a new word is assumed to mean something else; a new object if it is available; or a part, texture, or shape of a known one. Researchers are divided at present on the extent to which these biases are learned, or inherent.

Young children also frequently name objects at an intermediate level of abstraction known as the *basic object* level. That is, they will use the word *dog*, rather than the more specific *collie* or the more general, *animal*, or *flower* rather than *dandelion* or *plant*. This coincides with the naming practices of most parents, and seems to be the level of greatest utility for the two-year old.

Preschool years: the two-year old
Grammar: the two-word utterance

The first sentence is the transition that separates humans from other creatures. Most toddlers produce their first spontaneous two-word sentence at 18 to 24 months, usually once they have acquired between 50 and 500 words. Before their first sentence, they often achieve the effect of complex expressions by stringing together their simple words:

Book

Mine

Read

Then their first sentence puts these words under a single intonational envelope, with no pause. Their first sentences are not profound, but they represent a major

advance in the expression of meaning. The listener is also freed of some of the burden of interpretation and does not need to guess so much from context.

For children learning English, their first sentences are *telegraphic*, that is, content words predominate, primarily the nouns and verbs necessary in the situation. Words that have grammatical functions, but do not themselves make reference, such as articles, prepositions and auxiliary verbs, do not occur very often. The true character of this grammar is hotly debated. The fact that the function words and inflections appear variably for a protracted period of months leads some researchers to argue that the child really knows the grammar but has some kind of production limit that precludes saying extra words. On the other side, some researchers argue that the forms that do appear may be imitations, or particular learned fragments, and that the full grammar is not yet present. Tests of comprehension or judgment that might decide between these alternatives are very hard to undertake with two-year-old children, though the little work that does exist suggests children are sensitive to the items they omit in their own speech.

At the start, the child combines the single words into two-word strings that usually preserve the common order of parents' sentences in English. At the time the English-speaking child is producing many two-word utterances, comprehension tests show he can also distinguish between sentences that contrast in word order and hence meaning:

The dog licks the cat

The cat licks the dog.

Researchers using innovative techniques with preverbal infants have claimed infants understand basic word order contrasts before they learn to produce them. Infants who saw a choice of two brief movies along with spoken sentences preferred to look at the movie of the event that was congruent with the spoken sentence, where the only contrast was in word order.

Semantic relations

Most studies on early child language conclude that the child at the two-word stage is concerned with the expression of a small set of semantic relationships. The cross-linguistic study of children includes languages as remotely related as French, Samoan, Luo (spoken in Kenya), German, Finnish, and Cakchiquel (a Mayan language spoken in Guatemala). Two-year-old children learning all these languages expressed only a narrow range of the possible meanings that the adult language could express. All over the world, children apparently talk about the same meanings—or ideas—in their first sentences, despite the variety of forms in those languages. For example, the children refer to possession (Mommy dish, my coat), action-object sequences (hit ball, drop fork), attribute of an object (big truck, wet pants) or an object's location (cup shelf, teddy bed).

Debate has raged over how significant this finding of universal semantic relations is for the study of grammatical development. On the one hand, it might mean that building a grammar based on meaningful relations is a universal first step for language learning. On the other hand, there is the larger problem of how the child builds a grammar that resembles the adult's, because for true linguistic competence, the child needs to build a theory out of the right components: subjects, objects, noun phrases, verb phrases, and the rest. These abstract categories do not translate easily into semantic relations, if at all. To succeed at analyzing or parsing adult sentences into their true grammatical parts, the child must go beyond general meaning. The alternative interpretation of the findings about the first sentences is that children all over the world are constrained by their cognitive development to talk about the same ideas and that their doing so need not mean that their grammars are based solely on semantic relations. So the semantic analysis of children's early sentences offers fascinating data on the meanings children express at that age, but it is less clear that these semantic notions are the components out of which children's grammars are constructed. A weaker hypothesis about the role of semantics in the learning of grammar is that perhaps children exploit the correlation between certain grammatical notions, like subject, and certain semantic notions, like agent, to begin parsing adult sentences. The child could then proceed to analyze sentences by knowing already:

a. the meaning of the individual words

b. the conceptual structure of the event, namely that dog is the agent; bit is the action.

Some have proposed that the child may have some further, possibly innate, "hypotheses" that guide his code-cracking:

c. actions are usually verbs

d. things are usually nouns

e. agents are usually subjects.

Semantic notions then become vital bootstraps for the learning of grammar.

Preschool years: the three-year old
Shades of meaning

What is missing from the two-word stage are all the modulations of meaning, the fine tunings, which add immeasurably to the subtlety of what we can express. Consider the shades of meaning in the following sentences:

He played

He's playing

He was playing

He has played

He had played

He will play

He will have played

Not all languages make these distinctions explicitly, and some languages make distinctions that English does not. In the next stage of development of English, the extra little function words and inflections that modulate the meaning of the major syntactic relations make their appearance, though it is years until they are fully mastered. For English, it is common to measure the stage of language development by counting and then averaging the morphemes (words and inflections) in a child's set of utterances, and refer to that as the mean length of utterance (MLU). The inflections are surprisingly variable in children's utterances, sometimes present and sometimes absent even within the same stretch of conversation. According to psychologist R. Brown, "All these, like an intricate sort of ivy, begin to grow up between and among the major constituent blocks, the nouns and verbs, to which stage I is largely limited."

A classic error noticed in the acquisition of English inflections is the overgeneralization of plurals and past tenses. In each case, when the regular inflection begins to be mastered, it is overgeneralized to irregular forms, resulting in errors like *foots, sheeps, goed* and *eated.* In the case of the past tense, children usually begin by correctly using a few irregular forms like *fell* and *broke,* perhaps because these forms are frequent in the input and the child learns them by rote. At first they may not be fully analyzed as past tenses of the corresponding verbs *fall* and *break.* But when the child begins to produce regular past tense endings, the irregulars are sometimes also regularized (e.g. *falled* and *breaked*). Two kinds of overgeneralizations occur: one in which the -ed ending is attached to the root form of the irregular verb (e.g. *sing - singed*) and the other in which the ending is attached to the irregular past form (e.g. *broke -broked*).

Cross-linguistic work

An understanding of how children acquire grammatical morphemes is now thought to require a broader perspective than that obtained from studying English alone. A large research initiative has gathered data from children acquiring other languages, especially languages very different from English. Researchers have studied children acquiring Luo, Samoan, Kaluli, Hungarian, Sesotho and many others in an effort to understand the process of language acquisition in universal terms. One finding is that the telegraphic speech style of English children is not universal—in more heavily inflected languages like Italian, even the youngest speakers do not strip their sentences to the bare stems of nouns and verbs.

One of the purposes of the cross-linguistic work is to try to disentangle some of the variables that are confounded in a single language. For example: English-speaking children acquire the hypothetical (if...then statements) rather late, around four years of age, but the hypothetical form is complex in English grammar. It requires an ability to imagine an unreal situation. Cross-linguistic studies provide a way to tease these variables apart, for Russian has a very simple hypothetical form, though its meaning is as complex as the English version. Research shows that Russian children do not use this simple form until after they are about four years of age. Most morphemes vary along multiple dimensions: phonological, semantic and grammatical. The full program of research may reach fruition only when the massive matrix of possibilities across the world's languages can be entered into a computer, complete with detailed longitudinal data from children learning those languages.

Auxiliaries

Children's first sentences lack any auxiliaries or tense markers:

Me go home

Daddy have tea

and they also lack auxiliary-inversion for questions at this stage:

I ride train?

Sit chair?

They also lack a system for assigning nominative case to the subject, that is, adult sentences mark the subject as nominative:

Adult: *I want that book*

but children at this stage frequently use the accusative case:

Child: *Me want that book*

These facts lead some to conclude that young children's sentences lack the full syntactic structures typical of adult sentences, and undergo a radical restructuring as they develop. Others argue that the limitation is not so much at the level of knowledge of grammar, but merely performance limits, so preserving the continuity of form at an abstract level between child and adult.

In addition to learning the basic word order and inflectional system of the language, a child must learn how to produce sentences of different kinds: not just simple active declarative, but also negatives, questions, imperatives, passives and so forth. In English there are word order changes and auxiliary changes for these sentence modalities.

One type of question is called a yes/no question, for the simple reason that it requires a *yes* or a *no* answer. A second kind of question is called the Wh-question, so-called because it usually begins with the sequence Wh in English (in French, they are Qu-questions). Wh-questions do not require a simple yes or no response: instead they ask for information about one of the constituents in the sentence. *What, who, when, where, why,* and *how* all stand in for possible phrases in the sentence—the subject, or object, or a prepositional phrase. Discourse permits us to respond elliptically with only the missing constituent if we choose:

What is he buying?

Coffee.

Where is she going?

To the store.

How is she getting there?

By bike.

The structure of such questions is similar to that of yes/no questions because the auxiliary and subject are inverted, so that transformation is involved in both. In addition, the Wh-word is in initial position, though it stands for constituents in varied sentence positions. Linguistic evidence suggests that the Wh-word originated at another site in the structure and was moved there by a grammatical rule, called, appropriately, Wh-movement. Children's responses to such questions reveal the sophisticated nature of their grammatical knowledge.

Negation also involves the auxiliary component in the sentence, because for simple sentence negation, the negative is attached to the first member of the auxiliary, and may be contracted:

She isn't coming home.

He won't be having any.

How do children acquire these rules of English? When auxiliaries do emerge, it seems that they come in first in declarative sentences. Before children master the placement of the auxiliary, they ask questions using rising intonation. They may also pick up a few routine forms of yes/no questions, particularly in households that demand politeness from young children, as in:

May I have one?

When auxiliaries do begin to appear in initial position, what has the child learned? One of the claims made by modern linguistic theory is that the rules of natural languages are "structure dependent," that is, they always refer to structural units, constituents such as "noun phrase" or "auxiliary verb," not to other arbitrary units such as "the fifth word" or "the first word beginning with 'f'." The case of auxiliary inversion provides a nice illustration, used by Noam Chomsky to make this point. The child could hear sentence pairings such as:

The man is here

Is the man here?

The boy can swim

Can the boy swim?

The dog will bite

Will the dog bite?

and draw the conclusion that to make a question, you take the *third* word and move it to the front. Of course, that hypothesis would soon be disconfirmed by a pair such as:

The tall man will come

Will the tall man come?

not: *Man the tall will come?*

More likely, the child might form the rule "move the first word like *can, will, is,* etc. up to the front," which would fit all of the above and hundreds of other such sentences. However, that is not a structure-dependent rule, because it makes no reference to the grammatical role that word plays in the sentence. The only disconfirmation would come from the occasions when a subject relative clau*se appears before the auxiliary:*

The man who is the teacher will be coming tomorrow

Will the man who is the teacher be coming tomorrow?

but our earlier, structure-<u>in</u>dependent rule would produce:

Is the man who the teacher will be coming tomorrow?

The child who formulated the almost-adequate rule would fail in such circumstances, but no child has been observed to make the mistake. Hence even from the inadequate data that children receive, they formulate a complex, structure-dependent rule.

Wh-questions

Wh-questions appear among the child's first utterances, often in a routine form such as "Whazzat?" The forms are routines because they are invariant in form, but more varied productions are not slow to emerge in children's grammar. The first, stereotyped forms may be tied to particular functions or contexts, but genuine interrogatives are varied not only in form but in use.

Just as in yes/no questions, the auxiliary must be in front of the subject noun phrase in a Wh-question, and children seem to have more difficulty with auxiliary-inversion in Wh-questions than in yes/no questions. At the same time children can say:

Can he come?

they might say:

Why he can come?

failing to invert the auxiliary in the Wh-question.

What else does the child have to learn in Wh-questions? One factor concerns the link between the Wh-word and the "missing constituent." Certain of the Wh-words enter children's speech earlier than others, and there is some consistency across studies in that order: *What, who,* and *where* tend to emerge before *why* and *how,* with *when* coming later. Some have explained the order in terms of semantics, or rather concreteness, of the ideas contained in these words, since *when* and *how* depend upon cognitive developments of time and causality whereas *what* and *who* do not. The question *why* seems to be late for this reason: it is only through discourse that a child can determine the meaning of *why,* which may be the reason some young children ask it endlessly. It is also a question that rarely elicits a one-word answer, so it may be a way to keep the conversation going when you can't say much yourself!

Creativity

A feature that is markedly evident in young children is their **creativity** with language. Children, like adults, continually produce sentences they have not heard before, and one can more easily recognize that novelty in children because sometimes the ideas are rather strange. For example, after hearing many "tag questions" such as "That's nice, isn't it?" and "You're a good girl, aren't you?" and "You can open that, can't you?" a three-year-old figured out how to make her own tags, and used the rules to say, "Goosebumps are hairy legs, aren't they?" and "He's a punk rocker, isn't he?," which were definitely not sentences she had heard. In addition, the creative use is revealed because children overextend rules to exceptional cases, e.g., a child saying "My porridge is getting middle-sizeder" as he struggles through a huge bowl of oatmeal. It can also occur because children do not yet have the vocabulary for certain subtleties of expression. But the way that children fill these "lexical gaps" uses the same principles as adults who do the same thing. For example, an adult might use an "innovative verb" such as "I weekended in New York," and a child might similarly say, "I broomed her!" after pursuing a sibling with a broom. However, a child who said "You have to scale it first" as she put a bag on a scale was creating an innovation for which there is already an existing word—namely, weigh. The creativity of children's linguistic innovations has been emphasized because it demonstrates that children do not just imitate what they hear, but extract general rules and principles that allow them to form new expressions.

Later preschool years

Joining sentences

Once the child has mastered the fundamentals of sentence construction, what is left to learn? Actually, language would be very dull to listen to or read if we could just produce simple sentences with one verb at a time. Perhaps the first response of a novice to the field of child language is that the sentences children speak are short and not very complicated for a long period. Certainly when one measures the mean length of utterance of children younger than age four, it tends not to be very impressive, ranging from 1.0 to 4.0 morphemes per utterance. Yet by age four, the MLU (mean length of utterance) loses much of its usefulness as a measure, because children's utterances, like those of an adult, fluctuate in length dramatically depending on the circumstances of the conversation. Even before age four, there are rare, but significant, occurrences of surprising complexity, showing that the child is in command of a considerable amount of grammar when needed. The first sentences involving more than one "proposition" are simple coordinations, for instance two sentences joined by *and*. Later other conjunctions come in, such as *so, but, after,* or *because*. But embeddings are not much later: there is evidence of embedded structures even in the primitive talk of two-year-olds.

There are different kinds of embedded structures. One kind are *relative clauses*, clauses that are used to further specify a noun phrase:

*The man **who took the job** is coming to dinner.*

Here is a sample sentence from a child at 2;10 (2 years, 10 months), said in reference to playground equipment:

*I'm going on the one **that you're sitting on**.*

or the slightly aberrant:

*Where's a hammer **we nailed those nails in**?*

On the other hand are *complement* constructions, which can be considered the equivalent further specification of the verb phrase:

*The doctor decided **to perform the operation**.*

Again, a child at age 2;11 was observed to say:

*I don't like **Nicky share a banana**.*

*I'm going downstairs **to see what Nicky's watching**.*

Both kinds of embedding are means of packing information into a single sentence that would require multiple sentences (probably with lots of pointing) to convey the equivalent ideas. When children reach the stage at which they can control these and similar structures, they become capable of expressing a much wider variety of ideas and thoughts not dependent on the immediate environment for support, and an important further step is taken in being ready for literacy.

Researchers have used innovative procedures to elicit relative clause structures from children as young as two by arranging the situation to call for specification of a referent. In one procedure, for example, the child, the experimenter, and a confederate are playing with two identical toy bears. The experimenter makes one bear ride a bike. Then the confederate is blindfolded, and the child alone watches the experimenter make that same bear do another action, say jump. Then the blindfold is removed from the confederate and the child has to help him guess which bear did something. Children of two and three can say:

Pick the one that rode the bike.

If the literature on comprehension of relative clauses is considered, it appears that children below age five are in very poor control of relative clause sentences. The typical comprehension task uses an "act-out" procedure in which several small animals are provided to the child and he is asked to act out whatever the experimenter says. After a couple of simple warm-ups, e.g.,

Show me:

The lion hit the kangaroo

The dog jumped.

the child would be asked to act out relative clause structures in which there are no clues to meaning from the words alone, i.e., the syntax carries all the meaning:

The lion that hit the dog bit the turtle

The cat that the dog pushed licked the mouse.

When preschoolers are given such a task, their performance is usually fairly poor, suggesting that they continue to have difficulty reconstructing the speaker's meaning from complex structures: a problem perhaps in processing rather than grammar per se.

Similarly, even five- and six-year-olds continue to have trouble figuring out who did what to whom for sentences containing various kinds of complements:

Fred told Harry to wash the car.

Fred promised Harry to wash the car

Fred told Harry that he washed the car.

Fred told Harry after he washed the car.

The various "complement-taking" verbs in English fall into several distinct patterns, as do the complements themselves, so there is room for lots of confusion.

Finally, there are aspects of the pronoun system that may take several years to get straight. Pronouns in English have to have an "antecedent" (noun which is referred to by the pronoun) outside the sentence in which the pronoun occurs: you can't say, for example:

John hit him

and mean John hit himself. Reflexives like "himself," on the other hand, have to be in the same clause as their antecedent; you can't say:

John was wondering why Fred hit himself.

and have it mean that Fred hit John. Children's control over antecedents, particularly of pronouns, is still being acquired after age four or five when complex sentences are involved.

Later word learning

The child's vocabulary grows enormously in the age period two to five years, and vocabulary size is frequently used by researchers as an index of the child's development. In addition to learning many new nouns and verbs, the child must organize vocabulary, for example, into hierarchies: that Rover is also a dog, a corgi, an animal, a living thing and so on. The child also learns about opposites and relatedness—all necessary forms of connection among words in the "inner lexicon." The child also becomes better able to learn words from linguistic context alone, rapidly homing in on the meaning after only a few scattered exposures. This is a surprisingly effective process, though hardly fail-safe: after being told that screens were to stop flies from bringing germs into the house, one child concluded that germs were "things flies play with."

Discourse and reference

Researchers have been acutely aware that the child's language learning does not take place in a vacuum or a laboratory—it is enmeshed in the social relationships and circumstances of the child. The child uses language for communication with peers, siblings, parents, and increasingly, relative strangers. All of these individuals make special demands on the child in terms of their different status, knowledge, requirements of politeness, clarity or formality, to which the child must adjust and adapt, and the preschool child is only beginning this process of language socialization. Even four-year-olds adjust their style, pitch and sentence length when talking to younger children or infants rather than peers or older people, and in other cultures they master formal devices that acknowledge the status or group membership of different people. However, it is recognized that the three-year-old is rather poor at predicting what others know or think, and therefore will be rather egocentric in expressing himself. Especially when communicating across a barrier or over a telephone, the child of this age might be unable to supply the right kind of information to a listener. However, other researchers show that children become increasingly adept at "repairing" their own communicative breakdowns as they get older.

Narrative and literacy

The difficulty that children have with predicting what others already know or believe shows itself also in their attempts to produce narratives, that is, extended sentences that convey a story. Retelling a story is considerably easier than constructing one about witnessed events, but may need considerable "scaffolding" by a patient listener who structures it by asking leading questions. Skill in producing a coherent narrative is one of the culminating achievements of language acquisition, but it is acquired late and varies widely according to opportunity for practice and experience with stories. In part, this is because creating a narrative is a cultural event: different cultures have different rules for how stories are structured, which must be learned. At first, children tend to focus just on the actions, with little attention to the motives, or reasons, or consequences of those actions, and little overarching structure that might explain the events. Young children also fail to use the linguistic devices that maintain cohesion among referents, so they may switch from talking about one character to another and call them all "he," to the bewilderment of the listener. Reading and writing in the grade school years depend on this ability and nurture it further, and one of the best predictors of reading readiness is how much children were read to in the first few years. As children begin to read and write, there are further gains in their vocabulary (and new ways to acquire it) and new syntactic forms emerge that are relatively rare in speaking but play important roles in text, such as stage-setting and maintaining cohesion. Mastery of these devices requires a sensitivity to the reader's needs, and it is a lifelong developmental process.

For Further Study

Books

Berko-Gleason, J. *The Development of Language*. New York: Macmillan, 1993.

de Villiers, P., and J. de Villiers. *Early Language*. The Developing Child series. Cambridge, Mass.: Harvard University Press, 1979.

Fletcher, P., and B. MacWhinney. *The Handbook of Child Language*. Cambridge, Mass.:Blackwell Publishers, 1995.

Goodluck, H. *Language Acquisition: A Linguistic Introduction*. Cambridge, Mass.: Blackwell Publishers, 1991.

Pinker, S. *The Language Instinct*. New York: Morrow, 1994.

—Jill De Villiers, Ph.D.
Smith College

Language Disorder

Problem with any function of language and communication.

In adults, much of what is known about the organization of language functions in the brain has come from the study of patients with focal **brain** lesions. It has been known for hundreds of years that a left-hemisphere injury to the brain is more likely to cause language disturbance—**aphasia**—than a right hemisphere injury, especially but not exclusively in right-handed persons. For about a hundred years, certain areas in the adult left hemisphere—Broca's area in the posterior frontal lobe,

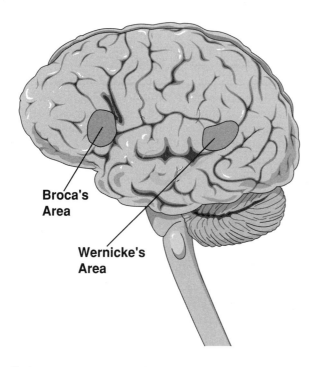

Brain map

and Wernicke's area in the temporal lobe—have been identified as centrally involved in language functions. However, researchers in the field of adult aphasia are divided over the exact role these brain areas play in language processing and production. Damage to Broca's area results in marked problems with language fluency; with shortened sentences, impaired flow of speech, poor control of rhythm and intonation (known as prosody); and a telegraphic style, with missing inflections and function words. In contrast, the speech of Wernicke's aphasics is fluent and often rapid, but with relatively empty content and many neologisms (invented words) and word substitutions. It was initially believed that the two areas were responsible for output (Broca's) versus input (Wernicke's), but research does not confirm such a simple split.

Other theories ask whether the two areas might be differentially involved in syntax versus semantics, or phonology versus the lexicon, but the picture is not clear. Some have argued that adult aphasic patients, once they are stable after their injury or stroke, employ many compensatory devices that conceal or disguise the central character of their language difficulties. It then becomes more difficult to assess what is missing or disturbed because the difficulties are overlaid by new strategies, and perhaps new areas of the brain taking over functions for the damaged areas.

Infants and young children who suffer focal brain lesions in advance of acquiring language provide valuable information to neuroscientists who want to know how "plastic" the developing brain is with respect to language functions. For instance, is the left hemisphere uniquely equipped for language, or could the right hemisphere do as well? What if Broca's or Wernicke's areas were damaged before language was acquired? Thirty years ago a review of literature on children who had incurred brain lesions suggested that, unlike the case of adults, recovery from language disruption after left-brain damage was rapid and without lasting effect. Researchers concluded that the two hemispheres of the brain were equipotential for language until around puberty, and that this allowed young brain-damaged children to compensate with their undamaged right hemisphere.

However, several studies suggested that left-brain damage caused greater disruption to language than right-sided damage even in the youngest subjects. Children known to be using only their right hemisphere for language (because they had undergone removal of the left hemisphere for congenital abnormalities) demonstrated subtle syntactic deficits on careful linguistic testing, but the deficits failed to show in ordinary conversational analysis. Almost all of these studies were retrospective, that is, they looked at the performance of children at an older age who had suffered an early lesion. Furthermore, the technology for scanning the brain and locating the lesion site, then carefully matching the subjects, was much less developed.

With the invention of new technologies including CT scans and Magnetic Resonance Imaging (MRI), several studies have been conducted to look prospectively at the language development of children with focal, defined lesions specifically in the traditional language areas. There is surprising concordance among the studies in their results: all of them find initial (but variable) delays in the onset of lexical, syntactic, and morphological development followed by remarkably similar progress after about age two to three years. Lasting deficits have not been noticed in these children. Surprisingly, there are also no dramatic effects of laterality: lesions to either side of the brain seem to produce virtually the same effects. However, most of the data comes from conversational analysis or relatively unstructured testing, and these children have not been followed until school age. Until those detailed studies are extended, it is difficult to reconcile the differing results of the retrospective and prospective studies. Nevertheless, the findings suggest remarkable plasticity and robustness of language in spite of brain lesions that would devastate an adult's system.

For Further Study

Books

Byers Brown, B., and M. Edwards. *Developmental Disorders of Language.* San Diego: Singular Publishing, 1989.

Miller, J. *Research on Child Language Disorders: A Decade of Progress.* Austin, TX: Pro-ed, 1991.

—Jill De Villiers, Ph.D.
Smith College

Large Motor Control *see* **Gross Motor Skills**

Latchkey Children

A child who must spend part of the day unsupervised at home while his parents are working.

The term "latchkey children" was coined by the media to refer to children who wore a housekey around their necks for safekeeping. Other names for this group of children have included "children in self-care," "children of working parents," "unsupervised children," or "children on their own." However, none of these labels offers an unprejudiced description of the situation experienced by children who are at home when a parent is absent.

The need for child care after school is a relatively new phenomena. In the 1960s, only 19% of mothers with school-aged children were employed full-time. By the 1980s, 60% of such mothers were employed and the numbers continue to grow. Despite this trend, society has not yet provided a set of clear expectations about parental supervision and its importance. In the United States, failing to be present to look after a preschool child constitutes child neglect. However, school-age children are increasingly viewed as capable of self-care as they mature. In many states, it is legal to leave children eight years of age and older in self-care. Most laws regarding child neglect make reference to supervision "that fails to meet community standards." However, no clear community standards exist describing when and under what circumstances children can be left alone or in the care of other children.

Surveys suggest that some latchkey children are left alone only for a few minutes each day (e.g., the school bus drops the child off at 3:45 and the parent returns home at 4:00 p.m.) or for only one day a week. In contrast, some children return home, do homework, supervise siblings, fix them dinner, and put them to bed before the parent returns home from work in the evening.

Parents' and children's satisfaction with self-care seems linked to several factors such as (1) the children's age, (2) the parents' belief about working outside the home, (3) parental unconventionality (more conservative parents are less happy with self-care arrangements), and (4) the child's separate social network. In addition, the degree of isolation children experience and the safety of the neighborhood also seem to influence the level of satisfaction with self-care. Some parents supervise by telephone, with their children checking in as soon as they enter the home and periodically calling throughout the afternoon. Other children may have a grandmother, aunt, or neighbor who lives nearby whom the children can contact. The availability of adult company, judgment, and information in part determines the self-care experience, even when there is no adult actually in residence.

Another issue is the safety of the neighborhood. Some children in self-care feel safe and confident in their surroundings. In other neighborhoods, children must lock themselves in and remain indoors for safety's sake. For these children, the absence of a parental **caregiver** may considerably change their experience.

There are many potential positive as well as negative outcomes of self-care. Children may become more responsible and capable because of self-care. Many take pride in their ability to contribute to the family by managing their own supervision after school. However, in some cases negative outcomes overshadow the positive. Some latchkey children have reported feeling frightened and lonely without adult supervision. However, larger scale, representative studies of children in self-care show that many children are typically not frightened nor unduly lonely during self-care. In fact, many children enjoy their time alone in the house.

When left to themselves, latchkey children appear to make more unhealthy choices than children with more adult supervision. One article in *Pediatrics*, a prestigious medical magazine, asked, "Are we fattening our children in front of the television?" and the answer was a resounding "yes." Unsupervised children pick foods high in fat, sugar, and salt, which are frequently advertised on television. The unhealthy food choices, in addition to the absence of healthy activity, could happen in any family, but appear to be more likely when the child is left without an adult to monitor the snacks and activities selected.

Older latchkey children are also more likely to become involved in **smoking,** alcohol, drugs, and early sexual experiences. Interestingly, it is not adult presence, per se, that appears to make a difference. One study showed that adolescents who were required to return home and call the parent were no more likely than adolescents whose parents were home to engage in sexual behavior and substance abuse.

Childhood injury is an even more dangerous outcome when there is a lack of supervision. Injuries kill more children than the next nine leading causes of death combined, and children may be at greater risk if they are unsupervised. Drowning, being burned by matches, and pedestrian injury after playing in the streets are all major killers of children, injuries that may be preventable with caregiver supervision.

There are many more options to latchkey status than there were even a few years ago. Many schools now have after-school activities such as the "Adventure Clubs" sponsored by the YMCA that offer affordable child care on the school premises. Many **day care** centers that once focused solely on preschool-age child care are now offering services to bus children from school to the child care center after school. Other communities have arranged co-ops, whereby several parents exchange days of child care with one another.

As experience continues to grow within the area of self-care, more definitive standards are likely to develop to help parents determine which children will do best in self-care. Currently, the best advice for parents is to role play various high-risk situations that might arise, to ensure that the child knows how to respond (asking the child to act out rather than recite the correct behavior is important). The presence of an adult nearby or by telephone is also helpful. Gradually increasing the amount of responsibility a child assumes at the appropriate rate is not only good parenting, but also the hallmark of self-care.

For Further Study

Books

Kleeberg, Irene Cumming. *Latchkey Kid.* New York: F. Watts, 1985.

Swan, Helen L., and Victoria Houston. *Alone After School: A Self-Care Guide for Latchkey Children and Their Parents.* Englewood Cliffs, NJ: Prentice-Hall, 1985.

Periodicals

Hansen, Ronald J., and Joyce Price. "As Recent Crimes Show, Children Remain Most Vulnerable Victims." *Insight on the News* 13, June 9, 1997, pp. 42+.

Ingram, Leah. "Staying Home Alone. (Eight to 12 Years). *Parenting* 11, March 1997, p. 160.

Audiovisual Recordings

Changing Families, Challenges, and Opportunities. Columbus, OH: Ohio Cooperative Extension Service, The Ohio State University, 1988.
(Four audiocassettes).

Home Alone: Tips for Latchkey Children and Their Parents. Wadsworth, OH: Fred Productions, 1991.
(One 90-minute videocassette).

—Lizette Peterson-Homer
University of Missouri

Late Developer

Imprecise term describing a child whose development seems to lag behind that of his peers.

Laypersons use the terms "late developer" or "late bloomer" to describe the child or adolescent whose development is at the lower range of normal for his or her chronological age. The terms are imprecise, since they are used to describe any developmental lag, whether indicated by poor academic performance or a lag in physical, emotional, psychological, or social development.

Law of Effect

Principle associated with learning and behavior developed by American psychologist Edward Thorndike.

One of the first principles of learning was the law of effect developed by American psychologist Edward Thorndike. The law of effect states that behavior that leads to a satisfying outcome is likely to be repeated; behaviors that lead to undesired outcomes are less likely to be repeated. Prior to Thorndike's assertion of the law of effect, many psychologists interested in behavior attributed learning to the process of reasoning. Thorndike theorized that animals learned new behaviors through trial and error. From his observations, Thorndike concluded that an animal makes an association between a behavior and a positive or satisfying outcome and draws on this association for future behavior. Alternatively, when an animal engages in a behavior that does not have a positive outcome, it is less likely to repeat that behavior.

Initially, Thorndike believed that negative outcomes produced negative associations similar to the positive associations affiliated with positive outcomes. Later, however, he modified his view, believing that negative outcomes were ineffective in shaping behavior, and rather, in Thorndike's view, led instead to unpredictable behavior.

The law of exercise, another of Thorndike's principles, states that responses that occur under a specific set of circumstances become strongly associated with those circumstances. Thorndike believed that the combination of these two laws explained the development of all behavior patterns. He believed there was no need to consider the thought process in considering how behavior is learned, but that all learning could be explained by positive and negative outcomes.

For Further Study

Books

Clifford, G. J., *Edward L. Thorndike: The Sane Positivist.* Middletown, PA: Wesleyan Univeristy Press, 1984.

Mackintosh, N. J. *Conditioning and Associative Learning.* New York: Oxford University Press, 1983.

Lazy Eye *see* **Amblyopia**

Leach, Penelope (1937–)

Pediatrician and author.

Penelope Leach is best known for her popular books offering practical advice on child care and development for both physical and psychological needs. Leach attended Cambridge University and the London School of Economics where she received her Ph.D. in psychology in 1964. She was a research officer for the Medical Research Council, Unit for the Study of Child Development in London from 1965–71, and has been a medical editor for Penguin books and a research consultant at the University of Bristol International Centre for Child Studies since 1984. Her early research addressed the effects of various parental strategies and approaches to child rearing on the developing personality of the child. Later she investigated the effects of children on their parents as well as various aspects of adolescent development. She has brought her work to the public and to policy makers in an extensive series of popular press books and television productions. In her advice to parents, Leach advocates individualized approaches to child rearing, doing things "by the baby" instead of "by the book" (Leach, 1989). She is a Fellow of the British Psychological Society and an advocate for the support of children and families.

For Further Study

Books

Leach, P. *Babyhood: Infant Development from Birth to Two Years.* New York: Knopf, 1974, 1983.

———.*Who Cares? A New Deal for Mothers and Their Small Children.* New York: Penguin, 1979.

———. *Your Growing Child: From Babyhood Through Adolescence.* New York: Knopf, 1986.

———. *Your Baby and Child: From Birth to Age Five.* New York: Knopf, 1978, 1989.

———. *The First Six Months: Getting Together with Your Baby.* New York: Knopf, 1986.

———. *Children First.* New York: Knopf, 1994.

Periodicals

"British Child Psychologist Penelope Leach." *Current Biography* 55, August 1994, pp. 27+.

Kinkead, Gwen. "Penelope Leach." *The New York Times Magazine,* April 10, 1994 p. 32.

—Doreen Arcus, Ph.D.
University of Massachusetts Lowell

Lead Poisoning

A toxic condition that results from the ingestion of lead, typically occurring in young children.

Lead poisoning occurs when small amounts of lead, usually in the air or dust, are ingested over a period of time. Its victims are chiefly young children who chew on furniture and woodwork painted with lead-based paints or who eat dust and soil that has been contaminated. Ten percent of the ingested lead is absorbed by the body; children with iron deficiencies can absorb as much as 50%. High lead levels in the body decrease the production of heme, the iron compound in the blood, resulting in **anemia**. Unchecked, the anemia prevents the normal rate of brain and cell activity resulting in stunted physical growth, **learning disabilities** and behavioral problems. Recent studies suggest that lead poisoning is a factor in juvenile delinquency as well. Abnormally high lead levels also cause the loss of large amounts of amino acids, carbohydrates, and salts through the urine, resulting in kidney failure. In the most severe cases, the brain swells (lead encephalopathy), followed by **seizures** and death.

Early symptoms of lead poisoning include fatigue, paleness, constipation, loss of appetite, irritability, anemia, sudden behavioral changes, loss of short-term memory, slowing of mental development, and sleep disorders. In the final stages before the onset of lead encephalopathy, victims experience vomiting, abdominal pain (lead colic), headaches, clumsiness, and muscle weakness.

In the 1970s, lead-based paints and leaded gasoline were banned in the United States. However, lead particles from gasoline are still found in soil and many older inner-city dwellings have not been stripped of their leaded paint. Drinking water in older homes may also be passing through old lead-containing pipes. Experts estimate that three million preschool children in the United States have elevated levels of lead. The highest incidence, 36%, occurs among low-income African American children living in industrialized cities. Seventeen percent of Hispanic American children have elevated

LEADERSHIP

levels. The figure is only 4% for white, non-city-dwelling children. The high figures for inner-city children is exacerbated by the fact that many also suffer from iron-deficiency. In mid-1996, the Centers for Disease Control (CDC) detected unhealthy levels of lead in imported metal miniblinds, putting middle-class children at risk as well. According to the CDC, exposure to sunlight causes the lead used as a binding agent on the blinds to break down and mingle with the dust on the slats. Tests are now being conducted on other imported plastic and metal merchandise such as patio furniture and playground equipment.

The CDC recommends that all children under the age of six be tested annually. Many school systems have instituted this testing as part of their health screening. Parents who suspect that their children have ingested lead particles should have them tested immediately. Severe cases are treated with chelation therapy that binds the lead to tiny particles that are then filtered out of the bloodstream by the kidneys and eliminated in the urine. Because the effects of lead poisoning develop gradually over time, every child who tests positive for lead poisoning should undergo neuropsychological testing by the age of five and have his or her progress monitored throughout childhood and adolescence.

When a diagnosis is positive, the lead in the building where the poisoning occurred must be safely eliminated before the child returns. Children should not be present in the building during this procedure. Strip the walls and/or woodwork with liquid paint remover, covering the floor with drop cloths to catch the paint chips and dust. The surfaces should then be patched, sealed and repainted with lead-free paint or covered with wallpaper or paneling. Dispose of the drop cloths and wash the floors. Furniture and toys painted with leaded paint should be discarded or stripped and repainted in the same fashion.

Parents and child-care providers should also take care not to use lead or pewter cooking utensils, lead-glazed pottery or lead-lined storage containers.

For Further Study

Books

Brody, Jane E. "Aggressiveness and Delinquency in Boys is Linked to Lead in Bones." *The New York Times*, February 7, 1996, p. C9.

Hilgers, Laura. "Lead." *Parenting* 10, November 1996, pp. 155–61.

Laliberte, Richard. "Lead Alert! An Update on one of the Most Potent—and Pervasive—Poisons in Your Home." *Parents Magazine* 72, March 1997, pp. 52–56.

Lamb, Yannick Rice. "Lowdown on Lead." *Essence* 27, August 1996, p. 104.

PREVENTING LEAD POISONING IN THE HOME

- Encourage children to wash their hands, especially before snacks and meals. Children who suck their thumbs while sleeping should always wash their hands before naps and at bedtime.
- Wash pacifiers and toys regularly, particularly if young children still put objects in their mouths.
- To avoid tracking lead-contaminated soil indoors, leave shoes at the door.
- Serve foods high in calcium and iron. Iron-deficient children absorb more lead. Vitamin C improves iron absorption, so serve foods high in Vitamin C with foods high in iron. For example, a glass of orange juice at breakfast will improve the absorption of iron from a bowl of fortified cereal.
- Never use hot tap water for cooking, and always run cold water for 60 seconds before drinking—even longer if you haven't used the faucet for a few hours or overnight.
- If your home was built before 1978, do not undertake any remodeling that could disturb painted surfaces without first testing for the prescence of lead paint.

Organizations

National Lead Information Center
Address: 1025 Connecticut Ave., NW
Washington, DC 20036
Telephone: (800) 424-LEAD

Leadership

The ability to take initiative in planning, organizing, and managing group activities, projects, and games.

In any group of children or adults, there are those who step forward to organize people and events to achieve a specific result. In organized activities, leaders can be designated and, in informal contexts, such as children's play groups, they may emerge naturally. What makes certain people into leaders is open to debate. Thus Luella Cole and Irma Nelson Hall have written that leadership "seems to consist of a cluster of traits, a few inborn but most of them acquired or at least developed by contact with the environment." Leaders have their own leadership style, and that style may not transfer from one situation to another.

Psychologists have also defined leadership as a mentality, as opposed to aptitude, the assumption being that mentalities can be acquired. For example, as John E. Anderson has observed, parents often play a crucial role in fostering a leadership mentality in their children. According to Anderson, when strength of mind and independent thinking are encouraged, "children don't succumb to peer pressure; they follow their own beliefs." While defining leadership mentality in general terms, Anderson recognizes that children's leadership behavior will depend on their interests; therefore, he advises sensitivity toward the child's chosen area of leadership: for example, a leader of a discussion group may be uncomfortable playing games.

In a 1993 research review, Ron Maynard underscored the importance of a child's ability to use his or her characteristic "leadership style." Researchers have identified two distinct types of leaders: "idea generators" and "social facilitators." They function equally in the preschool years, but the two groups later separate. The "facilitators" gain ascendance in elementary school and are eclipsed by the "idea generators" in early adolescence. The groups do not necessarily have to compete, however. For example, an introverted "idea generator" can learn the fundamental skills needed for successful social interaction, thereby safeguarding his or her feelings of self-worth without the compulsion to compete with the "facilitator."

Child psychologists who study girls, and particularly educators and parents advocating equal-opportunity education for girls, have remarked that girls with leadership potential often have to struggle with various prejudices, which also include the notion that leadership is a "male" characteristic. In a study of 304 fourth-, fifth-, and six-graders enrolled in 16 Girl Scout troops, Cynthia A. Edwards found that in an all-female group, leaders consistently display characteristic qualities such as organizational skills and independent thinking. Significantly, election to leadership posts was based on perceived managerial skills, while "feminine" qualities, such as empathic behavior, were generally not taken into account. However, in examining the research on mixed (male-female) groups, Edwards has found studies that show "that the presence of male group members, even in the minority, suppresses the verbal expression and leadership behavior of female group members." The fact that leadership behavior can be suppressed would seem to strengthen the argument that leadership is, indeed, a learned behavior. A study by T. Sharpe, M. Brown, and K. Crider measured the effects of consistent positive reinforcement, favoring skills such as leadership, sportsmanship, and conflict resolution, on two urban elementary physical education classes. The researchers found that the focus on positive skills caused a significant increase in leadership and conflict-resolution behavior. These results seem to support the idea, discussed by Maynard, that leadership behavior can be non-competitive (different individuals exercising leadership in different areas) and also conducive to group cohesion, as children developing their strengths learn to replace conflict with collaborative behavior.

Although leaders display qualities they are born with, most leadership behaviors are learned. Parents and teachers can encourage the development of independent thinking and organizational abilities in children. Individual children have their own interests and leadership styles, however, and may not show leadership qualities in every context. Experts emphasize that learning to be an effective leader also means learning when to be a good follower. Knowing this distinction is an important step toward adulthood.

For Further Study

Books

Cole, Luella, and Irma Nelson Hall. *Psychology of Adolescence.* 7th ed. New York: Holt, Rinehart and Winston, 1970.

Periodicals

Anderson, John E. "By Knowing These Eight Secrets You Can . . . Make Your Child A Leader." *Reader's Digest* 143, no. 1855, July 1993, pp. 19–26.

Edwards, Cynthia A. "Leadership in Groups of School-Age Girls." *Developmental Psychology* 30, no. 6, November 1994, pp. 920–27.

Maynard, Ron. "Nurturing Leadership: How Children's Style Differ." *Chatelaine* 66, no. 5, May 1993, pp. 32.

Sharpe, T., M. Browne, and K. Crider. "The Effects of A Sportsmanship Curriculum Intervention on Generalized Positive Social Behavior of Urban Elementary School Students." *Journal of Applied Behavior Analysis* 28, 1995, pp. 401–16.

—Zoran Minderovic

Learned Helplessness

An apathetic attitude stemming from the conviction that one's actions do not have the power to affect one's situation.

The concept of learned helplessness was developed in the 1960s and 1970s by Martin Seligman (1942–) at the University of Pennsylvania. He found that animals receiving electric shocks, which they had no ability to prevent or avoid, were unable to act in subsequent situations where avoidance or escape was possible. Extending the ramifications of these findings to humans, Seligman and his colleagues found that human motivation to initiate responses is also undermined by a lack of control over one's surroundings. Further research has shown that learned helplessness disrupts normal development and learning and leads to emotional disturbances, especially **depression.**

Learned helplessness in humans can begin very early in life if infants see no correlation between actions and their outcome. Institutionalized infants, as well as those suffering from maternal deprivation or inadequate mothering, are especially at risk for learned helplessness due to the lack of adult responses to their actions. It is also possible for mothers who feel helpless to pass this quality on to their children. Learned helplessness in children, as in adults, can lead to anxiety or depression, and it can be especially damaging very early in life, for the sense of mastery over one's environment is an important foundation for future emotional development. Learned helplessness can also hamper education: a child who fails repeatedly in school will eventually stop trying, convinced that there is nothing he or she can do to succeed.

In the course of studying learned helplessness in humans, Seligman found that it tends to be associated with certain ways of thinking about events that form what he termed a person's "explanatory style." The three major components of explanatory style associated with learned helplessness are permanence, pervasiveness, and personalization. Permanence refers to the belief that negative events and/or their causes are permanent, even when evidence, logic, and past experience indicate that they are probably temporary ("Amy hates me and will never be my friend again" vs. "Amy is angry with me today"; "I'll never be good at math"). Pervasiveness refers to the tendency to generalize so that negative features of one situation are thought to extend to others as well ("I'm stupid" vs. "I failed a math test" or "nobody likes me" vs. "Janet didn't invite me to her party"). Personalization, the third component of explanatory style, refers to whether one tends to attribute negative events to one's own flaws or to outside circumstances or other people. While it is important to take responsibility for one's mistakes, persons suffering from learned helplessness tend to blame themselves for everything, a tendency associated with low **self-esteem** and depression. The other elements of explanatory style—permanence and pervasiveness—can be used as gauges to assess whether the degree of self-blame over a particular event or situation is realistic and appropriate.

Seligman believes it is possible to change people's explanatory styles to replace learned helplessness with "learned optimism." To combat (or even prevent) learned helplessness in both adults and children, he has successfully used techniques similar to those used in cognitive therapy with persons suffering from depression. These include identifying negative interpretations of events, evaluating their accuracy, generating more accurate interpretations, and decatastrophizing (countering the tendency to imagine the worst possible consequences for an event). He has also devised exercises to help children overcome negative explanatory style (one that tends toward permanent, pervasive, and personalized responses to negative situations). Other resources for promoting learned optimism in children include teaching them to dispute their own negative thoughts and promoting their problem-solving and social skills.

Seligman claims that parents can also promote learned optimism in children who are too young for the types of techniques outlined above by applauding and encouraging their mastery of new situations and letting them have as much control as possible in everyday activities such as dressing and eating. In addition, parents influence the degree of optimism in their youngsters through their own attitudes toward life and their explanatory styles, which can be transmitted even to very young children.

For Further Study

Books

Seligman, Martin. *Helplessness: On Development, Depression, and Death.* New York: W.H. Freeman, 1975.

———. *The Optimistic Child.* New York: HarperCollins, 1995.

———. *Learned Optimism.* New York: A.A. Knopf, 1991.

....

Learning Disability

A disorder that causes problems in speaking, listening, reading, writing, or mathematical ability. (Also Specific Developmental Disorder).

A learning disability is a disorder that inhibits or interferes with the skills of learning, including speaking, listening, **reading,** writing, or mathematical ability. Legally, a learning disabled child is one whose level of academic achievement is two or more years below the standard for his age and IQ level. It is estimated that anywhere from 5–20% of school-age children in the United States, mostly boys, suffer from learning disabilities (currently, most sources place this figure at 20%). Often, learning disabilities appear together with other disorders, such as **attention deficit/hyperactivity disorder** (ADHD). They are thought to be caused by irregularities in the functioning of certain parts of the brain. Evidence suggests that these irregularities are often inherited (a child is more likely to develop a learning disability if other family members have them). However, learning disabilities are also associated with certain conditions occurring during fetal development or birth, including maternal use of alcohol, drugs, and tobacco, exposure to infection, injury during birth, low birth weight, and sensory deprivation.

Aside from underachievement, other warning signs that a child may have a learning disability include overall lack of organization, forgetfulness, taking unusually long amounts of time to complete assignments, and a negative attitude toward school and schoolwork. In the classroom, the child's teacher may observe one or more of the following characteristics: difficulty paying attention, unusual sloppiness and disorganization, social withdrawal, difficulty working independently, and trouble switching from one activity to another. In addition to the preceding signs, which relate directly to school and schoolwork, certain general behavioral and emotional features often accompany learning disabilities. These include impulsiveness, restlessness, distractibility, poor physical coordination, low tolerance for frustration, low **self-esteem, daydreaming,** inattentiveness, and anger or sadness.

Types of learning disabilities

Learning disabilities are associated with brain dysfunctions that affect a number of basic skills. Perhaps the most fundamental is sensory-perceptual ability—the capacity to take in and process information through the senses. Difficulties involving vision, hearing, and touch will have an adverse effect on learning. Although learning is usually considered a mental rather than a physical pursuit, it involves motor skills, and it can also be impaired by problems with motor development. Other basic skills fundamental to learning include memory, attention, and language abilities.

The three most common academic skill areas affected by learning disabilities are reading, writing, and arithmetic. Some sources estimate that between 60–80% of children diagnosed with learning disabilities have reading as their only or main problem area. Learning disabilities involving reading have traditionally been known as **dyslexia;** currently the preferred term is developmental reading disorder. A wide array of problems is associated with reading disorders, including difficulty identifying groups of letters, problems relating letters to sounds, reversals and other errors involving letter position, chaotic spelling, trouble with syllabication, failure to recognize words, hesitant oral reading, and word-by-word rather than contextual reading. Writing disabilities, known as dysgraphia, include problems with letter formation and writing layout on the page, repetitions and omissions, punctuation and capitalization errors, "mirror writing," and a variety of spelling problems. Children with dysgraphia typically labor at written work much longer than their classmates, only to produce large, uneven writing that would be appropriate for a much younger child.

Learning abilities involving math skills, generally referred to as dyscalcula (or dyscalculia), usually become apparent later than reading and writing problems—often at about the age of eight. Children with dyscalcula may have trouble counting, reading and writing numbers, understanding basic math concepts, mastering calculations, and measuring. This type of disability may also involve problems with nonverbal learning, including spatial organization.

Assessment

The first step in dealing with a learning disability is assessment by one or more qualified professionals, such as a learning specialist with a master's or doctoral degree, a psychologist, or a psychiatrist. The evaluation setting may be the child's school, a community mental health center, an outpatient clinic affiliated with a hospital or university, or a professional practitioner's private office. The person performing the assessment gathers comprehensive background information about the child and the family and administers several types of testing. Psychological testing consists of IQ tests to assess a child's verbal and nonverbal **intelligence** and projective tests to evaluate his emotional state. Educational tests evaluate academic skills in basic areas including reading, writing, and arithmetic. Neuropsychological tests determine possible inefficiencies in brain functioning by assessing motor skills, perception, **memory,** and language. After the testing is completed, a follow-up session is scheduled to discuss the results. At this time, referral may be made to other professionals, such as a speech-language pathologist, audiologist, ophthalmologist, or psychiatrist.

Treatment

The principal forms of treatment for learning disabilities are remedial education and **psychotherapy.** Either may be provided alone, the two may be provided simultaneously, or one may follow the other. Schools are required by law to provide specialized instruction for children with learning disabilities. Remediation may take place privately with a tutor or in a school resource center. A remediator works with the child individually, often devising strategies to circumvent the barriers caused by the disability. A child with dyscalcula, for example, may be shown a "shortcut" or "trick" that involves memorizing a spatial pattern or design and then superimposing it on calculations of a specific type, such as double-digit multiplication problems. The most important aspect of remediation is finding new ways to solve old problems. In this respect, remediation diverges from ordinary tutoring methods that use drill and repetition, which are ineffective in dealing with learning disabilities. The earlier remediation is begun, the more effective it will be. At the same time that they are receiving remedial help, children with learning disabilities spend as much time as possible in the regular classroom.

While remediation addresses the obstacles created by the learning disability itself, psychotherapy deals with the emotional and behavioral problems associated with the condition. The difficulties caused by learning disabilities are bound to affect a child's emotional state and behavior. The inability to succeed at tasks that pose no unusual problems for one's peers creates a variety of unpleasant feelings, including shame, doubt, embarrassment, frustration, anger, confusion, fear, and sadness. These feelings pose several dangers if they are allowed to persist over time. First, they may aggravate the disability: excessive **stress** can interfere with the performance of many tasks, especially those that are difficult to begin with. In addition, other, previously developed abilities may suffer as well, further eroding the child's self-confidence. Finally, destructive emotional and behavioral patterns that begin in response to a learning disability may become entrenched and extend to other areas of a child's life. Both psychoanalytic and behaviorally oriented methods are used in therapy for children with learning disabilities.

The sensitivity developed over the past two decades to the needs of students with learning disabilities has extended to college campuses, virtually all of which have special resource and advocacy centers for students with disabilities, including learning disabilities. Many learning disabled students have been accommodated by special measures such as extra time on exams and classroom note takers. However, this trend has recently produced a backlash at some colleges by persons who are concerned with declining academic standards and who question whether the increasing claims of learning disabilities among college students—which have doubled since 1988—are all justified. In 1995 Jon Westling, newly appointed president of Boston University, known for its progressive attitude policies regarding learning disabilities, aroused widespread controversy by requiring learning disabled students to be retested and revoking some of the accommodations that had previously been provided to them. In 1997 the university was sued by ten learning-disabled students who faced the loss of special assistance that had previously been provided to them.

For Further Study

Books

Clayton, Lawrence, and Jaydene Morrison. *Coping with a Learning Disability.* New York: Rosen Publishing Group, 1992. [Juvenile]

Cummings, Rhoda Woods, and Gary Fisher. *The Survival Guide for Teenagers with LD.* Minneapolis: Free Spirit Publishers, 1993.

Getman, Gerald N. *Smart in Everything—Except School.* Santa Ana, CA: VisionExtension, 1992.

Mangrum, Charles T., and Stephen S. Strichart. *Peterson's Colleges with Programs for Students with Learning Disabilities,* 4th ed. Princeton: Peterson's, 1994.

Novick, Barbara Z., and Maureen M. Arnold. *Why Is My Child Having Trouble at School?: A Parent's Guide to Learning Disabilities.* New York: Villard Books, 1991.

Tuttle, Cheryl Gerson, and Gerald A. Tuttle, eds. *Challenging Voices: Writings By, For, and About People with Learning Disabilities.* Los Angeles: Lowell House, 1995.

Wong, Y.L., ed. *Learning About Learning Disabilities.* San Diego: Academic Press, 1991.

Organizations

Association for Children and Adults with Learning Disabilities
Address: 4900 Girard Rd.
Pittsburgh, PA 15227-1444
Telephone: (412) 881-2253

National Center for Learning Disabilities
Address: 99 Park Ave.
New York, NY 10016
Telephone: (212) 687-7211

Left-handed *see* **Handedness**

. . . .

Leukemia

A set of related cancers that form in the bone marrow and other blood-producing organs.

Leukemia is named after the leukocytes, white blood cells which mutate before maturity and become cancerous. These cells reproduce rapidly, suppressing production of normal white cells that are essential to fighting infection in the body, and red cells that are needed to carry oxygen in the blood. **Cancer** cells may spread to the liver, spleen, lymph nodes, genitals, or the brain.

After accidents, leukemia is the leading cause of death for children ages 2–15. It is the most common form of cancer among children, accounting for up to one-third of childhood cancers. Of 28,000 cases diagnosed per year, 2,500 are children. The incidence of leukemia peaks between the ages of 3–5 for whites, but remains constant up until age 20 for non-white populations. There are several types of leukemia, depending on the type of blood cell affected and the course of development. It may be *chronic*, slowly progressing with few symptoms for up to 20 years or more, or *acute*, with sudden onset and rapid progression of symptoms requiring immediate hospitalization and treatment. Most childhood leukemia is acute: 75% of cases are of the acute lymphocytic type, 20% are acute myelocytic, and 5% are chronic myelocytic ("cytic"= of the cell). Chromosomal abnormalities predispose children to develop leukemia, and **Down**

syndrome children in particular are 30 times more likely than others to be leukemic. Long-term exposure or direct contact with chemicals found in some herbicides and pesticides has been shown to induce leukemia, and many identified chemicals were banned during the 1970s. Studies have also attributed some leukemia to long-term exposure to high-voltage power lines (due to their magnetic fields). A 1996 report by the National Research Council found no conclusive evidence linking power lines to cancers, but did acknowledge an unexplained link between leukemia and the high magnetic fields that the lines produce (See **Electric and magnetic fields**).

Early symptoms of leukemia are high **fever**, recurrent infections, bleeding of the gums or nose, bruising, bone pain or tenderness, fatigue, headaches, and swelling in the neck, armpit, or groin. Diagnosis will be based on a blood sample and confirmed by a bone marrow **biopsy**, where a syringe is inserted into the spine. Until the 1960s leukemia was almost always fatal—within a matter of months for the acute forms. Yet, since the development and specialization of chemo-(drug), radiation(x ray), and transfusion therapies, a large proportion of childhood leukemia is now curable. Estimates range from 50–70% survival rates for the most common form, acute lymphocytic leukemia (ALL). Children diagnosed between the ages of 3–9 have the best prognosis.

The primary issue in treating leukemia is to kill the cancerous blood cells while preserving the healthy ones. Treatment involves three basic stages: *induction, consolidation*, and *maintenance*. The patient may take antibiotics throughout the process in order to fight infection. During the *induction* phase the goal is to induce remisssion, i.e., to stop cancer cells from multiplying and to drastically lower the percentage of eixsting ones through "rapid cell kill." The patient is exposed to extremely high doses of chemotherapy, either orally or by injection, or radiation therapy, where x rays are directed at tumorous areas. Because the drugs kill healthy white cells as well as cancerous ones, the patient will become extremely vulnerable to bacterial and fungal infections as the immune system is weakened.

The primary side effects of the medication itself are hair loss and nausea, which can sometimes be severe. After remission is achieved, during the *consolidation* phase the goal is essentially to reactivate the patient's immune system. This may be done with further chemotherapy (sometimes using different drugs) or by a bone-marrow transplant, which introduces new, healthy white cells. Generally bone marrow transplants are not attempted until a relapse has occured and chemotherapy has been found ineffective. If a transplant is necessary, marrow from a compatible donor—ideally a sibling, or from the patient's own body will be used. Unfortunately, about 5–10% of transplant recipients die from the transplant itself,

due to the body's rejection of foreign cells (known as graft vs. host rejection) and other complications. A newer form of transplant, where the patient's own marrow is removed, "cleaned" of cancerous cells and then reinjected into the body avoids the graft-host problem, but its efficacy is disputed.

The final phase of leukemia treatment, *maintenance*, lasts from one to three years, during which the patient stays under surveillance and may receive periodic chemotherapy, transfusions, and radiation. During this phase the child's hair will usually grow back, other side effects subside, and he or she can return to school. If a relapse occurs, the consolidation phase may begin again and some form of transplant used, but after a certain point the level of toxicity entailed in treating the leukemia would be equal to or greater than the damage done by the cancer itself. Treatment is usually stopped after two years, and if relapse occurs, the disease is allowed to take its course.

For Further Study

Books

Johnson, F. Leonard, and Marc Miller. *Shannon: A Book for Parents of Children with Leukemia*. New York: Hawthorn Books, 1975.

Baker, Lynn S., et al. *You and Leukemia: A Day at A Time*. Philadelphia: Saunders, 1978.

Organizations

Leukemia Society of America
Telephone: toll-free (800) 955-4LSA [955-4572]
(A national voluntary health agency dedicated to curing leukemia and related cancers—lymphoma, multiple myloma and Hodgkin's disease—and to improving the quality of life of patients and their families. Call for local chapter information.)

National Childhood Cancer Foundation
Address: 440 E. Huntington Drive, Suite 300
P.O. Box 60012
Arcadia, CA 91066-6012
Telephone: toll-free (800) 458-6223
Website: http://www.nccf.org/
(A non-profit organization that supports pediatric cancer treatment and research projects at over 115 medical institutions in the United States, Canada, and Australia.)

Lincoln-Oseretsky Motor Development Scale

Assesses the development of motor skills.

The Lincoln-Oseretsky Motor Development Scale is an individually administered test that assesses the development of motor skills in children and adults. Areas covered include **fine** and **gross motor skills,** finger dexterity and speed, and hand-eye coordination. The test consists of 36 tasks arranged in order of increasing difficulty. These include walking backwards, standing on one foot, touching one's nose, jumping over a rope, throwing and catching a ball, putting coins in a box, jumping and clapping, balancing on tiptoe while opening and closing one's hands, and balancing a rod vertically. Norms for each part of the test are provided for children aged 6-14 with percentiles.

For Further Study

Books

McCullough, Virginia. *Testing and Your Child: What You Should Know About 150 of the Most Common Medical, Educational, and Psychological Tests.* New York: Plume, 1992.

Walsh, W. Bruce, and Nancy E. Betz. *Tests and Assessment.* 2nd ed. Englewood Cliffs, NJ: Prentice Hall, 1990.

Lisping

A disorder of speech articulation involving the inability to pronounce one or more sibilant consonant sounds, usually s or z, correctly.

Lisping is a speech disorder characterized by the inability to pronounce the sounds of s or z, known as the sibilant consonants, correctly. Usually *th* sounds are substituted for the sibilants; the word "lisp," for example, would be pronounced "lithp" by someone with this speech disorder. Sometimes there are also problems with *sh* and *ch* sounds. Many children lisp at certain stages of speech development, especially when they lose their front primary teeth. This frontal or interdental lisp, produced when the tongue protrudes through the front teeth, is the most familiar type of lisp. Sibilant production may be interfered with in a number of other ways as well. These are all classified as lisping and include excessive pressure by the tongue against the teeth; the tongue held too far back along the midline of the palate; and a "substitute hiss" produced in the throat or larynx.

Lisping has a variety of causes, both physiological and psychological. Physiological causes include structural irregularities of the tongue, palate, or teeth (including abnormalities in the number or position of teeth) and mild hearing loss involving high frequencies. In some cases, a child with no physical abnormality will develop a lisp by imitating another child or an adult who lisps. Lisping is also associated with immaturity: in some cases children will deliberately adopt a babyish lisp as a form of psychological regression. Unless it has psychological causes, lisping in children under the age of eight is considered a part of normal speech development and is usu-

ally not a cause for concern. However, if a child eight years of age or older lisps, evaluation by a speech-language pathologist is generally recommended. If untreated, lisping can persist into adulthood.

For Further Study

Books

Barach, Carol. *Help Me Say It: A Parent's Guide to Speech Problems.* New York: Harper & Row, 1983.

Cantwell, Dennis P. *Developmental Speech and Language Disorders.* New York: Guilford Press, 1987.

Hanson, Marvin L. *Articulation.* Philadelphia: Saunders, 1983.

Lass, N. J., L. V. McReynolds, and J. L. Northern. *Handbook on Speech-Language Pathology and Audiology.* Philadelphia: B. C. Decker, 1988.

Shames, G., and E. Wiig, eds. *Human Communication Disorders: An Introduction.* Columbus, OH: Charles Merrill Publishing Co., 1982.

Sommers, Ronald K. *Articulation Disorders.* Englewood Cliffs, NJ: 1983.

Organizations

American Speech-Language-Hearing Association
Address: 10801 Rockville Pike
Rockville, MD 20785
Telephone: (301) 897-5700

Literacy

The ability to read and write.

Declining literacy in the United States has been an increasing cause for concern in recent decades. The Department of Education's National Adult Literacy survey, released in 1993, surveyed a demographic cross section of 27,000 Americans over the age of 16 and found that nearly 50% were functionally illiterate (lacking the reading and writing skills to function effectively in the workplace). Of these, almost half were barely able to read or write at all, while the rest lacked literacy skills beyond the fifth-grade level. The literacy level of adults between the ages of 21 and 25 had dropped 14% since the publication of a similar survey in 1985. The country's literacy crisis has also been documented by declining **SAT** scores over the past 30 years, especially on the verbal portion of the test.

Literacy and the schools

Numerous reasons have been cited for the rising illiteracy rate in the United States, including such social and cultural factors as overcrowded classrooms, television, drugs, the breakdown of the American family, and the growing ethnic diversity of the student population. The American education system itself has been criticized from a variety of viewpoints. Following the lead of Rudolf Flesch's 1955 best-seller *Why Johnny Can't Read,* some experts have blamed the switch from **phonics** to the word recognition teaching method. Others cite neglectful teaching of basic grammar, syntax, and spelling skills and the "dumbing down" of textbooks since World War II (the average 12th-grade literature textbook has been found to be simpler than those used by prewar 7th and 8th graders). Most recently, controversy has arisen over the adoption of the holistic **whole-language** approach, which introduces reading in the context of children's literature and, in some cases, allows students to invent their own spelling systems, which are gradually corrected through reading and instruction. In a backlash against the perceived failure of these programs to provide students with adequate reading skills, parents and educators in some areas of the country have once again advocated a renewed emphasis on phonics instruction.

Literacy and the family

Although schools are responsible for formal reading instruction, families play a crucial role in a child's acquisition of literacy skills. Parents who value language and literacy are likely to pass on this quality to their children, while the acquisition of literary skills is more difficult for children from homes where reading is a low priority. One of the greatest problems posed by the current high rate of functional illiteracy in the United States is that the children of illiterate parents are at risk for educational failure. In addition to providing a negative role model, parents who are illiterate are unable to read to their children or support their school participation in such routine ways as responding to teachers' notes or helping with homework. Children of high school dropouts are six times more likely than their peers to drop out of high school themselves. In response to this problem, family literacy centers have multiplied throughout the nation—their number grew from 500 to over 5,000 in the 10 years between 1985 and 1995. Recent studies have found that such programs have made a dramatic difference in helping at-risk students avoid having to repeat grades in school.

Lack of cultural responsiveness by educators has been cited as a cause of literacy problems among ethnic minorities. It is important for children to have continuity between the early at-home learning they do with their parents—who are their first language teachers—and their later experiences at school. Strategies for insuring this kind of continuity include having teachers familiarize themselves with the speech patterns and learning styles of the different ethnic groups they teach.

Reading out loud

Of the various things parents can do to help improve their children's language skills, one of the most important is reading out loud to them, even after they are old enough to read by themselves. Many writers and other language experts have lamented the decline of oral reading, which was once a popular pastime among young and old alike. According to a 1990 survey, only 20% of parents read to their children on a daily basis, while 42% read to them two to three times a week. Reading aloud stretches a child's imagination and attention span; provides new information; enriches vocabulary; exposes children to good grammar; improves listening comprehension; and provides a positive role model.

Infancy. Any child who can be talked to can be read to as well. In fact, researchers have demonstrated that infants can distinguish passages that have been read to them in utero. In infancy, the most important component of reading aloud is simply the stimulating and reassuring sound of the parent's voice. Books should be chosen to stimulate sight and hearing. Over the first months of life, the infant takes an increasingly active role in the ritual of reading, changing from a passive listener to one who turns the pages and points to pictures. Frequent short readings are recommended, as an infant's attention span on books is only about three minutes.

Toddlerhood. Picture books are an excellent way to help toddlers begin learning to name familiar objects. This is the stage when children first acquire favorite books. Experts have pointed out that as boring as the constant repetition may be to adults, the child may really be finding something new in the book with every reading. Repetition also improves the child's memory, vocabulary, and sequencing abilities. At this stage, children are drawn to books that provide reassurance, humor, predictability, and characters with whom they can identify.

Preschool and school age. As the child continues to mature, her attention span may be expanded by choosing longer books—including books with chapters—that can be read over the course of several days. School-age children can benefit by a cross-disciplinary approach that encourages outside investigation of topics that are brought up in their reading material, such as a project that calls for locating the settings of their books on maps. It is also important for students to have an adequate opportunity to discuss stories that are read to them. Even in the upper grades, many picture books retain their fascination. Older children (and, indeed, adults) can always find new levels of meaning in books that they read when they were younger. At the same time, children in the upper elementary grades can also be introduced to short novels as read-aloud material. Reading aloud need not stop with the advent of adolescence: in-class reading of such texts as poems, magazines articles, and newspaper columns can open up new areas of interest for older students to pursue further on their own.

Family activities to promote literacy

It is helpful for parents to keep up with subjects that children are reading about on their own so they can discuss them together. Parents can also transmit a love of reading to their children by providing a positive example and being active readers themselves. Children who see their parents caught up in an absorbing novel or reading about a favorite hobby will be more likely to pursue their own interests through books.

Although reading is generally a solitary pursuit, literacy can be enhanced through group activities involving the whole family. Even an ordinary activity like dinner table conversation can improve language skills, and experts say that parents should not talk down to their children by avoiding big words, which can help build a child's vocabulary. Parents can make language acquisition fun for their children through word games and even playful activities based on such mundane reading matter as product labels and road signs. Another important family activity is the regular visit to the neighborhood library. In addition to checking out books, children can be encouraged to participate in activities such as book clubs and special readings.

In addition to instilling in their children a genuine enjoyment of reading, parents can also emphasize the importance of literacy in making sense of the world and even in making it a better place. Children can be encouraged to keep up with current events through children's magazines or children's pages of the local newspaper. Educators also recommend having children write letters to public officials and letters to the editor about public issues and causes that arouse their concern.

For Further Study

Books

Chall, Jeanne. *Learning to Read: The Great Debate.* New York: McGraw-Hill, 1983.

Flesch, Rudolf. *Why Johnny Still Can't Read: A New Look at the Scandal of Our Schools.* New York: Harper & Row, 1981.

Leonhardt, Mary. *Parents Who Love Reading, Kids Who Don't.* New York: Crown Publishers, 1993.

Lipson, Eden Ross. *The New York Times Parent's Guide to the Best Books for Children.* New York: Random House, 1988.

McCuen, Gary E. *Illiteracy in America.* Hudson, WI: GEM Publications, 1988.

Morrow, L. M. *Literacy Development in the Early Years.* Boston: Allyn and Bacon, 1993.

Trelease, Jim. *The Read-Aloud Handbook.* 4th ed. New York: Penguin Books, 1995.

Organizations

National Clearinghouse on Literacy Education
  Address: 1118 22nd St. NW

Washington, DC 20037
  Telephone: (202) 429-9292
Literacy Volunteers of America
  Address: 5795 Widewaters Parkway
Syracuse, NY 13214
  Telephone: (315) 445-8000
Project Literacy U.S. (PLUS)
  Address: Box 2
4802 Fifth Ave.
Pittsburgh, PA 15213
The National Center for Family Literacy
  Address: Waterfront Plaza, Suite 200
325 W. Main St.
Louisville, KY 40202-4251
  Telephone: (592) 584-1133

Liver Development and Function

The largest of the body's organs, with the greatest number of functions.

The liver is the largest of the body's organs. It produces major proteins and chemicals, purifies the blood, converts food to energy and stores it in the form of glucose, and excretes unwanted substances. One of the primary chemicals produced by the liver is bile, which facilitates the digestion of fats in the small intestine. The liver is present by the third week after conception and begins basic functioning by the sixth or eighth week. However, the liver's ability to break down bilirubin and bile acids is still rudimentary at birth. Development continues until sometime between the ages of six months to one year when the liver reaches adult-level functioning.

Jaundice, brought on by the buildup of bilirubin in the bile, is a common feature of liver dysfunction. It is characterized by yellow skin and yellow in the whites of the eyes. Newborns are the most susceptible because liver function is still immature. In many cases, newborn jaundice is a harmless and short-lived form called physiologic jaundice that disappears in a few days. However, 15% of newborns with jaundice require treatment. Jaundice in older children generally signals an underlying disease.

The most common liver diseases among children and adolescence are biliary atresia, hepatitis, Reye's syndrome, alpha-1-antitrypsin deficiency, galactosemia, and Wilson's disease. Biliary atresia is a severe, non-hereditary defect in the ducts that carry bile away from the liver. It is present in one of every 25,000 live births. Twice as many girls as boys are affected. The cause is not known but thought to result from in utero viral blood infection, a metabolic defect, or a biological poison in the bile duct cells. In affected infants, jaundice occurs within three to six weeks after birth. The liver is enlarged; the abdomen is swollen and tender to the touch. The infant's stool is generally putty-colored and sticky. Urine is caramel-colored. Sometimes a surgical technique called the Kasai procedure can replace the damaged ducts with a clear section of the child's intestine. However, this procedure is only effective in 50% of the cases. A liver transplant is the only way to completely correct biliary atresia.

Hepatitis, an inflammation of the liver, is primarily caused by a viral infection contracted by eating food or drinking water contaminated with human excrement. Hepatitis can also occur from the ingestion of excess chemicals or toxic substances. Children in **day care** are on the Centers for Disease Control and Prevention's high risk list for Hepatitis A. Acute cases usually dissipate in six months. Hepatitis B is the more severe form, particularly for infants. A vaccine is available for susceptible children, particularly those on dialysis or babies born to women with Hepatitis B. Children with **Down syndrome** are also at risk to contract Hepatitis B. The virus develops slowly with fever, headache, muscle aches, loss of appetite, and an itchy rash. Symptoms then increase to nausea, vomiting, abdominal and joint pain, and foul breath.

Reye's syndrome is a serious condition leading to the rapid deterioration of the liver and the development of encephalopathy (brain disease). The ammonia-processing properties of the liver are affected, causing the ammonia to accumulate and pass into the bloodstream and brain. It can affect children from the age of one through adolescence, and generally occurs during the winter months. Children with the **chicken pox**, influenza and other viral infections are particularly at risk. Reye's syndrome usually develops two to seven days after the virus's onset. A child might exhibit forceful vomiting, drowsiness, hallucinations, delirium, and unusually aggressive or uncooperative behavior. Twenty to thirty percent of children with severe cases of Reye's syndrome die from extensive brain damage. There is strong evidence that aspirin can contribute to the risk, therefore parents are advised to use alternative pain and fever relievers in the treatment of viruses.

Galactosemia is an inherited enzyme deficiency affecting the digestion of milk sugars. The sugars build up in the liver, spread to other organs and, if left untreated, lead to cirrhosis, **cataracts**, and brain damage. It is often confused with lactose intolerance. The affected child may exhibit vomiting, weight loss, and lethargy. Treatment is the complete removal of milk from the child's diet as well as many fruits and vegetables that contain galactose.

Wilson's disease is a rare inherited abnormality caused by the accumulation of copper in the liver, resulting in cirrhosis and brain damage. Although present at birth, the symptoms may take five years to surface. When the copper invades the red blood cells, severe **anemia** re-

sults. Affected children may have a gold-brown or gray-green ring at the edge of the cornea. Treatment includes restricting the ingestion of copper-rich foods such as shellfish, organ meats, legumes, nuts, whole grain cereals, and chocolate; and the administering of the drug penicillamine (known commercially as Cuprunine or Depen).

Alpha-1-antitrypsin deficiency is the most common genetic cause of liver disease in children. Although it is present in one out of every 2,000 births in the United States, only 10–20% of affected children will develop liver disease. Symptoms in the infant include jaundice, abdominal swelling, and inefficient feeding. When it occurs in childhood or adolescence, symptoms include fatigue, poor appetite, abdominal swelling, and leg swelling. Although alpha-1-antitrypsin deficiency cannot be cured, it can be treated through a regiment of multiple vitamins and vitamins E, D, and K to provide essential nutrients. If liver failure develops, a transplant is recommended.

For Further Study

Organizations
Alpha One National Association
   Address: 1829 Portland Avenue S.
   Minneapolis, MN 55404
   Telephone: toll-free (800) 925-7421; 612/871-7332
   FAX: (612) 871-9441
American Liver Foundation
   Address: 1425 Pompton Avenue
   Cedar Grove, NJ 07009
   Telephone: toll-free (800) 465-4827; (201) 256-2550
   FAX: (201) 356-3214
Children's Liver Foundation, Inc.
   Address: 76 S. Orange Avenue, Suite 202
   South Orange, NJ 07040
   Telephone: (201) 761-1111
Parents of Galactosemic Children
   Address: 20981 Solano Way
   Boca Raton, FL 33433
   Telephone: (407) 852-0266
Wilson's Disease Association
   Address: P.O. Box 75324
   Washington, DC 20013
   Telephone: (703) 636-3003; (703) 636-3014

—Mary McNulty

Locus of Control

A personality orientation characterized either by the belief that one can control events by one's own efforts (internal locus of control) or that the future is determined by forces outside one's control (external locus of control).

If a child with an internal locus of control does badly on a test, she is likely to blame either her own lack of ability or preparation for the test. By comparison, a child with an external locus of control will tend to explain a low grade by saying that the test was too hard or that the teacher graded unfairly. The concept of locus of control was developed by psychologist Julian Rotter, who devised the Internal-External Locus of Control Scale (I-E) to assess this dimension of personality. Studies have found that this test is a valid predictor of behavior typically associated with locus of control.

Links have been found between locus of control and behavior patterns in a number of different areas. Adults and children with an internal locus of control are inclined to take responsibility for their actions, are not easily influenced by the opinions of others, and tend to do better at tasks when they can work at their own pace. By comparison, people with an external locus of control tend to blame outside circumstances for their mistakes and credit their successes to luck rather than to their own efforts. They are readily influenced by the opinions of others and are more likely to pay attention to the status of the opinion-holder, while people with an internal locus of control pay more attention to the content of the opinion regardless of who holds it. Some researchers have claimed that "internals" tend to be more intelligent and more success-oriented than "externals." In the elementary grades, children with an internal locus of control have been found to earn higher grades, although there are conflicting reports about whether there is a relationship between college grades and locus of control. There is also a relationship between a child's locus of control and his or her ability to delay gratification (to forgo an immediate pleasure or desire in order to be rewarded with a more substantial one later). In middle childhood, children with an internal locus of control are relatively successful in the **delay of gratification,** while children with an external locus of control are likely to make less of an effort to exert self-control in the present because they doubt their ability to influence events in the future.

Although people can be classified comparatively as "internals" or "externals," chronological development within each individual generally proceeds in the direction of an internal locus control. As infants and children grow older they feel increasingly competent to control events in their lives. Consequently, they move from being more externally focused to a more internal locus.

For Further Study

Books

Bem, Allen P. *Personality Theories.* Boston: Allyn and Bacon, 1994.

Burger, Jerry M. *Personality.* Pacific Grove, CA: Brooks/Cole Publishing Company, 1993.

Logical Thinking

The ability to understand and to incorporate the rules of basic logical inference in everyday activities.

Regarded as a universal human trait, the ability to think logically, following the rules of logical inference, has traditionally been defined as a higher cognitive skill, typically beyond the ken of a very young child. The field of cognitive child psychology was dominated for more than half a century by the Swiss philosopher and psychologist **Jean Piaget**, whose seminal studies are considered fundamental. Piaget identified four stages of cognitive development: during the *sensory-motor stage* (ages 0–2), the child learns to experience the world physically and attains a rudimentary grasp of symbols; in the *preoperational stage* (ages 2–7), symbols are used, but thought is still "preoperational," which means that the child does not understand that a logical, or mathematical, operation can be reversed; the *concrete operations stage* (ages 6 or 7–11) ushers in logical thinking: children, for instance, understand principles such as cause and effect; the *formal operations stage* (12–adulthood), introduces abstract thinking, i.e., thought operations that do not need to relate to concrete concepts and phenomena.

Logical thinking, in Piaget's developmental scheme, is operational, which means that it does not appear before the concrete operations stage. While students of child cognition generally agree with Piaget's developmental milestones, subsequent research in the area has led researchers to question the idea that some logical thinking cannot appear in the preoperational stage. For example, Olivier Houdè and Camilo Charron tested a group of 72 children between the ages of 5 and 8, giving them various tasks related to classes of objects, and found that children who could not perform extensional logic tasks were nevertheless able to practice intensional logic. (Intension defines the properties of a class, while extension determines who or what can be a member of a particular class; if the intension of a class is "red objects," the extension will include any particular object that happens to be red.) However, Piaget knew that preoperational children could practice intensional logic, but, in his view, incomplete logical thought was, by definition, pre-logical. For example, children who understand the meaning (intensionality) of a "red objects" class may decide not to include certain red objects--for reasons that the experimenter would define as illogical (e.g.: "it's too little").

Houdè and Charron have identified an "operational proto-logic" in children whom Piaget would define as pre-logical. Instead of arbitrarily promoting purely intensional thinking to the rank of full-fledged (extensional and intensional) logical thought, Houdè and Charron decided to investigate the mental processes underlying seemingly illogical behavior. In a series of experiments involving children aged 5–8, a group straddling the preoperational/operational boundary, the two researchers focused on the intensional logicians who failed the extensional logic (inclusion). Clearly, the act of not including some red object in the "red objects" class was, in a strictly Piagetian sense, illogical, or, more precisely, illogical behavior, but was that behavior determined by irrational thinking? To their surprise, they found, particularly in a modified form of the "partition" experiment (Piaget and Garcia, 1987), that, when shown the drawing of a circle (B) divided into two by a line (the two subclasses being A and A'), A' may be ignored as a subclass of B, not because of illogical thinking, but because A is more compelling from the point of view of perception. According to Pascual-Leone (Pascual-Leone, 1988), there is a misleading scheme underlying the perception of B, and a subclass is excluded. According to Houdè and Charron, the child understands the intensional logic, or meaning, of the "red objects" class, but stumbles at the extensional, or inclusion, level because of perceptual factors. Thus, the undeniable Piagetian shift, around the age of seven years, from non-inclusive to inclusive behavior does not indicate a quantum leap from pre-logical to logical thinking, but, rather, reflects the presence of an inhibiting mechanism, whereby the confusing effect of perception on cognition is neutralized. Thus, as Houdè and Charron have remarked, a non-inclusive six-year-old may have an inefficient inhibiting mechanism. These findings, although suggesting a continuum model of cognitive development, as opposed to the Piagetian idea of a quantum leap from pre-logical to logical thinking, does not, in fact, question the foundations of Piaget's essentially developmental theory of cognition. Piaget himself, in his search for the origins of logical thinking, studied very young children, ever mindful of the relevance of other mental, and non-mental, factors and processes to the emergence of logical thought. Finally, Piaget's work was the foundation from which emerged the insight, corroborated by empirical observation, that the very young child is already a logician.

Philosophers specializing in the study of childhood have found that the logical repertoire of young children is not limited to intensional logic. Many utterances made by children, particularly statements involving the concepts of possibility and necessity, exhibit a grasp, albeit rudimentary, of modal logic, i.e., the branch of logic which formulates rules for propositions about possibility and necessity (Matthews, 1980). The fact that the discourse of young children fits easily into the formal context of modal logic, which is related to intensional logic, indicates that the children's logical aptitude may yield new surprises. Building on the rich legacy of Piaget's work, researchers have significantly expanded the field of cog-

nitive development, gaining critical insights which will further elucidate the human paradigm. The crucial relevance of Piagetian and post-Piagetian studies for the inquiry concerning logical thinking in children lies in the fact that these studies have shed light on the important role played by non-logical, and non-mental, factors in the formation of logical thought.

For Further Study

Books

Inhelder, Bärbel, and Jean Piaget. *The Early Growth of Logic in the Child: Classification and Seriation.* London: Routledge and Kegan Paul, 1964.

Matthews, Gareth B. *Philosophy and the Young Child.* Cambridge: Harvard University Press, 1980.

Periodicals

Garcia, R. "Logique extensionnelle et logique intensionnelle." In Jean Piaget and R. Garcia, eds., *Vers une logique des significations.* Geneva: Murionde, 1987.

Houdè, Olivier, and Camilo Charron. "Catègorisation et logique intensionnelle chez l'enfant." *L'annèe psychologique* 95, March 1995, pp. 63-86.

Pascal-Leone, J. "Organismic Processes for Neo-Piagetian Theories: A Dialectical Causal Account of Cognitive Development." In A. Demetriou, ed., *The Neo-Piagetian Theories of Cognitive Development: Toward an Integration.* Amsterdam: North-Holland, 1988.

—Zoran Minderovic

Longitudinal Study

Research method used to study changes over time.

Researchers in such fields as **developmental psychology** use longitudinal studies to study changes in individual or group behavior over an extended period of time by repeatedly monitoring the same subjects. In longitudinal research, results are recorded for the same group of subjects, referred to as a cohort, throughout the course of the study.

An example of a longitudinal study might be an examination of the effects of preschool attendance on later school performance. The researchers would select two groups of children—one comprised of children who attend preschool, and the other comprised of children who had no preschool experience prior to attending kindergarten. These children would be evaluated at different points during their school career. The longitudinal study allows the researcher to focus on these children as they mature and record developmental patterns across time. A disadvantage of the longitudinal study is that researchers must be engaged in the study over a period of years and risk losing some of their research subjects, who may discontinue their participation for any number of reasons. Another disadvantage of the longitudinal study reflects the fact that some of the changes or behaviors observed during the study may be the effects of the assessment process itself. In addition to the longitudinal study, some researchers may employ the cross-sectional study method. In this method, the subjects, or cohort, are drawn from different groups and are studied at the same point in time.

Lung Development and Breathing Disorders

By taking in oxygen from the air and expelling carbon dioxide, the lungs play a crucial role in maintaining life. The oxygen gathered by the lungs enters the blood as it circulates and is distributed to cells throughout the body. Of all the body's organs, the lungs, which are not yet fully mature at birth, account for the greatest number of health problems in infants and young children, including viral and bacterial infections, **asthma,** and obstruction from swallowing or inhaling foreign objects and substances.

During the prenatal stage, the lungs are among the last organs to finish developing. The surfactant coating that keeps them from sticking together isn't formed until the last month or two of gestation. The air sacs (alveoli) at the ends of the bronchial tubes are formed last and continue developing for some time after birth: the lungs of infants have only one-tenth as many air sacs as those of adults. The unborn baby, who is suspended in fluid, does not need lungs yet because the placenta exchanges oxygen and carbon dioxide, performing the task the lungs will later assume. The lungs themselves are also filled with fluid, most of which is expelled during the birth process. After birth, the chest expands and takes in air for the first time as the infant takes her first breath. After the first few breaths, the lungs should be fully expanded, and the air sacs fully inflated within an hour. Deep breathing begins about 30 seconds after birth, and respiration should total 30 to 60 breaths per minute by the time the infant is 90 minutes old. The lungs are pale pink at birth, eventually becoming darker as a result of inhaling dust and other particles.

Newborns

Some babies need help breathing at birth, a condition known as perinatal **asphyxia**, which requires emergency treatment. Any liquids blocking the baby's airway are removed, and the infant is supplied with oxygen. In most cases, the initial gasp of oxygen is enough to initiate breathing. Sometimes a tracheal tube and/or artificial respiration are necessary. Asphyxia in newborns has been linked to low birth weight, late deliveries, and flattening or twisting of the umbilical cord during labor. An infant's risk of asphyxia is lower today than in the past thanks to medical advances that help physicians identify babies at risk for asphyxia before birth, enabling doctors to take precautions before or shortly after the baby is born. If the infant starts breathing within the first five minutes, lasting damage can be averted. In some cases where an infant is known to be at risk for asphyxia, an emergency delivery may be attempted either by forceps or cesarean section.

Newborns not suffering from asphyxia may still undergo acute respiratory distress from various causes. The most widespread is hyaline membrane disease, also known as Respiratory Distress Syndrome (RDS). Usually found in premature babies, it is caused by a lack of surfactant lining in the lungs, preventing the alveoli from functioning normally. At one time this condition was a leading cause of mortality in newborns, accounting for over 25,000 infant deaths per year. Advances in neonatal care since 1970 have increased the chances of survival from about 30% to over 75%. With the current treatment, which involves administering oxygen and intravenous fluids and using a breathing machine when necessary, the infant's condition usually improves dramatically within days. Another cause of respiratory distress in newborns is fetal lung fluid that is not properly absorbed at birth. Oxygen may need to be administered, but the fluid is usually absorbed within 24 hours. Meconium aspiration poses yet another danger for newborns. Meconium, the contents of the intestines before birth, can be aspirated at birth if it is expelled into the amniotic fluid, obstructing the infant's airway and threatening to cut off respiration. Meconium aspiration accounts for between 1 and 2% of all newborn deaths.

Several congenital defects can impair breathing, including tracheomalacia, in which the structures that support the airways are underdeveloped, causing them to narrow and become blocked; tracheal stenosis, a narrowing of the trachea itself due to cartilage, malformed arteries, cysts, and other causes; and disorders of the alveoli and their blood cells. Other congenital obstructions include choanal atresia, which obstructs the airway at the back of the nose, and obstructions of the larynx (voice box). In addition to obstructive disorders, infants sometimes suffer from problems with the central nervous system mechanism that controls breathing. Infants with apnea periodically stop breathing, a condition that can be triggered by an infection, a metabolic or cardiovascular disorder, maternal drug use, or a variety of other causes. Some cases of **apnea**, which is especially common in premature babies, resolve on their own. A related disorder is **Sudden Infant Death Syndrome** (SIDS), also known as crib death, in which an infant dies suddenly for no known reason. In most cases, an apparently healthy child is put to bed at night and found dead in the morning. Occurring in infants between the ages of one week and 12 months, SIDS claims 7,000 infants in the United States every year. While the cause of SIDS is not known, it is often classified as a respiratory disorder because the infant apparently stops breathing. Many cases occur in infants with mild colds or infections, and low birth weight and maternal smoking are known to be risk factors. In recent years, a connection has been found between SIDS and soft bedding that may trap carbon dioxide near the baby's face. There also appears to be a correlation between SIDS and babies who sleep on their stomachs. For this reason, the **American Academy of Pediatrics** now recommends that infants be put to sleep on their backs or sides.

Other respiratory disorders that can affect newborns include pulmonary edema (buildup of fluid in the lungs); neonatal pneumonia (usually caused by inhaling streptocuccus bacteria at birth); pulmonary hemorrhage (internal bleeding that fills a large part of the lung); congenital diaphragmatic hernias (in which the intestines protrude into the chest of the fetus, interfering with lung development); and obstruction caused by cardiovascular abnormalities.

Infants and children

Infants and children of all ages are subject to the most widespread respiratory disorder: the upper respiratory tract infection known as the common cold. Colds are caused by viruses transmitted through the air by sneezing and coughing or through touched surfaces that have had virus germs deposited on them by someone with a cold. Children get more colds than adults—often as many as three to nine in a single year. Symptoms—including sore throat, sneezing, nasal congestion, a runny nose, cough, or laryngitis—may end in three or four days, or they may last 10 days or longer. While the elusive cure for the common cold has yet to be found, acetaminophen is generally recommended to bring down any associated fever. Another common illness associated with respiratory tract symptoms is influenza (flu). This viral infection is generally divided into three types—A, B, and C (C is the mildest; A is the most severe and long-lasting). Unlike colds, the flu can occur in epidemics, and it can lead to dangerous pulmonary complications. In addition to the upper and lower respiratory symptoms that characterize colds, flu symptoms can also include headaches, a high fever with chills, muscles aches, loss of appetite, and weakness. The flu can also produce gastrointestinal symptoms. Although the flu generally has to run its course—usually within five days—it should be monitored careful-

ly because it can lead to secondary sinus or ear infections, and sometimes even to pneumonia.

Croup is an inflammation of the air passages that lead to the lungs. The larynx, trachea, or bronchi may be affected. In children under the age of three all three are typically involved, and the infection is a viral one. Symptoms include a "barking" cough, noisy (stridorous) breathing, breathing with difficulty, wheezing, and hoarseness. Croup can be dangerous because it can severely obstruct the breathing of young children, who have smaller airways than older children or adults. Signs of serious respiratory obstruction—requiring emergency medical treatment—include rapid, difficult breathing, inability to speak, drooling, increasing restlessness, sweating, and a rapid pulse. The most severe form of croup, epiglottitis, can completely block a child's breathing in four to 12 hours. It is treated by placing a tube in the trachea and administering oxygen.

It is not uncommon for a cold to lead to **bronchitis,** a lower respiratory inflammation of the trachea and bronchial tubes. When the larynx is also affected, the condition is known as laryngotracheobronchitis. Bronchitis can be caused by viruses, bacteria, or **allergies.** Acute bronchitis, usually caused by a cold virus, is a common childhood disease, especially in children under the age of four. It begins with a dry, hacking cough lasting up to three days, followed by a loose cough that produces thick mucous or sputum and that worsens at night. Since the virus itself cannot be treated with medication, treatment is limited to controlling the symptoms with either a cough suppressant such as dextromethorphan for a dry, hacking cough or an expectorant such as guaifenesin to help thin the sputum of a loose cough so it can be expelled, unclogging the airways. Children with bronchitis also needs to get plenty of rest so that the body can fight the infection. In cases where bronchial inflammation is caused by a bacterial infection, antibiotics such as erythromycin can be prescribed.

Bronchitis also occurs as a chronic ailment, with symptoms persisting over several weeks or longer or recurring frequently. In children, this type of bronchitis is generally caused by allergies (as opposed to adults, in whom it is often caused by smoking). The most effective way to treat chronic bronchitis in children is to identify any allergies that may be causing it and by avoiding the foods or other substances that trigger them. In addition, antihistamines can control the body's reaction to allergens, and, in the case of certain moderate to severe allergies, allergy shots can be an effective treatment method. Measures that can help prevent children from getting bronchitis include frequent hand washing to prevent the spread of germs and eliminating smoking from the home. Infants whose parents smoke are four times as likely to get bronchitis as those in non-smoking households.

Another lower respiratory inflammation that affects children (primarily infants between 2 and 10 months old) is bronchiolitis, a viral infection of the small airways that branch off the bronchi. The bronchioles swell and thicken, obstructing the air supply to the alveoli and making breathing difficult. Usually, this condition clears up by itself within a few days, but severe cases may require medical attention, including hospitalization to administer oxygen and hydration. In bronchiectasis, a condition arising from chronic inflammation of the airway (from infections or other causes), a portion of the bronchial tree is destroyed, resulting in a heavy sputum-producing cough and breathing difficulty. It is treated by antibiotics to clear up any residual infection, drainage of the sputum, and, in severe cases, surgical removal of the affected area.

Pneumonia, a serious lung inflammation that can be contracted by infants and children, has a variety of possible causes. It can be caused by a number of viruses, as well as bacteria including staphylococcus, chlamydia, and pneumococcus. (Newborns can acquire it from bacteria in the mother's body.) More rarely, it is caused by chemicals that are inhaled and damage the lungs. The most universal symptom of pneumonia is coughing. Other symptoms vary with the type of pneumonia and may include rapid breathing, chest pain, a high fever, and (in the case of viral pneumonia) vomiting. Since the introduction of **antibiotics**, pneumonia is no longer the health scourge it once was, but it is important for it to be correctly diagnosed (in an office examination that includes listening to chest sounds and possibly an x ray) and treated. Newborns with pneumonia are usually hospitalized.

Asthma is a chronic, reversible respiratory disorder that involves obstruction and swelling of the airways to the lungs. The main symptoms of asthma are coughing, wheezing, and shortness of breath; other possible symptoms include fatigue, anxiety, and tightness in the chest. Nine to 10 million Americans suffer from asthma, about half of them children under the age of 16. In addition to allergens such as pollen, animal dander, dust, and foods, asthma can be triggered by a number of other factors, including certain activities (aerobic exercises such as running) and irritants such as tobacco smoke and certain chemical substances. It is possible to control asthma by avoiding known allergens and irritants, using medications that can prevent or alleviate the symptoms of asthma attacks, and receiving allergy shots to bolster the body's tolerance to allergens. Children often outgrow asthma when they reach adolescence or adulthood: in more than half, the condition resolves completely, while 10% only have occasional asthma attacks as adults.

Among the most serious childhood disorders affecting the lungs is **cystic fibrosis,** a genetic disease that disrupts the functioning of mucus-producing glands throughout the body, including the lungs. The condition results in abnormally thick, sticky mucus secretions that, in the case of the lungs, accumulate and interfere with normal respiration, also leading to chronic infections such as bronchitis and pneumonia and eventual deterioration of the lungs. (In the digestive system, these secretions prevent important digestive enzymes from the pancreas from reaching the intestines, impairing normal digestion.) Signs of cystic fibrosis include both digestive abnormalities (as well as the resulting weight loss and malnutrition) and respiratory symptoms, such as coughing and shortness of breath. Treatment consists of antibiotics to prevent respiratory infections, therapy to help loosen and expel excess phlegm, and enzyme supplements to aid digestion. The outlook for sufferers of cystic fibrosis is improving as new medications and improved methods of care are developed. The gene that causes the disease was isolated in 1989, opening the possibility of eventually conquering it through gene therapy.

After almost being eradicated in the United States in the 1950s, **tuberculosis** (TB) has become a cause for renewed concern since the 1980s, resurfacing primarily in certain high-risk groups (immigrants from Southeast Asia, the urban poor, and AIDS victims). Especially troublesome is the appearance of strains of tuberculosis that are resistant to the standard medications used to combat the disease, a development that occurs when patients do not complete the full course of treatment, allowing their infections to persist and become drug-resistant. Once contracted, tuberculosis can remain latent for some time, although skin scratch tests can detect it even in this phase. Once the disease becomes active, it causes coughing, fever, fatigue, and weight loss and is detectable by a chest x ray and/or sputum culture. Once medication is begun, patients with the normal non-resistant forms of the illness become contagion-free in a matter of weeks, although it takes about two years of drug therapy for a complete cure. TB tests to detect the disease in its latent form are part of routine **well-baby exams** and are usually performed at the age of 12–15 months, before a child starts school, and during the teenage years.

In addition to the specific disorders discussed above, a common cause of lower respiratory problems in children is the aspiration of foreign objects. Although infants and young children swallow a wide variety of objects, some of the most common ones are bones, coins, nuts, and safety pins. Large objects can obstruct airways; smaller ones may go unnoticed at first but later cause a number of problems, including infection, inflammation, overinflation, and even partial collapse of the lungs. Many but not all aspirated objects are visible in an x ray.

For Further Study

Books

de Vries, Jan. *Asthma and Bronchitis*. Edinburgh: Mainstream Publishers, 1991.

Haas, Francois, and Sheila Sperber Haas. *The Chronic Bronchitis and Emphysema Handbook*. New York: Wiley, 1990.

Levitzky, Michael B. *Pulmonary Physiology*. New York: McGraw-Hill, 1986.

National Institutes of Health. *Pediatric Respiratory Disorders*. Bethesda, MD: Division of Lung Diseases, National Institutes of Health, 1986.

Organizations

American Lung Association
Address: 1740 Broadway
New York, NY 10019
Telephone: (212) 315-8700

Asthma and Allergy Foundation of America
Address: 1125 15th Street NW, Suite 512
Washington DC 20005
Telephone: (202) 466-7643

Cystic Fibrosis Foundation
Address: 6931 Arlington Road, Suite 200
Bethesda, MD 20814
Telephone: (301) 951-4422; (800) FIGHTCF [344-4823]

Lying

Intentional misrepresentation of reality.

Lying is an intentional misrepresentation of reality, as distinguished from the innocent **fantasy** common to preschoolers whose notion of truth and falsehood has yet to develop clearly.

Very young children do not understand the difference between truth and falsehood. Preschoolers often engage in wishful thinking, fantasy, and the embellishment of reality with no intention of deliberate deceit. Children as young as five years old may recognize different types of lies and their relative severity, but it is not until about age seven that most children learn the basic meaning of honesty. At that point, lying becomes intentional.

Children lie for a variety of reasons. Rather than focus on the lie as the primary problem, adult caregivers should instead try to determine the reason(s) for the lie. It is important for adults to remember that in nearly every case children lie to save face, not to show disrespect for the adult. Children with low self-esteem will often embellish the truth, or fabricate completely false stories, in order to boost their image in their own eyes and others'. If a child believes that his or her self is "bad" or "worthless," he or she will create a false self to cover up the truth. False selves require a great deal of lying to maintain. Shame-filled children will lie when caught in wrongdoing, whether accidental or purposeful, to avoid the shame of exposure. Children will also lie simply to dissociate themselves from something painful or to avoid punishment.

Lying also results from a child's frustration with certain rules imposed by adults. If a parent requires that homework be done before a child can go out to play, the child may lie about completing the homework in order to circumvent a frustrating rule. Children may simply not like certain rules, or they may not accept the adults' right to set the rules. They therefore break the rules, then lie to avoid facing the consequences, or to avoid being caught so they can continue to break the rules. When a child lies to evade adult-imposed rules, it is necessary for the adult(s) to discuss the rules with the child and negotiate a mutually acceptable settlement. Children are much more likely to follow negotiated rules than imposed ones. This is particularly important with older children and teens.

If lying is not addressed at all, children will not develop a clear sense of truth and falsehood, nor an understanding of the importance of honesty in personal and social relationships. Children's natural sense of right and wrong will eventually be deadened if they do not receive consistently appropriate cues from the adults in their lives. When adults ignore lying, or even reward it by allowing children to get what they want by lying, children can become desensitized to their guilt. A child with a desensitized conscience may grow into an adult with little self-control.

It is extremely difficult for adults to teach children the importance of honesty when those adults frequently lie themselves. Children learn more through modeling than through any other form of instruction. If parents and teachers regularly engage in lying, whether "half-truths," "white lies," or out-and-out deceptions, children will learn that lying is acceptable, no matter what adults say. In today's climate of dishonest politics and corrupt religious leaders, many children grow up with a contempt for talk of "honesty" by adults. They see the same politicians who promote a return to traditional values like honesty indicted for lying on their tax returns or to a congressional investigation committee. Less blatant forms of lying, such as misleading campaign advertisements and partisan propaganda, are a common and even integral part of politics the world over. Highly visible religious leaders who preach fidelity and honesty are caught embezzling funds or hiring prostitutes.

See also **Discipline**, **Moral development**

For Further Study

Books

Ford, Charles V. *Lies! Lies! Lies! The Psychology of Deceit*. Washington, DC: American Psychiatric Press, 1996.

Kurtines, William M, and Jacob L. Gewirtz. *Moral Development: An Introduction.* Boston: Allyn and Bacon, 1995.

Schulman, Michael, and Eva Mekler. *Bringing Up a Moral Child: A New Approach for Teaching Your Child to Be Kind, Just, and Responsible.* New York: Doubleday, 1994.

Sears, William, M.D. *The Discipline Book: Everything You Need to Know to Have a Better-Behaved Child—From Birth to Age 10.* 1st ed. Boston: Little, Brown and Co., 1995.

Wyckoff, Jerry. *How to Discipline Your Six-to-Twelve Year Old: Without Losing Your Mind.* 1st ed. New York: Doubleday, 1991.

Periodicals

DeMott, Benjamin. "Morality Plays." *Harper's Magazine* 289, no. 1735, December 1994, pp. 67–76.

—Dianne K. Daeg de Mott

Lymphatic System

System that filters harmful substances from fluids surrounding the tissues of the human body.

The lymphatic system is the body's network of organs, ducts, and tissues that filter harmful substances out of the fluid that surrounds body tissues. The primary lymphatic organs are the thymus and bone marrow, which produce lymphocytes. Although the thymus is critical for T-cell development in children, it begins to shrink as they progress toward adulthood. The secondary lymphatic organs are the spleen, appendix, tonsils, adenoids, lymph nodes, and Peyer's patches in the small intestine. The tonsils reach full size at around age seven, gradually shrinking until adulthood. In the past, tonsils and adenoids were routinely removed surgically in most children. In the 1980s and 1990s, tonsils are not removed unless the child experiences repeated infections of the tonsils (tonsillitis). For most children, removal of tonsils is routine and is performed on an outpatient basis without an overnight hospital stay.

Lymphocytes are a type of white blood cell that is highly concentrated in lymphatic fluid. This clear fluid, also called lymph, travels through the lymphatic vessels connecting the lymphatic organs. The terminal lymphatic vessels feed into the thoracic duct that returns body fluids to the heart prior to blood reoxygenation. The reincorporated fluid originates in the bloodstream, bathes organs and tissues, and is returned to the bloodstream after passing through lymphatic filters that function as part of the body's defense system against infection and **cancer.**

Lymph nodes, primarily clustered in the neck, armpits, and pelvic area, are the system's battle stations against infection. Lymph nodes are connected to one another by lymphatic vessels. It is in the nodes and other secondary organs where white blood cells engulf and destroy debris to prevent them from reentering the bloodstream.

Lymphatic diseases

Although lymph nodes commonly enlarge to fight infection, an overwhelming infection can leave a lymph node and travel through the lymphatic system to other nodes and even to other body tissues. Cancer can spread very easily through the lymph system, but different cancers vary in how soon they attack the nodes.

For Further Study

Books

Alberts, B., D. Bray, J. Lewis, M. Raff, K. Roberts, and J. Watson, eds. *Molecular Biology of the Cell.* 3d ed. New York: Garland Publishing, 1994.

Rhoads, R., and R. Pflanzer, eds. *Physiology.* 2d ed. New York: Saunders College Publishing, 1992.

Maccoby, Eleanor Emmons (1917–)

American psychologist and educator.

Most widely known for her work in the psychology of sex differences, Eleanor Maccoby has achieved a distinguished career as an educator as well. She spent eight years in the 1950s as a lecturer and research associate in social relations at Harvard University. Later, she joined the faculty at Stanford University and eventually became chairman of the psychology department.

Eleanor Emmons was born May 15, 1916, in Tacoma, Washington, to Harry Eugene and Viva May Emmons. She married Nathan Maccoby in 1938, received her bachelor's degree from the University of Washington in 1939, and then traveled to Washington, D.C., where she spent the years during World War II working for a government agency. Returning to her studies at the University of Michigan, Maccoby earned her master's degree in 1949 and her Ph.D. in 1950. She spent the next eight years at Harvard University in Cambridge, Massachusetts, before moving to Stanford University in California, where she served as a professor and chairman of the psychology department from 1973–76.

Although Eleanor Maccoby's interests lay primarily in studying the social factors that influence human development, she also considered the interweaving contributions of other factors, such as biological and cognitive processes. In fact, for her doctoral dissertation, which she completed under the guidance of B.F. Skinner, she conducted experiments in learning and reinforcement.

After finishing her doctoral work, Maccoby joined Robert Sears, then a professor of social relations at Harvard, in a large-scale study investigating whether certain parental practices were related to children's personality characteristics. This study resulted in an influential book, *Patterns of Child Rearing.* Maccoby's work led her to believe that identification was an important moderating variable in the development of personality. This notion was supported in her work in parent-child socialization and also in studies of children's identification with film characters.

Maccoby's interest in children and research never flagged. Even while deeply involved in this socialization project, she conducted studies on the effects of television on children, identifying the kinds of activities that were displaced when families acquired televisions, and other studies of the influence of neighborhood cohesion on delinquency rates in low-income areas. She found that neighborhoods in low-income, "at risk" areas had lower rates of juvenile delinquency when they were relatively tightly knit and, simply put, people looked out for one another and one another's children.

After moving to Stanford, Maccoby added studies of developmental changes in attention to her areas of study. She and her colleagues demonstrated that as they grew, children improved first in the ability to attend to a single message in the presence of distractions, and then in the ability to divide attention between simultaneously competing stimuli.

It was also at Stanford that Maccoby began a long association with Carol Nagy Jacklin that would result in the work for which she is most well known. Jacklin and Maccoby studied differences and similarities in boys and girls, using a thorough review of available literature as well as original research. Their 1974 book, *The Psychology of Sex Differences,* represented an unparalleled synthesis of research in the area of sex differences in development, and, given the political climate of the 1970s, stimulated much discussion. Maccoby and Jacklin were simultaneously criticized for being too biological, not biological enough, giving too much credence to socialization pressures, and not giving enough credence to social forces.

Interestingly, however, Maccoby and Jacklin offered a third possibility for forces that shape differences between the sexes that reflected Maccoby's earlier interests in cognition and identification. They argued that, in addi-

[aside] MACROCEPHALY

tion to being influenced by their biology and the social environment around them, children engaged in "self-socialization." The authors suggested that in this proactive process, children themselves draw inferences from the roles and behaviors in which they see men and women, boys and girls engaging. Depending on their developmental level, children then use these inferences to guide their own behavior.

Maccoby's published works reflect her abiding interest in the social development of children and differences between the sexes. Maccoby has received many honors and awards during her career. They include the Gores Award for excellence in teaching from Stanford (1981); a research award from the American Educational Research Association (1984); an award recognizing her research from the Society for Research in Child Development (1987); and the Distinguished Scientific Contribution Award from the American Psychological Association (1988). She was elected to the National Academy of Sciences in 1993.

For Further Study

Books

Maccoby, E. "Eleanor E. Maccoby." In *A History of Psychology in Autobiography*. G. Lindzey, ed. Stanford, CA: Stanford University Press, 1989.
———. *Social Development: Psychological Growth and the Parent-Child Relationship*. New York: Harcourt, Brace and Jovanovich, 1980.
Maccoby, E., and C.N. Jacklin. *Psychology of Sex Differences*. Stanford: Stanford Univesity Press, 1974.
Maccoby, E., and R.H. Mnookin. *Dividing the Child: Social and Legal Dilemmas of Custody*. Cambridge, MA: Harvard University Press, 1992.

—Doreen Arcus, Ph.D.
Harvard University

Macrocephaly

A congenital disorder characterized by abnormally large-sized head and brain in relation to the rest of the body.

Also called macrocephalia and megalocephaly, macrocephaly is diagnosed when the circumference of the head is more than two standard deviations above average for the child's age, sex, race, and period of gestation. The fontanelle (soft spot) of the newborn is wide, but facial features are usually normal. Macrocephaly is distinguished from **hydrocephalus** in that there is no intracranial pressure. The disorder can result from a defect in formation during the embryonic stage, or as a result of certain degenerative diseases such as Schilder's disease, Greenfield's disease, or congenital lipoidosis. Mental de-

ficiency, seizures, and movement disorders are common in macrocephalic children.

When mental deficiency and the attendant diseases or disorders are severe, the child may be placed on a life-support system. When the mental deficiency is less severe, the child may be diagnosed with minimal brain dysfunction or as neurologically handicapped. Minimal brain dysfunction can include any or all of the following: **memory** and language problems, neuromotor functioning problems, and behavior and social problems. The degree of dysfunction will help the parents determine whether the child can continue to live at home and what type of schooling is appropriate. Parents and teachers need to be cognizant of the nature of the child's dysfunction. What was once seen as laziness and lack of motivation on the child's part has now begun to be recognized as a medical condition that can be corrected or modified through **psychotherapy**. Sometimes, though, a child may suffer several years of frustrating failure and abnormal development or behavior before the problem is recognized and he or she is properly diagnosed.

Before devising a plan of psychotherapy, the mental health professional needs a full record of the child's neurological development. Depending on the child's particular weaknesses, the program might include techniques for enhancing concentration, improving sensory and perceptual learning, and managing anger and violence. **Drug therapy** may also be prescribed. Anticonvulsant medications can keep **seizures** under control, and physical therapy can help with movement disorders. Children with **attention deficit/hyperactivity disorder (ADHD)** are usually given **methylphenidate**, commonly known as Ritalin. Parents should be aware of the possible side effects of these drugs as well as drug interactions.

For Further Study

Books

Gattozzi, Ruth. *What's Wrong with My Child?* New York: McGraw-Hill, 1986.

Periodicals

Levine, Melvin D. "Childhood Neurodevelopmental Dysfunction and Learning Disorders." *Harvard Mental Health Letter* 12, no. 1, July 1995, p. 5.

Organizations

American Association on Mental Retardation
Address: 1719 Kalorama Road, NW
Washington, DC 20009-2683
Telephone: (202) 387-1968; toll-free (800) 424-3688
Association of Birth Defect Children
Address: 827 Irma Avenue
Orlando, FL 32803
Telephone: (407) 245-7035; toll-free (800) 313-2232
Abiding Hearts
Address: P.O. Box 5245

Bozeman, MT 59717
Telephone: (406) 587-7471
FAX: (406) 587-7197
March of Dimes Birth Defects Foundation
Address: 1275 Mamaroneck Avenue
White Plains, NY 10605
Telephone: (914) 428-7100
FAX: (914) 997-4763

Mainstreaming *see* **Inclusive Classrooms**

Maladjusted Child *see* **Adjustment Disorders**

Malignancy

A cancerous tumor.

A malignant **tumor**—in contrast to a benign tumor—is one that spreads throughout the tissues or organ in which it originates and expands to other parts of the body as well (metastasizes). A malignant tumor is usually life-threatening, causing death if it remains untreated. If treated, the spread of a malignant tumor may be slowed or even arrested. Depending on the amount of tissue damage prior to treatment, tissue or organ function may be compromised.

> *See also* **Biopsy, Cancer,** and **Tumor.**

Malnutrition *see* **Nutrition**

Manic Depression *see* **Bipolar Disorder**

Manual Dexterity *see* **Fine Motor Skills**

Maslow's Hierarchy of Needs

Theory of human motivation

The hierarchy of needs is a theory about the needs that motivate all humans developed by Abraham Maslow, a central figure in humanistic psychology and in the human potential movement. Maslow began to work out this theory of human motivation in the 1940s, and first published his thoughts in *Motivation and Human Personality* in 1954. Rejecting the determinism of both the psychoanalytic and behaviorist approaches, Maslow took an optimistic approach to human behavior that emphasized developing one's full potential. He based his studies on successful historical and contemporary figures whom he considered "self-actualizers," including Thomas Jefferson (1743–1826), Abraham Lincoln (1809–

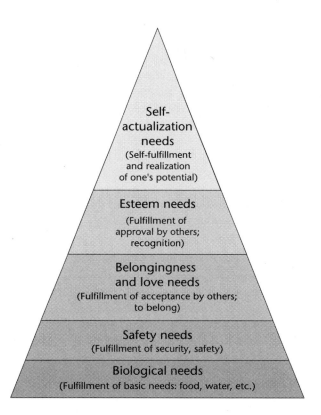

Maslow's hierarchy of needs.

1865), Jane Addams (1860–1935), Albert Einstein (1879–1955), and Eleanor Roosevelt (1884–1962). In addition to drawing up a list of the common traits of these individuals, Maslow placed self-actualization at the peak of his hierarchy of human motivations, the concept for which he is best known today.

This hierarchy is usually depicted as a pyramid with five levels, ranging from the most basic needs at the bottom to the most complex and sophisticated at the top. From bottom to top, the levels are biological needs (food, water, shelter); safety; belongingness and love; the need to be esteemed by others; and self-actualization, the need to realize one's full potential. According to Maslow, the needs at each level must be met before one can progress to the next level. Maslow considered fewer than one percent of the population to be self-actualized individuals. However, he believed that all human beings still possessed an innate (if unmet) need to reach this state.

During the 1950s and 1960s, Maslow became associated with the movement known as humanistic psychology, which he also referred to as the Third Force because it offered an alternative to the prevailing schools of **psychoanalysis** and **behaviorism** in both theory and therapeutic practice. Maslow rejected the idea that human behavior was determined by childhood events or conditioning and believed that the goal of **psychotherapy** was to remove the obstacles that prevented clients from self-actualizing.

As humanistic psychology gave birth to the human potential movement of the 1960s, Maslow became one of its central figures, lecturing at the Esalen Institute at Big Sur, California. In 1967–68, Maslow served as president of the **American Psychological Association**. Prior to his death in 1970, Maslow published over 100 articles in magazines and professional journals. His books include *Toward a Psychology of Being* (1962), *Religions, Values, and Peak Experiences* (1964), *Eupsychian Management* (1965), *The Psychology of Science* (1966), and a posthumous collection of papers entitled *The Farther Reaches of Human Nature* (1971).

Further Reading

Books

Hoffman, Edward. *The Right to be Human: A Biography of Abraham Maslow.* Los Angeles: Tarcher, 1988.

Masturbation

The erotic stimulation of one's own genitals.

Between 60 and 90% of adolescent boys and 40% of girls masturbate. Although people's attitudes about masturbation differ widely, there is no evidence that masturbation is in any way physically harmful. For many people, masturbation is an opportunity for private sexual exploration before deciding whether to engage in sexual activity with another person.

For Further Study

Books

McCoy, Kathy, and Charles Wibbelsman. *The New Teenage Body Book.* New York: The Body Press (Putnam), 1992.

—Gail B. Slap, M.D.
University of Pennsylvania School of Medicine

McCarthy Scales of Children's Abilities (MSCA)

Assesses the cognitive development and motor skills of young children.

An individually administered test that assesses the **cognitive development** and motor skills of children aged 2½–8½. The length of the testing session is about 45 minutes for children under the age of 5 and an hour for older children. A wide range of puzzles, toys, and game-like activities is used to evaluate each child according to five different scales. The Verbal Scale, consisting of 5 subtests, assesses comprehension and use of language. The Quantitative Scale (3 subtests) measures mathematical ability. The Perceptual-Performance Scale (7 subtests) evaluates a child's ability to conceptualize and reason without words. The Memory Scale (4 subtests) tests short-term recall of words, numbers, pictures, and tonal sequences. Finally, the Motor Scale (5 subtests) assesses both gross and fine motor coordination. In addition to individual scores for each scale, the Verbal, Quantitative, and Perceptual-Performance Scales are combined to yield the General Cognitive Scale, an index of overall intellectual functioning expressed as a Mental Age Equivalent between 1-½ and 12-½ years. Besides indicating overall cognitive development, the McCarthy Scales are useful for determining strengths and weaknesses in specific areas. Parts of this test are included in the McCarthy Screening Test, used to assess school readiness in the early grades.

For Further Study

Books

Cohen, Libby G., and Loraine J. Spenciner. *Assessment of Young Children.* New York: Longman, 1994.

McCullough, Virginia. *Testing and Your Child: What You Should Know About 150 of the Most Common Medical, Educational, and Psychological Tests.* New York: Plume, 1992.

Wortham, Sue Clark. *Tests and Measurement in Early Childhood Education.* Columbus: Merrill Publishing Co., 1990.

Mathematics/Mathematical Ability

Study of numbers and their operations.

Skill with mathematics is as important as literacy for daily living. Mathematics are used daily—to keep score in sports, to calculate the amount of change due when making a purchase, to measure a room for wallpapering, etc. While most parents find it enjoyable to read with their young children, few would describe sharing math experiences in the same positive terms. Social scientists report that Americans are the only citizens of developed nations that describe themselves as "not good at math," and point to supporting evidence from standardized tests administered worldwide—U.S. students rank below those of many other nations in math proficiency.

In 1989, the National Council of Teachers of Mathematics (NCTM, founded in 1920) issued "Curriculum and Evaluation Standards for School Mathematics" establishing a plan for mathematics education reform in the

RANKINGS BY COUNTRY OF STUDENTS' MATH SCORES IN THIRD INTERNATIONAL MATHEMATICS AND SCIENCE STUDY (TIMSS)	
8th graders	**4th graders**
1. Singapore	1. Singapore
2. Korea	2. Korea
3. Japan	3. Japan
4. Hong Kong	4. Hong Kong
5. Belgium	5. Netherlands*
6. Czech Republic	6. Czech Republic
7. Slovak Republic	7. Austria
8. Switzerland	8. Slovenia* Note: Average scores for test-takers from Slovenia (8) to Israel (14) are not significantly different.
9. Netherlands*	9. Ireland
10. Slovenia*	10. Hungary*
28. United States	11. Australia*
	12. United States
	13. Canada
	14. Israel*

* Indicates countries that do not adhere to international standards (students tested may be over the age, for example)

elementary grades. "Professional Standards for Teaching Mathematics" followed in 1991, offering ways mathematics teachers can create an effective learning environment and establishing standards for evaluation. In 1995, "Assessment Standards for School Mathematics" was published to provide criteria for judging the quality of mathematics assessment.

These three documents propose a mathematics curriculum with the following features:

- More extensive study of mathematical ideas and concepts and their uses in today's world;

- Learning that shifts toward more active student involvement with mathematics, including mathematical problems that relate to their world, and the use of a variety of mathematical tools for solving those problems;

- Creating classrooms that are stimulating learning environments in which all students have the opportunity to reach their full mathematical potential;

- Assessment practices that shift toward student evaluations that are continuous and based on many sources.

The standards proposed by the NCTM state that children will:

- Be engaged in discovering mathematics, not just doing problems in a book;

- Have the opportunity to explore, investigate, estimate, question, predict, and test their ideas about math;

- Explore and develop understanding for math concepts using materials they can touch and feel, either natural or manufactured;

- Be guided by the teacher in learning (i.e., the teacher will not dictate how mathematics problems must be solved);

- Have many opportunities to look at math in terms of daily life and to see the connections among math topics such as between geometry and numbers.

GENDER DIFFERENCES IN MATH

In the late 1970s, political scientists Sheila Tobias and others called attention to the trend for girls to avoid and feel anxiety about math, a fact she attributed to social conditioning. Girls historically were discouraged from pursuing mathematics by teachers, peers, and parents.

In the early 1990s, two studies suggested that there might be differences in how boys and girls approach mathematics problems. One study, conducted by researchers at Johns Hopkins University, examined differences in mathematical reasoning using the School and College Ability Test (SCAT). The SCAT includes 50 pairs of quantities to compare, and the test-takers must decide whether one is larger than the other or whether the two are equal, or whether there is not enough information. Groups of students in second through sixth grade who had been identified as "high ability" (97th percentile or above on either the verbal or quantitative sections of the California Achievement Test) participated in the study. The boys scored higher than the girls overall, and the average difference between male and female scores was the same for all grade levels included in the study. Another study by Australian researchers at the University of New South Wales and La Trobe University gave 10th-graders 36 algebraic word problems and asked them to group the problems according to the following criteria: whether there was sufficient information to solve the problem; insufficient information; or irrelevant information along with sufficient information. (There were 12 problems in each category.) Students were grouped into ability groups according to prior test scores. Boys and girls performed equally well in identifying problems containing sufficient information, but boys were more able than girls to detect problems that had irrelevant information, or those that had missing information. Next, the researchers asked the students to solve the problems. Girls performed as well as boys in solving problems that had sufficient information, but no irrelevant information. On the problems that contained irrelevant information, girls did not perform as well as boys. The researchers offered tentative conclusions that perhaps girls are less able to differentiate between relevant and irrelevant information, and thus allow irrelevant information to confuse their problem-solving process. The researchers hypothesized that this tendency to consider all information relevant may reflect girls' assumption that test designers would not give facts that were unnecessary to reaching a solution.

Some researchers have argued that offering all-girl math classes is an effective way to improve girls' achievement by allowing them to develop their problem-solving skills in an environment that fosters concentration. Others feel this deprives girls of the opportunity to learn from and compete with boys, who are often among the strongest math students.

In June 1997, President Bill Clinton held a Rose Garden ceremony at the White House to recognize the improvement in U.S. fourth-graders' ranking among their peers around the world in math and science, based on results from the Third International Mathematics and Science Study (TIMSS). U.S. fourth graders averaged 63% correct answers to the items on the test, compared to 59% average correct for the students from all 26 countries who took the test. Results from the eighth-grade TIMSS were released in November 1996: U.S. eighth graders averaged 80% correct answers, compared to 83% for eight graders from 41 countries who took the test. The ranking of U.S. fourth graders was 11th out of 26, and U.S. eighth graders ranked 28th out of 41. The accompanying table lists the rankings for TIMSS. In 1998–99, further results from TIMSS are scheduled to be released, including information on teaching techniques, use of calculators for math computation, and other educational practices worldwide. By examining the teaching strategies used in those countries where students outperform U.S. students in math, educators and curriculum development specialists may be able to address areas of weakness in American classrooms.

President Bill Clinton's education agenda presented during his 1997 "State of the Union" address called for all students to master challenging mathematics, including the foundations of algebra and geometry, by the end of eighth grade.

To succeed in higher level mathematics, and even to solve complex problems encountered in daily life, students must acquire the skills necessary to use mathematics with ease. Students must master procedures (addition and division, for example), but they must also understand the problem-solving strategies that apply to mathematical procedures and concepts. Effective school curricula are designed to build student's critical, creative, and logical problem-solving abilities. The National Commission on Teaching and America's Future made this strong statement in its report, *What Matters Most*, "Today's society

PERIODICALS FOR STUDENTS

Dynamath, published by Scholastic Press School Division.
For children in grade 5 (appropriate for grades 4-6)

Games Junior (ages 7 and above) magazine, P.O. Box 10147, Des Moines, IA 50347.
Older children may enjoy *Games* magazine, available from the same address.

Math Power, published by Scholastic Press School Division.
For children in grade 3 and above.

Puzzlemania, published by Highlights, P.O. Box 18201, Columbus, OH 43218-0101.
Includes spatial reasoning, logical thinking, and word puzzles.

Zillions, published by Consumer Reports, P.O. Box 44861, Boulder, CO 80322.
Children's version of *Consumer Reports,* focusing on products of interest to young people. Illustrates data gathering and analysis.

---

has little room for those who cannot read, write, and compute proficiently."

Parents can support the development of math skills by making math a family activity, much the same as reading. Opportunities for math practice include adding prices while shopping, calculating the amount of discount of sale items, calculating the price per ounce of grocery items, and practicing estimating the temperature in Celsius when hearing the weather report. While traveling, devise "mental math" games that the family can play together. Use the clock to give practice in addition and working with fractions.

When parents express positive attitudes toward math—and avoid making negative observations about the subject—they are helping their children to keep an open willingness to succeed in math. Even when a parent feels unable to help with math homework, he or she should avoid expressions of failure or inability. By helping the child construct strategies for getting help—using the school's tutoring center or asking the teacher for extra help—the parent is showing the child that math is a subject that can be tackled, and that there are pathways to success.

For Further Study

Books

Kanter, Patsy F. *Helping Your Child Learn Math.* Washington, DC: U.S. Department of Education, Office of Educational Research and Improvement, 1992.

Martinez, Joseph G. *Math Without Fear: A Guide for Preventing Math Anxiety in Children.* Boston: Allyn and Bacon, 1996.

Measuring What Counts: A Conceptual Guide for Mathematics Assessment. Washington, DC: National Academy Press, 1993.

Sternberg, Robert J., and Talia Ben-Zeev. (eds.) *The Nature of Mathematical Thinking.* Mahwah, NJ: L. Erlbaum Associates, 1996.

Tobias, Sheila. *Math Anxiety.* New York: W.W. Norton, 1995.

Vinton, Layne T. *Math Assessment: Grades 5–6.* Huntington Beach, CA: Teacher Created Materials, 1994.

———. *Math Assessment: Grades 1–2.* Huntington Beach, CA: Teacher Created Materials, 1994.

———. *Math Assessment: Grades 3–4.* Huntington Beach, CA: Teacher Created Materials, 1994.

Periodicals

Kloosterman, Peter, et al. "Students' Beliefs about Mathematics: A Three-Year Study." *Elementary School Journal* 97, September 1996, pp. 39–56.

"The Learning Lag: You Can't Blame TV. (Third International Mathematics and Science Study Finds That American Students are Far below Japanese.)" *U.S. News and World Report* 121, December 2, 1996, p. 16.

"The Quest for Qualified Teachers." *U.S. News and World Report* 121, September 23, 1996, p. 19.

Audiovisual Recordings

Get Ready to Read. Get Ready for Math. Racine, WI: Golden Book Video, 1989.
(One 54-minute videocassette.)

Organizations

National Council of Teachers of Mathematics (NCTM)
Address: 1906 Association Drive
Reston, VA 22091-1593
Telephone: toll-free (800) 235-7566; (703) 620-9840
FAX-on-demand line: toll-free 24-hours a day (800) 220-8483 (order information to be sent by fax)
Website: www.nctm.org

Measles *see* **Rubeola**

Mediation *see* **Peer Mediation**

Medical Tests

Evaluations done to provide information on health and to assist in identification of a condition or diagnosis of disease or injury.

Medical tests are used to provide information to health care providers about a person's health status. Some tests require the collection of a specimen, as in a urine test, blood test, or **biopsy**. Some tests, such as an ear canal check or assessment of the heart and lung function using a stethoscope, are simple and non-invasive. Others, such as x rays and ultrasound tests, require a visit to a special laboratory, and may or may not carry risks and side effects.

Health care personnel are required by law to obtain what is referred to as "informed consent" before performing any invasive medical test or procedure. This means that the health care professional must describe the test or procedure that he or she is suggesting the patient undergo, explain the risks posed by the test itself, outline what information the test will yield, and what benefits are expected from the test results. Children are not able to evaluate such information for themselves, so their parents or legal **guardians** will be responsible for obtaining and evaluating all aspects of the test or procedure and for making the decision to consent to it.

HOME MEDICAL TESTING CHECKLIST

- Check expiration date.
- Store test properly, being cautious about appropriate temperature.
- Read all instructions carefully and completely before performing the test.
- Consult a pharmacist or the toll-free number included with the product if any aspect of the procedure is unclear.
- Follow the instructions precisely. Don't skip steps, and follow timing instructions exactly, using a stopwatch or watch that counts seconds.
- Follow the guidelines for testing, which may include such things as avoidance of physical activity or a period of fasting.
- Keep accurate records of the date, conditions, and outcome of the test.
- If symptoms persist, consult a physician or other medical practitioner.

Following the tests, patients (and the parents or guardians of minor children) are entitled to receive a clear, comprehensible explanation of the test results. Legal access to test results varies from state to state, but in general a person's medical records are afforded protection under privacy laws. Many states allow patients to have full access to their own medical records, although in some cases a court order is required. If a doctor is not providing parents with complete and accurate information about their child's condition and treatment, in many cases parents are legally entitled to go to court to get the information they need. However, it is likely that such communication problems would indicate a change of physician would be appropriate.

Tests can give false results in a percentage of cases. Most experts recommend that a test be repeated before any major treatment regimen is begun. When a test result is positive, especially when the condition or disease being tested for is serious, it is appropriate to repeat the test using a different laboratory. Tests are performed by human technicians, using sophisticated equipment in many cases. Opportunities for procedural, specimen-handling, interpretation, and other errors can occur at many points during the process. Therefore, parents should be cautious and diligent in gathering information about any medical tests being performed on their children, and about action being taken based on the results.

Home medical tests

There are a number of medical tests that are manufactured and sold for consumers to perform at home. These range from blood glucose monitoring for people with **diabetes mellitus** to screening tests for indicators of diseases or conditions that may or may not have symptoms present. All home testing kits sold in the United States must receive approval by the Food and Drug Administration (FDA). Among those available are tests to monitor cholesterol; to screen for HIV, the virus that causes AIDS; to monitor blood presure; to monitor ovulation; and to detect hidden fecal blood (a possible indicator of rectal or colon disease). In 1997, the FDA approved an at-home drug testing kit aimed at concerned parents who want to be able to confirm (or rule out) their children's use of illegal drugs. Parents can also invest in an at-home ear examination kit, enabling a parent to examine a child's ears with an otoscope, similar to the one the family's pediatrician uses to examine the ear canal. The kit includes a booklet of color photos for the parent to use in determining whether the child may have an ear infection.

Medical tests that can be performed at home afford the patient control over and understanding of the functioning of his or her body. Supermarkets and drug stores report increases in sales of at-home kits that test for body fat, blood pressure, ovulation, and **pregnancy**. In 1996, sales of home diagnostic and monitoring products totaled about $1.2 billion, an increase of about 15% over 1995.

For Further Study

Books

Pinckney, Cathey. *Do-It-Yourself Medical Testing: 240 Tests You Can Perform At Home.* New York: Facts on File, 1989.

———. *The Patient's Guide to Medical Tests.* New York: Facts on File, 1986.

Shtasel, Philip. *Medical Tests and Diagnostic Procedure: A Patient's Guide to Just What the Doctor Ordered.* New York: Harper and Row, 1990.

Periodicals

Lieberman, Adrienne B. "Understanding Prenatal Tests." *American Baby* 58, November 1996, pp. 32+.

"Medical Test Kits." *Consumer Reports* 61, December 15, 1996, pp. 219+.

Tippit, Sarah. "Home Medical Tests." *Better Homes and Gardens* 75, January 1997, pp. 50+.

Audiovisual Recording

The HIV Test?: An Informed Decision. Los Angeles: Churchill Media, 1991.

(One 10-minute videotape and one discussion guide.)

Meeting Street School Screening Test

Identifies possible learning disorders.

The Meeting Street School Screening Test is an individually administered test that identifies possible learning disorders in kindergartners and first graders (ages 5–7-½). The test is divided into three subtests with five tasks apiece. One focuses on motor skills and evaluates finger dexterity, imitation of hand gestures, and the ability to hop, skip, and move on command. A second subtest assesses visual skills and consists of copying geometric figures and letters, drawing on request, and tapping blocks in a sequence. The language portion of the test evaluates repetition of short phrases, sentences, and nonsense words; counting forward and backward; chronological sequencing; and describing an abstract picture. A behavior rating scale and book of norms are used in scoring the test.

For Further Study

Books

Cohen, Libby G., and Loraine J. Spenciner. *Assessment of Young Children.* New York: Longman, 1994.

Hart, Diane. *Authentic Assessment: a Handbook for Educators.* Menlo Park, CA: Addison-Wesley Pub. Co., 1994.

McCullough, Virginia. *Testing and Your Child: What You Should Know About 150 of the Most Common Medical, Educational, and Psychological Tests.* New York: Plume, 1992.

Wortham, Sue Clark. *Tests and Measurement in Early Childhood Education.* Columbus: Merrill Publishing Co., 1990.

Memory

The abilities to recall what has been experienced or learned.

Memory refers to the abilities to store and retrieve information for later use. How memories are stored and then recalled is not fully understood by scientists, although new evidence is helping them to develop theories.

Researchers believe that regions in the temporal and frontal cortex, and the hippocampus are critical for various forms of memory.

It is now believed that (1) conscious recall of facts, called declarative memory, (2) memory of the time and place of an event, called episodic memory, and (3) memory of a previously learned motor habit, called procedural memory, involve different mechanisms. In addition, implicit memory, which is not conscious, involves recognition of prior experience. Further, the duration of a memory trace is important. Working memory, popularly referred to as short-term memory, lasts for about 20–30 seconds. Working memory is the moment-to-moment memory function—the brain's ability to keep track of two activities at once, such as opening the mail while talking on the phone. Researchers have found that working memory deteriorates noticeably for most people in their 40s, but cannot explain why. Amnesia, or damage to the memory, is caused by any number of factors, including viral infection, head injury, near drowning or suffocation, or any other event that deprives the brain of oxygen for a period of time.

Infancy

Studies indicate that by six months, infants have developed memory skills to recall some experiences. In fact, as early as six weeks of age, some infants stare more intensely at unfamiliar objects, a behavior researchers interpret as evidence that infants can distinguish the unfamiliar from the familiar.

Researchers studying older infants between 12 and 24 months have found that they are beginning to develop the memory necessary to recall specific events. This recall ability is stronger when the event has been experienced more than once. Hints, cues, or reminders also improve the young child's ability to retrieve a memory.

Researchers believe that working memory involves complex interactions of different areas of the brain—one for visual memories and another for verbal memories. In the early 1970s, researchers at UCLA gathered evidence that the prefrontal cortex, the region of the brain just beneath the forehead, was stimulated when monkeys looked for a hidden item. In the late 1980s, researchers at Yale University expanded upon this experiment to confirm the prefrontal cell activity during experiments with monkeys.

In 1993, activity in the prefrontal regions of the brain refined the identification of object identity memories and spatial relationship memories. This led to the development of a model for working memory that features parallel areas processing different types of sensory memory information. Researchers at the National Institute of Mental Health, using positron emission tomography (PET) to map neuronal activity, found that working memory for facial features and for locations are centered in different areas of the pre-

FALSE AND RECOVERED MEMORIES

As of the late 1990s, research into recovered memories was characterized by tremendous controversy. A leading researcher in this subject, Elizabeth Loftus, conducted studies on over 20,000 subjects, and pointed to evidence she felt was convincing that memory is both fragile and unreliable. Her work supported the notion that eyewitness accounts of events are often inaccurate, and that false memories can be created through suggestion in approximately 25% of the population. Loftus's work calls into question the validity of memories that are recovered under coaching or questioning; such memories have provided the basis for countless lawsuits brought against adults who are accused of molesting children. Her research has shown that emotional state—either low points, such as boredom or sleepiness or high points, such as stress or trauma—decrease the reliability of memory. She has also shown that experiencing violent and traumatic events decrease the accuracy of memory. Loftus theorizes that memory is suggestible and deteriorates over time. In her classic study, known as "Lost in the Shopping Mall," she demonstrated that subjects—children and teenagers—could be induced to remember being lost in a mall at an early age, even though it never actually happened, by simply questioning them about it as if it had happened.

One of the problems with the recovery of repressed memories is the very process of recovery. Many individuals recover memories while in therapy, under hypnosis, or in some other situation where the possibility of suggestion is powerful. In the late 1990s, in responses to the swelling controversy over recovered memories, the American Medical Association, American Psychiatric Association, and American Psychological Association all issued guidelines to help practitioners deal with reports of recovered memories, especially of sexual abuse during childhood. In general, most physicians, psychiatrists, and psychologists suggest that recovered memories be corroborated through external investigation, and that alternative explanations for the existence of the memories be considered before any legal action be taken based on them.

False memory syndrome is dividing the field of professional psychotherapy. Some psychotherapists believe that to question the interpretation of and belief in recovered memories is to undermine the possibility of the existence of repression; others see the challenge to recovered memories as a sign of society's refusal to confront a serious problem with child abuse and abuse of women. Others contend that there are no psychoanalytic theories to support forgetting of traumatic events, or their detailed recall after the passage of time.

frontal cortex. University of Michigan research teams corroborated this evidence that working memory for spatial relations is centered in a different location from working memory for verbal information.

As of the late 1990s, the evidence seems to indicate that the prefrontal cortex is the site of working memory. To perform this function, however, it must interact with the areas of the brain that receive sensory input. As available imaging and other research techniques become more refined, researchers will also refine their understanding of how the memory works. Memories that can be retrieved when needed (one's phone number, for example) appear to be coordinated through the hippocampus deep in the core of the brain, while other types of memories are handled by other areas.

For Further Study

Books

Baddeley, Alan, Barbara A. Wilson, and Fraser Watts. (eds.) *Handbook of Memory Disorders.* New York: Wiley and Sons, 1995.

Bartlett, Frederic C. *Remembering: A Study in Experimental and Social Psychology.* New York: Cambridge University Press, 1995.

Cohen, Neal J. *Memory, Amnesia, and the Hippocampal System.* Cambridge: MIT Press, 1993.

Damasio, Antonio. *Descartes' Error: Emotion, Reason, and the Human Brain.* New York: G.P. Putnam, 1994.

DeFelice, Stephen L., and Sue Nirenberg. *Memory Loss.* Secaucus, NJ: L. Stuart, 1987.

Schacter, Daniel L. *Searching for Memory: The Brain, the Mind, and the Past.* New York: Basic Books, 1996.

Periodicals

Bauer, Patricia J. "What Do Infants Recall of Their Lives? Memory for Specific Events by One- and Two-Year-Olds." *American Psychologist* 51, January 1996, pp. 29–41.

Bogartz, Richard S. "Measuring Infant Memory." *Developmental Review* 16, September 1996, pp. 284–300.

"Doctors Record Signals of Brain Cells Linked to Memory." *New York Times* 146, May 24, 1997, p. 8.

Hall, Nancy W. "Your Baby's Amazing Memory: New Research Reveals How Much Infants Remember." *Parents Magazine* 72, March 1997, pp. 90+.

Kepler, Lynne. "Thinking About Memory and the Brain." *Instructor* 106, November-December 1996, pp. 46+.

Lemonick, Michael D. "Glimpses of the Mind." *Time* 146, July 17, 1995, pp. 44+.

Robins, Trevor W. "Refining the Taxonomy of Memory." *Science* 273, September 6, 1996, pp. 1353+.

Wickelgren, Ingrid. "Getting a Grasp on Working Memory." *Science* 275, March 14, 1997, pp. 1580+.

For Further Study on False and Recovered Memory

Books

Bass, Ellen, and Laura Davis. *The Courage to Heal.* 3rd edition, New York: HarperCollins, 1994.

Loftus, Elizabeth, and Katherine Ketcham. *The Myth of Repressed Memory.* New York: St. Martin's Press, 1994.

Organizations and Organization Reports

Report on Memories of Child Abuse. Chicago: American Medical Association, 1994.

Memories of Sexual Abuse. Washington, DC: American Psychiatric Association, fact sheet, 1994.

Report of the Working Group on Investigation of Memories of Childhood Abuse. Washington, DC: American Psychological Association, 1995.

False Memory Syndrome Foundation
Address: 3401 Market St., Suite 130
Philadelphia, PA 19104-3315
Telephone: (215) 387-1865

Periodicals

Meier, Sue A., and Pamela Freyd. "Are Recovered Memories of Childhood Sexual Abuse Reliable?" *Health* 8, May-June 1994, p. 24.

Menarche

The first menstrual period, which occurs at an average age of 12.8 years for girls in the United States

The age at which girls begin to menstruate varies widely and may be influenced by a number of factors, most notably the percentage of body fat. Anywhere from 10.8 years old to 14.6 years old is considered normal. In the months preceding menarche, many girls experience a small amount of clear or whitish vaginal discharge, an indication that the first period will soon take place. Family history plays an important role in determining when a girl's periods will start. For example, mothers who started to menstruate early will often have daughters who also start early. In most girls, menarche occurs at about two years after the beginning of breast development and one year after the growth spurt. For the first year or so after menarche, a girl's ovaries do not release eggs into the fallopian tubes.

See also **Amenorrhea, Menstruation**

For Further Study

Books

Bell, Ruth, et al. *Changing Bodies, Changing Lives.* New York: Vintage, 1988.

Organizations

American College of Obstetricians and Gynecologists
Address: 409 12th Street
Washington, DC 20024
(Brochures about menstruation and other topics)

—Gail B. Slap, M.D.
University of Pennsylvania School of Medicine

Meningitis

An inflammation of the meninges, most often caused by infection.

Meningitis is a potentially fatal inflammation of the meninges, membranes which encase the brain and spinal cord. Meningitis is most commonly caused by an infection of bacteria, viruses, or fungi, although there can be other causes, including bleeding into the meninges, **cancer**, or diseases of the immune system. The inflammation causes swelling of the **brain**, whose fragile tissues are pressed against the skull. Brain cells in these areas can become damaged and eventually die.

The most classic symptoms of meningitis include fever, headache, vomiting, photophobia (extreme sensitivity to light), irritability, lethargy, and a stiff neck. The disease progresses with **seizures**, confusion, and eventually coma. Infants, however, may not show these signs. A baby's immune system is not yet developed enough to mount a fever in response to infection, so fever may be absent. Some infants with meningitis may have seizures as their only identifiable symptom.

The origin of an infection leading to meningitis varies according to an individual's age, habits, living environment, and health status. In newborns, the most common agents of meningitis are those contracted from the mother, including Group B streptococci, *Escherichia coli*, and *Listeria monocytogenes*. Older children are more frequently infected by *Haemophilus influenzae*, *Neisseria meningitidis*, and *Streptococcus pneumoniae*, while adults are infected by *S. pneumoniae* and *N. meningitidis*. *N. meningitidis* is the only organism that can cause epidemics of meningitis. Epidemics of meningitis can occur in crowded conditions, such as when a child in a **day care** falls ill with *N. meningitidis* meningitis and exposes other children and workers to the infection.

Viral causes of meningitis include **herpes simplex**, **mumps** and measles, **chicken pox**, **rabies**, and a number of viruses which are acquired through the bite of infected mosquitoes. Non-bacterial, or inflammatory, meningitis is most often caused by a virus, but can also be triggered by some medications. Inflammatory meningitis can also be caused by the presence of certain atypical cells in the cerebrospinal fluid (CSF). Other causes of meningitis include fungal infections, malignancies, and syphilis. Patients with AIDS (Acquired Immunodeficiency Syndrome) are more susceptible to certain infectious causes of meningitis, including certain fungal agents, as well as by the agent that causes **tuberculosis**.

Meningitis can damage the brain in several ways. The agent of infection can damage the brain tissue directly or cause swelling of brain tissue, compressing it against the inner surface of the skull. Swelling of the meninges may interfere with the normal absorption of cerebrospinal fluid by blood vessels, causing accumulation of the fluid and resultant pressure on the brain. Inflammation may reduce the blood-brain barrier's effectiveness in preventing the passage of toxic substances into brain tissue.

The most frequent long-term effects of meningitis include deafness and blindness, due to compression of specific nerves and parts of the brain controlling hearing and sight. Patients can also develop seizures. In addition, scarring of the meninges may result in obstruction of the normal flow of cerebrospinal fluid, causing it to accumulate.

Diagnosis can be verified by certain manipulations of the patient's head; for example, lowering the head (chin toward chest) is very painful for a patient with meningitis. However, the most important diagnostic test is the lumbar puncture (LP), commonly known as the spinal tap. This procedure involves the insertion of a needle into a space between the vertebrae in the lower back, and the withdrawal of a small amount of cerebrospinal fluid. Abnormally low levels of glucose, a normal ingredient of the fluid, indicate bacterial meningitis. Another indicator of meningitis is the presence of white blood cells in the cerebrospinal fluid

Antibiotic medications (forms of penicillins and cephalosporins, for example) are the crucial element of treatment against bacterial meningitis. Because the blood-brain barrier prevents passage of most substances into the brain, medications must be delivered intravenously in very high doses. Antiviral medications are administered in the case of viral meningitis, and antifungal medications are available as well. Other treatments for meningitis involve decreasing inflammation with steroids, and monitoring the balance of fluids, glucose, sodium, potassium, oxygen, and carbon dioxide in the patient's system. Patients who develop seizures also need medications to halt the seizures and prevent their return.

Many cases of meningitis can be prevented. A series of vaccines against *Haemophilus influenzae*, started at the age of two months, has greatly reduced the incidence of that form of meningitis. Vaccines also exist against *Neisseria meningitidis* and *Streptococcus pneumoniae*, but these vaccines are recommended only for individuals who have particular susceptibility to those organisms, due to certain immune deficiencies, lack of a spleen, or **sickle-cell anemia.** Because *N. meningitidis* is known to cause epidemics, people who have close contact with a known carrier are treated with Rifampin, which generally stops the spread of the disease. Mothers with certain risk factors may be treated with antibiotics during labor, to prevent the passage of microorganisms (particularly Group B streptococcus) which may cause meningitis in the newborn.

For Further Study

Books
Krugman, Saul, et al. *Infectious Diseases of Children.* St. Louis: Mosby Year Book, 1992.

Audiovisual Recordings
Meningitis. Evanston, IL: Altschul Group Corporation, 1996. (One 13-1/2 minute videocassette.)

. . . .
▌ Menstruation

The periodic sloughing off of the uterine lining (endometrium) during a woman's reproductive years.

Approximately once a month, women of childbearing age experience a bloody vaginal discharge known as menstruation. The onset of menstruation (**menarche**) usually occurs sometime between 11 and 15 years of age (average age is 12.8). The average menstrual cycle lasts approximately 28 days, although anywhere between 20 and 36 days is considered normal. (The menstrual cycle is measured from the first day of one period to the first day of the following period.) Monthly menstruation continues until a woman reaches menopause, which ordinarily occurs between the ages of 45 and 50.

Menstruation is the result of complex hormonal interactions. During the typical menstrual cycle, the ovaries produce estrogen and progesterone, which cause ovulation to occur and the lining of the uterus (endometrium) to build up. If sexual intercourse takes place and a sperm fertilizes the egg (ovum) as it moves through the fallopian tube, the fertilized egg will implant itself in the endometrium and begin developing into a fetus. If no fertilized egg has implanted itself in the endometrium, the secretion of progesterone from the ovaries declines, which causes the endometrium to be sloughed off. Menstruation usually occurs two weeks after ovulation, although irregular periods

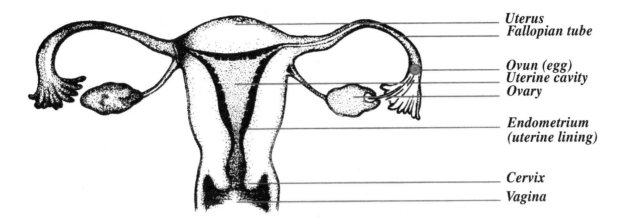

Uterus
Fallopian tube

Ovun (egg)
Uterine cavity
Ovary

Endometrium
(uterine lining)

Cervix
Vagina

Female reproductive system

are common in early adolescence, and menstruation often takes place without ovulation (anovulatory menstrual bleeding). For many girls, it takes a year or two to establish a predictable menstrual pattern. Even after **adolescence**, a number of physical and emotional factors can throw off the timing of menstruation. These include relationship problems, starting a new job or school, and weight change, among others.

Dysfunctional uterine bleeding (DUB)

Dysfunctional uterine bleeding (DUB) is heavy or prolonged bleeding, usually anovulatory. Heavy bleeding is defined as more than 15 soaked pads or tampons per period, and prolonged bleeding as bleeding that lasts for more than 8–10 days. Although DUB is very common in the first couple of years after menarche, it can be very frightening and should always be reported to a physician. DUB accompanied by dizziness and low blood pressure should be considered a medical emergency. DUB has a number of causes, including hormonal imbalance, **sexually transmitted diseases**, ectopic **pregnancy**, hypothyroidism, ovarian cysts, and uterine fibroids or polyps.

Dysmenorrhea

Dysmenorrhea (painful menstruation) is the most common gynecological problem reported by adolescents and the leading cause of absence from school and work. Approximately 75% of women have some degree of pain associated with menstruation, most commonly cramping in the lower abdomen which is most severe on the first day or two of a period. Leg and back pain are also common, as are diarrhea, nausea, fatigue, and headache.

Dysmenorrhea is usually not indicative of serious underlying medical problems. The term *primary dysmenorrhea* refers to painful periods that are not attributable to any abnormality of the reproductive system. Primary dysmenorrhea is most often caused by prostaglandins

(fatty acids) produced in the uterus which cause contractions of the uterus and blood vessels. Prostaglandins may also increase sensitivity to pain. Over-the-counter medications, especially those containing ibuprofen, are often effective for the treatment of primary dysmenorrhea. If non-prescription medication is not effective, a physician may prescribe a drug called a prostaglandin inhibitor. In some cases, an oral contraceptive may be prescribed to prevent ovulation and reduce prostaglandin production.

The term *secondary dysmenorrhea* refers to painful periods caused by an abnormality of the ovaries, uterus, fallopian tubes, or vagina. If dysmenorrhea does not respond to medication, a physician will investigate other possible causes. The medical evaluation might include ultrasonography (a picture similar to an x ray created by sound waves) or laparoscopy (a minor surgical procedure). Among adolescents, the most common cause of secondary dysmenorhea is a condition called endometriosis. In endometriosis, cells from the uterine lining (the endometrium) travel to other places in the abdomen such as the fallopian tubes. Other conditions that can lead to dysmenorrhea during adolescence include tumors, malformations, cysts, or inflammation caused by sexually transmitted diseases (STDs).

See also **Amenorrhea; Menarche; Ovum; Toxic Shock Syndrome**

For Further Study

Books

Avraham, Regina. *The Reproductive System.* New York : Chelsea House, 1991.

Bell, Ruth, et al. *Changing Bodies, Changing Lives.* New York: Vintage, 1988.

McCoy, Kathy, and Charles Wibbelsman. *The New Teenage Body Book.* New York: The Body Press (Putnam), 1992.

—Gail B. Slap, M.D.
University of Pennsylvania School of Medicine

Mental Age *see* **Intelligence**

Mental Deficiency *see* **Mental Retardation**

Mental Disorder

Imprecise term, primarily used by laypeople, to refer to mental conditions.

This term is widely used, but has no precise definition. In fact, many mental health professionals feel the implied distinction between mental and physical disorders oversimplifies the reality. There is considerable research into the physical aspects of mental disorders and, alternatively, the mental aspects of physical disorders. Mental disorder has been defined as a behavioral or psychological syndrome that is associated with distress or disability (ability to function normally in activities of daily living) or with an increased risk of pain, disability, loss of freedom, or death. The classification of the person (schizophrenic, bulimic, alcoholic) with the disorder is common in everyday discourse, but professionals stress that it is more accurate to classify the disorder (e.g., **schizophrenia, bulimia, alcoholism**) rather than the individual who has it. In addition, classification of a mental disorder does not imply that the condition does not have physical and/or biological components.

Mental Retardation

Below-average intellectual abilities that are present before the age of 18 and interfere with developmental processes and with the ability to function normally in daily life (adaptive behavior).

The term mental retardation is commonly used to refer to people with an **intelligence quotient** (IQ) below 70. An IQ of 80-130 is considered the normal range, and 100 is considered average. According to the definition in the **American Psychiatric Association**'s *Diagnostic and Statistical Manual* (DSM-IV), a mentally retarded person is significantly limited in at least two of the following areas: self-care, communication, home living, social/interpersonal skills, self-direction, use of community resources, functional academic skills, work, leisure, health, and safety. Mental retardation affects roughly 1% of the American population. According to the U.S. Department of Education, about 11% of school-aged children were enrolled in special education programs for students with mental retardation.

There are four categories of mental retardation: mild, moderate, severe, and profound. The roughly 80% of retarded persons who are classified as mildly retarded have an IQ between 50 or 55 and 70. Mild retardation, which may not be detected in early childhood, usually involves little sensorimotor impairment. Persons in this category can be educated up to a sixth-grade level. With adequate vocational guidance, they can live and work productively in the community as adults, either independently or with some degree of supervision.

About 10% of retarded persons are classified as moderately retarded, with IQs generally between 35 and 50. Although they usually do not progress beyond the second-grade level academically, as adults they can take care of themselves within supervised settings and perform unskilled or semiskilled work.

Persons with severe retardation, who account for 3-4% of the retarded population, have serious language and motor impairment. They usually do not speak in early childhood but can learn communication and basic self-care during the school years. Their language skills may be limited to the most basic functional words necessary to meet their daily needs. As adults, they live either with their families, in group homes, or, when necessary, in facilities that can provide skilled medical or nursing care.

Profound retardation, which accounts for 1-2% of the retarded population, is usually associated with a neurological condition. It is characterized by severe sensorimotor difficulties beginning in early childhood and serious long-term limitations on both communication and the ability to care for oneself. Some profoundly retarded individuals are never able to speak or to be toilet trained. Most need constant care throughout their lives.

In addition to the categories of mild, moderate, severe, and profound retardation, separate categories are sometimes used to designate those retarded persons who can benefit from some degree of academic training. Those designated "educable mentally retarded" (EMR) can handle academic work at a third- to sixth-grade level, and usually have IQs that fall between 50 and 75. The "trainable mentally retarded" (TMR) have IQs of between 30 and 50 and can progress as far as second-grade

RATE OF MENTAL RETARDATION AMONG SCHOOL-AGED CHILDREN BY U.S. STATE, 1993

State	Children aged 6-17 with mental retardation per 1,000 population	State	Children aged 6-17 with mental retardation per 1,000 population
Alabama	31.4	Montana	7.1
Alaska	5.0	Nebraska	15.3
Arizona	7.7	Nevada	6.6
Arkansas	23.1	New Hampshire	4.0
California	4.5	New Jersey	3.2
Colorado	4.2	New Mexico	5.6
Connecticut	7.1	New York	5.7
Delaware	14.4	North Carolina	19.5
District of Columbia	13.5	North Dakota	8.9
Florida	14.8	Ohio	22.5
Georgia	20.0	Oklahoma	19.7
Hawaii	8.0	Oregon	7.6
Idaho	12.1	Pennsylvania	14.0
Illinois	10.4	Rhode Island	5.9
Indiana	17.8	South Carolina	21.9
Iowa	21.2	South Dakota	9.3
Kansas	10.9	Tennessee	14.3
Kentucky	25.5	Texas	6.4
Louisiana	12.9	Utah	6.9
Maine	6.2	Vermont	11.8
Maryland	6.5	Virginia	11.8
Massachusetts	13.8	Washington	8.3
Michigan	10.3	West Virginia	21.1
Minnesota	11.1	Wisconsin	4.6
Mississippi	12.9	Wyoming	5.7
Missouri	12.5		

level work. It is important to note that IQ scores are not foolproof ways of detecting the abilities and potential of mentally retarded children. Some children with lower IQs ultimately prove to be more capable of leading independent, productive lives than others who score higher. Factors such as emotional support, medical attention, and vocational training can play as great a role as IQ in determining the future of a retarded child.

Causes of mental retardation

There are many different causes of mental retardation, both biological and environmental. In about 5% of cases, retardation is transmitted genetically, usually through chromosomal abnormalities, such as **Down syndrome** or **fragile X syndrome.** Down syndrome occurs when there is an extra chromosome in the 21st pair of chromosomes (known as **trisomy** 21). People with Down syndrome have 47 chromosomes instead of the normal 46. The disorder occurs in one out of every 600–700 births worldwide. Women over 35 are at greater risk of bearing a child with Down syndrome than younger women, and Down syndrome births are over 20 times more likely in women over 45 than in those under the age of 30. Children and adults with Down syndrome demonstrate both mental and motor retardation. Most are severely retarded, with IQs between 20 and 49, and prone to a number of physical problems, including poor vision, hearing and heart defects, and low resistance to respiratory infections. Individuals with Down syndrome (formerly called mongoloidism) also have distinctive physical features, including upward-slanting, almond-shaped eyes and a short, stocky build with a short neck and a smaller than average skull, which is usually flat in back.

Besides Down syndrome, the chromosomal condition that most commonly causes mental retardation is fragile X syndrome, in which a segment of the chromosome that determines gender is abnormal. Fragile X syndrome primarily affects males, in whom the incidence of the condition is 1 in 1,000, as opposed to 1 in 2,500 for females. Males with fragile X syndrome tend to have long, thin faces with prominent ears and jaws, and they often have characteristics of **autism.** Some researchers suspect that as many as 15% of people diagnosed with autism actually have fragile X syndrome. About 20% of genetically caused mental retardation results from single gene mutations, including **Tay-Sachs disease, phenylketonuria (PKU),** and metachromatic leukodystrophy.

Mental retardation may be caused by problems that occur during pregnancy and birth, including maternal nutritional deficiencies, toxemia, infections such as **rubella,** maternal phenylketonuria (even if the **fetus** doesn't have the condition), use of drugs or alcohol, maternal injury during **pregnancy,** extreme prematurity, low birth weight, perinatal injury, or lack of oxygen at birth. Retardation can also be the result of medical conditions and injuries that occur after birth, including metabolic disorders, severe childhood malnutrition, prolonged high fever, near drowning, lead poisoning, severe mental disorders such as autism, and infections such as meningitis that affect the brain. Environmental factors influencing mental retardation include deprivation of physical or emotional nurturance and stimulation. Altogether, there are hundreds of possible causes of, or factors contributing to, mental retardation.

Mentally retarded people are more prone to both physical and mental disorders than the general population. Some of the conditions that cause mental retardation may also be characterized by **seizures,** hearing problems, congenital heart defects, and other symptoms. Mental disorders are much more common among the mentally retarded than among the general population: an estimated one million Americans have some degree of mental retardation as well as a mental disorder of some kind. The most severely retarded appear to be most at risk for mental disorders, and the more severe the retardation the more serious the disorder. Diagnosis and treatment of these disorders can be especially difficult due to communication problems. In addition, mental illness in the retarded may also be caused by the stresses, frustrations, and loneliness they encounter in daily life. **Depression,** for example, is a common disorder of the mentally retarded, and one that often goes undiagnosed. In spite of their limited intellectual capabilities, retarded children realize that they are different and that other people are often uncomfortable around them. Professional counseling, along with parental love and attention, can help a retarded child maintain a positive self-image, which is crucial to the ability to function effectively with family, peers, and in the larger community.

Preventive measures

Some types of mental retardation can be prevented through genetic counseling to determine the risk of a couple having a retarded baby. Other prenatal preventative measures include ensuring that a pregnant mother has adequate **nutrition** and **immunization** against infectious diseases; monitoring to screen for fetal abnormalities that are associated with mental retardation; and reduced use of drugs and alcohol by women during pregnancy. Following the birth of a child, the chances of retardation can be reduced by maintaining good nutrition for both the nursing mother and the young child; avoiding environmental hazards such as lead; and providing the child with emotional, intellectual, and social stimulation.

Another important preventative measure is early detection of certain metabolic and nutritional conditions that result in mental retardation following a period of degeneration. Screening for certain disorders is mandatory in most states. Hypothyroidism, which affects 1 in 4,000 infants born in the United States, can be prevented if a thyroid hormone is administered by the first month of an infant's life. However, if the condition goes untreated, it will cause impaired mental development in 20% of affected children by the age of three months, and in 50% by the age of six months. Phenylketonuria (PKU) prevents an infant from metabolizing the amino acid phenylalanine. Reducing the amount of this substance in an infant's diet can prevent retardation. Infants with galactosemia lack the enzyme needed to convert the sugar galactose to glucose. Avoiding milk and certain other dairy products prevents galactose from accumulating in the blood and eventually interfering with the child's normal mental development. However, none of the preceding measures can be taken if the conditions involved are not detected, and most are undetectable without screening.

The symptoms of mental retardation are usually evident by a child's first or second year. In the case of Down syndrome, which involves distinctive physical characteristics, a diagnosis can usually be made shortly after birth. Mentally retarded children lag behind their peers in developmental milestones such as sitting up, smiling, walking, and talking. They often demonstrate lower than normal levels of interest in their environment and responsiveness to others, and they are slower than other children in reacting to visual or auditory stimulation. By the time a child reaches the age of two or three, retardation can be determined using physical and psychological tests. Testing is important at this age if a child shows signs of possible retardation because alternate causes, such as impaired hearing, may be found and treated.

There is no cure for mental retardation once it has occurred. Treatment programs are geared toward helping retarded children reach their own full potential, not toward helping them catch up with their peers who aren't retarded. Nevertheless, this type of habilitative intervention can prepare most retarded people to lead fulfilling and productive lives as active members of their communities. All states are required by law to offer early intervention programs for mentally retarded children from the time they are born. The sooner the diagnosis of mental retardation is made, the more the child can be helped. With mentally retarded infants, the treatment emphasis is on sensorimotor development, which can be stimulated by exercises and special types of play. It is required that special education programs be available for retarded children starting at three years of age. These programs concentrate on essential self-care, such as feeding, dressing, and toilet training. There is also specialized help available for language and communication difficulties and physical disabilities. As children grow older, training in daily living skills, as well as academic subjects, is offered.

Counseling and therapy are another important type of treatment for the mentally retarded. Retarded children as a group are prone to behavioral problems caused by short attention spans, low tolerance for frustration, and poor impulse control. **Behavior therapy** with a mental health professional can help combat negative behavior patterns and replace them with more functional ones. A counselor or therapist can also help retarded children cope with the low **self-esteem** that often results from the realization that they are different from other children, including siblings. Counseling can also be valuable for the family of a retarded child to help parents cope with painful feelings about the child's condition, and with the extra time and patience needed for the care and education of a special-needs child. Siblings may need to talk about the pressures they face, such as accepting the extra time and attention their parents must devote to a retarded brother or sister. Sometimes parents have trouble bonding with an infant who is retarded and need professional help and reassurance to establish a close and loving relationship.

Current social and health care policies encourage keeping mentally retarded persons in their own homes or in informal group home settings rather than institutions. The variety of social and mental health services available to the mentally retarded, including pre-vocational and vocational training, are geared toward making this possible.

For Further Study

Books

Beirne-Smith, Mary, et al., eds. *Mental Retardation.* New York: Merrill, 1994.

Drew, Clifford J. *Retardation: A Life Cycle Approach.* Columbus: Merrill, 1988.

Grossman, Herbert J., et al, eds. *AMA Handbook on Mental Retardation.* Chicago: American Medical Association, 1987.

Matson, Johnny L., and James A. Mulick, eds. *Handbook of Mental Retardation.* New York: Pergamon Press, 1991.

Organizations

American Association on Mental Deficiency (AAMD)
Address: 1719 Kalorama Rd. NW
Washington, DC 20009
Telephone: (202) 387-1968

Association for Retarded Citizens (ARC)
Address: P.O. Box 6109
Arlington, TX 76005
Telephone: (817) 640-0204

National Down Syndrome Congress
Address: 1800 Dempster
Park Ridge, IL 60068-1146
Telephone: (708) 823-7550

Merrill-Palmer Scales of Mental Development

Intelligence test.

The Merrill-Palmer Scales of Mental Development is an **intelligence** test for children aged 18 months-4 years that can be used to supplement or substitute for the **Stanford-Binet** test. Its 19 subtests cover language skills, motor skills, manual dexterity, and matching ability. They require both oral responses and tasks involving a variety of materials including pegboards, formboards, cubes, Kohs design blocks, buttons, scissors, sticks, and strings. The following comprise about half of the Merrill-Palmer scales: the Color Matching Test; Buttoning Test; Stick and String, and Scissors tests; Language Test; Picture Formboards 1, 2, and 3; Nested Cubes; Copying Test; Pyramid Test; and Little Pink Tower Test. The remaining Merrill-Palmer subtests are the Wallin Pegboards A and B; Mare-Foal Formboard; Seguin-Goddard Formboard; Pintner-Manikin Test; Decroly Matching Game; Woodworth-Wells Association Test; and the **Kohs Block Design Test**. Resistance to the testing situation is taken into account in scoring. The test is accompanied by a detailed list of factors that can influence a child's willingness to cooperate, and refused or omitted items are considered when arriving at the total score, which may then be converted and reported in a variety of ways, including mental age and percentile ranking.

For Further Study

Books

Cohen, Libby G., and Loraine J. Spenciner. *Assessment of Young Children.* New York: Longman, 1994.

McCullough, Virginia. *Testing and Your Child: What You Should Know About 150 of the Most Common Medical, Educational, and Psychological Tests.* New York: Plume, 1992.

Wortham, Sue Clark. *Tests and Measurement in Early Childhood Education.* Columbus: Merrill Publishing Co., 1990.

Metamemory

High-level memory skill defined as the ability to remember to remember.

Memory development is one aspect of a child's cognitive development. Memory skills, such as grouping similar bits of information together, using acronyms or other mnemonic devices, are characteristics of older children, adolescents, and adults. (For example, a child learning the names of the planets in the solar system may use the initial letters of the words in this sentence to recall the planets: *My very educated mother just sold us nine pizzas* for *Mercury, Venus, Earth, Mars, Jupiter, Saturn, Uranus, Neptune, Pluto.*) Metamemory is the skill to remember that one needs to recall something for a specific purpose. This skill is one of the most advanced in the developing child's memory repertoire.

For Further Study

Books

Antaki, Charles and Alan Lewis, eds. *Mental Mirrors: Metacognition in Social Knowledge and Communication.* Beverly Hills: Sage, 1986.

Moely, Barbara E. *Teachers' Expectations for Memory and Metamemory Skills of Elementary School Children.* Washington, DC: National Institute of Education, 1985.

Sweeney, Dee. *Meet Your Mind.* Washington, DC: Office of Educational Research and Improvement, 1994.

Volk, Tyler. *Metapatterns across Space, Time, and Mind.* New York: Columbia University Press, 1995.

Methylphenidate

The generic name for the drug Ritalin, the most commonly prescribed medication for treating children with attention deficit/hyperactivity disorder (ADHD).

A central nervous system stimulant, methylphenidate is also used to control **narcolepsy**, a condition characterized by an overpowering desire to sleep. Methylphenidate comes in short- and long-acting tablets. The latter should be swallowed whole, never broken into smaller pieces or chewed.

Initially methylphenidate is prescribed in two daily doses of 0.25 mg each, taken at breakfast and lunch times. The dosage is gradually increased until the daily amount reaches 1.0 mg. The dosages should be strictly followed and always accompanied by a meal or snack. The primary side effect of methylphenidate is growth suppression. Others include irritability, restlessness, agitation, nausea, and headaches. Occasionally it causes sleeplessness, in which case the last dosage of the day should be a short-action tablet. Physicians often recommend regular drug-free periods to combat these effects. In many cases, the child only takes methylphenidate during the school year.

Persons taking methylphenidate should be aware of the possible adverse interactions with the following drugs: amphetamines, appetite suppressants, caffeine, chlophedianol, cocaine, asthma medication, cold, sinus and hay fever medications, nabilone, pemoline, monoamine oxidase inhibitors, and pimozide. Methylphenidate is also affected by **epilepsy**, **Tourette's**

syndrome, glaucoma, high blood pressure, psychosis, severe anxiety, and **tics**. Methylphenidate can be addictive and dosage should be tapered off gradually. Signs of physical dependency include the need to increase the dosage in order to achieve results, mental **depression**, unusual behavior, and unusual tiredness or weakness. Some medical professionals believe that methylphenidate is prescribed too often. They call for better diagnostic procedures conducted by trained personnel rather than relying primarily on subjective observations by parents and teachers.

For Further Study

Publications

Advice for the Patient: Drug Information in Lay Language. Edition 16. USP DI-Volume II, 1996.

Metropolitan Achievement Tests

Achievement tests that assess general language skills, arithmetic skills, and reading comprehension.

The Metropolitan Achievement Tests feature a battery of group-administered achievement tests that assess general language and arithmetic skills, and **reading** comprehension. Results are often given as grade equivalents (such as Instructional Reading Level, or IRL, which indicates the optimal reading level at which a student can learn). The tests are administered at all grade levels, K-12, and can last from 1-½ hours (kindergarten) to over four hours for grades 6–12. The complete assessment battery covers five disciplines: reading, mathematics, language (i.e.writing), science, and social studies. The reading test includes a vocabulary component and a comprehension section consisting of passages followed by multiple-choice questions. The mathematics test includes a section on concepts and problem solving which assesses mastery of strategies including estimating, classification, working backwards, finding a pattern, reasoning logically, and using probability. The procedures portion of the mathematics test (not always included) consists of computation both with and without a context. The language test gives the student a writing task to complete for a specific audience, with the main steps in the writing process—prewriting (brainstorming, organizing, etc.), composing, and editing—built into the test. The Metropolitan Achievement Test's science portion stresses process skills and reasoning ability within life science, physical science, and earth science, with minimal emphasis on memorization of facts. The test contains illustrations including traditional laboratory activities and equipment, charts, and graphs. The social studies test in-cludes questions on geography, history, culture, political science, and economics, and emphasizes critical thinking and research skills.

For Further Study

Books

Hart, Diane. *Authentic Assessment: A Handbook for Educators.* Menlo Park, CA: Addison-Wesley Pub. Co., 1994.

McCullough, Virginia. *Testing and Your Child: What You Should Know About 150 of the Most Common Medical, Educational, and Psychological Tests.* New York: Plume, 1992.

Metropolitan Readiness Tests

Battery of tests for prekindergarten to first grade that assesses the development of language and mathematical skills necessary for early school learning.

The Metropolitan Readiness Tests are a widely used battery of tests for prekindergarten to first grade. These tests assess the development of language and mathematical skills necessary for early school learning. They are generally used not as an admissions test but as an aid to class placement and sometimes to help determine promotion to the first or second grade. The tests, which can be administered individually or in groups, take 80 to 100 minutes and are given in four to seven sittings. There are two different forms, or levels, which partially overlap. Level One, which assesses pre-reading abilities, is used with four-year-olds in preschool but may also be given up to the middle of kindergarten. It consists of subtests (called composites) evaluating auditory **memory**, beginning consonants, letter recognition, visual matching, school language and listening, and quantitative language. Level Two, which measures skills needed for beginning reading and mathematics, is used from the middle of kindergarten to early in the first grade. Skills assessed include beginning consonants, sound-letter correspondence, visual matching, finding patterns, school language, listening, quantitative concepts, and quantitative operations. Results of the Metropolitan Readiness Tests are reported as a raw score, a national performance rating, and a percentile ranking.

For Further Study

Books

Cohen, Libby G., and Loraine J. Spenciner. *Assessment of Young Children.* New York: Longman, 1994.

McCullough, Virginia. *Testing and Your Child: What You Should Know About 150 of the Most Common Medical, Educational, and Psychological Tests.* New York: Plume, 1992.

Wortham, Sue Clark. *Tests and Measurement in Early Childhood Education.* Columbus: Merrill Publishing Co., 1990.

Microcephaly

A birth defect characterized by an abnormally small head, a receding forehead, and large ears and nose. The condition often signals an abnormally small brain and the presence of other disorders such as **cerebral palsy.**

Microcephaly can be caused by genetic and chromosomal abnormalities, or by environmental factors such as prenatal radiation exposure, prenatal infections (**rubella**, toxoplasmosis), and maternal drug use. Women with **phenylketonuria (PKU)** who do not maintain a low-protein diet during pregnancy are also at risk for having babies with microcephaly.

Microcephaly is occasionally obvious at birth, particularly if the fontanelle, or soft spot, is closed. It is typically diagnosed by measuring the circumference of the baby's head. Sometimes this measurement can be taken in utero through ultrasound waves. The child's physical growth is usually retarded, and he or she suffers delays in speech and mental development. Some children have seizures, crossed eyes, and spastic paralysis.

The treatment for a microcephalic child is essentially therapeutic, depending on the attending disabilities. The parents may need to learn special feeding techniques if the child's swallowing techniques are underdeveloped. Physical therapy can improve the child's coordination and strengthen or relax the muscles. **Seizures** and involuntary movements can be prevented by drugs such as anticonvulsants and muscle relaxers. Wheelchairs and orthopedic devices can aid mobility. Speech therapy can help the child to overcome communication difficulties.

For Further Study

Organizations

March of Dimes Birth Defects Foundation
Address: 1275 Mamaroneck Avenue
White Plains, NY 10605
Telephone: (914) 428-7100
FAX: (914) 997-4763

Center for Children with Chronic Illness and Disability
Address: Box 721 WMHC
420 Delaware SE
Minneapolis, MN 55455
Telephone: (612) 626-4032
FAX: (612) 626-2134

Association of Birth Defect Children
Address: 827 Irma Avenue
Orlando, FL 32803
Telephone: (407) 245-7035; toll-free (800) 313-2232

Minnesota Multiphasic Personality Inventory

Gathers information on personality, attitudes, and mental health.

The Minnesota Multiphasic Personality Inventory is a test used to gather information on personality, attitudes, and mental health of persons aged 16 or older and to aid in clinical diagnosis. It consists of 556 true-false questions, with different formats available for individual and group use. The MMPI is untimed and can take anywhere from 45 minutes to 2 hours to complete. This is normally done in a single session, but can be extended to a second session if necessary. Specific conditions or syndromes that the test can help identify include hypochondriasis, **depression**, hysteria, paranoia, and **schizophrenia**. Raw scores based on deviations from standard responses are entered on personality profile forms to obtain the individual results. There is also a validity scale to thwart attempts to "fake" the test. Because the MMPI is a complex test whose results can sometimes be ambiguous (and/or skewed by various factors), professionals tend to be cautious in interpreting it, often preferring broad descriptions to specific psychiatric diagnoses, unless these are supported by further testing and observable behavior. A sixth-grade reading level is required in order to take the test. However, a tape-recorded version is available for those with limited literacy, visual impairments, or other problems.

For Further Study

Books

Aylward, Elizabeth H. *Understanding Children's Testing: Psychological Testing.* Austin, TX: Pro-Ed, 1991.

Blau, Theodore H. *The Psychological Examination of the Child.* New York: J. Wiley & Sons, 1991.

Knoff, Howard M. *The Assessment of Child and Adolescent Personality.* New York: Guilford Press, 1986.

McCullough, Virginia. *Testing and Your Child: What You Should Know About 150 of the Most Common Medical, Educational, and Psychological Tests.* New York: Plume, 1992.

O'Neill, Audrey Myerson. *Clinical Inference: How to Draw Meaningful Conclusions from Psychological Tests.* Brandon, VT: Clinical Psychology Publishing Co., 1993.

Walsh, W. Bruce, and Nancy E. Betz. *Tests and Assessment.* 2nd ed. Englewood Cliffs, NJ: Prentice Hall, 1990.

Wodrich, David L., and Sally A. Kush. *Children's Psychological Testing: A Guide for Nonpsychologists.* 2nd ed. Baltimore, MD: Brookes Publishing Co., 1990.

MMR vaccine *see* **Immunization**

Montessori Method

A progressive system of education for early childhood through adolescence developed in the first half of the twentieth century by Maria Montessori (1870–1952), an Italian physician turned educator.

Maria Montessori's educational methods are based on individualized, self-directed study, with children choosing the activities they want to work on and proceeding at their own pace, either alone or in small groups, using specially devised instructional materials that allow them to monitor and correct their own errors. The cornerstone of the method is the enjoyment and satisfaction that are produced when children's natural love of learning is respected and allowed to flourish without the regimentation of traditional instructional systems.

Historical background

Maria Montessori pursued a lifelong interest in human development, first as a physician and later as an educator. The first woman in Italy to be awarded a degree in medicine, she began developing her educational methods while working with retarded children in the Orthophrenic School from 1898 to 1900. After a number of these children made sufficient progress to pass examinations administered to children of normal ability, Montessori turned her attention to general education. In 1907 she took charge of a day care program for children of tenement dwellers in Rome, designed primarily to keep the unruly preschoolers out of trouble. Her Casa dei Bambini (Children's House) inaugurated two decades of developing educational methods by careful observation and a continual process of trial and error. In addition to the intellectual progress made by Montessori's pupils when they were free to engage in activities that interested them and to learn at their own pace, the children also showed impressive and unexpected gains in social development, becoming calmer, kinder, more disciplined, and more independent. As more schools were opened and Montessori's methods were used with children of middle-class and wealthy families, interest in her educational innovations grew throughout Italy and abroad.

By 1909 Montessori had published an account of her work at the Casa dei Bambini, and she later wrote numerous articles and books that drew on her classroom experiences for the formulation of educational theories and principles. The Association Montessori Internationale was founded in 1929, with Montessori serving as president until her death. After working as a government inspector of schools in the 1920s, Montessori left Italy for Spain in 1934, eventually moving to the Netherlands, where she died in 1952.

By 1912 Montessori's ideas had gained attention in the United States. In that year an English translation of her first book was published, and the first Montessori school in the U.S. was opened in Tarrytown, New York. However, after an initial burst of activity, interest in Montessori's methods fell into a decline that lasted for several decades, due largely to their divergence from the contemporary theories of American psychologists and educators, which downplayed the role of environmental factors in the development of **intelligence.** Montessori education has enjoyed a resurgence in the U.S. since the 1950s, and its methods are practiced and adapted today in public as well as private and parochial education.

Montessori's theory of child development

The philosophy of linear development underlies traditional methods of education (i.e., children get a little smarter every year). Montessori believed that intellectual development takes place in four distinct periods called "planes" that correspond to the chronological stages of birth to age 6, 6–12, 12–18, and 18–24. Moreover, development within each of these planes surges and then declines, with the developmental peaks occurring at the ages of 3, 9, 15, and 21. Montessori's ideas resemble those of the Swiss psychologist **Jean Piaget** in that she believed the nature of intelligence and learning is qualitatively different at each stage of development. For example, she contrasted the rapid, instinctive learning of children up to the age of six with the more deliberate learning styles of older children and adults. She labeled preschoolers' ability to "soak up" aspects of their environments the "Absorbent Mind." Also like Piaget, she theorized that accomplishments at each stage build on those of the previous ones, and that inadequate development at any stage will influence the ability to carry out the developmental tasks of later stages.

Another one of Montessori's basic concepts is that of "sensitive periods," distinct but overlapping age ranges that are most favorable for development in specific areas. According to Montessori, the ages of one to five constitute a sensitive period for development through the five senses. She thought it important for children of this age to have educational experiences that exercise the senses as fully as possible. The sensitive period for language, when children are acutely sensitive to sounds and able to discriminate between them, occurs between the ages of three months and five or five-and-one-half years. A sensitive period for order, when children want things to follow familiar and reassuring patterns that allow them to organize their experiences, lasts roughly from the first birthday to the age of three. According to Montessori, the upsets of the "terrible twos," which seem so disorderly, are often exaggerated reactions to small disruptions in order not perceived by adults. Next comes the sensitive period for "small details," around the age of two, when children tend to focus on a single aspect of an object or situation more readily than on the whole. According to Montessori, this period develops the powers of observation as well as the ability to concentrate on one thing for an extended period of time. During the following sensitive period, occurring roughly between the ages of two-and-one-half and four, children develop their motor coordination through a tendency to perform and repeat a variety of everyday motions, an activity that may appear pointless to adults but is actually helping children learn to control the movements of their bodies. During the final sensitive period, children develop their social skills by attentiveness to the feelings and behavior of others. During this period, they progress from parallel to cooperative play and are introduced to standard social rules, such as those involved in table manners.

The educational system

Education in a Montessori classroom is "self-activated": each child takes the initiative in choosing from a range of available materials and activities in a carefully prepared classroom environment. The teacher has a much less intrusive role than in a conventional classroom, basically acting as an observer who allows the children to learn on their own with the aid of the prepared materials and provides help only when it is needed. This educational framework fosters the development of self-discipline, confidence, competence, and problem-solving skills.

The classroom

A Montessori classroom is readily distinguishable from a conventional one. Instead of rows of desks, children work individually, or in groups at several tables or on the floor. At the elementary level, three age levels mingle in a single classroom, allowing younger children to learn by observing older ones. Children ages 6 to 9 are in one classroom, and ages 9 through 12 in another. Activities center around a series of learning games, which progress in complexity, moving from the concrete to the abstract. These games utilize cardboard, wooden, cloth, and metal materials designed to teach children about such concepts as size, shape, weight, texture, color, and sound. They are designed to automatically provide children with feedback that allows them to correct their own errors. Although livelier than an ordinary classroom, the Montessori environment is an orderly and industrious one, with children totally absorbed in their tasks, at which they can work uninterrupted for hours at a time if they choose. Montessori believed that interruptions, even for such worthwhile activities as gym or music, do not allow children to achieve their full learning potential, so her teaching method calls for two uninterrupted three-hour periods every day in which the children pursue their educational activities, one in the morning and one in the afternoon. In addition to the prepared educational materials, the typical Montessori classroom at the elementary level also includes items such as dishes, kitchen utensils, and plants, which aid in the development of gross and fine motor abilities by making everyday domestic activities part of the educational setting. Motor, sensory, and intellectual activities are integrated in the Montessori curriculum, so that, for example, reading begins on the sensory and motor levels with sandpaper letters and movable alphabets. Computers have been introduced into Montessori classrooms, although they are used primarily by older children because it is feared that heavy computer use by young children would use up valuable time needed for more basic pursuits, such as manipulating objects and writing, that are crucial to the types of learning they need to do.

The Montessori teacher

The role of the teacher in a Montessori classroom is very different from that of conventional teachers, who lead an entire class in a single activity for which they issue directions and allot a specific amount of time. Allowing students to work at their own pace, either singly or in groups, Montessori teachers are both observers and facilitators. They do not force unwanted assistance on their students, instead giving them the opportunity to make discoveries on their own and being available to help them when they get stuck and need further guidance. They keep track of each student's progress through careful observation and detailed record-keeping to help advise them in ways that ensure the best possible use of the teaching materials provided. Due to the self-motivating nature of the Montessori **curriculum**, they do not need to rely on the system of reward and punishment that characterizes most formalized instruction. They also do not have to devote large amounts of energy to **discipline,** for the Montessori system fosters a spirit of cooperation and self-discipline. Children learn self-control at the primary level, ages three to six, and, at the elementary level, are able to apply it to group work as well. To qualify as Montessori teachers, instructors take a training course devised by Maria Montessori, usually administered as a nine-month graduate program following the acquisition of a degree in education. They must learn about all the different levels of development, not just the one pertaining to the level they want to teach. All major subject areas are covered, and trainees are familiarized with the classroom teaching materials. At the end of the program they must pass both oral and written examinations.

Montessori education in the U. S. today

The past 30 years have seen the founding of over 3,000 Montessori schools affiliated with either a national or international Montessori association, as well as many others without such affiliations. Initially most Montessori schools were established at the primary level for children aged three to six, but many private schools have extended their programs to the elementary-school level, especially since the 1980s. The 1990s have seen many programs extend even further upward through the ages of 12–15 and also downward to include parent-child programs for children under the age of three. Public school programs are generally offered in one of two formats, as magnet school programs or as charter schools funded by the states and operated independently from local school districts. Like private schools, public programs, which typically began with kindergarten and first grade only, have also extended their range, expanding to cover more of the elementary grades and also offering classes at the **preschool** level by obtaining funding through **Head Start** grants. Children in Montessori programs, including children from low-income families, have consistently scored higher than their peers on standardized tests and have shown above-average development of the personal skills necessary to classroom success. Montessori magnet schools consistently have long waiting lists, often containing hundreds of names.

One of the challenges facing Montessori educators is working out the details of programs for adolescents and young adults ages 12–24, for which Maria Montessori was only able to formulate a theoretical framework but not develop specific programs based on day-to-day teaching experience. Another challenge is maintaining the quality of Montessori education as programs proliferate and expand. To help meet this goal, a number of different Montessori organizations have jointly formed the Montessori Accreditation Council for Teacher Education (MACTE), which has the mission of maintaining a supply of qualified, dedicated professionals to staff Montessori programs throughout the country. The ultimate goal of Montessori educators is to make Montessori programs available to all children regardless of socioeconomic background, a goal that comes closer to reality as the success of these programs is repeatedly demonstrated to parents, educators, and government officials on the local, state, and federal levels.

For Further Study

Books

Gerhardt-Seele, Peter. *The Computer and the Child, A Montessori Approach.* Rockville, MD: Computer Science Press, 1985.

Gettman, David. *Basic Montessori: Learning Activities for Under-Fives.* New York: St. Martin's Press, 1987.

Lillard, Paula Polk. *Montessori Today: A Comprehensive Approach to Education from Birth to Adulthood.* New York: Schocken Books, 1996.

Montessori, Maria. *From Childhood to Adolescence.* New York: Schocken Books, 1973.

———. *The Child, Society, and the World.* Oxford: Clio Press, 1989.

Organizations

Association Montessori Internationale (U.S. Branch Office)
Address: 170 W. Schofield
Rochester, NY 14617
Telephone: (716) 544-6709

Montessori Accreditation Council for Teacher Education (MACTE)
Address: 17583 Oak Tree
Fountain Valley, CA 92708

Montessori, Maria (1870–1952)

Innovative Italian educator.

Maria Montessori is best known for the progressive method of education that bears her name. She earned her medical degree from the University of Rome in 1894, the first Italian woman to do so. A psychiatrist by training, Montessorri worked with deprived and retarded children at the Orthophrenic School in Rome starting in 1899. Her observations of the educational challenges facing these children lead to the formulation of her theories of cognitive development and early childhood education. As she observed the progress of pupils previously considered to be uneducable, Montessori pondered the poor performance of normal children in regular schools. These schools, she concluded, were unable to address the individual educational needs of children and therefore stifled, rather than encouraged, learning. She described children in standard classrooms as butterflies mounted on pins, wings motionless with useless knowledge. To see whether her ideas could be adapted to the education of normal children, Montessori opened her own school in 1907, the Casa dei Bambini, for 3-7-year-olds living in the tenements of Rome.

Montessori believed that children learn what they are ready to learn, and that there may be considerable differences among children in what phase they might be going through and to what materials they might be receptive at any given time. Therefore, Montessori individualized her educational method. Children were free to work at their own pace and to choose what they would like to do and where they would like to do it without competition with others. The materials in Montessori's classrooms reflected her value in self selected and pursued activity, training of the senses through the manipulation of physical objects, and individualized cognitive growth facilitated by items that allowed the child to monitor and correct his or her own errors—boards in which pegs of various shapes were to be fitted into corresponding holes, lacing boards, and sandpaper alphabets so that children could feel the letters as they worked with them while beginning to read

Maria Montessori

and write, for example. While other schools at the beginning of the 20th century emphasized rote learning and "toeing the line," self absorption in discovery and mastery tasks was the trademark of Montessori classrooms. Still, her classrooms combined this seemingly playful self direction with Montessori self discipline and respect for authority. Continued effort and progress was sustained by the satisfaction and enjoyment children received from mastering tasks and from engaging in activities they themselves have chosen. Montessori believed that these methods would lead to maximal independence for each child from dressing him or herself to organizing his or her day.

Interestingly, Montessori's educational approach also reflected the Darwinian notion that the development of each individual is a microcosm of the development of the entire species, or that "Ontogeny recapitulates phylogeny." She therefore advocated that even young children be taught to grow plants and tend animals so that, like their agrarian ancestors, they would ultimately achieve the highest level of civilization.

In 1922 Montessori became the government inspector of schools in Italy. She left Italy in 1934, traveled, and eventually moved to the Netherlands where she died in 1952. Maria Montessori left behind a rich legacy. Her educational approach to young and special needs children quickly became a popular progressive alternative to traditional classrooms. Today Montessori schools are common in many communities, and even traditional approaches to education embrace many of Montessori's ideas.

For Further Study

Books

Britton, L. *Montessori Play and Learn.* New York: Crown, 1992.

Hainstock, E.G. *Teaching Montessori in the Home: The Preschool Years.* New York: NAL-Dutto, 1976.

Hainstock, E.G. *Teaching Montessori in the Home: The School Years.* New York: NAL-Dutton, 1989.

Montessori, M. *The Montessori Method.* 1939

Montessori, M. *The Secret of Childhood.* New York: Ballantine, 1982.

Montessori, M. *Spontaneous Activity in Education.* Cambridge,MA: Robert Bentley, 1964.

Organizations

American Montessori Society
  Address: 150 Fifth Avenue, Suite 203
  New York, NY 10011
  Telephone: (212) 924-3209

—Doreen Arcus, Ph.D.
University of Massachusetts Lowell

Moral Development

The formation of a system of underlying assumptions about standards and principles that govern moral decisions.

Moral development involves the formation of a system of values on which to base decisions concerning "right" and "wrong, " or "good" and "bad." **Values** are underlying assumptions about standards that govern moral decisions.

Although morality has been a topic of discussion since the beginning of human civilization, the scientific study of moral development did not begin in earnest until the late 1950s. Lawrence Kohlberg (1927–1987), an American psychologist building upon **Jean Piaget**'s work in cognitive reasoning, posited six stages of moral development in his 1958 doctoral thesis. Since that time, morality and moral development have become acceptable subjects of scientific research. Prior to Kohlberg's work, the prevailing positivist view claimed that science should be "value-free"—that morality had no place in scientific studies. By choosing to study moral development scientifically, Kohlberg broke through the positivist boundary and established morality as a legitimate subject of scientific research.

There are several approaches to the study of moral development, which are categorized in a variety of ways. Briefly, the **social learning theory** approach claims that humans develop morality by learning the rules of acceptable behavior from their external environment (an essentially behaviorist approach). Psychoanalytic theory proposes instead that morality develops through humans' conflict between their instinctual drives and the demands of society. Cognitive development theories view morality as an outgrowth of cognition, or reasoning, whereas personality theories are holistic in their approach, taking into account all the factors that contribute to human development.

The differences between these approaches rest on two questions: 1) where do humans begin on their moral journey; and 2) where do we end up? In other words, how moral are infants at birth? And how is "moral maturity" defined? What is the ideal morality to which we aspire? The contrasting philosophies at the heart of the answers to these questions determine the essential perspective of each moral development theory. Those who believe infants are born with no moral sense tend towards social learning or behaviorist theories (as all morality must therefore be learned from the external environment). Others who believe humans are innately aggressive and completely self-oriented are more likely to accept psychoanalytic theories (where morality is the learned management of socially destructive internal drives). Those who believe it is our reasoning abilities that separate us from the rest of creation will find cognitive development theories the most attractive, while those who view humans as holistic beings who are born with a full range of potentialities will most likely be drawn to personality theories.

What constitutes "mature morality" is a subject of great controversy. Each society develops its own set of norms and standards for acceptable behavior, leading many to say that morality is entirely culturally conditioned. Does this mean there are no universal truths, no cross-cultural standards for human behavior? The debate over this question fuels the critiques of many moral development theories. Kohlberg's six stages of moral development, for example, have been criticized for elevating Western, urban, intellectual (upper class) understandings of morality, while discrediting rural, tribal, working class, or Eastern moral understandings. (See **Kohlberg's theory of moral reasoning.**) Feminists have pointed out potential sexist elements in moral development theories devised by male researchers using male subjects only (such as Kohlberg's early work). Because

women's experience in the world is different from men's (in every culture), it would stand to reason that women's moral development might differ from men's, perhaps in significant ways.

Definitions of what is or is not moral are currently in a state of upheaval within individual societies as well as, at least, in the Western world. Controversies rage over the morality of warfare (especially nuclear), ecological conservation, genetic research and manipulation, alternative fertility and childbearing methods, abortion, sexuality, pornography, drug use, euthanasia, racism, sexism, and human rights issues, among others. Determining the limits of moral behavior becomes increasingly difficult as human capabilities, choices, and responsibilities proliferate with advances in technology and scientific knowledge. For example, prenatal testing techniques that determine birth defects in utero force parents to make new moral choices about whether to birth a child. Other examples of recently created moral questions abound in modern-day society.

Therefore, the study of moral development is lively today. The rise in crime, drug and alcohol abuse, gang violence, teen parenthood, and **suicide** in recent years in Western society has also caused a rise in concern over morality and moral development. Parents and teachers want to know how to raise moral children, and they turn to moral development theorists to find the answers. Freudian personality theories became more widely known to the Western public in the 1960s and were understood to imply that repression of a child's natural drives would lead to neuroses. Many parents and teachers were therefore afraid to **discipline** their children, and permissiveness became the rule. **Cognitive development** theories did little to change things, as they focus on reasoning and disregard behavior. (After a great deal of criticism in this regard, Kohlberg and other cognitive development theorists did begin to include moral actions in their discussions and education programs, but their emphasis is still on reasoning alone.) Behaviorist theories, with their complete denial of free will in moral decision-making, are unattractive to many and require such precise, dedicated, behavior modification techniques to succeed that few people are able to apply them in real-life situations.

The continuing breakdown of society, however, is beginning to persuade people that permissiveness is not the answer and another approach must be found. Schools are returning to "character education" programs, popular in the 1920s and 1930s, where certain "virtues" such as honesty, fairness, and loyalty, are taught to students along with the regular academic subjects. Unfortunately, there is little or no agreement as to which "virtues" are important and what exactly each "virtue" means. For example, when a student expresses dislike of another student, is she or he practicing the virtue of "fairness" or, rather, being insensitive to another's feelings? If a student refuses to salute the flag, is he or she betraying the virtue of "loyalty" or, rather, being loyal to some higher moral precept? These complex questions plague "character education" programs today, and their effectiveness remains in dispute.

Another approach to moral education that became popular in the 1960s and 1970s is known as "values clarification" or "values modification. " The purpose of these programs is to guide students to establish (or discern) their own system of values on which to base their moral decisions. Students are also taught that others may have different values systems, and that they must be tolerant of those differences. The advantages of this approach are that it promotes self-investigation and awareness and the development of internal moral motivations (which are more reliable than external motivations), and prevents fanaticism, authoritarianism, and moral coercion. The disadvantage is that it encourages moral relativism, the belief that "anything goes." Pushed to its extreme, it creates social chaos because no one can be held to any universal (or societal) moral standard. "Values clarification" is generally seen today to be a valuable *component* of moral education, but incomplete on its own.

Lawrence Kohlberg devised a moral education program in the 1960s based on his cognitive development theory. Called the Just Community program, it utilizes age-appropriate (or stage-appropriate) discussions of moral dilemmas, democratic rule-making, and the creation of a community context where students and teachers can *act* on their moral decisions. Just Community programs have been established in schools, prisons, and other institutions with a fair amount of success. Exposure to moral questions and the opportunity to practice moral behavior in a supportive community appear to foster deeper moral reasoning and more constructive behavior.

Overall, democratic family and school systems are much more likely to promote the development of internal self-controls and moral growth than are authoritarian or permissive systems. Permissive systems fail to instill *any* controls, while authoritarian systems instill only fear of punishment, which is not an effective deterrent unless there is a real chance of being caught (punishment can even become a reward for immoral behavior when it is the only attention a person ever gets). True moral behavior involves a number of internal processes that are best developed through warm, caring parenting with clear and consistent expectations, emphasis on the reinforcement of positive behaviors (rather than the punishment of negative ones), modeling of moral behavior by adults, and creation of opportunities for the child to practice moral reasoning and actions.

As previously stated, there is disagreement as to the exact motivations involved in moral behavior. Whatever the motivations, however, the internal processes remain the same.

The Four Component model describes them as follows:

1) moral sensitivity = empathy (identifying with another's experience) and cognition of the effect of various possible actions on others;

2) moral judgment = choosing which action is the most moral;

3) moral motivation = deciding to behave in the moral way, as opposed to other options; and

4) implementation = carrying out the chosen moral action.

According to personal (social) goal theory, moral (or prosocial) behavior is motivated by the desire to satisfy a variety of personal and social goals, some of which are self-oriented (selfish), and some of which are other-oriented (altruistic). The four major internal motivations for moral behavior as presented by personal (social) goal theorists are: 1) empathy; 2) the belief that people are valuable in and of themselves and therefore should be helped; 3) the desire to fulfill moral rules; and 4) self-interest. In social domain theory, moral reasoning is said to develop within particular social "domains": 1) moral (e.g., welfare, justice, rights); 2) social-conventional (social rules for the orderly function of society); and 3) personal (pure self-interest, exempt from social or moral rules).

Most people in fact have more than one moral "voice" and shift among them depending on the situation. In one context, a person may respond out of empathy and place care for one person over concern for social rules. In a different context, that same person might instead insist on following social rules for the good of society, even though someone may suffer because of it. People also show a lack of consistent morality by sometimes choosing to act in a way that they know is not moral, while continuing to consider themselves "moral" people. This discrepancy between moral judgment (perceiving an act as morally right or wrong) and moral choice (deciding whether to act in the morally "right" way) can be explained in a number of ways, any one of which may be true in a given situation:

- weakness of will (the person is overwhelmed by desire);

- weakness of conscience (guilt feelings are not strong enough to overcome tempation); or

- limited/flexible morality (some latitude allowed in moral behavior while still maintaining a "moral" identity).

The Moral Balance model proposes that most humans operate out of a limited or flexible morality. Rather than expecting moral perfection from ourselves or others, we set certain limits beyond which we cannot go. Within those limits, however, there is some flexibility in moral decision-making. Actions such as taking coins left in the change-box of a public telephone may be deemed acceptable (though not perfectly moral), while stealing money from an open, unattended cash register is not. Many factors are involved in the determination of moral acceptability from situation to situation, and the limits on moral behavior are often slippery. If given proper encouragement and the opportunity to practice a coherent inner sense of morality, however, most people will develop a balanced morality to guide their day-to-day interactions with their world.

For Further Study

Books

Crittenden, Paul. *Learning to be Moral: Philosophical Thoughts About Moral Development*. Atlantic Highlands, NJ: Humanities Press International, 1990.

Gilligan, Carol. *In a Different Voice: Psychological Theory and Women's Development*. Cambridge: Harvard University Press, 1982.

Kohlberg, Lawrence. *Essays on Moral Development, I: The Philosophy of Moral Development: Moral Stages and the Idea of Justice*. San Francisco: Harper & Row, 1981.

———. *Essays on Moral Development, II: The Psychology of Moral Development*. San Francisco: Harper & Row, 1984.

———. *Child Psychology and Childhood Education: A Cognitive-Developmental View*. New York: Longman, 1987.

Kurtines, William M., and Jacob L. Gewirtz, eds. *Moral Development: An Introduction*. Boston: Allyn and Bacon, 1995.

Power, F. C., Ann Higgins, and Lawrence Kohlberg. *Lawrence Kohlberg's Approach to Moral Education: A Study of Three Democratic High Schools*. New York: Columbia University Press, 1989.

Schulman, Michael, and Eva Mekler. *Bringing Up a Moral Child: A New Approach for Teaching Your Child to Be Kind, Just, and Responsible*, rev. ed. New York: Main Street Books/Doubleday, 1994.

Organizations

Developmental Studies Center
Address: 2000 Embarcadero, Suite 305
Oakland, CA 94606-5300
Telephone: (510) 533-0213; toll-free (800) 666-7270
[Researches and creates programs (such as the Reading for Real program for elementary school students) concerning children's moral, social, and intellectual development.]

Center for the Advancement of Ethics and Character
Address: Boston University School of Education
605 Commonwealth Ave., Room 356
Boston, MA 02215
Telephone: (617) 353-3262
FAX: (617) 353-3924

(Provides information on the teacher's role in students' moral development.)

Educators for Social Responsibility (ESR)
Address: 23 Garden St.
Cambridge, MA 02138
Telephone: toll-free (800) 370-2515
(Provides curriculum materials, teacher training, and information on character education, conflict resolution, and violence prevention.)

The Heartwood Institute
Address: 425 N. Craig St., Suite 302
Pittsburgh, PA 15213
Telephone: toll-free (800) 432-7810
(Offers the Heartwood Program, a literature-based curriculum that teaches children seven "universal values": courage, loyalty, justice, respect, hope, honesty, and love.)

—Dianne K. Daeg de Mott

Moro Reflex *see* **Neonatal Reflexes**

Morpheme *see* **Language Development**

Motherese or Parentese

Pattern of speaking used by a caretaker when talking to an infant.

Motherese, or parentese, is the name given to the pattern of speech used by caretakers (mothers and other adults) when talking to infants. It is characterized by higher pitch, slower tempo, and wider fluctuations in intonation than that used in normal conversation with older children or adults. Motherese is employed by **caregivers** worldwide in interacting with infants. Although most researchers believe that the motherese speech pattern is not essential for the infant's language acquisition, it does attract the infant's attention and get him or her to focus on spoken language. In addition, motherese may draw attention to certain language features (patterns of emphasis, relationship of words to affect) that help infants learn. A feature of motherese—repeating what the infant or child attempts to say—is effective in encouraging the use of language in communication.

In the mid-1980s, studies at Stanford University demonstrated that infants preferred listening to motherese, with its pattern of exaggerated tone and slower tempo, over adult conversation. Other studies at the University of Washington found that caregivers saturate their motherese speech pattern with vowels. The researchers concluded that this feature of motherese helps to form the infant's perceptual categories for his or her native language.

For Further Study

Books

Kuhl, Patricia K. "Perceptions of Speech and Sound in Early Infancy." In *Handbook of Infant Perception: Volume 2.* New York: Academic Press, 1987.

Welker, J. F., and J. E. Pegg. "Infant Speech Perception and Phonological Acquisition." In *Phonological Development: Models, Research, Implications.* Timonium, MD: York, 1992.

Periodicals

Fernald, Anne. "Four-month-old Infants Prefer to Listen to Motherese." *Infant Behavior and Development* 8, 1985, pp. 303–306.

"How to Talk 'Parentese' to Your Child." *Newsweek,* Spring/Summer 1997, p. 21.

Motor Development *see* **Fine Motor** and **Gross Motor Skills**

Mourning *see* **Death and Mourning**

Multicultural Education/Curriculum

The education philosophy and methodology aiming to replace a dominant cultural paradigm in the classroom with a multiplicity of views reflecting the students' cultural backgrounds.

Multicultural education is essentially an effort to translate a pluralistic world view into educational practices and theories. Thus, a multicultural curriculum, unlike traditional programs, strives to present more than one perspective of a historical event or a cultural phenomenon. For example, Christopher Columbus's expedition to America, defined as "discovery" in traditional textbooks with a Eurocentric bias, appears in a different light to the "discovered" populations. Responding to criticism that pluralism in education may impoverish the current curriculum, multiculturalists have argued that multicultural education actually enriches the curriculum. James A. Banks writes: "Rather than excluding Western civilization from the curriculum, multiculturalists want a more truthful, complex, and diverse version of the West taught in the schools. They want the curriculum to describe the way in which African, Asian, and indigenous cultures have influenced and interacted with Western civilization."

The presence of multiculturalism in American education is undeniable, but it is still a minority movement. With the growing awareness of the multi-ethnic nature of American society, educators have challenged the "melting-pot" principle, observing that the traditional concept of "Americanization" really means conformity to a white, Eurocentric cultural model. Yet, while multicultural education seems appropriate for a multi-ethnic society, many obstacles have hindered the development of formal multicultural educational programs. Chief among them is the opinion that multicultural education would do away with the classics of art and literature, impoverishing the curriculum, and depriving the students of essential knowledge. However, others have argued for the benefits of multicultural education as an active approach to learning, which encourages the learner to construct his or her own knowledge.

Multiculturalism is not a new phenomenon, emerging after World War II, in part as a reaction to Nazi ideas of racial, ethnic, and cultural supremacy. However, as Banks notes, multicultural "education itself is a product of the West"—which implies that the idea of cultural pluralism and tolerance is woven into the founding ideals of Western education, which include freedom, equality, and humanism. In the 1960s, multicultural education as a movement strongly benefitted from society's growing awareness that the monocultural paradigm was not working. According to Thomas J. La Belle and Christopher R. Ward, four factors contributed to the rise of multicultural education in the 1960s, namely, "the civil rights movement, a rise in ethnic consciousness, a more critical analysis of textbooks and other materials, and the loss of belief in theories of cultural deprivation." While theories of cultural deprivation defined minority cultures as failing to conform to a standard, multicultural theory in the 1960s embraced the idea of difference, eliminating the concepts of superiority and inferiority. Enjoying significant government support in the late 1970s, multicultural education faced funding problems in the 1980s, and funding continues to be the principal challenge in the 1990s.

In designing multicultural curricula, educators have often favored an approach whereby the traditional curriculum is enriched and modified by new elements. Banks advocates a gradual, four-stage transformation of the curriculum. The first, the contributions approach, focuses on a particular minority culture's heroes and holidays; the second level, known as the additive approach, introduces new concepts and themes without changing the curriculum's essential structure; the third level, called the transformative approach, enables students to view issues and events from a minority culture's point of view; and the fourth level, the social action approach, encourages students to address social problems caused by a one-dimensional perception of culture. For example, a teacher can, using the transformative approach when presenting a unit in American history, ask her students to describe the "Westward Movement" from the point of the Lakota Sioux, whose homeland was invaded by white settlers. In addition, the study of folklore provides the teacher with numerous lessons in multiculturalism that can be used in the classroom. In a class exercise suggested by Bette Bosma, students read two or three stories from different cultural traditions in which the same theme is developed. If the theme is laziness, the elementary school teacher can introduce *The Lazies: Tales of the People of Russia* by the Russian-American translator and storyteller Mirra Ginsburg, and ask the students to compare a particular story with a similar tale from a non-European source. By focusing on the similarity, students realize that literature, including oral and written traditions, contains motifs and ideas which are shared by more than one culture. Furthermore, in higher grades, it may suffice to study the profound and pervasive influence of a work such as *The Arabian Nights* on Western literature to realize that even national literatures are best approached from a multicultural point of view.

For Further Study

Books

Banks, James A. *An Introduction to Multicultural Education.* Boston: Allyn and Bacon, 1994.

Bishop, Rudine Sims, ed. *Kaleidoscope: A Multicultural Booklist for Grades K-8.* Urbana: National Council of Teachers of English, 1994.

Bosma, Bette. *Fairy Tales, Fables, Legends, and Myths: Using Folk Literature in Your Classroom.* 2nd ed. New York: Teachers College Press, 1992.

La Belle, Thomas J., and Christopher R. Ward. *Multiculturalism and Education: Diversity and Its Impact on Schools and Society.* Albany: State University of New York Press, 1994.

Periodicals

Phillips, Anne. "Who's Afraid of Multiculturalism?" *Dissent,* Winter 1997, pp. 57-63.

—Zoran Minderovic

Multiparent Family *see* **Family**

Mumps

A viral infection that causes swelling of the salivary glands, the glands that produce saliva in the mouth, for which there is a vaccine available.

Most children are immunized against mumps when they receive the MMR vaccine (measles, mumps, **rubella**) at about 15 months and between 11 and 12 years of age. (*See* **immunization** for recommended schedule.)

The mumps virus is transmitted by airborne droplets, spread when an infected person (or an uninfected carrier) coughs or sneezes. The virus infects a person by passing through the respiratory system and settling in the salivary glands, most often the parotid gland located in front of the ear and just above the jawline. Most infected people—though not all—experience swelling on the side of one or both cheeks, and the area will be sensitive to the touch. Eating will cause pain, since it stimulates the salivary glands. Infected individuals may also have a **fever** lasting from three to five days. In addition to swelling of the salivary glands, there may be some swelling in the joints and, in boys, of the testes.

Contagious period: An infected individual is contagious for several days before the swelling of the glands becomes apparent, and will continue to be contagious for at least ten days after the first sign of swelling (or until the swelling is completely gone).

Treatment: There is no specific treatment for mumps, aside from rest, drinking liquids, and taking acetaminophen for fever. Citrus and other strong flavors that stimulate the salivary glands should be avoided. Foods that are soft and easy to chew and swallow are recommended to minimize the demands on the infected glands. Other infections besides mumps can cause inflammation of the salivary glands. If a child who has been immunized against mumps (or one who has previously had mumps) presents mumps-like symptoms, a **pediatrician** should be contacted to determine the cause.

For Further Study

Books

Bellet, Paul S. *The Diagnostic Approach to Common Symptoms and Signs in Infants, Children, and Adolescents.* New York: Lea and Febiger, 1989.

Garwood, John, and Amanda Bennett. *Your Child's Symptoms.* New York: Berkeley Books, 1995.

Organizations

American Academy of Pediatrics, Division of Publications
Address: 141 Northwest Point Blvd., P. O. Box 927
Elk Grove Village, IL 60009-0927
(Publishes brochures on most immunizations and childhood diseases, and a 24-page booklet for parents that includes forms for tracking immunizations and other health-related information.)

National Institute of Allergy and Infectious Diseases (NIAID)
Address: 9000 Rockville Pike
NIH Building 31, Room 7A50
Bethesda, MD 20892-2520
(Arm of the National Institutes of Health that deals with allergies and infectious diseases.)

Muscular Dystrophy

A category of inherited, incurable, and often life-threatening diseases in which the limb and trunk muscles deteriorate.

The major types of muscular dystrophy (MD) are Duchenne, limb-girdle, facioscapulohumeral (FSH), Becker, and myotonic. In the United States, 250,000 people are affected by muscular dystrophy, with boys disproportionally represented at the rate of one in every 4,000 births.

Duchenne, the most severe form of muscular dystrophy, is passed exclusively by a defective gene in the mother to her son. A woman with the defective gene has a 50% chance of bearing a son with Duchenne muscular dystrophy. Female children of carrier mothers have a 50% chance of being carriers themselves. In this disease, the muscles of the lower body and spine are affected first; onset is in early childhood between the ages of two and six years. Nearly one-half of all Duchenne victims do not walk until after they reach 18 months old. When they do begin walking, it is usually with a waddling or swaying gait. The child will also have difficulty getting up from the floor or standing on one foot and may tire easily. A child with Duchenne MD has a tendency to walk on the toes, which causes the pelvis to tilt forward, resulting in lordosis, a hollowing of the back. The disease also creates muscle enlargement, especially in the calf. Dental problems, such as a widening of the jaw and spaces between the teeth, are also common. The child's arms are usually not affected until the latter stages of the disease.

Most victims of Duchenne MD lose the ability to walk between the ages of 10 and 13. This will result in bone deformities, **scoliosis,** and deterioration of the respiratory muscles. The child may also suffer from constipation due to constant sitting. Death usually results from respiratory infection or heart failure. Borderline **mental retardation** and slowed intellectual development occasionally accompany Duchenne MD. However, many patients have above-average **intelligence**.

Limb-girdle muscular dystrophy describes a group of diseases that affect the muscles in the pelvic area and manifests itself in late childhood to middle age. Its effects range from mild to debilitating. An early onset of limb-girdle muscular dystrophy usually signals a swift and severe case. It shares the toe walking and muscle enlargement features characteristic of Duchenne. However, the heart and mental development are usually not affected. Limb-girdle MD is passed on to boys when the defective gene is carried by both parents.

Facioscapulohumeral (FSH) muscular dystrophy is a mild form of the disease involving the muscles of the shoulders, upper back, and face. It appears in adolescence, affecting both boys and girls. FSH is inherited from a parent who also suffers from FSH. Victims' face muscles tend to weaken first; they cannot close their eyes tightly, purse their lips to blow, or puff out their cheeks. This is followed by a weakening of the shoulder and upper back muscles, making it difficult for the child to raise his arms, or to lift objects. The shoulder blades push upward towards the head, creating a "terracing" characteristic.

Becker muscular dystrophy is similar to Duchenne in that it is passed to sons from mothers possessing the defective gene. The symptoms are also similar to Duchenne and occur between two and 16 years of age. Victims of Becker MD generally walk until adulthood and live into their 30s and even 50s. Heart complications are rare.

Myotonic dystrophy, also known as Steinert's disease, attacks the eyes, heart, and testes. Its most telling characteristic is the inability of the muscles to relax after sudden, vigorous exertion.

Three laboratory tests are administered to determine the existence of muscular dystrophy. A blood test can pick up proteins leaked by the muscles even before muscle weakness occurs. An electromyogram will register certain tracings if muscles are diseased. A **biopsy** of muscle tissue can also detect the condition.

Because no cure exists for muscular dystrophy, the focus of parents and medical professionals is to help the patient maintain his mobility as long as possible and to remain an active member of society. The child should be encouraged to exercise the affected muscles, even during periods of illness. Parents should also work closely with teachers to provide a positive educational environment for the child. Time allowances should be made to accommodate the child's difficulty in turning textbook pages, grasping a pencil or pen, and traveling within the classroom and school buildings. Participation in physical education classes should be allowed as much as possible. Even if the child cannot play a particular game, he can keep score or be involved in other ways.

Muscular dystrophy is an extremely difficult challenge for a young person to face, and emotional support is of utmost importance. Summer camps operated by the Muscular Dystrophy Association have been very effective in building **self-esteem** in MD patients. Parents and other family members may find encouragement in joining support groups.

For Further Study

Books

Corrick, James A. *Muscular Dystrophy.* New York: F. Watts, 1992.

Donsbach, Kurt W., and H. Rudolph Alsleben. *Multiple Sclerosis, Muscular Dystrophy and ALS.* USA: Rockland Corporation, 1993.

Audiovisual Recordings

Goodgold, Joseph. *The Doctor Talks to You About Muscular Dystrophy.* Bayside, NY: Soundwords, Inc., 1981. (One 39-minute audiocassette.)

Organizations

Muscular Dystrophy Association
> **Address:** 3300 E. Sunrise Drive
> Tucson, AZ 85718-3208
> **Telephone:** toll-free (800) 572-1717

—Mary McNulty

Music and Musical Ability

Exposure to music and active participation in music making can enrich a child's life both immediately and over the long term, fostering creativity and self-expression, transmitting cultural values, and contributing to physical, intellectual, and social development. After years of cutbacks, school districts throughout the country are restoring programs in music and the other arts. In 1980 only two states mandated instruction in the arts as a requirement for graduation; now 28 do. Research has shown that listening to music has beneficial short- and long-term effects on abstract reasoning ability. The most publicized study is the one associated with the so-called "Mozart effect," in which college students who had listened to a Mozart piano sonata scored eight points higher than a control group on portions of an IQ test. In other research, the cognitive skills of preschool and elementary school-age children have shown improvement in response to music instruction. The renewed interest in integrating music into the school curriculum has also been influenced by the work of psychologist Howard Gardner, who, in his groundbreaking study *Frames of Mind,* challenged the limitations of traditional concepts of intelligence, listing musical ability as one of seven basic types of **intelligence** that need to be nurtured and exercised.

Development of musical aptitude

A child's involvement with music begins even before birth. Studies have shown that the behavior of newborns changes when they are exposed to melodies sung or played to them during the third trimester of **pregnancy.** Newborns are sensitive to both the pitch and volume of sounds, and they even react differently to different styles of music. In the first months of life, infants already have an impressive ability to discriminate among different pitches, and by the age of three months a baby can repeat specific pitches with a high degree of accuracy. An infant's sense of pitch also plays a role in speech development by making adult speech patterns more readily understandable, beginning with the exaggerated pitches and rhythms of baby talk, or **"motherese,"** and extending to the pitch characteristics of ordinary adult speech, such as the tendency for voices to rise at the end of a question. An appreciation and understanding of the musical structures that predominate in one's own culture also begin in infancy. Six-month-olds can discriminate tonal relationships in a wide variety of musical scales, including those used in cultures vastly different from their own. By the age of one year, however, this openness has begun to disappear as infants' musical expectations become shaped by the acoustic intervals that characterize the music of their own culture.

Infants make their first rudimentary attempts at singing as early as eight months of age with musical babbling and show the ability to repeat distinct pitch patterns by 12 months. Coordination of movement and rhythm develops by the age of 18 months, as does the ability to repeat specific melodic intervals (as opposed to single pitches). When actual singing does begin, usually between the second and third years, words are learned first, followed by rhythm, and then pitch. By the age of five, a child has acquired a repertoire of songs. Kindergartners can typically recognize musical phrases and understand the concepts of tempo (whether music is fast and slow) and dynamics (loud and soft). Seven-year-olds can identify pitch differences as small as a quarter tone. A sensitivity to the concept of tonality (what key a piece is in) develops between the ages of five and eight, together with the ability to recognize harmonic changes, and is manifested in the ability to differentiate major from minor keys, recognize when a melody has been transposed into a different key, or identify an incomplete cadence (one that fails to resolve to the tonic, or "home tone").

A special musical talent that is now thought to be influenced by both heredity and environment is perfect pitch, the ability to recognize the exact pitch of any sound and, in return, to accurately produce any pitch without being given a starting pitch as a reference point. (Someone who can sing a given pitch *with* the aid of such a reference point—also a special and valuable skill—is said to have relative pitch.) Although many trained musicians do not have perfect pitch, musical training does foster the development of this talent, which is much more prevalent among trained musicians than among the general population. Recent studies have found that perfect pitch tends to run in families. Researchers plan on studying the DNA of some of these families in hopes of isolating the specific gene that carries this gift.

Fostering music appreciation

One of the best ways for parents to foster an appreciation for music in their children is to provide a positive role model by demonstrating a love for it themselves, exposing their children to recorded music and concerts and, when they are very young, singing to and with them at home.

Infancy

Babies who are exposed to music at home are often able to sing even before they start talking. From the beginning, parents can enhance the bonding process by singing to their infants. Young infants the world over prefer lullabies and other quiet songs with a narrow range of pitches and simple, repetitive melodic patterns. By the middle of the first year, livelier songs can be added, including interactive songs such as "Old McDonald," in which the baby can participate by making sounds or rhythmic movements. Favorite songs often include those with lyrics about animals, including animal noises, and parts of the body, which can be touched in rhythm to the song. Singing can calm infants, provide an accompaniment to familiar routines, and reinforce mastery of new words. Infants can also benefit from exposure to recorded music, musical mobiles, and musical toys, such as stuffed animals that play a song. Between the ages of six and nine months, they can begin playing with musical toys activated by turning knobs or other types of manipulation.

Toddlerhood

Toddlers love imitating sounds and moving to music. Parents should not be alarmed if a toddler cannot sing in tune or keep a beat accurately, as these are abilities that often develop later. Musical development can be enhanced by listening to a variety of music, especially lively music, which toddlers especially enjoy, and playing musical games that involve both song and movement. Toddlers can also use simple rhythm instruments, such as beating on drums or makeshift percussion instruments, shaking maracas (real or homemade), and jangling bells. Toddlers can be sung to (and with) at many times throughout the day, even when riding in the car.

Preschool

Preschoolers can play vocal pitch-matching games and begin learning to recognize the sounds of different musical instruments and associating them with their pictures. If there is a piano in the household, they can begin experimenting with it. Games that involve clapping and moving to music, and also "freezing" when the music stops, are popular at this age. Awareness of musical form also develops as children become able to master songs in which verses alternate with a chorus. Preschoolers can also begin learning simple anecdotes about specific composers and pieces.

Several systematic group approaches to musical training, all imported from abroad, begin at the preschool level. The most well known is the Suzuki Talent Education program, begun by the Japanese educator Shinichi

Suzuki as a method for teaching the violin, but later extended to piano and other instruments. Suzuki's "mother tongue" approach teaches music to children in a sequence of steps that is modeled on the way they learn language; listening comes first, followed by imitation and, finally, reading and writing. Children first listen to recordings of pieces they are to study and then learn them by rote, and the study of musical notation is worked into the lessons later. Parents, who attend both the private lessons and monthly ensemble classes, take part in practice sessions and actually learn to play along with their children. Regular ensemble playing with other youngsters is an integral part of the program.

Another program originated by the Japanese is the Yamaha music education program, which provides a background in both classical and popular music. Children progress through a two-year sequence of instruction between the ages of four and six in classes of eight to 12, with parents attending all activities and helping their children at home as well. Activities include singing and whole-body movement, with an introduction to the keyboard but no formal instruction in piano or other instruments.

Dalcroze Eurhythmics, developed at the Geneva Conservatory of Music by Emile Jacques-Dalcroze, stresses physical movement and creativity. Children learn about the elements of music—melody and dynamics as well as rhythm—through natural, improvised movements. They also study sight-singing with *solfege* syllables (do-re-mi, etc.), ear training, and keyboard improvisation. Dalcroze training is offered through special programs, often under the auspices of a music school. Some private teachers also use its techniques for teaching rhythm.

Two other methods, both developed by well-known 20th-century European composers, include the use of folk songs as an introduction to music. The Orff Schulwerk approach, introduced in the 1950s by German composer Carl Orff, emphasizes dance and other rhythm activities, making use of both folk songs and speech patterns familiar through nursery rhymes and children's games. It is also known for the special percussion instruments developed by Orff that can produce both rhythms and melody. Many music educators in public and private schools use Orff's methods as part of their teaching approach. The other modern composer to create a system of music education was the Hungarian Zoltan Kodaly, whose approach, developed in the 1920s, was first introduced to the United States in the 1960s. Created for children aged three and up, it focuses mainly on developing a good ear and rhythmic sense through singing, making use of the nursery songs and folk music of a child's native country. Children learn to read and write music through singing, after which instrumental activities are introduced.

School-age

In the elementary grades children can be taken to young people's concerts, which feature appropriately short, colorful pieces that hold their attention in programs that are significantly shorter than those performed for adults. They can also start becoming familiar with different types and periods of music by listening to recorded music at home and reading short books about music and composers. After the age of six or seven, children mature in ways that are conducive to beginning private instrumental study. Mastery of new skills becomes an important goal, one they are willing and able to work toward through practice, including practice that involves repetition. Their **fine motor skills** continue to develop, resulting in increased speed and dexterity and, by the age of nine, increased ability to use their hands independently. Hand-eye coordination also improves.

Performance adds an important dimension to the musical experience of children in the elementary grades. Many children naturally enjoy performing, and giving them a head start while they are young can reduce their experience of stage fright at later ages, when they are naturally more self-conscious. Children who are taking lessons can play in recitals organized by their private teacher or by the music school where they take lessons. All children can perform in school vocal or instrumental programs. Other activities, such as Sunday school or summer camp, can provide additional opportunities to perform, both as a solo and with an ensemble.

Adolescence

By adolescence young people have usually begun developing musical interests of their own, often including various forms of popular music. They may begin building their own CD and/or tape collections. Parental attempts to restrict their children's taste in music at this point are not constructive, and all efforts should go toward broadening rather than limiting their musical experience. Interests in different types of music can coexist, and a love of classical music or jazz, especially when nurtured by instruction and active participation, can survive a teenager's enthusiasm for the latest rock group. Teenagers can attend classical music concerts and participate in performing ensembles at school. Participation in student orchestras, marching bands, or choirs can promote self-discipline, teamwork, and social skills. Musical theater productions can become the high point of the school year, giving teenagers valuable performing experience. Young people with a serious interest in classical music can attend music camps, enter competitions through their schools or through local musical organiza-

tions, participate in musical activities through their church, and join music clubs.

Music lessons

Although children receive varying amounts of music instruction in school, private study of a musical instrument produces a proficiency in and understanding of music beyond what can be provided in a classroom setting. Private music lessons also encourage confidence, self-discipline, an ability to use time efficiently, and the development of both intellectual and motor skills. Private instruction also protects a child from the bad habits that can develop when people attempt to play instruments on their own without the benefit of close individual supervision. Bad playing habits, especially those developed over extended periods of time, can significantly delay progress on an instrument once private lessons are started. Depending on the instrument and teaching method, young people begin private music lessons at any point from the age of three through high school. Research has shown that the method of instruction is less important than the student's attitude and level of commitment, the relationship between the teacher and the student, and the degree of parental commitment and support.

Children can begin studying most instruments while they are in elementary school but should not start voice lessons until adolescence (age 12–14 for girls, 15–17 for boys). Because of individual differences in rates of physical and mental maturation, it is impossible to specify exact ages at which all children should begin study. However, some general guidelines are possible. Piano, violin, and recorder can be begun at the youngest ages, although quarter-size or half-size violins are needed for young children. With the Suzuki method of instruction, discussed above, children begin instrumental study at earlier ages than with other methods. It is possible for Suzuki instruction to begin as early as three or four years of age because of several distinctive features: students begin playing by ear before developing the ability to read notes; parents participate in lessons and practice sessions; and students do much of their playing in groups. Because most other types of instruction rely on playing from music right away, children cannot begin lessons until they are old enough to start reading music, usually around the same time they are beginning to read and write in school.

Conventional lessons on piano and violin (using a quarter-size instrument) can generally be begun at the age of six or seven. A child can begin playing a half-size cello as early as seven years of age. The study of woodwind and brass instruments (flute, clarinet, piccolo, oboe, bassoon, trumpet), which makes demands on a child's still-developing lung capacity, begins somewhat later, usually around the ages of 10 or 11, with trombone and French horn study generally beginning around the age of 13. Acoustic guitar lessons can be begun at the age of eight or nine; electric guitar, harp and viola at 11 or 12; and double-bass at about 13. To find a teacher, parents should ask for referrals from other parents whose children are taking lessons and/or from local musicians, including the music teacher at their child's school. A qualified teacher should have a degree in music. Membership in professional organizations is another possible criteria in looking for a qualified teacher. However, as many as 73% of music instructors, including many fine teachers, do not belong to such groups. The teacher should be willing to discuss his or her teaching philosophy and methods with parents and establish a good rapport with the child.

The greatest challenge in making music lessons work is maintaining a consistent practice schedule. Practicing an instrument on a daily basis regardless of one's mood, schedule, or energy level requires greater self-discipline than most other activities a child engages in. It is a solitary, repetitive task that usually requires extended periods of time before significant results are seen. Practicing can be done much more effectively if the teacher gives the student pointers on how to practice, rather than just instructions on what to practice. Although practicing should not become a steady source of conflict between parents and children, parents do need to provide a certain amount of coaxing and encouragement on a regular basis. It is helpful to set up a regular practice routine so that practicing becomes an integral part of a child's daily schedule.

For Further Study

Books

deBeer, Sarah, ed. *Open Ears: Musical Adventures for a New Generation.* Roslyn, NY: Ellipsis Kids, 1995.

Ben-Tovim, Atarah. *Children and Music: A Handbook for Parents, Teachers, and Others Interested in the Musical Welfare of Children..* London: Adam and Charles Black, 1979.

———. *The Right Instrument for Your Child: Practical Guide for Parents and Teachers.* New York: William and Co., 1985.

Bloom, B. S. *Developing Talent in Young People.* New York: Balantine, 1985.

Chroninger, Ruby. *Teach Your Kids About Music: An Activity Handbook for Parents and Teachers Using Children's Literature.* New York: Walker & Co., 1994.

Fuller, Cheri. *How to Grow a Young Music Lover: Helping Your Child Discover and Enjoy the World of Music.* Wheaton, IL: Harold Shaw Publishers, 1994.

Judy, Stephanie. *Making Music for the Joy of It: Enhancing Creativity, Skills, and Musical Confidence.* Los Angeles: Jeremy P. Tarcher, 1990.

Kavanaugh, Patrick. *Raising Musical Kids.* Ann Arbor: Servant Publications, 1995.

———. *A Taste for the Classics.* Nashville, TN: Sparrow Press, 1993.

Nichol, Barbara. *Beethoven Lives Upstairs.* New York: Orchard Books, 1993. [Juvenile]

Seeger, Ruth Crawford. *American Folk Songs for Children in Home, School, and Nursery School: A Book for Children, Parents, and Teachers.* New York: Doubleday, Zephyr, 1980.

Van Kampen, Vlasta. *Orchestranimals.* New York: Scholastic, Inc.,1989. [Juvenile]

Ventura, P. *Great Composers.* New York: G. P. Putnam, 1988. [Juvenile]

Organizations

Music Teachers National Association
Address: 441 Vine St., Suite 505
Cincinnati, OH 45202

Myelinization

A developmental process whereby a protective fatty material wraps around nerve cells.

Myelinization is a gradual developmental process whereby a protective, fatty material called myelin wraps around nerve cells in the peripheral and central nervous system. The myelin sheath protects the nerve fibers in much the same way as insulation covering electrical wiring. Although the process can take up to 10 years to reach completion, the bulk of myelinization occurs during the fetal and infancy stages.

Several degenerative diseases can result when the myelin sheath is destroyed. The most common is multiple sclerosis (MS), which affects 250,000 people in the United States. MS occurs when deviant white blood cells destroy the myelin layers. Sclerotic plaque forms on the fibers, short-circuiting electrical signals in the nervous system. Victims of the disease may suffer recurring episodes of numbness and muscle weakness, uncontrollable tremors, slurred speech, loss of bowel and bladder control, **memory** lapses, and/or paralysis. A vaccine is currently under development and some victims have responded favorably to bee venom therapy.

Adrenoleukodystrophy (ALD) is caused by an enzyme deficiency that fails to break down very long chain fatty acids, or VLCFAs, that are found in foods and produced by the body. When the VLCFAs build up, they attack the myelin sheath. Affecting one or two out of every 100,000 people in the United States, boys between the ages of five and 10 are the most susceptible. Victims quickly lose their sight and speech; death usually follows quickly. A highly purified oil has been developed by the parents of one young victim that fools the body into slowing the production of VLCFAs.

Transverse myelitis is a sudden inflammation of the myelin sheath that results in the loss of motor control and sensation below the level of attack. The cause is unknown but often occurs after a viral infection. It usually begins with severe back pain, followed by muscle weakness, flaccid paralysis, bladder and bowel dysfunction, and progressive spasticity. Eighty-five to 90% of its victims recover all or most of their functioning.

Canavan disease, a rare and fatal **brain** disorder brought on by myelin destruction, primarily affects Jewish infants. Although appearing normal at birth, affected babies become severely retarded quickly and usually die by the age of two or three. A blood test is available to test prospective parents for the hereditary gene.

For Further Study

Books

Duncan, I. D., R. P. Skoff, and D. Colman. *Myelination and Dysmyelination.* New York: New York: New York Academy of Sciences, 1990.

Organizations

Myelin Messenger Newsletter
    Address: HC-29 Box 686
    Stable Lane
    Prescott, AZ 86301-7435
    Telephone: (602) 776-7556

The Myelin Project
    Address: 1747 Pennsylvania Avenue NW, Suite 950
    Washington, DC 20006
    Telephone: toll-free (800) 869-3546

The National Foundation for Jewish Genetic Diseases
    Address: 250 Park Avenue, Suite 1000
    New York, NY 10017
    Telephone: (212) 371-1030

National Multiple Sclerosis Society
    Address: 733 Third Avenue, 6th Floor
    New York, NY 10017-3288
    Telephone: (212) 986-3240; toll-free (800) 532-7667

United Leukodystrophy Foundation
    Address: 2304 Highland Drive
    Sycamore, Il 60178
    Telephone: toll-free (800) 728-5483

Nail Biting

A generally harmless nervous habit of biting or chewing the fingernails.

Children's nervous habits, including nail biting, are common. Nail biting is in most cases harmless and is best ignored. The most problematic side effect of nail biting (and other nervous habits such as **thumb-sucking** and nose-picking) is social ostracism—the child may be teased by her or his peers, and adults observing a nail-biting child may conclude that he or she is insecure or stressed. In addition, the sight of fingernails chewed to the ends of the fingers is unattractive.

About 30% of children ages 7–10 bite their nails. Although the habit may subside during adolescence, researchers at the University of Wisconsin estimated that 20% of college students bite their nails at some time during their college years.

HELPING A CHILD TO BREAK THE NAIL-BITING HABIT

Do's

Choose a time to focus on nail biting when the child is feeling healthy and happy.

If the habit has become a touchy family or social issue, agree on a "free period," a period of time during which parents will not raise the subject with the child. This may help the child prepare psychologically to break the habit by eliminating any negative attention.

Discuss objectively the positive and negative consequences of the habit.

Raise awareness by placing mirrors where the child can see herself engaging in nail-biting.

Help the child think of an alternate behavior. For example, the child could keep a small ball handy to squeeze whenever the urge to nail-bite occurs; alternatively, he or she could concentrate on gripping something such as a book or the edge of a table or desk.

To help him or her become aware of engaging in the habit, the child could wear gloves or socks over the hands during the times when nail biting is the most likely to occur.

For public situations, less obvious than wearing gloves or socks is to apply colorful bandages to the fingertips. Commercial products that have strong, unappealing flavors can also be applied to the nails.

Don'ts

Don't focus on the nail biting when your child is sick or has just experienced a frustration, failure, or major life change.

Avoid punishing the child for engaging in nail biting.

Avoid discussing the nail biting in public.

Don't demand that the child stop nail biting.

Don't physically stop the nail biting by slapping the hand away

Don't expect the nail biting habit (or any habit) to be broken immediately. A strategy that involves several steps with intermediate rewards is more likely to be effective at breaking a habit.

Nervous habits often begin as comfort habits in infancy. When an infant feels anxious, frustrated, hungry, or tired, a familiar, often repetitive or rhythmic, activity can be calming. For many children these habits persist into childhood. For others, the habit begins during the later preschool and early elementary school years. At some point, some older children and adolescents become concerned about their appearance and are motivated to stop the habit to avoid the unsightly nails that result from nail biting.

For Further Study

Books

Azrin, Nathan. *Habit Control in a Day.* New York: Simon and Schuster, 1977.

Smith, Frederick Henry. *Nail-Biting: The Beatable Habit.* Provo, UT: Brigham Young University Press, 1980.

Periodicals

Eberlein, Tamara. "Nervous Habits." *Redbook* 182, April 1994, pp. 178+.

Thompson, Andrea. "Those Nervous Habits." *Good House-keeping* 221, September 1994, pp. 165+.

Names, Socially Desirable

Significance of personal name.

Finding an appropriate name for a child is one of the first tasks new parents assume. For some, the effort begins well before the child is born. Other parents decide on a name after birth, when they have an impression of the child. Some names are dictated by family tradition, such as taking on the name of a parent or other relative. A name may also be given according to some circumstance surrounding the birth, as when a child is named after a season or month of the year or after the doctor performing the delivery. Names can be dictated by fashion, some parents may name their children after their favorite movie and television stars.

In the early 1900s, Agnes and Charles were among the most popular names for babies. As of the mid-1990s, the names in the accompanying table were the five most popular for boys and girls

Names with significant religious meaning are also frequently chosen. A child's name may be chosen by whim or after long deliberation, but in either case, the decision has a life long effect on the child. A child's name is important to his or her self-image. Names convey impressions of personality, and people are likely to attach their image of the name to the child bearing it. Some names, for example, sound exceedingly feminine or masculine, while others are intellectual or sporty. Associations with particular names may change because of

FIVE MOST POPULAR NAMES	
Boys	**Girls**
Michael	Jessica
Daniel	Ashley
Matthew	Samantha
Christopher	Emily
Nicholas	Sarah

prominent people who bear them, the development of new slang terms, or world events that focus attention on a specific region. Many studies have been conducted rating particular first names for qualities they imply, such as cheerfulness, health, achievement, authority, and passiveness. Several names that seemed to imply positive qualities tend to be the most conventional or popular, such as John, Michael, Jennifer, or Lisa. One study found children with the most popular names were also the most popular kids, and that children with odd names were not as well liked. Adults have also been shown to judge people based on name prejudices. One study gave teachers a set of fictitious papers to grade. Some of the papers were said to be by children with popular names and others by children with odd or unpopular names. Though all the papers were judged by the researchers to be roughly comparable in quality, the teachers graded the papers by the children with popular names significantly higher than those by the oddly named children. Other studies have found people with unconventional names have a higher incidence of psychiatric disorders and criminality. However, people who are socially prominent also seem to have a high incidence of unusual names, with many successful business executives and politicians apparently overcoming the stigma of their rare names.

Some research findings on the social effects of names may not hold true for today's children, since there is a departure from conventional names. The name John may be more rare in the nursery school of the 1990s than the name Gideon. In some communities, a unique, invented name is popular, and children in those communities may have very different name prejudices than those noted earlier by researchers. Since name fads quickly change, research on the qualities of particular names can become outdated. Research, however, does show that the connotations of names are very important, and should be kept in mind by conscientious parents.

Parents desiring to give their child a name that is both socially acceptable and a little unusual, or that follows family tradition, may succeed by pairing an exotic first name with an more common middle name. A child may also go by a nickname or a shortened version of an unconventional first name. Nicknames often have connotations entirely different from the names they are derived from; Nicolai may choose to go by Nick, or Edith by Edie. When unconventional names are the trend, though, children may feel far less social stigma regarding their names than earlier generations.

For Further Study

Books

Anderson, Christopher P. *The Name Game.* New York: Simon and Schuster, 1977.

Mehrabian, Albert, *The Name Game: The Decision that Lasts a Lifetime.* Bethesda, Maryland: National Press Books, 1990.

Rosenkrantz, Linda. *Last Word on First Names.* New York: St. Martin's Press, 1997.

Periodicals

Doyle, Brian. "Naming: A Name Is a Thing of Immense Power." *America* 170, No. 16, May 7, 1994, pp. 10–12.

Sagert, Kelly. "Angela Barbara, Cheri." *Hopscotch* 8, No. 2, August–September 1996, p. 20–22.

"Top 5 Baby Names." *Time for Kids* 1, no. 16, February 16, 1996, pp. 2+.

— A. Woodward

Narcissism

Excessive preoccupation with self and lack of empathy for others.

Narcissism is the personality trait that features an exaggerated sense of the person's own importance and abilities. People with this trait believe themselves to be uniquely gifted and commonly engage in fantasies of fabulous success, power, or fame. Arrogant and egotistical, narcissistics are often snobs, defining themselves by their ability to associate with (or purchase the services of) the "best" people. They expect special treatment and concessions from others. Paradoxically, these individuals are generally insecure and have low **self-esteem.** They require considerable admiration from others and find it difficult to cope with criticism. Adversity or criticism may cause the narcissistic person to either counterattack in anger or withdraw socially. Because narcissistic individuals cannot cope with setbacks or failure, they often avoid risks and situations in which defeat is a possibility.

Another common characteristic of narcissistic individuals is envy and the expectation that others are envi-

ous as well. The self-aggrandizement and self-absorption of narcissistic individuals is accompanied by a pronounced lack of interest in and empathy for others. They expect people to be devoted to them but have no impulse to reciprocate, being unable to identify with the feelings of others or anticipate their needs. Narcissistic people often enter into relationships based on what other people can do for them.

During **adolescence,** when the individual is making the transition from childhood to adulthood, many demonstrate aspects of narcissism. These **traits,** related to the adolescent's need to develop his or her own sense of self, do not necessarily develop into the disorder that psychologists have studied for decades, known as narcissistic personality disorder. In 1898, Havelock Ellis (1859–1939) was the first psychologist to address narcissism in a published work. Sigmund Freud claimed that sexual perversion is linked to the narcissistic substitution of the self for one's mother as the primary love object in infancy. In 1933, psychoanalyst Wilhelm Reich (1897–1957) described the "phallic-narcissistic" personality type in terms that foreshadow the present-day definition: self-assured, arrogant, and disdainful. In 1969, Theodore Milton specified five criteria for narcissistic personality disorder in the third edition of the *Diagnostic and Statistical Manual of Mental* Disorders (DSM-III): (1) inflated self-image; (2) exploitative; (3) cognitive expansiveness; (4) insouciant temperament; and (5) deficient social conscience.

The person with narcissistic personality disorder experiences a powerful need to be admired and seems consumed with his or her own interests and feelings. Individuals with this disorder have little or no empathy for others and an inflated sense of their own importance and of the significance of their achievements. It is common for persons with this disorder to compare themselves to famous people of achievement and to express surprise when others do not share or voice the same perception. They feel entitled to great praise, attention, and deferential treatment by others, and have difficulty understanding or acknowledging the needs of others. They envy others and imagine that others are envious of them. The person with narcissistic personality disorder has no patience with others, and quickly strays from situations where he or she is not the center of attention and conversation. According to *DSM-IV,* narcissistic personality disorder affects less than 1% of the general population. Of those, between half and three-fourths are male.

Secondary features of narcissistic personality disorder include feelings of shame or humiliation, **depression,** and mania. Narcissistic personality disorder has also been linked to **anorexia nervosa,** substance-related disorders (especially cocaine abuse), and other personality disorders.

For Further Study

Books

Masterson, James F. *The Emerging Self: A Developmental, Self, and Object Relations Approach to the Treatment of the Closet Narcissistic Disorder.* New York: Brunner/Mazel, 1993.

Sandler, Joseph, Ethel Spector Person, and Peter Fonagy, eds. *Freud's "On Narcissism—an Introduction."* New Haven, CT: Yale University Press, 1991.

Westen, Drew. *Self and Society: Narcissism, Collectivism, and the Development of Morals.* New York: Cambridge University Press, 1985.

Narcolepsy

A sleep disorder whose primary symptom is irresistible attacks of sleepiness during the daytime.

Narcolepsy, which usually begins in adolescence or early adulthood, affects about one in every 1,000 persons and is equally common in males and females. The **sleep** attacks, which can occur anywhere from six to 20 times a day, usually last about 10 to 20 minutes but can persist for as long as two to three hours. Narcolepsy is diagnosed if sleep attacks occur every day for at least three months (although most people treated for the disorder suffer from it for a much longer period of time—often years—before seeking help). In addition to the sleep attacks, persons suffering from narcolepsy often display several other characteristic symptoms. The most debilitating of these is cataplexy, a sudden loss of muscle tone that can affect a part or all of the body. Cataplectic attacks range from a sagging jaw or drooping head to a total collapse that causes the person to fall to the ground. Affecting about 70% of narcoleptics, they are usually triggered by strong emotions, ranging from fear and anger to excitement and amusement (laughter often provokes cataplectic attacks). Respiration is not affected, and full consciousness is maintained throughout the episode. Usually the attacks only last a few seconds, after which normal muscle strength returns. Other symptoms of narcolepsy include vivid dreamlike imagery while waking or falling asleep, episodes of sleep paralysis (in which the person wakes but is temporarily unable to move), and automatic behavior (sleepwalking-type actions which are performed without the person's conscious knowledge).

The cause of narcolepsy is not known, but sleep researchers believe it comes from a malfunction of the mechanism in the brain that regulates sleeping and waking, especially the regulation of REM (rapid eye movement) sleep, the part of the sleep cycle associated with dreaming. It is also known that there is a hereditary component to narcolepsy: having a narcoleptic parent dramatically increases one's chances of developing the disorder, from the normal 1 in 1,000 to 1 in 20. In recent research, a genetic marker has been found in the blood of over 95% of narcolepsy sufferers who were tested for it. Narcolepsy may also develop as a consequence of brain damage caused by injury or disease.

Narcolepsy is a chronic illness that lasts throughout a person's lifetime and has no known cure. Napping during the daytime can reduce the number of sleep attacks by lessening sleepiness. For those severely affected by the disorder, stimulants such as **methylphenidate** (Ritalin) and Dexedrine have been prescribed to ward off sleep attacks. Cataplexy—thought to be a partial intrusion of REM sleep into the waking state—has been treated with medications known to suppress REM sleep, such as tricyclic **antidepressants**. Doctors have had good results with another medication, the experimental drug gamma-hydroxybutyrate, prescribed for narcoleptics to improve the quality of their nighttime sleep, which is usually fitful and fragmented. The resulting improvement of nighttime sleep has had marked success in the reduction (and in some cases complete remission) of symptoms, including both daytime sleep attacks and cataplexy. To avoid the potential danger and embarrassment of cataleptic episodes, some persons with narcolepsy try to control the emotions that trigger them, even avoiding situations that are likely to bring on these emotions.

Narcolepsy has a crippling effect on the lives of those afflicted with it, causing disruption, embarrassment, and, potentially, danger in their everyday lives and interfering with both work and family life. Self-help groups sponsored by the American Narcolepsy Association (and a similar group in Canada) offer support to narcoleptics and their families. These organizations also work to help raise public awareness about the disorder.

For Further Study

Books

Dement, William C. *The Sleepwatchers.* Stanford: Stanford Alumni Association, 1992.

Dotto, Lydia. *Losing Sleep: How Your Sleeping Habits Affect Your Life.* New York: William Morrow, 1990.

Ince, Susan. *Sleep Disturbances.* Boston: Harvard Medical School, Health Publications Groups, 1995.

Organizations

American Narcolepsy Association
Address: 425 California Street, Suite 201
San Francisco, CA 94104
Telephone: (415) 788-4793

Narcotic Drugs

A category of addictive drugs that reduce the perception of pain and induce euphoria.

A narcotic is a depressant that produces a stuporous state in the person who takes it. Narcotics, while often inducing a state of euphoria or feeling of extreme well being, are powerfully addictive. The body quickly builds a tolerance to narcotics, so that greater doses are required to achieve the same effect. Because of their addictive qualities, most countries have strict laws regarding the production and distribution of narcotics.

Historically, the term narcotic was used to refer to the drugs known as opiates. Opium, morphine, codeine, and heroin are the most important opiate alkaloids—compounds extracted from the milky latex contained in the unripe seedpods of the opium poppy. Opium, the first of the opiates to be widely used, was a common folk medicine for centuries, often leading to addiction for the user. The invention of the hypodermic needle during the mid-19th century allowed opiates to be delivered directly into the blood stream, thereby dramatically increasing their effect. By the late 20th century, the legal definition of a narcotic drug had been expanded to include such non-opiate addictive drugs as cocaine and cannabis.

Narcotic drugs decrease the user's perception of pain and alter his or her reaction to pain. For this reason, narcotics—primarily codeine and morphine—are prescribed legitimately as pain killers. In a medical setting, they are referred to as narcotic analgesics. For pain relief, scientists have developed opioids, which are synthetic drugs with morphine-like properties. Some common synthetic opioids include meperidine (trade name Demerol) and methadone, a drug often used to treat heroin addiction. The use of methadone as a treatment for addiction is controversial, however, since methadone itself is addicting.

Scientists have attempted to develop ways to use the pain-killing properties of narcotics while counteracting their addictive qualitites. Such investigations have led to the discovery of narcotic receptors in the brain, and of the body's own natural pain-killing substances, called endorphins. Narcotics behave like endorphins and act on, or bind to, the receptors to produce their associated effects. Substances known as narcotic or opioid antagonists are drugs that block the actions of narcotics and are used to reverse the side effects of narcotic abuse or an overdose. A new class of drugs, a mixture of opioids and opioid antagonists, has been developed so that patients can be relieved of pain without the addictive or other unpleasant side effects associated with narcotics.

Narcotic drugs are among those substances used illegally, or abused, by adolescents. Some estimate that as many as 90% of adult drug addicts began a pattern of substance abuse during adolescence.

See also **Pain and Pain Management**

For Further Study

Books

Sanberg, Paul R. *Prescription Narcotics: The Addictive Painkillers.* New York: Chelsea House, 1986.

Traub, James. *The Billion-Dollar Connection: The International Drug Trade.* New York: J. Messner, 1982.

Willette, Robert E., and Gene Barnett, eds. *Narcotic Antagonists: Naltrexone Pharmacochemistry and Sustained-Release Preparations.* DHHS Publications No. ADM 81-102 490 1, NIDA Research Monograph No. 28. Rockville, MD: U.S. Department of Health and Human Services, Public Health Service, 1981.

National Association of Developmental Disabilities Councils

The National Association of Developmental Disabilities Councils (NADDC) is a national organization which represents Developmental Disabilities (DD) Councils, appointed by the governor of each state, to plan, advocate and work for change on behalf of people with developmental disabilities and their families. NADDC is an effective member of the Consortium for Citizens with Disabilities, a coalition of more than 100 national disability organizations. The mission of the NADDC is to promote national policy which enables individuals with developmental disabilities and their families to make choices regarding the quality of their lives and to exercise control over their participation in the community. The NADDC provides support and assistance to member Councils at the state and national levels.

NADDC was created in 1974 by DD Councils to aid them in carrying out their mandated responsibilities under the Developmental Disabilities Assistance and Bill of Rights Act and to be their representative voice in Washington. NADDC acts as the standard-bearer for people with DD and the state councils that represent them, obtains increased funding for the DD Basic State Grant Program, and mobilizes DD councils by means of *Alerts* on various topics including long term services, health care, housing, and the like.

At the state level, NADDC helps DD Councils solve problems in management and in systems advocacy and build their capacities to improve the lives of people with developmental disabilities. NADDC publishes *Highlights,* a monthly newsletter which informs DD Councils on current federal policy and lists critical issues and activities nationwide.

For Further Study

Organizations

National Association of Developmental Disabilities Councils (NADDC)
Address: 1234 Massachusetts Avenue, NW, Suite 103
Washington, DC 20005
Telephone: (202) 347-1234

National Association of School Psychologists

Organization of school psychologists and related professionals, with members in the United States and 25 other countries.

The National Association of School Psychologists (NASP) has over 18,000 members from the United States and abroad. Founded in 1969, NASP is dedicated to serving the mental health and educational needs of school age children and adolescents. Members are school psychologists or professionals in related fields. The association encourages professional development and provides publications, meetings, workshops, and seminars for its members, and maintains a resource library and a placement service for school psychologists. In addition, NASP plays an activist role on behalf of school-age children, issuing position statements and resolutions to its membership, the general public, and government officials at all levels on such issues as violence in media and toys; legislative priorities; advocacy for appropriate educational services for all children; corporal **punishment;** and racism, prejudice, and discrimination.

NASP operates a national certification program for school psychologists. In addition, NASP is approved by the **American Psychological Association** and the National Board of Certified Counselors to provide continuing education for psychologists and National Certified Counselors. This allows participants in NASP's convention workshops and regional workshops to apply these sessions to their state's requirements for renewal of professional licenses.

For Further Study

Organizations

National Association of School Psychologists
Address: 4340 East-West Highway, Suite 402
Bethesda, MD 20814-4411
Telephone: (301) 657-0270

National Committee to Prevent Child Abuse

The National Committee to Prevent Child Abuse (NCPCA) is a volunteer-based organization of concerned citizens in the corporate, civic, lay, and professional communities working together to prevent child abuse. Its mission is to gain a nationwide commitment to prevent child abuse through the creation of sound policies, and awareness and prevention programs. It believes in the right of every child to have a safe and nurturing home, with parents who are adequately educated and supported in the art of good parenting.

The NCPCA membership consists of 67 chapters with affiliates throughout the states. Its goals include a fully aware and informed public, a more complete body of knowledge on child abuse prevention, services available for all, and an informed, well-equipped nationwide network of **child abuse** prevention organizations.

The Committee defines child abuse as one or more of the following: physical abuse, neglect, sexual abuse, and emotional maltreatment. A current area of concern for the NCPCA is the body of multicultural and multiethnic issues that place some children at greater risk for abuse. NCPCA acts as an advocate for children, their families, and abuse prevention.

Much of the work of the NCPCA is concentrated in the areas of research, training, and public awareness, and findings are made available to its members in a monthly memo. Among its many services, NCPCA also publishes monographs, booklets, and pamphlets, furnishes technical assistance and consulting services, sponsors workshops and seminars, and provides training for professionals and volunteers.

For Further Study

Organizations

National Committee to Prevent Child Abuse
Address: 332 South Michigan Avenue, Suite 1600
Chicago, IL 60604-4357
Telephone: (312) 663-3520
TDD: (312) 663-3540

National Institute of Mental Health

U.S. government agency that conducts and supports research on mental illness and mental health.

The National Institute of Mental Health (NIMH) is the U.S. government agency that conducts and supports research on mental illness and mental health. NIMH is a component of the National Institutes of Health (NIH). Areas of research include the **brain**, behavior and mental health services. NIMH is dedicated to improving the mental health of the American people, fostering better understanding, diagnosis, treatment, and rehabilitation of mental and brain disorders, and preventing mental illness.

In order to carry out its mission, NIMH supports research by awarding NIMH grants to scientists working in universities or other research facilities to study all aspects of mental illness from biological to social, and by identifying specific areas where research is needed. NIMH also supports a large in-house research program on the causes of and new treatments for mental illnesses. In addition, it collects and disseminates statistical information to scientists and researchers, trains scientists to fill needed research positions, and prepares and distributes a wide variety of written materials, audiovisual materials, and educational exhibits.

Among the key areas of research interest for NIMH are neuroscience and behavioral science, including sciences basic to the understanding of the anatomical and chemical basis of brain disorders; and the most prevalent mental disorders and their causes and prevention, such as **schizophrenia,** mood disorders, anxiety disorders, **eating disorders,** and Alzheimer's disease.

The National Institute of Mental Health communicates current research, diagnosis and treatment information to professionals and the public through conferences, symposia and meetings, and works closely with professional and voluntary organizations and other federal agencies.

For Further Study

Organizations
National Institute of Mental Health
    Address: Information Resources and Inquiries Branch
    5600 Fishers Lane, Room 7C-02
    Rockville, MD 20857
    Telephone: (301) 443-4513

Nativism

The belief that learning and behavior are strongly influenced by innate characteristics.

Nativism has its roots in the teachings of the Greek philosopher Plato, who believed that from birth infants have an understanding of such concepts as beauty and truth. Immanuel Kant (1724–1804) believed that human thinking has certain inborn understandings or structures, like cause and effect, that are used to impose order on ex-

perience. Since the 1960s, psychologists have demonstrated considerable interest in the inborn emotional characteristics of infants. It is generally agreed by experts that individuals exhibit differences in emotions or motivations that are present in infancy, are biologically based, and may be genetic.

In its pure form, nativism postulates that an individual is predisposed from birth to a certain path in life because of the aptitudes and limitations he or she posseses at birth. The nativists minimize the influence learning can assert over these innate abilities. In philosophy and psychology, **empiricism** is the theory that represents the opposite point of view to nativism.

Natural Childbirth *see* **Birth**

Neck-Righting Reflex *see* **Neonatal Reflexes**

Negativism

A tendency to resist complying with directions or suggestions.

Negativism is a behavior characterized by the tendency to resist direction from others, and the refusal to comply with requests. Negativism appears and wanes at various stages of a child's development. Active negativism, that is, behavior characterized by doing the opposite of what is being asked, is commonly encountered with young children. For example, a parent may ask a toddler to come away from the playground to return home; on hearing these instructions, the toddler demonstrates active negativism by running away.

Infant studies have revealed that negativism develops during the first year of life, and resurfaces during toddlerhood and again during adolescence. Negativism is used by adolescents as a way to assert their autonomy from their parents, and to control their own behavior. When negativism does not diminish, it becomes a characteristic of the individual's personality. Negativism is an aspect of one of the essential features of **oppositional-defiant disorder**, characterized by a pattern of behavior that is defiant, negativistic, and hostile toward authority figures. However, for the majority of children who display negativism, the behavior will pass with further development.

For Further Study

Books
Baker, Lynne Rudder. *Explaining Attitudes: A Practical Approach to the Mind.* New York: Cambridge University Press, 1995.

Craighead, Linda W. *Cognitive and Behavioral Interventions: An Empirical Approach to Mental Health Problems.* Boston: Allyn and Bacon, 1994.

Eagly, Alice Hendrickson. *The Psychology of Attitudes.* Fort Worth, TX: Harcourt Brace Jovanovich, 1993.

Miller, William R. *Motivational Enhancement Therapy Manual.* Rockville, MD: National Institutes of Health, National Institute on Alcohol Abuse and Alcoholism, 1995.

Solnit, Albert J., Peter B. Neubauer, Samuel Abrams, and A. Scott Dowling. *The Psychoanalytic Study of the Child.* New Haven, CT: Yale University Press, 1994.

Periodicals

Belsky, Jay. "Infant Positive and Negative Emotionality: One Dimension or Two?" *Developmental Psychology* 32, March 1996, pp. 289–98.

Wenar, Charles. "On Negativism." *Human Development* 25, January–February 1982, pp. 1–23.

Audiovisual Recordings

Touchpoints: The Brazelton Study, Volume 2: First Months Through One Year. New York: GoodTimes Home Video, 1992.
(One 45-minute videocassette.)

Neglect *see* **Child Abuse, Physical**

Neonatal Reflexes

Actions in response to specific stimuli that are present in newborn infants.

Neonatal reflexes are the reflexes that are present at birth. They are believed to be inborn and have predictable action patterns. Reflexes, more accurately described as unconditioned reflexes, are not learned or developed through experience. Normally developing neonates (infants up to about four weeks of age) are expected to respond to specific stimuli with a specific, predictable behavior or action. Any variation in, or absence of, response may be a sign of abnormality in development. Further testing of the infant is usually recommended when any response to a stimulus differs from the expected norm. Some neonatal reflexes disappear with maturation; other persist into adulthood.

Although reflex actions are complex, most reflexes can be simplified into four basic steps. In the first step, the stimulus is received by nerve endings involving one of the senses—taste, sight, smell, hearing, or touch. Secondly, the energy created by the stimulus is conducted through the nerves to the central nervous system. Next, the impulses generated by the stimulus are transmitted to the nerves that stimulate muscle action. Finally, the muscles, and sometimes certain glands, respond with an action.

Babinski reflex

The Babinski reflex is characterized by a fanning of all five toes and the stretching forward of the big toe when the bottom of the foot is stroked or tickled. It is a sign that the infant is neurologically normal. Usually around the age of one this reflex disappears completely. It is replaced with the plantar reflex found in young children and adults; this reflex involves curling of the toes in response to the stroking of the sole of the foot.

Blink reflex

The blink reflex is characterized by the involuntary blink of the eyes when an infant is subjected to a bright light, wind, or rapid approach of an object. This involuntary action protects the eyes and is therefore maintained throughout life.

False crawling reflex

When a newborn infant is placed on her stomach, she may begin to flex her arms and legs in a motion that simulates crawling. This action is due to the baby's natural curled-up position, which gradually changes over the days following birth. After about one week, the infant will be able to lie flat, and the false crawling movements will disappear.

Knee-jerk reflex

The knee-jerk, or patellar reflex, is a sign of a neurologically healthy baby; the neonate's lower leg and foot involuntarily kick upward or forward when the neonate is tapped on the tendon just below the patella (kneecap). This reflex prevails throughout maturation into adult life. It is checked by applying the stimulus tap to a young child or adult while he or she is in a sitting position. This reflex is so commonly known that the term "knee-jerk" response is an idiom for any reaction that seems to come automatically, with little or no thought.

Landau's reflex

At about three months of age, an infant will begin to display the Landau's reflex. When she is placed on her stomach face down, she will raise her head and arch her back. This reflex will persist until around the child's first birthday. Absence of this reflex suggests problems in motor development. The pediatrician may investigate further to rule out such problems as **cerebral palsy** and **mental retardation**.

Moro reflex

Also referred to as Moro's reflex, the startle reaction, or the embracing reflex, the Moro reflex is characterized by a "grabbing" motion if an infant is subjected to a loud noise or loss of support. The infant's arms and legs will extend and then come together. The infant's back will also arch, and the infant may cry. This reflex, like other neonatal reflexes, is the sign of a neurologically normal newborn infant. Between the ages of five and seven the child will lose this reflex; if the reflex persists, it is a sign of brain damage, neurological impairment, or motor reflex difficulties.

Neck-righting reflex

The stimulus for this reflex, which turns the neonate's head to one side, is applied when the neonate is lying on his or her back facing upward. The neonate's reflex response is to turn his or her shoulders and body in the same direction as the head. This reflex disappears after a few weeks; if it persists after infancy, it may indicate abnormal development of the central nervous system.

Palmar grasp reflex

The palmar grasp reflex is characterized by the grasping of an object that is placed crosswise on the palm of a newborn infant, or neonate. Like the other neonatal reflexes, it is a sign of normal neurological development. Immediately following birth, the hand grip of this reflex is strong enough to support the baby's weight. Within a few hours, this strength will begin to wane, and the reflex usually fades completely after three to four months.

Rage reflex

The rage reflex is the newborn infant's reponse to having his or her movements suddenly restrained. The infant responds by strongly resisting the restraint, developing redness in the face, or crying. Like the other neonatal reflexes, the rage reflex is a sign of normal neurological development. This reflex tends to diminish in intensity before six months of age.

Rooting reflex

When a newborn infant's cheek is touched or stroked, she will respond automatically by turning her head toward that side and beginning to suck. This is the reflex that allows the newborn to turn toward the mother's nipple to begin **breastfeeding**. Usually during the first six months of life, but sometimes as late as 12 months of age, this reflex disappears. The rooting reflex is the sign of a neurologically normal neonate.

Sucking reflex

The sucking reflex occurs when the mouth of the neonate has been stimulated. It is strongest in the first three to five months of life, and is one of the signs of a neurologically healthy infant.

Walking reflex

The walking reflex is characterized by stepping motions resembling walking when the newborn infant is held upright with contact between the feet and a resisting surface. This reflex will disappear within about a week, usually recurs between eleven and sixteen months, and is a sign of a neurologically normal infant.

For Further Study

Books

Biracree, Tom, and Nancy Biracree. *The Parents' Book of Facts: Child Development from Birth to Age Five.* New York: Facts on File, 1989.

Driscoll, Jeanne. *Taking Care of Your New Baby: A Guide to Infant Care.* Garden City Park, NY: Avery Publishing Group, 1996.

Audiovisual Recordings

Brazelton on Parenting: Newborn Topics. Columbus, OH: Ross Laboratories, 1992.
(One 52-minute videocasette.)

Nervous Tic *see* Tic Disorders

Night Terrors

Also referred to as pavor nocturnus, a childhood sleep disorder featuring behavior that appears to be intense fear.

Night terrors, known medically as *pavor nocturnus,* are episodes that apparently occur during the non-dreaming stages of **sleep** in some children. Episodes of night terrors are most common in the preschool and early school years. Night terrors usually occur within an hour or two after the child has fallen asleep, and generally do not recur with any frequency or regularity. Many children experience only one episode of night terrors, and few experience more than three or four such episodes over the whole course of childhood. A parent or **caregiver** witnessing an episode of night terrors, which usually lasts from ten to thirty minutes, will find the behavior unsettling. The child sits up abruptly in bed, appears to be extremely upset, cries out or screams, breathes heavily, and perspires. He or she might also thrash about, kicking, and his or her eyes may bulge out, seemingly in fear of something. The child does not wake during the episode, although his or her eyes will be open, and he or she will be unresponsive to any offers of comfort. The child falls back to sleep, and will have no memory of the occurrence. Night terrors have not been shown to have any link to personality or emotional disorders, although they may be related to a specific feeling of fear that the child has experienced, such as being startled by someone leaping at him or her from behind a chair, or the sight of someone fainting or having an accident.

For Further Study

Books

Beaudet, Denise. *Encountering the Monster: Pathways in Children's Dreams.* New York: CrossroadContinuum, 1990.

Lansky, Vicki. *Getting Your Child to Sleep—and Back to Sleep: Tips for Parents of Infants, Toddlers, and Preschoolers.* Deephaven, MN: Book Peddlers, 1991.

Thorpy, Michael. *The Encyclopedia of Sleep and Sleep Disorders.* New York: Facts of File, 1990.

Organizations

Association of Sleep Disorders Centers (ASDC)
   Address: 602 Second Street, SW
   Rochester, MN 55902
   (Professional organization of specialists in sleep disorders; publishes the journal *Sleep.*)

Nightmares

A frightening dream that occurs during REM (rapid eye movement) sleep.

Nightmares—frightening dreams—are the most common type of sleep disturbance in early childhood. They are distinguished from **night terrors** *(pavor nocturnus),* another childhood sleep disturbance, by the fact that night terrors occur during a different phase of sleep and do not involve dreaming. Nightmares are thought to be caused by a central nervous system response, and are related to other parasomnias such as sleepwalking.

Nightmares begin between the ages of 18 months and three years and increase in frequency and intensity around the ages of four and five years. Children this age have an exceptionally vivid fantasy life that carries over into their sleep. Their nightmares are typically characterized by feelings of danger and helplessness and often involve fleeing from monsters or wild animals. It is not unusual for a normal child this age to have nightmares as often as once or twice a week. The increase in nightmares among preschoolers reflects not only their capacity for vivid fantasy but also the fact that as they become increasingly active, their daily lives hold more opportunities for frightening experiences, and growing interaction with peers and siblings produces added potential for conflict and tension. **Separation anxiety** and exposure to frightening programs on television are additional sources of emotional turbulence.

When children have nightmares, parents generally spend some time holding and reassuring them; a parent may explain that the events in the nightmare are not real and can't hurt the child. (Although some parents take the opposite tack and pretend to scare away the monster or whatever else was frightening the child in the nightmare.) The lights in the bedroom can be turned on, as a child's familiar bedroom surroundings can have a calming effect. Sometimes it is more effective for the child to leave the bedroom and go to another part of the house for a while (although some experts caution against letting children sleep in the parents' bed in order to avoid having this become a habit). Parents can help reduce their children's nightmares by making sure that they are not under unusual or excessive **stress** in the daytime, which includes monitoring their television viewing and perhaps even eliminating it in the evening. A soothing evening ritual that calms a child at bedtime—such as a snack and a bedtime story or quiet game—may also reduce the frequency or intensity of nightmares.

Although nightmares are frequent in preschoolers, a child this age should not be having them every night. Excessive nightmares indicate stress that may call for professional counseling. The **American Psychiatric Association's** *Diagnostic and Statistical Manual (DSM-IV)* recognizes an anxiety disorder characterized by persistent, severe nightmares (Nightmare Disorder, formerly Dream Anxiety Disorder) but cautions that intense nightmares are normal in children between the ages of 3 and 5, in whom this diagnosis is only warranted if there is significant distress and if the nightmares interfere with other aspects of daily life. *DSM-IV* points out that between 10 and 50% of all young children have nightmares that are severe enough to alarm their parents. Generally, Nightmare Disorder is found only in children who have experienced severe psychological stress.

Although the intense nightmares of the preschool period abate after the age of five, children continue to experience more nightmares than adults until about the age of 10, after which there is a marked decline in their frequency. The average college student has between four and eight nightmares per year, and this figure generally drops to one or two in adults.

For Further Study

Books

Ferber, Richard. *Solve Your Child's Sleep Problems.* New York: Simon and Schuster, 1985.

Lansky, Vicki. *Getting Your Child to Sleep—and Back to Sleep: Tips for Parents of Infants, Toddlers, and Preschoolers.* Deephaven, MN: Book Peddlers, 1991.

Nongraded Schools

Nongraded schools teach children in multiage classrooms, instead of separating them into the traditional grade levels.

Nongraded schools have become increasingly popular in the 1990s, particularly among elementary school educators, though some school districts have applied multiage teaching to junior high and high school students as well. The typical multiage classroom in a nongraded school includes students who are one or two years apart in age, for example, combining first, second, and third graders, or fifth and sixth graders. Because children are at widely varying skill levels in the multiage group, the curriculum is usually altered. One common approach is to teach thematic units—on dinosaurs or measuring, for example—and students read, write, and work on math projects relating to the unit at a level appropriate to their ability. Schools using this kind of curriculum usually replace traditional letter grade evaluations with narrative assessments that report a child's strengths and weaknesses, as well as academic progress. Many nongraded schools also keep children with the same teacher for two or three years consecutively. The teacher and students can get to know each other better than in a traditional graded school, and the students may exhibit more family-like relations.

There are several reasons school districts use nongraded schools. Some school districts have low enrollment and can fill schools more efficiently if grade levels are combined. In some areas, teachers and administrators simply believe in the effectiveness of multiage classrooms. Several states, including Kentucky, Mississippi, and Oregon, have passed laws requiring multiage classrooms for at least certain levels—usually primary schools.

Though the long-term effects of nongraded schools on students have not been assessed, the majority of studies report that students generally excel in them. Children in multiage classrooms have been found to perform better academically than their peers in traditional schools. There is also a host of social advantages to the multiage approach. Classrooms using the unit approach to curriculum allow students to progress at their own rates. Underachievers may be more comfortable, because they suffer less stigma than in a traditional classroom. Gifted students are not held back by the learning rate of the rest of the class. Students learn to cooperate, and older or more advanced students may gain valuable leadership skills from helping other children. Younger or more immature children benefit from the role models they have in the older children, and teachers report fewer cliques and less bullying in multiage groups. Many teachers also like the rapport they develop with students they stay with for several years. Parents too have found they develop a stronger relationship with their children's teacher. According to some research, students who may have the most difficulty in a traditional school do better in a nongraded school. One study identifies boys, African Americans, **underachievers,** and students from poorer families as those likely to perform better and feel better about themselves in nongraded schools. These students score better on achievement tests than their peers, and the improve-ment is greater the longer they stay in a nongraded program.

For Further Study

Books

Anderson, Robert H., and Barbara Nelson Pavan. *Nongradedness: Helping It to Happen.* Lancaster, Pennsylvania: Technomic Press, 1993.

Kasten, W. C., and B. K. Clarke. *The Multiage Classroom.* Katonah, New York: Richard C. Owen, 1993.

—A. Woodward

Nutrition

The process by which humans take in and utilize food; also the study of diet as it relates to health.

Good nutrition in childhood lays the foundation for good health throughout a person's lifetime. With the proliferation of fast food restaurants, the number of junk food commercials on television, and the increased trend toward eating out, it is more difficult than ever for parents to ensure that their children maintain a nutritious diet. In recent decades, increasing affluence and the widespread availability of vitamin-enriched foods have shifted the focus of nutritional concerns in the United States from obtaining minimum requirements to cutting down on harmful elements in one's diet. According to a 1988 report from the office of the U.S. Surgeon General, health problems are more likely to be caused by nutritional excesses and imbalances than by deficiencies. In other words, parents need to be as concerned about high levels of fat, **cholesterol**, sugar, and salt as about adequate intake of vitamins, minerals, and other nutrients.

Recommended restrictions

The **American Academy of Pediatrics,** the National Academy of Sciences, the American Heart Association, and other nutrition-oriented organizations agree that fat should not account for more than 30% of the calorie intake of children over the age of two, and saturated fat should account for under 10%. The main dietary sources of saturated fat include whole milk, cheese, hot dogs, and luncheon meats. Recommendations for dietary change include switching to 1% or skim milk, low-fat cheese, and meats from which the fat can be trimmed. (Since fat is important for growth, experts also caution that fat intake should not be lowered to under 25% of daily calorie intake, and that parents of children under two should not restrict fat in their diets.) Hardening of the arteries and heart disease have been linked not only to the conversion of saturated fats into cholesterol but also to cholesterol that comes directly from food (dietary cholesterol), often found in the same foods that are high in saturated fat. Egg yolks are the primary source of dietary cholesterol, and their consumption should be monitored in children as in adults.

The amount of refined sugar in children's diets—typically accounting for 14% of calorie intake by adolescence—is another cause for concern. Although sugar is known to cause tooth decay and also may be associated with behavior problems, the greatest danger in consuming foods high in added sugar is that these "empty calories" will replace the more nutritious foods that children need in order to maintain good health. (Soft drinks, perhaps the single greatest source of refined sugar in the diet of children and teenagers, get virtually all their calories from sugar and offer no nutrients whatsoever.) Children can only eat large amounts of sweets in addition to more nutritious foods by overeating, which leads to excess weight and, potentially, **obesity.**

Another element that needs to be restricted in children's diets is the intake of sodium through salted foods. Sodium has been closely linked to hypertension (high blood pressure), which increases a person's risk of heart disease and strokes. It has been determined that 18-year-olds need only 500 milligrams of sodium daily. However, the average two-year-old already consumes more than five times that amount (2,670 milligrams), and this figure rises to 3,670 milligrams by the age of 17. The National Academy of Sciences recommends limiting sodium intake to 2,400 milligrams daily (if possible, 1,800 milligrams). Contrary to what most people might think, the vast majority of sodium enters a person's diet through salt that is added in food preparation rather than table salt used when a person is eating. The best way for parents to cut down on the amount of salt in their children's diets is to reduce their consumption of processed foods and increase the proportion of daily calorie intake that comes from such natural foods as fruits, vegetables, and grains.

In addition to limiting the amounts of fat, cholesterol, salt, and sugar in their children's diets, health authorities also recommend that parents concerned about nutrition ensure that children obtain a generous supply of complex carbohydrates (found in such foods as beans, potatoes, whole-grain foods, and pasta) and have at least five servings of fresh fruits and vegetables daily.

Obtaining adequate nutrition and eating a balanced diet involve different concerns and challenges at every stage of a child's development.

Infancy

The first nutritional decision that must be made for a child is whether to breastfeed or bottle-feed. Breast milk is generally considered the best food for an infant up to the age of six to nine months. A 1994 report by the office of the U.S. Surgeon General called breast milk "the food

of choice for infants." It has virtually all the nutrients that babies need, and in the right balance. In addition, it contains important antibodies that help protect infants from infection at a time when their own immune systems are not yet fully developed. Not only does **breastfeeding** lower the likelihood of certain infectious diseases, such as **meningitis,** in infancy, it has also been found that older children and adults who were breastfed have a lower incidence of a number of chronic conditions, including **diabetes, celiac sprue disease**, and inflammatory bowel disease. In addition, it is virtually unknown for a baby to have an allergic reaction to breast milk, and breastfed babies are less likely to develop other allergies later on. Today over half of all American women breastfeed their babies at birth, compared with only about 25% in the early 1970s.

The composition of breast milk actually changes during the first two weeks after a baby is born. Initially, it consists largely of colostrum, a substance that has more protein than complete breast milk and lower amounts of fat and sugar. It is also rich in the antibody immunoglobin A, which helps protect against infections. By the tenth day after birth, the regular breast milk, containing more carbohydrates and fat and less protein, is produced. The amounts of carbohydrates and fat will gradually continue to increase, as will the quantity of the milk itself, to match the needs of the growing baby. Not only does breast milk change over time, its composition also changes while an infant is nursing. It gradually becomes higher in fat and thus more filling, acting as a curb on the baby's appetite to prevent overfeeding. Although most full-term infants get all the necessary nutrients from breastfeeding, some may need supplements of vitamins D and K.

Women who are either unable to breastfeed (a small minority of mothers) or who choose not to do so usually feed their babies formula made from cow's milk—generally reconstituted skim milk with vegetable oils added to substitute for the missing butterfat, which is difficult for infants to digest. Lactose (milk sugar) is also added, and some formulas contain whey protein as well. For infants who demonstrate sensitivity to cow's milk, formulas based on soy protein are available.

Breast milk or formula provides all the nutrients an infant needs up to the age of four to six months. Contrary to past beliefs, it has been found that not only do babies not need solid foods before that time, introducing solids too early may lead to food allergies or overfeeding. Cow's milk, which cannot be adequately digested by infants and can cause gastrointestinal bleeding, should not be introduced until a child is a year old. As the first solid food, pediatricians often recommend cereal made from a grain other than wheat (rice is a favorite). Parents are commonly advised to introduce new foods one at a time and about a week apart in order to identify any foods that may produce allergic sensitivity. The first solid foods may be either commercial baby food or strained foods prepared at home. Today commercial baby foods are healthier than in the past, thanks to the actions of consumer groups and professional associations that protested the manufacturers' former inclusion of additives such as monosodium glutamate, sugar, and salt to make their products more flavorful for parental taste-testing (although the infants themselves couldn't tell the difference). Although these ingredients have been omitted, parents still need to watch out for fillers, such as modified food starch, which companies are required to list on the label of every jar of baby food.

Once solid foods have been introduced, infants still need to receive most of their nourishment from either breast milk or formula during their first year. A major difference between nutritional needs in infancy and those later in life is that infants have a greater requirement for fat in their diet to promote the dramatic growth and development—especially brain development—that takes place during this stage of life. Babies need both more nutrients and more calories per pound of body weight than adults do.

Toddlerhood

During a child's second year, her growth rate slows dramatically compared to the prior period. In the first year, her birth weight tripled, her length increased by 50%, and the size of her brain doubled. Now it will take several years for her weight to even double. She will grow in spurts, with each spurt followed by a period of weight gain. This decreased growth leads to a decreased demand for food, often manifested in a newfound pickiness. "Food jags," where a child eats only certain foods—or even only one food—begin to occur at this age, often with an insistence on particular rituals, such as using only a certain plate or eating the food in a certain order. In spite of parental concern about the decreased food intake—and even the refusal to eat some meals at all—toddlers do manage to regulate their food intake adequately, and parents are widely advised against engaging in struggles with their toddlers over eating or completely finishing meals. As long as a child consumes an adequate, varied diet over a period of several days, parents are cautioned against becoming unduly concerned over a single day of unbalanced eating. Turning meals into battles over control can result in unhealthy eating habits that can last a lifetime. Toddlers need to eat more than three times a day—either five or six small meals, or three major ones with snacks in between. However, they should not spend most of the day eating, which prevents them from being truly hungry (and willing to try new foods) at mealtime and can encourage the development of obesity later.

Nutrition should be a concern for parents choosing a day care center. Visiting a center at mealtime can reveal whether it serves junk food high in fat, sugar, and salt or nutritious meals featuring fresh fruits and vegetables, whole grains, lean fish and meat, and low-fat dairy products. The federal government encourages good nutrition in day care centers and home-based programs through the USDA's Child Care Food Program. A center's participation in this program indicates a concern for the nutrition of the children it cares for.

Preschool

Preschoolers are still growing relatively slowly. Their weight increases about 12% between the ages of three and five, although their appearance changes considerably as they lose the baby fat of infancy and toddlerhood. They are still picky eaters, generally eating less—and less consistently—than their parents would like. Although their fat requirement is not as high as that of infants, preschoolers still require more fat and fewer carbohydrates than adults. Fat is needed both for growth and for regulation of body temperature (young children need to burn more calories than adults do to stay warm). Also needed for growth is protein—preschoolers need proportionately more than twice as much as adults. If the nutritional recommendations of the National Academy of Sciences are followed, a preschooler's diet will consist of 40% carbohydrates, 35% fats, 20% protein, and 5% fiber.

Between the ages of three and five, children's tastes expand considerably, and they are willing to consider foods they would have refused as toddlers (although, like toddlers, they can still be quirky eaters). Four-year-olds can generally eat whatever foods the rest of the family is having. Preschoolers still can't eat enough at three meals to meet their nutritional needs, and nutritious snacks are important. By this age, children's food choices can be strongly influenced by others. This means they will imitate good eating habits they see practiced by their parents, but they can also be easily swayed by television commercials for the latest deep-fried snack food or sugar-coated cereal. Experts on children's nutrition and media experts recommend that parents watch food commercials with their children and point out some of the forms of manipulation used, such as showing fruit on commercials for breakfast cereals to give the impression of healthfulness, although the cereals themselves contain little or no fruit. Peggy Charren, the founder of the activist group **Action for Children's Television**, has suggested that children create parodies of TV food commercials, which can be filmed using home videorecorders.

School age

The diet of school-age children, like that of preschoolers, should contain (in the following order of importance) carbohydrates, fat, and protein. A

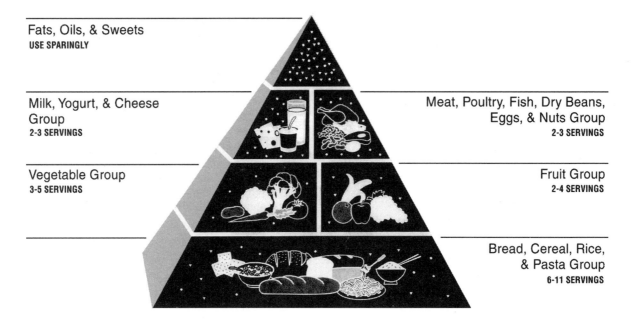

Fats, Oils, & Sweets
USE SPARINGLY

Milk, Yogurt, & Cheese
Group
2-3 SERVINGS

Meat, Poultry, Fish, Dry Beans,
Eggs, & Nuts Group
2-3 SERVINGS

Vegetable Group
3-5 SERVINGS

Fruit Group
2-4 SERVINGS

Bread, Cereal, Rice,
& Pasta Group
6-11 SERVINGS

Food pyramid with recommended dietary guidelines.

recommended proportion of these nutrients is 55% of the daily calorie intake from carbohydrates, 30% from fats, and 15% from protein. Once children begin spending a full day in school, a substantial, nutritious breakfast becomes more important than ever. Breakfast has been shown to affect the concentration and performance of elementary school children. Ideally, a balanced breakfast for a school-age child contains food high in protein as well as fruit and bread or another form of grain.

A major change affecting the nutrition of school-age children is the growth of opportunities to eat outside the home (and away from parental control). The carefully packed homemade lunch may be traded for a salty snack or cupcake, and parts of it may be discarded, even without any trading involved. Vending machines and stores offer more temptations. In addition, school lunch programs differ widely in quality—even the nutritional value of a single food, such as a hamburger, can vary significantly depending on how it is prepared and what ingredients are used. Nutrition experts recommend that parents concerned about their children's diet become actively involved in assessing the lunch menus offered at their children's schools and, if they are found wanting, agitating for change. Their efforts can be directed toward the food services director, school officials, and even local and state government officials. (For example, a 1989 California law mandates the development of nutritional guidelines for school breakfasts and lunches by the state department of education.) The federally funded National School Lunch Program ensures that lunches in participat-

ing schools provide one-third of a child's daily nutritional requirements. (It specifies foods from each of the four major food groups, including minimum amounts of meat, fruit, vegetables, grains, and milk.)

Adolescence

Adolescence brings its own set of nutritional needs and challenges. Beginning with the preteen years, children undergo their most intensive period of physical growth since infancy and need more food than at any other stage of life, particularly if they participate in sports. Teenagers—especially teenage boys—are notorious for being able to empty the refrigerator of food, usually without gaining excess weight. Early adolescence in particular is a time of increased nutritional requirements for girls, who experience their greatest growth spurt at this time and also begin menstruating. It is difficult for weight-conscious teenage girls to eat enough to satisfy their minimum daily iron requirement of 18 milligrams, and they should try to eat either foods that are naturally rich in iron, such as turkey, beef, liver, and beans, or foods made from iron-enriched cereals. Adequate calcium intake is essential for the rapidly growing bones of teenagers, but milk has often been replaced by soft drinks as the beverage of choice among this age group. Parents should encourage adolescents—especially adolescent girls—to eat other foods rich in calcium, such as cheese, salmon, and broccoli.

As adolescents grow more independent, the number of meals and snacks eaten away from home increases as they spend more and more time with friends and take increased responsibility for arranging their own meals (with fast foods, soft drinks, and sweets often prominent on the menu). In addition to the natural appeal of these foods, peer pressure contributes to the choice of a diet soft drink over milk or juice, or pizza over broccoli. Although parents can't control the eating habits of their teenagers, they can influence them by consistently making nutritious foods available at home and, at least in some cases, by discussing the benefits of good nutrition with them, especially if a relative or friend has had an illness, such as heart disease or colon **cancer**, that has known links to diet.

Food allergies

A special problem that may affect childhood nutrition is the presence of food **allergies,** which are more common in children than in adults. They are most likely to begin when a child is very young and the immune system is still sensitive—most begin in infancy. Food allergies also tend to run in families: if one parent has food allergies, a child has a 40% likelihood of developing one. This figure rises to 75% if both parents have allergic sensitivities to food. Common symptoms of food allergies include hives, rashes, swelling of the eyes, lips, and mouth, respiratory symptoms, and digestive problems. Foods that most often produce allergic reactions in infants are cow's milk, soy products, and citrus fruits. Other common childhood allergens include wheat, nuts, chocolate, strawberries, tomatoes, corn, and seafood. A widely used method for detecting food allergies is to temporarily place children on diets free of known allergy-causing foods and then add one "suspect" food at a time for a week or so and observe the reaction. Once the causes of food allergies are known, the best treatment method is to remove those foods from the child's diet. If the causes of a food allergy cannot be determined, antihistamines can be used to reduce the symptoms of allergic reactions. In time, childhood food allergies are often outgrown.

Feeding a child with food allergies is a challenging but not impossible task for parents. A variety of foods can be substituted for those to which a child is allergic: soy products for milk and other dairy products; carob for chocolate; and, in the case of wheat allergies, products or flour made from grains such as rice or oats. Although it can be difficult for allergic children to forgo the offending foods when they are away from home, the desire to prevent a recurrence of allergic symptoms is generally a powerful incentive. In addition, parents can sometimes provide a special snack or treat for them to take along— sometimes even a non-allergic treat that a child may share with the group so he doesn't have to feel different from everyone else.

Vitamin and mineral supplements

Many authorities, including the American Academy of Pediatrics, agree that healthy children receiving a well-balanced diet do not need to take nutritional supplements. Nevertheless, some pediatricians still recommend vitamins for children until they are eating solid foods. Special situations that may call for supplements include vitamin K deficiencies in low birthweight babies; iron deficiency in young children or adolescent girls; weight-reduction or allergy diets that may cause vitamin deficiencies; vitamin B_{12} deficiencies in children from strict vegetarian families who do not receive animal protein from dairy products; and various illnesses, including metabolic disorders. Recommendations for supplements are universally accompanied by the precaution that they should not be considered substitutes for an adequate diet.

For Further Study

Books

Hess, Mary Abbott. *A Healthy Head Start: A Worry-Free Guide to Feeding Young Children.* New York: Henry Holt, 1990.

Jacobson, Michael F., and Bruce Maxwell. *What Are We Feeding Our Kids?* New York: Workman Publishing, 1994.

Kleinman, Ronald E. *What Should I Feed My Kids?: The Pediatrician's Guide to Safe and Healthy Food and Growth.* New York: Ballantine, Books, 1996.

Powter, Susan. *Hey Mom! I'm Hungry: Great-tasting, Low-fat, Easy Recipes to Feed Your Family.* New York: Simon and Schuster, 1997.

Juvenile Books

Berenstain, Stan. *The Berenstain Bears and Too Much Junk Food.* New York: Random House, 1985.

Sharmat, Mitchell. *Gregory the Terrible Eater.* New York: Four Winds Press, 1980.

Stock, Catherine. *Alexander's Midnight Snack.* New York: Clarion, 1988.

Organizations

American Dietetic Association
    Address: 216 W. Jackson Blvd. Suite 800
    Chicago, IL 60606-6995
    Telephone: toll-free (800) 877-1600; (312) 899-0040
    Website: www.eatright.org
Center for Science in the Public Interest
    Address: 1875 Connecticut Ave. NW, Suite 300
    Washington, DC 20009-5728
    (Sponsors "Kids Against Junk Food," nationwide network of elementary and high school student activists.)
Human Nutrition Information Service
    Address: U. S. Department of Agriculture
    6505 Belcrest Rd., Room 360
    Hyattsville, MD 20782
    Telephone: (301) 436-7725
Office of Consumer Affairs, Food and Drug Administration
    Address: 5600 Fishers Lane
    Rockville, MD 20857
    Telephone: (301) 443-1544

Obesity

Term describing a condition where the ratio of body fat to total body mass is higher than accepted norms.

Obesity is a relative term used to describe the condition where the ratio of body fat, which is measurable, to total body mass is higher than the accepted norm. (*Obesity* and *overweight* are often used interchangeably, but their technical definitions are different. Overweight refers to an excess of body weight that includes all tissues—fat, bone, and muscle. Obesity refers specifically to an excess of body fat.) Body fat is about 15% of total body mass for the normal adult male and about 20–25% for the normal adult female. A general rule of thumb is that an individual is probably obese when his or her weight exceeds the maximum weight on standardized height and weight charts by more than 20%. However, during childhood and adolescence, when the body is growing and developing, the proportion of body fat is slightly higher than for a mature adult. In addition, the proportion of body fat fluctuates during various stages of growth.

The percent of U.S. children who are overweight is estimated to be between 20–30%, but there is no firm definition of obesity for children and adolescents. The body mass index (BMI) and average weight-for-height charts provide general guidelines. Pediatricians and parents should evaluate an individual child's weight in the context of his stage of growth, level of physical activity, and general dietary habits. Richard P. Troiano, a researcher at the Centers for Disease Control and Prevention, encourages parents and physicians to observe children and adolescents in their environment over time, and cautions against making weight a disease. Adults should help children see the relationship between eating and exercise choices and weight.

Infancy through school age

Some babies are born obese, chiefly the result of diabetic mothers, obese mothers, or mothers with excessive pregnancy weight gains. The causes of neonatal obesity are therefore obvious; excessive insulin produced by the fetus itself in the first case and an excessive supply of transplacental nutrients in the latter cases. Neonatal obesity does not necessarily translate into childhood or later obesity, but there is an increased probability if the obese neonate is born into (or adopted into) an obese family.

Some babies actually become obese because of infant-care workers, grandmothers, or other parent-surrogates. Such care-giving individuals may simply value infant obesity ("a nice plump baby"), or they may use the bottle to quiet the infant, or to demonstrate their own competence as child-rearers. Because infants who are obese on their first birthday may be physically delayed in crawling and walking, they are therefore delayed in attaining the increased energy expenditure that ordinarily goes with toddler-stage activity.

Children of obese parents are more likely to become obese during childhood, and the presence of additional obese family members greatly increases that likelihood. Many studies have shown that the probability of childhood obesity rises with the number of obese family members (including both siblings and grandparents in the count). Though demonstrably familial, childhood and later obesity is not necessarily genetic, as evidenced by adoption studies. Normal weight children adopted into obese families are far more likely to become obese themselves.

Adolescence

Adolescent obesity, in turn, is of particular interest because it is more common for girls than boys, and for low-income adolescent girls in particular. In recent years adolescent obesity has become far more common among girls of Black, Mexican American, Native American and Pacific Island origin.

Though separate childhood-onset, adolescent-onset, and adult-onset obesities have been postulated longitudinal studies that identify the age of onset show that obese people stem from similarly obese family-lines but that the adult-onset obese are especially likely to be of low **socioeconomic status** (SES). Furthermore, obesity may be encouraged by significant partners and peers as well.

In-depth longitudinal studies of the juvenile-onset obese also show parental and peer encouragement to overeat and even deliberate overfeeding of obese children. Concern for the **nutrition** of obese children carries over to adolescence where some pediatricians may be reluctant to recommend caloric reduction ("intervention") for fear of delaying growth, even when the typical obese adolescent is developmentally well advanced over age-peers!

At all ages, after the first year, obese boys and girls are taller than their nonobese peers, by as much as 10 centimeters at the end of the first decade. Obese boys and girls are also advanced in skeletal maturation (measured as "bone-age"), so they stop growing earlier. Sexual maturation is also advanced in obese boys and girls. It is not uncommon for obese girls to evidence precocious **menarche,** (early onset of **menstruation**), sometimes even before the tenth year of life.

It is of course necessary to distinguish between the chronic (or habitual) obese and the newly obese, for the former are much more difficult to restore to a nonobese state and tend to come from families with a larger number of risk factors for obesity. It is also useful to distinguish between the formerly obese and the habitually obese, for the formerly obese are much more likely to revert to obesity (and to come from high-risk families). Summer camps specializing in habitually obese children, especially obese girls, have little long-term success in reducing the level of obesity and a high degree of recidivism for habitual overeating and under-exercise. As an additional problem, parental separation and **divorce** or other psychological stressors may stimulate compensatory overeating in previously nonobese children. Moreover, obese teenagers and (increasingly) obese preteens may combine periods of binge eating and caloric deprivation, leading variously to **bulimia** and **anorexia nervosa.**

For Further Study

Books

Hansen, B.C. (eds.). *Controversies in Obesity*. New York: Praeger Publishers, 1983.

Marin, Roselyn. *Helping Obese Children: Weight Control Groups That Really Work*. Montreal: Learning Publications, 1990.

Rotatori, Anthony F., and Robert A. Fox. *Obesity in Children and Youth: Measurement, Characteristics, Causes, and Treatment*. Springfield, IL: Thomas, 1989.

OBESITY IS A DISEASE

In 1995, the Institute of Medicine published a report that described obesity as a "complex, multifactorial disease of appetite regulation and energy metabolism." The report cited the following outcomes from even relatively moderate weight losses:

- Lower blood pressure (and related lower risk of heart attack and stroke)
- Reduce abnormally high levels of blood glucose
- Lower blood levels of cholesterol and triglycerides (and related lower risk of cardiovascular disease)
- Reduce sleep apnea
- Decrease risk of osteoarthritis of weight-bearing joints
- Decrease depression
- Increase **self-esteem**

Source: "Weighing the Options: Criteria for Evaluating Weight-Management Programs." Washington, DC: Institute of Medicine, telephone: (800) 624-6242.

Periodicals

Garn, S.M. "Continuities and Changes in Fatness from Infancy through Adulthood." *Current Problems in Pediatrics* 15(2), 1985, pp. 1–47.

Garn, S.M. "Family-Line and Socioeconomic Factors in Fatness and Obesity." *Nutrition Reviews* 44, 1986, pp. 381–86.

Garn, S.M., T.V. Sullivan, and V.M. Hawthorne. "The Juvenile-Onset, Adolescent-Onset and Adult-Onset Obese." *International Journal of Obesity* 15, 1991, pp. 105–110.

Larkin, Marilynn. "Losing Weight Safely." *FDA Consumer* 30, January–February 1996, pp. 16–21.

—Stanley Garn, Ph.D.
University of Michigan

Obsessive-Compulsive Disorder

Mental illness characterized by the recurrence of intrusive, anxiety-producing thoughts (obsessions) accompanied by repeated attempts to suppress these thoughts through the performance of certain irrational, often ritualistic, behaviors (compulsions).

Obsessive-compulsive disorder is classified as a mental illness, and is characterized by the recurrence of intrusive, anxiety-producing thoughts (obsessions). The person with obsessive-compulsive disorder repeatedly and consistently tries to suppress these thoughts through the performance of certain irrational, often ritualistic, behaviors (compulsions).

Symptoms

Although there are marked similarities between cases, no two people experience this anxiety disorder in exactly the same way. In one common form of obsessive-compulsive disorder (OCD), an exaggerated fear of contamination (the obsession) leads to washing one's hands so much that they become raw (the compulsion). Other common manifestations of OCD involve sorting, checking, and counting compulsions. Checking compulsions seem to be more common among men, whereas washing is more common among women. Another type of OCD is **trichotillomania**, the compulsion to pull hair. The compulsive behavior is usually not related in any logical way to the obsessive fear, or else it is clearly excessive (as in the case of hand-washing).

Everyone engages in these types of behavior to a certain extent—counting steps as we walk up them, double-checking to make sure we've turned off the oven or locked the door—but in a person with OCD, such behaviors are so greatly exaggerated that they interfere with relationships and day-to-day functioning at school or work. A child with a counting compulsion, for example, might not be able to listen to what the teacher is saying because he or she is too busy counting the syllables of the teacher's words as they are spoken.

These are some of the signs that a child might be suffering from OCD:

- *Avoidance of scissors or other sharp objects.* A child might be obsessed with fears of hurting herself or others.

- *Chronic lateness or the appearance of dawdling.* A child could be performing checking rituals (e.g., repeatedly making sure all her school supplies are in her bookbag).

- *Daydreaming or preoccupation.* A child might actually be counting or balancing things mentally.

- *Inordinate amounts of time spent in the bathroom.* A child could be involved in a hand-washing ritual.

- *Late schoolwork.* A child might be repeatedly checking her work.

- *Papers with holes erased in them.* This might also indicate a checking ritual.

- *Secretive and defensive behavior.* People with OCD will go to extreme lengths in order not to reveal or give up their compulsions.

Although people with OCD realize that their thought processes are irrational, they are unable to control their compulsions, and they become painfully embarrassed when a bizarre behavior is discovered. Usually certain behaviors called rituals are repeated in response to an obsession. Rituals only temporarily reduce discomfort or anxiety caused by an obsession, and thus they must be repeated frequently. However, the fear that something terrible will happen if a ritual is discontinued often locks OCD sufferers into a life ruled by what appears to be superstition.

Causes

Sigmund Freud attributed obsessive-compulsive disorder to traumatic **toilet training** and, although not supported by any empirical evidence, this theory was widely accepted for many years. Current research, however, indicates that OCD is neurobiological in origin, and researchers have found physical differences between the brains of OCD sufferers and those without the disorder. Specifically, neurons in the brains of OCD patients appear to be overly sensitive to *serotonin*, the chemical which transmits signals in the brain. A recent study at the National Institute of Mental Health suggests a link between childhood streptococcal infections and the onset of OCD. Other research indicates that a predisposition for OCD is probably inherited. It is possible that physical or mental stresses can precipitate the onset of OCD in people with a predisposition towards it. Puberty also appears to trigger the disorder in some people.

Prevalence

Once considered rare, OCD is now believed to affect between 5 and 6 million Americans (2 to 3% of the population), which makes it almost as common as **asthma** or **diabetes mellitus**. Among mental disorders, OCD is the fourth most prevalent (after **phobias**, substance abuse, and **depression**). In more than one-third of cases, onset of OCD occurs in childhood or adolescence. Although the disorder occurs equally among adults of both genders, among children it is three times more common in boys than girls.

Treatment

Fewer than one in five OCD sufferers receive professional help; the typical OCD patient suffers for seven years before seeking treatment. Many times, OCD is diagnosed when a patient sees a professional for another problem, often depression. Major depression affects close to one-third of patients with obsessive-compulsive disorder.

In recent years, a new family of **antidepressant** medications called *selective serotonin reuptake inhibitors* (SSRIs) has revolutionized the treatment of obsessive-compulsive disorder. These drugs include clomipramine

(Anafranil), fluoxetine (Prozac), fluvoxamine (Luvox), and sertraline (Zoloft). They work by altering the level of serotonin available to transmit signals in the brain. Thanks to these medications, the overwhelming majority of OCD sufferers (75 to 90%) can be successfully treated.

In addition to medication, an extreme type of behavior therapy is sometimes used in patients with OCD. In *exposure-response prevention* therapy, a patient slowly gives up his or her compulsive behaviors with the help of a therapist. Someone with a hand-washing compulsion, for example, would have to touch something perceived as unclean and then refrain from washing his/her hands. The resulting extreme anxiety eventually diminishes when the patient realizes that nothing terrible is going to happen.

For Further Study

Books

Rapoport, Judith L. *The Boy Who Couldn't Stop Washing: The Experience and Treatment of Obsessive-Compulsive Disorder.* New York: E.P. Dutton, 1989.

Organizations

The Obsessive-Compulsive Foundation Inc.
   Address: P.O. Box 70
   Milford, CT 06460-0070
   Telephone: toll-free (800) NEWS-4-OCD; (203) 878-5669
   Website: http://pages.prodigy.com/alwillen/ocf.html
Obsessive Compulsive Anonymous (OCA)
   Address: P.O. Box 215
   New Hyde Park, NY 11040
   Telephone: (516) 741-4901
The Obsessive Compulsive Information Center
   Address: Dean Foundation for Health, Research and Education
   8000 Excelsior Drive, Suite 302
   Madison, WI 53717-1914
   Telephone: (608) 836-8070

Internet Site:

Website: http://www.fairlite.com/ocd

Occupational Therapist

A professional who promotes health, enhances development, and increases independent functioning in children and adults through activities involving work, play, and self-care.

Occupational therapists help persons with both physical and emotional problems as well as learning difficulties. Although occupational therapy was initially associated with reintegrating veterans of World Wars I and II into the work force, the term "occupation" used in the context of this profession actually refers to any activity with which persons occupy their time, including—for children—play and school.

Occupational therapists undergo a rigorous training program. Four-year undergraduate programs, offered by many institutions, include courses in anatomy, psychology, and the theory and practice of occupational therapy. In addition, occupational therapists must complete six to nine months of clinical training. After graduation, most take a national examination to qualify as a Registered Occupational Therapist (R.O.T.). Occupational therapists work in various settings, including hospitals, nursing homes, rehabilitation centers, schools, day care centers, and patients' homes.

It is estimated that as many as 35% of occupational therapists work with children, many receiving specialized pediatric training in graduate programs. Much occupational therapy with children is based on giving children the physical, mental, and emotional benefits of performing various activities by turning them into play. For example, a special safety seat can help a previously resistant infant enjoy splashing and playing at bath time. One occupational therapist has gotten older children to enjoy being sprayed and scrubbed by devising a "car wash" for them to crawl through, complete with a "hot wax" lotion.

A pediatrician can often help parents choose an occupational therapist for their child. Before therapy can begin, the therapist evaluates the child through observation, discussion with parents, and, often, special assessment tests such as the **Bayley Scales of Infant Development** or the Knox Play Scale. Occupational therapists generally use one of two major treatment approaches with children: developmental or functional therapy. Developmental therapy is geared toward helping children achieve normal developmental milestones. A commonly used traditional method associated with this approach is neurodevelopmental therapy (NDT), which was developed in the 1950s by a neurologist and a physical therapist. It helps children with disorders, such as **cerebral palsy,** that affect muscle tone, making muscles either too tight (spastic) or loose and floppy (hypotonic). Treatment involves helping parents handle children with such disorders in ways that promote more normal muscle tone and helping the children themselves develop healthier, less restricted movement patterns. Occupational therapists are trained in NDT as part of their formal studies, although many of those specializing in pediatric occupational therapy receive additional training, including an eight-week certification course offered by the Neurodevelopmental Treatment Association.

A newer approach to developmental occupational therapy is the sensory integration method developed in the 1960s by Dr. A. Jean Ayres. Sensory integration is based on the idea that certain types of developmental problems are caused by neurological difficulties in processing information taken in by the senses. Usually used to treat children with **learning disabilities,** it has also been effective for other types of disorders, including cerebral palsy and **autism.** This approach concentrates primarily on three senses: touch and two that are not among the commonly listed "five senses"—the vestibular sense and proprioception. The vestibular sense, regulated by fluid levels in the inner ear, controls bodily movement and is important in balance and coordination. Proprioception, which is closely linked to the vestibular sense, is the perception of one's body position—the sense that allows people to touch their noses or comb their hair. Difficulties with sensory integration are most often caused by problems with the central nervous system and may appear as over- or under-sensitivity to touch, problems learning new sensorimotor skills, language delays, or an abnormally high or low level of activity.

The idea behind the sensory integration approach is to improve the way sensory messages are processed by the brain through activities that require a child to provide a specific reaction to controlled sensory input. Therapy sessions are usually scheduled once or twice a week for six months or more. There is still controversy surrounding the effectiveness of sensory integration therapy, and many pediatricians are not aware of this approach. A special organization, Sensory Integration International in California, works to promote awareness of this therapy. Occupation therapists often use it in conjunction with other techniques as part of a more comprehensive therapeutic program.

In contrast to developmental occupational therapy, functional therapy concentrates on teaching a child self-care activities, such as eating and dressing. Within this pragmatic context, however, therapy encourages children to develop new skills and practice the ones they already have. Special devices often aid in this process, such as splints to position parts of the body to function as effectively as possible, or such devices as a dish with a non-slip bottom that can't slide away from a child who is working on using a spoon properly. Physical problems commonly addressed in functional occupational therapy include limited motion, weakness, and lack of endurance; weakness on one side of the body; and poor coordination. This type of therapy is also used to increase the independence of the mentally retarded and help blind children master their environment.

For Further Study

Books

Ayres, A. Jean. *Sensory Integration and the Child.* Los Angeles: Western Psychological Services, 1979.

Breines, Estelle. *Occupational Therapy Activities from Clay to Computers: Theory and Practice.* Philadelphia: F. A. Davis Company, 1995.

Clancy, Helen, and Michele J. Clark. *Occupational Therapy with Children.* New York: Churchill Livingstone, 1990.

Pratt, P.N., and A.S. Allen. *Occupational Therapy for Children,* 2d ed. St. Louis: C.V. Mosby, 1989.

Semmler, Caryl J. *Early Occupational Therapy Intervention: Neonates to Three Years.* Gaithersburg, MD.: Aspen Publishers, 1990.

Organizations

The American Occupational Therapy Association
   Address: 1383 Piccard Drive
   P.O. Box 1725
   Rockville, MD 20850
Sensory Integration International
   Address: 1402 Cravens Ave.
   Torrance, CA 90501

....

Ontogenetic Development

The development of the individual.

Ontogenetic development describes the process of development of the individual from conception through the fetal stage through birth and growth to adulthood. It encompasses all aspects of development, including physical, emotional, and intellectual development.

....

Operant Conditioning

Approach to human learning based on the premise that human intelligence and will operate on the environment rather than merely respond to the environment's stimuli.

Operant conditioning is an elaboration of **classical conditioning.** Operant conditioning holds that human learning is more complex than the model developed by Ivan Pavlov (1849–1936) and involves human intelligence and will operating (thus its name) on its environment rather than being a slave to stimuli.

The Pavlovian model of classical conditioning was revolutionary in its time but eventually came to be seen as limited in its application to most human behavior, which is far more complex than a series of automatic responses to various stimuli. B.F. Skinner (1904–1990) elaborated on this concept by introducing the idea of consequences into the behaviorist formula of human learning. Pavlov's classical conditioning explained behavior strictly in terms of stimuli, demonstrating a causal relationship between stimuli and behavior. In Pavlov's model, humans responded to stimuli in specific, predictable ways. According to Skinner, however, behavior is seen as far more complex, allowing for the introduction of choice and free will. According to operant conditioning, the likelihood that a behavior will be repeated depends to a great degree on the amount of pleasure (or pain) that behavior has caused or brought about in the past. Skinner also added to the vocabulary of **behaviorism** the concepts of negative and positive reinforcer and of **punishment.**

According to the Skinner model of operant conditioning humans learn behaviors based on a trial and error process whereby they remember what behaviors elicited positive, or pleasurable, responses and which elicited negative ones. He derived these theories from observing the behaviors of rats and pigeons isolated in what have come to be known as Skinner boxes. Inside the boxes, rats that had been deprived of food were presented with a lever that, when pushed, would drop a pellet of food into the cage. Of course, the rat wouldn't know this, and so the first time it hit the lever, it was a purely accidental, the result of what Skinner called random trial and error behavior. Eventually, however, the rat would "learn" that hitting the lever resulted in the appearance of food and it would continue doing so. Receiving the food, then, in the language of operant conditioning, is considered the reinforcer while hitting the lever becomes the operant, the way the organism operates on its environment.

Skinner's model of operant conditioning broke down reinforcements into four kinds to study the effects these various "schedules of reinforcement" would have on behavior. These schedules are: fixed interval, variable interval, fixed ration, and variable ration. In a fixed interval schedule experiment, the lever in the rat's box would only provide food at a specific rate, regardless of how often the rat pulled the lever. In other words, food would be provided every 60 seconds. Eventually, the rat adapts to this schedule, pushing the lever with greater frequency approximately every 60 seconds. In variable interval experiments, the lever becomes active at random intervals. Rats presented with this problem adapt by pressing the lever less frequently but at more regular intervals. An experiment using a fixed ratio schedule uses a lever that becomes active only after the rat pulls it a specific number of times, and in a variable ration experiment the number of pulls between activity is random. Behavior of the rats adapts to these conditions and is adjusted to provide the most rewards.

The real-world ramifications of operant conditioning experiments are easy to imagine, and many of the experiments described would probably sound very familiar to parents who use such systems of rewards and punishments on a daily basis with their children whether they've ever heard of B.F. Skinner. His model has been used by learning theorists of various sorts to describe all kinds of human behaviors. Since the 1960s, however, behaviorism has taken a back seat to cognitive theories of learning, although few dispute the elementary tenets of operant conditioning and their use in the acquisition of rudimentary adaptive behaviors.

For Further Study

Books

Blackman, Derek E. *Operant Conditioning: An Experimental Analysis of Behaviour.* London: Methuen, 1974.

Mackintosh, Nicholas John. *Conditioning and Associative Learning.* New York: Oxford University Press, 1983.

Smith, Terry L. *Behavior and Its Causes: Philosophical Foundations of Operant Psychology.* Boston: Kluwer Academic Publishers, 1994.

Oppositional-Defiant Disorder

A form of antisocial behavior disorder characterized by opposition to authority figures such as parents and teachers, and by excessive anger and hostility.

Depending on the population, 2–6% of children have oppositional-defiant disorder. Oppositional-defiant disorder is similar to **conduct disorder,** without the more severe behavior components of aggression, property destruction, deceit, and theft. Oppositional-defiant children often go on to develop conduct disorder. Many children, especially during transitional periods such as preschool and adolescence, exhibit transient oppositional behavior towards parents and peers that will decline as they mature. If oppositional behavior is initiated during adolescence in particular it is probably part of the child's process of individuation, and should not be mistaken for a disorder. Children with oppositional-defiant disorder (1) are oppositional much more frequently than other children of their age and (2) increase their oppositional behaviors rather than decrease them with age. Disobedience and hostility usually appear first in the home environment, and may or may not ever emerge in school settings. Oppositional-defiant disorder is more common in families where there is marital discord, where a parent has a history of an antisocial, mood, or attention disorder, and where child rearing practices are either harsh (punishing), inconsistent (a succession of different **caregivers**), or neglectful.

Criteria for diagnosis

According to the *Diagnostic and Statistical Manual of Mental Disorders (DSM-IV),* oppositional-defiant disorder is diagnosed when (1) there is a pattern of defiant, disobedient, and hostile behavior towards authority figures lasting for at least six months, including frequent occurrence of at least four of the following behaviors; (2) the child exhibits the behaviors more frequently than other individuals of the same age or developmental level.

The child with oppositional-defiant disorder will:

- often lose his or her temper
- often argue with adults
- defy or refuse to comply with requests or rules
- deliberately do things that annoy other people
- blame others for his or her own mistakes
- be touchy or easily annoyed
- be angry and resentful
- be spiteful or vindictive

Care should be taken to distinguish oppositional-defiant behavior that results from other problems, such as mood or psychotic disorders, **attention deficit/hyperactivity disorder, mental retardation,** and language disorders.

See also **Antisocial behavior; Conduct disorder**

For Further Study

Books

Bernstein, Neil I. *Treating the Unmanageable Adolescent: A Guide to Oppositional Defiant and Conduct Disorders.* Northvale, NJ: Jason Aronson, 1997.

Price, Jerome A. *Power and Compassion: Working with Difficult Adolescents and Abused Parents.* New York: Guilford Press, 1996.

Wenning, Kenneth. *Winning Cooperation from Your Child!: A Comprehensive Method to Stop Defiant and Aggressive Behavior in Children.* Northvale, NJ: J. Aronson, 1996.

Orthodontics

The diagnosis, prevention, and treatment of dental and facial irregularities caused by misalignment of the teeth and jaw.

About 70% of people experience some form of malocclusion (literally "bad bite"), or poor positioning of the teeth. In Class I malocclusion the bite is even; that is, the top teeth line up with the bottom ones, but the teeth are crooked, crowded, or turned. In Class II malocclusion, also called "buck teeth," there is an overbite, in which the upper teeth extend past the top of the lower teeth, and in Class III malocclusion there is an underbite, in which the lower teeth extend past the bottom of the upper teeth. Untreated malocclusion can cause periodontal disease, digestive problems (due to the inability to chew food properly), and facial distortion. An orthodontist, who has at least two years training after dental school, performs dental manipulations to straighten the teeth and their relationship to the jaw.

There are two types of orthodontic treatment, which take place at different phases of **dental development** and involve different techniques. Interceptive orthodontics

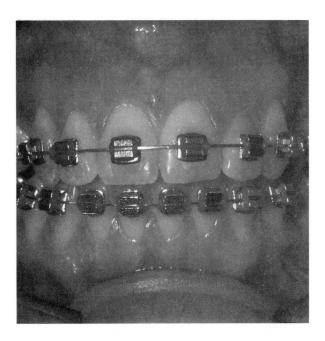

Braces are used by orthodontists to correct the bite and properly align the permanent teeth.

take place at around ages six to eight, before the permanent teeth emerge and while the jaw is growing the fastest. The goal of interceptive treatment is to make room for the permanent teeth, and a treatment usually lasts from three to 14 months. The orthodontist may expand the palate (roof of the mouth) and begin to correct over- and underbites. Appliances used to correct these problems may include a palatal expander, to enlarge the mouth, or a facebow, to make more room for crowded teeth. A facebow, a wire apparatus attached to the teeth and around the back of the head, is used to push the molars back to make room for front teeth, and must be worn 12 hours a day. Good interceptive treatment, like the use of these appliances, can reduce the length of full orthodontic treatment or even prevent the need for such treatment.

The second phase, full orthodontics, takes place between ages 12 and 18, after the permanent teeth have emerged. Braces (orthodontia) are the primary appliance used to correct the bite and properly align the permanent teeth. Orthodontists disagree on the optimal age to initiate full orthodontia. The teeth become more firmly embedded in the mouth as the adolescent grows, yet the jaw is continuing to grow and change. The interaction between these factors influences the effect of braces. The length of time the braces must be worn varies between a year and two and a half years. After the braces are removed, a removable retainer must be worn continuously for approximately a year and then inserted several nights a week. Ideally a retainer will be worn periodically until jaw growth stops at around age 24.

OVUM

Full orthodontic treatment usually costs anywhere from $3,000 to $7,000, although less expensive treatment may be obtained through dental schools. On the adolescent's first visit to the orthodontist, a full examination will be performed in order to discover any special problems and recommend orthodontic treatment, if any. During the records appointment, x rays, a casting of the bite, and photographs of the face will be taken. Using these records, the orthodontist will build a model of the mouth and determine a treatment plan. The plan and associated costs will be presented during the consultation appointment. At this time any concerns should be raised and questions should be asked about how the braces will affect the child's lifestyle. If the patient opts to get the braces, the orthodontist will insert separators between the back molars to be worn for two weeks.

Brace installation takes about two and a half hours. Teeth must be polished, measured, and dried before braces are installed. Braces are made in several designs and styles, varying in type of metal, length of time worn, degree of comfort, cost, and the "profile" they present. Lower profile braces are more comfortable and less visible to others. The lowest profile braces are lingual braces, worn behind the teeth. Lingual braces are not recommended for the average adolescent as they create speech problems and must be worn twice as long as regular braces. Components of the braces can be colored or flavored. Braces themselves consist of bands that are cemented around the back molars, buccal tubes that attach to the bands, and wires that attach to the tubes. Brackets are glued onto the front and side teeth, along with plastic ligature to hold the wires. Rubber bands may also be attached to make particular adjustments.

As the teeth shift during the first few days after installation, wires that rub against the mouth may need to be adjusted or cut. Wax can be applied to lessen the abrasion against the lips. Special mouthguards are available for athletics and for playing wind instruments. Salt water eases the pain, which will disappear after several days. Regular maintenance of the braces involves a visit to the orthodontist every three to six weeks for examination, tightening, or replacement of wires.

With current innovations in materials and design, braces are much less painful and intrusive than in the past. The primary variable in determining the effectiveness of full orthodontic treatment is patient involvement. Extra care must be taken to brush the teeth after every meal in order to remove food particles that lodge in the braces. The orthodontist can also prescribe a gel that reduces plaque and gum bleeding, which the patient can apply after brushing. A disinfecting mouthwash should also be used to inhibit growth of bacteria and control bad breath. Rubber bands must be taken out before meals and replaced with new ones afterwards, and must also be re-

placed before sleep. Headgear and/or a retainer must be worn according to the orthodontist's prescription. If this is not done, the teeth can take longer to correctly align or corrections that have been achieved can be reversed.

See also **Dental Development**

For Further Study

Books
Foster, Malcolm S. *Protecting Our Children's Teeth: A Guide to Quality Dental Care from Infancy Through Age Twelve.* New York: Insight Books, 1992.

Organizations
American Academy of Pediatric Dentistry
Address: 211 E. Chicago Ave., Suite 700
Chicago, IL 60611-2616
American Association of Orthodontists
Address: 401 North Lindbergh Boulevard
St. Louis, MO 63141-7816
Telephone: (314) 993-1700
American Dental Association
Address: 211 E. Chicago Avenue
Chicago, IL 60611
Telephone: (312) 440-2500

Ovum

The ovum, also called the egg, is the microscopic female sex cell. Its nucleus contains the chromosomes, which bear the hereditary material of the female parent.

Before birth, the ovaries of a female human contain all the eggs (ova) she will produce in her lifetime, up to 300,000. Beginning at **menarche** and during each normal menstrual cycle, an ovum develops in a fluid-filled cyst called a follicle. Ovulation is said to occur when the follicle ruptures and releases the egg from the ovary into the fallopian tube.

If sexual intercourse takes place, a sperm can fertilize the ovum, in which case **pregnancy** will result. Over the nine months of pregnancy, a single-celled ovum evolves into a fully developed human. If an ovum is not fertilized, it will be discharged through the vagina along with the monthly menstrual discharge.

See also **Sperm cell (spermatozoon)**

For Further Study

Books
Avraham, Regina. *The Reproductive System.* New York: Chelsea House, 1991.

—Gail B. Slap, M.D.
University of Pennsylvania School of Medicine

P

Pacifier

An artificial nipple designed for infants to suck, and which has a soothing effect.

Infants have a strong desire to suck, which may not be entirely fulfilled while feeding. Both the newborn and older infant are often soothed by sucking. Some babies suck their thumbs, while others take readily to a pacifier.

Pacifiers are often most effective in the child's first few months, when **colic** and fussiness are at their peak. Many babies who like pacifiers early on will spit them out when they become five or six months old, as the need for sucking lessens.

Pacifiers come in several different types. The shape of the nipple may be long, short, with a ball-shaped end, or flattened. There seems to be no evidence that one shape is better than another, but a baby may prefer one type. A tiny pacifier may be appropriate for a low-birth weight or premature baby. It is important that the nipple be firmly attached to the shield, so that it cannot come off and possibly choke a child. The shield should be large enough so that the child cannot get the whole pacifier into his or her mouth. When a baby is teething, parents should check the pacifier nipple for damage since it can be torn by emerging teeth. Many parents hang the pacifier on a string around the child's neck to prevent it from dropping or getting lost. This will keep the pacifier clean as well, but the string presents a danger if the child gets entangled in it. A child should never wear a pacifier on a string to bed.

There may be some disadvantages to using a pacifier. A baby who sucks on a pacifier at night may wake up crying several times during the night because the pacifier has fallen out of his or her mouth. Parents may need to encourage some alternate comfort at night. For a baby who is constantly quieted with a pacifier during the day, there may be a danger of the baby not getting adequate stimulation. That is, a baby who can be comforted with a pacifier might not be exposed to other methods of comfort, such as being held or taken for a walk. Some research has shown that babies display less exploratory visual behavior while sucking on a pacifier. That is, they look around less and may appear less alert. One recent study in England showed a correlation between pacifier use and lowered IQ scores. The researchers offered several hypotheses that might explain their finding. They reasoned that use of a pacifier may result in the baby receiving less mental stimulation and encouragement to learn and explore. A placid baby who is easily quieted with a pacifier gets less parental attention than a fussy child who challenges the parents to find other means to calm her. However, these are suggestions arising from a small body of research. There seems to be no evidence that use of a pacifier is itself directly harmful.

For Further Study

Books
Biracree, Tom, and Nancy Biracree. *The Parents' Book of Facts: Child Development From Birth to Age Five.* New York Facts on File, 1989.

Driscoll, Jeanne. *Taking Care of Your New Baby: A guide to Infant Care.* Garden City Park, NY: Avery Publishing Group, 1996.

Periodicals
Gale, Catharine R., and Christopher N. Martyn. "Breastfeeding, Dummy Use, and Adult Intelligence." *The Lancet,* April 20, 1996, pp. 1072–76.

Palmar Grasp Reflex *see* **Neonatal Reflexes**

Pain and Pain Management

The diagnosis and treatment of various kinds of pain; ethical issues involved in providing, or more commonly, withholding such treatment.

In 1994, the *New England Journal of Medicine* published a forum on ethical questions concerning pain management in children. The forum began its discussion by acknowledging that the medical community at large fails to provide effective pain relief for children and infants. The forum cited recent studies which found that "pain can be relieved effectively in 90 percent of patients but is not relieved effectively in 80 percent of patients." In children the failure to relieve pain is even more pronounced. Forum participants cited a study which found that postoperative analgesics were administered to children far more infrequently, or in lower doses, than to adults—even when both had undergone the same operation.

The forum considered several issues regarding the medical establishment's reluctance to provide pain relief for children and arrived at some interesting conclusions. For one, it stated that "Denial of relief from pain that is proportionate to the expressed need for such relief must be judged an unjustified harm, unless such deprivation serves a substantially greater good." It characterized as "undocumented lore" the belief among practitioners that giving narcotic painkillers to children could lead to a life of drug addiction. The forum implored pediatricians to rely instead on empirical data, none of which has found a link between opioid treatment of pain and drug addiction. Finally, acknowledging that research published in journals often has little impact on actual doctor practices, participants in the forum concluded their discussion with a call for "specific administrative interventions" to eradicate the currently inadequate standards of pain management for infants and children. The authors encourage "pressure from parents" to force doctors to take a child's expressions of pain as seriously as they would an adult's.

Infancy

By the time a fetus is 30 weeks old, the central nervous system has developed sufficiently to process and transmit pain messages. Infants have the internal networks to process pain, but they can feel more intense pain since the pain inhibiting mechanisms of their bodies have not fully developed. Infants are also more likely to suffer from unrelieved pain simply because they are unable to communicate their distress. A further complication is that many doctors believe children either don't feel pain as intensely as adults or won't remember having experienced it, and as such will only suffer in the instant. As Jane Brody pointed out a 1995 *New York Times* column, this belief accounts for the common procedure of simply restraining infants and young children about to undergo a painful procedure. Also, until recently, premature infants who needed surgical procedures were given only minimal **anesthesia**. Recent studies, however, have changed these practices, and medical personnel hotly debate how much and in what instances infants should be medicated against pain.

Discerning the level of pain experienced by infants is, of course, very difficult since they are unable to verbally communicate their distress. Bernadette Carter, in her book *Child and Infant Pain*, discusses several strategies for pain measurement in infants based on behavioral and physiological data. Behavioral data for measuring infant pain include measuring facial expressions, body movements/rigidity, and levels of crying. Sociologists and anthropologists have long known that facial expressions have universal significance. Several researchers have used this knowledge to devise facial expression coding systems to assist doctors in measuring pain. Two of the most common are the Neonatal Facial Coding System and the Facial Action Coding System. These systems have slightly varying conclusions as to how infant facial expressions relate to specific levels of pain, but both concluded that tightly closed eyes and open mouths can be regarded as good indications of infant pain. Crying is difficult to relate to a level of pain, since an infant's cry can mean several things, but research has found that adults tend to be able to discern hunger and other cries from cries of pain. Research into body movement has also shown some promise for pain measurement, finding that rapid foot movement is a fairly reliable indication of suffering.

The use of pain-killing drugs in infants is controversial, and many doctors are reluctant to prescribe opioids for fear of provoking respiratory depression, especially in very young infants. Recent research, however, has suggested that with the types of pain that call for opioid intervention in children older than two months, reasonable use of opioids is usually medically safe. However, there can be side effects, and pediatric nurses should watch for their onset. Among non-opioid pain relievers, **aspirin** is to be avoided because of the risk of Reye's syndrome. **Acetaminophen** is the most popular non-opioid, anti-inflammatory analgesic for children. It is widely used, generally considered safe, and is available in a variety of formulations. Non-drug pain management techniques are also available and vary, depending on the degree and duration of pain, from the simple use of **pacifiers** and reassuring touch to such non-traditional methods as acupuncture and aromatherapy—although the latter have seldom been used with infants.

Toddlerhood to school-aged children

Pain assessment in toddlers, preschoolers, and school-aged children faces some of the same problems associated with infants, but is made considerably easier by the children's increasing communicative sophistication. Several methods of assessment have been developed, including facial expression scales (like those for infants) as well as other techniques that allow the child to report his or her level of pain. These methods include questionnaires, diaries, games, diagrams, and several types of scales.

Pain management strategies for toddlers need not involve drugs. Recent studies have explored the possibility of using children's imagination and playfulness to help them relieve their own pain. These strategies work best when the pain is short-lived (like getting an injection or having a bandage removed) or low-level, such as the pain associated with common childhood illnesses. To alleviate short-lived pain, parents can tell their children that they have the power to make the pain go away by simply turning it off in their minds, just like they would turn off a light. Or, it has been suggested, children can be given a specific task to perform, like blowing as hard as they can when the doctor is about to inject them. The blowing directs their attention away from the pain and fear of the needle. There are a variety of such techniques which play on the high level of suggestibility in young children. In 1994, a study was conducted in which 77 children aged four to seven were told to pretend they were blowing bubbles while being given an injection. The study found that they reported experiencing significantly less pain than the control group.

There are also ways to incorporate play into pain management. Children can be given the opportunity to play doctor before receiving an injection. Another method is to allow children to see a procedure performed on another child, on video, before it is performed on them. In many cases, this latter strategy dramatically relieves anxiety about a procedure, such as a cast removal, which generally causes little, if any, pain aside from the child's fear. Parents also should not show their own apprehension of medical procedures in front of their children; like everything else, a child models much of her behavior from her parents'. As Dr. Gina French, a fellow in behavioral pediatrics at the Ohio State University College of Medicine told *Prevention* magazine, "Most kids don't have a lot of experience with shots, and much of their anticipated fear has been taught to them."

Surprisingly little research has been done in the area of pain relievers specifically designed for children. This again goes back to the medical community's long-standing reluctance to administer narcotic pain relievers to children. Drug companies are unlikely to devote the large amounts of money needed to develop new drugs for children if doctors are not willing to use them. However, in recent years some companies have begun to produce childhood pain relievers. One of the first was Anesta Corporation, which in the early 1990s began production of an opiate called fentanyl (marketed under the brand name Oralet). It was the first narcotic ever tested and approved specifically for children and was sold as a lollipop. This marketing strategy, despite the protest it provoked, was intended to make the drug more palatable to children, who are often resistant to orally administered liquids delivered in a medical setting. Many doctors, relying on the

"undocumented lore" decried by the *New England Journal of Medicine,* suggested that linking candy and opiates in the mind of a child was dubious. Another recently developed drug, EMLA Cream, is a topical anesthetic that can be applied to a child's skin. It deadens nerve endings, making the insertion of IVs or more difficult procedures, such as spinal taps or bone marrow aspiration, significantly less painful. Midazolam (Versed) is also commonly used in a diluted form to calm and sedate children before a procedure, although it is not technically approved for such use. Over-the-counter analgesics, such as acetaminophen and ibuprofen, are also commonly used.

For Further Study

Books
Carter, Bernadette. *Child and Infant Pain: Principles of Nursing Care and Management.* London: Chapman and Hall, 1994.

Periodicals
Brody, Jane. "Personal Health Column." *New York Times,* October 25, 1995, and November 1, 1995 (two-part article), pp. B7 & C13.

Muson, Marty. "Save the Wails." *Prevention,* December 1994, p. 38.

Stevens, Bonnie, and C. Celeste Johnson. "Pain in the Infant: Theoretical and Conceptual Issues." *Maternal-Child Nursing Journal,* January-March 1993, pp. 3–13.

Walso, Gary, et al. "Pain, Hurt, and Harm: The Ethics of Pain Control in Infants and Children." *New England Journal of Medicine,* August 25, 1994, pp. 541–44.

Williams, Rebecca D. "Calming Fears, Easing Pain." *FDA Consumer,* October 1994, p. 16.

Parens Patriae

Legal term describing the state's power to act on behalf of certain individuals.

This term, which in Latin literally means "parent of the state," refers to a rule, derived from the English common law, empowering the monarch to act as guardian and protector of persons—e.g., children and mentally incompetent individuals—under what is known as "legal disability." In the United States, where the states hold parens patriae authority, state attorney generals in certain cases act on behalf of state residents in need of legal protection. Typically, parens patriae power is used to protect a child who has no legal **guardian**. However, since a significant 1839 Pennsylvania court ruling which upheld a mother's decision to have her daughter committed, despite the father's petition for her release, parens patriae power has been invoked, unjustly, according to some writers, to over-rule a parent's custodial rights.

For Further Study

Books

Chesler, Phyllis. *Mothers on Trial: The Battle for Children and Custody.* New York: McGraw-Hill, 1986.

Parent-Child Relationships

The relationship, over the full extent of a child's development, between parent and child.

Of the many different relationships we form over the course of the life span, the relationship between parent and child is among the most important. Not surprisingly, students of child development have devoted considerable attention to the parent-child relationship, in order to understand how it develops and functions over the lifespan. Among the many questions researchers examine are those concerning normative changes in the parent-child relationship over the course of development (e.g., How does the parent-child relationship change during adolescence?), the impact of variations in the parent-child relationship on the child's behavior and functioning (e.g., Which types of discipline are most effective during the preschool years?), and the effects of the parent-child relationship on the parent (e.g., How are adults affected by parenthood?).

Infancy

A baby cries, a parent feeds her; a baby snuggles, a parent hugs her. Day after day, night after night, mothers and fathers feed, burp, wash, change, dress, and hold their babies. Out of these interactions, feelings and expectations grow. The baby feels distressed and hungry, then satisfied; the parent feels tenderness, joy, annoyance, exhaustion, pleasure. Gradually, the baby begins to expect that her parent will care for her when she cries. Gradually, parents respond to and even anticipate their baby's needs. These elements form the basis for a developing relationship, a combination of behaviors, interactions, feelings, and expectations that are unique to a particular parent and a particular child.

By the end of the first year, most infants who are cared for in families develop an **attachment** relationship, usually with the primary caretaker. This relationship is central to the child's development.

Developmental psychologists have studied attachment in infancy mainly by watching how infants react when they are separated from, and then reunited with, their caregiver (usually one of the infant's parents). An experimental laboratory procedure called the **Strange Situation** is the most common assessment. Researchers have been particularly interested in understanding individual differences in the quality of attachment is inferred

from behavior in the Strange Situation. The majority of children develop a *secure attachment*: when reunited with their **caregiver** after a temporary absence of several minutes, they greet her in two distinctive ways. If distressed, they want to be picked up and find comfort in her arms; if content, they smile, talk to her, or show her a toy. In contrast, some children with an *insecure attachment* want to be picked up, but they are not comforted; they kick or push away. Others seem indifferent to the caregiver's return, and ignore her when she returns.

The quality of the infant's attachment seems to be predictive of aspects of later development. Youngsters who emerge from infancy with a secure attachment stand a better chance of developing happy, competent relationships with others. The attachment relationship not only forms the emotional basis for the continued development of the parent-child relationship, but can serve as a foundation upon which subsequent social relationships are built.

Researchers disagree about the origins of a secure attachment relationship. One account focuses on the way caregivers behave toward their infants. According to this view, the key element is the caregiver's sensitivity in responding to the infant's signals. Secure infants have mothers who sensitively read their infant's cues and respond appropriately to their needs.

Another perspective emphasizes the temperament of the infants. A secure attachment is more easily formed between a caregiver and an infant with an easier disposition, or **temperament,** than between a caregiver and an infant who is characteristically negative, fearful, or not especially sociable. In this respect, security of attachment may reflect what the infant is like rather than how the caregiver behaves. Most likely, the early parent-child relationship is the product both of what the infant *and* caregiver bring to it.

Toddlerhood

When children move from infancy into toddlerhood, the parent-child relationship begins to change its focus. During infancy, the primary function of the parent-child relationship is nurturance and predictability, and much of the relationship revolves around the day-to-day demands of caregiving: feeding, sleeping, toileting, bathing. The attachment relationship develops out of these day-to-day interactions.

As youngsters begin to talk and become more mobile during the second and third years of life, however, parents usually attempt to shape their child's social behavior. In essence, parents become teachers as well as nurturers, providers of guidance as well as affection. The process of socialization—preparing the youngster to function as a member of a social group—implicit during most of the first two years of life, becomes explicit as the child moves toward his or her third birthday.

Socialization has been an important focus of research in child development for well over 60 years. Initially, researchers focused on particular child-rearing practices—including types of **discipline** and approaches to **toilet training** and **weaning**—in an effort to link specific parenting practices to aspects of the child's development. Findings from this research were inconsistent and not especially informative. Over time, such efforts gave way to research that emphasized the overall emotional climate of the parent-child relationship, instead of discrete parenting practices.

A number of studies conducted during the past 30 years have pointed to two overarching dimensions of the parent-child relationship that appear to be systematically linked to the child's psychological development: how responsive the parents are, and how demanding they are. Responsive parents are warm and accepting toward their children, enjoying them and trying to see things from their perspective. In contrast, parents who are low in responsiveness tend to be aloof, rejecting, or critical. They show little pleasure in their children and are often insensitive to their emotional needs. Demanding parents maintain consistent standards for their child's behavior. In contrast, parents who are insufficiently demanding are too lenient; they exercise minimal control, provide little guidance, and often yield to their child's demands. Children's healthy psychological development is facilitated when the parents are both responsive and moderately demanding.

During toddlerhood, children often begin to assert their desire for autonomy by challenging their parents. Sometimes, the child's newfound assertiveness during the "terrible twos" can put a strain on the parent-child relationship. It is important that parents recognize that this behavior is normal for the toddler, and that the healthy development of independence is facilitated by a parent-child relationship that provides support and structure for the child's developing sense of autonomy. In many regards, the security of the initial attachment between infant and parent provides the child with the emotional wherewithal to begin exploring the world outside the parent-child relationship.

Preschool

Many researchers study the ways in which responsiveness and demandingness interact to form a general tone, or climate, in the household. Using this sort of approach, experts have identified four main parenting styles that typically emerge during the preschool years: authoritative, authoritarian, indulgent, and disengaged. Although no parent is absolutely consistent across situations and over time, parents do seem to follow some general tendencies in their approach to childrearing, and

it is possible to describe a parent-child relationship in terms of the prevailing style of parenting employed. These descriptions can be used to provide guidelines for both professionals and parents interested in understanding how variations in the parent-child relationship affect the child's development.

Authoritative parents are both responsive and demanding; they are firm, but they discipline with love and affection, rather than power, and they are likely to explain rules and expectations to their children instead of simply asserting them. *Authoritarian* parents are also highly demanding, but they are not less responsive; authoritarian parents tend to be strict disciplinarians, frequently relying on physical punishment and the withdrawal of affection to shape their child's behavior. *Indulgent* parents are responsive, but not especially demanding; they have few expectations of their children and impose little discipline. *Disengaged* parents are neither responsive nor demanding. They may be neglectful or unaware of the child's needs for affection and discipline.

What makes a parent more likely to use one style as opposed to another? Ultimately, the parenting style a parent employs is shaped by many factors: the parent's developmental history, education, and personality, the child's behavior, and the immediate and broader context of the parent's life. Thus, the parent's behavior vis-a-vis the child is influenced by such things as work, marriage, family finances, and other factors likely to affect the parent's behavior and psychological well-being. In addition, systematic comparisons of parenting practices among families living in different circumstances teach us that parents in different cultures, from different social classes, and from different ethnic groups rear their children differently.

Nevertheless, research has shown that aspects of children's behavior and psychological development are linked to the style of parenting with which they have been raised. Generally speaking, preschoolers with authoritative parents tend to be curious about new situations, focused and skilled at play, self-reliant, self-controlled, and cheerful. Children who are routinely treated in an authoritarian way tend to be moody, unhappy, fearful, withdrawn, unspontaneous, and irritable. Children of permissive parents tend to be low in both social responsibility and independence, but they are usually more cheerful than the conflicted and irritable children of authoritarian parents. Finally, children whose parents are disengaged tend to have a higher proportion of psychological difficulties than other youngsters.

School age

During the elementary school years, the child becomes increasingly interested in peers, but this should not be taken as a sign of disinterest in the parent-child relationship. Rather, with the natural broadening of psychosocial and cognitive abilities, the child's social world expands to include more people and settings beyond the home environment. The parent-child relationship continues to remain the most important influence on the child's development. Generally speaking, children whose parents are both responsive and demanding continue to thrive psychologically and socially during the middle childhood years.

The parenting styles that first become apparent during the preschool years continue to influence development across middle childhood. Over the course of childhood, parents' styles tend to remain the same, and their effects on the child quite similar. Children of authoritative parents tend to be socially competent, responsible, successful in school, and high in **self-esteem.** The authoritarian style, with its perfectionism, rigidity, and harsh **discipline,** continues to affect children adversely, with these youngsters generally rated lower than their peers in appropriate social assertiveness, cognitive ability, competence, and self-esteem, but higher in aggression. Children of permissive parents also tend to be more aggressive than their peers, but also more impulsive, less self-reliant, and less responsible. Children raised in disengaged homes continue to have the most difficulty, and show more behavior problems.

The natural tendency is to think of the parent-child relationship as a one-way street, with the parent influencing the child. But in actuality the relationship is reciprocal and bidirectional. During the school years especially, the parent-child relationship is influenced not only by the child's parents but by the child. In most families, patterns of interaction between parent and child are well established by the elementary school years. Overly harsh parenting, for example, often leads to aggressive behavior in children, leading children to join antisocial peer groups, further heightening their aggressiveness. This, in turn, may provoke harsher parenting, leading to further aggressiveness in the child, and so on. Authoritative parenting, in contrast, helps children develop self-reliance and social competence, which, of course, makes it easier for parents to rear their child in an authoritative, reasoned fashion. Continued authoritativeness on the part of the parent contributes to increased competence in the child, and so on. Rather than trying to solve the "which came first" puzzle—the parenting or the child's characteristics—it is more useful to think of parenting as a process and the parent-child relationship as one part of an intricate social system.

Much research has examined how the child's development is affected by such factors as **divorce,** remarriage, and parental (especially, maternal) employment. As a rule, these studies show that the quality of the parent-child relationship is a more important influence on

the child's psychological development than changes in the structure or composition of the household. Generally speaking, parenting that is responsive and demanding is associated with healthier child development regardless of the parent's marital status or employment situation. If changes in the parent's marital status or work life disrupt the parent-child relationship, however, short-term effects on the child's behavior are likely to be seen. One goal of professionals who work with families under stress is to help them re-establish healthy patterns of parent-child interaction.

Adolescence

Early adolescence marks an important turning point in the parent-child relationship. As the child enters **adolescence,** the biological, cognitive, and emotional changes of the period spark transformations in the parent-child relationship. In many families, the transition into adolescence coincides with the parent's transition into midlife, and this, too, may introduce additional challenges into the family system that spill over into the parent-child relationship.

Early adolescence is a time during which the child's urges for independence may challenge parents' authority, as the young adolescent strives to establish a sense of emotional autonomy, or *individuation.* And much like toddlerhood, many parents find early adolescence to be a difficult period requiring a fair amount of adaptation. But, as is also the case with toddlerhood, research shows that most families are able to cope with these adaptational demands successfully. Adolescents fare best, and their family relationships are happiest, in households in which parents are both supportive and are accepting of the child's needs for more psychological independence.

Although the significance of peer relationships grows during adolescence, the parent-child relationship maintains its importance for the psychological development of the child. As in previous eras, authoritative parenting—parenting that combines warmth and firmness—seems to have the most positive impact on the youngster's development. Research shows that over time, adolescents who have been reared authoritatively continue to show more success in school, better psychological development, and fewer behavior problems than their counterparts from other types of homes. Youngsters whose parents are disengaged continue to show the most difficulty.

It is widely assumed that conflict between parents and children is an inherent feature of family life in adolescence, but systematic research on the so-called "generation gap" indicates that the phenomenon has been exaggerated in the popular media. Early adolescence may be a time of heightened bickering and somewhat diminished closeness in the parent-child relationship, but most disagreements between parents and young teenagers are over fairly mundane matters, and most teenagers and parents agree on the essentials. Nevertheless, the increased frequency with which these squabbles occur may take its toll on parents' mental health, especially on the mothers'. This period appears to be temporary, however, and most parents and adolescents are able to establish a comfortable working relationship by the beginning of high school. Indeed, by late adolescence most children report feeling as close to their parents as they did during elementary school.

For Further Study

Books

Bornstein, M., ed. *Handbook of Parenting.* Hillsdale, NJ: Erlbaum, 1995.

—Laurence Steinberg, Ph.D.
Temple University

Parent Locator Service (PLS)

A service of the Office of Child Support Enforcement to find missing parents.

Parent Locator Service (PLS) is a service that custodial parents can use to locate missing parents, usually to obtain child support payments, but in some cases, to find a non-custodial parent who has kidnapped a child. The PLS relies on federal government records such as computer databases, income tax, and Social Security earnings and benefits records. At the state level, the PLS uses motor vehicle registration, driver's license, welfare, police and prison, and worker's compensation records. The PLS is operated by the Office of Child Support Enforcement (OCSE), established in 1975 as a branch of the U.S. Department of Health and Human Services to help enforce payment of court-ordered child support. Working through a network of regional and state agencies, the OCSE uses the Parent Locator Service and other investigative techniques to locate the missing parent.

Parent-Teacher Conferences

Regularly scheduled meeting between a student's parent(s) and teacher to discuss his or her progress.

The parent-teacher conference is an opportunity for parents to get a glimpse into the school lives of their children. Although many parents are involved in their children's schools, either as members of a parent-teacher organizations, such as PTA, or as volunteers (in a variety of areas), many more have little or no contact other than the parent-teacher conference.

Some parents are reluctant to attend parent-teacher conferences. Such parents are often anxious about schools because of their own negative experiences as children or because they fear they will be perceived as meddlesome. Often, however, an invitation from a teacher to come in for a meeting will be sufficient to break the ice. More and more teachers are now producing newsletters for children to take home (or having the students produce the newsletters) to inform parents about educational activities. Many schools also offer adult education, recreation, and entertainment events to encourage parents to become more involved in the school setting.

Most school systems require teachers to hold conferences with parents. Both teachers and parents benefit from planning how they will use the time together. The *Education Digest,* a journal directed at K–12 teachers, suggests that teachers carefully consider a range of areas before a parent arrives. These include providing samples of student work, identifying weaknesses and strengths, discussing the student's overall abilities in critical and creative thinking (rather than just grades), discussing social skills and peer relations, and identifying areas for growth and suggestions for strategies parents can use at home to support their child's success in school. In addition, productive parent-teacher conferences provide opportunities for the teacher to receive information about their students' home lives. Teachers can share what they know about the student, and should be prepared to listen to what parents have to say as well. It is vital that teachers assume a non-threatening, non-judgmental stance in listening to parents' views, since parents may find the conference intimidating.

To make the parent-teacher conference less threatening, parents can also prepare in advance. It is common for parents to interpret criticism of their child as an assault on their parenting skills and can react defensively. To set the tone for a productive conference, parents can prepare by discussing the school experience with their child. Parents can take time prior to and during the conference to ask their child for a self-evaluation; objectively review report cards and grades on homework to gain accurate sense of the child's academic performance; maintain openness to the teacher's evaluation, even if it contradicts the parent's own point of view; and strive to use non-threatening and open-minded language and body language.

Alternative approaches

Many school districts evaluate the process of parent-teacher conference and monitor the academic research related to this aspect of the education process. Some alternative approaches to the parent-teacher conference that

TEACHERS ASSESS STUDENTS IN RELATION TO PEERS

Fred White, a first grade teacher from New York City, told *Better Homes and Gardens,* "Parents look at their children with different eyes. That's the way it should be. Teachers, on the other hand, are more objective, less partial. While we certainly see each child as an individual, we also have the benefit of seeing many more kids of the same age every day. That gives us a basis for seeing where one particular seven-year-old is in relationship to other seven-year-olds."

are being tested by school districts in the late 1990s include triangular conferences, home conferences, and portfolio assessment.

Triangular conferences

A triangular conference involves the student, the parent(s), and the teacher. This idea is relatively new but is praised on many fronts because it tends to keep the conversation focused on the needs and progress of the student, thus minimizing the opportunity for either the teacher or the parent(s) to become defensive. The student takes responsibility for sharing his or her progress, and describes his or her assessment of achievements. In most situations, the teacher helps the student prepare in advance, encouraging him or her to select samples of work that he or she feels is representative of his or her learning.

Home conferences

Although it is not feasible in every school system—such as large rural or even suburban school districts—urban school districts, typically geographically compact, may arrange for home conferences for parents and teachers. To minimize safety and security concerns, these home conferences are often carried out by pairs of teachers who visit the parents in their home. Such conferences alleviate anxiety parents may have about entering a school building; they also help teachers become aware of any situations at home that may affect the student.

Portfolio assessment

A portfolio is a collection of student-selected examples of his or her work. The portfolio, considered by those in educational research as an alternative assessment method, can be designed to reflect work in progress or to highlight the student's completed efforts. The portfolio can be used to fulfill several educational objectives, such as improvement of learning or measuring achievement. One of the goals of such alternative assessments is to enable the teacher to address individual student differences.

In the parent-teacher conference setting, the portfolio may provide the basis for the discussion. When the student is present at the conference, he or she shares the items in the portfolio and discusses why each piece represents a notable milestone in his or her educational progress. By using the portfolio—with or without the student present at the conference—the teacher is able to direct the focus on the student's own perception of his or her progress.

Troubleshooting

When a problem develops between the teacher and parent(s), it is important for both parties to maintain the student's education and growth as priorities. Some school districts make school personnel available to serve as mediators when conflict develops between parents and teachers. Counselors, assistant principals, department heads, and senior teachers are among those who could mediate disagreements.

For Further Study

Periodicals

"Beyond the Brief Encounter," *NEA Today* 15, October 1996, p. 22.

D'Auria, John. "Tremors We Should Not Ignore," *Daedalus* 124, Fall 1995, pp. 149–52.

Enoch, Steven W. "Better Parent-Teacher Conferences," *Education Digest* 52, April 1996, pp. 48–51.

Johns, Mary Sue. "The New Crusade: Parent Involvement," *School Arts* 94, December 1994, pp. 16–18.

Kennedy, Marge. "Talking to Teachers," *Better Homes and Gardens,* November 1995, pp. 36–38.

Moyers, Suzanne. "Giving Students a Voice at Conference Time." *Instructor* 104, October 1994, pp. 64+.

Rich, Dorothy. "Win Over the No-Shows," *Instructor* 105, January/February 1996.

"Seven Ways You Can Improve Your School," *Redbook,* April 1996, pp. 70–76.

Pavor Nocturnus *see* **Night Terrors**

Peabody Picture Vocabulary Test

A language skills test that measures comprehension but doesn't require a child to produce words.

In administering the Peabody Picture Vocabulary Test, the examiner says a word, and the child is asked to point to the one of four pictures on a page that corresponds to the word spoken. The sequence of words progresses from easy to more complex, but the test is only continued to the limit of the child's ability. Performance is measured by comparison with that of other children in the same age group, and test results are expressed

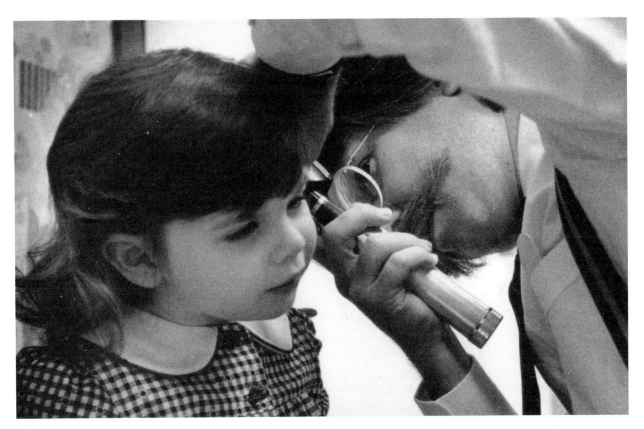

Parents rely on their pediatrician for support and advice as well as medical care.

as a percentile ranking and an educational age equivalent. Because the Peabody picture test requires no verbal response, it can be administered to very young children, children for whom English is a second language, and to children with **language disorders.**

For Further Study

Books

Cohen, Libby G., and Loraine J. Spenciner. *Assessment of Young Children.* New York: Longman, 1994.

McCullough, Virginia. *Testing and Your Child: What You Should Know About 150 of the Most Common Medical, Educational, and Psychological Tests.* New York: Plume, 1992.

Wortham, Sue Clark. *Tests and Measurement in Early Childhood Education.* Columbus: Merrill Publishing Co., 1990.

Pediatrician

A physician who specializes in the treatment of children from birth through adolescence.

A pediatrician is a physician who has taken extra training in the development and diseases of infants, children, adolescents, and young adults through age 21. Parents are advised to begin the process of selecting a pediatrician about three months before their baby is due to be born. Most obstetricians will assist with the referral, and the **American Academy of Pediatrics** also offers a referral service. Other parents may also have recommendations and advice to offer. Because new parents will rely on their pediatrician for support and advice as well as medical care, it is important that they feel comfortable with the personality and style of the pediatrician they choose. Many parents interview more than one pediatrician before making the final selection. It is necessary to designate a pediatrician before the baby is born, so that he or she can examine the newborn in the hospital shortly after birth.

Pediatricians receive extensive training that begins with four years of medical school. A three-year residency—special training in pediatrics—follows. (The resident works under the supervision of an experienced physician or team of physicians to acquire the knowledge and skills necessary to diagnose and treat childhood illnesses, diseases, and conditions.) Following the completion of the residency, the newly trained pediatrician is eligible to take the written examination offered by the American Board of Pediatrics. When the pediatrician passes the certification exam, he or she receives a certificate—which most will frame and display on the wall of their office—and earns the right to use the initials FAAP (Fellow of the American Academy of Pediatrics) after his or her name. Only pediatricians that have passed the certification examination can join the American Academy of Pediatrics. As of 1997, there were over 48,000 board-certified pediatricians who were members of the Academy.

Some pediatricians then elect to pursue more study in a specific area of pediatrics—known as a subspecialty. Subspecialties include: adolescent medicine; allergy/immunology; ambulatory pediatrics; behavioral/developmental pediatrics; cardiology; child development; community pediatrics; critical care; dermatology; developmental biology; developmental disabilities; emergency medicine; endocrinology (glands and diabetes); gastroenterology; general academic pediatrics/epidemiology; genetics/dysmorphology (inherited diseases); hematology/oncology (blood disorders/childhood cancers); immunology; infectious disease; metabolism; neonatal/perinatal medicine; nephrology (kidneys); neurology (nervous system); nutrition; pathology; pharmacology/toxicology; public health/preventive medicine; pulmonology; radiology; rheumatology; and teratology.

Parents may also need to call on a medical specialist—such as an ophthalmologist or surgeon—who has received special training in pediatrics.

Pediatricians are called on to provide a variety of services to families, including diagnosing illness, prescribing treatment, counseling families, monitoring the growing child's physical, mental, and social development, and advising adolescents on a range of emotional and social issues. Pediatricians may also participate in research, advocacy for social and legislative changes to benefit all children, and in public education on issues like **nutrition,** injury and disease prevention, and in providing guidelines for safe participation in athletics.

For Further Study

Books

Brazelton, T. Berry. *Doctor and Child.* New York: Dell Publishing Co., 1978.

Markel, Howard. *The Practical Pediatrician: The A to Z Guide to Your Child's Health, Behavior, and Safety.* New York: W.H. Freeman and Co., 1996.

Nathanson, Laura Walther. *The Portable Pediatrician's Guide to Kids 5–12.* New York: HarperPerennial, 1996.

Shelov, Steven P. *Caring for Your Baby and Young Child: Birth to Age 5.* Chicago: American Academy of Pediatrics, 1991.

Periodicals

Greenspan, Peter, and Suzanne Levert. "Pediatricians and Parents." *Parenting* 10, December–January 1996, pp. 45+.

Koop, C. Everett. "The Tiniest Patients." *Newsweek* special edition, Spring–Summer 1997, p. 51.

Shifrin, Donald L. "Choosing Your Baby's Doctor." *American Baby* 58, February 1996, pp. 16+.

Spock, Benjamin. "How to Pick Your Child's First Doctor." *Parenting* 10, April 1996, pp. 112+.

Organizations

American Academy of Pediatrics
  Address: 141 Northwest Point Blvd.
  Elk Grove Village, IL 60007-1098
  Telephone: (847) 228-5005
  FAX: (847) 228-5097
  website: www.aap.org
  e-mail: kidsdocs@aap.org
  (Offers a pediatrician referral service. Parents may request a referral by sending a self-addressed, stamped envelope, specifying geographic area and pediatric specialty, if appropriate.)

Peer Acceptance

The degree to which a child or adolescent is socially accepted by peers; the level of peer popularity. The ease with which a child or adolescent can initiatice and maintain satisfactory peer relationships. The opposite of peer rejection.

Peer acceptance is measured by the quality rather than the quantity of a child or adolescent's relationships. While the number of friends varies among children and over time as a child develops, peer acceptance is often established as early as preschool. Factors such as physical attractiveness, cultural traits, and disabilities affect the level of peer acceptance, with a child's degree of social competence being the best predictor of peer acceptance. Children who are peer-accepted or popular have fewer problems in middle and high school, and teens who are peer-accepted have fewer emotional and social adjustment problems as adults. Peer-accepted children may be shy or assertive, but they often have well-developed communication skills. Peer-accepted children tend to:

- Correctly interpret other children's body language and tone of voice. Well-liked children can distinguish subtleties in emotions. For example, they can distinguish between anger directed toward them versus toward a parent.

- Directly respond to the statements and gestures of other children. Well-liked children will say other children's names, establish eye contact, and use touch to get attention.

- Give reasons for their own statements and gestures (actions). For example, well-liked children will explain why they want to do something the other child does not want to do.

A CLOSER LOOK AT TWO SUBSPECIALTIES

Adolescent medicine

Adolescent medicine became a subspecialty in November 1994, when the first certification examination was offered by the American Board of Pediatrics and the American Board of Internal Medicine. To qualify for the certification exam, a pediatrician must complete a three-year fellowship.

Approximately 1,000 physicians in the United States treat primarily adolescents, representing an estimated 1–2% of the total number of physicians treating teenagers. The certification was created to provide care for adolescents, and to recognize the fact that many pediatricians and primary care physicians feel they are not prepared to deal with some of the challenges of adolescent health care, such as eating disorders, depression, HIV infection, and other reproductive and sexuality concerns. Physicians have been specializing in treatment of adolescents since the 1970s, and some feel the certification could prove to be a disincentive to physicians entering the field, since certification is unlikely to translate into higher earnings.

Surgery: fetal and pediatric

The subspecialty of surgery known as fetal and pediatric surgery involves special training in surgical techniques for **fetuses** in utero and children under age three, and is a relatively recent area of medical phenomenon. Two examples of technological advances in this area include open heart surgery, orthopaedic surgery, and organ transplantation in infants. C. Everett Koop, U.S. Surgeon General from 1981–89, began his career in pediatric surgery in the 1940s, when there was no official designation for the specialty. Writing in *Newsweek* magazine in 1997, Koop reports "When I left pediatric surgery 35 years later [in the 1980s], the former mortality rate of 95% [for certain birth defects] had become the *survival* rate. "I can't think of anything in medicine that brings more joy than intervening surgically in the life of an otherwise doomed newborn, and changing a congenital death sentence into the prospect of more than 70 years of life." Pediatric surgeons—once they mastered the delicate art of pediatric anesthesiology—developed procedures for repairing hernias, correcting deformed limbs, treating **hydrocephalus,** closing **spina bifida**, and repairing **cleft lips** and **palates**

- Cooperate with, show tact towards, and compromise with other children, demonstrating the willingness to subordinate the self by modifying behavior and opinions in the interests of others. For example, when joining a new group where a conversation is already in progress, well-liked children will listen first, establishing a tentative presence in the group before speaking (even if it is to change the subject).

These skills are crucial in initiating and maintaining relationships, and in resolving conflicts. By contrast, rejected children tend either towards aggressive, **antisocial behavior,** or withdrawn, depressive behavior. They also don't listen well, tend not to offer reasons for their behavior, don't positively reinforce their peers, and have trouble cooperating. Antisocial children will interrupt people, dominate other children, and either verbally or physically attack them. Depressive or withdrawn children may be excessively reserved, submissive, anxious, and inhibited. Competitiveness or dominance by itself is not necesarily indicative of low peer acceptance. In fact, popular children tend to have the characteristics of both competitiveness and friendliness.

Although biological predisposition may be a factor in a child's social competence and level of peer acceptance, environmental factors are also extremely important. Some of the factors contributing to peer acceptance include (1) during infancy, the quality of **attachment** between mother or primary **caregiver** and child; (2) during childhood, the quantity and quality of opportunities for interaction with different types of peers in different environments (in the family, at school, church, camp, activity centers, in sports, or in the neighborhood); (3) the type of parenting style. A highly nurturant but moderately controlling "authoritative" parenting style is associated with the highest levels of social competence. By contrast, a low nurturant, highly controlling "authoritarian" parenting style is associated with children's aggressiveness, while the high nurturant but low-controlling "permissive" style is associated with failure to take responsibility for behavior.

Children learn to relate to peers by engaging in peer relationships. Often a vicious circle develops where a rejected child is given fewer and fewer opportunities by his peers to relate and thereby learn new skills. Lack of opportunity to participate normally in peer interaction is especially problematic for children who differ in some obvious way, either culturally, racially, or through some mental or physical disability. Issues of peer acceptance should be addressed as early as possible in order to prevent loss of self-confidence and **self-esteem.**

In addition to providing direct social skills training or counseling for the child with peer acceptance problems, parents and teachers can create opportunities for non-threatening social interaction to occur. Though children should never be forced to play together (this can create the rejection it is intended to remedy), popular and less-popular preschoolers can be encouraged to interact with one another. For example, a less sociable child may be encouraged to answer and ask questions of others. Older children should be provided opportunities to interact in smaller groups and in one-on-one situations, where it may be easier to try out new behaviors and make up for social mistakes. Shy or withdrawn children can be encouraged to develop outside interests that will place them in structured contact with others. In school, peer helping programs and collaborative learning provide opportunities for popular and less-popular children to work together. Ideally, collaboration should highlight the less-popular students' strengths, such as special interests and talents, rather than weaknesses. At any age, the smallest positive change in behavior should be reinforced with attention and praise.

For Further Study

Books

Asher, S. R., and J. D. Coie, eds. *Peer Rejection in Childhood.* New York: Cambridge University Press, 1990.

Goleman, Daniel. *Emotional Intelligence.* New York: Bantam Books, 1995.

Ramsey, P.G. *Making Friends in School: Promoting Peer Relationships in Early Childhood.* New York: Teacher's College Press, 1991.

Selman, R. *The Growth of Interpersonal Understanding.* New York: Academic Press, 1980.

Periodicals

Bhavnagari, Navaz Peshotan, and Barbara G. Samuels. "Making and Keeping Friends: A Thematic Unit to Promote Understanding of Peer Relationships in Young Children." *Childhood Education* 72, Summer 1996, pp. 219+.

Kreidler, William J. "How Can I Make Friends?" *Instructor* 106, March 1997, pp. 74+.

Peer Mediation

A process by which students act as mediators to resolve disputes among themselves. A form of conflict resolution used to address student disagreements and low-level disciplinary problems in schools.

Peer mediation is a form of **conflict resolution** based on integrative negotiation and mediation. Disputing parties converse with the goal of finding a mutually satisfying solution to their disagreement, and a neutral third party facilitates the resolution process. The salient feature of peer mediation as opposed to traditional discipline measures and other forms of conflict resolution is that, outside of the initial training and ongoing support

services for students, the mediation process is entirely carried out by students and for students. Due to the rise of violence in schools, the sharp increase in serious crime committed by youths, and the increasing awareness of the need for social skills instruction in education, peer mediation programs exploded in the 1980s. In 1984, when the National Association for Mediation in Education (NAME) was formed, there were about 50 mediation programs in school districts nationwide. Eleven years later NAME reported over 5,000 programs across the country. Peer mediation programs that have gained national stature include the early Educators for Social Responsibility program, San Francisco's Community Board program, New York's School Mediators Alternative Resolution Team (SMART), and New Mexico's Center for Dispute Resolution.

Purposes of peer mediation

In accordance with the principles of conflict resolution, peer mediation programs start with the assumption that conflict is a natural part of life that should neither be avoided nor allowed to escalate into verbal or physical violence. Equally important is the idea that children and adolescents need a venue in which they are allowed to practically apply the conflict resolution skills they are taught. Peer mediation programs vary widely in their scope and function within a school or system. In some schools, mediation is offered as an alternative to traditional disciplinary measures for low-level disruptive behavior. For example, students who swear at each other or initiate fights might agree to participate in mediation rather than being referred to the playground supervisor or principal. In other schools, mediation takes place in addition to disciplinary measures. In either case, peer mediation is intended to prevent the escalation of conflict. Serious violations of rules or violent attacks are not usually addressed through mediation.

Although peer mediation is primarily carried out by students, at least a few staff members and teachers are actively involved in training and facilitation. Ideally, peer mediation will encourage a culture of open communication and peaceful solutions to conflict. According to the NAME, five of the most common purposes of a school mediation program are:

1. to increase communication among students, teachers, administrators, and parents.

2. to reduce school violence, vandalism, and suspensions.

3. to encourage children, adolescents, and teens to resolve their own disputes by developing listening, critical thinking, and problem-solving skills.

4. to teach peaceful resolution of differences, a skill needed to live in a multicultural world.

PEER MEDIATION PROCESS

The process varies, but most programs use the following general format:

I. Introduction—The mediator introduces him or herself and explains the rules. The mediator tries to make the disputants feel comfortable.

II. Identifying the Problem—The mediator listens to each party describe the problem and writes down an agreed-upon "agenda" that includes all the elements of a dispute.

III. Identifying Facts and Feelings—The disputants tell their sides of the story to each other. The goal is to "surface" all of the underlying facts and feelings pertaining to the problem. The mediator asks many questions with the goal of helping to refocus the problem by viewing it differently.

IV. Generating Options—The mediator asks both parties to brainstorm how they might solve the problem. The mediator writes down all the solutions, marking the ones that are mutually agreed upon. If none are forthcoming, participants return to previous steps. Sometimes, individual sessions with each disputant and the mediator are necessary.

V. Agreement—The mediator writes a contract using the solutions to which both parties agree, and everyone signs it.

VI. Follow-Up—After a period of time the former disputants will report back to the mediator on whether the contract is being upheld by both parties.

5. to motivate students' interest in conflict resolution, justice, and the American legal system, and encourage active citizenship.

Training of peer mediators

Programs vary in whether they train all the students in the school to act as mediators, or only as a "cadre" of selected students. The cadre approach may be used initially with the intention of expanding later. Mediators either volunteer or are nominated by teachers or other students; often, students who are "troublemakers" turn out to be the best mediators. Many programs have a required conflict resolution course sometime during the middle school years. Training is done by teachers, counseling staff, or outside consultants, and ranges from the semester-long course (15–20 hours of training), to a two-day workshop for middle or high school students, to a three-hour workshop for elementary students. Through discussion and role play, students learn conflict resolution skills such as active listening, cooperation in achieving a goal, acceptance of differences, problem-solving, anger management, and methods of maintaining neutrality as a mediator. They also practice the structured mediation process they will be following in actual dispute resolution.

The mediation session

Elementary mediators usually work in teams, visiting designated school areas and responding to signs of antagonism between students as they arise. They will approach the disputants, ask if they need help, and take them aside for mediation, if the students agree. Middle and high school programs may employ resident mediators in the cafeteria or public areas, using a more formal procedure for students to refer themselves or others for mediation. There is usually a separate mediation room or rooms set up to facilitate private communication among the disputants and the mediator.

It is essential that disputants voluntarily agree to participate in mediation, and ground rules for the process prohibit name-calling or interrupting someone who is talking.

Success of peer mediation programs

It is difficult to measure the success of peer mediation programs. Almost all teachers and administrators report that their programs are extremely successful, and that they perceive a more positive climate and see less destructive behavior in the school. When measuring success in reaching or maintaining agreement between disputants, rates vary between 58–93%. A few studies show reductions in suspension rates, suspension rates for fighting, or incidence of fighting by as much as 50%. Even elementary students learn and retain the knowledge of conflict resolution techniques, and those who participate in mediation, either as mediators or as disputants, benefit from the experience. The NAME found that peer mediation programs reduce the amount of teacher and administrator time spent on discipline, reduce violence and crime in schools, and increase the **self-esteem** and academic achievement of students trained as mediators.

One critical factor in the success of peer mediation programs is the active support of the school principal, and in some cases of the local community. A comprehensive planning process is necessary to outline goals and administrative accountability for each phase of the program. Provision for the ongoing support of the peer mediators is especially important. At minimum, a weekly meeting should be held for the students to debrief, engage in guided reflection, and receive continued training.

A PEER MEDIATOR IN ACTION

Roslyn wasn't sure it would work. She had explained the ground rules in her *Introduction* speech and recorded all the elements of the dispute in the *Identifying the Problem* phase, just as she had been taught in peer mediation training. What had happened was that one of the disputants in this session, Tera, thought that the other disputant, Sarah, had stolen her purse earlier that morning. Later, when Sarah gave Tera a dirty look ("dogged her out") in the cafeteria fourth period, Tera's suspicions were confirmed—she thought. So, Tera got in line behind Sarah and pushed her to the floor when the bell rang.

When they were first given the options of going to the principal or to resolve the conflict through peer mediation, Sarah said she preferred to go to the principal. Roslyn thought this was typical of the victim of an attack who had never been through mediation before. Mediation appeared to be a way for the attacker to avoid punishment. But in this case Tera was also a victim—of theft.

Roslyn felt sure she could help them forgive each other's dirty looks and the attack. She had been through situations like this before, and found it was almost miraculous the way that helping disputants put things in perspective could change their attitudes. But Tera was out for blood. Though she was talking to Sarah and Roslyn, she was not actually facing them in her seat. Roslyn was worried about her. How could they determine whether Sarah stole the purse, and in any case prove it to Tera's satisfaction? What they needed was a courtroom instead of this mediation kidstuff.

Roslyn decided to remind the disputants of the mediation ground rule that everything, including information about the theft, is kept confidential unless it poses a danger. Then she launched into the next phase of the mediation, *Identifying Facts and Feelings.* She began to feel more comfortable as she recalled her goal in this phase: to uncover everything pertaining in any way to the dispute or the disputants' feelings about the dispute. She had to get Tera and Sarah to talk.

It took all of fifth period to get through the next phase. Although she was uncertain whether she would be able to help Tera and Sarah resolve their dispute, Roslyn's skilled questioning uncovered more than was first apparent. It turned out there were two other elements in the dispute, a sophomore named Anthony who was Sarah's ex-boyfriend and Tera's friend, and a bottle of nail polish that looked like Tera's but wasn't. Unknown to Tera, Anthony told Sarah that Tera had accused her of the theft, which was why Sarah had dogged Tera in the cafeteria. The bottle of nail polish was out on Sarah's table, and when Tera saw it she was positive it was hers.

By that time they were able to discuss how the facts had been distorted by both girls, based on their assumptions about what was true. Neither of them had spoken directly with the other, only with Anthony.

(Continued)

One of the reasons for the success of peer mediation is the fact that it is student-run. Children and adolescents build a culture of positive peer pressure within which they can begin to establish independence from adult guidance. When given the opportunity, they are capable of using their own judgment to creatively solve disputes, and often their solutions are less punitive than those of adults. Research shows that children's solutions to conflict are more aggressive when adults are present. As children grow older they rely increasingly on their peers as models and measures of correct behavior. The potential judgment of peers during the mediation process may have a higher degree of moral significance to a teen than would the same judgment coming from an adult. In peer mediation, students have the opportunity to conform to positive social standards without sacrificing their identification with the peer group.

For Further Study

Books

Ferrara, Judith M. *Peer Mediation: Finding a Way to Care.* York, ME: Stenhouse Publishing, 1996.

Robertson, Gwendolyn. *School-Based Peer Mediation Programs: A Natural Extension of Developmental Guidance Programs.* Gorham, ME: University of Southern Maine, 1991.

Sorenson, Don L. *Conflict Resolution and Mediation for Peer Helpers.* Minneapolis, MN: Educational Media Corporation, 1992.

Townley, A., and M. Lee. *Training for Trainers: Staff Development in Conflict Resolution Skills.* Amherst, MA: National Association for Mediation in Education, 1993.

Wolowiec, Jack, ed. *Everybody Wins: Mediation in the Schools,* Chicago: American Bar Association, 1994.

A PEER MEDIATOR IN ACTION (cont.)

Sarah and Tera also began to realize that their feelings about him were also influencing their assumptions about each other.

Roslyn felt it was necessary to move on to the next phase, *Generating Options*. It was difficult because Tera's first brainstorm was that Sarah could return the purse and Tera would forgive her. Though she personally believed that Sarah had not stolen it, Roslyn wrote it down on the board. Sarah suggested Tera could find the real thief and have him or her apologize to Tera. They seemed to be back at the beginning. Then Sarah, fed up, suggested they could take it to the principal. She said that she wanted to be relieved of the blame for the theft of the purse, and the principal was the only one who could do that.

Roslyn looked at Tera, who was much calmer now than she had been at the beginning. As Roslyn was writing down "Take it to the principal" on the board, Tera asked Sarah why she wanted to do that when she'd only get into trouble. She looked Sarah straight in the eye, and said, "You said that when we were in the cafeteria, didn't you? You really want the truth to come out, don't you? Maybe you're not the one who did it."

"It's about time you see that," Sarah said, and a small smile appeared on her face. The tension melted as Tera smiled back.

"Is this the solution you both agree on, then?" Roslyn asked, giving them an opportunity to clarify the change that had just happened.

Sarah said, "We don't have to, if Tera's willing to drop me as her suspect."

"I think I'll be going by myself, to try to get to the bottom of this," Tera said. "I know it wasn't you."

"OK, so what solution do you both agree on?"

They wrote up a contract *(Agreement Phase)* specifying that each girl would always confront the other one directly about any suspicions she had or rumors she had heard about the other, especially information obtained from friends such as Anthony. Sarah and Tera wanted to bring Anthony in for another mediation session with all of them together, but Roslyn suggested he might be more willing to come if they approached him individually to hold separate mediation sessions with each of them. Also, Sarah agreed to go with Tera to report the stolen purse.

After they set the follow-up dates *(Follow-Up Phase)* and put the chairs and easel back, Roslyn felt pleased with herself and with the disputants. The students themselves had achieved an agreement without involving the principal.

Organizations

American Bar Association
   Address: Special Committee on Dispute Resolution
   1800 M Street, NW
   Washington, DC 20036

Educators for Social Responsibility
   Address: 475 Riverside Drive, Room 450
   New York, NY 10115

National Association for Mediation in Education (NAME)
   Address: 205 Hampshire House
   Box 33635
   University of Massachusetts
   Amherst, MA 01003-3635
   Telephone: (413) 545-2462

School Initiatives Program
   Address: Community Board Center for Policy and
   Training

149 Ninth Street
San Francisco, CA94103

School Mediation Associates
   Address: 702 Green Street #8
   Cambridge, MA 02139

. . . .

Peer Pressure

The influence of the social group on an individual.

Peers are the individuals with whom a child or adolescent identifies, who are usually but not always of the same age-group. Peer pressure occurs when the individual experiences implicit or explicit persuasion, sometimes amounting to coercion, to adopt similar values, beliefs, and goals, or to participate in the same activities as those in the peer group.

Although it is usually conceived of as primarily a negative influence acting on adolescents or teens, peer pressure can be a positive influence as well, and it can act on children at any age, depending on their level of contact with others. The influence of peer pressure is usually addressed in relation to the relative influence of the family on an individual. Some characteristics that peer groups offer and which families may be lacking are: (1) a strong belief structure; (2) a clear system of rules; and (3) communication and discussion about taboo subjects such as drugs, sex, and religion.

Peer pressure is strongly associated with level of academic success, drug and substance use, and gender role conformity. The level of peer influence increases with age, and resistance to peer influence often declines as the child gains independence from the family or caretakers, yet has not fully formed an autonomous identity. One study in particular confirms other research findings that the values of the peer group with whom the high schooler spends the most time are a stronger factor in the student's level of academic success than the values, attitudes, and support provided by the family. Compared to others who started high school with the same grades, students whose families were not especially supportive but who spent time with an academically oriented peer group were successful, while those students whose families stressed academics but who spent time with peers whose orientation was not academic performed less well.

The peer pressure study contradicts prevailing ideas about the influence of families on the success of racial and cultural minorities such as Asians and African Americans. While some Asian families were not especially involved in their children's education, the students, who found little social support of any type, tended to band together in academic study groups. Conversely, African American students, whose families tended to be highly involved in and supportive of education, were subjected to intense peer pressure not to perform academically. According to the study, the African American peer groups associated the activities of studying and spending time at the library with "white" behavior, and adopted the idea that the student who gets good grades, participates in school activities, or speaks Standard English is betraying his racial heritage and community. Consequently, gifted students "dumb-down" as they make the choice between academics and "fitting in." Research suggests that this type of peer pressure contributes to a decline in the grades of African American students (especially males) as early as the first through fourth grades.

Peer pressure similarly compels students of all ethnic backgrounds to engage in other at-risk behaviors such as cigarette **smoking, truancy,** drug use, sexual activity, fighting, theft, and daredevil stunts. Again, peer group values and attitudes influence, more strongly than do family values, the level of teenage alcohol use. Regardless of the parenting style, peer pressure also influences the degree to which children, especially girls, conform to expected gender roles. Up until about grade six, girls' performance in science and math are on par with that of boys, but during adolescence girls' test scores and level of expressed interest declines. The tendency is to abandon competition with boys in favor of placing more emphasis on relationships and on physical appearance.

Ideally the child, adolescent, or teen should make decisions based on a combination of values internalized from the family, values derived from thinking independently, and values derived from friends and other role models. In order to achieve this balance, rather than attempting to minimize peer influence, families and schools must provide strong alternative beliefs, patterns of behavior, and encourage formation of peer groups that engage in positive academic, athletic, artistic, and social activities.

Parents

In order to rival their children's peers, parents should convey a strong, clear (not necessarily rigid) value structure and open avenues of communication early in life, while the child is first being exposed to the group persuasions of preschoolers. In situations where decisions might be made about peer pressure, parents who are hesitant to discourage their children's independence and individuality often send vague messages or no message at all to the child about their perspective on the matter. Voicing parental opinion provides guidance, which the child can choose to accept or reject in future situations. In turn, the knowledge that the child is being guided on important matters gives parents a sense of confidence when the child succumbs to the numerous small, inconsequential peer pressures concerning interests, toys, and styles of dress throughout grade school.

In a positive sense, peer pressure provides the motivation to try different behaviors, which may just as quickly disappear. But if the child has few alternative sources of communication, emotional support, or self-esteem, undesirable behaviors may be continued for the positive peer reinforcement they bring. The period of greatest risk is when adolescents enter high school. Just as their **self-esteem** lowers (especially girls) and their daily pressures increase, they are introduced to older peer groups who engage in new activities. Adolescent exploration of some sexual and substance-using activities can be circumvented by establishing policies of open communication between the parents or caregivers and the adolescent or teen. It should be made clear that the parent or other adult is willing to discuss virtually any subject matter and listen to the child's point of view, which is not the equivalent to condoning or allowing the associated behaviors to occur. Knowing the child's close friends and their parents, being informed about the social situations the teen is confronted with, and being familiar with teen-age trends also help in anticipating problems and maintaining intergenerational communication.

Adolescents

Adults may vary in their level of independence from groups, the degree to which they follow the crowd, but even the most popular, independent teen feels the strong effect of peer pressure. Techniques of resisting teen peer pressure include:

1. Observe people and the groups with whom they socialize. Observe what they do and the consequences of their actions. When someone tries to argue "everyone's doing it," you can prove otherwise. Make choices about who you spend time with, instead of joining a group just because it's there.

2. Avoid situations that present problems—parties with drugs, being alone with a boyfriend or girlfriend who might pressure you.

3. Communicate: Say "No" forcefully and with eye contact. (If you do not believe yourself, they will not either.) Talk about it. Find someone who feels the same way you do.

4. Anticipate what your friends will say or do and decide beforehand how you will react. Consider all the alternatives, including the consequences of doing it their way. Is it a matter of wearing something you do not like, or is it a matter of damaging your body?

5. If you find yourself anticipating conflict too often, seriously think about finding a new friend or set of friends. Start off gradually, spending less and less time with the person who is pressuring you.

6. Know yourself. Know what moods might make you more susceptible to negative peer influence. Know (or figure out) what activities build your self-esteem. Know why you are doing whatever you do everyday—be aware of your actions.

Schools

Two primary areas in which schools can discourage negative peer pressure and encourage formation of positive peer groups are in peer leader programs and in collaborative learning practices. Virtually every school trains student peer leaders to participate in counseling, support groups, drug or violence prevention programs, or peer mentoring and tutoring programs. For these programs, students are trained in cognitive awareness, goal setting, problem identification, decision-making, and communication skills in order to lead, coach, and support other students. Peer leader programs implicitly combat

peer pressure as the students act as positive role models for other teens.

With collaborative learning techniques, teachers require students to work together to solve problems, answer questions, create and deliver presentations, and provide feedback to each other on individual work. When they are well-planned, collaborative activities have been shown to increase levels of academic engagement, increasing students' self-esteem and achievement. Effective collaborative learning groups essentially create new peer groups in the classroom, offering the students new patterns of peer communication and sometimes new value systems.

For Further Study

Books

Bernard, B. *The Case for Peers.* Portland, OR: Northwest Regional Educational Laboratory, 1990.

Feller, Robyn M. *Everything You Need to Know About Peer Pressure.* New York: Rosen Publishing Group, 1995.

Friar, Linda and Penelope B. Grenoble. *Teaching Your Child to Handle Peer Pressure.* Chicago: Contemporary Books, 1988.

Juvonen, Jaana, and Kathryn R. Wentzel, eds. *Social Motivation: Understanding Children's School Adjustment.* New York: Cambridge University Press, 1996.

Kageler, Len. *Helping Your Teenager Cope with Peer Pressure.* Loveland, CO: Family Tree, 1989.

Myrick, R.D., and D.L. Sorenson. *Peer Helping: A Practical Guide.* Minneapolis, MN: Educational Media Corporation, 1988.

Stienberg, Laurence, et al. *Beyond the Classroom: Why School Reform Has Failed and What Parents Need to Do.* New York: Simon and Schuster, 1996.

—Hallie Bourne

Perfectionism

The tendency to set unrealistically high standards for performance of oneself and others, along with the inability to accept mistakes or imperfections in matters of personal appearance, care of the home, or work; may be accompanied by an obsession with completeness, purity, or goodness.

Perfectionism is a psychological orientation which, depending on the severity, may have biological and/or environmental causes. To an educated observer, a perfectionist orientation is usually evident by the preschool years, though it may not cause problems until the college years. The perfectionist orientation has two components: impossibly high standards, and the behaviors intended to help achieve the standards and avoid mistakes. The high standards interfere with performance, and perfectionist behavior becomes an obstacle instead of a means to achieving the goal. For example, when a five-year-old who is learning to write repeatedly erases his lines because they are not exactly straight, he is exhibiting a perfectionistic tendency.

Due to obsessive effort and high standards of performance combined with natural gifts, perfectionists may be athletic, musical, academic, or social achievers, but they may equally as often be **underachievers.** Perfectionists engage in dichotomous thinking, believing that there is only one right outcome and one way to achieve that outcome. Dichotomous thinking causes indecisiveness, since according to the individual's perception a decision, once made, will be either entirely right or entirely wrong. Due to their exacting precision, they take an excessive amount of time to perform tasks. For example, the perfectionist kindergartner may produce two entirely straight lines out of ten attempts, but the emotional fatigue she experiences may hamper her future performance and detract from the value of the effort. Even small tasks become overwhelming, which leads to frustration, procrastination, and further anxiety caused by time constraints.

Perfectionists also pay selective attention to their own achievements, criticizing themselves for mistakes or failures, and downplaying their successes. Overwhelmed by anxiety about their future performance, they are unable to enjoy successes.

Perfectionist anxiety can cause headaches, digestive problems, muscle tension, and heart and vascular problems. Anxiety can also cause "blanking" or temporary **memory** losses before events such as musical performances or academic exams. Perfectionists also hesitate to try new activities for fear of being a beginner at an activity, even for a short period of time. Negative effects of perfectionism are felt especially when an individual is a perfectionist in all areas of life, rather than in one realm, such as an artistic or scientific pursuit, which might allow room for mistakes in other areas of life.

In extreme forms perfectionism may contribute to **depression** or be diagnosed as obsessive-compulsive personality disorder (which should be distinguished from the more serious **obsessive-compulsive disorder**). The more common syndromes of **anorexia nervosa** and **bulimia** can be considered an extreme form of perfectionism directed towards the body and its appearance. The irrational distortions of perception that can arise from abnormally high standards of "performance" (i.e., thinness) are evident in the anorexic's perception of her or himself as fat.

Perfectionist behavior functions essentially to control events. Conditions that place the child in a position of vulnerability and/or that require the child to take extra responsibility for events can contribute to perfectionism. First-born children, children with excessively critical parents, and children who have lost a parent or sibling all may be predisposed towards perfectionism. It is estimated that 15% of gifted children will struggle with perfectionism at some point in their lives. Although it may not be immediately evident, often there is a sense of vulnerability, inferiority, shame, or guilt behind perfectionist efforts. The perfectionist's continual high achievements and/or control over events do not lead to satisfaction because there is always something to criticize or worry about, or another goal to achieve. Some perfectionists are other-directed and subject others to impossibly high standards of performance and conduct, causing difficulties in interpersonal relationships. Because they cannot accept their own imperfections, they may adopt a falsely exaggerated self-esteem, which hides an intense insecurity. Other perfectionists subject their own emotions to excessive control, and have difficulty becoming intimate. The perfectionist may be afraid of exposing his imperfections to others, which also causes difficulty with intimacy.

Perfectionism is socially encouraged by the modern emphasis on accuracy of information and evidence of success in life. Practices such as assigning percentage grades to school assignments encourage children to aim for "100%" perfect performance without mistakes. It is important to emphasize the process of effort and learning as much as the number of mistakes a child makes in a given homework assignment or creative activity. Indeed, accepting and valuing children's work regardless of mistakes—from making the bed to buttering toast—is a basic function of parenting. To avoid any perfectionist tendencies, children must be given a deep sense of how much they are valued as persons regardless of their performance and behavior. They should also have the belief that failure is a fundamental experience in life, without which one cannot learn and grow.

The first step in moving away from a perfectionist orientation is to identify it and to examine the ways in which it manifests in an individual's life. Because the end results of perfectionist behavior—winning first prize, writing the perfect paper, or being the quietest child—provide so many rewards from teachers, parents, peers, and society in general, the specific ways that perfectionism inhibits the child or teen must be identified. This will probably involve discussion of time spent and of feelings and self-concept involved in the process of achieving some goal. Any judgmental thoughts aimed at self or others should be examined. Positive affirmations should be substituted for judgment, and the child's attention can be directed to other, more subtle, aspects of the experience,

FIVE PERSPECTIVES ON PERSONALITY DEVELOPMENT		
Perspective	**Assumed Processes**	**Primary Outcomes**
Temperament	Inherent physiological mechanisms	Ease of arousal, ability to regulate emotions and impulses, energy, reaction to unfamiliar people and events, dominant mood
Psychoanalytic	Conflict over sexual and hostile motives	Defenses, phobias, depressed mood
Attachment	Relation to the caretaker in the infant years	Control of impulse, social habits, security, anger, frustration tolerance, trust in others, capacity for love
Self	Interpretations of experience, identification	Guilt, shame, anxiety, self-confidence
Observed behavior	Acquired habits	Sociability, aggressive behavior, impulsivity, shyness, obedience

such as questions, feelings, and discoveries that are unrelated to performance.

It is important for the perfectionist to set and meet deadlines in order to experience the reward of finishing a task. If procrastination is a special problem, tasks should be broken down into smaller steps or goals to be accomplished, so that the task appears less overwhelming and the feeling of accomplishment can be experienced often as each task is completed. The perfectionist should also be encouraged to take risks simply for the sake of taking risks. A decision to take risks gives the perfectionist permission to be a beginner at a task, and allows him or her to voluntarily relinquish control of a situation. A significant illustration of the value of mistakes and taking risks is the fact that Babe Ruth held the record for the most strikeouts as well as for the most homeruns.

For Further Study

Books

Adderholdt-Elliott, M. R. *Perfectionism: What's Bad About Being Too Good*. Minneapolis: Free Spirit, 1987.

Bottner, B. *The World's Greatest Expert on Absolutely Everything...Is Crying*. New York: Dell Publishers. 1986.

Heide, F. & Chess, V. *Tales for the Perfect Child*. New York: Lothrop, Lee and Shepard Books, 1985.

Mallinger, A. E., & DeWyze, J. *Too Perfect: When Being in Control Gets Out of Control*. NY: Random House, 1993.

Manes, S. *Be a Perfect Person in Just Three Days*. New York: Bantam/Skylark Books, 1987.

Zadra, D. *Mistakes Are Great*. Mankato, MN: Creative Education, 1986.

 Perinatal Period

The period from 28 weeks after conception through one week after birth.

The perinatal period spans the last stage of pregnancy and the first days following birth. Approximately coinciding with the last trimester of pregnancy, the perinatal period features the final development and maturation of the **fetus.** At the onset of the perinatal period, the fetus is fully formed, with eyelids that open and close, a detectable heartbeat, and has demonstrated detectable movement for about one month. During the perinatal period, the internal organs will complete their formation and development, and the fetus will go from approximately two pounds to its birth weight of seven to eight pounds on average.

A **premature birth** is one that takes place during the first two months of the perinatal period.

Personality Development

The development of the beliefs, moods, and behaviors that differentiate among people.

The concept of personality refers to the profile of stable beliefs, moods, and behaviors that differentiate among children (and adults) who live in a particular society. The profiles that differentiate children across cultures of different historical times will not be the same because the most adaptive profiles vary with the values of the society and the historical era. An essay on personality development

IMPORTANT DERIVATIVES OF FOUR PROCESSES IN PERSONALITY DEVELOPMENT	
Process	**Outcome**
Identification	Expectation of success or failure, pride vs. shame
Ordinal position	Attitude toward legitimate authority
Social class	Feelings of entitlement and power vs. feeling of impotence and coercion
Parental socializations	Values the child holds for achievement, honesty, tolerance to others, responsibility, loyalty, control of aggression, guilt over failure

written 300 years ago by a New England Puritan would have listed piety as a major psychological **trait** but that would not be regarded as an important personality trait in contemporary America.

Contemporary theorists emphasize personality traits having to do with individualism, internalized conscience, sociability with strangers, the ability to control strong emotion and impulse, and personal achievement.

An important reason for the immaturity of our understanding of personality development is the heavy reliance on questionnaires that are filled out by parents of children or the responses of older children to questionnaires. Because there is less use of behavioral observations of children, our theories of personality development are not strong.

There are five different hypotheses regarding the early origins of personality (see accompanying table). One assumes that the child's inherited biology, usually called a temperamental bias, is an important basis for the child's later personality. Alexander Thomas and Stella Chess suggested there were nine temperamental dimensions along with three synthetic types they called the difficult child, the easy child, and the child who is slow to warm up to unfamiliarity. Longitudinal studies of children suggest that a shy and fearful style of reacting to challenge and novelty predicts, to a modest degree, an adult personality that is passive to challenge and introverted in mood.

A second hypothesis regarding personality development comes from Sigmund Freud's suggestion that variation in the sexual and aggressive aims of the id, which is biological in nature, combined with family experience, leads to the development of the ego and superego. Freud suggested that differences in parental socialization produced variation in anxiety which, in turn, leads to different personalities.

A third set of hypotheses emphasizes direct social experiences with parents. After World War II, Americans and Europeans held the more benevolent idealistic conception of the child that described growth as motivated by affectionate ties to others rather than by the narcissism and hostility implied by Freud's writings. **John Bowlby** contributed to this new emphasis on the infant's relationships with parents in his books on **attachment**. Bowlby argued that the nature of the infant's relationship to the caretakers and especially the mother created a profile of emotional reactions toward adults that might last indefinitely.

A fourth source of ideas for personality centers on whether or not it is necessary to posit a self that monitors, integrates, and initiates reaction. This idea traces itself to the Judeo-Christian assumption that it is necessary to award children a will so that they could be held responsible for their actions. A second basis is the discovery that children who had the same objective experiences develop different personality profiles because they construct different conceptions about themselves and others from the same experiences. The notion that each child imposes a personal interpretation to their experiences makes the concept of self critical to the child's personality.

An advantage of awarding importance to a concept of self and personality development is that the process of identification with parents and others gains in significance. All children wish to possess the qualities that their culture regards as good. Some of these qualities are the product of identification with each parent.

A final source of hypotheses regarding the origins of personality comes from inferences based on direct observations of a child's behavior. This strategy, which relies on induction, focuses on different characteristics at different ages. Infants differ in irritability, three-year-olds differ in **shyness**, and six-year-olds differ in seriousness of mood. A major problem with this approach is that each class of behavior can have different historical antecedents. Children who prefer to play alone rather than with others do so for a variety of reasons. Some might be temperamentally shy and are uneasy with other children while others might prefer solitary activity.

DEVELOPMENTAL CHANGES IN THE ORIGIN OF THE EMOTIONS TO BE REGULATED		
Emotion to be regulated	Source in child under 5 years	Source in child over 5 years
Fear/anxiety	Unfamiliarity	Identification, school failure, peer rejection
Anger/resentment	Frustration and punishment	Coercion, rejection, risk failure
Shame and guilt	Violations of parental standards	Failure to meet internalized standards

The current categories of child psychopathology influenced the behaviors that are chosen by scientists for study. Fearfulness and **conduct disorder** predominate in clinical referrals to psychiatrists and psychologists. A cluster of behaviors that includes avoidance of unfamiliar events and places, fear of dangerous animals, shyness with strangers, sensitivity to **punishment**, and extreme **guilt** is called the internalizing profile. The cluster that includes disobedience toward parent and teachers, aggression to peers, excessive dominance of other children, and impulsive decisions is called the externalizing profile. These children are most likely to be **at risk** for later juvenile delinquency. The association between inability of a three-year-old to inhibit socially inappropriate behavior and later **antisocial behavior** is the most reliable predictive relation between a characteristic scene in the young child and later personality trait.

Influences on Personality Development

The influence comes from a variety of **temperament** but especially ease of arousal, irritability, fearfulness, sociability, and activity level. The experiential contributions to personality include early attachment relations, parental socialization, identification with parents, class, and ethnic groups, experiences with other children, ordinal position in the family, physical attractiveness, and school success or failure, along with a number of unpredictable experiences like **divorce**, early parental death, mental illness in the family, and supporting relationships with relatives or teachers.

The most important personality profiles in a particular culture stem from the challenges to which the children of that culture must accommodate. Most children must deal with three classes of external challenges: (1) unfamiliarity, especially unfamiliar people, tasks, and situations; (2) request by legitimate authority or conformity to and acceptance of their standards, and (3) domination by or attack by other children. In addition, all children must learn to control two important families of emotions: anxiety, **fear**, and guilt, on the one hand, and on the other, anger, jealousy, and resentment.

Of the four important influences on personality—identification, ordinal position, social class, and parental socialization—identification is the most important. By six years of age, children assume that some of the characteristics of their parents belong to them and they experience vicariously the emotion that is appropriate to the parent's experience. A six-year-old girl identified with her mother will experience pride should mother win a prize or be praised by a friend. However, she will experience shame or anxiety if her mother is criticized or is rejected by friends. The process of identification has great relevance to personalty development.

The child's ordinal position in the family has its most important influence on receptivity to accepting or rejecting the requests and ideas of legitimate authority. First-born children in most families are most willing than later-borns to conform to the requests of authority. They are more strongly motivated to achieve in school, more conscientious, and less aggressive.

The child's social class affects the preparation and motivation for academic achievement. Children from middle-class families typically obtain higher grades in school than children of working or lower-class families because different value systems and practices are promoted by families from varied social class backgrounds.

The patterns of socialization used by parents also influence the child's personality. Baumrind suggests that parents could be classified as authoritative, authoritarian, or permissive. More competent and mature preschool children usually have authoritative parents who were nurturant but made maturity demands. Moderately self-reliant children who were a bit withdrawn have authoritarian parents who more often relied on coercive discipline. The least mature children have overly permissive parents who are nurturant but lack discipline.

For Further Study

Books

Ainsworth, M. B. S., M. C. Blehar, E. Waters, and S. Wall. *Patterns of Attachment*. Hillsdale, NJ: L. Erlbaum, 1978.

Bowlby, J. *Attachment*. New York: Basic Books, 1969.

———. *Separation: Anxiety and Anger.* New York: Basic Books, 1973.

———. *Loss: Sadness and Depression.* New York: Basic Books, 1980.

Erikson, E. H. *Childhood and Society.* New York: W. W. Norton, 1963.

Kagan, J. *Birth to Maturity.* New York: Wiley, 1962.

———. *Galen's Prophecy.* New York: Basic Books, 1994.

———. *The Nature of the Child.* rev. ed. New York: Basic Books, 1994.

Rothbart, M. K. "Temperament in Childhood." n G. A. Kohnstamm, J. E. Bates, and M. K. Rothbart, eds. *Temperament in Childhood.* New York: Wiley, 1989, pp. 59–73.

Thomas, A. and S. Chess. *Temperament and Development.* New York: Brunner Mazel, 1977.

—Jerome Kagan, Ph.D.
Harvard University

Pertussis

A serious, highly contagious disease caused by bacteria, for which there is a vaccine available.

Pertussis, or whooping cough, is a highly contagious disease caused by airborne bacteria. Pertussis is rarely seen in countries where **immunization** is widespread; however, prior to the availability of the vaccine, hundreds of thousands of cases of pertussis were reported in the United States each year. The name pertussis comes from the pertussis bacteria, which are spread when an infected person coughs, sneezes, or simply talks. Pertussis attacks the breathing passages, producing inflammation in the bronchial passages and narrowing the airways. Violent coughing and choking that interfere with eating, drinking, and in severe cases, breathing are the primary symptoms. The illness got its nickname—whooping cough—from the gasping deep breaths the pertussis patient takes between coughing episodes. Pertussis infections begin with symptoms similar to the common cold, but progress in a week or two, with the coughing becoming severe. A pediatrician should be consulted if pertussis symptoms appear. Pertussis should be suspected if the child is a young infant and has not been immunized. The symptoms persist for several weeks, contributing to the seriousness of the disease. Nearly 75% of pertussis cases reported worldwide are in children; half of those children affected will require hospitalization.

The pertussis vaccine (the "P" in DTP vaccine) has been the subject of great controversy because it had been linked to side effects ranging from mild to serious, including irritability, **seizures**, **fever**, and brain damage. The **American Academy of Pediatrics** urges all parents of healthy, normally developing infants and children to continue with the full course of immunizations despite the

very slight risk of serious side effects. The risk associated with the pertussis infection is much greater; one child in every thousand who contract pertussis dies. Some developed countries stopped giving the pertussis vaccine when the study results were first made public, and the incidence of pertussis has increased dramatically in those areas.

For Further Study

Organizations

National Institute of Allergy and Infectious Diseases (NIAID)
 Address: 9000 Rockville Pike
 NIH Building 31, Room 7A50
 Bethesda, MD 20892-2520
 Telephone: (301) 496-5717
 (Arm of the National Institutes of Health that deals with allergies and diseases.)

National Vaccine Information Center
 Address: 128 Branch Road
 Vienna, VA 22180

Pervasive Developmental Disorder (PDD)

A group of conditions involving serious impairment in several areas of development, including physical, behavioral, cognitive, social, and language development.

The incidence of pervasive development disorders (PDDs) in the general population is estimated at 1%. These disorders are thought to be genetically based, and there is no evidence linking them to environmental factors. Many children who are diagnosed with PDDs today would have been labeled psychotic or schizophrenic in the past. The most serious form of pervasive developmental disorder is **autism,** a congenital condition characterized by severely impaired social interaction, communication, and abstract thought, and often manifested by stereotyped and repetitive behavior patterns.

In addition to autism, several other conditions are considered pervasive developmental disorders by the **American Psychiatric Association.** Rett's disorder is characterized by physical, mental, and social impairment that appears between the ages of five months and four years in children whose development has been normal up to that point. Occurring only in girls, it involves impairment of coordination, repetitive movements, a slowing of head growth, and severe or profound **mental retardation,** as well as impaired social and communication skills. Childhood disintegrative disorder is marked by the deterioration of previously acquired physical, social, and communication skills after at least two years of normal development. It first appears between the ages of two and 10, usually at three or four years of age, and many of its symptoms resemble those of autism. Other names for this disorder are Heller's syndrome, dementia infantilis, and disintegrative psychosis. It sometimes appears in conjunction with a medical condition such as Schilder's disease, but usually no organic cause can be found.

Asperger's disorder includes many of the same social and behavioral impairments as autism, except for difficulties with language. Children with this disorder lack normal tools of social interaction, such as the ability to meet someone else's gaze, use appropriate body language and gestures, or react to another person's thoughts and feelings. Behavioral impairments include the repetitive, stereotyped motions and rigid adherence to routines that are characteristic of autism. Like childhood disintegrative disorder, Asperger's disorder is thought to be more common in males than females.

Research based on autopsies and magnetic resonance imaging (MRI) of live patients shows that PDDs are connected with specific abnormalities in the brain. These conditions are usually evident in early childhood and often cause some degree of mental retardation. They are not curable, but there are a variety of treatments that can alleviate specific symptoms and help children function better in daily life. Drugs like Prozac, Zoloft, and Luvox, all selective serotonin reuptake inhibitors (SSRIs), can reduce aggression and repetitive thoughts and improve social interaction. Attention problems and hyperactivity respond to psychostimulants, such as Ritalin, Dexedrine, and Cylert, which can make children more responsive to other types of intervention. **Behavior therapy** has helped children with PDDs minimize negative behavior, such as repetitive activities and persistent preoccupations, and group therapy has helped improve social skills.

Education is an important component in the treatment of PDDs. **Special education** programs that address all types of developmental problems—social, linguistic, and behavioral—are mandated by federal law and available to children from the ages of four or five. Even those children with PDDs who can be enrolled in regular classes can benefit from supplemental special instruction programs. Speech, language, and occupational therapy can help children with PDDs, including autism, function at the highest level possible. In many cases, appropriate education and therapy from the earliest age can save these children from institutionalization.

For Further Study

Books

Haskell, Simon H. *The Education of Children with Motor and Neurological Disabilities.* New York: Nichols, 1989.

Lewis, Vicky. *Development and Handicap.* New York: B. Blackwell, 1987.

Organizations

American Academy of Child and Adolescent Psychiatry
    Address: 3615 Wisconsin Avenue NW
    Washington, DC20016-7300
    Telephone: toll-free (800) 333-7636; (202) 966-7300
Federation of Families for Children Mental Health
    Address: 1021 Prince St.
    Alexandria, VA22314-2971
    Telephone: (703) 684-7710

Phenotype

Describes the observable traits resulting from the underlying genetic makeup of the individual.

Phenotype and **genotype** are companion terms that describe an individual's genetic makeup. The genotype is the complete description of an individual's genetic traits. The phenotype describes the outcome of the genotype, but may not always reveal the complete genotype. For example, the gene for blue eyes is recessive—both mother and father must contribute the gene for blue eyes to the child's genotype for the child to exhibit blue eyes in his or her phenotype. The child may have a recessive gene for blue eyes in his genotype, while having brown eyes in his phenotype. The differences in genotype (the underlying genetic makeup) and phenotype (the expression of the genetic makeup) are important in diagnosing and intervening in genetically transmitted diseases or syndromes caused by recessive genes.

See also **Genotype**

Phenylketonuria (PKU)

An inherited metabolic disease caused by a defect in the liver enzyme that prevents the conversion of the protein called phenylalanine into a useful form.

In phenylketonuria (PKU), a defect in the liver enzyme prevents the conversion of the protein called phenylalanine into a useful form. Instead, the phenylalanine builds up in the bloodstream and hampers normal brain development. If left untreated, a child with PKU will suffer **mental retardation** by the end of his or her first year, with the first signs of intellectual delay exhibited by six or seven months of age. Walking and talking are delayed; in some cases the child never accomplishes either. The retardation worsens until the age of six when brain growth is typically complete. One-third of untreated PKU children will suffer **seizures.**

Throughout most of the United States, a Guthrie PKU test is required for all newborns. It is conducted on blood pricked from the baby's heel. If a particular hospital does not routinely conduct this test, parents should request that their child be tested. One in every 16,000 infants is born with PKU. The incidence is highest among those of northern European descent; the lowest incidence occurs among those of Jewish, Asian, or African descents. The disease is equally distributed among boys and girls.

PKU is treated by a low-protein diet. Inattention to the dietary restrictions can result in behavioral disturbances and/or **learning disabilities**. The newborn diagnosed with PKU is immediately placed on a low-protein milk substitute. Recent studies suggest that PKU babies can be fed a controlled amount of breast milk. Once the child is ready for solid foods, the diet is primarily vegetarian. Meat, fish, poultry, eggs, and cheeses are prohibited. Protein substitutes are now available for peanut butter, breads, and breakfast foods such as waffles and pancakes. As yet, most private health insurance plans and public health programs do not reimburse for these protein substitutes with the exception of infant formula.

Affected children usually visit a PKU clinic every two to four months for a physical, a blood test, and a diet adjustment, if necessary. When the child enters school, adherence to the diet can be frustrating for both the parents and the child. Parents should involve the child in devising the food he or she wants in a way that fits the dietary restrictions. For example, hamburgers can be made with a low-protein mushroom mixture in the place of beef.

Medical experts differ on their recommendations for how long the low-protein diet is necessary. Some believe that once the myelin coating of the brain is complete at about five years of age, a regular diet is safe. Others recommend that the diet be followed throughout life. Many children shed the diet when they reach their teens. However, women of child-bearing age who are planning to become pregnant should maintain a low-protein diet. The high level of phenylalanine in their bloodstreams could have serious consequences for their unborn children. Although the recessive hereditary nature of the disease will prevent the child from having PKU, he or she is at high risk for mental retardation, **microcephaly** (an abnormally small head), low birth weight, and congenital heart disease if the mother does not regulate her protein intake.

One out of every 50 adults is a PKU carrier. Genetic testing can determine if the prospective parents are carriers. A prenatal PKU test is currently under development.

For Further Study

Periodicals

Magol, Marsha. "Food for Thought: Helping Your Child on a Special Diet Eat Right." *The Exceptional Parent* 25, August 1995, no. 8, p. 52.

Organizations

National PKU News
  Address: 6869 Woodlawn Avenue, NE, No. 111
  Seattle, WA98115
  Telephone: (206) 525-8140
Children's PKU Network
  Address: 10515 Vista Sorrento Parkway
  San Diego, CA92121
  Telephone: (619) 587-9421
  FAX: (619) 450-5034
National Phenylketonuria Foundation
  Address: 6301 Tejas Drive
  Pasadena, TX77503
  Telephone: (713) 487-4802

Phobia/Phobic Disorder

An intense, irrational, persistent fear that interferes with normal functioning or creates significant distress.

Ordinary **fears** are a normal part of childhood and can actually help children work through certain developmental issues. Universal fears in infancy include fear of strangers and of loud noises. Fear of certain animals is common between the ages of two and three, and subsequent years often bring fears of imaginary creatures (such as monsters under the bed) and of the dark. However, when fears cause a child to repeatedly avoid certain situations or when they persist for an unusually long time or occur at an inappropriate age, they are considered to be phobias. For clinical diagnosis of a phobia in a child or adolescent, the fear must persist for a period of at least six months. While adults with phobias are aware that their fears are exaggerated and unfounded, this is not always the case with children.

Phobias are the most common anxiety disorder in the United States, affecting an estimated 5–12% of the population. They can have a variety of possible causes. Some children have anxious **temperaments** that make them prone to develop phobias even when there is no discernible external cause, a fact that today's researchers and clinicians often view in terms of brain chemistry. Debilitating fears can also be learned. It is easy for parents to pass on their own fears to their children: parents who fear airplanes or thunderstorms often have children who do, too. Fear can also be directly learned through a traumatic incident: a child who has been bitten by a dog may come to fear all dogs.

There are many kinds of phobias. Specific phobias (formerly called simple phobias) involve a particular object, situation, or activity. These phobias fall into several categories: animal phobia (often involving dogs, snakes, or insects); blood-injection-injury phobia (fear of injections or of injuries that cause bleeding); situational phobia (fear of a particular closed-in space, such as an elevator or airplane); and natural environment phobia (fear of a natural setting or phenomenon, such as heights, storms, and water). Animal phobias usually begin in childhood, while blood-injection-injury phobias usually have their onset in adolescence or early adulthood. The average onset age for situational and environmental phobias tends to peak in childhood, subside, and then peak again in the mid-20s. As diverse as they are, specific phobias have certain elements in common; people affected by them experience intense anxiety when they have to confront the feared object or experience. The closer they are to it in space or time, and the slimmer the potential for escape, the stronger the anxiety. Their fear is strong enough to have physiological manifestations, including sweating, rapid or difficult breathing, and a racing heartbeat. Phobic persons will go to great pains to avoid the source of their discomfort and anxiety.

In addition to specific phobias, the other type of phobia that affects children is social phobia (also called social anxiety disorder), fear of social situations because of an irrational dread of embarrassing oneself. The phobia may be generalized, extending to all social interactions, or limited to specific situations. Often, the feared situation involves some type of performance, such as playing music or speaking in public. Some persons develop a phobia about performing certain commonplace activities, including eating and writing, when others are present; even using a public lavatory may become a cause of apprehension. The exaggerated fear of humiliating oneself by doing something stupid or embarrassing is so strong that it can make people afraid to take part in the most ordinary social exchange. As with specific phobias, persons with social phobia suffer anxiety severe enough to generate physical symptoms and often cope by avoiding the source of the anxiety (although this option is generally less available to children than to adults—often they have no choice and simply have to suffer through an anxiety-producing situation, whether it be a competition, music recital, or simply day-to-day school attendance.) The most widespread form of social phobia is fear of public speaking, followed by fear of dealing with strangers. Other types of fears, such as the fear of eating in front of strangers, are less common. Social phobia usually begins in adolescence, often preceded by a childhood history of **shyness**. While the shyness may have been manageable earlier in life, the increased social demands and stresses that beset even the average teenager can lead to phobia in those whose social skills were fragile to begin with. True social phobia, as opposed to mere shyness, is quite rare in young people, affecting only about 1% of children and adolescents.

Agoraphobia—the fear of being separated from a safe place or trusted person, or of being trapped in a place or situation from which a person fears it would be difficult to escape—is not a phobia of childhood or adolescence, except when it occurs in conjunction with panic disorder, which is itself rare in these age groups (it is thought to affect about 0.6% of high school students). The central feature of agoraphobia with panic disorder is avoidance of situations because it is feared they will bring on a panic attack (an episode of acute anxiety in which people experience an uncontrollable sense of impending disaster, often fearing that they are going to die or lose their minds). Physical symptoms include dizziness, nausea, a pounding heart, hyperventilation, and profuse sweating. A hallmark of panic disorder is fear of future attacks, and a person who has panic disorder with agoraphobia generally avoids public places that draw crowds, such as malls, theaters, and restaurants, fearing that escape in the event of an attack will be both difficult and embarrassing.

The most popular and effective treatment for phobias is **behavior therapy**, which approaches the phobia as an undesirable behavior to be unlearned. Most often it takes the form of systematic desensitization, a technique by which the phobic person is exposed to the feared stimulus in an extremely mild form and then with gradually increasing degrees of intensity. For example, a child who fears dogs may first be asked to look at pictures of dogs, then perhaps play with a stuffed dog or view a dog from afar, ultimately getting to the point when she is able to pet and play with dogs up close. Phobias also respond to treatment by medication, including anti-anxiety drugs such as Xanax and BuSpar and selective serotonin reuptake inhibitors (SSRIs), such as Prozac and Zoloft. Medication is especially helpful for social phobia, where it can help the child overcome her aversion to social interaction sufficiently to work with a therapist. When agoraphobia accompanies panic attacks, it also responds to cognitive-behavioral treatment for panic disorder, often in conjunction with anti-anxiety and anti-depressant medications similar to those prescribed for other phobias.

For Further Study

Books

Gold, M. S. *The Good News About Panic, Anxiety, and Phobias.* New York: Bantam Books, 1989.

Hecker, J. E., and G. L. Thorpe. *Agoraphobia and Panic: A Guide to Psychological Treatment.* Needham Heights, MA: Allyn and Bacon, 1992.

Peurifoy, Reneau. *Anxiety, Phobias, and Panic: Taking Charge and Conquering Fear,* 2nd ed. Citrus Heights, CA: LifeSkills Publications, 1992.

Markway, B. G., et. al. *Dying of Embarrassment: Help for Social Anxiety and Phobias.* Oakland, CA: New Harbinger Publications, 1992.

Ross, Jerilyn. *Triumph Over Fear.* New York: Bantam Books, 1994.

Phonics

A method of teaching beginners to read and pronounce words by having them relate letters to sounds.

Phonics is generally thought of as the traditional method of teaching someone how to read. Throughout the 20th century, its popularity has periodically risen and declined, but it has never been abandoned altogether. There are two main ways of incorporating phonics into the **reading** curriculum: the synthetic and analytic approaches. With the synthetic approach, children learn the 44 basic sounds that can be produced by the 26 letters of the English alphabet, and vocabulary words are only introduced when all the letter sounds have been mastered. Students are taught to sound out unfamiliar words one letter at a time based on their sounds. With the analytic method, students first acquire a basic vocabulary of words they know by sight and then study the relationships of letters and sounds by analyzing how they operate within these words.

Phonics is generally taught by dictation and drills and by testing students on their ability to spell individual words accurately. It relies on both visual and auditory memory, independent of meaning (which is used as one of the chief arguments against this method). Because auditory discrimination is so important in phonics, ear training, often in the form of listening games, is generally part of phonics programs. The various phonetic elements (long and short vowels and consonants) are introduced one at a time, often accompanied by keywords that reinforce memorization of each sound (such as "apple" for the short *a*). Another common technique in phonetics instruction is the use of word families (also called phonograms), a group of words that share a common beginning, middle, or ending sound (such as *all, ball, call,* etc.).

Phonics has been used universally throughout history to teach reading in languages that have alphabets. Formal phonics instruction was first introduced into school systems in the United States at the end of the 19th centu-

ry, eventually replacing the rote alphabet memorization that had prevailed before that time. A synthetic approach was employed, and diacritical marks over, through, or under letters were used to indicate long and short vowel sounds, silent letters, and other sounds. One popular practice was teaching long words by encouraging students to find familiar shorter words inside them.

After its introduction, phonics rapidly became the dominant mode of reading instruction and flourished until the 1920s, when it fell into disfavor. By that time, the "look-say" method of instruction (also called "see and say" or "whole word") based on memorizing whole words by sight had been adopted by a number of private schools and was rapidly gaining popularity in the most prestigious teacher-training institutions, including Columbia University and the University of Chicago. In 1929, the *Dick and Jane* readers, based on the new methods, were developed by Scott Foresman. In the succeeding years, other major educational publishers followed suit. By the 1930s, the whole word approach to reading had become the dominant system throughout the nation and it remained so until the early 1960s. Students read stories which gradually built up a vocabulary of words they could recognize on sight. By the end of each grade level, they were expected to be familiar with a specified number of words. In contrast to the synthetic phonics approach, comprehension and interpretation were part of the reading program from the beginning, and phonics drills in isolation from the reading of sentences or stories were discouraged.

In the 1950s, reading educators underwent a period of reassessment touched off by the 1955 publication of Rudolf Flesch's best-selling *Why Johnny Can't Read.* Arguing that reading competence among the nation's children and adults had suffered a serious decline, Flesch blamed the whole-word teaching method, advocating a return to synthetic phonics. The professional turmoil of the late 1950s and early 1960s produced a plethora of new theories and reading methods, including new phonics programs, methods based on linguistics, individualized reading instruction, the Language Experience approach, and a renewed interest in the **Montessori method** of teaching reading. Phonics was often introduced into the curriculum earlier and more directly than in the preceding decades and received more attention than it had in preceding years.

In the 1970s, instructional emphasis began shifting toward what would eventually become known as the **whole-language** approach, which advocated teaching reading in a literary context by using stories and poems that would interest and motivate youngsters and (in many cases) by downplaying the mechanical rote teaching of phonics. The 1990s has seen a renewed interest in phonics instruction, as parents and educators worry about declining reading abilities and test scores. However, many experts have supported a balanced approach that combines phonics with more holistic comprehension-based methods.

For Further Study

Books

Chall, Jeanne. *Learning to Read: The Great Debate.* New York: McGraw-Hill, 1983.

Fields, Harriette. *Phonics for the New Reader: Step-by-Step.* Firestone, CO: Words Publishing, 1991.

Flesch, Rudolf. *Why Johnny Can't Read—And What You Can Do About It.* New York: Harper & Row, 1955.

——— . *Why Johnny Still Can't Read: A New Look at the Scandal of Our Schools.* New York: Harper & Row, 1981.

McCuen, Gary E. *Illiteracy in America.* Hudson, WI: GEM Publications, 1988.

Vail, Priscilla L. *Common Ground: Whole Language and Phonics Working Together.* Rosemont, NJ: Modern Learning Press, 1991.

Organizations

Reading Reform Foundation
Address: 7054 East Indian School
Scottsdale, AZ 85251
Telephone: (602) 946-3567
(Organization interested in promoting use of phonics in teaching of reading.)

Jean Piaget

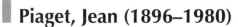

Piaget, Jean (1896–1980)

French psychologist, philosopher, and naturalist.

Jean Piaget is universally known for his studies of the development of **intelligence** in children. Although he is one of the creators of **child psychology** as it exists today, psychology was for him only a tool of epistemology (the theory of knowledge). He identified his domain as "genetic [i.e., developmental] epistemology." He thus studied the growth of children's capacity to think in abstract, logical terms, and of such categories as time, space, number, causality, and permanency, describing an invariable sequence of stages from birth through adolescence. A prolific author, he wrote over fifty books and hundreds of articles.

Piaget was born in 1896 in the French-speaking Swiss city of Neuchâtel, the son of an agnostic medievalist and a religious mother with socialist leanings. After completing a doctoral thesis in natural sciences (1918), and studies in psychology and philosophy in Zurich and Paris, he joined the Rousseau Institute of Geneva in 1921, which was founded by Edouard Claparède as a center for research on child development and education. He later taught experimental and **developmental psychology,** sociology, and history and philosophy of sciences, mainly at the University of Geneva. Piaget died in 1980. His interdisciplinary

International Center for Genetic Epistemology (established in 1955) closed in 1984.

As an adolescent, Piaget published numerous papers on the classification of mollusks. During World War I, he was active in socialist and Christian student groups, and sketched a theory of organic, psychological, and social phenomena aimed at providing a scientific basis for postwar reconstruction. Much of his later thinking built directly on his youthful speculations and values, but its empirical impetus derived from his own reaction against the metaphysical and mystical tendencies of his adolescence.

Piaget devised a "clinical method" that combined standard intelligence tests and open-ended conversations with school-age children. In his first five books, he studied children's language, reasoning, conceptions of the world, theories of causality, and moral judgment. He found that children are at first "egocentric" (incapable of taking another person's point of view) and attached to concrete appearances, but that they gradually move away from egocentrism and become capable of abstract thinking. Piaget's observations of his own children led to *The Origins of Intelligence* (1952) and *The Construction of Reality* (1954), where he describes how basic forms of intentionality, and of the categories of object, space, causality, and time evolve between the onset of the newborn's reflex activities and the emergence of language at

PLASTIC SURGERIES PERFORMED ON PATIENTS UNDER AGE 18 IN 1996		
Procedure	Total number	Percentage of patients (all ages)
Breast augmentation	1,172	1%
Breast reduction in males	1,319	22%
Ear surgery	2,470	34%
Nose reshaping	4,313	9%

about 18 months; *Play, Dreams, and Imitation* (1951), deals with the development of mental representation up to the age of six. In these three classics, Piaget expounded the notion of intelligence as a form of adaptation to the external world. Starting in the 1940s, Piaget and Bärbel Inhelder studied the development of logical and formal thought in various fields (conceptions of movement, speed, time, space, geometry, chance, and probability). One of his major works, *Introduction to Genetic Epistemology* (1950), remains untranslated.

Piaget and his collaborators created many original and ingenious problem-solving situations that became paradigms for research all of the world. In one famous experiment, children sat facing a scale model of three mountains and were asked to choose from a series of pictures the one that represents the mountains as seen by a doll sitting at other positions. Younger subjects systematically identified the doll's viewpoint with their own. Studies of "conservation" provide further notable examples: the child is presented with two identical balls of clay; the shape of one is modified, and the child is asked whether the amount, weight, or volume of clay has changed. Other situations involve manipulating blocks or pouring identical quantities of liquid in differently shaped containers.

Most of the research Piaget inspired is disconnected from the theoretical goals of genetic epistemology. His work had some direct impact on mathematical and moral education, and reinforced the belief that instruction must be adapted to the child's developmental level. But it is Piaget's investigative techniques, formulation of new problems, insightful observations, and emphasis on the development of cognitive capacities that form some of the bases of contemporary child psychology.

For Further Study

Books

Boden, M. *Jean Piaget*. Penguin Books, 1979.

Gruber, H., and J. Voneche, eds. *The Essential Piaget*. New York: Basic Books, 1977.

Piaget, J. *Genetic Epistemology*. Trans. E. Duckworth. New York: Norton, 1970.

Vidal, F. *Piaget Before Piaget*. Cambridge: Harvard University Press, 1994.

Plastic Surgery

Applications of plastic surgery in pediatrics have focused primarily on the correction of congenital deformities and repairing damage from traumatic injuries. To make plastic surgery (or any surgery) less risky for infants and young children, researchers have experimented with new techniques of **anesthesia.** In addition, plastic surgeons have sought to develop better techniques for the treatment and repair of skin damage resulting from burns, and improved techniques for the repair of congenital deformities of the hand and craniofacial reconstruction for repair of **cleft lip** and **palate,** one of the most common plastic surgeries for babies, children, and adolescents

A relatively small percentage of plastic surgery procedures are performed on patients under 18 for cosmetic purposes. These procedures include otoplasty (correcting prominent ears) and rhinoplasty (reshaping the nose); and breast augmentation and breast reduction. Data from the American Society of Plastic and Reconstructive Surgeons on cosmetic procedures performed on patients under age 18 are shown in the accompanying table..

For Further Study

Books

Hayes, Harry, ed. *An Anthology of Plastic Surgery*. Rockville, MD: Aspen Publishers, 1986.

Smith, James D., and Robert M. Bumsted, eds. *Pediatric Facial Plastic and Reconstructive Surgery*. Arlington Heights, IL: Lippincott-Raven, 1993.

Periodicals

"Local Heroes." *Time* 147, June 3, 1996, p. 20.

Richard, M.E. "Common Pediatric Craniofacial Reconstructions." *Nurse Clinician in North America* 29, December 1994, pp. 791–99. .

Sadove, A.M., and B.L. Eppley. "Pediatric Plastic Surgery." *Clinical Plastic Surgery* 23, January 1996, pp. 139–55.

Organizations

American Society of Plastic and Reconstructive Surgeons
Address: 444 East Algonquin Road
Arlington Hts., IL 60005
Telephone: (847) 228-9900
FAX: (847) 228-9131

Poisons and Toxins

Substances that cause illness or death in living things.

A poison is a chemical that causes some dysfunction, or toxic reaction, in a person or other living thing. By definition, a toxin is a poisonous chemical of biological origin, produced by a microorganism, plant, or animal. In common usage, however, the words poison and toxin are often used interchangeably. The study of poisons is called toxicology.

Individuals differ in their tolerance of potentially toxic chemicals, and children are much more sensitive to poisons than adults. Individuals who are extremely sensitive to poisoning by a particular chemical are said to be hypersensitive to that chemical. People are exposed daily to potentially toxic chemicals in the environment through food, medicine, water, and the atmosphere.

Toxicity

All chemicals have the potential to be toxic when the dose (or exposure) is large enough to affect the functioning of the organism. The Swiss physician and alchemist Paracelsus (1493–1541) wrote, "Dosage alone determines poisoning." Exposure to poisoning may be by ingesting (swallowing), inhaling, or injecting the substance; the poison may also be absorbed through the skin. Even benign household products can be toxic in large doses, especially to children. Smaller exposures to chemicals may be referred to as contamination, while larger exposures are referred to as poisoning; in an environmental context, the term pollution is used to describe the presence of chemicals.

Acute toxicity

Biochemical responses to exposure to chemicals range from mild irritation to loss of function, tissue damage, or death. When there is obvious tissue damage, illness, or death after a short-term exposure to a large dose of some chemical, the condition is referred to as acute toxicity. One index of acute toxicity is known as the LD_{50}, which is based on the dose of chemical that is required to kill one-half of a laboratory population of organisms during a short-term, controlled exposure. Even seemingly harmless substances—such as table sugar—can be toxic in high doses.

Some examples of acute toxicity levels for laboratory rats (measured in milligrams [mg] of chemical per kilogram [kg] of body weight) are shown in the table below

Chronic toxicity

When toxic effects of chemicals develop after a longer period of exposure to smaller concentrations than are required to cause acute poisoning, they are referred to as chronic toxicity. In humans, chronic toxicity may take the form of increased rate of **birth defects** and spontaneous **abortions** (miscarriages), **cancer,** and organ damage. Because of their relatively indeterminate nature and long-term lags in development, chronic toxicities are much more difficult to diagnose than acute toxicities.:

ACUTE TOXICITY LEVELS	
sucrose (table sugar)	30,000 mg/kg
ethanol (drinking alcohol)	13,700 mg/kg
glyphosate (a herbicide)	4,300 mg/kg
sodium chloride (table salt)	3,750 mg/kg
acetylsalicylic acid (aspirin)	1,700 mg/kg

Poisoning potential

In the home

For children, household chemicals pose the greatest threat for poisoning. Substances such as art supplies; cleaning and laundry products; cosmetics, medications, and vitamin supplements; and garden and automotive chemicals are all potentially hazardous, especially to young children.

In the environment

Many poisonous chemicals—such as metals and other elements—are present naturally in the environment, causing natural "pollution" in areas where minerals containing toxic elements, such as copper, lead, selenium, or arsenic are concentrated. The soil may contaminate plant material in areas, such as the semi-arid regions of the western United States, where the soil contains high concentrations of selenium. This element is absorbed by plants, causing them to become extremely poisonous to cattle that might eat their toxic foliage.

Other naturally occurring toxins are biochemicals that are synthesized by plants and animals as part of their system of defenses. Some of the most toxic chemicals known to science, such as tetrodotoxin, synthesized by the Japanese globe fish *(Spheroides rubripes),* occur in nature. Other examples of deadly biochemicals are snake and bee venoms and mushroom poisons.

See also **Lead Poisoning**

For Further Study

Books

Freedman, B. *Environmental Ecology.* 2nd ed. San Diego: Academic Press, 1995.

Klaassen, C., M. Amdur, and J. Doull. *Cassarett and Doull's Toxicology: The Basic Science of Poisons.* 4th ed. Boston: Little, Brown, 1991.

Lerner, Carol. *Dumb Cane and Daffodils: Poisonous Plants in the House and Garden.* New York: Morrow Junior Books, 1990.

Smith, R. P. *A Primer of Environmental Toxicology.* Philadelphia: Lea & Febiger, 1992.

Periodicals

Castleman, Michael. "What Is This Stuff?" *Sierra,* January–February 1995, vol. 80, no. 1, pp. 23+.

Israeloff, Roberta. "The Poison-Control Crisis." *Parents Magazine,* September 1995, vol. 70, no. 9, pp. 40+.

Jones, Laurie. "Federal Antidote? Stable Funding Needed to Keep Centers Running." *American Medical News,* November 14, 1994, vol. 37, no. 42, pp. 3+.

Organizations

Agency for Toxic Substances and Disease Registry
    Address: Public Affairs Office
    1600 Clifton Rd.
    Atlanta, GA 30333
    Telephone: (404) 639-0501

American Association of Poison Control Centers
    Address: 3201 New Mexico Avenue, NW, Suite 310
    Washington, DC 20016
    Telephone: (202) 362-7217

Art Hazards Information Center
    Address: Center for Safety in the Arts
    Five Beekman Street
    New York, NY10038
    Telephone: (212) 227-6220

Food and Drug Administration
    Address: Poison Prevention Materials (HFE-88)
    Rockville, MD 20857
    website: http://www.fda.gov

National Toxicity Program
    Address: National Institute of Environmental Health Sciences
    P.O. Box 12233, Mail Stop A0-02

Research Triangle Park, NC27709
Telephone: (919) 541-4482

Poliomyelitis

A serious disease, caused by a virus, that has become extremely rare because of widespread availability of vaccines developed in the 1950s.

Poliomyelitis, commonly known as polio, is a severe disease caused by an airborne virus that is spread from person to person through coughs, sneezes, or simply talking. In mild cases, the person experiences fever, sore throat, nausea, and pain and stiffness in the spine and legs. In more severe cases, known as paralytic polio, the disease can cause paralysis of some muscles of the body, and can cause death it its most serious cases. About half the individuals with paralytic polio suffer some permanent effects, such as lack of mobility, from the disease. Fortunately, the incidence of polio has become rare since vaccines became widely available in the 1950s. The most common vaccine in use in the late 1990s is the oral, live-virus vaccine, referred to as Oral Polio Vaccine (OPV) or Sabin Oral Vaccine. The advantages of OPV are that it provides a strong, permanent immunity to polio, and can be painlessly administered orally. An alternate vaccine is the inactivated polio vaccine or IPV, developed by Jonas Salk and first available to the public in 1954. The OPV is given by injection in the leg or arm, rather than administered orally, and provides a less vigorous immunity than the OPV.

For Further Study

Organizations

Gazette International Networking Institute (GINI)
    Address: 4502 Maryland Avenue
    St. Louis, MO 63108
    Telephone: (314) 361-0475
    (Organization for severely disabled people, such as polio victims, those with spinal cord injuries, and their families and caregivers. Publishes *Polio Network News.*)

March of Dimes Birth Defects Foundation
    Address: 1275 Mamoroneck Avenue
    White Plains, NY 10605
    Telephone: (914) 428-7100
    (Publishes information sheets on specific birth defects and related topics, including *Polio* and *Post Polio Muscle Atrophy.*)

Pregnancy

Period of time from conception to birth.

Pregnancy normally lasts 40 weeks and spans the time from the fertilization of a mother's egg to the **birth**

POISON EMERGENCIES: WHERE TO GET HELP

Poison control centers, located in many larger communities, provide a source of information on the toxicity of household chemicals, cleaning products, medications, garden, and hobby chemicals. The white pages of the local telephone directory will list the area poison control centers, which are typically staffed 24 hours a day, 365 days a year. Poison control centers are nonprofit operations with annual operating costs in the late 1990s estimated to be $111 million. Two studies—one conducted by the National Public Services Research Institute, a nonprofit policy analysis organization, and another by American Association of Poison Control Centers—found that poison control centers saved $7.75 and $8.25, respectively, in medical costs for every $1 spent. Sixty percent of the cases handled involve children under age six.

Poison control phone operators have information on the most common household chemicals, and reference texts and toxicological databases available to enable them to respond quickly to urgent requests for information. A caller to a poison control operator may or may not know the name of the substance that has been ingested. The poison-control operator will categorize the chemical—a lawn fertilizer, for example—and will provide advice based on knowledge of similar chemicals.

Swallowing a toxic substance is a fairly common household emergency, and families are advised to keep the poison control center telephone number near the phone, with other emergency numbers. A recommended treatment for many (but not all) situations where a person—usually a child—has swallowed something toxic is to administer syrup of ipecac to induce vomiting. Poison control experts recommend that all households keep syrup of ipecac on hand for such emergencies.

A division of the Centers for Disease Control and Prevention, the Agency for Toxic Substances and Disease Registry (ATSDR) provides information on toxic chemicals encountered at work or elsewhere in the environment. When the substance can be identified by name, an ATSDR toxicologist can analyze how serious any exposure might be. If the exposure is to an unknown substance, an ATSDR physician will request information on the details of the exposure and a description of any symptoms. ATSDR provides consulting services to poison control centers, investigates alleged contaminated industrial sites and incidents, and maintains a 24-hour hotline.

Another resource is the National Toxicology Program (NTP), a division of the National Institute for Environmental Health Sciences established in the late 1970s to test chemicals for general toxicity; carcinogenicity; reproductive, neurological, and immunological hazards; and other adverse health effects. Federal, state, and local agencies use NTP findings to develop regulations.

POISON CONTROL CENTERS	
Number in United States	75
Cases handled (1996)	2.2 million
Total regionally certified centers (24-hour accessible, highly trained staff, offer community outreach)	48
Percent of Americans with access to regional centers	87%
Percent of poisonings handled by centers that are manageable with telephone guidance	80%
Percent of poisonings handled by centers that involve children younger than 6	53 (1.1 million cases)
Health-care dollars saved for each dollar spent on centers	$8.25

Source: American Association of Poison Control Centers, Health Resources Services Administration, March 1997.

of her child. Pregnancy is divided into three trimesters, each lasting just over 3 months. The first trimester is called the development stage. All fetal organ systems are functioning by the end of this stage. During the second and third trimesters the developing baby is called a **fetus** and will begin growing rapidly in the womb. In the second trimester the heartbeat of the fetus is detectable by an ordinary stethoscope. By the third trimester fetal features are refined and the senses are alert.

During pregnancy a woman may experience fatigue, nausea, increased urination, and bloating, all normal signs that the body has begun the changes of early pregnancy. The fetus is most vulnerable during the organ system development phase of pregnancy. Inadequate diet, exposure to radiation, excessive heat, alcohol, smoke, or viruses increase the risk of genetic defects during this period.

Teenage pregnancy

In the United States pregnancy and birth rates among teenage girls are higher than in any other developing country. The birth rate for young teens (ages 15–17) has been steadily rising. From 1986 to 1991, the rate increased by nearly 30%. In 1991 alone, nearly 4 in 100 girls ages 15–17 had a baby, according to the March of Dimes. Both the short- and long-term impact of teenage pregnancy on mother, child, and society indicate the enormity of this problem. Poverty and teenage pregnancy appear to be directly related. Teenage mothers tend to come from families of lower economic status and become more likely to drop out of school during or after their pregnancy (one in three teen mothers drops out of high school). Infants born to a teenage mother are more likely to be premature or of low birth weight. Frequently these premature babies will suffer **developmental delays** and serious physical problems that will require frequent care. The child of a teenage mother is at greater risk for health problems such as neural tube defects, respiratory distress syndrome, and low birth weight for the following reason: teens are the least likely to get prenatal care, which is important in educating the mother regarding **nutrition**, lifestyle habits, and the prevention of common **birth defects.**

For Further Study

Books

Johnson, Robert., ed. *Mayo Clinic Complete Book of Pregnancy and Baby's First Year.* New York: William Morrow and Co., 1994.

Simkin, P., J. Whalley, and A. Keppler. *Pregnancy, Childbirth, and the Newborn: The Complete Guide.* New York: Meadowbrook Press, 1991.

Premarital Sexual Activity *see* **Adolescence; Sexually Transmitted Diseases**

Premature Birth

A birth that occurs before the 37th week of gestation

A birth that occurs before the 37th week of **pregnancy** is considered premature. Although researchers have long sought a way to prevent premature birth, an estimated 9% of infants are still born prematurely, costing the United States billions of dollars in health care expenditures annually. Neonatal intensive care costs for a premature infant generally range from $20,000 to $100,000, and a single day in a neonatal intensive care unit can cost as much as $3,000. While a direct cause cannot be pinpointed for most premature births, there are a number of known risk factors associated with early delivery. These include multiple **fetuses**, a weak cervix, a difficult pregnancy, fetal abnormalities, maternal infections and other health problems, and poor maternal **nutrition**. Certain maternal behaviors, including **smoking**, drug use, and alcohol consumption, are also known to increase the likelihood of premature birth. Physicians often advise pregnant women to avoid prolonged standing or lifting in order to have a better chance of carrying their babies to term.

Measures currently recommended by the medical community to prevent early labor include frequent prenatal check-ups, good nutrition, and adequate patient education and psychosocial support. Medications can often arrest premature labor by acting on the muscle cells of the uterus to suppress contractions. Even if a premature delivery cannot be averted altogether, it can be delayed. A delay of even 48 hours—even in a birth that may be two or three months premature—can make a significant difference. Within this time frame steroids administered to the mother can speed up development of the immature fetal lungs that pose one of the major health risks for the premature infant. This procedure helps most infants between the ages of 26 and 35 weeks and poses no serious risks to either the mother or the baby. If a combination of bed rest and medication can delay delivery of a 25-week-old fetus by even one week, its chances of survival increase 20 percent.

Premature infants have less body fat and thinner skin than full-term babies, and their skull bones are still soft, giving their heads a flattened appearance. (During delivery, their heads are often protected from vaginal compression and decompression by the use of forceps.) Their grasping, sucking, and gag reflexes are not fully developed (often complicating the feeding process), and their fragile central nervous systems tend to make them hypersensitive to sensory stimuli. Often they are unable to respond to more than one type of stimulus at a time—for example, touch and sound—without becoming overloaded. A premature infant's stage of development corresponds more closely to her gestational age rather than to her age since birth. Not only has she had fewer weeks or months to mature since conception, but there is also evidence that during times of acute danger to an infant's health—such as the period that a fragile newborn spends in neonatal intensive care—the physical maturation process is "put on hold" while the baby uses all her energy to fight for her life. Normal maturation does eventually occur, it just happens later.

Many premature infants require special care in a neonatal intensive care unit (NICU), where their heart function, breathing, blood pressure, and body temperature can be closely monitored, and oxygen, ventilators, and tube feeding are available. With the level of care available in these facilities, infants as young as 25 or 26 weeks can be helped to survive. Women who seem likely to deliver prematurely are often moved to hospitals with such units. NICUs have become more comfortable, welcoming places for both infant and parents than they often were in the past. Most infants are still kept in incubators, clear plastic enclosures that are temperature-controlled to accommodate the babies' need for extra warmth. However, bright lights, noise, and other stimuli are kept to a minimum to accommodate the infants' sensitive nervous systems, and they are handled slowly and gently. Parents are still encouraged to interact with their babies, feeding, changing, and holding them. Many NICUs take steps to further personalize the experience for both parents and hospital staff, such as giving the infants little knit hats with their names on them.

Because their internal organs have not finished developing, premature infants face a number of potential health risks, including a greater susceptibility to infection. The smallest infants (those weighing less than 3 lb, 5 oz at birth) are most likely to develop problems. The immature lungs of premature infants pose the most serious danger, especially the threat of respiratory distress syndrome, in which the air sacs cannot function adequately to exchange oxygen and carbon dioxide and may require oxygen and even a ventilator until they become stronger. **Apnea**, or interrupted breathing, is a common problem among premature infants because the nerve pathways that control breathing are not fully developed. The infants' immature livers also have trouble functioning, often resulting in **jaundice** and requiring special treatment, and an eye problem called retinopathy of prematurity can cause permanent vision impairment. Neurological conditions such as **cerebral palsy** are also a danger for premature babies.

Premature birth can cause significant emotional distress for parents. In addition to their concern over the health of the baby, parents (especially the mother) often experience guilt, feeling that there is something they could have done to prevent the early delivery. However, in spite of the connection between prematurity and

unhealthy maternal behavior such as smoking and drinking, many premature births occur to mothers who maintain good health habits and are in excellent condition throughout their pregnancies. The majority of premature infants become normal, healthy children and adults, although they do remain small for their ages during their first two or three years. In addition, their incidence of **learning disabilities** and **attention deficit/hyperactivity disorder (ADHD)** is higher than that for full-term babies.

For Further Study

Books

Jason, Janine, and Antonia van de Meer. *Parenting Your Premature Baby.* New York: Delta, 1990.

Lieberman, Adrienne B. *The Premie Parents' Handbook: A Lifeline for the New Parents of a Premature Baby.* New York: Dutton, 1984.

Pfister, Fred R., and Bernard Griesemer. *The Littlest Baby: A Handbook for Parents of Premature Children.* Englewood Cliffs, NJ: Prentice-Hall, 1983.

Stirt, Joseph A. *Baby.* Far Hills, NJ: New Horizon Press, 1992.

Organizations

International Childbirth Education Association, Inc.
  Address: P.O. Box 20048
  Minneapolis, MN 55420
  Telephone: (612) 854-8660

Maternal and Child Health Bureau
  Address: Parklawn Building, Room 18-05
  5600 Fishers Lane
  Rockville, MD 20857
  Telephone: (301) 443-2170

Maternity Center Association
  Address: 49 East 92nd Street
  New York, NY 10128
  Telephone: (212) 369-7300

Preschool

An early childhood setting in which children combine learning with play within a comprehensive program run by professionally trained adults.

In spite of the inclusion of the word *school* in *preschool*, preschools have traditionally been more concerned with social skills, emotional maturity, and **cognitive development** than with formal academic schooling. Although children are most commonly enrolled in preschool between the ages of three and five, those as young as two can attend. The term preschool is sometimes used interchangeably with nursery school and child care center. In 1990, 28.8% of three-year-olds and 49.1% of four-year-olds were enrolled in preschool programs, about twice what it had been a generation earlier. Reasons for this dramatic increase include a rise in the number of working mothers, a decline in the size of families (leading more parents to turn to preschools as a social outlet for their children), and a growing desire to give children a head start to help them compete academically later on.

Preschools vary widely in setting, affiliation, format, and educational philosophy. They may offer either all-day or half-day programs, either every day or several days a week. They may be completely independent, affiliated with a school or religious organization, or part of a nationwide chain. So-called lower schools, which are affiliated with private schools, maintain an educational philosophy in accord with the parent institution, although the children they enroll are often as likely to attend public school or even a different private school. A growing number of states have begun funding preschool programs offered at public schools, called pre-kindergarten (or pre-K) programs. They may be administered by the local school board or by an independent contractor paid by the state. Like private school programs, they may run for half a day or a full day. Preschools offered by a day care or child care center are generally all-day programs running from early morning to dinnertime or later to accommodate parents with full-time work schedules. Nursery schools, or play schools, usually offer half-day programs or even more flexible scheduling that allows a child to attend for a time period that the parents select. Cooperative (co-op) preschools are distinguished by the role that parents play. In return for lowered tuition costs, they assist trained teachers in supervising children and perform a variety of other administrative and physical tasks that keep the school going, such as serving on committees, repairing toys, and helping maintain the school building. A final type of preschool setting is **Head Start,** a free federally funded program for "at-risk" three- to five-year-olds from low-income families. These programs, available in all 50 states, are offered in a variety of formats, including both all-day and half-day programs, some of them held at the public school a child will eventually attend. Head Start programs in rural areas may be home based.

Whatever their format, preschools offer parents and children certain typical benefits. Working parents can give young children a level of care that is more stimulating to their social, emotional, physical, and cognitive development than leaving them with a babysitter. Through its structured play activities, a good preschool program can help children develop their **gross** and **fine motor skills,** improve their language and communication abilities, and exercise their **creativity.** Children, especially those with few playmates, can develop valuable social skills, learning to relate to other children their own age and interact in groups, as well as to relate to adults other than their parents. Preschool can promote **self-esteem,**

independence, and a sense of identity. It can also create a positive attitude toward the upcoming school experience.

However, in spite of their potential advantages, preschools are not for everyone, and there are several valid reasons against enrolling a child in one. While most youngsters enrolled in preschool experience a brief period of distress over separation from their parents, **separation anxiety** in some children is acute enough to indicate that they are not yet ready emotionally to make the transition from being looked after by a parent or other individual caregiver. In addition to tolerating separation from parents, three- and four-year-olds who are ready for preschool should be able to dress and feed themselves and express their needs verbally. Also, most programs for children this age expect them to be toilet trained. Preschool can be expensive, and some parents simply cannot afford it. Also, attending a preschool can do more harm than good if it is run by either authoritarian or overly permissive teachers. After investigating preschools in their area, parents may not find any to their liking and conclude that their child is better off being looked after at home and socializing with friends and neighbors.

In the 1980s, many parents began to approach the preschool experience as a form of accelerated education that could give their children a competitive edge by putting them on an academic "fast track." The so-called "hothousing" trend toward providing highly structured, intensive academic programs for preschool children has been decried by many respected child development authorities, including pediatrician and author **T. Berry Brazelton** and David Elkind, author of *The Hurried Child* and *Miseducation.* Critics of academic saturation programs have pointed out that the trend toward turning out "superkids" creates inappropriate expectations relative to the developmental level of most three- and four-year-olds, who cannot truly learn at an elementary-school level. They claim that what appears to be early learning is often little more than rote memorization that does less for children's real intellectual development than less structured traditional play activities that allow them to explore and experiment. Another common criticism is that any lasting academic gains made by hothousing are negligible, especially in light of the emotional stress often created by the pressure these programs place on children.

Parents choosing a preschool for their youngsters need to consider a number of factors in making their decision. If their state or locality has licensing requirements for preschools, they should know whether the facility is licensed. They should inquire about the background of the director and staff. Special training in child development or early-childhood education is more applicable to preschool teaching than experience teaching older children. Questions can also be asked about the age and background of teachers' aides, who spend a substantial amount of time with the children. Knowing the turnover rate of the staff can provide valuable insight into the quality and nature of the facility. The director should be able to describe the overall philosophy of the preschool and tell parents the ratio of teachers to children and the maximum group size for each age level. For two-year-olds, group sizes of between 8 and 10 are recommended, with at least one teacher for every five children. Recommendations for group size range up to 15 (with a teacher for every 7 to 10 children) for three-year-olds, and 20 (with a teacher for every 10 to 12 children) for four-year-olds. It is also appropriate for parents to inquire about a preschool's disciplinary philosophy and practices.

It is universally recommended that parents visit any preschool they are considering while it is in session before deciding to send a child there. The physical environment should be safe, spacious enough for vigorous exercise, and clean (although not perfectly neat). Parents should note whether there is an adequate outdoor play area, either right outside the building or nearby. There should be a good selection of appropriate indoor and outdoor play equipment, including blocks, puzzles, sand, dress-up clothes, and tumbling mats for indoor play and climbing equipment, tricycles, and slides for outdoor play. Parents should also look for signs of ongoing creative and fine-motor activity, including a good supply of crayons, scissors, and paint brushes. The atmosphere of the preschool is also important. Parents should note whether the children are free to be active and enjoy themselves, but also whether it is clear that an adult is in control. Other items that merit attention are quality of food service (if applicable), provisions for medical emergencies, and fire safety.

Many preschools have phase-in programs to help minimize separation anxiety during a child's initial adjustment period. After an introductory parent-and-child visit to the facility, the preschool may have a teacher visit the child at home to help bridge the gulf between home and school and give parent, child, and teacher a chance to get acquainted. Children who are to attend preschool for a full day may go for a short period of an hour or two the first day, and then stay a little longer every succeeding day until the full day is attained. In addition, for the first several days or weeks after school begins, parents are often allowed to stay at the facility for all or part of the time their children are there.

For Further Study

Books

Brenner, Barbara. *The Preschool Handbook: Making the Most of Your Child's Education.* New York: Pantheon Books, 1990.

Church, Ellen Booth. *Everything You Always Wanted to Know about Preschool but Didn't Know Whom to Ask.* New York: Scholastic Books, 1996.

Elkind, David. *Miseducation: Preschoolers at Risk.* New York: Knopf, 1987.

Hechinger, Fred M., ed. *A Better Start: New Choices for Early Learning.* New York: Walker, 1986.

Hendrick, Joanne. *The Whole Child: Developmental Education for the Early Years.* 4th ed. Columbus, OH: Merrill Publishing Co., 1988.

Kagan, Sharon L., and Edward F. Zigler, eds. *Early Schooling: The National Debate.* New Haven: Yale University Press, 1987.

Kuklin, Susan. *Going to My Nursery School.* New York: Bradbury Press, 1990 [juvenile literature].

Organizations

National Association for the Education of Young Children. (NAEYC)
Address: 1834 Connecticut Ave. NW
Washington, DC 20009
Telephone: toll-free (800) 424-2460; (202) 232-8777

Parent Cooperative Preschools International, U.S. Office
Address: P.O. Box 31335
Phoenix, AZ 85046

Privacy, Child's Right to

Laws and guidelines concerning who should have access to a child's privacy.

Privacy is viewed in most democratic societies as a necessary element in the development of healthy, active individuals. The Fourth Amendment to the U.S. Constitution protects "the right of the people to be secure in their persons, houses, papers, and effects, against unreasonable searches and seizures." The amendment allows for search and seizure "upon probable cause, supported by oath or affirmation, and particularly describing the place to be searched, and the persons or things to seized." Many psychologists recognize that privacy is a cornerstone of a free society. In fact, prisons systematically eliminate privacy for their inmates to reinforce the fact that they have lost the privilege of control over their environment.

Children do not begin to understand issues of privacy until around the age of five or six. At this stage until age 10 or 11, parents can establish the atmosphere of mutual trust and communication that will carry the parent-child relationship through the pre-adolescent and adolescent years. Between ages 10 and 12, the pre-adolescent may want to establish his or her independence. Signs of this include a desire to keep his or her bedroom door closed and to seek privacy for telephone conversations, time with friends, and time alone. Parents should avoid challenging this behavior unless they have reason to suspect that the child is engaged in dangerous or destructive activities. However, they should establish clear rules about acceptable activities. Children should understand that if they breach their parents' trust, parents have both the right and the responsibility to challenge their privacy. By trusting the child in the preadolescent years, parents may minimize the chance that their child will become either secretive and rebellious or dependent and lacking in self-esteem.

Parents can also gather information about their children's world without intruding on their privacy by volunteering at their school; getting acquainted with teachers, principals, guidance counselors, and the school nurse; getting to know their children's friends and the friends' parents; and becoming involved in children's extracurricular activities by attending such events as concerts and sports activities. Many school systems routinely contact parents whose children cut classes or are absent. Parents can express their support of such policies and act immediately if the school contacts them about a problem.

Adolescents in the United States are especially sensitive to any actions that they feel may infringe on their privacy rights. In the late 1990s, concerns about access to inappropriate material on the Internet fostered a lively debate among adolescents, library users, parents, and concerned citizens about ways to limit access to pornographic, violent, or subversive material that is available through the Internet. Filters that limit access are especially offensive to adolescents, but libraries continue to seek ways to selectively access Internet sites, just as they selectively build their book, video, and audio collections.

Privacy at school

There are several aspects to privacy at school. Schools must balance their responsibility to maintain a safe, healthy environment for all students against the privacy rights of the individual student. In addition, schools control access to important personal information about their students. Since 1975, a number of legislative actions have been taken by the U.S. Congress, state, and local governments to address these privacy issues.

In 1976, the Family Educational Records Protection Act (FERPA) was passed to guarantee parents free access to their child's school records. FERPA, a federal law, grants the Secretary of Education the right to withhold federal funds from schools that deny parents access to their children's records. The Act provides specific guidelines for access to a student's records. Access is guaranteed to the following: parents; government officials for the purpose of auditing public assistance programs; researchers engaged in data gathering for studies of education, testing, curriculum, or other legitimate inquiry; and school administrators or officials of institutions who have been granted access by students or their parents as part of a college admission or employment application.

Many states have set guidelines for privacy protection and access to student records that often go beyond those established by FERPA. For example, some states allow communications between a student and certain school personnel to be kept confidential, even from parents. Examples might include discussion between a student and the school nurse relating to alcohol or drugs, or between a student and a counselor. Some states have provisions whereby the student or parents can designate information as confidential when communicating with the school, thus preventing access to that portion of the student's portfolio by any other parties. Many states have implemented specific guidelines to allow access to a student's records by both the custodial and non-custodial parent.

Random personal searches and drug testing

Random personal searches and drug testing of students have both been tested in state and federal courts. A court case in Washington state found that school officials must meet only a "reasonable suspicion" standard to justify a search, as distinct from the "probable cause" standard that is constitutionally required of law enforcement officials. Such suspicion must be particular to the individual being searched. U.S. Supreme Court Justice Antonin Scalia, writing for the majority opinion in a case that allowed random drug testing for school athletes, asserted that Fourth Amendment rights are different in public schools because athletes have less expectation of privacy and expose themselves to regulation by joining the team. The push for schools to be able to search and test has not abated, however. By the late 1990s, societal pressures had spurred schools to assume an aggressive strategy in the development of programs to stop violence and the use of alcohol and drugs in schools. School officials must develop reasonable policies in these two areas, since education law no longer provides a clear rule to follow in deciding when student searches and drug testing are permissible. Both sides of the debate on these issues usually agree that reasonable suspicion remains the general guideline.

Privacy protection for minors

The federal government is interested in protecting the privacy of minor children from exploitation by advertising and marketing concerns. Children are attractive consumers to retailers and other marketers. Online services, television, and other emerging media make it easier for marketers to advertise their products and services to children. The Federal Telecommunications Commission (FTC) investigates ways to protect the privacy of online service users, especially the privacy of children. The FTC monitors the techniques used by online marketers to gather and use information about potential customers.

Another aspect of privacy relates to researchers and others gathering information from children to use in studies. This issue became of interest to the U.S. Congress in 1995, when the Family Privacy Protection Act, HR 1271, passed the House of Representatives. Because the bill did not pass the Senate, it had not become law as of this writing. The bill was based on the notion that parents have a fundamental right to choose whether their children participate in research studies. Under the terms of the bill, researchers receiving federal funding would be required to obtain written consent from parents before using minors in studies involving such issues as weight management, tobacco, sexual behavior, illegal or **antisocial behavior,** psychological problems, and alcohol and illegal drug use. Sixteen federal agencies conduct or support research using human subjects. For example, the National Institute on Drug Abuse's "Monitoring the Future" survey obtains data on the substance abuse patterns of 50,000 eighth through tenth graders in 420 schools per year. Researchers opposed the bill, arguing that requirement would impede the federal government's ability to collect vital information. Over 30 leading medical and science advocacy groups, including the **American Psychological Association,** American Public Health Association, and the **American Academy of Pediatrics,** joined together to form the Research and Privacy Coalition to oppose the bill. Although the Family Privacy Protection Act is not law, it does reflect a growing concern among many citizens about who has access to information about minor children.

Both families and society must balance the child's need for privacy and independence against the society's need for order. Parents have the responsibility to supervise their minor children to keep them from harming themselves or others in society, while encouraging them to become independent decision-makers.

For Further Study

Periodicals

Caywood, Carolyn. "YA Confidential." *School Library Journal* 42, August 1996, p. 41.

Goode, Stephen. "Are Privacy Rights Still Inalienable?" *Insight on the News* 12, August 19, 1996, pp. 22+.

Kent, Christina. "New Bill Asks Written Parental Consent for Minors in Studies." *American Medical News* 39, June 17, 1996, pp. 3+.

Ross, Julie Ritzer. "Children's Issues Become Flashpoint in Broader Privacy Debate." *Stores* 78, December 1996, pp. 26+.

Sanchez, J.M. "Expelling the Fourth Amendment from American Schools." *Journal of Law and Education,* Summer 1992, pp. 381–412.

Scalia, Antonin, and Dave Kindred. "Should Schools Have the Right to Randomly Test Athletes for Drug Use?" *CQ Researcher* 5, September 22, 1995, pp. 841.

Service, Robert F. "Bill Threatens Child Survey Research." *Science* 268, May 19, 1995, pp. 967+.

Van Gelder, Lawrence. "Police Use of Yearbooks Draws Protests from the Schools." *The New York Times* 146, March 28, 1997, p. B7.

Warren, Andrea. "Should Parents Spy on Their Kids?" *Ladies Home Journal* 112, November 1995, pp. 114+.

Zirkel. Perry A. "Another Search for Student Rights." *Phi Delta Kappan* 75, May 1994, pp. 728+.

Private Speech

Speech patterns not intended for communication with others; "talking to oneself."

Many young children engage in a rich pattern of speech with **imaginary playmates** or in imagined settings. Researchers have found that certain characteristics of **creativity**—e.g., imagination and problem-solving—are reflected in preschool children's private speech. Studies have revealed that many young children use private speech to provide self-guidance while performing school and play tasks. The results of one study on private speech were presented in 1992 at the meeting of the American Educational Research Association. Twenty children from two kindergarten classrooms (one mixed-age, one same-age) were observed for four weeks, using a time-sampling procedure. Results using statistical analysis indicated private speech use varied in different physical and social situations. For example, children used more self-regulatory private speech when engaged in a specific task, compared to free play. They also used more private speech with what the researchers characterized as "intermediate teacher regulation," compared to very little structure or a great deal of structure. When younger classmates were present, children used more private speech than when they were with their peer group or with older students. Otherwise, the use of private speech did not appear to be influenced by the presence of other children or other adults.

The Russian psychologist Lev Vygotsky studied the relationship between thought and language. Vygotsky believed that children's private speech plays an important role in cognitive development. In his view, private speech allows the child (and older person, as well) to consciously direct the thought process.

Researchers have confirmed that private speech may continue through late adolescence. Teenagers often employ private speech utterances to describe activities they are engaging in or observing, and for self-guidance when confronted with a challenging task.

For Further Study

Periodicals

Behrend, Douglas A., et al. "A New Look at Children's Private Speech: The Effects of Age, Task Difficulty, and Parent Presence." *International Journal of Behavioral Development* 12, September 20, 1989, pp. 305–20.

Berk, Laura E. and Sarah T. Spuhl. "Maternal Interaction, Private Speech, and Task Performance in Preschool Children." *Early Childhood Research Quarterly* 10, June 1995, pp. 145–69.

Daugherty, Martha, and Jenny Logan. "Private Speech Assessment: A Medium for Studying the Cognitive Processes of Young Creative Children." *Early Child Development and Care* 115, January 1996, pp. 7–17.

Daugherty, Martha, et al. "Relationships among Private Speech and Creativity Measurements of Young Children." *Gifted Child Quarterly* 38, Winter 1994, pp. 21–26.

Diaz, Rafael M. and Jean R. Lowe. "The Private Speech of Young Children at Risk: A Test of Three Deficit Hypotheses." *Early Childhood Research Quarterly* 2, June 1987, pp. 181–194.

Duncan, Robert M. "An Examination of Vygotsky's Theory of Children's Private Speech." April 1991. Paper presented at the Biennial Meeting of the Society for Research in Child Development, Seattle, WA, April 18–20, 1991.

Goudena, Paul P. "The Social Nature of Private Speech of Preschoolers during Problem Solving." *International Journal of Behavioral Development* 10, June 1987, pp. 187–206.

Kronk, Carol Marie. "Private Speech in Adolescents." *Adolescence* 29, Winter 1994, pp. 781–804.

Manning, Brenda H., et al. "Young Children's Private Speech as a Precursor to Metacognitive Strategy Use during Task Engagement." *Discourse Processes* 17, March–April 1994, pp. 191–211.

Manning, Brenda H. and Stephen C. White. *Comparisons of Young Children's Private Speech Profiles: Analogical Versus Nonanalogical Reasoners.* A portion of this paper was presented at the Conference on Human Development, Richmond, VA, March 1990.

Smolucha, Larry and Francien Smolucha. "A Vygotskian Perspective on Critical Thinking." Proceedings, 29 November 1989. Paper presented at the Conference on Science and Technology for Education in the 1990s: Soviet and American Perspectives. Meadville, PA, April 6–7, 1989.

Psychoanalysis

A method of treatment for mental, emotional, and behavioral dysfunctions as developed by Sigmund Freud.

Developed in Vienna, Austria, by Sigmund Freud (1856–1939), psychoanalysis is based on an approach in which the therapist helps the patient better understand him- or herself through examination of the deep personal feelings, relationships, and events that have shaped motivations and behavior. Freud developed his theories during the end of the 19th and the early part of the 20th centuries in Vienna, Austria, where he was a practicing physician specializing in neurological disorders. Freud's interest originated in his medical practice when he encountered patients who were clearly suffering physical symptoms for which he could find no organic, or biological, cause. Freud's first attempt to get at the psychological cause of these patient's pain was through hypnosis, which he studied in Paris in 1885. He found the results to be less than he'd hoped, however, and soon borrowed from a Viennese contemporary the idea of getting a patient to simply talk about his or her problems. Freud expanded upon this practice, however, by creating the idea of "free association," in which a patient is encouraged to speak in a non-narrative, non-directed manner, with the hope that he or she will eventually reveal/uncover the unconscious heart of the problem. This sort of unbridled, undirected self-exploration became one of the signature tenets of psychoanalysis.

Continuing his research of the mind and the unconscious, Freud published *The Interpretation of Dreams* in 1900. In this work he outlined his ideas about the construction of the mind and human personality. This book was followed by the now basics of the Freudian canon: *The Psychopathology of Everyday Life* in 1904 and *A Case of Hysteria* and *Three Essays on the Theory of Sexuality,* both in 1905. By the second decade of the 20th century, Freud had become an internationally renowned thinker, and psychoanalysis had emerged as a significant intellectual achievement on par with the work of Albert Einstein in physics and in many ways comparable to the modernist movement in the visual arts. Psychoanalysis was in its prime and it became something of a fad to undergo psychoanalytic treatment among the Western world's elite.

Psychoanalysis and the development of personality

Freud believed that human personality was constructed of three parts: the id, the ego, and the superego. The id, according to this schema, is comprised largely of instinctual drives—for food and sex, for instance. These drives are essentially unconscious and result in satisfaction when they are fulfilled and frustration and anxiety when they are thwarted. The ego is linked to the id, but is the component that has undergone socialization and which recognizes that instant gratification of the id urges is not always possible. The superego acts in many ways like the ego, as a moderator of behavior; but whereas the ego moderates urges based on social constraints, the superego operates as an arbiter of right and wrong. It moderates the id's urges based on a moral code. Having theorized this framework of human personality, Freud used it to demonstrate how instinctual drives are inevitably confounded with strictly social codes (by the ego) and by notions of morality (by the superego). This conflict, psychoanalytic theory supposes, is at the heart of anxiety and neuroses.

In dealing with these conflicts, Freud's psychoanalytic theory suggests that the human mind constructs three forms of adaptive mechanisms: namely, **defense mechanisms**, neurotic symptoms, and dreams. Freud believed dreams were vivid representations of repressed urges: the id speaking out in wildly incongruous nighttime parables. He considered dreams to have two parts, the manifest content, the narrative that one is able to remember upon waking, and the latent content, the underlying, largely symbolic message. Because Freud believed dreams to represent unfulfilled longings of the id, psychoanalysis deals heavily with dream interpretation.

Psychoanalytic theory also sees various neurotic symptoms as symbolic acts representing the repressed longings of the id. For Freud, a neurotic symptom was what we now consider a psychosomatic disorder, some physical symptom that has a psychological, or in Freud's terms, neurological, origin. Psychoanalytic theory suggests that conditions like blindness, paralysis, and severe headaches can result from unfulfilled longings that the patient is unable to confront on a conscious level. Because of this inability, the patient develops some acceptable symptom, such as headaches, for which he or she can then seek medical attention.

The final adaptive mechanism Freud suggested are defense mechanisms. Freud identified several defense mechanisms, such as repression, displacement, denial, rationalization, projection, and identification. Each has its own peculiar dynamic but all work to distance a person from a conflict that is too difficult to confront realistically. These conflicts, according to psychoanalytic theory, originate during one of the four developmental stages Freud identified. These stages, and the infantile sexuality he identified as occurring within them, are some of the most controversial aspects of psychoanalytic theory. Freud suggested that adult neuroses was a result of and could be traced back to frustrated sexual gratification during these stages, which are: the oral stage, birth to one year; the anal stage, 1–3 years; the phallic stage, 3–5 years; and latency, five years to puberty. Each of these stages is in turn divided into sub-stages. In each of the major stages, the infant has sexual needs which, because of social mores, are left largely unfulfilled, causing neuroses to originate.

It is during the phallic stage that Freud hypothesized the development of the Oedipus complex, easily the most renowned and controversial theoretical construction of the Freudian canon. The Oedipus complex suggests that during the phallic stage, a child begins associating his

FREUD AND FALSE MEMORIES

Is it possible to "recover" buried memories? Did Freud engage in planting false memories in his patients? Sigmund Freud introduced the concept of repression into psychoanalytic theory and its validity is still very much debated. He described repression as "...the function of rejecting and keeping something out of consciousness." He theorized that people repress, or intentionally forget, painful memories to protect their conscious minds from experiencing them again. Most therapists would agree that memory is subjective and that the actual details of memories are clouded through time, but whether people actually repress memories is up for debate. It is not scientifically possible to prove whether repression actually occurs. Perhaps for this reason, therapists have traditionally placed more emphasis on the emotional quality of memories, rather than the actual details. Freud himself emphasized emotion over content in his discussions of repression.

However, some therapists have been accused of helping their patients "remember" things that never happened. The false memory debate involves people who believe they were abused (sexually or otherwise) as children, have forgotten or repressed the memory, and are then able to "recover" it through therapy. The controversy lies in the fact that some people claim that therapists are leading their patients to give them certain answers. In some cases it could be that the patient did actually suffer some emotional trauma as a child and is, with the guidance of the therapist, applying an abuse scenario to the painful memories. According to Frederick Crows, author of *The Memory Wars*, Freud often harassed his patients into accepting his sometimes strange or even incorrect interpretations of what they told him. The power of suggestion in hypnosis is an accepted fact, but there may be evidence that the therapy session can also be a highly suggestible environment as well. If a therapist suggests that a patient might have been abused, it is easy for the patient to believe it to be so. The legal ramifications of this are enormous, with people's lives and reputations sometimes ruined because of so-called recovered memories.

genitals with sexual pleasure and becomes erotically attracted the parent of the opposite sex while at the same time developing an intense jealousy of the same-sex parent. While Freud's original theory excludes consideration of females, his contemporary, Carl Jung (1875–1961), expanded this particular dynamic and theorized an Electra complex for women in which the same psychodrama of erotic attraction and jealousy is played out from the young girl's point of view.

Freud's critics

From nearly the beginning, Freud and his construction of psychoanalytic theory have faced intense criticism. His most famous dissenter is Jung, his former disciple. Jung split with Freud in 1913 over a variety of issues including, but certainly not limited to, Freud's emphasis on infantile sexuality. Jung had a different view of the construction of human personality, for instance, and had different ideas about how dreams should be interpreted and viewed as part of psychoanalysis. **Alfred Adler,** another disciple of Freud, broke with the master over infantile sexuality, positing a view that infants and children are driven primarily by a need for self-affirmation rather than sexual gratification. In modern times, Freud has been the target of criticism from many corners. Feminists especially criticize his understanding of "hysteria" and his theory of Oedipal conflict.

Although traditional Freudian psychoanalysis is not frequently used with children, long-term therapy for problems of childhood and adolescence may be based on an approach that shares the Freudian emphasis on uncovering unconscious motivations and breaking down defenses. Many therapists feel that psychoanalysis is the most effective technique to identify and deal with internal conflicts and feelings that contribute to dysfunctional behavior. Through psychoanalysis, the patient increases his understanding of himself and his internal conflicts so that they will no longer exert as much influence on mental and emotional health.

With younger children, the psychoanalytic process takes place through play. Young children, guided in play by a therapist, create situations in which their problems are represented. The therapist helps the child understand the feelings she expresses through her play scenarios, and assists the child in developing strategies for changing behavior. Older children and adolescents can be encouraged to talk about their feelings and the situations that are causing them problems.

For Further Study

Books

Coles, Robert. *Anna Freud: The Dream of Psychoanalysis.* Reading, MA: Addison-Wesley Publishing Company, Inc., 1992.

Doft, Norma. *When Your Child Needs Help: A Parent's Guide to Therapy for Children.* New York: Crown Paperbacks, 1992.

Fishman, Katharine Davis. *Behind the One-Way Mirror: Psychotherapy and Children.* New York: Bantam Books, 1995.

Kazdin, Alan E. *Child Psychotherapy: Developing and Identifying Effective Treatments.* New York: Pergamon Press, 1988.

Kendall, Philip C., ed. *Child and Adolescent Psychotherapy: Cognitive Behavioral Procedures.* New York: Guilford Press, 1991.

Turecki, Stanley. *The Emotional Problems of Normal Children.* New York: Bantam Books, 1994.

Organizations

American Academy of Child and Adolescent Psychiatry
Address: 3615 Wisconsin Avenue, NW
Washington, DC 20016
Telephone: (202) 966-7300

American Psychological Association
Address: 1200 17th Street, NW
Washington, DC 20002
Telephone: (202) 336-5500
website: www.apa.org
(Publishes *A Child's First Book About Play Therapy.*)

Psychotherapy

The treatment of mental or emotional disorders and adjustment problems through the use of psychological techniques rather than through physical or biological means.

Psychoanalysis, the first modern form of psychotherapy, was called the "talking cure," and the many varieties of therapy practiced today are still characterized by their common dependence on a verbal exchange between the counselor or therapist and the person seeking help. The therapeutic interaction is characterized by mutual trust, with the goal of helping individuals change destructive or unhealthy behaviors, thoughts, and emotions.

For a child, psychotherapy can bolster hope and **self-esteem,** improve mastery and coping abilities, change maladaptive behavior patterns, and facilitate normal developmental processes. Childhood emotional and behavioral problems that have been treated through psychotherapy include adjustment problems at school; **attention deficit/hyperactivity disorder;** anxiety and **depression;** conduct problems; **obsessive-compulsive behavior; eating disorders; enuresis; autism; child abuse;** and post-traumatic stress disorder. Severe problems that require immediate professional attention include severe, uncontrollable anxiety; hallucinations and other bizarre behavior; dangerous actions such as arson and other forms of violent aggression; and suicidal behavior.

A major distinguishing feature of psychotherapy for children is the role played by the parents, who choose the therapist (in most cases), provide information that aids in the initial assessment, and may be asked to participate in therapy sessions. While therapists generally respect the privacy of children, as they respect that of adult clients, patient confidentiality may be breached if circumstances warrant notifying a parent about activities or feelings that pose a potential danger to the child. Most of the basic therapeutic approaches used with adults are also used with children, but they are adjusted for the child's age, mental and emotional development, and language skills. It is common for experienced therapists to combine several different approaches or techniques. The most effective therapy for a child may be either time-limited (generally six months or less) or long-term, depending on the severity of his or her problems.

Psychodynamic approach

Although Freudian psychoanalysis is rarely used with children, individual, long-term therapy may be based on a psychodynamic treatment approach that shares the Freudian emphasis on uncovering unconscious motivations and breaking down defenses. Therapy sessions may be scheduled once or even twice a week for a year or more. This type of therapy is appropriate when internal conflicts contribute significantly to a child's problems. Play therapy, which has been called "the playing cure," is generally used with young children to help them express their repressed emotions and resolve their inner conflicts. Repressed feelings are allowed to emerge as the child symbolically acts them out using dolls, puppets, games, and storytelling. Infants as young as 15 months of age have responded to play therapy.

Behavioral techniques

In contrast to the psychodynamic approach, behavior-oriented therapy is geared toward helping children see their problems as learned behaviors that can be modified, without looking for unconscious motivations or hidden meanings. According to the theory behind this approach, once behavior is changed, feelings will change as well. Probably the best-known type of **behavioral therapy** is behavior modification, which focuses on eliminating undesirable habits by providing positive reinforcement for the more desirable behaviors. **Timeouts** are an example of negative reinforcement; accumulating tokens that can be exchanged for a reward (such as a movie) is an example of positive reinforcement.

Another behavioral technique is systematic desensitization, in which people are deliberately and gradually exposed to a feared object or experience to help them overcome their fears. A child who is afraid of dogs may first be given a toy dog to play with, then be exposed to a real dog seen at a distance, and eventually work up to the point of interacting with dogs at close range. Relaxation training is another popular form of behavior therapy. Through such techniques as deep breathing, visualization, and progressive muscle relaxation, youngsters learn to control fear and anxiety. Relaxation training can be particularly helpful with **separation anxiety** and sleep problems.

Cognitive methods

Some behavior-oriented therapy methods are used to alter not only overt behavior, but also the thought patterns that drive it. This type of treatment is known as **cognitive-behavior therapy** (or just cognitive therapy). Its goal is to help people break out of distorted, harmful patterns of thinking and replace them with healthier ones. Common examples of negative thought patterns include magnifiying or minimizing the extent of a problem; "all or nothing" thinking (i.e., a child regards himself as either perfect or worthless); overgeneralization (arriving at broad conclusions based on one incident, for example); and personalization (continually seeing oneself as the cause or focus of events).

In cognitive-behavioral therapy, a therapist may talk to the child, pointing out illogical thought patterns, or use a variety of techniques, such as thought substitution, in which a frightening or otherwise negative thought is driven out by substituting a pleasant thought in its place. Thus, a child who is afraid that monsters will attack her when she falls asleep may be encouraged to concentrate on winning first place in the school spelling bee. Children may also be taught to use positive self-talk, a repetition of positive statements similar to the affirmations used by adults. A child who is afraid of walking to school alone may be encouraged to repeat to himself: "I'm six and I'm a brave boy." Cognitive therapy may take a more fanciful turn with very young children, who can benefit from such techniques as positive magical thinking, which makes use of their vivid imaginations to conjure up imaginary companions who can protect them, or such products as a magical eraser that can get rid of monsters. Cognitive therapy is usually provided on a short-term basis (generally 10–20 sessions).

Family and group therapy

Family therapy has proven effective in treating a number of childhood emotional and adjustment problems. While the child's immediate complaint is the initial focus of attention, the ultimate goal of family therapy is to improve the interaction between all family members and enhance communication and coping skills on a long-term basis (although therapy itself need not cover an extended time period). Group therapy, which is often combined with individual therapy, offers the support and companionship of other children of the same age at a time when a youngster may be having difficulty reaching out to his or her peers because of emotional problems. It can be especially effective because children often confide in each other more readily than in adults. Problems that respond well to group therapy include social aggression or withdrawal and difficulties with problem-solving.

With adolescents, group therapy is a useful approach for eating disorders and substance abuse.

Group therapy can be employed with children of all ages. Structured play—a central component of individual therapy for young children—is also utilized in group therapy with youngsters whose verbal skills are not yet well developed. More sophisticated games, as well as crafts, can also be part of the therapeutic experience for school-age children. Hyperactive or aggressive children and those who have displayed anti-social behaviors that may endanger others should not participate in group therapy.

Other approaches

Children who are too emotionally fragile to respond well to the active approaches outlined above may be helped by supportive therapy, in which the main goal is simply to provide the child with a positive, supportive, and stable relationship with an adult she can trust. Group therapy, which is sometimes offered by schools, can be effective, especially for children who are having trouble relating to their peers.

Another important resource is family therapy, which involves at least one other member of the child's family and often the entire family. A specialized form of family therapy is infant therapy, used with children from infancy through the age of three. Thanks to modern research into children's early **emotional development**, clinicians can diagnose and intervene in parent-child interactions that may cause problems later. The therapist observes the pattern of interaction between parent and child and recommends ways of modifying parental behavior. In one survey, researchers found that 10–15% of infants brought to pediatricians' offices suffered from mild emotional problems, including irritability, withdrawal, attachment problems, and sleep disorders, that respond to short-term treatment.

If the adult or adults in a child's life are seriously troubled, the best way to help the child may be for the adults to seek treatment for themselves.

Choosing a therapist

A variety of mental health professionals work with children, including pediatric social workers, school counselors, child psychiatrists, and child psychologists. The most common way of finding a therapist is through a referral, often from the family's internist or pediatrician or from the parent of another child who has undergone therapy (especially therapy for a similar or related problem). Other resources for referrals include members of the clergy, psychology or psychiatry departments of local hospitals (especially children's hospitals), and local chapters of professional organizations.

Initially, parents should inquire about the therapist's professional background (including licensing); learn

ANNA FREUD: PIONEER AND CHAMPION OF CHILDREN

Anna Freud (1895–1982), a pioneer in the application of psychoanalysis to the treatment of children and daughter of the founder of psychoanalysis, Sigmund Freud.

Anna Freud believed that the psychological development of children progresses through a series of stages, best understood by direct observations of children as they grow. To support her study of child development, Freud founded a nursery school where she applied her understanding of the psychoanalytic process to the treatment of childhood mental illness. In 1946, she published *The Psychoanalytic Treatment of Children,* and in 1947 founded the Hampstead Child Therapy Course and Clinic in London, providing training for child psychologists and teachers in the psychological and emotional development of children.

what kinds of patients he or she usually treats; and become familiar with the therapist's office policies and fees and the standard procedures for new clients. Parents should also find out what role the therapist expects them to play in the treatment process. The initial visit may involve only the child, or it may include other family members as well. This visit is an opportunity for the therapist to make a preliminary assessment of the child's situation and needs, and for the parents to form an initial impression of the therapist. It is important for the child to feel comfortable with the therapist either initially or at least after a few sessions.

Therapy is terminated when the treatment goals have been met or if the parents and/or therapist conclude that it isn't working. It can be effective to phase out treatment by gradually reducing the frequency of therapy sessions. Even after regular therapy has ended, the child may return for periodic follow-up and reassessment sessions.

For Further Study

Books

Doft, Norma. *When Your Child Needs Help: A Parent's Guide to Therapy for Children.* New York: Crown Paperbacks, 1992.

Engler, Jack, and Daniel Goleman. *The Consumer's Guide to Psychotherapy.* New York: Fireside, 1992.

Fishman, Katharine Davis. *Behind the One-Way Mirror: Psychotherapy and Children.* New York: Bantam Books, 1995.

Kazdin, Alan. E. *Child Psychotherapy: Developing and Identifying Effective Treatments.* New York: Pergamon Press, 1988.

Kendall, Philip C., ed. *Child and Adolescent Psychotherapy: Cognitive Behavioral Procedures.* New York: Guilford Press, 1991.

Turecki, Stanley. *The Emotional Problems of Normal Children.* New York: Bantam Books, 1994.

Organizations

American Academy of Child and Adolescent Psychiatry
Address: 3615 Wisconsin Avenue, NW
Washington, DC20016
Telephone: (202) 966-7300

American Psychological Association
Address: 1200 17th Street, NW
Washington, DC20002
Telephone: (202) 336-5500
Website: www.apa.org
(Publishes *A Child's First Book About Play Therapy.*)

Puberty

The process of physical growth and sexual maturation that signals the end of childhood and the advent of adolescence. (Also, the period during which this process takes place.)

The word *puberty* is derived from the Latin *pubertas,* which means adulthood. Puberty is initiated by hormonal changes triggered by a part of the brain called the hypothalamus, which stimulates the pituitary gland, which in turn activates other glands as well. These changes begin about a year before any of their results are visible. Both the male reproductive **hormone** testosterone and female hormone estrogen are present in children of both sexes. However, their balance changes at puberty, with girls producing relatively more estrogen and boys producing more testosterone.

Most experts suggest that parents begin short and casual discussions about puberty with their children by the age of seven or eight. Offering the child reading materials about puberty can impart information to the young person without the awkwardness that may characterize the parent-child conversations. Parents can then offer their children opportunities to ask questions or to discuss any aspects of puberty and sexuality that may arise from their reading.

The first obvious sign of puberty is a growth spurt that typically occurs in girls between the ages of 10 and 14 and in boys between 12 and 16. Between these ages both sexes grow about nine inches. The average girl gains about 38 pounds, and the average boy gains about 42. One reason for the awkwardness of adolescence is the fact that this growth spurt proceeds at different rates in different parts of the body. Hands and feet grow faster than arms and legs, which, in turn, lengthen before the torso does, all of which create the impression of gawkiness common to many teenagers. In addition, there can be temporary unevenness of growth on the two sides of the body, and even facial development is disproportionate, as the nose, lips, and ears grow before the head attains its full adult size. The growth spurt at puberty is not solely an external one. Various internal organs increase significantly in size, in some cases with observable consequences. Increases in heart and lung size and in the total volume of blood give adolescents increased strength and endurance for athletics and for recreational activities such as dancing. (During puberty, the heart doubles in size.) Teenagers' ravenous appetites are related to the increased capacity of the digestive system, and the decrease in respiratory problems (including **asthma**) is associated with the fact that the lymphoid system, which includes the tonsils and adenoids, actually shrinks in adolescence. Yet another change, the increase in secretions from the sebaceous glands, triggered by the growth hormone androgen, is responsible for acne, which affects about 75% of teenagers. The excess oil from these glands clogs pores, and they become inflamed, causing the reddening and swelling of acne.

Following the beginning of the growth spurt, the sexual organs begin to mature and secondary sex characteristics appear. In girls, the uterus and vagina become larger, and the lining of the vagina thickens. The first visible sign of sexual maturation is often the appearance of a small amount of colorless pubic hair shortly after the growth spurt begins. Over the next three years, the pubic hair becomes thicker, darker, coarser, and curlier and spreads to cover a larger area. Hair also develops under the arms, on the arms and legs (sufficiently so that most girls start shaving), and, to a slight degree, on the face. Around the age of 10 or 11, "breast buds," the first sign of breast development, appear. Full breast development takes about three or four years and is generally not complete until puberty is almost over. The single most dramatic sign of sexual maturation in girls is **menarche,** the onset of **menstruation,** which usually occurs after a girl's growth rate has peaked. In virtually all cases it occurs between the ages of 10 and 16, with the average age in the United States being 12.8 years. The first menstrual periods are usually anovulatory, meaning that they happen without ovulation. Periods remain irregular for a while, and for at least a year after menarche young women's fertility levels are very low, and they are prone to spontaneous abortions if they do conceive.

In boys, as in girls, the first outward sign of sexual maturation is often light-colored pubic hair around the time the growth spurt begins. The testes and scrotum begin to grow, and the scrotum darkens, thickens, and becomes pendulous. About a year after the testes begin to increase in size, the penis lengthens and widens, taking several years to reach its full size. Sperm production increases, and ejaculations—the male counterpart to menarche in girls—begin, occurring through nocturnal emission, **masturbation,** or sexual intercourse. (It takes from one to three years until ejaculations contain enough sperm for a boy to be really fertile.) Boys' pubic hair, like that of girls, gradually becomes thicker and curlier and covers a wider area, and facial hair appears, first in the mustache area above the upper lip and later at the sides of the face and on the chin. As a boy's larynx grows and the vocal cords lengthen, his voice drops (roughly an octave in pitch) and changes in quality. Although girls' voices also become lower, the change is more dramatic (and less controlled) in boys, whose voices occasionally break, producing an embarrassing high-pitched squeak.

The sequence and age range of the developmental changes associated with puberty can vary widely. Although most children begin puberty between the ages of 10 and 12, it can start at any age from 8 to 16. The most obvious determining factor is gender; on average, puberty arrives earlier for girls than boys. Heredity also appears to play an important role. Compared to an overall age range of 9 to 18 for menarche, the age difference for sisters averages only 13 months and for identical twins, less than 3 months. Body weight is a factor as well: puberty often begins earlier in heavier children of both sexes and later in thinner ones. The onset of menstruation, in particular, appears to be related to amounts of body fat. Girls with little body fat, especially athletes, often

HORMONE SURGE TRIGGERS PUBERTY

A point in child development known as adrenarche—the beginning of adrenal androgen acitivity—may represent the beginning of the process of puberty. Two University of Chicago researchers, Dr. Martha K. McClintock and Dr. Gilbert Herdt, believe that puberty is triggered by dihydroepiandrosterone (DHEA), a hormone produced by the adrenal glands. According to data the two gathered from three separate studies, DHEA levels begin to increase at around the age of six and reach a critical level around age ten. The researchers characterize these hormonal changes as triggering a number of cognitive, emotional, and social changes in around fourth or fifth grade. Students in these grades begin to engage in boy-girl teasing, exhibit a significant increase in abstract reasoning skills, and experience vulnerability to embarrassment. The three studies also gathered data on subjects' (who were mostly in their mid-30s) first recollected feelings of sexual attraction. The mean age reported by the subjects was around 10 or 11. This finding has led the researchers to postulate that sexual development moves along a continuum, beginning with attraction, progressing to desire, and leading to the willingness and readiness to act on the desire. Dr. McClintock, quoted in the *New York Times,* noted: "Our culture regards middle childhood as a time of hormonal quiescence. Freud called it 'latency.' But actually a great deal of activity is going on."

start menstruating at a later-than-average age. Over the past 100 years, puberty has tended to begin increasingly early in both sexes (a phenomenon called the *secular trend*). In 1997, the results of a study led by Dr. Marcia E. Herman-Giddens of University of North Carolina at Chapel Hill School of Public Health provided evidence that the average age of menarche was declining. Instead of occurring between the ages of 12 and 14, as is typical in the late 1990s, girls' first menstrual periods commonly appeared between the ages of 15 and 17 in the 19th century. Puberty in boys usually didn't begin until the ages of 15 or 16 (in the late 18th and early 19th centuries, boy sopranos in their mid-to-late teens still sang in church choirs). Explanations for this pattern have ranged from evolution to better health, especially as a consequence of improved nutrition.

An important aspect of puberty is the development of body image. Teenagers are often critical of their bodies during this period, either because they feel they are maturing too early or too late, or because they fail to match the stereotyped ideals of attractiveness for their sex (i.e., tall and muscular for men, fashionably thin for women). Girls who mature early have a hard time initially because they feel self-conscious and isolated, but they adjust well and even gain in status once their peers begin to catch up. Some research even suggests that girls who mature early may ultimately be better off than those who mature late because the turmoil of their early teenage years helps them develop coping skills that stand them in good stead later on. For boys, the relative positions of early and late maturers is reversed. Those who are already tall and athletic in junior high school feel better about themselves than those who remain short and skinny. Researchers have linked late physical maturation in boys to the development of both positive personality traits (humor, perceptiveness, flexibility, creativity, and leadership skills) and negative ones (restlessness and lack of poise). In most cases, adolescents gradually become more accepting of their bodies in the years following junior high school.

For Further Study

Books

Chirinian, Alain. *Boys' Puberty: An Illustrated Manual for Parents and Sons.* New York: Tom Doherty Associates, 1989.

Feldman, Shirley, and Glen R. Elliott, eds. *At the Threshold: The Developing Adolescent.* Cambridge, MA: Harvard University Press, 1990.

Hynes, Angela. *Puberty: An Illustrated Manual for Parents and Daughters.* New York: Tom Doherty Associates, 1989.

Jukes, Mavis. *It's a Girl Thing: How to Stay Healthy, Safe, and In Charge.* New York: A. Knopf, 1996.

Steinberg, Laurence, and Ann Levine. *You and Your Adolescent: A Parent's Guide for Ages 10–20.* New York: Harper & Row, 1990.

Periodicals

Gilbert, Susan. "Early Puberty Onset Seems Prevalent." *New York Times* 146, April 9, 1997, p. B12.

Marano, Hara Estroff. "Puberty May Start at 6 as Hormones Surge." *New York Times* 146, July 1, 1997, p. B9+.

Nathanson, Laura. "Prepuberty Coaching." *Parents Magazine* 72 (March 1997): pp. 110+.

Books (for teens)

Bell, Alison, and Lisa Rooney. *Your Body Yourself: A Guide to Your Changing Body.* Chicago: Contemporary Books, 1993.

Bourgeois, Paulette, and Martin Wolfish. *Changes in You and Me: A Book About Puberty, Mostly for Boys.* Kansas City: Andrews and McMeel, 1994.

———. *Changes in You and Me: A Book About Puberty, Mostly for Girls.* Kansas City: Andrews and McMeel, 1994.

Madaras, Lynda. *The What's Happening to My Body? Book for Boys: A Growing Up Guide for Parents and Sons.* New York: Newmarket Press, 1984.

———. *The What's Happening to My Body? Book for Girls: A Growing Up Guide for Parents and Daughters.* New York: Newmarket Press, 1988.

Solin, Sabrina. *The Seventeen Guide to Sex and Your Body.* New York: Simon and Schuster, 1996.

Audiovisual Recordings

Children's Television Workshop. *What Kids Want to Know About Sex and Growing Up.* Los Angeles, CA: Pacific Arts Video Publishing, 1992.
(One 60-minute videocassette and one 20-page parent's guide.)

What My Parents Didn't Tell Me. Saturn Productions, 1985.
(One 27-minute videocassette.)

What's Happening to Me? A Guide to Puberty. Los Angeles, CA: LCA, 1986.
(One 30-minute videocassette.)

Who Am I Now? Facts, Fibs and Fantasies About Puberty. Lake Success, NY: Tambrands, Inc., 1987.
(One 21-minute videocassette and one teacher's guide. Also one poster, three booklets, one information sheet, and various sample feminine hygiene products.)

Punishment

Penalty imposed on another as a result of unwanted behavior.

Punishment is often used as a synonym for **discipline,** but the two are not interchangeable. Discipline is a system of actions or interactions intended to create orderly behavior. Some disciplinary systems use punishment as a tool. Therefore, discipline does not always involve punishment, but punishment is sometimes a method of discipline. However, it is the child's interpretation of the punishment that is critical.

Punishment can be either physical or nonphysical. Behavior modification techniques, such as "logical consequences" or "**time-out,**" use rewards and nonphysical punishments to control behavior. Behavior modification is sometimes distinguished from punishment with the claim that it is "corrective" rather than "retaliatory, " but any time a penalty is imposed because of unwanted behavior, it is punitive. Physical punishments are used frequently in Western society, as well as elsewhere, despite controversy over their effects. Numerous studies have shown that using physical force to control behavior can lead to more resistance and aggression on the part of the child. However, many parents, teachers, psychologists, religious leaders, and others still believe that there is a place for physical punishment in effective discipline.

Most current promoters of punitive discipline in the United States, however, espouse nonviolent forms of control, or "mild" punishments, such as time-out, scolding and disapproval, natural and logical consequences, and penalties (restricting television viewing, for example).

Time-out is a behavior modification technique that has become quite popular in recent years. Used mostly on children between the ages of 2 and 12, it attempts to stop unwanted behavior by removing the child from all stimulation and attention. A certain room or chair is designated as the "time-out" place, and a child is ordered or carried there whenever he or she engages in a particular unwanted behavior. Time-out can be effective in modifying disruptive behaviors, like hitting, grabbing, talking back, or **tantrums.** Proponents of behavior modification claim that the child learns quickly to control his or her own behavior so as to avoid time-out. Detractors of punitive discipline argue that external controls do little to change internal motivations or attitudes. Children simply learn to resist or evade external controls.

Another technique of behavior modification involves "logical consequences. " Children often learn not to behave in certain ways through the *natural* consequences of their actions, such as getting burned when touching a hot stove. Parents and adult caregivers extend that form of learning by *arranging* consequences to children's actions. To be effective, these arranged consequences must be logically related to the action. For example, if a child does not complete his or her task of washing the dishes one night, the next night he or she must wash double the amount of dishes. Sometimes, natural consequences are too dangerous, so a parent arranges logical consequences instead. A child who rides her or his tricycle into the street cannot be allowed to be hit by a car (natural consequences), so instead the parent takes the tricycle away from the child for a week (logical consequences).

Behavior modification systems of discipline that use "mild" punishments suffer from a serious contradiction, however. Studies have clearly shown that in order for punishment to be effective it must happen *immediately* after the behavior, be *severe*, and occur *every time* the behavior occurs. Nonviolent punitive systems of discipline, on the other hand, recommend that parents not punish a child in anger (meaning parents must wait until their emotions cool down), and that the punishment be mild. This recommendation negates the first two requirements of effective punishment. The third requirement is impossible to fulfill, as parents are not constantly present with their children to witness every occurrence of the unwanted behavior.

Americans believe that severe physical punishment defeats its own purpose by modeling aggressive or physical behavior, the very behavior it is often attempting to correct. Studies have shown that violent punishment can produce aggression, anxiety, fear, paranoia, apathy, hatred, **depression**, delinquency, and self-destructive behaviors. Adults who were punished violently as children display an increased likelihood of criminal activity, domestic violence, and **suicide.**

For Further Study

Books

Clark, Lynn. *The Time-Out Solution: A Parent's Guide for Handling Everyday Behavior Problems.* Chicago: Contemporary Books, 1989.

Dobson, James. *Children at Risk: The Battle for the Hearts and Minds of Our Kids.* Dallas: Word Publishing, 1990.

———. *Dare to Discipline.* Wheaton, Illinois: Tyndale House, 1981. *The New Dare to Discipline.* Wheaton: Tyndale, 1992. (Conservative Christian approach to control-based discipline.)

———. *Parenting Isn't for Cowards: Dealing Confidently with the Frustrations of Child-Rearing.* Waco, TX: Word Books, 1987.

Dreikurs, Rudolf. *Logical Consequences: A New Approach to Discipline.* New York: Dutton, 1990.

Greven, Philip. *Spare the Child: The Religious Roots of Punishment and the Psychological Impact of Physical Abuse.* New York: Vintage Books, 1990.

McCord, Joan, ed. *Coercion and Punishment in Long-Term Perspectives.* Cambridge/New York: Cambridge University Press, 1995.

Straus, Murray, Richard Gelles, and Suzanne Steinmetz. *Behind Closed Doors: Violence in the American Family.* New York: Anchor Press/Doubleday, 1980.

Wright, Logan. *Parent Power.* New York: William Morrow, 1980.

—Dianne K. Daeg de Mott

Pyromania

Irresistible urge to start fires.

Little is known about pyromania. The term comes from the Greek words *pyr* (fire) and *mania* (madness). It is a rare condition, listed under the heading of **impulse control disorders.** Pyromania is not the same as arson (deliberate fire-setting), and not all arsonists (fire-setters) are pyromaniacs. Fires are often started by individuals with this disorder deliberately and with careful planning, rather than by accident. A key feature of this disorder is the presence of repeated association with fire, but with no evidence of a reason or motivation for the fire (such as profit or to hide criminal activity). Nearly all pyromaniacs are male. Pyromania may begin in childhood, but there is no conclusive data regarding the typical age of onset. Similarly, there is no documented link between fire-setting in childhood and adult pyromania.

See also **Impulse Control Disorders**

For Further Study

Books

Morrison, James. *DSM-IV Made Easy: The Clinician's Guide to Diagnosis.* New York: Guilford Press, 1995.

Quadriplegia

A complete paralysis of the arms, legs, and trunk, usually occurring after a severe injury to the spinal cord between the fifth and seventh vertebrae. Spastic quadriplegia is a condition present at birth often accompanied by vision problems, seizures, and mental retardation.

Treatment of quadriplegia includes physical and psychological therapy as well as mechanical support of any normal functions made impossible by blockage of the sympathetic nervous system. The quadriplegic patient needs assistance in maintaining respiration, proper body temperature, and bowel and urinary functions. Children born with spastic quadriplegia usually require perpetual, comprehensive care. The degree of **mental retardation** will dictate the level of the child's education and independence.

When quadriplegia occurs as the result of an injury, the patient will likely suffer a period of grief and/or **depression**. The sudden loss of control of nearly all bodily functions is devastating. Counseling should be provided to help the patient successfully progress through this stage. In severe injuries, parents and patients may consider the withdrawal of life support. Such decisions should not be made until the patient has completed rehabilitation, and all parties are made aware of the long-term physiological and psychological consequences of the injury.

Independence is of utmost concern to the quadriplegic, and every effort should be made to assist him or her in achieving it. Approximately 150,000 Americans are afflicted with quadriplegia, and many are able to lead independent lives through the use of electric wheelchairs and mouthsticks that facilitate the use of push-button telephones, cassette recorders, computers, and myriad other tools for modern living. Organizations such as the National Easter Seals Society are available to help patients and families design accessible living spaces. Helping Hands is a unique non-profit group that trains capuchin monkeys to assist quadriplegics. In 1994 a cough stimulator was invented that assists quadriplegics who have lost the cough reflex. A pocket-sized version is expected by the year 2000.

For Further Study

Periodicals

Exceptional Parent Magazine
> **Address:** 209 Harvard Street, Suite 303
> Brookline, MA 02146-5005
> **Telephone:** (617) 730-5800
> **FAX:** (617) 730-8742

Organizations

Helping Hands
> **Address:** Boston University School of Medicine
> 1505 Commonwealth Avenue
> Boston, MA 02135
> **Telephone:** (617) 787-4419

National Easter Seals Society
> **Address:** 230 W. Monroe Street
> Chicago, IL 60606
> **Telephone:** (312) 726-6200; toll-free (800) 786-7437
> **FAX:** (312) 726-1494

National Information Center for Children and Youth with Disabilities
> **Address:** P.O. Box 1492
> Washington, DC 20013
> **Telephone:** (202) 884-8200; toll-free (800) 695-0285
> **FAX:** (202) 884-8441

Rabies

A viral disease that is fatal in humans if not treated immediately. It typically spreads to humans from animals through a scratch or a bite and causes inflammation of the brain.

Although the vaccine first used in 1885 is widely used today, fatalities from rabies still occur. Most fatalities take place in Africa and Asia, but some also happen in the United States. Prevention of rabies in the United States can cost as high as $1 billion per year.

From animal to human

While many animal diseases cannot be passed from animal to humans, rabies can, and since ancient times it has been known as an easy traveler from one species to the next. The very name rabies, Latin for "rage" or "madness," suggests the fear early men and women must have had for the disease. For centuries no treatment existed, and the disease was left to run a rapid course leading to death.

This changed in 1885, when French scientist Louis Pasteur saved the life of a nine-year-old boy who had been attacked by a rabid dog. Pasteur used a live virus vaccine made from spinal cords of infected rabbits. To be effective, the vaccine needed to be administered 14 to 21 times.

The vaccine has since been refined and improved many times. Currently, two rabies vaccines are used in the United States. Yet rabies continues to plague most underdeveloped parts of the world, particularly regions without access to health care.

Rabies is caused by a number of different viruses that vary depending on the geographic area and species. While the viruses are different, the disease they cause is singular in its course. The bullet-shaped virus is spread when it comes in contact with broken skin or a mucous membrane. Initially, the virus begins to reproduce itself in muscle cells near the place of first contact. At this point, within the first five days or so, treatment by vaccination has a high rate of success.

Once the rabies virus passes to the central nervous system, **immunization** is no longer effective. When it moves into the brain, it replicates itself there before finally moving to other tissues such as the heart, lungs, liver, and salivary glands. Symptoms appear when the virus reaches the spinal cord.

Since rabies symptoms for humans and animals mirror each other, sick animals are an excellent guide to understanding the disease. The common symptoms are muscle spasms, confusion, sensitivity to bright light, and fever. In addition, a fear of water and so-called foaming of the mouth, a symptom that occurs due to difficulty in swallowing and abnormally active salivation, are present. The incubation period from the time one is exposed to rabies to the time the disease develops is usually one to two months, but it can take as long as seven years for symptoms to make their appearance.

Dogs, cats, and bats

The likelihood that certain animals will contract rabies varies from one location to the next. Dogs are one example. In areas where public health efforts to control rabies have been aggressive, dogs make up less than 5% of rabies cases in animals. These areas include the United States, most European countries, and Canada. However, dogs are the most common source of rabies in many countries. They make up at least 90% of reported cases of rabies in the developing countries of Africa, Asia, and many parts of Latin America. In these countries, public health efforts to control rabies have not been as aggressive. Other key carriers of rabies include the fox in Europe and Canada, the jackal in Africa, and the vampire bat in Latin America.

In the United States, raccoons comprised 60% of all reported rabies cases. A total number of 4,311 rabid raccoons was reported in 1992. The high number of these cases suggests an animal epidemic, or epizootic. The epizootic began when diseased raccoons were carried further south from Virginia and West Virginia. Since then, rabies in raccoons has spread up the eastern seaboard of the United States. Concentrations of animals with rabies include coyotes in southern Texas, skunks in California and in south and north central states, and gray foxes in southeastern Arizona. Bats throughout the United States also develop rabies. When rabies first enters a species, large numbers of animals die. When it has been exposed for a long period of time, the species adapts, and smaller numbers of animals die.

Rabies in humans

Few deaths from rabies have occurred in the United States in recent years. Between 1980 and the middle of 1994, a total of 19 people in the United States died of rabies, which, by comparison, is far fewer than the 200 Americans killed by lightning during the same period. Eight of these cases were acquired outside the United States, and of the 11 cases contracted in the United States, eight stemmed from bat-transmitted strains of rabies. Internationally, the statistics are much higher. According to the World Health Association, more than 33,000 people die each year from rabies. A majority of these cases stem from dog bites.

Different countries employ different strategies in the fight against rabies. The United States depends primarily on vaccination of domestic animals and on immunization following exposure to possibly rabid animals. In Great Britain, where rabies has never been established, a strict quarantine for all domestic animals entering the country is utilized.

Continental Europe, which has a long history of rabies, developed an aggressive program in the 1990s of airdropping a new vaccine for wild animals. The laboratory-engineered, live vaccine is mixed with pellets of food for red foxes, the primary carrier there. Public health officials have announced that fox rabies may be eliminated from western Europe by the end of the decade. The World Health Organization now intends to use the vaccine in parts of Africa. Trials of the new vaccine have also been conducted in the United States. However, concern over the cost of distributing the vaccine across large areas of the United States has prohibited extensive use of the substance. Such concerns also reflect the limited loss of human life due to rabies in the United States.

Although the United States has been largely successful in controlling rabies in humans, the disease remains present in the animal population. This is a constant reminder of the serious threat rabies could become without effective, on-going prevention.

For Further Study

Books

Kaplan, Colin, G.S. Turner, D. A. Warrell. *Rabies: The Facts.* (2d ed.) New York: Oxford University Press, 1986.

Rabies: A Warm Weather Hazard. Washington, DC: Department of Health and Human Services, 1987.

Smith, Jane S. *Patenting the Sun.* New York: William Morrow and Company, Inc., 1990.

Periodicals

Browne, Malcolm W. "Rabies, Rampant in U. S., Yields to Vaccine in Europe." *The New York Times,* July 5, 1994, p. C1.

Cantor, Scott B., Richard D. Clover, and Robert F. Thompson. "A Decision-Analytic Approach to Postexposure Rabies Prophylaxis." *American Journal of Public Health* 84, no. 7. July 1994, pp 1144–48.

Clark, Ross. "Mad Dogs and Englishmen." *The Spectator,* August 20, 1994, pp. 16–17.

Corey, Lawrence. "Rabies, Rhabdoviruses, and Marburg-Like Agents." *In Harrison's Principles of Internal Medicine* 1. Edited by Kurt J. Isselbacher, et al. 13th ed. New York: McGraw-Hill Inc., 1994.

Fishbein, Daniel B., and Laura E. Robinson. "Rabies." *The New England Journal of Medicine* 329, no. 22, November 25, 1993, pp.1632–38.

—Karen L. Rice, M.A.

Rage Reflex *see* Neonatal Reflexes

Rationalization *see* Defense Mechanisms

....

Reading

Interpreting written language and translating it into words and sentences that convey thoughts and ideas.

Reading is the recognition of printed letters and their interpretation as words and sentences. Words are used to convey, for example, information, instructions, warnings, and traffic directions. For most people in modern societies, the skill of reading is practiced numerous times during the course of a day.

Reading is a complex process involving vision and many cognitive and **memory** skills. Infants and toddlers begin to gain an understanding of the relationship between printed letters, words, and their meanings when someone reads aloud to them. Vocabulary is developed through the process of hearing language spoken in context; young children who enter school with rich vocabularies are more likely to be successful in learning to read.

Most schools begin to teach the skills of reading in kindergarten. Students' readiness for reading depends on a number of factors, including previous experiences, mental and **emotional development**, spoken language skills, interests, and motivation. To help build motivation, parents and teachers should select reading materials that appeal to the new reader's interests, which will vary considerably from child to child. Reading readiness tests are used by educators of young children to evaluate whether a child is developmentally ready to learn to read. Reading readiness tests assess the child's ability to use language in his or her own speech and the ability to understand spoken language. These tests also evaluate a child's ability to perceive differences in line drawings or other visual symbols and his or her attention and general responsiveness to a story or other engaging spoken language. In assessing readiness, the test evaluates whether the child's experiences up to the point of testing have prepared him or her for the next stage in learning. Recent research has indicated that test results from assessment of young children should be used as only one among many factors for decision-making, because young children change rapidly.

Difficulties in learning to read take many forms. **Dyslexia** and other learning disabilities affect the prospective reader's ability to accurately interpret the printed word.

Continuity is important for beginning readers. Some children experience difficulty when advancing from one grade to the next, because the new teacher's approach is different from that used the previous year. Children who move from one school district to another may experience similar difficulties; teachers should be attentive to the needs of new students in this critical area of education.

Educators refer to the word-interpretation errors children make while learning to read as miscues. Common miscues of the beginning reader include skipping a word or substituting a similar, known word for an unknown word. Students whose first language is not the language of their classroom experience the dual challenge of learning to read while learning to speak and understand the language at the same time. Many schools have provisions for bilingual education or (in the United States) English as a Second Language (ESL) classes to provide these students with extra support and instruction in all aspects of communication.

Reading skill is required for success in almost every subject in school and for many activities of adult life. Therefore, educators monitor reading progress carefully and employ a number of strategies to help readers who are having difficulty or who are reluctant to read. Reading is taught by two basic methods: **phonics** and **whole language**. Both systems have advantages and disadvantages, and many educators favor employing strategies using both methods to teach reading.

KEY READING SKILLS

- Perception: Is the reader able to recognize the printed combinations of letters as words?

- Comprehension: Does the reader understand and remember what he or she has read?

- Speed or rate: How fast is the reader reading?

- Scanning ability: Scanning or "survey reading" is a useful skill when the reader is looking for information quickly. Does the reader have the skill needed to quickly skim the content of a section of printed material?

- Techniques used to read new words, known as word-attack skills: How successful are the strategies the child uses when encountering a new, unfamiliar word?

- Vocabulary: How is the child's active vocabulary (words that a child can use independently) developing? Is the passive vocabulary (words that a child can decipher and understand in context, but does not use) growing? Is the number of words the child can read and recognize—known as "sight words"—growing? Similarly, is the sight vocabulary—the words the reader can recognize and understand without consulting a dictionary—growing?

Word-recognition strategies taught to young readers (known as "word-attack" skills) include sight words (those words recognized by the configuration of their letters), context clues (analyzing other parts of the passage to "figure out" the unknown word), phonics ("sounding out"), and structural analysis (looking for recognizable morphemes, or parts of words). Reading specialists estimate that competent readers have the ability to recognize about 250 words by their shape alone. Context clues, including illustrations, are important aides for beginning readers that draw on past experiences and knowledge to help the young reader add new words to his or her reading vocabulary. Phonics helps the beginning reader to see relationships between the printed letters and their spoken sounds. Most teachers begin teaching the consonant sounds, followed by the consonant blends or combinations (sh, cl, or th, for example). Vowel sounds are introduced as new words are added to the student's reading vocabulary.

Beginning readers typically read aloud to an adult, a peer, or to other members of a reading group. As a child's reading ability improves, he or she will begin silent reading, sometimes forming the words without speaking them, or whispering, as the transition to silent reading is accomplished.

A number of systems—termed readability measures—have been developed to convey the relative difficulty of reading material. Readability includes a number of assessments of printed materials, including average number of words per sentence, average number of syllables per word, number of complex sentences per paragraph or page, number of abstract ideas, use of pronouns, and the sophistication of the vocabulary used. The readability is expressed as a reading level, usually in terms of reading material typically included in specific grade level curricula. Thus, reference is made to reading material at the "third-grade" or "fifth grade level," for example.

For Further Study

Books

Chall, Jeanne. *Learning to Read: The Great Debate.* New York: McGraw-Hill, 1983.

Flesch, Rudolf. *Why Johnny Still Can't Read: A New Look at the Scandal of Our Schools.* New York: Harper & Row, 1981.

Jacobs, Vicki A., and Luke E. Baldwin. *The Reading Crisis: Why Poor Children Fall Behind.* Cambridge, MA: Harvard University Press, 1990.

Leonhardt, Mary. *Parents Who Love Reading, Kids Who Don't.* New York: Crown Publishers, 1993.

Lipson, Eden Ross. *The New York Times Parent's Guide to the Best Books for Children.* New York: Random House, 1988.

McClain, Joan Brooks, and Gillian Dowley McNamee. *Early Literacy.* Cambridge, MA: Harvard University Press, 1990.

McCuen, Gary E. *Illiteracy in America.* Hudson, WI: GEM Publications, 1988.

Morrow, L. M. *Literacy Development in the Early Years.* Boston: Allyn and Bacon, 1993.

Rudman, Masha K., et al. *For Love of Reading: A Parent's Guide to Encouraging Young Readers and Writers from Infancy through Age 5.* New York: Consumer Reports Books, 1988.

Trelease, Jim. *The Read-Aloud Handbook.* 4th ed. New York: Penguin Books, 1995.

Vail, Priscilla L. *Common Ground: Whole Language and Phonics Working Together.* Rosemont, NJ: Modern Learning Press, 1991.

Organizations

National Clearinghouse on Literacy Education
   Address: 1118 22nd St. NW
   Washington, DC 20037
   Telephone: (202) 429-9292

Literacy Volunteers of America
   Address: 5795 Widewaters Parkway
   Syracuse, NY 13214
   Telephone: (315) 445-8000

LITERATURE FOR CHILDREN

In the 1980s, teachers began to replace basal readers—books with controlled vocabulary—with books of children's literature for the teaching of reading. Proponents of literature-based curricula cite many advantages to using this approach. Literature features interesting stories and characters, both of which help to motivate beginners to learn to read. Literature also helps children understand social relationships. When a reader relates a fictional character's decisions and actions to his own experiences, he is learning about social and moral decisions of real life.

The following organizations offer reading lists for readers of all skill levels:

American Library Association,
   Young Adult Services Division (ALA-YASD)
   Address: 50 East Huron
   Chicago, IL 60611
   Telephone: (312) 944-6780

Books for Children
   Address: Consumer Information Center
   Department 109N
   Pueblo, CO 81002
   (Publishes a list of the year's best books for preschool through middle school readers.)

Great Books Foundation
   Address: 40 East Huron
   Chicago, IL 60611
   Telephone: toll-free (800) 222-5870
   (312) 332-5870
   (Discussion materials on classic literature for groups of all ages.)

Project Literacy U.S. (PLUS)
   Address: Box 2
   4802 Fifth Ave.
   Pittsburgh, PA 15213

The National Center for Family Literacy
   Address: Waterfront Plaza, Suite 200
   325 W. Main St.
   Louisville, KY 40202-4251
   Telephone: (592) 584-1133

Reading Is Fundamental (RIF)
   Address: 600 Maryland Avenue, SW, Suite 500
   Washington, DC 20560
   Telephone: (202) 287-3220

Reading Reform Foundation
  Address: 7054 East Indian School
  Scottsdale, AZ 85251
  Telephone: (602) 946-3567

Reasoning *see* **Deductive Reasoning** *and* **Inductive Reasoning**

Recommended Dietary Allowance (RDA)

Recommendations for dietary intake of specific amounts of essential substances for healthy growth.

Recommended Dietary Allowance (RDA), is a set of recommendations for dietary intake of specific amounts of essential substances for healthy growth.

The Food and Nutrition Board of the National Research Council suggests ingestion of specific amounts of essential substances for the body to function normally. These amounts are estimates, and are updated regularly (usually about every five years) to reflect new research findings. The Food and Nutrition Board began preparing these guidelines in 1941, with the first set of Recommended Dietary Allowances published in 1943. The eighth edition of the guidelines, published in 1974, established the defininition of recommended dietary allowances as follows: *"the levels of intake of essential nutrients that, on the basis of scientific knowledge, are judged by the Food and Nutrition Board to be adequate to meet the known nutrient needs of practically all healthy persons."*

RDAs are distinct from, but related to, the Reference Daily Intake (RDI) developed by the Food and Drug Administration to be used in food labelling. RDI replaced the term U.S. Recommended Daily Allowances, which was used until new food labelling regulations went into effect in late 1992. All packaged foods were required to bear the new term on labels as of May 1994. Because RDAs and RDIs are widely used, it is important to understand generally how to interpret them. The recommended allowances for nutrients are amounts intended to be consumed as part of a normal diet, and are neither minimum requirements nor optimal levels of intake; it is not possible based on current research to set such specific guidelines, nor to set a specific amount that would apply to all individuals. Rather, RDAs are safe and adequate levels of intake that reflect current knowledge.

The recommended dietary allowances for infants, children, and adolescents are prepared by the National Research Council.

For Further Study

National Research Council. *Recommended Dietary Allowances.* 10th ed. Washington, DC: National Academy Press, 1989.

Reflex *see* **Neonatal Reflexes**

Regression *see* **Defense Mechanisms**

Reinforcement *see* **Operant Conditioning**

Repression *see* **Defense Mechanisms**

Retardation *see* **Mental Retardation** *and* **Familial Retardation**

Retention in School

Repeating an academic year of school.

A significant number of high school freshmen in the United States have repeated at least one grade. In most cases, teachers recommend retention for one of three reasons: developmental immaturity that has resulted in learning difficulties; emotional immaturity that has resulted in severely disruptive behavior; or failure to pass standardized proficiency or achievement tests at the end of specific years.

Some teachers believe that retaining a student is the best thing parents and teachers can do for the child. Many of these teachers are in early elementary education where maturity factors are of primary concern. Students begin school at such an early age, many teachers argue, that it is unrealistic to expect them all to have the emotional maturity to succeed in structured learning regimens. Marie Ubelhart, who has taught kindergarten and early elementary school in New Jersey, expressed these sentiments in a debate published in the journal *NEA Today.* Ubelhart, who has recommended retention for many students, says, "Youngsters who should be retained but aren't usually move through each grade slowly, losing more academic ground each year. Falling so far behind makes them feel stupid, and they develop a dislike for themselves." She says that in her own experience she has seen that holding students back, especially at the early stages of education, is beneficial. Ubelhart cites the case of one of her students who repeated a grade, and went on to win an academic award as a senior in high school.

Anecdotal evidence aside, psychological studies of retention have proved otherwise. In most of the research conducted on the outcomes of retention, it has been concluded that retention, even at the elementary level, does not result in improved academic achievement among low-achieving students. Short-term outcomes (the period of time immediately following the retention) may be temporary improvement in academic achievement, but that decreases over time. Researchers have found remedial instruction or other types of individualized intervention more likely to result in improved academic achievement. In addition, retention is controversial because male and minority students are much more likely to be retained.

In the early 1990s, a landmark study was completed that examined the practice of grade retention over the course of 60 years. It concluded that students who repeat a grade do no better than similar students who are passed on to the next grade. Other researchers have found that students who are retained are 30% more likely to drop out of school. One reason often cited for the increase in drop-out rate is that repeating a grade does not automatically improve the student's chances of learning; he or she is usually placed into a classroom no different from the one in which they were in the year before. The implication underlying the retention process is that the problem lies with the student, not with the curriculum or method of instruction.

In fact, undiagnosed learning problems have been shown by researchers to be a factor in a significant number of retentions. In the early 1990s, researchers collected data on a population of elementary students who were evaluated for learning problems. Two-thirds were determined to have a **learning disability** (LD). Of those so diagnosed, over 70% had been retained at least once, with minority students the most likely to be retained before being evaluated for learning disability.

Another reason educators have begun to reconsider the values of retention is the social stigma attached to being held back, which can be devastating to students. In 1990, *Ladies Home Journal* reported the results of a study that showed that among six- to nine-year-olds "the prospect of repeating was more stressful than wetting their pants in class or being caught stealing." The only things these children reported as being more stressful than repeating a grade was going blind or losing a parent. The students even reported that losing a sibling would be less stressful than being held back.

An alternative to retention is delaying a child's entry into kindergarten in order to give her an extra year of pre-school. More common in suburban school districts, the idea is to allow children, especially those who would be young among their peers in kindergarten (birthdays falling near the cutoff date for school entry), to gain maturity and a greater likelihood of success in kindergarten. The practice is believed to reduce the need for retention in the future. A study published in 1995 in the journal *Remedial and Special Education* examined retention and the use of **special education** services for students in a school

district that had practiced delayed entry into kindergarten (just over 8% of all students). The researchers found that students who delayed school entry were more likely to be boys, and were placed in special education programs more often, but that they were not any more likely to be retained than their peers, who entered school the year they were qualified chronologically to do so.

Despite research finding that retention does not appear to help learning difficulties, there is the problem of what to do with a child who is, for whatever reason, unprepared to move on to the next grade. Schools feel social pressure to adhere to academic standards, while at the same time being fully aware of the studies which show that, by and large, retention is counter-productive. Many frustrated educators compare the social pressure to retain students to the social pressure for tougher crime laws: the laws make people feel better, but they don't really address the core issues and, inevitably, the problems continue.

In recent years, some schools have been experimenting with variations on retention. In the New York City school system, for example, retention became a major problem after the state instituted standardized tests administered at the end of the fourth and the seventh grade. These tests were imposed on the schools by the state legislature in response to demands by constituents who were exasperated with poor academic performance. Students who failed to pass these tests were automatically retained, resulting in a significant increase in both the number of students repeating grades, and the number of students and parents who were dissatisfied with the public schools. Beginning in the early 1990s, however, New York City announced that it would stop automatic retention and institute a system of tutoring and remedial summer programs for students who didn't pass the standardized tests. In Dade County, Florida, which faced a similar problem, the school system has instituted an early intervention program that begins warning parents early in the year if their child is having problems that might result in retention. Other school districts have instituted tutoring centers or "special needs centers" where students at all achievement levels can go to do special work. Gifted students can do independent work and students having trouble can be tutored, either by peer tutors or by faculty in the centers.

Although many school districts involve parents in the decision to retain, in most communities the school system has the right to make the decision, with or without the parent's support. However, most experts support the idea that parents who are opposed to the decision to retain their child should make their concerns known. Parents should survey other local school systems, both public and private, to see their policies on retention. Parents should also request evidence supporting a retention

REDSHIRTING

The term "redshirting" is used in a situation where students are retained to improve performance in a nonacademic area, namely sports. Regardless of academic performance, a student is retained, usually in junior high, to increase his or her likelihood of winning a college athletic scholarship. In addition, retention of strong athletes allows the school to build teams of older, bigger athletes. In some communities, this type of activity may be unofficially sanctioned. In these cases, the retention is usually carried out with the knowledge and support of the student and his family, and is not likely to carry a social stigma, as would be the case if the retention were for academic reasons.

decision, including details of their child's academic performance, standardized test results, or other pertinent factors, such as the student's emotional maturity. The National Association of School Psychologists (NASP) offers a brochure for concerned parents entitled "Should My Child Repeat a Grade?" as well as other literature concerning this issue.

For Further Study

Books

Gilmore, June. *The Rape of Childhood: No Time to Be a Kid.* J&J Publishing, 1990.

Shephard, Lorrie, ed. *Flunking Grades: Research and Policies on Retention.* Falmer Press, 1989.

Periodicals

Barnett, Katherine P., et al. "Grade Retention Among Students with Learning Disabilities." *Psychology in the Schools* 33, October 1996, pp. 285–93.

Bergin, David A., Vicki L. Osburn, and John R. Cryan. "Influence of Child Independence, Gender, and Birthdate on Kindergarten Teachers' Recommendations for Retention." *Journal of Research in Childhood Education* 10, Spring/Summer 1996, pp. 152–59.

Diegmueller, Karen. "Charges of Redshirting in Louisiana Prompting Questions of Values. *Education Week* 15, April 3, 1996, pp. 1+.

Fishel, Elizabeth. "Should Kids Be Held back? *Parenting* 8, April 1994, pp. 39+.

May, Deborah C., Deborah King Kundert, and Donna Brent. "Does Delayed School Entry Reduce Later Grade Retentions and Use of Special Education Services?" *Remedial and Special Education* 16, September 1995, pp. 288–94.

Plostker-Herman, Candace. "When Kids Flunk: Should Your Child Repeat a Grade." *Better Homes and Gardens* 69, June 1991, p. 26.

Solorzano, Lucia, and Andrea Atkins. "Will Staying Back Help or Hurt*?" Ladies Home Journal* 107, September 1990, p. 80.

Ubelhart, Marie E., And Pam Walkup. "Do Good Teachers Flunk Kids?" *NEA Today* 12, March 1994, p. 39.

Walters, Deneen M., and Sherry B. Borgers. "Student Retention: Is It Effective?" *The School Counselor* 42, March 1995, pp. 300–10.

Organizations

National Association of School Psychologists
Address: 8455 Colesville Rd. Suite 1000
Silver Spring, MD 20910
National Committee for Citizens in Education
Telephone: (800) 638-9675

Reye Syndrome *see* **Encephalitis**

....

▌ Rh Factor

An antigen found on the red blood cells of most people. Individuals with the Rh factor are considered as Rh positive, while those without the Rh factor are considered Rh negative.

Rh factor, like the blood types A, B, and O, is inherited from one's parents. Through a simple blood test, blood type and the presence of the Rh factor can be determined. About 85% of white Americans and 95% of African Americans are Rh positive. A person's state of health is not affected by the presence or absence of Rh factor.

Importance of the Rh factor

The Rh factor, a blood protein, plays a critical role in some pregnancies. If an Rh negative woman is pregnant with a fetus who is Rh positive, her body will produce antibodies against the fetus's blood. This can cause Rh disease, also known as hemolytic disease of the newborn, or erythroblastosis fetalis, in the baby. In severe cases, Rh disease leads to brain damage and even death.

Rh factor is important only during a **pregnancy** in which an Rh negative woman is carrying an Rh positive **fetus**. This can occur when an Rh negative woman conceives a baby with an Rh positive man. The gene for Rh positive blood is dominant over the gene for Rh negative blood, so their baby will be Rh positive. If the Rh positive father also carries the gene for Rh negative blood, his children have a 50% chance of inheriting Rh negative blood and a 50% chance of inheriting Rh positive blood. If both parents are Rh negative, their offspring will always be Rh negative. In order to protect their future children from Rh disease, all women of childbearing age should know their Rh status before becoming pregnant.

Rh factor in pregnancy

The conditions allowing for Rh disease are established when the blood of an Rh negative mother is exposed to the Rh positive blood of her first baby, prompting the mother's immune system to build up antibodies to fight the foreign blood protein. Since this exposure usually occurs at birth, the first child is generally unaffected, but any fetus the mother carries afterward will develop Rh disease unless preventative measures are taken. Mixing of blood also occurs during an **abortion** or miscarriage and results in the same sensitization. Certain prenatal tests, such as **amniocentesis** and chorionic villi sampling, can also result in maternal exposure to fetal blood.

The attack of a mother's antibodies on the red blood cells of her Rh positive fetus results in several serious conditions. The first, **anemia**, refers to a reduction in red blood cells and is marked by weakness and fatigue. Another consequence is the buildup of a reddish yellow fluid called bilirubin, which in turn causes **jaundice**. If the bilirubin level gets high enough, brain damage can result. The most severe form of Rh disease, called hydrops fetalis, is marked by profound anemia and edema. Infants with hydrops fetalis are usually stillborn or only survive a few hours after birth.

Treatment for Rh disease

Since 1968 a vaccine has existed which prevents sensitization from even occurring. The vaccine is considered the best way to eliminate Rh disease because it prevents the mother's body from making antibodies against the fetus's blood. The vaccine, called Rh immune globulin (RhoGAM), is available by injection. RhoGAM blocks the action of the antibodies and prevents the mother's antibodies from attacking the baby's blood. To be effective, the vaccine must be given any time fetal blood mixes with maternal blood: after birth, abortion, miscarriage, or prenatal tests like amniocentesis and chorionic villus sampling. The vaccine is typically given within 72 hours of any of these events. Since mixing of the blood may occur during the last three months of pregnancy, some health care providers recommend receiving the vaccine at 28 weeks of pregnancy.

If a woman has become sensitized during a previous pregnancy, she can still take steps to prevent future babies who are Rh positive from developing Rh disease. Unfortunately, once the harmful antibodies are in a woman's blood, they cannot be removed.

A pregnant woman who has already been sensitized from a previous pregnancy should be carefully monitored throughout her pregnancy for the level of antibodies in her blood. As long as the antibody levels remain relatively low, no problem exists. However, if those levels rise, the fetus will need special attention. High antibody levels indicate that the fetus's red blood cells are being attacked and destroyed.

In these circumstances, the fetus will need a blood transfusion while it is still in the uterus. Two or three transfusions may be necessary before the baby is born. If the fetus shows signs of illness close to its anticipated birth, the physician may elect to deliver the baby early, either through an induced **birth** or cesarean section. The baby will then receive a transfusion after birth.

Eliminating Rh disease

Until the introduction of RhoGAM, Rh disease could not be prevented. Prior to widespread use of the vaccine in the early 1970s, researchers reported that approximately 45 babies per 10,000 births developed Rh disease yearly. The number of newborns with Rh disease has dropped dramatically ever since the introduction of the vaccine; about 10 per 10,000 in the early 1990s. The prevention of Rh disease is one of the triumphs of modern medicine.

Nevertheless, a relatively high number of newborns with Rh disease are still delivered each year in the United States. Clearly, the disease is not completely eradicated. Further steps must be taken since this is a preventable disease. The majority of Rh disease cases of are the result of women not receiving the vaccine at the appropriate time. Poor women, particularly those without health insurance, are the ones most at risk for inadequate prenatal care. Older women may have become sensitized before the vaccine was available. Foreign-born women may not have had access to the vaccine. With further diligence, health care providers hope to eradicate Rh disease.

For Further Study

Books

Planning for Pregnancy, Birth, and Beyond. Washington, DC: American College of Obstetricians and Gynecologists, 1990.

Reuben, Carolyn. *The Healthy Baby Book.* New York: Jeremy P. Tarcher/Perigee Books, 1992.

Rich, Laurie A. *When Pregnancy Isn't Perfect.* New York: Dutton, 1991.

Periodicals

Heins, Henry C. "Should You Worry About Rh Disease?" *American Baby,* April 1992, p. 24.

—Karen L. Rice, M.A.

Ritalin *see* **Methylphenidate**

....

▌ Rite of Passage

A ceremony or event marking the passage from one social status or developmental state to another.

The Belgian anthropologist Arnold van Gennep, who first coined the term early in the 20th century, noted a three-part pattern in transitions between life stages: 1) an initial phase, during which the individual is isolated from the community; 2) a period of disorder or confusion (called the liminal period), during which his or her former identity is broken down; and 3) the individual's reincorporation into the community once he or she has made the passage to a new stage of existence and a new identity.

One of the most important transitions in the life cycle is the passage from childhood to adulthood. Ceremonies marking this event were common in pre-industrial societies and are still practiced in a number of non-Western cultures, whose coming-of-age or initiation rituals generally follow the pattern outlined by van Gennep. For males, these rituals often consist of some kind of test and include **circumcision.** Boys belonging to the Masai tribes of East Africa become warriors between the ages of 12 and 16 after a ritual in which a group of initiates is isolated, their heads shaved, and then circumcised. The Kikuyu of Kenya were traditionally circumcised and adopted by ritual parents at around the age of 15. Isolated in groups for a period of eight days, they sang, danced, and ate special ceremonial foods.

Ritual coming-of-age ceremonies for girls were traditionally associated with the onset of **menstruation.** However, in contrast to males, young women were generally isolated individually (usually for about one week), after which they often participated in activities literally or symbolically related to their future status as homemakers. (Carib girls in Surinam were made to handle a tuft of burning cotton as a reminder that they would always need to keep their hands busy.) Finally, they would be adorned with jewelry and special clothing and have festivities held in their honor. One female rite of passage still practiced in parts of Africa has drawn protests throughout the international community: among the Masai and other groups, female circumcision (genital mutilation) is considered the main ritual marking a young woman's transition to adulthood, a sign that she is ready to marry and procreate. While some tribal groups cling to certain practices such as this one, others have modified their rituals to accord with contemporary life. For example, many African males undergo ritual circumcision in a clinic under local **anesthesia** and, contrary to traditional practice, do not immediately assume full adult responsibilities, remaining instead in their parents' home and finishing school.

In the United States, as in many other Western cultures, there is no clear-cut point at which a young person becomes an adult and, therefore, no single definitive rite of passage marking the transition to adulthood. Another reason cited for the absence of such a ritual is that such rites are typically religious in nature, and the United States has no official religion. In fact, the closest approximations to traditional rites of passage in the United States are the Judeo-Christian religious ceremonies of confirmation and bar/bat mitzvah.

Protestants consider the confirmation a reaffirmation of the religious promises made for the infant at baptism. The **bar mitzvah** marks the point at which a Jewish boy, at the age of 13, enters into full adult participation in the religious life of his community. He is deemed qualified to be counted as part of a *minyan* (the quorum of 10 men needed for public prayer) and can begin wearing religious symbols called *tefillin* (phylacteries) and fully observing the ritual fast days of the Jewish calendar.

The **bat mitzvah**, a 20th-century innovation, is a similar ceremony for Jewish girls when they turn 12. Bar and bat mitzvah are also terms referring to the altered status that the young person automatically attains at the age of 12 or 13, with or without the ceremony (although the ceremony is always an integral part of the occasion for observant Jews, especially the bar mitzvah). A bar or bat mitzvah is not only something one has, but it is also something one becomes. Traditionally, the lives of boys in the strictly Orthodox Jewish communities of Eastern Europe underwent a significant change once they reached the age of 13. They were sent out of town to special schools (yeshivas) for advanced religious study and returned home only for major holidays. Except for these visits, many young men never lived with their families again. Although almost all Jews, including modern Orthodox Jews, have abandoned this practice, Hasidim and other strictly Orthodox groups still maintain it in the various countries where they reside, including the United States.

Although there is no universal rite of passage for American teenagers, a number of different milestones do carry symbolic connotations of adulthood. These include getting a driver's license and getting one's first job. Two special rituals for young women that were once common but have faded in popularity are the "sweet sixteen" party and the debutante ball. Both of these events (especially the latter) served a function similar to that of more traditional female initiation rituals: announcing the young woman's availability for dating and marriage. Two symbolic events accompany the end of secondary schooling: the prom and high school graduation. The high school graduation, which may be the closest thing Americans have to a definitive coming-of-age ritual, involves a standardized formal ceremony, including speeches, music, and a procession. In addition, the initiates are spatially separated from the rest of the community (i.e., their parents), which they rejoin after the ceremony. Other experiences commonly associated with coming-of-age include joining the military, getting married, and getting one's first full-time job.

Aside from the lack of a clearly defined point of entry into adulthood, another difference between modern industrialized societies and those with clear rites of passage is that in the latter there is usually no equivalent to the prolonged period of **adolescence** common in developed countries. Initiates of the Masai and the Kikuyu tribes, for example, start out as children and become adults. Some have viewed the entire period of adolescence in modern cultures as analogous to the disorienting middle stage of van Gennep's classic three-part scheme: an extended period of transition characterized by uncertainty and confusion that eventually leads to the adult taking his or her place in society.

For Further Study

Books

Kaplan, Louise J. *Adolescence: The Farewell to Childhood.* New York: Simon and Schuster, 1984.

Liptak, Karen. *Coming-of-Age: Traditions and Rituals Around the World.* Millbrook Press, 1994.

Schlegel, Alice. *Adolescence: An Anthropological Inquiry.* New York: Free Press, 1991.

van Gennep, Arnold. *The Rites of Passage.* Chicago: University of Chicago Press, 1960.

Rivalry, Sibling *see* **Birth Order**

Rogers, Fred McFeely (1928–)

American television producer of educational television programs for children.

Fred Rogers is best known as the quiet host of a popular and long-running children's public television program "Mister Rogers' Neighborhood." He graduated from Rollins College with a degree in music composition in 1952. Rogers first saw television in the 1950s while a college student and disapproved of the slapstick aimed at children. He decided to pursue a career in this field to provide higher quality programming for children's television.

After working for the National Broadcasting Company, Rogers was invited to work on a live children's program for National Education Television. Rogers co-produced, wrote, composed, and functioned as puppeteer and organist for the "Children's Corner" from 1953–62. Rogers produced and hosted "Misterogers" for the Canadian Broadcasting Company from 1962–64, and was executive producer and host of the popular "Misterrogers' Neighborhood" (later, "Mister Rogers' Neighborhood") for the Public Broadcasting Company from 1965–75. Attending class during lunch hours and evenings, Rogers was ordained a Presbyterian minister with a charge to serve families and children through the mass media. He graduated magna cum laude from Pittsburgh Theological Seminary in 1962. Later he pursued

graduate work in child development at the University of Pittsburgh from 1964–67.

Rogers continually sought to convey a message of affirmation to young children. He credits his grandfather, Fred Brooks McFeely, with the signature quotation from his television show, "I like you, just the way you are." He arranges his program to combine reality and fantasy, providing educational excursions to various places in the neighborhood as well as visits to the puppets that inhabit "Make Believe" and act out children's issues including jealousies, fears, and everyday moral dilemmas.

In addition to his work in television, Rogers has written a number of children's books including a First Experience series in which Rogers addresses such topics as the New Baby, Moving, Fighting, Going to the Doctor, Going to Daycare, and Going to the Potty. His books address common childhood fears and anxieties with respect and reassurance, reflecting the tone and message of his television show. Rogers has been the recipient of numerous awards and honors for his contributions to children's television.

For Further Study

Books

Collins, Mark, and Margaret Mary Kimmel, eds. *Mister Rogers' Neighborhood: Children, Television, and Fred Rogers.* Pittsburgh, PA: University of Pittsburgh Press, 1996.

DiFranco, JoAnn, and Anthony DiFranco. *Mister Rogers: Good Neighbor to America's Children.* Minneapolis, MN: Dillon Press, 1983.

Rogers, Fred. *Mr. Rogers Talks with Parents.* Berkley, 1985.

Rogers, Fred, and B. Head. *The Mister Roger's Playbook: Insights and Activities for Parents and Children.* Berkley, 1986.

Rogers, Fred. *You Are Special: Words of Wisdom from America's Most Beloved Neighbor.* New York: Viking, 1994.

—Doreen Arcus, Ph.D.
University of Massachusetts Lowell

Role Playing

The act of putting oneself in another person's position in an attempt to see his or her point of view in a situation.

Also referred to as role taking or perspective taking.

In role playing, participants take the position of someone else to "act" the part of that person in a particular situation. Parents, teachers, and therapists all use role playing in varying degrees of formality to help a child develop empathy. Children often benefit from trying to see a situation from the point of view of someone else, such as a friend or sibling, especially when involved in an argument or conflict.

Even infants appear to be capable of empathy and simple perspective taking. When an infant observes another infant or family member display outward signs of being upset or hurt, the infant often mirrors those emotions, becoming distressed also. Within the first year of life, infants are able to practice taking turns for short periods with parent, sibling, or caretaker. Many researchers feel that the infant's ability to share feelings and empathize is evidence that these social behaviors are innate rather than learned. Researchers who have studied brain functioning and the family history of people with severe social behavior deficits seems to confirm this view.

Teachers often use role playing or perspective taking in discussing literature. Even the youngest students and beginning readers can examine picture-book characters' facial expressions in order to express empathy. Older readers can discuss a character's motive and attempt to understand the situation from that character's point of view. Psychodrama, a technique used in group therapy, involves reenacting life situations with different people taking the roles of the participants. With the guidance of a therapist, individuals participating in psychodrama, a formalized form of role playing, may gain insights into others' feelings, or into their own responses to the behavior of others.

For Further Study

Books

Hawley, Robert C. *Value Exploration through Role Playing: Practical Strategies for Use in the Classroom.* New York: Hart Publishing Co., 1975.

Jones, Ken. *Interactive Learning Events.* New York: Nichols Publishing, 1988.

Parisi, Lynn. *Creative Role-Playing Exercises in Science.* Boulder, CO: Social Science Education Consortium, 1986.

Sawyer, R. Keith. *Pretend Play as Improvisation.* Mahwah, NJ: L. Erlbaum, 1997.

Shaftel, Fannie R. *Role Playing in the Curriculum.* Englewood Cliffs, NJ: Prentice-Hall, 1982.

Van Ments, Morry. *The Effective Use of Role-Play: A Handbook for Teachers and Trainers.* New York: Nichols Publishing, 1989.

Rooting Reflex *see* **Neonatal Reflexes**

Rorschach Psychodiagnostic Test

Assesses personality structure and identifies emotional problems.

The Rorschach Psychodiagnostic Test, also known as the Rorschach Technique and popularly as the "Inkblot Test," is the most widely used projective psychological test. It is generally administered to adolescents and adults but can be used with children as young as three years of age. The Rorschach is used to assess personality structure and identify emotional problems. The test provides information about a child's thought processes, perceptions, motivations, and attitude toward his or her environment, and it can detect internal and external pressures and conflicts as well as illogical or psychotic thought patterns. It can aid in diagnosing and treating a wide range of psychological problems and psychiatric disorders. The untimed, individually administered test consists of interpreting a series of 10 inkblots. The child is shown the inkblots on separate cards and asked a set of standard questions about what he or she sees. Responses are tabulated, put in summary form, and scored according to a set of criteria. Hermann Rorschach, who pioneered the test in 1921, did not provide a comprehensive scoring system, but many different ones have since been developed. The most thorough and widely used is the Exner system, called "The Rorschach: A Comprehensive System." Many consider it the most objective and reliable method of scoring the test. The Rorschach is generally used as part of a battery of tests and must be administered by a trained psychologist.

For Further Study

Books

Knoff, Howard M. *The Assessment of Child and Adolescent Personality.* New York: Guilford Press, 1986.

Leichtman, Martin. *The Rorschach: A Developmental Perspective.* Analytic Press, 1996.

McCullough, Virginia. *Testing and Your Child: What You Should Know About 150 of the Most Common Medical, Educational, and Psychological Tests.* New York: Plume, 1992.

Shore, Milton F., Patrick J. Brice, and Barbara G. Love. *When Your Child Needs Testing: What Parents, Teachers, and Other Helpers Need to Know about Psychological Testing.* New York: Crossroad, 1992.

Wortham, Sue Clark. *Tests and Measurement in Early Childhood Education.* Columbus: Merrill Publishing Co., 1990.

Roseola Infantum

Mild viral disease of infancy and childhood characterized by high fever and enlarged lymph node.

Also called exanthem subitum, sixth disease, and/or Zahorsky's disease.

Roseola infantum is a mild viral disease affecting infants and young children between the ages of 6–18 months. It is characterized by an abrupt high **fever** of 104°F (40°C) or higher, mild pharyngitis (inflammation of the pharynx), a runny nose, and enlarged lymph nodes.

The high fever may cause convulsions; if this occurs, a physician should be consulted immediately. The fever subsides after four to five days, followed by a faint, flat, pink rash on the neck, body, and thighs. A white circle may appear around the individual spots. Depending on the severity of the disease, the rash can last from several hours to two days.

Treatment includes bed rest, fluids, and medication to reduce the fever.

For Further Study

Books

Brown, Jeffrey L. *The Complete Parents' Guide to Telephone Medicine: A Ready Reference for Childhood Illnesses, Common Emergencies, Newborn Infant Care, Psychological and Behavior Problems.* New York: Putnam, 1988.

Infectious Diseases of Children. 9th ed. St. Louis: Mosby, 1992.

Rubella

A highly contagious disease, also known as German or three-day measles, for which there is a vaccine available.

Rubella, or German measles, is caused by the rubella virus. Since 1969, an **immunization** has been given to nearly all children in industrialized countries. German measles is a highly contagious disease caused by the rubella virus. It is spread through air-borne droplets introduced into the environment when an infected person coughs, sneezes, or even talks. In 1969, a vaccine was introduced that has nearly eliminated German measles from Westernized countries. When young children are infected, the symptoms are usually a mild, low-grade **fever** for one or two days and a rash on the face or neck for about three days. As children get older, infection with rubella causes more severe symptoms, including swollen glands in the neck and stiffness in the joints. The rubella virus can cause serious **birth defects** if a woman contracts it during **pregnancy**. In the 1960s, thousands of babies were either miscarried or born with birth defects including deformed limbs, blindness, deafness, abnormally small brains, and **mental retardation** due to German measles. Any unimmunized woman considering pregnancy should receive the vaccine at least three months prior to getting pregnant. The rubella vaccine is normally given at 15 months of age in combination with the vaccines for measles and **mumps**.

See also **Immunization.**

For Further Study

Organizations

National Institute of Allergy and Infectious Diseases (NIADID)
   Address: 9000 Rockville Pike
   NIH Building 31, Room 7A50
   Bethesda, MD 20892-2520
   Telephone: (301) 496-5717
   (Arm of the National Institutes of Health that deals with allergies and diseases.)
National Vaccine Information Center
   Address: 128 Branch Road
   Vienna, VA 22180

Rubeola

A highly contagious disease, also known as measles, for which there is a vaccine available.

Rubeola, also known as measles, is a serious and highly contagious disease. It is spread by airborne droplets that are introduced into the atmosphere when an infected person sneezes or coughs. The symptoms of measles are a rash over most of the body, high **fever**, cough, runny nose, and watery eyes. The symptoms generally persist for up to two weeks. A small percentage (approximately 10%) of children with measles develop more serious symptoms, such as ear infection, pneumonia, **diarrhea**, and **seizures**. In rare instances, measles can result in **encephalitis** (inflammation of the brain), brain damage, and in extremely rare instances, death. A vaccine against measles has been widely available since 1963, and epidemics are rare. In the 1990s, a few outbreaks of measles were attributed to relaxed attitudes about **immunization**, since the disease seems to be under control. Rubeola, like **rubella** (German measles) is especially threatening to unborn fetuses. If a woman contracts rubeola during pregnancy, miscarriage, **premature birth**, or birth defects can result. Any woman considering pregnancy should verify her immunization against rubeola, rubella, and mumps. The combination vaccine (**MMR vaccine**) is often given at about age 15 months, and between 11 and 12 years of age.

See also **Immunization.**

For Further Study

Organizations

National Institute of Allergy and Infectious Diseases (NIADID)
   Address: 9000 Rockville Pike
   NIH Building 31, Room 7A50
   Bethesda, MD 20892-2520
   Telephone: (301) 496-5717
   (Arm of the National Institutes of Health that deals with allergies and diseases.)

National Vaccine Information Center
  Address: 128 Branch Road
Vienna, VA 22180

Running Away

Being absent from home at least overnight without permission from a parent or caretaker.

Every year an estimated one to two million teenagers in the United States run away from home. Most return voluntarily within a few days. Some are aided by police and social agencies and eventually return home or are placed in alternative stable environments. About one-fourth become homeless street kids with no permanent source of adult support. They are exposed to sexual exploitation, drug addiction, violent crime, and the other harmful mental and physical effects of homelessness. Runaways include "throwaways," who leave with the overt or tacit approval of parents or caretakers, and "push-outs," who are turned out by parents who don't want them, as well as teens who run away because they have become dissatisfied with their home life.

Results of a research study released in 1990 provided the following estimates for the United States:

RUNAWAY, "THROWAWAY," AND MISSING CHILDREN	
Estimated number of runaways annually	450,000
Estimated percent of runaways who are are physically or sexually abused while away from home	11%
Estimated number of "throw-aways" annually	127,000
Estimated number of children lost, injured, or otherwise missing	438,000
Estimated number abducted by non-family members	4,600
Estimated number abducted by family members	354,100

The grim realities of street life belie the traditional romantic notions of adventure found in the novels of Mark Twain or Charles Dickens. Rather than seeking adventures, most of today's runaways are running from intolerable domestic situations. It has been estimated that at least 60–70% of these young people are fleeing from families in which they have been mentally, physically, or

LEGISLATIVE TIMELINE

1982 Missing Children's Act: Enabled the entry of missing child information into the FBI's national crime computer (NCIC).

1984 Missing Children's Assistance Act: Mandated a national resource center to address child abduction and exploitation. The private, nonprofit National Center for Missing and Exploited Children (NCMEC) was established in cooperation with the U.S. Department of Justice, to find missing children and prevent child victimization. Created a 24-hour hotline (1-800-THE-LOST).

1990 National Child Search Assistance Act: Mandating an immediate police report and NCIC entry for missing children cases.

Results

In 1982, there were 154,341 missing person reports in NCIC.

Since 1984, National Center for Missing and Exploited Children has handled 700,000 calls; trained 126,000 professionals; disseminated 7,600,000 publications; and played a role in the recovery of 24,000 youngsters.

In 1993, there were 868,345 missing person reports; FBI estimated that 85–90% involved children.

sexually abused. Historically, attention to the role played by a child's family environment in the treatment of a runaway is relatively new. In past eras, runaways themselves were uniformly blamed for their situation and seen as hostile and destructive lawbreakers who needed to be reformed. In the 19th century they were generally sent to reform schools that were similar to prisons. Even after the establishment of the juvenile justice system toward the end of the 19th century, most runaways were regarded as delinquents, and the home situations from which they had fled received little scrutiny. In the early and mid-20th century, the prevailing view of runaways underwent a partial shift in emphasis from crime to pathology. Early versions of the **American Psychiatric Association**'s *Diagnostic and Statistical Manual* included "runaway reaction" as a **mental disorder**. (In subsequent editions it was reclassified within the category of under-socialized nonaggressive personal conduct disorder.)

In the 1960s, with the growth of the hippie subculture and the associated "youth rebellion," the number of teen runaways increased dramatically, drawing attention to the risks these youths faced on the streets. Growing public concern over their fate was reflected in the 1974 passage of the Runaway Youth Act, which funded a program to establish a network of centers for runaways. Increased attention to the plight of these young people revealed the dangers of child prostitution and pornography they faced on the streets. It also began to change the public image of runaways from that of thrill-seekers to that of young people from families in crisis fleeing intolerable conditions with no place else to go. This perception of runaways has become influential in both public opinion and government policy.

Researchers have identified several common characteristics of the abusive family environments that prompt young people to run away. These include financial troubles, sexual abuse, alcohol and drug abuse, physical and verbal abuse, and tolerance of deviant behavior. Besides outright physical or sexual abuse, runaways may be reacting to persistent tension between family members, including parental fighting or competition among siblings (especially step-siblings), feelings of rejection by their families, or authoritarian parenting that allows too little room for normal self-expression or social life.

Young people who run away and do not return home may remain on the street, go to a shelter, or be placed in foster homes by welfare agencies. Some eventually join the armed services or take jobs that keep them on the road, such as carnival or sales work. Others end up in jails or mental institutions. Those who remain on the streets have few options that would provide them with decent living conditions. Their age, lack of work experience, and uncompleted education make it difficult to find a job, especially one that pays more than minimum wage. It is common for both male and female runaways living on the streets to steal, panhandle, deal and abuse drugs, engage in prostitution, and pose for pornographic pictures. For shelter they may stay with strangers, spend nights in bus stations, all-night coffee shops, and other public places, or stow away in empty or abandoned buildings, or even in stairwells. Many never get off the streets, becoming part of the adult homeless population.

The estimated 500 runaway shelters and youth crisis centers in the United States offer not only a safe shelter but also food, counseling, and advocacy services, which help young people deal with parents, police, and the courts. Many also provide educational and vocational assistance. However, shelters do set certain conditions for accepting runaways, the most common being parental notification. This is an obstacle for some young people who do not want their parents contacted, even though the shelter does not pressure them to return home. One problem that has occurred at some shelters is sexual molestation by staff members. Even the highly respected founder of the Covenant House network of youth shelters, Father Bruce Ritter, has been accused of molestation by former clients. Nevertheless, many young people have had positive experiences at shelters, which they either find on their own or are sent to by the legal or welfare systems.

Since the 1970s hotlines have been available to help runaways and their families. The Runaway Hotline and the National Runaway Switchboard are widely used 24-hour help lines that offer crisis counseling and referrals to service agencies that can provide food, shelter, medical aid, and other types of help. The National Runaway Switchboard will put runaways and their parents in touch without revealing the location from which the teenager is calling.

For Further Study

Books

Cutler, Evan Karl. *Runaway Me: A Survivor's Story.* Fort Collins, CO: Blooming Press, 1994.

Hyde, Margaret O., and Lawrence E. Hyde. *Missing Children.* New York: Franklin Watts, 1985.

Janus, Mark-David, et. al. *Adolescent Runaways: Causes and Consequences.* Lexington, MA: D.C. Heath, 1987.

Resener, Carl R., and Judy Hall. *Kids on the Street.* Nashville: Broadman Press, 1992.

Organizations

National Runaway Switchboard
Telephone: toll-free hotline (800) 621-4000; (312) 880-9860.

Runaway Hotline
Address: P.O. Box 12428
Austin, TX 78711
Telephone: toll-free hotline (800) 231-6946; (512) 463-2000

Covenant House
Telephone: toll-free (800) 999-9999
(Referrals and counseling for youth in need)

National Center for Missing and Exploited Children (NCMEC)
24-hour toll-free hotline: (800) THE-LOST [(800) 843-5678].

National Clearinghouse on Runaway and Homeless Youth
Address: P.O. Box 13505
Silver Spring, MD 20911-3505
Telephone: (301) 608-8098

National Network of Runaway and Homeless Youth Services
Address: 1319 F Street NW, Suite 201
Washington, DC 20004
Telephone: (202) 783-7949

S

Safety

Keeping children from injuries and hazards.

Keeping children safe involves removing hazards from their environment and using protective safety equipment to prevent or minimize injuries from accidents. Unintentional injury is a serious threat to children as these 1991 statistics from the National Center for Health Statistics illustrate: each year approximately 7,250 children are killed and another 50,000 are permanently disabled from injuries that could have been prevented. Parents, **caregivers,** and school personnel should continually monitor the indoor and outdoor environments for safety and should teach children about safety practices.

Safety at home

Every room in the house may feature hazards for infants, toddlers, and young children. Parents should begin **childproofing** as soon as their infant is able to sit and roll, so that by the time he or she is crawling, their home environment will be welcoming and safe. By looking at each room with an eye for potential hazards, parents can anticipate problems and correct them or compensate for them. For example, accidents involving electrical outlets can be prevented by covering all unused outlets with inexpensive covers. Drapery and blind cords are potential hazards, and should be tied up well out of reach of young children. Door knobs can be fitted with special covers that prevent small hands from turning them and opening the door.

The kitchen, considered to be the most dangerous room in the house, is more difficult to keep hazard-free when it is cluttered. Parents should try to keep the kitchen surfaces as clean and clutter-free as possible to minimize the potential for an accident. Parents should devise ways to keep the child safely away from potential danger, such as using safety gates to keep a child under two from wandering into the kitchen. (Parents should make sure that the gate itself is not a hazard; accordion-style gates

Children should be taught always to wear a helmet when biking or in-line skating.

should never be used, since children can get their heads stuck in the V-shaped or diamond-shaped openings. Vertical slats on a gate should have no more than 2-3/8 inches of space between them.)

Children should be warned about the dangers of hiding in appliances, since they pose a potential for suffocation if a child were to become trapped inside. Parents may want to consider installing a Velcro-strap safety latch on all appliance doors to prevent children from opening them. The doors and other surfaces of appliances should be kept free of hazards as well. Children could choke if they put refrigerator magnets into their mouths, so parents should remove all small magnets from appliance surfaces. The dishwasher may also pose a hazard. Scalding hot water may back up into the sink when the dishwasher is running; therefore, parents should never bathe a child in the kitchen sink while the dishwasher is operating.

The stove is an obvious source of potential danger from burns and scalds. The recommended safety practice of keeping the handles of pots and pans turned away from the stove's edges is especially important in households with toddlers and young children. Food that is appealing to children, such as cereals and snacks, should be stored in cabinets away from the stove. Likewise, the fire extinguisher, an important item of safety equipment that all households should have, should be stored out of reach of small children.

When the infant has mastered sitting up unsupported, he or she may be fed using a high chair. The high chair is also a good way to keep the child restrained and safe while parents work in the kitchen. The seat belt restraint in the high chair, with a strap that goes between the child's legs, must be used every time the child sits in the chair. The high chair tray does not provide sufficient security to prevent the child from slipping out of or standing up in the highchair.

There are many poisons in the kitchen—cleaning agents, furniture polish, detergents, insect repellents and pesticides—that must be kept out of reach of children. Safety latches should be installed on the doors of any cabinet that contains hazardous substances. In case of an accidental poisoning, the telephone number of the local poison control center should be posted near all telephones, along with the family's own address and telephone number.

The bathroom is another site for potential accidents for young children. Families should keep the toilet cover down at all times to prevent accidental drowning; a safety latch is available to keep the lid down and secure. Children under age five should not be left unattended in the bathtub, since drowning can occur in the few minutes it takes to answer the telephone. Medications should be kept well out of the reach of young children, and in child-proof containers.

Safety for travel and play

Most states require that children use a child safety seat when traveling in a motor vehicle. In fact, many hospitals will not discharge mothers and infants unless the infant will be transported in an approved car seat. In 1997, there were widespread news reports about the possibility of injury for short-stature adults and children from the deployment of auto airbags. The National Highway Traffic Safety Administration recommended that laws be enacted by the state governments (traffic safety laws fall under the jurisdiction of individual states) so that infants and children under age 13 must be seated in the rear seats only when traveling by car; child safety seats for young infants should be installed in the rear seat and facing the back of the car. Older toddlers and young children may use a booster-type child safety seat, facing forward in the rear auto seat.

For children who enjoy biking and in-line skating, parents should require that appropriate safety equipment be used, and that safety rules be observed. The police department in many communities offer a program to teach five-year-olds rules of safe pedestrian and bicycle travel. These "Safety Town" programs provide an opportunity for children to practice strategies for crossing the street, interacting with strangers, fire emergency, and bicycle travel in a controlled and safe setting. If such a program is available, parents should consider enrolling their children, where they will have opportunities to meet and learn from a friendly police officer.

For Further Study

Books

Breitenbach, Robert J., Janet B. Carnes, and Judy A. Hammond. *Baby Seats, Safety Belts, and You!* 2nd ed. Washington, DC: U. S. Department of Transportation, National Highway Traffic Safety Administration.

Dlugokencky, Peter. *The Child Safety Handbook: A Parent's Guide to Avoiding Hidden Household Hazards.* Farmingdale, NY: Blue Island Press, 1995.

Periodicals

"Baby Equipment (Evaluation)." *Consumer Guide Magazine* 616, December 6, 1996, pp. 433+.

"Child Safety Seats (1997 Buying Guide)." *Consumer Reports* 61, December 16, 1996, pp. 311+.

Johnson, Maija. "Care-Seat Savvy." *Parents Magazine* 72, June 1997, pp. 55+.

Martinex, Anne, Erin Albert, and Kristen Bruno. "Car Seat Do's and Don'ts." *Parenting* 10, April 1996, p. 163.

Mickalide, Angela D. "Creating Safer Environments for Children." *Childhood Education* 70, no. 5, Annual 1994, pp. 263+.

Audiovisual Recordings

Baby Care Basics. Columbus, OH: Ross Laboratories, 1992. (One 49-minute videotape, including a segment on car seats.)

Children and Child Safety. Cincinnati, OH: WCPO-TV, 1996. (One 12-½ minute videotape.)

Protecting Your Newborn. Washington, DC: National Highway Traffic Safety Commission, 1997.

(One 26-minute videotape. Includes information on keeping children safe in cars with airbags.)

Organizations

Center for Injury Prevention
Address: 1007 Ellis Street
Stevens Point, WI 54481
Telephone: toll free (800) 344-7580
FAX: (715) 341-8400

Children's Safety Network
Address: National Injury and Violence Prevention Resource Center
Education Development Center, Inc.
55 Chapel Street
Newton, MA 02158-1060
Telephone: (617) 969-7101, ext. 2207
FAX: (617) 244-3436
website: http://www.edc.org/HHD/csn/index.html

National Safe Kids Campaign
Address: 1301 Pennsylvania Avenue, NW, Suite 1000
Washington, DC 20004
Website: safekids.org
e-mail comments to: info@safekids.org
(Coalition of state and local organizations to implement community-based strategies focusing on child occupant protection, bicycle safety, residential fire detection, and scald and burn prevention.)

The ABC's of Safe and Healthy Child Care: An On-line Handbook for Child Care Providers
website: http://www.cdc.gov:80/ncidod/hip/abc/abc.htm
(This site is maintained through cooperation of agencies of the U.S. Public Health Service, including: Centers for Disease Control and Prevention, National Center for Infectious Diseases, Hospital Infections Program, and Epidemiology Program Office.)

SAT

Measures verbal and mathematical abilities and achievement in specific subject areas.

The SAT, known until 1997 as the Scholastic Assessment Test and prior to that as the Scholastic Aptitude Test, changed its name and format in March 1994. (SAT tests are also referred to informally as College Entrance Examination Boards or College Boards.) The SAT is still a series of group-administered tests of verbal and mathematical abilities as well as achievement in a variety of subject areas. It is offered on Saturday mornings seven months of the year at locations across the country and used by over 2,000 colleges and universities to aid in assessing a student's ability to do college-level work. Intended as a useful standard for comparing the abilities of students from widely different cultural backgrounds and types of schools, the test can also help students, their parents, and guidance counselors make decisions in the college application process. The two major components of

the test are SAT I: Reasoning Test and SAT II: Subject Tests (formerly called Achievement Tests). SAT I—the part of the test that is most important and that all students take—is, as before, a three-hour multiple-choice test.

The Test of Standard Written English, which formerly comprised a half-hour section of the SAT, has been eliminated, and the new version consists of three verbal reasoning and three mathematical reasoning sections. However, not all of these are half-hour sections. For both the verbal and math components, two sections take 30 minutes, and the third takes only 15. This brings the total test time to 2-½ hours. The remaining half hour is devoted to an experimental section (now called the Equating section), which can be either a math or a verbal section and isn't counted in the students score (the catch is that he or she doesn't know which one is the Equating section while taking the test).

The Verbal Reasoning in the new SAT no longer contains antonym questions, and a greater emphasis has been placed on reading comprehension (now called Critical Reading), which, in some cases, requires the student to answer questions on two different passages instead of just one. As before, the Verbal Reasoning sections also include sentence completion and analogy questions. The Mathematical Reasoning sections consist of multiple-choice questions covering arithmetic, algebra, and geometry; quantitative comparison (which are also multiple choice); and a section of problems requiring students to come up with their own answers. Students are allowed (and encouraged) to use calculators for the math sections.

SAT II includes a variety of subject tests in English, foreign languages, math, history and social studies, and the sciences. SAT I and II cannot be taken on the same day. Raw SAT scores based on the number of correct answers minus a fraction of a point for each wrong answer (the "guessing penalty") are converted using a scale ranging from 200 to 800, with separate scores provided for the verbal and math sections (and for each subject test in SAT II). Scores are reported, about six weeks after the test date, to students and their high schools, and to colleges of their choice.

The SAT has been criticized on grounds of cultural and gender bias, charges that the revised version has attempted to respond to. The widespread use of test preparation courses and services for the SAT has also generated controversy, with detractors arguing that the test is unfair to economically disadvantaged students, who have limited access to coaching.

For Further Study

Books

Crouse, James, and Dale Trusheim. *The Case Against the SAT.* Chicago: University of Chicago Press, 1988.

Hanford, George H. *Life with the SAT: Assessing Our Young People and Our Times.* New York: College Entrance Examination Board, 1991.

United States Congress. House Committee on the Judiciary. *Sex and Race Differences on Standardized Tests: Oversight Hearings Before the Subcommittee on Civil and Constitutional Rights of the Committee on the Judiciary.* Washington, DC: U.S. Government Printing Office, 1989.

Wildemuth, Barbara M. *ERIC Digests: Coaching for Tests.* Princeton, NJ: ERIC Clearinghouse on Tests, Measurement, and Evaluation: Educational Testing Service, 1983.

Audiovisual Recordings

Look Inside the SAT I: Test Prep from the Test Makers. New York: College Entrance Examination Board, 1994. (One videocassette)

Savant Syndrome

Below normal intelligence combined with a special talent or ability in a specific area.

Also known as autistic savant or idiot savant.

Children who display savant syndrome have traditionally been referred to as idiot, retarded, or autistic savant. (The negative connotations of the term "idiot" have led to the disuse of idiot savant; because the syndrome is often associated with **autism,** the latter term is more frequently heard.) Persons with savant syndrome have an exceptional talent or skill in a particular area, such as the ability to process mathematical calculations at a phenomenal speed. These individuals have been the subject of much scientific study, although the nature and cause of their seemingly contradictory abilities is not well understood. Savant syndrome affects more males than females.

Savant skills occur in a number of different areas, including music, visual arts, and mathematics. Experts believe that the most common skills demonstrated by savants is extraordinary memory. Persons with savant syndrome may be able to memorize extensive amounts of data in such areas as sports statistics, population figures, or historical and biographical data. One particular type of memorization common to those with savant syndrome is the ability to calculate what day of the week a particular date fell on or will fall on.

For Further Study

Books

Howe, Michael J. *Fragments of Genius: The Strange Feats of Idiots Savants.* London: Routledge, 1989.

Obler, L. K., and D. Fein (eds.) *The Exceptional Brain: Neuropsychology of Talent and Special Abilities.* New York: Guilford Press, 1988.

Treffert, D. A. *Extraordinary People.* New York: Harper and Row, 1989.

Periodicals

Sacks, Oliver. "Prodigies." *The New Yorker* 70, January 9, 1995, pp. 44+.

Scarlet Fever

An acute, contagious, bacterial disease characterized by sore throat, fever, enlarged lymph nodes, and a bright red, non-itchy rash. Also called scarlatina.

Scarlet fever occurs most often during the winter months. Children between the ages of three and 12 are the most susceptible. It is extremely contagious, spread by coughs and sneezes.

Scarlet fever comes on suddenly with a **fever** of 103°F (39.4°C) or higher, accompanied by a sore throat, physical weakness, headache, nausea, and stomachache. The high fever may cause convulsions.

Twelve to 48 hours after the onset of fever, a fine, rough rash (often likened to sandpaper or sunburn with goosebumps) appears in the armpits and groin and on the neck and inner thighs. It then spreads out to the chest, back, arms, and legs. The roof of the mouth may also break out, and the throat and tonsils appear bright red. The child's tongue is first covered with a white, fuzzy coating before changing to bright red. The rash lasts two to three days and then the skin begins to peel off in flakes, scales, and sheets. The face is usually the first to peel. The peeling lasts from three to eight weeks depending on the severity of the case.

The rash of scarlet fever is often confused with that of the measles (**rubeola**), German measles (**rubella), toxic shock syndrome,** heat rash, or sunburn. Therefore, the child should be seen by a physician on the first day that the rash breaks out. The doctor takes a throat culture to verify a strep infection and then prescribes an antibiotic. While the fever lasts, the child needs plenty of rest, fluids, and a fever-reducing medication. If left untreated, scarlet fever can lead to a middle-ear infection and/or abscess of the tonsils. In rare cases, the disease results in rheumatic fever and nephritis (inflammation of the kidneys).

For Further Study

Books

Fry, John, and Gerald Sandler. *Common Diseases: Their Nature, Prevalence, and Care.* (5th ed.) Boston: Kluwer Academic Publishers, 1993.

Hamann, Barbara P. *Disease: Identification, Prevention, and Control.* St. Louis: Mosby, 1994.

Schizophrenia

A mental illness characterized by disordered thinking, delusions, hallucinations, emotional disturbance, and withdrawal from reality.

Some experts view schizophrenia as a group of related illnesses with similar characteristics. The condition affects between one-half and one percent of the world's population, occurring with equal frequency in males and females (although the onset of symptoms is usually earlier in males). Between 1 and 2% of Americans are thought to be afflicted with schizophrenia—at least 2.5 million at any given time, with an estimated 100,000 to 200,000 new cases every year. Although the name "schizophrenia," coined in 1911 by Swiss psychologist Eugene Bleuler (1857–1939), is associated with the idea of a "split" mind, the disorder is different from a "split personality" (**dissociative identity disorder**), with which it is frequently confused. Schizophrenia is commonly thought to disproportionately affect people in the lowest socioeconomic groups, although some claim that socially disadvantaged persons with schizophrenia are only more visible than their more privileged counterparts, not more numerous. In the United States, schizophrenics occupy more hospital beds than patients suffering from **cancer**, heart disease, or **diabetes**. At any given time, they account for up to half the beds in long-term care facilities and 40% of the treatment days. With the aid of antipsychotic medication to control delusions and hallucinations, about 70% of schizophrenics are able to function in society.

Causes of schizophrenia

While the exact cause of schizophrenia is not known, it is believed to be caused by a combination of physiological and environmental factors. Studies have shown that there is clearly a hereditary component to the disorder. Family members of schizophrenics are ten times more prone to schizophrenia than the general population, and identical twins of schizophrenics have a 46% likelihood of having the illness themselves. Relatives of schizophrenics also tend to have milder psychological disorders with some of the same symptoms as schizophrenia, such as suspicion, communication problems, and eccentric behavior.

In the years following World War II, many doctors blamed schizophrenia on bad parenting. In recent years, however, advanced neurological research has strengthened the case for a physiological basis for the disease. It has been discovered that the brains of schizophrenics have certain features in common, including smaller volume, reduced blood flow to certain areas, and enlargement of the ventricles (cavities filled with fluid that are found at the brain's center). Over the past decade much attention has focused on the connection between schizophrenia and neurotransmitters, the chemicals that transmit nerve impulses within the brain. One such chemical—dopamine—has been found to play an especially important role in the disease. Additional research has concentrated on how and when the brain abnormalities that characterize the disorder develop. Some are believed to originate prenatally for a variety of reasons, including trauma, viral infections, malnutrition during pregnancy, or a difference in Rh blood factor between the fetus and the mother. Environmental factors associated with schizophrenia include birth complications, viral infections during infancy, and head injuries in childhood. While the notion of child rearing practices causing schizophrenia has been largely discredited, there is evidence that certain family dynamics do contribute to the likelihood of relapse in persons who already have shown symptoms of the disease.

Types of schizophrenia

Schizophrenia is generally divided into four types. The most prevalent, found in some 40% of affected persons, is paranoid schizophrenia, characterized by delusions and hallucinations centering on persecution, and by feelings of jealousy and grandiosity. Other possible symptoms include argumentativeness, anger, and violence. Catatonic schizophrenia is known primarily for its catatonic state, in which persons retain fixed and sometimes bizarre positions for extended periods of time without moving or speaking. However, catatonic schizophrenics may also experience periods of restless movement. In disorganized, or hebephronic, schizophrenia, the patient is incoherent, with flat or inappropriate emotions, disorganized behavior, and bizarre, stereotyped movements and grimaces. Catatonic and disorganized schizophrenia affect far fewer people than paranoid schizophrenia. Most schizophrenics not diagnosed as paranoid schizophrenics fall into the large category of undifferentiated schizophrenia (the fourth type), which consists of variations of the disorder that do not correspond to the criteria of the other three types. Generally, symptoms of any type of schizophrenia must be present for six months before a diagnosis can be made. Over the long term, about one-third of patients experience recovery or remission.

The initial symptoms of schizophrenia usually occur between the ages of 16 and 30, with some variation depending on the type. (The average age of hospital admission for the disease is between 28 and 34.) Disorganized schizophrenia tends to begin early, usually in adolescence or young adulthood, while paranoid schizophrenia tends to start later, usually after the age of 25 or 30. The onset of acute symptoms is referred to as the first psychotic break, or break from reality. In general, the earlier the onset of symptoms, the more severe the illness will be. Before the disease becomes full-blown, schizophrenics may go through a period called the prodromal stage, lasting about a year, when they experience behavioral changes that precede and are less dramatic than those of the acute stage. These may include social withdrawal, trouble concentrating or sleeping, neglect of personal grooming and hygiene, and eccentric behavior.

The prodromal stage is followed by the acute phase of the disease, which is characterized by "positive" symptoms and requires medical intervention. During this stage, three-fourths of schizophrenics experience delusions—illogical and bizarre beliefs that are held despite objections. A typical delusion might be a belief that the afflicted person is under the control of a sinister force located in the sewer system that dictates his every move and thought. Hallucinations are another common symptom of acute schizophrenia. These may be auditory (hearing voices) or tactile (feeling as though worms are crawling over one's skin). The acute phase of schizophrenia is also characterized by incoherent thinking, rambling or discontinuous speech, use of nonsense words, and odd physical behavior, including grimacing, pacing, and unusual postures. Persons in the grip of acute schizophrenia may also become violent, although often this violence is directed at themselves—it is estimated that 15–20% of schizophrenics commit **suicide** out of despair over their condition or because the voices they hear "tell" them to do so, and up to 35% attempt to take their own lives or seriously consider doing so. In addition, between 25 and 50% of people with schizophrenia abuse drugs or alcohol. As the positive symptoms of the acute phase subside, they may give way to the negative symptoms of what is called residual schizophrenia. These include flat or inappropriate emotions; an inability to experience pleasure (anhedonia); lack of motivation; reduced attention span; lack of interest in one's surroundings; and social withdrawal.

In rare cases, schizophrenia may have its onset during childhood. Childhood schizophrenia has been known to appear as early as five years of age. Occurring primarily in males, it is characterized by the same symptoms as adult schizophrenia. Diagnosis of schizophrenia in children can be difficult because delusions and hallucinations may be mistaken for childhood **fantasies**. Other signs of schizophrenia in children include moodiness, problems relating to others, attention difficulties, and difficulty dealing with change. It is important for the condition to be diagnosed as early as possible. The longer the symptoms last, the less well they respond to treatment. Even when treated, schizophrenia interferes with normal development in children and adolescents and makes new learning difficult.

Researchers have found correlations between childhood behavior and the onset of schizophrenia in adulthood. A 30-year longitudinal research project studied over 4,000 people born within a single week in 1946 in order to document any unusual developmental patterns observed in those children who later became schizophrenic. It was found that a disproportionate number of them learned to sit, stand, and walk late. They were also twice as likely as their peers to have speech disorders at the age of six and to have played alone when they were young. Home movies have enabled other researchers to collect information about the childhood characteristics of adult schizophrenics. One study found that the routine physical movements of these children tended to be slightly abnormal in ways that most parents wouldn't suspect were associated with a major mental illness and that the children also tended to show fear and anger to an unusual degree.

Treatment

Schizophrenia has historically been very difficult to treat, usually requiring hospitalization during its acute stage. In recent decades, antipsychotic drugs have become the most important component of treatment. They can control delusions and hallucinations, improve thought coherence, and, if taken on a long-term maintenance basis, prevent relapses. However, antipsychotic drugs don't work for all schizophrenics, and their use has been complicated by side effects, such as akathisia (motor restlessness), dystonia (rigidity of the neck muscles), and tardive dyskinesia (uncontrollable repeated movements of the tongue and the muscles of the face and neck). In addition, many schizophrenics resist taking medication, some because of the side effects, others because they may feel better and mistakenly decide they don't need the drugs anymore, or because being dependent on medication in order to function makes them feel bad about themselves. The tendency of schizophrenics to discontinue medication is very harmful. Each time a schizophrenic goes off medication, the symptoms of the disease return with greater severity, and the effectiveness of the drugs is reduced.

Low doses of antipsychotic medication have been used successfully with children and adolescents, especially when administered shortly after the onset of symptoms. Their rate of effectiveness in children between the ages of 5 and 12 has been found to be as high as 80%. Until recently, the drugs most often prescribed for schizophrenia have been neuroleptics such as Haldol, Prolixin, Thorazine, and Mellaril. A major breakthrough in the treatment of schizophrenia occurred in 1990 with the introduction of the drug clozapine to the U.S. market. Clozapine, which affects the neurotransmitters in the brain (specifically serotonin and dopamine), has been dramatically successful in relieving both positive and negative symptoms of schizophrenia, especially in patients in whom other medications have not been effective. However, even clozapine doesn't work for all patients. In addition, about 1% of those who take it develop agranulocytosis, a potentially fatal blood disease, within the first year of use, and all patients on clozapine must be monitored regularly for this side effect. (Clozapine was first developed decades ago but couldn't be introduced until it became possible to screen for this disorder.) The screening itself is expensive, creating another problem for those using the drug. Risperidone, a new, safer medication that offers benefits similar to those of clozapine, was introduced in 1994 and is now the most frequently prescribed antipsychotic medication in the United States. Olanzapine, another in the new generation of schizophrenia drugs, received FDA approval in the fall of 1996, and more medications are under development. Electroconvulsive therapy (ECT, also called electric shock treatments) has been utilized to relieve symptoms of catatonia and **depression** in schizophrenics, especially in cases where medication is not effective.

Although medication is the most important part of treatment, **psychotherapy** can also play an important role in helping schizophrenics manage anxiety and deal with interpersonal relationships, and treatment for the disorder usually consists of a combination of medication, therapy, and various types of rehabilitation. **Family therapy** has worked well for many patients, educating both patients and their families about the nature of schizophrenia and helping them in their cooperative effort to cope with the disorder.

For Further Study

Books

Atkinson, Jacqueline M. *Schizophrenia: A Guide to What It Is and What Can Be Done to Help.* San Bernardino, CA: R. Reginald Borgo Press, 1989.

Hoffer, Abram, and Humphry Osmond. *How to Live with Schizophrenia.* New York: Carol Publishing Group, 1992.

Lidz, Theodore. *The Origin and Treatment of Schizophrenic Disorders.* International Universities Press, 1990.

Mueser, Kim T., and Susan Gingerich. *Coping with Schizophrenia: A Guide for Families.* Oakland: New Harbinger Press, 1994.

Peschel, Enid. *Neurobiological Disorders in Children and Adolescents.* San Francisco: Jossey-Bass, 1992.

Walsh, Maryellen. *Schizophrenia: Straight Talk for Families and Friends.* New York: William Morrow, 1985.

Organizations

American Schizophrenia Association
    Address: 900 North Federal Highway, Suite 330
    Boca Raton, FL 33432
    Telephone: (407) 393-6167

National Alliance for Research on Schizophrenia and Depression
    Address: 60 Cutter Mill Rd., Suite 200
    Great Neck, NY 11202
    Telephone: (516) 829-0091

Schizophrenics Anonymous
    Address: 1209 California Rd.
    Eastchester, NY 10709
    Telephone: (914) 337-2252

Scholastic Assessment Test *see* **SAT**

School Phobia/School Refusal

Reluctance or refusal to attend school.

School phobia is an imprecise, general term used to describe a situation in which a child is reluctant to go to school. According to the **American Academy of Child and Adolescent Psychiatry,** refusal to go to school is most common in the period from preschool through second grade. In most cases, school phobia is a symptom of an educational, social, or emotional problem the child is experiencing.

The child with school phobia develops a pattern of predictable behavior. At first, the child may begin the day complaining that he is too sick to go to school, with a headache, sore throat, stomachache, or other symptom. After the parent agrees that the child may stay home from school, he begins to feel better, although his symptoms often do not completely disappear. By the next morning, the symptoms are back in full intensity. When the child repeats this pattern, or simply refuses to go to school without complaining of any symptoms of illness—on a chronic and consistent basis—school phobia is considered to have evolved into school refusal (or school refusal syndrome).

School refusal is a diagnostic criterion for **separation anxiety** disorder, a mental condition characterized by abnormally high anxiety concerning possible or actual separation from parents or other individuals to whom the child is attached. When school refusal is related to separation anxiety disorder, it is likely that the child will also display aversion to other activities (after-school clubs and sports, birthday parties, summer camp) that involve being away from the person to whom the child is attached. In addition, he may cling to the person, and refuse to allow her out of his sight for even short periods of time. Children experiencing separation anxiety disorder and school refusal may express feelings of fear when left alone in a room.

Refusal to go to school may begin as a result of any of the following stresses: birth of a sibling; death of a family member, close friend, or pet; change in school, such as a new teacher; loss of a friend due to a move or change in school; or a change in family, such as **divorce** or remarriage. It may also follow summer vacation or holiday break, when the young child has spent more time with her primary **caregiver**.

Almost every child will display behavior to avoid going to school—for academic or social reasons—at some point during his school career. In these cases, the situation the child is trying to avoid is usually temporary—an argument with a friend, the threat of a bully, or the consequences of a missed homework assignment, for example. When the avoidance of school becomes a chronic pattern the child may develop serious social and academic problems. A professional counselor or child psychiatrist working with the child's teacher and other school personnel can all support the family in overcoming a child's refusal to go to school.

Returning the child to school is the highest priority so that disruption to the child's educational and emotional development is minimized. Depending on the severity of the fears that produced the symptom of school refusal, ongoing counseling or psychiatric treatment may be necessary for a length of time, even after the child is successfully back in school.

For Further Study

Books

Kahn, Jack. *Unwillingly to School.* New York: Pergamon Press, 1981.

School Vouchers

A program to provide government money to parents to subsidize tuition for their children at private schools.

School voucher systems have been proposed in several states and cities across the nation and is part of a larger movement toward school choice. The choice movement advocates abolishing strict school district lines, allowing parents to enroll their children in any public school in the area, creating so-called "magnet" schools with special programs to attract bright students and similar "charter" schools with more autonomy than a traditional public school. School vouchers, therefore, extend the choice concept. Using a voucher of state money to subsidize tuition, parents would also be able to send their children to private or religious schools. While other aspects of the school choice agenda have been implemented in many school districts, including Los Angeles and Chicago, the voucher system has encountered both legal problems and lack of voter support. A California referendum on school vouchers failed in 1993. The first

functioning school choice program, in the Milwaukee school district, remains experimental and limited in scope.

The Milwaukee program began in 1990. At first, it provided money only for lower-income parents to send their children to private, nonsecular schools. Religious schools were not covered because of issues regarding separation of church and state. But the space at nonsecular schools was limited, so in 1995 the Milwaukee voucher system was expanded to include church-run schools as well. The expanded program met immediate legal challenges, and its implementation was blocked by the State Supreme Court. The issue is still not settled.

Even a voucher system that does not include religious schools raises many legal problems. Any school receiving government funds through vouchers is liable to government regulation. A private school participating in the voucher program would likely be required to comply with state and federal laws regarding discrimination, freedom of religion, freedom of speech, due process, and other civil liberties. This means that private schools that distinguish themselves by strict behavior codes, distinctive religious doctrines, or censorship of student expression would be open to legal challenges. Private schools accepting vouchers may also be required to perform more extensive student testing to ensure accountability.

Many critics of the school voucher system fear that compliance with government regulations would eventually transform private schools into quasi-public schools, losing their uniqueness, and the attributes that made them attractive to parents would be eroded. Other critics of voucher plans are afraid that public schools would be harmed. If parents can send their children to private schools, there will be less incentive to repair the many faults of public school systems.

Critics see voucher plans as a way for government to abandon its mission to provide free public education for all, and it is unclear whether districts can save money through voucher plans. Private schools are usually less expensive to run than public schools because teacher salaries are lower, and autonomous schools require less bureaucracy. The bureaucratic requirements would likely change, though, if vouchers were used. Teachers' salary expectations may change also if the nature of the school changes. Some fear that taxpayers would end up supporting two school systems under a voucher program, one public and one private. Voucher systems will likely continue to be controversial until they are more fully tested.

For Further Study

Books

Doyle, Denis P., and Chester E. Finn, Jr. *Educational Quality and Family Choice: Toward a Statewide Public School*

Voucher Plan. Washington, DC: National Institute of Education, 1983.

Harmer, David. *School Choice: Why We Need It, How We Get It.* Washington, DC: Cato Institue, 1994.

McGroarty, Daniel. *Break These Chains: The Battle for School Choice.* Rocklin, California: Prima Publishing, 1996.

Skillen, James W. (ed.) *The School-Choice Controversy: What Is Constitutional?* Washington, DC: Center for Public Justice, 1993.

—A. Woodward

Scoliosis

Abnormal curvature of the spine.

Beginning in childhood or adolescence, scoliosis curves the spine so that the shape of the body is distorted. The disease can cause pain, deformity, and other medical problems if not properly treated. Scoliosis is defined medically as a sideways (lateral) spinal curvature of eleven degrees or more. Only lateral curvatures constitute scoliosis, as distinct from an excessive rounding of the back with rounded shoulders and sunken chest (hyperkyphosis) or an abnormal forward curve of the lower back (hyperlordosis, also called swayback). Scoliosis eventually pulls the rib cage out of its normal position, crowding the ribs inside the curve and pulling those outside it apart. If severe enough, it can damage internal organs and impair breathing. In cases where scoliosis is painful, the pain is generally increased by bending, extended standing, and heavy work.

The lateral curvatures of scoliosis are either C- or S-shaped. The C-shaped right thoracic curve shifts the ribs on the right side and can squeeze the heart and lungs. Lower C-shaped curves include the thoracolumbar curve, stretching from the thoracic vertebrae to the lumbar region, and the lumbar curve, which twists the hips. The most common S-shaped curve is the double major curve, which consists of a curve in the chest area and one going in the opposite direction in the lumbar area. S-shaped curves generally cause less deformity because the two parts balance each other out somewhat. The spinal curvatures of scoliosis are measured by a method known as Cobb's angle, which is the angle created by the intersection of lines perpendicular to the top and bottom vertebrae of the curve. Having a standard of measurement allows for accurate and consistent communication between physicians. It also allows the progress of a single patient to be accurately tracked over time.

Roughly 80% of scoliosis cases are idiopathic, meaning that they have no known cause. The remainder are caused by a variety of conditions, including **birth defects,** chronically poor posture, uneven leg lengths, acci-

dental injuries, nerve and muscle diseases such as **muscular dystrophy** and poliomyelitis, and diseases of the connective tissues, such as Marfan's syndrome and osteogenesis imperfecta. Idiopathic scoliosis is known to have a hereditary component.

While idiopathic scoliosis usually appears in adolescence, the disorder may also begin in childhood or infancy. When it occurs in infants, it affects males more frequently than females, at a ratio of 3:2. Unlike scoliosis that is diagnosed at later ages, infantile idiopathic scoliosis (onset between birth and 3 years of age) usually corrects itself. Although scoliosis at this age is virtually unknown in the United States and Canada, it is as common as the adolescent form in other parts of the world. In contrast to infantile scoliosis, the juvenile variety (onset between ages four to 10) is equally common among boys and girls and, like the adolescent variety, shows a hereditary influence. Scoliosis is most likely to become apparent during the growth spurts between ages 10 and 15, when it strikes 2–3% of young people. In this age group, girls are affected three times as often as boys and are 10 times more likely than boys to have spinal curvatures of 30 degrees or more.

Early warning signs of scoliosis are generally provided by children's posture and the fit of their clothes. One hip or shoulder might be higher than the other, and the head may tilt, or a shoulder blade protrude. One arm may look longer than the other, or there may be asymmetric creases at the waist. When the child bends over, the ribs tend to form a hump on one side. Uneven hemlines or pant legs are other common clues. When signs of scoliosis appear, prompt diagnosis is important. Early treatment with a brace can prevent the need for surgery later on. Many states require schools to have screening programs for scoliosis, and the **American Academy of Pediatrics** recommends that physicians check youngsters for the condition during routine office visits every other year between the ages of 10 and 16. The Scoliosis Research Society and the American Academy of Orthopedic Surgeons recommend screening girls at the ages of 10 and 12 and boys at either 13 or 14. When scoliosis is suspected, a physician performs a detailed examination, including x rays, to determine the shape and severity of the spinal curvature.

Treatment of scoliosis ranges from simple monitoring to surgery. Decisions about treatment are based on the age, gender, and general health of the child, as well as the severity and nature of the curvature. Mild curvatures under 25 degrees often require no treatment other than periodic examinations and x rays to monitor the condition. Special exercises may also be recommended to help strengthen the back. Only 20% of mild spinal curvatures worsen, and only 3 in 1,000 become serious enough to require treatment. Treatment of moderate curves, 25 to 40

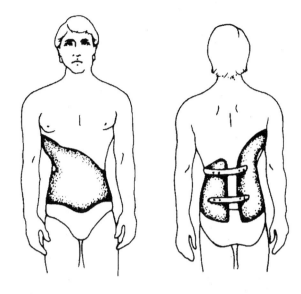

A custom-made brace hugs the torso beneath the underarms to correct scoliosis. Source: *FDA Consumer,* July–August 1994.

degrees, varies depending on the age of the patient. The younger the patient is at the onset of symptoms, the more severe the curves are likely to become.

The treatment for moderate scoliosis in children who are still growing is a lightweight brace, custom molded to fit the body, that can be worn for 16–24 hours a day. These braces, which come up only as high as the underarms and usually don't show underneath clothing, have proven 85% effective in arresting spinal curvatures. They can be removed for showering and swimming, and they allow for a much higher activity level than the traditional braces. If the curvature is high up in the spine, a full torso brace may be most effective, although young people are more reluctant to wear these.

An alternative treatment for moderate scoliosis is electronic stimulation ("electronic bracing"), in which electrodes are placed on the skin during sleep, stimulating the muscles to contract and straighten the spine. Like conventional braces, electrosurface stimulation only works for curvatures under 40 degrees, and in patients whose bones are still growing. While some researchers have found this method 80% effective in halting the progress of scoliosis curves, others have questioned its effectiveness.

For treatment of severe scoliosis (curves of 40–50 degrees) surgery may be necessary, especially if the curve continues to worsen even with a brace or there is pain that does not respond to treatment. Only about one of 100 cases of scoliosis is serious enough to warrant surgery. It is estimated that as many as a third of all spinal operations are for severe scoliosis. The most common operation is the Harrington rod technique, in which metal hooks attached to the vertebrae at the top and bottom of the curve hold metal rods that straighten the spine and hold it in place. Small bone fragments taken from the hip or ribs are inserted between the vertebrae, promoting the growth of solid bone which then fuses the vertebrae together within six to eight months. A brace or body cast is worn for a period of weeks or months after the operation. Newer surgical techniques that are gaining popularity include the use of two rods to provide additional balance and more correction of the curve; use of wires instead of hooks to hold the rods in place; and the Luque method, in which numerous wires pass through the neural canal and are attached to slim rods on either side of the curve. These newer methods require shorter periods of hospitalization, and patients may not need to wear body casts during the recovery period. Scoliosis is not outgrown in adulthood. Adults with the condition should have their spinal curvatures monitored by a physician at least once a year.

For Further Study

Books

American Physical Therapy Association. *Scoliosis: An Anthology.* Alexandria, VA: American Physical Therapy Association, 1984.

Caillet, Rene. *Scoliosis: Diagnosis and Management.* Philadelphia: F.A. David, 1975.

Sachs, Elizabeth-Ann. *Just Like Always.* New York: Atheneum, 1981. [juvenile fiction]

Schommer, Nancy. *Stopping Scoliosis: The Complete Guide to Diagnosis and Treatment.* New York: Doubleday, 1987.

Periodicals

Farley, Dixie. "Correcting the Curved Spine of Scoliosis." *FDA Consumer* 28, July–August 1994, pp. 26–28.

Organizations

American Academy of Orthopaedic Surgeons
   Address: 6300 N. River Road
   Rosemont, IL 60018-4262
   Telephone: toll-free (800) 346-2267

National Scoliosis Foundation, Inc.
   Address: 72 Mt. Auburn St.
   Watertown, MA 02172
   Telephone: (617) 926-0390

Scoliosis Association, Inc.
   Address: P.O. Box 811705
   Boca Raton, FL 333481-1705
   Telephone: toll-free (800) 800-0669

Scoliosis Research Society
   Address: 6300 N. River Road, Suite 727
   Rosemont, IL 60018
   Telephone: (708) 698-1627

Security Objects

A soft, clingable object like a blanket that provides the child with security and comfort in mildly or moderately fearful situations.

Security objects are items, usually soft and easily held or carried, that offer a young child comfort. Security objects are also referred to as attachment objects, inanimate attachment agents, nonsocial attachments, comfort habits, transitional objects, not-me possessions, substitute objects, cuddlies, treasured possessions, soothers, pacifiers, special soft objects, Linus phenomenon, and security blankets.

Early history

In the 1940s, attachment to a special object was regarded as a childhood fetish reflecting pathology in the relationship between the mother and her child (Wulff, 1946). D. W. Winnicott (1953), however, regarded the object as necessary for normal development: it was a "transitional" experience, intermediate between the infant's ability to distinguish the inner subjective world from outside reality. **John Bowlby** considered transitional objects to be a "substitute" for the absent mother, and he deemed the child's attachment to them normal and even desirable.

Nevertheless, throughout the 1970s, but progressively less in the 1980s and 1990s, a stigma remained attached to children who hugged a blanket in times of stress. The popular—but now generally discredited—stereotype was that these children, being overly anxious and insecure, were better off without their blanket. As a result, the blanket was often taken away from the child, sometimes forcibly, just when it could have been beneficial. Although some disagreement and inconsistency persist in the research literature, there is no justification for such drastic actions. Evidence does not support ascribing psychopathology to children just because they demonstrate an attachment to a security object. Blanket-attached children appear to be neither more nor less maladjusted or insecure than other children.

Theoretical underpinnings

Three current theories pertain to nonsocial attachment. Psychoanalytic theory surmises that it is created as a necessary transition between the child's outside and inside worlds once the child has formed a sufficient relationship with the mother. It helps augment feelings of personal control and continuity of the self. Ethological theory argues that the comfort object substitutes for the mother and should form only if **attachment** to the mother is secure. **Social learning theory** states that the physical characteristics of the object (softness, warmth, fuzziness, etc.) can be rewarding per se. Furthermore, if the mother's nurturing and distress-reducing presence is

associated with the inanimate object, attachment behaviors toward the object may ensue. Because the child is able to control a security object more readily than the mother, attachment to it should begin to develop relatively independently of the mother.

It is not, however, clear from any of these theories why some children engage in comfort habits while others do not. Child-rearing practices are frequently cited as contributing factors, especially children's sleeping arrangements and parental behavior at bedtime, but evidence has largely been inconclusive. Cultural and socioeconomic factors have received stronger support, although, again, the exact mechanisms underlying the differential acquisition of nonsocial attachments remain unclear. A mother's sensitivity to her children's security needs may be relevant, but the quality of the mother-child relationship seems not to be. However, preliminary evidence suggests that the security of a child's attachment to the mother does predict how a security object will be used in novel situations.

One problem in evaluating attachments to objects is the lack of uniformity in definitions and criteria. Divergent theoretical positions as well as cultural backgrounds have brought forth a variety of interpretations. Another complication involves the unreliability of adults' recollections about former treasured possessions. In studies attempting to link older children's or adults' current behaviors with their previous relationships to a special object, they—or their parents—are requested to recall details. However, such retrospective reports may misrepresent actual events. When college students and their mothers were questioned, 24% of the pairs disagreed totally about whether there had been a childhood attachment, and an additional 19% disagreed on what the object was (Mahalski, 1982). In a follow-up study one year later, 18% of the students contradicted their earlier statements about having had a security object! Clearly, mothers' concurrent reports and investigators' direct observations are necessary to generate reliable information about security objects.

Cultural issues

Despite current theoretical assertions that attachment to transitional objects is normal and almost universal, it should be pointed out that this attachment is culture-specific. For instance, in the United States, 60% of children have at least a mild degree of attachment to a soft, inanimate object some time during their life, and 32% exhibit strong attachment (Passman and Halonen, 1979). The incidence of attachments to soft objects in the Netherlands, New Zealand, and Sweden is comparable to that in the United States. Korean children have substantially fewer attachments to blankets (18%) than do American children, but Korean-born children living in the United

States display an intermediate percentage (34%). Only 5% of rural Italian children have transitional objects, compared to 31% of urban Romans and 62% of foreign children living in Rome. However, just 16% of Londoners' children have a special security object.

Developmental trends

In a cross-sectional investigation surveying the mothers of almost 700 children in the United States through their first 63 months of life, R. H. Passman and J. S. Halonen (1979) examined children's attachments to various classes of objects. The percentage of children who are not attached to any object remains relatively stable throughout the first three years, averaging around 40%, with a low of 28% at three months of age. From 33 months, it rises consistently to a high of 84% at 63 months. The number of children having at least a slight attachment to a favorite *hard* toy (like blocks or a toy truck) remains steady and low through the first four years, averaging approximately 14%, but then drops swiftly toward 0% through 63 months. Attachment to a **pacifier** peaks early at three months, with 66% reported as having at least some attachment. Pacifier usage declines quickly through the first 18 months, after which attachments are extremely unusual (averaging under 3%) through 63 months. Attachment to blankets begins at a later age than it does to pacifiers. Mild attachment to a blanket is rare at 3 months (8%), but increases somewhat through 15 months (22%), peaks rapidly at 18 months (60%), stays near this level through 39 months (57%), tapers off to 40% at 48 months, and falls suddenly to 16% through 63 months. Simultaneous attachment to both a pacifier and a blanket is infrequent; it rises from 4% at 3 months to 12% at 9 months, remains at a relative plateau through 21 months, then drops sharply, averaging about 1% thereafter. Passman and Halonen also investigated children's intense attachments to these objects and found similar patterns with respect to age. At three months, 16% are strongly attached to pacifiers. Strong attachment to blankets peaks at 18 and 24 months (32%), stays near this high level through 39 months, and diminishes steadily to 8% through 63 months. Generally in the United States, attachments to various objects are now regarded as conventional throughout the first five years of life.

Advantages of having security objects

Being attached to a security object can be beneficial to a child. Left in an unfamiliar playroom with a supportive agent (mother or transitional object), children played, explored, and refrained from crying more so than did children who had their favorite hard toy or who had no supportive agent available (Passman & Weisberg, 1975). Thus, children's attachment to a special soft object is something qualitatively different from their relationship with a noncuddly toy. The blanket provided comfort as well as the mother did—but only if the children were attached to it; nonattached children entering the room with their blanket adapted relatively poorly, with greater dismay. The security blanket, therefore, is aptly named; it indeed provides security to those attached to it.

Because security objects may serve as a substitute for the mother in her absence, they can be employed practically by parents, teachers, doctors, **babysitters,** and other professionals. Besides facilitating separation from the mother or father, the attachment object can promote interactions with strangers. At bedtime, it can soothe and facilitate sleep. A study by G. J. Ybarra, R. H. Passman, and C. Eisenberg found that during a routine third-year pediatric examination, the security object enhanced rapport with the examining nurse. Children attached to a blanket who were allowed access to it were rated as less distressed and experienced less physiological stress—as evidenced by heart rate and systolic blood pressure—than children undergoing the medical evaluation without their security object. The comfort provided by a blanket in novel situations has even been shown to enhance children's learning (Passman, 1977).

Alternatives to blankets

A variety of soft objects besides the blanket (e.g., diapers, pillow cases, sheepskins, soft toys, stuffed animals, dolls, napkins, handkerchiefs) may also provide security. Furthermore, research has shown that representations of the mother (e.g., films, videotapes, photographs, audiotapes of her) can also help children's adjustment. Although most children are thought to respond to their special object through touching or sucking, merely seeing (or hearing) it seems sufficient. Even an object as tactile as the security blanket does not have to be touched; visual contact alone evokes its soothing effects. For children too young for an attachment to a blanket, the pacifier seems to share many of the same functional characteristics (although its origins may be different).

Limitations

The positive effects of an attachment to an object have restrictions. If the situation is particularly arousing or threatening, the attachment object can be less effective in providing security than the child's mother.

For Further Study

Books

Greenberg, Mark T., Dante Cicchetti, and E. Mark Cummings, eds. *Attachment in the Preschool Years: Theory, Research, and Intervention.* Chicago: University of Chicago Press, 1990.

Periodicals

Adams, R. E., and R. H. Passman. "Effects of Visual and Auditory Aspects of Mothers and Strangers on the Play and Exploration of Children." *Developmental Psychology* 15, 1979, pp. 269–74.

Haslam, N. "Temperament and the Transitional Object." *Child Psychiatry and Human Development* 22, 1992, pp. 237–47.

Hong, K. M., and B. D. Townes. "Infants' Attachment to Inanimate Objects: A Cross-Cultural Study." *Journal of the American Academy of Child Psychiatry* 15, 1976, pp. 49–61.

Mahalski, P. "The Reliability of Memories for Attachment to Special, Soft Objects During Childhood." *Journal of the American Academy of Child Psychiatry* 21, 1982, pp. 465–67.

Mahalski, P. A., P. A. Silva, and G. F. S. Spears. "Children's Attachment to Soft Objects at Bedtime, Child Rearing, and Child Development." *Journal of the American Academy of Child Psychiatry* 24, 1985, pp. 442–46.

Passman, R. H. "Arousal-Reducing Properties of Attachment Objects: Testing the Functional Limits of the Security Blanket Relative to the Mother." *Developmental Psychology* 12, 1976, pp. 468–69.

———. "Providing Attachment Objects to Facilitate Learning and Reduce Distress: Effects of Mothers and Security Blankets." *Developmental Psychology* 13, 1977, pp. 25–28.

———. "Attachments to Inanimate Objects: Are Children Who Have Security Blankets Insecure?" *Journal of Consulting and Clinical Psychology* 55, 1987, pp. 825–30.

Passman, R. H., and R. E. Adams. "Preferences for Mothers and Security Blankets and Their Effectiveness as Reinforcers for Young Children's Behavior." *Journal of Child Psychology and Psychiatry* 23, 1982, pp. 223–36.

Passman, R. H., and J. S. Halonen. "A Developmental Survey of Young Children's Attachments to Inanimate Objects." *Journal of Genetic Psychology* 134, 1979, pp. 165–78.

Passman, R. H., and L. A. Lautmann. "Fathers', Mothers', and Security Blankets' Effects on the Responsiveness of Young Children during Projective Testing." *Journal of Consulting and Clinical Psychology* 50, 1982, pp. 310–12.

Passman, R. H., and P. Weisberg. "Mothers and Blankets as Agents for Promoting Play and Exploration by Young Children in a Novel Environment: The Effects of Social and Nonsocial Attachment Objects." *Developmental Psychology* 11, 1975, pp. 170–77.

Van IJzendoorn, M. H., F. A. Goosens, L. W. C. Tavecchio, M. M. Vergeer, and F. O. A. Hubbard. "Attachments to Soft Objects: Its Relationship with Attachment to the Mother and with Thumbsucking." *Child Psychiatry and Human Development* 14, 1983, pp. 97–105.

Winnicott, D. W. "Transitional Objects and Transitional Phenomena: A Study of the First Not-Me Possession." *International Journal of Psycho-analysis* 34, 1953, pp. 89–97.

Wulff, M. "Fetishism and Object Choice in Early Childhood." *Psychoanalytic Quarterly* 15, 1946, pp. 450–71.

—Richard H. Passman, Ph.D.
University of Wisconsin-Milwaukee

Seizures

A temporary series of uncontrollable muscle spasms brought on by unusual electrical activity in the brain.

Also known as convulsion, clonic seizure, or tonic-clonic seizure.

A seizure is characterized by a sudden episode of uncontrollable brain activity. The intense, involuntary muscular contractions that often accompany seizures are referred to as convulsions. Seizures normally last three to five minutes, with a period of unconsciousness that may last for up to 30 minutes.

Seizures can result from a chronic condition, such as **epilepsy.** Alternatively, convulsions may be related to an acute condition, such as a high fever, adverse reaction to medication, or infection. In childhood, the most common cause of convulsion, or seizure, is high fever. Seizures triggered by fever are referred to as febrile seizures. Seizures can also result from **encephalitis, meningitis,** otitis media (middle ear infection), or from the ingestion of large doses of drugs, such as **antidepressants** or stimulants.

There are two types of seizures: grand mal and petit mal. Grand mal seizures involve intense contractions of the muscles of the trunk and limbs. Immediately prior to the seizure, the patient may have some indication that it is imminent. During the seizure the patient becomes unconscious and experiences generalized muscle contractions, known as clonic seizures, that may distort the body. Thrashing movements of the limbs follow, caused by opposing sets of muscles alternating in contractions (hence, the other name for grand mal seizures: tonic-clonic seizures). The patient may also lose bladder control. When the seizure ceases, usually after three to five minutes, the patient may remain unconscious for up to half an hour. Upon waking, he or she may not remember having had a seizure and may be confused.

Petit mal seizures last approximately 30 seconds, during which the patient may experience subtle signs of irregular brain activity before returning to normal activity. Signs of petit mal seizures include blinking, staring into space, or pausing in conversation. Petit mal seizures are hereditary, and only occur only in children and adolescents under age 20. The seizures may occur several times a day, usually when the patient is quiet. After **puberty**, petit mal seizures usually disappear or are replaced by grand mal seizures.

Status epilepticus is a very rare but potentially life-threatening condition in which grand mal seizures occur in rapid succession with no period of recovery between them. The patient may have difficulty breathing and experience a dangerous rise in blood pressure. Status epilepticus can be triggered by abruptly discontinuing medication prescribed for epilepsy, or by alcohol withdrawal.

Although observing a child experiencing a seizure can be alarming, the incident itself rarely leads to serious injury or complications. People of all ages who experience seizures are more adversely affected by misconceptions and stigma attached to seizures than by the seizure itself. For many individuals, the unpredictableness and loss of control over one's body are the most difficult aspects of seizure. Adolescents, particularly susceptible to seizure associated with epilepsy, may find the loss of control and dependence on others especially disturbing. Adolescents (and adults) with epilepsy are restricted from participating in certain activities, such as driving a car or riding a motorcycle, scuba diving, and gymnastics.

Seizures associated with epilepsy can usually be controlled with anticonvulsant medication. Education and consistent medication will help the patient adjust to seizure activity and carry on a normal life, with some restrictions. Occasionally, an adolescent who does not respond to medication may find relief in a surgical procedure to remove brain tissues.

Children who experience even one episode of febrile seizure (associated with high fever) were formerly treated with anticonvulsant medication as a preventive measure. The National Institutes of Health issued a recommendation in the 1980s that this practice be discontinued, except in cases where there is some indication that seizures are likely to recur, such as with a child with a family history of epilepsy or a nervous system impairment.

Pseudoseizures resemble seizures but are not caused by a physical disorder of the brain. The physical process of a pseudoseizure may be identical to a real seizure, including staring unresponsively, stiffening, and rhythmic jerking. If brain activity were monitored during a pseudoseizure, the brain wave tracing would not show the changes that are characteristic of epileptic seizures. Researchers believe that, in some cases, pseudoseizures may be related to dissociative disorders. Although there are many causes for pseudoseizures, many studies indicate that physical or sexual abuse may be one of the most common causes. In fact, patients with dissociative disorders often report experiencing pseudoseizures, which may be the symptom that led them to seek treatment.

For Further Study

Books

Freeman, John Mark, Eileen P. G. Vining, and Diana J. Pillas. *Seizures and Epilepsy in Childhood: A Guide for Parents.* Baltimore: The John Hopkins University Press, 1990.

Tuttle, Heather. *Living with Seizures.* Rootstown, OH: Tuttle Press, 1995. [juvenile]

WHAT TO DO WHEN YOUR CHILD HAS A SEIZURE

Many children experience a seizure at some time during childhood. Febrile seizures can be controlled through medication, frequent sponge baths, and by encouraging fluid intake. When a child, adolescent, or adult begins to experience a seizure, observers should quickly remove any hard, sharp, or otherwise dangerous objects from the area, and ease the person to the floor or ground. There is no need to restrain the person during the episode—it is a myth that a person will swallow his or her tongue during a seizure—and nothing should be placed inside the person's mouth. When the muscle contractions subside, let the person rest. If the seizure was triggered by fever, sponge the person gently with tepid water, not cold water or alcohol, and offer frequent sips of cool beverages. As soon as the child is comfortable, contact a pediatrician to discuss the episode.

Organizations

American Epilepsy Foundation
Address: 638 Prospect Avenue
Hartford, CT 06105-2498
Telephone: (203) 232-4825

Epilepsy Foundation of America
Address: 4351 Garden City Drive
Landover, MD 20785
Telephone: toll-free (800) 332-1000

Self-Conscious Emotions

Emotions such as guilt, pride, shame, and hubris.

Succeeding or failing to meet the standards, rules, and goals of one's group or society determines how well an individual forms relationships with other members of the group. Living up to one's own internalized set of standards—or failing to live up to them—is the basis of complex emotions. The so-called self-conscious emotions, such as **guilt**, pride, shame, and hubris, require a fairly sophisticated level of intellectual development. To feel them, individuals must have a sense of self as well as a set of standards. They must also have notions of what constitutes success and failure, and the capacity to evaluate their own behavior.

Because these emotions are complex, they have generally been thought of as adult emotions. But very little research had, until recently, been done to confirm this.

Research has now shown that children start to develop self-conscious emotions surprisingly early in life. Before a child reaches the third birthday, he or she has started to manifest these emotions in some form.

Self-conscious emotions are difficult to study. For one thing, there are no clear elicitors of these emotions. Joy registers predictably on a baby's face at the approach of a parent, and fear appears at the approach of a stranger. But what situation is guaranteed to elicit pride or shame, guilt or embarrassment? These emotions are so dependent on a person's own experience, expectations, and culture, that it is difficult to design uniform experiments.

Some psychoanalysts, notably Sigmund Freud and Erik Erikson, argued that there must be some universal elicitors of shame, such as failure at **toilet training** or exposure of the backside. But the idea of an automatic noncognitive elicitor does not make much sense. Cognitive processes are likely to be the elicitors of these complex emotions. It is the way people think or what they think about that becomes the elicitor of pride, shame, guilt, or embarrassment. There may be a one-to-one correspondence between certain thoughts and certain emotions; however, in the case of self-conscious emotions, the elicitor is a cognitive event. This does not mean that the earlier primary emotions are elicited by noncognitive events. Cognitive factors may play a role in eliciting any emotion, but the nature of the cognitive events is much less articulated and differentiated in the primary than in the self-conscious emotions.

Those who study self-conscious emotions have begun to determine the role of the self in such emotions, and in particular the age at which the notion of self emerges in childhood.

Recently, models of these emotions are beginning to emerge. These models provide testable distinctions between often confused emotions, such as guilt and shame. Moreover, nonverbal tools for studying these emotions in children are being developed. As a result, models exist to explain when and how self-conscious emotions develop.

The self-conscious emotions depend on the development of a number of cognitive skills. First, individuals must absorb a set of standards, rules, and goals. Second, they must have a sense of self. And finally, they must be able to evaluate the self with regard to those standards, rules, and goals and then make a determination of success or failure.

As a first step in self-evaluation, a person has to decide whether a particular event is the result of his or her own action. If, for example, an object breaks while you are using it, you might blame yourself for breaking it, or you might decide the object was faulty. If you place the blame on yourself, you are making an internal attribution. If you decide the object was defective, then you are making an external attribution. If you don't blame yourself, chances are you will give the matter no more thought. But if you do blame yourself, you are likely to go on to the next step of evaluation.

Whether a person is inclined to make an internal or an external attribution depends on the situation and on the individual's own characteristics. Some people are likely to blame themselves no matter what happens. Dweck and Legget (1988) studied children's attitudes toward their academic records. They found that some children attributed their success or failure to external forces. Others were likely to evaluate success and failure in terms of their own actions. Interestingly, strong sex differences emerged: boys are more apt to hold themselves responsible for their success and others for their failure, whereas girls are apt to do the opposite.

Psychologists still do not entirely understand how people decide what constitutes success and failure after they have assumed responsibility for an event. This aspect of self-evaluation is particularly important because the same standards, rules, and goals can result in radically different feelings, depending on whether success or failure is attributed to oneself. Sometimes people assess their actions in ways that do not conform to the evaluation that others might give them. Many factors are involved in producing inaccurate or unique evaluations. These include early failures in the self system, leading to narcissistic disorders, harsh socialization experience, and high levels of reward for success or punishment for failure. The evaluation of one's own behavior in terms of success and failure plays a very important role in shaping an individual's goals and new plans.

In a final evaluation step, an individual determines whether success or failure is global or specific. Global attributions come about when a person is inclined to focus on the total self. Some individuals, some of the time, attribute the success or failure of a particular action to the total self: they use such self-evaluative phrases as "I am bad (or good)." On such occasions, the focus is not on the behavior but on the self, both as object and as subject. Using such global attribution results in thinking of nothing else but the self. During these times, especially when the global evaluation is negative, a person becomes confused and speechless. The individual is unable to act and is driven away from action, wanting to hide or disappear.

In some situations individuals make specific attributions, focusing on specific actions. Thus, it is not the total self that has done something wrong or good; instead, a particular behavior is judged. At such times individuals will use such evaluative phrases as, "What I did was wrong, and I must not do it again." Notice that the individual's focus here is not on the totality of the self but on the specific behavior of the self in a specific situation.

The tendency to make global or specific attributions may be a personality style. Global attributions for negative events are generally uncorrelated with global attributions for positive events. It is only when positive or negative events are taken into account that relatively stable and consistent attributional patterns are observed. Some individuals are likely to be stable in their global and specific evaluations under most conditions of success or failure. Such factors are thought to have important consequences for a variety of fixed personality patterns. For example, Beck (1979) and others have found that depressed individuals are likely to make stable, negative, global attributions, whereas nondepressed individuals are less likely to be stable in their global attributions.

Shame and guilt

An important determinant of whether shame or guilt follows failure to live up to a standard is whether a person believes he could have avoided the violating act. If not, shame is likely. If the person feels he could have done otherwise, guilt is likely to occur.

Shame or guilt occurs when an individual judges his or her actions as a failure in regard to his or her standards, rules, and goals and then makes a global attribution. The person wishes to hide, disappear, or die (Lewis, 1992; Nathanson, 1987). It is a highly negative and painful state that also disrupts ongoing behavior and causes confusion in thought and an inability to speak. The body of the shamed person seems to shrink, as if to disappear from the eye of the self or others. Because of the intensity of this emotional state, and the global attack on the self system, all that individuals can do when presented with such a state is to attempt to rid themselves of it. Its global nature, however, makes it very difficult to dissipate.

The power of shame drives people to employ strategies to rid themselves of this feeling. These strategies may generate behavior that is generally considered abnormal. Some people readjust their notions of success and failure, at least as they apply to their own actions. The narcissistic personality, for example, perceives its actions to be successful while others perceive them as failure. The narcissist is characterized by an exaggerated sense of his or her own accomplishments and is likely to appear hubristic. But underlying the bombast is an attempt to avoid the exaggerated shame the narcissist may really feel. In contrast to the narcissist, a depressed person may be acutely aware of shame and feel helpless, hopeless, and worthless.

Shame and guilt is not produced by any specific situation, but rather by an individual's interpretation of an event. Even more important is the observation that shame is not necessarily related to whether the event is public or private. Although many theorists hold that shame is a public failure, this need not be so. Failure attributed to the self can be public or private, and can center around moral as well as social action.

Guilt is produced when an individual evaluates his or her behavior as a failure, but focuses on the specific features of the self that led to the failure. A guilty person is likely to feel responsible and try to repair the failure. Guilty individuals are pained by their evaluation of failure. Guilt is often associated with a corrective action that the individual can take (but does not necessarily take) to repair the failure and prevent it from happening again (Barrett, 1995; Tangney, 1990). In guilt, the self is differentiated from the object.

Hubris and pride

Self-consciousness is not entirely a negative feeling. Self-evaluation can also lead to positive and even overly positive emotions. Hubris, defined as exaggerated pride or self-confidence, is an example of the latter. Hubris is the emotion elicited when success with regard to one's standards, rules, and goals is applied to a person's entire self. People inclined to be hubristic evaluate their actions positively and then say to themselves: "I have succeeded. I am a success." Often, hubris is considered an undesirable trait to be avoided.

Hubris is difficult to sustain because of its globality. The feeling is generated by a nonspecific action. Because such a feeling is alluring, yet transient, people prone to hubris ultimately derive little satisfaction from the emotion. Consequently, they seek out and invent situations like to repeat this emotional state. According to Morrison (1989), this can be done either by altering their standards, rules, and goals or by reevaluating what constitutes success.

An individual who considers himself or herself globally successful may be viewed with disdain by others. Often the hubristic person is described as "puffed up" or, in extreme cases, grandiose or narcissistic. The hubristic person may be perceived as insolent or contemptuous. Hubristic people have difficulty in interpersonal relations, since their hubris likely makes them insensitive to the wishes, needs, and desires of others, leading to interpersonal conflict. Moreover, given the contemptuousness associated with hubris, other people are likely to be shamed by the nature of the actions of the hubristic person. Narcissists often derive pleasure in shaming others by claiming their superiority.

If hubris is the global emotion that follows a positive assessment of an action, then pride is the specific emotion. A person experiencing pride feels joyful at the successful outcome of a particular action, thought, or feeling. Here the focus of pleasure is specific and related to a particular behavior. In pride, the self and object are separated, as in guilt, and unlike shame and hubris, where subject and object are fused. Heckhausen (1984, 1987) and Stipek et al. (1992) have made a particularly apt comparison between pride and achievement motivation, where succeeding at a particular goal motivates activity. Because the positive state engendered by pride is associated with a particular action, individuals are able to reproduce the emotion: pride's specific focus allows for action.

Shyness and embarrassment

In addition to the emotions already discussed, two others bear mention—embarrassment and shyness, which are frequently confused. Some consider shyness to be sheepishness, bashfulness, uneasiness, or psychological discomfort in social situations. According to this definition, shyness is related to fear and is a nonevaluative emotion precipitated by an individual's discomfort with others. Such a description fits Buss's (1980) notion of shyness as an emotional response elicited by experiences of novelty or conspicuousness. For Buss (1980), shyness and fear are closely related and represent fear of others. One way of distinguishing shyness from shame, with which it is sometimes confused, is that it appears much earlier in childhood than either shame or guilt.

This approach to shyness seems reasonable because it fits with other notions relating the self to others, or what we might call the "social self." Eysenck (1954) has characterized people as social or asocial by genetic disposition, and recently Kagan, Reznick, and Snidman (1988) have pointed out the physiological responses of children they call "inhibited." Inhibited children are withdrawn, are uncomfortable in social situations, and appear fearful. Shyness may be a dispositional factor not related to self-evaluation. Rather, it may simply be the discomfort of being in the company of other social objects; in other words, it is the opposite of sociability.

If shyness does not seem to rely on self-evaluation, embarrassment often does. It is important, however, to distinguish among types of embarrassment. Sometimes, the self-consciousness of shyness can lead a person to become embarrassed (Buss, 1980). In certain situations of exposure, people become embarrassed, but this is not related to negative evaluation. Perhaps the best example of this is the case of a compliment. A speaker might feel embarrassed after a particularly flattering introduction. Surprisingly, praise, rather than the displeasure resulting from negative evaluation, elicits such embarrassment.

Another example of this type of embarrassment can be seen in people's reactions to public display. When people observe someone looking at them, they are apt to become self-conscious, look away, and touch or adjust their bodies. Women being observed often adjust or touch their hair. Men may adjust their clothes or change

their body posture. In few cases do the observed people look sad; if anything, they appear pleased by the attention. The combination of a briefly averted gaze and nervous touching characterizes the first type of embarrassment.

A related example of embarrassment from exposure can be seen in the work of Lewis et al. (1991) which demonstrates that embarrassment can be elicited just by exposure. In their experiment, a professor, announcing that he is going to randomly point to a student, and shows that pointing is random and does not reflect a judgment about the person, closes his eyes and points. The pointing invariably elicits embarrassment in the student selected, even though the student has done nothing, good or bad, to deserve attention.

In each of these examples, there is no negative evaluation of the self in regard to standards, rules, and goals. Nevertheless, work with children has shown that a sense of self is a prerequisite for feeling embarrassment (Lewis et al., 1989). In these situations, it is difficult to imagine embarrassment as related to shame. Since praise cannot readily lead to an evaluation of failure, it is likely that embarrassment resulting from compliments, from being looked at, and from being pointed to, has more to do with the exposure of the self than with evaluation. Situations other than praise come to mind, in which a negative evaluation is inferred (perhaps incorrectly). Take, for example, walking into a crowded meeting room before the speaker has started to talk. It is possible to arrive on time only to find people already seated. When walking into the room, eyes turn toward you, and you may experience embarrassment. One could say that there is a negative self-evaluation: "I should have been earlier, I should not have made noise." However, the experience of embarrassment in this case may not be elicited by negative self-evaluation, but simply by public exposure.

In contrast, a second type of embarrassment is closely related to shame and is therefore dependent on self-evaluation. For Izard (1977) and Tomkins (1963), embarrassment is distinguished from shame by the intensity of the latter. Whereas shame appears to be strong and disruptive, embarrassment is clearly less intense and does not involve disruption of thought and language. Furthermore, people who are embarrassed do not assume the posture of someone wishing to hide, disappear, or die. In fact, their bodies reflect an ambivalent approach and avoidance posture. Am embarrassed person alternatively looks at people and then looks away, smiling all the while. In contrast, the shamed person rarely smiles while averting his or her gaze. Thus, from a behavioral point of view, shame and embarrassment appear to be different.

The difference in intensity can probably be attributed to the nature of the failed standard, rule, or goal. Some standards are more or less associated with the core of self; for one person failure at driving a car is less important than failing to help someone. Failures associated with less important and less central standards, rules, and goals result in embarrassment rather than shame.

The study of self-conscious emotions has only recently begun. The model outlined here offers an opportunity to consider and to define carefully some of the self-conscious emotions. Unless we develop a more accurate taxonomy, we will be unable to proceed in our study of these emotions. Given the renewed interest in emotional life, it is now appropriate to consider these more complex emotions rather than the primary ones. Moreover, as others have pointed out, these self-conscious emotions are intimately connected with other emotions, such as anger and sadness. Finally, given the place of self-evaluation in adult life, it seems clear that the self-conscious evaluative emotions are likely to stand in the center of our emotional life.

For Further Study

Books

Barrett, K.. "A Functionalist Approach to Shame and Guilt." In J. Tangney and K. Fischer (Eds.), *Self-Conscious Emotions*. New York: Guilford, 1995, pp. 25-63.

Beck, A. T. *Cognitive Therapy and the Emotional Disorders.* New York: Times Mirror, 1979.

Buss, A.H. *Self Consciousness and Social Anxiety."* San Francisco: W.H. Freeman, 1980.

Eysenck, H.J. *The Psychology of Politics.* London, England: Routledge & Kegan Paul, 1954.

Heckhausen, H. "Emotional Components of Action: Their Ontogeny as Reflected in Achievement Behavior." In D. Glitz and J. F. Wohlwill (Eds.), *Curiosity, Imagination and Play: On the Development of Spontaneous Cognitive and Motivational Processes.* Hillsdale, NJ: Erlbaum, 1987, pp. 326-348.

Izard, C. *Human Emotions.* New York: Plenum Press, 1977.

Lewis, M. *Shame, the Exposed Self.* New York: The Free Press, 1992.

Morrison, A.P. *Shame: The Underside of Narcissism.* Hillsdale, NJ: Analytic Press, 1989.

Nathanson, D.L. (eds.). *The Many Faces of Shame.* New York: Gilford Press, 1987.

Tangney, J.P., and K.W. Fischer (Eds.). *Self-Conscious Emotions: Shame, Guilt and Pride.* New York: Guilford, 1995.

Tomkins, S.S. *Affect, Imagery, and Consciousness: Volume 2: The Negative Affects.* New York: Springer, 1963.

Periodicals

Dweck, C. S., and E. L. Leggett. "A Social Cognitive Approach to Motivation and Personality." *Psychological Review* 95, 1988, pp. 256–273.

Edelman, R. J., and S. E. Hampson. "The Recognition of Embarrassment." *Personality and Social Psychology Bulletin* 7, 1981, pp. 109–116.

Ferguson, T. J., and H. Stegge. "Children's Understanding of Guilt and Shame." *Child Development* 62, 1991, pp. 827–839.

Kagan, J., and N. Snidman. "Biological Bases of Childhood Shyness." *Science* 240, 1988, pp. 167–171.

Lewis, M., M. W. Sullivan, and P. Barone. "Changes in Embarrassment as a Function of Age, Sex, and Situation." *British Journal of Developmental Psychology* 9, 1991, pp. 485–492.

Lewis, M., M. W. Sullivan, C. Stanger, and M. Weiss. "Self-Development and Self-Conscious Emotions." *Child Development* 60, 1989, pp. 146–156.

Stipek, D. J., and S. McClintic. "Self-Evaluation in Young Children." *Monographs of the Society for Research in Child Development* 57 (Serial No. 226), 1992.

Tangney, J. P. "Assessing Individual Differences in Proneness to Shame and Guilt: Development of the Self-Conscious Affect and Attribution Inventory." *Journal of Personality and Social Psychology* 59, 1990, pp. 102–111.

—Michael Lewis
Robert Wood Johnson Medical School

Self-Esteem

Considered an important component of emotional health, self-esteem encompasses both self-confidence and self-acceptance.

Experiences at home, at school, and with peers can all build or diminish a child's self-esteem. Psychologists and child-care authorities who write about self-esteem generally discuss it in terms of two key components: the feeling of being loved and accepted by others and a sense of competence and mastery in performing tasks and solving problems independently.

The value placed on self-esteem by the mental health profession over the past 30 years has been critiqued by psychologist Martin Seligman. Seligman claims in order for children to feel good about themselves, they must feel that they are able to do things well. He claims that trying to shield children from feelings of sadness, frustration, and anxiety when they fail robs them of the motivation to persist in difficult tasks until they succeed. It is precisely such success in the face of difficulties that can truly make them feel good about themselves. Seligman believes that this attempt to cushion children against unpleasant emotions is in large part responsible for an increase in the prevalence of **depression** since the 1950s, an increase that he associates with a conditioned sense of helplessness.

Like Seligman, pediatrician and child-care expert **T. Berry Brazelton** emphasizes that children develop self-esteem through the sense of competence and mastery that comes from tackling and triumphing over challenges, even modest ones. He believes that parents can boost children's self-esteem even in infancy by giving them an active and autonomous role in casual play. As infants and toddlers advance to self-care activities, such as beginning to feed themselves, Brazelton encourages parents to let children complete tasks for themselves, however imperfectly, rather than jumping in and providing help. For example, he suggests allowing children to pick up small bits of food at the age of eight months even if they drop some, and letting them hold their own bottles at 12 months. Like Seligman, Brazelton emphasizes the value of leaving a child to work through a problem for herself, trying out different approaches to a task until she succeeds. For a child accustomed to learning by trial and error, frustration can serve as a source of motivation and energy rather than an obstacle. Brazelton also emphasizes the importance of encouraging the child in her endeavors and providing positive reinforcement when a goal is achieved.

In spite of his emphasis on the development of competence, Brazelton does advise parents to address their children in a positive way to reinforce feelings of love and acceptance. Among the harmful negative examples he points out are belittling comparisons with siblings ("Why can't you be more like your brother?") and threats of abandonment ("If you don't stop that right now, I'm leaving you here!"). Various experts have noted that when parental communication is consistently delivered in a negative style it becomes internalized, and children start to practice negative "self-talk," generating their own negative messages. In addition to their verbal communication style, parents also express acceptance and affirmation by showing physical affection and being good listeners, which makes children feel important and cared about.

Social critics have pointed out that it can be more difficult for children in the United States and other modern industrialized nations to achieve a sense of competence than it was for their counterparts in earlier historical periods. Children in the past, or in modern developing countries, participated actively in the economic life of the community, helping their families by doing some of the same jobs performed by adults. Today's children, especially in urban areas, perform little "useful" work and thus have few opportunities to master tasks that contribute to the welfare of their families and the community as a whole. In addition, their competence at the tasks that are demanded of them is continually challenged by competition in school, athletics, and other areas.

Self-esteem comes from different sources for children at different stages of development. The development of self-esteem in young children is heavily influenced by parental attitudes and behavior. Supportive parental behavior, including the encouragement and praise of mastery, as well as the child's internalization of the parents' own attitudes toward success and failure, are the most powerful factors in the development of self-esteem in early childhood. Later, older children's experiences outside the home—in school and with peers—become increasingly important in determining their self-esteem. Schools can influence their students' self-esteem through the attitudes they foster toward competition and diversity and their recognition of achievement in academics, sports, and the arts. By middle childhood, friendships have assumed a pivotal role in a child's life. Studies have shown that school-age youngsters spend more time with their friends than they spend doing homework, watching television, or playing alone. In addition, the amount of time they interact with their parents is greatly reduced from when they were younger. At this stage, social acceptance by a child's peer group plays a major role in developing and maintaining self-esteem.

The physical and emotional changes that take place in **adolescence**, especially early adolescence, present new challenges to a child's self-esteem. Boys whose growth spurt comes late compare themselves with peers who have matured early and seem more athletic, masculine, and confident. In contrast, early physical maturation can be embarrassing for girls, who feel gawky and self-conscious in their newly developed bodies. Both boys and girls expend inordinate amounts of time and energy on personal grooming, spending long periods of time in the bathroom until they have achieved the kind of look they want. Fitting in with their peers becomes more important than ever to their self-esteem, and, in later adolescence, relationships with the opposite sex can become a major source of confidence or insecurity. Up to a certain point, adolescents need to gain a sense of competence by making and learning from their own mistakes and by being held accountable for their own actions.

For Further Study

Books

Anderson, Eugene, George Redman, and Charlotte Rogers. *Self-Esteem for Tots to Teens: Five Principles for Raising Confident Children.* New York: Simon and Schuster, 1984.

Clark, Aminah, Harris Clemes, and Reynold Bean. *How to Raise Teenagers' Self-Esteem.* San Jose: Price/Stein/Sloan Publishing, 1985.

Gillett, Richard. *Change Your Mind, Change Your World: A Practical Guide to Turning Limiting Beliefs into Positive Realities.* New York: Simon & Schuster, 1992.

Hart, Louise. *The Winning Family: Increasing Self-Esteem in Your Children.* Berkeley: Celestial Arts, 1993.

Kutner, Lawrence. *Parent and Child: Getting through to Each Other.* New York: Morrow, 1991.

AGGRESSIVENESS VS. ASSERTIVENESS

Many people fail to distinguish between assertiveness and aggressiveness. Behaviorist psychologists view assertiveness as a complex set of behaviors, both verbal and non-verbal. Assertive behavior is often correlated with high self-esteem. To a child, assertiveness is an abstract concept: the first-grader who is terrorized by a bully is too busy dealing with such feelings as shame and fear to even think about being assertive. Furthermore, even when assertiveness is explained to a child, i.e., when he is told by a teacher that walking away from a fight can be an assertive act, this positive message is sometimes undermined by conflicting societal messages such as "fight like a man." This prompts some children, and some adults, to seek self-assertion in aggression. Instead of firmly demanding that a toy be returned, for example, a child might punch and grab the toy away from another child.

While assertiveness may be viewed favorably by parents and educators, psychologists specializing in childhood and adolescence have noticed that behavioral and attitudinal changes leading to assertiveness often provoke a strong negative response. Society may claim to support assertiveness in children, but this is not always proven in reality. For example, an educator, baffled by a child's to refusal to accept a particular opinion, may find the student insolent and label her difficult. Furthermore, feminist psychologists have pointed out that assertiveness is hardly a gender-neutral phenomenon. Researchers have found that it is generally easier for boys to be assertive than girls. In one study Rosemary Leonard found that while boys generally get away with demonstratively defiant behavior, girls provoke anger when they reject a request by saying "No" in an unemotional way. According to Leonard, assertiveness training for girls must incorporate ways of overcoming primary socialization, which encourages girls to be compliant and obedient.

Parents who want to encourage assertive behavior in children and adolescents can find help through assertive training programs that specialize in working with young people. Parents can also help their children become more assertive by helping them distinguish between legitimate and unreasonable requests from authority figures. Manuel J. Smith, for example, recommends that parents discuss the extent of teacher's authority with their children, so that they can evaluate whether a request from a teacher is legitimate or whether they need to disobey the teacher in order to assert themselves.

Leman, Kevin. *Bringing Up Kids Without Tearing Them Down.* New York: Delacorte Press, 1993.

Seligman, Martin E. P. *The Optimistic Child.* Boston: Houghton Mifflin Co., 1995.

Smith, Manuel. *Yes, I Can Say No: A Parent's Guide to Assertiveness Training for Children.* New York: Arbor House, 1986.

Periodicals

Lazarus, A. A. "On Assertive Behavior: A Brief Note." *Behavior Therapy* 4, 1973, pp. 697-99.

Leonard, Rosemary. " 'I'm Just A Girl Who Can't Say "No" ': A Gender Difference in Children's Perception of Refusals." *Feminism and Psychology* 5, August 1995, pp. 315-28.

Audiovisual Recordings

Allert, Adrienne. *Rearing Secure Children: Are You Building Your Children's Self-Esteem?* Skokie, IL: Parents Resource Network, 1988.

Self-Instructional Training *see* **Behavior Modification**

Sensitive Period *see* **Critical Period**

Separation Anxiety

Distress reaction to the absence of the parent or caregiver.

Separation anxiety emerges according to a developmental timetable during the second half year in human infants. This development reflects advancing cognitive maturation, rather than the onset of problem behaviors.

As illustrated in the accompanying figure, infants from cultures as diverse as Kalahari bushmen, Israeli kibbutzim, and Guatemalan Indians display quite similar patterns in their response to maternal separation, which peaks at the end of the first year and gradually becomes less frequent and less intense throughout later infancy and the preschool years. This fact has been interpreted to mean that the one-year-old is alerted by the absence of the parent and tries to understand that discrete event. If it fails, **fear** is created and the child cries.

Cultural practices have an impact on separation anxiety. Infants who remain in constant contact with their mothers may show an earlier onset of separation anxiety, and possibly more intense and longer periods of reactivity. For example, Japanese infants who are tested in **Mary Ainsworth**'s **Strange Situation** show more intense reac-

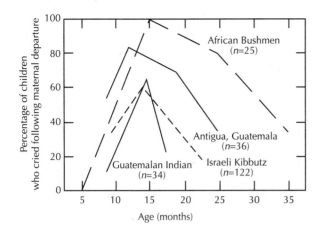

Children who cried during separation (in percent). These graphs show the course of separation distress in children of the African Bushmen, the Guatemalan Indians, lower-class families from Antigua, Guatemala, and infants from an Israeli kibbutz.

tions to the separation, presumably as a result of cultural norms prescribing constant contact between mother and infant for the first several years of life.

Like separation anxiety, researchers who observe infant emotions and behavior in the first month or two of life generally agree that no specific fear reaction is present at this early stage. Rather, infants become distressed due to unpleasant stimulation involving pain, discomfort, or hunger.

Typically researchers have found that by five to six months, if a stranger stares in silence at an infant, the infant will often return the look and after about 30 seconds begin to cry. Bronson has termed this distress reaction to a stranger's sober face "wariness." Because of the gradual building up of tension in the infant, Bronson interprets the emotional distress as a reaction to the failure to assimilate the unfamiliar face to a more familar schema. In another words, the older infant can distinguish between familiar and unfamiliar faces, tries to understand the distinction, and becomes upset if the new face does not match the now familiar pattern.

A few months later, infants may react immediately to strangers, especially if approached suddenly or picked up by the stranger. This fear reaction, which can be readily elicited in most infants between seven and twelve months, has been called stranger distress or **stranger anxiety.**

The context and qualitative aspects of the stranger's approach are critical in determining how an infant might respond. If the stranger approaches slowly when the **caregiver** is nearby, smiling and speaking softly, offering a toy, the infant will often show interest or joy, and distress is unlikely. Also, the degree of distress shown by

an infant to the silent intrusion of the stranger varies greatly from baby to baby, a finding that many believe to be rooted in the **temperament** of the infant. Finally, if the infant finds the stranger's approach to be ambiguous, the caregiver's reaction will often influence the infant's response. Should the parent smile and warmly greet the new person, the older infant will often use these emotional reactions as cues for how to respond.

Stranger distress was originally described by Rene Spitz as an emotion that suddenly appears in all infants at about 8 months. While we now understand how important a role context and cognition play in determining this response, there is nevertheless evidence suggesting a precise timetable for its emergence across different cultures, including Uganda, Hopi Indian, and the United States. A genetic basis has also been shown by twin research, with identical **twins** showing more similar onset of stranger distress than fraternal twins. Rather than indicating emotional difficulties, the emergence of a fear of strangers in the second half of the first year is an indicator of **cognitive development**. For example, EEG and heart rate patterns in human infants both show a major developmental shift at this time in response to the presentation of threatening stimuli.

As infants acquire more experience in dealing with unfamiliar persons at family outings, visits to the home, or in **day care**, they no longer become distressed at the sight of a stranger. Young children show a wide variety of responses depending on the situation, their past experiences, and their level of sociability. Parents will want to encourage their child's natural curiosity and friendliness, while at the same time teaching them that they should always rely on parental guidance and approval in dealing with strangers.

The study of these two common fears of infancy underscores the important links between emotion and cognition. Discrepancy theories originating in the work of Hebb and **Jean Piaget** provide an account of the steps in the development of this basic emotional system in infancy and demonstrate its dependence on perceptual and cognitive development. In addition, the importance of context and meaning have been clearly shown in the work of Jerome Kagan, Alan Sroufe, and others to be the hallmark of the mature fear response, as distinct from the general distress of early infancy.

While stranger distress and separation anxiety are normal for one-year-old infants, should a parent become concerned if they persist into the toddler or preschool years? The key to answering this question depends upon the nature of the child's response, its intensity, and persistence over time. For example, it is commonplace for young preschoolers to show some distress at separation from their parents during the first week or two of daycare in a new setting. Typically this settling in period does not last too long. If a preschooler persists in showing excessive separation anxiety even after several weeks at a new preschool and this interferes with the child's participation with peers and teachers, parents should consult with the teacher and other child care professionals. Childhood anxieties of this sort are generally quite responsive to treatment, and this may be a better option than waiting for the problem to resolve itself.

—Peter LaFreniere
University of Maine Orono

See also **Stranger Anxiety**

Sexually Transmitted Diseases (STDs)

Viral and bacterial infections passed from one person to another through sexual contact.

Adolescence is the period of transition from childhood to adulthood when profound changes occur. This period of tremendous change fulfills important developmental tasks in which the adolescent develops formal operational thought, builds cognitive decision-making skills, forms a sense of self-identity, and expresses the need for autonomy and individuation from the family.

Adolescence is also a time of opportunities and risk, when many health behaviors are established. Although many of these behaviors are health-promoting, some are health-compromising, resulting in increasingly high rates of adolescent morbidity and mortality. For example, initiation of sexual intercourse and experimentation with alcohol and drugs are normative adolescent behaviors. However, these behaviors often result in negative health outcomes such as the acquisition of sexually transmitted diseases (STDs), including the fatal human immunodeficiency virus (HIV). As a consequence of STDs, many adolescents experience serious health problems that often alter the course of their adult lives, including infertility, difficult pregnancy, genital and cervical cancer, neonatal transmission of infections, and AIDS (acquired immunodeficiency syndrome).

The acquisition and transmission of STDs among adolescents are influenced by complex interrelationships among sociodemographic, biologic, psychosocial, and behavioral factors. For example, many STD-related risk markers (e.g., age, gender, race/ethnicity) correlate with more fundamental determinants of risk status (e.g., access to health care, living in communities with high prevalence of STDs) to influence adolescents' risk for STDs.

Developmental factors such as pubertal timing, **self-esteem**, and peer affiliation may also increase their risk of exposure to STDs. An assessment of these interrelationships are critical to preventing and controlling STDs in adolescents, yet they are poorly defined and understood. Moreover, since behavior is the common means by which STDs occur, an important first step in fighting STDs is to understand the prevalence and patterns of risk behaviors as well as the psychosocial context in which these behaviors occur.

Epidemiology of STDs, including AIDS and HIV

STDs among sexually experienced adolescents occur at alarmingly high rates. One-fourth of the estimated 12 million new cases reported annually occur among adolescents between ages 15 and 19 years. Moreover, since many STDs are asymptomatic, they are often undiagnosed and untreated, thus increasing their potential for proliferation among adolescents.

Prevalent bacterial STD infections

Gonorrhea and chlamydia, the most prevalent bacterial STDs, disproportionately affect adolescents. The rates of gonorrhea in adolescents, 15 to 19 years of age, have declined since 1990, but they continue to be higher than rates for any five-year age group between 20 and 44 years, particularly among women and African Americans.

Age- and race/ethnic-specific national data for chlamydial infections are not currently available, however, numerous prevalence studies have shown rates to be highest among adolescents and young adults under 25 years of age, many of whom are minorities. Rates of chlamydia reported by gender indicate that women, overall, have higher rates than men due in large part to increased efforts in screening women for asymptomatic chlamydial infections. The low rates of chlamydia for men suggest that the sexual partners of women diagnosed with chlamydia are not being diagnosed or treated. Chlamydia is the most pervasive and destructive STD that threatens the reproductive health of women. It has been detected in more than 10% of sexually experienced women during screening.

Prevalent viral STD infections

Similar to bacterial STDs, genital herpes simplex virus (HSV-2) and human papillomavirus (HPV) occur at alarming rates among sexually experienced adolescents. Although AIDS is currently rare in adolescents, the rate of HIV infection is thought to be more prevalent. Unfortunately, there are no effective cures for these infections despite their sequelae of negative reproductive morbidity, including neonatal transmission of these infections, cervical and genital cancer, and even premature death. Studies indicate that one in six Americans is infected

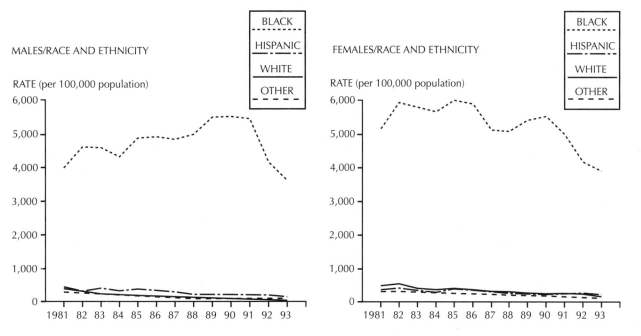

Gonorrhea in U.S. males aged 15–19 by race and ethnicity, 1981–93; and, gonorrhea in U.S. females aged 15–19 by race and ethnicity, 1981–93.

with HSV-2, reflecting a nine-fold increase in the last three decades. Prevalence of HSV-2 in adolescents and young adults vary by the demographic and behavioral characteristics of the populations studied as well as the diagnostic methods used. Recent studies indicate that approximately 4% of Caucasians and 17% of African Americans are infected with HSV-2 by the end of their teenage years. One study of young pregnant women of low income status found an HSV-2 infection rate of 11% in women 15 to 19 years of age and 22% in women 25 to 29 years of age.

HPV causes genital warts and is associated with cervical, genital, and anal cancer many years after the first infection. Prevalence studies found higher rates of HPV among women of younger age, indicating that HPV is the most common STD infection currently affecting adolescent women.

Recent surveillance data indicate that 441,528 cases of AIDS have been diagnosed in the United States through December 1994. Although this rate is of epidemic proportions, adolescents ages 13 to 19 years represent 1,965 cases, or less than one percent of the total cases. Males comprise 1,304 cases and females comprise 661 cases. The reported number of AIDS cases may not reflect the actual rate of HIV infection among adolescents since the incubation period is long and varied. It is probable that many of the 81,645 young adults, ages 20 to 29 years, who are diagnosed with AIDS acquired HIV during their teen years. Most adolescents with AIDS were infected as a result of high risk sexual and sub-

stance use behaviors. Studies also indicate that African American and Latino teens are overrepresented among persons with AIDS relative to their proportion in the population. Although these epidemiological statistics on AIDS in the United States provide a descriptive overview of the prevalence and patterns of HIV exposure in adolescents, the extent of asymptomatic HIV infection remains largely unknown.

Biologic factors associated with STD risk

Both men and women suffer serious health consequences from STD infection, including infertility, cancer and HIV; however, women are disproportionately affected due to a number of biologic factors. For example, it is well known that the transmission of STDs is more efficient from men to women than from women to men. With just one unprotected sexual encounter with an infected partner, a woman is twice as likely than a man to acquire gonorrhea or chlamydia. Also, differences in the types of STDs may influence STD transmissibility; with one exposure of unprotected sexual intercourse, a woman has a one percent chance of acquiring HIV, a 30% chance of acquiring herpes, and 50% chance of contracting gonorrhea. Adolescent women may also be particularly vulnerable to exposure to STD infections since, biologically, they have more "immature" ectopic tissue on the endocervix that potentially increases the likelihood of acquiring certain STDs. Adolescent women also have "immature" or unchallenged local immune systems that make them more vulnerable to STD infections.

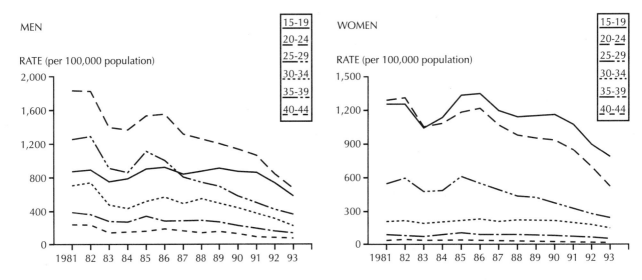

Gonorrhea rates for U.S. men aged 15–44, 1981–93; and, gonorrhea rates for U.S. women aged 15–44, 1981–93.

In summary, the prevalence data on STDs, HIV, and AIDS in adolescents indicate that younger women, gay and bisexual teens, poor, urban, and racial/ethnic minority young people have higher rates of STDs and HIV relative to their peers. Primary prevention of initial STD infections through prevention and risk reduction programs are essential for stemming the tide of these sexually acquired diseases. Moreover, secondary prevention through screening **at risk** adolescents for asymptomatic STD infections and effectively treating the index case and his or her sexual contact(s) are the most effective means of eliminating long-term medical and psychosocial consequences from STDs.

Behavioral factors associated with STD risk

Although biologic factors play an important role in the transmission of STDs, it is also the health-risking behaviors of adolescents that place them at increased risk for exposure to STDs. Therefore, to more fully understand adolescents' risk for STDs, it is imperative to understand the risk behaviors that are associated with STD infections as well as the psychosocial context in which these behaviors occur. Behavioral risk factors include the age of sexual activity, number of sexual partners, use of contraceptives, and use of alcohol and drugs.

Sexual activity

Early initiation of sexual intercourse has been associated with high risk sexual activities, including ineffective use of contraceptives, multiple sex partners over a short period of time, high risk sex partners, and acquisition of STDs and their consequences of cervical cancer and dysplasia. More adolescents are initiating sexual intercourse at younger ages today than over the previous three decades and placing themselves at risk for STDs at younger ages than ever before. The average age of first sexual intercourse is between the age of 16 and 17 years for adolescent men and between the age of 17 and 18 years for adolescent women, and has been found to be as young as age 12 in some high risk populations. Research on adolescents' decision to initiate sexual intercourse indicates an interaction betwen biological and social factors. However, much remains unknown about the interactions between **hormones**, behavior, and social factors.

The Youth Risk Behavior Surveillance System (YRBSS), a self-reported survey of a national representative sample of high school students in grades 9 to 12, indicate that 53% of the students reported having had sex. Of these students, 38% reported sexual experience during the three months prior to the survey. Prevalence rates of sexual experience differed by race/ethnicity and gender. African American students were significantly more likely (89% of males and 70% of females) than Caucasian (49% of males and 47% of females) and Latino (64% of males and 48% of females) students to have engaged in sexual intercourse. Rates for adolescent women increased significantly between grades 9 and 12, but for men the rates increased significantly between grades 10 and 12. Moreover, data from the National Survey of Family Growth (NSFG), a large-scale national survey of women ages 15 to 44 years, reveal that family income is associated with adolescents' decision to engage in sexual intercourse; adolescents from poor and low income families are more likely to report an earlier age of sexual experience than their counterparts from higher income families.

In addition to early sexual activity, many adolescents have multiple sex partners within a short period of time in a pattern of serial monogamy which also increases their risk of acquiring STD for two important reasons: it increases the likelihood of being exposed to a sexually transmitted pathogen, and it may reflect poor choices of sexual partners. Among the sexually experienced high school students responding to the YRBSS, 19% reported having four or more sex partners. Having had multiple sex partners was noted more frequently among African American students (59% of males and 27% of females), compared to Latino (26% of males and 11% of females) and Caucasian (15% of males and 13% of females) students. This behavior increased exponentially with increasing age and grade. Other national data indicate that by the time young sexually experienced women reach their early twenties, 71% have had more than one sex partner and 21% have had six or more sex partners. On the average young men report having had more sex partners since their first sexual encounter, compared to young women of similar ages, due in part to a longer length of time in which they have been sexually active. A study of adolescents and young adults ages 12 to 20 years who were seeking care at an urban public STD clinic found that the mean number of sex partners among males was 33 and 9 for females.

Involuntary sexual intercourse such as sexual coercion and sexual abuse may occur more commonly among adolescents, especially younger adolescent women, and often pose a potential risk for acquisition of STDs; 74% of young women who experienced sexual intercourse before age 14, and 60% of young women who experienced sexual intercourse before age 15, reported engaging in sexual intercourse involuntarily. A study on the effects of child abuse (i.e., incest, extra-familial sexual abuse, and physical abuse) on adolescent males showed a strong association between abuse and a number of risk-taking behaviors, such as forcing female sexual partners into having sexual intercourse and drinking alcohol prior to sexual intercourse. Moreover, when sexual intercourse is intermittent, as it is with most sexually experienced adolescents, they are less likely to take proper measures to safeguard against STDs.

Contraceptive use

Sexually experienced adolescents are also at risk for STDs because of their patterns of contraceptive use, especially their use of barrier-method contraceptives. The increasingly high rates of negative reproductive morbidities in adolescents suggest that they do not use effective methods to reduce their risk of STDs or unintended pregnancies. Sexual abstinence is the only sure method of eliminating risk for STDs, however, when used consistently and correctly, **condoms** offer the best protection against acquisition of STDs, including HIV. Even when condoms are used improperly they reduce the risk of acquiring infections by 50%.

The overall reported use of contraceptives, particularly condoms, has increased among adolescents in the last decade. Data from the YRBSS reveal that 53% of the students who reported sexual activity in the three months prior to the survey also reported using condoms during their last sexual encounter; this behavior was more common among males of virtually all ages and racial/ethnic groups. In contrast, data from the NSFG indicate that 32% of adolescent women ages 15 to 19 years reported use of contraceptives. Of these women, 52% reported use of the pill, 44% reported use of condoms, and none of the women reported use of IUDs or diaphragms. It appears that while the use of oral contraceptives provides some protection against the development of gonococcal and nongonococcal forms of PID, it may increase the risk of chlamydial endocervical infections.

Differences in the types and patterns of contraceptive use by race/ethnicity, age, and **socioeconomic status** have also been noted. In general, with age and sexual experience, use of oral contraceptives increases and condom use decreases. This trend, however, is not true for Latinas. Among contraceptive users, African American and Latina adolescent women are less likely to use a barrier-method of **contraception** compared to their Caucasian counterparts, but African American women are more likely to use oral contraceptives. Also, adolescent women of higher income are more likely than young women of lower income to use oral contraceptives. These factors are related to access and utilization of medical services for reproductive health care. Thus, providing *all* sexually experienced adolescents with reproductive health counseling and education about the importance of consistently and correctly using barrier-method contraceptives such as condoms may play a crucial role in reducing their risk of acquiring and transmitting STDs.

Alcohol and drug use

Use of alcohol and drugs is prevalent among adolescents, and thus poses a significant threat to their health. One-third of high school youth responding to the YRBSS have used marijuana at least once in their lifetime with 18% of these students reporting use of this substance within 30 days before the survey. Cocaine was used at least once by 5% of the students and currently (prior 30 days) by 2%. Three percent of the high school population used crack or free-base forms of cocaine and nearly 2% reported injecting illegal drugs at some point during their life. However, the substance of choice, by far, is alcohol; 81% of students had at least one drink at some point in time and nearly half (48%) consumed alcohol in the 30 days prior to the survey. Among the current alcohol users, 30% had five or more drinks on at least one occasion, suggesting that a sizeable proportion of the students are periodic heavy drinkers. Grade, age, and gender differences were noted for lifetime and current use of alcohol and other illicit substances. In general, students in higher grade levels (grades 11 and 12) and males were more likely to use all substances. Racial/ethnic differences in use of substances were also found. Heavy use of alcohol was most prevalent among Caucasian and Latino males and females, while marijuana use was most common among African American and Latino males, but cocaine was most frequently used by Latino males and females, and Caucasian males indicated a greater likelihood of injecting illicit drugs.

Although these data strongly suggest that adolescents are at increased risk for social and physical morbidities, and even premature mortality because of their use of alcohol and other illicit substances, they underrepresent the actual prevalence of substance use among all adolescents. Teens who have dropped out or who are repeatedly absent from school and those who are homeless or otherwise disenfranchised are not represented by the reported data; many of these teens are potentially at higher risk for STDs because of their substance use behavior.

Co-occurrence of behaviors associated with STD risk

Risk behaviors that are associated with the acquisition and transmission of STDs are prevalent and are interrelated among adolescents. For example, use of alcohol and other illicit substances has been associated with an early age of sexual activity, frequent sexual activity, multiple sex partners, and inconsistent or no use of condoms. However, little is known about the specific mechanisms which determine these relationships.

A recent study found that substance use prior to sexual intercourse is related to a number of risk-taking behaviors: sexual intercourse with a casual acquaintance, lack of communication about use of condoms or previous sexual experiences, and no use of condoms. This association remained significant regardless of demographic factors, sexual experience and dispositional factors such as adventure and thrill seeking. It appears that early intervention to prevent the use and abuse of alcohol and other substances may significantly decrease their risk of acquiring STDs.

Psychosocial factors associated with STD risk

In the absence of a cure for viral STDs or vaccines to safeguard against bacterial STDs (except hepatitis B), effective strategies to prevent or modify risk behaviors associated with sexually acquired infections is paramount. In order to develop such strategies, it is imperative to also understand the psychosocial context in which STD-related behaviors occur. For example, it is important to understand which factors influence adolescents' selection of sexual partners as well as the processes that influence their contraceptive decisions, in particular, how use of condoms is negotiated.

One study of college students examined the relationship between sexual behavior, substance use, and specific constructs from social cognitive theory (i.e., perceptions of self-efficacy, vulnerability to HIV risk, social norms, negative outcome expectancies of condoms, and knowledge of HIV risk and prevention). The results indicate that although young men expected more negative outcomes of condom use and were more likely to have sexual intercourse under the influence of alcohol and other drugs, young women reported perceptions of higher self-efficacy to practice safer sex. The study further revealed that perceptions of higher self-efficacy to engage in safer-sexual behaviors, perceptions of fewer negative outcomes of condom use, and less frequent alcohol and drug use with sexual intercourse were the best predictors of safer-sexual behaviors.

A conceptual model to evaluate STD risk

The information, motivation, and behavioral skills (IMB) model is one method of evaluating risk for STDs. This model posits that information, motivation, and behavior are the primary determinants of AIDS-related preventive behavior. Specifically, the model asserts that *information* regarding the transmission of HIV and information concerning specific methods of preventing HIV (e.g., condom use, decreasing the number of partners) are necessary prerequisites of reducing risk behaviors. *Motivation* to change risk behaviors is another determinant of prevention and affects whether a person acts on his or her knowledge of the transmission and prevention of HIV. The IMB contends that motivation to engage in prevention behaviors is a function of one's attitudes toward the behavior and of subjective norms regarding prevention behaviors. Other critical factors which are hypothesized to influence motivation to engage in prevention behaviors are perceived vulnerability to acquiring HIV, perceived costs and benefits of engaging in prevention behaviors, intention to engage in prevention behaviors regarding HIV, as well as characteristics of the sex partner and/or the sexual relationship (e.g., primary vs. secondary partner). *Behavioral skills* for engaging in specific prevention behaviors are a third determinant of prevention; it affects whether a knowledgeable, highly motivated person will be able to change his or her behavior to prevent HIV. Important skills required to engage in prevention behaviors include the ability to effectively communicate with one's sex partner about safer-sex, refusal to engage in unsafe sexual practices, to properly use barrier-method contraceptives, and the ability to exit a situation when prevention behaviors are not possible. In addition, individuals who are able to practice prevention skills are presumed to have a strong self-belief (self-efficacy) in their ability to practice these prevention behavioral skills. Overall, the IMB asserts that information and motivation "trigger" behavioral skills to affect the initiation and maintenance of HIV prevention behaviors.

Strategies to prevent and reduce STD risk

Prevention of high risk sexual, contraceptive, and substance use behaviors through cognitive-behavioral skills training and prevention and risk reduction counseling programs are our primary hope for decreasing the high incidence of STDs in adolescents. Prevention and risk reduction strategies should be developed and implemented in settings where most adolescents can be reached, including schools or community-based programs where there are multiple opportunities to intervene with adolescents or clinical settings where one-to-one risk reduction counseling can occur and actual risk can be assessed.

Cognitive-behavioral skills building interventions

In order to prevent new STD infections, adolescents must not only be informed about the risk and prevention of STDs, they must also have skills to resist **peer pressure**, negotiate the use of condoms, and project the future consequences of their behaviors. In addition, prevention of STDs in adolescents requires that they have the necessary means, resources and social support to develop self-regulative skills and self-efficacy to effectively reduce their risk of disease transmission. Such cognitive-behavioral skills building programs have been shown to be effective in building skills, delaying the onset of sexual activity, and changing high risk behaviors associated with pregnancy, STDs, and HIV infection. Moreover, cognitive-behavioral skills building programs should be immediate, sustained, and cost-effective. Specifically, these programs should be designed to: increase knowledge about the prevention and transmission of STDs and their consequences; formulate realistic attitudes and perceptions about personal susceptibility to acquiring infections; enhance self-efficacy and self-motivation; monitor and regulate STD-related risk behaviors; address the role of social peer norms; and develop appropriate decision-making, problem-solving, and communication skills.

Prevention and risk reduction counseling

Counseling strategies to prevent and reduce the risk of STDs should be conducted in a confidential and non-judgmental manner that is both developmental and culturally appropriate for the adolescent. It should focus on a number of key elements such as: maintenance and support of healthy sexual behaviors (e.g., delaying initiation of sexual intercourse, limiting the number of sexual partners); use of barrier-method contraceptives (e.g., condoms, diaphragms, spermicide); routine medical care and advice (e.g., seeking medical care if he or she has participated in high risk behavior); compliance with

treatment recommendations (e.g., taking all medications as directed); and encouraging sex partners to seek medical care. Adolescents should also be informed about the myths and misconceptions of acquiring STDs. Moreover, adolescents should receive anticipatory guidance to assist them in defining appropriate options and alternatives to engaging in high risk behaviors. The ability to implement prevention and risk reduction programs is limited by the setting and the lack of time that is allocated for these efforts.

Conclusions

The rates of STDs among sexually experienced adolescents are currently very high. They occur most frequently in younger adolescent women and poor, urban minorities. Many more adolescents are at increased risk for exposure to STDs, including HIV, because of health-risking behaviors such as initiation of sexual intercourse at a young age, having multiple sex partners in a short period of time, ineffective use of contraceptives, and frequent use of alcohol and other illicit substances. These behaviors are prevalent and occur together. Thus, strategies to prevent further spread of STDs must target these multiple risk factors. Moreover, prevention and risk reduction strategies should be based on appropriate theoretical and conceptual frameworks that account for individual differences and be culturally sensitive and developmentally appropriate for the target population. Importantly, prevention strategies should specifically dispel myths and misconceptions about STDs, address psychosocial contextual factors such self-efficacy and peer influences, and aggressively provide skills which are necessary to enact STD-prevention behaviors. Finally, these programs should be on-going and conducted in a variety of settings where most adolescents can be reached.

For Further Study

Books

Boyer, C. B. "Psychosocial, Behavioral, and Educational Factors in Preventing Sexually Tranxmitted Diseases." In: Schydlower, M., and M. A. Shafer. (eds.), *Adolescent Medicine: State of the Art Reviews: AIDS and Other Sexually Transmitted Diseases.* Vol I(3). Philadelphia: Hanley & Belfus, Inc., 1990, pp. 597–613.

Millstein, S. G., A. C. Petersen, and E. O. Nightingale. "Adolescent Health Promotion: Rationale, Goals, and Objectives." In: Millstein, S.G., Petersen, A.C., Nightingale, E.O. (eds). *Promoting the Health of Adolescents: New Directions for the Twenty-First Century.* New York: Oxford University Press, 1993.

The Alan Guttmacher Institute. *Sex and America's Teenagers.* New York: New York, 1994.

Periodicals

Crowe, L. C., and W. H. George. "Alcohol and Human Sexuality: Review and Integration." *Psychol Bull* 105, 1989, pp. 374–86.

Fisher, J. D., and W. A. Fisher. "Changing AIDS Risk Behavior." *Psychol Bull* 111, 1992, pp. 455–74.

Fisher, W. A. "Understanding and Preventing Adolescent Pregnancy and Sexually Transmissible Disease/AIDS." In: Edwards, J., R. S. Tinsdale, C. Heath, and E. J. Posavac, eds. *Social Influence Processes and Prevention*. New York: Plenum, 1990, pp. 71–101.

Kipke, M. D., C. B. Boyer, and K. Hein. "An Evaluation of an AIDS Risk Reduction Education and Skills Training (ARREST) Program." *Journal of Adolesc Health* 14, 1993, pp. 533–39.

Millstein, S. G., E. O. Nightingale, A. C. Petersen, A. M. Mortimer, and D. A. Hamburg. "Promoting the Healthy Development of Adolescents." *JAMA* 269, 1993, pp. 1413–15.

Strunin, L., and R. Hingson. "Alcohol, Drugs and Adolescent Sexual Behavior." *International Journal of Addiction* 27, 1992, pp.129–146.

Vincent, M., A. Clearie, and M. Schluchter. "Reducing Adolescent Pregnancy through School and Community-Based Education." *JAMA* 257, 1987, pp. 3382–86.

—Cherie B. Boyer, Ph.D.
Department of Pediatrics,
Division of Adolescent Medicine
University of California, San Francisco

Shame *see* Self-Conscious Emotions

Shaping

A gradual, behavior modification technique in which successive approximations to the desired behavior is rewarded.

Shaping, or behavior-shaping, is a variant of **operant conditioning.** Instead of waiting for a subject to exhibit a desired behavior, any behavior leading to the target behavior is rewarded. For example, B. F. Skinner (1904–1990) discovered that, in order to train a rat to push a lever, any movement in the direction of the lever had to be rewarded, until finally, the rat was trained to push a lever. Once the target behavior is reached, however, no other behavior is rewarded. In other words, the subject behavior is shaped, or molded, into the desired form.

Although rejected by many orientations within the field of psychology, behavioral techniques, particularly shaping, are widely used as therapeutic tools for the treatment of various disorders, especially those affecting verbal behavior. For example, behavior shaping has been used to treat selective, or elective, mutism, a condition manifested by an otherwise normal child's refusal to speak in school. Using candy and toys as a reward (Masten, Stacks, Caldwell-Colbert, and Jackson, 1996), a therapist succeeded in eliciting speech from an eight-year-old selective mute Mexican American boy.

Therapists have also relied on behavior shaping in treating cases of severe **autism** in children. While autistic children respond to such stimulus objects as toys and musical instruments, it is difficult to elicit speech from them. However, researchers (Koegel, O'Dell, and Dunlap, 1988) have noted that behavior shaping is more effective when speech *attempts* are reinforced than when speech production is expected. When unsuccessful efforts to produce speech are rewarded, the child feels inspired to make a greater effort, which may lead to actual speech.

While recognizing the effectiveness of behavior shaping in the laboratory and in therapy, experts, particularly psychologists who do not subscribe to **behaviorism,** have questioned the long-term validity of induced behavior change. For example, researchers have noted that people have a tendency to revert to old behavior patterns, particularly when the new behavior is not rewarded any more. In many cases, as Alfie Kohn has written (Kohn, 1993), behavior-shaping techniques used in school, instead of motivating a child to succeed, actually create nothing more than a craving for further rewards.

For Further Study

Books

Kohn, Alfie. *Punished by Rewards: The Trouble with Gold Stars, Incentive Plans, A's, Praise, and other Bribes.* Boston: Houghton Mifflin, 1993.

Nye, Robert D. *The Legacy of B. F. Skinner: Concepts and Perspectives, Controversies and Misunderstandings.* Pacific Grove, CA: Brooks/Cole, 1992.

Periodicals

Koegel, R. L., and M. Mentis. "Motivation in Childhood Autism: Can They or Won't They?" *Journal of Child Psychology and Psychiatry* 26, 1985, pp. 185–91.

Koegel, Robert L., Mary O'Dell, and Glen Dunlap. "Producing Speech Use in Nonverbal Autistic Children by Reinforcing Attempts." *Journal of Autism and Developmental Disorders* 18, no. 4, December 1988, pp. 525–38.

Masten, William G., James R. Stacks, A. Toy Caldwell-Colbert, and Jacqueline Jackson. "Behavioral Treatment of a Selective Mute Mexican-American Boy." *Psychology in the Schools* 33, no. 1, January 1996, pp. 56–60.

Skinner, B. F. "Can Psychology Be a Science of the Mind?" *American Psychologist* 45, no. 11, November 1990, pp. 1206–10.

—Zoran Minderovic

Shyness

The tendency to avoid or be timid or subdued with unfamiliar children or adults.

Shyness first appears around the first birthday, when the capacity to experience **fear** to discrepant events matures. During the first year or two children raised under most family circumstances who are extremely shy behave this way because of a temperamental bias to react with withdrawal to unfamiliar events. When the unfamiliar event is meeting a stranger, the child is called shy. However, as children grow, other reasons for shyness emerge and many five and six-year-old children can show shyness without any special temperamental predisposition. Some children are shy because they feel that they are physically unattractive, others are shy because they have failed to attain proper achievement levels in school, and other children are shy because of shame over aspects of their family, including poverty or mental illness.

Kenneth Rubin of the University of Maryland studies shyness in children and notes that some children appear shy because they prefer to play alone but these children are not anxious over interacting with other children. They merely prefer what Rubin calls autonomous play. Other children play alone because they are anxious. Rubin calls these children reticent, and their apparent shyness is due to apprehension and uncertainty over interacting with other children. The vast majority of children who are extremely shy in the first five or six years of life will conquer their shyness and by the time they are adolescents will not be particularly shy. A small proportion, perhaps no more than 10%, of children who are extremely shy in the preschool years will retain this quality and have an introverted personality style during **adolescence**.

Psychological research that follows large numbers of children from very early childhood to adulthood has found that a tendency to be shy with others is one of the most stable traits that is preserved from the first three of four years of life through young adulthood. Shyness is much more stable from age three through age twenty, than aggressive behavior, **tantrums**, a concern with neatness, and a large number of other traits.

For Further Study

Books

Izard, C. *Human Emotions.* New York: Plenum Press, 1977.

Kagan, Jerome. *Galen's Prophecy: Temperament in Human Nature.* New York: Basic Books, 1994.

Kohnstamm, Geldolph A., John E. Bates, and Mary Klevjord Rothbart. eds. *Temperament in Childhood.* New York: Wiley, 1989.

Tangney, J. P., and K.W. Fischer, ed. *Self-Conscious Emotions: Shame, Guilt and Pride.* New York: Guilford, 1995.

Zimbardo, Philip G. *The Shy Child: A Parent's Guide to Preventing and Overcoming Shyness from Infancy to Adulthood.* New York: McGraw-Hill, 1981.

Periodicals

Kagan, J., and N. Snidman. "Biological Bases of Childhood Shyness." *Science* 240, 1988, pp. 167–171.

—Jerome Kagan
Harvard University

Siblings *see* **Birth Order**

Sickle-Cell Anemia

An inherited disease characterized by periods of relative health alternating with episodes of severe illness caused when sickle-shaped red blood cells block small blood vessels.

Sickle-cell anemia is a genetic disorder that causes the victim's red blood cells to become stiff and sickle-shaped. The disease causes a variety of symptoms, the most prominent of which are crises, caused when the misshapen cells block small capillaries, preventing the flow of oxygen to limbs and organs. This blockage is called sludging. The crises range from mild bone aches to debilitating body pain and can last up to a week. In the most severe cases, stroke can occur. Currently, there is no cure for the disease.

A child with sickle-cell anemia has inherited one copy of the defective gene from each parent. Two sickle-cell carriers have a 25% chance of having a child with sickle-cell and a 50% chance of having a child with the defective gene. In the United States, the illness is prevalent among African Americans, although people of Middle Eastern, Mediterranean, and Indian descent are also at risk. One of every 10 black Americans carries a single gene for sickle-cell anemia; one in every 500 (50,000–70,000 people) carries two genes and thus suffers from the disease. Those at risk can be tested for the presence of the gene. A hemoglobin electrophoresis test determines if someone is a carrier, and **amniocentesis** can detect the presence of sickle-cell anemia in a **fetus**. Newborn screening is mandated in approximately 40 states and can be requested if not done routinely.

Symptoms of sickle-cell anemia usually appear when the child is about three months old. The child will suffer from painful swelling of the hands or feet. By one year of age the child may refuse to walk. During the first five years of life, infection is a primary concern, particularly if sludging occurs in the spleen, preventing it from filtering out bacteria. Parents should be alert for any signs of infection, such as fever, poor feeding, fussiness and irritability, vomiting, and diarrhea. If infection is present, **antibiotics** are needed to head off possible fatal complications.

After the age of five, the child has acquired a number of natural immunities, and the danger of infection lessens. During the early school years, the sickle-cell patient will experience periodic sludging in the large bones of the body. In adolescence the danger of complications returns as major organs become susceptible to sludging. During crises, blood can pool in the spleen and destroy its tissue. Sickle-cell victims may also have enlarged hearts. Teenagers with sickle-cell are generally two to four years behind in physical development, which can be a source of anxiety to young people. Young women with sickle-cell anemia usually do not suffer from infertility, but any pregnancy should be handled with caution.

Aggressive research and treatment in recent years have made it possible for sickle-cell anemia patients to live long and productive lives. For young children, a pneumococcal vaccine and antibiotic therapy is recommended. When sludging episodes are mild, the child can be made comfortable with over-the-counter pain medications, rest, and fluids. More severe crises may require hospitalization for stronger pain relief such as spinal anesthetics. Blood transfusions also offer temporary relief from sludging crises. Although bone-marrow transplants have been effective in a few, very rare cases, the procedure is still under study as a possible cure for the disease. Transplants carry a 10% risk of death and the drugs used to destroy the old bone marrow can result in infertility.

For Further Study

Books

LeVert, Suzanne. *When Your Child Has a Chronic Illness.* New York: Dell, 1995.

Mankad, Vipul N., and R. Blaine Moore. *Sickle Cell Disease: Pathophysiology, Diagnosis, and Management.* Westport, CT: Praeger, 1992.

Serjeant, Graham R. *Sickle Cell Disease.* 2nd ed. New York: Oxford University Press, 1992.

Ujamaa, Dawud R. *Back to Our Roots: Cooking for Control of Sickle Cell Anemia and Cancer Prevention.* Decatur, GA: Al Maidah Publications, 1995.

Periodicals and publications

Agyemang-Badu, Nana Akua. "Sickle-cell and Your Child." *Essence* 25, January 1995, no. 9, p. 101.

U.S. Department of Health and Human Services, Public Health Service, Agency for Health Care Policy and Research. *Sickle Cell Disease in Newborns and Infants: A Guide for Parents.* Superintendent of Documents, Rockville, MD; Washington, DC: U.S. Government Printing Office, 1993.

Audio and video recordings

Invisible Illness: Living with Sickle Cell Anemia. Evanston, IL: Altschul Group Corporation 1993. [13-minute videorecording]
(This video, designed especially for children and teens, explains the disease of sickle-cell anemia and its invisible side effects. Narrated by young people with sickle-cell anemia, this firsthand account reveals the most common symptom of the disease, the intense pain, and how sufferers try to mentally work through the pain.)

Organizations

National Association for Sickle Cell Disease
Address: 3460 Wilshire Boulevard, Suite 1012
Los Angeles, CA 90010
Telephone: (800) 421-8453
The Sickle Cell Disease Association of America, Inc.
Address: 200 Corporate Pointe, Suite 208
Los Angeles, CA 90043
Telephone: (800) 421-8453
Sickle Cell Disease Research Foundation
Address: 4401 South Crenshaw Boulevard, Suite 208
Los Angeles, CA 90043
Telephone: (213) 299-3600

—Mary McNulty

Sign Language *see* **American Sign Language**

. . . .
Skeletal Development

Development of the bones of the human body.

Scientists who study the development of the human being from conception to birth begin calling the **embryo** a **fetus** around eight weeks after conception, when the first bone cells appear. The beginnings of the skeletal system begins prior to this, however. In the third week after conception, the notochord—a rod-like structure along the back of the embryo that will later become the spine, spinal cord, and brain—develops, followed in the fourth week by the first signs of arms and legs. Between the fifth and eighth weeks, the limbs (first the arms, hands, and fingers, followed by the legs, feet, and toes) begin to extend and take on a definite shape. By the end of the fifth week, the embryo has doubled in size and has grown a tail-like structure that will become the coccyx, or lowermost tip of the backbone. By the seventh week it is about 2 cm (1 in) long and facial features are visible. At this stage, the 206 bones of the human body—tubular, round, and flat—are all set down, in surprisingly adult form. However, the process of osteogenesis—development of bone—has not progressed to the point where the bones will become "bony." Indeed, ossification—the process whereby tissue hardens completely and becomes bone—of most bony nuclei of the long bones and round bones does not take place until after birth. It is therefore commonly but incorrectly stated in many elementary texts that the infant and child have more bones than adults do; this is a conceptual error resulting from confusing ossification centers (more than one bony spot that will spread and merge with other similar bony spots to form one bone mass) with anatomical bones.

Bone growth is more complicated than simple elongation or simple enlargement. Most long bones or tubular bones add in width on the outside by a process scientists refer to as *subperiosteal apposition* (layers added to those already existing), while losing bone on the inside by *endosteal resorption* (breaking down and reabsorbing material at the center of a mass). At the same time, long or tubular bones gain in length by additions to the epiphyseal plate (the surface at the end of the bone). As they elongate, bones of this type go through a process, remodeling, where they change in outer shape as well.

The individual bones of the skull grow by circumferential apposition (adding layers at the circumference), while gaining in thickness by adding layers (apposition) at the surface with simultaneous resorption at the inner surface. By this process, the skull expands and becomes thicker while allowing for more brain space within.

Linear growth of the long bones continues until the bone is completely hardened. At birth, long bones have more than one ossification center. These grow during childhood until the epiphyseal plates (at the ends of the bone) becomes fused with the shaft of the long bone, known as the diaphysis. This process is stimulated by the hormones produced by the testes and ovaries, which provide the developmental signal that the linear growth of the long bones should reach completion, or full development. Compact cortical bone, representing about 80% of the mature skeleton, supports the body, and features extra thickness at the midpoint in long bones to prevent the bones from bending. Cancellous bone, whose porous structure with small cavities resembles sponge, predominates in the pelvis and the 33 vertebrae from the neck to the tailbone.

Both round and flat bones of the skeleton are capable of continued growth throughout life. Deficiencies in bone growth may be caused by insufficient thyroid hormone or growth hormone (hypopituitarism). Conversely, hyperpituitarism (too much growth hormone) before puberty results in bone overgrowth, and, if left untreated, giantism, characterized by statures of eight feet (244 cm) or greater.

During childhood, bones are growing rapidly. Bone growth is fueled by a positive energy balance, created by a well-balanced diet and healthy living environment. Even in circumstances of severe malnutrition, there may be some formation of new bone; however, it will occur while bone formed earlier is deteriorating. During protein malnutrition, bone growth is largely halted and existing bone is cannibalized by the body as a source of protein. Both conditions exist in low-income families worldwide. Bone growth may also be limited by vitamin D deficiency, resulting in rickets in children (osteomalacia in adults) and other conditions characterized by insufficient dietary calcium.

With growing concern about adult osteoporosis, it is important to realize that the mass of skeleton built during childhood and into early adulthood constitutes bone banked against inevitable later withdrawals. For this reason there is much interest in the proposition that a calcium intake over 1500 mg per day may build a greater skeletal mass. However, this proposition, currently favored in the United States, is met with great skepticism in the United Kingdom. Moreover, calcium intakes during childhood are far greater in the United States than in most countries, but there is no particular evidence that the adult North American skeleton has a greater bone density (bone mass divided by bone volume).

Ossification centers and their development

The many ossification centers of the body—hand, foot, knee, elbow, and pelvis, for example—are not visible by radiography (x rays) until they begin to mineralize or ossify, even though they are actually present long before such mineralization begins. The age at appearance of individual centers then becomes a useful measure of skeletal development and especially in the form of "bone age" assessments of the hand, foot, or knee. Such assessments, made by taking a series of radiographs and comparing them against appropriate standards are both highly reliable and useful estimates of the stage of physical development. Bone age assessments are therefore used in pediatric evaluation, especially when malnutrition, malabsorption, food intolerance, or endocrinopathies (such as hypopituitarism or hypothyroidism) are suspected. Bone age assessments also have forensic application (estimating the chronological age of skeletal or cadaver material). In addition, bone age assessments provide data for making age assessments for children whose birth date in unknown, birth certificate does not exist, or is suspected of being inaccurate. Families adopting infants or children from countries where there has been socioeconomic stress may find bone age assessment helpful in establishing the chronological age their adopted child has attained.

The normal variability of skeletal age is about ±10% of attained chronological age. Thus, some chronological 12-year-olds may be assessed as 14 in terms of skeletal development, while others may be assessed as 10. Bone age is useful in projecting final stature; research has shown that it is more meaningful in making such projections than chronological age alone.

DISORDERS AND DEFICIENCY DISEASES OF THE SKELETON

Disorder	Characteristic	Cause	Treatment
Giantism	Excessive bone growth.	Hyperpituitarism before puberty (too much growth hormone)	Inhibit pituitary hormone production
Osteogenesis imperfecta; also known as brittle bone disease	Limbs and joints fracture under slight pressure (even walking puts too much pressure on fragile bones)	Genetic condition	Incurable; treatment prescribes restricted activity to minimize stress on bones and joints
Osteomalacia	Softening of the bones in adults	Lack of vitamin D	
Rickets	Soft and/or deformed bones	Inability to absorb calcium due to lack of vitamin D	

The question of long-bone growth and completion is of particular concern to parents children whose growth falls at the outside edges of the normal range. Long-bone growth may be accelerated by growth hormone administration if given by age nine, without speeding the timing of completion of long-bone growth, known as epiphyseal union.

Factors affecting bone growth and remodeling

Bone growth, bone remodeling, and the timing of skeletal maturation are all profoundly affected by nutritional status throughout the growing period. In bone remodeling, complex chemical signals prompt cells called osteoclasts to break down and remove (resorb) old bone, and others called osteoblasts to deposit new bone. Many elements influence bone remodeling, including whether the bone is weight-bearing, vitamin D intake, growth factors, and production of various hormones, including estrogen, thyroid, parathyroid, and calcitonin. Thus, poorly nourished boys and girls may be delayed in linear bone growth, diminished in all bone widths, later in the appearance of ossification centers, and delayed in epiphyseal union (completion of long-bone-growth). Children living in poverty worldwide may exhibit evidence of smaller amounts of incremental growth of all long bones and vertebrae, and delay in epiphyseal union. Conversely, obese boys and girls evidence greater growth in bone lengths and widths, earlier appearance of ossification centers, and earlier completion of epiphyseal union. In other words, obese children grow more, though for a shorter time period, because of their elevated caloric and nutrient intake.

Beyond simple caloric malnutrition due to inadequate food intake, there is also a protein-calorie malnutrition. In protein-calorie malnutrition, lower rates of bone formation may be exceeded by higher rates of bone loss. Thus children and adolescents with protein-calorie malnutrition may show a marked thinning of the outer walls of tubular bones, and an increased incidence and prevalence of bone fractures as a result. Excessive bone loss in protein-calorie malnutrition is also common in juvenile and adolescent cases of **anorexia nervosa**. Individuals with this condition show diminished bone density (bone mass/bone width). Researchers have also found that high levels of sodium in an the diet of girls ages 8–13 can significantly increase calcium lost. This effect is particularly powerful in girls whose calcium intake is less than the recommended 1500 mg—the amount in five glasses of milk—per day.

Girls mature earlier than boys, grow for a shorter time, and ultimately have shorter overall bone lengths by about seven percent. Adolescent girls are, in general, shorter-legged than adolescent boys; this proportional difference is also reflected in the hand and foot skeletons as well. Thus, even at comparable stature, females are shorter-legged and shorter-handed than boys; in addition, girls' bones are more gracile (narrower) than boys, and are therefore more affected by adult bone loss.

There are major genetically determined differences in relative growth rates of individual bones—in both length and width. Bone widths in general parallel differences in muscle mass and overall "frame size." The sequence of ossification of the bony nuclei also differs significantly from child to child, and the different sequences are controlled by genetics. Differences in growth patterns even among siblings confirms this genetic component. There are also major population differences in skeletal proportions and bone sizes and ratios. Children and adults of African ancestry have relatively longer bones in their hands and feet; the same bones in children and adults of Japanese, Korean, and Chinese ancestry are relatively shorter.

For Further Study

Books

Iscan, Mehmet Yasar, ed. *Age Markers in the Human Skeleton.* Springfield, IL: Charles C. Thomas, 1989.

Parker, Steve. *Skeleton.* New York: Alfred A. Knopf, 1988.

Roche, Alex F., Jean Roberts, and Peter V. Hamill. *Skeletal Maturity of Youths 12–17 Years: Racial, Geographic Area, and Socioeconomic Differentials.* Hyattsville, MD: Department of Health, Education, and Welfare, Public Health Service, Health Resources Administration, National Center for Health Statistics, 1978.

Walker, Richard. *The Visual Dictionary of the Skeleton.* New York: Dorling Kindersley, 1995.

Periodicals

Farley, Dixie. "New Ways to Heal Broken Bones." *FDA Consumer* 30, April 1996, pp. 14+.

Garn, Stanley M., C.G. Rohman, and F. N. Silverman. "Radiographic Standards for Postnatal Ossification and Tooth Calcification." *Medical Radiography and Photography* 43, pp. 45–66, 1967.

Munson, Marty, and Susan Flagg Godbey. "Calling All Calcium: Salt Can Curb Preteen Bone Buidling." *Prevention* 48, June 1996, p. 42.

Audiovisual Recordings

Skeletal System. 2d ed. Northbrook, IL: Coronet Films & Video, 1980.
    (One 12-minute videocassette.)

Skeleton: Eyewitness Skeleton. BBC Lionheart Television, 1994.
    (One 35-minute videocassette.)

—Stanley M. Garn, Ph.D.
University of Michigan

Sleep

The natural, periodic suspension of consciousness needed to revive the body.

There is no one acceptable pattern of sleep for all children. As a child develops from infancy through childhood and adolescence, sleep patterns change. In addition, there are also differences between the sleep needs of children at the same stage of development; some children naturally sleep for a shorter period of time, while others need a greater than average amount of sleep. The vast majority of children get enough sleep to meet their needs. As long as a child's sleep pattern is consistent, and she does not exhibit signs of excessive sleepiness or fatigue during the daytime, the quantity and quality of her sleep are probably adequate.

Infancy

Newborn infants sleep in short periods throughout the day and night, totaling up to 18 hours out of every 24. Like all human sleep, the sleep of young infants is divided into two types, non-REM sleep, which gradually progresses through four stages of increasingly deep sleep, and REM (rapid eye movement) sleep, the lighter sleep during which dreaming occurs. About half of a newborn's sleep time is spent in REM sleep. These are the periods when infants are most likely to squirm, yawn, or make soft noises in their sleep, and also the times when they are most easily awakened. As children grow older, their need for REM sleep declines, and it accounts for an increasingly smaller percentage of their nightly sleep time. For example, a toddler spends only about 30% of his sleep time in REM sleep, in contrast to the newborn's 50%. Corresponding to this gradual reduction in REM sleep, dreaming decreases dramatically as children get older. Infants spend about 40% of their sleep time dreaming, as opposed to 20% for adults. Infants have a cycle of REM and non-REM sleep that typically lasts 90 minutes, and they rise to a near-waking state every three to four hours. This cycle sets the pattern for night-time feedings, which typically occur at about 2:00 and 6:00 AM. Later, babies become able to comfort themselves during these near-awakenings, and their sleep cycles gradually become longer until they eventually sleep through the night.

By the age of two months, an infant's sleep has concentrated itself into a less diffuse schedule of regular naps. By three months, 70% of babies are able to get most of their sleep in one nighttime stretch, going through several consecutive cycles of REM and non-REM sleep. This number rises to 83% by the age of six months and 90% by one year. By four months of age, most infants can sleep through a 12-hour stretch with only one awakening. In the first months of life, environmental stressors and emotional issues do not intrude on an infant's sleep, and babies basically go to sleep whenever they are sleepy, unless they are hungry or in pain. By the end of the first year, however, external factors such as excitement or anxiety can keep a child from falling asleep naturally. During this time, she is learning the new skills of sitting, crawling, and walking, and the daytime excitement of mastering these activities can spill over into the night, creating a temporary regression in sleep patterns.

Toddlerhood and preschool age

By the age of one year, there can also be active resistance to going to bed, either because of reluctance to give up the stimulation and fun of being awake or because of fears and anxieties. Bedtime may trigger **separation anxiety**—the fear that while the child is asleep, he will lose or be abandoned by his parents—or other nighttime fears, such as fear of the dark or **fantasies** about monsters under the bed or in the closet. Between the ages of one and three years, children develop various strategies for resisting being put to bed—asking for another kiss, another story, a glass of water, or anything else they think will delay the final goodnight. They may also want to sleep in the parents' bed. For these children, it is helpful to get them to wind down, both mentally and physically, so they are ready for sleep. Comforting, enjoyable bedtime routines, such as a snack, a warm bath, a bedtime story, or a ritual of saying goodnight to the child's toys, can help a child calm down from the day's activities and mentally prepare for nighttime separation from parents.

Sleep problems caused by separation anxiety usually peak in the second and third year and end by the fourth. The worst of a child's resistance to bedtime is usually over by about the age of three years. Sometime after the age of three, bedtime can also be made more attractive by the replacement of the child's crib with a youth- or adult-sized bed and the creation of an appealing bedroom environment. During this period, the primary disruption of a child's sleep usually comes from **nightmares**, which are most prevalent between the ages of three and five, occurring as often as once or twice a week. Even though they can be upsetting, nightmares, especially at these ages, when the child's vivid daytime fantasy life is carried over into sleep, are not a cause for concern unless a child has the same nightmare repeatedly within a short period of time. Another form of sleep disturbance sometimes confused with nightmares is **night terror**, which is most common in children between the ages of six months to four years and is characterized by screaming, thrashing, sweating, rapid breathing, and confusion. Night terrors usually occur early in the night, often about two hours after a child falls asleep. Unlike nightmares, which are dreams and occur during REM sleep, night terrors occur during deep, non-REM sleep and are thought to be caused by a central nervous system response to momentary physical pain or discomfort, as opposed to nightmares, which are psychological in origin. Night terrors are most closely related to parasomnias, conditions such as sleepwalking in which normal daytime activities are performed during sleep. After the age of five, **enuresis** or bedwetting, is also classified as a parasomnia. These conditions, which are most common in early and middle childhood, are usually outgrown, with the exception of tooth grinding, which may persist into adulthood. During the preschool years, daytime napping decreases, and most children give up the daytime nap by the age of four or five, making do with about 11 hours of sleep at night.

School age and adolescence

In contrast to toddlers, who need a total of 12 to 14 hours of sleep a day (including naps), school-age children only need to sleep between 10 and 11 hours.

At any age, a child's sleep may be temporarily disturbed by life events that disrupt her routine, such as moving to a new house, starting a new school, or even sleeping in a new room. Sleeplessness that persists for more than a few nights, though, merits the attention of a physician. Sometimes an underlying physical problem, such as an ear infection, can be discovered. In rare cases a youngster can suffer from childhood-onset insomnia, a condition thought to be related to the functioning of the central nervous system. It is difficult to treat but can respond to tricyclic **antidepressants** such as amitriptyline (Elavil) or imipramine (Tofranil). This type of insomnia generally persists into adulthood.

A major factor affecting sleep in adolescence is the teenager's desire to assert his independence by setting his own sleep schedule, generally going to bed late to accommodate increased social activities. In combination with a natural slowdown of the biological clock that delays sleep onset time, the typical adolescent lifestyle results in increasingly late bedtimes, difficulty awakening, and daytime sleepiness. The additional responsibilities of increased schoolwork and part-time jobs add to the pressures to stay up late, although the resulting loss of sleep only makes it harder to keep up. The teenager's sleep schedule is further worsened by the tendency to catch up on lost sleep by sleeping in on weekends, further disrupting the sleep cycle. Abuse of street drugs or prescription medications, such as tranquilizers, causes additional sleep problems, often leading to the onset of insomnia that persists into adulthood.

Adolescents' sleep schedules can become even more chaotic in college. If students move away from home, they are no longer influenced by the sleep schedules of other family members, which may be more regular. In addition, staggered daytime class schedules may accommodate the recovery of lost sleep time by increased napping. While evidence of sleep loss in adolescence is usually attributable to the poor sleep schedule described above, parents and other adults who are in contact with teenagers need to be aware that various psychological disorders that can affect sleep, such as **depression**, often have their onset in late adolescence. In rare cases, for instance, excessive daytime sleepiness may be a sign of **narcolepsy,** a serious sleep disorder, rather than an ordinary deficit caused by a poor sleep schedule.

For Further Study

Books

Eberlein, Tamara. *Sleep: How to Teach Your Child to Sleep Like a Baby.* New York: Pocket Books, 1996.

Ferber, Richard. *Solve Your Child's Sleep Problems.* New York: Simon and Schuster, 1985.

Huntley, Rebecca. *The Sleep Book for Tired Parents.* Seattle: Parenting Press, 1991.

Lansky, Vicki. *Getting Your Child to Sleep—and Back to Sleep: Tips for Parents of Infants, Toddlers, and Preschoolers.* Deephaven, MN: Book Peddlers, 1991.

Mindell, Jodi A. *Sleeping Through the Night: How to Get a Good Night's Sleep for You and Your Baby.* New York: HarperCollins, 1997.

Sleep Disorders

Problems involving disruption in sleep pattern or inability to sleep.

Sleep is a period of decreased activity and muscle relaxation, characterized by patterns of deep sleep (where brain waves are slower, called non-rapid eye movement sleep) alternating with dreaming sleep, known as rapid eye movement (REM) sleep. Sleep restores energy to the body, especially to the brain and nervous system.

Sleep disorders common in childhood include **enuresis** (bedwetting), pavor nocturnus (**night terrors**), and **somnabulism** (sleepwalking). Less common in children are insomnia (sleeplessness, trouble falling, and staying asleep), and **narcolepsy** (difficulty staying awake).

Sleepwalking *see* Somnabulism

Small for Gestational Age

Small for gestational age (SGA) describes infants who weigh less than they should given their gestational age (the weeks they have spent in the uterus).

SGA infants can be premature, full-term, or post-term; such infants are simply not as large as would be predicted by their maturity. Experts differ on whether the cutoff for being small for gestational age (SGA) should be the third percentile or the tenth percentile for weight. Being SGA is not a disease in itself, but rather a risk factor for developing problems during the **perinatal period** as a result of having experienced smaller-than-expected growth in the womb.

Causes

Although underlying fetal problems cause some infants to be SGA, in the vast majority of SGA infants, the condition is caused by an inadequate supply of oxygen or nutrients before birth. Uterine environmental problems that can lead to SGA include:

- illness in the mother, such as severe high blood pressure, severe heart disease or vascular disease, or gastrointestinal ailments severe enough to result in malnutrition in the mother

- toxins such as **smoking**, alcohol, and certain abuse of drugs

- poor transport of oxygen to the fetus, such as infants born at high altitude, or mothers who have unusual types of hemoglobin (i.e., sickle-cell hemoglobin).

These uterine environment problems are by far the most common causes of underweight infants, but a number of fetal problems may also cause inadequate growth. These problems include chromosomal abnormalities (e.g., **Turner syndrome**, **trisomy** 21); certain malformation syndromes (e.g., **dwarfism**, diGeorge syndrome); and multiple gestations, including twinning. (Even healthy **twins**, however, are smaller on average than single births of the same gestational age; additionally, sometimes there will be a condition known as twin-twin transfusion, in which one twin receives most of the blood supply from the placenta and the second twin is short-changed and thus stunted.)

Complications

With improved methods of prenatal fetal monitoring, many cases of intrauterine growth retardation can be ascertained prior to delivery. This is important because a number of perinatal problems must be anticipated and dealt with promptly in an SGA newborn.

SGA babies have poor fat supplies and poor stores of glycogen (an energy-storing molecule). They are thus prone to **hypoglycemia** (low blood sugar) in the hours after birth and often have trouble maintaining a normal body temperature. SGA infants also have high rates of intra-partum distress and **asphyxia** at the time of birth because they do not tolerate the stresses of labor and delivery as well as infants who are appropriate for gestational age (AGA). Subtle neurological problems may be present at the time of birth, including tremor and abnormal reflex patterns. SGA infants may also have increased blood viscosity and calcium abnormalities in the hours following birth.

Prognosis

Long-term prognosis depends on the severity of the growth retardation they experience, the timing of the intrauterine insult, and whether brain growth (as measured by head growth) is affected or relatively spared.

—Marta M. Vielhaber, M.D.

Small Motor Development *see* **Fine Motor Skills**

Smiling

The development of smiling in the first months of life is an important indicator of an infant's level of social and cognitive functioning. Babies are born with a smiling reflex that is unrelated to any social impulse, a conclusion confirmed by the fact their earliest smiles, appearing within days of birth, occur almost solely while they are asleep. Researchers have described these early smiles as simple reactions to fluctuations in arousal: the relaxation produced when arousal reaches a modest threshold level and then declines produces a slight smile. If the arousal is too strong, relaxation doesn't occur soon enough to produce this smile. A physiological basis has been found for the contrast between this reflexive smiling and the social smiling that comes later: newborn smiles are associated with the lower brain regions, while social smiles involve the higher mental activities of the cerebral cortex. Newborn smiles (also called "sleep smiles") have been observed in infants whose cerebral cortexes are largely undeveloped or even missing entirely due to congenital abnormalities.

Social smiling, which occurs in response to the behavior of another person, usually begins between the ages of six and eight weeks. Initially, it is a response to pleasurable interaction with others in general rather than to a particular person. Although infants at this age do recognize their mothers, this recognition is not reflected in their smiles—they will smile as readily at the faces of others, including strangers. They will even smile at unpleasant-looking or unresponsive faces. According to child development experts, the pleasure shown by social smiling at this stage comes from an infant's satisfaction at having made sense of the world by recognizing a familiar object (a toy or mobile, or the human face in general, rather than a particular face), a phenomenon that has been termed recognitory assimilation. Laughter quickly follows the initiation of social smiling, often between the ages of two and three months. At this stage, babies will laugh at many of the same things that make them smile, with the laugh representing an intensification of the plea-

sure they feel. Social smiling in response to particular faces occurs at four or five months of age, when infants stop smiling at strangers and reserve their smiles for their mothers and other familiar persons.

Even before true social smiling begins, infants' smiles serve a social purpose by making their parents more attentive and affectionate toward them, which in turn helps the infants feel loved and secure. This pattern of reciprocal response helps lay the foundation for normal social development and parent-child **bonding**. Another way in which smiling holds a significance that extends beyond its underlying impulses is that through experience infants come to regard it as a way of manipulating their environment. Babies whose smiles elicit favorable responses, such as being picked up or being smiled at in return, learn that they can have an effect on their environment, and they are encouraged to smile even more. When smiling elicits no response, infants feel powerless and become depressed and unresponsive.

For Further Study

Books

Bornstein, Marc H. *Development in Infancy: An Introduction.* New York: McGraw-Hill, 1992.

Brazelton, T. Berry, and Bertrand G. Cramer. *The Earliest Relationship: Parents, Infants, and the Drama of Early Attachment.* Reading, MA: Addison-Wesley, 1990.

Damon, William. *Social and Personality Development: Infancy through Adolescence.* New York: W.W. Norton, 1983.

Smoking

Use of cigarettes and other tobacco products to engage in a habit that almost always leads to addiction.

Every day 3,000 young people light up their first cigarette; every year a million teenagers become regular smokers. Adolescent smoking has risen steadily throughout the 1990s, following a sharp decline in the 1970s that leveled off in the 1980s. A 1994 report by the office of the U.S. Surgeon General found that approximately 28% of teens smoked in 1991 and 1992. By 1995 a survey of high school students released by the Centers for Disease Control and Prevention found that the prevalence of teen smoking had increased to 34.8%. The study also found that smoking was most prevalent among white teenagers (38%), followed by Hispanics (34%), and blacks (19%). In addition to smoking more, teenagers are also starting to smoke earlier. The average teen smokes his or her first cigarette at the age of 13, becoming a regular smoker at 14-½. A 1996 survey by the Public Health Service found that 21% of eighth graders and 30% of tenth graders surveyed smoked.

The harmful effects of teenage smoking are known to be both short-term and long-term. During **adolescence**, smoking interferes with ongoing lung growth and development, preventing the attainment of full lung function. Teenagers who smoke are less fit than their non-smoking peers and more apt to experience shortness of breath, dizziness, coughing, and excess phlegm in their lungs. They are also more vulnerable to colds, flu, pneumonia, and other respiratory problems. Smoking for even a short time can produce a chronic smoker's cough. In addition to respiratory problems and a diminished level of overall well-being in adolescence, teenage smoking is also responsible for health problems in adulthood.

It is estimated that one-third of the teenagers who start smoking each year will eventually die of diseases related to tobacco use—diseases that will shorten their lives by an average of 12–15 years. Cigarette smoking is a major risk factor for cardiovascular disease, including coronary heart disease, atherosclerosis (hardening of the arteries), and stroke. The 1994 Surgeon General's report links teenage smoking to cardiovascular disease in both adolescents and adults. The same report cites evidence that the length of time a person has smoked has a greater impact on the risk of developing lung cancer and other smoking-related cancers than the number of cigarettes smoked—in other words, starting to smoke at an early age is an even greater health risk than being a heavy smoker.

Several factors have been cited as inducements for teenagers to begin smoking. It is generally agreed that the most important is **peer pressure.** Having friends who smoke makes smoking appear desirable to teens and makes them feel different or left out if they don't smoke also. (Many teenagers overestimate the prevalence of teen smoking.) At parties or in other social situations, smoking can help teenagers mask or cope with feelings of insecurity or self-consciousness. They also use it—as adults do—to help them cope with a broad range of stressors and negative feelings. Other factors cited as playing a role in teenage smoking include curiosity, boredom, and the desire to rebel against parents and other authority figures. Teenagers are much less likely to model parental smoking behavior than that of their peers. The main impact parents can have on teen smoking is to actively discourage their children from smoking by discussing its harmful effects and to be supportive of their children in other areas of their lives.

The 6.2 billion dollars that the tobacco industry spends every year on advertising has also been shown to have a significant effect on teenage smoking. In spite of industry denials, teenagers are a crucial market for cigarette manufacturers. Since the vast majority of people who smoke start before the age of 18, this is the prime period during which tobacco companies must make their

SECOND HAND SMOKE

The health risks to teens who use cigarettes are well documented, but studies in the late 1990s revealed another risk. Children and teens who live with a smoker are also at risk due to exposure to second hand smoke. The American Academy of Pediatrics report the following findings:

Mothers who smoke during pregnancy have a 50% higher risk of giving birth to a mentally retarded infant; if the mother smokes one pack of cigarettes or more per day, the risk increases to 75%.

Between 354,000 and 2.2 million middle-ear infections in children each year are linked to second hand smoke.

Children of smokers are twice as likely to need tonsillectomies.

Household smoking causes an estimated 307,000–522,000 cases of asthma in children under 15.

Bronchitis due to secondhand smoke in children under five is linked to household smoking in an estimated 260,000–436,000 cases annually; cases of pneumonia in those under age five are linked to secondhand smoke in 115,000–190,000 cases per year.

Between 284–360 children die each year from smoking-related fires and respiratory-tract illnesses due to second hand smoke .

appeal to potential new customers. And now more than ever they need these customers to replace the many adults lost to the market every year through quitting (in addition to those who die). Although cigarette advertising has been banned on radio and television since 1971, the tobacco industry can still target young people in print ads and, increasingly, through sponsorship of sporting events, concerts, and other types of entertainment. Today's print ads rely more heavily on images than slogans or information, representing smokers as young, healthy, energetic, and stylish. The Surgeon General's report suggests that cigarette ads work not only by associating smoking with a positive self-image but also by making it seem pervasive.

Although it is illegal to sell tobacco to minors, most teenagers report having little trouble obtaining cigarettes. Of the adolescents questioned in the 1995 Centers for Disease Control Youth Risk Behavior Survey, 40% said they regularly bought cigarettes in stores. Thirty-three percent reported borrowing them from others, while another 16% said they usually gave someone else money to buy cigarettes for them. About 4% said they stole cigarettes, and 2% reported buying them from vending machines. In response to the easy availability of tobacco to teenagers, the Food and Drug Administration has included in its new anti-smoking program a regulation requiring store employees to request that all cigarette purchasers who appear to be under 27 years of age provide proof that they are at least 18. This measure, which went into effect at the end of February 1997, will be monitored through undercover inspection, and any merchant found selling cigarettes to a minor will receive a warning and be fined $250 for any subsequent violation.

As the next step in the FDA's program to cut teenage smoking in half within seven years, regulations aimed at the marketing of cigarettes to teenagers were slated to take effect in August of 1997. These include the banning of cigarette advertising on billboards within 1,000 feet of a school or playground; an attempt to reduce the appeal of tobacco to young people by restricting all outdoor cigarette advertising (and advertising in magazines frequently read by teenagers) to black and white ads with no pictures; and a ban on printing the logos of cigarette brands on athletic clothing such as baseball caps, T-shirts, and gym bags. As of August 1998 cigarette manufacturers were to be prohibited from displaying brand names (as opposed to corporate logos) at sporting events.

Although nicotine is considered by some to be as addictive as cocaine, most teen smokers tell themselves that they will be able to control their use of cigarettes. This is usually not the case. Two-thirds of young people who smoke have made at least one failed attempt at quitting. Seventy percent regret having started smoking. Symptoms of withdrawal from nicotine include irritability, anxiety, mood swings, difficulty concentrating, insomnia, depression, headaches, and changes in appetite. Smokers commonly have to try quitting between 7 and 17 times before they succeed. Both the American Lung Association and the American Medical Association (AMA) have launched programs to help teens stop smoking. Additional programs target younger children to prevent them from starting to smoke. The AMA targets children with a superhero called "The Extinguisher," who visits schools and is featured in comic books. A joint outreach program—Teens Against Tobacco Use—has been developed by the American Cancer Society, the American Heart Association, and the American Lung Association. Groups of four teens aged 14 through 17 work with children in grades four through six to inform them about the negative aspects of smoking and serve as positive role models.

Teenage smokers can also obtain help and support from their family physicians, who may be able to prescribe medications that can ease withdrawal symptoms.

Call-in hotlines and support groups such as Nicotine Anonymous are also available.

For Further Study

Books

Glantz, Stanton A., et al. *The Cigarette Papers.* Berkeley and Los Angeles: University of California Press, 1996.

Institute of Medicine. *Growing Up Tobacco Free.* Washington, DC: National Academy Press, 1994.

Schwebel, Robert. *Saying No Is Not Enough: What to Say and How to Listen to Your Kids About Alcohol, Tobacco and Other Drugs—A Positive Prevention Guide for Parents.* New York: Newmarket Press, 1997.

U.S. Department of Health and Human Services. *Preventing Tobacco Use Among Young People: A Report of the Surgeon General.* Atlanta, GA: U.S. Department of Health and Human Services, Public Health Service, Centers for Disease Control and Prevention, Office on Smoking and Health, 1994.

Wekesser, Carol, ed. *Smoking.* Current Controversies series. San Diego, CA: Greenhaven Press, 1997.

Periodicals

"When Parents Puff." *U.S. News and World Report* 120, no. 16, April 22, 1996, p. 22.

Organizations

American Cancer Society
   Address: 316 Pennsylvania Ave. SE
   Washington, DC 20003
   Telephone: (202) 546-1682
American Lung Association
   Address: 1740 Broadway
   New York, NY 10019-4374
   Telephone: (212) 315-8700
Stop Teen-Age Addiction to Tobacco (STAT)
   Address: 511 E. Columbus Ave.
   Springfield, MA 01105
   Telephone: (413) 72-STAT ([413]-732-7828)

Social Class *see* **Socioeconomic Status**

Social Competence

Mastering the social, emotional, and cognitive skills and behaviors needed to succeed as a member of society.

Social competence refers to the social, emotional, and cognitive skills and behaviors that children need for successful social adaptation. Despite this simple definition, social competence is an elusive concept, because the skills and behaviors required for healthy social development vary with the age of the child and with the demands of particular situations. A socially competent preschool child behaves in a much different manner than a socially competent adolescent; conversely, the same behaviors (e.g., aggression, shyness) have different implications for social adaptation depending upon the age of the child and the particulars of the social context.

A child's social competence depends upon a number of factors including the child's social skills, social awareness, and self-confidence. Social skills is a term used to describe the child's knowledge of and ability to use a variety of social behaviors that are appropriate to a given interpersonal situation and that are pleasing to others in each situation. The capacity to inhibit egocentric, impulsive, or negative social behavior is also a reflection of a child's social skills. The term emotional intelligence refers to the child's ability to understand others' emotions, perceive subtle social cues, "read" complex social situations, and demonstrate insight about others' motivations and goals. Children who have a wide repertoire of social skills and who are socially aware and perceptive are likely to be socially competent. Social competence is the broader term used to describe a child's social effectiveness—a child's ability to establish and maintain high quality and mutually satisfying relationships and to avoid negative treatment or victimization from others. In addition to social skills and emotional intelligence, factors such as the child's self-confidence or social anxiety can affect his/her social competence. Social competence can also be affected by the social context and the extent to which there is a good match between the child's skills, interests, and abilities and those of the other children in his/her environment. For example, a quiet and studious boy may appear socially incompetent in a peer group full of raucous athletes, but may do fine socially if a better peer group "niche" can be found for him, such as a group of peers who share his interests in quiet games or computers.

Importance of social competence

Whereas parents are the primary source of social and emotional support for children during the first years of life, in later years peers begin to play a significant complementary and unique role in promoting child social-emotional development. Increasingly with age, peers rather than parents become preferred companions, providing important sources of entertainment and support. In the context of peer interactions, young children engage in **fantasy** play that allows them to assume different roles, learn to take another person's perspective, and develop an understanding of the social rules and conventions of their culture. In addition, relationships with peers typically involve more give-and-take than relationships with adults, and thus provide an opportunity for the development of social competencies such as cooperation and negotiation. During adolescence, peer relations become particularly important for children. A key developmental task of adolescence is the formation of an identity—a sense of the kind of person you are and the kind of person

you want to be. Adolescents "try on" different social roles as they interact with peers, and peers serve as a social "stepping stone" as adolescents move away from their emotional dependence upon their parents and toward autonomous functioning as an adult. In many ways, then, childhood peer relations serve as "training grounds" for future interpersonal relations, providing children with opportunities to learn about reciprocity and intimacy. These skills are associated with effective interpersonal relations in adult life, including relations with co-workers and with romantic partners.

When children experience serious difficulties in the domain of peer relations, the development of social competencies may be threatened. Rejection or victimization by peers may become a source of significant stress to children, contributing to feelings of loneliness and low **self-esteem**. In addition, peer rejection can escalate in a negative developmental spiral. That is, when children with poor social skills become rejected, they are often excluded from positive interactions with peers—interactions that are critical for the learning of social skills. Rejected children typically have fewer options in terms of play partners and friends than do accepted children. Observations of rejected children have revealed that they spend more time playing alone and interacting in smaller groups than their more popular peers. In addition, the companions of rejected children tend to be younger or more unpopular than the companions of accepted children. Exclusion from a normal peer group can deprive rejected children of opportunities to develop adaptive social behaviors. Hence, the social competence deficits of rejected children may increase over time, along with feelings of social anxiety and inadequacy.

Social competence deficits and peer rejection

Many children experience difficulties getting along with peers at some point during their youth. Sometimes these problems are short-lived and for some children the effects of being left out or teased by classmates are transitory. For other children, however, being ignored or rejected by peers may be a lasting problem that has lifelong consequences, such as a dislike for school, poor self-esteem, social withdrawal, and difficulties with adult relationships.

Considerable research has been undertaken to try to understand why some children experience serious and long-lasting difficulties in the area of peer relations. To explore factors leading to peer difficulties, researchers typically employ the sociometric method to identify children who are or are not successful with peers. In this method, children in a classroom or a group are asked to list children who they like most and those who they like least. Children who receive many positive ("like most") nominations and few negative ("like least") nominations are classified as "popular;" those who receive few positive and few negative nominations are designated "neglected," and those who receive few positive and many negative nominations are classified as "rejected."

Evidence compiled from studies using child interviews, direct observations, and teacher ratings all suggest that popular children exhibit high levels of social competence. They are friendly and cooperative and engage readily in conversation. Peers describe them as helpful, nice, understanding, attractive, and good at games. Popular and socially competent children are able to consider others' perspectives, can sustain their attention to the play task, and are able to "keep their cool" in situations involving conflict. They are agreeable and have good problem-solving skills. Socially competent children are also sensitive to the nuances of "play etiquette." They enter a group using diplomatic strategies, such as commenting upon the ongoing activity and asking permission to join in. They uphold standards of equity and show good sportsmanship, making them good companions and fun play partners.

Children who have problems making friends, those who are either "neglected" or "rejected" sociometrically, often show deficits in social skills. One of the most common reasons for friendship problems is behavior that annoys other children. Children, like adults, do not like behavior that is bossy, self-centered, or disruptive. It is simply not fun to play with someone who doesn't share or doesn't follow the rules. Sometimes children who have learning problems or attention problems can have trouble making friends, because they find it hard to understand and follow the rules of games. Children who get angry easily and lose their temper when things don't go their way can also have a hard time getting along with others. Children who are rejected by peers often have difficulties focusing their attention and controlling their behavior. They may show high rates of noncompliance, interference with others, or aggression (teasing or fighting). Peers often describe rejected classmates as disruptive, short-tempered, unattractive, and likely to brag, to start fights, and to get in trouble with the teacher.

Not all aggressive children are rejected by their peers. Children are particularly likely to become rejected if they show a wide range of conduct problems, including disruptive, hyperactive, and disagreeable behaviors in addition to physical aggression. Socially competent children who are aggressive tend to use aggression in a way that is accepted by peers (e.g., fighting back when provoked), whereas the aggressive acts of rejected children include **tantrums,** verbal insults, cheating, or tattling. In addition, aggressive children are more likely to be rejected if they are hyperactive, immature, and lacking in positive social skills.

Children can also have friendship problems because they are very shy and feel uncomfortable and unsure of themselves around others. Sometimes children are ignored or teased by classmates because there is something "different" about them that sets them apart from other children. When children are shy in the classroom and ignored by children, becoming classified as "neglected," it does not necessarily indicate deficits in social competence. Many neglected children have friendships outside of the classroom setting, and their neglected status is simply a reflection of their quiet attitude and low profile in the classroom. Developmentally, peer neglect is not a very stable classification, and many neglected children develop more confidence as they move into classrooms with more familiar or more compatible peers. However, some shy children are highly anxious socially, and uncomfortable around peers in many situations. Shy, passive children who are actively disliked and rejected by classmates often become teased and victimized. These children often do have deficits in core areas of social competence that have a negative impact on their social development. For example, many are emotionally dependent on adults, and immature in their social behavior. They may be inattentive, moody, depressed, or emotionally volatile, making it difficult for them to sustain positive play interactions with others.

The long-term consequences of sustained peer rejection can be quite serious. Often, deficits in social competence and peer rejection coincide with other emotional and behavioral problems, including attention deficits, aggression, and **depression**. The importance of social competence and satisfying social relations is life-long. Studies of adults have revealed that friendship is a critical source of social support that protects against the negative effects of life stress. People with few friends are at elevated risk for depression and anxiety.

Childhood peer rejection predicts a variety of difficulties in later life, including school problems, mental health disorders, and **antisocial behavior**. In fact, in one study, peer rejection proved to be a more sensitive predictor of later mental health problems than school records, achievement, and IQ scores or teacher ratings.

It appears, then, that positive peer relations play an important role in supporting the process of healthy social and **emotional development**. Problematic peer relations are associated with both concurrent and future maladjustment of children, and hence warrant serious attention from parents and professionals working with children. When assessing the possible factors contributing to a child's social difficulties and when planning remedial interventions, it is important to understand developmental processes associated with social competence and peer relations.

Developmental changes and social competence

The key markers of social competence listed in the previous section are remarkably consistent across the developmental periods of the preschool years, middle childhood, and adolescence. Across these developmental periods, prosocial skills (friendly, cooperative, helpful behaviors) and self-control skills (anger management, negotiation skills, problem-solving skills) are key facets of social competence. In addition, however, developmental changes occur in the structure and quality of peer interactions which affect the complexity of skills contributing to social competence. That is, as children grow, their preferences for play change, and the thinking skills and language skills that provide a foundation for social competence also change. Hence, the kinds of interactions that children have with peers change qualitatively and quantitatively with development.

The ways in which children spend their time together, for example, changes with development. During the preschool years, social competence involves the ability to separate from parents and engage with peers in shared play activities, particularly fantasy play. As preschool children are just learning to coordinate their social behavior, their interactions are often short and marked by frequent squabbles, and friendships are less stable than at later developmental stages. In addition, physical rough-and-tumble play is common, particularly among boys.

By grade school, children begin to develop an interest in sports, structured board games, and group games with complex sets of rules. Being able to understand and follow game rules and being able to handle competition in appropriate ways (e.g., being a good sport) become important skills for social competence. Children play primarily in same-sex groups of friends, and expect more stability in their friendships. Loyalty and dependability become important qualities of good friends.

During the preadolescent and early adolescent years, communication (including sending notes, calling on the phone, and "hanging out") becomes a major focus for peer interactions. Increasingly, social competence involves the willingness and ability to share thoughts and feelings with one another, especially for girls. When adolescent friends squabble, their conflicts typically center around issues such as gossiping, disclosing secrets, or loyalty and perceived betrayal. It is at this stage that friends and romantic partners consistently rival parents as the primary sources of intimacy and social support.

In addition to developmental changes in the content and focus of peer relations, development brings changes in the structure of peer relations. During the preschool and early grade school years, children are primarily focused on group acceptance and having companions to spend time with and play with. However, during the mid- dle to late grade school years, children begin to distinguish "regular" friends from "best" friends. The establishment of close, best friendships is an important developmental milestone. That is, in addition to gaining acceptance from a group of peers, one of the hallmarks of social competence is the ability to form and maintain satisfying close friendships. Many of the positive characteristics that promote popularity (such as cooperativeness, friendliness, and consideration for others) also assist children in developing and maintaining friendships. Friendships emerge when children share similar activities and interests and, in addition, when they develop a positive and mutual bond between them. Group acceptance and close friendships follow different timetables and serve different developmental functions, with the need for group acceptance emerging during the early grade school years and filling a need for belonging, and the need for close friends emerging in preadolescence to meet newfound needs for affection, alliance, and intimacy outside the family. Key features of close friendships are reciprocity and similarity, mutual intimacy, and social support.

A third major shift in the complexity of peer relations involves the changing role of **cliques** and crowds. Grade school children often have little conception of peer groups. For example, when we interviewed fifth graders and asked them about groups at their school, a typical reply was, "what do you mean, reading groups?" In contrast, by eighth grade, children had distinct ideas about groups at their school, responding to our questions with labels such as "the jocks, the brains, the nerds." The recognition of cliques and crowds as organizational structures of the peer group usually emerges during early adolescence. In part, the understanding of cliques reflects a cognitive advance, as children in adolescence are able to use formal operational thinking to consider abstract ideas such as "cliques" and apply them to their thinking about peers. In part, the rise of cliques in the organizational structure of peer groups reflects the structure of American schools, which typically transition from small elementary schools to large middle schools or junior high schools around sixth or seventh grade. The change in the school context has a large impact on the nature of the peer group, as the typical middle school or junior high school peer group involves a very large and diverse set of peers. In the context of this large group, children associate with smaller networks of familiar classmates. Typically, the grouping into friendship networks takes place on the basis of shared interests, activities, and attitudes. Children in the same friendship networks influence each other in matters of dress, behavior, and language, leading to identifiable characteristics of group members that become the basis for group labels (e.g., jocks or brains).

From an emotional standpoint, adolescents are focused on developing a sense of themselves and in sorting out how their identities fit (or do not fit) with the expectations of others and the social niches available to them. As a correlate to identity formation, adolescents become keenly aware of group peer norms and increasingly seek to associate with peers and use peer standards to evaluate their own and other's social behavior. Whereas in grade school peer status referred to one's state of acceptance or rejection from the classroom group, by adolescence one's peer status is complicated by the nature of the various groups toward which one may seek and attain (or be refused) membership status. In other words, in addition to finding friends, adolescents often worry about their placement in the larger social structure of cliques and crowds.

The increased level of social awareness and self-consciousness that accompanies the advanced social reasoning of adolescence and the increased importance that adolescents place on peer acceptance may strengthen the impact of perceived peer rejection on emotional adjustment and self-concept. Social ostracism or self-imposed isolation my also become a more important determinant of peer rejection during adolescence than at younger ages.

At all ages, the treatment a child receives from peers may influence his or her social adaptation. Once rejected by peers, disliked children may find themselves excluded from peer activities and exposed to ostracism, or more severely to victimization by peers. Peers may develop negatively biased attitudes and expectations for rejected children and treat these children differently (with more counteraggression and hostility) than they treat their well-accepted peers. Children who are particularly stressed by the academic demands of school, such as those aggressive-rejected children with attentional deficits or hyperactive behaviors, may be at increased risk for negative interactions with teachers and peers. Over time, teachers tend to become less positive and less contingent in their reactions to these problematic students, decreasing their effectiveness at managing social behavior.

During the preadolescent and later adolescent years, the combination of ostracism from conventional peer groups and the evolution of peer group cliques and crowds can be problematic for rejected children. That is, adolescents who feel pushed out of the conventional peer groups may begin to affiliate with defiant peers. As cliques of deviant peers form in adolescence, these groups may begin to exert a strong influence on children, shaping their attitudes and social behaviors and increasing the likelihood of future antisocial and deviant behavior. Particularly in adolescence, youth turn to their peer groups for guidance in matters of dress code, social behavior, social attitudes, and identity formation. In peer networks containing many members who exhibit high rates of aggression, group norms are likely to be accepting of aggression. Hence, although affiliations with deviant peers may provide companionship and support, the "cost" of such affiliations may be great, in terms of their negative influence exacerbating antisocial behavior and attitudes. Preadolescent children who form friendships with antisocial peers appear to be at heightened risk for later antisocial behavior, including delinquency, drug use, and school dropout.

Family contributions to social competence

Because the family is the primary context for social development, there are a number of ways in which family interaction patterns may help or hinder the development of children's social competence. Some researchers have speculated that the origins of social competence can be found in infancy, in the quality of the parent-child **attachment** relationship. Studies have shown that babies whose parents are consistent and sensitive in their responses to distress are less irritable, less anxious, and better emotionally regulated. By contrast, parents who are inconsistent and insensitive to their infants' signals are more likely to have anxious, irritable babies who are difficult to soothe. These children may learn both to model their parents' insensitivity and to rely on intrusive, demanding behavior of their own in order to get attention. If they then generalize these socially incompetent behaviors to their peer interactions, peer rejection may result.

As children get older, family interaction styles and the ways in which parents discipline may play a primary role in the development of noncompliant or aggressive behaviors in children. In families where parents are extremely demanding and use inconsistent, harsh, and punitive **discipline** strategies, family interaction patterns are frequently characterized by escalation and conflict, and children often exhibit behavior problems. When children generalize the aggressive and oppositional behavior that they have learned at home to their interactions with peers, other children often reject them. Indeed, research has revealed that aggressive behavior is the common link between harsh, inconsistent discipline and rejection by peers.

By contrast, parents of popular children are typically more positive and less demanding with their children than parents of unpopular children. In addition, parents of popular children "set a good example" by modeling appropriate social interactions, and assist their children by arranging opportunities for peer interaction, carefully supervising these experiences, and providing helpful feedback about conflict resolution and making friends.

Child characteristics and social competence

In addition to family interaction patterns and various aspects of the parent-child relationship, children's own thoughts, feelings, and attitudes may influence their social behavior. Research has revealed that many rejected children make impulsive, inaccurate, and incomplete judgments about how to behave in social situations and are lacking in social problem-solving skills. They may make numerous errors in processing social information, including misinterpretation of other people's motives and behavior, setting social goals for themselves that are unrealistic or inappropriate, and making poor decisions about their own conduct in social situations. For example, aggressive children are more likely to interpret an accidental push or bump from a peer as intentionally hostile, and respond accordingly. Similarly, socially incompetent children are often more interested in "getting even" with peers for injustices than they are in finding positive solutions to social problems, and expect that aggressive, coercive strategies will lead to desired outcomes.

Many children who are rejected by peers have lower self-esteem, feel lonelier, and are more dissatisfied with their social situations than are average or popular children. These feelings can cause them to give up and avoid social situations, which can in turn exacerbate their peer problems. Interestingly, not all rejected children feel badly about their social difficulties. Studies have shown that aggressive-rejected children, who tend to blame outside factors for their peer problems, are less likely to express distress than withdrawn-rejected children, who often attribute their problems to themselves.

Assessing social competence

There is an important difference between not being "popular" and having friendship problems. Some children are outgoing and have many friends. Other children are quite content with just a good friend or two. Either one of these friendship patterns is fine. Distinguishing "normative" friendship problems from problematic peer relations that signal serious deficits in social competence is an important goal of assessment. There are several key signs that a child's peer difficulties may be more serious and long-lasting rather than temporary. First, the nature of the child's social behavior is important. If children behave aggressively with peers, act bossy and domineering, or are disruptive and impulsive at school, they are more likely to have stable and long-lasting peer difficulties than are children who are simply shy. Children who display aggressive or disruptive behavior often have many discouraging experiences at school, including discipline problems and learning difficulties as well as poor peer relations. School adjustment can be a downhill slide for these children as teachers may get discouraged and peers may get angered by their behaviors. Peers may attempt to "get back" at these children by teasing, which only increases the frustrations and helplessness experienced by aggressive, disruptive children.

Second, children who are actively disliked, teased, or ostracized by peers are at more risk than children who are simply ignored. It is not necessary for a child to be popular in order to gain the advantages of peer support. When children are ignored by peers and are neither disliked nor liked, teachers and parents can take steps to foster friendship development and peer support. When children are actively disliked by peers and the victims of teasing or ostracism, the task is harder for parents and teachers and the likelihood of the child reestablishing positive peer relations without help is slimmer.

Third, the stability and chronicity of peer problems should be considered. It is not unusual for children to experience short-term social difficulties when they are moving into new peer situations, such as a new school or a new classroom. Peer problems may also emerge if children are distressed about other changes in their lives, such as a reaction to parental conflict or the birth of a sibling. When peer problems emerge at a time that corresponds to other family or situational changes, they may serve as signals to let parents and teachers know that the child needs extra support at that time. When peer problems have been stable and have existed for a long time, more extensive intervention focused on improving peer relations may be needed.

There is a variety of methods available for the assessment of social competence. When choosing a particular assessment strategy, it is important to consider the nature of a particular child's problem. Some children have difficulty with all types of social relationships, while others do well in their neighborhoods or in one-on-one friendships but experience problems with the peer group at school. When problems occur in the school setting, teachers and other school personnel who have opportunities to see children interacting in several peer group situations (such as the classroom, playground, and lunchroom) are often the best first step in assessment. Teachers can often provide information about how children treat and are treated by peers, and can also offer opinions about how typical or unusual a child's peer problems are relative to others of the same age. Teacher assessments can include behavioral checklists and rating scales and direct observations of specific social behaviors.

Similarly, parents can also provide information about children's social competence. Parents can help to identify problem behaviors such as aggression, withdrawal, and noncompliance that may interfere with social skills. In addition, parents are usually more aware than teachers of their children's social activities outside of school, such as their participation in sports, clubs, or hobbies.

Because they do not have access to the full range of situations in which children interact, however, teachers and parents may not always be the best source of information on children's peer problems. In some cases, it is most helpful to get information directly from peers themselves. One method of obtaining such information is the use of sociometric ratings and nominations. With these procedures, all of the children in a classroom are asked to rate how much they like to play with or spend time with each of their classmates. In addition, they nominate specific peers with whom they particularly like or dislike, and may be asked to identify peers who exhibit particular behavioral characteristics (e.g., nice, aggressive, shy, etc.). The sociometric method, although cumbersome to administer, identifies children who are popular, rejected, and neglected by their peers more accurately than parent or teacher reports, and provides useful information about the reasons for peer dislike.

A third approach to assessment of social competence involves children's self-reports. Although input from parents, teachers, and peers can provide valuable insight into children's social behavior and their status within the peer group, information regarding children's thoughts, feelings, and perceptions of their social situations can be obtained only by asking the children themselves. Depending upon the age of the child, information about social competence can be obtained through the use of questionnaires and rating scales that measure children's self-perceptions of their peer relations, the use of stories and hypothetical social situations to elicit information about the child's social reasoning, or simply talking with children to determine their perspectives on their social situations.

Because children may have different experiences in different kinds of peer settings and because no one particular method of assessment is entirely reliable or complete, it is desirable to use a variety of sources when attempting to assess children's social competence. Teacher, parent, peer, and self-reports may yield distinct but complementary information, and hence, by gathering multiple perspectives, a more complete picture of a child's social strengths and weaknesses can be obtained.

Interventions to promote social competence

Different strategies may be needed to help children develop social competencies and establish positive peer relations depending upon the age of the child and the type of peer problem being experienced. Different children have different needs when it comes to helping them get along better with others and making friends. The age of the child, the kinds of behaviors that are part of the problem, the reasons for the friendship problem—all of these may affect the helping strategy.

One strategy involves social skill training. Observations have revealed that children who are well-liked by peers typically show helpful, courteous, and considerate behavior. The purpose of social skill training is to help unpopular children learn to treat their peers in positive ways. The specific skills taught in different programs vary depending upon the age and type of child involved. Commonly taught skills include helping, sharing, and cooperation. Often children are taught how to enter a group, how to be a good group participant, how to be a fair player (e.g., following rules, taking turns), and how to have a conversation with peers. The skills might also include anger management, negotiation, and conflict resolution skills. Problem solving skills (e.g., identifying the problem, considering alternative solutions, choosing a solution and making a plan) are often included in social skill training programs. Sometimes social skill training is done individually with children, but often it is done in a small group. A particular skill concept is discussed, and children may watch a short film or hear a story that illustrates the usefulness of the skill. They then have the opportunity to practice the skill during activities or roleplays with other children in the group. A trained group leader helps guide the children in their use of the skill and provides support and positive feedback to help children become more natural and spontaneous in socially skillful behavior.

Another intervention strategy focuses on helping children who are having trouble getting along with others because of angry, aggressive, or bossy behavior. It can be difficult to suppress aggressive and disruptive behaviors in peer settings for several reasons. For one thing, these behaviors often "work" in the sense that they can be instrumental in achieving desired goals. By complaining loudly, hitting, or otherwise using force or noise, children may be able to get access to a toy they want or they may be able to get peers to stop doing something noxious to them. In this type of situation, an adult's expressed disapproval may suppress the behavior, but the behavior is likely to emerge again in situations where an adult supervisor is not present. Often contracts and point systems are used to suppress aggressive behavior and bossiness; however, positive skill training must be used in conjunction with behavior management in order to provide the child with alternative skills to use in situations requiring negotiations with peers. Often parents are included in programs to help children develop better anger management skills and to help children reduce fighting. Trained counselors, educators, or psychologists work with parents to help them find positive discipline strategies and positive communication skills to promote child anger management and conflict resolution skills.

A third helping strategy focuses on finding a good social "niche" for the child. Large, unstructured peer group settings (such as recess) are particularly difficult situations for many of the children who have peer problems. These children need more structured, smaller peer interaction setting in which an adult's support is available to guide positive peer interaction. Finding a good social "niche" for some children can be a difficult task, but an important one. Sometimes a teacher can organize cooperative learning groups that help an isolated child make friends in the classroom. Sometimes parents can help by inviting potential friends over to play or getting their child involved in a social activity outside of school that is rewarding (such as scouting, church group, sports groups). Providing positive opportunities for friendship development is important, as it provides children with an appropriate and positive learning environment for the development of social competence.

For Further Study

Books

Asher, Steven R., et al. *Children's Social Development: Information for Teachers and Parents.* Urbana, IL: ERIC Clearinghouse on Elementary and Early Childhood Education, University of Illinois, 1987.

———— and J. D. Coie. (eds.) *Peer Rejection in Childhood.* Cambridge, Eng.: Cambridge University Press, 1990.

———— and John M. Gottman. (eds.) *The Development of Children's Friendships.* Cambridge , Eng.: Cambridge University Press, 1981.

Berndt, Thomas J., and Gary W. Ladd. (eds.) *Peer Relationships in Child Development.* New York: Wiley, 1989.

Bierman, Karen L. "Improving the Peer Relationships of Rejected Children." In Lahey, B. and A. Kazdin (eds.), *Advances in Clinical Child Psychology.* New York: Plenum, l989, pp. 53–84.

Bukowski, William M., Andrew Newcomb, and Willard W. Hartup. (eds.) *The Company They Keep: Friendship During Childhood and Adolescence.* New York: Cambridge University Press, 1996.

Coie, J. D. and G. K. Koeppl. "Adapting Intervention to the Problems of Aggressive and Disruptive Children." In Asher, S. R. & J. D. Coie. (eds.) *Peer Rejection in Childhood.* New York: Cambridge University Press, l990, pp. 275–308.

Dodge, K. A. "Problems in Social Relationships." In Mash, E. and R. Barkley (eds.) *Treatment of Childhood Disorders.* New York: Guilford Press, l989, pp. 222–44.

Olweus, D. "Victimization by Peers: Antecedents and Long-Term Outcomes." In Rubin, Kenneth H. and J.B. Asendorpf (eds.) *Social Withdrawal, Inhibition and Shyness in Childhood.* Hillsdale, NJ: Erlbaum, 1993, pp. 315–344.

Parke, R. D., and G. W. Ladd. *Family-Peer Relationships: Modes of Linkage.* Hillsdale, NJ: Erlbaum, 1992.

Pepler, Debra J., and Kenneth H. Rubin. (eds.) *The Development and Treatment of Childhood Aggression.* Hillsdale, NJ: L. Erlbaum, 1991.

Rubin, K. H. and S. L Stewart. "Social Withdrawal." In Mash, E.J., and R. A.Barkley. (eds.) *Child Psychopathology.* New York: Guilford, 1996, pp. 277–310.

Schneider, B., K. H. Rubin, and J. E. Ledingham, (eds.) *Children's Peer Relations: Issues in Assessment and Intervention* New York: Springer-Verlag, 1985.

Periodicals

Cicchetti, Dante, and William M. Bukowski. "Developmental Processes in Peer Relations and Psychopathology." *Development and Psychopathology* 7, 1995, pp. 587–89.

Crick, N. R., and K. A. Dodge. "A Review and Reformulation of Social Information-Processing Mechanisms in Children's Social Adjustment." *Psychological Bulletin* 115, 1994, pp. 74–101.

Dodge, K. A., and R. R. Murphy. "The Assessment of Social Competence in Adolescents." *Advances in Child Behavior Analysis and Therapy* 3, 1984, pp. 61–96.

Hartup, Willard W. "Social Relationships and Their Developmental Significance." *American Psychologist* 44, 1989, pp. 120–26.

Parker, J., and S. R. Asher. "Peer Acceptance and Later Personal Adjustment: Are Low-Accepted Children at Risk?" *Psychological Bulletin* 102, no. 3, 1987, pp. 357–89.

—Janet A. Welsh, Ph.D. and Karen L. Bierman, Ph.D.
The Pennsylvania State University

Social Learning Theory

A theory, first proposed in the late 1960s, which posits that children learn through a process of interactions with their environments and their caregivers.

In the early 1960s, researchers who had become disillusioned with the radical **behaviorism** of theorists like B.F. Skinner began to look for theories that would explain the process of learning without relying on the behaviorist model. That model, pioneered by **John Watson**, Ivan Pavlov, and Skinner, was developed by studying the effects of conditioning on animals. With the cognitive revolution of the late 1950s, however, researchers began to acknowledge the faults of such an approach to studying human learning. The difference being, of course, that when dealing with human children, "instructors" are dealing with an organism whose capacity to think is equal to their own. That is, radical behaviorism fails in application to humans because children are not, as some behaviorists like to assert, empty vessels simply waiting to be filled with correct social instruction. Social learning theory is an expansion upon strict behaviorism but differs in that the child is understood to have broad interpretive skills and is not simply responding by instinct to parental cues and instructions.

Social learning theorists, having rejected reinforcement and association as the sole constructors of knowledge, offered new theories about how we acquire knowledge of the world. One such theory states that children learn by imitation, by observing the consequences of certain behaviors and by the exposure to the thinking of others. A child learns by: *attending* to a model; *remembering* what is they have seen and heard; *reproducing* the model behavior at an appropriate time; and being *reinforced* for accurately performing the behavior.

Clearly, this schema differs from classical behaviorism in that it requires that the learner understand the context of a behavior. In classical behaviorist studies of animal behavior, the response of the learner is always within the context of a specific reinforcement. Pavlov's dogs were trained to salivate at the sound of a bell rather than the appearance of food. In the schema presented above, a child learns to soothe a crying playmate with calming words and light touches because she has seen this done to either herself or others and then *makes the decision* to repeat the performance in a socially appropriate context, or, in some cases, doesn't.

This is the heart of social learning theory: humans exhibit wide latitude in choosing which behaviors to imitate and which to ignore. In reacting to any given situation, children, and indeed all people, engage in a complex process that not only involves behaviorist principles, but also such factors as ethics, morals, and a person's understanding of his or her role in the world. Social learning theorists conceive of this interaction as involving three elements: the person (P), behavior (B), and environment (E). According to this conception, people learn by filtering all experience through their own interpretations in relation to their environments. This theory is known as reciprocal determinism. It highlights the importance and limitations of subjectivity in the creation of personal belief systems, or personal narratives. These belief systems—a person's understanding of how the world works and his or her place among these complex workings—drastically impact one's responses to the world.

A final tenet of social learning theory holds that the successful integration of a personal belief system and behavior in response to that system leads to feelings of competence or self-mastery, a belief that one is "in charge" of one's relations to and understanding of the world. This feeling of mastery is brought about in a variety of ways, including verbal instructions (a parent telling a child she can accomplish some difficult task) and imitation, but it relies most heavily on personal experience, or what social learning theorists call enactive attainment. Children learn to rely on their skills and on their ability to think through problems by being given the opportunity to do so successfully. This kind of reinforcement, the experience of having achieved something, is, according to social learning theory, the most powerful form of learning in humans.

For Further Study

Books

Bandura, Albert. *Social Learning.* Englewood Cliffs, NJ: Prentice Hall, 1977.

Fiske, Susan T., and Shelley E. Taylor. *Social Cognition.* New York: McGraw Hill, 1991.

 # Social Referencing

The process by which infants seek out and interpret the emotional responses of their parents to form their own emotional understanding of unfamiliar events, objects, or persons.

The concept of social referencing in children has been the subject of increasing study over the last quarter century, as developmental psychologists seek to understand the formation of emotion in infants and children. Research in this area has sought to understand how children learn to respond emotionally to various events, how they learn to interpret the emotional responses of others, and how they form ideas about appropriateness of emotional displays.

Studies have shown that beginning in early infancy, children begin looking at their parents for cues about how to respond to various situations, persons, and stimuli. Researchers have concluded that this kind of social referencing generally occurs in situations of high ambiguity, when infants are presented with novel, startling, or otherwise unfamiliar occurrences. Social referencing in early infancy has been broken down into a four-stage process by a group of researchers in the 1980s (Klinnert, et al, 1983). After conducting several studies, they constructed a sequence beginning with 1) the ability to recognize emotional expressions; 2) the ability to understand emotional expressions; 3) the ability to respond to emotional expression; and 4) the ability to alter behavior in response to emotional expressions.

While little is known for certain about how social referencing develops, researchers have suggested several hypotheses. The question at the heart of the debate is to what extent infants attach the emotional responses of their parents to the object, or referent, of the message. If an infant is uncertain about how to react to a strange adult, he checks the expression of a nearby parent. The question is whether the infant is simply imitating the parent's reaction or whether he understands the reaction is related to this stranger. Researchers who suggest the latter speak of social referencing in early infancy as a generalized process of mood modification, whereby infants' emotions are spurred almost by contagion. Other researchers suggest that infants are simply imitating parental responses and do not feel or understand the emotion they are modeling.

In a 1988 study conducted at Vanderbilt University, researchers sought to resolve these questions about the nature of social referencing by studying infants ages 6 to 22 months to determine under what conditions they reference parents, how they interpret the information gained in referencing, and to what extent they modified their behavior in accordance with that information. They found that, as they develop, infants use social referencing in varying ways. When confronted with a novel situation or an unfamiliar toy, the youngest infants were found to be less concerned with looking at their mothers' faces than they were with simply making sure the mother was there. This, the researchers hypothesized, suggests that very young infants are not so much referencing their mothers for emotional cues about how to respond, but simply checking to see that their mother was nearby when confronted with ambiguous or fearful situations. Infants older than 10 months began looking specifically at their mothers' faces when referencing, leading researchers to believe that it is at about this age that true social referencing begins.

The study also found that younger infants were more likely to continue looking at their mother if she was expressing positive emotions rather than negative. Older infants gazed longer at apprehensive or negative responses. Significantly, younger infants were also found to be less affected by a parent's reaction, so that while they gazed longer at positive expressions than negative, fearful reactions to a new toy expressed by a parent had little effect on their willingness to play with the toy. In infants 14 to 22 months, fearful expressions had the effect of decreasing their likelihood of playing with an unfamiliar toy. In infants approaching two years, fearful expressions had the opposite effect.

Overall, the study's authors found that both the hypotheses mentioned above, that infants simply imitate emotions or that they assume them through contagion, were flawed. Neither hypothesis could account for the age-specific variables in responses they had observed. Instead, they suggest that the children were using the parent's response to interpret the event in a way that was meaningful to them. This interpretation suggests that children are more cognitively aware of the meanings of emotional expressions and how to react to them than previous theorists have been willing to concede. It also suggests that infants are capable of interpreting something as subtle as context in measuring the seriousness of a parental cue.

See also **Developmental Psychology; Emotional Development**

For Further Study

Books

Klinnert, M., et al. "Social Referencing: Emotional Expressions as Behavior Regulators." In *Emotion: Theory, Research, and Experience: Vol. 2. Emotions in Early Development.* Academic Press, Orlando, FL.

Periodicals

Walden, Tedra A., and Tamra A. Ogan. "The Development of Social Referencing." *Child Development* 59 (1988): 1230–40.

Social-Emotional Giftedness *see* **Invulnerables**

Sociobiology

A term coined by the eminent entomologist Edward O. Wilson to define a field of study combining biology and social sciences.

In his 1975 work, *Sociobiology: The New Synthesis,* entomologist Edward O. Wilson first coined the term "sociobiology" to create a new field of study combining biology and social sciences, especially anthropology and sociology. Sociobiologists study the biological nature of human behavior and personality according to the tenet that all social behavior has a biological basis.

The field of sociobiology has not been widely accepted by contemporary theorists of personality and culture. The trend of social thought for several decades has been that humans are by and large responsible for their personal behaviors and for the ways they interact with others and with society as a whole. Wilson and other sociobiological theorists consider many human behaviors to be genetically based, including aggression, mother-child bond, language, the taboo against incest, sexual division of labor, altruism, allegiance, conformity, xenophobia, genocide, ethics, love, spite, and other emotions.

Traditional social scientists, however, debate sociobiology. Feminists have been particularly critical of the new field's view on gender roles. Feminists believe that gender roles are culturally determined. Sociobiologists see gender roles as basic human traits and point out that in almost no culture in the history of the world have women, for example, taken the role of sexual aggressor or exhibited a propensity to collect harems of sexually active men—two human traits that appear in nearly every culture.

Sociobiologists point to the mother-child bond as one of the prime examples of genetically based behavior. According to sociobiologists, the **attachment** a mother feels for her infant is a genetically programmed response to the biological need to continue the human gene pool.

While this is almost certainly true to some extent, many psychologists and those in the various fields of social science argue otherwise. They point out that non-genetic mothers in contemporary society, for example, adoptive parents and step-mothers, demonstrate a bond just as deep as those between genetic mothers and their children.

Sociobiologists have also tried to explain the prevalence of gender stereotypes across different cultures. As children approach school age in Western culture, their experiences become more social and less domestic as they spend a great deal of time away from home with people other than their parents. During this time, children start to identify with their same-sex peers and learn stereotypical gender roles whether or not these roles are enforced in the home. Sociobiologists believe the current trend to avoid gender-marking is a wasted effort since gender roles are an intractable part of human nature.

Young boys tend to be aggressive in their play, while young girls tend to be reflective, or, to use a term widely applied in sociobiology, coy. This tendency is also seen in other primates and occurs across a variety of human cultures. It is therefore logical to assume that a young boy is naturally predisposed to aggressive behavior while a young girl is naturally predisposed to less violent modes of play. It is also widely held that boys and girls have different intellectual capacities, with boys being more adept at spatial reasoning and girls at verbal. There are reams of standardized test score data backing up such assertions, but it is not clear whether such differences are genetically determined.

Sociobiologists do not claim that aggression in males is acceptable. Even though male domination seems to be the predominant form of social organization, organized societies are not in any way obliged to defer to it. Social structures have for thousands of years modified what might be considered "natural" behaviors. Murder is an example. In preliterate societies murder is sanctioned under a variety of conditions. Human sacrifice, for example, used to play a large role in preliterate societies. But as societies develop, these "natural" tendencies are, necessarily, curbed. Instinctive behavior is replaced by social behavior because a culture sees social behavior as more desirable. While sociobiology may predict patterns of behavior in young children, there is no reason to believe that these tendencies cannot or should not be altered.

If there is any stage of life that most exemplifies the ideas of sociobiologists, it is **adolescence**. During this period, **hormones** are changing the body at a pace unmatched during any time in life, and with those changes in physical appearance, behavior also changes. Boys and girls take on social roles during adolescence that are radically different from their roles as children.

Some sociobiologists believe that many of the problems adolescents face in constructing their adult identities have a basis in evolution. There is increasing evidence, for instance, that certain adolescents are genetically predisposed to fall into clinical **depressions**. Genetic research has shown that many people suffering depression share a genetic abnormality that may only "turn on" if confronted with certain overwhelming social problems such as those faced by adolescents. There is also evidence that a predisposition to drugs and alcohol dependency is genetically determined. Recent studies have found links between several biological functions and anti-social and criminal behavior among adolescents. Included in this list are a slowly developing frontal lobe system in the brain, a variety of genes, a faulty autonomic nervous system, abnormal blood sugar levels, deviant brain waves, and hyperactivity. So, while specific behaviors are not linked to a specific gene or to evolutionary adaptation, a propensity to behave in a certain way, in the absence of more socially acceptable alternatives, may have a partial foundation in biology.

For Further Study

Books

Wilson, Edward. *Sociobiology—the New Synthesis.* Cambridge, MA: Harvard University Press, 1975

Periodicals

de Wal, Frans B.M. "The Biological Basis of Behavior." *The Chronicle of Higher Education,* June 14, 1996, p. B1.

Horgan, John. "The New Social Darwinists." *Scientific American*, October, 1995, p. 174.

———. "Revisiting Old Battlefields." *Scientific American,* April 1994, p. 36.

"Irven DeVore." *Omni* (interview) June 1993, p. 69.

Laying, Anthony. "Why Don't We Act Like the Opposite Sex?" *USA Today,* January 1993, p. 87.

Socioeconomic Status (SES)

Relative economic and social ranking of an individual or family.

An assessment of an individual or family's relative economic and social ranking comprises the socioeconomic status. Many organizations use an assessment of a family's financial resources—referred to as a means test—as a way to qualify the person or family for certain programs, such as government assistance programs and financial aid for education. Means tests are used by social service agencies, colleges and universities, private and parochial schools, and other agencies providing programs for children and in determining eligibility for financial aid.

A key qualifier used by U.S. government agencies is the poverty level. For a family to be considered as living in poverty, the Department of Health and Human Services establishes income guidelines every year.

Poverty guidelines for 1997

For 1997, the following income levels were set as the "poverty line" for the 48 contiguous states and the District of Columbia.

Number of family members	Maximum household income to be considered "living in poverty"
One	$7,890
Two	$10,610
Three	$13,330
Four	$16,050
Five	$18,770
Six	$21,490
Seven	$24,210
Eight	$26,930

For families with more than eight members add $2,720 for each additional member.
Source: *Federal Register* 62 (March 10, 1997): 10857.

For Further Study

Books

Berger, Joseph, et al. *Status Characteristics and Social Interaction: An Expectation-States Approach.* New York: Elsevier Scientific, 1977.

Ellis, Lee. *Social Stratification and Socioeconomic Inequality.* Westport, CT: Praeger, 1993.

Soiling *see* Encopresis

Somnabulism

Also known as sleepwalking, a common disorder among children that involves getting out of bed and moving about while still asleep.

Somnabulism, or sleepwalking, affects an estimated 15% of children in the early school years. It is similar to pavor nocturnus (**night terrors**) in that it occurs during the non-dreaming stage of sleep, usually within an hour or two of going to bed. The sleepwalking child feels an intense need to take action and may appear alert, pur-

poseful, or anxious as he moves about. For many years, people believed that it was dangerous to waken a sleepwalker, but there is no basis for this view. There is, however, little reason to waken a sleepwalking child, and it may be impossible to do so. Sleepwalking children should be gently guided back to bed, and will usually be cooperative in this effort. Episodes of sleepwalking may be signs of a child's heightened anxiety about something. Parents should give careful consideration to events and environmental changes that may have triggered the onset of sleepwalking. If sleepwalking is common among family members, it is more likely that the child may respond to even slight increases in anxiety with sleepwalking behavior.

Special Education

Educational instruction or social services designed or modified to assist individuals with disabilities.

Special education refers to a range of services, including social work services and rehabilitative counseling, provided to individuals with disabilities from ages 3–21 through the public school system, including instruction given in the classroom, at home, or in institutions. Special education classes are taught by teachers with professional certification. Some teachers specialize in working with children with **learning disabilities** or multiple handicaps, and instruction may take place within a regular school or a residential school for students with disabilities.

In 1975 the **Education for All Handicapped Children Act** (EHCA, PL 94-142) mandated that states provide a "free and appropriate public education" (FAPE) to all students, including those with physical, mental, or behavioral disabilities. This special education must include a comprehensive screening and diagnosis by a multi-disciplinary team and the development of an annual Individualized Education Plan (IEP) for each student, outlining academic and behavioral goals, services to be provided, and methods of evaluation. The student's parents must consent to initial screening and must be invited to participate in all phases of the process. Besides the unprecedented move in guaranteeing free comprehensive services to children with special needs, the act was revolutionary in that it specified that special education take place in the "least restrictive environment" (LRE). In 1991 the Individuals with Disabilities Education Act (IDEA) provided federal assistance to state and local agencies to implement EHCA and made some revisions including: requiring that the disability status of the special-needs student be reevaluated every three years; adding the category of learning disabled as a qualifying disability; and further interpreting the LRE clause to require that the special-needs student be educated "to the maximum extent appropriate" with children who are not disabled. Services are available to individuals ages 2–21, and states are required to seek and initiate contact with qualifying individuals.

During the nearly 20 years after the passage of special education laws (1977–94), the rate of enrollment in public special education programs increased by 46%, while total enrollment in public schools declined 2%. In 1994 12% of students enrolled in public schools or institutions were in special education programs. Much of the increase took place after 1991, when children identified with learning disabilities dominated special education classrooms: in 1994 learning disabled students made up 5% of total enrollment, falling short of just half of all special education students. Children's disabilities are defined under 13 categories: **autism,** blindness, visual impairment, deafness, hearing impairment, deaf-blindness, orthopedic (movement) impairments, multiple handicaps (several disabilities), **mental retardation** (also called developmental disability), serious emotional disturbance, speech and language disorders, specific learning disabilities (e.g., **dyslexia**), and specialized health care needs (e.g., oxygen dependence). Traumatic brain injury also qualifies. Of students enrolled in special education programs in 1994, 45% were learning disabled; 19% had speech and language disorders; 10% were mentally retarded; 8% were deaf or hearing impaired; 8% were seriously emotionally disturbed; and 8% had other disabilities

Screening and evaluation

In order to qualify for special education a child must be diagnosed as having a disability and the disability must be found to "adversely affect educational performance" so as to require special services. There is wide variability in the way students are referred and evaluated for special education. For children with severe disabilities the physician and parents identify and refer the child to special education. Other disabilities or deficits in the child's developing physical and cognitive abilities may be identified by teacher and parent observation or revealed by academic or developmental tests. Most districts have standardized programs to screen large numbers of children between kindergarten and third grade. Other disabilities may be subtle or compensated for, such as dyslexia, and may not be discovered until demands on the student increase in college. After referral, a meeting is held to determine whether the child should be "assessed" or "evaluated" to determine the type of disability he or she may have. Tests will attempt to identify the cognitive (academic), social, or physical tasks which the child has difficulty performing, and why the difficul-

ty exists, i.e., what disability or disabilities are present. Tests may include: reading, writing, spelling, and math tests; psychological or intelligence tests; speech and language; vision and hearing tests; or an examination by a doctor. Parents must consent to all testing, evaluation, and placement, and can appeal most decisions if they disagree with the conclusions.

Over- and under-referral

There is some concern about over- or under-referral in particular disability categories. Mild disabilities are especially difficult to diagnose. Since special education laws went into effect the enrollment of students diagnosed with mental retardation and speech and language disorders decreased sharply while those with learning disabilities increased. The changes reflect a social consciousness about the stigma of labeling and fundamental changes in the way people view disabilities. Yet, under-referral of mental retardation in particular may reflect schools' realistic fear of litigation. Others are concerned about over referral for mild disabilities (learning and behavioral disorders) as a method of classroom management. Thirty-four states require some method of pre-referral intervention. If a teacher suspects a disability, he or she must consult with a team of teachers and develop alternate methods of effectively addressing the student's problems, through modifications in instruction or classroom environment, before the school will consider special education referral.

Race

There is a concern that minority students are disproportionately represented in special education, mostly with learning disabilities. In 1993 white, learning-disabled students made up 5% of total enrollment in special education. The corresponding percentage of black students (proportionate to their representation in the total population) would be 0.5%, but African American students with learning disabilities make up 6% of total enrollment. There is no consensus on the exact diagnosis of specific learning disabilities, and the same treatment goals and teaching strategies are used for all types of learning disabilities. Often psychologists will continue testing until they "find" a learning disability for which a student can receive special instruction. Criticism can be levied from both sides against this practice: white, low-achieving students do not receive special attention they need, and black students are segregated and labeled incorrectly.

Location of services, mainstreaming, and inclusion

Before passage of the EHCA and IDEA, many disabled children were either not provided public education services at all, were in residential settings, or at best in separate day schools. In addition to providing special ed-

Individualized Educational Plan (IEP)

After a student is evaluated as having a disability that interferes with learning, an interdisciplinary team of special education teachers, general education teachers, a social worker, school psychologist or other therapist, the parents, and ideally the student will develop an Individualized Education Plan (IEP) for the student which is reviewed and revised annually. The IEP serves to

(1) identify existing abilities and skills

(2) plan cognitive (reading, math) and behavioral (self-discipline, social skills, physical mobility) objectives unique to the student, and

(3) outline specific actions that will be taken to achieve the objectives.

The IEP describes exactly what services will be provided to assist the student in attaining the objectives. Services include curriculum modifications like lowered reading level materials, social skills training, technological adaptations like a Braille typewriter, computer-assisted instruction, wide doorways, and teacher services like tutored instruction, group instruction in a resource room, counseling services, or physical therapy. Objectives also include the means of evaluating the student's achievements over specified periods, and when the next review or transition will occur. IEPs vary widely in length and complexity according to the type of disability. Good IEP objectives are based on the child's needs, are mutually agreed upon by parents, teachers, and counselors, support activities that are typical of other students in the same age-group, promote school and community membership, and clearly facilitate the student's long-range life goals.

ucation in regular public school buildings, the stipulation that special-needs children be educated in the "least restrictive environment" led to the practice of mainstreaming. Mainstreaming is the policy of placing special education students in regular classrooms as much as possible, and using resource rooms where the student receives special tutoring, review, and instruction. In 1993, 40% of children received instruction primarily in regular classrooms, 30% in resource rooms, 24% in separate, special education classrooms, and the remaining 6% in public or private day schools and residential facilities. Students with speech or language impairments (80%) were most likely to be in general education classrooms.

Mentally retarded and multiple-handicapped students (7% of each group) were the least likely to be in general education classrooms.

The type of contact special education teachers have with students varies according to district resources and student population. Some teachers, such as visual impairment specialists, may serve a whole region, tutoring a specific student only once a week. Others teach entire special education classes, providing general education teachers with support, ideas, and resources for mainstreamed pupils. Inclusion, sometimes considered the logical goal of mainstreaming, is total integration of special education students and services into the general education classroom, where special education teachers collaborate with general education teachers to teach the entire class. Full inclusion of all special education students would require restructuring of several traditional educational policies. To the extent that it necessitates extensive continuing collaboration between special education teachers, general education teachers, and support paraprofessionals, and requires restructuring of curricula and lessons, full inclusion represents a revolution in educational methods. Research on existing programs suggests that for inclusion to be successful certain attitudes and beliefs must be held and certain resources must be available:

- The general education teacher must believe the special-needs student can succeed

- The school must be committed to accepting responsibility for the learning outcomes of special education students

- Parents must be informed and supportive

- Services and physical accommodations must be adequate for the student's needs

- The principal must understand the needs of special education students

- Enough teacher and staff hours must be devoted to the child's care

- Continuing staff development and technical assistance must be provided

- Evaluation procedures must be clear

- Special education teachers must be part of the entire planning process

- A team approach is used by teachers and other specialists

- A variety of instructional arrangements must be available (team teaching, ability grouping, peer tutoring)

Matriculation and employment

In 1992, 44% of special education students graduated with a diploma, 13% graduated with a certificate (including GED finished by age 21), 22% dropped out, and

21% exited school for other reasons. The highest dropout category was seriously emotionally disturbed students at 35%. The lowest was deaf-blind students, only 4% of whom dropped out. Graduation and employment rates for students with disabilities rose over the two decades after the passage of EHCA and IDEA and other disability legislation such as the Americans with Disabilities Act. Yet depending on the disability, as many as 45–70% of disabled adults were still unemployed in the early 1990s. People with learning disabilities and speech disorders have the lowest rates of unemployment. Because 77% of students take **vocational education** classes, a comprehensive vocational assessment, including assessment of independent living skills, is necessary. The assessment may take place at a regional center and follow an adult rehabilitation model. Assessments should take place several times in the course of a student's school career.

Gifted and talented

Gifted and talented children are those who demonstrate special abilities, aptitude, or **creativity.** Often they will express themselves primarily in one area such as humanities, sciences, mathematics, art, music, or leadership. Gifted and talented students are not usually considered clients of special education. There is no federal mandate or regular funding to support gifted and talented students, although about half of the states have programs for the gifted and talented. As a percentage of total public school enrollment, students in gifted and talented programs range from 1–2% in Idaho, Nevada, Alabama, and Washington to over 10% in Hawaii, Maryland, Michigan, Nebraska, Ohio, Wisconsin, and South Carolina.

In addition to special counseling, grade skipping, taking summer or correspondence courses, or early graduation, there are a variety of adaptations that can be made to serve the needs of gifted students. Adaptations can be made to the content, the process, or the products of learning. Some strategies include:

Acceleration–Raising the academic level of assignments and giving the student reading material at a higher level of difficulty.

Telescoping–Reducing the time allowed the student to cover given content. For example, a teacher could give the student two successive mathematics chapters to complete in the ordinary time period used to cover one chapter.

Compacting–Testing to determine how much of a certain content unit the student knows already and custom designing a curriculum to fill in the gaps. Students can then use the gained time for creative or exploratory activities.

Independent study–Allowing the student to choose his or her own focus, plan research, present material, and evaluate the process.

Tiered assignments–Preparing assignments at different levels for different students. Asking more complex and higher order questions in assignments for gifted and talented students.

Other tools for pacing the learning of gifted and talented students are portfolios and learning centers. Several commercially prepared curricula that provide structured exploratory and design projects are also available.

For Further Study

Books

Adelman, H., and L. Taylor. *Learning Problems and Learning Disabilities*. Pacific, CA: Brooks, 1993.

Algozzine, B. et al. *Behaviorally Disordered? Assessment for Identification and Instruction*. Reston, VA: The Council for Exceptional Children, 1991.

Council of Administrators of Special Education. *Student Access: A Resource Guide for Educators, Section 504 of the Rehabilitation Act of 1973*. Albuquerque, NM: Author, 1991.

Cummins, J. *Bilingualism and Special Education: Issues in Assessment and Pedagogy*. Clevedon, England: Multilingual Matters. Co-published in the U.S. by College-Hill Press, San Diego, 1994.

Cook, L., and M. Friend. *Interactions: Collaboration Skills for School Professionals*. White Plains, NY: Longman Publishing, 1992.

Council for Exceptional Children, Department of Public Policy. *The Rights of Children with Disabilities under ADA and Section 504: A Comparison to IDEA*. Reston, VA: Author, 1994.

Giangreco, M. F., et al. *Choosing Options and Accommodations for Children: A Guide to Planning Inclusive Education*. Baltimore: Paul H. Brookes, 1993.

Gutkin, T. B., and C. R. Reynolds, eds. *The Handbook of School Psychology*. 2nd ed. New York: Wiley, 1990.

Hallahan, D., and J. Kaufmann. *Exceptional Children*. Englewood Cliffs, NJ: Prentice Hall, 1991.

Hunt, N., and K. Marshall. *Exceptional Children and Youth*. Boston, MA: Houghton Mifflin Co., 1994.

Levinson, E. M. *Transdisciplinary Vocational Assessment: Issues in School-Based Programs*. Brandon, VT: Clinical Psychology Publishing Co., 1993.

Marder, C., and R. D'Amico. *How Well Are Youth with Disabilities Really Doing? A Comparison of Youth with Disabilities and Youth in General*. Menlo Park, CA: SRI International, 1992.

National Center for Education Statistics. *Products Avaialbe from the National Center for Education Statistics*. Washington, DC: NCES, 1997.

Stoner, G., et al. *Interventions for Achievement and Behavior Problems*. Silver Spring, MD: National Association of School Psychologists, 1991.

U.S. Department of Education. *Eighteenth Annual Report to Congress on the Implementation of the Individuals with Disabilities Act.* Washington, DC: Office of Special Education Programs, 1996.

Wang, M. C., et al. *The Handbook of Special Education: Research and Practice.* Vols 1 & 2. Oxford, England: Pergamon Press, 1987.

Organizations

American Coalition of Citizens with Disabilities
Address: 1012 Fourteenth Street, NW
Washington, DC 20005

Association for Children and Adults with Learning Disabilities
Address: 4156 Library Road
Pittsburgh, PA 15234

National Information Center for Handicapped Children and Youth
Address: 155 Wilson Boulevard, Suite 508
Arlington, VA 22209

National Center for Education Statistics
Address: 555 New Jersey Ave., NW
Washington, DC 20208-5574
website: nces.gov

The Council for Exceptional Children
Address: 1920 Association Drive
Reston, VA 22091
Telephone: (703) 620-3660

Learning Disabilities Association of America
Address: 4156 Library Road
Pittsburgh, PA 15234
Telephone: (412) 341-1515

Specific Language Impairment (SLI)

Describes a condition of markedly delayed language development in the absence of any apparent handicapping conditions.

Many different terms have been used to describe the disorder of childhood characterized by markedly delayed language development in the absence of any apparent handicapping conditions such as deafness, **autism**, or **mental retardation**. It is sometimes called childhood dysphasia, or developmental **language disorder**. Much research since the 1960s has attempted to identify clinical subtypes of the disorder. These include *verbal auditory agnosia* and *specific language impairment*. Some children have a very precise difficulty in processing speech, called *verbal auditory agnosia*, that may be due to an underlying pathology in the temporal lobes of the brain. The most prevalent sub-type of childhood language disorder, *phonosyntactic disorder*, is now commonly termed *specific language impairment* or *SLI*. These children have a disorder specifically affecting inflectional morphology and syntax.

Very little is known about the cause or origin (referred to as *etiology*) of specific language impairment, though evidence is growing that the underlying condition may be a form of brain abnormality, not obvious with existing diagnostic technologies: SLI children do not have clear brain lesions or marked anatomical differences in either brain hemisphere. However, there is some indication of a familial pattern in SLI, with clinicians noting patterns across generations. It is more common in boys than girls. As of the 1990s, research suggests a possible genetic link, though there are still many problems in identifying such a gene. Sometimes the siblings of an affected child show milder forms of the difficulty, complicating the picture. One of the major stumbling blocks is the definition of the disorder, because the population of children with language impairments is still much more heterogeneous than required to support a search for a gene.

Children with SLI usually begin to talk at roughly the same age as normal children but are markedly slower in the progress they make. They seem to have particular problems with inflection and word forms (inflectional morphology), such as leaving off endings as in the past tense verb form. This problem persists much longer than early childhood, often into the grade school years and beyond, where the children encounter renewed difficulties in reading and writing. The SLI child has also been observed to have difficulties learning language "incidentally," that is, in picking up a new word from context, or generalizing a new syntactic form. This is in decided contrast to the normal child's case, where incidental learning and generalization are the hallmarks of language acquisition. Children with SLI are not necessarily cognitively impaired, and are not withdrawn or socially aloof like the autistic child.

Some investigators have attributed the SLI child's difficulty with speech sounds (a *phonological* problem), suggesting that inflection and word forms (morphology) such as endings are vulnerable because those items are so fleeting and unstressed in speech. It is not that the child is deaf in general, but that he has a specific difficulty discriminating speech sounds.

Other researchers have argued that this difficulty is not specific to speech but reflects a general perceptual difficulty with the processing of rapidly timed events, of which speech is the most taxing example. The left hemisphere of the brain seems to be specialized for processing rapid acoustic events, so perhaps the SLI child has a unique difficulty with that part of the brain. Yet phonology does not seem to be the whole problem because the child may be quite good at articulation or speech perception per se. Instead, it is argued that the child may have a linguistic difficulty with morphology, going beyond the sounds themselves. Cross-linguistic work supports a more refined perspective that suggests certain kinds of inflectional morphology, especially those associated with the verb, may be more likely to be disrupted than others. If so, that would suggest the problem is not just phonological and not just inflectional. Given the centrality of the verb to sentence structure, the difficulty causes pervasive problems.

Whatever the final identification of the linguistic problem, researchers are curious to discover how such a specific disorder could come about: is a language "module" of the brain somehow compromised in these children? The puzzle is that children with very precise lesions of the usual language areas somehow overcome those difficulties more easily than the SLI child who presents no such dramatic brain abnormalities.

The child with SLI becomes increasingly aware of his difficulties with language and may lose spontaneity and avoid conversation as he gets older. Intensive language intervention can allow these children to make considerable gains, with modeling of appropriate linguistic forms producing more gains than simply "enriching" the child's language environment. Early identification is thus seen as very important for intervention. One procedure for children aged 24 to 36 months asks parents to complete a standardized questionnaire in which they check off the vocabulary the child knows, and write down examples of the child's two-word sentences. If the child has fewer than 50 words and no two-word sentences, that is an indication of risk for language disorder. Estimates of true SLI vary according to the age of identification: some experts argue that as many as 10% of 2-year-olds may have a specific language impairment, but by age 3 or 4, that percentage drops considerably, presumably because some difficulties resolve themselves. The incidence in the general population is estimated at about 1%.

For Further Study

Books

Gleason, Jean Berko. *The Development of Language.* (4th ed.) Boston: Allyn and Bacon, 1996.

Peterson, Harold A. *Appraisal and Diagnosis of Speech and Language Disorders.* (3rd ed.) Englewood Cliffs, NJ: Prentice Hall, 1994.

Taylor, Orlando L. *Nature of Communication Disorders in Culturally and Linguistically Diverse Populations.* San Diego: College-Hill Press, 1986.

—Jill De Villiers, Ph.D.
Smith College

Speech Development *see* Language Development

Speech Perception

The ability to hear and understand speech.

Speech perception, the process by which we employ cognitive, motor, and sensory processes to hear and understand speech, is a product of innate preparation ("nature") and sensitivity to experience ("nurture") as demonstrated in infants' abilities to perceive speech. Studies of infants from birth have shown that they respond to speech signals in a special way, suggesting a strong innate component to language. Other research has shown the strong effect of environment on language acquisition by proving that the language an infant listens to during the first year of life enables the child to begin producing a distinct set of sounds (babbling) specific to the language spoken by its parents.

Since the 1950s, great strides have been made in research on the acoustics of speech (i.e., how sound is produced by the human vocal tract). It has been demonstrated how certain physiologic gestures used during speech produce specific sounds and which speech features are sufficient for the listener to determine the phonetic identity of these sound units. Speech prosody (the pitch, rhythm, tempo, stress, and intonation of speech) also plays a critical role in infants' ability to perceive language. Two other distinct aspects of perception—segmentation (the ability to break the spoken language signal into the parts that make up words) and normalization (the ability to perceive words spoken by different speakers, at different rates, and in different phonetic contexts as the same)—are also essential components of speech perception demonstrated at an early age by infants.

In addition to the acoustic analysis of the incoming messages of spoken language, two other sources of information are used to understand speech: "bottom-up" and "top-down". In the former, we receive auditory information, convert it into a neural signal and process the phonetic feature information. In the latter, we use stored information about language and the world to make sense of the speech. Perception occurs when both sources of information interact to make only one alternative plausible to the listener who then perceives a specific message.

In order to understand how bottom-up processing works in the absence of a knowledge base providing top-down information, researchers have studied infant speech perception using two techniques: high-amplitude sucking (HAS) and head-turn (HT). In HAS, infants from 1 to 4 months of age suck on a **pacifier** connected with a pressure transducer which measures the pressure changes caused by sucking responses when a speech sound is presented. Head turn conditioning is used to test infants between 6 months and one year of age. With this technique, a child is trained to turn his or her head when a speech sound, repeated once every second as a background stimulus, is changed to a comparison speech sound. When the head is turned during the presentation of the comparison stimulus, the child is rewarded with a visual stimulus of a toy which makes a sound.

As a result of studies using these techniques, it has been shown that infants at the earliest ages have the ability to discriminate phonetic contrasts (/bat/ and /pat/) and prosodic changes such as intonation contours in speech. However, to understand speech, more than the ability to discriminate between sounds is needed; speech must be perceptually organized into phonetic categories, ignoring some differences and listening to others.

To measure categorical perception, adults were asked to discriminate between a series of sounds varying in equal steps in acoustic dimension from /ra/ to /la/. As predicted by the categorical perception phenomenon, their discrimination improved at the boundary between the two phonetic categories. However, adult listeners could do this only for sounds in their native language. The discovery that categorical perception was language-specific suggested that it might be a learned behavior. This prompted researchers to question if categorical perception was the result of experience with language. If so, young infants could not be expected to show it, while older infants, who had experienced language, might be expected to do so.

Using the sucking technique, this study revealed that at birth, infants' discrimination of /pa/ and /ba/ was categorical not only with the perception of sounds in their native language but also with sounds from foreign languages as if the infants heard all the phonetic distinctions used in all languages. But if this "language-general" speech perception ability of infants later became "language-specific" speech perception in adults, when and by what process did this change occur? To answer this question, researchers began to study the perception of phonetic prototypes (i.e., the "best" members of a phonetic category).

Under the assumption that sound prototypes exist in speech categories, adults were asked to judge the category "goodness" of a sampling of one hundred instances of the vowel /i/ using a scale from 1 to 7. Results indicated evidence of a vowel prototype for /i/ but also showed that phonetic prototypes or "best" vowels differed for speakers of different languages. Further perceptual testing revealed an even more unique occurrence: sounds that were close to a prototype could not be distinguished from the prototype, even though they were physically different. It appeared as if the prototype perceptually assimilated nearby sounds like a magnet, attracting the other sounds in that category. Dubbed the perceptual magnet effect, this theory offered a possible explanation of why adult

speakers of a given language can no longer hear certain phonetic distinctions as is the case with Japanese speakers who have difficulty discriminating between /r/ and /l/; the Japanese prototype is something that is acoustically similar to both sounds and results in their assimilation by the Japanese prototype.

To discover whether infants are born with all the prototypes of all languages and whether language experience then eliminates those prototypes which are not reinforced, an experiment in which 6-month-old American infants listened to English was performed (Kuhl, 1991). It confirmed the perceptual magnet effect but left the question of the role of language experience unresolved. When a study was conducted (Kuhl, Williams, Lacerda, Stevens & Lindblom, 1992) with listeners from two different languages (English and Swedish) on the same vowel prototypes it was demonstrated that the perceptual magnet effect is strongly affected by exposure to a specific language.

The Native Language Magnet (NLM) theory grew out of the research on the development of speech perception. Simply stated, it explains how infants at birth can hear all of the phonetic distinctions used in the world's languages. However, during the first year of life, prior to the acquisition of word meaning and contrastive phonology, infants begin to perceive speech by forming mental representations or perceptual maps of the speech they hear in their environment. These representations, stored in the brain, constitute the beginnings of language-specific speech perception and serve as a blueprint which guides infants' attempts to produce speech. The native language magnet effect works to partition the infant's perceptual space in a way that conforms to phonetic categories in the language that is heard. Sounds in the spoken language that are close to a given magnet or prototype are perceptually pulled into the magnet and thus assimilated, and not discriminated, by the listener. As the perceptual space surrounding a category prototype or magnet shrinks, it takes a very large acoustic difference for the listener to hear that sound. However, a very small acoustic difference in the region of a nonprototype can be heard easily. Thus the developing magnet pulls sounds that were once discriminable toward a single magnet, making them no longer discriminable and changing the infant's perception of speech.

—Patricia Kuhl, Ph.D.
University of Washington

For Further Study

Books

Aitchison, Jean. *The Seeds of Speech: Language Origin and Evolution.* New York: Cambridge University Press, 1996.

Kuhl, Patricia K, Ph.D. "Speech Perception." Introduction to *Communication Sciences and Disorders*. San Diego: Singular Publishing Group, Inc.

———. *Learning and Representation in Speech and Language*. Philadelphia: Current Biology Ltd.

Speech-Language Pathology

Treatment for the improvement or cure of communication disorders, including both speech problems and language disorders.

Formerly referred to as speech therapy, the techniques, strategies, and interventions designed to improve or correct communication disorders are known as speech-language pathology. Both speech disorders, which involve difficulty in producing the sounds of language, and **language disorders,** which involve difficulty in understanding language or using words in spoken communication, are treated by speech-language pathologists.

In 1993 there were nearly 70,000 speech-language pathologists in the United States certified by the American Speech-Language-Hearing Association (ASHA). Speech disorders treated by speech-language pathologists include voice disorders (abnormalities in pitch, volume, vocal quality, or resonance or duration of sounds), articulation disorders (problems producing speech sounds), and fluency disorders (impairment in the normal rate or rhythm of speech, such as **stuttering**). Language disorders in children involve the comprehension or use of spoken or written language. They may represent an isolated problem, or they may be associated with **mental retardation, autism,** hearing impairment, or acquired **aphasia.** Speech-language pathologists participate in the screening, assessment, and treatment of patients.

Children with isolated speech disorders are often helped by articulation therapy, in which they practice repeating specific sounds, words, phrases, and sentences. For stuttering and other fluency disorders, a popular treatment method is fluency training, which develops coordination between speech and breathing, slows down the rate of speech, and develops the ability to prolong syllables. A child may practice saying a single word fluently and then gradually add more words, slowly increasing the amount and difficulty of speech that can be mastered without stuttering. The speaking situations can gradually be made more challenging as well, starting with speaking alone to the pathologist and ending with speaking to a group of people. Delayed auditory feedback (DAF), in which stutterers hear an echo of their own speech sounds, has also been effective in treating stuttering. When a speech problem is caused by serious or multiple disabilities, a neurodevelopmental approach, which

inhibits certain reflexes to promote normal movement, is often preferred. Other techniques used in speech therapy include the motor-kinesthetic approach and biofeedback, which helps children know whether the sounds they are producing are faulty or correct. For children with severe communication disorders, speech pathologists can assist with alternate means of communication, such as manual signing and computer-synthesized speech.

The majority of speech-language pathologists work in educational institutions, many of them in public elementary schools. They are also found at both residential health care facilities and over 300 outpatient clinics that specialize in communication disorders and are often affiliated with hospitals and universities. Professional training programs in speech-language pathology are offered at both the undergraduate and graduate levels. Undergraduate training may include classes in biology, anatomy, psychology, linguistics, education, and **special education**. Most clinicians hold a master's degree in communications sciences and disorders from a program accredited by the ASHA.

Diagnosis and treatment

Pediatrician and author **T. Berry Brazelton** has recommended early evaluation for speech or communication disorders in young children who show any of the following signs:

1) no intelligible speech by two years of age

2) nasal or high-pitched speech sounds

3) utterances without facial expression

4) lack of responsiveness when spoken to or looked at

5) continual repetition of adult speech without variation or modification.

Children may receive speech therapy either through their public school or privately. Speech impairment qualifies as a disability under PL 94-142, the federal law mandating education for the disabled. Most communities have school speech pathologists. There is no cost to the family whose child receives therapy in public school. It is convenient; children often have the opportunity to work in groups, and the speech pathologist has easy access to child's classroom teacher. At a speech and hearing clinic, on the other hand, earlier intervention is possible, and parents can often work more closely with the speech pathologist than they could under a school program.

Parents seeking speech therapy for their children are advised to look for a clinician with certification by the American Speech-Language-Hearing Association who is favorably recommended by current or former clients, has good rapport with children, and is willing to speak openly and clearly with parents about the child's condition and progress and the treatment methods employed. Active involvement by parents is an essential component of an effective speech pathology program. Many programs require parents to attend special educational sessions with the clinician, and they may be encouraged to attend the child's therapy sessions as well. They may also be instructed or advised on specific activities they can pursue at home as a supplement to the sessions with the clinician.

For Further Study

Books

Flower, R. M. *Delivery of Speech-Language Pathology and Audiology Services*. Baltimore, MD: Williams and Wilkins, 1986.

Hicks, Patricia Larkins. *Opportunities in Speech-Language Pathology Careers*. Lincolnwood, IL: VGM Career Horizons, 1996.

Lass, N. J., L. V. McReynolds, and J. L. Northern. *Handbook on Speech-Language Pathology and Audiology*. Philadelphia: B. C. Decker, 1988.

Organizations

American Academy of Private Practice in Speech-Language Pathology and Audiology
Address: 7349 Topanga Canyon Boulevard
Canoga Park, CA 91303

American Speech-Language-Hearing Association
Address: 10801 Rockville Pike
Rockville, MD 20785
Telephone: (301) 897-5700

Infant and Family Special Interest Group
Address: Box 1776 SIUE
Edwardsville, IL 62026

National Black Association for Speech, Language and Hearing
Address: 3542 Gentry Ridge Court
Silver Spring, MD 20904

Sperm Cell (Spermatozoon)

The sperm cell, or spermatozoon, is the male sex cell. Its nucleus contains the chromosomes, which bear the hereditary material of the male parent.

The sperm cell (spermatozoon) is smaller than the female sex cell (the **ovum**). The sperm cell has a tail-like flagellum, which gives it a shape like a tadpole and allows for motility (movement). Beginning at **puberty**, millions of microscopic spermatozoa are produced in the testes. It takes 46 days for the testes to produce a sperm cell, but millions are produced simultaneously. Sperm are stored in the semen, a milky fluid in the *seminal vesicles* and the *vas deferens*. During ejaculation, semen is released through the urethra, a tube that runs through the penis. If ejaculation takes place during sexual intercourse, sperm can travel through the female uterus and into the fallopian tubes. If an egg is present in either of

the fallopian tubes, a single sperm can fertilize it and **pregnancy** will result. Half of the chromosomes in the resulting zygote (fertilized egg) come from the ovum and half from the sperm.

See also **Ovum**

For Further Study

Books

Avraham, Regina. *The Reproductive System*. New York: Chelsea House, 1991.

—Gail B. Slap, M.D.
University of Pennsylvania School of Medicine

Spirituality in Children

A child's inner life expressed through thoughts, feelings, and yearnings related to the ultimate questions about life, death, and reality.

Often discussed in the context of religion, the subject of children's spirituality is nevertheless a separate, and arguably more general, topic. In fact, according to experts, children's spirituality not only transcends the idea of particular religious denomination or tradition, but also goes beyond religion itself, as is evidenced by the spiritual concerns of children, and people in general, who are defined as "not religious." According to the noted child psychiatrist and author **Robert Coles**, there is nothing exceptional or unusual about children's spirituality: unless suppressed through abuse, a child's spirituality naturally develops by an innate feeling of wonderment and fascination. In his numerous conversations with children about their spiritual concerns, Coles has noted that regardless of their cultural and religious background, children feel a profound desire to understand the universe and their place in it, and that desire, articulated through words, gestures, songs, and drawings, remains constant. Furthermore, children, often combining spiritual musings with ethical concerns—e.g., wondering why there is injustice in the world—often express a wish to influence the entire universe in an effort to improve the world.

Commenting on his conversations with two eight-year-old girls with different backgrounds (Hopi and Irish American), Coles noted that the girls, despite the differences in their religious backgrounds, had similar spiritual concerns and aspirations. According to Coles, both girls find in themselves a human strength, striving "every once in a while to break the confines of self, of society, of time and space, even of faith" (Coles, 1990). While Coles's young interlocutors used different sets of symbols to express their spirituality, the Catholic girl dreaming about Christ's return, and her Hopi counterpart contemplating a joyful reunion of all humankind, their reactions to reality reflected a deep desire to live in harmony with the universe.

As researchers have observed, the phenomenon of children's spirituality eludes the traditional conceptual and methodological apparatus of psychology or theology. Spiritual concerns, i.e., questions pertaining to life, death, birth, rebirth, and the universe in all its immensity do not, it seems, directly depend on cognitive and verbal development. Indeed, it is possible to trace the development of children's religious consciousness, as David Elkind has done, noting how, for example, as children mature, their prayers shift from being self-centered to altruistic. But spirituality, undefinable as a process, defies the theoretical strictures of child development. In other words, there is something timeless about children's spirituality. Thus children often wonder about God without any intellectual, or historical, understanding of the concept "God." Children have the ability to tackle difficult philosophical and theological questions almost unknowingly, focusing on the idea itself, while sidestepping the logical sequences prescribed by rational discourse. Gareth B. Matthews has criticized **Jean Piaget** for dismissing a nine-year-old girl's insistence that God must exist because he has a name. According to Piaget, the child shows her inability to dissociate names from objects. Matthews demonstrates that the little girl's reasoning is logically correct and in accordance with a long philosophical and theological tradition of thinking about God.

Whatever the parents' attitude toward their child's spiritual aspirations, spirituality is an unavoidable issue in every family: the question of his or her origin, which every child asks, essentially pertains to spirituality.

According to Erik Erikson, trust "born of care is, in fact, the touchstone of the *actuality* of a given religion." Erikson uses the term "religion," but his insight about care and trust can easily apply to spirituality in general. While there is no formula for a healthy spiritual life, caring parents will, by inspiring a fundamental sense of trust and by respecting the spiritual aspects of birth, enable their children to freely develop a sense of spirituality and manifest it through a passionate and fulfilling involvement in life. Declaring that spirituality affirms children's humanity and enhances their ability to understand life's mysteries, Robert Coles advises parents to encourage a child's natural sense of wonderment and curiosity about spiritual issues. By their nature, children ask probing questions, and this desire to know, Coles affirms, "is also part of the **moral development** of children—a way for them to find a set of beliefs and ideals to guide their daily lives, a way for them to gain command of their behavior."

For Further Study

Books

Coles, Robert. *The Spiritual Life of Children.* Boston: Houghton Mifflin, 1990.

Elkind, David. *The Child's Reality: Three Developmental Themes.* Hillsdale, NJ: Lawrence Erlbaum Associates, 1978.

Erikson, Erik. *Childhood and Society.* 2nd rev. ed. New York: W. W. Norton, 1963.

Matthews, Gareth B. *Philosophy and the Young Child.* Cambridge: Harvard University Press, 1980.

Prather, Hugh, and Gayle Prather. *Spiritual Parenting: A Guide to Understanding Nurturing the Heart of Your Child.* New York: Three Rivers Press, 1996.

Rizzuto, Ana-Maria. *The Birth of the Living God: A Psychoanalytic Study.* Chicago: University of Chicago Press, 1979.

Periodicals

Coles, Robert. "The Spirit Within." *Parenting,* December-January 1996, pp. 116–18.

—Zoran Minderovic

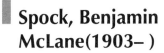

Spock, Benjamin McLane(1903–)

American pediatrician, psychiatrist, and author.

In a controversial book that sold more than 30 million copies in the three decades following its publication in 1946, **pediatrician** Benjamin Spock changed the way American parents raised their babies. *The Common Sense Book of Baby and Child Care*, based on Spock's ten years of pediatric practice and psychoanalytic training, gave parents permission to use **pacifiers**, maintain flexible feeding schedules, and show ample affection to their babies. All were considered radical ideas at the time and, many believed, led to permissiveness that produced undisciplined, out-of-control behavior. The controversy created by the book catapulted Spock to fame, making him a worldwide child-rearing icon and prompting him to branch out in his career to include teaching and political activism.

Benjamin McLane Spock was born the eldest of six children in 1903 in New Haven, Connecticut. His father was a railroad lawyer whom Spock describes as "grave" and "just," who commuted by trolley to his job and left most of the household and child-rearing duties to his wife. Spock's mother, the dominant influence in her son's life even many years later, rarely relied on any type of physical **punishment** for **discipline**. Rather, she controlled her children by instilling a strong sense of **guilt**. Spock credits his mother with encouraging him to read and inspiring him and his siblings to succeed later in life: "She had a great sense of humor and delighted her children and her friends with stories about things she found amusing or ridiculous. She was a terrific mimic. She inspired her children with idealism and a drive to serve—five out of six of us became teachers or psychologists."

After two years of schooling at the prestigious Andover Academy, Spock enrolled at Yale University where, as part of the school's varsity crew team, he won an Olympic gold medal in Paris in 1924. He earned an undergraduate degree in English literature and then, inspired by his summer job at a small home for crippled children, he began medical school. Two years at Yale's medical school were followed by a final two years at Columbia University, where he was at the top of his class both years. Now married—he and his wife Jane were married for 48 years before divorcing—Spock interned for two years at Presbyterian Hospital in New York. A subsequent one-year residency at New York Nursery and Child's Hospital led to what Spock has called "the most independent decision of my life:" accepting a residency in psychiatry at New York Hospital.

As he started his own pediatric practice, Spock began psychoanalytic training and quickly saw a link between the medical and psychological aspects of treating children and helping their parents cope with their responsibilities. When he learned "that mothers were delighted to find a pediatrician interested in such common problems as thumb sucking and resistance to weaning or toilet training, I decided to stay in pediatrics. That was a momentous decision."

The publication of *The Common Sense Book of Baby and Child Care* led to teaching positions for Spock at Wayne State University in Detroit, Children's Hospital of the East Bay in Oakland and the Mayo Clinic in Minnesota, and an administrative position at the University of Pittsburgh. Before he retired in 1967, Spock spent 12 years at Western Reserve University (now Case Western Reserve University) in Cleveland in the departments of psychiatry and pediatrics. Almost everywhere he went, he experienced some resistance from physicians uncomfortable with the psychoanalytic theories he used to supplement traditional medical norms.

In 1962, Spock joined the board of the National Committee for a Sane Nuclear Policy, prompted by his belief that the world's children were both physically and psychologically endangered by nuclear testing and the threat of nuclear war. It was just the beginning of Spock's life as a political activist. In 1968 he was convicted of conspiracy for his anti-Vietnam War activities, a conviction that later was overturned on appeal. In 1972,

he ran for president, a candidate of the small People's Party. He received 80,000 votes in ten states.

Spock continued to write and speak, often about what he considered disturbing changes in society, such as increases in **divorce,** teen **pregnancy**, **suicide,** substance abuse, and violence. He remarried in 1976 to Mary Morgan, and she began to manage his speaking, writing, and consulting activities. Speaking with pride of his diverse career, all related to children's health, Spock says that people need to "realize that child care, the happiness of the family, the feelings of adults and children, and cultural and neighborhood activities are the most vital aspects of existence."

For Further Study

Books

Spock, Benjamin. *Spock on Spock.* New York: Pantheon Books, 1989.

———. *The Common Sense Book of Baby and Child Care.* New York: Duell, Sloan, and Pearce, 1946.

———. *Baby and Child Care. Revised and Updated.* New York: Pocket Books, 1985.

———. *A Better World for Our Children.* Bethesda, MD: National Press Books, 1994.

▌Sports

Games and individual activities involving physical skills.

A child will have many opportunities to participate in sports throughout his or her developing years and into adolescence. The level of a child's participation in sports, how he or she performs, or whether he or she enjoys playing is greatly influenced by adults' attitudes toward the physical and emotional aspects of the activity.

Infancy

The amount of athletic activity that an infant is capable of participating in is limited. Still, many parents worry about their child's motor skill development and how they can help develop these skills. The **American Academy of Pediatrics** (AAP) advises parents that normal play with adults is more than enough physical stimulus to encourage normal development of motor skills. In years of research, no one has produced any evidence that increased stimulation of infants increases development of motor skills in later years.

Swimming is perhaps the only sport infants are really able to participate in. While infants instinctively hold their breath when immersed in water, pediatricians warn that they also swallow water, which can produce hazardous side effects. The AAP advises that infants should not participate in swimming activities until they are at least four months old.

Toddlerhood and preschool

Children at this stage of development are naturally curious and exploratory, leading them to develop independence skills such as walking and talking. These should be encouraged by adults, as should frequent interaction with other children their own age. Athletic activity at this age should be free-form and spontaneous, with adult interference or direction held to a minimum. The AAP suggests that adult intervention—such as teaching a child to throw and catch a baseball—has little effect on later motor development, and they warn that the repetition of such practicing will often stifle the natural urge to play creatively. It has also been shown that until the ages of 5–7, young children's vision is not sufficiently developed to follow objects that are moving quickly through their line of sight, such as thrown balls.

Appropriate athletic activities for children of this age are dance, rudimentary gymnastics (tumbling), and swimming. Of course, free-form play with peers is probably most important, both for its socializing effect and for the creative expression it offers.

School-age

By the age of five or six, children begin developing motor skills rapidly. However, learning complex rules is often difficult and trying to teach a child a sport requiring a great deal of instruction (baseball, football, soccer) may only cause frustration and a lack of interest. A child's inability in these areas can also cause a sense of failure and provoke a life-long aversion to organized sports. Most pediatricians suggest that complex, team sports that require coaching or memorization should be postponed until a child reaches the age of nine or ten. One good way to get a child interested in sports during these years is to engage in physical activity the whole family can participate in, such as taking long walks or bicycle rides.

Adolescence

By the time a child reaches **adolescence,** his or her interest in sports is most likely at its peak. Children of this age often collect sports memorabilia, wear clothes resembling the uniforms of their favorite players, and spend larger amounts of time watching and talking about sports.

In 1993, the *Journal of the American Medical Association* reported on a study that found participation in school athletics programs substantially reduced the likelihood that adolescents would begin **smoking.** The national study surveyed more than 11,000 students from across the country and found that the "ratios of regular and heavy smoking decreased substantially with increasing number of sports played." Speculating as to the rea-

sons for this dramatic statistical revelation, the authors of the study suggested a series of social factors associated with athletics, including increased **self-esteem,** counseling from coaches about the dangers of smoking, decreased **peer pressure**, and a realistic understanding of reduced athletic performance as the result of smoking. The study further suggested that the culture of organized athletics values conservative appearance and behavior more so than other adolescent cultures.

Minorities and women also benefit socially from participation in high school sports. A 1993 Harris survey reported that the main reason women and minorities participated was to become more productive, better adjusted people and, many also said, to help them pay for their college education. The Harris survey found that 70% of African Americans say athletics helps keep them focused on academic work; 44% say it helps them to become better citizens; and 65% say it helps them avoid drugs. One other rarely considered benefit of high school athletics is that the playing field is often the only place where different cultures meet. The Harris survey found that 76% of all athletes polled said they had become friends with someone from a different racial group while participating in a high school sport.

The social benefits of athletics are especially important for young girls. In fact, it has been argued that girls are more in need of the benefits of athletics than boys. Adolescent girls tend to have lower self-esteem than boys, and many suffer from the false belief that their bodies are useful only to the extent that they are attractive to men. Statistics compiled by the Women's Sports Foundation also demonstrate that girl athletes receive substantial benefits from participation in sports. They found that girls who participated in school athletics are 92% less likely to use drugs, including tobacco and alcohol, and 80% less likely to get pregnant. Additionally, they are three times more likely to graduate from college.

Society also benefits from school athletic programs in ways that are not immediately apparent. One such benefit, according to an article in the *Sporting News,* is decrease in juvenile crime, which is most prevalent between the hours of 3:00 and 6:00 p.m., when many students are left on their own. These are also the hours generally occupied by high school sports, often the only constructive activity available to students after school.

Despite the numerous benefits athletics brings to children, there are negative aspects as well. While sports are routinely credited with helping boys and girls build self-esteem, practice team work, and respect authority, over-intense competition and pressure to succeed from parents, coaches, and peers can also damage young people, both physically and psychologically.

Often, a competitive drive, coupled with over-eager coaches or insistent peers, can drive young athletes to compete even when they are injured. At the 1996 Summer Olympics in Atlanta, for instance, Kerri Strug, a teenage girl on the U.S. gymnastics team, became a sort of national hero for continuing to compete while injured. Young people will often interpret cultural messages like this to mean that one should continue competing even with pain.

To help reduce the chances of being injured, several organizations have begun advocating the use of more protective gear in organized sports for children. The January-February 1996 issue of *Public Health Reports* published the results of a study conducted by the U.S. Department of Health and Human Services calling for wider use of protective head and mouth gear for all organized athletics for children. The journal cited a recent study which estimated that as many as one-third of all dental injuries in children are sports-related. As evidence of the effectiveness of using protective head-gear, the article pointed out that prior to a 1962 rule requiring high school football players to wear helmets and mouthguards, 50% percent of all injuries were to the face or mouth. That figure has since dropped to 1.4%. Youths participating in football and hockey are perhaps the most likely to be provided with protective devices, but baseball and soccer players are also at risk for injuries, and are less likely to wear protective gear.

In 1994, *Science World* reported the surprising results of a study done on sports injury rates among high school athletes. The study, conducted over 13 years and surveying 60,000 high school athletes, arrived at the startling conclusion that the high school sport with the highest rates of injury was girls' cross country running, which had 36% more injuries than boys' football. Explaining the findings, the study's author, Stephen Rice, suggested that biological and social factors play a role but reminded readers that "cross country is a contact sport." He said that the contact runners have with the ground can be just as damaging as the contact received on the football field, if not more so.

The other major factor to consider when enrolling a child in organized athletics is the sometimes adverse effects competitive pressure can have on a child. This is a major problem in the United States, where professional athletes are some of the most admired and highly paid people in the country. Many parents and coaches have dreams of developing the next Michael Jordan or Jackie Joyner-Kersey and can push a child beyond his or her capacity, leading to physical injury and psychological problems. Another drawback to consider is that many sports, such as football, wrestling, and gymnastics, have rigid weight requirements that can often lead young athletes to manipulate their body weight with drugs and severe diets

or eating binges. In 1995, *Sports Illustrated* reported that officials of a suburban Chicago youth football league routinely gave diuretics to athletes as young as 10 to help them meet weight requirements. The story broke when the mother of a 12-year-old told her pediatrician that her son had taken drastic measures to lose 12 pounds in three days. After being confronted by the pediatrician, the boy's coach freely admitted that he had given the boy Lasix, a diuretic that, used incorrectly, can cause heart failure, kidney problems, coma, and, in some cases, death. When the story was picked up by the *Chicago Tribune,* the paper heard from several parents defending such practices, saying that if a child wants to take such drastic actions and his or her parents approve, it's perfectly okay.

This attitude on the parts of coaches and parents is cited as one of the main reasons 75% of children drop out of organized athletics by the age of 15, according a study published in *Family Circle* in 1996. The study was conducted by Michigan State University's Institute for the Study of Youth Sports and found that the major reason children dropped out of sports was "coaches who yelled or played favorites." Students also reported too much emphasis was placed on winning. In many cases, coaches' drive to win can lead to instances of **child abuse**, and the popular press has in recent years reported several frightening stories of bullying coaches. One child advocate was quoted in *Family Circle* as saying, "Ridiculing kids and embarrassing them in front of their peers and parents is child abuse. You don't have to hit a kid to inflict deep wounds."

In 1995, *McCalls* magazine published an article of do's and don'ts for families to help them use athletics as a unifying, family-building force, rather than allowing it to become an overriding consumer of family time or a point of contention or pressure when a child doesn't live up to parental expectations. The article also addressed the touchy issue of non-athletic children. Many children simply aren't interested in sports, and parents should respect the wishes of a child who shows no interest in sports. Other activities such as skiing, bicycling, running, and swimming, which do not emphasisize competition, may be more attractive to some children.

For Further Study

Books and Publications

American Academy of Pediatrics. *Sports Medicine: Health Care for Young Athletes.* Elk Grove Village, IL: American Academy of Pediatrics, 1991.

Duff, John D. *Youth Sports Injuries: A Medical Handbook for Parents and Coaches.* New York: Macmillan, 1992.

The President's Council of Physical Fitness and Sports 1985. *National School Population Fitness Survey.* Washington,

SPORTS-RELATED BRAIN INJURY IN THE UNITED STATES

The Centers for Disease Control estimate that 300,000 traumatic brain injuries (TBIs) related to sports occur each year. Parents and coaches are advised by the American Academy of Neurology to become familiar with the classifications of head concussion and the related treatment so that if such an injury occurs during a sporting event, the proper action can be taken.

Grade 1 Concussion

Definition: Transient confusion, no loss of consciousness, and mental status abnormalities for less than 15 minutes.

Treatment: The athlete should be removed from the sports activity and examined immediately and at five-minute intervals. If symptoms disappear after fifteen minutes, the athlete may return to the activity. If the athlete receives a second concussion the same day, he or she should be removed from sports activities for at least one week.

Grade 2 Concussion

Definition: Transient confusion, no loss of consciousness, and mental status abnormalities for more than 15 minutes.

Management: The athlete should be removed from sports activity and examined frequently to assess the progress of symptoms. If the symptoms get worse or persist for more than one week, more extensive diagnostic evaluation should be made. The athlete should not return to sports activity until he or she has been free of symptoms for at least one week. If the Grade 2 concussion followed a Grade 1 concussion on the same day, the athlete should not participate in sports activity until he or she has been free of symptoms for two weeks.

Grade 3 Concussion

Definition: Brief (seconds) or prolonged (minutes or longer) loss of consciousness.

Management: If the loss of consciousness was brief, the athlete should be removed from sports activity until he or she has been free of symptoms for one full week, and for two full week if loss of consciousness was prolonged. If still unconscious or if abnormal neurologic signs are present at the time of initial evaluation, the athlete should be transported by ambulance to the nearest hospital. This athlete should not participate in sports activity until he or she is free of symptoms for one full month. If further diagnosis by computer tomography or magnetic resonance imaging reveals signs of brain swelling, contusion, or other intracranial problem, the athlete should at least not return to sports for the season, and should be discouraged from further participation in contact sports.

D.C.: HHS-Office of the Assistant Secretary for Health, 1986.

Periodicals

"A Sad Tale from Youth Sports." *Sports Illustrated,* October 9, 1995.

Dash, Judi. "Is Your Child's Coach a Tyrant?" *Family Circle,* April 23, 1996.

Escobedo, Luis G., et al. "Sports Participation, Age at Smoking Initiation, and the Risk of Smoking Among High School Students." *Journal of the American Medical Association,* March 17, 1993.

Freiman, Chana. "Achy Athletes." *Science World,* March 11, 1994.

Lapchick, Richard. "School Sports is a Safety Net for Youths." *The Sporting News,* March 25, 1996.

Nowjack-Raymer, Ruth, and Helen C. Gift. "Use of Mouthguards and Headgear in Organized Sports by School-aged Children." *Public Health Reports,* January-February 1996.

Standard Progressive Matrices (SPM)

Assesses intelligence nonverbally in children and adults.

The Standard Progressive Matrices (SPM) is a group or individually administered test that nonverbally assesses **intelligence** in children and adults through abstract reasoning tasks. It is sometimes called Raven's, although the SPM is only one of three tests that together comprise Raven's Progressive Matrices. Appropriate for ages 8–65, the SPM consists of 60 problems (five sets of 12), all of which involve completing a pattern or figure with a part missing by choosing the correct missing piece from among six alternatives. Patterns are arranged in order of increasing difficulty. The test is untimed but generally takes 15–45 minutes and results in a raw score which is then converted to a percentile ranking. The test can be given to hearing- and speech-impaired children, as well as non-English speakers. The Standard Progressive Matrices is usually used as part of a battery of diagnostic tests, often with the Mill Hill Vocabulary Scales. The SPM is part of a series of three tests (Raven's Progressive Matrices) for persons of varying ages and/or abilities, all consisting of the same kind of nonverbal reasoning problems. The SPM is considered an "average"-level test for the general population. The Coloured Progressive Matrices (CPM), which includes the two easiest sets from the SPM and a dozen other questions of similar difficulty, is designed for 5- to 11-year-olds, persons with mental or physical handicaps, and non-English speakers. The Advanced Progressive Matrices (APM) is generally for ages 11 to adult or, specifically, for gifted students. It consists of a practice and screening test (Set I) and a 36-problem series for use with persons of above-average intellectual ability.

For Further Study

Books

McCullough, Virginia. *Testing and Your Child: What You Should Know About 150 of the Most Common Medical, Educational, and Psychological Tests.* New York: Plume, 1992.

Shore, Milton F., Patrick J. Brice, and Barbara G. Love. *When Your Child Needs Testing: What Parents, Teachers, and Other Helpers Need to Know about Psychological Testing.* New York: Crossroad, 1992.

Walsh, W. Bruce, and Nancy E. Betz. *Tests and Assessment.* 2nd ed. Englewood Cliffs, NJ: Prentice Hall, 1990.

Stanford-Binet Intelligence Scale

Widely used intelligence test.

The oldest and most influential intelligence test, devised in 1916 by Stanford psychologist Lewis Terman (1877–1956), using the 1908 Binet-Simon model. Although some of its concepts, such as mental age and **intelligence quotient**, are questioned by many today, the test is still widely used to assess **cognitive development**, and often to determine placement in special education classes. Most recently revised in 1986, it can be used with children ages 2 to adult. Consisting of questions and short tasks arranged from easy to difficult, the Stanford-Binet measures a wide variety of verbal and nonverbal skills. Its 15 tests are divided into the following four cognitive areas: 1) verbal reasoning (vocabulary, comprehension, absurdities, verbal relations); 2) quantitative reasoning (math, number series, equation building); 3) abstract/visual reasoning (pattern analysis, matrices, pa-

per folding and cutting, copying); and 4) short-term memory (memory for sentences, digits, and objects, and bead memory). While the child's attitude and behavior during the test are noted, they are not used to determine the result, which is arrived at by converting a single raw score for the entire test to a figure indicating "mental age" (the average age of a child achieving that score). A formula is then used to arrive at the intelligence quotient, or IQ. An IQ of 100 means that the child's chronological and mental ages match. Traditionally, IQ scores of 90–109 are considered average, scores below 70 indicate **mental retardation**, and scores of 140 or above place a child into the "gifted" category.

For Further Study

Books

McCullough, Virginia. *Testing and Your Child: What You Should Know About 150 of the Most Common Medical, Educational, and Psychological Tests.* New York: Plume, 1992.

Shore, Milton F., Patrick J. Brice, and Barbara G. Love. *When Your Child Needs Testing: What Parents, Teachers, and Other Helpers Need to Know about Psychological Testing.* New York: Crossroad, 1992.

Walsh, W. Bruce, and Nancy E. Betz. *Tests and Assessment.* 2nd ed. Englewood Cliffs, NJ: Prentice Hall, 1990.

Startle Reaction *see* **Neonatal Reflexes**

Stealing

Taking property belonging to someone else.

Stealing is defined as taking another person's property without permission. Very young children do not understand the concept of personal property. When they see something they want, they simply take it. Young children generally take things for immediate use only, whereas older children will take them "for keeps." Since they have no sense of personal property, young children should not be accused of stealing when they take another person's things without permission. However, the concept of stealing should be explained right from the start, even before the child can understand. If a parent or teacher (or other adult) simply tells the child, "Don't take Sally's crayon," the child will believe only that taking Sally's crayon is wrong, while taking a crayon from Juan, or a cookie from Sally, is okay. A child must be told repeatedly that stealing in general is wrong in order to develop an understanding of the broader issue.

Most children have a basic sense of "mine" and "not mine" by the age of two and can therefore begin to learn respect for other people's possessions. However, a true understanding of the hurtful nature of stealing does not begin to develop until about age five to seven. At this age, children are deterred from stealing mostly by their fear of parental disapproval. Internal motivations of conscience and **guilt** do not develop until the middle childhood years. Once the recognition of property boundaries appears, stealing becomes an intentional act which must be addressed more deliberately.

Children steal for a number of reasons. Young children, or older children who have not developed sufficient self-control, may steal to achieve instant gratification when an object cannot be obtained immediately by honest means. Others steal to gain a sense of power, to acquire status with peers who resist authority, to get attention, to take revenge on someone who has hurt them, to alleviate **boredom,** or to vent unresolved feelings of anger or fear. Children who steal are often expressing displaced feelings of anxiety, rage, or alienation resulting from a disruption in their life, such as their parents' **divorce** or remarriage.

People who feel excluded or disconnected from society have fewer qualms about stealing, because they have no sense of respect, trust, or responsibility in relation to the community. They may even purposely steal in retaliation for the pain they feel society has inflicted on them. Studies have shown a direct correlation between stealing and alienation. Community-building programs in American high schools have greatly reduced the incidence of theft by developing a sense of community among the students and faculty. When a child feels integrally connected with a community, he or she will support all members of that community. Stealing becomes unthinkable in a mutually supportive environment.

While there is no correlation between stealing and social or economic class (members of lower, middle, and upper classes all steal), attitudes toward stealing and its consequences are class-specific. People in lower socioeconomic classes tend to steal material goods by direct, hands-on theft, while members of the middle and upper classes lean more towards "white-collar" crimes such as embezzlement and insider trading. In studies with high school students, lower- and working-class students who were raised in an environment where sheer survival was an issue felt that stealing was a much more serious crime than **cheating,** whereas middle- and upper-class students who were raised in an academically oriented environment felt that cheating, the theft of knowledge, was much worse than stealing. In terms of consequences (at least in Western society), lower-class crimes of theft are much more severely punished than upper-class, "white-collar" crimes.

A child who is caught stealing for the first time should be treated compassionately; the main focus

should be on the reason(s) for the act rather than on the act itself. Parents, teachers, or other adult care givers need to discern if the child lacks self-control, is angry (and with whom), needs attention, is bored, feels pressured by peers to cross boundaries, feels or is alienated from her or his community, has poor **self-esteem,** or needs to develop more positive moral values. A habitual stealer is expressing a serious internal problem that needs close attention. Children at risk of becoming habitual stealers are individuals with low self-esteem; strong desires and weak self-control (impulsive); a lack of sensitivity to others, or who are angry, bored, or disconnected; spend a great deal of time alone; or have recently experienced a significant disruption in their lives. Stealing is a behavior problem, not a character problem. The behavior can be corrected if the underlying difficulty is resolved.

See also **Moral Development; Discipline**

For Further Study

Books

Kurtines, William M., and Jacob L. Gewirtz. *Moral Development: An Introduction.* Boston: Allyn and Bacon, 1995.

Schulman, Michael, and Eva Mekler. *Bringing Up a Moral Child: A New Approach for Teaching Your Child to Be Kind, Just, and Responsible.* New York: Doubleday, 1994.

Sears, William. *The Discipline Book: Everything You Need to Know to Have a Better-Behaved Child—From Birth to Age 10,* 1st ed. Boston: Little, Brown and Co., 1995.

Wyckoff, Jerry. *How to Discipline Your Six-to-Twelve Year Old: Without Losing Your Mind,* 1st ed. New York: Doubleday, 1991.

—Dianne K. Daeg de Mott

Stepping Reflex *see* **Neonatal Reflexes**

Stimulant Drugs

Also called psychostimulants, drugs that produce increased levels of mental and physical energy and alertness and an elevated mood by stimulating the central nervous system.

Stimulants are used for the treatment of certain psychiatric conditions and also used (and abused) for recreational purposes, enhanced levels of energy, and weight loss. They may be prescription or over-the-counter medications, illegal street drugs, or ingredients in commonly ingested substances, such as the caffeine in coffee or the nicotine in cigarettes. Whatever their form, stimulants increase respiration, heart rate, and blood pressure, and their abuse can cause adverse physical effects and endanger a person's health and even his or her life. An overdose of stimulants can result in chest pains, convulsions, paralysis, coma, and death.

Caffeine and nicotine

The most commonly used stimulant (and the most widely consumed drug) in the United States is caffeine. Found in coffee, tea, soft drinks, chocolate, and drugs, including pain relievers, diet pills, and cold and allergy medications, caffeine belongs to a family of drugs called methylxanthines. It works by disrupting the action of a neurotransmitter called adenosine. Since caffeine is usually consumed in food, it normally enters the body through the gastrointestinal system, passing from the intestines into the blood, which circulates it through the body. It reaches its maximum effect within 30–60 seconds from the time it is consumed, although it remains in the body for several hours. Caffeine is addictive. People who consume it regularly develop a tolerance for it, meaning that they need to ingest progressively greater amounts to continue getting the same effect. (Thus, diet pills containing caffeine lose their effectiveness after a few days, when a tolerance is established.) Caffeine causes physical dependence, producing withdrawal symptoms including anxiety, headaches, and fatigue when its use is discontinued. People who stop using caffeine also experience a craving for it, which is a sign of psychological dependence. In addition to their sugar content, another reason for parents to limit the amount of chocolate and soft drinks their children consume is that excess caffeine can lead to restless, uncontrolled behavior. It is generally agreed that daily caffeine consumption equal to the amount contained in one cup of coffee or soft drink (under 240 milligrams) is probably harmless, but that consumption over 600 milligrams (the amount in four cups of coffee) can cause anxiety, sleep and digestive disorders, a rapid heartbeat, and other health problems. The National College Athletic Association has limited the amount of caffeine that its players can consume.

Besides caffeine, the other stimulant widely ingested is the nicotine consumed in smoking. Both caffeine and nicotine are classified as secondary stimulants because, unlike drugs such as amphetamines and cocaine, they affect the sympathetic nervous system more than the central nervous system. Also unlike stimulants that are abused for recreational purposes, caffeine and nicotine produce only an increased energy level but not a feeling of intoxication. Nicotine acts mostly as a stimulant in new users, but long-term users claim that it relaxes them. Teenage smoking has been rising steadily throughout the 1990s. A 1995 survey of high school students by the Centers for Disease Control and Prevention found that on average 34.8% of teenagers smoke. Like users of other addictive substances, teen smokers start out thinking they will be able to control their use of cigarettes, but two-thirds of young people who smoke have tried to quit and failed. Nicotine withdrawal symptoms include anxiety, irritability, insomnia, depression, headaches, mood swings, difficulty concentrating, and changes in appetite. Teen smokers who want to quit can obtain help from support groups such as Nicotine Anonymous and call-in hotlines and from their family physicians, who may prescribe medications to reduce withdrawal symptoms.

Stimulants used for therapeutic purposes

Stimulant drugs have long been used to treat psychological disorders. In the past psychiatrists used certain stimulants as **antidepressants**, but today this practice is confined primarily to seriously depressed patients who have failed to respond to either **psychotherapy** or to the wide range of other antidepressants that are currently available (and that, unlike stimulants, are not addictive). Today the primary therapeutic use of stimulants is the treatment of **attention deficit/hyperactivity disorder** (ADHD) in children, and the most widely used drug is Ritalin (**methylphenidate**). Ritalin works by facilitating the release of the neurotransmitter norepinephrine, which improves alertness, attention span, and the ability to focus. Hyperactive children taking Ritalin are less impulsive, have better self-control, and make fewer errors in their schoolwork. They also get along better with their peers. Developed in 1956, Ritalin has been tested in over 200 studies—more than any other drug used for children. It is officially approved by the FDA for use in treating ADHD. Daily dosage of the medication (usually administered two or three times a day) ranges from 10 milligrams to as high as 80, with most children taking between 30 and 70 milligrams a day. Although it is generally considered safe and effective for the treatment of ADHD, there is still controversy surrounding the frequency with which this medication—whose use by children doubled between 1988 and 1994—is prescribed. Side effects include insomnia, appetite loss, and stomach pains. Ritalin may also produce withdrawal symptoms, including headache, irritability, nausea, and abnormal chewing movements and movements of the tongue. Ritalin can also interfere with a child's rate of growth, and some physicians recommend a "drug holiday" of several weeks a year for children taking the medication to help them catch up on growth that may have been delayed by the drug (and also to assess their condition). Other stimulants used for ADHD (usually when Ritalin doesn't work or produces too many negative side effects) are Dexedrine and Cyclert (pemoline), a stimulant similar to Ritalin. Psychiatrists also prescribe Ritalin, Cyclert, and Dexedrine to improve attention span and reduce hyperactivity in children with **pervasive developmental disorder** (PDD) and **autism.** An important effect of this treatment is that it makes these children more receptive to psychotherapy. Ritalin and other stimulants have also been prescribed to prevent daytime sleep episodes in persons suffering from severe **narcolepsy.**

Abuse of illegal stimulants

The primary illegal stimulants used for recreational purposes are amphetamines and cocaine. Street names for various types of amphetamines include speed, uppers, dexies, bennies, ice, L.A. ice, Ecstasy, and crank. Amphetamines produce an effect similar to that of the hormone adrenaline, making its users feel awake, alert, and energetic. Drugs of this type were abused by young people as early as the 1930s, when it was popular to tear the medicated strip out of Benzedrine nasal inhalers and ingest them directly or in coffee. By the 1950s and 1960s amphetamines were widely used by people who needed to keep themselves awake through the night, such as truck drivers and jazz musicians, or by athletes for extra energy. Many young people used them to stay awake when they needed to cram for tests or complete school assignments. It is estimated that up to half the amphetamines sold by drug companies in the 1960s were sold illegally. After the government imposed controls on the manufacture of these drugs, they began to be produced illegally in home laboratories. Not only are these preparations vulnerable to contamination, they are often diluted by manufacturers and dealers. Many supposed amphetamines sold on the street contain mostly caffeine and other drugs, with a very small percentage of amphetamine or even none at all.

The use of amphetamines declined in the 1980s as cocaine became the drug of choice. However, in the 1990s methamphetamine (traditionally known as speed) has become newly popular, especially among middle-class suburban teenagers, in a crystalline form—known as ice, L.A. ice, or crank—that can either be smoked or snorted like cocaine. Smoking methamphetamine first became fashionable in Hawaii. Use of the drug then became widespread in California, and now it is increasing in other parts of the country. A 1994 survey conducted at the University of Michigan found that more high school seniors had used methamphetamine than cocaine. In 1993 alone, the number of emergency room admissions related to the use of this drug increased by 61%. Crank is much cheaper to produce than cocaine, so its manufacturers realize a larger profit (a pound can be produced for $700 and sold for as much as $225,000). Users like it because it reaches the brain almost immediately, and its effects last longer than those of cocaine. It produces feelings of alertness, euphoria, and increased energy. Like other amphetamines, crank also decreases appetite and promotes weight loss, making it attractive to young women, who represent 50% of the teenage market for the drug.

People taking methamphetamine, which remains in the body for as long as four days, quickly establish a tolerance for the drug and require ever greater amounts to experience the same effect. Users can become addicted within four to six months. Side effects of the drug include a dry mouth, sweating, diarrhea, insomnia, anxiety, and blurred vision. Severe reactions can include hallucinations (called "tweaking"), paranoia, and speech disorders, all of which may persist for up to two days after use of the drug. In addition to physical addiction, amphetamines produce a psychological dependency on the euphoric effects produced by these drugs, especially since when they wear off they are followed by a "crash" that produces a depression so severe it can lead to **suicide**.

A related stimulant, which is derived from methamphetamine, is MDMA, also known as Ecstasy. MDMA combines the characteristics of a stimulant and a psychedelic drug, producing hallucinations and enhanced feelings of sociability and closeness to others. It is less addictive than amphetamines but more dangerous. Persons have died from taking this drug; some had preexisting heart conditions, but others had no known medical problems. MDMA causes brain damage, and its use can lead to the development of panic disorder.

Cocaine is a stimulant made from the leaves of the coca plant. Its street names include coke, snow, toot, blow, stardust, nose candy, and flake. When the pure drug was first extracted from the leaves in the 19th century, its harmful effects—including addiction—weren't known, and early in the 20th century it was legally sold in medicines and soft drinks, including Coca-Cola, which originally contained small amounts of the substance (from which its name is derived). Cocaine use has been illegal since 1914. Until the 1970s it was not widely used, except among some members of the arts community. At first cocaine was largely used in a diluted powder form that was inhaled. Eventually, more potent smokable forms were developed, first "freebase" then "crack," which has been widely used since the 1980s. In 1988 the *National Household Survey on Drug Abuse* reported that 1 in 10 Americans had used cocaine. Of young adults between the ages of 18 and 25, one in four reported having used cocaine at some point. Cocaine also became visible as a substance abused by celebrities, including actor John Belushi (who died of a cocaine-heroin overdose), comedian Richard Pryor (who was badly burned freebasing cocaine), and Washington, D.C. mayor Marion Barry, who was forced to resign from office but later reelected. In 1991 a government study found that 15% of high school seniors and 21% of college students had tried cocaine, and cocaine use by teenagers has continued to increase significantly through the 1990s.

Cocaine produces a physical addiction by affecting the brain's chemistry and a psychological addiction because users become dependent on the confident, euphoric feeling it creates to help them cope with the stresses of daily life. Possible negative reactions to large doses of cocaine use include hallucinations, paranoia, aggressive behavior, and even psychotic "breaks" with reality. Cocaine can cause heart problems, **seizures**, strokes, and comas. Reactions to withdrawal from the drug are so severe that most users are unable to quit without professional help. Withdrawal symptoms, which may last for weeks, include muscle pains and spasms, shaking, fatigue, and reduced mental function. Both inpatient and outpatient programs are available to treat persons for cocaine addiction. Although such programs are costly, treatment expenses for teenagers are often covered by their parents' health insurance plans or HMOs. Some treatment facilities also have provisions to waive fees for a certain number of low-income patients.

For Further Study

Books

Carroll, Marilyn. *Cocaine and Crack. The Drug Library.* Springfield, NJ: Enslow Publishers, 1994.

Chomet, Julian. *Speed and Amphetamines.* New York: Franklin Watts, 1990.

Cole, L. *Never Too Young to Die: The Death of Len Bias.* New York: Pantheon, 1989.

DeBenedette, Valerie. *Caffeine.* The Drug Library. Springfield, NJ: Enslow Publishers, 1996.

Jahanson, C.E. *Cocaine: A New Epidemic.* New York: Main Line Book Co., 1992.

Lukas, Scott E. *Amphetamines: Danger in the Fast Lane.* New York: Chelsea House, 1985.

Salzman, Bernard. *The Handbook of Psychiatric Drugs.* New York: Henry Holt, 1996.

Schwebel, Robert. *Saying No Is Not Enough: What to Say and How to Listen to Your Kids About Alcohol, Tobacco and Other Drugs—A Positive Prevention Guide for Parents.* New York: Newmarket Press, 1997.

Ullman, Robert. *Ritalin-Free Kids: Safe and Effective Homeopathic Medicines for ADD and Other Behavioral and Learning Problems.* Rocklin, CA: Prima Publishing, 1996.

U.S. Department of Health and Human Services. *Preventing Tobacco Use Among Young People: A Report of the Surgeon General.* Atlanta, GA: U.S. Department of Health and Human Services, Public Health Service, Centers for Disease Control and Prevention, Office on Smoking and Health, 1994.

Organizations

Drug Abuse Clearinghouse
  Address: P.O. Box 2345
  Rockville, MD 20847-2345
  Telephone: (301) 443-6500; toll-free (800) 729-6686

National Cocaine Hotline
  Telephone: toll-free (800) COCAINE

Stop Teen-Age Addiction to Tobacco (STAT)
  Address: 511 E. Columbus Ave.
  Springfield, MA 01105
  Telephone: (413) 732-STAT ([413] 732-7828

▌ Strabismus

An eye disorder characterized by crossed or misaligned eyes.

Strabismus is an eye problem affecting approximately 5% of children. It is more common among children born prematurely and children with **cerebral palsy**. It may be evident in the first months of life, or begin when the child is between two and three years old. Beyond this age, onset of strabismus is rare. Strabismus is diagnosed by looking at a child's eyes. Parents should be aware that an infant may often appear to have temporarily crossed eyes, because the muscles that control eye movements are still developing. If a child is older than six months and seems to have persistently crossed eyes, the child may have strabismus. Sometimes the eyes do not cross in, but may look outward, upward, or downward. The eyes may be more or less turned depending on the angle of the child's gaze, and the turn may not be constant, but appear intermittently. A child who persistently tilts her head or turns her face may also be exhibiting a warning sign of strabismus.

Because the eyes are not properly aligned in the child with strabismus, the child cannot focus properly and may have double vision. To compensate for this, the child may use only one eye, and vision in the other does not develop normally. This leads to **amblyopia,** or lazy eye. Therefore, it is important to catch strabismus early and begin treatment.

In examining a child for strabismus, an ophthalmologist will check for any underlying organic problem such as a **tumor, cataracts,** or atrophy of the optic nerve. Then the doctor may measure the refraction of the eyes to fit corrective lenses. Some children can be treated successfully for strabismus with prescription glasses. If one eye is substantially weaker than the other, the child may be treated with an eye patch. The patch is worn over the stronger eye so the weaker eye develops. If glasses do not cure the strabismus, the child may then need surgery to align the eye.

For Further Study

Books

Collins, James F. *Your Eyes: An Owner's Guide.* Englewood Cliffs, NJ: Prentice-Hall, 1995.

Savage, Stephen. *Eyes.* New York: Thomson Learning, 1995.

Showers, Paul. *Look at Your Eyes.* New York: HarperCollins Publishers, 1992.

Zinn, Walter J., and Herbert Solomon. *Complete Guide to Eyecare, Eyeglasses and Contact Lenses.* Hollywood, FL: Lifetime Books, 1995.

Organizations

American Academy of Ophthalmology
  Address: P.O. Box 7424
  San Francisco, CA 92120-7424
National Eye Institute
  Address: Building 31, Room 6A32
  Bethesda, MD 20892
  Telephone: (301) 496-5248

—A. Woodward

Strange Situation

A research technique developed by American psychologist Mary Ainsworth and used in the assessment of attachment.

The Strange Situation procedure, developed by American psychologist **Mary Ainsworth,** is widely used in child development research. The goal of the Strange Situation procedure was to provide an environment that would arouse in the infant both the motivation to explore and the urge to seek security. An observer (often a researcher or therapist) takes a mother and her child (usually around the age of 12 months) to an unfamiliar room containing toys. A series of eight separations and reunions are staged involving mild, but cumulative, stress for the infant (see accompanying table). Separation in such an unfamiliar setting would also likely activate the child's **attachment** system and allow for a direct test of its functioning. Although no single behavior can be used to assess the quality of the infant's attachment to the **caregiver,** the pattern of the infant's responses to the changing situation is of interest to psychologists. The validation of the procedure and its scoring method were grounded in the naturalistic observation of the child's exploration, crying, and proximity-seeking in the home.

Ainsworth's research revealed key individual differences among children, demonstrated by the child's reaction to the mother's return. Ainsworth categorized these responses into three major types:

(A) Anxious/avoidant—the child may not be distressed at the mother's departure and may avoid or turn away from her on her return;

(B) Securely attached—the child is distressed by the mother's departure and easily soothed by her on her return;

(C) Anxious/resistant—the child may stay extremely close to the mother during the first few minutes and become highly distressed at her departure. When she returns, the child will simultaneously seek both comfort and distance from the mother. The child's behavior will be characterized by crying and reaching to be held and then attempting to leave once picked up.

Using the Strange Situation procedure, many researchers have studied the development of child attachment to the mother and to other caregivers. However, there continues to be much debate about the origins of the child's reaction in the Strange Situation, and about what factors influence the development of an infant's attachment relationships.

For Further Study

Books

Ainsworth, M. *Infancy in Uganda: Infant Care and the Growth of Love.* Baltimore: Johns Hopkins University Press, 1967.

Ainsworth, M., M. C. Blehar, E. Waters, and S. Wall. *Patterns of Attachment: A Psychological Study of the Strange Situation.* Hillsdale, NJ: Earlbaum, 1978.

Bowlby, J. *A Secure Base: Parent-Child Attachment and Healthy Human Development.* New York: Basic Books, 1988.

Sroufe, L. A., and J. Fleeson. "Attachment and the Construction of Relationships." In Hartup, W. and Z. Rubin, eds. *Relationships and Development.* Hillsdale, NJ: Erlbaum, 1986, pp. 51–71.

Periodicals

Ainsworth, M., and S. M. Bell. "Infant Crying and Maternal Responsiveness." In *Child Development,* 1171–90.

Silver, Nan. "The ABCs of Intimacy." *Parents Magazine* 71, June 1996, p. 72+.

Spock, Benjamin. "Mommy, Don't Go!" *Parenting* 10, June-July 1996, pp. 86+.

Stranger Anxiety

Fear of people with whom a child is not familiar.

An infant learns to recognize her parents within the first few months of birth by sight, sound, and even smell. Up until six months, a baby will usually seem interested in other adults as well, engaging in games such as peek-a-boo. After six months, many babies undergo a period of fear and unhappiness around anyone except their parents. The child may burst into tears if an unknown person makes eye contact or shriek if left even momentarily in the care of an unfamiliar person. This stranger anxiety is a normal part of a child's **cognitive development;** the baby has learned to differentiate her caretakers from other people and exhibits her strong preference for familiar faces. Stranger anxiety begins around eight or nine months and generally lasts into the child's second year.

Stranger anxiety can be upsetting to friends and relatives, who may feel rebuffed by a suddenly shy child. The baby may reject a **babysitter** she was previously comfortable with or grow hysterical when relatives visit. It can also be a trying time for the child's parents; the baby may reject the parent who is not the principal **caregiver**. Furthermore, the child may be particularly upset around people who look different to her—perhaps people with glasses, men with beards, or people of an unfamiliar skin tone. Parents should respect the child's fear as much as possible, and allow her to approach people as she is able. Extra time should be spent with the child when dropping her off at a babysitter or relative's house. The new face should be introduced slowly. If the child does not want to be hugged by or sit with a relative, it is unwise to force her. Eventually the child will outgrow his fear, and may become more sociable later.

For Further Study

Books

Greenberg, Mark T., Dante Cicchetti, and E. Mark Cummings. *Attachment in the Preschool Years: Theory, Research, and Intervention.* Chicago: University of Chicago Press, 1990.

Watkins, Kathleen Pullan. *Parent-child Attachment: A Guide to Research.* New York: Garland Publishing, 1987.

Periodicals

Spock, Benjamin. "Mommy, Don't Go!" *Parenting* (10): June-July 1996, pp. 86+.

Sroufe, L. A. and J. Fleeson. "Attachment and the Construction of Relationships." In Hartup, W. and Z. Rubin (Eds.) *Relationships and Development.* Hillsdale, NJ: Erlbaum, 1986, pp. 51–71.

Wingate, Carrie. "Separation Distress." *American Baby* (58): May 1996. pp. 20+.

Strep Throat

Strep throat (streptococcal pharyngitis) is a throat infection caused by a bacteria called Group A beta-hemolytic streptococcus (GAS).

Symptoms

A child with a streptococcal throat infection may experience one or more of the following symptoms: sore throat, throat pain upon swallowing, fever, headache, or abdominal pain (with or without vomiting). Symptoms not typical of strep throat include nasal congestion, hoarseness, cough, or diarrhea; these symptoms are often indicators that a child's illness is caused by something else, commonly a viral syndrome.

In a child with strep throat, the tonsils and pharynx will appear reddened, sometimes to the point of being almost hemorrhagic, and exudates (pus) may be seen. The anterior cervical lymph nodes (the lymph nodes in the front of the neck, below the ear and just behind the jaw) may be tender or swollen, and the uvula in the back of the throat or the soft palate may have a red, rash-like appearance. Some children and adults with a GAS infection of the throat develop a highly characteristic skin rash known as **scarlet fever**. The diagnosis of strep throat is made with a throat culture, or in recent years, with rapid antigen detection tests or gene probe tests, both of which, like throat cultures, are performed on material obtained from swabbing the throat and tonsils.

At present, the treatment and outcome for streptococcal pharyngitis is the same whether a scarlet fever rash is present. However, some authorities believe that decades ago, scarlet fever may have represented a more severe disease that sometimes resulted in serious illness and even death.

Complications

Local complications of untreated strep throat can include infections of the sinuses, mastoids (bones behind the ear), and lymph nodes. The most serious complication of untreated streptococcal pharyngitis is a late immunologic complication known as rheumatic fever. This problem can occur several weeks after strep throat and cause inflammation of the heart valves with subsequent scarring. Glomerulonephritis (a kidney inflammation resulting in blood and protein in the urine) can also follow a GAS infection of the throat several weeks later, but is quite rare.

Treatment

To reduce the risk of complications and prevent transmission to others, streptococcal pharyngitis should be treated with an **antibiotic**, most often penicillin (either injectable or oral). For patients allergic to penicillin, erythromycin is the primary drug used. In addition to treatment of the infection itself, the discomfort of strep throat may be alleviated with over-the-counter analgesics (such as acetaminophen). After treatment with antibiotics, some children will continue to have throat cultures that are positive for GAS, and re-culturing asymptomatic patients after antibiotic therapy is not recommended.

Prevention

Antibiotics are sometimes used to prevent GAS pharyngitis in patients who have had rheumatic fever. If such patients contract strep throat again, they will experience exacerbations of their valvular disease and additional scarring; for this reason, they must be given streptococcal prophylaxis lifelong, which can be in the form of either monthly injections of long-acting penicillin or a daily oral antibiotic dose.

For Further Study

Books

Berger, Melvin. *Germs Make Me Sick!* New York: HarperCollins, 1995. [juvenile]

Weinberg, Winkler G. *No Germs Allowed!: How to Avoid Infectious Diseases at Home and on the Road.* New Brunswick, NJ: Rutgers University Press, 1996.

—Marta M. Vielhaber, M.D.

Stress

Disturbance in the physiology of the individual.

Among psychologists and psychiatrists, stress refers to a psychological reaction within the person to events that generate strong emotion that cannot be easily regulated; for other social scientists, the term stress is used to describe a disturbance in the individual's physiology. These two definitions of stress are not identical. For example, a fall from a tree that leads to a broken arm creates physiological changes in a child that would be regarded as stressful, for there is a cascade of biological events that occurs in such an act of harm to the child. However, many children who have had such falls are not necessarily psychologically upset, anxious, or fearful, even though there was a physiological stress reaction.

On the other hand, a child who believes his parent does not like him, experiences rejection from a friend, or is feeling guilt over violating a moral standard will experience unpleasant psychological feelings that disrupt ordinary functioning. That disruption is a result of a psychological stress. This definition of stress need not involve any strong cascade of physiological changes, as occurred in the fall that leads to a broken arm. Nonetheless, psychiatrists and psychologists would say in the second instance that the child was experiencing stress.

A problem with understanding the effects of either physiological or psychological stress more completely is that there are no sensitive techniques to ascertain the private reactions that are occurring in the child's body or mind. Many scientists make the assumption that certain events will produce stress in the child, recognizing that in some cases the event will not be stressful. For example, most sociologists, psychologists, and psychiatrists assume that death of a parent, marital strife, separation and **divorce**, abuse, rejection by a close friend, and chronic failure in school will create stress in the child. Although this assumption is reasonable there is no one-to-one relationship between the occurrence of those and similar external events and a physiological or psychological reaction of stress within the child.

Hans Selye is credited with introducing the importance of the concept of stress. Selye discovered that if an individual is under chronic physiological stress there are permanent changes that occur in the body leading to a compromised immunity and a reduced resistance to many forms of disease. Thus college students who are stressed during final examination periods will show a lowered resistance to getting colds and other minor infectious diseases.

For Further Study

Books

Carter, Frank, and Peter Cheesman. *Anxiety in Childhood and Adolescence: Encouraging Self-Help through Relaxation Training.* New York: Croom Helm, 1988.

Kendall, Philip C., et al. *Anxiety Disorders in Youth: Cognitive-Behavioral Interventions.* New York: Pergamon Press, 1991.

Newman, Susan. *Don't be S.A.D.: A Teenage Guide to Handling Stress, Anxiety and Depression.* Englewood Cliffs, NJ: J. Messner, 1991.

Organizations

National Institute of Mental Health (NIMH)
Telephone: toll-free information services for panic and other anxiety disorders: (800) 647-2642
NIMH Public Inquiries
Address: 5600 Fishers Lane, Rm. 7C-02
Rockville, MD 20857

—Jerome Kagan
Harvard University

Stuttering

A speech disorder characterized by a lack of normal fluency.

A person who stutters repeats words and parts of words, prolongs sounds, has difficulty producing sounds (usually at the beginning of words or groups of words), and generally speaks in fragmented phrases. ("Stuttering" and "stammering" are synonymous. The former is used more frequently in the United States, while the latter is the preferred term in Britain.) Due to the frustration and embarrassment caused by this problem, stuttering is usually accompanied by anxiety about speaking. It is estimated that stuttering affects about one percent of the general population in the world's industrialized nations—2.5 million people in the United States alone. It is much more common in males than females: the ratio is generally thought to be about four to one (and according to some estimates may even be as high as nine to one). About four-fifths of children who stutter outgrow the problem by adulthood, in some cases spontaneously and in others with treatment. Stuttering usually begins between the ages of two and seven; it is very rare for it to occur in an adolescent or adult who has no history—even a brief one—of childhood stuttering. Except for cases where it results from brain damage, no physical basis can normally be found for the disorder.

Stuttering was long regarded as an emotional disorder (or as a symptom of one), but this view has been largely abandoned by today's researchers and speech pathologists. It is known that the condition has a genetic component. Children whose parents have a childhood history of stuttering, even if they have outgrown it, are more likely than other children to stutter. If one identical twin stutters, there is a 77% likelihood that the other one will, too. Experts have speculated that the timing of the three functions involved in speech—respiration, articulation, and use of the larynx (or voice box) to produce sound—may be different in stutterers than in persons who speak normally. Through the use of brain scans, neurologists have been able to contribute valuable information to what is known about the physiological basis of stuttering. It has been found that when people stutter, the areas of the brain that control physical movement go into overdrive while parts of the cortex (the brain's outer layer) that are instrumental in controlling the content and organization of speech remain abnormally inactive.

In addition to a better understanding of the physical aspects of stuttering, there have also been advances in analyzing the environmental influences that lead a child to stutter. Foremost among these is parental behavior in relation to children's speech. When children are first learning to communicate verbally, their speech is very far from the normal fluency of adults (and even older children). It is common for their speech to be punctuated by many of the same types of interruptions that characterize stuttering: hesitation, repetition or prolongation of sounds, and a generally fragmented flow of speech. A major difference, however, between this normal lack of fluency (called dysfluency) and stuttering is that very young children do not know there is anything wrong with their speech. When a parent corrects the child's speech or attempts to speak for him, the possible feelings of failure and parental disapproval can create anxiety that worsens this transient dysfluency and causes it to become chronic.

Parents of young children who show dysfluency in their speech are advised to avoid any action that will make the child think there is something wrong, such as showing disapproval or concern over the child's speech, mentioning the term "stuttering," or asking him to slow down or say something again the correct way (which usually backfires because the child becomes anxious and the speech actually worsens). On the other hand, it can be helpful to note if there are particular situations associated with the dysfluency and to refrain from asking or expecting the child to speak in these or any other situa-

tions that seem likely to produce unusual anxiety. Other positive actions that parents can take at this stage include being patient and calm when listening to their children speak and speaking in an unhurried manner themselves. It is especially helpful to make sure the pause before answering after the child speaks is long enough so that the conversation has an unhurried pace, and the child feels he doesn't have to rush to answer. By grade school, it is often too late to prevent stuttering. However, there are still ways that parents can still help a child who stutters. In general, a relaxed parenting style can help reduce stuttering, while inflexibility and perfectionism can exacerbate it, as can conflicts within the family. As with younger children, awareness of the situations that either exacerbate and reduce stuttering is helpful. Perhaps the most intriguing aspect of stuttering, in both children and adults, is the fact that under certain circumstances it disappears. Children who stutter should be encouraged to participate in activities that generally tend to eliminate the problem, including group singing, reciting from memory, and play-acting.

There are two basic methods of treating stuttering. One is fluency training, which attempts to totally eradicate the stutter and replace it with normal speech, using exercises that help coordinate speech and breathing, slow down the rate of speech, and prolong syllables. One technique used with children is a method that involves saying a single word fluently and then gradually adding words to slowly increase the length and complexity of speech that can be mastered without stuttering. Often, more challenging speaking situations are gradually introduced as well. For example, a child may progress from speaking together with the speech pathologist to speaking alone, followed by speaking to other people individually and, finally, to a group. A technological aid that has been effective in fluency training is the use of delayed auditory feedback (DAF), in which the stutterer hears an echo of his own speech sounds. For some reason, this disruption, which would make it harder for most people to speak, tends to produce fluent speech in stutterers. Once DAF has been used to get the stutterer accustomed to what it feels like to speak normally, the speech pathologist gradually reduces the amount of feedback delay until it is eliminated and the stutterer is still speaking fluently.

Fluency training generally works best with young children. Older children and adolescents may be more successful with another treatment method, in which true fluency is not attained but the impulse to stutter is controlled in ways that makes speech much clearer and less hesitant. A "hard stutter" is replaced with an "easy stutter" in which, for example, the first sound of a word may be prolonged or repeated very softly. The speech produced this way may sound somewhat halting or deliberate but it will not sound like stuttering, and it is considered a great improvement by those stutterers who master it. As with fluency training, this method requires diligent practice under the guidance of a qualified speech pathologist.

Speech language pathology, commonly referred to as speech therapy, is offered in a variety of settings. Speech impairment is considered a disability under Public Law 94-142, the federal law governing education for the handicapped. Most communities have school speech pathologists who can assess and work with children who stutter. In addition to the obvious financial advantages, therapy in public school has the advantage of convenience. The child may be able to work in a group with other children who have the same problem, and it is easy for the speech therapist to consult with the child's classroom teacher. However, some mild cases of stuttering may not qualify for school treatment, and parents may need to seek private treatment, often at a speech and hearing clinic. The early intervention that private treatment makes possible for children under school age can also be an advantage, as can the opportunity for parents to work more closely with the speech therapist than they could ordinarily do under a school program.

For Further Study

Books

Bloodstein, Oliver. *A Handbook on Stuttering.* 5th ed. San Diego: Singular Publishing Group, 1995.

Conture, Edward G., and Jane Fraser, eds. *Stuttering and Your Child: Questions and Answers.* Memphis, TN: Speech Foundation of America, 1990.

Peters, Theodore J. *Stuttering: An Integrated Approach to Its Nature and Treatment.* Baltimore: Williams and Wilkins, 1991.

Schwartz, Martin F. *Stop Stuttering.* New York: Harper and Row, 1986.

Van Riper, C. *The Nature of Stuttering,* 2nd ed. Englewood Cliffs, NJ: Prentice-Hall, 1982.

Wells, G. Beverly. *Stuttering Treatment: A Comprehensive Clinical Guide.* Englewood Cliffs, NJ: Prentice-Hall, 1987.

Periodicals

"Acclaimed Actor James Earl Jones Reveals That He Still Occasionally Has Stuttering Problems." *Jet* 87 (10), January 16, 1995, p. 27.

Audiovisual Recordings

Conture, Edward G., et al. *Stuttering and Your Child: A Videotape for Parents.* Memphis, TN: Stuttering Foundation of America, 1994.
(One 29-minute videocassette.)

Do You Stutter: Straight Talk for Teens. Memphis, TN: The Foundation, 1996.
(One 34-minute videocassette and one 80-page book.)

Naylor, Rex, with Randy Taylor. *A Look at Stuttering.* Silver Spring, MD: Center for Compassion, 1992.
(One 28-minute videocassette.)

Taylor, Randy. *Stuttering with Friends.* Silver Spring, MD: The Center for Compassion, 1993.
(One 25-minute videocassette.)

Organizations

American Speech-Language-Hearing Association (ASHA)
Address: 10801 Rockville Pike
Rockville, MD 20852
Telephone: (301) 897-5700

Speech Foundation of America
Address: P. O. Bos 11749
Memphis, TN 38111
Telephone: (901) 452-0995

Sudden Infant Death Syndrome (SIDS)

Also referred to as crib death or cot death.

The sudden, unexpected death of a seemingly normal, healthy infant under one year of age that remains unexplained after a thorough postmortem investigation, including an autopsy and a review of the case history.

In the United States, sudden infant death syndroms (SIDS) is the leading cause of postneonatal deaths (those occurring between the ages of 28 days and one year). According to the National Center for Health Statistics, at least 4,000 infants in the United States die of SIDS every year, or 1.03 per 1,000 live births. (In the late 1990s, many sources placed the annual total number of deaths as high as 6,000 due to possible under-reporting.) Ninety percent of SIDS deaths occur during the first six months of life, mostly between the ages of two and four months. SIDS also occurs about 1.5 times more frequently in boys than girls.

Understanding SIDS

Studies have identified many risk factors for SIDS, but the actual cause of the disorder remains a mystery. Although investigators are still not sure whether the immediate cause of SIDS deaths is respiratory failure or cardiac arrest, patterns of infant sleep, breathing, and arousal are a major focus of current research. It is known that young infants often stop breathing for short periods of time, then gasp and start again. Some researchers and physicians believe that SIDS involves a flaw in the mechanism, perhaps controlled by the central nervous system, that is responsible for re-starting breathing. Aside from its occurrence during sleep, the other most striking feature of SIDS is its narrow age distribution, which has prompted researchers to examine the developmental changes that take place during this period, especially between the ages of two and four months, when most SIDS deaths occur. A growing number of experts believe that rather than a single cause, there are a number of different conditions that can cause or contribute to SIDS. This picture is complicated still further by the interaction of possible physical abnormalities with a number of environmental and developmental factors known to increase the risk of SIDS. Premature infants, and low birth weight babies generally, are known to be at increased risk of developing SIDS, as are infants born to teenage mothers, poor mothers, and mothers who for any reason have had inadequate prenatal care. Other risk factors include maternal **smoking** during **pregnancy**, exposure to smoking in the home after birth, formula feeding rather than **breastfeeding**, and prior death of a sibling from SIDS (although this is thought to be due to shared environmental risk factors rather than genetic predisposition). The rate of SIDS in African American infants is twice as high as that of Caucasians, a fact attributed to the lower quality of prenatal care received by many African American mothers. Many SIDS deaths occur in babies who have recently had colds (a possible reason that SIDS is most prevalent in winter—the time when upper respiratory infections are most frequent).

SIDS and sleep habits

Thus far, the most significant risk factor discovered for SIDS is placing babies to sleep in a prone position (on their stomachs). Studies have reported that anywhere from 28–52% of infants who die of SIDS are found lying face down. Another finding reinforcing the connection between SIDS and front-sleeping is the fact that SIDS rates are higher in Western cultures, where women have traditionally placed children on their stomachs, than in Eastern ones, where infants usually sleep on their backs. The cause-effect relationship between front-sleeping and SIDS is not fully understood. However, it is known that when infants sleep on their backs they are more prone to arousal, and SIDS is often thought to involve a failure to rouse from sleep. In addition, front-sleeping raises a baby's temperature, and overheating is another risk factor for the disorder.

In the 1990s a number of countries initiated campaigns aimed at getting parents to put their infants to sleep on their backs or sides. In the United States, the **American Academy of Pediatrics** (AAP) in 1992 issued an official recommendation that infants be put to bed on their backs (supine position) or on their sides (lateral position). In 1994 the Public Health Service launched its "Back to Sleep" campaign, targeting parents, other care givers, and health care personnel with brochures advocating supine or lateral infant sleeping and also including information about other risk factors for SIDS. By the mid-1990s it was apparent that this and similar campaigns

world wide had had a significant—in many cases dramatic—impact in reducing the number of deaths from SIDS. In a number of countries the incidence of SIDS dropped by 50% or more. SIDS deaths in Great Britain were reduced by 91% between 1989 and 1992; in Denmark they declined by 72% between 1991 and 1993; and they were reduced by 45% in New Zealand between 1989 and 1992.

In the United States, the AAP recommendations reduced the incidence of front-sleeping in infants from over 70% in 1992 to 24% in 1996. A decline in SIDS rates, already observed in the 1980s, tripled its previous pace between 1990 and 1994, with SIDS deaths falling 10–15% between 1992 and 1994. Preliminary 1995 figures from the National Center for Health Statistics place the incidence of SIDS at fewer than 1 per 1,000 live births (compared to 1.3 in 1990 and 1.5 in 1980). Links between SIDS and other aspects of an infant's sleep environment have also emerged in recent years. The best known is the finding that soft, padded sleep surfaces can endanger infants by obstructing breathing or creating air pockets that trap their expelled carbon dioxide, which they can then inhale.

Recent research also suggests that co-sleeping (having an infant sleep with the mother in her bed) can help regulate an infant's sleep pattern in ways that reduce the risk of SIDS. (Like supine infant sleeping, co-sleeping is also prevalent among Asian populations, which have a low incidence of SIDS.) Infants who share their mothers' beds become accustomed to frequent minor arousals when the mother shifts position, and their own sleep tends to be lighter and more even than that of infants who sleep alone in their cribs and are more prone to the heavier, but sporadic, breathing that stops and then starts up again with a gasp. Experts speculate that this lighter sleep not only makes it less likely for an infant to stop breathing but also that such an infant, with the "practice" gained from more frequent arousals every night, can be aroused more easily when any respiratory distress does occur. In addition, infants who co-sleep with their mothers are naturally more likely to sleep on their backs or sides, which also reduces the risk of SIDS.

In December 1996 the American Academy of Pediatrics issued the following updated recommendations regarding infant sleep: 1) Infants should be put to sleep in a nonprone position. The supine position (on their backs) is safest, but sleeping on their sides can also significantly reduce the risk of SIDS. When infants sleep on their sides, the bottom arm should be extended to prevent them from rolling over on to their stomachs. 2) Soft sleeping surfaces should be avoided, and a sleeping infant should not be placed on soft objects such as pillows or quilts. 3) It may be better for parents, with the guidance of their pediatrician, to depart from these recommendations in the case of infants with certain health problems, such as gastroesophageal reflux (GER). 4) Infants should spend some time lying on their stomachs when they are awake and supervised by an adult.

Other precautions parents can take include obtaining adequate prenatal care; avoiding exposing infants to cigarette smoke, either pre- or postnatally; breastfeeding instead of formula feeding; and not allowing an infant to become overheated while sleeping. Another measure taken by some parents is the use of a portable battery-operated monitor that sounds an alarm in response to significant deviations in infants' respiration or heart rates while they are asleep. Monitoring is based on the belief that if parents can quickly reach an infant who has stopped breathing, they can either get him breathing again themselves or call for emergency assistance. There has been no substantiated link between monitoring and the decrease in SIDS, and infants have, in fact, died while being monitored. Nevertheless, monitors provide peace of mind for many parents, especially those who have lost a previous infant to SIDS or whose baby has special risk factors for the disorder. Medical opinion is generally in favor of monitoring only for newborns who have had episodes of **apnea** (cessation of breathing) or for any infant who has had a precipitous, life-threatening interruption of breathing or cardiovascular function.

The grieving process

Losing a child—a traumatic experience for any parent—is especially difficult for those who lose a child to SIDS because the death is so sudden and its cause cannot be determined. Parents of a child who dies of SIDS are forever missing the sense of closure that come from a sympathetic and detailed medical explanation of their infant's death. Although such an understanding doesn't lessen their loss, it can serve an important function in the healing process, one that is denied to SIDS parents. In addition to the emotions that normally accompany grief, such as denial, anger, and guilt, SIDS parents may experience certain other reactions unique to their situation. They may become fearful that another unexpected disaster will strike them or members of their families. After the death of a child from SIDS, parents often become overprotective of the infant's older siblings, and of any children born subsequently. Some fear having another child, due to misgivings that the tragedy they have experienced may repeat itself. Parents of children who die of SIDS often make major changes in their lives during the period following the death, such as relocating or changing jobs, as a way to avoid confronting painful memories or even to try protecting themselves against the SIDS death of another baby by changing the circumstances of their lives as much as possible.

SIDS deaths place a great strain on marriages. Parents' individual ways of coping with their grief may prevent them from giving each other the support they need, creating an emotional distance between them. Nevertheless, the **divorce** rate among SIDS parents appears to be no higher than that for the general population, and in one survey half the respondents reported that their marriages had ultimately been strengthened by the experience. A SIDS death also has a significant effect on the infant's siblings. Young children often experience developmental regressions in **toilet training** or other areas. Some fear going to sleep, which they associate with the death of their baby brother or sister. As with any death in the family, children need to be reassured that they are not guilty in any way. Many pose difficult questions to their parents, wanting to know why the baby died or where he has gone, or even whether they are going to die, too. Children may also come to feel jealous of the attention paid to the infant who has died, or resentful of the disruption the death has caused in their family's life. Most parents report that their way of caring for their remaining children changes after the family experiences a SIDS death. Having young children (or infants born later on) sleep with them at night makes some parents feel more confident of preventing a second tragedy from occurring. In addition to overprotecting their children and worrying about their health, SIDS parents may also spoil them and find it hard to say "no" to their requests. On the positive side, many parents simply value their remaining children more, spend more time with them, and become closer to them. In a minority of cases, however, the reverse happens, and parents feel emotionally distant from their surviving children. In addition, fear of being hurt sometimes makes it difficult to bond with babies born later.

Many parents of infants who die of SIDS are helped by participating in local support groups, where they can share their feelings and experiences with others who have undergone the same experience. Counseling can also be beneficial, especially with a mental health professional experienced in dealing with parental grief.

For Further Study

Books

Corr, Charles A. *Sudden Infant Death Syndrome: Who Can Help and How.* New York: Springer Publishing Co., 1991.

Culbertson, Jan L., Henry F. Krous, and R. Debra Bendell, eds. *Sudden Infant Death Syndrome.* Baltimore: Johns Hopkins University Press, 1988.

Defrain, John, et al. *Sudden Infant Death: Enduring the Loss.* Lexington, MA: D. C. Heath, 1991.

Guntheroth, Warren G. *Crib Death: Sudden Infant Death Syndrome.* Mount Kisco, NY: Futura, 1982.

Harper, Ronald M., and Howard J. Hoffman, eds. *Sudden Infant Death Syndrome: Risk Factors and Basic Mechanisms.* New York: PMA Publishing Group, 1988.

Horchler, Joani Nelson. *The SIDS Survival Guide: Information and Comfort for Grieving Family and Friends and Professionals Who Seek to Help Them.* Hyattsville, MD: SIDS Educational Services, 1994.

Sears, William. *SIDS: A Parent's Guide to Understanding and Preventing Sudden Infant Death Syndrome.* Boston: Little, Brown, 1995.

Organizations

Back to Sleep

Telephone: toll-free (800) 505-CRIB

National SIDS Resource Center

Address: 2070 Chain Bridge Rd. Suite 450
Vienna, VA 22182

Telephone: (703) 821-8955

internet: info@circsol.com; www.circsol.com/sids.

(Professional and consumer education materials, including *Information Exchange* newsletter, information sheets, and bibliography. Database searches on specific topics related to SIDS.)

SIDS Alliance

Address: 1314 Bedford Ave., Suite 210
Baltimore, MD 21208

Telephone: toll-free (800) 221-SIDS

internet: sids@charm.net

(Funding for SIDS research, bereavement support, information for expectant and new parents. Affiliates in thirty-five states.)

Sun Protection

Protection from the damaging ultraviolet rays of sunlight.

Scientists have found a strong link between exposure to direct and reflected sunlight and a number of health risks. Ultraviolet (UV) radiation, a component of sunlight, causes damage to the skin and increases the risk of skin **cancer.** UV radiation comes in two forms—ultraviolet A (UVA) and ultraviolet B (UVB). UVB is the radiation sunscreens are designed to screen out. The United States Food and Drug Administration has not approved a rating system for UVA protection because experts have not reached a consensus as to what constitutes a good test. Manufacturers can claim protection against "broad spectrum" radiation if their product contains one of the following ingredients: benzophenone, oxybenzone, sulisobenzone, titanium dioxide, zinc oxide, and butyl ethoxydibenzolmethane (also called avobenzone and known by the trade name Parsol 1789).

One of the factors that increases the risk of skin cancer is the number of sunburns experienced during childhood. For the first six months of life, infants should be protected from all sun exposure, according to recommendations from the American Medical Association and the American Cancer Society. The AMA studies predict that one in six of all individuals born in the late 1980s and

ULTRAVIOLET RADIATION INDEX NUMBER	
U.S. Weather UV Index	**Exposure Level**
0–2	minimal
3–4	low
5–6	moderate
7–8	high
9–10+	very high

1990s will develop skin cancer at some point in their lives, compared with one in 1,500 for those individuals born in the late 1940s and 1950s. This increase is due to many factors, including the deterioration of the earth's protective ozone layer, the trend toward wearing lighter clothes that leave more skin surface exposed, and the increase in the amount of time people spend outdoors.

In the late 1990s, about one million new cases of skin cancer were being diagnosed each year. Dermatologists reported that skin cancer was as common as all other cancers combined. From 1980–89, the incidence of skin cancer increased dramatically; melanoma skin cancer increased 21%, and non-melanoma (basal cell and squamous cell) skin cancer increased 65%. The accompanying tables provide information on risk factors and the National Weather Service UV level index rating system. The UV index is routinely reported in major cities in the United States, and is included in weather forecasts on television and radio. By monitoring the UV levels in the geographic area, residents can respond with the appropriate degree of protection necessary.

Sunscreens are rated by a sun protection factor, or SPF, which is a multiplier of the amount of time the skin can be exposed to the sun before experiencing sunburn. The American Academy of Dermatology recommends that everyone use a broad-spectrum sunscreen having a sun protection factor (SPF) of at least 15. The Academy also recommends that consumers check sunscreen labels for ingredients that protect from UVA rays as well as UVB. It is important to note that the SPF is not cumulative; in other words, reapplying a sunscreen after being in the sun for a period of time does not extend the sun protection factor; it will only replenish the protection that may have been washed away by perspiration or during swimming. The only way to get protection for a longer period of sun exposure is to choose a sunscreen with a higher SPF factor.

While sunscreens protect against sunburn, they do not necessarily prevent skin cancer. Even when a person

SKIN CANCER RISK FACTOR RATING

Characteristic	Check if yes
Hair color: blond or red	
Eye color: blue, gray, or green	
Skin freckles easily	
Skin has many moles	
Two or more blistering sunburns in childhood	
Spent significant time in a tropical climate as a child	
Family history of skin cancer	
Work outdoors	
Significant amount of time in recreation outdoors	
Spend significant time sunbathing	
Go to tanning parlors or use a sunlamp	
Assign one point to every item	
8–11 "yes" answers	*High risk* Limit your time in the sun, always wear a sunscreen outdoors, and use protective clothing and a hat.
4–7 "yes" answers	*Increased risk* Use a sunscreen and hat regularly. Avoid exposure at midday when the sun is most intense.
1–3 "yes" answers	*Still at risk* Use a sunscreen regularly.

Adapted from *FDA Consumer*, July–August 1995.

uses sunscreen for the purpose of spending more time in the sun, the skin can still collect damaging radiation. Dermatologists advise wearing protective clothing and head covering during the midday hours (from 10 A.M. to 3 P.M.), and the consistent use of sunscreens year-round. To protect children from the damaging effects of the sun, apply sunscreens with an SPF of at least 15 and encourage them to wear hats with visors. It is also recommended that even young children wear sunglasses that are designated as providing protection from UV radiation. Although many children may want to play outdoors wearing little clothing, parents should encourage them to keep as much skin area covered by clothing as possible.

New fabrics are being produced that are comfortably lightweight but also offer protection from UV radiation. As these fabrics are used to a greater degree, parents can watch clothing labelling for this protection factor.

For Further Study

Books

Greeley, Alexandra. *Dodging the Rays.* Rockville, MD: U.S. Food and Drug Administration, 1995.

Lowe, Nicholas J., ed. *Physician's Guide to Sunscreens.* New York: Dekker, 1991.

Robins, Perry. *Sun Sense.* New York: Skin Cancer Foundation, 1990.

Siegel, Mary-Ellen. *Safe in the Sun.* New York: Walker, 1990.

Periodicals

Reed, Charles. "How to Beat the Heat." *American Baby* 58, August 1996, p. 8.

Strange, Carolyn. "Thwarting Skin Cancer with Sun Sense." *FDA Consumer* 29, July-August 1995, pp. 10–13.

Audiovisual Recordings

Skin Cancer. Columbus, OH: The Institute, 1994.
　　(One 6-½ minute videocassette.)

Skin Cancer: Preventable and Curable. New York: Skin Care Foundation, 1990.
(One videocassette.)

Organizations

American Academy of Dermatology
Address: 930 North Meacham Rd.
Schaumburg, IL 60173-4965
Mailing address: P.O. Bo 4014
Schaumburg, IL 60168-4014
Telephone: (847) 330-0230
website: www.aad.org
(Includes public information and patient education, including "Safe Sun Tips")

Suicide/Suicidal Behavior

Alternative terms: Deliberate self-harm

The phenomenon of deliberate self-harm, often with a wish to die.

Suicide is the third leading cause of death among adolescents, occurring at a rate of 10.8 per 100,000 among 15–19 year olds in 1992. Suicide is much less common among 10–14 year olds, at 1.7 per 100,000, although the rate of suicide has increased dramatically since 1950 among all age groups. Suicide attempts are much more common, occurring in 2% of adolescent girls and 1% of adolescent boys per year. Significant suicidal ideation (with a plan to commit suicide or intent to die) is more common, occurring in 5–10% of child and adolescent youth.

The suicide completion rate is about four times higher in males than females, while the rate of attempt is two to three times higher in females than males. Completed suicide may be greater among males because of their tendency to utilize methods of more potential lethality. The rate of suicide also varies according to victims' race. Highest are Native Americans and whites. The suicide rate among African American males increased dramatically in the 1980s, and now approaches 80% of the white male suicide rate.

In the United States, the most common method for completed suicide is firearms, followed by hanging, carbon monoxide, and jumping. A gun in the house, particularly a loaded gun, appears to increase the risk for completed suicide, even in those youth without other obvious risk factors for suicide. Among suicide attempters, the two most common methods are overdose and wrist-cutting.

The most common precipitants for suicidal behavior among children and adolescents involve interpersonal conflict or loss, most frequently with parents or romantic attachment figures. Family discord, physical or sexual abuse, and an upcoming legal or disciplinary crisis are also commonly associated with completed and attempted suicide. Adolescents who complete suicide show relatively high suicidal intent (wish to die), although many are intoxicated at the time of death. The most serious suicide attempters leave suicide notes, show evidence of planning, and use an irreversible method. Most adolescent suicide attempts, though, are of relatively low intent and lethality, and only a minority actually want to die. Usually, suicide attempters want to escape psychological pain or unbearable circumstances, gain attention, influence others, or communicate strong feelings, such as anger or love.

Risk factors

The vast majority of both suicide attempters and completers have evidence of at least one major psychiatric disorder. These disorders are most often affective disorders, causing changes in moods or emotions. Major depressive disorder is the single biggest risk factor for attempted or completed suicide, with the risk heightened even further by comorbid anxiety, substance abuse, or **conduct disorder.** Bipolar affective disorder also conveys increased risk for completed and attempted suicide. There is an average of seven years between the onset of disorder and completed suicide in adolescence, so repeated suicide threats or attempts are common. Youths who attempt suicide feel hopeless, are impulsive, and have poor problem-solving and social skills. Children with other illnesses may also face an increased risk of suicidal behavior. For example, children with **epilepsy** have a higher suicide rate, which may be related to the side effects of the drug phenobarbital.

Family history and environment are also risk factors for suicide. The relatives of both suicide attempters and completers have high prevalences of affective disorder, substance abuse, assaultive behavior, suicide, and suicide attempts. The tendency for suicidal behavior appears to be passed on independently of the transmission of psychiatric disorders, and may be more closely related to the tendency for impulsive aggression. The family environments of suicide attempters and completers have been described as discordant, with greater exposure to family violence, including physical and sexual abuse. Both have also been exposed to suicidal behavior. Studies of friends and siblings of suicide victims show they tend not to imitate the act, suggesting that increased risk is related more to distant exposure. For example, media publicity about fictional or true suicides have been shown consistently to increase the risk for suicide and suicidal behavior.

Repeated suicide attempts are common, but rates vary. Follow-up studies ranging from one to 12 years found a re-attempt rate among adolescents of between 6% and 15% per year, with the greatest risk within the first three months after the initial attempt. Factors associated with a higher reattempt rate included chronic and severe psychopathology (**depression** and substance abuse), hostility and aggression, non-compliance with treatment, poor level of social adaptation, family discord, abuse, or neglect, and parental psychopathology. The risk for completed suicide ranges from 0.7% per year among males and 0.1% per year among females seen in an emergency room for an overdose. Among psychiatric inpatients after a 10–15 year follow-up, the risks are higher, 10% for males and 2.9% for females.

Suicidal ideation, or thinking about suicide, is even more common than suicidal behavior. Suicidal ideation spans a continuum from non-specific thoughts, for example, "life is not worth living," to specific ideation. Community surveys indicate that between 12 and 25% of primary and high school children have some form of suicidal ideation, whereas 5–10% have suicidal ideation with a plan or intent to make a suicide attempt. Not surprisingly, specific ideation is more closely associated with risk for attempted suicide, and frequently occurs with other risk factors.

Developmental issues

Suicidal behavior is rare in prepubertal children, probably because of their relative inability to plan and execute a suicide attempt. Psychiatric risk factors, such as depression and substance abuse, become more frequent in adolescence, contributing to the increase in the frequency of suicidal behavior in older children. The emergence of conflicts with parents and with boy/girlfriends and legal or disciplinary problems are frequently associated with suicidal behavior. Some view the transition from primary to middle school as particularly stressful, especially for girls. Finally, parental monitoring and supervision decrease with increasing age, so that adolescents may be more likely to experience emotional difficulties without parents' knowledge.

Care of suicidal patients

The first step in the care of a suicidal patient is to determine the degree of suicidal risk and the appropriate level of care. It is critical to obtain a no-suicide contract with the patient and family, in which the patient promises to refrain from self-destructive behavior and to notify the professional or caregiver if he or she does feel suicidal again. Treatment of the suicidal youngster should proceed on four levels: (1) removal of firearms and dangerous medications from the home; (2) treatment of the underlying psychiatric disorders; (3) remediation of social and problem-solving skills; and (4) family education about psychiatric problems and suicidal risk.

For Further Study

Books

Cytryn, Leon, and Donald H. McKnew. *Growing Up Sad: Childhood Depression and Its Treatment.* New York: Norton, 1996.

Periodicals

Brent, D. A. "Risk Factors for Adolescent Suicide and Suicidal Behavior: Mental and Substance Abuse Disorders, Family Environmental Factors, and Life Stress." *Suicide Life-Threat Behavior* 25, 1995, pp. 52–63.

Brent, D. A., J. A. Perper, C. E. Goldstein, D. J. Kolko, M. J. Allan, C.J. Allman, and J. P. Zelenak. "Risk Factors for Adolescent Suicide: A Comparison of Adolescent Suicide Victims with Suicidal Inpatients." *Archives of General Psychiatry* 45, 1988, pp. 581–88.

Lewinsohn, P. M., P. Rohde, and J. R. Seeley. "Adolescent Suicidal Ideation and Attempts: Prevalence, Risk Factors, and Clinical Implications." *Clinical Psychology: Science and Practice* 3, 1996, pp. 25–46.

Shaffer, D., M. S. Gould, P. Fisher, P. Trautman, D. Moreau, M. Kleinman, and M. Flory. "Psychiatric Diagnosis in Child and Adolescent Suicide." *Archives of General Psychiatry* 53, 1996, pp. 339–48.

—David A. Brent, M.D.
Western Psychiatric Institute & Clinic

Sweat Test

A test, used in the diagnosis of cycstic fibrosis, that measures the level of sodium and chloride excretions from the sweat glands.

The sweat test is used in the diagnosis of **cystic fibrosis** (CF), an incurable, inherited disease that affects the sweat glands, as well as glands in the lungs, intestines, bile duct, and pancreas. The test is administered as soon as CF is suspected, either because of a family history or symptoms such as frequent colds, recurrent lung infections, recurrent diarrhea, difficulty absorbing food, and slower-than-normal growth. Because early diagnosis and treatment can often ease the severity of the disease, sweat tests may be administered as early as the first week of life. However, this is recommended only when a family history of CF exists or symptoms specific to the disease are exhibited. Sweat tests should never be given for minor breathing problems. Because siblings of CF patients carry a 25% chance of having the disease, they should also be tested.

For infants, the test is done on the right thigh; for children, the right forearm is used. After the area is washed and dried, two metal electrodes are attached and fastened with straps. Two gauze pads, one soaked in salt water and the other in pilocarpine to induce sweating, are placed under the electrodes. A tiny electric current is sent for five to 10 minutes to carry the pilocarpine into the skin. The child should only feel a slight tingling or tickling. Although there is virtually no risk of electrical shock from a sweat test, it should never be conducted on the left side of the body. Nor should it be given in the chest area. The current should come from a battery-powered unit rather than from a direct current.

After the electrodes are removed, the skin is cleansed and dried again. A dry gauze pad or piece of filter paper covered with a sheet of clear plastic is taped to the area where the pilocarpine was applied. The gauze or filter paper, called a sweat patch, is weighed before application. After 30–45 minutes, the plastic is removed and the gauze or paper is placed in a sealed bottle. The test area may be red and sweaty for several hours after the test. In the lab the sweat patch will be weighed and analyzed for sodium and chloride content. A sodium level above 90 milliequivalents per milliliter and a chloride level above 60 is indicative of cystic fibrosis.

For Further Study

Books

Bellet, Paul S. *The Diagnostic Approach to Common Symptoms and Signs in Infants, Children, and Adolescents.* Philadelphia: Lea & Febiger, 1989.

Garwood, John, and Amanda Bennett. *Your Child's Symptoms.* New York: Berkeley Books, 1995.

Harris, Ann, and Maurice Super. *Cystic Fibrosis: The Facts.* New York: Oxford University Press, 1987.

Organizations

Cystic Fibrosis Foundation
    Address: 6931 Arlington Road
    Bethesda, MD 20814
    Telephone: toll-free (800) 344-4823

Swimming

Swimming is an enjoyable aerobic activity that can help children develop strength, flexibility, and endurance. A 1991 study found that the hundreds of thousands of young people enrolled in organized swim programs throughout the United States are thinner, stronger, and in better health than their nonswimming peers in a nation where 34% of children are reportedly overweight and up to half do not receive enough aerobic exercise to maintain adequate cardiovascular fitness. Participation in swimming programs also promotes self-discipline and responsibility and develops regular exercise habits that can benefit children throughout their lives. Swimming is especially well-suited for children because it results in fewer injuries than any other sport. It takes place in a safe

Participation in swimming programs also promotes self-discipline and responsibility and develops regular exercise habits that can benefit children throughout their lives.

environment and does not place undue stress on growing tendons, joints, and bones. The rhythmic breathing and lung expansion involved in swimming provide relief for children with **asthma**, and swimming can be an important form of exercise and a valuable source of accomplishment and **self-esteem** for young people with a wide range of physical disabilities.

Although there is universal agreement that swimming is beneficial for children, opinion is split when it comes to the value and advisability of swim lessons for infants and toddlers. This issue has caused controversy as the number of infant swim programs has increased in recent years. Proponents of teaching infants to swim have claimed that babies as young as six months old can be taught to swim sufficiently to be considered "pool safe"—able to swim to the side of a pool unassisted if they accidentally fall into the water or mistakenly jump or wander into deep water. It has also been claimed that early swimming advances a child's **motor development** and promotes good health. Proponents of early swimming point out that very young infants placed in water will automatically keep themselves afloat by paddling and that early lessons take advantage of this "swimming reflex," which disappears after about six months. Opponents of infant swimming say that this type of paddling isn't really swimming, and that an infant who engages in it could actually drown at any time. The **American Academy of Pediatrics** cautions against swimming lessons for children under the age of four, claiming that children this young will forget their training in an emergency and that early lessons are actually a hazard because they may lull parents into exercising reduced vigilance when their children are in the water.

Whether actual swimming lessons are pursued, infants and toddlers can become comfortable in water through games played in the bathtub or shower (with careful adult supervision) and water orientation classes with their parents at a local community pool or YMCA. Phillip Whitten, author of the *Complete Book of Swimming,* recommends beginning lessons at the age of four or five. Suggested criteria for choosing a program include instructor certification by the YMCA, American Red Cross, or National Safety Council; the presence of a lifeguard during classes; and a comfortably low ratio of students to teachers (six to one for beginners; ten to one for intermediate and advanced swimmers). Early swimming skills for young students include kicking while holding onto a kicking board; dog paddling and blowing bubbles; learning to float; opening one's eyes underwater; and kicking while floating on one's back. Once they have mastered these early steps, children are ready to learn the proper arm and breathing techniques for freestyle swimming and, later, the strokes used in competitive swimming: the butterfly, backstroke, and breaststroke.

There are currently over 220,000 young people between the ages of 8 and 18 enrolled in the United States Swimming (USS) competitive age-group program, as well as hundreds of thousands more participating in similar programs through a variety of local organizations, including YMCAs, Jewish community centers, and country clubs. In addition to the immediate and long-term benefits to the young people who participate, these programs have helped make the United States a top contender in competitive swimming at the international level since the 1950s. There are five standard age groups in the USS program: 10 and under, 11 and 12, 13 and 14, 15 and 16, and 17 and 18. (Many areas also have an "eight-and-under" group.) Boys and girls train together but compete separately, and they are rated separately for every event according to national standards ranging from C (lowest) to AAAA (highest). Within every age group, children and adolescents compete against others in their own rating group. The top swimmers at the local level go on to compete for championships at the regional and junior national levels, and the top swimmers in the oldest group are also eligible for competition in the senior national meets. The United States Swimming program has produced world and Olympic champions such as Mark Spitz, Janet Evans, Jenny Thompson, and Pablo Morales.

Competitive swimming promotes physical fitness, independence, and self-confidence, as well as a comfortable, healthy relationship with members of the opposite sex. Even though swimmers have less time for school-

work, their training makes them able to focus better, and they can usually get more done than their peers in a shorter amount of time. However, swim competitions also involve inevitable disappointments, and attendance at training sessions and meets requires a substantial commitment of time and effort by both children and their families and impinges on the time available for normal socializing. In addition, parents can become overly caught up in the competitive aspect of the sport and place undue pressure on their children to perform well.

Children's participation in all water activities requires **safety** precautions by both children and their parents. Every year, drowning takes the lives of approximately 600 children in the United States under the age of five and about 220 children between the ages of five and nine. (The American Academy of Pediatrics reports that about one-fourth of the older children who drown know how to swim.) The single most important safety precaution is making sure that young children playing in or near water are watched continuously: a child can go under in 10–20 seconds without making a sound. In an emergency, anyone who is not a strong swimmer should run for help rather than attempting a rescue on his own. General water safety measures also include never diving into water without being sure of its depth; never pushing anyone into the water; and keeping children from running, fighting, or riding tricycles at the edge of a pool. It is also important to keep the gates to backyard pools locked when children are not supposed to play there. Other ways to make a backyard pool safer include leaving kicking boards and buoys in the water around the clock; keeping a telephone with emergency numbers near the pool area; and keeping the water clean with pool-cleaning equipment to reduce the health risk in case water is swallowed during an emergency.

One traditional safety precaution that is now largely discounted is the popular prohibition on swimming within 30 minutes after eating. Many physicians now say that it is no more dangerous for children to swim after eating than it is for them to engage in other active pursuits.

For Further Study

Books

Bory, Eva. *Teach Your Child to Swim: An Instructional Guide to the Basics of Swimming.* New York: Simon & Schuster, 1993.

Delzeit, Linda. *Swimming Made Fun and Easy: Step by Step Advice for Beginning and Advanced Swimmers.* Dubuque, IL: Kendall/Hunt Publishing Co., 1991.

Langendorfer, Stephen, and Lawrence D. Bruya. *Aquatic Readiness: Developing Water Competence in Young Children.* Champaign, IL: Human Kinetics Publishers, 1995.

National Swimming Pool Safety Committee. *Children Aren't Waterproof.* National Swimming Pool Safety Committee, U.S. Product Safety Commission. Washington, DC, 1987.

Whitten, Phillip. *The Complete Book of Swimming.* New York: Random House, 1994.

Syphilis

A sexually transmitted disease that, if untreated, can cause permanent damage to the heart and central nervous system.

Syphilis is a **sexually transmitted disease** (STDs) caused by an organism called *Treponema pallidum.* The incidence of syphilis among adolescents has risen dramatically in recent years, yet because most adolescents infected with syphilis have no symptoms, the growing nature of the problem is not obvious. Syphilis is spread by sexual intercourse, by kissing, and by touching infected sores. Left untreated, syphilis can cause serious permanent damage to the **heart** and to the central nervous system. For these reasons, all sexually active adolescents should be routinely screened for syphilis with a blood test called VDRL or RPR.

At the onset of infection, a painless sore called a chancre sometimes appears, usually in the genital area. If an adolescent infected with syphilis develops a chancre, it will disappear in a few weeks even without treatment. The disease, however, will continue to progress.

Syphilis is treated with penicillin or another **antibiotic,** either injected or by mouth. All sexual partners should also be tested for syphilis, and an adolescent being treated for syphilis should abstain from sexual activity. Follow-up blood tests should be performed every three months to confirm that the cure is complete.

For Further Study

Organizations

National Sexually Transmitted Disease Hotline
   Telephone: toll-free (800) 227-8922
   (Free information and clinic referrals)

Books

Daugirdas, John T., M.D. *STD, Sexually Transmitted Diseases, Including HIV/AIDS.* Hinsdale, IL: Medtext, 1992.

System of Multicultural Pluralistic Assessment (SOMPA)

Assesses cognitive abilities, sensorimotor skills, and adaptive behavior.

Ths System of Multicultural Pluralistic Assessment is a system for assessing the cognitive abilities, sensorimotor skills, and adaptive behavior of children from diverse cultural backgrounds. Based on the premise that cultural, linguistic, and health factors must be taken into account when assessing a child's performance, SOMPA estimates academic potential by considering these aspects of a child's experience. The test, which is suitable for children ages 5–11, consists of two parts, one for the child and one for the parents. The Parent Interview, available in both English and Spanish, takes place in the home with the child's primary caregiver and has three components: Sociocultural Scales; the Adaptive Behavior Inventory for Children (ABIC); and Health History Inventories. The Student Assessment includes the following tests and tasks: Physical Dexterity Tasks; the **Bender Visual Motor Gestalt Test**; Weight by Height, Visual Acuity, and Auditory Acuity; and either the **Wechsler Intelligence Scale** for Children (WISC-R) or the Wechsler Preschool and Primary Scale of Intelligence (WPPSI). Student Assessment materials are collected in the school. SOMPA is untimed, but the Parent Interview generally takes about 20 minutes and the Student Assessment activities about an hour. Test results need to be interpreted by a psychologist or a trained assessment team. Separate norms are provided for black, white, and Hispanic children.

For Further Study

Books

McCullough, Virginia. *Testing and Your Child: What You Should Know About 150 of the Most Common Medical, Educational, and Psychological Tests.* New York: Plume, 1992.

Shore, Milton F., Patrick J. Brice, and Barbara G. Love. *When Your Child Needs Testing: What Parents, Teachers, and Other Helpers Need to Know about Psychological Testing.* New York: Crossroad, 1992.

Walsh, W. Bruce, and Nancy E. Betz. *Tests and Assessment.* 2nd ed. Englewood Cliffs, NJ: Prentice Hall, 1990.

Tantrums

Also called temper tantrums.

In young children, an episode of extreme anger and frustration characterized by crying, screaming, and violent body motions, including throwing things, falling to the floor, and banging one's head, hands, and feet against the floor.

Tantrums, which can occur by the age of 15 months, are most frequent between the ages of 1½ and 3. Every child has them at some point, and active, strong-willed youngsters may have as many as one or two a week. Generally, tantrums are primarily an expression of loss of control rather than an attempt at manipulation (although the latter can also be involved).

Two-year-olds are at a stage of development fraught with frustration. They have not acquired the verbal skills necessary to adequately express their emotions or even, in many situations, to make themselves understood. In addition, they can only use words to demand what they want, not to negotiate for it. They love to explore, but often they don't understand which places or objects are off limits and get scolded as a result. Although they are developing rapidly, they still lack the motor skills to do many things they would like to. They want to be independent but still require continued supervision and assistance, and their preferences are often ignored or refused by their **caregivers**. There is also a great deal of ambivalence and indecision associated with this stage of life, meaning that there is internal conflict as well as tension between the toddler and her environment. A tantrum occurs because the small child, who is still learning to cope with her feelings, is simply unable to contain strong emotions of anger, frustration, or disappointment. In some cases, children are actively discouraged from showing these feelings, which creates even more tension.

Aside from taking any measures needed to prevent danger to the child, a parent should ignore the tantrum and let it run its course. If the upset has occurred over something the child wants and has been denied, it is tempting to give in to her wishes, but this can be harmful because it teaches her that she can get what she wants by having a tantrum. Tantrums are especially unsettling for parents when they occur in a public place, which is frequently the case. Children become overstimulated more easily in busy public spaces such as the supermarket or mall and may also use the tantrum as an attempt to regain parental attention that is focused elsewhere. In spite of their embarrassment, parents should treat a public tantrum in essentially the same way they treat one at home. Whenever possible, they should remove the child to the car or some other private space to avoid inconveniencing others and attracting any more unwelcome attention, after which they should ignore the tantrum and let it run its course.

While a parent cannot stop tantrums once they are in progress, it is sometimes possible to prevent them by being alert to certain danger signs, especially fatigue and irritability, and changing plans to give the child a needed rest or change of scene. For example, a child who is getting cranky at a party or other event at which the parent is present can be taken home early. The archetypal shopping tantrum over the candy bar at the checkout counter or the elaborate toy can sometimes be countered by proposing an alternative treat or purchase instead of the flat denial that sends the child into a tantrum. Emotional upsets that occur when children are left with a **babysitter** or at **daycare** can be alleviated by preparing the child in advance for the separation and having her become familiar with the babysitter or daycare setting ahead of time. Keeping walking trips short can prevent tantrums over a child's demand to be carried.

For Further Study

Books

Eastman, Meg. *Taming the Dragon in Your Child: Solutions for Breaking the Cycle of Family Anger.* New York: Wiley, 1994.

Eisenberg, Arlene. *What to Expect the First Year.* New York: Workman Publishing, 1988.

LaFarge, Ann E. *Tantrums: Secrets to Calming the Storm.* New York: Pocket Books, 1996.

Leach, Penelope. *Your Baby and Child from Birth to Age Five.* New York: Knopf, 1989.

Ruben, Douglas H. *Bratbusters! Say Goodbye to Tantrums and Disobedience.* El Paso, TX: Skidmore-Roth Publishers, 1992.

Spock, Benjamin. *Dr. Spock's Baby and Child Care.* New York: Dutton, 1992.

Tay-Sachs Disease

A genetically transmitted disease of the central nervous system.

Tay-Sachs disease is a fatal childhood degenerative disease of the central nervous system that is genetically transmitted and found primarily among Jews of Eastern European ancestry (Ashkenazim). Tay-Sachs is caused by the absence of a particular enzyme, hexosaminidase (hex-A). Without hex-A, fatty substances (lipids) build up in the brain and interfere with the functioning of the central nervous system. The disease is named for two doctors who were pioneers in identifying and describing it. In 1881, Warren Tay, a British ophthalmologist, first noted the red spot on the retina that is a distinctive mark of the disorder. In the United States, neurologist Bernard Sachs identified the cause of the illness and discovered its prevalence among Ashkenazic Jews in 1887.

Although the disease is already present *in utero,* the symptoms do not usually become apparent until the child is about five or six months old, at which point development is arrested and starts to regress. The child stops crawling and becomes unable to sit, push himself up, or perform other simple motor activities. He becomes easily startled, exhibiting an abnormal jerking motion (myoclonus), begins to lose his vision, and develops respiratory problems. By the second year of the disease, there is severe deterioration, including blindness, paralysis, deafness, seizures, and dementia, followed by death, usually between the ages of three and five.

Tay-Sachs is transmitted by a recessive gene present in both parents, even though they do not have the disease themselves. For the disease to be passed on, both parents must be carriers. However, if even one parent is a carrier, the child has a 50% chance of also being a carrier. If both parents are carriers, their child has a 25% chance of being born with the disease. Although Tay-Sachs has been reported among other groups, including Amish and Italian Catholics, it is primarily found in Jews of Eastern European descent, in whom it is 100 times more frequent than in the general population. The average person has a one in 300 chance of being a carrier; an Ashkenazic Jew's chance of carrying the disease is about one in 30.

In the early 1970s, a pilot program was set up for genetic screening of potential Tay-Sachs carriers, who have visibly lower levels of the hex-A enzyme than non-carriers, although they have enough to prevent the lipid build-up that produces the disease. Testing centers were set up in Baltimore, Maryland, and an extensive educational campaign was launched in the Jewish community. More than 60,000 couples had their blood tested for levels of hex-A, and the screening identified a number of carriers of the disease. Since then, the International Tay-Sachs Disease Testing, Quality Control, and Data Collection Center has established and monitored testing centers throughout the world, and nearly one million young adults, both Jews and non-Jews, have been tested for the disease. The incidence of Tay-Sachs in the United States and Canada has plummeted from 60 new cases per year before 1970 to only three to five cases by the early 1990s—a 90% reduction. Couples who are carriers, and who decide to conceive, can learn in advance through **amniocentesis** whether their child will have the disease. More than 100 hospitals and clinics throughout the United States provide genetic screening for Tay-Sachs on an ongoing basis. Currently, approximately 62,000 persons worldwide are tested for the disease each year, 35,000 of them in the United States. Due to dramatic effectiveness of this testing program in reducing the incidence of the disease, it is considered a model for the application of genetic screening programs for other diseases.

One surprising discovery has been that the prevalence of Tay-Sachs disease among French-Canadian Catholics, which had received little attention until very recently, is roughly equal to that of Ashkenazic Jews. In a medical breakthrough of special significance for Catholic couples, who are unwilling to abort a pregnancy for religious reasons, a physician in Virginia has developed a procedure for screening an egg fertilized in a laboratory to determine if the child will be born with the disease. If it is found to be healthy, the pre-**embryo** can then be implanted in the mother's womb, and the parents can be assured of giving birth to a healthy baby.

At present there is no treatment for Tay-Sachs. Attempts to inject patients with the missing enzyme hex-A have failed because the substance was not absorbed by the brain after entering the bloodstream. Research on a cure is currently underway in the United States, Europe, and South Africa, with new hope provided by ongoing advances in molecular genetics and other relevant fields. The National Tay-Sachs and Allied Diseases Association (NTSAD), founded in 1958, promotes research, testing, and public education about the disease.

For Further Study

Books

Brown, Fern G. *Hereditary Diseases*. New York: Franklin Watts, 1987.

Organizations

National Tay-Sachs and Allied Diseases Association, Inc.
Address: 385 Elliot Street
Newton, MA 02164
Telephone: (617) 964-5508
(Booklets available from the National Tay-Sachs and Allied Diseases Association include "What Every Family Should Know," and "Services to Families.")
Center for Jewish Genetic Disease, Division of Medical Genetics of Mount Sinai Medical Center
Address: 100 Street at Fifth Avenue
New York, NY 10029
Telephone: (212) 241-6947

Teacher Training/Competency

Education and training required for teacher certification.

Each of the 50 states has specific qualifications for becoming a teacher and enforces a system of certification and licensure for public school teaching. While these qualifications vary, all require at least a bachelor's degree and some specialized training. Many states also require teachers to train as substitutes or in an apprentice role for a prescribed period. Still, there is a growing sense that teachers are not qualified, or not as qualified as they could be. Remarkably, this feeling is even prevalent among teachers themselves. A 1990 study reported in *Comparative Education* found that only 47% of natural sciences teachers felt that they themselves were qualified to teach their courses. The same study found that in England 80% felt qualified, 95% of Japanese natural science teachers considered themselves qualified, and in Germany 91% felt qualified. Similarly, only 42% of American teachers felt qualified to teach their math assignments. While these numbers at first may appear shocking, they reflect a widespread concern that has been voiced from various arenas over the last couple of decades: American public education is facing tremendous challenges.

One reason often cited for the failings of American public education is the relatively low status afforded teachers in our highly commercialized, highly corporate culture. In other industrialized countries, teachers are held in much higher esteem and are correspondingly paid at a much higher rate. During the 1980s, American teachers' salaries were roughly equal to that of the average factory worker. Canadian teachers during the same period earned 40% more than the average factory worker,

Danish teachers earned 28% more, and Japanese teachers earned 77% more than the average factory worker. In considering these figures, it is important to keep in mind that factory workers in most other industrialized countries earn much better livings than factory workers in the United States, where the power of labor has been on the decline for some years.

Low cultural esteem and low pay combine to force many highly qualified and highly educated people to turn away from careers in teaching in the United States. The cream of the academic crop may seek more lucrative careers. A 1991 survey of college graduates who had taken the Armed Forces Qualifying Test showed that graduates with the lowest IQs were more than twice as likely to go into education than those with the highest IQs.

Critics who observe teacher training note the relative ease of acceptance to American universities. In most industrialized countries of Western Europe and Japan, high school students must pass one or more difficult, highly competitive examinations to be granted entrance to the university system. These exams are much more rigorous than anything American students must pass, and they determine at a quite young age whether a student has the intellectual skills necessary for college entrance. In the United States, on the other hand, many state-funded universities have open admissions policies, which basically means that if you have a high school diploma you can be admitted to the university. While this attitude follows the American ideal of equality of opportunity and strikes many people as a more just and humane system than the Western European/Japanese model of academic and social stratification, it produces high school and college graduates with minimal reading and writing skills. This system also produces a large number of college dropouts. In the U.S., only about half of the students who enter four-year colleges earn a degree within six years.

In the area of technology and its useful application, U.S. teachers also face problems of competency. **Computers** have been in American classrooms for more than a decade now, but teachers still struggle to understand their usefulness. At first, many computers were simply glorified **video games** and typewriters, which many students were more adept with than their teachers. In the last several years, with the proliferation of the Internet, however, this has started to change. Computers have been recognized as valuable tools for research and instruction. Yet, teacher training on the use of new technology is inadequate in most cases. Often, teachers are trained in software or hardware but not given adequate instruction on applying this knowledge to student tasks. In a 1995 survey conducted by *Electronic Learning* magazine, teachers reported that 66% of their recent training sessions were on software packages or the workings of hardware, while only 21% focused on **curriculum**. Fourteen percent of teachers reported that they are "not very satisfied" with the level of training they were receiving in computer technology. Forty-six percent of teachers reported that they received no compensation for attending training sessions, and only 17% reported that they could consider such sessions part of their mandatory continuing education requirements.

Solutions

Of course, many teachers are highly qualified and committed to their careers, despite these social and cultural disincentives. Despite the grim picture many critics paint, there are many proposals for fixing the crisis. One is that teacher certification standards should be stiffened. In some states, economic incentives are used to encourage teachers to pursue graduate training in the subject they teach. (Almost no states require, for instance, that science teachers have advanced degrees in science.) Some people have even suggested that teachers be required to have a degree in the subject they teach along with their teaching degree. This suggestion has problems, however, considering the low pay offered to teachers in the United States. In 1994, Congress passed Goals 2000: Educate America Act, a broad, non-binding resolution outlining the federal governments' vision of where public education should be headed in the year 2000. Goal Four of the Act deals with teacher education and professional development, and focuses on curriculum and reforms in teacher training.

Another approach to school reform is privatization, advocated by free marketeers from Congress and the business world. Turning the schools over to the private sector, they maintain, would lead, among other things, to better trained teachers. One such advocate, Philip Geiger, president of Education Alternatives, suggests what he euphemistically refers to as "rightsizing" the teaching force while instituting broad programs of professional development. He writes, in a 1996 issue of *American School and University,* "The private sector has learned that productivity and profits can grow when downsizing is accompanied by increased spending for training." He, and many privatization advocates like him, believe that the increased profits downsizing has brought to the corporate world are equivalent to higher quality education in school systems. Some of Geiger's solutions to cost-effective staff development include working lunch meetings, organizing research teams among teachers, having teachers trade classrooms to get a feel for other subjects and approaches, and having teachers teach each other.

For Further Study

Books

Sikula, John, et al. *Handbook of Research on Teacher Education.* 2nd ed. New York: Macmillan, 1996.

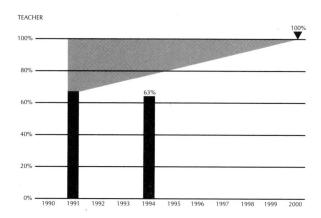

TEACHER

Goals 2000: Educate America Act. In 1991, the goal was set by the US Department of Education to have 100% of high school teachers holding degrees in the subject they teach. By 1994, only 63% of the high school teachers held such degrees, a 3% loss from 1991.

HIGH SCHOOL TEACHERS WITH DEGREES IN THE MAIN SUBJECT THEY TEACH			
Goal	**Baseline (1991)**	**1994**	**Goal for 2000**
Teachers, percent of total	66%	63%	100%

Note: Includes secondary school teachers whose main teaching assignment was in mathematics, science, English, social studies, fine arts, foreign language, or special education.

Source: National Education Goals Panel, 1996.

Periodicals

Geiger, Philip. "The Politics of Professional Development," *American School and University* 68, April 1996, p. 40.

"Good Kopp or Bad Kopp: The Hubbub over Teach for America," *New Yorker* 70, October 17, 1994, pp. 46–47.

McAdams, Richard. "Teaching Our Teachers: Lessons from Abroad," *The Clearing House* 68, July/August 1995, pp. 353–55.

Siegel, Jessica. "The State of Teacher Training," *Electronic Learning* 14, May/June 1995, pp. 43–51.

Television and Aggression

The effect of television violence on children has been studied extensively since the 1950s, and most researchers agree that what children see on television does cause behavioral changes. In 1982, the National Institute of Mental Health concluded that there was no question that television violence causes aggression; in 1992, the **American Psychological Association** concurred. In response to such findings, the television industry has pledged on several occasions to cut back on violent programming. Nevertheless, violent acts continue to appear in children's programs.

The average American child watches 27 hours of television a week. Many television programs that depict violent behavior are broadcast during hours when children are most likely to be watching. According to a study conducted by the National Coalition on Television Violence in 1992, some prime time television programs average at least one violent act per minute, while children's cartoons average 32 violent acts per hour. The **American Academy of Pediatrics** concluded that the number of violent acts on television tripled during the 1980s, and in 1993 the American Psychological Association estimated that the average child will have seen 8,000 murders and 100,000 acts of violence on television before finishing elementary school.

Although there have been cases of "copy-cat" crimes, where an actual murder or **suicide** is said to have been triggered by a specific television incident, a direct correlation between what a person sees and does is difficult to prove. Since the 1950s more than 3,000 studies have been dedicated to tracing more indirect links between actual violence and televised violence. Some researchers have employed a laboratory setting where children watched either violent cartoons or more passive children's programming, and then measured the children's agressiveness. Much research has been done comparing communities without television (such as a town in a remote part of Canada) to similar communities with television. Researchers have also compared crime rates and indicators of violence and aggression in communities before and after television became available. Such studies concluded that verbal and physical aggressiveness increased in children exposed to television. One long-term study, carried out by a psychiatrist at the University of Michigan, tracked hundreds of children from age eight to age 30, and the ones who watched the most television were the most aggressive, were more likely to be convicted of a serious crime, and were prone to use violence to punish their children.

Other studies have found concomitant effects. Children may become more aggressive as well as more fearful of becoming a victim of violence. Children may also become desensitized to violence and not react to help someone who is in trouble. Not only does exposure to television violence stimultate antisocial behavior in children, it also seems to block prosocial, altruistic behavior.

Other researchers note a difference between the way violence is depicted on television and in movies, and the way violence is portrayed in literature, from fairy tales to Shakespeare, noting that television violence often seems to be without consequences. It is not portrayed as tragic or symbolic and seems an easy solution to a difficult situation. There is little differentiation between a hero's and a villain's use of violence, and realisitc portrayals of injured victims and perpetrators, grieving relatives and friends, as well as other tragic consequences of violence are often not dramatized. Children who absorb these lessons from television may not realize that violence hurts, and they may not be aware that there are nonviolent means to resolving a conflict.

In the face of such accumulated evidence—that exposure to television violence has a variety of harmful effects on children—parents may wonder what they can do. There have been recurring attempts by public interest groups to censor television violence or to persuade television industry executives to agree to censor themselves. Such campaigns run into problems, not only with issues of free speech, but also with accountability, as the television industry claims to be providing what their viewers want and to be reflecting a violent society, rather than creating one. Since television is broadcast indiscriminately, not just to children or parents of children, any attempt to regulate what some people watch will impinge on the freedom of others to view what they want. Some recent proposals for federal regulation of television violence, short of direct censorship, advocate a ratings system, similar to that for movies, which will include warnings, before broadcasts, about the possible ill effects of viewing violence. Consumer groups have also called for a public health campaign in schools to help children deal with the issues of violence and aggressive behavior.

It is also possible for parents to block out television programs they do not want their children to see. Since 1984, all cable companies have been required to offer a lock box that prevents certain programs from being received. These locking devices are becoming more sophisticated, with the advent of the so-called "V-chip"—a computer chip that can be programmed to block out programs with violent content.

Several groups, such as the National Parent Teacher Association (NPTA) and the American Academy of Pediatrics, have issued guidelines for parents concerned about what their children see on televison. Both organizations recommend that children be limited to no more than one or two hours of television a day, and that parents watch TV with their children. Parents can discuss any violent acts they see on television, explain to their children that violent stunts are faked, and encourage children to watch nonviolent shows. Parents can complain to local television stations about programs or incidents that trouble them. With proper supervision, parents can limit the amount of violence their children are exposed to, and help children put television violence into its proper context.

For Further Study

Books

Huesmann, L. Rowell, and Leonard D. Eron, eds. *Television and the Aggressive Child: A Cross National Comparison.* Hillsdale, New Jersey: Lawrence Erlbaum Associates, 1986.

Reiss, Albert J. Jr., and Jeffrey A. Roth, eds. *Understanding and Preventing Violence.* Washington, DC: National Academy Press, 1993.

—A. Woodward

Temper Tantrums *see* **Tantrums**

Temperament

Individual differences in human motivation and emotion that appear early in life.

Psychologists have long argued about what causes differences in personality. In earlier centuries, theorists like Galen have invoked nature, claiming that a difference in the humours or fluids in the bodies was responsible for personality. During most of the twentieth century, political ideology, discoveries about the learning or conditioning capabilities of infants, and the emergence of psychoanalytic theory, which emphasized the importance of early experience, all combined to discredit biological explanations for human motivation and emotion. Nurture and socialization became the explanations of favor.

In the latter half of this century, there has been a resurgence of interest in the contribution of temperament to children's development. Although a number of theorists have their own distinctive definitions, temperament is generally agreed to be a source of individual differences in emotions or motivations (i.e., not cognitive or intellectual) that are biologically based and inherent in the individual, that may be genetic, and that appear early in life. Temperament may be considered the biological contribution to personality. It is a predisposition that allows two individuals to experience the same objective event very differently within the range of normal behavior and development. Temperament is a source of individual differences, not abnormalities or psychopathologies.

Many factors have lead to this renewed interest in the idea of temperament. Scientists have uncovered the role of many neurochemicals in the brain and their link to behavior. Studies on animals have identified genetically mediated strain differences in physiology and behavior

that have provided clues about human temperament. Certainly, one of the most important influences was the work of two clinicians whose interest was in the role of temperament in mental health.

The New York Longitudinal Study. Suspecting that inherent individual differences among their young patients contributed to their developmental path. Child psychiatrists Alexander Thomas and Stella Chess designed a study that would challenge the nature-nurture dichotomy. Beginning in 1956, Thomas and Chess collected longitudinal data from over 100 children, following them from infancy through early adulthood. Using extensive clinical interviews to gather information about children's behavior as well as parents' values and expectations, they examined the **goodness of fit** between the individual child and his or her environment.

Even in infancy, the investigators found that children could be rated on each of nine dimensions: activity level, rhythmicity or regularity in biological functions like eating and sleeping, the tendency to approach or withdraw, adaptability, threshold of responsiveness (degree of stimulation required to evoke a response from the child), intensity or energy level of reactions, quality of mood, distractibility and attention span, and persistence. Moreover, the pattern of children's ratings on each of these nine dimensions combined to distinguish three major temperamental types.

About 40% of the NYLS sample displayed a profile marked by regularity, ease of approach to new stimuli, adaptability to change, mild to moderate mood intensity, and a preponderance of positive mood. This profile characterizes what Thomas and Chess call the easy child.

About 10% of children showed a very different profile and were called difficult children. They had irregular patterns of eating and sleeping, withdrew negatively to new stimuli, did not adapt easily to change, and were of intense mood which was often negative.

Children who were slow-to-warm-up comprised the third temperamental group, about 15% of the sample. These children tended to withdraw negatively from new stimuli and had difficulty adapting to change, but their reactions were of mild intensity and would gradually become neutral or positive with repeated exposures to the new event or item.

Clearly, these three temperamental types did not include all of the variation seen in children across the entire sample. About one-third of the children showed mixed profiles. Nonetheless, these temperamental classifications have become highly influential in child development research. Perhaps, however, the greatest contribution of the NYLS was the emphasis on "goodness of fit," that is, that the temperament of the child alone was not the most important consideration in the child's growth and development, but the extent to which that temperament fit with the values, expectations, and style of the child's family.

Trait approaches. Many approaches to the study of temperament are **trait** approaches that assume that temperamental qualities can be rated on continuous dimensions across individuals. David Buss and Robert Plomin consider temperament to be heritable, stable personality profiles, that is, profiles that are genetically influenced and relatively unchanging over time. They have used maternal questionnaires to gather information on children's emotionality, activity, and sociability, traits they regard as the fundamental dimensions of temperament. Interestingly, Buss and Plomin have suggested that children who are rated as extreme on these dimensions may be qualitatively different from those more toward the middle.

Basic emotions are at the core of H. Hill Goldsmith and Joseph Campos's conception of temperament. They describe temperament as individual differences in the likelihood of experiencing and expressing the primary emotions. Goldsmith and Campos, however, emphasize the temporal and intensive characteristics in addition to frequency of emotional experience, i.e., how quickly and how intensely does a child feel an emotional response?

Mary Rothbart has emphasized reactivity and self regulation as core processes in organizing temperamental profiles. These processes, she believes, can be seen in infant behaviors—smiling, distress to limitations, fear, activity level, soothability, and duration of orienting. Her Infant Behavior Questionnaire is one of the most widely used methods of infant temperament assessment.

Goldsmith and Rothbart have collaborated to develop an assessment tool to gauge temperamental dimension based on systematic observations of behaviors elicited under standard laboratory conditions (for example, how does a child react to a mechanical spider?). The development of an observational protocol to assess temperamental characteristics offers an advantage over reliance on questionnaires. When parents describe their children's behavior, they do so from a subjective frame of mind and their reports include many sources of information so that reports of the child's behavior are not independent from the parent's biases, values, or expectations.

Type approaches. Another major approach to the study of temperament assumes that the critical distinctions are among types of people characterized by different profiles of behaviors. Even though the behaviors can be rated on continuous scales, their combinations create temperamental categories of children. An analogy can be found in the measurement of sex-related hormones in the blood; any child's scores could be placed on a continuous scale. However, the combinations of these hormones are characteristic of two categorically different types of child: boys and girls.

Jerome Kagan and his colleagues have studied two types of children, their development through adolescence, and the infant profiles that predict the emergent behavior at later ages. At early ages, inhibited children cling to their mothers and may cry and hesitate when confronted with unfamiliar persons or events. These children appear to be timid and shy, and comprise about 20% of volunteer Caucasian samples. Uninhibited children, on the other hand, approach new events and persons without hesitation or trepidation. They appear fearless and sociable, and comprise about 40% of volunteer samples.

Observations of these children over time indicate that these characteristic profiles tend to continue, although the display of temperamental tendencies varies in accordance with the child's developmental level. An older inhibited child or teen, for example, may not cling to his or her mother or cry when coming to an unfamiliar laboratory, but may hesitate to talk to the examiner and may smile infrequently.

Interestingly, the behavioral profiles of these children are accompanied by physiologic profiles that implicate involvement of sites in the brain and nervous system that contribute to fear and arousal reactions. Inhibited, compared to uninhibited, children tend to have higher and more stable heart rates, higher levels of stress-related hormones like cortisol and norephinephrine, larger changes in blood pressure in response to stressors, and more tension in the physical parameters of the voice when speaking under conditions of mild cognitive stress. These differences support the contention that there are biological contributions to these temperamental categories.

Although young infants are not sufficiently mature to demonstrate timidity in response to novelty, the reactivity of the nervous system sites—presumed to underlie inhibited and uninhibited temperaments—may be stimulated at early ages. When infants are exposed to variation in sights and sounds, some become aroused and demonstrate this arousal by moving their arms and legs and fretting or crying. Other infants remain calm motorically and do not cry. Those who are highly reactive to stimulation tend to become inhibited in their reactions to novelty and uncertainty at later ages. Those whose reactivity level is low in infancy tend to grow into children who are able to remain relaxed in novel situations so that they appear outgoing and uninhibited.

Malleability. It is important to remember that continuity of temperamental profiles from infancy through later ages is a group phenomenon, that is, individual children may change and become more or less inhibited while the groups of children remain distinct on average. Neither temperament nor biology is destiny. Temperament and environment both influence development, although there are few studies of the interaction of these two sources of influence.

In one such study, Doreen Arcus observed infants in their homes over the first year. She found that young infants who were highly reactive were less likely to become timid and inhibited one-year-olds when their mothers were firm and direct in their limit-setting behavior in response to infant transgressions like pulling at plants or getting into the cat food. Conversely, high reactive infants tended to become fearful and inhibited when their mothers were highly permissive and indirect in their discipline. When high reactive children learned to cope with the minor stresses of discipline in the warmth and security of their homes, they were, apparently, better able to cope with the stress of unfamiliar situations at a later age.

Temperaments have also been thought to moderate the effects of certain kinds of experiences. For example, in her longitudinal study of children at risk for developmental problems, Emmy Werner found that an easy, sociable temperament tended to provide a protective buffer for children growing up in difficult circumstances. How might temperament shield a child from negative environmental effects? Children who are sociable and adaptable are likely to evoke positive reactions from individuals in the environment and to establish alliances with teachers or other adults. These children are not too timid to ask for help when they need it. Acknowledging the interactions of both temperament and environment during development should make possible continued progress in our understanding of the intricate multiple influences of children's lives and growth.

For Further Study

Books

Arcus, D. (forthcoming). *The Roles of Temperament and Family Experience in Early Development.*

Buss, D. and R. Plomin. *Temperament: Early Developing Personality Traits.* Hillsdale, New Jersey: Erlbaum, 1984.

Campos, J.J., K.C. Barrett, M.E. Lamb, H.H. Goldsmith, and C. Stenberg. "Socio-Emotional Development." In M.M. Haith and J.J. Campos (eds.), Infancy and Developmental Psychobiology vol. 2, *Handbook of Child Psychology* edited by P.H. Mussen, New York: John Wiley, 1983, p. 783-915.

Chess, S. and A. Thomas. *Origins and Evolution of Behavior Disorders: From Infancy to Early Adult Life.* Cambridge, MA: Harvard, 1987.

Goldsmith, H.H., and J.J. Campos. "Fundamental Issues in the Study of Early Temperament." In M.E. Lamb and A. Brown (eds.), *Advances in Developmental Psychology,* Hillsdale, New Jersey: L. Erlbaum, 1986, p. 231-283.

Kagan, J. *Galen's Prophecy.* New York: Basic, 1994.

Rothbart, M.K. "Temperament in Childhood." In G.A. Kohnstamm, J.E. Bates, and M.K. Rothbart (eds.). *Temperament in Childhood.* Chichester: Wiley, 1989, p. 59-76.

Thomas, A. and S. Chess. *Temperament and Development.* New York: Brunner Mazel, 1977.

Werner, E.E., and R.S. Smith. *Vulnerable but Invincible: A Longitudinal Study of Resilient Children and Youth.* New York: McGraw-Hill, 1982.

—Doreen Arcus, Ph.D.
University of Massachusetts Lowell

Teratogen

Environmental agent that interrupts the normal development of an organism, especially a fetus.

A teratogen, also referred to as a teratogenic agent, is an environmental agent that can cause abnormalities in a developing organism, resulting in either fetal death or congenital abnormality. The human **fetus** is separated from the mother by the placental barrier, but the barrier is imperfect and permits a number of chemical and infectious agents to pass to the fetus. Well-known teratogens include (but are not limited to) alcohol, vitamin A and retinoic acid in excessive doses, the **rubella** virus, the syphilis bacterium, and high levels of ionizing radiation. In the 1960s, it was discovered that the tranquilizer **thalidomide** had serious side effects when taken during pregnancy. Although thalidomide was never sold legally in the United States, it was available elsewhere in the world and prescribed freely during the 1940s and 1960s. It was later shown to induce **birth defects,** especially severe limb abnormalities known as phocomelia, in children whose mothers took the drug.

In the 1970s, a study of birth defects among babies born to women who had taken lithium during at least the first trimester of pregnancy seemed to link lithium to birth defects, especially in congenital cardiovascular abnormalities. However, subsequent studies in the 1990s have questioned the adverse effects of lithium on fetal development. Today, many physicians treating pregnant women who take lithium as medication for a **bipolar disorder** carefully weigh the risk posed by lithium against the effects of discontinuing medication.

For Further Study

Books

Fine, Ralph. *The Great Drug Deception.* New York: Stein and Day, 1972.

Kelley-Buchanan, Christine. *Peace of Mind During Pregnancy: An A–Z Guide to the Substances that Could Affect Your Unborn Baby.* New York: Dell Publishing, 1989.

Roskies, Ethel. *Abnormality and Normality: The Mothering of Thalidomide Children.* Ithaca, New York: Cornell University, 1972.

Test Anxiety

A condition characterized by persistent anxiety in test situations that is severe enough to seriously interfere with performance.

Physical symptoms of test anxiety include a rapid heartbeat, dry mouth, sweating, stomach ache, dizziness, and desire to urinate. The anxiety interferes with concentration and **memory**, making it difficult or impossible to recall previously memorized material and resulting in test performance that does not accurately reflect a child's intelligence or the amount of effort spent preparing for the exam. Often, the memorized material is recalled once the test is over and the child leaves the classroom.

Young people with text anxiety are usually conscientious students who work hard and have high expectations of themselves. The condition may begin with inadequate performance on a particular test, which then creates a general fear of the testing situation that hampers future performance, creating a vicious cycle of anxiety and low scores. Very creative students may develop test anxiety when unorthodox responses to questions result in low grades that make them question their own abilities and intelligence. Test anxiety can interfere significantly with a child's academic accomplishment and impair confidence and **self-esteem**. Parents of children who are suffering from this condition should try to get them to talk about it (often they don't tell anyone, and parents and teachers think the cause of their low test grades is underpreparation). Sometimes teachers are willing to consider alternative testing procedures, such as oral exams instead of written tests. In some cases, test anxiety can be reduced or eliminated by having a child work on test-taking skills, such as strategies for answering different types of questions, and then hone them through practice testing (including timed testing if this is a source of apprehension). Both creating and taking practice tests can help defuse anxiety by demystifying the test experience. If the problem doesn't improve, the child's pediatrician may recommend treatment by a behavior therapist aimed at changing the way a child thinks about and responds to tests.

Behavior and **cognitive behavior therapy** offer a variety of strategies to counter test anxiety. A more positive mental image of tests can be developed by having the child pretend to take a test while "playing school" with a friend or sibling, using props such as books, pencils, notebooks, and makeshift classroom furniture. Mental imagery can also be used, with the child imagining herself in a test situation while she is in a relaxed state in order to begin associating feelings of relaxation with test taking. This technique can be worked into a program of gradual desensitization, in which the child develops the ability to remain relaxed while experiencing a sequence of increasingly anxiety-producing situations related to test taking. A typical sequence might be: 1) imagine taking a test; 2) take various kinds of mock tests; 3) practice taking a timed test; 4) sit in the classroom where an actual test will be given and imagine you are taking it; and 5) take an actual untimed test. A list of positive statements ("self-talk" or "affirmations") can be created to counter anxiety, such as "I have studied and I know the material well," "this test is only one part of my grade," and "if I take a deep breath I will remember what I have studied." These can be taken to school on a note card at test time and, with teacher permission, they can be displayed on the desk and the student can be instructed to repeat them to help counter anxiety.

Other techniques that have been used to treat test anxiety include hypnotherapy and biofeedback. The beta blocker Inderal, taken on an as-needed basis, has helped adolescents overcome anxiety in test situations.

For Further Study

Books

Erwin, Bette, and Elza Teresa Dinwiddie. *Test Without Trauma: How to Overcome Test Anxiety and Score Higher on Every Test.* New York: Grosset and Dunlap, 1983.

Hayes, Jeri, ed. *How to Get Better Test Scores [Grades 3-4; 5-6; 7-8].* New York: Random House, 1991.

Testing *see* **Assessment**

Test of Adolescent Language (TOAL)

Assesses language skills and acquired vocabulary.

The Test of Adolescent Language is an individually administered test of language skills and acquired vocabulary for students in grades 6–12. It can aid in identifying specific areas where students need help and in diagnosing **learning disabilities**. There are eight subtests with questions requiring both oral and written responses and involving a variety of activities, such as matching words and pictures, identifying similar sentence structures, and using words in sentences. The test yields composite scores in the following 10 areas: listening, speaking, reading, writing, spoken language, written language, vocabulary, grammar, receptive language, and expressive language. Results are converted from raw scores to percentile rankings and expressed as an Adolescent Language Quotient (ALQ). The test is untimed and usually takes about 1-½ hours.

For Further Study

Books

McCullough, Virginia. *Testing and Your Child: What You Should Know About 150 of the Most Common Medical, Educational, and Psychological Tests.* New York: Plume, 1992.

Shore, Milton F., Patrick J. Brice, and Barbara G. Love. *When Your Child Needs Testing: What Parents, Teachers, and Other Helpers Need to Know about Psychological Testing.* New York: Crossroad, 1992.

Walsh, W. Bruce, and Nancy E. Betz. *Tests and Assessment.* 2nd ed. Englewood Cliffs, NJ: Prentice Hall, 1990.

Wodrich, David L., and Sally A. Kush. *Children's Psychological Testing: A Guide for Nonpsychologists.* 2nd ed. Baltimore, MD: Brookes Publishing Co., 1990.

Test of Language Development (TOLD)

Assesses spoken language skills.

The Test of Language Development (TOLD) is an individually administered oral-response test that assesses the spoken language skills of children ages 4–12. The Primary Version is used with ages 4-8 years and 11 months. The Intermediate level is for ages 8 1/2 to nearly 13. TOLD is sometimes used as a language achievement test but mostly given to identify strengths and areas that need work and to aid in diagnosing mental retardation as well as speech delays, articulation problems, and other language disorders. The 170-item test involves a variety of activities including defining words, pronunciation, word/picture identification, and sentence imitation. Seven subtests cover the following areas: Picture Vocabulary (25 questions), Oral Vocabulary (20 questions), Grammatic Understanding (25 questions), Sentence Imitation (30 questions), Grammatic Completion (30 questions), Word Articulation (20 questions), and Word Discrimination (20 questions). The test is untimed but usually takes 40 minutes. Results are reported in terms of standard scores, percentile rankings, age equivalents, and a language quotient. Subtest scores are combined to produce assessments in the following areas: overall spoken language; listening (receptive language); speaking (expressive language); semantics (word meanings); and syntax (grammar).

For Further Study

Books

McCullough, Virginia. *Testing and Your Child: What You Should Know About 150 of the Most Common Medical,*

Educational, and Psychological Tests. New York: Plume, 1992.

Shore, Milton F., Patrick J. Brice, and Barbara G. Love. *When Your Child Needs Testing: What Parents, Teachers, and Other Helpers Need to Know about Psychological Testing.* New York: Crossroad, 1992.

Wodrich, David L., and Sally A. Kush. *Children's Psychological Testing: A Guide for Nonpsychologists.* 2nd ed. Baltimore, MD: Brookes Publishing Co., 1990.

Testosterone

Testosterone, the principal male sex hormone, is produced in the testes.

Testosterone, an androgen, is necessary for the development of external genitals in the male fetus. In addition, increased levels of testosterone in males during **puberty** trigger the development of secondary sexual characteristics such as facial hair and a deepening voice. If the testes are not able to produce adequate amounts of testosterone, puberty does not occur. The testes may be damaged by injury, illness (mumps), chemotherapy, or radiation therapy. In **Klinefelter's syndrome**, which occurs in one in 600 males, the testes do not develop normally. In order to induce and maintain male secondary sex characteristics, adolescents with Klinefelter's and other conditions that prevent the testes from producing adequate amounts of testosterone must be treated with synthetic testosterone.

For Further Study

Books

Avraham, Regina. *The Reproductive System.* New York: Chelsea House, 1991.

—Gail B. Slap, M.D.
University of Pennsylvania School of Medicine

Tests of General Educational Development (GED)

Measures literacy and computational skills compared to most high school graduates.

The Tests of General Education Development are a battery of tests designed to measure an individual's literacy and computational skills against those of most high school graduates, and a requirement for a General Equivalency Degree. The GED test was first developed in 1942 to help veterans who hadn't finished high school. Today about 800,000 people, mostly civilians, take the test each year and roughly 70% pass. The GED is offered at special testing centers throughout the United States, and each state sets its own standard for passing, although a passing grade is generally supposed to indicate that an individual's skills are equivalent to those of the upper two-thirds of the students currently graduating from American high schools. The American Council on Education, which sponsors the tests, stresses that they are geared toward broad concepts and general knowledge rather than memorization of precise facts and definitions to avoid penalizing those who have been out of school for a while. The latest version of the GED was introduced in 1988. It consists of five parts containing five-item multiple-choice questions (except for an essay section that is new in this version of the test). The Writing Skills test consists of a grammar section and the writing sample, a 200-word essay on an assigned topic. The Social Studies section covers history, economics, political science, geography, and behavioral science. The Science section is equally divided between life and physical science. A section on Interpreting Literature and the Arts (formerly Reading) consists of questions on both popular literature and on 19th- and 20th-century classics. Half the questions on the Mathematics test are on arithmetic while the other half covers algebra and geometry. GED test results are converted from raw scores to standard scores ranging from 20 to 80 for each test. To pass the GED in most states, an individual must get a minimum total standard score of 225 on all five tests with no score under 35 on any single test. Persons who fail one or more of the tests can retake only those sections for a passing score.

For Further Study

Books

McCullough, Virginia. *Testing and Your Child: What You Should Know About 150 of the Most Common Medical, Educational, and Psychological Tests.* New York: Plume, 1992.

Shore, Milton F., Patrick J. Brice, and Barbara G. Love. *When Your Child Needs Testing: What Parents, Teachers, and Other Helpers Need to Know about Psychological Testing.* New York: Crossroad, 1992.

Walsh, W. Bruce, and Nancy E. Betz. *Tests and Assessment.* 2nd ed. Englewood Cliffs, NJ: Prentice Hall, 1990.

Wodrich, David L., and Sally A. Kush. *Children's Psychological Testing: A Guide for Nonpsychologists.* 2nd ed. Baltimore, MD: Brookes Publishing Co., 1990.

Tetanus

A serious disease characterized by painful spasms of all muscles.

Tetanus is caused by bacteria that are present everywhere in the environment and enter the body through a cut or open wound. It causes serious, painful spasms of all muscles in the body. Tetanus takes its nickname, lockjaw, from its most serious and advanced symptom—immobilization of the jaw, preventing the infected person from opening his or her mouth and from swallowing.

A vaccine to protect against tetanus is routinely administered during childhood in three doses, with the first dose at around four months of age. (*See* **Immunization.**) Further immunization against tetanus is needed, administered at ten-year intervals, through adulthood.

For Further Study

Organizations

National Institute of Allergy and Infectious Diseases (NIAID)
  Address: 9000 Rockville Pike
  NIG Building 31, Room 7A50
  Bethesda, MD 20892-2529
  Telephone: (301) 496-5717

Thalidomide

A drug known to cause severe birth defects that was never approved for use in the United States, but widely available elsewhere in the 1950s and 60s as a sedative and for treatment of nausea during pregnancy.

Thalidomide was sold in Europe, notably West Germany and Britain, in 1958. It was available without a prescription, and was advertised as a safe sedative. Pregnant women were among those who bought it on the advice of their doctors that it would lessen nausea and provide a safe aid for sleeping. Within the next three years, 12,000 infants were born in Europe and Canada with serious deformities, including missing or misshapen limbs, spinal cord defects, **cleft lip** or **palate,** eye and ear defects, and severe defects of the heart, lungs, kidneys, and digestive systems. By the end of 1961, thalidomide had been identified as the common link in thousands of these **birth defects.** (In early 1961, thalidomide was licensed for sale in Canada, but it was never approved for sale in the United States.) Thalidomide was withdrawn from the market in Europe before the end of 1961, and from the market in Canada by early 1962.

Over three decades later, scientists are reevaluating the use of thalidomide for the treatment of such diseases as **cancer** and AIDS. Thalidomide stops new blood vessels from forming, which may be effective in shrinking cancerous tumors. It also slows the production of a specific protein that the body uses to fight infection and tumors. When levels of this protein become too high, it causes **fever,** weight loss, and inflammation. By slowing the production of this protein, thalidomide may be effective in treating mouth and throat ulcers in AIDS patients and a potentially deadly immune system reaction in bone marrow transplant patients. Testing is not yet complete, but researchers believe thalidomide may be effective in treating wasting disease (severe weight loss) in AIDS patients, rheumatoid **arthritis,** lupus, Crohn's disease, and multiple sclerosis. In fact, as of the late 1990s in Canada, about 180 patients a year receive thalidomide under controlled conditions to treat marrow-transplant complications, lupus, and AIDS-related ulcers and wasting disease.

For Further Study

Periodicals

Chartrand, Sabra. "Drug Makers Test Thalidomide As a Treatment for Inflammations That Accompany Serious Diseases." *The New York Times* 146, February 24, 1997, p. C2.

Elash, Anita. "Thalidomide Is Back; A Horror Drug from the '60s May Find New Uses." *Maclean's* 110, March 10, 1997, p. 48.

Nemecek, Sasha. "Transforming Hyde into Jekyll; Researchers Redesign Thalidomide." *Scientific American* 273, November 1995, pp. 20–22.

Thematic Apperception Test

Assesses personality.

The Thematic Apperception Test is an untimed, individually administered psychological test used for personality assessment. Suitable for ages 14–40, it is used to identify dominant drives, emotions, and conflicts, as well as levels of emotional maturity, observational skills, imagination, and **creativity**. The subject is shown a series of pictures, one at a time, and asked to make up a story about each one, and his or her responses are evaluated by a trained psychologist. The test is usually given in two sessions, with 10 pictures shown in each one. Sessions are untimed but generally last about an hour. (For children ages 3–10, see **Children's Apperception Test.**)

For Further Study

Books

McCullough, Virginia. *Testing and Your Child: What You Should Know About 150 of the Most Common Medical, Educational, and Psychological Tests.* New York: Plume, 1992.

Shore, Milton F., Patrick J. Brice, and Barbara G. Love. *When Your Child Needs Testing: What Parents, Teachers, and Other Helpers Need to Know about Psychological Testing.* New York: Crossroad, 1992.

Walsh, W. Bruce, and Nancy E. Betz. *Tests and Assessment.* 2nd ed. Englewood Cliffs, NJ: Prentice Hall, 1990.

Wodrich, David L., and Sally A. Kush. *Children's Psychological Testing: A Guide for Nonpsychologists.* 2nd ed. Baltimore, MD: Brookes Publishing Co., 1990.

Thumb Sucking

A harmless childhood habit of sucking the thumb for comfort.

About half of all children suck their thumbs during infancy, with most starting in the first months of life. Ultrasound pictures of intrauterine life have even shown fetuses sucking their thumbs. Infants explore their world by putting objects in their mouths and sucking on them. Thumb sucking appears to be a natural habit of children in all parts of the world. Sucking the thumb is soothing for a small child, and many children continue this habit for comfort and security into the early school years. Thumb sucking is most prevalent in children under two, and most children give up the habit on their own by age four.

Thumb sucking by itself is not a cause or symptom of physical or psychological problems. It is not known why some children suck their thumbs longer than others. More girls than boys suck their thumbs beyond age two. Researchers speculate that boys receive stronger negative messages from parents and peers that thumb sucking is infantile and not acceptable. Thumb sucking offers security to a child, but this behavior does not imply that the child is insecure. Most children have some sort of self-comforting ritual that may involve sucking the thumb, fingers, or a **pacifier**; pulling or twisting their hair; or stroking or sucking a soft toy or blanket. These are all normal habits of infancy that are eventually outgrown.

Some 19-century physicians feared a variety of consequences from thumb sucking, such as weak moral character, and earlier generations of parents were advised to break this habit forcibly. Parents were sometimes asked to place mechanical constraints on their children's hands to keep their thumbs out of their mouths. Children's thumbs were sometimes coated with a bitter substance, taped, or covered with gloves. It was also considered necessary to shame and humiliate the thumb sucker. Modern doctors find few negative health effects of thumb sucking, even if prolonged, and parents are urged to let their children outgrow the habit on their own. Thumb sucking may be more of a problem for the parent than the child, if the parent is unsettled by the behavior. But weaning a young child from the habit before he or she is ready is usually difficult, and may only prolong the thumb sucking.

There are a few cases where thumb sucking may become a problem. If a school-age child sucks his or her thumb and is teased by classmates, the child may wish to quit, and need help, either from the parents or a counselor. Some dentists warn of misalignment of permanent teeth of a child of five or six sucks the thumb with a lot of pressure on the teeth. Not all dentists agree, however, that thumb sucking is harmful to teeth development. But if a child's dentist sees evidence that thumb sucking is causing a particular problem, the child may need to be urged to quit. If the child is having trouble quitting the habit, parents may be able to help with positive reinforcement. The child can be given a sticker or small reward for a day spent without thumb sucking. Parents can also help the child find something else to do with her hands when she has the urge to suck her thumb. Parents should avoid negative pressure on children to stop sucking their thumbs; this habit is eventually outgrown by all children. In extreme cases, some dentists can prescribe an oral device to alter the shape of the roof of the child's mouth, so that it is unpleasant for the child to continue sucking. An aluminum thumb brace has also been invented to deter children from sucking their thumbs.

For Further Study

Books

Azrin, Nathan. *Habit Control in a Day.* New York: Simon and Schuster, 1977.

Eisenberg, Arlene. *What to Expect the First Year.* New York: Workman Publishing, 1988.

Leach, Penelope. *Your Baby and Child from Birth to Age Five.* New York: Knopf, 1989.

Spock, Benjamin. *Dr. Spock's Baby and Child Care.* New York: Dutton, 1992.

Periodicals

Eberlein, Tamara. "Nervous Habits." *Redbook* 182, April 1994, pp. 178+.

Thompson, Andrea. "Those Nervous Habits." *Good Housekeeping* 221, September 1994, pp. 165+.

Tic Disorder

Sudden, repetitive, involuntary muscular movement or vocal pattern.

Tic disorders feature involuntary repetitive (but non-rhythmic) patterns, and may be either motor tics (muscle movements) or vocal tics. Although tics are involuntary, the individual with a tic disorder can often repress the tic for a period of time. The occurrences of tics appear to be more likely when the individual is under stress or concentrating on a task, such as reading or writing. Most tics seem to nearly disappear during sleep.

The *Diagnostic and Statistical Manual of Mental Disorders,* 4th edition, lists the following examples:

Both motor and vocal tics may be categorized as simple or complex, although the distinction between the two is not precise. Generally, a simple motor tic involves only one part of the body, while a complex tic is more involved and takes the form of some recognizable action. They also include imitating the actions of others and making involuntary obscene gestures. Complex vocal tics involve recognizable words or animal sounds as op-

EXAMPLES OF SIMPLE AND COMPLEX TICS

	Simple	Complex
Motor tics	eye blinking	facial gestures
	neck jerking	grooming behaviors
	shoulder shrugging	jumping
	facial grimacing	touching
	repeated coughing	stamping
		sniffing an object
		echokinesis, i.e., imitation of someone else's movements
Vocal tics	throat clearing	repeating words or phrases out of context
	grunting	coprolalia, i.e., use of socially unacceptable words, usually obscene
	sniffing	palilalia, i.e., repeating one's own sounds or words
	snorting	echolalia, i.e., repeating the last word, sound, or phrase heard
	barking	

posed to simple noises. These may include the repetition of short phrases, such as "Oh, boy," the repetition of a single word, repetition of the words of others, called **echolalia**, or involuntary swearing, known as coprolalia.

The health care professional will distinguish a tic disorder from other categories of involuntary movements, such as those that are related to other problems such as medical conditions, alcohol or drug abuse, side effects from medication, or other behavior or psychological disorders. When a tic disorder has been diagnosed, further definition of the nature and scope of the tic will be made. Factors such as age at onset and duration of the tic will be taken into account.

Transient tic disorder

As the name implies, transient tic disorder is characterized by motor or vocal tics that are not permanent and appear before age 18. The tic occurs many times a day for at least four weeks, but dissipates after no more than 12 consecutive months. Persons with transient tic disorder experience impairment in social and school settings. When the tic lasts longer than 12 months, the diagnosis may be **Tourette syndrome** or chronic motor or tic disorder.

Chronic motor or tic disorder

Chronic motor or vocal tic disorder features tics that persist for more than 12 consecutive months. The factor that distinguishes this disorder from Tourette's is that only one type of tic—motor or vocal, not both—is present. The other factors for diagnosis are the same. These include tics that first appear before age 18, occur many times a day, and persist for longer than one year. (Periods of up to three months with no tic occurrences do not rule out tic disorders). The person with chronic tic disorder is adversely affected in his or her ability to function in social or school settings because of the tic, although the impairment is usually less than for Tourette syndrome.

School-aged children with any tic disorder may have problems functioning in social and school settings. It is not uncommon for them to experience other learning difficulties such as **attention deficit/hyperactivity disorder,** or problems with visual motor integration or auditory processing. Parents and educators should be alert to warning signs of learning problems related to tic disorders to prepare for intervention and remedial help.

For Further Study

Publications

Davidovicz, Herman, et al. *Fact Sheets on Tourette Syndrome.* Bayside, NY: Tourette Syndrome Association, Inc., 1994. (Set of three fact sheets, "Learning Problems and the TS Child," "Specific Classroom Strategies and Techniques for Students with Tourette Syndrome," "Techniques To Aid Students with TS in Completing Written Assignments.")

Organizations

Tourette Syndrome Association, Inc.
    Address: 42-40 Bell Blvd.
    Bayside, NY 11361–2874

Time on Task *see* **Attention**

Time-Out Procedure

A technique in which a child is removed from activity and forced to sit alone for a few minutes, in order to calm down.

The time-out has become an increasingly popular method of dealing with children's inappropriate behavior. If a child becomes too aggressive or angry, the parent or caregiver may remove the child from the upsetting situation. Parents may have a special place in the home for time-outs—in the child's room, in a certain chair, or on a rug in an out-of-the-way place. The child may be allowed to end the time-out when he or she is ready or told to stay in the time-out place for a specific length of time. The time should be very short—a couple of minutes—as most young children cannot easily comprehend longer time spans.

The time-out is not used as a **punishment** so much as a time for the child to try to regain control of emotions. Some children can accomplish this by themselves, and being removed from a stressful play situation is all that they need. Other children may not be able to recover their equilibrium without help from an adult. The parent or caregiver may ask the child to try to calm down alone in the time-out spot, and then give attention only after the child has made some effort.

Children under three may not be mature enough to comprehend a time-out. Time-outs are more effective with preschool-age children. If time-outs are used in a preschool or daycare situation, parents may want to discuss this with the teachers or **caregivers**. It should be clear that the time-out is not punitive, and a child should not feel humiliated for having a time-out. The time-out area should not be a constraining or frightening place, such as a locked closet. The time-out should serve to teach the child to manage strong feelings safely, and after he or she has done so, the child should be praised for calming down.

There may be other techniques parents or caregivers can use before a time-out becomes necessary. If an activity is too stressful to one or more children, it may be better for all to end the activity. Changing the situation may restore tempers more readily than a spell of reflection. If children are fighting because they are hungry or tired, then that need should be addressed. Children may benefit most from a time-out if the issues of aggression or out-of-control behavior have been discussed at a time when the child was not upset. Though the goal of time-out may be to teach the child to take responsibility for controlling his or her own behavior, this may not be possible without support and comfort from parents or other concerned adults.

For Further Study

Books

Clark, Lynn. *The Time-Out Solution: A Parent's Guide for Handling Everyday Behavior Problems.* Chicago: Contemporary Books, 1989.

Corwin, Donna G. *The Time-Out Prescription: A Parent's Guide to Positive and Loving Discipline.* Chicago: Contemporary Books, 1996.

Hill, Barbara Albers. *Time-Out for Children.* Garden City Park, NY: Avery Publishing Group, 1997.

—A. Woodward

Timidity *see* **Self-Conscious Emotions, Temperament, Withdrawal Behavior**

Toilet Training

The process of learning to control the bowel and bladder and use the bathroom for elimination.

Most children are toilet trained by the age of two or two-and-a-half. Bowel control comes before bladder control, and daytime training is achieved before a child stays dry at night. Child care experts today recommend a more easy-going, low-pressure approach than was often used in the past. It has been found that when parents wait until their toddler has attained the greatest possible degree of readiness, the process is easier, faster, and accompanied by fewer lapses. The emphasis is on letting the child proceed at his own pace, motivated by the desire to be grown up and imitate his parents. Measures that may cause pressure and anxiety are avoided.

Children achieve some control over the sphincter—the muscle that controls elimination—as early as 9 months of age, and are able to cooperate in controlling themselves to some degree by the age of 12 to 15 months. However, most experts consider any training before the age of 18 months to be premature. When children are ready to be toilet trained, they exhibit certain signs of readiness, usually between the ages of two and three years. Unlike infants, they know when they are urinating or defecating and may assume certain postures or become quiet when they are about to move their bowels. They have also learned the vocabulary their family uses for elimination. Another sign is a sense of fastidiousness and desire for order that appears at this stage of development. Children are likely to ask parents to change their dirty diapers right away, and they show a general interest in orderliness that can be harnessed for purposes of toilet training. A child this age also has a pronounced desire to imitate the parent of the same sex, a trait that can be used to advantage in enticing her to use the toilet.

Pediatrician and author **T. Berry Brazelton** recommends the following steps in toilet training a child. A potty should be purchased for the bathroom floor, and the child should spend some time sitting on it, first in her clothes and then with her diaper off. The connection between what she is doing on her small potty and what the adults and siblings do on the big potty should be emphasized. Next, she should be brought to the potty with a dirty diaper and the contents should be placed in it so she can see that this is where they belong. Finally, the child can be placed on the potty if she's ready to try using it. Once the connection between the potty and the toilet has been established, the potty can be taken from the bathroom and placed where the child has easy, private access to it, for example in her bedroom or, during the summer months, in the backyard. Once she starts using it, her diapers or training pants can be left off for increasing periods of time. Some accidents will occur, and these should be treated casually.

Children are not ready for nighttime training until they can stay dry all day, or at least for four to six hours. Girls usually reach this point before boys; some girls begin to stay dry at naptime and even, occasionally, at night before the age of two. After the age of two, dry nights become more frequent: 45% of girls and 35% of boys stay dry at night at the ages of two to three. With many children, nighttime training is not done until the age of three and, in many cases, not complete until four or five. The signal from the child's bladder has to be strong enough to wake him from sleep and get him to the bathroom at least once or twice a night. As many as 25% of children have relapses after they have been dry at night for six months or longer, usually due to a temporary stressor. In a minority of children, nighttime bladder control doesn't develop until after the age of five; this often occurs in families where there is a history of **enuresis** (bedwetting).

Brazelton and other authorities on child care emphasize that toilet training should be "child-oriented." It should occur when the child is physically and emotionally ready, interested, and motivated, and it should be the child who determines the pace. If anxiety or resistance is shown at any point in the process, the parent should back off: the experience should not take the form of a power struggle between parent and child. One potential negative effect of parental coercion is that the child can hold back bowel movements, resulting in **constipation.** This in turn makes elimination uncomfortable and even painful, creating even greater reluctance and resistance on the part of the child. Severe cases of constipation can cause painful anal fissures, fecal soiling (**encopresis**), or rectal enlargement. Special measures may be required (on the advice of a pediatrician), including enemas and stool softeners. Unusual delays in toilet training normal children, or regressions to soiling, generally indicate family stress and/or underlying emotional problems and may require counseling to be effectively resolved.

The basic parental strategy of encouraging and rewarding a child's progress toward bowel and bladder control can be enhanced by certain techniques and aids. Having the child model proper toileting by "teaching" a doll or stuffed toy to use the toilet is often an effective learning device. Special read-aloud books about toilet training are popular, as are videos. Small rewards can also be offered for progress in toilet training. For many children, simply progressing from diapers to training pants and then to regular underpants is an incentive and reward in itself. The example set by other children, such as friends and older siblings, can also be a powerful motivator.

For Further Study

Books

Faull, Jan. *Mommy! I Have to Go Potty!: A Parent's Guide to Toilet Training.* Hemet, CA: Raefield-Roberts, 1996.

Frankel, Alona. *Once Upon a Potty.* Barron, 1987.

Lansky, Vicki. *Toilet Training: A Practical Guide to Daytime and Nighttime Training.* New York: Bantam, 1993.

Van Pelt, Katie. *Potty Training Your Baby: A Practical Guide for Easier Toilet Training.* Garden City Park, NY: Avery Publishing Group, 1996.

Audiovisual Recordings

It's Potty Time. Learning Through Entertainment, Inc., 1991. (One videocassette. Telephone toll-free (800) 445-5142.)

Tonic Neck Relex *see* **Neonatal Reflexes**

"Tough Love"

A behavior-modification approach to discipline.

"Tough love" is a phrase popularized in the late 1970s and early 1980s in the United States and Canada to describe a form of parenting or guidance for troubled children that holds the children responsible for their actions and compassionately forces them to face the consequences. The tough love movement was founded in the early 1980s by Phyllis and David York in the Philadelphia, Pennsylvania, area after their experiences with their troubled teenage daughter. Finding a lack of support in the social service, psychiatric, and criminal justice systems, the Yorks formed a group, known as Toughlove, with other parents of troubled teens. The Toughlove movement caught on quickly: the number of groups rose from a mere half a dozen in the Philadelphia region in 1981 to over 1,000 worldwide by the mid-1990s. Although the Toughlove movement is intentionally decentralized, there is a national network center in Doylestown, Pennsylvania, called Toughlove International.

"Tough love" is a response to children who are already involved in destructive and/or dangerous activities. The Toughlove Network is not a child-rearing clinic but rather a crisis-treatment center. Parents who have lost the respect of their children are guided to a firmer, more effective approach to parenting by other parents who have faced similar situations. The parents in Toughlove groups support each other in their efforts to regain authority in their homes. Others in the group will be present during planned confrontations, accompany parents to meetings with school or police officials, or even take others' children into their own homes while resolutions to conflicts are being worked out. In effect, Toughlove groups act as surrogate extended families in a society where most families have become isolated into nuclear units, many with only one parent.

The tough love approach to crisis treatment avoids blame, dealing with the present situation only, not its possible causes in the past. Treatment is always based on action: parents are guided and encouraged to take specific actions to address the situation, rather than simply blowing off steam by talking about it, or distracting themselves with over-analysis. Parents are empowered through the intentional decentralization and lack of hierarchical authority structure in Toughlove groups to act on their own and reclaim their personal authority. By helping parents gain or regain self-respect, tough love helps the entire family regain its necessary balance.

While tough love encourages individual empowerment and responsibility, Toughlove groups also provide much-needed support to both parents and children. The Toughlove movement emphasizes cooperation in all things, between parents, relatives, teachers, friends' parents, and the children themselves. Toughlove groups also reach out to the wider community, forging connections with social service agencies, police departments, juvenile detention centers, schools, and others to create cooperative solutions to troubled teenage behaviors. Working together, Toughlove groups in the United States, Canada, and elsewhere in the world have established drug rehabilitation centers for youths, alternative schools, and group homes. To be effective, "tough love" must be supported by others involved in the teens' lives. Otherwise, the teens simply escape the consequences of their actions by turning to an ally.

Phyllis and David York, along with counselor and educator Ted Wachtel, describe "tough love" and the tough love movement in their books *Toughlove* and *Toughlove Solutions.* Crises such as unhealthy sexual activity, incest, drug and alcohol abuse, physical abuse of parents and/or other family members, **running away**, and **suicide** are addressed, as well as potential discipline problems involved with blended and step-families, adopted children, single parents, and divorce and ex-spouses. Attention is also given to problems specific to grandparenting.

For Further Study

Books

York, Phyllis, David York, and Ted Wachtel. *Toughlove*. Garden City, NY: Doubleday and Co., 1982.

———. *Toughlove Solutions*. Garden City, NY: Doubleday and Co., 1984.

Organizations

Toughlove International

Address: P.O. Box 1069
Doylestown, PA 18901
Telephone: toll-free (800) 333-1069; (215) 348-7090

—Dianne K. Daeg de Mott

Tourette Syndrome

A genetic, neurological disorder characterized by motor and vocal tics and associated behavioral features including obsessions and compulsions and hyperactivity.

Tourette syndrome (TS) affects roughly one in every 2,500 persons. The incidence of the condition is at least three times higher in males than in females. Historically, Tourette syndrome has been a largely misunderstood condition; it has been identified as demonic possession, **epilepsy**, **schizophrenia**, and other mental disorders and was formerly thought to be the result of emotional problems due to faulty childrearing. The condition was first identified as a physiological disorder in 1885 by the French neurologist Gilles de la Tourette. Although the causes of Tourette syndrome are still not fully understood, researchers have made substantial progress in understanding and treating the condition.

Symptoms

Tics—sudden, repetitive, involuntary muscular movements—are the hallmark of Tourette syndrome, appearing in two forms: motor and vocal tics. Motor tics are uncontrollable body movements, such as blinking, grimacing, shrugging, or tossing one's head. Vocal tics, which involve the muscles that produce speech, take the form of uncontrolled speech and involuntary noises, including snorting, hissing, yelping, sniffing, grunting, throat-clearing, and yelling. For a diagnosis of Tourette syndrome to be made, the *Diagnostic and Statistical Manual (DSM-IV)* of the **American Psychiatric Association** specifies criteria, including multiple motor tics and at least one vocal tic, occurring numerous times every day or almost daily for a period of over one year, with no tic-free period longer than three months, and onset of symptoms before the age of 18. There are two basic types of tics: simple and complex. Simple tics are isolated movements (such as blinking, kicking, or twitching) that involve only one part of the body. Complex tics are more involved and take the form of recognizable actions, such as poking, hitting, biting, and grooming behaviors (such as smoothing one's hair). They also include imitating the actions of others and making involuntary obscene gestures. Complex vocal tics involve recognizable words (or animal sounds) as opposed to simple noises. These may include the repetition of short phrases, such as "Oh, boy," the repetition of a single word, repetition of the words of others (echolalia), or involuntary swearing (coprolalia), which is one of the most publicized symptoms of the disorder, although it affects fewer than 10% of people with TS.

Besides tics, there are several types of behavior often associated with Tourette syndrome. At least half the persons affected with TS show symptoms **of obsessive-compulsive disorder** (OCD), a psychological condition that involves repeated intrusive and senseless thoughts (obsessions) and repetitive behavior (compulsions) intended to stop them. An obsession may be an ordinary but inappropriately intense desire (such as a preoccupation with visiting a certain store) or an outlandish idea, such as a wish to walk across the dinner table or touch a stranger. Compulsions are pointless activities that a person with OCD can't help repeating, such as turning lights on and off, counting things over and over, or arranging objects in a certain pattern. OCD symptoms can be extremely debilitating, taking time away from normal pursuits, including schoolwork and social activities. The other major behavior disorder associated with Tourette syndrome is **attention deficit/hyperactivity disorder** (ADHD), whose symptoms include hyperactivity, inability to concentrate, and **impulse control disorders**. Some persons with Tourette syndrome have both OCD and ADHD.

Causes and onset of Tourette syndrome

Tourette syndrome, once thought to be caused by psychological problems, is now known to be a genetic disorder. About 90% of children with TS have a family history of TS or related disorders, such as other conditions involving tics. Some persons are genetic carriers of Tourette syndrome without actually having symptoms themselves (these are almost always females; roughly 99% of males who carry the genetic tendency toward the disorder develop symptoms). The biological basis for Tourette syndrome is an imbalance in the brain's neurotransmitters, chemicals that transport messages between nerve cells. The main neurotransmitter affected in people with TS is dopamine, which controls movement. Research has shown that two other neurotransmitters, norepinephrine and serotonin, also play a role in the condition. In addition, imaging techniques, such as brain scans, have shown abnormalities in the size and functioning of certain parts of the brain in persons affected by TS.

Symptoms of Tourette syndrome usually appear before the age of 18. Children with TS develop their first tics at the age of six or seven but show other signs of the disorder, including sleep problems, language difficulties, and oppositional behavior, in early childhood, often by the age of two or three. TS usually starts with a single tic, often in the head area (most frequently repeated blinking). The initial tics are generally simple motor tics in the head and upper extremities. As the disorder progresses, the tics gradually move downward to include the torso and lower extremities. Vocal tics usually begin at about the age of nine; complex vocal tics such as coprolalia are among the last to appear. Tics in people with TS are suppressed under certain conditions, usually during sleep and when an individual is engaged in an activity that requires intense concentration. In some cases, children with TS can even manage to keep their tics under control voluntarily in situations where they fear embarrassment, although this takes an immense effort and afterwards the suppressed tics emerge with even greater force than usual. The symptoms of Tourette syndrome increase through childhood and peak during adolescence, after which their intensity usually decreases. An estimated 20–30% of all children with TS outgrow the condition entirely by adulthood.

Treatment

Although there is no medical cure for Tourette syndrome, medications can relieve many of its symptoms. Currently, the medications of choice for the suppression of tics are antihypertensives, notably Catapres, which reduces tics by 60% in most patients with only minor side effects. Related drugs that have proven effective in tic suppression are Tenex, another antihypertensive, and Klonopin, an antianxiety medication. Another class of drugs, the neuroleptics (including Haldol, Orap, and Prolixin) are even more effective than antihypertensives in suppressing tics, but for most children their advantages are outweighed by side effects, including concentration and memory impairment, weight gain, and drowsiness.

In addition to drugs used for the suppression of tics, additional medications are used to treat other behavioral symptoms associated with Tourette syndrome. **Antidepressants** such as Prozac and Anafranil are effective in treating obsessive compulsive symptoms, and ADHD is commonly treated with Ritalin or other stimulants. Combining these different types of medications can be a difficult balancing act, and their effects need to be carefully monitored by both parents and physician. For example, the Ritalin used for ADHD may worsen a child's tics, and tricyclic antidepressants such as Norpramin and Anafranil may have to be considered as an alternative treatment for ADHD symptoms. Another symptom of Tourette syndrome that is sometimes treated with medi-

TOURETTE SYNDROME ASSOCIATION, INC.

The Tourette Syndrome Association (TSA) is a national voluntary non-profit membership organization whose mission it is to identify the cause, find the cure for and control the effects of Tourette Syndrome (TS). TS is a neurological disorder characterized by various motor and vocal tics, ranging from mild to severe. Members of TSA include those with the disorder, their families, and other interested and concerned individuals.

The Tourette Syndrome Association was founded in 1972 in order to disseminate information to interested individuals, health professionals and agencies in the fields of education and government and to coordinate support groups for affected individuals and their families. TSA also funds research to find the cause of TS and its ultimate cure and to find improved medications and treatments. Today its membership includes many thousands of individuals and organizations.

The activities of TSA are diverse, ranging from support and counseling to the publication of educational materials. For instance, TSA offers direct help to families in crisis situations through its National Service Response Team. In addition, the Association maintains a data base of those diagnosed with TS, sponsors a Brain Bank Program for collection of tissue needed for research, and maintains a state-by-state list of doctors who diagnose and treat TS. The Association also represents the interests of members to the government on crucial policy issues.

The Tourette Syndrome Association, Inc. has available an extensive list of publications and video tapes concerning symptoms, diagnosis and treatment options for TS discussed in detail. TSA also publishes a quarterly newsletter outlining the latest treatments, research programs and scientific discoveries.

cation is uncontrolled aggression, which may be decreased by Tegretol or lithium carbonate. Although medications are universally considered the first line of treatment for Tourette syndrome, relaxation techniques, including self-hypnosis, can also be very helpful in reducing symptoms of the disorder, which worsen with tension. Physical activity is also an excellent way for children with TS to reduce tension and work off their extra energy.

Effects on schoolwork

In spite of the variety of possible symptoms associated with Tourette syndrome, about half of all children who have the disorder require only minor adjustments in order to function successfully in school. The rest require special educational programs to accommodate their needs. TS can disrupt a child's schoolwork in a number of different ways. Tics can make it difficult to concentrate or to perform certain tasks. Ironically, the effort required to suppress them can be just as disruptive because it requires so much energy. Tics can also interfere with the normal school experience by impeding the development of social skills if youngsters feel ostracized by their peers because of their unusual behavior. OCD symptoms also interfere with school performance because preoccupation with obsessive thoughts and the time spent performing compulsive actions make it difficult for children to concentrate on and complete their academic tasks. Children whose TS symptoms include ADHD have trouble with the organizational and concentration skills and the self-control needed for successful performance in school. Fortunately, medication helps alleviate tics and symptoms of OCD and ADHD in many children, giving them a better chance of succeeding in school. However, about 40% of children with Tourette syndrome often have additional **learning disabilities** that require attention, including problems with reading, math, handwriting, and spelling. In many children with TS, educational problems peak between the ages of 11 and 13 and then gradually decrease in severity. Parents of children with Tourette syndrome whose symptoms interfere with their ability to learn in a regular classroom environment should become familiar with their children's rights to an individualized education program under Public Law 94-142, the 1975 federal law aimed at insuring an adequate education for children with special needs.

For Further Study

Books

Baton Rouge Tourette's Support Group. *Toughing Out Tourette's*. Baton Rouge, LA: Baton Rouge Tourette's Support Group, 1989.

Buehrens, Adam. *Hi, I'm Adam*. Duarte, CA: Hope Press, 1991. [Juvenile]

Bruun, Ruth Dowling, and Bertel Bruun. *A Mind of Its Own: Tourette's Syndrome, A Story and a Guide*. New York: Oxford University Press, 1994.

Comings, David. *Tourette Syndrome and Human Behavior*. Duarte, CA: Hope Press, 1990.

Fowler, Rick. *The Unwelcome Companion: An Insider's View of Tourette Syndrome*. Cashiers, NC: Silver Run Publications, 1995.

Haerle, Tracy, ed. *Children with Tourette Syndrome: A Parents' Guide*. Rockville, MD: Woodbine House, 1992.

Koplewicz, Harold. *It's Nobody's Fault: New Hope and Help for Difficult Children and Their Parents*. New York: Random House, 1996.

Kurlan, Roger, ed. *Handbook of Tourette's Syndrome and Related Tic and Behavioral Disorders*. New York: M. Dekker, 1993.

Seligman, Adam, and John S. Hilkevich, eds. *Don't Think About Monkeys: Extraordinary Stories by People with Tourette Syndrome*. Duarte, Calif.: Hope Press, 1992.

Organizations

Tourette Syndrome Association, Inc.
    Address: 42-40 Bell Boulevard
    Bayside, NY 11361-2820
    Telephone: toll-free (800) 237-0717; (718) 224-2999

Tourette Syndrome Clinic
    Address: City of Hope National Medical Center
    1500 E. Duarte Rd.
    Duarte, CA 91010
    Telephone: (818) 359-8111

Toxic Shock Syndrome (TSS)

Toxic shock syndrome (TSS) is a rare but sometimes fatal disease that occurs mainly in menstruating women who use tampons.

Toxic shock syndrome (TSS) is caused by a toxin-producing strain of bacteria called *Staphylococcus aureus* that can accumulate in the vagina during **menstruation**. Women who use high-absorbency tampons or leave a tampon in place for an extended period are at increased risk for TSS. There have also been several reported cases of TSS associated with the use of the contraceptive sponge or diaphragm. Treatment of TSS usually involves a hospital stay with intravenous fluids, **antibiotics**, and flushing of the vagina to reduce the level of toxin-producing bacteria. A teenager who experiences an episode of TSS faces a 30% chance of a repeat episode sometime in the future.

TSS is characterized by the following symptoms during menstruation:

- sudden high fever (over 101°F); nausea, vomiting, or diarrhea; blotchy, red rash that resembles sunburn; sudden drop in blood pressure (usually indicated by lightheadedness or fainting); lethargy or disorientation; severe muscle ache; and redness of the eyes, mouth, throat, or vagina.

Any woman who experiences these symptoms during tampon use should remove the tampon immediately and seek medical attention.

—Gail B. Slap, M.D.
University of Pennsylvania School of Medicine

Toys

Physical items used in play.

An estimated 2.6 billion toys are sold in the United States each year. Toys can support cognitive growth, development of **fine motor** and **gross motor skills**, and improve problem-solving and attention. The child may find extended periods of play with a toy, whether it was purchased in a store or found in the home (recycled plastic containers and empty spools of thread, for example). Most children will be happy to play with a few favorite toys—the size of the toy inventory is not critical to successful play. Parents and others who choose toys for children should take into account the following characteristics of the child for whom the toy is intended: age and developmental stage; his or her interests; ease of use of the toy (is adult supervision required); presence of younger siblings for whom the toy could pose a hazard; and whether the toy is designed for independent play or group play.

Labeling for age

The Consumer Product Safety Commission has developed guidelines for age grading of toys and related products. Most toy manufacturers use these guidelines in labeling toys and games for age-appropriateness. Manufacturers also consider recommendations of experts in child development regarding the stages of physical, emotional, and intellectual development.

Four main criteria are considered in establishing age guidelines:

- Physical skills: can the child manipulate and play with the features of the toy as it was designed?

- Understanding: can the child understand how to use the toy?

- Interest: is the toy of interest to a child of a particular age?

- Safety: is the toy safe for a child at this particular stage?

Labeling for safety

The Consumer Product Safety Commission has established a number of regulations related to toy **safety**. These are published by the American Society for Testing and Measurement (ASTM) under the safety standard known as ASTM F963. This standard is voluntary, but the majority of U.S. toy manufacturers comply with its guidelines. In fact, many incorporate a message about the toy's compliance with ASTM F963 on the toy packaging.

Infants and toddlers

Toy manufacturers consider the size of toy parts—which are likely to be put into the mouth by an older in-

TOYS FOR CHILDREN UNDER THREE

Because the youngest children are the most at risk with unsafe toys, parents and others who purchase toys for this age group should educate themselves about safety and developmental issues related to toys. Age ranges listed on product labels provide general guidelines; developmental differences among children should also be considered.

The examples listed below are generally appropriate for the age ranges provided.

Age range	Toys
1–3 months	Activity centers and mobiles attached to the crib; rattles
4–6 months	Large balls, large stacking blocks
7–9 months	Nesting boxes and cylinders; pop-up toys; high chair toys
10–12 months	Push or pull toys for the beginning walker
13–15 months	Toy telephone, toy radio; toy stroller
16–18 months	Simple toy musical instruments; pouring activities with sand or water
19–21 months	Rocking horse; easy puzzles; simple matching shapes toys
22–24 months	Make believe toys (lawn mower, kitchen appliances, doll furniture, trucks)
2–3 years	Small tricycle; kiddie basketball hoop; toy woodworking set

fant or toddler—in designing toys. Anyone purchasing a toy for the youngest children must take the choking hazard seriously and make appropriate selections. When a new toy is brought into the home or childcare setting, all wrapping material should be promptly discarded. Plastic wrapping in particular may pose a suffocation hazard to the youngest children.

The U.S. government maintains statistics on toy-related injuries and deaths. Many accidents involving toys are not caused by the toy itself; for example, a child may trip over a toy that was not put away after play. When an unsafe toy reaches the marketplace, U.S. government inspectors may discover it and order its recall; additionally, vigilant parents and caregivers can observations about toy safety to the Consumer Product Safety Commission. Manufacturers routinely cooperate with the Consumer Product Safety Commission in recalling products that are deemed unsafe or dangerous. Examples of toy recall notices issued during June and July 1997 include:

Toy description	Problem or flaw	Hazard
Toy jewelry sets	necklaces and bracelets break easily, releasing small beads; earring clasps come off easily	small beads can be inhaled, leading to death clasps are choking hazard
Water rocket toy	rockets can break apart from water pressure during filling	serious injury from flying broken rocket pieces
Infant toy	not labeled with warning about strangulation risk	strangulation risk if hung across crib or playpen
Chinese jump ropes	Metal crimp joining two ends of rope may fail	Rope may snap back if it breaks during use, causing injury to a child
Stuffed animals	Eyes may come off	Small eye parts are a choking hazard

Preschool and school-aged children

In January 1995, the U.S. Congress passed a law requiring that toys and games for young children (ages three to six) carry a warning about **choking** hazards. If the toy or game includes small parts, marbles, or balloons, the toy must be marked that it is not appropriate for children under the age of three. Toys or parts for children this age must be able to pass through a tube approximating a child's throat diameter. Beyond toddlerhood, children begin to develop their own ideas about play activities and the toys that they want. They will be influenced by what they see advertised on television and by their peers. Toy fads and television show tie-ins can be powerfully persuasive to children. Parents may experience their first opportunities to teach about **peer pressure** and independent decision-making over toy requests. Toys should be selected to stimulate play and related cognitive and physical development; fad toys are less likely to sustain play activity and support development beyond the fad stage.

For Further Study

Books

Auerbach, Stevanne. *The Toy Chest: A Sourcebook of Toys for Children.* Secaucus, NJ: Lyle Stuart, 1986.

Boehn, Helen F. *The Right Toys: A Guide to Selecting the Best Toys for Children.* New York: Bantam Books, 1986.

Fraser, Antonia. *A History of Toys.* New York: Delacorte Press, 1966.

Lederman, Ellen F. *Developmental Toys and Equipment: A Practical Guide to Selection and Utilization.* Springfield, IL: C.C. Thomas, 1986.

Periodicals

Laudan, Larry. "It's Not the Toys, Stupid. (Toys Are Not Major Cause of Children's Injuries)." *Consumers' Research Magazine* 80, February 1997, p. 36.

Audiovisual Recordings

Selecting Appropriate Toys. Derry, NH: Chip Taylor Communications, 1991.
(One 15-minute videocassette, produced by Baltimore County Public Schools.)

Organizations

American Toy Institute, Inc.
(Educational arm of the Toy Manufacturers of America, Inc.)
Address: 200 Fifth Avenue, Suite 740
New York, NY 10010
(Publishes the *TMA Guide to Toys and Play*)

Consumer Product Safety Commission
Address: Washington, DC 20207
To report an unsafe consumer product (not limited to toys)
Telephone: toll-free hotline (800) 638-2772 or (800) 638-8270 (hearing impaired)
e-mail: infocpsc.gov
website: http://www.cpsc.gov

Tracking *see* **Ability Grouping**

Trait

A stable, relatively permanent characteristic.

In psychology, trait describes a characteristic that is unchanging and predictable. For example, shyness is a trait that is usually stable in an individual's personality. Another example is talkativeness. A child who is talkative is likely to continue this characteristic throughout the various stages of development.

There are some temperamental traits that researchers believe to be innate—that is, the infant possesses a basis for developing the trait at birth.

Other traits are acquired through learning, such as the tendencies toward tidiness or untidiness. Determining whether a trait is inborn or acquired is difficult, and many psychologists and others study various human traits to gather evidence to help provide insight into this question.

Some researchers are interested in the acquired traits that enable an individual to function effectively in society. These traits, known as socially adaptive traits, enable the individual to participate in society as a member of a couple, family, club, school class, or sports team. Examples of these traits are cooperation, motivation, and willingness to share. The counterpart to socially adaptive traits, socially maladaptive traits, prevent the individual from effectively participating in groups. Examples of socially maladaptive traits are deception, **antisocial behavior**, and extreme selfishness.

Transitional Object *see* **Security Objects**

Transsexualism

Condition where an individual wishes to live as if he or she were of the opposite gender, sometimes seeking surgical procedures to change from one sex to the other.

Transsexualism, a condition in which the individual defines him or herself as male or female in opposition to their physical gender, or feels strongly that he or she wants to live as a member of the other gender, is rare. By some estimates, no more than 1 person in 350,000 believes he or she was born the wrong gender.

As these few people progress through childhood, their inability to relate to their own gender identity increases. Some seek the advice of a physician, and by the time they reach early adulthood, begin to take medical action to alter their gender. Since more males than females are diagnosed as transsexuals, it is more common for males to receive hormone treatment to develop secondary sex characteristics, such as breasts. In some cases, a surgical procedure is performed to alter the male sex organs to physically complete the transformation from one gender to the other.

At the Netherlands Institute for Brain Research in Amsterdam, scientists studied six male-to-female transsexuals and found evidence that a section of the hypothalamus that controls sexual function appeared to be more like the type found in women than that found in men. Because human **embryos** destined to become males differentiate early in the development process, the Netherlands study raises the question of whether the developing embryo could receive mixed hormonal signals to portions of the brain and the developing genitalia. Thus, as of the late 1990s, research seems to indicate that there may be physical reasons for transsexualism.

For Further Study

Periodicals

Glausiusz, Josie. "Transsexual Brains." *Discover* 17, January 1996, p. 83.

Gorman, Christine. "Trapped in the Body of a Man?" *Time* 146, November 13, 1995, pp. 94+.

Trichotillomania

Uncontrollable or overwhelming urge to pull out one's own hair.

This pattern of recurrent hair-pulling results in noticeable hair loss. Individuals with this disorder most commonly pull hair from the scalp, eyebrows, and eyelashes, although any area of the body where hair grows can be involved. Hair-pulling may increase during periods of stress, but is also frequent during periods of calm or relaxation. This behavior often begins around ages 5–8; another common period of onset of this disorder is at age 13. Some individuals may experience this disorder spasmodically over periods of weeks or months; other have continuous symptoms for many years.

See also **Impulse Control Disorder.**

Trisomy

Chromosomal abnormalities that cause birth defects including Down syndrome.

Chromosomes in the human body generally come in pairs. Most people have 23 pairs of chromosomes, for a total of 46. When an extra chromosome is present in one of the pairs (resulting in three instead of two), the abnormality is labeled trisomy. Scientists have numbered the 23 pairs of human chromosome, and the trisomy abnormality may occur in several different chromosomes. For example, when the trisomy abnormality occurs in chromosome 21, the result is **Down syndrome.** Babies born with Down syndrome usually survive into adulthood.

Other chromosomal abnormalities are trisomy 13, Patau's syndrome, and trisomy 18, Edward's syndrome. Both are relatively rare but serious conditions that cause severe mental retardation and physical deformities. Babies born with either of these trisomies usually do not survive beyond their first year.

For Further Study

Organizations

Support Organization for Trisomy13/18 (SOFT)
    Address: 5030 Cole
    Pocatello, ID 93202
    (Organization for families of children with trisomy 13 or 18. Publishes a newsletter, *SOFT Touch,* and a book, *Trisomy 18: Book for Families.*)

Truancy

Failure to attend school regularly without parents' approval.

In the 1990s, truancy has become a serious problem in many communities worldwide. The U.S. Department of Justice reports that 80% of those in prison were at one time truants. The percent of juvenile offenders who started as truants is even higher, approaching 95%.

The majority of the states in the United States require that students attend school until at least the age of 16. All states have laws governing compulsory education, and noncompliance results in penalties for the parent(s) or guardian of the truant student. Obviously, the state's objective is to educate its young people so that they will become capable, employable citizens. Although fines and jail terms for parents are prescribed if truancy becomes chronic, most states provide for mediation and counseling to return the student to school, and many are seeking positive incentives to combine with the penalties.

In the late 1990s, there were more than 51 million students in U. S. public and private schools, and the number was expected to continue to grow at least through 2010. The rising number of students combined with an increase in juvenile crime underline the urgent need for initiatives to keep young people in school, off drugs, and away from weapons and violence. Most experts believe that truancy is the first step toward involvement in crime and violence. For many truant students, feelings of academic inadequacy, **peer pressure,** chaotic family life, and feelings of hopelessness about future employment prospects lead them to give up on school.

Schools can introduce incentives for attendance and punishments for non-attendance. In 1996, a study conducted by the Rand Corporation evaluated programs designed to divert young people from crime. One of the most effective provided cash and other incentives to induce students to stay in school until graduation. The researchers estimated that incentives and other early intervention programs to keep students in school save enough money (by not having to arrest, process, and in-carcerate juvenile offenders) to pay for themselves. In Peoria, Arizona, a Phoenix suburb, the city prosecutor estimates that it costs about $15,000 per year to house a juvenile delinquent for one year, and the cost of a diversion program is about $1,000 per child. Since the program, which is known as Project AIM (Attendance Is Mandatory), was begun in 1994, truancy has been reduced by 92%. (Prior to initiating the program, 17% of the school population had truancy problems.) The features of Project AIM are: after three unexcused absences, the truant student's parents receive a letter. After five unexcused absences, the truant is referred to the city prosecutor's office and a criminal complaint is filed. The truant and his or her family choose between two options. The first is to pay a $200 fine plus have a police record; the second involves participating in counseling, training, and a support group. Since 1994, 72% of the truants went back to school after the initial letter was sent. The prosecutor reports that **gang** activity, violent crime by juveniles, and crimes against children diminished after the program was begun.

In July 1996, the U. S. Department of Education, under the direction of then-Secretary Richard Riley, published the *Manual to Combat Truancy,* and announced the availability of $300,000-$500,000 grants to school districts for programs to address truancy problems. While there are no reliable data on truancy, the *Manual to Combat Truancy* stated that, in some U.S. cities, truant students number in the thousands on any given school day. It also cited reports from major urban centers. Pittsburgh, Pennsylvania schools reported 3,500 students, or 12% of all students were absent on an average school day; 70% of those were unexcused. Milwaukee, Wisconsin, reported 4,000 unexcused absences on an average school day. Miami, Florida, reported that over 70% of 13–16-year-olds prosecuted for crimes were truant.

Communities where anti-truancy programs have been successful use a combination of incentives and sanctions to keep students in school. In the *Manual to Combat Truancy,* five key points are defined for minimizing truancy. The critical first step is to involve parents in all aspects of truancy prevention. To stop truants, the school must be able to provide parents with notification of their child's absence on the day the absence occurs. Schools are advised to create an efficient attendance-tracking system, and to communicate students' absences to parents immediately.

Second, schools must have firm policies on the consequences for truancy, and all students should be aware of the sanctions that will be imposed if they are absent without an excuse. Some states have found that linking truancy to the student's driver's license or grades effectively reduces unexcused absences. Others have invoked a daytime curfew, allowing police to question any young person not in school during school hours.

Third, parents must take responsibility for keeping their children in school. Most state laws impose fines or jail terms on parents of truants. Alternatively, some states are investigating ways to use incentives. Maryland and Oklahoma, for example, have found that linking eligibility for public assistance to truancy can be an effective way to capture parents' interest in keeping their children in school. Another positive incentive provides increased eligibility for services to families whose children attend school regularly. Many communities also offer effective parenting courses and family counseling.

Fourth, the vigil to eliminate causes of truancy must be ongoing. The root causes of truancy are complex and varied, and can include drug use, membership in a peer group of truants, lack of direction in education or work, poor academic performance, and violence at or near school. By analyzing the reasons students are truant, the school administration may be able to correct or improve the problem and reduce truancy. For example, if students stay away from school because of inadequate academic skills, special tutoring programs may be initiated. If students have concerns about violence near the school, the administration may request increased security from the police for the surrounding neighborhood. Local business can be enlisted to support school-to-work programs to help students make the transition to employment.

Finally, a close link with law enforcement, juvenile court, and family court officials may lead to creative solutions for truancy. Some communities have authorized the police to patrol neighborhoods where truant youth are likely to be spend the school hours. In Milwaukee, Wisconsin, police take the truant youth to a Boys and Girls Club center for counseling. In New Haven, Connecticut, the Stay-in-School program targets middle school students who have just begun to have problems. Youth and attorney mentors are assigned to each student for support, with accountability to a truancy court.

Government programs will continue to provide support to communities to combat truancy. Local school administrations, law enforcement, and family services agencies can learn from the experiences of other communities in designing their own program to keep students in school.

For Further Study

Books

Altenbaugh, Richard J., et al. *Caring For Kids: A Critical Study of Urban School Leavers.* Washington, DC: Falmer Press, 1995.

Gabb, Sean. "Truancy in the United States," in *Issues in School Attendance and Truancy,* Dennis O'Keefe and Pat Stoll, eds. London: Pitman Press, 1995.

Greenwood, Peter. *Diverting Children from a Life of Crime: Measuring Costs and Benefits.* Santa Monica: Rand Corporation, 1996.

Hersov, Lionel, and Ian Berg. *Out of School: Modern Perspectives in Truancy and School Refusal.* London: John Wiley and Sons, Ltd., 1980.

U.S. Department of Education Safe and Drug-Free Schools Office. *Manual to Combat Truancy.* Washington, DC: U.S. Department of Education, 1996. To order, call toll-free (800) 624-0100.

Periodicals

Greenwood, Peter, Karyn Model, C. Peter Rydell, and James Chiesa. "The Economic Benefits of Diverting Children From Crime." *Challenge* 3, no. 5, Sept–Oct 1996, 42+.

Audiovisual Recordings

Mattox, Phil, and E. TY Gardner, producers. *Why School Is Important.* Charleston, WV: Cambridge Research Group, 1990. (One 30-minute videocassette and one manual.)

 Tuberculosis

A chronic, infectious disease primarily attacking the lungs.

Tuberculosis (TB) is an chronic, infectious disease caused by *Mycobacterium tuberculosis* that primarily attacks the lungs. The tubercle bacillus is transmitted by droplets when an infected person coughs or sneezes. It is not spread through kissing or other physical contact. Children nearly always contract the disease from an infected adult.

The TB-infected areas of the lungs become dry and cheese-like, eventually hardening into scar tissue. The severity of the attack depends on whether the bacteria spreads from the lungs to other parts of the body. Tuberculin infection in the blood, the meninges (membranes around the brain and spinal cord), or the kidneys are the most serious. Children between the ages of six and 24 months are the most susceptible to **meningitis;** it is the chief cause of tuberculin death among children.

In 1987, there were one to two cases of tuberculosis for every 10,000 people in the United States. By 1993, the Centers for Disease Control's Division of Tuberculosis Elimination was reporting significant increases in the incidence of TB among children under 15. The AIDS epidemic and antibiotic-resistant strains of TB have also contributed to the rise in the number of TB cases. The highest incidence occur on the East Coast, the Southeast, and the Southwest.

Early symptoms include unusual fatigue, loss of weight, headache, coughing, and irritability. The child may have night sweats and cough up blood. In advanced stages, the patient will suffer persistent coughing, breathlessness, and fever. Many times TB is not diagnosed and becomes dormant; this is known as initial tuberculosis. In severe cases among young children between the ages of two and four, initial TB can be fatal. The disease can reoccur, or reactivate, during adolescence when resistance is low, and may disappear on its own or develop into serious lung disease.

Tuberculosis is nearly always diagnosed by tuberculin skin tests, although one can also be diagnosed by chest x rays and analysis of sputum smears and cultures. The most common tuberculin skin test is the Mantoux test, which consists of injecting a small amount of protein from the tubercle bacillus into the forearm. A reddening and swelling of the area after 24–72 hours signals the presence of TB. However, a negative result may not necessarily exclude a diagnosis of TB.

The disease is treated with a regimen of strong antibiotics such as Refampin and Isoniazid for six months to two years. Because some strains of the disease are unusually drug-resistant, cultures are grown from the patient's bacteria and tested with a variety of drugs to determine the most effective treatment. In cases of strong drug-resistant strains, the child may undergo surgery to remove the infected areas. The recent appearance of multi-drug-resistant tuberculosis (MDR TB) is prompting the CDC to reexamine the benefits of a vaccination against TB.

Infants with TB are usually hospitalized but children and teenagers can generally lead active lives within two weeks of beginning medication. It is imperative that the mediation prescribed be taken faithfully.

Stopping the spread of tuberculosis is the most effective way of preventing its incidence among children. All adults who work with children should be screened regularly. In most communities, children are tested when they reach their first birthday and then at one-to-three year intervals throughout the school years. The medical profession is divided on the issue of screening; some physicians believe that the screening should be focused in areas of common occurrence or within high-risk populations such as foreign-born children. The practice of relying on parents to report results of the skin testing has also come under criticism from some members of the medical community.

For Further Study

Books

Landau, Elaine. *Tuberculosis*. New York: F. Watts, 1995.

Tuberculosis. Bethesda, MD: U.S. Dept. of Health and Human Services, Public Health Service, National Institutes of Health, 1981.

Organizations

American Lung Association
  Address: 1740 Broadway
  New York, NY 10019
  Telephone: (212) 315-8700
The National Medical and Research Center, Global Leader in Lung, Allergic and Immune Diseases
  Address: 1400 Jackson Street
  Denver, Colorado 80206
  Telephone: (303) 398-1079

—Mary McNulty

Tumor

Mass of abnormally growing cells.

Tumor is the term applied to any collection of abnormally growing cells. In most instances, tumors are solid, although health care professionals use the term *solid tumor* specifically to describe a localized mass of abnormally growing tissue. Solid tumors that are cancerous are termed malignant; those that are not cancerous are termed benign.

See also **Biopsy; Cancer; Malignancy**

Turner Syndrome

A genetic disorder caused by a missing X chromosome that occurs only in females.

Victims of Turner syndrome are characterized by short stature, absence of secondary sexual characteristics, infertility, and a number of other physical abnormalities. The condition was first identified in 1928 by Dr. Henry H. Turner, for whom it is named. The underlying chromosomal defect was discovered in 1959. Turner syndrome occurs in approximately one out of every 2,500 live births. However, all but 2% of **fetus**es affected by the disorder are miscarried. Of all the chromosomal abnormalities that result in spontaneous **abortion** or miscarriage, Turner syndrome is the most common, accounting for about 20% of all miscarriages.

Most women with Turner syndrome are under 5 feet (1.5 m) tall , averaging 4 feet 7 inches (1.4 m). They have a distinctive appearance that may include the following characteristics: puffiness of the hands and feet in the first year of life; cross-eyes; a short, webbed neck and a small chin; a pronounced bending outward of the elbows; short fingers and toes; curved, underdeveloped nails; birthmarks; and a broad chest with widely spaced nipples. In addition to these visible signs, common features of the condition include **hypertension,** thyroid disorders, osteoporosis, and abnormalities of the heart, kidney, or urinary tract. Women with Turner syndrome are born with underdeveloped ovaries that are eventually replaced by connective tissue. Because of the resulting lack of sex **hormones**, they do not have menstrual periods and their breasts remain undeveloped, although they may develop underarm and pubic hair. Turner syndrome does not affect intelligence, although persons with the condition have poor spatial perception and mathematical aptitude, often accompanied by **learning disabilities.**

About one-third of women with Turner syndrome are diagnosed within six weeks of birth, one-third are diagnosed in childhood, and the remaining third are diagnosed in adolescence when they fail to mature sexually. Two types of treatment have been effective in alleviating the symptoms of Turner syndrome. With early diagnosis, growth hormone can help women affected by the condition come closer to attaining a normal height. Once full growth has been achieved, the administration of sex hormones can produce breast development and **menstruation**. In 1986 hormone treatments enabled two women with Turner syndrome to bear children with the aid of in vitro fertilization. Persons with Turner syndrome have normal life expectancies and can lead independent and productive lives.

See also **Genetic Disorders**

For Further Study

Audiovisual Recordings

Turner Syndrome. North York, Ontario: Turner's Syndrome Society, 1989.

Organizations

Turner's Syndrome Society, Inc.
    Address: 814 Glencairn Avenue
    North York, Ontario M6B 2A3
    Canada
    Telephone: toll-free (800) 465-6744; (416) 781-2086; (416) 781-7245

Tutor

A person hired to give individual help to a student in a particular subject.

Hiring a tutor or sending a child to a private tutoring center is becoming a popular option for parents. Though using tutors is traditionally associated with older children, such as with a high school student in danger of failing a subject, elementary school children can also benefit from a tutor. The number of tutors being hired for younger children is increasing. This may indicate decreasing parents' satisfaction with the way their children are taught in school, or it may be that parents want to provide extra resources to enrich their children's early education. Parents may also decide to hire a tutor if their child is not picking up basic skills in the classroom. The child's teacher may alert the parent that his child needs extra help, and may be able to recommend tutors in the area.

Professional tutors, or solo tutoring, can be quite costly—from about $25 to $40 an hour. A high school or college student may be more affordable for a younger child. In selecting a tutor, parents should evaluate several factors:

1.) if the tutor has experience helping children in a particular subject area;

2.) whether the tutor can come to the child's home, or whether the child can go to the tutor's home; and

3.) whether the tutor motivates the student with positive encouragement.

One of the fastest-growing trends in education is the private tutoring company, or learning center, which teaches children individually or in small groups after school. Long popular in Japan, the number of these tutoring centers is rising quickly in both Canada and the U.S. The three leading companies are Sylvan Learning Systems. Huntington Learning Centers, and the Japan-based Kumon Math and Learning Centers. They charge either an hourly or monthly fee. Students may enroll in these tutoring centers for remedial help, but many students who are already doing well also enroll to enhance or gain extra skills. The private tutoring companies have their own worksheets and homework. Many of these companies work on a rewards system, giving children tokens for completed assignments, which they can redeem for prizes.

In both Canada and the U.S., private tutoring companies have been hired by public school systems to boost students' skills. In most cases, the tutors help with remedial math and reading. Initial feedback suggests that this method helps improve students' test scores, and this combination of private industry and public education is becoming more common.

For Further Study

Books

Gallop, Catharine M. *Individual Tutoring: A Realistic and Effective Solution for Children's Learning Difficulties.* Springfield, IL: C.C. Thomas, 1988.

MacDonald, Ross B. *The Master Tutor: A Guidebook for More Effective Tutoring.* Williamsville, NY: Cambridge Stratford Study Skills Institute, 1994.

Shelton, Leslie. *Excellence for All: A New Tutor Training Model: LSCA Title VI Final Performance Report..* Washington, DC: U.S. Dept. of Education, Office of Educational Research and Improvement, Educational Resources Information Center, 1990.

Twins

Two children born at the same birth.

Identical, or onozygotic, twins are of the same sex and are genetically and physically similar because they both come from one ovum, which, after fertilization, divides in two and develops into two separate individuals. Fraternal, or dizygotic, twins occur when the mother produces two eggs in one monthly cycle and both eggs are fertilized. The conceptions may take place on two separate occasions and could involve different fathers. Fraternal twins, who are no more genetically alike than ordinary siblings, may be of the same or different sex and may bear some similarity of appearance. Fraternal twinning appears to be passed on by the female members of a family: if the mother is a fraternal twin herself, has fraternal twin siblings or fraternal twin relatives on her side of the family, or has already given birth to fraternal twins (one in twenty chance), her chances of giving birth to fraternal twins are approximaly five times as great.

Between 1980 and 1994, the number of twin births in the United States increased by 42%, from 68,339 to 97,064. The twin birth rate (i.e, the number of twin births to total live births) increased 30%, from 18.9 to 24.6 per 1,000 live births. According to data gathered by the Centers for Disease Control, there is considerable variation among the states in number and rate of twin births. In 1994, for example, the twin birth rate ranged from 19.8 in Idaho and New Mexico to 27.7 in Connecticut and Massachusetts. One factor that may influence multiple births in a state is whether the state provides insurance coverage for procedures such as **in vitro fertilization** (IVF) and other treatments to improve fertility. During 1992–1994, 11 states mandated such benefits.

The CDC is also studying whether maternal age has any correlation with the rate of twins births. The data seems to suggest that mothers in states with rates of twin births higher than the overall rate for the United States are older on average, and mothers in states with rates of twin births lower than the overall rate for the United States are younger.

Ethnicity is another factor that may correlate to the twin birth rate. For 1994, the twin birth rate among non-Hispanic white mothers was 24.3; among non-Hispanic black mothers, 28.3; and among Hispanic mothers, 18.6.

Twin birth rate may also affect other statistics related to infant health. The accompanying table illustrates some key statistics on twin births.

KEY FACTS ABOUT TWIN BIRTHS

Factor	Incidence
Twins births	2% of all births
Low birthweight twins	17% of all low birthweight infants
Infant deaths in twins	12% of all infant deaths
Twin births in Japan	0.7% of all births
Twin births among Yoruba people of Nigeria	4% of all births
White mother, U.S. (non-Hispanic)	twin birth rate 24.3 per 1,000 births
Black mother, U.S. (non-Hispanic)	twin birth rate 28.3 per 1,000 births
Hispanic mother, U.S.	twin birth rate 18.6 per 1,000 births

While the rate of identical twin births is stable for all ages of childbearing women, the chance of any mother bearing fraternal twins increases from the age of 15 to 39 and then drops after age 40. For women of all ages, the more children they have had previously, the more likely they are to bear twins. Since the 1960s, fertility drugs have also been linked to the chances of producing twins. The majority of research indicates that fathers' genes have little effect on the chances of producing twins.

There are four types of monozygotic twins, determined by the manner in which the fertilized egg, or zygote, divides and the stage at which this occurs. Two independent embryonic structures may be produced immediately at division, or the zygote may form two inner cell masses, with each developing into an embryo. A late or incomplete division may produce conjoined, or Siamese twins. As the zygote develops, it is encased in membranes, the inner of which is called the amnion, and the outer one the chorion. Among monozygotic twins, either or both of these membranes may be either separate or shared, as may the placenta. Together, the arrangement of these membranes and the placenta occurs in four possible permutations. Among dizygotic twins, each one has separate amnion and chorion membranes, although the placenta may be shared. Ascertaining zygosity, or the genetic make up of twins, can be done by analyzing the placenta(s) to determine if it is a single placenta with a single membrane or a double placenta, which account for one-third of identical twins and all fraternal twins. In the case of same-sex twins with two placentas, a **DNA** or blood test can determine whether they share the same genes or blood groups.

The scientific study of twins, pioneered by Francis Galton in 1876, is one effective means of determining genetic influences on human behavior. The most widely used method of comparison is comparing monozygotic and dizygotic twins for concordance and discordance of traits. Concordant traits are those possessed by either both or neither of a pair of twins; discordant traits are possessed by only one of the pair. Monozygotic twins who are discordant for a particular trait can be compared with each other with reference to other traits. This type of study has provided valuable information on the causes of **schizophrenia.**

Another common type of twin research compares monozygotic twins reared together with those reared apart, providing valuable information about the role of environment in determining behavior. In general, monozygotic twins reared apart are found to bear more similarities to each other than to their respective adoptive parents or siblings. This finding demonstrates the interaction between the effects of environment and genetic predispositions on an individual's psychological development.

For Further Study

Books

Albi, Linda. *Mothering Twins: From Hearing the News to Beyond the Terrible Twos.* New York: Simon & Schuster, 1993.

Bryan, Elizabeth M. *Twins, Triplets, and More: Their Nature, Development, and Care.* New York: St. Martin's Press, 1992.

Clegg, A., and A. Woolett. *Twins from Conception to Five Years.* New York: Van Nostrand Reinhold, 1983.

Gromada, Karen Kerkhoff, and Mary C. Hurlburt. *Keys to Parenting Twins.* Hauppauge, NY : Barron's, 1992.

Leigh, G. *All About Twins: A Handbook for Parents.* Boston: Routledge and Keegan Paul, 1983.

Theroux, Rosemary T., and Josephine F. Tingley. *The Care of Twin Children: A Common Sense Guide for Parents.* 2nd ed. Chicago: Center for the Study of Multiple Birth, 1984.

Periodicals

Bouchard, Thomas J. "Genes, Environment, and Personality." *Science* 264, June 17, 1994, pp. 1700+.

Lykken, D.T., T.J. Bouchard Jr., M. McGue, and A. Tellegen. "Heritability of Interests: a Twin Study." *Journal of Applied Psychology* 78, August 1993, pp. 649+.

"State-specific Variation in Rates of Twin Births—United States, 1992–1994." *JAMA, The Journal of the American Medical Association* 277, March 19, 1997, p. 878.

Wright, Lawrence. "Double Mystery: Recent Research into the Nature of Twins Is Reversing Many of Our Most Fundamental Convictions About Why We Are Who We Are." *The New Yorker* 71, August 7, 1995, pp. 44+.

Organizations

Center for the Study of Multiple Births
   Address: 333 E. Superior St., Suite 463-5
   1415 Green Run Lane
   Reston, VA 22090

International Twins Association
   Address: 114 N. Lafayette Drive
   Muncie, IN 47303

National Organization of Mothers of Twins Clubs, INc.
   Address: P. O. Box 23188
   Albuquerque, NM 87192-1188
   Telephone: (505) 275-0955

Twins Foundation
   Address: P. O. Box 6043
   Providence, RI 02940
   Telephone: (401) 729-1000

Twins Magazine
   Address: 5350 S. Roslyn Street, Suite 400
   Englewood, CO 80111-2125
   Telephone: toll-free (888)55-TWINS [558-9467]; (303) 290-8500

Underachiever

Also referred to as a latent achiever, a person whose performance is significantly below that which would be predicted by educators.

An underachiever's performance in academic studies falls significantly below his scores on standardized tests of aptitude or ability. A student may also be considered to be underachieving based on the educator's evaluation of her learning potential in relation to the quality of the work she does on class assignments.

There are many explanations for achievement that falls below evaluated potential. Some problems may be the educational experience itself: bright students may be bored by class assignments, and therefore do not give them much attention; or a student's learning style may conflict with the method of instruction used in his school. Underachievers may also have **learning disabilities** that prevent them from making full use of their capabilities. Family factors may also contribute to a pattern of underachievement in a variety of ways. When parents' expectations are low or nonexistent (the family doesn't expect the student to do more than pass), the student may work "just hard enough"—well below his full potential—to get by. When a student's peer group does not value academic achievement, **peer pressure** may be another factor contributing to underachievement.

Caregivers, educators, and the student, can all work together to counter underachievement. First, working with the family and school personnel, the student must understand the factors that contribute to low academic achievement. Factors may include poor time management, self-defeating thought patterns ("I could never get a B in science."), weak writing skills, poor (or no) study environment (i.e., homework done while watching television), friends or role models who do not value academic performance, or self-destructive habits like alcohol or drug abuse. Next, the student needs to acknowledge that she could be more successful in school. Parents and teachers can help the student compile a list of strengths, both academic and other, that she can build upon. They can also help direct the student to peer groups (through clubs, sports, or other extracurricular activities) that support academic success. In addition, role models can be presented to the student to help her focus on the possibilities in academic life, rather than the limitations. Finally, where necessary, families can seek counseling and treatment for problems such as alcohol abuse that prevent the student from focusing on school.

For Further Study

Books

Griffin, Robert S. *Underachievers in Secondary School: Education Off the Mark.* Hillsdale, NJ: Lawrence Erlbaum Associates, 1988.

Holt, John. *How Children Fail.* Revised edition. Reading, MA: Addison-Wesley Publishing Company, 1995.

Lehr, Judy Brown. *At-Risk, Low-Achieving Students in the Classroom.* Washington, DC: National Education Association, 1988.

Thiel, Ann, Richard Thiel, and Penelope B. Grenoble. *When Your Child Isn't Doing Well in School.* Chicago: Contemporary Books, 1988.

Varma, Ved. *How and Why Children Fail.* Philadelphia: J. Kingsley, 1993.

Undesirable Language

Verbal expression that affects the listener negatively.

The term "undesirable language" refers to words and grammar that: (a) are judged to have a negative impact on listeners or (b) cause listeners to make negative evaluative judgments about speakers. In common, everyday language "undesirable speech" is more specifically understood as speaking "dirty words" or "curse words." "Curse words" are an important aspect of emotional expression, but they create problems for children when they use them in the wrong context.

Undesirable speech encompasses words categorized as obscenity, profanity, blasphemy, name calling, vulgarity, epithets, insults, slang, sexual harassment, and verbal abuse. Undesirable words in American English tend to relate to sex *(fuck)*, religion *(hell)*, deviance *(whore)*, body parts *(prick)*, body products *(piss)*, disgust items *(pus)*, ethnic/racial/gender discrimination *(nigger)*, cultural taboos *(motherfucker)*, and animal imagery *(cock)*.

Speech standards

Communicating with others is grounded in a set of standards regarding what is acceptable or not acceptable in public. Speech patterns vary according to national and local standards. National speech standards are exemplified by news reporters in electronic or print media and by speakers engaged in formal business interactions. Federal and state laws prohibit offensive speech, such as obscenity and harassment. Speakers also conform to regional dialect standards and community preferences for speech patterns and vocabulary. And finally at the local level, one's group affiliations (cliques, prestige groups, ingroups) further define preferred language.

Teachers and parents guide children to acquire conventional speech so that they will "sound educated" and have access to desirable jobs and social circles. Many parents worry that when their child curses, it reflects badly on them. Frequently, though, children use unconventional speech to rebel against authority figures or to identify with different reference groups that use slang, obscenity, or racist speech. In spite of teachers' and parents' pleas for conventional speech, cursing seems essential to many American adolescents to express their emotions.

Language, emotion, and context

Human communication is conducted through different levels of formality. Speech styles range from very informal to very formal. Undesirable speech is usually informal and nonstandard. The acceptability of cursing or emotional speech depends heavily on the context in which it appears. Informal speech is acceptable in informal contexts but not formal ones. One easily imagines emotional speech in heated playground arguments or in sexual situations. Not only is emotional speech acceptable to the speakers in sexual or aggressive contexts, the absence of emotional language in these situations would seem odd. On the other hand, such emotional language would not be acceptable in a classroom or public place.

It is not effective to divide words into two-level categories like good versus bad or naughty versus nice since all speech is contextual. Some gray areas exist between speech that seems clearly acceptable and that which seems clearly unacceptable. It is more effective to conceptualize speech as a three-category system. First, there is *acceptable* speech, which is standard or conventional speech like that used in media broadcasts. Acceptable speech will prove appropriate in most contexts. At the other end of the spectrum is *unacceptable* speech, which violates federal or state laws or community standards. Unacceptable speech includes sexual harassment, obscenity, fighting words, and discriminatory speech. The gray area is *inappropriate* speech, which includes language that can be offensive when used in the "wrong" context; for example, a young child gets angry and curses in his classroom. While his angry curse words might be appropriate with peers in a playground dispute, it is not appropriate in a classroom setting.

Why do children use offensive language?

Research on language acquisition indicates that the use of curse words is frequent and normal in childhood (see Berges, Neiderbach, Rubin, Sharpe & Tesler, 1983). Americans hear curse words on a daily basis and most use vulgarities in informal language. Most adults, though, do not view childhood cursing as appropriate.

Knowing why and when children curse allows adults to develop strategies to deal with cursing episodes. Cursing is more likely in certain predictable contexts. Offensive words are highly probable in sex talk, joking, storytelling, name calling, insulting, racial/gender discrimination, emotional expressions (surprise, anger, elation), to establish one's personal identity, and in acts of verbal aggression, bullying, and gang-related violence. Children will also curse to defend themselves in disputes.

Pathological cursing

While normal cursing is primarily under a speaker's voluntary control, compulsive cursing is not. Compulsive cursing, or **coprolalia**, is often the result of neurological conditions such as **Tourette syndrome** (TS), frontal lobe damage, **epilepsy**, **schizophrenia**, dementia, Alzheimer's disease, and **mental retardation**. Children and adolescents are common victims of TS, and one-third exhibit coprolalia.

Developmental issues

American children encounter cursing in everyday life and in the popular media. Children's cursing is normal and undergoes predictable shifts with cognitive development, sexual development, and social interaction. Cursing evolves with a child's need to communicate thoughts and feelings. While American English has hundreds of words to express emotion, the cursing lexicon is small. The spoken cursing lexicon during childhood is about 20-30 words and expands to 50-60 words by adulthood (Jay, 1992). While some curse words are used frequently and consistently throughout a speaker's life *(shit),* other terms are more likely to only occur in childhood *(fraidy cat, poo-poo head)* and later fall from usage.

From a parenting perspective, one needs to understand how cursing is acquired and used in society. It would seem wise when examining and responding to any child's cursing to keep a few strategies in mind: figure out why the child is cursing, act in his best interest, help the child express emotions, be prepared to talk about matters of sexuality and language in general terms. Be prepared for cursing to evolve with development and help children learn the contexts where emotional expressions are appropriate.

Toddlers

Toddlers repeat single, offensive words when they first learn to speak, about the end of the first year. However, they are merely imitating what adults or siblings are saying around them. Ignoring cursing at this stage will extinguish it.

Preschoolers

During the preschool period one can hear offensive language used to express humor, anger, or frustration, in temper tantrums, for attention seeking, and in taunting and name calling. Preschoolers pick up language habits at home and in school settings. Offensive words that are reinforced by peers, siblings, and adults will be repeated, generally. Gender differences in cursing are minimal; preschool boys and girls use roughly the same lexicon of curse words.

Behavior modification strategies such as reinforcing acceptable speech and ignoring or punishing unacceptable speech will control cursing episodes by preschoolers. Adults would want to be attentive to their own language and serve as good role models.

School-aged children

During elementary school, children's sense of humor, sense of self, emerging sexual awareness, joke telling, and story telling rituals are associated with undesirable speech. School-aged children are particularly fond of scatology (references to feces and elimination), talking about sex, and improving their sense of humor. Gender differences in speech rituals appear here (see Thorne, 1993), with some becoming stable in adolescence. Girls use less offensive words and swear less frequently than boys. At this age most cursing is used to express anger and frustration. Adults can encourage children to adopt communication habits grounded in good character traits such as reason, respect, and responsibility. For example, name calling is hurtful to others not because a child used a "bad" word but because such names are disrespectful to others.

Adolescents

The use of undesirable speech reaches a peak in adolescence. Adolescents will experiment with identity, seek negative attention, rebel against authority figures, and question rules, boundaries, and social norms. Offensive humor becomes abstract, socially and politically. Conflicts with authority figures (parents, teachers, adults) and peers can produce cursing quite readily. Some teens undergoing stressful life events or identity crises (antisocial or deviant personalities) will use offensive speech to distance themselves from outsiders.

It is important to realize that many adult-adolescent conflicts arise as adolescents explore boundaries and personal identity. Teens have the ability to use and understand offensive language, but they need to see that using conventional language is instrumental in gaining access to jobs and social groups. Cursing in the wrong context can produce negative consequences, such as failing a job interview or losing a job. Adults can help teenagers by modeling good communication skills.

Other factors that influence speech

Children generally learn language through experience with local speakers. Negative role models, abusive adults or siblings, and neighborhood language norms directly affect one's lexicon. Popular culture and media (television, film, radio, music) are also involved.

Ample anecdotal evidence suggests that today's children are using offensive language more frequently than ever before, but so are adults. This is a reflection of social changes such as: changing media standards, increasing acceptance of sexuality and sexual expression, decreased influence of organized religion, changing roles for women and the family, relaxing styles of dress and etiquette, increasing daily stress, increasing anonymity, and decreasing sense of community responsibility. Cursing has evolved as an aspect of human emotional expression. Adults can help children by being open about matters of sexuality and language by teaching them about the contexts where such emotional expressions are appropriate.

For Further Study
Books

Berges, E., S. Neiderbach, B. Rubin, E. Sharpe, R. Tesler. *Children and Sex: The Parents Speak.* New York, NY: Facts on File, 1983.

Jay, T. B. *Cursing in America.* Philadelphia, PA: John Benjamins Pub. Co., 1992.

———. *What to Do When Your Students Talk Dirty.* San Jose, CA: Resource Publications, Inc., 1996.

———. *What to Do When Your Kids Talk Dirty.* San Jose, CA: Resource Publications, Inc., 1997.

Thorne, B. *Gender Play: Girls and Boys in School.* New Brunswick, NJ: Rutgers University Press, 1993.

—Timothy Jay
North Adams State University

Ungraded Schools *see* **Nongraded Schools**

Urination *see* **Kidney Function and Urological Disorders** and **Toilet Training**

Varicella

Disease commonly known as chicken pox.

Varicella, commonly known as **chicken pox**, is a highly contagious disease for which a vaccine became available in the 1990s.

Veneral Disease *see* **Sexually Transmitted Diseases**

Video Games

Electronic, interactive games known for their vibrant colors and complex graphics.

First mass-marketed in the 1970s, video games are played by installing cartridges into a game box connected by wire to a television set. They then manipulate a joystick or buttons to control the actions of a character or series of characters as the imaginary characters face obstacles displayed on the screen. Video games, designed chiefly to appeal to children and adolescents, are also played in arcades and on small, hand-held screens.

It has been estimated that more than 50 million homes in the United States have one or more of the most popular game systems—Sega, Nintendo, and Sony—including as many as 80% of families with boys ages 8–16. Few children have not been exposed to some form of video games, and access to the games is readily available in all walks of life.

Video games for home use proved popular from the start. Children are particularly attracted to them for a variety of reasons. The fantasy characters and situations appeal to young imaginations and provide an escape from everyday routine and the stresses presented by parents, friends, and school. In addition, the games give children a level of control they don't experience in real life as the characters on the screen respond to their commands.

Players also receive immediate rewards for making the right moves. Most games can be played at a variety of skill levels so that every player can progress to a higher level.

The popularity of video games has been matched by the controversy they have sparked among parents, psychologists, and educators. The most prevalent objection results from the violent themes and characters that predominate in most video games. A 1989 study by the National Coalition on Television Violence (NCTV) found that, of the 95 most popular home video games, 58% were war games and 83% featured violent themes. As technology has improved to allow the games to show more realistic situations and characters, debate has escalated about the potential effects of video games on children's behavior. One NCTV study, which monitored the playground behavior of eight- to ten-year-olds immediately after playing a laser-weapon game, found an 80% increase in fighting. There is also added concern that repeated exposure to violence desensitizes children to its effects. Other experts—and video game manufacturers—contend that negative effects have not been proven adequately and, in fact, playing such games gives players an avenue for the harmless release of stress and aggression.

Public pressure prompted some video game manufacturers in the early 1990s to begin labeling games to warn consumers about violent or sexually explicit content. In 1994, in response to considerable political pressure and the possibility of a federal rating agency, the industry created its own rating system. Generally, ratings are assigned based on their suitability for various age groups. An "Early Childhood" designation on a game box indicates that the game is suitable for players ages three and older, and there is no violence, sexual content, or profanity. "Kids to Adults" is for players ages six and older and may contain minimal violence or crude language. A "Teen" game for ages 13 and up may contain violence, profanity, and mild sexual themes. A "Mature" rating is considered suitable only for ages 17 and older, and may include more intense violence, profanity, and mature sexual themes. "Adults Only" games may include graphic descriptions of sex and violence.

While most consumers applaud the institution of the rating system, critics contend that its effectiveness is compromised by some retailers' unwillingness to screen buyers. Some video-game retailers continue to sell inappropriate games to underage buyers in spite of the ratings. The ratings themselves attract many underage buyers to the most inappropriate products, which makes sales procedures especially important to enforce. In addition, critics argue, the ratings may prompt many parents to abdicate their own responsibility for monitoring their children's activities.

The issue of gender bias in video games is another area of considerable debate. Not only are the themes of most video games male-oriented—sports and combat—female characters in the games are portrayed as victims to be rescued by the male hero or objects of violence or sexual desire. The typical female video game character rarely initiates action and is often scantily dressed. Some have argued that the predominantly male themes and passive, sexual female characters will help perpetuate male dominance in everyday life as well as in technology-related industries. There has been a move in recent years to create more games that will appeal to girls as well as to create more gender-neutral games like the popular "Mario" and "Sonic" titles.

Besides the socialization concerns presented by video games, medical concerns were also raised in the early 1990s, when video games were linked to epileptic seizures experienced by some 50 children. About a third of the children had experienced previous seizures, and there was some question about whether the seizures they experienced were actually related to playing or watching a video game. Two large studies later reported that the children who experienced video game-related seizures (VGRS) were particularly sensitive to light and that the video games with their flashing lights merely precipitated, rather than caused, the seizures. Sitting too close to the screen could exacerbate the effects of the light sensitivity, as could the increasingly complex graphic technology featured in today's games. Patients with **epilepsy** are not thought to be particularly susceptible to VRGS, and no lasting neurological damage has been linked to these seizures.

Despite the controversy surrounding video games, positive benefits have also been noted: development of hand-eye coordination, increase in concentration, logical thinking skills, healthy **competition** among children as well as socialization skills gained from sharing strategies, and heightened **self-esteem** resulting from successful performances.

The educational potential and use of video games remains untapped, and many believe that technological advances will allow the development of more complex educational software to accompany the already dazzling video displays. In the future, many hope that video games will encompass both entertainment and education.

See also **Television and Aggression**

For Further Study

Periodicals
Adler, Tina. "Seizures Strike Some Video Gamesters." *Science News* 145, no. 17, April 23, 1994.

Alaimo, Dan. "Industry Mulls More Games for Girls." *Supermarket News* 44, no. 25, June 20, 1994.

Brody, Herb. "Video Games That Teach?" *Technology Review* 96, no.8, November-December 1993.

Jehlen, Alain. "A Patron for Videogames." *Technology Review* 97, no. 6, August-September 1994.

Jukes, Peter. "The Sonic Boom." *New Statesman & Society* 6, no. 259, July 2, 1993.

Munson, Marty. "Kids and Vids: Many Children Like the Nice Stuff Better." *Prevention* 47, no. 12, December 1995.

Silver, Marc. "The Rating Game." *U.S. News & World Report* 117, no. 20, November 21, 1994.

Trenite, D.G.A. Kasteleijn-Nolst. "Video-game Epilepsy." *The Lancet* 344, no. 8930, October 22, 1994.

—Mary Anne Klasen

The Vineland Social Maturity Scale

Measures social competence, self-help skills, and adaptive behavior.

The Vineland Social Maturity Scale measures social competence, self-help skills, and adaptive behavior from infancy to adulthood. It is used in planning for therapy and/or individualized instruction for persons with **mental retardation** or emotional disorders. The Vineland scale, which can be used from birth up to the age of 30, consists of a 117-item interview with a parent or other primary caregiver. (There is also a classroom version for ages 3–12 that can be completed by a teacher.) Personal and social skills are evaluated in the following areas: daily living skills (general self-help, eating, dressing); communication (listening, speaking, writing); motor skills (fine and gross, including locomotion); socialization (interpersonal relationships, play and leisure, and coping skills); occupational skills; and self-direction. (An optional Maladaptive Behavior scale is also available.) The test is untimed and takes 20–30 minutes. Raw scores are converted to an age equivalent score (expressed as social age) and a social quotient. A Spanish-language edition is also available.

For Further Study

Books

McCullough, Virginia. *Testing and Your Child: What You Should Know About 150 of the Most Common Medical, Educational, and Psychological Tests.* New York: Plume, 1992.

Shore, Milton F., Patrick J. Brice, and Barbara G. Love. *When Your Child Needs Testing: What Parents, Teachers, and Other Helpers Need to Know about Psychological Testing.* New York: Crossroad, 1992.

Walsh, W. Bruce, and Nancy E. Betz. *Tests and Assessment.* 2nd ed. Englewood Cliffs, NJ: Prentice Hall, 1990.

Wodrich, David L., and Sally A. Kush. *Children's Psychological Testing: A Guide for Nonpsychologists.* 2nd ed. Baltimore, MD: Brookes Publishing Co., 1990.

Wortham, Sue Clark. *Tests and Measurement in Early Childhood Education.* Columbus: Merrill Publishing Co., 1990.

Vitamins and Minerals

Groups of nutrients that the human body needs in order to remain healthy and function normally.

Vitamins are organic substances, small amounts of which are needed for certain biochemical reactions in the human body. Minerals are inorganic compounds also needed for a variety of bodily functions.

Vitamins

Because the human body does not synthesize vitamins (at least not in the quantities needed), they must be obtained either through food or through nutritional supplements. Vitamins help the body use fats, proteins, minerals, and carbohydrates. They perform numerous functions, including fighting infections, maintaining mental alertness, helping with blood clotting, forming red blood cells, and promoting good vision. Although medical experts recommend obtaining one's necessary allowance of vitamins by eating a balanced diet, nutritional supplements are very popular among Americans, many of whom fear that their regular diets do not provide them with the nutrients they need to stay healthy. Over half of all Americans say they use vitamin supplements on a daily basis. There are 13 known vitamins, which can be divided into two categories: fat-soluble and water-soluble. The fat-soluble vitamins—A, D, E, and K—dissolve in fat but not in water. After being absorbed, they are stored by the body, creating reserves that can be called upon when needed. However, because they are fat-soluble, these vitamins also pose a relatively high risk of toxicity if taken in large amounts.

Vitamin A occurs in two forms. Retinol, found in meat and dairy products, can be used immediately, while beta-carotene, found in plants, must be converted to vitamin A in the body. Vitamin A is essential for proper vision and normal bone growth and also aids the immune and reproductive systems. Recent research has linked beta-carotene, once regarded as merely a raw material needed for vitamin A, to the prevention of vision disorders, cancer, cardiovascular disease, and other health problems. Beta-carotene is found in yellow and orange vegetables and green leafy vegetables. Animal products containing vitamin A include milk, cheese, butter, egg yolks, fish, and liver.

Unlike other vitamins, *vitamin D* can be synthesized by the body. Ultraviolet light activates the manufacture of this vitamin by the skin. With enough exposure to the sun, people can manufacture as much vitamin D as they need. This vitamin helps the body absorb calcium and phosphorus, helps the pancreas produce insulin, and plays a role in the immune system. Foods are not an important natural source of vitamin D, although some fish, dairy, and meat products contain amounts of vitamin D. The main dietary sources for this vitamin are foods that have been artificially fortified.

Vitamin E is one of a group of vitamins called *antioxidants* that have received a great deal of attention in recent times (the other antioxidants are vitamin C and beta-carotene). Antioxidants protect cells from damage by free radicals, substances produced whenever the body uses oxygen. Researchers have claimed that antioxidants protect against chronic disease, including **cancer**, cardiovascular disease, and **cataracts**, as well as aging. Besides being an antioxidant itself, vitamin E also protects the body's supply of the antioxidants vitamin C and beta-carotene. Vitamin E is found in vegetable oils, wheat germ, whole grains, and green leafy vegetables. Although vitamin E deficiency is very rare in the United States, premature or low birth-weight babies tend to have low levels of this vitamin, and physicians sometimes recommend vitamin E supplements in these cases.

Vitamin K is important for blood clotting and is thought to be necessary for bone formation. Newborn babies are routinely given vitamin K to prevent abnormal bleeding. This vitamin is found in meat, dairy products, and green leafy vegetables. Because the intestines play a role in the production of vitamin K, people with gastrointestinal disorders have an above average likelihood of being deficient in this vitamin.

The water-soluble vitamins are vitamin C and those belonging to the B complex—B_1 (thiamin), B_2 (riboflavin), B_3 (niacin), B_5 (pantothenic acid), B_6 (pyridoxine), B_{12} (cyanocobalamin), biotin, and folic acid. These vitamins dissolve easily in water and are only stored in the body in small quantities (surpluses of these vitamins are eliminated in the urine). While water-soluble vitamins pose less danger of toxicity than fat-soluble ones, it is easier to develop deficiencies of these vitamins.

Vitamin C (ascorbic acid) has long been touted as a remedy for the common cold due to its role in strengthening the immune system, but it also performs many other functions to keep the body healthy. It helps in the processing of carbohydrates and the production of fats and proteins, promotes healing, aids in the formation of connective tissue, and stimulates production of certain hormones and brain chemicals. In addition, it is one of the antioxidants that protect the body from damage by free radicals. Vitamin C is often recommended for maintaining health in times of stress. It is found in citrus fruits, strawberries, melons, and other types of fruit, as well as green vegetables, tomatoes, potatoes, and, in more modest amounts, in meat, fish, and dairy products. It is present in greater quantities in fresh vegetables than cooked ones.

The eight vitamins of the *B complex* aid the body's metabolism, often with two or more of them working together. All are relatively non-toxic because they are water-soluble. Common functions of several B vitamins include maintaining the nervous system, providing energy, and assisting in the production of red and white blood cells. Each individual B vitamin also performs a variety of special functions, from B_1 (thiamin), which removes excess lactic acid from the body, to folic acid, which aids in fetal and infant development. Niacin (vitamin B_3) has gained popularity due to research showing that it can help control blood cholesterol levels. Certain types of food are rich sources for several of the B vitamins: meat (especially organ meat such as liver and kidney), poultry, fish, wheat germ, yeast, and, in some cases, legumes (soybeans and peas), spinach, and dairy products.

Minerals

Although vitamins generally receive more attention than minerals, the body actually needs larger amounts of certain minerals—called macrominerals—than the amounts of vitamins it requires to stay healthy. The seven macrominerals, all required in amounts of 100 mg or more a day, are calcium, magnesium, phosphorus, sodium, potassium, chloride, and sulfur. In addition, there are 10 microminerals, also called "trace elements," of which the body requires only very small amounts. These are cobalt, iron, zinc, iodine, copper, fluorine, manganese, chromium, selenium, and molybdenum. In spite of the small requirements for these minerals—in some cases considerably less than 1 mg—they are all needed if good health is to be maintained.

Iron, which plays an important role in carrying oxygen to the tissues, has long been the mineral best known to the general public because of its connection with **anemia.** Iron-fortified, multivitamin supplements have been popular for decades. Women are especially at risk for iron deficiency because iron is lost during **menstruation,** especially by women who bleed heavily. Good dietary sources of iron are red meat, liver, dark green leafy vegetables, and legumes. In addition, many foods are fortified with iron.

Calcium, which is necessary for healthy bones and teeth, is the body's most plentiful mineral, accounting for about 2% of the average person's body weight. This mineral is also needed for muscle contraction, blood clotting, and the release of neurotransmitters, which carry impulses throughout the nervous system. The main dietary sources of calcium are dairy products. Other good sources of calcium are green leafy vegetables, beans, and nuts. Many foods, including orange juice, breakfast cereal, and bread, are available fortified with calcium.

Zinc is an important mineral found in all the cells of the body. It is necessary for normal physical growth in children and is also known for promoting healing and fighting infections. Zinc deficiencies in pregnant women can interfere with normal fetal development. Animal products—especially meat and seafood—are the main dietary source of zinc. *Magnesium,* which activates over 300 of the body's enzymes, is needed for muscle relaxation. It is thought to reduce hypertension and lessen the damage from heart attacks. *Selenium,* another important mineral, is an antioxidant believed capable of preventing heart attacks and reducing the risk of certain types of cancer.

Children's vitamin and mineral requirements

The **American Academy of Pediatrics** recommends that children obtain the vitamins they need by eating a well-balanced diet rather than through nutritional supplements. The group has stated that "healthy children receiving a normal, well-balanced diet should not need vitamin supplements over and above the recommended dietary allowances." However, some physicians still recommend vitamins for children until they are eating solid foods.

Infancy. Low birth-weight babies (those weighing less than 5.5 lb [2.5 g]) may require supplements due to vitamin deficiencies. Newborn babies generally have low levels of vitamin K, and it is standard practice for physicians to provide injections of this vitamin. Physicians may recommend vitamin supplementation in infancy during periods of rapid growth, or due to certain dietary factors, such as the use of powdered milk or goat's milk. Vitamins A and D are often recommended for breast-fed babies. Because they go through periods of rapid growth, infants also have aspecial need for iron. Babies are born with reserves of iron, which are enhanced by natural iron from breast milk or iron supplements in formula. By the age of six months, the infant's diet should include cereal, meat, and other foods that contain iron. Physicians routinely test hemoglobin levels in infants at the age of nine months to check for anemia.

School age. Some experts believe that supplements can be beneficial for older children since many may not eat well-balanced diets, either because their parents do not provide them or because the children are finicky eaters. Supplements are often recommended for children on weight-reduction diets. Children in strict vegetarian families who do not receive animal protein from dairy products may have a greater than average need for vitamin supplements, especially vitamin B_{12}. Other situations that may make nutritional supplements necessary include dietary restrictions due to food **allergies,** and metabolic or other disorders. A study conducted at the University of Washington in Seattle and published in the *Journal of the American Dietetic Association* found that children between the ages of 3-½ and 9 are most likely to be deficient in folic acid and vitamin B_6. Iron and zinc—trace elements that promote normal growth—have also been cited as nutrients lacking in the diets of many children. All experts who recommend supplements emphasize the fact that in almost all cases they should be considered as insurance rather than as a substitute for an adequate diet.

Adolescence. Due to the rapid growth spurts and the bad eating habits that are common at this age, adolescents may develop some vitamin deficiencies. Teenage girls, in particular, may be deficient in iron.

Nutritional supplements: precautions and toxicity

The benefits of many nutritional supplements for children are compromised by the fact that they contain refined sugar or artificial sweeteners. It is possible to find alternatives to these products, especially in health food stores, which often carry liquid vitamin formulas sweetened with honey or rice syrup. Nutritional supplements are best administered with meals (usually afterward, except in the case of a purely mineral supplement, which should be given before). Parents need to treat nutritional supplements with the same caution as other pills in the household, as an accidental overdose can be serious or even fatal, especially when it involves supplements that contain iron.

Adverse reactions have been reported for the following vitamins in the dosages listed: vitamin A (over 25,000 international units [IU] or more daily for several months); vitamin B_6 (200–500 mg daily for several months); vitamin C (doses above 1,000 mg daily for long periods of time); vitamin D (more than 5,000 IU a day for several weeks); and zinc (more than 20 mg a day for over a month).

See also **Nutrition; Recommended Dietary Allowances.**

For Further Study

Books

Davis, Adelle. *Let's Have Healthy Children.* New York: Harcourt, Brace Jovanovitch, 1972.

Elliot, Rose. *Vegetarian Mother and Baby Book: A Complete Guide to Nutrition, Health, and Diet During Pregnancy and After.* New York: Pantheon Books, 1984.

Lieberman, Shari, and Nancy Bruning. *The Real Vitamin and Mineral Book.* Garden City Park, NY.: Avery Publishing Group, 1990.

Smith, Lendon H. *Foods for Healthy Kids.* New York: McGraw Hill, 1981.

U.S. Pharmacopeia. *The USP Guide to Vitamins and Minerals.* New York: Avon Books, 1996.

Ulene, Art, and Val Ulene. *The Vitamin Strategy.* Berkeley: The Ulysses Press, 1994.

Vocational Education

At the secondary school level, a curricular track, program, or course designed to prepare students to enter the work force immediately after high school in a skilled occupation, as opposed to college preparatory or academic programs..

Vocational education courses have been a distinct part of the public high school system since the Smith Hughes Act of 1917. The height of enrollment in vocational education (voc ed) classes was during the 1970s when approximately 15% of students majored in voc ed. During the 1980s enrollment declined as federal funding was entirely cut off and voc ed programs were downsized or eliminated. In the 1990s most students take at least one voc ed class, about 10% take a voc ed track, 30% a college preparatory track, and 60% follow neither track. There are three types of voc ed courses: consumer and homemaking classes which prepare students for daily living; general labor courses that teach skills valuable across many occupations, for example, word processing; and job-specific classes which may cover any of the following occupational areas: agriculture; business and office; marketing and distribution; health; occupational home economics; trade and industry; and technical and communications

OCCUPATION PROGRAMS WITH THE HIGHEST PARTICIPATION	
Business	56%
Trade and industry	35%
Technical and communications	23%

Source: *Vocational Eduation Journal,* May 1995, pp. 28–31.

Vocational education classes tend to be smaller, with an average of 17 students as opposed to 22 in non-vocational classes. During the 1990s the most popular classes in terms of number of credits taken were in the areas of business and office, trade and industry, and technical and communications. The most popular concentrations for a full voc ed major were in the fields of health and technical and communications. A higher than average number of students from special populations tends to enroll in voc ed courses: students with disabilities, with low socioeconomic backgrounds, and low GPAs tend to take voc ed classes. Eighty percent of **special education** students take a voc ed track in high school. Some studies show that low-achieving students in voc ed programs increase their reading abilities faster and perform higher on standardized math exams than their low-achieving counterparts in regular comprehensive programs.

Vocational education programs vary widely in number, type, and diversity of courses offered, in their access to technical and industrial resources, and in the level of exposure they provide students to real-world work environments. Only about one-third of voc ed programs require students to concentrate in an occupational area, even though studies show that students who concentrate are more likely to obtain jobs matching their training. In 1993 only 40% of voc ed graduates found jobs matching their training. Performance standards by which voc ed programs are measured also vary. Programs are measured by rates of placement and continuing education, rates of enrollment, employer satisfaction, student satisfaction, employability skills attainment, and the cost of the program.

The most comprehensive vocational education programs are coop, youth apprenticeship, and mentoring programs in which students participate in paid employment. These programs declined sharply during the 1980s, but the 1994 School-to-Work Opportunities Act was passed with the goal of reinvigorating such programs. The primary difference between coop and apprenticeship programs is that apprenticeships lead to a certificate of competency in those areas which have defined skill standards. In these school-to-work programs students generally acquire basic skills through a few years of school-based instruction and then spend at least their senior year working half-time in a paid job. Students work part of the week and attend classes during off hours, or else alternate periods of full-time work or school. Supervision is provided by both a voc ed teacher and by a workplace mentor, both of whom monitor and evaluate the student's learning. Ideally, each work placement will demand progressively higher levels of responsibility, and students will have ample opportunities for guided reflection on their experience.

SPECIAL POPULATIONS PARTICIPATING IN VOCATIONAL EDUCATION	
Student characteristics	Occupation-specific course credits*
Four or more credits in remedial coursework	4.0 credits
Handicapped	3.5 credits
Household in lowest socioeconomic status quartile	3.2 credits
Grade-point average less than 1.6	3.1 credits

*Average number of occupation-specific credits for all high school graduates is 2.5.
Source: *Vocational Education Journal,* May 1995, pp. 28–31.

Developments in vocational education

Traditional vocational education programs were organized around manual labor woodshops, metalworking, and machine shops. But in the 1990s as information and communication-oriented fields expanded, many industrial arts classrooms were replaced by computers, televisions, VCRs and other electronic equipment. Furthermore, the average worker today is expected to have some management and presentation skills, in addition to technical skills. In 1965 an auto mechanic could master 500 pages of information and be prepared to fix almost any car. To gain a similar mastery of automobiles in the 1990s would require learning 500,000 pages of material. Thus, auto mechanics, like most productive workers today, also need skills in locating information and in decision-making. In light of the demands of the 20th-century workforce, several pieces of legislation in the 1990s focused on reinvigorating and improving vocational education programs in three major areas:

- establishment of voluntary industry-based skills standards for most occupations;

- integration of academic and vocational education curricula; and

- emphasis on providing quality vocational education to all students, including special populations.

The 1990s legislation required establishment of state-level performance measures for vocational education programs funded by federal monies. One example of a program that addresses all three developments in vocational education is the Tech Prep program. Organized by broad career clusters such as Health and Human Services, Engineering and Industrial Training, Information Systems, tech prep programs are composed of a two-to-three year curriculum of instruction in the basic principles of science, math, communications, and social policies that form the backbone of a particular cluster. Under this program both college prep and voc ed students would take classes together. One student might be planning for career in medical school and another might have the goal of obtaining a position as a nurse's aide immediately after graduation.

Academies and magnet schools also exemplify integration of academic and vocational education coursework, particularly in urban areas. Academies are schools within schools that concentrate on one vocational area and provide a high level of structure. Students take all their voc ed classes from the same teachers for two to three years. Magnet schools such as aviation high schools, fashion high schools, and the Chicago High School for Agricultural Sciences operate independently and offer a less structured program than academies.

For Further Study

Books

Allum, K. F. *Finding One's Way: Career Guidance for Disadvantaged Youth.* Washington, DC: US Department of Labor, Employment, and Training Administration, 1993.

Grub, W. N. ed. *Education Through Occupations: Integrating Academic and Vocational Education in American High Schools (Vols. 1 & 2).* New York: Teachers College Press, 1995.

Levesque, Karen, et al. *Vocational Education in the United States: The Early 1990s.* Washington, DC: US Department of Education, National Center for Education Statistics, November 1995.

Levinson, E. M. *Transdisciplinary Vocational Assessment: Issues in School Based Programs.* Brandon, VT: Clinical Psychology Publishing Co., 1993.

National Occupational Information Coordinating Committee (NOICC). *National Career Development Guidelines.* Portland, OR: Northwest Regional Educational Laboratory, 1989.

Secretary's Commission on Achieving Necessary Skills. *What Work Requires of Schools.* Washington, DC: US Department of Labor, 1991.

Stern, D., et al. *Career Academies: Partnerships for Reconstructing American High Schools.* San Francisco: Jossey-Bass, 1992.

Organizations

National Center for Research in Vocational Education
Address: University of California at Berkeley
1995 University Avenue, Suite 375
Berkeley, CA 94704-1058
Telephone: toll free (800) 762-4093

█ Vomiting

Forcibly disgorging the contents of the stomach through the mouth.

Vomiting in children has a wide range of causes, from ordinary cases of stomach flu that spontaneously resolve within days to serious disorders of the digestive tract and other problems. The most common danger associated with vomiting is dehydration, especially when the vomiting is accompanied by **fever** and **diarrhea.** Severe, repeated vomiting can also strain the esophagus and stomach and cause internal bleeding or shock. If it becomes chronic, vomiting can also disrupt a child's metabolism and slow growth. Another concern is the danger that vomit will be aspirated into the lungs, which can lead to pneumonia.

Infancy

Vomiting should be distinguished from the spitting up (gastrointestinal reflux) that is common in infants. Unlike the forcible reverse peristalsis of vomiting, spitting up is a free discharge of the stomach contents resulting from rapid feeding or overfeeding, or simply from the fact that in the first six months the entrance to an infant's stomach isn't tight enough to keep all its contents down all the time. Unless there are other problems associated with it, spitting up does not pose any danger and is considered normal for infants under 15 months.

Infants with chronic vomiting may also have a condition that results when the esophogeal sphincter, the valve between the esophagus and stomach, allows the stomach contents to flow back into the esophagus. This problem, usually outgrown within the first year, can be alleviated by burping the infant frequently and by leaving the infant in an upright or semi-upright position for at least 30 minutes following a feeding. For bottlefed babies, thickening the formula with baby cereal may help.

In contrast, persistent vomiting in an infant may indicate a serious disorder, including some that require surgery. An example is pyloric stenosis, a narrowing of the passageway between the stomach and small intestine caused by a thickening of the surrounding muscle. (Abnormal narrowing of a digestive system passageway is known as *stenosis;* the pyloric sphincter connects the stomach and small intestine.) The hallmark of pyloric stenosis is projectile vomiting, usually within 15 to 30 minutes of feeding. Most infants with pyloric stenosis begin to exhibit projectile vomiting sometime between two weeks and four months. Pyloric stenosis is the most common surgically correctable cause of vomiting, occurring in approximately one out of every 250 births. (It is four times more common in boys than girls.) Similarly, anal stenosis is the condition in which the anus is too small to allow the passage of fecal material.

Vomiting in infants and young children may also be caused by other congenital conditions that require surgery, including atresia, in which the esophagus or another part of the gastrointestinal tract fails to open properly; Hirschsprung's disease, in which some of the nerve cells that regulate normal bowel activity are missing; and intussusception, in which part of the small intestine "telescopes" onto itself, with one section sliding over another. Intussusception usually occurs between the ages of 6 months and 2 years.

The most common cause of vomiting in children is gastroenteritis (stomach flu), which is caused by a virus in over 90% of cases. In gastroenteritis, vomiting is usually accompanied by diarrhea, which increases the danger of dehydration, making it important for the lost body fluids to be replaced, preferably with a specially prepared oral rehydration solution. About one to two hours after the last vomiting episode, offer the child a few sips of cool water. Follow this every half hour with a few sips of water or other clear liquid such as sugar water or gelatin water (one-half to one teaspoon of sugar or flavored gelatin in about four ounces of water). Commercially prepared solutions, sold under such names as Naturalyte, Pedialyte, and Rehydralyte, contain a combination of water and electrolytes in the form of citric acid, potassium citrate, potassium sorbate, potassium benzoate, and sodium chloride, usually with fruit flavoring. These fluids are regulated by the Food and Drug Administration (FDA) as medical foods. Food can gradually be reintroduced when the vomiting starts to subside. In most cases of gastroenteritis, the vomiting lasts between 12 and 24 hours with moderate abdominal pain and little or no fever.

When an infant or young child is vomiting, it is important to keep his head turned to the side or face down over a basin or towel to minimize the possibility of inhaling the vomitus (material being vomited) into the lungs.

Two serious causes of chronic vomiting in children of any age are malrotation and volvulus. Malrotation (as its name suggests) refers to a congenital abnormality in the rotation which normally occurs in the fetus as the gastrointestinal tract develops. Malrotation allows portions of the intestine to become twisted, causing intermittent vomiting. This twisting can even destroy a portion of the intestine by cutting off its blood supply, a condition known as volvulus, characterized by abdominal pain and persistent vomiting. Both malrotation and volvulus require surgical treatment. (Volvulus is considered a surgical emergency.)

In addition to the flu, vomiting is associated with other infectious diseases, including pneumonia, **meningitis,** urinary tract infections, and intestinal infections—including food poisoning—caused by bacteria such as campylobacter, *E. coli,* shigella, and staphylococcus. Other medical causes of vomiting include migraine headaches, disorders of the central nervous system, brain tumors, hepatitis, **appendicitis,** ulcers, metabolic disorders, and food **allergies.**

An environmentally related cause of vomiting is motion sickness in response to travel by car, airplane, boat, or other form of transport. The symptoms—which include headache, pallor, and sweating in addition to vomiting—are believed to be triggered by the vestibular apparatus in the inner ear, which is responsible for balance and spatial orientation. Many physicians discourage the use of antinausea medications (antiemetics), especially for young children, because of possible side effects which can be intensified by dehydration.

After age five, abdominal pain and vomiting is also a common response to emotional upset—either distress or excitement. In children, vomiting may be triggered by any one or combination of factors such as anxiety, anticipation over an upcoming event, feelings of unhappiness, disappointment, or anger. In female adolescents, chronic vomiting can be sign of an **eating disorder** or **pregnancy.** If a child exhibits recurring abdominal pain and vomiting accompanied by change in behavior, emotional triggers for the digestive problems should be considered. A pediatrician, teacher, or child psychologist can provide insight into the root of the emotional upset if the problem persists.

For Further Study

Books

Maryon-Davis, Alan, and Steven Parker. *Food and Digestion.* New York: F. Watts, 1990.

Peikin, Steven R. *Gastrointestinal Health.* New York: HarperCollins, 1991.

Videorecordings

Gut Feelings: Health Talks at the Cleveland Clinic. Cleveland, OH : Cleveland Clinic Foundation, 1996.
(Two-hour video on digestive disorders.)

Organizations

American Digestive Disease Society
Address: 7720 Wisconsin Avenue, NW
Bethesda, MD 20814
Telephone: (301) 223-0179
(Organization for people with digestive diseases. Provides information and referral; offers counseling; publications include *Living Healthy,* booklets, and books on special diets to manage various digestive disorders.)

Voucher System *see* **School Vouchers**

Watson, John Broadus (1878–1958)

American psychologist and founder of behaviorism.

John Broadus Watson is best known as the founder of **behaviorism**, which he defined as an experimental branch of natural science aimed at the prediction and control of behavior. Its model was based on Ivan Pavlov's studies of conditioned reflex: every conduct is a response to a stimulus or to a complex set of stimulus situations. From birth, a few stimuli elicit definite reactions. But most behaviors are conditioned; they result from the association of unconditioned stimuli to other stimuli.

Watson was born in 1878 to a poor, rural South Carolina family. His mother was a pious Baptist; his father left the family in 1891. After taking a traditional classical curriculum at Furman University, he studied philosophy at the University of Chicago. Disappointed with John Dewey's teaching, he began work in animal psychology, and received his Ph.D. in 1903. Watson was a professor at Johns Hopkins University from 1908 to 1920, when he was dismissed because of his relationship with a graduate student, Rosalie Rayner. He divorced his wife, married Rosalie, and had a successful career in advertising. In 1957, he was awarded a gold medal by the **American Psychological Association** (of which he had been the youngest president, in 1915). Watson died in 1958.

Developmental issues were crucial for behaviorism. According to Watson, unhealthy adult personalities resulted from habit systems carried over from infancy. Early childhood was key, and a detailed knowledge of child development was indispensable for designing a behavioral social technology. The significance of childhood and child-study for behaviorism is summed up in Watson's most famous statement: "Give me a dozen healthy infants . . . and my own specified world to bring them up in and I'll guarantee to take any one at random and train him to become any type of specialist I might select . . . regardless of his talents, penchants, tendencies, abilities, vocations, and the race of his ancestors."

By 1917 Watson had focused his research on children. He carried out pioneering observational and experimental work on newborns and infants, produced *Experimental Investigation of Babies* (1919), one of the first psychology films done in the United States, wrote the best-selling manual *Psychological Care of Infant and Child*, and became a popular child-rearing expert. Much of his research was directed at distinguishing unlearned from learned behavior. Observations of hundreds of babies revealed that sneezing, hiccoughing, crying, erection of penis, voiding of urine, defection, smiling, certain eye movements and motor reactions, feeding responses, grasping, and blinking were unlearned, but that they began to become conditioned a few hours after birth. Crawling, **swimming**, and **handedness** appeared to be learned. Watson also traced the beginnings of language to unlearned vocal sounds, and found that three forms of emotional ("visceral") response can be elicited at birth be three sets of stimuli: fear (by loss of support and loud sounds; Watson did not notice that his conditioning fear of fire through burning alone contradicted his view), rage (by hampering of bodily movement), and love (by stroking of the skin, tickling, gentle rocking, patting). Just as there was no innate fear of darkness, there was no instinctive love of the child for the mother; all "visceral habits" were shaped by conditioning. In one of the most controversial experiments of all psychology, Watson conditioned eleven-month-old "little Albert" to fear furry objects; this case was for him proof that complex behavior develops by conditioning out of simple unlearned responses.

Watson considered the ultimate aim of psychology to be the adjustment of individual needs to the needs of society. He encouraged parents to approach childrearing as a professional application of behaviorism. *Psychological Care of Infant and Child* (1928) is dedicated "to the first mother who brings up a happy child." Such a child would be an autonomous, fearless, self-reliant, adaptable, problem-solving being, who does not cry unless physically hurt, is absorbed in work and play, and has no great attachments to any place or person. Watson warned against the dangers of "too much mother love," and advocated strict routines and a tight control over the child's environment and behavior. His disapproval of thumb-sucking, masturbation, and homosexuality was not moral, but practical, and he encouraged parents to be honest about sex. He agreed with psychoanalysts on the importance of sexuality. Partly because of the premature end to Watson's university career, his views did not have a decisive influence on academic child psychology. They contributed, however, to professionalizing childbearing, and bolstered contemporary arguments, by Fred and John Dewey for example, on the determining lifelong effects of early development.

For Further Study

Books

Buckley, K.W. *Mechanical Man. John Broadus Watson and the Beginnings of Behaviorism.* New York: Guilford Press, 1989.

Cohen, D. *Behaviorism.* [1924, 1930], New York: W.W. Norton, 1970.

———. *Psychological Care of Infant and Child.* New York: W.W. Norton, 1928.

———. *J.B. Watson: The Founder of Behaviorism.* London: Routledge & Kegan Paul, 1979.

Weaning

The process of decreasing breastfeeding and introducing other replacement forms of nutrition to a baby or toddler, such as bottlefeeding, cupfeeding, and solid foods.

Weaning can occur at widely varying ages, according to culture, family, and individual circumstances. The average age for weaning is 4.20 years worldwide, but in the United States babies are usually weaned after the first year, and quite often after only five or six months of age. A survey of mothers in the United States practicing extended breastfeeding reported an average weaning age of 2.75 years. Generally, exclusive **breastfeeding** is recommended for the first six months, and either formula or breast milk should constitute 75% of the babies' diet during at least the first year.

Weaning should be initiated at an otherwise nonstressful time, and should be done gradually over a period of months. Abrupt weaning is not recommended, because it is traumatic for the baby and may cause **depression** and breast mastitis in the mother. If for some reason breast milk becomes abruptly unavailable, a feeding tube should be introduced and the baby held in the familiar nursing position while feeding. To begin weaning, systematically eliminate feedings to no more than one feeding every three days. The process can be continued until feedings become rare and eventually stop.

An alternative to mother-led weaning is baby-led weaning, where breastfeeding continues until the baby voluntarily stops. The average age for baby-led weaning is about 2.50 years. A policy many mothers find successful is "don't offer and don't refuse." Mothers can start to offer liquids from a cup instead of offering the breast at feeding times unless the baby gives a clear signal that he or she wants to be breastfed. For babies over nine months the feeding can be replaced by solid food or drink. Reading, singing, or other close personal time can also be substituted for time usually spent breastfeeding.

With decreased stimulation of the breasts lactation should naturally diminish, but if breast engorgement should still occur, milk can be artificially expressed to reduce pressure. This, however, interferes with the weaning process and will prolong the period of lactation.

For Further Study

Books

Eisenberg, A., et al. *What to Expect the First Year.* New York: Workman Pub., 1989.

La Leche League International Staff, eds. *The Womanly Art of Breastfeeding: Thirty-Fifth Anniversary Edition.* New York: NAL-Dutton, 1991.

Wechsler Intelligence Scales

Series of intelligence tests.

A widely used series of **intelligence** tests developed by clinical psychologist David Wechsler. Their most distinctive feature is their division into a verbal section and a nonverbal (or "performance") section, with separate scores available for each one. Verbal intelligence, the component most often associated with academic success, implies the ability to think in abstract terms using either words or mathematical symbols. Performance intelligence suggests the ability to perceive relationships and fit separate parts together logically into a whole. The inclusion of the performance section in the Wechsler scales is especially helpful in assessing the cognitive ability of non-native speakers and children with speech and language disorders. The test can be of particular value to school psychologists screening for specific learning disabilities because of the number of specific subtests that make up each section. The Wechsler Preschool and Primary Scales of Intelligence (WPPSI) have traditionally been geared toward children ages 4–6, although the newest version of the test (WPPSI-III, 1989) extends the age range down to 3 years and upward to 7 years 3 months. The Verbal section covers the following areas: general information (food, money, the body, etc.); vocabulary (definitions of increasing difficulty); comprehension (responses to questions); arithmetic (adding, subtracting, counting); sentences (repeating progressively longer sentences); and similarities (responding to questions such as "How are a pen and pencil alike?"). The Performance section includes picture completion; copying geometric designs; using blocks to reproduce designs; working through a maze; and building an "animal house" from a model.

The Wechsler Intelligence Scale for Children (WISC), now in its second revision (WISC-III, 1991), is designed for children and adolescents ages 6–16. Its makeup is similar to that of the Preschool Scale. Differences include the following: geometric designs are replaced by assembly of three-dimensional objects; children arrange groups of pictures to tell simple stories; they are asked to remember and repeat lists of digits; a coding exercise is performed in place of the animal house; and mazes are a subtest. For all of the Wechsler scales (which also include the Wechsler Adult Intelligence Scale, or WAIS), separate verbal and performance scores, as well as a total score, are computed. These are then converted using a scale divided into categories (such as average and superior), and the final score is generally given as one of these categories rather than as a number or percentile ranking.

For Further Study

Books

McCullough, Virginia. *Testing and Your Child: What You Should Know About 150 of the Most Common Medical, Educational, and Psychological Tests.* New York: Plume, 1992.

Shore, Milton F., Patrick J. Brice, and Barbara G. Love. *When Your Child Needs Testing: What Parents, Teachers, and Other Helpers Need to Know about Psychological Testing.* New York: Crossroad, 1992.

Walsh, W. Bruce, and Nancy E. Betz. *Tests and Assessment.* 2nd ed. Englewood Cliffs, NJ: Prentice Hall, 1990.

Well Baby Examination

Examinations held regularly during the first two years of life during which the pediatrician can monitor and advise on the baby's growth and development.

The **American Academy of Pediatrics** recommends the newborn infant see a doctor for a check-up at birth, one, two, four, six, nine, 12, 15, 18, and 24 months, and annually thereafter. Most pediatricians follow this schedule, or some variation of it, in prescribing a check-up regimen for their patients.

The features of a well-baby examination or "check-up" include:

Taking a history. During this stage, the physician or an assistant will ask the parents a number of questions. Topics include developmental milestones, interactions with peers and adults, sleeping patterns, and eating habits. Examples are "Are there any changes or concerns that have come up since the last visit?;" "How is the child functioning in child-care?;" "How is the relationship with peers?" The pediatrician (or his assistant) will observe the parents and the infant for signs of distress or difficulties with adjustment. In addition, they will be alert for any signs of child abuse.

Performing a physical examination. At every visit, the child will be examined by the physician, usually conducted on a child undressed to his or her diaper or underwear. Parents should discuss this aspect of the routine with the older infant and toddler prior to the visit, so that he or she is prepared to remove his or her clothes. The child will be measured, weighed, and have temperature and blood pressure recorded. Infants will have head circumference measured as well. The pediatrician will also check the eyes, ears, mouth, and throat; heart and lung rates; abdomen for unusual masses or enlargements; genitalia for anything unusual; arm and leg movement; and reflexes.

Answering parents' questions. The pediatrician may solicit questions by asking, "Do you have any concerns?" Some parents bring written questions, so that they will not forget to ask something they want more information about.

Explaining expected developmental pattern to parents. The pediatrician can help parents understand their child's next stage of development by explaining what stages are coming next, and by forewarning parents of difficulties that typically arise. The pediatrician also discusses behavior, **nutrition**, and safety issues, recommending **childproofing** strategies and emphasizing car seat use, for example.

Administering developmental and medical tests and **immunizations***.* Many pediatricians order various tests, such as urinalysis, tuberculin test, and blood tests during the first two years. The American Academy of Pediatrics recommends **cholesterol** screening of children over age two whose parents have a history of cardiovascular disease before age 55, or have blood cholesterol levels above 240mg/dl. Because there are a number of controversial factors influencing the value of cholesterol screening, as of the late 1990s the AAP did not recommend universal cholesterol screening.

For Further Study

Books

Eisenberg, Arlene. *What to Expect the First Year.* New York: Workman Publishing, 1988.

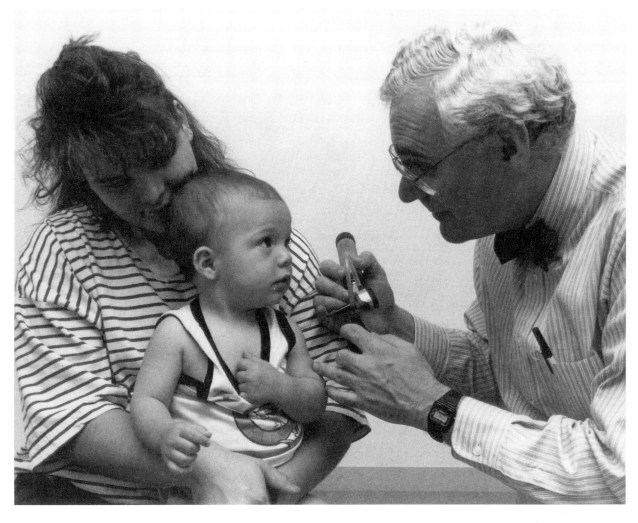

During the well-baby examination, the pediatrician talks with the mother about the baby's development.

Leach, Penelope. *Your Baby and Child from Birth to Age Five.* New York: Knopf, 1989.

Spock, Benjamin. *Dr. Spock's Baby and Child Care.* New York: Dutton, 1992.

Periodicals

Shelov, Steven P. "A Visit to the Pediatrician." *Good House-keeping* 219, September 1994, p. 180+.

Wise, Nicole. "Well-Baby Visits." *Parenting* 10, March 1996, p. 134.

Whole Language

Refers to a method of literacy instruction which is based on the theory that children can learn written language (reading and writing) as effortlessly as they learn spoken language.

Proponents of whole language believe that, if children are immersed in a print-rich environment from an early age, reading and writing skills will develop natural-ly. This hands-off philosophy is in direct opposition to traditional language instruction programs that teach children to associate sounds with the individual letters that make up words. In such traditional phonics-based programs, children are taught to "decode" unfamiliar words by sounding them out. Some pure-phonics programs (such as the widely advertised commercial product "Hooked on Phonics") go so far as to teach letter-sound associations completely separate from any meaningful context.

In contrast to **phonics**-based programs, the whole-language method emphasizes whole-word recognition skills. Teachers in whole-language kindergarten class-rooms often read aloud to children from "big books" (oversized versions of children's books), pointing to each printed word as it is spoken. Rather than using basal reading texts with limited vocabularies, reading selections come from the canon of "authentic" children's literature. After several readings of the same big book, a child might begin to recite the words along with the teacher. In this way, according to the whole-language theorists, children learn to recognize whole words in context.

Another essential component of whole language is the incorporation of literature "across the curriculum" rather than the isolation of literature in a separate language arts program. For example, if a first-grade class were studying bats, there might be a shelf full of books in the classroom about bats, including current fiction titles such as *Stellaluna* by Janell Cannon.

The whole-language approach is used in approximately 20-25% of elementary-school reading programs in the United States, with an even greater number adopting at least some of the techniques of whole language. The movement gained momentum in the 1980s with the publication of *What's Whole in Whole Language* by University of Arizona education professor Kenneth Goodman. Most teachers' colleges and university-level education departments now advocate the whole-language ideology, and a number of state education agencies have also adopted the whole-language philosophy in some form or other.

Despite its widespread use, the whole-language approach is by no means welcomed by all parents and educators. The so-called "great debate" over phonics versus its alternatives has been going on for more than a century in this country. In the 1950s, Rudolf Flesch's bestselling book, *Why Johnny Can't Read*, swung public opinion in the direction of phonics-based instruction. But in the late 1970s, however, phonics was being criticized for making learning to read a joyless chore. In the 1990s the "back to basics" movement in education cited lower reading scores among U.S. schoolchildren as evidence that whole language is a failure. Children from socially and economically disadvantaged backgrounds appear to be particularly vulnerable in strictly whole-language classrooms because they do not receive as much informal letter-sound instruction at home as their middle-class peers do. Several states (most notably California and Texas) are in the process of reconsidering their policies on reading instruction.

In the midst of this debate, there are some who believe a compromise between pure whole language and pure phonics might be the most prudent approach to literacy instruction. Researchers such as Marilyn Adams advocate using a combination of instructional methods and adapting them to individual children's needs.

Preschool

Whole language methodologies are often implemented before formal **reading** instruction begins simply by stocking the preschool classroom with ample materials for "reading" and "writing." The housekeeping center in a print-rich preschool classroom might include a telephone directory for children to "look up" phone numbers and paper and pencil for children to "write"

grocery lists. Children playing "office" or "post office" might pretend to address envelopes. In this manner, preschoolers have numerous opportunities to practice literacy skills in a natural way simply by imitating the actions of adults in their lives.

School age

In addition to being read to from "big books," children in whole-language kindergarten classrooms write on a regular basis, even before they know the conventional spellings of words. Using this "invented spelling" a child in such a classroom might write a journal entry that reads: "Mi dg haz a yelo coler and a grn lees" (My dog has a yellow collar and a green leash). In addition, children in whole-language classrooms often collaborate on writing projects, creating their own "big books."

Even in first and second grade, teachers in whole-language classrooms overlook misspellings or misreadings. If a child reading out loud from a book says "chair" when the word in print is actually "seat," the teacher does not "correct" him or her. Rather, such misreadings are viewed as a natural step on the road to reading competency.

Adolescence

One innovative use of whole-language reading instruction is the Literature Project, a program that uses literature to help build **self-esteem** in adolescents with learning and behavior problems. In its original conception, the Literature Project was devised to improve reading skills and self-perception in female juvenile offenders through the reading of books about women who embodied such qualities as courage, loyalty, and tolerance. Because the program was so successful in this population, it has been adapted for use with other adolescents.

For Further Study

Books

Adams, Marilyn J. *Beginning to Read: Thinking and Learning About Print.* Cambridge, MA: MIT Press, 1990.

Commission on Reading. *Becoming a Nation of Readers.* Pittsburgh: National Academy of Education, 1984.

Flesch, Rudolf. *Why Johnny Can't Read.* New York: Harper, 1955.

Goodman, Kenneth S. *What's Whole in Whole Language: A Parent-Teacher Guide.* Portsmouth, NH: Heinemann, 1986.

Wide Range Achievement Test (WRAT-R)

Measures basic academic skills.

The Wide Range Achievement Test is a test of basic academic skills for ages 5–adult, covering **reading** (word recognition and pronunciation), written spelling, and arithmetic. It is used for educational placement, identification of strengths, weaknesses, and possible learning problems, and as a tool in planning remedial programs. Used in conjunction with behavior or intelligence tests, such as the Wechsler Scales, it can also aid in providing information about personality. The test is given at two levels: Level I (ages 5–11) and Level II (12–adult). It consists of three paper-and-pencil subtests with 50–100 items each, arranged in order of increasing difficulty. The Reading subtest consists of recognizing and naming letters and pronouncing printed words. The Spelling subtest includes copying marks resembling letters, writing one's name, and printing words, and the Arithmetic section involves counting, reading number symbols, and oral and written computation. The test is normed by age rather than grade. Raw scores for each subtest are converted to percentile rankings, standard scores, and grade equivalents. The Spelling and Arithmetic sections can be given either individually or in groups, but the Reading subtest must be administered individually. Large-print editions of WRAT-R are available for use with visually impaired children.

For Further Study

Books

McCullough, Virginia. *Testing and Your Child: What You Should Know About 150 of the Most Common Medical, Educational, and Psychological Tests.* New York: Plume, 1992.

Shore, Milton F., Patrick J. Brice, and Barbara G. Love. *When Your Child Needs Testing: What Parents, Teachers, and Other Helpers Need to Know about Psychological Testing.* New York: Crossroad, 1992.

Walsh, W. Bruce, and Nancy E. Betz. *Tests and Assessment.* 2nd ed. Englewood Cliffs, NJ: Prentice Hall, 1990.

Williams Syndrome

A rare genetic disorder first described by J.C.P. Williams of New Zealand, characterized by an abnormality on chromosome seven.

Williams syndrome (WS) is a genetic disorder first described by J.C.P. Williams of New Zealand. It is estimated to occur in about 1 in 20,000 births. Research has indicated that individuals with Williams syndrome have a chromosomal abnormality. A blood test technique known as the fluorescent *in situ* hybridization (FISH) may be used to detect the deletion of the elastin gene on chromosome #7 of the individual's DNA. This chromosomal abnormality confirms the diagnosis of Williams syndrome. Williams syndrome is present from birth, although it often remains undiagnosed until a later stage of

PERCENT OF INFANTS WITH WILLIAMS SYNDROME WHO DISPLAY SPECIFIC MEDICAL OR DEVELOPMENTAL DIFFICULTIES	
Symptom	**Percent of infants with Williams syndrome exhibiting symptom**
Failure to thrive	81%
Congenital heart defects	79%
Feeding difficulty	71%
Colic	67%
Constipation	43%
Vomiting	40%
Chronic ear infections	38%
Inguinal hernia	38%
Umbilical hernia	14%
Hypercalcemia	4–6%

Source: Williams Syndrome Association, 1997.

development. After a child has missed several developmental milestones, the pediatrician may refer him or her to a specialist for diagnosis. **Developmental delays** that are typical include delay in sitting or walking. Also commonly observed are poor fine motor coordination and delayed development in language (although individuals with WS go on to develop excellent language skills). After reviewing the child's medical and family history, physical condition, and observing the child's behavior, a specialist in **birth defects** may identify symptoms of Williams syndrome. In many cases, a heart murmur or suspected heart disorder may lead a cardiologist to suspect Williams syndrome, since an estimated 70–75% of people with Williams syndrom have mild to severe cardiovascular problems.

Diagnosis and treatment

Williams syndrome cannot be cured, but the ensuing symptoms, developmental delays, learning problems, and behaviors can be treated. There is a wide variation in the number and severity of symptoms among the individuals with Williams syndrome.

Specialists who can be helpful in diagnosing and treating Williams syndrome include

- cardiologist, to diagnose and prescribe treatment for heart or circulatory problems;

- endocrinologist, to prescribe treatment if elevated calcium levels are detected in infancy;

- pediatric radiologist, to conduct diagnostic renal and bladder ultrasound tests to diagnose and prescribe treatment for any abnormalities present; and

- occupational therapist, to assess development delays and prescribe a plan for therapy to acquire skills necessary for daily living.

Physical characteristics typical of Williams syndrome include a broad forehead, puffiness around the eyes, stellate eye pattern (in blue-eyed children), upturned nose, depressed nasal bridge, full lips, widely spaced teeth, and small chin. In addition, a child with Williams syndrome often exhibits one or more of these characteristics: sloping shoulders, and elongated neck. Many individuals with Williams syndrome have heart disorders, typically supravalvular aortic stenosis (narrowing) and pulmonary stenosis. Kidney and bladder problems are also common. Poor muscle tone and problems with the skeletal joints become evident as a person with Williams syndrome moves into adolescence.

Infancy and toddlerhood

Williams syndrome babies typically have low weight at birth, and are often diagnosed as **failure to thrive.** Elevated levels of calcium in the blood (hypercalcemia) may develop in infancy, but it usually is resolved within the first two years. Digestive system symptoms such as vomiting, constipation, and feeding difficulties may contribute to a misdiagnosis in the first months after birth. The infant may not be able to settle in a normal sleep pattern, and may seem to be extremely sensitive to noise (hyperacusis or sensitive hearing), exhibiting agitation or distress when exposed to high-pitched sounds, such as electrical appliances, motors, and loud bangs. This sensitivity most often goes away or diminishes greatly.

School age

By the time the child with Williams syndrome is ready to enter school, mild to severe learning difficulties may appear, including impulsiveness and poor concentration. Contributing to classroom difficulties are problems with vision and spatial relations. Concepts involving numbers—especially math and time—appear to be more difficult. In the later elementary school years, a child with Williams syndrome will be more adept at producing language than at comprehending it. Poor muscle tone and development will continue to contribute to difficulties with **gross** and **fine motor skills.** The Williams syndrome child has difficulty forming relationships with his or her peers, preferring the company of younger children or adults. Throughout childhood, the child with Williams syndrome may exhibit deficits in the ability to reason and in self-help skills.

Children with Williams syndrome are overly social and outgoing and are inappropriately friendly to adults and unwary of strangers. Williams syndrome children are talkative, with intense enthusiasm bordering on obsession for topics that interest them.

Adolescence

As the child with Williams syndrome approaches full adult growth and maturity, he or she is typically shorter than average height with progressive physical problems, including increasing potential for hypertension. In most cases, the adolescent and adult with Williams syndrome will require multidisciplinary care, with continued medical assessment to diagnose and treat medical complications early. The ability to live independently and to work are usually not limited by the physical problems, which are treated successfully in the majority of cases. Rather, psychological characteristics and the ability to behave appropriately in social settings are more likely to prevent the individual from living and functioning completely on his or her own. However, each year more individuals with William syndrome are able to living independently in supervised apartment settings.

For Further Study

Organizations

Williams Syndrome Association Inc.
    Address: P.O. Box 297
    Clawson, Michigan 48017-0297
    Telephone: (248) 541-3630
    website: www.williams-syndrome.org
Canadian Association for Williams Syndrome
    Address: P.O. Box 2115
    Vancouver, British Columbia V6B 3T5

—Reviewed by Williams Syndrome Association

Withdrawal Behavior

Tendency to avoid either unfamiliar persons, locations, or situations.

Withdrawal behavior is characterized by the tendency to avoid the unfamiliar, either people, places, or situations. Though withdrawal, or avoidance, can be the result of a temperamental tendency toward inhibition to unfamiliar events, anxiety over the anticipation of a critical evaluation of the child, or a conditioned avoidant response, often called a **phobia,** can produce withdrawal. These are three different mechanisms, each of which can mediate withdrawal behavior in the child. The withdrawal or avoidance that is seen in the preschool years is, most of the time, due to a temperamental bias that makes some children uncertain over unfamiliar events. During later childhood, withdrawal or avoidance occurs to very specific events, like lightening, animals, insects, or foods. At this state, withdrawal is usually not the result of a temperamental bias, but more often is due to conditioning experiences in which the child had a painful or frightening experience in association with the even he avoids.

A small group of children who appear withdrawn may have serious mental illness, including **schizophrenia** or **autism**. However, these are relatively rare illnesses and therefore the average child who appears withdrawn will probably not be afflicted with these problems.

—Jerome Kagan
Harvard University

Working Mothers

More mothers in the United States are working today than ever before. In 1993, 58% of mothers with children under the age of six, and nearly 75% of those with children between the ages of six and eighteen were part of the paid labor force. Although the number of single mothers, who are dependent solely on their own income, is steadily increasing, a growing percentage of married women living with their husbands are working as well (40% worked full time in 1992, compared with 16% in 1970). The rapid influx of women into the labor force that began in the 1970s was marked by the confidence of many women in their ability to successfully maintain both a career and a family. Throughout the 1970s and 1980s the dominant image of the working mother was the "Supermom," juggling meetings, reports, and presentations with birthday parties, science projects, and soccer games. With growing numbers of women confronting the competing pressures of work and home life, observers predicted that these women's needs would be accommodated by significant changes in how things were managed on both fronts: a domestic revolution in the roles of the sexes at home and a major shift toward enlightened attitudes and policies toward women in the workplace. Although there have been some changes, they have not been substantial enough to prevent many working mothers from feeling that the price for "having it all" is too high. In the '90s working mothers are increasingly expressing disenchantment with the "Supermom" ideal and looking for alternatives to help them create a better balance between work and family.

The "Mommy track"

Working mothers in many fields experience conflicts between motherhood and professional advancement. Many report that their professional aspirations are not taken as seriously by colleagues or superiors once they have children. In particular, if they quit working for a time to stay home with their children, the gap in their resumes is regarded with suspicion. One study found that the earnings of women with MBAs who took even nine months off after their children were born were still 17% lower 10 years later than those of employees with similar qualifications but no comparable gap in their employment record. Some women feel too threatened by the repercussions of time off the job to even take a maternity leave; others report problems on reentering the workforce after such a leave. Women in highly competitive professions are especially reluctant to lighten their work loads or schedules for fear that such measures will signal a lower level of commitment or ability than that of their peers, and they will be automatically assigned to the infamous "Mommy track." Many women—both with and without children—in traditionally male professions still earn lower salaries and carry greater workloads than those of male colleagues with comparable credentials and work experience because of the perception that they are not the "breadwinners" in their families.

Working two shifts

On the home front, married working mothers, even those whose husbands espouse an egalitarian philosophy, still find themselves saddled with most of the housework and child care responsibilities. In effect, they often have the equivalent of two jobs, a phenomenon expressed in the title of Arlie Hochschild's highly regarded study *The Second Shift,* which reported that the husbands of working mothers shoulder, on average, one third of the couple's household duties. Hochschild also noted that the tasks performed most often by men, such as repairs and home maintenance chores, can often be done at their convenience, as opposed to women's duties, such as cooking, which must be done on a daily basis and at specific times, giving women less control over their schedules. In 1990 a survey of 5,000 couples found that only 50% of husbands take out the garbage, 38% do laundry, and 14% iron. Working mothers also receive less help than ever from their children, with one important exception— working single mothers, whose children help out at home twice as much as children in other families. In addition, they often work at tasks traditionally done by the opposite sex: boys cook, clean, and babysit; girls help with home repairs and yard work. A supplementary benefit of this development is that the daughters of single mothers have a greater than average likelihood of entering traditionally male professions offering higher pay and better opportunities for advancement.

Day care arrangements

More than eight million school-age and fifteen million preschool-age children are placed in the charge of substitute care givers during the hours their mothers are working. The major options for child care include staggered work hours that allow parents to meet all child care needs themselves; care by relatives or close friends; hiring a **babysitter** or housekeeper; and **day care** in a private home or at public facilities, including day care centers, nursery schools, and company-sponsored programs. In 1990, provisions for children under the age of five were split almost equally between in-home care by parents or other relatives and out-of-home care by non-relatives. The percentage of child care provided by day care centers had increased from 6% in 1965 to 28% in 1990, partly because the influx of women into the workforce had narrowed the pool of female relatives and friends available to take care of other people's children. In the past two decades, employment by day care centers has increased over 250%, representing a gain of almost 400,000 new jobs. However, a 1995 survey found that only 10% of the nation's 681 major employers offered on-site care programs to their employees.

Alternative work arrangements

Given the failure of either home or workplace demands to ease significantly, working mothers routinely sacrifice time for themselves, and many report high levels of stress, anxiety, and fatigue. In addition, many still feel torn between the conflicting demands of family and career and feel guilty for not being able to spend more time with their children. Increasing numbers of working mothers also feel responsible for helping their own aging parents as they develop health problems and become less able to handle their own affairs. (And parents traditionally place greater demands on grown daughters than on sons.) In addition, working mothers are often expected to assume most of the responsibility in family emergencies, such as the illness of a child, which periodically disrupt their already overloaded schedules.

Dissatisfied with the pressures and sacrifices of combining mothering with full-time work, many women have sought alternatives that allow them to relax the hectic pace of their lives but still maintain jobs and careers. According to one study, the number of companies offering some type of employment flexibility to their workers rose from 51% in 1990 to 73% in 1995. Fifty-five percent offered flex-time, while 51% offered part-time work. Mothers who work part-time gain more flexibility and more time with their children, as well as time to devote to their own needs. They are able to be there when their children get home from school, attend school plays and

other functions, and take their children to doctor appointments without facing conflicts at work. However, part-time work also has disadvantages, even aside from the cut in pay. Many part-timers carry workloads disproportionate to the number of hours they put in, sometimes being required to be available by phone to clients or colleagues during their hours at home. They may also face the resentment of co-workers on a nine-to-five schedule, and part-time work, like time taken off the job, usually places women at a disadvantage in terms of professional advancement. Promotions come later, and the "fast-track" positions are often out of reach altogether.

An employment arrangement that is becoming increasingly popular is job sharing, in which two people jointly fill one full-time position. They may alternate their hours in a variety of ways depending on what arrangement best suits the personal and professional needs of both women. For example, one pair of job sharers may work alternate days, while another arrangement may have each woman working two days in a row and part of a third day. Job sharing opens up a wider arena of employment than that normally available to holders of traditional part-time jobs, and unlike most part-time employees, women who job share generally receive benefits, prorated in accordance with the number of hours each works. For working mothers another advantage of job sharing is that women who job share often cover for each other when unusual family needs arise. In successful job sharing arrangements, the partners have a cooperative, supportive relationship, staying in close touch to maintain continuity on the job. One study found that the number of companies with job sharing arrangements almost doubled between 1992 and 1994.

The computer revolution has made possible yet another alternative work option for mothers seeking extra time and a more flexible schedule: telecommuting, or working from home. According to reports in both the *Wall Street Journal* and the *New York Times,* telecommuting is the fastest-growing type of alternative work arrangement in the United States today. It can replace either all or part of one's hours at the workplace, and a telecommuter can work either part- or full-time. Telecommuters receive and send documents via their company's computer networks and can be available, if necessary, by e-mail, voice mail, and pager. Even when a telecommuting employee is expected to adhere to fixed work hours, the arrangement still provides a significant savings in time spent dressing for work, commuting back and forth, and socializing with other employees. Experts caution, however, that a woman who works at home should not expect to simultaneously take care of her children. Telecommuting mothers are advised to arrange for child care during their working hours and to be disciplined in maintaining boundaries between their work and their family life. Like other alternative work arrangements, telecommuting can result in a loss of professional status, due to the prejudices of colleagues and superiors and also to the networking opportunities lost while working at home. In addition, some employers try to change the employment status of telecommuters to that of independent contractor, resulting in a loss of benefits.

A final option for working mothers who want a challenging but flexible work schedule is self-employment, a rapidly growing career option for women. While the number of entrepreneurs in the United States increased 56% overall in the 1980s, the number of female entrepreneurs grew 82%. It is estimated that women will start 2.5 million companies in the 1990s and that they will own half of all American businesses by the year 2000. In the early 1990s home-based businesses started by women were the fastest-growing type of small business. The number of women employed in these ventures tripled between 1985 and 1991. Self-employment can accommodate a wide range of skills and employment backgrounds, from cooking and crafts to consulting and tax law. Self-employed women working at home may put in long hours and those leaving high-powered corporate jobs usually earn less money, at least initially, but they gain flexibility and control over their schedules. Like telecommuters, self-employed women need to make day care arrangements and be able to mentally and physically maintain boundaries between their business and personal lives. Fortunately, start-up costs for home-based businesses are relatively low. For women requiring assistance, low-interest loans can be obtained through the Small Business Administration, which also runs a variety of training and networking programs for female entrepreneurs. A number of states also offer programs that aid women-owned businesses.

For Further Study

Books

Byalick, Marcia, and Linda Saslow. *The Three-Career Couple: Mastering the Art of Juggling Work, Home, and Family.* Princeton, NJ: Peterson's, 1993.

Christenson, Kathleen. *Women and Home-Based Work: The Unspoken Contract.* New York: Henry Holt, 1988.

Gerson, Kathleen. *Hard Choices: How Women Decide about Work, Career, and Motherhood.* Berkeley: University of California Press, 1985.

Hays, Sharon. *The Cultural Contradictions of Motherhood.* New Haven: Yale University Press, 1996.

Hochschild, Arlie, with Anne Machung. *The Second Shift: Working Parents and the Revolution at Home.* New York: Viking, 1989.

Jones, Jacqueline. *Labor of Love, Labor of Sorrow: Black Women, Work, and the Family from Slavery to the Present.* New York: Basic Books, 1985.

Mahony, Rhona. *Kidding Ourselves: Breadwinning, Babies, and Bargaining Power.* New York: HarperCollins, 1995.

Polakow, Valerie. *Lives on the Edge: Single Mothers and Their Children in the Other America.* Chicago: University of Chicago Press, 1993.

Swiss, Deborah J., and Judith P. Walker. *Women and the Work/ Family Dilemma.* New York: John Wiley & Sons, 1993.

Weisberg, Anne C., and Carol A. Buckler. *Everything a Working Mother Needs to Know.* New York: Doubleday, 1994.

Organizations

9 to 5: National Association of Working Women
    Address: 1430 W. Peachtree St., Suite 610
    Atlanta, GA 30310
    Telephone: toll-free hotline (800) 522-0925; (414) 274-0925

Families and Work Institute.
    Address: 330 Seventh Ave.
    New York, NY 10001
    Telephone: (212) 465-2044

Mothers' Home Business Network
    Address: P.O. Box 423A
    East Meadow, NY 11554
    Telephone: (516) 997-7394

National Association of Women Business Owners (NAWBO)
    Address: 1377 K Street NW
    Washington, DC 20005
    Telephone: (301) 608-2590

New Ways to Work
    Address: 149 Ninth St.
    San Francisco, CA 94103
    Telephone: (415) 552-1000

Small Business Administration, Office of Women's Business Ownership
    Address: 409 Third Street SW
    Washington, DC 20416
    Telephone: (202) 205-6673

Working Women Count Honor Roll
    Telephone: toll-free (800) 827-5335
    (Department of Labor program to share information about innovative employment arrangements for working women.)

Year-Round School

Refers to a reorganization of the traditional 180-day school calendar so that children attend school in every season of the year.

In year-round schools, children attend all year with more frequent, shorter breaks taking the place of the 10-week summer vacation characteristic of the traditional calendar. A typical schedule would feature three-week "intersessions" between ten-week academic blocks.

"Year-round" schooling is also the term frequently used to describe what is more accurately called "extended-year" schooling. Extended-year schools may operate on a similar year-round schedule, but their calendars include more days of instruction. Instead of going to school for around 180 days per year, children enrolled in extended-year systems typically attend classes for 200 or more days. In 1995, it was estimated that more than 1.5 million children in the United States attended year-round schools, about five times the number in 1985.

The framework for the traditional school schedule in the United States, with its 180 days and long summer vacation, was set in the more agrarian culture of the 18th and early 19th centuries. Because children were needed to perform vital functions on family farms during the late spring and summer, schooling was relegated to cooler weather months. Even as times changed and society became more industrialized, the tradition became ingrained in American culture. Women, who had not yet begun to work outside the home in large numbers, were available to care for younger children during the long summer break. Families scheduled vacations and other recreational activities around the summer months. Because of the long-standing tradition, proposals to institute year-round schooling, with or without added days of instruction, typically are met with vociferous debate.

Many opponents of year-round schooling simply object to breaking tradition. Others point to more substantive pitfalls. Teachers who want to study for advanced degrees or enrichment would lose their chance at concentrated study. Summer recreational opportunities—camps, swimming pools, water parks—would be lost to children. The organizations that operate such activities would suffer financially and jobs would be lost. For most communities, the financial burden presented by year-round schools is another major objection. Teacher salaries and training costs would increase, as would the cost of operating schools year.

Those in favor of extending the school calendar point to many benefits of such a move. Because large numbers of women now work outside the home, many parents are faced with the dilemma of finding safe, stimulating, and affordable child care during the summer. Year-round schools would ease some of that burden. All-season schooling would present special benefits to inner-city areas where weak, at-home support for education is common and drop-out rates are high. Teachers would experience less stress and burn-out because of the more frequent breaks. School buildings, targets for vandals during the summer, would be easier to maintain if continuously occupied. Vacations would be cheaper and easier for parents to schedule because they would be available several times per year, not just during peak seasons. And overcrowding could be eased by scheduling students on rotating on-off schedules throughout the year.

The educational value of traditional versus year-round or extended-year schools is perhaps the most hotly debated topic. Supporters of a calendar change contend that most teachers currently spend an inordinate amount of time at the beginning of each school year reviewing the previous year's material. Many of today's students fail to retain much of their learning over the long summer break. Shorter breaks would improve continuity and thus increase learning. Remediation would also be facilitated by more constant instruction. Instead of waiting for the traditional "summer school" to assist children who need extra instruction, those opportunities could be offered during each "intersession."

Advocates of extended-year education blame the outdated school calendar for the poor performance of

DAYS IN SCHOOL YEAR WORLDWIDE	
Country	**Days in standard school year**
Japan	243
South Korea	220
Israel, Luxembourg	216
Netherlands, Scotland, Thailand	200
England, Hungary	192
Swaziland	191
Finland, New Zealand, Nigeria	190
France	185
Spain, Sweden, United States	180

American students on standardized tests administered worldwide. In fact, most children in the United States attend school fewer days per year than children in almost any industrialized country in the world. For example, the school year runs 243 days in Japan, up to 240 in Germany, 220 in South Korea, and 216 in Israel. By the time Japanese teens have completed 12th grade, they would have spent the equivalent of at least three more years in school than their U.S. counterparts. Standardized test results typically show Japanese scores far superior to American. For example, some tests show 98% of Japanese children score better than American children on math and science. The accompanying table provides the average humber of school days per year in selected countries.

Supporters of the current system state that poor scores by students in the United States are the result of inadequate curriculum rather than lack of class time. Some estimate that more than half of classroom time in

the United States is devoted to nonacademic courses rather than core courses like English, math, and science. Strengthening the curriculum, holding teachers to more stringent standards, and requiring students to do more homework, some experts contend, will do more to increase test scores than extending the school calendar.

Opinion polls throughout the years show that, while year-round and extended-year schooling are still controversial, more Americans are supporting some type of change in the educational system. The Gallup polling organization has been asking questions about the subject since the late 1940s. In 1989, for the first time, more people supported increasing classroom time than opposed it. Some states are gradually adding small numbers of days to their calendars, and as of 1993, some year-round schools were operating in at least 32 states in more than 300 school districts and 1,500 schools.

For Further Study

Books

Berliner, David C., and Bruce J. Biddle. *The Manufactured Crisis: Myths, Fraud and the Attack on America's Public Schools.* Reading, MA: Addison-Wesley Publishing Co., 1995.

Cetron, Marvin and Margaret Gayle. *Educational Renaissance: Our Schools at the Turn of the Century.* New York: St. Martin's Press, 1991.

Periodicals

Allis, Sam. "Why 180 Days Aren't Enough." *Time* 138, no. 9, September 2, 1991.

Barrett, Michael J. "The Case for More School Days." *The Atlantic* 266, no. 5, November 1990, pp. 78+.

Forbes, Steve. "Quality Time." *Forbes* 154, no. 6, September 12, 1994, pp. 25+.

Tawasha, Mary Ann. "Breaking Away from the Agrarian School Calendar: Can 30 More Days Make a Difference?" *Omni* 17, no. 7, April 1995, p 20.

Tice, R. Dean. "Year-round Schools: What Do They Mean for Parks and Recreation?" *Parks & Recreation* 28, no. 11, November 1993, p. 2.

"How Not to Be Outclassed Abroad." *U.S. News & World Report* 108, no. 7, February 19, 1990, p. 12.

Warrick-Harris, Elaine. "Year-round School: The Best Thing Since Sliced Bread." *Childhood Education* 71, no. 5, annual 1995, pp. 282+.

BIBLIOGRAPHY

A

Aaseng, Nathan. *Cerebral Palsy.* New York: F. Watts, 1991.

Ackerman, Robert J., Ph.D., and Dee Graham. *Too Old to Cry: Abused Teens in Today's America.* Blue Ridge Summit, Pennsylvania: TAB Books, 1990.

Adams, Marilyn J. *Beginning to Read: Thinking and Learning About Print.* Cambridge, MA: MIT Press, 1990.

Adderholdt-Elliott, M. R. *Perfectionism: What's Bad About Being Too Good.* Minneapolis: Free Spirit, 1987.

Adelman, H., and L. Taylor. *Learning Problems and Learning Disabilities.* Pacific, CA: Brooks, 1993.

Adler, Bill, Jr. *Tell Me a Fairy Tale: A Parent's Guide to Telling Magical and Mythical Stories.* New York: Penguin, 1995.

Ainsworth, Frank, and Leon C. Fulcher, eds. *Group Care for Children: Concept and Issues.* New York: Tavistock, 1981.

Ainsworth, M. *Infancy in Uganda: Infant Care and the Growth of Love.* Baltimore: Johns Hopkins University Press, 1967.

——, M. C. Blehar, E. Waters, and S. Wall. *Patterns of Attachment: A Psychological Study of the Strange Situation.* Hillsdale, NJ: Earlbaum, 1978.

Aitchison, Jean. *The Seeds of Speech: Language Origin and Evolution.* New York: Cambridge University Press, 1996.

Alan Guttmacher Institute. *Sex and America's Teenagers.* New York: New York, 1994.

Alba, Richard D. *Ethnic Identity: The Transformation of White America.* New Haven: Yale University Press, 1990.

Algozzine, B., et al. *Behaviorally Disordered? Assessment for Identification and Instruction.* Reston, VA: The Council for Exceptional Children, 1991.

Allum, K. F. *Finding One's Way: Career Guidance for Disadvantaged Youth.* Washington, DC: US Department of Labor, Employment, and Training Administration, 1993.

Almonte, Paul. *The Immune System.* Crestwood House; Maxwell Macmillan Canada; Macmillan International, 1991.

Alvino, James, and the editors of *Gifted Children Monthly. Parents' Guide to Raising a Gifted Child: Recognizing and Developing Your Child's Potential.* Boston: Little, Brown, 1985.

——, and the editors of *Gifted Children Monthly. Parents' Guide to Raising a Gifted Toddler: Recognizing and Developing the Potential of Your Child from Birth to Five Years.* Boston: Little, Brown, 1989.

Amabile, Teresa M. *Growing Up Creative: Nurturing a Lifetime of Creativity.* New York: Crown Publishers, 1989.

——. *The Social Psychology of Creativity.* New York: Springer-Verlag, 1983.

American Academy of Pediatrics. *Sports Medicine: Health Care for Young Athletes.* Elk Grove Village, IL: American Academy of Pediatrics, 1991.

American Physical Therapy Association. *Scoliosis: An Anthology*. Alexandria, Va.: American Physical Therapy Association, 1984.

Ames, Louise Bates. *Arnold Gesell: Themes of His Work*. New York: Human Sciences Press, 1989.

———. *He Hit Me First: When Brothers and Sisters Fight*. New York: Warner Books, 1989.

Andersen, Hans Christian. *Andersen's Fairy Tales*. Trans. by L. W. Kingsland. Oxford: Oxford University Press, 1985.

Anderson, Clifford. *The Stages of Life: A Groundbreaking Discovery: The Steps to Psychological Maturity*. New York: Atlantic Monthly Press, 1995.

Anderson, Eugene, George Redman, and Charlotte Rogers. *Self-Esteem for Tots to Teens: Five Principles for Raising Confident Children*. New York: Simon and Schuster, 1984.

Anderson, Robert H., and Barbara Nelson Pavan. *Nongradedness: Helping It to Happen*. Lancaster, Pennsylvania: Technomic Press, 1993.

Annunziata, Jane, and Phyllis Jacobson-Kram. *Solving Your Problems Together: Family Therapy for the Whole Family*. Washington, DC: American Psychological Association, 1994.

Antaki, Charles and Alan Lewis, eds. *Mental Mirrors: Metacognition in Social Knowledge and Communication*. Beverly Hills: Sage, 1986.

Arcus, D. (forthcoming). *The Roles of Temperament and Family Experience in Early Development*.

Asher, S. R., and J. D. Coie, eds. *Peer Rejection in Childhood*. New York: Cambridge University Press, 1990.

Atkinson, Jacqueline M. *Schizophrenia: A Guide to What It Is and What Can Be Done to Help*. San Bernardino, CA: R. Reginald Borgo Press, 1989.

Avraham, Regina. *The Reproductive System*. New York : Chelsea House, 1991.

Axelrod, R.M. *The Evolution of Cooperation*. New York: Basic Books, 1984.

Aylward, Elizabeth H. *Understanding Children's Testing: Psychological Testing*. Austin, TX: Pro-Ed, 1991.

Ayres, A. Jean. *Sensory Integration and the Child*. Los Angeles: Western Psychological Services, 1979.

Azarnoff, Pat, ed. *Preparation of Young Healthy Children for Possible Hospitalization: The Issues*. Santa Monica: Pediatric Projects, 1983.

Azrin, Nathan. *Habit Control in a Day*. New York: Simon and Schuster, 1977.

———, and V.A. Besalel. *A Parent's Guide to Bedwetting Control*. New York: Pocket Books, 1981.

B

Bandura, Albert. *Social Learning*. Englewood Cliffs, NJ: Prentice Hall, 1977.

Banks, James A. *An Introduction to Multicultural Education*. Boston: Allyn and Bacon, 1994.

Barr, Murray Llewellyn. *The Human Nervous System: An Anatomical Viewpoint*. 6th ed. Philadelphia, PA: Lippincott, 1993.

Bass, Ellen, and Kate Kaufman. *Free Your Mind: The Book for Gay, Lesbian, and Bisexual Youth—and Their Allies*. New York: HarperPerennial, 1996.

Bauer, Caroline Feller. *New Handbook for Storytellers*. Chicago: American Library Association, 1993.

Baugh, John. *Black Street Speech: Its History, Structure, and Survival*. Austin: University of Texas Press, 1983.

Bean, Constance A. *Methods of Childbirth*, 2nd ed. Garden City, New York: Doubleday, 1990.

Bean, Reynold. *How to Develop Your Children's Creativity*. Los Angeles: Price Stern Sloan, 1992.

Beck, Aaron. *Cognitive Therapy and the Emotional Disorders*. New York: International Universities Press, 1976.

Beckelman, Laurie. *Body Blues*. New York: Crestwood House, 1994 [juvenile literature].

Bee, Helen L. *Lifespan Development*. New York: HarperCollins Publishers, 1994.

———. *The Developing Child*. 7th ed. New York: HarperCollins College Publishers, 1995.

Beirne-Smith, Mary, et al., eds. *Mental Retardation*. New York: Merrill, 1994.

Bell, Alison, and Lisa Rooney. *Your Body Yourself: A Guide to Your Changing Body.* Chicago: Contemporary Books, 1993.

Bell, Ruth, et al. *Changing Bodies, Changing Lives.* New York: Vintage, 1988.

Bellet, Paul S. *The Diagnostic Approach to Common Symptoms and Signs in Infants, Children, and Adolescents.* Philadelphia: Lea & Febiger, 1989.

Berch, Daniel B., and Bruce G. Bender. *Sex Chromosome Abnormalities and Human Behavior: Psychological Studies.* Boulder: Westview Press, 1990.

Berenstain, Stan. *The Berenstain Bears and the In-Crowd.* New York: Random House, 1989.

Berezin, Judith. *The Complete Guide to Choosing Child Care.* New York: Random House, 1990.

Berger, Joseph, et al. *Status Characteristics and Social Interaction: An Expectation-States Approach.* New York: Elsevier Scientific, 1977.

Berges, E., S. Neiderbach, B. Rubin, E. Sharpe, R. Tesler. *Children and Sex: The Parents Speak.* New York, NY: Facts on File, 1983.

Berko-Gleason, J. *The Development of Language.* New York: Macmillan, 1993.

Berkowitz, Samuel. *The Cleft Palate Story: A Primer for Parents of Children with Cleft Lip and Palate.* Chicago: Quintessence Books, 1994.

Berliner, David C., and Bruce J. Biddle. *The Manufactured Crisis: Myths, Fraud and the Attack on America's Public Schools.* Reading, Mass.: Addison-Wesley Publishing Co., 1995.

Bernard, B. *The Case for Peers.* Portland, OR: Northwest Regional Educational Laboratory, 1990.

Bernstein, Neil I. *Treating the Unmanageable Adolescent: A Guide to Oppositional Defiant and Conduct Disorders.* Northvale, NJ: Jason Aronson, 1997.

Berry, James R. *Why You Feel Hot, Why You Feel Cold: Your Body's Temperature.* Boston: Little, Brown, 1973.

Bettelheim, Bruno. *The Uses of Enchantment: The Meaning and Importance of Fairy Tales.* New York: Vintage Books, 1977.

Biracree, Tom, and Nancy Biracree. *The Parents' Book of Facts: Child Development from Birth to Age Five.* New York: Facts on File, 1989.

Bishop, Rudine Sims, ed. *Kaleidoscope: A Multicultural Booklist for Grades K-8.* Urbana: National Council of Teachers of English, 1994.

Bjorklund, Barbara R., and David F. Bjorklund. *Parents [TM] Book of Discipline.* New York: Ballantine Books, 1990.

Blackman, Derek E. *Operant Conditioning: An Experimental Analysis of Behaviour.* London: Methuen, 1974.

Blau, Theodore H. *The Psychological Examination of the Child.* New York: J. Wiley & Sons, 1991.

Bloch, Dorothy. *So the Witch Won't Eat Me: Fantasy and the Child's Fear of Infanticide.* New York: Grove Press, 1978.

Block, Martin E. *A Teacher's Guide to Including Students With Disabilities in Regular Physical Education.* Baltimore: Brookes, 1994.

Blomquist, Geraldine M. *Coping as a Foster Child.* New York: Rosen Publishing, 1992.

Bloodstein, Oliver. *A Handbook on Stuttering.* 5th ed. San Diego: Singular Publishing Group, 1995.

Blume, Sheila B. *What You Can Do to Prevent Fetal Alcohol Syndrome: A Professional's Guide.* Minneapolis: Johnson Institute, 1992.

Boden, M. *Jean Piaget.* Penguin Books, 1979.

Bolick, Nancy O'Keefe. *How to Survive Your Parents' Divorce.* New York: Franklin Watts, 1994.

Borman, Kathryn M. and Nancy P. Greenman. eds. *Changing American Education: Recapturing the Past or Inventing the Future?* Albany: State University of New York Press, 1994.

Bornstein, M., ed. *Handbook of Parenting.* Hillsdale, NJ: Erlbaum, 1995.

Bosma, Bette. *Fairy Tales, Fables, Legends, and Myths: Using Folk Literature in Your Classroom.* 2nd ed. New York: Teachers College Press, 1992.

Bottigheimer, Ruth B. *Fairy Tales and Society.* Philadelphia: University of Pennsylvania Press, 1986.

Bottner, B. *The World's Greatest Expert on Absolutely Everything...Is Crying.* New York: Dell Publishers. 1986.

Bourgeois, Paulette, and Martin Wolfish. *Changes in You and Me: A Book About Puberty, Mostly for Boys.* Kansas City: Andrews and McMeel, 1994.

Bowen-Woodward, Kathryn. *Coping With a Negative Body-Image.* New York: Rosen Publishing Group, 1989.

Bowlby, John. *Attachment and Loss. Vol. 1: Attachment.* New York: Basic Books, 1969.

———. *Attachment and Loss. Vol. 2: Separation: Anxiety and Anger.* New York: Basic Books, 1973.

———. *Attachment and Loss. Vol. 3: Loss: Sadness and Depression.* New York: Basic Books, 1980.

———. *A Secure Base: Parent-Child Attachment and Healthy Human Development.* New York: Basic Books, 1988.

Bowler, Rosemary F., ed. *Annals of Dyslexia.* Baltimore, Md.: The Orton Dyslexia Society, 1983.

Boyd-Franklin, Nancy. *Black Families in Therapy.* New York: Guilford Press, 1989.

Boyer, C.B. "Psychosocial, Behavioral, and Educational Factors in Preventing Sexually Tranxmitted Diseases." In: Schydlower, M., and M.A. Shafer. (eds.), *Adolescent Medicine: State of the Art Reviews: AIDS and Other Sexually Transmitted Diseases.* Vol I(3). Philadelphia: Hanley & Belfus, Inc., 1990, pp. 597–613.

Brace, Edward R., and John P. Pacanowski. *Childhood Symptoms: Every Parent's Guide to Illnesses.* New York: HarperPerennial, 1992.

Bradley, Robert A. *Husband–Coached Childbirth.* New York: Harper and Row, 1981.

Braly, James, M.D. and Laura Torbet. *Dr. Braly's Food Allergy and Nutrition Revolution.* New Canaan, CT: Keats Publishing, 1992.

Branch, Taylor. *Parting the Waters: America in the King Years, 1954–1963.* New York: Simon and Schuster, 1988.

Bregman, Albert S. *Auditory Scene Analysis: The Perceptual Organization of Sound.* Cambridge, MA: MIT Press, 1990.

Breines, Estelle. *Occupational Therapy Activities from Clay to Computers: Theory and Practice.* Philadelphia: F. A. Davis Company, 1995.

Breitenbach, Robert J., Janet B. Carnes, Judy A. Hammond. *Baby Seats, Safety Belts, and You!* 2nd ed. Washington, DC: U. S. Department of Transportation, National Highway Traffic Safety Administration.

Brenner, Barbara. *The Preschool Handbook: Making the Most of Your Child's Education.* New York: Pantheon Books, 1990.

Bridge, R. Gary. *The Determinants of Educational Outcomes: The Impact of Families, Peers, Teachers, and Schools.* Cambridge, MA: Ballinger Publishing Co., 1979.

Briggs, John. *Fire in the Crucible: The Alchemy of Creative Genius.* New York: St. Martin's Press, 1988.

Britton, L. *Montessori Play and Learn.* New York: Crown, 1992.

Brown, Christy. *My Left Foot.* New York, Simon and Schuster, 1955.

Brown, Fern G. *Hereditary Diseases.* New York: Franklin Watts, 1987.

Brown, Jeffrey L. *The Complete Parents' Guide to Telephone Medicine: A Ready Reference for Childhood Illnesses, Common Emergencies, Newborn Infant Care, Psychological and Behavior Problems.* New York: Putnam, 1988.

Brown, Jeffrey. *No More Monsters in the Closet: Teaching Your Child to Overcome Everyday Fears and Phobias.* New York: Crown Paperbacks, 1995.

Bruner, Jerome. *On Knowing: Essays for the Left Hand.* Cambridge, MA: Belknap Press, 1979.

———. *Studies in Cognitive Growth: A Collaboration at the Center for Cognitive Studies.* New York: Wiley, 1966.

Buckingham, R. W. *Care of the Dying Child: A Practical Guide for Those Who Help Others.* New York: Continuum, 1989.

Buckley, K.W. *Mechanical Man. John Broadus Watson and the Beginnings of Behaviorism.* New York: Guilford Press, 1989.

Burman, Erica. *Deconstructing Developmental Psychology.* New York: Routledge, 1994.

Buss, A.H. *Self Consciousness and Social Anxiety.* San Francisco: W.H. Freeman, 1980.

Buss, D. and R. Plomin. *Temperament: Early Developing Personality Traits.* Hillsdale, New Jersey: Erlbaum, 1984.

Byrne, Kevin P. *Understanding and Managing Cholesterol: A Guide for Wellness Professionals.* Champaign, IL: Human Kinetics Books, 1991.

C

Caillet, Rene. *Scoliosis: Diagnosis and Management.* Philadelphia: F.A. David, 1975.

Campbell, Joseph, ed. *The Portable [Carl] Jung.* New York: Viking, 1971.

Candland, Douglas Keith. *Feral Children and Clever Animals: Reflections on Human Nature.* New York: Oxford University Press, 1993.

Capossela, Cappy, and Sheila Warnock. *Share the Care: How to Organize a Group to Care for Someone Who Is Seriously Ill.* New York: Simon and Schuster, 1995.

Caris, Timothy N. *Understanding Hypertension: Causes and Treatments.* New York: Basic Books, 1986.

Carroll, Marilyn. *Cocaine and Crack. The Drug Library.* Springfield, NJ: Enslow Publishers, 1994.

Carruthers, Peter. *Human Knowledge and Human Nature: A New Introduction to an Ancient Debate.* New York: Oxford University Press, 1992.

Carson, Lillian. *The Essential Grandparent: A Guide for Making a Difference.* Deerfield Beach, FL: Health Communications, 1996.

Carter, Bernadette. *Child and Infant Pain: Principles of Nursing Care and Management.* London: Chapman and Hall, 1994.

Carter, Maggie. *Training Teachers: A Harvest of Theory and Practice.* Redleaf Press, 1994.

Cash, Thomas F. *What Do You See When You Look in the Mirror?: Helping Yourself to a Positive Body Image.* New York: Bantam Books, 1995.

Cattell, Raymond B. *Personality and Learning Theory.* Springer Publishing, 1979.

Cetron, Marvin and Margaret Gayle. *Educational Renaissance: Our Schools at the Turn of the Century.* New York: St. Martin's Press, 1991.

Chall, Jeanne. *Learning to Read: The Great Debate.* New York: McGraw-Hill, 1983.

Chandler, Louis A., and Virginia J. Johnson. *Using Projective Techniques with Children: A Guide to Clinical Assessment.* Springfield, IL: C.C. Thomas, 1991.

Chavez, Linda. *Out of the Barrio: Toward a New Politics of Hispanic Assimilation.* New York: Basic Books, 1991.

Cherlin, Andrew J., and Frank F. Furstenberg, Jr. *The New American Grandparent: A Place in the Family, A Life Apart.* New York: Basic Books, 1986.

Chess, S. and A. Thomas. *Origins and Evolution of Behavior Disorders: From Infancy to Early Adult Life.* Cambridge, MA: Harvard, 1987.

Chirinian, Alain. *Boys' Puberty: An Illustrated Manual for Parents and Sons.* New York: Tom Doherty Associates, 1989.

Chodorow, Nancy. *The Reproduction of Mothering: Psychoanalysis and the Sociology of Gender.* Berkeley: University of Berkeley Press, 1978.

Chomet, Julian. *Speed and Amphetamines.* New York: Franklin Watts, 1990.

Church, Ellen Booth. *Everything You Always Wanted to Know about Preschool but Didn't Know Whom to Ask.* New York: Scholastic Books, 1996.

Clancy, Helen, and Michele J. Clark. *Occupational Therapy with Children.* New York: Churchill Livingstone, 1990.

Clark, Aminah, Harris Clemes, and Reynold Bean. *How to Raise Teenagers' Self-Esteem.* San Jose: Price/Stein/Sloan Publishing, 1985.

Clark, Barbara. *Growing Up Gifted,* 3rd ed. Columbus, Oh.: Merrill Publishing Co., 1988.

Clark, Catherine, Alan Dyson, and Alan Millward, eds. *Towards Inclusive Schools?* New York: Teachers College Press, 1995.

Clark, Charlotte. *Inside Manic-Depression: The True Story of One Victim's Triumph over Despair.* Sunnyside Press, 1993.

Clark, Cindy Dell. *Flights of Fancy, Leaps of Faith: Children's Myths in Contemporary America.* Chicago: University of Chicago Press, 1995.

Clark, Lynn. *The Time-Out Solution: A Parent's Guide for Handling Everyday Behavior Problems.* Chicago: Contemporary Books, 1989.

Clayman, Charles B., ed. *The Human Body: An Illustrated Guide to Its Structure, 1st American ed.* New York: Dorling Kindersley Publishing, 1995.

Cohen, D. *Behaviorism.* [1924, 1930], New York: W.W. Norton, 1970.

———. *J.B. Watson: The Founder of Behaviorism.* London: Routledge & Kegan Paul, 1979.

———. *Psychological Care of Infant and Child.* New York: W.W. Norton, 1928.

Cohen, Libby G., and Loraine J. Spenciner. *Assessment of Young Children.* New York: Longman, 1994.

Cole, L. *Never Too Young to Die: The Death of Len Bias.* New York: Pantheon, 1989.

Coles, Robert. *Anna Freud: The Dream of Psychoanalysis.* Reading, MA: Addison-Wesley Publishing Company, Inc., 1992.

———. *The Mind's Fate: A Psychiatrist Looks at His Profession.* Boston: Little, Brown and Co., 1975.

———. *The Spiritual Life of Children.* Boston: Houghton Mifflin, 1990.

Commission on Reading. *Becoming a Nation of Readers.* Pittsburgh: National Academy of Education, 1984.

Conture, Edward G., and Jane Fraser, eds. *Stuttering and Your Child: Questions and Answers.* Memphis, TN: Speech Foundation of America, 1990.

Cook, Allan R. *Immune System Disorders Sourcebook: Basic Information for the Layperson.* Detroit, MI: Omnigraphics, 1996.

Cook, L., and M. Friend. *Interactions: Collaboration Skills for School Professionals.* White Plains, NY: Longman Publishing, 1992.

Cook, Ruth E., Annette Tessier, and M. Diane Klein. *Adapting Early Childhood Curricula for Children in Inclusive Settings.* 4th ed. Englewood Cliffs, NJ: Merrill, 1996.

Cook, William. *Tracking Down Hidden Food Allergies.* Jackson, TN: Professional Books, 1980.

Copeland, Lennie. *The Lice-Buster Book: What To Do When Your Child Comes Home With Head Lice!* Mill Valley, California: Authentic Pictures, 1995.

Corbett, Margaret-Ann and Jerrilyn H. Meyer. *The Adolescent and Pregnancy.* Boston: Blackwell Scientific Publications, 1987.

Coren, Stanley. *The Left-Hander Syndrome: The Causes and Consequences of Left-Handedness.* New York: Vintage Books, 1993.

———, and L.M. Ward. *Sensation and Perception.* 3rd ed. San Diego: Harcourt Brace Jovanovich, 1989.

Corr, Charles A. *Sudden Infant Death Syndrome: Who Can Help and How.* New York: Springer Publishing Co., 1991.

Corrick, James A. *Muscular Dystrophy.* New York: F. Watts, 1992.

Costa, Paul T., and Thomas A. Widiger, eds. *Personality Disorders and the Five-Factor Model of Personality.* Washington, DC: American Psychological Association, 1994.

Costin, Carolyn. *Your Dieting Daughter: Is She Dying for Attention?* New York: Brunner/Mazel, 1997.

Council for Exceptional Children, Department of Public Policy. *The Rights of Children with Disabilities under ADA and Section 504: A Comparison to IDEA.* Reston, VA: Author, 1994.

Council of Administrators of Special Education. *Student Access: A Resource Guide for Educators, Section 504 of the Rehabilitation Act of 1973.* Albuquerque, NM: Author, 1991.

Crandall, Richard, and Thomas Crosson, eds. *Dwarfism: The Family and Professional Guide.* Irvine, CA: Short Stature Foundation and Information Center, 1994.

Crawford, James. *Hold Your Tongue: Bilingualism and the Politics of "English-Only."* Reading, MA: Addison-Wesley Publishing Co., 1992.

Crittenden, Paul. *Learning to Be Moral: Philosophical Thoughts About Moral Development.* New Jersey: Humanities Press International, 1990.

Culbertson, Jan L., and Diane J. Willis, eds. *Testing Young Children: A Reference Guide for Developmental, Psychoeducational, and Psychosocial Assessments.* Austin, TX: PRO-ED, Inc., 1993.

———, Henry F. Krous, and R. Debra Bendell, eds. *Sudden Infant Death Syndrome.* Baltimore: Johns Hopkins University Press, 1988.

Cummins, J. *Bilingualism and Special Education: Issues in Assessment and Pedagogy.* Clevedon, England: Multilingual Matters. Co-published in the U.S. by College-Hill Press, San Diego, 1994.

Cunningham, Cliff. *Down's Syndrome: An Introduction for Parents.* Cambridge, MA: Brookline Books, 1988.

Cutler, Evan Karl. *Runaway Me: A Survivor's Story.* Fort Collins, CO: Blooming Press, 1994.

Cytryn, Leon, and Donald H. McKnew. *Growing Up Sad: Childhood Depression and Its Treatment.* New York: Norton, 1996.

D

D'Augelli, Anthony R., and Charlotte J. Patterson. *Lesbian, Gay, and Bisexual Identities Over the Lifespan: Psychological Perspectives.* New York: Oxford University Press, 1995.

Dana, N., and A. Price. *Successful Breastfeeding: A Practical Guide for Nursing Mothers.* New York: Meadowbrook, 1985.

Dance, Sandy. *Picture Interpretation: A Symbolic Approach.* Singapore; River Edge, NJ: World Scientific, 1995.

Dash, Judi. "Is Your Child's Coach a Tyrant?" *Family Circle,* April 23, 1996.

Daugirdas, John T., M.D. *STD, Sexually Transmitted Diseases, Including HIV/AIDS.* Hinsdale, IL: Medtext, 1992.

Davidson, Mayer B. *Diabetes Mellitus: Diagnosis and Treatment.* New York: Churchill Livingstone, 1991.

Davies, Nancy Millichap. *Foster Care.* New York: Franklin Watts, 1994.

Davis, Adelle. *Let's Have Healthy Children.* New York: Harcourt, Brace Jovanovitch, 1972.

Davis, Diane. *Reaching Out to Children with FAS/FAE: A Handbook for Teachers, Counselors, and Parents Who Work with Children Affected by Fetal Alcohol Syndrome and Fetal Alcohol Effects.* West Nyack, NY: Prentice Hall, 1994.

Davis, G. P., and E. Park, eds. *The Heart: The Living Pump.* Washington, DC: U. S. News Books, 1981.

de Villiers, P., and J. de Villiers. *Early Language.* The Developing Child series. Cambridge, Mass.: Harvard University Press, 1979.

De Wardener, H.E. *The Kidney: An Outline of Normal and Abnormal Function.* New York: Churchill Livingstone, 1985.

DeBenedette, Valerie. *Caffeine.* The Drug Library. Springfield, NJ: Enslow Publishers, 1996.

Defrain, John, et al. *Sudden Infant Death: Enduring the Loss.* Lexington, MA: D. C. Heath, 1991.

Deikman, Arthur J. *The Wrong Way Home: Uncovering the Patterns of Cult Behavior in American Society.* Boston: Beacon Press, 1991.

Deleuze, Gilles. *Empiricism and Subjectivity: An Essay on Hume's Theory of Human Nature.* New York: Columbia University Press, 1991.

Deluca, Helen R. *Mountains to Climb.* Huron, OH: Cambric Press, 1983. (Biography)

Delzeit, Linda. *Swimming Made Fun and Easy: Step by Step Advice for Beginning and Advanced Swimmers.* Dubuque, IL: Kendall/Hunt Publishing Co., 1991.

Dement, William C. *The Sleepwatchers.* Stanford: Stanford Alumni Association, 1992.

Denny, M. Ray. *Comparative Psychology: Research in Animal Behavior.* Homewood, IL: Dorsey Press, 1970.

Deutsch, M. *The Resolution of Conflict: Constructive and Destructive Processes.* New Haven, CT: Yale University Press, 1989.

Diagnostic and Statistical Manual of Mental Disorders, 4th edition. Washington, DC: American Psychiatric Association, 1994.

Diamant, Anita. *The New Jewish Baby Book: Names, Ceremonies, Customs.* Woodstock, VT: Jewish Lights, 1993.

Diamant, Louis, and Richard D. McAnulty, ed. *The Psychology of Sexual Orientation, Behavior, and Identity: A Handbook.* Westport, CT: Greenwood Press, 1995.

Diamond, Barbara. *Bat Mitzvah: A Jewish Girl's Coming of Age.* New York: Viking, 1995.

Dick-Read, Grantley. *Childbirth Without Fear.* New York: Harper and Row, 1984.

Dillingham, Maud. *It's 1995. Do You Know How Your Children Are?* Santa Monica, CA: Times Books, 1995.

Division of Maternal and Child Health. *Surgeon General's Workshop on Breastfeeding and Human Lactation.* Washington, DC: Bureau of Health Care Delivery and Assistance, 1991.

Dlugokencky, Peter. *The Child Safety Handbook: A Parent's Guide to Avoiding Hidden Household Hazards.* Farmingdale, NY: Blue Island Press, 1995.

Dobson, James. *Children at Risk: The Battle for the Hearts and Minds of Our Kids.* Dallas: Word Publishing, 1990.

———. *Dare to Discipline.* Wheaton, IL: Tyndale House, 1981. *The New Dare to Discipline.* Wheaton: Tyndale, 1992.

———. *Parenting Isn't for Cowards: Dealing Confidently with the Frustrations of Child-Rearing.* Waco, TX: Word Books, 1987.

Dodson, Fitzhugh. *How to Grandparent.* New York: Harper & Row, 1981.

Doft, Norma. *When Your Child Needs Help: A Parent's Guide to Therapy for Children.* New York: Crown Paperbacks, 1992.

Donahoe, John W., and David C. Palmer. *Learning and Complex Behavior.* Boston: Allyn and Bacon, 1994.

Donsbach, Kurt W., and H. Rudolph Alsleben. *Multiple Sclerosis, Muscular Dystrophy and ALS.* USA: Rockland Corporation, 1993.

Doran, Kevin. *What Is a Person: The Concept and the Implications for Ethics.* Lewiston, NY: E. Mellen Press, 1989.

Dorris, Michael. *The Broken Cord.* New York: Harper and Row, 1989.

Dosick, Wayne. *Golden Rules: The Ten Ethical Values Parents Need to Teach Their Children.* San Francisco: HarperCollins, 1995.

Dotto, Lydia. *Losing Sleep: How Your Sleeping Habits Affect Your Life.* New York: William Morrow, 1990.

Down's Syndrome. March of Dimes/Birth Defects Foundation, 1993.

Doyle, Denis P., Chester E. Finn, Jr. *Educational Quality and Family Choice: Toward a State-wide Public School Voucher Plan.* Washington, DC: National Institute of Education, 1983.

Drake, Susan M. *Planning Integrated Curriculum: the Call to Adventure.* Alexandria, VA: Association for Supervision and Curriculum Development, 1993.

Dreikurs, Rudolf. *Logical Consequences: A New Approach to Discipline.* New York: Dutton, 1990.

Drew, Clifford J. *Retardation: A Life Cycle Approach.* Columbus: Merrill, 1988.

Drinking During Pregnancy: Fetal Alcohol Syndrome and Fetal Alcohol Effects. March of Dimes/Birth Defects Foundation, 1991.

Driscoll, Jeanne. *Taking Care of Your New Baby: A Guide to Infant Care.* Garden City Park, NY: Avery Publishing Group, 1996.

Drotar, Dennis, ed. *New Directions in Failure to Thrive: Implications for Research and Practice.* New York: Plenum Press, 1985. Based on the proceedings of the National Institute of Mental Health Workshop held October 9–10, 1984.

Dryden, Windy, ed. *The Essential Albert Ellis: Seminal Writings on Psychotherapy.* New York: Springer, 1990.

DSM-IV Sourcebook. Washington, DC: American Psychiatric Association, 1994. In five volumes, contains documentation of all work leading to criteria published in *DSM-IV,* and includes executive summaries of the rationales for final decisions made in compiling the work.

Duff, John D. *Youth Sports Injuries: A Medical Handbook for Parents and Coaches.* New York: Macmillan, 1992.

Duke, Patty. *Call Me Anna.* New York: Bantam, 1987.

Dunn, Judy. *From One Child to Two.* New York: Fawcett Columbine, 1995.

E

Eastman, Meg. *Taming the Dragon in Your Child: Solutions for Breaking the Cycle of Family Anger.* New York: Wiley, 1994.

Eberlein, Tamara. *Sleep: How to Teach Your Child to Sleep Like a Baby.* New York: Pocket Books, 1996.

Eckert, Helen M. *Motor Development.* 3rd ed. Indianapolis, IN: Benchmark Press, 1987.

Edelson, Edward. *The Immune System.* New York: Chelsea House, 1989.

Edelstein, Susan B. *Children with Prenatal Alcohol and/or Other Drug Exposure: Weighing the Risks of Adoption.* Washington, DC: CWLA Press, 1995.

Efron, Benjamin, and Alvan D. Rubin. *Coming of Age: Your Bar/Bat Mitzvah.* New York: Union of American Hebrew Congregations, 1977.

Eiger, M. S., and S. W. Olds. *The Complete Book of Breastfeeding,* rev. ed. New York: Bantam, 1985.

Eisenberg, A., et al. *What to Expect the First Year.* New York: Workman Pub., 1989.

Eisman, Eugene and Diane Batshaw Eisman. *Your Child and Cholesterol.* Hollywood, FL: Fell, 1990.

Ekkehard, Othmer. *Life on a Roller Coaster: Coping with the Ups and Downs of Mood Disorders.* Pia Press, 1989.

Elia, Irene. *The Female Animal.* New York: Henry Holt, 1988.

Elkind, David. *All Grown Up and No Place to Go: Teenagers in Crisis.* Reading, MA: Addison-Wesley, 1984.

———. *The Child's Reality: Three Developmental Themes.* Hillsdale, NJ: Lawrence Erlbaum Associates, 1978.

———. *The Hurried Child: Growing Up Too Fast Too Soon.* Reading, MA: Addison-Wesley, 1988.

———. *Miseducation: Preschoolers at Risk.* New York: Knopf, 1987.

Elliot, Rose. *Vegetarian Mother and Baby Book: A Complete Guide to Nutrition, Health, and Diet During Pregnancy and After.* New York: Pantheon Books, 1984.

Elliott, Ruth and Jim Savage. *The Complete Guide to In-Home Childcare.* New York: Prentice-Hall, 1988.

———. *Minding the Kids: A Practical Guide to Employing Nannies, Care Givers, Babysitters, and Au Pairs.* 1st ed. New York: Prentice Hall Press, 1990.

Ellis, Lee. *Social Stratification and Socioeconomic Inequality.* Westport, CT: Praeger, 1993.

Engler, Jack, and Daniel Goleman. *The Consumer's Guide to Psychotherapy.* New York: Fireside, 1992.

English, Fenwick W. *Deciding What To Teach and Test: Developing, Aligning, and Auditing the Curriculum.* Newbury Park, CA: Corwin Press, 1992.

Erikson, Erik. *Childhood and Society.* 2nd rev. ed. New York: W. W. Norton, 1963.

———. *Identity and the Life Cycle.* New York: W. W. Norton, 1980.

———. *Identity, Youth and Crisis.* New York: W. W. Norton, 1968.

Erwin, Bette, and Elza Teresa Dinwiddie. *Test Without Trauma: How to Overcome Test Anxiety and Score Higher on Every Test.* New York: Grosset and Dunlap, 1983.

Escobedo, Luis G., et al. "Sports Participation, Age at Smoking Initiation, and the Risk of Smoking Among High School Students." *Journal of the American Medical Association,* March 17, 1993.

Eyer, Diane E. *Mother-Infant Bonding: A Scientific Fiction.* New Haven, CT: Yale University Press, 1992.

Eysenck, H. J. *The Intelligence Controversy.* New York: Wiley, 1981.

———. *The IQ Argument: Race, Intelligence, and Education.* Library Press, 1971.

———. *The Psychology of Politics.* London, England: Routledge & Kegan Paul, 1954.

———, and Michael Eysenck. *Personality and Individual Differences.* New York: Plenum Press, 1985.

F

Feindler, Eva L. *Adolescent Anger Control: Cognitive-Behavioral Techniques.* New York: Pergamon Press, 1986.

———, and Grace R. Kalfus, eds. *Adolescent Behavior Therapy Handbook.* New York: Springer, 1990.

Feldman, B. Robert. *The Complete Book of Children's Allergies.* New York: Times Books, 1986.

Feldman, Shirley, and Glen R. Elliott, eds. *At the Threshold: The Developing Adolescent.* Cambridge, MA: Harvard University Press, 1990.

Feller, Robyn M. *Everything You Need to Know About Peer Pressure.* New York: Rosen Publishing Group, 1995.

Ferber, Richard. *Solve Your Child's Sleep Problems.* New York: Simon and Schuster, 1985.

Ferrara, Judith M. *Peer Mediation: Finding a Way to Care.* York, ME: Stenhouse Publishing, 1996.

Fields, Harriette. *Phonics for the New Reader: Step-by-Step.* Firestone, CO: Words Publishing, 1991.

Fine, Ralph. *The Great Drug Deception.* New York: Stein and Day, 1972.

Fink, Aaron J. *Circumcision: A Parent's Decision for Life.* Mountain View, CA: Kavanah, 1988.

Firestone, Robert W., and Joyce Catlett. *Psychological Defenses in Everyday Life.* New York: Human Sciences Press, 1989.

Fishel, Elizabeth. *Sisters: Shared Histories, Lifelong Ties.* Berkeley: Conari Press, 1994.

Fisher, Arthur, and the editors of Time-Life books. *The Healthy Heart.* Alexandria, VA: Time-Life Books, 1981.

Fishman, Katharine Davis. *Behind the One-Way Mirror: Psychotherapy and Children.* New York: Bantam Books, 1995.

Fiske, Susan T., and Shelley E. Taylor. *Social Cognition.* New York: McGraw Hill, 1991.

Fitness for Life: Childhood to Maturity. Alexandria, VA: Time-Life Books, 1989.

Flesch, Rudolf. *Why Johnny Can't Read.* New York: Harper, 1955.

———. *Why Johnny Can't Read—And What You Can Do About It.* New York: Harper & Row, 1955.

———. *Why Johnny Still Can't Read: A New Look at the Scandal of Our Schools.* New York: Harper & Row, 1981.

Fletcher, P., and B. MacWhinney. *The Handbook of Child Language.* Cambridge, MA: Blackwell Publishers, 1995.

Flower, R. M. *Delivery of Speech-Language Pathology and Audiology Services.* Baltimore, MD: Williams and Wilkins, 1986.

Fogerty, Mary Jayne. *Babysitter's Companion: A Fill-in-the-blank Book for All Names, Numbers, Times, and Places You Want the Babysitter, Mother's Helper, or Anyone Who Takes Care of Your Kids to Know.* Berkeley, CA: Tricycle Press, 1994.

Folstein, Susan E. *Huntington's Disease: A Disorder of Families.* Baltimore: Johns Hopkins University Press, 1989.

Foster, Malcolm S. *Protecting Our Children's Teeth: A Guide to Quality Dental Care from Infancy through Age Twelve.* New York: Insight Books, 1992.

Fraser, Steven. *The Bell Curve Wars: Race, Intelligence, and the Future of America.* New York: Basic Books, 1995.

Freeman, John M., et al. *Seizures and Epilepsy in Childhood: A Guide for Parents.* Baltimore: The Johns Hopkins University Press, 1990.

Freud, Anna. *The Ego and the Mechanisms of Defense.* New York: International Universities Press, 1966.

Freud, Sigmund. *An Outline of Psychoanalysis.* New York: Norton, 1987.

Friar, Linda and Penelope B. Grenoble. *Teaching Your Child to Handle Peer Pressure.* Chicago: Contemporary Books, 1988.

Friedland, Bruce. *Personality Disorders.* New York: Chelsea House, 1991.

Froemer, Margot Joan. *Surviving Childhood Cancer: A Guide for Families.* Washington, DC: American Psychiatric Press, Inc., 1995.

Fry, John, and Gerald Sandler. *Common Diseases: Their Nature, Prevalence, and Care.* (5th ed.) Boston: Kluwer Academic Publishers, 1993.

Fuchs, Lynn S. *Connecting Performance Assessment to Instruction: Comparison of Behavioral Assessment, Mastery, Learning, Curriculum-based Measurement, and Performance Assessment.* Reston, VA: ERIC Clearinghouse on Disabilities and Gifted Education, the Council for Exceptional Children; Office of Educational Research and Improvement, Educational Resources Information Center, 1995. Available from Washington, DC: U.S. Government Printing Office, 1995.

G

Gaes, Geralyn, Craig Gaes, and Philip Bashe. *You Don't Have to Die: A Family's Guide to Surviv-*

ing Childhood Cancer. New York: Villard Books, 1992.

Galaburda, A., ed. *Dyslexia and Development: Neurobiological Aspects of Extraordinary Brains.* Cambridge, MA: Harvard UP, 1993.

Galanter, Marc. *Cults: Faith, Healing, and Coercion.* New York: Oxford Univ. Press, 1989.

Galper, Miriam. *Long Distance Parenting: A Guide for Divorced Parents.* New York: Signet, 1989.

Galvin, Matthew. *Clouds and Clocks: A Story for Children Who Soil.* New York: Magination Press, 1989. [juvenile fiction]

Garbarino, D., E. Guttman, and J.W. Seeley. *The Psychologically Battered Child: Strategies for Identification, Assessment, and Intervention.* San Francisco: Jossey-Bass, 1988.

Garber, Marjorie. *Vice Versa: Bisexuality and the Eroticism of Everyday Life.* New York: Simon & Schuster, 1995.

Gardner, Howard. *Creating Minds.* New York: Basic Books, 1993.

———. *Frames of Mind: The Theory of Multiple Intelligences.* New York: Basic Books, 1983.

———. *Multiple Intelligences: The Theory in Practice.* New York: Basic Books, 1993.

———. *The Unschooled Mind: How Children Learn and How Schools Should Teach.* New York: Basic Books, 1991.

Gardner, Richard. *The Boys and Girls Book About Divorce.* Northvale, N.J.: Aronson, 1992.

Gardner, Sandra. *Street Gangs in America.* New York: Franklin Watts, 1992.

Garwood, John, and Amanda Bennett. *Your Child's Symptoms.* New York: Berkeley Books, 1995.

Gaskin, Ina May. *Babies, Breastfeeding and Bonding,* South Hadley, MA: Bergin & Garvey, 1987.

Gattozzi, Ruth, Ph.D. *Wha's Wrong with My Child?* New York: McGraw-Hill, 1986.

Gauvain, Mary, and Michael Cole. *Readings on the Development of Children.* New York: Scientific American Books, 1993.

Gaynor, Jessica, and Chris Hatcher. *The Psychology of Child Firesetting: Detection and Intervention.* New York: Bruner/Mazel, 1987.

Gemelli, Ralph J. *Normal Child and Adolescent Development.* Washington, DC: American Psychiatric Press, 1996.

Genishi, Celia. ed. *Ways of Assessing Children and Curriculum: Stories of Early Childhood Practice.* New York: Teachers College Press, 1992.

Gershwin, M. Eric, and Edwin L. Klingelhofer. *Conquering Your Child's Allergies.* Reading, MA: Addison-Wesley, 1989.

Gewirtzman, Garry. *Smooth as a Baby's Bottom: A Dermatologist's Complete Guide to Your Child's Skin.* Hollywood, FL: Frederick Fell, 1988.

Giangreco, M.F., et al. *Choosing Options and Accommodations for Children: A Guide to Planning Inclusive Education.* Baltimore: Paul H. Brookes, 1993.

Gifford, Bernard R., and Mary Catherine O'Connor. (eds.) *Changing Assessments: Alternative Views of Aptitude, Achievement, and Instruction.* Boston: Kluwer Academic Publishers, 1992.

Gill, D. *Violence Against Children: Physical Child Abuse in the United States.* Cambridge, MA: Harvard, 1970.

Gilligan, Carol. *In a Different Voice: Psychological Theory and Women's Development.* Cambridge, Massachusetts: Harvard University Press, 1982.

Gilmore, June. *The Rape of Childhood: No Time to Be a Kid.* J&J Publishing, 1990.

Ginsburg, Herbert, and Sylvia Opper. *Piaget's Theory of Intellectual Development.* 3rd ed. Englewood Cliffs, NJ: Prentice-Hall, 1988.

Girard, K., and S. Koch. *Conflict Resolution in the Schools: A Manual for Educators.* San Francisco: Jossey-Bass, Inc., 1996.

Glantz, Stanton A., et al. *The Cigarette Papers.* Berkeley and Los Angeles: University of California Press, 1996.

Gleason, Jean Berko. *The Development of Language.* (4th ed.) Boston: Allyn and Bacon, 1996.

Glover, Bob, and Jack Shepherd. *The Family Fitness Handbook.* New York: Penguin Books, 1989.

Goland, Susan K. *The Joys and Challenges of Raising a Gifted Child.* New York: Prentice Hall Press, 1991.

Gold, Lois. *Between Love and Hate: A Guide to Civilized Divorce.* New York: Plenum Press, 1992.

Gold, M. S. *The Good News About Panic, Anxiety, and Phobias.* New York: Bantam Books, 1989.

Goldhammer, John. *Under the Influence: The Destructive Effects of Group Dynamics.* Amherst, NY: Prometheus Books, 1996.

Goldsmith, H. H., and J. J. Campos. "Fundamental Issues in the Study of Early Temperament." In M.E. Lamb and A. Brown (eds.), *Advances in Developmental Psychology*, Hillsdale, New Jersey: L. Erlbaum, 1986, p. 231-283.

Goldstein, Joseph, et al. *The Best Interests of the Child: The Least Detrimental Alternative.* New York: Free Press, 1996.

Goldsworthy, Candace L. *Developmental Reading Disorders: A Language-Based Treatment Approach.* San Diego: Singular Publishing Group, 1996.

Goleman, Daniel. *Emotional Intelligence.* New York: Bantam Books, 1995.

———. *Vital Lies, Simple Truths: The Psychology of Self-Deception.* New York: Simon and Schuster, 1985.

Golombok, Susan, and Robyn Fivush. *Gender Development.* Cambridge: Cambridge University Press, 1994.

Goodluck, H. *Language Acquisition: A Linguistic Introduction.* Cambridge, MA: Blackwell Publishers, 1991.

Goodman, Kenneth S. *What's Whole in Whole Language: A Parent-Teacher Guide.* Portsmouth, NH: Heinemann, 1986.

Gootman, Marilyn E. *The Loving Parents' Guide to Discipline: How to Teach Your Child to Behave—With Kindness, Understanding and Respect.* New York: Berkley Books, 1995.

Gordon, Neil F. *Diabetes: Your Exercise Guide.* Dallas: Human Kinetics, 1993.

Gordon, Thomas. *Discipline that Works: Promoting Self-Discipline in Children.* New York: Plume, 1991.

Gottfried, Allen W. et al. *Gifted IQ: Early Developmental Aspects.* New York: Plenum Press, 1994.

Graham, Norma Van Surdam. *Visual Pattern Analyzers.* New York: Oxford University Press, 1989.

Greenberg, Jack. *Crusaders in the Courts: How a Dedicated Band of Lawyers Fought for the Civil Rights Revolution.* New York: Basic Books, 1994.

Greenberg, Keith Elliot. *Out of the Gang.* Minneapolis, MN: Lerner Publications, 1992.

Greenberg, Mark T., Dante Cicchetti, and E. Mark Cummings. *Attachment in the Preschool Years: Theory, Research, and Intervention.* Chicago: University of Chicago Press, 1990.

Greenberg, Polly. *What Do I Do When My Children Don't Get Along?* New York: Scholastic, 1997.

Greene, Caroline. *The Babysitter's Handbook.* New York: Dorling Kindersley, 1995.

Greenspan, P. S. *Practical Guilt: Moral Dilemmas, Emotions, and Social Norms.* New York/Oxford: Oxford University Press, 1995.

Greven, Philip. *Spare the Child: The Religious Roots of Punishment and the Psychological Impact of Physical Abuse.* New York: Vintage Books, 1990.

Gribbin, John. *In Search of the Double Helix.* New York: McGraw-Hill, 1985.

Griffin, Robert S. *Underachievers in Secondary School: Education Off the Mark.* Hillsdale, NJ: Lawrence Erlbaum Associates, 1988.

Grisanti, Mary Lee, Dian G. Smith, and Charles Flatter. *Parents' Guide to Understanding Discipline: Infancy Through Preteen.* New York: Prentice Hall, 1990.

Grossman, Herbert J., et al, eds. *AMA Handbook on Mental Retardation.* Chicago: American Medical Association, 1987.

Groves, B.M. "Children Who Witness Violence." In S. Parker & B. Zuckerman (Eds.) *Behavioral and Developmental Pediatrics: A Handbook for Primary Care.* Boston: Little-Brown, 1994.

Grub, W.N. ed. *Education Through Occupations: Integrating Academic and Vocational Education in American High Schools (Vols. 1 & 2).* New York: Teachers College Press, 1995.

Gruber, H., and J. Voneche, eds. *The Essential Piaget.* New York: Basic Books, 1977.

Guilford, J. P. *The Nature of Human Intelligence.* New York: McGraw-Hill, 1967.

Gunter, Mary Alice, Thomas H. Estes, and Jan Schwab. *Instruction: A Models Approach.* 2nd ed. Boston: Allyn and Bacon, 1995.

Guntheroth, Warren G. *Crib Death: Sudden Infant Death Syndrome.* Mount Kisco, NY: Futura, 1982.

Guterson, David. *Family Matters: Why Home-schooling Makes Sense.* New York: Harcourt Brace Jovanovich, 1992.

Gutkin, T.B., and C.R. Reynolds, eds. *The Handbook of School Psychology.* 2nd ed. New York: Wiley, 1990.

H

Hainstock, E.G. *Teaching Montessori in the Home: The Preschool Years.* New York: NAL-Dutto, 1976.

Hall, Brian, Janet Kalven, Larry Rosen, and Bruce Taylor, eds. *Readings in Value Development.* Ramsey, New Jersey: Paulist Press, 1982.

Hall, Calvin S. *A Primer of Freudian Psychology.* New York: Harper and Row, 1982.

Hall, Granville Stanley. *Adolescence: Its Psychology and its Relations to Physiology, Anthropology, Sociology, Sex, Crime, Religion and Education.* 2 vols., New York: Appleton, 1908.

————. *Life and Confessions of a Psychologist.* New York: Appleton, 1923.

Hall, Katy. *Skeleton! Skeleton!* New York: Platt and Munk, 1991.

Hallahan, D., and J. Kaufmann. *Exceptional Children.* Englewood Cliffs, NJ: Prentice Hall, 1991.

Hamann, Barbara P. *Disease: Identification, Prevention, and Control.* St. Louis: Mosby, 1994.

Hamilton, Virginia. *The People Could Fly: American Black Folktales.* New York: Knopf, 1985.

Handel, Stephen. *Listening: An Introduction to the Perception of Auditory Events.* Cambridge, MA: MIT Press, 1989.

Hansen, B. C., ed. *Controversies in Obesity.* New York: Praeger Publishers, 1983.

Harlan, Judith. *Bilingualism in the United States: Conflict and Controversy.* New York: Franklin Watts, 1991.

Harlow, Harry. *Learning to Love.* New York: Aronson, 1974.

Harmer, David. *School Choice: Why We Need It, How We Get It.* Washington, DC: Cato Institue, 1994.

Harper, Ronald M., and Howard J. Hoffman, eds. *Sudden Infant Death Syndrome: Risk Factors and Basic Mechanisms.* New York: PMA Publishing Group, 1988.

Harris, Ann, and Maurice Super. *Cystic Fibrosis: The Facts.* New York: Oxford University Press, 1987.

Hart, Diane. *Authentic Assessment: A Handbook for Educators.* Menlo Park, CA: Addison-Wesley Pub. Co., 1994.

Hart, Louise. *The Winning Family: Increasing Self-Esteem in Your Children.* Berkeley: Celestial Arts, 1993.

Haskell, Simon H. *The Education of Children with Motor and Neurological Disabilities.* New York: Nichols, 1989.

Haviland, Virginia, ed. *The Fairy Tale Treasury.* New York: Dell, 1986. [Preschool-grade 4]

Hawley, Robert C. *Value Exploration through Role Playing: Practical Strategies for Use in the Classroom.* New York: Hart Publishing Co., 1975.

Hayes, Jeri, ed. *How to Get Better Test Scores [Grades 3-4; 5-6; 7-8].* New York: Random House, 1991.

Hechinger, Fred M., ed. *A Better Start: New Choices for Early Learning.* New York: Walker, 1986.

Hecker, J. E., and G. L. Thorpe. *Agoraphobia and Panic: A Guide to Psychological Treatment.* Needham Heights, MA: Allyn and Bacon, 1992.

Heide, F. & Chess, V. *Tales for the Perfect Child.* New York: Lothrop, Lee and Shepard Books, 1985.

Helfer, Ray E., M.D., and Ruth S. Kempe, MD., eds. *The Battered Child.* Chicago: The University of Chicago Press, 1987.

Hendrick, Joanne. *The Whole Child: Developmental Education for the Early Years.* 4th ed. Columbus, OH: Merrill Publishing Co., 1988.

Herrnstein, Richard J., and Charles Murray. *The Bell Curve: Intelligence and Class Structure in American Life.* New York: Free Press, 1994.

Hess, Mary Abbott. *A Healthy Head Start: A Worry-Free Guide to Feeding Young Children.* New York: Henry Holt, 1990.

Hicks, Patricia Larkins. *Opportunities in Speech-Language Pathology Careers.* Lincolnwood, IL: VGM Career Horizons, 1996.

Hinde, Robert. *Animal Behaviour: A Synthesis of Ethology and Comparative Psychology.* New York: McGraw Hill, 1966.

———. *Biological Bases of Human Social Relationships.* New York: McGraw-Hill, 1974.

———. *Toward Understanding Relationships.* London: Academic Press, 1979.

Hirsch, E. D., Jr. *The Schools We Need and Why We Don't Have Them. Books to Build On: A Grade-By-Grade Resource Guide For Parents and Teachers.* New York: Delta, 1996.

———, and John Holdren. *What Your Fifth Grader Needs to Know: Fundamentals of a Good Fifth Grade Education.* New York: Doubleday, 1993.

———. *What Your First Grader Needs to Know: Fundamentals of a Good First Grade Education.* New York: Doubleday, 1997.

———. *What Your Fourth Grader Needs to Know: Fundamentals of a Good Fourth Grade Education.* New York: Doubleday, 1994.

———. *What Your Kindergartner Needs to Know: Preparing Your Child for a Lifetime of Learning.* New York: Doubleday, 1996.

———. *What Your Second Grader Needs to Know: Fundamentals of a Good Second Grade Education.* New York: Dell, 1993.

———. *What Your Third Grader Needs to Know: Fundamentals of a Good Third Grade Education.* New York: Delta, 1992.

———, Joseph Kett, and James Trefil. *Cultural Literacy: What Every American Needs to Know, What Literate Americans Know.* New York: Vintage Books, 1988.

———, William G. Rowland, Jr., and Michael Stanford, eds. *A First Dictionary of Cultural Literacy: What Our Children Need to Know.* 2nd ed. Boston: Houghton Mifflin, 1996.

Hoffer, Abram, and Humphry Osmond. *How to Live with Schizophrenia.* New York: Carol Publishing Group, 1992.

Hoffman, M. L. "Development of Prosocial Motivation: Empathy and Guilt." In *The Development of Prosocial Behavior*, edited by N. Eisenberg, 218-231. New York: Academic Press, 1982.

Holt, John. *How Children Fail.* Revised edition. Reading, MA: Addison-Wesley Publishing Company, 1995.

Hoppert, Rita. *Rings, Swings, and Climbing Things.* Chicago: Contemporary Books, 1985.

Horchler, Joani Nelson. *The SIDS Survival Guide: Information and Comfort for Grieving Family and Friends and Professionals Who Seek to Help Them.* Hyattsville, MD: SIDS Educational Services, 1994.

Howe, Michael J. *Fragments of Genius: The Strange Feats of Idiots Savants.* London: Routledge, 1989.

———. *The Origins of Exceptional Abilities,* Cambridge, MA: Basil Blackwell, 1990.

Hubbard, Ruth. *A Workshop of the Possible: Nurturing Children's Creative Development.* York, ME: Stenhouse, 1996.

Huckaby, Elizabeth. *Crisis at Central High: Little Rock, 1957–58.* Baton Rouge: Louisiana State Univ. Press, 1980.

Huesmann, L. Rowell, and Leonard D. Eron, eds. *Television and the Aggressive Child: A Cross National Comparison.* Hillsdale, New Jersey: Lawrence Erlbaum Associates, 1986.

Huggins, K. *The Nursing Mother's Companion,* rev. ed. Boston: Harvard Common, 1990.

Hunt, N., and K. Marshall. *Exceptional Children and Youth.* Boston, MA: Houghton Mifflin Co., 1994.

Huntley, Rebecca. *The Sleep Book for Tired Parents.* Seattle: Parenting Press, 1991.

Hutchins, Loraine, and Lani Kaahumanu, eds. *Bi Any Other Name: Bisexual People Speak Out.* Boston: Alyson Publications, 1991.

Hyde, Margaret O., and Lawrence E. Hyde. *Cancer in the Young: A Sense of Hope.* Philadelphia: Westminster Press, 1985.

Hynes, Angela. *Puberty: An Illustrated Manual for Parents and Daughters.* New York: Tom Doherty Associates, 1989.

I

Ikeda, Joanne P., and Priscilla Naworski. *Am I Fat?: Helping Young Children Accept Differences in Body Size: Suggestions For Teachers, Parents, And Care Providers of Children to Age 10.* Santa Cruz, CA: ETR Associates, 1992.

Ince, Susan. *Sleep Disturbances.* Boston: Harvard Medical School, Health Publications Groups, 1995.

Infectious Diseases of Children. (9th ed.) St. Louis: Mosby, 1992.

Inhelder, B. *The Diagnosis of Reasoning in the Mentally Retarded* [1943]. Trans. by W. B. Stephens, et al. New York: J. Day, 1968.

Institute of Medicine. *Growing Up Tobacco Free.* Washington, DC: National Academy Press, 1994.

Izard, C. *Human Emotions.* New York: Plenum Press, 1977.

J

Jablow, Martha M. *A Parent's Guide to Eating Disorders and Obesity.* New York: Delta Publishing, 1992.

Jacobs, Vicki A., and Luke E. Baldwin. *The Reading Crisis: Why Poor Children Fall Behind.* Cambridge, MA: Harvard University Press, 1990.

Jacobson, Michael F., and Bruce Maxwell. *What Are We Feeding Our Kids?* New York: Workman Publishing, 1994.

Jahanson, C.E. *Cocaine: A New Epidemic.* New York: Main Line Book Co., 1992.

Jamison, Kay. *Touched by Fire: Manic-Depressive Illness and the Artistic Temperament.* New York: Free Press, 1993.

Janowitz, Henry D. *Your Gut Feelings: A Complete Guide to Living Better with Intestinal Problems.* New York: Oxford Univ. Press, 1994.

Janus, Mark-David, et. al. *Adolescent Runaways: Causes and Consequences.* Lexington, MA: D.C. Heath, 1987.

Jason, Janine, and Antonia van de Meer. *Parenting Your Premature Baby.* New York: Delta, 1990.

Jay, T. B. *Cursing in America.* Philadelphia, PA: John Benjamins Pub. Co., 1992.

———. *What to Do When Your Kids Talk Dirty.* San Jose, CA: Resource Publications, Inc., 1997.

———. *What to Do When Your Students Talk Dirty.* San Jose, CA: Resource Publications, Inc., 1996.

Jeffrey, Lorraine. *Hearing Loss and Tinnitus.* New York: Sterling Publishing, 1995.

Johnson, Joan J. *The Cult Movement.* New York: Franklin Watts, 1984.

Johnson, Robert., ed. *Mayo Clinic Complete Book of Pregnancy and Baby's First Year.* New York: William Morrow and Co., 1994.

Jones, Ken. *Interactive Learning Events.* New York: Nichols Publishing, 1988.

Jones, Reginald L., ed. *Psychoeducational Assessment of Minority Group Children: A Casebook.* Richmond, CA: Cobb & Henry, 1988.

Jorde, L., J. Carey, and R. White. *Medical Genetics.* St. Louis: Mosby, 1995.

Joseph, Stephen M. *Mommy! Daddy! I'm Afraid: Help Your Children Overcome Fears That Hold Them Back in School and at Play.* New York: Collier Books, 1979.

Jukes, Mavis. *It's a Girl Thing: How to Stay Healthy, Safe, and In Charge.* New York: A. Knopf, 1996.

Juvonen, Jaana, and Kathryn R. Wentzel, eds. *Social Motivation: Understanding Children's School Adjustment.* New York: Cambridge University Press, 1996.

K

Kagan, Jerome. *Galen's Prophecy.* New York: Basic, 1994.

————. *The Nature of the Child.* New York: Basic Books, 1976.

Kagan, Sharon L., and Edward F. Zigler, eds. *Early Schooling: The National Debate.* New Haven: Yale University Press, 1987.

Kageler, Len. *Helping Your Teenager Cope with Peer Pressure.* Loveland, CO: Family Tree, 1989.

Kahana, Eva, David E. Biegel, and May Wykle. *Family Caregiving Across the Lifespan.* Thousand Oaks, CA: Sage Publications, 1994.

Kahn, Jack. *Unwillingly to School.* New York: Pergamon Press, 1981.

Kail, Robert V., and John C. Cavanaugh. *Human Development.* Pacific Grove, CA: Brooks/Cole, 1996.

Kalter, Neil. *Growing Up with Divorce: Helping Your Child Avoid Immediate and Later Emotional Problems.* New York: Free Press, 1990.

Kaplan, Colin, G.S. Turner, D. A. Warrell. *Rabies: The Facts.* (2d ed.) New York: Oxford University Press, 1986.

Kaplan, Louise J. *Adolescence: The Farewell to Childhood.* New York: Simon and Schuster, 1984.

Karmel, Marjorie. *Thank you, Dr. Lamaze.* New York: Harper and Row, 1993.

Kaslow, Florence W., ed. *Handbook of Relational Diagnosis and Dysfunctional Family Patterns.* New York: John Wiley, 1996.

Kasten, W.C., and B. K. Clarke. *The Multiage Classroom.* Katonah, New York: Richard C. Owen, 1993.

Katz, A. M. *Physiology of the Heart.* New York: Raven Press, 1992.

Kazdin, Alan E. *Child Psychotherapy: Developing and Identifying Effective Treatments.* New York: Pergamon Press, 1988.

————. *Conduct Disorders in Childhood and Adolescence.* Newbury Park, CA: Sage Publications, 1995.

Kellerman, Jonathan. *Helping the Fearful Child: A Parent's Guide to Everyday and Problem Anxieties.* New York: Norton, 1981.

Kelley-Buchanan, Christine. *Peace of Mind During Pregnancy: An A–Z Guide to the Substances that Could Affect Your Unborn Baby.* New York: Dell Publishing, 1989.

Kendall, Philip C., ed. *Child and Adolescent Psychotherapy: Cognitive Behavioral Procedures.* New York: Guilford Press, 1991.

Kernberg, Paulina F., et al. *Children with Conduct Disorders: A Psychotherapy Manual.* New York: Basic Books, 1991.

Kilby, Donald. *Manual of Safe Sex.* Philadelphia: Decker, 1986.

Kingore, Bertie W. *Portfolios: Enriching and Assessing All Students, Identifying the Gifted Grades K-6.* Des Moines, IA: Leadership Publishers, 1993.

Klaus, Marshall H., John H. Kennell, and Phyllis H. Klaus. *Bonding: Building the Foundations of Secure Attachment and Independence.* Reading, MA: Addison-Wesley, 1995.

Klein, Fritz, M.D. *The Bisexual Option*, 2nd ed. New York: The Haworth Press, 1993.

Kleinman, Ronald E. *What Should I Feed My Kids?: The Pediatrician's Guide to Safe and Healthy Food and Growth.* New York: Ballantine, Books, 1996.

Kline, Paul. *Intelligence: The Psychometric View.* London: Routledge, 1991.

Kluger, Matthew J. *Fever: Its Biology, Evolution, and Function.* Princeton, NJ: Princeton University Press, 1979.

Knobil, Ernst, and Neill, Jimmy D., eds. *The Physiology of Reproduction*, 2nd ed. New York: Raven Press, 1994.

Knoff, Howard M. *The Assessment of Child and Adolescent Personality.* New York: Guilford Press, 1986.

Knox, Mike. *Gangsta in the House: Understanding Gang Culture.* Troy, MI: Momentum Books, 1995.

Kohlberg, Lawrence. *Child Psychology and Childhood Education: A Cognitive-Developmental View.* New York: Longman, 1987.

————. *Essays on Moral Development, I: The Philosophy of Moral Development: Moral Stages and the Idea of Justice.* San Francisco: Harper & Row, 1981.

————. *Essays on Moral Development, II: The Psychology of Moral Development.* San Francisco: Harper & Row, 1984.

Kohn, Alfie. *Punished by Rewards: The Trouble with Gold Stars, Incentive Plans, A's, Praise, and other Bribes.* Boston: Houghton Mifflin, 1993.

Koplewicz, Harold S. *It's Nobody's Fault: New Hope and Help for Difficult Children and Their Parents.* New York: Times Books, 1996.

Kornhaber, Arthur. *Grandparent Power! How to Strengthen the Vital Connection Among Grandparents, Parents, and Children.* New York: Crown Publishers, 1994.

Kowalski, Robert E. *Cholesterol & Children.* New York: Harper & Row, 1988.

Koziol, Leonard F., Chris E. Stout, and Douglas H. Ruben, eds. *Handbook of Childhood Impulse Disorders and ADHD: Theory and Practice.* Springfield, IL: C.C. Thomas, 1993.

Krause, Harry D. *Child Law: Parent, Chld, and State.* New York: New York Universty Press, 1992.

Kreidler, W.J. *Creative Conflict Resolution: More Than 200 Activities for Keeping Peace in the Classroom—K–6.* Glenview, IL: Scortt, Foresman, 1984.

Krementz, Jill. *How It Feels When Parents Divorce.* New York: Knopf, 1984. (For ages 8–14)

Krugman, Saul, et al. *Infectious Diseases of Children.* St. Louis: Mosby Year Book, 1992.

Kubler-Ross, E. *On Children and Death.* New York: Macmillan, 1983.

Kuhl, Patricia K, Ph.D. *Learning and Representation in Speech and Language.* Philadelphia: Current Biology Ltd.

Kuklin, Susan. *Thinking Big: The Story of a Young Dwarf.* New York: Lothrop, Lee & Shepard Books, 1986. (Illustrated book for young people.)

Kurtines, William M., and Jacob L. Gewirtz, eds. *Moral Development: An Introduction.* Boston: Allyn and Bacon, 1995.

L

La Belle, Thomas J., and Christopher R. Ward. *Multiculturalism and Education: Diversity and Its Impact on Schools and Society.* Albany: State University of New York Press, 1994.

La Leche League International Staff, eds. *The Womanly Art of Breastfeeding: Thirty-Fifth Anniversary Edition.* New York: NAL-Dutton, 1991.

LaFarge, Ann E. *Tantrums: Secrets to Calming the Storm.* New York: Pocket Books, 1996.

Lam, J.A. *The Impact of Conflict Resolution Programs on Schools: A Review and Synthesis of the Evidence.* 2nd edition. Amherst, MA: National Association for Mediation in Education, 1989.

Lamb, Michael E., and Abraham Sagi, eds. *Fatherhood and Family Policy.* Hillsdale, NJ: L. Erlbaum Associates, 1983.

Lanckton, Alice Keidan. *The Bar Mitzvah Mother's Manual.* New York: Hippocrene Books, 1986.

Landau, B., and L. Gleitman. *Language and Experience: Evidence from the Blind Child.* Cambridge, MA: Harvard University Press, 1985.

Lang, Paul. *The English Language Debate: One Nation, One Language!* Springfield, NJ: Enslow Publishers, Inc., 1995.

Langendorfer, Stephen, and Lawrence D. Bruya. *Aquatic Readiness: Developing Water Competence in Young Children.* Champaign, IL: Human Kinetics Publishers, 1995.

Lansky, Vicki. *Getting Your Child to Sleep—and Back to Sleep: Tips for Parents of Infants, Toddlers, and Preschoolers.* Deephaven, MN: Book Peddlers, 1991.

———. *Vicki Lansky's Divorce Book for Parents: Helping Your Children Cope with Divorce and Its Aftermath.* New York: Penguin Books, 1989.

Lass, N. J., L. V. McReynolds, and J. L. Northern. *Handbook on Speech-Language Pathology and Audiology.* Philadelphia: B. C. Decker, 1988.

Lauer, Ronald M., Richard B. Shekelle. (eds) *Childhood Prevention of Atherosclerosis and Hypertension.* New York: Raven Press, 1980.

Lavi, Zvi. *Kibbutz Members Study Kibbutz Children.* New York: Greenwood Press, 1990.

Leckert, Bruce, with L. Weinberger. *Up From Boredom . . . Down From Fear.* New York: R. Marek, 1980.

Lee, Victor, and Prajna Das Gupta., eds. *Children's Cognitive and Language Development.* Cambridge, MA: Blackwell Publishers, 1995.

Lehr, Judy Brown. *At-Risk, Low-Achieving Students in the Classroom.* Washington, DC: National Education Association, 1988.

Leichtman, Martin. *The Rorschach: A Developmental Perspective.* Analytic Press, 1996.

Lejeune, Jirtma. *The Concentration Can: When Does Human Life Begin?* San Francisco: Ignatius Press, 1992.

Leman, Kevin. *Bringing Up Kids Without Tearing Them Down.* New York: Delacorte Press, 1993.

Leneman, Helen. *Bar/Bat Mitzvah Basics.* Woodstock, Vt.: Jewish Lights Publishing, 1996.

Leonard, Robin, and Stephen Elias. *Family Law,* 3rd ed. Berkeley: Nolo Press, 1994.

Leonhardt, Mary. *Parents Who Love Reading, Kids Who Don't.* New York: Crown Publishers, 1993.

Lerch, Harold A., and Christine B. Stopka. *Developmental Motor Activities for All Children: From Theory to Practice.* Dubuque, IA: Brown and Benchmark, 1992.

LeVert, Suzanne. *When Your Child Has a Chronic Illness.* New York: Dell, 1995.

Levesque, Karen, et al. *Vocational Education in the United States: The Early 1990s.* Washington, DC: US Department of Education, National Center for Education Statistics, November 1995.

Levinson, E.M. *Transdisciplinary Vocational Assessment: Issues in School-Based Programs.* Brandon, VT: Clinical Psychology Publishing Co., 1993.

Lewis, M. *Shame, the Exposed Self.* New York: The Free Press, 1992.

Lewis, Vicky. *Development and Handicap.* New York: B. Blackwell, 1987.

Lickona, Thomas. *Educating for Character: How Our Schools Can Teach Respect and Responsibility.* New York: Bantam Books, 1991.

Lidz, Theodore. *The Origin and Treatment of Schizophrenic Disorders.* International Universities Press, 1990.

Lieberman, Adrienne B. *The Premie Parents' Handbook: A Lifeline for the New Parents of a Premature Baby.* New York: Dutton, 1984.

Lieberman, Shari, and Nancy Bruning. *The Real Vitamin and Mineral Book.* Garden City Park, NY.: Avery Publishing Group, 1990.

Lillard, Paula Polk. *Montessori Today: A Comprehensive Approach to Education from Birth to Adulthood.* New York: Schocken Books, 1996.

Lindzey, G. ed. *A History of Psychology in Autobiography.* Stanford, CA: Stanford University Press, 1989.

Lipson, Eden Ross. *The New York Times Parent's Guide to the Best Books for Children.* New York: Random House, 1988.

Lipson, Marjorie Y., and Karen K. Wixson. *Assessment and Instruction of Reading Disability: An Interactive Approach.* New York: HarperCollins, 1991.

Liptak, Karen. *Coming-of-Age: Traditions and Rituals Around the World.* Millbrook Press, 1994.

Little, M. *The Endocrine System.* New York: Chelsea House Publishers, 1990.

Lloyd, Barbara B. *Gender Identities and Education: The Impact of Starting School.* New York: St. Martin's Press, 1992.

Lobby, Ted. *Jessica and the Wolf: A Story for Children Who Have Bad Dreams.* New York: Magination Press, 1990.

Lorenz, Konrad. *The Foundation of Ethology.* New York: Springer-Verlag, 1981.

Love, Susan M. *Dr. Susan Love's Breast Book.* Reading, MA: Addison-Wesley, 1995.

Low Birth Weight. March of Dimes/Birth Defects Foundation, 1991.

Lowe, Paula C. *Care Pooling: How to Get the Help You Need to Care for the Ones You Love.* San Francisco: Berrett-Koehler Publishers, 1993.

Lukas, Scott E. *Amphetamines: Danger in the Fast Lane.* New York: Chelsea House, 1985.

Lyster, Mimi E. *Child Custody: Building Agreements That Work.* Berkeley: Nolo Press, 1995.

M

Maag, John W. *Parenting without Punishment: Making Problem Behavior Work for You.* Philadelphia, PA: Charles Press, 1996.

Maccoby, E. *Social Development: Psychological Growth and the Parent-Child Relationship.* New York: Harcourt, Brace and Jovanovich, 1980.

———, and C. N. Jacklin. *Psychology of Sex Differences.* Stanford: Stanford Univesity Press, 1974.

———, and R.H. Mnookin. *Dividing the Child: Social and Legal Dilemmas of Custody.* Cambridge, MA: Harvard University Press, 1992.

Mackintosh, Nicholas John. *Conditioning and Associative Learning.* New York: Oxford University Press, 1983.

MacNamara, Roger D. *Creating Abuse-Free Caregiving Environments for Children, the Disabled, and the Elderly: Preparing, Supervising, and Managing Caregivers for the Emotional Impact of Their Responsibilities.* Springfield, IL: C.C. Thomas, 1992.

Madaras, Lynda. *The What's Happening to My Body? Book for Boys: A Growing Up Guide for Parents and Sons.* New York: Newmarket Press, 1984.

Madaras, Lynda. *The What's Happening to My Body? Book for Girls: A Growing Up Guide for Parents and Daughters.* New York: Newmarket Press, 1988.

Mahoney, Michael J., ed. *Cognition and Psychotherapy.* New York: Plenum Press, 1985.

Mallet, Carl-Heinz. *Fairy Tales and Children.* New York: Schocken, 1984.

Mallinger, A. E., & DeWyze, J. *Too Perfect: When Being in Control Gets Out of Control.* NY: Random House, 1993.

Maloney, Michael and Rachel Kranz. *Straight Talk About Eating Disorders.* New York: Facts on File, 1991.

Manes, S. *Be a Perfect Person in Just Three Days.* New York: Bantam/Skylark Books, 1987.

Mango, Karin. *Hearing Loss.* New York: Franklin Watts, 1991.

Mankad, Vipul N., and R. Blaine Moore. *Sickle Cell Disease: Pathophysiology, Diagnosis, and Management.* Westport, CT: Praeger, 1992.

Manzo, Ula C. *Literacy Disorders: Holistic Diagnosis and Remediation.* Fort Worth: Harcourt, Brace Jovanovitch, 1993.

Marder, C., and R. D'Amico. *How Well Are Youth with Disabilities Really Doing? A Comparison of Youth with Disabilities and Youth in General.* Menlo Park, CA: SRI International, 1992.

Marin, Roselyn. *Helping Obese Children: Weight Control Groups That Really Work.* Montreal: Learning Publications, 1990.

Markway, B.G., et. al. *Dying of Embarrassment: Help for Social Anxiety and Phobias.* Oakland, CA: New Harbinger Publications, 1992.

Martin, B. *Scientific Knowledge in Controversy: The Social Dynamic of the Fluoridation Debate.* Albany, New York: State University of New York Press, 1991.

Martin, Frederick. *Introduction to Audiology.* 4th ed. New Jersey: Prentice Hall, 1991.

Martin, Garry. *Behavior Modification: What It Is and How to Do It.* Englewood Cliffs, NJ: Prentice-Hall, 1988.

Martorano, Joseph T., and John P. Kildahl. *Beyond Negative Thinking: Breaking the Cycle of Depressing and Anxious Thoughts.* New York: Insight Books, 1989.

Maryon-Davis, Alan and Steven Parker. *Food and Digestion.* New York: F. Watts, 1990.

Masterson, James F. *The Emerging Self: A Developmental, Self, and Object Relations Approach to the Treatment of the Closet Narcissistic Disorder.* New York: Burnner/Mazel, 1993.

Matson, Johnny L., and James A. Mulick, eds. *Handbook of Mental Retardation.* New York: Pergamon Press, 1991.

Matthews, Gareth B. *Philosophy and the Young Child.* Cambridge: Harvard University Press, 1980.

Maxon, Antonia. *The Hearing-Impaired Child: Infancy through High School Years.* Boston: Andover Medical Publishers, 1992.

McClain, Joan Brooks, and Gillian Dowley McNamee. *Early Literacy.* Cambridge, MA: Harvard University Press, 1990.

McCord, Joan, ed. *Coercion and Punishment in Long-Term Perspectives.* Cambridge/New York: Cambridge University Press, 1995.

McCoy, Kathy, and Charles Wibbelsman. *The New Teenage Body Book.* New York: The Body Press (Putnam), 1992.

McCuen, Gary E. *Illiteracy in America.* Hudson, WI: GEM Publications, 1988.

———, ed. *Born Hooked: Poisoned in the Womb.* 2nd ed. Hudson, WI: G.E. McCuen Publications, 1994.

McCullough, Virginia. *Testing and Your Child: What You Should Know About 150 of the Most Common Medical, Educational, and Psychological Tests.* New York: Plume, 1992.

McDermott, John F. *The Complete Book on Sibling Rivalry.* New York: Putnam, 1987.

McGrath, Elizabeth Z. *The Art of Ethics: A Psychology of Ethical Beliefs.* Chicago: Loyola University Press, 1994.

McGroarty, Daniel. *Break These Chains: The Battle for School Choice.* Rocklin, California: Prima Publishing, 1996.

McNeil, John D. *Curriculum: A Comprehensive Introduction.* 4th ed. Glenview, IL: Scott, Foresman/Little, Brown Higher Education, 1990.

McShane, John. *Cognitive Development: An Information Processing Approach.* Oxford, Eng.: B. Blackwell, 1991.

Meier, Kenneth J., Joseph Stewart, Jr., and Robert E. England. *Race, Class, and Education: The Politics of Second-Generation Discrimination.* Madison: University of Wisconsin Press, 1989.

Meier, Scott T. *The Chronic Crisis in Psychological Measurement and Assessment: A Historical Survey.* San Diego: Academic Press, 1994.

Melton, J. Gordon. *Encyclopedia Handbook of Cults in America.* Garland, 1986.

Mensh, Elaine, and Harry Mensh. *The IQ Mythology: Class, Race, Gender, and Inequality.* Carbondale, IL: Southern Illinois University Press, 1991.

Messerly, John G. *An Introduction to Ethical Theories.* Lanham, MD: University Press of America, 1995.

Middleton-Moz, Jane. *Shame and Guilt: Masters of Disguise.* Deerfield Beach, Florida: Health Communications, 1990.

Miles. T. R. *Dyslexia.* Philadelphia: Open University Press, 1990.

Millstein, S.G., A.C. Petersen, and E.O. Nightingale. "Adolescent Health Promotion: Rationale, Goals, and Objectives." In: Millstein, S.G., Petersen, A.C., Nightingale, E.O. (eds). *Promoting the Health of Adolescents: New Directions for the Twenty-First Century.* New York: Oxford University Press, 1993.

Milunsky, Aubrey. *Choices Not Chances: An Essential Guide to Your Hereditary and Health.* Boston: Little, Brown, 1989.

Mindell, Jodi A. *Sleeping Through the Night: How to Get a Good Night's Sleep for You and Your Baby.* New York: HarperCollins, 1997.

Minuchin, Salvador. *Family Therapy Techniques.* Cambridge: Harvard University Press, 1981.

Mitford, Jessica. *The American Way of Birth.* New York: Dutton, 1992.

Moely, Barbara E. *Teachers' Expectations for Memory and Metamemory Skills of Elementary School Children.* Washington, DC: National Institute of Education, 1985.

Moller, Karlind T., Clark D. Starr, and Sylvia A. Johnson. *A Parent's Guide to Cleft Lip and Palate.* Minneapolis: University of Minnesota Press, 1990.

Montessori, M. *The Montessori Method.* 1939.

———. *The Secret of Childhood.* New York: Ballantine, 1982.

———. *Spontaneous Activity in Education.* Cambridge, MA: Robert Bentley, 1964.

Monti, Daniel. *Wannabe: Gangs in Suburbs and Schools.* Cambridge, MA: Blackwell, 1994.

Moore, Lorraine. *Inclusion, A Practical Guide for Parents: Tools to Enhance Your Child's Success in Learning.* Minnetonka, MN: Peytral Publications, 1996.

Moore, Raymond, and Dorothy Moore. *The Successful Homeschool Family Handbook.* Nashville: Thomas Nelson Publishers, 1994.

Morris, Richard J. *Behavior Modification with Exceptional Children: Principles and Practices.* Glenview, IL: Scott Foresman, 1985.

Morrison, A.P. *Shame: The Underside of Narcissism.* Hillsdale, NJ: Analytic Press, 1989.

Morrow, L. M. *Literacy Development in the Early Years.* Boston: Allyn and Bacon, 1993.

Mortensen, Karen Vibeke. *Form and Content in Children's Human Figure Drawings: Development, Sex Differences, and Body Experience.* New York: New York University Press, 1991.

Mueser, Kim T., and Susan Gingerich. *Coping with Schizophrenia: A Guide for Families.* Oakland: New Harbinger Press, 1994.

Munster, Andrew M. and staff of Baltimore Regional Burn Center. *Severe Burns: A Family Guide to Medical and Emotional Recovery.* Baltimore: Johns Hopkins University Press, 1993.

Musetto, Andrew P. *Dilemmas in Child Custody: Family Conflicts and Their Resolution.* Chicago: Nelson-Hall, 1982.

Mussen, P. H. "Infancy and Developmental Psychobiology." *Handbook of Child Psychology.* New York: John Wiley, 1983.

Myrick, R.D., and D.L. Sorenson. *Peer Helping: A Practical Guide.* Minneapolis, MN: Educational Media Corporation, 1988.

N

Nathanson, D.L. (eds.). *The Many Faces of Shame.* New York: Gilford Press, 1987.

National Cancer Institute. *Tips for Teenagers with Cancer.* Bethesda, MD: U.S. Department of Health and Human Services, 1987.

National Center for Education Statistics. *Products Avaialbe from the National Center for Education Statistics.* Washington, DC: NCES, 1997.

National Institutes of Health. *What You Need to Know about Wilms' Tumor.* National Institutes of Health, Public Health Service, U.S. Dept. of Health and Human Services, 1983.

National Occupational Information Coordinating Committee (NOICC). *National Career Development Guidelines.* Portland, OR: Northwest Regional Educational Laboratory, 1989.

National Research Council Committee on Toxicology. *Health Effects of Ingested Fluoride.* Washington, DC: National Academy Press, 1993.

National Swimming Pool Safety Committee. *Children Aren't Waterproof.* National Swimming Pool Safety Committee, U.S. Product Safety Commission. Washington, DC, 1987.

Neal, Margaret B., et al. *Balancing Work and Caregiving for Children, Adults, and Elders.* Newbury Park, CA: Sage Publications, 1993.

Nelsen, Jane. *Positive Discipline,* rev. ed. New York: Ballantine Books, 1996.

Nevitt, Amy. *Fetal Alcohol Syndrome.* New York: Rosen Publishing Group, 1996.

Nichols, Michael P., and Richard C. Schwartz. *Family Therapy: Concepts and Methods.* Boston: Allyn and Bacon, 1991.

Norman R. Bernstein, Alan Jeffry Breslau, and Jean Ann Graham, eds. *Coping Strategies for Burn Survivors and Their Families.* New York: Praeger, 1988.

Nowjack-Raymer, Ruth, and Helen C. Gift. "Use of Mouthguards and Headgear in Organized Sports by School-aged Children." *Public Health Reports,* January-February 1996.

Nye, Robert D. *The Legacy of B. F. Skinner: Concepts and Perspectives, Controversies and Misunderstandings.* Pacific Grove, CA: Brooks/Cole, 1992.

————. *Three Psychologies: Perspectives from Freud, Skinner, and Rogers.* 4th ed. Pacific Grove, CA: Brooks/Cole Pub. Co., 1992.

O

O'Neill, Audrey Myerson. *Clinical Inference: How to Draw Meaningful Conclusions from Psychological Tests.* Brandon, VT: Clinical Psychology Publishing Co., 1993.

Obler, L.K., and D. Fein (eds.) *The Exceptional Brain: Neuropsychology of Talent and Special Abilities.* New York: Guilford Press, 1988.

Oliver, Marilyn Tower. *Gangs: Trouble in the Streets.* Springfield, NJ: Enslow Publishers, 1995.

Orr, Eleanor Wilson. *Twice as Less: Black English and the Performance of Black Students in Mathematics and Science.* New York: Norton, 1987.

P

Paley, Vivian. *Bad Guys Don't Have Birthdays: Fantasy Play at Four.* Chicago: University of Chicago Press, 1988.

Parisi, Lynn. *Creative Role-Playing Exercises in Science.* Boulder, CO: Social Science Education Consortium, 1986.

Parker, M., ed. *Steroid Hormone Action.* New York: IRL Press, 1993.

Parkes, C.M., and J. Stevenson-Hinde, eds. *The Place of Attachment in Human Behavior.* New York: Basic Books, 1982.

Patel, Nalin M. *The Doctor's Guide to Your Digestive System.* Champaign, IL: N.M.P. Publishing, 1988.

Pavel, Monique. *Fundamentals of Pattern Recognition.* 2nd ed. New York: M. Dekker, 1993.

Peck, Lee A. *Coping with Cliques.* New York: Rosen Publishing Group, 1992.

Pedersen, Anne, and Peggy McNamara, eds. *Schooling at Home: Parents, Kids, and Learning.* Santa Fe: John Muir Publications, 1990.

Peikin, Steven R. *Gastrointestinal Health.* New York: HarperCollins, 1991.

Pelaka, Beverly. *Don't Settle for Less: A Woman's Guide to Getting a Fair Divorce and Custody Settlement.* New York: Doubleday, 1994.

Perry, Susan. *Playing Smart: A Parent's Guide to Enriching, Offbeat Learning Activities for Ages Four to Fourteen.* Minneapolis, MN: Free Spirit Publishing, 1990.

Peschel, Enid. *Neurobiological Disorders in Children and Adolescents.* San Francisco: Jossey-Bass, 1992.

Peters, Theodore J. *Stuttering: An Integrated Approach to Its Nature and Treatment.* Baltimore: Williams and Wilkins, 1991.

Peterson, Harold A. *Appraisal and Diagnosis of Speech and Language Disorders.* (3rd ed.) Englewood Cliffs, NJ: Prentice Hall, 1994.

Peurifoy, Reneau. *Anxiety, Phobias, and Panic: Taking Charge and Conquering Fear,* 2nd. ed. Citrus Heights, CA: LifeSkills Publications, 1992.

Pfister, Fred R., and Bernard Griesemer. *The Littlest Baby: A Handbook for Parents of Premature Children.* Englewood Cliffs, NJ: Prentice-Hall, 1983.

Phelps, Ethel Johnston. *The Maid of the North: Feminist Folk Tales from Around the World.* New York: Holt, 1981.

Phillips, Dennis H. *Living with Huntington's Disease: A Book for Patients and Families.* Madison: University of Wisconsin Press, 1981.

Phillips, Sidney F. *Diarrhea: Infectious and Other Causes.* Washington, D.C.: National Digestive Diseases Information Clearinghouse, U.S. Dept. of Health and Human Services, 1995.

Piaget, Jean. *Genetic Epistemology.* Trans. E. Duckworth. New York: Norton, 1970.

———, and Barbel Inhelder. *The Growth of Logical Thinking from Childhood to Adolescence.* New York: Basic Books, 1958.

Pinckney, Cathey. *Do-It-Yourself Medical Testing: 240 Tests You Can Perform At Home.* New York: Facts on File, 1989.

———. *The Patient's Guide to Medical Tests.* New York: Facts on File, 1986.

Pinker, S. *The Language Instinct.* New York: Morrow, 1994.

Planning for Pregnancy, Birth, and Beyond. Washington, DC: American College of Obstetricians and Gynecologists, 1990.

Plomin, R. *Nature and Nurture.* Pacific Grove, CA: Brooks/Cole Publishing, 1990.

Poarch, John E. *Limits: The Keystone of Emotional Growth.* Muncie, IN: Accelerated Development Inc., 1990.

Pojman, Louis P. *Ethics: Discovering Right and Wrong.* Belmont, CA: Wadsworth Publishing, 1990.

Porter, Rosalie Pedalino. *Forked Tongue: The Politics of Bilingual Education.* New York: Basic Books, 1990.

Posner, George J. and Alan N. Rudnitsky. *Course Design: A Guide to Curriculum Development for Teachers.* 4th ed. New York: Longman, 1994.

Postley, John E., and Janet Barton. *The Allergy Discovery Diet: A Rotation Diet for Discovering Your Allergies to Food.* New York: Doubleday, 1990.

Power, F. C., Ann Higgins, and Lawrence Kohlberg. *Lawrence Kohlberg's Approach to Moral Education: A Study of Three Democratic High Schools.* New York: Columbia University Press, 1989.

Powers, Gene R. *Cleft Palate.* Austin, TX: PRO-ED, 1986.

Powter, Susan. *Hey Mom! I'm Hungry: Great-tasting, Low-fat, Easy Recipes to Feed Your Family.* New York: Simon and Schuster, 1997.

Prather, Hugh, and Gayle Prather. *Spiritual Parenting: A Guide to Understanding Nurturing the Heart of Your Child.* New York: Three Rivers Press, 1996.

Pratt, P.N., and A.S. Allen. *Occupational Therapy for Children*, 2d ed. St. Louis: C.V. Mosby, 1989.

President's Council of Physical Fitness and Sports 1985. *National School Population Fitness Survey.* Washington, D.C.: HHS-Office of the Assistant Secretary for Health, 1986.

Price, Jerome A. *Power and Compassion: Working with Difficult Adolescents and Abused Parents.* New York: Guilford Press, 1996.

Pueschel, Siegfried. *Down Syndrome: Toward a Brighter Future.* Baltimore: Paul H. Brookes, 1990.

R

Rabies: A Warm Weather Hazard. Washington, DC: Department of Health and Human Services, 1987.

Rachlin, Howard. *Introduction to Modern Behaviorism.* 3rd ed. New York: Freeman, 1991.

Ramsey, P.G. *Making Friends in School: Promoting Peer Relationships in Early Childhood.* New York: Teacher's College Press, 1991.

Rapoport, Judith L. *The Boy Who Couldn't Stop Washing: The Experience and Treatment of Obsessive-Compulsive Disorder.* 1st ed. New York: E.P. Dutton, 1989.

Raths, Louis, M. Harmin, and S. Simon. *Values and Teaching.* Columbus, OH: Charles E. Merrill Publishing Company, 1966.

Ravitch, Diane. *The Schools We Deserve: Reflections on the Educational Crises of Our Time.* New York: Basic Books, 1985.

Rees, Michael K. *The Complete Family Guide to Living with High Blood Pressure.* Englewood Cliffs, NJ: Prentice-Hall, 1980.

Reiss, Albert J. Jr., and Jeffrey A. Roth, eds. *Understanding and Preventing Violence.* Washington, DC: National Academy Press, 1993.

Resener, Carl R., and Judy Hall. *Kids on the Street.* Nashville: Broadman Press, 1992.

Resetak, Richard M. *Receptors.* New York: Bantam Books, 1994.

Reuben, Carolyn. *The Healthy Baby Book.* New York: Jeremy P. Tarcher/Perigee Books, 1992.

Rich, Laurie A. *When Pregnancy Isn't Perfect.* New York: Dutton, 1991.

Rider, Anthony Olen. *The Firesetter: A Psychological Profile.* Washington, D.C.: Federal Bureau of Investigation, U.S. Department of Justice, 1984.

Rizzuto, Ana-Maria. *The Birth of the Living God: A Psychoanalytic Study.* Chicago: University of Chicago Press, 1979.

Roberts, Michael C. *Handbook of Pediatric Psychology.* 2nd ed. New York: Guilford Press, 1995.

Robertson, Gwendolyn. *School-Based Peer Mediation Programs: A Natural Extension of Developmental Guidance Programs.* Gorham, ME: University of Southern Maine, 1991.

Rockwell, Anne. *The Three Bears and 15 Other Stories.* New York: HarperCollins, 1975. [Preschool-grade 1]

Rodriguez, Richard. *Hunger of Memory: The Education of Richard Rodriguez.* New York: Bantam Books, 1983.

Rogers, F. *Mr. Rogers Talks with Parents.* Berkley, 1985.

———. *You Are Special: Words of Wisdom from America's Most Beloved Neighbor.* New York: Viking, 1994.

———, and B. Head. (1986). *The Mister Roger's Playbook: Insights and Activities for Parents and Children.* Berkley, 1986.

Romberg, Henry C. *Bris Milah: A Book About the Jewish Ritual of Circumcision.* New York: Feldheim Publishers, 1982.

Romberg, Rosemary. *Circumcision: The Painful Dilemma.* South Hadley, MA: Bergin and Garvey, 1985.

Rose, Sharon, Cris Stevens, et al. *Bisexual Horizons: Politics, Histories, Lives.* London: Lawrence & Wishart, 1996.

Rosen, Marcia. *Test Your Baby's I.Q.* Englewood Cliffs, NJ: Prentice-Hall, 1986.

Roskies, Ethel. *Abnormality and Normality: The Mothering of Thalidomide Children.* Ithaca, New York: Cornell University, 1972.

Ross, D. G. *Stanley Hall: The Psychologist as Prophet.* Chicago: University of Chicago Press, 1972.

Ross, Jerilyn. *Triumph Over Fear.* New York: Bantam Books, 1994.

Ross, Linda M., ed. *Communication Disorders Sourcebook: Basic Information About Deafness and Hearing Loss, Speech and Language Disorders, Voice Disorders, Balance and Vestibular Disorders, and Disorders of Smell, Taste, and Touch.* Detroit, MI: Omnigraphics, 1995.

Rotatori, Anthony F., and Robert A. Fox. *Obesity in Children and Youth: Measurement, Characteristics, Causes, and Treatment.* Springfield, IL: Thomas, 1989.

Rothbart, M.K. "Temperament in Childhood." In G.A. Kohnstamm, J.E. Bates, and M.K. Rothbart (eds.). *Temperament in Childhood.* New York: Wiley, 1989, p. 59-76.

Roush, Jackson, and Noel D. Matkin, eds. *Infants and Toddlers with Hearing Loss: Family-Centered Assessment and Intervention.* Baltimore: York Press, 1994.

Ruben, Douglas H. *Bratbusters! Say Goodbye to Tantrums and Disobedience.* El Paso, TX: Skidmore-Roth Publishers, 1992.

Rudman, Masha K., et al. *For Love of Reading: A Parent's Guide to Encouraging Young Readers and Writers from Infancy through Age 5.* New York: Consumer Reports Books, 1988.

S

Sachs, Elizabeth-Ann. *Just Like Always.* New York: Atheneum, 1981. [juvenile fiction]

Sadker, David, and Myra Sadker. *Failing at Fairness: How America's Schools Cheat Girls.* New York: Scribner's, 1994.

Salander, James M. *Hypertension: Reducing Your Risk.* New York: Bantam, 1993.

Salkin, Jeffrey K. *Putting God on the Guest List: How to Reclaim the Spiritual Meaning of Your Child's Bar or Bat Mizvah.* Woodstock, VT: Jewish Lights Publishing, 1992.

Salzman, Bernard. *The Handbook of Psychiatric Drugs.* New York: Henry Holt, 1996.

Sameroff, Arnold J., and Marshall M. Haith, eds. *The Five to Seven Year Shift: The Age of Reason and Responsibility.* Chicago: University of Chicago Press, 1991.

Sanberg, Paul R. *Prescription Narcotics: The Addictive Painkillers.* New York: Chelsea House, 1986.

Sanders, Pete. *Feeling Safe.* New York: Gloucester Press, 1988.

Sandler, Joseph, Ethel Spector Person, and Peter Fonagy, eds. *Freud's "On Narcissism—an Introduction."* New Haven, CT: Yale University Press, 1991.

Sanford, Doris. *Yes, I Can!: Challenging Cerebral.* Sisters, OR: Multnomah Press, 1992. [juvenile literature]

Satir, Virginia. *Conjoint Family Therapy.* Palo Alto: Science and Behavior Books, 1983.

Saunders, Jeraldine and Harvey M. Ross. *Hypoglycemia: The Disease Your Doctor Won't Treat.* New York: Pinnacle Books, 1980.

Sawyer, R. Keith. *Pretend Play as Improvisation.* Mahwah, NJ: L. Erlbaum, 1997.

Scala, James. *Eating Right for a Bad Gut: The Complete Nutritional Guide to Ileitis, Colitis, Crohn's Disease, and Inflammatory Bowel Disease.* New York: Plume, 1992.

Schaefer, C.K. *Childhood Encopresis and Enuresis.* New York: Von Nostrand Rheinehold, 1979.

Scharf, M.B. *Waking Up Dry.* Cincinnati: Writer's Digest Books, 1986.

Schindler, Lydia Woods. *The Immune System: How It Works.* Bethesda, MD: U. S. National Institutes of Health, 1993.

Schlegel, Alice. *Adolescence: An Anthropological Inquiry.* New York: Free Press, 1991.

Schleichkorn, Jay. *Coping with Cerebral Palsy: Answers to Questions Parents Often Ask.* 2nd ed. Austin, TX: PRO-ED, 1993.

Schmittroth, Linda. *Statistical Record of Children.* Detroit: Gale Research, 1994.

Schneider, Phyllis. *Parents Book of Infant Colic.* New York: Ballantine Books, 1990.

Schommer, Nancy. *Stopping Scoliosis: The Complete Guide to Diagnosis and Treatment.* New York: Doubleday, 1987.

Schrier, Robert W. *Diseases of the Kidney.* 4th ed. Boston: Little, Brown, 1988.

Schulman, Michael, and Eva Mekler. *Bringing Up a Moral Child: A New Approach for Teaching Your Child to Be Kind, Just, and Responsible.* New York: Doubleday, 1994.

Schwartz, Martin F. *Stop Stuttering.* New York: Harper and Row, 1986.

Schwartz, Sue, ed. *Choices in Deafness: A Parents' Guide to Communication Options.* 2nd ed. Bethesda, MD: Woodbine House, 1996.

Schwebel, Robert. *Saying No Is Not Enough: What to Say and How to Listen to Your Kids About Alcohol, Tobacco and Other Drugs—A Positive Prevention Guide for Parents.* New York: Newmarket Press, 1997.

Sciacca, Fran. *Cliques and Clones: Facing Peer Pressure.* Grand Rapids, MI: Zondervan, 1992.

Sears, William, *The Discipline Book: Everything You Need to Know to Have a Better-Behaved Child—From Birth to Age 10,* 1st ed. Boston: Little, Brown and Co., 1995.

———. *SIDS: A Parent's Guide to Understanding and Preventing Sudden Infant Death Syndrome.* Boston: Little, Brown, 1995.

Secretary's Commission on Achieving Necessary Skills. *What Work Requires of Schools.* Washington, DC: US Department of Labor, 1991.

Seligman, Daniel. *A Question of Intelligence: The IQ Debate in America.* New York: Birch Lane Press, 1992.

Seligman, Martin E. P. *The Optimistic Child.* Boston: Houghton Mifflin Co., 1995.

Selman, R. *The Growth of Interpersonal Understanding.* New York: Academic Press, 1980.

Semmler, Caryl J. *Early Occupational Therapy Intervention: Neonates to Three Years.* Gaithersburg, MD.: Aspen Publishers, 1990.

Serjeant, Graham R. *Sickle Cell Disease.* 2nd ed. New York: Oxford University Press, 1992.

Service, F. John, ed. *Hypoglycemic Disorders: Pathogenesis, Diagnosis, and Treatment.* Boston: G.K. Hall, 1983.

Shaftel, Fannie R. *Role Playing in the Curriculum.* Englewood Cliffs, NJ: Prentice-Hall, 1982.

Shapiro, Burton L. and Ralph C. Heussner, Jr. *A Parent's Guide to Cystic Fibrosis.* Minneapolis: University of Minnesota Press, 1990.

Shapiro, Howard I. *The New Birth-Control Book: A Complete Guide for Men and Women.* New York: Prentice Hall Press, 1988.

Shapiro, Kenneth Joel. *The Experience of Introversion.* Durham, NC: Duke University. Press, 1975.

Shapiro, Robert. *Sharing the Children: How to Resolve Custody Problems and Get On with Your Life.* Bethesda, MD: Adler & Adler, 1988.

Sheehy, Gail. *Passages: Predictable Crises of Adult Life.* New York: E. P. Dutton, 1976.

Shellenberger, Susie. *Lockers, Lunch Lines, Chemistry, and Cliques.* Minneapolis, MN: Bethany House Publishers, 1995.

Shephard, Lorrie, ed. *Flunking Grades: Research and Policies on Retention.* Falmer Press, 1989.

Shimberg, Elaine Fantle. *Relief from IBS.* New York: M. Evans, 1988.

Sholevar, G. Pirooz, ed. *Conduct Disorders in Children and Adolescents.* Washington, DC: American Psychiatric Press, 1995.

Shore, Milton F., Patrick J. Brice, and Barbara G. Love. *When Your Child Needs Testing: What Parents, Teachers, and Other Helpers Need to Know about Psychological Testing.* New York: Crossroad, 1992.

Shtasel, Philip. *Medical Tests and Diagnostic Procedure: A Patient's Guide to Just What the Doctor Ordered.* New York: Harper and Row, 1990.

Sikula, John, et al. *Handbook of Research on Teacher Education.* 2nd ed. New York: Macmillan, 1996.

Silber, Sherman J. *How to Get Pregnant with the New Technology.* New York: Warner Books, 1991.

Siminerio, Linda M., and Jean Betschart. *Children with Diabetes.* Alexandria, VA: American Diabetes Association, 1986.

Simkin, P., J. Whalley, and A. Keppler. *Pregnancy, Childbirth, and the Newborn: The Complete Guide.* New York: Meadowbrook Press, 1991.

Simon, Paul. *The Tongue-Tied American: Confronting the Foreign Language Crisis.* New York: Continuum, 1980.

Simon, S., L. Howe, and H. Kirschenbaum. *Values Clarification.* New York: Hart, 1972.

Singer, Peter. *Making Babies: The New Science and Ethics of Conception*. New York: C. Scribner's Sons, 1985.

Singh, Joseph. *Wolf Children and Feral Man*. Hamden, CT: Archon Books, 1966.

Skillen, James W. (ed.) *The School-Choice Controversy: What Is Constitutional?* Washington, DC: Center for Public Justice, 1993.

Slap, Gail B., and Martha M. Jablow. *Teenage Health Care*. New York: Pocket Books, 1994.

Slater, John G., ed. *Bertrand Russell, 1927–42: A Fresh Look at Empiricism*. New York: Routledge, 1996.

Smilansky, S. *On Death: Helping Children Understand and Cope*. New York: Peter Lang Publishing, 1987.

Smith, Frederick Henry. *Nail-Biting: The Beatable Habit*. Provo, UT: Brigham Young University Press, 1980.

Smith, Jane S. *Patenting the Sun*. New York: William Morrow and Company, Inc., 1990.

Smith, Lendon H. *Foods for Healthy Kids*. New York: McGraw Hill, 1981.

Smith, Terry L. *Behavior and Its Causes: Philosophical Foundations of Operant Psychology*. Boston: Kluwer Academic Publishers, 1994.

Smitherman, Geneva. *Talkin and Testifyin: The Language of Black America*. Detroit: Wayne State University Press, 1986.

Smutny, Joan F., Kathleen Veenker, and Stephen Veenker. *Your Gifted Child: How to Recognize and Develop the Special Talents in Your Child from Birth to Age Seven*. New York: Facts on File, 1989.

Solin, Sabrina. *The Seventeen Guide to Sex and Your Body*. New York: Simon and Schuster, 1996.

Sorenson, Don L. *Conflict Resolution and Mediation for Peer Helpers*. Minneapolis, MN: Educational Media Corporation, 1992.

Spiro, Melford E. *Children of the Kibbutz*. Cambridge, MA: Harard University Press, 1975.

Spock, Benjamin. *Baby and Child Care. Revised and Updated*. New York: Pocket Books, 1985.

———. *A Better World for Our Children*. Bethesda, MD: National Press Books, 1994.

———. *The Common Sense Book of Baby and Child Care*. New York: Duell, Sloan, and Pearce, 1946.

———. *Spock on Spock*. New York: Pantheon Books, 1989.

Sroufe, L. Alan, Robert G. Cooper, and Mary E. Marshall. *Child Development*. New York: Random House, 1987.

St. John, N. H. *School Desegregation: Outcomes for Children*. New York: Wiley, 1975.

Staddon, John. *Behaviorism: Mind, Mechanism and Society*. London: Duckworth, 1993.

Stanton-Jones, Kristina. *An Introduction to Dance Movement in Therapy in Psychiatry*. London: Routledge, 1992.

Starr, Philip. *Cleft Lip and/or Palate: Behavioral Effects from Infancy to Adulthood*. Springfield, IL: Charles C. Thomas, 1983.

Stein, D. J., ed. *Impulsivity and Aggression*. Chichester, NY: Wiley, 1995.

Steinberg, Laurence, et al. *Beyond the Classroom: Why School Reform Has Failed and What Parents Need to Do*. New York: Simon and Schuster, 1996.

———, and Ann Levine. *You and Your Adolescent: A Parent's Guide for Ages 10–20*. New York: Harper & Row, 1990.

Steinberg, Marlene. *Handbook for the Assessment of Dissociation: A Clinical Guide*. Washington, DC: American Psychiatric Press, 1995.

Stern, D., Raby M. and Dayton, C. *Career Academies: Partnerships for Reconstructing American High Schools*. San Francisco: Jossey-Bass, 1992.

Sternberg, R. J. *Beyond IQ: A Triarchic Theory of Human Intelligence*. Cambridge, Eng.: Cambridge University Press, 1985.

———. *The Nature of Creativity*. New York: Cambridge University Press, 1988.

———, and Janet E. Davidson, eds. *Conceptions of Giftedness*. London: Cambridge University Press, 1986.

Stevens, Richard. *Erik Erikson: An Introduction*. New York: St. Martin's, 1983.

Stine, G., ed. *The New Human Genetics*. Dubuque, IA: Wm. C. Brown, 1989.

Stirt, Joseph A. *Baby.* Far Hills, NJ: New Horizon Press, 1992.

Stoner, G., et al. *Interventions for Achievement and Behavior Problems.* Silver Spring, MD: National Association of School Psychologists, 1991.

Stouffer, Dennis J. *Journey Through Hell: Stories of Burn Survivors' Reconstruction of Self and Identity.* Lanham, MD: Rowman & Littlefield, 1994.

Stratton, Kathleen, Cynthia Howe, and Frederick Battaglia. *Fetal Alcohol Syndrome: Diagnosis, Epidemiology, Prevention, and Treatment.* Washington, DC: National Academy Press, 1997.

Straus, Murray, Richard Gelles, and Suzanne Steinmetz. *Behind Closed Doors: Violence in the American Family.* New York: Anchor Press/ Doubleday, 1980.

Stray-Gundersen, ed. *Babies with Down Syndrome: A New Parents Guide.* Woodbine House, 1986.

Strean, Herbert S., and Lucy Freeman. *Raising Cain: How to Help Your Children Achieve a Happy Sibling Relationship.* New York: Facts on File Publications, 1988.

Strom, Charles. *Heredity and Ability: How Genetics Affects Your Child and What You Can Do About It.* New York: Plenum Press, 1990.

Sugden, David A. *Problems in Movement Skill Development.* Columbia, SC: University of South Carolina Press, 1990.

The Super Sitter. Washington, DC: U.S. Consumer Product Safety Commission, 1994.

Sweeney, Dee. *Meet Your Mind.* Washington, DC: Office of Educational Research and Improvement, 1994.

T

Tangney, J.P., and K.W. Fischer (Eds.). *Self-Conscious Emotions: Shame, Guilt and Pride.* New York: Guilford, 1995.

Tanner, Laurel N., ed. *Critical Issues in Curriculum.* Chicago: University of Chicago Press, 1988.

Taubman, Bruce. *Curing Infant Colic: The 7-Minute Program for Soothing the Fussy Baby.* New York: Bantam Books, 1990.

Tauscher, Ellen O. *The Childcare Sourcebook: The Complete Guide to Finding and Managing Nannies, Au Pairs, Babysitters, Day Care, and After-School Programs.* New York: Macmillan, 1996.

Taylor, Hanni U. *Standard English, Black English, and Bidialectism: A Controversy.* New York: P. Lang, 1989.

Taylor, Orlando L. *Nature of Communication Disorders in Culturally and Linguistically Diverse Populations.* San Diego: College-Hill Press, 1986.

Temple, Christine. *The Brain.* London: Penguin Books, 1993.

Terkel, Susan Neiburg. *Ethics.* New York: Lodestar Books, 1992.

Texas Heart Institute. *Heart Owner's Handbook.* New York: John Wiley & Sons, 1996.

Therman, Eva. *Human Chromosomes: Structure, Behavior, and Effects.* New York: Springer-Verlag, 1993.

Thiel, Ann, Richard Thiel, and Penelope B. Grenoble. *When Your Child Isn't Doing Well in School.* Chicago: Contemporary Books, 1988.

Thomas, A. and S. Chess. *Temperament and Development.* New York: Brunner Mazel, 1977.

Thomas, Jerry R., ed. *Motor Development in Childhood and Adolescence.* Minneapolis, MN: Burgess Publishing Co., 1984.

Thomas, R. Murray. *Comparing Theories of Child Development.* 3rd ed. Belmont, CA: Wadsworth Publishing Company, 1992.

Thompson, W. Grant. *The Angry Gut: Coping with Colitis and Crohn's Disease.* New York: Plenum Press, 1993.

Thorne, B. *Gender Play: Girls and Boys in School.* New Brunswick, NJ: Rutgers University Press, 1993.

Todd, James T., and Edward K. Morris. *Modern Perspectives on B.F. Skinner and Contemporary Behaviorism.* Westport, CT: Greenwood Press, 1995.

———. *Modern Perspectives on John B. Watson and Classical Behaviorism.* Westport, CT: Greenwood Press, 1994.

Tomkins, S.S. *Affect, Imagery, and Consciousness: Volume 2: The Negative Affects.* New York: Springer, 1963.

Torrance, E. P. *Guiding Creative Talent.* Englewood Cliffs, NJ: Prentice-Hall, 1962.

Townley, A., and M. Lee. *Training for Trainers: Staff Development in Conflict Resolution Skills.* Amherst, MA: National Association for Mediation in Education, 1993.

Traub, James. *The Billion-Dollar Connection: The International Drug Trade.* New York: J. Messner, 1982.

Treffert, D.A. *Extraordinary People.* New York: Harper and Row, 1989.

Trelease, Jim. *The Read-Aloud Handbook.* 4th ed. New York: Penguin Books, 1995.

Trillin, Alice. *Dear Bruno.* New York: The New Press, 1996.

Trombetta, C. *Edouard Claparède psicologo,* Rome, Italy: Armando, 1989.

Turecki, Stanley. *The Emotional Problems of Normal Children.* New York: Bantam Books, 1994.

Tuttle, Heather. *Living with Seizures.* Rootstown, OH: Tuttle Press, 1995. [juvenile]

U

U.S. Department of Education. *Eighteenth Annual Report to Congress on the Implementation of the Individuals with Disabilities Act.* Washington, DC: Office of Special Education Programs, 1996.

U.S. Department of Health and Human Services, Committee to Coordinate Environmental Health and Related Programs. Ad Hoc Subcommittee on Fluoride. *Review of Fluoride Benefits and Risks: Report of the Ad Hoc Subcommittee on Fluoride.* Washington, DC: Public Health Service, Department of Health and Human Services, 1991.

———. Public Health Service, *Seventh Annual Report on Carcinogens, Summary 1994.* National Institute of Environmental Health Sciences: Research Triangle Park, North Carolina, 1995.

———. *Preventing Tobacco Use Among Young People: A Report of the Surgeon General.* At-

lanta, GA: U.S. Department of Health and Human Services, Public Health Service, Centers for Disease Control and Prevention, Office on Smoking and Health, 1994.

U.S. Pharmacopeia. *The USP Guide to Vitamins and Minerals.* New York: Avon Books, 1996.

Ujamaa, Dawud R. *Back to Our Roots: Cooking for Control of Sickle Cell Anemia and Cancer Prevention.* Decatur, GA: Al Maidah Publications, 1995.

Ulene, Art, and Val Ulene. *The Vitamin Strategy.* Berkeley: The Ulysses Press, 1994.

Ullman, Robert. *Ritalin-Free Kids: Safe and Effective Homeopathic Medicines for ADD and Other Behavioral and Learning Problems.* Rocklin, CA: Prima Publishing, 1996.

Uzgiris, Ina C., and J. McVicker Hunt. eds. *Infant Performance and Experience: New Findings with the Ordinal Scales.* Urbana, IL: University of Illinois Press, 1987.

V

Vail, Priscilla L. *Common Ground: Whole Language and Phonics Working Together.* Rosemont, NJ: Modern Learning Press, 1991.

Van Gennep, Arnold. *The Rites of Passage.* Chicago: University of Chicago Press, 1960.

Van Ments, Morry. *The Effective Use of Role-Play: A Handbook for Teachers and Trainers.* New York: Nichols Publishing, 1989.

Van Riper, C. *The Nature of Stuttering,* 2nd ed. Englewood Cliffs, NJ: Prentice-Hall, 1982.

Varma, Ved. *How and Why Children Fail.* Philadelphia: J. Kingsley, 1993.

Vasta, Ross, Marshall M. Haith, and Scott A. Miller. *Child Psychology: The Modern Science.* New York: J. Wiley & Sons, 1992.

Vaughan, Christopher. *How Life Begins: The Science of Life in the Womb.* New York: Times Books, 1996.

Vidal, F. *Piaget Before Piaget.* Cambridge: Harvard University Press, 1994.

Virtue, Doreen. *My Kids Don't Live with Me Anymore: Coping with the Custody Crisis.* Minneapolis: Compcare, 1988.

Volk, Tyler. *Metapatterns across Space, Time, and Mind.* New York: Columbia University Press, 1995.

W

Wallerstein, Judith S. *Second Chances: Men, Women, and Children a Decade after Divorce.* New York: Ticknor & Fields, 1989.

———, and Joan Kelly. *Surviving the Break-Up: How Children Cope with Divorce.* New York: Basic Books, 1980.

Walsh, Maryellen. *Schizophrenia: Straight Talk for Families and Friends.* New York: William Morrow, 1985.

Walsh, W. Bruce, and Nancy E. Betz. *Tests and Assessment.* 2nd ed. Englewood Cliffs, NJ: Prentice Hall, 1990.

Walsh, William. *The Food Allergy Book.* St. Paul, MN: ACA Publications, 1995.

Walters, Marianne, et. al. *The Invisible Web: Gender Patterns in Family Relationships.* New York: Guilford Press, 1988.

Wang, M.C., et al. *The Handbook of Special Education: Research and Practice.* Vols 1 & 2. Oxford, England: Pergamon Press, 1987.

Warren, Paul, and Frank Minirth. *Things That Go Bump in the Night: How to Help Children Resolve Their Natural Fears.* Nashville, TN: T. Nelson Publishers, 1992. (This book also addresses Christian aspects of fear.)

Warshak, Richard A. *The Custody Revolution: The Father Factor and the Motherhood Mystique.* New York: Poseidon Press, 1992.

Watkins, Kathleen Pullan. *Parent-child Attachment: A Guide to Research.* New York: Garland Publishing, 1987.

Webb, Margot. *Coping with Street Gangs.* New York: Rosen Publishing Group, 1992.

Webb, N. B., ed. *Helping Bereaved Children: A Handbook for Practitioners.* New York: Guilford Press, 1993.

Wechsler, Harlan J. *What's So Bad About Guilt? Learning to Live With It Since We Can't Live Without It.* New York: Simon and Schuster, 1990.

Weinberg, Martin S., Colin J. Williams, and Douglas W. Pryor. *Dual Attraction: Understanding Bisexuality.* New York: Oxford University Press, 1994.

Weissbluth, Marc. *Crybabies: Coping With Colic.* New York: Arbor House, 1984.

Wekesser, Carol, ed. *Smoking.* Current Controversies series. San Diego, CA: Greenhaven Press, 1997.

Weller, Charles and Brian Richard Boylan. *How to Live with Hypoglycemia.* Garden City, NY: Doubleday, 1968.

Wells, G. Beverly. *Stuttering Treatment: A Comprehensive Clinical Guide.* Englewood Cliffs, NJ: Prentice-Hall, 1987.

Wenning, Kenneth. *Winning Cooperation from Your Child!: A Comprehensive Method to Stop Defiant and Aggressive Behavior in Children.* Northvale, NJ: J. Aronson, 1996.

Werner, E.E., and R.S. Smith. *Vulnerable but Invincible: A Longitudinal Study of Resilient Children and Youth.* New York: McGraw-Hill, 1982.

Westen, Drew. *Self and Society: Narcissism, Collectivism, and the Development of Morals.* New York: Cambridge University Press, 1985.

Westwood, Peter S. *Commonsense Methods for Children with Special Needs: Strategies for the Regular Classroom.* 2nd ed. London; New York: Routledge, 1993.

Whitford, G.M. *The Metabolism and Toxicity of Fluoride.* Basel, New York: Karger, 1989.

Whitten, Phillip. *The Complete Book of Swimming.* New York: Random House, 1994.

Wicka, Donna Konkel. *Advice to Parents of a Cleft Palate Child.* 2d ed. Springfield, IL: Thomas, 1982.

Williams, Juan. *Eyes on the Prize: America's Civil Rights Years.* New York: Viking, 1987.

Wilson, Edward. *Sociobiology—the New Synthesis.* Cambridge, MA: Harvard University Press, 1975

Windell, James. *Children Who Say No When You Want Them to Say Yes: Failsafe Discipline Strategies for Stubborn and Oppositional Children and Teens.* New York: Macmillan, 1996.

Wodrich, David L., and Sally A. Kush. *Children's Psychological Testing: A Guide for Nonpsy-*

chologists. 2nd ed. Baltimore, MD: Brookes Publishing Co., 1990.

Wolff, Angelika. *Mom! I Broke My Arm!* New York: Lion Press, 1969.

Wolowiec, Jack, ed. *Everybody Wins: Mediation in the Schools*, Chicago: American Bar Association, 1994.

Wolpe, Joseph. *Life Without Fear.* Oakland, CA: Harbinger, 1988.

Wolpert, L. *The Triumph of the Embryo.* Oxford: Oxford University Press, 1991.

Wood, Judy W. *Adapting Instruction for Mainstreamed and At-Risk Students.* 2nd ed. New York: Maxwell Macmillan, 1992.

Wortham, Sue Clark. *Tests and Measurement in Early Childhood Education.* Columbus: Merrill Publishing Co., 1990.

Wright, Logan. *Parent Power.* New York: William Morrow, 1980.

Wyckoff, Jerry. *How to Discipline Your Six-to-Twelve Year Old: Without Losing Your Mind*, 1st ed. New York: Doubleday, 1991.

Wynn, Sidney K. and Alfred L. Miller, editors. *A Practical Guide to Cleft Lip and Palate Birth Defects: Helpful, Practical Information and Answers for Parents, Physicians, Nurses, and Other Professionals.* Springfield, IL: Thomas, 1984.

Y

Yoder, Eileen Rhude. *Allergy-Free Cooking: How to Survive the Elimination Diet and Eat Happily Ever After.* New York: Addison-Wesley, 1987.

Yolen, Jane, ed. *Favorite Folk Tales from Around the World.* New York: Pantheon, 1986. [Grades 6 and up]

Young, Carol. *Crying For Help: How to Cure Your Baby of Colic.* New York: Thorsons, 1986.

Z

Zadra, D. *Mistakes Are Great.* Mankato, MN: Creative Education, 1986.

Zaret, B., et al, eds. *Yale University School of Medicine Heart Book.* New York: Hearst Books, 1992.

Zigler, Edward F. and Mary E. Lang. *Child Care Choices: Balancing the Needs of Children, Families, and Society.* New York: The Free Press, 1991.

———, and Susan Muenchow. *Head Start: The Inside Story of America's Most Successful Educational Experiment.* New York: Basic Books, 1992.

———, and Matia Finn-Stevenson. *Children in a Changing World: Development and Social Issues.* 2d ed. Pacific Grove, CA: Brooks/Cole Publishing Company, 1993.

INDEX

A

AARP Grandparent Information Center 322
AASK. *See* Adopt A Special Kid
ABA Center on Children and the Law 2, 149
Abandonment 1–2
Abduction 148
Abecedarian Project 247
Ability grouping 2–3
    assessment and 62
Abortion 3–4
    spontaneous 38, 290
AboutFace 160
Absolutism, ethics and 268
Abstract thinking, in adolescence 11
Academy of Sports Dentistry
    recommendations on mouth protectors 206
Accidents
    childproofing 150
    infant mortality and 369
    latchkey children and 400
Accreditation, school 33
Acculturation 4–5
Acetaminophen 5
    dosage table 5
    fever and 292
    herpes simplex and 340
    pain and pain management 480
Acetylsalicylic acid 61
Achievement, recognition of 561
Achievement tests 545
    Kaufman Assessment Battery for Children (KABC) 379
Achilles Track Club Youth Program 272

Achondroplasia. *See* Dwarfism
Acne 5–7
Acting out 7
Action for Children's Television 7–8
Acute lymphocytic leukemia (ALL) 407
Acyclovir 138, 340
Adaptation 8
Adaptive Behavior Scale for Infants and Early Childhood (ABSI) 8–9
ADD. *See* Attention deficit/hyperactivity disorder *and* Autosomal dominant disease
Addiction 578
Adenosine deaminase deficiency (ADD) 308
Adjustment disorders 9, 17, 208
Adler, Alfred 10, 102
Adolescence 10–15, 575
    abortion and 3
    abused children and 141
    adjustment disorders and 9
    adjustment in adoptees 17
    alcohol use 22, 567, 569
    allowances and money management 32
    amenorrhea 34
    anemia 42
    antisocial behavior 49
    anxiety 9
    appendicitis 56
    arthritis 58
    as the period of transition 564
    assertiveness 562
    asthma 66
    at-risk students 66
    attention deficit/hyperactivity disorder 76
    autoimmune disorders 80
    bar/bat mitzvah 84
    battered child syndrome 86

behavioral risk factors 566, 568

bipolar disorder 97

body image 107

boredom 109

breast enlargement in boys 117

bullying 124

cancer, kidneys 381

celiac sprue disease 135

child psychology and 149

chlamydia 152

cleft lip and palate 160

cliques 161

conduct disorders and 172

contraceptive use 567

diabetes mellitus 219

divorce and 233

Down syndrome and 237

drug use 567, 569

eating disorders and 45, 123, 249

epilepsy and 266

Erikson's theory and 267

fears during 288

fetal alcohol effects and 291

friendships 299

gangs 301

giftedness and 313

girls and self-esteem 304

gonorrhea 319

growth spurt 11

heart disease 338

herpes simplex 339

Huntington's disease and 350

identity formation 581

idiopathic scoliosis 551

impulse control disorders 363

institutionalization and 371

intermittent explosive disorders 364

kibbutz life 380

kidney tumor 381

latchkey children 399

lead poisoning and 402

maturation rates 574

onset of pathological gambling 301

peer pressure during 13

population projections (table) 10

pregnancy 240, 249, 369

psoriasis 81

rheumatic fever 80

seizures 555

self-esteem in 304, 561

sexual abuse and 143

sexually transmitted diseases 564–569

shyness 571

sickle-cell anemia in 571

sleep patterns 575–576

smoking 578–579

social competence 580

sports 602

steroid use during 39

Adolescent medicine 489

Adopt A Special Kid 18

Adoption 15–18

acknowledging birth heritage 17

child custody laws 146

interracial 15

outcomes 17

types 16

Voluntary Cooperative Information System 17

Adoption Assistance and Child Welfare Reform Act 16, 296

Adoptive Families of America 18

Adrenals 345

Advocates for Better Child Support (ABC'S) 2

Affect 18–19

African Americans 567–568

bone growth 575

contraceptive use 567

drug/alcohol use 568

prevalent bacterial STD infections 564

sickle-cell anemia, incidence 571

sexual experience 566

smoking incidence 578

viral STD infections 564–565

Age, anatomical 40–41

Aggression 172, 580

abused children and 140

adoptees and 17

alcohol use and 27

bullying 124

exercise and 272

hospitalization and 349

imaginary playmates and 357
television and 628–629
tests for 151
television and 629
vs. assertiveness 562
Aid to Dependent Children 1
AIDS 358, 564–565, 568
Ainsworth, Mary 19–20
    attachment 69
    John Bowlby and 112
Airbags 544
Aircrib 88–89
Akathisia 548
Albert Ellis Institute 163
Albinism 308
Albright's hereditary osteodystrophy 309
    small for gestational age and 577
Alcohol use 566–567, 569
    abuse 548
    alienation and 25, 28
    as behavioral risk factor 49, 567, 569
    at-risk students 66
    bipolar disorder and 97
    by children, warning signs 26
    child abuse and 144
    maternal, infant mortality and 369
    users 567
    See also Alcoholism
Alcoholics Anonymous 27–28
Alcoholism 20–28
    adverse social consequences 23
    aversive conditioning and 82
    dependency symptoms 23
    escapist drinking coping motives 23
    gender differences in adolescence 22
    risk factors 24
    withdrawal 556
Alexander Graham Bell Association 336
Alexia 28
Allele 28
Allen cards, eye exams and 274
Allergies 28–31
    allergens 29
    asthma and 65
    bronchitis and 121
    eggs and MMR vaccine 361

    failure to thrive and 278
    food 31
    treatment 29
Allowance 31–32
Alopecia 32
Alpha Fetoprotein (AFP) Test 32–33, 38
Alport's syndrome 381
Alternative assessments 62
Amabile, Teresa 185
Amblyopia 33
Amenorrhea 34, 116
American Academy of Child and Adolescent
    Psychiatry (AACAP) 35, 82, 89, 91,
    163, 549
American Academy of Child Psychiatry. See
    Academy of Child and Adolescent Psy-
    chiatry
American Academy of Dermatology 619
American Academy of Ophthalmology 275
American Academy of Orthopaedic Surgeons
    551–552
American Academy of Pediatrics 35–36, 40,
    487, 551
    child abuse 145
    recommendations on breastfeeding 117
    recommendations on CPR 130
    recommendations on diet and cholesterol
        154
    recommendations on DTP vaccine 361
    recommendations on exercise 272
    recommendations on fluoride 295
    recommendations on HiB vaccine 327
    recommendations for immunization 360
    statistics on chicken pox 138
    television violence and 629
American Academy of Private Practice in
    Speech-Language Pathology and Audi-
    ology 599
American Adoption Congress 18
American Allergy Association 31
American Association for Marriage and Family
    Therapy 285
American Association for the Advancement of
    Science, founding 134
American Association of Certified Allergists 31
American Association of Kidney Patients

INDEX

(AAKP) 383

American Association of University Women (AAUW), study on gender bias 304

American Bar Association Center on Children and the Law 149

American Cancer Society 116, 129–130, 580

American Civil Liberties Union, character education and 137

American Cleft Palate Craniofacial Association (ACPCA) 161

American Coalition of Citizens with Disabilities 136

American College of Obstetricians and Gynecologists 35, 39

American Dance Therapy Association 272

American Dental Association, recommendations on fluoride 295

American Diabetes Association 352

American Educational Research Association 515

American Epilepsy Foundation 266, 556

American Family Therapy Association 285

American Heart Association 580

American Journal of Psychiatry 36

American Juvenile Arthritis Foundation 59

American Kidney Fund 383

American Lung Association 580

American Medical Association (AMA) 35, 580

American Psychiatric Association 36, 363–364

American Psychological Association 36–37, 344, 422, 460

classification of adjustment disorders 9

Division 15, educational psychology 253

television and aggression 629

American Psychologist 36

American Public Welfare Association 17

American Red Cross 83, 130

American Schizophrenia Association 549

American Sign Language 37, 336, 379

American Society for Adolescent Psychiatry 163

American Society of Anesthetists 43

American Society of Human Genetics 310

American Speech-Language-Hearing Association 161, 408, 599

American Urological Association 383

Ameslan. *See* American Sign Language

Amitriptyline (Elavil) 576

Amniocentesis 32, 38–39, 100, 571

fragile X syndrome and 298

genetic counseling and 312

risks 38

Tay-Sachs disease and 626

Anabolic steroids 39

Anaclitic depression 39–40

Anaphylactic shock. *See* Anaphylaxis

Anaphylaxis 31, 40, 44, 47

Anatomical age 40–41

Andersen, Hans Christian 279

Anderson, John E. 403

Androgens 6

Androgyny 41

Anemia 41–43, 106, 111

anoxia, and 46

apnea and 56

autoimmune disorders 81

jaundice and 377

juvenile rheumatoid arthritis 58

lead poisoning and 401

Anesthesia 43–45, 96

in infancy 480

Anger 560

Anhedonia 548

Anomia 45, 55

Anorexia nervosa 45–46, 107, 574

cognitive behavior therapy and 162

Anoxia 46

Antibiotics 46–47, 57, 572

allergic reactions 47

anaphylaxis and 40

bronchitis and 120

ear infection and 246

infant mortality and 369

therapy 572

treatment for chlamydia 152

treatment for gonorrhea 319

treatment for infectious arthritis 59

urinary tract infections 381

Antibodies 359

Anticonvulsant medication 556

Antidepressants 47–48, 210

anxiety and 53

attention deficit/hyperactivity disorder 76
breastfeeding 119
enuresis and 264
tricyclic 576
Antidiuretic hormone (ADH) 264, 345
Antigen-displaying-macrophages 359
Antipsychotic drugs 97, 548
Anti-smoking program 580
Antisocial behavior 48–51
cognitive behavior therapy and 162
fetal alcohol effects and 291
television violence and 629
Antisocial personality disorder 28, 48, 51–52
Anxiety 28, 52–53, 91
adjustment disorder and 9
anorexia nervosa and 46
bulimia nervosa 123
conduct disorders 172
failure to thrive and 278
family therapy 284
fantasy and 285
impulse control disorders and 364
sleep and 575
test 633
Anxiety disorder 52
Anxiety Disorders Association of America 53, 612
APA Monitor 36
APC *See* Antigen-displaying-macrophages
Apgar Score 53–54, 60
Apgar, Virginia 54
Aphasia 54–55, 397
anomia 45
communication board 166
jargon 55
Aplastic anemia 42
Apnea 55–56, 263
Appendicitis 56–57
Appropriate for gestational age (AGA) 577
Apraxia 57
Aptitudes Research Project 186
Art therapy 238
Arthritis 57–59, 61, 80
chlamydia and 152
Arthritis Foundation, The 59
Artificial insemination 315

Artificial respiration 59, 130
Asbestos 60
Asocial characterization 559
Asperger's disorder 501
Asphyxia 577
cerebral palsy and 135
neonatorum 60–61
infant mortality and 369
Aspirin 61
allergy to 31
fever and 292
Reye's syndrome and 261
rheumatic fever and 80
treatment for arthritis 58
Assertiveness 562
Assessment 61–64
alternative 62
attitude inventory 63
authentic 62
basal age 86
creativity 185–186
diabetes mellitus diagnosis 219
educational age and 251
Education for All Handicapped Children
Act 251
Goodenough-Harris Drawing Test 320
halo effect 63
influence of Barbel Inhelder 371
intelligence 185, 252, 320, 372–375
interviews 63
Iowa Tests of Basic Skills 376
Iowa Tests of Educational Development
(ITED) 376
Kaufman Assessment Battery for Children
(KABC) 379
Kohs Block Design Test 385
learning disabilities and 405
multiple intelligences and 252
observer bias 63
performance 62
personality 151
Piaget's studies of 505
portfolio 62
projective tests 63
questionnaires 63
of reading skills 303

Association for the Advancement of Behavior Therapy 82, 89, 91, 162–163

Association for Children and Adults with Learning Disabilities 406

Association for Persons with Severe Handicaps, The (TASH) 367

Association for the Care of Children's Health 349

Association of Medical Superintendents of American Institutions for the Insane. *See* American Psychiatric Association

Association of Retarded Citizens (ARC) 367

Asthma 29, 30, 64–66
    allergies and 213
    puberty and 521

Asthma and Allergy Foundation of America 66

Ataxia 68–69
    cerebral palsy and 136

Atherosclerosis 579

Athetoid cerebral palsy 136

Athletics. *See* Sports

Atresia 110

At-risk students 66–68
    alternative schools and 33
    identification 87
    tracking and dropping out 2

Attachment 41
    Ainsworth, Mary 19
    child abuse and 139
    critical period and 188
    Harlow's research 332
    Hinde, Robert 340
    infant and caregiver 69–74
    security objects and 553

Attachment, Separation, and Loss 112

Attention deficit/hyperactivity disorder 17, 74–77, 88, 209
    among adoptees 17
    antisocial behavior 48
    Attention Deficit Disorder Association 77
    behavior therapy and 91
    cognitive behavior therapy and 162
    drug therapy 239
    figure-ground discrimination and 293
    fragile X syndrome and 299

Attention span 9, 74

Attitude inventory 63

Attribution theory 77

Au pair 132

Audiometry, hearing assessment 335

Auditory Discrimination Test 77

Authoritarian parent. *See* Parent-child relationships

Autism 78–79, 89, 308, 500, 546, 570
    Bettelheim, Bruno and 93
    communication board 166
    drug therapy 239
    echolalia and 250
    fragile X syndrome and 299

Autistic savant. *See* Savant syndrome

Autoerotic behavior 14

Autoimmune disorders 57, 79–81

Autoimmune hemolytic anemia 81

Autonomy 269, 564

Autonomy vs. shame and doubt 267

Autosomal dominant disease 308

Average 82

Aversive conditioning 82, 90

B

Babbling 388, 391

Babinski reflex 462

Babysitter 83–84, 103, 554
    definition 132
    tantrums and 625

Back to Sleep 617

Bacterial infections 358, 564

Bacterial STD infection 564, 568

BAER. *See* Brainstem auditory-evoked response

Baldwin, J. Mark 134

Barnett, W. Steven 248

Basal age 86

Battered child syndrome 86–87, 139, 145

Bayley scales of infant development 87

B-cell lymphocyte 359

Beck, Aaron 161

Bedwetting. *See* Enuresis

Beery-Buktenica Test 88

Behavior 550
  alcohol-related 20
  childhood attachment 553
  developmental patterns and schizophrenia 548
  health 564, 566–569
  homeless children 340
  induced change 570
  motivation 560
  negative social 581
  parental 561
  prevention 568
  risk and sexually transmitted diseases 568–569
Behavior management
  acting out and 7
  fetal alcohol effects and 291
Behavior modification 88–90, 524, 570
Behavior of Organisms, The 88
Behavior therapy 82, 89–91
Behaviorism 91–92, 252, 562, 570
Bell Curve, The 281, 372
Bell, Alexander Graham 134
Bender Visual Motor Gestalt Test (Bender-Gestalt) 92
Benton Visual Retention Test 92
Bettelheim, Bruno 93, 280
Bi-Bi. *See* Bilingual-Bicultural
Bicycle safety 543–544
Bile 377
Bilingual-bicultural approach, hearing loss and 336
Bilingualism/bilingual education 93–95, 388
Bilirubin 377
Bilirubin test 95
Binet, Alfred 95–96, 252, 372–373
Binge-purge episode 123
Binocular vision 211, 274
Biofeedback 90
Biological parent 96
Biopsy 96, 128
  celiac sprue disease 135
  for leukemia 407
Bipolar disorder 96–97
Birth 97–99
  anoxia during 46

Caesarian 61
  father-child relationships 286
  in vitro fertilization and 365
Birth defects 99–102, 551
  bowel disorders 110
  embryo 255
  infant mortality and 369
  kidney abnormalities 381
Birth order 102–104, 499
Birthmark 99
Bisexuality 104–105, 566
Bladder inflammation 381
Blank slate 388
Bleuler, Eugene 547
Blood 80, 105–106
Blood disorders 41, 105–106, 572
Blood transfusions 572
Bob Jones University Press 342
Body image 106–107
  anorexia nervosa and 45
  during puberty 523
Boehm Test of Basic Concepts 107
Bonding 107–109
  failure to thrive and 278
Bone cancer 128
Bone growth 573
  age assessment 573
  brittle bone disease 574
  cells 572
  deficiencies in 573
  density 573–574
  factors affecting 574
  fractures 574
  genetic differences in rates 574
  overgrowth 573
  remodeling, factors affecting 574
Bone marrow 358
  transplant 42, 128, 572
Boredom 109–110
  cheating and 137
Born to Rebel: Birth Order, Family Dynamics, and Creative Lives 102
Bowel and bladder control. *See* Bowel Disorders; Digestive Disorders; Encopresis; Enuresis; Kidney Function and Urological Disorders; *and* Toilet Training

Bowel disorders 110–112
Bowlby, John 112–113, 498, 553
  attachment 69
  influence on Mary Ainsworth 19
Boys and Girls Clubs of America 301
Brain 113–114
  abnormalities 547
  anoxia 46
  aphasia and 54
  autism and 78
  cancer 128
  concussion 604
  cysts, cerebral palsy and 135
  damage, asphyxia neonatorum 61
  development 373, 572
  injury, traumatic (TBI), sports-related 604
  jaundice and 377
  lesions and language disorders 398
  stem 113
  See also Cerebellum *and* Cerebrum
Brainstem auditory-evoked response (BAER) 335
Brazelton Neonatal Behavioral Assessment Scale (BNBAS). *See* Brazelton Neonatal Test
Brazelton Neonatal Test 114–116
Brazelton, T. Berry 512, 560–561
Breast development 11, 116
Breast enlargement in adolescent boys 116–117, 383
Breastfeeding 117–119
  effect on ear infections 246
Breuer, Josef 133
Brigance Diagnostic Inventory of Early Development 120
Broadbent, D. E. 370
Broadbent's theory of attention 370
Broca, Paul Pierre 330
Broca's aphasia 55
Broca's area 397
Bronchitis 120–121
Bronchodilators 66, 120
Bronfenbrenner, Urie 41
Brown v. Board of Education 121–123, 212
Bruner, Jerome 216
Bulimia nervosa 107, 123

cognitive behavior therapy 162
perfectionism and 496
Bullies 124–125, 562
Burns 125–126, 544
Busing 122, 126, 212

C

Caesarian birth 61
Calcitonin 574
Calcium
  abnormalities 577
  absorption inability 574
  insufficient dietary 573
  intake 573
  loss 574
Caldeira, John 357
California Achievement Tests (CAT) 127
Caloric malnutrition 574
Cancer 60, 127–130, 547, 565
  anal 565
  biopsy 96
  bone 128
  brain 128
  carcinogens 130
  causes of 129
  cervical 349
  epidemiology and 265
  immune system and 358
  immunization against polio and 361
  incidence in childhood 127
  kidney 381
  leukemia 128
  liver, hepatitis B virus and 338
  lymphoma 128
  psychological treatment 129
  skin and exposure to sun 129, 617
  smoking-related 579
  steroid use and 39
  See also Chemotherapy
Cancer Information Service 130
Car seats 544
Cardiac arrhythmias, asthma and 66
Cardiopulmonary resuscitation (CPR) 59, 130

Cardiovascular disease 66, 579

Carditis 80

Caregiver 48, 103, 131–133
    child abuse and 139, 141, 143
    father-child relationships 287

CAT. *See* California Achievement Test *and*
    Children's Apperception Test

CAT scan 128

Cataracts 33, 133, 178

Catatonic schizophrenia 547, 549

Catharsis 133

Cattell Infant Intelligence Scale 134

Cattell, James McKeen 134

Caucasian 567–568
    contraceptive use 567
    drug/alcohol use 568
    prevalence rates of sexual experience 566
    smoking incidence 578
    viral STD infections 564

Ceiling age 86

Celiac sprue disease 110, 134–135

Center for Injury Prevention 545

Center for Jewish Genetic Disease 627

Center for Media Education 8

Center for the 4th and 5th R's (Respect and Re-
    sponsibility) 137

Centers for Disease Control and Prevention 42,
    281, 578
    birth defects 100
    fetal alcohol syndrome 290
    lead poisoning and 402
    1995 Youth Risk Behavior Survey 579

Central nervous system 56, 68, 626

Cerebellum 68, 113–114

Cerebral palsy 135–136
    developmental delay and 214
    early intervention and 248
    familial mental retardation and 281

Cerebrum 113

Certification
    for babysitters 83
    teachers 627

Cervical cancer 180–181, 564, 566

CF. *See* Cystic fibrosis

Chalazion 275

Character education 137

Character Counts Coalition 137

Charren, Peggy 7

Charter schools 550

Cheating 137–138

Chemotherapy 32, 127, 239

Chess, Stella 320

Chicken pox 138–139
    encephalitis and 260
    fever and 292
    immune system and 359, 362
    vaccine 362

Child abuse 567
    adoption and 18
    antisocial behavior and 48, 51
    attention deficit/hyperactivity disorder 75
    battered child syndrome 86–87
    Childhelp National Abuse Hotline 87
    coaches 603
    emotional 143
    enuresis and 263
    failure to thrive 279
    family therapy 284
    fetal alcohol effects and 290
    impulse control disorders and 363
    institutionalization and 371
    National Association of School Psycholo-
        gists 460
    neglect 139, 143
    physical 139–142, 241
    pyromania and 363
    sexual and emotional 143–146

Child custody. *See* Custody

Child psychology 10, 149–150, 383, 562

Child support
    enforcement 1
    Child Support Recovery Act, 1992 1

Child Welfare League of America 18, 372

Childhood, febrile seizures 555

Childhood diseases and illnesses. *See* Diseases
    and illnesses of childhood

Childhood disintegrative disorder 500

Childhood schizophrenia 548

Childhood Vaccine Injury Act 150, 360

Childproofing 150–151, 543, 544
    crawling stage and 184
    to prevent choking 152

Children and Adults with Attention Deficit Disorder 77
Children of alcoholics (COA) 21, 25
Children of the Dream 93
Children's Aid Society of New York City 15
Children's Apperception Test (CAT) 151
Children's Defense Fund 372
 estimates of school-aged homeless 341
 statistics on caregivers 131
Children's Hospice International 130
Children's Rights Council (CRC) 2, 149
Children's Safety Network 545
Children's Television Act, 1990 8
Chi-square test 320
Chlamydia 152, 564–565, 567
Chodorow, Nancy 306
Choking 46, 152–153, 645
Cholesterol 153–154, 338
Cholos. *See* Gangs
Chomsky, Noam 92, 387
Chores 155
Chromosomal abnormalities 577
Chronological age 573
Cigarette advertising 579
Circumcision 155–156
Civil liberties 550
Civil rights 15, 121–123, 212
Claparède, Eduoard 156–157
Classical conditioning 8, 90–91, 157–158
Cleft lip and palate 100, 158–161, 248, 335
Cleft Palate Foundation (CPF) 161
Clinton, President Bill 94, 137
Cliques 161, 267
 in adolescence 13
 gangs and 302
Clonic seizure 555
Clozapine 548
Clubfoot 100
Cobb's angle 551
Cocaine 567–568, 580
Coccyx 572
Cochlear implant 336
Cognitive behavior therapy 90, 161–163, 633
Cognitive development 163–164
 adolescence and 11
 ethnic identity and 271
 gender constancy and 305
 hearing loss and 335
Cognitive-behavioral skills training 569
Cold sores 312, 339
Coles, Robert Martin 165
Colic 165, 189, 479
Colitis 111, 222
College Boards. *See* SAT
College Entrance Examination Boards. *See* SAT
Colostrum 118
Comfort habits 553
Communication disorders 166–169
Communication board 78, 136, 166
Communication skills 9, 569
 assessment of 77
 at-risk students 68
 family therapy 284
Compact cortical bone 573
Competition 561, 602
 between and among siblings 103
Computers in education 169–170, 627
Concept formation 170–171
Concussion, sports and 604
Conditioning
 aversive 90
 classical 91
 operant 90
Condom 171–172, 179
 female 178
 use 567–569
Conduct disorder 51, 172–173
 antisocial behavior and 50
 cognitive behavior therapy and 162
Conduction aphasia 55
Conference, Parent-teacher 485–486
Conflict resolution 173–175
Conformity 175–176
Conjunctivitis 46, 176
 chlamydia and 152
 gonorrhea and 319
Constipation 110, 176–177
 appendicitis 57
 bulimia nervosa 123
 encopresis and 262
Contact dermatitis 30

Contact lenses 133, 177–178
Contraception 178–181
 barrier-method 567–568
 as behavioral risk factor 567
 contraceptive use 566–569
 by race/ethnicity, age, and socioeconomic status 567
Contract, in behavior modification 90
Convergent thinking 181–182, 185–186
Convulsions 555
Cooperation 103, 581
Co-parent 181–182
Core curriculum 182
Core Knowledge Foundation 182–183
Coronary heart disease 579
Co-sleeping 615
Council for Children with Behavior Disorders (CCBD) 367
Council for Exceptional Children (CEC) 367–368
Council for Learning Disabilities 244
Counseling 3, 550
Counterconditioning 183
CP. *See* Cerebral palsy
CPR. *See* Cardiopulmonary Resuscitation
Crack use 567
Crawling 183–184
 choking hazards and 152
Creativity 184–186
 Creativity Assessment Packet 187
 Creativity Attitude Survey (CAS) 187
 fantasy and 285
 genius and 312
 imaginary playmates and 357
 language development and 395
 preschool and 512
 private speech and 515
 tests of 186–188
Critical period 188–189
Crohn's Colitis Foundation of America, Inc. 112, 223
Crohn's disease 111, 222
Crying in infants 189–190
CSF. *See* Cerebrospinal fluid
Cults 9, 190–191
 child sexual abuse and 143

Cultural bias, SAT 545
Cultural differences, Kohlberg's theory and 385
Culture-fair test 191–192
Curriculum 192–194
 ability grouping and 2
 core 182
 Just Community program for moral development 384
 technology and 627
Custodial interference 148
Custody 1, 146–149, 194–196
 biological parent 96
 contested 147
 Custody Action for Lesbian Mothers 149
 grandparents and 321
 Grandparents As Parents 322
 joint 146
 laws regulating child 146
 temporary 146
 Uniform Child Custody Jurisdiction Act 148
Cyanosis 101
Cyclosporine, in autoimmune disorder treatment 81
Cystic fibrosis 110, 196–198, 308
 asthma and 65
 diarrhea and 222
Cystitis 381
Cytokines 359

D

Dairy products 465
Dance movement therapy 272
Darwin, Charles 372
Dating 14
Day care 86, 199–200
 ear infections and 246
 intellectual development and 316
 latchkey children vs. 400
 tantrums and 625
Daydreaming 200–201
Deadbeat dad. *See* Abandonment
Deafness 55, 289

Deafness Research Foundation 336
See also Hearing development and impairment
Death and mourning 49, 201–202,368
Decision-making skills 564, 569
Deductive reasoning 202–203
Defense mechanisms 203–204
    acting out 7
    antisocial behavior and 49
    fear and 287
Delay of gratification 205
Delusions 547–548
Dementia infantilis 501
Dental development 205–207
Deoxyribonucleic acid (DNA) 234–235
Dependent personality disorder 207
Depression 96, 207–211, 549, 558, 560
    adjustment disorder and 9
    alcohol use and 23
    anaclitic 39
    anorexia nervosa and 46
    antidepressants 47
    anxiety and 52
    at-risk students 67
    boredom and 109
    cancer and 129
    child abuse and 141
    cognitive behavior therapy 162
    conduct disorders 172
    drug therapy 239
    impulse control disorders 364
    in adoptees 17
    medication 47
    mental retardation and 434
    narcissism and 457
    perfectionism and 496
    postpartum 278
    reaction to divorce 233
    sleep patterns and 576
    suicide and 620
    treatment 47
Depth perception 135, 211
Dermatitis, contact 30
Desegregation 211–213
    Brown v. Board of Education 121
    busing 126

Desensitization 29, 90, 121, 213–214
Development, cognitive 11, 163–164, 271, 305, 335
Developmental delay 214–215
    early detection 87
    fetal alcohol effects 291
    fragile X syndrome 299
Developmental psychology 215–216
Developmental quotient 216
Developmental reading disorder 216–218
Dewey, John 251
Dextromethorphan 120
Diabetes insipidus 345
Diabetes mellitus 80, 218–220, 356, 547
    enuresis and 263
    home medical tests and 426
Diabetic ketoacidosis 352
Diagnostic and Statistical Manual of Mental Disorders (DSM-IV) 220–221
Dialysis, kidney 382
Diaper rash 221–222
Diaphragm 180, 567, 569
Diaphysis 573
Diarrhea 222–223
    and celiac sprue disease 135
    anorexia nervosa and 46
    See also Bowel disorders *and* Digestive disorders
Diencephalon 113
Diet 29, 99, 135, 154
DiGeorge syndrome 577
Digestive disorders 224–226
    anorexia nervosa and 46
    celiac sprue disease 134–135
    constipation 176
    failure to thrive 277
    gasteroenteritis 224, 577
Diphtheria 226–227
    vaccine 360
Diplegia, cerebral palsy 136
Disaster Response Network 36
Discipline 227–229
    alternative schools and 33
    cheating and 138
    grandparents and 321
Disconnection aphasias 55

Discrimination 550
Diseases and illnesses of childhood
    bronchitis 120
    cancer 127–130
    celiac sprue disease 134–135
    cerebral palsy and 135
    chicken pox 138–139
    immunization 360
    rubella 546
    rubeola 546
    scarlatina 546
    scarlet fever 546
Disorganized (hebephronic) schizophrenia 547
Disruptive behavior disorders 48
Dissatisfied Parents Together (DPT) 363
Disseminated gonococcal infection 319
Dissociative disorders 231, 556
Dissociative Identity Disorder/Multiple Personality Disorder 86, 229–231, 547
Divergent thinking 186, 231–232
    creativity and 185
    intelligence and 374
Diversity 561
Divorce 232–234, 283, 550
    abandonment and 1
    antisocial behavior following 49
    family therapy 284
Dogs, Pavlov's 90
Dopamine 547–548
Down syndrome 32, 102, 235–238, 646
    amniocentesis and 38
    cataracts and 133
    early intervention and 248
    familial mental retardation 281
    genetic disorders 309
    hearing impairment and 335
    language delay and 389
    mental retardation and 434
    tests for 38
Draw-a-Man test 320
Draw-a-Person test 238, 320
Draw-a-Woman test 320
Dreaming 575
Dropout Alert Scale (DAS) 66
Drowning 400, 544
Drug abuse 548

antidepressant ingestion 555
bipolar disorder and 97
maternal, infant mortality and 369
small for gestational age and 577
stimulant ingestion 555
Drug testing 514
Drug therapy 239–240
    enuresis and 264
    Huntington's disease 350
    macrocephaly 420
    schizophrenia 548
    treatment for epilepsy 266
Drug use 566, 568
    as behavioral risk factor 567, 569
    sleep disruption and 576
Drugs 6, 606–609
DTP vaccine 150, 360
DTVP. See Frostig Developmental Test of Visual Perception
Due process 550
Dunn, Judith 300
Dwarfism 101, 240–241, 308, 577
Dyseidetic disorder 217
Dysentery 111
Dysfunctional family 241–242
Dysgraphia 55
Dyslexia 216, 242–244
Dysphasia 55
Dysphonetic disorder 217
Dysplasia 566
Dysthymic disorder 208
Dystonia 548

E

Ear 245–247
Ear infection 246, 335
Eardrum 245
Early childhood education 247
Early Growth of Logic in the Child, The 370
Early intervention 248–249, 335
Earphones, effect on hearing 246
East African Institute of Social Research, Kampala, Uganda 19

Eating disorders 249
  anorexia nervosa 45–46, 107, 162, 574
  art therapy and 238
  bulimia nervosa 123
  dysfunctional family and 241
  family therapy 284
  perfectionism and 496
Ebonics 249–250
ECE. *See* Early childhood education
ECG. *See* Electrocardiograph
Echolalia 78, 250
Eczema 29–30
Education
  early childhood 247
Education Alternatives 628
Education for All Handicapped Children Act
    250–251, 366
  speech therapy and 598, 614
Educational age 251
Educational psychology 251–253
Educators for Social Responsibility 493
Edward's syndrome 309, 646
Egocentrism 12
EKG. *See* Electrocardiogram
Electra complex 305
Electric and magnetic fields 253–254, 407
Electric shock treatments 549
Electrical outlets, safety 543
Electrocardiogram (EKG) 47, 337
Electrocardiograph (ECG). *See* Electrocardio-
    gram (EKG)
Electroconvulsive therapy (ECT) 82, 549
Electroencephalogram (EEG) 114, 265
Electronic bracing 552
Elementary and Secondary Education Act 247
Elementary School Pupil Adjustment Scale
    (ESPAS) 66
Elimination diet 29, 254–255
Elkind, David 512
Ellis, Albert 161
Ellis, Havelock 457
Embarrassment 559
Embryo 255–256, 380, 572
  custody of 146
  in vitro fertilization 365
Emotional abuse 143

Emotional development 256–260, 560, 581
  in adolescence 12
  developmental delays and 214
  giftedness and 317
  sleep and 575
Empiricism 260
Empty Fortress, The 93
Encephalitis 138, 260–261, 555
Encephalopathy, lead 401
Encopresis 261–262
Endocrine glands 345
Endocrinopathies 573
Endosteal resorption 573
English as a Second Language 93–94
English First 94
English-Only movement 93
Enteropathy, gluten-induced. *See* Celiac sprue
    disease
Entwisle, Doris 247
Enuresis 88, 90, 262–264, 381, 576
  alarms 82
  aversive conditioning and 82
  family therapy 284
  sexual abuse and 143
  wetness alarms 264
Environmental factors
  effects on intelligence 374
  infant mortality and 369
  sleep and 575
Environmental Protection Agency 130
Epidemiology 265
Epiglottitis, *Haemophilus influenzae* type B
    327, 361
Epilepsy 265–266, 555
  Epilepsy Foundation of America 266, 556
  Huntington's disease and 350
Epinephrine 31, 40
Equality Nationwide for Unwed Fathers 149
Erikson, Erik 266, 557, 600
  influence on child psychology 149
  views on adolescence 12
Esalen Institute 422
ESL. *See* English as a Second Language
Estrogen 34, 574
Ethical development 269, 366
Ethics 268–270

Ethnic identity 270–272
Ethnocentricism 325
Ethologist 8
Eustachian tube 246
Ewing's sarcoma 128
Excitement, sleep and 575
Exercise 116, 272–273
    anorexia nervosa and 45
    cerebral palsy and 272
    handicapped children and 272
    muscular dystrophy and 272
    role in amenorrhea 34
    treatment for arthritis 58
    treatment for diabetes mellitus 219
    treatment of enuresis 264
Expectorants 120
Exposure therapy 90
External locus of control 77
Externalizing disorders 273
Extinction, in behavior modification 90
Extra-curricular activities
    at-risk students and 67
Extroversion 273–274
Eye and vision development 274–275
    amblyopia 33
    binocular 211, 274
    cataracts and 133
    cerebral palsy and 135
    conjunctivitis 176
    contact lenses 177
    eye inflammation 58
    eyelid problems 275
    shaken baby syndrome 143
Eysenck, Hans
    views on extroversion 273

F

Facial features development 572
Failing at Fairness: How America's Schools Cheat Girls 304
Failure 557–560
    self-esteem and 561
Failure to thrive (FTT) 277–279

fetal alcohol effects 290
Fairy tales 279–281
False crawling reflex 462
False memory. *See* Memories, recovered
Familial retardation 281–282
Family
    babysitter and 83
    battered child syndrome 86
    dynamics 547
    ethnic identity and 271
    expression of emotion 18
    income and sexually active adolescents 566
    low-income, and bone growth 573
    security 103
    violence 139
Family Service Association of America 284
Family therapy 284–285, 549
    antisocial behavior and 51
    anxiety and 52
    fetal alcohol effects 291
    pyromania and 364
Fantasy 285
    in adolescence 14
    fairy tales 279–281
    play 581
Father-child relationship 286–287
Favoritism 103
Fear 52, 287–288
    fantasy and 285
    of the dark 576
Febrile convulsion 293
Febrile seizures 555
Federation of Families for Children's Mental Health 82, 91
Federation of Parents and Friend of Lesbians and Gays 344
Felony, child custody and 148
Feral children 289
Fetal Alcohol Effect (FAE) and Fetal Alcohol Syndrome (FAS) 21, 99, 289–291
    developmental delay and 214
Fetus 292, 572
    amniocentesis and 38
    biological parent of 96
    father-child relationships 286
    fetal alcohol syndrome 290

hearing development 334
    problems 577
Fever 292–293
    anoxia and 46
    chicken pox and 138
    DPT vaccine and 361
    ear infection and 246
    genital herpes and 312
    immune system and 359
    juvenile rheumatoid arthritis 58
    leukemia and 407
    MMR vaccine and 361
Fight or flight response 8, 52
Fighting 103
Figure-ground perception 293
    Frostig Developmental Test of Visual Perception 300
Fine motor skills 294–295
    cerebral palsy and 135
    preschool and 512
    tests of 87–88, 120
First aid 125
First-born children 102
Flesch, Rudolph 409, 504
Fluoridation 295–296
Fluorosis 295
Flynn effect, intelligence tests and 374
Folic acid 100, 135
Folk tales. *See* Fairy tales
Food allergies. *See* Allergies
Food and Drug Administration 361, 580
Food intolerance 573
Food poisoning 358
Foster care 86, 139, 296–297
Foundation for Children with Learning Disabilities 244
Fourteenth Amendment, U.S. Constitution 121
Fracture 297–298
    child abuse and 145
Fragile X syndrome 298–299
    language delay and 389
    vs. autism 78
Frames of Mind 252
Frede, Ellen 247
Free association 133
Freedom of religion 550

Freedom of speech 550
Freud, Anna 520
Freud, Sigmund 89, 133, 305, 327, 520, 557
    influence on Alfred Adler 10
    influence on child psychology 149
    influence on developmental psychology 215
    psychoanalysis and 516
    views on bisexuality 104
Friedreich's ataxia 68
Friedreich's Ataxia Group in America (FAGA) 68
Friendship 299–300, 561
    adolescence and 12
Frostig Developmental Test of Visual Perception 300
FTT. *See* Failure to thrive
Fungi 358

G

Galactorrhea 116
Galactosemia 308
Galen, views on temperament 630
Gallstones, cholesterol and 154
Galton, Sir Francis 372
Gambling, pathological 301, 363
Gandhi 385
Gangs 9, 301–303
    at-risk students 67
    female 302
Gardner, Howard 252, 373–374
Gastrointestinal ailments. *See* Bowel Disorders; Digestive Disorders
Gates-MacGinitie Reading Tests (GMRT) 303
Gates-McKillop-Horowitz Reading Diagnostic Tests 304
Gay men, child custody and 148
Gay adolescents 566
GED. *See* Test of General Educational Development
Geiger, Philip 628
Gender, androgyny and 41
Gender bias
    education and 304–305

SAT 545
  video games and 658
Gender constancy 305
Gender differences
  alcohol use 22
  assertiveness 562
  attention deficit/hyperactivity disorder 75
  bullying 124
  chlamydia symptoms 152
  conduct disorders 172
  dwarfism 240
  dyslexia 242
  emotional development 260
  friendships in adolescence 299
  friendships in school-age years 299
  giftedness and 317
  Gilligan's view 384
  gonorrhea 319
  impulse control disorders 363
  in mathematics 424
  juvenile ankylosing spondylitis 59
  kleptomania 383
  leadership 403
  lupus 80
  sexual experience 566
  sports 602
  trichotillomania 364
  views of Maccoby on 419
  x-linked genetic disorders 309
Gender identity 287, 305–306
Generalized anxiety disorder 91
Genetic disorders 307–310, 571
  Hurler's syndrome 351
  juvenile rheumatoid arthritis 57
  Sickle-cell anemia 307
  Tay-Sachs disease and 626
  tests for 38
Genetics and genetic counseling 28, 310–312
  amniocentesis 38
  behavior and 311
  cancer and 129
  growth rates and 574
  Tay-Sachs disease and 626
Genital cancer 564
Genital deformities 381
Genital herpes simplex virus (HSV-2) 312, 564

Genital warts 565
Genius 312–314
Genotype 307, 314
German measles. *See* Rubella
Gesell Development Schedules 216, 314–315
Gesell, Arnold 216, 252, 314
Gestation period 315
Gestational age 315
Giantism 573–574
Giftedness 315–318
  introverson and 376
  tests for 379
Gilligan, Carol, views on Kohlberg 384
Girls Clubs of America, and Boys Clubs 301
Glaucoma 308, 318
Global aphasia 55
Glomerulonephritis 381
Gluten Intolerance Group of North America 112
Gluten intolerance. *See* Celiac sprue disease
Glycogen 577
Goals 2000: Educate America Act 628
Goiter 318–319
Goltz's syndrome 309
Gonadotropin releasing hormone (GRH) 347
Gonococcal forms of PID 567
Gonorrhea 319, 564–565
Goodenough-Harris Drawing Test 320
Goodness of fit 320
Gould, Stephen Jay 374
Governess 132
Grand mal seizures 265, 555
Grandparents 320–322
  child custody laws and 147
  family therapy 284
  giftedness and 316
  Grandparents As Parents (GAP) 322
  Grandparents United for Children's Rights 322
Gray Oral Reading Test (GORT-R) 322
GRH. *See* Gonadotropin releasing hormone
Grimm's Fairy Tales 280
Gross motor skills 322–324
  cerebral palsy and 135
  tests of 87, 120
Group homes 282, 371
Group norms 324–325

Growth hormone 345, 573–574
 deficiency 241, 308
Growth of Logical Thinking from Childhood to Adolescence, The 370
Growth patterns, genetics and 575
Guaifenesin 120
Guardian 325
 battered child syndrome and 86
Guessing penalty 545
Guilford, J.P. 185
Guilt 325–326, 556, 558
 abused child and 144
 cheating and 137
 Erickson's theory and 267
 impulse control disorders and 363
Gusella, James, DNA marker for Huntington's disease 350
Gynecomastia. *See* Breast enlargement in adolescent boys

H

Habituation 327
Haemophilus infections
 Haemophilus influenzae type B (HiB) 327, 361
 immunization 360
Hair loss 32
Hair-pulling, compulsive. *See* Trichotillomania
Hall, Granville Stanley 252, 327–328
Hallucinations 547–548
Hallucinogens 328–330
Halo effect 63
Handedness 330–331
Hand-eye coordination 331–332
Handicapped children
 Education for All Handicapped Children Act 250
 institutionalization 371
Hansel and Gretel 280
Harelip. *See* Cleft lip
Harlow, Harry F. 332–333
Hartup, Willard W. 41
HBV. *See* Hepatitis B virus

HD. *See* Huntington's disease
Head lice 333
Head Start 247, 334, 512
Head turning reflex. *See* Neonatal reflexes
Headstart 291
Health behaviors 564
Hearing development and impairment 334–337
 cerebral palsy and 135
 classifications of loss 335
 ear infection and 246
 hearing aids 336
 language delay and 389
 noise exposure and 246
 sensorineural 335
Heart 337–338
 cholesterol and 153
 defects, congenital 100
 disease 547, 577
Heat rash 546
Heimlich manuever for choking 153
Hemiplegia, cerebral palsy 136
Hemodialysis 382
Hemoglobin electrophoresis test 571
Hepatitis, infectious arthritis and 59
Hepatitis B 568
Hereditary Disease Foundation 350
Heredity
 birth defects 99
 schizophrena and 547
 See also Genetics and genetic counseling
Hermaphroditism 339
Hernandez, Donald 248
Herpes Resource Center (HRC), an affiliate of American Social Health Association 340
Herpes simplex virus (HSV) 339
 cold sores 312, 339
 conjunctivitis and 176
 encephalitis and 260
Herrnstein, Richard J. 372
HiB. *See* Haemophilus influenzae type B
High blood pressure. *See* Hypertension
High chair safety 544
High fever 555
High school
 ability grouping in 2

Hinde, Robert A. 340
    John Bowlby and 112
Hirschsprung's disease 110
Hispanics 578
    smoking incidence 578
Histamines 29
HIV infection 565, 567
    exposure in adolescence 565
    prevention behavior 568–569
    risk behavior 568–569
Hives 29–30
    anaphylaxis and 40
Hodgkin's disease 128
Hold-back. *See* Retention in school
Holt, John 342
Home School Legal Defense Association 343
Home schooling 342–343
Home Study International 342
Homeless children 568
    academic problems 340
    antisocial personality disorder and 51
Homosexuality 343–345
    child custody and 148
Hormone therapy. *See* Anabolic steroids
Hormones 345–347
    acne and 6
    adolescence and 11
    breastfeeding 118
    fetal 98
    oxytocin 98
Hospitalism. *See* Anaclitic Depression
Hospitalization 347–349
Houston Parent Child Center 247
"How Schools Shortchange Girls" 304
Howes, Carolyn 299
HPV. *See* Human papilloma virus
Hubris 556, 558
Human immunodeficiency virus (HIV) 564
    See also AIDS
Human Papilloma Virus (HPV) 349, 564
Human potential movement 421
Huntington, George 349
Huntington's chorea *See* Huntington's Disease
Huntington's disease 308, 349–350
Huntington's Disease Society of America, Inc.
    350

Hurler, Gertrud 351
Hurler's syndrome 351
Hydrocephalus 100, 351–352
Hyperactivity 74
    crying and fussing 189
    fetal alcohol effects 291
Hyperfractionation 128
Hyperglycemia 352–353
Hyperkyphosis 551
Hyperlordosis 551
Hyperpituitarism 573–574
Hypersensitivity 189
Hypertension 353, 577
    antidepressants 47
    steroid use and 39
Hypnosis 90, 133
    psychoanalysis and 516
    treatment for impulse control disorders 364
Hypnotism
    Binet's views on 95
Hypoglycemia 219, 356, 577
    bulimia nervosa 123
Hypopituitarism 573
    dental development and 206
Hypothalamus 345
    role in amenorrhea 34
Hypothyroidism 573
    dental development and 206
Hypoxia 46, 356
    infant mortality and 369

I

Identical twins 547
Identity
    formation of 581
Identity vs. role confusion 267
Idiot savant. *See* Savant syndrome
IEP. *See* Individualized Educational Plan
Imaginary playmate 285, 357
    fantasy 285
Imipramine (Tofranil) 576
Immigration, bilingualism 93
Immune system 357–360

chicken pox and 138
immunization against polio and 361
Immunization 360–363
  against allergens 213
  chicken pox vaccine 138
  for rubella 540
  Haemophilus influenza type B conjugate
    vaccine 361
  Head Start enrollees 334
  immune system and 359
  infant mortality and 369
  National Vaccine Injury Act 150
  pertussis (whooping cough) vaccine 360
  schedule 362
  travel and 363
Implant, contraceptive 179
Implosive therapy 90
Impulse control disorder 363–365
In loco parentis 365
In vitro fertilization 315, 365–366
  biological parent and 96
  ethical issues 366
  Tay-Sachs disease and 626
Inanimate attachment agents 553
Incest 567
Inclusion *See* Inclusive classrooms
Inclusive classroom 136, 366–368
Incontinentia pigmenti 309
Individualized Educational Plan (IEP) 120, 250,
    367
  attention deficit/hyperactivity disorder 76
  cerebral palsy and 136
  dyslexia and 243
Individuals with Disabilities Education Act
    (IDEA) 136, 366
Individuation 13, 564
Inductive reasoning 368, 370
Industry vs. inferiority 267
Infancy 318, 575
  adaptation and 8
  alcoholism and 21
  allergies 29
  anemia 42
  anoxia 46
  apnea 56
  asphyxia neonatorum 60

asthma 65
battered child syndrome 86
boredom 109
cataracts and 133
Cattell Infant Intelligence Scale 134
celiac sprue disease 135
chicken pox in 138
child abuse 139
cleft lip and palate 159
colic 165
constipation 177
contact lenses 178
crawling 184
crying and fussing 189
death in 368
developmental tests 87
diabetes mellitus in 219
diarrhea 222
digestive disorders 224
divorce and 232
DTP vaccine 360
emotional development 256
empathy 539
Erikson's theory and 267
eye and vision development 274
failure to thrive 277–278
fear in 287
fears during 288
fetal alcohol effects diagnosed 290
fetal alcohol syndrome 290
fine motor coordination 294
giftedness and 313
glaucoma 318
gross motor skills 323
habituation 327
Harlow's research 332
hearing 334
heart disease and 338
hepatitis B 338, 361
herpes simplex 339
Hinde's research 340
idiopathic scoliosis 551
immunizations 360–361
jaundice in 377
kibbutz life 380
language development and 390

memory 427

mother-infant bonding 108

obesity 471

pacifier 479

pain and pain management 480

parent-child relationships during 482

polio vaccine 361

safety 543

self-esteem 561

sleep patterns 575

swimming 602, 620

Tay-Sachs disease 626

toys 644

transitional object 553

urination 380

viral infects during 547

vomiting 224

Infant and Family Special Interest Group 599

Infant Behavior Record 87

Infant mortality 368–370

Infantile idiopathic scoliosis 551

Infants

SGA 577

Infants and Mothers 116

Infection 571

antibiotics 46

ear, hearing impairment and 335

infant mortality and 369

neonatal transmission of 564

sickle-cell anemia and 571

Infectious arthritis 59

Inferiority complex 10

Infertility 564–565, 572

Inflammation

immune system and 359

Inflammatory bowel disease (IBD) 111

Influenza

infant mortality and 369

Information processing theory 164, 370

Information, motivation, and behavioral skills
    (IMB) model

evaluating risk for STDs 568

Inhelder, Barbel 370–371

Initiative vs. guilt 267

Injection, contraceptive 179

In-line skating 544

Insect bites

allergy to 31

anaphylaxis and 40

Insecurity 579

Insomnia 576

asthma and 66

childhood-onset 576

Institute for Rational-Emotive Behavior Thera-
    py. *See* Albert Ellis Institute

Institute for the Study of Youth Sports 603

Institutionalization/institutionalized children
    90, 371–372

Insulin 218

shock 356

Insulin-dependent diabetes (type I) 219

Integration 211

Intelligence 95, 289, 372–373

Goodenough-Harris Drawing Test 320

learning disabilities and 405

Piaget's studies of 505

Intelligence quotient (IQ) 186, 252, 373–375

Intelligence tests

Kaufman Assessment Battery for Children
    (KABC) 379

Kohs Block Design Test 385

Merrill-Palmer Scales of Mental Develop-
    ment 134, 436

Standard Progressive Matrices (SPM) 604

Stanford-Binet Intelligence Scale 134, 163,
    316, 605

Terman, Lewis 96, 163, 252, 605

Wechsler Intelligence Scales 316, 373, 666–
    667

Intelligence, multiple 373

Intermittent explosive disorder 363–364, 375

Internal locus of control 77

International Childbirth Education Association
    119

International Lactation Consultant Association
    (ILCA) 119

International Nanny Association 131–133

International Tay-Sachs Disease Testing, Qual-
    ity Control, and Data Collection Center
    626

Interpersonal relations 558, 581

Interviews 63

INDEX

Intra-partum distress 577
Intrauterine growth retardation 577
Intrinsic motivation 185
Introversion 375–376
Intussusception 110
Invulnerables 376
Iowa Tests of Basic Skills (ITBS) 376
Iowa Tests of Educational Development (ITED) 376
Iron-deficiency anemia 41
Irritable bowel syndrome 222
Israel, kibbutz 379
Itard, Jean-Marc-Gaspard 289
IUDs 567

J

James, William 251
Jaundice 42, 95, 377–378
Jensen, Arthur 374
Johnson, Lyndon B. 334
Joint Authority for Jewish Zionist Education 380
Joint Custody Association 2, 149
Joslin Diabetes Center 353
Jung, Carl 327
Junk Food. *See* Nutrition
Just community approach 384
Juvenile ankylosing spondylitis 59
Juvenile delinquency. *See* Truancy
Juvenile Diabetes Foundation 353
Juvenile rheumatoid arthritis (JRA) 57–59, 80

K

Kaufman Assessment Battery for Children (KABC) 379
Kempe, C. Henry, child abuse researcher 145
Kennell, John 108
Ketoacidosis 219, 352
Kibbutz 93, 379–380
Kibbutz Program Center 380

Kidney function and urological disorders 380–383
    asphyxia neonatorum 61
    hormones and 345
    lead poisoning and 402
    scarlet fever and 546
    stones 382
    tumor 128
Kinesthetic approach 217
Kinsey, Alfred, view on bisexuality 104
Kitchen safety, childproofing 151
Klaus, Marshall 108
Klein Sexual Orientation Grid 104
Klein, Fritz, views on bisexuality 104
Kleptomania 363, 383
Klinefelter's syndrome 310, 383
Knee-jerk reflex 383
Kohlberg, Lawrence 305, 383
Kohlberg's theory of moral reasoning 383–385
Kohs Block Design Test 385
Ku Klux Klan 122

L

La Leche League International 119
Labeling 103
Labor 97
Lactation 98
LAD. *See* Language Acquisition Device
Lamaze method 99
Landau's reflex. *See* Neonatal Reflexes
Language acquisition 92, 387
    autism and 78
    communication board 166
    communicatoin skills and disorders 166
    developmental delay and 214
    ear infection and 246
    sign language 389
Language Acquisition Device (LAD) 387–388
Language delay 168, 388–390
    fragile X syndrome and 299

Language development 252, 390–397
 expressive style 388
 fairy tales and 280 ·
 fetal alcohol effects and 291
 referential style 388
Language disorder 397–399
 anomia 45
 aphasia 54
Language, undesirable 653
Laparoscopic surgery
 appendectomy 57
Last-born children 102
Latchkey children 399–400
Late developer 400
Lateral spinal curvature 551
Latino/Latina 567–568
 contraceptive use 567
 drug/alcohol use 568
 sexual experience in adolescence 566
 viral STD infections 565
Laughter 18
Law of effect 91, 400–401
Law of exercise 91, 400
Leach, Penelope 401
Lead encephalopathy 401
Lead poisoning 401–402
Leadership 274, 403
Learned helplessness 403–404
Learning disabilities 367, 404–406
 cerebral palsy and 135
 Frostig Developmental Test of Visual Perception 300
 impulse control disorders and 364
 inclusive classrooms and 366
 pyromania and 364
Learning Disabilities Association of America
 (LDA) 367
Left-handed. See Handedness
Lesbians, child custody and 148
Leukemia 106, 128, 406–407
 Down syndrome and 235
 immunization against polio and 361
Limb development 572
Lincoln-Oseretsky Motor Development Scale
 407–408
Linear bone growth 574

Linguistic isolation
 ebonics and 250
Linnaeus, Carl 289
Linus phenomenon 553
Lipreading 336
Lisping 408
Literacy 408–410
 language development and 397
Literacy Volunteers of America 532
Liver development and function 410–411
 cholesterol manufacture 153
 hepatitis B and liver disease 361
 hepatitis B virus and 338
 jaundice and 377
 Reye's syndrome 261
Lithium, to treat bipolar disorder 97
Locke, John 260
Lockjaw
 DTP vaccine 360
 immunization 360
Locomotion 323
Locus of control 411–412
 attribution theory 77
Logical thinking 412–413
Logorrhea 55
Long-bone
 growth and completion 574
Longitudinal study 413–414
Lorenz, Konrad 188
Love Is Not Enough 93
Low birth weight 32, 99, 577
 asphyxia neonatorum 60
 attention deficit/hyperactivity disorder 75
 infant mortality and 369
Lumbar curve 551
Lung cancer 579
Lung development and breathing disorders
 414–417
 asphyxia neonatorum 61
 smoking and 579
Lupus 80
Luque method 552
Lying 417–418
 cognitive behavior therapy and 162
 conduct disorders and 172
Lyme disease 59

Lymph nodes 358
Lymphatic system 418
Lymphatic vessels 358
Lymphoma 128
Lysozyme 358

M

Maccoby, Eleanor Emmons 419–420
Macrocephaly 420–421
Macrophages 358
MAGIC Foundation for Children's Growth 279
Magnet schools 3, 550
Magnetic resonance imaging (MRI) 54, 114
Magnetoencephalography (MEG) 114
Mainstreaming 253
    See also Inclusive classrooms
Major Depressive Disorder (MDD) 208
Malabsorption 573
Malformation syndromes 577
Malignancy 421
Malnourishment
    failure to thrive and 277
Malnutrition 577
    bone growth and 573
    during pregnancy 547
Malocclusions 207
Manic-depressive illness. See Bipolar disorder
Manually coded English 336
March of Dimes Birth Defects Foundation 139
Marfan's syndrome 308, 551
Marijuana use 567–568
Maslow, Abraham 421
Maslow's hierarchy of needs 421–422
Masturbation 14, 422
    Down syndrome and 237
Mathematical ability 422–425
Mathematics 422–425
    at-risk students 66
Maturation
    by sex 574
Matzinger, Polly 357
McCarthy Scales of Children's Abilities
        (MSCA) 422

McGrath, Elizabeth 269
Mead, Margaret 316
Mean length of utterance (MLU) 393
Measles 546
    vaccine 361
Mediator
    child custody cases 148
Medical tests 425–427
Medulla 113
Meeting Street School Screening Test 427
Megaloblastic anemia 43
Mellaril 548
Melting Pot, The 5
Memory 92, 370, 427–429
    child abuse and 141
    extraordinary 546
    tests of 87
Memory, recovered 428–429
    Freud and 517
Menarche 11, 429
    delayed 34
Meningitis 429–430, 555
    apnea and 56
    Haemophilus influenza type B and 327, 361
    immunization 360
Menstruation 430–432
    amenorrhea 34–35
    anemia 42
Mental age 96
    IQ tests and 373
Mental health 460
Mental illness 547–548
Mental retardation 92, 99–100, 432–435
    anaclitic depression and 39
    by state, table 433
    cerebral palsy and 135
    communication board 166
    cultural-familial 281
    failure to thrive 277
    familial 281
    fetal alcohol syndrome 290
    fragile X syndrome 299
    language delay 389
    misconceptions about epilepsy and 266
    tests for 96, 379
Mercury, birth defects and 99

Merrill-Palmer Scales of Mental Development 134, 436

Metacognition, adolescence and 12

Metamemory 436

Methadone 459

Methylphenidate 91, 436–437

Metropolitan Achievement Tests 437

Metropolitan Readiness Tests 437

MI. *See* Multiple intelligences

Microcephaly 438

Micro-orchidism, primary 383

Middle children 102

Middle ear infection 546, 555

Milestones
    language development 388

Milwaukee Project 247

Milwaukee voucher system 550

Miniblinds, lead levels in 402

Minnesota Multiphasic Personality Inventory 438

Minorities
    prevalent bacterial STD infections 564, 569

Mismeasure of Man, The 374

MLU. *See* Mean length of utterance

MMR vaccine 361
    National Vaccine Injury Compensation Program 150

Moldova, pesticide use and 360

Money management. *See* Allowance

Monitoring the Future Studies 22

Monocular depth cue 211

Montessori method 188, 439–441

Montessori, Maria 188, 441–442
    feral children 289

Mood swings 19, 96
    bulimia nervosa 123
    steroid use and 39

Moral agency 269

Moral awareness 269

Moral development 442–445
    character education 137
    stages of 228
    views of Kohlberg 383

Morbidity, adolescent 564, 567–568

Moro reflex 462

Morphine 459

Mortality
    adolescent 564
    premature 568

Mother's helper 132

Mother-child relationship 19, 553–554
    alcohol use and 21

Motherese 445–446
    language acquisition device and 387

Mother-infant interaction 327

Mothers of Asthmatics, Inc. 66

Motivation 185, 559, 569
    frustration as a source of 561
    STD risk 568
    theory of Abraham Maslow 421

Motor development
    developmental delay 214
    Tay-Sachs disease and 626
    tests of 134

Mouth protectors 206

Mouth-to-mouth resuscitation 59

Mucopolysaccharidosis (MPS) 351

Mucous membranes
    immune system and 358

Multicultural education curriculum 446–447

Multicultural Education, Training, and Advocacy, Inc. 95

Multifactorial genetic disorders 309

Multiple gestations 577

Multiple intelligences 252, 373

Mumps
    encephalitis and 261
    immunization 360
    infectious arthritis and 59
    MMR vaccine 361

Murray, Charles 372

Muscle mass, genetics and 574

Muscular dystrophy 96, 308, 448–449, 551

Mutism 570

Myasthenia gravis 275

Myelinization 452–453

Myringotomy
    treatment for ear infection 335

NAACP 121
Nail biting 455–456
    aversive conditioning and 82
Names, socially desirable 456–457
Nanny 132
Naps 575–576
Narcissism 457–458
Narcissistic disorders 557
Narcissistic personality 558
Narcolepsy 458, 577
Narcotic drugs 459
Narcotic lollipop 481
NASP *See* National Association of School Psychologists
Nation at Risk: The Imperative for Educational Reform 66
National Academy of Sciences
    bilingualism and 94
National Academy of Television Arts and Sciences 7
National Adoption Center 18
National Adoption Information Clearinghouse 18
National Alliance for Research on Schizophrenia and Depression 549
National Association for Bilingual Education (NABE) 95
National Association for Hearing and Speech Action 336
National Association for Legal Support of Alternative Schools (NALSAS) 33
National Association for Mediation in Education (NAME) 174
National Association of Anorexia Nervosa and Associated Disorders (ANAD) 46, 123, 249
National Association of Black Social Workers 15
National Association of Broadcasters 7
National Association of Developmental Disabilities Councils (NADDC) 459–460
National Association of Homes and Services for Children 372

National Association of School Psychologists 460
    address and telephone 460
National Ataxia Foundation (NAF) 69
National Black Association for Speech, Language and Hearing 599
National Black Womens' Health Project 370
National Board of Certified Counselors 460
National Capital Poison Control Center 42
National Center for Family Literacy 532
National Center for Health Statistics
    failure to thrive 277
National Center for Learning Disabilities 406
National Center for Missing and Exploited Children 341
National Center for the Early Childhood Work Force 133
National Center on Child Abuse Prevention Research 145
National Center on Educational Restructuring and Inclusion (NCERI) 368
National Clearinghouse on Literacy Education 532
National Certified Counselor 460
National Clearinghouse on Runaway and Homeless Youth 341
National Coalition Against Domestic Violence 87
National Coalition of Alternative Community Schools (NCACS) 33
National Coalition on Television Violence 629
National Committee for Prevention of Child Abuse 87
National Committee to Prevent Child Abuse (NCPCA) 460
National Council for Single Adoptive Parents 18
National Council on Alcohol and Drug Dependence, Inc. 28
National Council on Child Abuse and Family Violence 87
National Council on Education Standards and Testing 62
National Council on Education Statistics (NCES) 67
National Digestive Diseases Information Clear-

inghouse 112, 223

National Down Syndrome Congress 435

National Eating Disorders Organization 46, 123, 249

National Education Association 33

National Eye Institute 34, 133, 275

National Federation of Parents and Friends of Gays 344

National Gay and Lesbian Task Force 344

National Head Start Association 334

National Heart, Lung, and Blood Institute Information Center 106

National Highway Traffic Safety Administration 544

National Homeschool Association 343

National Information Center for Children and Youth for Disabilities, The (NICHCY) 367–368

National Information Center for Children and Youth with Disabilities 251

National Institute of Allergy and Infectious Diseases (NIAID) 139, 327, 338, 340, 363, 447

immune system research 357

National Institute of Diabetes, Digestive, and Kidney Diseases 383

National Institute of Drug Abuse
survey 22

National Institute of Mental Health 53, 344, 460–461, 612

Antisocial and Violent Behavior Branch 52

study on television and aggression 629

National Institute of Neurological Disorders and Stroke (NINDS) 69

National Institute on Alcohol Abuse and Alcoholism (NIAAA) 28

National Institute on the Education of At-Risk Students 68

National Institutes of Health 40, 556

National Kidney Foundation, Inc. 383

National Law Center on Homelessness and Poverty 341

National Lead Information Center 402

National Network of Runaway and Homeless Youth Services 341

National Research Council 407

National Runaway Switchboard 87

National Safe Kids Campaign 545

National Safety Council
statistics on home accidents 150

National Scoliosis Foundation, Inc. 552

National Sexually Transmitted Disease Hotline 152, 319, 349

National SIDS Resource Center 617

National Survey of Family Growth (NSFG) 566

National Tay-Sachs and Allied Diseases Association (NTSAD) 626

National Vaccine Information Center 150, 363

National Vaccine Injury Compensation Program (NVICP) 150

National Victim Center 87

National Youth Gang Information Center 303

Nativism 461

Natural selection 8

Nature vs. nurture 289

NBAS. *See* Neonatal Behavioral Assessment Scale

Near-awakenings 575

Nebulizer, asthma treatment 66

Neck-righting reflex 463

Negative reinforcement 89

Negativism 461–462

Neglect, child 143–144
victims of, and foster care 297

Negotiation 581

Neighborhood
influence on latchkey children 399

Neonatal Behavioral Assessment Scale (NBAS). *See* Brazelton Neonatal Test

Neonatal deaths 368

Neonatal reflexes 462–463

Neo-Nazi gangs 302

Nephritis 381, 546

Nephroblastoma 128, 381

Netherlands Institute for Brain Research 646

Neurosis. *See* Anxiety

Neurotransmitters 547

Neutrophils 358

New baby, introduction 103

Newborn screening 571

Nicotine 580
withdrawal symptoms 580

Nicotine Anonymous 580
Night terrors 463–464, 576
Nightmares 464, 576
Night-time feedings 575
NIMH. *See* National Institute of Mental Health
Nongonococcal forms of PID 567
Nongraded schools 464–465
Non-insulin-dependent diabetes (type II) 219
Non-organic failure to thrive 277
Non-REM sleep 575–576
Nonsocial attachments 553
Norms, age 134
Not-me possessions 553
Notochord 572
Nurse
    nursery 132
    pediatric oncology 129
Nurse-midwife 98
Nutrition 465–469
    cancer and 129
    effect on intelligence 375
    latchkey children and 399

O

Oberti v. Board of Education of the Borough of Clementon School District 367
Obesity 471–472
    bone growth and 574
Observer bias 63
Obsessive-compulsive disorder (OCD) 52, 88, 91, 473–474
    impulse control disorders and 364
Obstructions
    intestinal 110
Occupational therapist 474–475
Oedipus complex 305
Olanzapine 549
Olympic Games 39
On Learning to Read 93
On the Origin of Species 372
Oncology. *See* Cancer
Ontogenetic development 475
Open adoption 16

Open spine. *See* Spina bifida
Operant conditioning 475–476, 570
    adaptation and 8
    behavior modification and 88
Operational thought 564
Ophthalmologist 275
Oppositional-defiant disorder 48, 209, 476
Oral contraceptives 179–180, 567
Oral herpes 339
Oral hypersensitivity 277
Oral-facial-digital syndrome 309
Organic failure to thrive 277
Organizations
    AARP Grandparent Information Center 322
    ABA Center on Children and the Law 2, 149
    AboutFace 160
    Advocates for Better Child Support (ABC'S) 2
    Albert Ellis Institute 163
    Alexander Graham Bell Association 336
    American Academy of Child and Adolescent Psychiatry 82, 89, 91, 163
    American Academy of Ophthalmology 275
    American Academy of Pediatrics 130, 145, 629
    American Academy of Private Practice in Speech-Language Pathology and Audiology 599
    American Allergy Association 31
    American Assocation for Marriage and Family Therapy 285
    American Association for the Advancement of Science 134
    American Association of Certified Allergists 31
    American Association of Kidney Patients (AAKP) 383
    American Cancer Society 116, 129
    American Cleft Palate Craniofacial Association (ACPCA) 161
    American Coalition of Citizens with Disabilities 136
    American College of Obstetricians and Gynecologists 35, 39
    American Dance Therapy Association 272
    American Diabetes Association 352

American Epilepsy Foundation 266

American Family Therapy Association 285

American Juvenile Arthritis Foundation 59

American Kidney Foundation 383

American Psychiatric Association 36

American Psychological Association 37, 344

American Society for Adolescent Psychiatry 163

American Society of Anesthetists 43

American Society of Human Genetics 310

American Speech-Language-Hearing Association 161, 599

American Urological Association 383

Anxiety Disorders Association of America 53, 612

Arthritis Foundation, The 59

Association for Advancement of Behavior Therapy 163

Association for Children and Adults with Learning Disabilities 406

Association for Persons with Severe Handicaps, The (TASH) 367

Association for the Advancement of Behavior Therapy 82, 89, 91, 162

Association for the Care of Children's Health 349

Association for the Severely Handicapped 136

Association of Retarded Citizens (ARC) 367

Asthma and Allergy Foundation of America 66

Attention Deficit Disorder Association 77

Boys and Girls Clubs of America 301

Cancer Information Service 130

Center for Jewish Genetic Disease 627

Center for the 4th and 5th R's (Respect and Responsibility 137

Character Counts Coalition 137

Child Welfare League of America 372

Children and Adults with Attention Deficit Disorder 77

Children's Defense Fund 372

Children's Rights Council (CRC) 2

Cleft Palate Foundation (CPF) 161

Council for Children with Behavior Disorders (CCBD) 367

Council for Exceptional Children (CEC) 367–368

Council for Learning Disabilities 244

Crohn's Colitis Foundation of America, Inc. 112, 223

Custody Action for Lesbian Mothers 149

Deafness Research Foundation 336

Dissatisfied Parents Together (DPT) 363

English First 94

Environmental Protection Agency 130

Epilepsy Foundation of America 266

Equality Nationwide for Unwed Fathers 149

Family Service Association of America 284

Federation of Families for Children's Mental Health 82, 91

Federation of Parents and Friend of Lesbians and Gays 344

Foundation for Children with Learning Disabilities 244

Friedreich's Ataxia Group in America (FA-GA) 68

Gluten Intolerance Group of North America 112

Grandparents As Parents (GAP) 322

Grandparents United for Children's Rights 322

Hearing Aid Helpline 336

Herpes Resource Center (HRC) 340

Home School Legal Defense Association 343

Huntington's Disease Society of America, Inc. 350

Infant and Family Special Interest Group 599

Institute for the Study of Youth Sports 603

International Childbirth Education Association 119

International Lactation Consultant Association (ILCA) 119

International Nanny Association 133

International Tay-Sachs Disease Testing, Quality Control, and Data Collection Center 626

Joint Authority for Jewish Zionist Education 380

Joint Custody Association 2, 149

Joslin Diabetes Center 353

Juvenile Diabetes Foundation 353

Kibbutz Program Center 380

Ku Klux Klan 122

La Leche League International 119

Learning Disabilities Association of America (LDA) 367

MAGIC Foundation for Children's Growth 279

March of Dimes Birth Defects Foundation 139

Mothers of Asthmatics, Inc. 66

Multicultural Education, Training, and Advocacy, Inc. 95

National Academy of Sciences 94

National Association for Bilingual Education (NABE) 95

National Association for Hearing and Speech Action 336

National Association for Legal Support of Alternative Schools (NALSAS) 33

National Association for Mediation in Education (NAME) 174

National Association of Anorexia Nervosa and Associated Disorders (ANAD) 46, 123, 249

National Association of Homes and Services for Children 372

National Association of School Psychologists 460

National Ataxia Foundation (NAF) 69

National Black Association for Speech, Language and Hearing 599

National Black Womens' Health Project 370

National Center for Learning Disabilities 406

National Center for Missing and Exploited Children 341

National Center for the Early Childhood Work Force 133

National Center on Child Abuse Prevention Research 145

National Center on Educational Restructur-

ing and Inclusion (NCERI) 368

National Clearinghouse on Runaway and Homeless Youth 341

National Coalition of Alternative Community Schools (NCACS) 33

National Coalition on Television Violence 629

National Committee for Prevention of Child Abuse 87

National Council on Education Standards and Testing 62

National Council on Education Statistics (NCES) 67

National Digestive Diseases Information Clearinghouse 112, 223

National Eating Disorders Organization 46, 123

National Education Association 33

National Eye Institute 34, 133, 275

National Federation of Parents and Friends of Gays 344

National Gay and Lesbian Task Force 344

National Head Start Association 334

National Heart, Lung, and Blood Institute Information Center 106

National Homeschool Association 343

National Information Center for Children and Youth with Disabilities, The (NICHCY) 251, 367–368

National Institute of Allergy and Infectious Diseases (NIAID) 139, 357, 363, 447

National Institute of Diabetes, Digestive, and Kidney Diseases 383

National Institute of Mental Health (NIMH) 53, 344, 612

National Institute of Neurological Disorders and Stroke (NINDS) 69

National Institute on the Education of At-Risk Students 68

National Institutes of Health 52

National Kidney Foundation, Inc. 383

National Law Center of Homeless and Poverty 341

National Lead Information Center 402

National Network of Runaway and Homeless Youth Services 341

National Sexually Transmitted Disease Hotline 349

National Tay-Sachs and Allied Diseases Association (NTSAD) 626

National Vaccine Information Center 150, 363

National Vaccine Injury Compensation Program (NVICP) 150

National Youth Gang Information Center 303

Orton Dyslexia Society 244

Parents and Friends of Lesbians and Gays 344

Parents Sharing Custody (PSC) 2, 149

Ronald McDonald House 130

Sex Information and Education Counsel of the United States 345

Step Family Foundation (SFF) 284

U.S. English 94–95

United Cerebral Palsy Association 136

Wide Smiles 161

Women's Health Network 370

World Resources Institute 360

Young Kibbutz Movement 380

Organized gangs 301

Orthodontia

braces and fluoride 295

Orthodontics 477–478

dental development and 207

Orton Dyslexia Society 244

Orton-Gillingham method 217

Ossification 572–573

Osteoblasts 574

Osteoclasts 574

Osteogenesis 572

Osteogenesis imperfecta 551, 574

Osteomalacia 573–574

Osteoporosis

adult 573

amenorrhea and 34

Osteosarcoma 128

Otitis media 246, 555

hearing impairment and 335

with effusion (OME) 246

Ovaries 345, 573

Overweight vs. obese 471

Ovum 478

in vitro fertilization 365

Oxygen

inadequate prenatal supply 577

Oxygen deprivation

infant mortality and 369

Oxytocin 98, 345

P

Pacifier 479, 553–554

as a security object 554

crying and fussing 189

pain and pain management 480

use during breastfeeding 118

Pain and pain management 479–481

anesthesia and 43

Palmar grasp reflex 294, 463

Panadol®. *See* Acetaminophen

Pancreas 345

Panic

fear and 287

panic attack 53

panic disorder 52

Paranoid schizophrenia 547

Parasites 111, 358

Parathyroid 345, 574

Parens patriae 481

Parent

androgyny 41

as primary source of social and emotional support 581

custodial 146

equitable 146

in vitro fertilization and 366

legal definition for custody purposes 146

noncustodial 1, 146

psychological 146

response to alcohol use 27

single 1

See also Parent-child relationships

Parent expectations

cheating and 137

Parent Locator Service (PLS) 485
Parent organizations. *See* Organizations
Parent's helper 132
Parental attention 103
Parent-child relationships 482–485
    adjustment disorder and 9
    communication style 445–446, 561
    crying and fussing and 189
    drinking practices and 21
    ethics and 270
Parentese 445–446
Parents and Friends of Lesbians and Gays 344
Parents Sharing Custody (PSC) 2, 149
Parent-teacher conference 485–486
    triangular conference 486
Parkes, Colin Murray
    John Bowlby and 112
Patau's syndrome 309, 646
Paternity suit 96
Pathogens 46
Pathological gambling. *See* Gambling, pathological
Pavlov, Ivan 90–91
    operant conditioning 475
Pavlov's dogs 90
Pavor nocturnus 486, 591
    See also Night terrors
Peabody Picture Vocabulary Test 486–487
Pearson, Karl 320
Pediatric oncology. *See* Cancer
Pediatrician 487–488
    eye exams and 274
    immunizations 360
    views on exercise 272
Pediculosis 333
Peer acceptance 488–490
    cheating and 137
    Down syndrome and 237
    gangs and 302
Peer group
    niche 581
    self-esteem and 561
    social norms 569
    STDs and 564
Peer mediation 174, 490–493
Peer pressure 18, 493–495, 569

adolescent smoking and 579
alcohol use and 25
at-risk students and 67
cliques and 161
in adolescence 13
Peer relations
    abused children and 140
    antisocial behavior and 50
    battered children and 86
    depression and 47
    in adolescence 13
    sexual abuse and 143
Peer-group rejection 581
Peers, fantasy and 285
Pelvic inflammatory disease 319
    chlamydia and 152
Penicillin 47
    allergy to 31
Perfectionism 495–497
    anorexia nervosa and 45
    gifted children and 317
    impulse control disorders and 364
Performance assessment 62
Perinatal period 497
    risk factor 577
Perinatal problems 577
Peritonitis 56
Personality development 215
    psychoanalysis and 516
Personality disorders 97
Personality style 558
Perspective taking. *See* Role playing
Pertussis 120
    DTP vaccine 360
    immunization 360
Pervasive Developmental Disorder (PDD) 75, 500–501
    See also Autism
Pesticides, immune system and 360
Petit mal seizures 265, 555
Peyer's patches 358
Phenotype 307, 501
Phenylketonuria (PKU) 308, 501–502
Phobia/phobic disorder 28, 88, 502–504
    behavior therapy and 90
Phocomelia 100

Phonics 217, 504–505
    ebonics and 249
    literacy and 409
Phototherapy
    for jaundice 377
Physical abuse 567
    dissociative disorders 556
Physiological stress 554
Piaget, Jean 163, 216, 280, 305, 370, 505–506
    influence on child psychology 149
    influence on developmental psychology 215
    influence on Kohlberg 384
Pineal gland 345
Pinel, Philippe 289
Pinkeye. *See* Conjunctivitis
Pituitary gland 345
    role in amenorrhea 34
Pituitary hormone production 574
Placenta 46, 98, 577
Planned Parenthood 4
Plastic surgery 506–507
Play
    hospitalization and 348
    imaginative 186
    pain and pain management 481
Playmate, imaginary 357
Plessy v. Ferguson 121, 212
Pneumococcal vaccine 572
Pneumonia 358
    complications from chicken pox 138
    infant mortality and 369
    vs. bronchitis 120
Poisons and toxins 507–509, 544
Polio 508, 551
    encephalitis and 260
    National Vaccine Injury Compensation Program 150
    vaccine 361
Pollen, immune system and 359
Polycythemia 106
Polydactyly 308
Pool safety, childproofing 151
Portfolio assessment 62, 486
Positive reinforcement 89, 103
Positron emission tomography (PET) 76, 114
Post Traumatic Stress Disorder

sexual abuse and 144
Postlingual hearing impairment 335
Postneonatal deaths 368
Post-term 577
Post-traumatic stress disorder (PTSD) 52
Post-traumatic stress syndrome
    impulse control disorders 364
Poverty
    child abuse and 141
    infant mortality and 369
Praise 103, 559, 561
Pregnancy 508–510
    abortion and 3
    alcohol use and 24
    amniocentesis 38
    diabetes mellitus and 219
    difficult 564
    fetal alcohol effects 290
    infant mortality and 369
    Rh factor 535
    risk behavior 569
    sexual abstinence 567
    sickle-cell anemia and 572
    unintended 567
Prelingual hearing impairment 335
Premature birth 99, 510–511
    amniocentesis and 38
    apnea 56
    asthma and 65
    cerebral palsy and 135
    jaundice and 377
Premature death 564
Prenatal care 98
Prenatal development
    anoxia 46
    familial mental retardation 281
    kidneys 380
Prenatal fetal monitoring 577
Prenatal tests
    amniocentesis 38
Preschool 511–513
Preschool and Kindergarten Interest Descriptor (PRIDE) 187
Preschool years 351
    acting out during 7
    adaptation and 8

allergies 29

anemia 42

appendicitis 56

arthritis 58

asthma 65

autism 78

batttered child syndrome 86

boredom 109

Brigance Diagnostic Inventory of Early Development 120

bullying 124

cancer, kidneys 381

cheating during 137

child abuse during 140

child abuse, physical 140

choosing a preschool 512

contact lenses and 178

deaf children and language delay 389

digestive disorders 224

diseases of 546

divorce and 233

Down syndrome and 236

emotional development 258

enuresis 262

epilepsy and 266

Erikson's theory and 267

fairy tales and 280

fears during 288

fine motor skills 294

giftedness and 313

gross motor development 323

hand-eye coordination 332

imaginary playmate in 357

kibbutz life 380

kidney tumor 381

language acquisition device 387–388

language development and 392

later language development 395

nightmares 464

nutrition 467

obesity 471

private speech and 515

rheumatic fever 80

school phobia 549

sleep patterns 576

social competence 580

sports 602

tantrums 625

tests 120

Title I 247

toys 645

vocabulary development 397

President's Council on Physical Fitness 272

Prevention and risk reduction counseling programs 210, 569

Pride 556, 558–559

Primary emotions 560

Privacy, child's right to 513–515

Private schools 550

Private speech 515–516

Privatization of schools 628

Problem-solving skills 569

Pro-choice, abortion and 3

Prodigy. *See* Genius

Prodromal stage 548

Progesterone challenge test 34

Progressive Education Association 93

Projective tests 63

Project Literacy U.S. (PLUS) 532

Prolixin 548

Prosody, language disorders and 398

Protein-calorie malnutrition 574

Prozac. *See* Selective serotonin reuptake inhibitors

Pseudoseizures 556

Psoriasis 81

Psychedelic. *See* Hallucinogens

Psychiatric News 36

PsychINFO 37

Psychoanalysis 133, 516–518
family therapy 284

Psychoanalytic Society 10

Psychoanalytic theory, security objects 553

Psychodynamic approach 519

Psychological assessment 63–64

Psychological Corporation 134

Psychological Review 134

Psychology of Sex Differences 419

Psychopathology 499

Psychotherapist 7

Psychotherapy 133, 518–521
bulimia nervosa 123

depression and 210

impulse control disorders and 364

views of Abraham Maslow 421

Ptosis 275

Puberty 11, 116, 521–523, 573–574

alcohol use 26

amenorrhea 34

anorexia nervosa and 45

autoimmune disorders 80

breast enlargement in boys 117

gender identity and 305

immune system and 358

Klinefelter's syndrome 383

seizures and 266

STDs and 564

Pubic hair 11

Public display 559

Public exposure 559

Public Health Service 578

Public Law 94-142 *See* Education for All Handicapped Children Act

Public schools 550

Pulitzer Prize

Erik Erikson and 268

Punishment 89, 92, 523–524

child abuse and 141

development of ethics and 270

Kohlberg's views on 384

Pyelonephritis 381

Pyloric stenosis 110, 224

Pyromania 363, 524–525

Q

Quadriplegia 527

cerebral palsy 136

Quality time 103

Questionnaires 63

Questions

language development and 395

R

Rabies 529–530

immunizations and 363

Race/ethnicity 568

contraceptive use 567

prevalence rates of sexual experience 566

Radiation therapy 32

for cancer 127

hyperfractionation 128

side effects 128

Radiography (x-rays) 573

Radon

exposure to and cancer 129

Rage reflex 463

Rational-emotive therapy (RET) 161

Readiness

tests of 127

Reading 530–533

Reading Is Fundamental (RIF) 532

Reading problems

assessment of 322

Reading Reform Foundation 533

Rebellion

adolescent 579

Recessive genetic disorders 308

Reciprocity 581

Recommended Dietary Allowances (RDA) 533

Redshirting 535

Regular Education Initiative (REI) 367

Reinforcement

family therapy 285

negative 89, 92

positive 89, 92

Relativism, ethics and 268

Relaxation training 90–91

Religious doctrines 550

Religious schools 550

REM (rapid eye movement) sleep 575

Remarriage 550

Remediation, learning disabilities and 405

Renal failure 382

Reproductive health 564, 567

Rescue breathing 59

Residual schizophrenia 548

Respiratory distress syndrome 369
Respiratory problems 29
    anaphylaxis and 40
    asbestos and 60
    asthma 30, 64–66
    bronchitis 120
    rhinitis 30
Retention in school 340, 533–535
    early childhood education and 247
Retinoblastoma (Rb) 308
Rett's disorder 500
Reviving Ophelia 10
Rewards, development of ethics and 270
Reye's syndrome 261
    acetaminophen and 5
    aspirin and 61
    fever and 292
    pain and pain management 480
Rh factor 106, 535–536, 547
    anemia and 41
    juvenile rheumatoid arthritis 58
Rheumatic fever 80
Rhinitis 30
Richet, Charles-Robert 40
Rickets 573–574
Risk-taking behaviors 567
Risperidone 549
Ritalin. *See* Methylphenidate
Rite of passage 536–538
Roe v. Wade, 1973 4
Rogers, Fred McFeely 538
Role playing 538–539
Rollerblades. *See* In-line skating
Ronald McDonald House 130
Rooting reflex 463
Rorschach Psychodiagnostic Test 63, 185, 539
Roseola infantum 539–540
Rubella (German measles) 99, 135, 540, 546
    during pregnancy 99
    diabetes mellitus and 219
    hearing loss and 335
    vaccine 360–361
Rubeola 540–541
    vaccine 361
Running away 541–542
    abused children and 141

battered children and 87
institutionalization and 371

S

Sabin oral vaccine 361
Sabin, Albert Bruce 361
Sachs, Bernard 626
Sadness 560
Safer-sexual behaviors 568
Safety 543–545
    at home 543–544
    bathroom childproofing 151
    bedroom childproofing 151
    childproofing 150
    choking prevention 152
    first aid classes 153
    for travel and play 544
    gates 543
    kitchen childproofing 151
    pool childproofing 151
    procedures for babysitters 83
SAT 545, 549
    Critical Reading 545
    Equating section 545
    Mathematical Reasoning sections 545
    Test of Standard Written English 545
    Verbal Reasoning section 545
Satir, Virginia 285
Savant skills 546
Savant syndrome 546, 546
    intelligence and 373
SCA. *See* Sickle-cell anemia
Scald prevention 126
Scales for Rating the Behavioral Characteristics
        of Superior Students (SRBCSS) 187
Scarlatina 546
Scarlet fever 546
    automimmunie disorders and 80
    complications 546
    symptoms 546
Scavenger gangs 301
Schizophrenia 28, 97, 173, 547–549
    echolalia and 250

Schizophrenics Anonymous 549
Scholastic Aptitude Test *see* SAT
Scholastic Assessment Test *see* SAT
School-age years
    abused children and 140
    adjustment in adoptees 17
    alcoholism and 21
    allergies 29
    appendicitis 56
    arthritis 58
    assertiveness 562
    asthma 66
    at-risk students 66
    attitudes toward academic records 557
    battered child syndrome 86
    boredom 109
    bullying 124
    cerebral palsy and 136
    cleft lip and palate 160
    cliques 161
    conduct disorder and 172
    constipation and 177
    contact lenses and 178
    developmental reading disorder 217
    digestive disorders 224
    divorce and 233
    diseases of 546
    Down syndrome and 237
    enuresis 262
    epilepsy and 266
    Erikson's theory and 267
    exercise 272
    fairy tales 280
    fears during 288
    fetal alcohol syndrome and 291
    fine motor skills 295
    friendships 299
    giftedness and 313
    gross motor skills 324
    hand-eye coordination 332
    herpes simplex 339
    Hurler's syndrome 351
    imaginary playmate 357
    impulse control disorders 363
    kibbutz life 380
    locus of control 77
    pain and pain management 480
    psoriasis 81
    rheumatic fever 80
    sleep patterns 576
    sports 602
    trichotillomania and 364
    Tourette syndrome 641
    toys 645
School and Society, The 252
School choice movement 550
School dropouts 568
School Initiatives Program 493
School Mediation Associates 493
School Mediators Alternative Resolution Team
    (SMART) 490
School phobia 549–550
    fear 287
    fetal alcohol syndrome and 291
    triggers of 549
School vouchers 550–551
Schools
    alternative 33
    busing 126
    conflict resolution and 174
    self-esteem and 561
Schumm, Jeanne Shay 368
Scoliosis 551–552
Scoliosis Association, Inc. 552
Scoliosis Research Society 551–552
Screening Assessment for Gifted Elementary
    Students (SAGES) 187
Security objects 553–555
    benefits 554
    blankets 553–554
    cultural issues 553
    limitations 554
Seizures 555–556
    apnea and 56
    asphyxia neonatorum 60
    asthma and 66
    DTP vaccine and 360–361
    encephalitis 261
    epilepsy and 265
    fever and 293
    grand mal 265
    hypoglycemia and 356

Jacksonian 265
related to vaccine administration 150
restrictions 556
treatment 556
Selective serotonin re-uptake inhibitors (SSRIs) 47, 363
pyromania and 364
Self-acceptance 560
Self-actualization 421
Self-care children. *See* Latchkey children
Self-concept 107
Self-confidence 558, 560, 581
Self-conscious emotions 18, 406, 556–560, 579
in adolescence 12
cheating and 137
elicitors 557
learning disabilities and 406
role of self 557
Self-efficacy 568–569
Self-esteem 86, 560–562, 581
antisocial behavior and 49
assertiveness and 562
attention deficit/hyperactivity disorder 75
bullies 124
eating disorders and 249
family therapy and 285
gender bias and 304
in adolescence 12
minority students and 212
newborn introduction 103
STDs and 564
two key components of 560
Self-evaluation 558–560
external attribution 557
global attribution 557
internal attribution 557
specific attribution 557
Self-identity 564
Self-image 579
Self-injury
during seizure 266
Self-motivation 569
Self-mutilation 364
Self-regulative skills 569
Self-talk 561
Seligman, Martin 560

Selman, Robert 300
Selye, Hans 612
Semantic relations
language development and 392
Sensory stimulation 8
Separation anxiety 52, 287, 576
disorder 88, 90, 549
divorce and 232
fear and 287
hospitalization and 348
parental nighttime 576
psychotherapy 519
Septicemia 106
Serotonin 364, 548
Serving Homeless Children 340
Sex and America's Teenagers 4
Sex Information and Education Counsel of the United States 345
Sexual abuse 143, 556–567
dissociative disorders 556
extra-familial 567
Sexual activity
age as risk factor 566–568
coercion 567
high risk 565
Sexual intercourse
during high school years 14
involuntary 567
Sexual orientation 104–105, 343–345, 566
child custody and 148
Sexuality, adolescence and 11
Sexually Transmitted Diseases (STDs) 564–570
alcohol use and 24
behavioral factors and risk 566
biologic factors and risk 566
chlamydia 152
condom use to protect against 171
contraception and 178
epidemiology of 564–565
evaluating risk 568
health consequences of 565
herpes simplex 339
hotline 152
long-term medical and psychosocial consequences from 566

myths and misconceptions about 569
psychosocial factors and risk 568
risk markers 564
risk prevention strategies 569
risk status 564
transmissibility 565
SFD. *See* Small for Date
SGA. *See* Small for Gestational Age
Shaken baby syndrome 143
Shame 556–559
    Erikson's theory and 267
    power of 558
Shaping 570
Sharing 103
Shaywitz, Sally E. 216
Shigellosis 111
Shoplifting vs. kleptomania 383
Shunt, treatment for hydrocephalus 100, 352
Shyness 52, 559, 571, 580
Siblings
    attention deficit/hyperactivity disorder 76
    birth order and 102
    cancer patients 129
    family therapy 284
    gender identity and 305
    growth patterns 575
    kidney donation 382
    rivalry 103–104
Sickle-cell anemia 42, 101, 308, 571–575
    enuresis and 263
    symptoms of 571
Sickle-cell hemoglobin 577
Side effects
    contraceptives and 180
    DTP vaccine 360
    hepatitis B vaccine 361
    leukemia treatment 407
    MMR vaccine 361
Siegler, Robert 370
Silverman, Linda 376
Simon, Theodore 96
Skating, in-line 543–544
Skeletal development 572–575
    disorders and deficiency diseases 574
Skin
    allergies 30
    disorders
    immune system and 358
    jaundice 377
    problems 29
Skin rash
    juvenile rheumatoid arthritis 58
    lupus 80
Skinheads 302
Skinner Box 88
Skinner, B. F. 88, 90, 91, 92, 163, 252
    daughter of 88
Sleep 575–577
    childhood pattern of 575
    cycles 575
    disorders 577
    disturbances 103
    loss of 576
    problems 576
    sleeplessness 576
    types of 575
Sleepwalking. *See* Somnabulism
Sludging episodes 572
Small for date (SFD) 315
Small for gestational age (SGA) 315, 577–578
Smiling 578
Smoking 578–580
    asthma and 65
    aversive conditioning and 82
    exposure in childhood and cancer 129
    harmful effects of 579
    maternal, and asphyxia neonatorum 60
    maternal, and birth defects 99
    second-hand and cancer 129
    second-hand and ear infection 246
    small for gestational age and 577
Social anxiety 581
Social awareness 581
Social characterization 559
Social competence 580–587
    at-risk students 67
Social learning theory 49, 370, 587–588
    security objects 553
Social norms, sexual behavior and 568
Social policy, abused children and 145
Social referencing 588–589
Social-emotional development 581

Society for the Prevention of Cruelty to Children, founding 145
Sociobiology 589–590
Socioeconomic status (SES) 545, 590–591
    at-risk students 66
    bone growth 574
    cheating and 138
    child abuse and 139, 141
    early childhood education and 248
    eligibility for Head Start 334
    failure to thrive 279
    familial mental retardation 281
    gangs and 302
    intelligence and 372
    mental illness and 547
    obesity and 472
    personality development 499
Sodium, calcium loss and 574
Somnabulism 576, 591
SOMPA. *See* System of Multicultural Pluralistic Assessment
Spastic cerebral palsy 136
Spearman, Charles 372
Special education 591–595
    antisocial behavior and 50
    cerebral palsy and 136
    child abuse and 139
    Education for All Handicapped Children 250
    fetal alcohol effects and 291
    inclusive classrooms vs. 366
Specific developmental disorder *See* Learning disability
Specific language impairment (SLI) 595–596
Speech disorders 45, 54, 397–399, 548, 595–596
Speech perception 596–598
Speech therapy. *See* Speech-language pathology
Speech, private 515–516
Speech-language pathology 45, 168, 247, 598–599
    Auditory Discrimination Test 78
    speech-language pathologist 55
Sperm 599
    in vitro fertilization 365

Spermicide 179–180, 569
Spina bifida 33, 100
    amniocentesis and 38
    tests for 38
Spinal anesthetics 572
Spinal curvatures 551–552
Spine development 572
Spirituality 599–600
Spitz, René 39
Spleen 358
"Split personality" 547
Spock, Benjamin McLane 115, 600–601
Sponge, contraceptive 179
Sports 601–604
    anabolic steroids and 39
    competition 561
    gender differences 602
    participation by children with arthritis 59
Standard Progressive Matrices (SPM) 604
Stanford-Binet Intelligence Scale 134, 163, 316, 605
Statistics, measures of central tendency 82
Status epilepticus 266, 555
STD. *See* Sexually Transmitted Diseases
Stealing 605–606
Steinberg, Robert 374
Step Family Foundation (SFF) 284
Stepparent 15, 146
Stereotypes
    giftedness and 317
    group norms and 325
Sterility 56
Stern, William 373
Sternberg, Robert 372
Steroid drugs
    acne and 6
    immunization against polio and 361
    See also Anabolic steroids
Stigma
    security objects 553
    seizures 556
Still's disease. *See* Juvenile rheumatoid arthritis
Stimulant drugs 606–609
Stocker, Clare 300
Stop Teen-Age Addiction to Tobacco (STAT)

580
Storytelling 280
Strabismus 33, 609–610
Strange situation 20, 610
Stranger anxiety 610–611
    attachment and 70
Strep infection 546
Strep throat 611–612
    antibiotics 46
    autoimmune disorders and 80
Stress 612
    learning disabilities and 406
    role in amenorrhea 34
Stroke 571, 579
Structure-of-intellect (SI) model 186
Student Sensitivity Index 66
Stuttering 612–614
Stye, of the eye 275
Subperiosteal apposition 573
Substance abuse 173
    antisocial behavior and 49
    antisocial personality disorder and 51
    at-risk students 66
    attention deficit/hyperactivity disorder 75
    bipolar 97
    high risk behaviors 565
Substitute objects 553
Success 557–558
    self-esteem and 561
    self-evaluation and 557
Sucking reflex 463
Sudden Infant Death Syndrome (SIDS) 360,
        614–617
    apnea and 56
    infant mortality and 369
Suffocation 543
Suicidal behavior 619–620
Suicidal thoughts 7
    abused child 86
    adjustment disorders and 9
    alcohol use and 24
Suicide 97, 105, 548
    among victims of bullies 124
    anorexia nervosa and 46
    antisocial behavior and risk of 49
    Huntington's disease and 350

violence on television and 629
Sulfa drugs
    allergy to 31
Sulloway, Frank J. 102
Sun protection 617–619
Sun protection factor 129
Sunburn 546
Support groups
    attention deficit/hyperactivity disorder 76
    bulimia nervosa 123
    for children with arthritis 59
Surgeon General 579
Surgery
    fetal and pediatric 488
    for infant cataracts 133
    glaucoma 318
    to correct cleft lip and palate 100
    to correct club foot 100
    to correct ptosis 275
    to treat cancer 127
Swayback 551
Sweat test 620–621
Swimming 58, 602, 621–623
Symptoms
    adjustment disorder with depressed mood
        208
    bone cancer 128
    celiac sprue disease 135
    cerebral palsy 135
    chicken pox 138
    chlamydia 152
    concussion 604
    conduct disorder 172
    crying and fussing as 189
    depression 209
    digestive disorders 224
    diphtheria 226
    dyslexia and 243
    dysthymic disorder 208
    encephalitis 261
    epilepsy and 265
    genital herpes 312
    glaucoma 318
    gonorrhea 319
    Huntington's disease 350
    kidney tumor 129

leukemia 407

lymphoma 128

major depressive disorder (MDD) 208

oppositional-defiant disorder 209

pertussis 500

post-traumatic stress disorder and sexual abuse 144

roseola infantum 539

scarlet fever 546

strep throat 611

Tay-Sachs disease 626

Tourette syndrome 641

Syphilis 623

Syracuse Family Development Research Program 247

System of Multicultural Pluralistic Assessment (SOMPA) 92, 623

Systematic lupus erythematosus 80

T

Tabula rasa 260, 388

Talipes cavus 100

Talipes valgus 100

Talipes varus 100

Talmud 84

Tanner stages of breast development 116

Tantrums 625–626

    abused children and 140

    babysitters and 83

    fetal alcohol effects and 291

Tardive dyskinesia 548

Tattoos, gangs and 301

Taxes, child custody and 148

Tay, Warren 626

Tay-Sachs disease 101, 308, 626–627

    amniocentesis and 38

TB. *See* Tuberculosis

T-cell lymphocyte 358–359

Teacher competency 627

Teacher training 627–628

Teachers

    gender bias and 304

    inclusive classrooms and 367

Teens Against Tobacco Use 580

Teething. *See* Dental development

Television

    Action for Children's Television 7

    advertising and alcohol 26

    Afterschool Special 7

    aggression and 628–630

    imaginary playmates and 357

    parental censoring 629

Temper, intermittent explosive disorder 364

Temper tantrums. *See* Tantrums

Temperament 630–632

    child abuse and 139

    crying and fussing 189

    extroversion and 273

    failure to thrive 279

    father-child relationships 287

Tempra®. *See* Acetaminophen

Teratogen 632–633

Teratogenic agent. *See* Teratogen

Terman, Lewis 96, 163, 252, 605

Test anxiety 633

Test of Adolescent Language (TOAL) 633

Test of Creative Potential (TCP) 187

Test of Language Development (TOLD) 634

Test of Visual-Motor Integration. *See* Beery-Buktenica Test

Test preparation courses 545

Testes 11, 345

    cancer and 129

    hormones 573

    testicles, undescended 381

Testing 62–64

    See also Assessment; Intelligence tests

Testosterone 11, 345, 634

Tests

    Alpha Fetoprotein Test 32

    alternative assessment 62

    amniocentesis 38

    anesthesia 43

    assignment of tasks 64

    attitude inventory 63

    Auditory Discrimination Test 77

    basal age 86

    Bayley Scales of Infant Development 87

    Beery-Buktenica 88–89

Bender Visual Motor Gestalt Test 92

Benton Visual Retention Test 92

bilirubin test 95

blood 95

blood, for appendicitis 57

Brigance Diagnostic Inventory of Early Development 120

California Achievement Tests 127

Cattell Infant Intelligence Scale 134

ceiling age 86

cheating 137

Children's Apperception Test (CAT) 63, 151

cholesterol profile 154

communication skills 77

criterion-referenced 61

diagnosing Tay-Sachs disease 102

diagnostic 38

Dropout Alert Scale (DAS) 66

effect of bilingual education 94

Elementary School Pupil Adjustment Scale (ESPAS) 66

fine motor skills 120

for allergies 30

for amenorrhea 34

for diabetes mellitus 219

Gates-MacGinitie Reading 303

Gates-McKillop-Horowitz Reading Diagnostic Tests 304

gross motor skills 120

infant health 53–54

Kaufman Assessment Battery for Children 379

Kohs Block Design Test 385

math skills 120

medical 95, 425–427

Merrill-Palmer Scales of Mental Development 134

neonatal 95

norm-referenced 61

prenatal 38

preschool screening 120

projective tests 63

Standard Progressive Matrices (SPM) 604

standardized 61

Stanford-Binet Intelligence Scale 134

Student Sensitivity Index 66

System of Multicultural Pluralistic Assessment (SOMPA) 92, 623

Tay-Sachs disease 626

Thematic Apperception Test (TAT) 63

Tests of General Educational Development (GED) 634–635

Tetanus

DTP vaccine 360

immunization 360

Thalassemia 42, 308

Thalidomide 99, 635–636

The ABC's of Safe and Healthy Child Care An On-line Hand 545

Thematic Apperception Test (TAT) 63, 636

Therapy, dysfunctional family and 242

Third International Mathematics and Science Study (TIMSS) 424

Thomas, Alexander 320

Thoracolumbar curve 551

Thorazine 548

Thorndike, Edward 91, 252

law of effect and 400

law of exercise 400

Three-day measles. See Rubella

Thrill seeking 568

Thumb sucking 364, 636–637

Thymus 345, 358

Thyroid 345, 574

goiter and 318

hormone 573

Tic disorder 637–638

Tourette syndrome 641

Time on task. see Attention

Time-out procedure 89, 90, 103, 141, 638

family therapy 285

Timidity. See Self-Conscious Emotions and Temperament

TIMSS. See Third International Mathematics and Science Study

Title I, Elementary and Secondary Education Act 247

TOAL. See Test of Adolescent Language

Tobacco 578–579

Toddlerhood

allergies 29

anemia 42

appendicitis 56

asthma 66

boredom 109

cancer, kidneys 381

child abuse in 140

choking and 152

cleft lip and palate 159

constipation 177

developmenta delay and 214

digestive disorders 224

divorce and 232

Down syndrome 236

DTP vaccine 360

emotional development 257

Erikson's theory and 267

failure to thrive 278

fantasy and 285

fear in 287

fears during 288

fetal alcohol effects diagnosed 291

fine motor skills and 294

glaucoma 318

gross motor skills 323

hand-eye coordination 332

hepatitis B 338

herpes simplex 339

Hurler's syndrome 351

immunization 360–361

kibbutz life 380

kidney tumor 381

language acquisition device 387–388

language development and 391

MMR vaccine 361

nutrition 467

obesity 471

pain and pain management 480

parent-child relationship during 482

polio vaccine 361

safety 544

security needs 553

self-esteem 561

sleep patterns 576

sports 602

swimming 622

tantrums 625

toys 644

Toilet training 557, 639–640

child abuse and 140

constipation and 177

encopresis 262

fetal alcohol effects and 291

obsessive-compulsive disorder and 473

TOLD. *See* Test of Language Development

Tonic Neck Relex. *See* Neonatal reflexes

Tonic-clonic seizure 555

Tonsils 358, 546

Tooth grinding 576

Total communication, hearing impairment and 336

Tough love 640–641

Tourette syndrome 641–642

developmental delay and 214

drug therapy 239

echolalia and 250

Tourette Syndrome Association 642

Toxic shock syndrome 180, 546, 643

Toxicity, iron 42

Toys 643–645

choking hazard and 152

effect on hearing 246

television advertising of 7

Tracking. *See* Ability grouping

Trait 645–646

Tranquilizer use, sleep disruption and 576

Transcortical sensory aphasia 55

Transitional Bilingual Education 94

Transitional object. *See* Security object

Transplants 382, 572

Transsexualism 306, 646

Trauma 547

Treacher-Collins syndrome, hearing impairment and 335

Treatment

depression 209

diarrhea 223

ear infection 335

encephalitis 261

enuresis 263

genital herpes 312

gonorrhea 319

head lice 333

herpes simplex 340

Huntington's disease 350

intermittent explosive disorder 364

leukemia 407

obsessive-compulsive disorder 473

pervasive personality disorder 501

phenylketonuria 502

phobias 503

Rh disease 536

strep throat 611

stuttering 613

syphilis 623

Tourette syndrome 642

Tremor 577

Trichotillomania 363, 646

Tricophagia 364

Tricyclid antidepressants 47

Trisomy 235, 309, 577, 646

Tronick, Edward 116

Truancy 647–648

abused children and 141

at-risk students 66

conduct disorders and 172

Truants from Life 93

Trust vs. mistrust 267

TS. *See* Tourette syndrome

TSS. *See* Toxic shock syndrome

Tuberculosis 648–649

immune system and 359

test, recommended age for 362

Tumor 34, 116, 649

kidney 381

liver or pancreas, jaundice and 377

Turner syndrome 240, 577

Tutor 650

cancer patients and 129

high-achieving student as 3

Twinning 577

Twins

bipolar disorder 97

bisexuality and 104

genetic disorders and 309

Twin-twin transfusion 577

Two-word sentences 388, 392

Tylenol®. *See* Acetaminophen

Tympanometry, hearing assessment 335

U

U.S. English 94–95

U.S. Surgeon General 578

Ultrasound testing 100

Underachiever 653

Ungraded schools. *See* Nongraded Schools

UNICEF 117

Uniform Child Custody Jurisdiction Act 148

United Cerebral Palsy Association 136

University of Southern California, study on gangs 301

Urethritis 381

Urination. *See* Enuresis; Kidney Development and Urological Disorders; Toilet Training

Urological disorders 380–381

Uses of Enchantment 93

Uterine environmental problems 577

Uterus 11

V

Vaccine. *See* Immunization

VAKT (visual, auditory, kinesthetic, tactual) 217

Values 137, 324

Varicella zoster vaccine (VZV) 362

Vascular disease 577

Vaughn, Sharon 368

V-chip and television 629

Verbal communication. *See* Language development style

Video games 627, 657–658

Vineland Social Maturity Scale 658–659

Violence

aggression and 628–630

gang-related 301

television and 628–630

Viral infections 358, 564, 568

Vision development. *See* Eye and vision development

Visualization 52, 288

Vitamin D 573–574
Vitamin supplements 469
Vitamins and minerals 469, 573–574, 659–661
VMI. *See* Beery-Buktenica Test
Vocabulary 397
Vocational education 2, 67, 291, 661–663
Voice change. *See* Adolescence
Vomiting 110, 224, 663–664
   appendicitis and 57
   asthma and 66
   bulimia nervosa 123
   celiac sprue disease and 135
   hyoglycemia and 356
Vouchers. *See* School vouchers
Vygotsky, Lev 515

W

Walden Two 92
Walking reflex 463
Watson, John Broadus 81, 163, 260, 665–666
Weaning 103, 666
Wechsler Intelligence Scales 316, 373, 666–667
Wechsler, David 373
Weight 99
   attention deficit/hyperactivity disorder 76
   bipolar disorder 97
Weightlifters, anabolic steroids 39
Well-baby examination 667–668
Wepman's Auditory Discrimination Test. *See*
   Auditory Discrimination Test
Werner's syndrome 308
Wernicke, Carl 330
Wernicke's aphasia 55
Wernicke's area 398
Westling, Jon 406
Wheezing 29, 30, 64
Whole language 252, 409, 668–669
Whooping cough. *See* Pertussis
Wide Range Achievement Test 669–670
Wide Smiles 161
Will, Madeline 367
Williams syndrome 389, 670–671

Wilms' tumor 128, 381
Winnicott, D. W. 553
Wisconsin State Supreme Court 550
Women 672–674
   adolescent contraceptive use 567
   body image 106–107
   sexual experience 567
   STD infections 564–565, 569
   sickle-cell anemia in 572
   See also Puberty; Contraception; Gender
      bias
Women's Health Network 370
Women's Sports Foundation 602
Word blindness. *See* Alexia
Word deafness 55
Working mothers 672–674
World Health Organization 117
World Resources Institute, research 360
Worthy Wage Campaign 133

X

XLGD. *See* X-linked genetic disorders
X-linked genetic disorders 309

Y

Year-round school 675–676
Young Kibbutz Movement 380
Youth Risk Behavior Surveillance System
   (YRBSS) 566–567
YRBSS. *See* Youth Risk Behavior Surveillance
   System

Z

Zigler, Edward, child abuse researcher 145
Zigmond, Naomi 368

     GALE ENCYCLOPEDIA OF CHILDHOOD AND ADOLESCENCE